Anda Lee Seat
Flower Mound High School, Texas

Deborah Grebel-Becker
Flower Mound High School, Texas

Ways of the World

A Global History with Sources

FIFTH EDITION

FOR THE AP® WORLD HISTORY: MODERN COURSE

SINCE 1200 C.E.

Robert W. Strayer
The College at Brockport: State University of New York

Eric W. Nelson
Missouri State University

bedford, freeman & worth
publishers

Boston | New York

Vice President, Social Sciences and High School: Shani Fisher
Executive Program Director, High School: Ann Heath
Program Manager, History & Government: Lee Benjamins
Associate Editor: Kelly Noll
Assistant Editor: Sophie Dora Tulchin
Executive Development Editor for Media: Lisa Samols
Senior Media Editor: Justin Perry
Associate Media Editor: Michael Emig
Director, High School Marketing: Janie Pierce-Bratcher
Senior Marketing Manager: Claire Brantley
Marketing Assistant: Brianna DiGeronimo
Senior Director, Content Management Enhancement: Tracey Kuehn
Senior Managing Editor: Michael Granger
Executive Content Project Manager: Christina Horn
Senior Workflow Project Manager: Lisa McDowell
Production Supervisor: Jose Olivera
Director of Design, Content Management: Diana Blume
Text Design: Jerilyn DiCarlo
Cover Design: William Boardman
Director, Rights and Permissions: Hilary Newman
Text Permissions Researcher: Elaine Kosta, Lumina Datamatics, Inc.
Executive Permissions Editor: Cecilia Varas
Director of Digital Production: Keri deManigold
Lead Media Project Manager: Jodi Isman
Copyeditor: Susan Zorn
Composition: Lumina Datamatics, Inc.
Printing and Binding: King Printing Co., Inc.

Library of Congress Control Number: 2022949186

ISBN 978-1-319-40930-2 (Student Edition)
ISBN 978-1-319-49380-6 (Teacher's Edition)
ISBN 978-1-319-49399-8 (Teacher's Edition e-book)

Printed in the United States of America.

1 2 3 4 5 6   28 27 26 25 24 23

Acknowledgments

Text acknowledgments and copyrights appear at the back of the book on page 929, which constitutes an extension of the copyright page. Art acknowledgments and copyrights appear on the same page as the art selections they cover.

AP® is a trademark registered by the College Board, which is not affiliated with, and does not endorse, this product.

For information, write: BFW Publishers, 120 Broadway, New York, NY 10271
hsmarketing@bfwpub.com

About the Teacher's Edition Authors

Anda Lee Seat

ANDA LEE SEAT
Flower Mound High School, Texas
Anda Lee has more than thirty-five years of teaching experience. She has presented on topics in AP® World History at state and national conferences. In addition to teaching AP® World History, she is currently Social Studies Department chair and a Table Leader for the AP® World History reading.

Deborah Brebel-Becker

DEBORAH GREBEL-BECKER
Flower Mound High School, Texas
Deborah has taught high school World History for thirteen years and AP® World History for eleven years and is a Reader for the AP® World History Exam. She has presented on topics in AP® World History at state and national conferences. She is also the University Interscholastic League Social Studies coach at Flower Mound.

With Previous Contributions by

JAY HARMON
Houston Christian High School, Texas

BARBARA BRUN-OZUNA
Paschal High School, Texas

CHRISTINE CUSTRED
Edmond Memorial High School, Oklahoma

MONTY ARMSTRONG
Cerritos High School, California

GWEN DURALEK
Franklin High School, New Jersey

CHRISTINA SHIVELY
Cypress Ranch High School, Texas

Teaching AP® World History: Modern

An Introduction

ANDA LEE SEAT
Flower Mound High School, Texas

DEBORAH GREBEL-BECKER
Flower Mound High School, Texas

JAY HARMON
Houston Christian High School, Texas

Maybe you decided to teach AP® World History: Modern after thoroughly researching the pros and cons of this challenging course. Maybe you were told yesterday that you will be teaching AP® World History: Modern tomorrow. Maybe you're coming back to the course after several years away from AP® World History. Or perhaps you have taught the course for several years but are new to this particular textbook. However you arrived, we welcome you to this exciting teaching journey. We wrote this book with you in mind, to ensure you are not simply surviving but also thriving while on this adventure we all share.

This section is your guide to teaching the AP® World History: Modern course. Here we offer some essential background on the AP® World History: Modern course and exam, along with suggestions for pacing, assessment, teaching, and projects. We also suggest ways that you can prepare for the exam throughout the year and offer ideas on what you can do after the exam in May.

Projects and handouts referenced in this introduction and throughout this Teacher's Edition can be found in the Teacher's Resource Materials, accessed through the book's digital platform, or by clicking on the **TRM** icons in the Teacher's Edition e-book.

Prepare to Teach AP® World History: Modern

If you are new to this course, welcome! Teaching AP® World History: Modern has been a rewarding experience for many teachers, and we hope it will be for you as well.

We suggest that you first familiarize yourself with the most recent AP® World History: Modern Exam and the current AP® World History: Modern Course and Exam Description, described below. We also suggest that you register as soon as possible for a College Board–approved workshop — see the section "Course Audit and Professional Development" (page TE-5) to learn more.

AP® World History: Modern Redesigns and Revisions

In fall 2016, the AP® World History course was redesigned to conform to the new skill-driven model previously implemented in AP® U.S. History (2014) and AP® European History (2015). This redesign shifted the fundamental focus of the course from knowing content to using content to demonstrate skills. In fall 2019, the course was revised to become AP® World History: Modern. The course now begins in ca. 1200 (with the exception of the foundations of world religions and major processes that straddle that date) and was restructured in terms of historical skills and content. In short: there has been a lot of change to adjust to. You may find it helpful to incorporate a "Unit 0" to start the course, which we have put together in Chapter 1. Here's where we are at the time of publication:

About the AP® World History: Modern Exam

The AP® World History Modern Exam currently consists of two sections:

Section 1 (95 minutes; 60 percent of the total exam score)

- 55 multiple-choice questions (55 minutes; 40 percent of the total exam score)
- 3 short-answer questions chosen from 4 options (40 minutes total; 20 percent of the total exam score)

Section 2 (100 minutes; 40 percent of the total exam score)

- 1 document-based question (DBQ) (60 minutes; 25 percent of the total exam score)
- 1 long essay question chosen from 3 options on the same theme (40 minutes; 15 percent of the total exam score)

The **multiple-choice questions** are designed to assess a student's ability to employ reasoning skills using historical evidence, so all multiple-choice questions are stimulus-based and organized in groups of two to five questions per stimulus. Some questions do not ask directly about the stimulus but use the historical situation of the stimulus as a topic.

The **short-answer questions** ask students to apply specific historical thinking skills to historical source material and historical problems. Question 1 is a primary source stimulus-based question, while Question 2 is a secondary source stimulus-based question. Questions 3 and 4, from which students choose one to respond to, are nonstimulus questions. They do not require students to develop a thesis.

The **document-based question** will include events and processes from between the years 1450 and 2001 and requires the analysis of seven historical sources. Note that the DBQ will provide seven documents, fewer sources than previously given in the AP® World History Exam.

For **long essay questions,** students will be given the option to select from three questions with prompts on the same theme (such as Continuity and Change), but with different time periods and topics. They will write a thesis-based essay using relevant historical evidence to support their thesis.

Further course information can be found in the Course Framework. More information on the exam, including rubrics and a complete sample exam, can be found in the AP® World History: Modern Course and Exam Description.

If your APWH® class, like ours, consists mostly of sophomores, you may be introducing them to a course and exam format that they will see again in AP® U.S. History or AP® European History. Let them know that if they conquer the skills required in APWHM®, the skills will carry over to the other two AP® history courses.

Course Audit and Professional Development

In addition to the Course Framework, the following resources are available to all teachers of AP® World History: Modern. Taking advantage of these resources will help prepare you for success in the classroom. Remember that we said you needed to register for an AP® workshop ASAP? Start reading here!

- **College Board–Approved AP® Summer Institutes (Workshops).** These weeklong seminars are held all over the United States and in some international locations. They are led by College Board–endorsed, veteran APWHM® consultants and are the best way to learn about the course. In the summer institutes, you will receive an abundance of teaching materials and ideas and will connect with other AP® World History: Modern teachers. If you cannot schedule a week in the summer, consider attending the many two-day College Board–approved workshops offered in the fall and spring. Find a location near you on College Board's AP® Central website.
- **AP® World History: Modern Teacher Community Forum.** This online teacher-driven forum sponsored by the College Board can be found at apcommunity .collegeboard.org. Here you can ask questions, get advice, and share resources. Think of this resource as a friendly faculty room where you can stand on a chair and yell "Help!" The authors of this Teacher's Edition are members of this group.
- **AP® Course Audit.** All AP® course syllabi must be approved by the College Board for a student to receive official AP® credit. The College Board has provided many online resources to guide you through this process. You will find them on the course page on the AP® Central site.

Pace Your Course

Melding content and skills is the biggest challenge of any history course. Teaching AP® World History: Modern is a particularly complex proposition that involves guiding students in the study of the past and showing them how to use analytical skills to discover history on their own. Reading, thinking, and writing are the most important components of the process. This Teacher's Edition will help you provide the tools your students need to succeed on the AP® World History: Modern Exam and to think like historians.

Due to the comparative and thematic nature of the AP® course and this textbook, you will find that the themes and concepts connect across the chapters—like major routes of exchange. Don't be puzzled when you see major historical concepts flow from one time period into the next. That's by design, and it's at the heart of this course and this book.

It may seem a daunting task to teach content, skills, themes, and concepts in a way that is logical, engaging, and effective in preparing students. It may seem downright scary if you are used to starting your course at the beginning of human history and now must begin your course at 1200. But rest assured that we have worked hard to support your planning, pacing, and instruction through this Teacher's Edition.

Before each chapter in this Teacher's Edition is a detailed pacing guide for that chapter. These are more than just pacing guides. They provide the following:

- Day-by-day pacing, assuming 50-minute classes
- Suggested reading assignments
- Alignment to AP® Learning Objectives and Essential Knowledge statements
- Suggested assignments and assessments: these are meant to be a "menu" of assignments you can choose from: you need not do them all
- Coverage notes from the authors of this Teacher's Edition

You might choose to follow those pacing guides faithfully, or you might use them as a guide when creating your own syllabus. Either way, a fully editable version is available in the Teacher's Resource Materials **TRM**. Adjust it to work best for you, your school, and your students.

Generally speaking, it's a good idea to write your syllabus backwards—create a stopping point in late April, and then work your way back chapter by chapter to the first week of classes in the fall. About twice a month, plug in a "catch-up day" so you can adjust for unforeseen events outside of your control, like that surprise pep rally.

Remember to build time into your calendar for practicing analysis and writing skills. (More on this and "sandwiches" below.) It's best to do skill development as you go through the content, and you will find many support materials in this Teacher's Edition to help you along the way, including AP® Skills Workshops.

Assess throughout the Year

It's important to assess your students' progress regularly. In addition, these assessments become exam practice. Here is one way to structure a typical unit:

- Assign a chapter to read and a date for a brief reading quiz to be given 3 or 4 days after a chapter is first assigned, if you are using a traditional schedule. Reading quizzes can be given using the end-of-chapter review questions, or the AP® Exam Practice at the end of each chapter.
- Review the quiz with students to see if they have questions. In this way, you are going over the material in the textbook with students, who are taking notes on what they missed. Quizzes, like homework, can count as minor grades for the term.
- Unit tests, like quizzes, can consist of free-response questions found at the end of each period of the book, or multiple-choice items from the test bank. You may also choose to give a unit test with a combination of multiple-choice items and short-answer questions from the test bank. You can also draw on questions from the AP® Classroom question bank. A three-chapter test should have no more than about thirty multiple-choice questions and one writing item, like a short-answer question. The idea is to focus on the main processes and connections in world history, not on "gotcha" questions. Plus, you don't want to spend all your nights grading essays! After returning the graded tests, allow time for students to ask questions and take notes on what they missed.
- Semester exams are a good way to utilize AP®-style practice exams. There is one at the end of the book. This text also includes an accompanying test bank, which offers additional AP®-style exams. You can also find released AP® Exams through AP® Classroom.

While you can use writing for unit tests, you might consider a writing assignment for each chapter instead, to be done in class. These can include short-answer practice and LEQ and DBQ writing assignments. For more on writing practice, see the section "Writing, Writing, Writing" (page TE-9). The best way to help students learn good essay skills is by being there in class to guide them as they write.

Minor grades can include the following:

- Reading and/or online quizzes
- Group and individual work such as historical comparisons, Continuity and Change practice, document analysis, essay writing, maps, and so on—see the wraparound material in this Teacher's Edition for specific suggestions.

Major grades can include the following:

- Unit tests
- Large projects such as vacation reading assignments, major map projects, or DBQ projects (see below)

Help Students Use the Text

As overwhelming as the AP® World History: Modern course may seem to teach, it is even more overwhelming to students with little or no experience in world history. Other courses may have encouraged students to memorize a lot of information about events, but in this course they are expected to make connections and comparisons, conduct analyses, and draw conclusions. The first step to success is being an active reader. For example:

The Sandwich Method

In your first week of class, teach students the "sandwich method" of reading the text. Each chapter is designed like a sandwich—with a top, a bottom, and a middle.

1. First, students should look at the beginning of the chapter. That's the top layer of bread on the chapter sandwich. There is a chapter introduction and an outline that shows the most important ideas in the chapter. These will help students prepare for taking notes.

2. Then, students should flip to the back of the chapter. That's the bottom layer of bread in the chapter sandwich. There is a list of important vocabulary words from the chapter and a set of guiding questions. The Chapter Review questions highlight the most important concepts in the chapter. Remind students that they will find the vocabulary definitions and answers to the essays as they read the chapter and take notes. There are other instructional components at the back of the chapter: AP® Skills Workshops, AP® Looking Again, AP® Working with Evidence (a primary source feature that trains them for the DBQ), AP® Historians' Voices (a secondary source feature with training for SAQs), and AP® Exam Practice. Make students aware of these resources and what purpose they serve.

3. Finally, students should begin reading the "narrative" of the chapter, which is the middle of the reading sandwich. They should take notes as they read, and make sure they can answer the questions in the margins and the Finding the Main Point questions that begin each section.

Reading and Taking Notes

We find that high schoolers don't always come to our classes with the best study skills, and they are not always convinced that their teacher knows the way to teach them. So for them and for you, here is a list of some helpful reading and note-taking tips from other successful AP® World History: Modern students:

- History textbooks can help you set up outline notes with the topics and subtopics in each chapter. There is a short lesson on taking notes in Chapter 2 that your teacher may find helpful to go through with you in class (page 69).
- Look for the following vital items in your textbook and make sure to take notes on them:
  - Lists
  - Changes and continuities
  - Causes and effects of the changes and continuities
  - Thematic words such as "political," "social," "economic," "gender roles," "technology," and "the environment"—and the information that accompanies these words
  - Any comparisons—similarities or differences—between cultures
- Read while you are alert. Never read in bed.
- Look for hints from the text that tell you this is important. A context clue might be "Perhaps the most important reason . . . "
- Read for shorter times more frequently rather than longer times less frequently. This will help you absorb information. For example, it is better to read 10–20 minutes a few times a day than an hour every few days.

Use Additional Projects

Longer projects are useful for working on writing skills and for practicing DBQs. They can also be used as vacation assignments or for consuming the days after the AP® Exam. Moreover, longer projects can give creative students a chance to shine.

You will find suggestions for longer projects and activities in the chapter wraparound material in this Teacher's Edition. There are also several useful long projects available in the Teacher's

Resource Materials associated with this introduction. These projects can be downloaded from the book's digital platform, or by clicking this link in the Teacher's Edition e-book:

TRM **Preface Resources**

Map Project

In the Teacher's Resource Materials you will find a six-part map project from the beginnings of agriculture to the present. Shape the time frame of the project to fit the years of the course you are teaching. You can use this project throughout the year or at the end of the course as part of your review.

TRM **Map Project**

Make Your Own DBQ

Look again in the Teacher's Resource Materials for a project that asks students to pair up and then write their own DBQ. The project includes detailed instructions for how to research, construct, and write a DBQ and includes a list of essay prompts. Jay Harmon's instructions to you include the procedure and suggested assessment strategies. This is a good project to assign early in the second semester.

TRM **Make Your Own DBQ**

End-of-Year Projects

You can find two suggested end-of-year projects in the Teacher's Resource Materials. These projects allow students to work on their own, with a partner, or with a small group to explore topics in world history that interest them and were maybe skimmed over during the year. You can assign at least one of these projects after the exam as an interesting way to close out the year.

TRM **End-of-Year Projects**

Exam Prep Begins on Day One

Earlier in this introduction, we suggested that you conclude your textbook instruction by late April so that you will have time for exam preparation and review. But make no mistake, your prep begins way before that. In fact, every day of your course is preparation for the AP® World History: Modern Exam in May. Each interaction between you and your students should focus on the following core goals:

- Enhancing student understanding of important trends, events, and connections in world history
- Increasing student ability to analyze historical information and primary sources
- Improving student capacity to convey skills and reasoning in short-answer and essay formats

If a lesson you plan does not fulfill one or more of these goals, you should revise it. At a loss on how to teach a certain goal? Look to the strategies in the Planning Pages and chapter wraparound material of this text, or post your question to the AP® community.

To help your students do their best on the AP® World History: Modern Exam, consider the following strategies for writing practice and short-term and long-term review.

Writing, Writing, Writing

It is essential that students get a great deal of practice writing responses to document-based questions, long essay questions, and short-answer questions. Although the exam has gone through some changes, you can adapt many questions from previously released APWH®

Exams to use as practice with your students. This is a strategy employed by every AP® teacher we know. Some released questions are referenced throughout the Teacher's Edition at appropriate points, and many have recommended replacements that are in line with the current format of the AP® Exam. Moreover, every chapter contains numerous prompts to give students practice writing free-response questions of every sort.

A good rule of thumb is to try to incorporate at least one SAQ per week and one LEQ and one DBQ per month. However, it can also be beneficial to students to do "mini-practices" of specific writing elements throughout the year, especially if you don't have time to write or grade six to seven full essays. In the fall semester, start by showing the class how to respond to a short-answer question. Introduce the long essay and the various forms it can take. Later, tackle a DBQ or LEQ in small groups. By the end of the first semester, students should be writing DBQ essays on their own. This next bit of advice is important for students who were likely raised on computers and cell phones: require them to write their essays by hand, in ink—not on a keyboard and not with pencil—to get them used to the real testing conditions in May.

To help teach students how to write a DBQ and an LEQ, there are AP® Skills Workshops in each chapter that can be used to either introduce skills or deepen and reinforce skills that you introduced earlier on. We also offer your students our advice on the following items found in the **TRM**.

> **TRM** **How to DBQ**
> **TRM** **How to LEQ**

Long-Term Review Strategies

It is important to review topics and themes throughout the year. Conducting reviews throughout the year also helps increase student confidence. Here are some ideas you can implement to make sure your students review and retain what they have learned:

- Hold a "review day" at the end of every major era to help students organize their understanding of what they recently learned and, just as important, to make connections to themes and trends in previous eras.
- Ask students to generate multiple-choice questions and free-response questions in small groups and collate them into a class review packet.
- Throughout this Teacher's Edition, you will find numerous activities that ask students to make comparison charts, fill in maps with information, and create timelines. Suggest that students keep this work in a review notebook, and ask students to share their review materials with a study group.

Practice for all questions that require writing—SAQ, DBQ, and LEQ—is vital for student success on the exam. These assignments should reflect the style and rigor of the AP® World History: Modern Exam. You will find examples of practice questions throughout *Ways of the World* and at apcentral.collegeboard.com.

Short-Term Review Strategies

Now we circle back to what you should do in late April. As exam day approaches, it's important to set aside a chunk of time for review—most of us veteran AP® World History teachers recommend 2–3 weeks. Below are some suggestions for how to approach this final review period.

- A chronological approach works best; focus on one major era at a time over 2 or 3 days.
- Give students multiple-choice questions they created throughout the school year (or from the test bank), and have them practice writing short-answer and essay responses that

they then peer-review. There are many options for essay practice in *Ways of the World*; earmark those you didn't use during the year so you can return to them.

- If at all possible, and certainly if you did not do this at midterm, give students the opportunity to complete a full-length AP® World History practice exam 2 or 3 weeks before the actual exam. It is important for them to have the experience of answering fifty-five stimulus-based multiple-choice questions, three short-answer questions, one document-based question, and one long essay question in one sitting. This "dress rehearsal" will help them become familiar with the challenges of sitting through the 3-plus-hour exam. Grade the multiple-choice questions and give them the results before they leave the practice exam so they can start studying their weak areas of knowledge. During the next class, review the short-answer and essay questions and review the components of a good answer. Remember: there is a practice exam at the end of this book, more AP®-style questions in the test bank, and previous exam questions available from the College Board. Lots to choose from.
- The day before the exam, do what you know works with your students to help them remain calm and focused. They may request a more formal review led by you, or they may prefer quizzing one another in small groups. Some teachers show a video from the History channel, such as The Epic History of Everyday Things. Others have a class party to shake out some of the nerves and cobwebs.
- Provide a checklist of final preparations for the exam, including the following:
  - Get a full night's sleep.
  - Eat a good breakfast.
  - Budget enough time to get to the exam site early, to get comfortable and organized before the test is administered.
  - Bring two #2 pencils with good erasers and two blue or black ink pens.
  - Bring a photo ID for checking in.
  - Pack water and a snack for the break.
  - Bring a light sweater or jacket in case the testing room is cold.

Use Time after the Exam to Promote Course Goals

Depending on your school calendar, you may have a few weeks or more than a month of class time after the exam. Tell your students well ahead of time what will be expected of them after the exam, and use assignments to promote the academic goals of the course. The following are just a few of the many possibilities for how to use this time:

- Assign groups to make videos or binders with advice for next year's students.
- Ask students to design review activities or games that could help next year's students prepare for the exam.
- Present in-depth lessons on favorite subjects that you could not get to during the year.
- Take a field trip to a local art or natural history museum.
- Assign one or more of the suggested research projects from the Teacher's Edition that you did not get to during the year, such as taking a gallery walk or researching an important archeological site.
- Have students design a historical "vacation" to send you on, allowing students to go more in-depth on historical topics they are interested in.
- Show a movie with historical relevance and ask students to comment on it from a world history perspective. This can be an old film, a newer costume drama, or even a popular feature-length animated film with a historical setting.

Final Advice

While this course may seem formidable, especially to a teacher new to AP® World History: Modern, it is not only doable but very rewarding as you guide students in their study of world history. As you head into this great adventure that is teaching AP® World History: Modern, keep in mind that you don't need to teach everything in world history; focus on the big ideas from the AP® Course and Exam Description. The chapters of this textbook do a great job of outlining those big ideas and making it feel more manageable. We have designed the lessons in this Teacher's Edition to help guide you through your first years of teaching the course, but please feel free to pick and choose (or even modify) the activities so they work best for you and your students. The more comfortable you become with the course, the better you will know what works best for your students. Finally, and some would say most importantly, take care of yourself and your students. Value progress over perfection and celebrate the little victories that pop up throughout the year.

We wish you all the best in your teaching journey.

Anda Lee Seat
Flower Mound, Texas

Deborah Grebel-Becker
Flower Mound, Texas

Jay Harmon
Houston, Texas

Reviewers

In any enterprise of significance, "it takes a village," as they say. Among the privileges and delights of writing and revising this book has been the opportunity to interact with our fellow villagers. We are grateful to the community of fellow historians who contributed their expertise to the building of this textbook program. We especially thank our colleagues Bryan Brinkman, Tonia E. Tinsley, and John F. Chuchiak IV for their translations for our primary source features. We offer our thanks to the following reviewers:

Dorian Borbonus, University of Dayton
Matthew Conn, Eastern Michigan University
Adrianna L. Ernstberger, Marian University
Andrei Gandila, University of Alabama at Huntsville
MayaLisa Holzman, Oregon State University
Toby Huff, Harvard University
Jeremy LaBuff, Northern Arizona University
Susan Maneck, Jackson State University
Dean Pavlakis, Carroll College

Charles V. Reed, Elizabeth City State University
Kimberly B. Sherman, Cape Fear Community College
Ira Spar, Ramapo College of New Jersey
Bianka Rhodes Stumpf, Central Carolina Community College
Jeanne M. Vloyanetes, Brookdale Community College
Erin Warford, Hilbert College
Tara S. Wood, Ball State University

We also offer our thanks to the following AP® Skills Workshop reviewers:

Henry Bryson, Leto High School, FL
Austin Chlapecka, Brookland High School, AR
Mason Logerot, Pflugerville High School, TX

Aiesha H. McFadden, Frisco Centennial High School, TX
Chad Smith, MacArthur High School, TX

We are especially grateful to the village of AP® instructors who lent us their suggestions on improving this textbook program. Participants in our survey included the following:

Dennis Abline, Roxboro Community School, NC
Charlie Acheson, Ellensburg High School, WA
Lauren Adams, Coahulla Creek High School, GA
Lindsay Alger, Heritage Christian School, IN
Krystle Ammann, Millville Senior High School, NJ
Erik Anderson, Magnolia Science Academy #1, CA
Kirstin Anderson, Gertz-Ressler High School, CA
Chris Baran, Boonsboro High School, MD
Eric Beckman, Anoka High School, MN
Sarah Belton, Scarborough High School, ME
George Beltran, Alice High School, TX
Tiffanie Bemoll, Ed W. Clark High School, NV
Nikole Brasch, West Point High School, AZ
Kim Brown, Coral Reef Senior High School, FL
Michael Burns, Bellevue High School, WA
Sean Carlson, The Pine School, FL
Summer Clauer, Mountain View High School, AR
Barry Coe, Millennium 6–12 Collegiate Academy, FL
Kimberly Coil, Francis Howell North High School, MO
Jim Crouch, Oak Harbor High School, WA
Mike Denman, West Mesa High School, NM
Janis Dinda, Delton Kellogg High School, MI
Colin Dinsmore, Sherando High School, VA
David DiTucci, Suncoast Polytechnical High School, FL
Donald D'Orto Jr., Lake Nona High School, FL
Megan Dover, Desert Ridge High School/Global Academy, AZ
Thomas Eilerts, Prospect High School, CA
Shagufta Ellam, McNeil High School, TX
Daniel Eubanks, Lufkin High School, TX
James Furno, Ridge Community High School, FL

Robert Gearhart, Gallup High School, NM
Dustin George, Madison Highland Prep, AZ
Tim Gildea, Saint Mary's High School, CA
Sam Greene, Camas High School, WA
Michael Hamilton, Leilehua High School, HI
Benjamin Haynes, Lake Nona High School, FL
Alexandra Hobgood, Franklin Academy, NC
Eric Hocker, Trinity High School, PA
Stan Honeycutt, The Woodlands College Park High School, TX
Laura Huffman, Cannon School, NC
Mattye Hulin, Mount Zion High School, GA
Marjorie Hunter, Academies of West Memphis, AR
Erin Jackson, Norcross High School, GA
Thomas Johnson, The Williston Northampton School, MA
Michele Jones, Palm Desert High School, CA
Katy King, Greenfield School, NC
David Kleb, Harmony Science Academy–Pflugerville, TX
Melanie Krob, Isidore Newman School, LA
Andy Lanigan, St. Francis High School, NY
Ashley Ligon, Miller Grove High School, GA
Teresa M. Lucas, Sickles High School, FL
Jeff MacGuinness, York High School, VA
Janet Mann, Hiram Johnson High School, CA
Belinda Matheney, Rector High School, AR
Susan Maynor, North Carolina Virtual Public School, NC
Jennifer McDaniel, Houston County High School, GA
Alicia Moore, Rosemount High School, MN
Sean Moughty, Rye High School, NY
Tia Murchie-Beyma, Compass Homeschool Enrichment, VA
Jennifer Myer, Coral Reef High School, FL

Erica Niemi, Zemmer 8–9 Campus, MI
Priscilla No, Roosevelt High School, HI
Allison Osweiler, Regina High School, IA
Lindsey Pahs, Chaparral High School, CO
Michael Papciak, Vista Murrieta High School, CA
Wendy Payan, Sierra Vista High School, CA
Robert Perez, John A. Ferguson Senior High School, FL
Aaron Pickering, Oak Ridge High School, TN
Teresa Posey, Thomson High School, GA
Denise Rappoport, Sacred Heart Academy, NY
Kristine Rauh, Queens Gateway to Health Sciences
    Secondary School (Q680), NY
Kaitlyn Reuter, Hyde Park High School, TX
Enrique Romero, Lyndon B. Johnson High School, TX
Matthew Ryan, Academy of Richmond County, GA
Ben Salba, Chattahoochee High School, GA
Chad Sandford, Central High School, NH

Greg Schams, Central High School, WI
Karen Schwarzl, Deer Lakes High School, PA
Jonathan Seyfried, Sandia High School, NM
Bethann Shaffer, Shamokin Area High School, PA
Tyrone Shaw, McKinley Technology High School, DC
Jessica Short, Cibola High School, NM
Rebekah Smith, Wakeland High School, TX
Brook Smith, Strong Rock Christian School, GA
Emily Stevens, Pace Academy, GA
Philip Sutherland, Francis Lewis High School, NY
Jaime Thompson, Middletown High School, MD
Ainhoa Tollinche, St. Brendan High School, FL
Joshua Twery, Broadway High School, VA
George Vlahakis, Rich South Fine Arts Campus, IL
Sneha Walia, Boston Latin Academy, MA
Michael Wyka, Citrus High School, FL
Ryan Zerkel, Anchor Bay High School, MI

To all of our fellow villagers, we offer deep thanks for an immensely rewarding experience. We are grateful beyond measure.

Robert Strayer
Eric Nelson

How to Use
This Teacher's Edition

Prepare with Ease

This Teacher's Edition was developed to be your ultimate teaching tool. Every tip, activity, and reference was written with one thing in mind: to provide support and guidance to help you teach a successful AP® World History: Modern course. By using this Teacher's Edition and accompanying Teacher's Resource Materials **TRM**, you will have at your fingertips everything you need to be effective and efficient in your AP® World History instruction.

Teaching AP® World History: Modern

An Introduction

ANDA LEE SEAT
Flower Mound High School, Texas

DEBORAH GREBEL-BECKER
Flower Mound High School, Texas

JAY HARMON
Houston Christian High School, Texas

Maybe you decided to teach AP® World History: Modern after thoroughly researching the pros and cons of this challenging course. Maybe you were told yesterday that you will be teaching AP® World History: Modern tomorrow. Maybe you're coming back to the course after several years away from AP® World History. Or perhaps you have taught the course for several years but are new to this particular textbook. However you arrived, we welcome you to this exciting teaching journey. We wrote this book with you in mind, to ensure you are not simply surviving but also thriving while on this adventure we all share.

This section is your guide to teaching the AP® World History: Modern course. Here we offer some essential background on the AP® World History: Modern course and exam, along with suggestions for pacing, assessment, teaching, and projects. We also suggest ways that you can prepare for the exam throughout the year and offer ideas on what you can do after the exam in May.

Projects and handouts referenced in this introduction and throughout this Teacher's Edition can be found in the Teacher's Resource Materials, accessed through the book's digital platform, or by clicking on the **TRM** icons in the Teacher's Edition e-book.

Prepare to Teach AP® World History: Modern

If you are new to this course, welcome! Teaching AP® World History: Modern has been a rewarding experience for many teachers, and we hope it will be for you as well.

We suggest that you first familiarize yourself with the most recent AP® World History: Modern Exam and the current AP® World History: Modern Course and Exam Description, described below. We also suggest that you register as soon as possible for a College Board–approved workshop—see the section "Course Audit and Professional Development" (page TE-5) to learn more.

AP® World History: Modern Redesigns and Revisions

In fall 2016, the AP® World History course was redesigned to conform to the new skill-driven model previously implemented in AP® U.S. History (2014) and AP® European History (2015). This redesign shifted the fundamental focus of the course from knowing content to

TE-4   TEACHING AP® WORLD HISTORY: MODERN

Before you begin working with this text, review the introduction **Teaching AP® World History: Modern**. This overview by the Teacher's Edition authors provides valuable tips for course preparation, suggestions on course planning and pacing, class projects, and exam review information to help you prepare your students for the rigors of reading and writing in this college-level course.

2 States and Civilizations
A Global Tapestry, 1200–1450

AP® Overview for Chapter 2

Chapter 2 corresponds with Unit 1: The Global Tapestry, ca. 1200 to ca. 1450, and covers Asia, Europe, and the Americas, officially beginning the material tested for AP® World History: Modern. This course is typically a high school student's first exposure to these regions prior to 1450. The material in this chapter is rich with historical information and images that will expose students to the civilizations that developed during this time period in Asia, Europe, and the Americas. Students should begin to use their AP® World History: Modern skills to compare the civilizations in this chapter. Examining the religious, economic, political, and social aspects of these civilizations will allow students to go deeper into the skills that the AP® World History: Modern course seeks to develop.

Chapter 2 Essential Activity

It's important for students to know the regions of the world and which states, empires, and kingdoms belong to those regions in order to be successful on the exam. Essay prompts and short-answer questions frequently ask students to discuss regions as well as specific states. Creating annotated maps can be a helpful way of getting students to know what states belong to a region and to learn the characteristics of those states. Give students two blank maps: one of Eurasia (including the Mediterranean region, the Middle East, and the Indian Ocean) and one of the Americas. To help with geography, ask students to identify the civilizations of the Global Tapestry (look at the Unit 1 section of the AP® World History: Modern Course and Exam Description to create a list of civilizations), as well as regions, continents, and important geographic features. After they have labeled their maps, have the students create note boxes on their map that connect to each of the civilizations on the map. In each box, they should take notes on the following AP® Themes:

- Governance
- Social Interactions and Organization
- Cultural Developments and Interactions
- Technology and Innovation
- Economic Systems
- Humans and the Environment

These annotated maps will be used throughout Chapter 2 as students learn about each civilization. For blank maps that you can use with this activity, download **Map 2A: Europe, Asia, and Africa** and **Map 2B: The Americas** from the Resources section of the book's digital platform or click on the linked TRM buttons in the Teacher's Edition e-book.

Differentiation

If you want to differentiate the Chapter 2 Essential Activity and have students practice presentation skills, follow the "Must Do, Should Do, Strive For" model below.

- Must Do: Students should label their maps so that they know the civilizations and geography of different regions of the world, and they should be able to identify the political structures, social hierarchies and gender roles, cultures, innovations and technologies, economic structures, and interactions with the environment for at least one of the civilizations in their notes (you may want to assign the civilizations if you choose to do the "Must Do, Should Do, Strive For" with your class).
- Should Do: Students should be able to, either on their own or in a group of three to four people, create a short presentation on one of the civilizations from the annotated map. Presentations can be created digitally (Google Slides, PowerPoint, Prezi, etc.) or on a poster. Students should be able to present the main ideas of the civilization to the class and include pictures and images to help illustrate the information. To help students access information f[...] presentations online [...]
- Strive For: For stude[...] front of their peers, g[...] their slides or poster[...] about their assigned [...]

TRM Map 2A: Europe[...]
TRM Map 2B: The A[...]

> As you prepare your lessons, look to each chapter's **Planning Pages** for help with relevant resources, pacing guides, and alignment information. Need to move quickly through a chapter? The Essential Activity is the least you should do to cover chapter content.

Chapter 2 Resources

TRM AP® Skills Workshop Activity Handout: Claims
TRM Chapter 2 DBQ Activity Handout
TRM Chapter 2 Guided Reading
TRM Chapter 2 Lecture Presentation Slides
TRM Chapter 2 Outline
TRM Chapter 2 Suggested Responses to Questions
TRM Eric's Activity 2: Interpreting Visual Sources
TRM Handout 2.1: Comparison Chart for China and Islamic World Politics and Technology
TRM Handout 2.2: Chart for Economic, Cultural, and Political Characteristics of Ottoman Empire
TRM Handout 2.3: Continuity and Change Chart for the Islamic World

TRM Handout 2.4: Causation Chart for Religious Toleration in al-Andalus
TRM Handout 2.5: Thematic Chart for Swahili City-States
TRM Handout 2.6: Comparison Chart for Pre-Renaissance and Renaissance Art
TRM Handout 2.7: Comparison Chart for the Aztec and Inca
TRM Map 2A: Europe, Asia, and Africa
TRM Map 2B: The Americas
TRM Note-Taking Tips Lecture Slides
TRM Writing Organizer for LEQ Practice

Pacing Guide

Below is a pacing guide for the AP® World History: Modern course beginning in ca. 1200 C.E. This pacing guide is based on a schedule with 120 sessions of 50 minutes each before the AP® Exam. It is meant as a place to start. If you have a different number of sessions before the exam, you can modify the pacing to suit your needs.

Day	Pages Assigned	AP® Topic	AP® Theme	Suggested Assignments	Coverage Notes
1	Read pages 69–73 to the third paragraph about China's economic revolution	1.1	CDI GOV	Chapter 2 Essential Activity Teaching Idea: AP® Exam Strategies on page 69 Eric's Activity 2: Interpreting Visual Sources on page 70 Building AP® Skills: Making Connections: Comparison on pages 72 and 73	While the first two days of this chapter focus on the Song dynasty, students will need to know a little bit about the Sui and Tang dynasties to contextualize the Song and to show continuity and change in government practices. Consider giving students a short homework assignment on those dynasties to help them.
2	Read pages 73–75 starting at the third paragraph about China's economic revolution	1.1	CDI ECN SIO	Chapter 2 Essential Activity AP® Working with Evidence: Social Patterns in Tang and Song China Apply the Tip on page 74	This part of the chapter focuses heavily on Song China's economic developments, role in trade, and the innovations happening in China. These are all important concepts to teach about Song China.
3	Read pages 76–79 to "The Worlds of Southeast Asia"	1.1	CDI GOV ECN SIO	Chapter 2 Essential Activity Apply the Tip on page 76 Building AP® Skills: Making Connections: Comparison on page 79	It's more important to focus on the impact China had on Korea and Japan than on the specifics of these societies. It may be helpful to incorporate the impact China had on these countries into your lesson on their characteristics.
4	Read pages 79–81 starting from "The Worlds of Southeast Asia"	1.1 1.3	CDI GOV ECN SIO	Chapter 2 Essential Activity Building AP® Skills: Making Connections: Comparison on page 80 Exploring AP® Themes: ECN and GOV on page 80	With the section on Vietnam, it's important to focus more on the impact China had on society and what elements Vietnam borrowed from China. The second part of this section looks at Southeast Asian states that were influenced by trade on the Indian Ocean. It may be good to revisit these states when teaching about the Indian Ocean trade network in Unit 2.

Expert Advice and Creative Ideas at Your Fingertips

In the margins of the chapters, you will find teaching notes that correspond to the student edition text at point-of-use. You will find the following note types:

- **AP® CLASSROOM** These notes point out key resources from the College Board and ideal places to use them for AP® practice in your classroom.

- **APPLY THE TIP** These notes suggest activities and discussion topics to expand the AP® Exam Tips in the student edition.

- **BUILDING AP® SKILLS** These notes discuss how to teach and practice AP® Historical Thinking Skills and Reasoning Processes, which are key building blocks for student success in the course and on the exam.

- **EXPLORING AP® THEMES** These notes suggest ways to help students draw thematic connections across sections and across chapters.

- **TEACHING IDEA** These notes provide engaging ways to enrich your classroom experience, from class discussion topics to curated videos and articles.

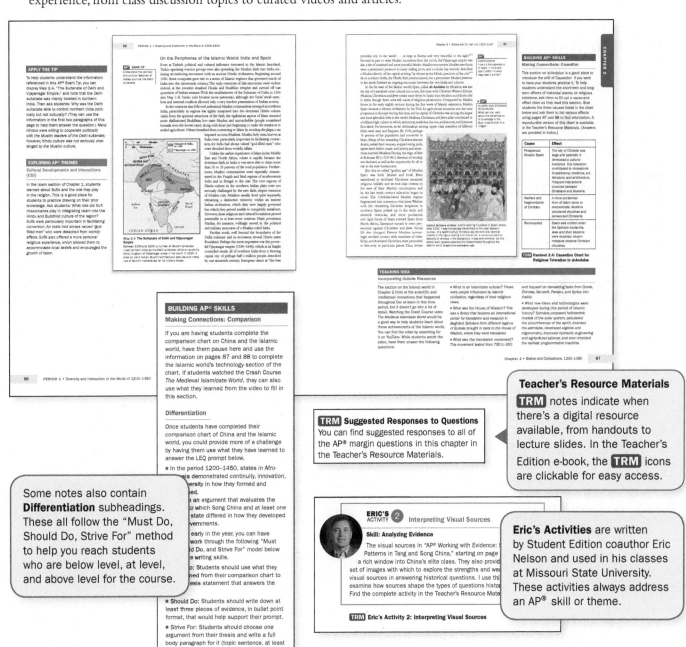

Some notes also contain **Differentiation** subheadings. These all follow the "Must Do, Should Do, Strive For" method to help you reach students who are below level, at level, and above level for the course.

Teacher's Resource Materials TRM notes indicate when there's a digital resource available, from handouts to lecture slides. In the Teacher's Edition e-book, the TRM icons are clickable for easy access.

Eric's Activities are written by Student Edition coauthor Eric Nelson and used in his classes at Missouri State University. These activities always address an AP® skill or theme.

Reach Students Anywhere

Find these and more resources online in our unique multimedia products.

 # Digital Options

Access the mobile-compatible student edition e-book, the *Thinking through Sources* reader, the Teacher's Edition e-book, and the Teacher's Resource Materials all in one convenient place on the program's digital platform.

The program's digital platform comes equipped with LearningCurve, an adaptive and automatically graded learning tool that guides students to content comprehension.

Test Bank

The Test Bank contains hundreds of helpful content review questions as well as additional AP®-style questions for exam practice.

About the Authors

Robert W. Strayer (Ph.D., University of Wisconsin) brings wide experience in world history to the writing of *Ways of the World*. His teaching career began in Ethiopia, where he taught high school world history for two years as part of the Peace Corps. At the university level, he taught African, Soviet, and world history for many years at the College at Brockport: State University of New York, where he received the Chancellor's Awards for Excellence in Teaching and for Excellence in Scholarship. In 1998 he was visiting professor of world and Soviet history at the University of Canterbury in Christchurch, New Zealand. Since moving to California in 2002, he has taught world history at the University of California, Santa Cruz; California State University, Monterey Bay; and Cabrillo College. He is a longtime member of the World History Association and served on its Executive Committee. He has also participated in various AP® World History gatherings, including two years as a reader. His publications include *Kenya: Focus on Nationalism, The Making of Mission Communities in East Africa, The Making of the Modern World, Why Did the Soviet Union Collapse?*, and *The Communist Experiment*.

Jerry Burke

Eric W. Nelson (D.Phil., Oxford University) is a professor of history at Missouri State University. He is an experienced teacher who has won a number of awards, including the Missouri Governor's Award for Teaching Excellence in 2011 and the CASE and Carnegie Foundation for the Advancement of Teaching Professor of the Year Award for Missouri in 2012. His publications include *Layered Landscapes: Early Modern Religious Space across Faith and Cultures, The Legacy of Iconoclasm: Religious War and the Relic Landscape of Tours, Blois and Vendôme*, and *The Jesuits and the Monarchy: Catholic Reform and Political Authority in France*.

Jesse Scheve/Missouri State University

About the AP® Edition Contributors

HENRY BRYSON
Leto High School ▪ Florida

AP® Skills Workshops
Henry has taught AP® World History and AP® Psychology for ten years. He is a Reader for the AP® World History Exam and has created AP® World History Daily Videos for AP® Classroom. In 2018 Henry was awarded the Hillsborough County Social Studies Teacher of Year Award. He enjoys spending time with his family, hiking, kayaking, barbeque, and traveling to new places.

AUSTIN CHLAPECKA
Brookland High School ▪ Arkansas

AP® Working with Evidence
Austin has taught AP® World History, AP® U.S. History, and AP® U.S. Government and Politics for nine years. He has also served as a Reader for both AP® World History and AP® U.S. History. Austin was an AP® Daily Video instructor for AP® World History and currently teaches at Brookland High School. Austin also is an adjunct instructor at Arkansas State University–Newport. At Brookland, he serves as the sponsor for Model United Nations and quiz bowl. In his free time, Austin enjoys spending time with his family, running, and reading.

ENAYE ENGLENTON
McDonogh School ▪ Maryland

Diversity, Equity, & Inclusion Sensitivity Reviewer
Enaye Englenton is a veteran history and social sciences teacher with over twenty years of classroom experience, most recently at Tampa Preparatory School in Florida, where she served as the History and Social Sciences Department Chair (2008–2016) and led institutional diversity, equity, and inclusion initiatives. She currently serves as the Director of Equity and Inclusion at the McDonogh School in Maryland. Enaye has a M.A. in International and Multicultural Education from the University of San Francisco and a B.A. in Political Science from Golden Gate University. She has taught Ancient World History, AP® World History, Caribbean History, U.S. Politics, Global Affairs, and AP® Psychology. Enaye is an experienced Table Leader, Question Leader, and Exam Leader at the AP® World Reading, and she has created AP® World History Daily Videos for AP® Classroom. She served on the Teacher Advisory Board for the Florida Holocaust Museum in St. Petersburg, FL (2007–2016), and was elected to the World History Association (WHA) Executive Council in 2022. She has been an active member of the WHA since 2013 and most recently co-presented a teaching workshop titled "Decentering the West in World History" at the 2021 WHA Annual Conference. Beyond being a world history enthusiast, Enaye enjoys travel and exploring the National Parks!

JONATHAN HENDERSON
Forsyth Central High School ▪ Georgia

**AP® Margin Notes
and Questions,
AP® Practice Exam**

Jonathan Henderson has taught AP® World History since 2002. He has twenty-five years of secondary teaching experience and also teaches at the University of North Georgia. He is a Reader for the AP® World History Exam, a College Board consultant, and part of the College Board's Instructional Design Team for World History.

MASON LOGEROT
Pflugerville High School ▪ Texas

**AP® Margin Notes
and Questions**

Mason Logerot has taught in Austin, Texas, since 2003 and has taught AP® History courses since 2008, most recently at Pflugerville High School. Since 2015 he has traveled around the country as an AP® World History consultant for the College Board and as a curriculum and video developer for AP® Classroom. He has also served as a Table Leader and Question Leader for the AP® World History Exam. When he is not in the classroom or on the road, you will find Mason running, biking, or playing soccer in the backyard with his wife, two boys, and two dogs.

AIESHA H. McFADDEN
Frisco Centennial High School ▪ Texas

AP® Skills Workshops

Aiesha McFadden has been teaching AP® World History since 2015. She has been an AP® Reader for several years, an AP® Daily content creator and moderator, a standard-setting panelist with the College Board for AP® World History, and has served as a district curriculum writer for multiple years. Aiesha has also taught Humanities (a blended two-year English and AP® World History course), AP® European History, and high school and college U.S. History for several years, and she has participated in relevant AP® History forums. When she is not teaching or reading the latest history monograph, Aiesha is busy traveling the world with her husband and son or playing with her two labs, Lucy and Poppy.

CHAD SMITH
MacArthur High School ▪ Texas

AP® Working with Evidence

Chad Smith has taught at MacArthur High School in Irving, Texas, for over twelve years. He began teaching AP® World History in 2012 and is an AP® World History Reader, APSI leader, and College Board consultant. During the COVID-19 pandemic, Chad helped create daily live stream lessons called AP® Live, and he later helped develop the AP® Daily Videos found in AP® Classroom. Chad also serves as the Coordinator for Texas Christian University's Institute for Teaching Excellence in Middle School Social Studies. Though he loves historical content, Chad's real passion for teaching comes in finding ways to scaffold and differentiate transferable skills to diverse learners. When he's not working, you can often find him on a patio enjoying a Texas sunset with some chips and salsa.

Brief Contents

Contents

photo: Bibliothèque
Nationale de France,
Paris, France/© BnF, Dist.
RMN–Grand Palais/Art
Resource, NY

2 States and Civilizations: A Global Tapestry 1200–1450   69

3 Connections and Interactions: Networks of Exchange 1200–1450   133

photo: Royal Collection Trust © Her Majesty Queen Elizabeth II, 2020/ Bridgeman Images

photo: Gianni Dagli Orti/
Shutterstock

photo: Archives Charmet/
Bridgeman Images

---

photo: Photo Josse/
Leemage/Getty Images

8 Revolutions of Industrialization 1750–1900   441

photo: Gianni Dagli Orti/ Shutterstock

photo: Bridgeman Images

10 Colonial Encounters in Asia, Africa, and Oceania 1750–1950 549

photo: TopFoto

photo: PhotoQuest/Getty Images

photo: SIMON MAINA/
AFP/Getty Images

photo: Image created by Reto Stockli, Nazmi El Saleous, and Marit Jentoft-Nilsen, NASA GSFC

How to Get the Most from This Program

Put history in context with opening features for each of AP® World History's four chronological periods

THE BIG PICTURE

Toward Modernity . . . or Not?

For the sake of clarity and coherence, historians often characterize a particular period of time in a brief phrase such as "the age of First Civilizations" or "the era of revolutions." Though useful and even necessary, such capsule descriptions vastly oversimplify what actually happened. Historical reality is always more messy, more complicated, and more uncertain than any shorthand label can convey. Such is surely the case when we examine the three centuries spanning the years from roughly 1450 to 1750, commonly labeled the "early modern era."

> Begin your study of each period by reading the **Big Picture** essay as an overview of what you will study in that time period.

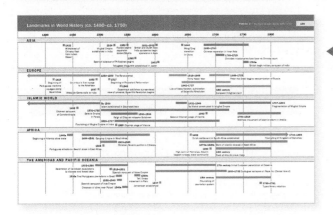

> Refer as often as needed to the **Landmarks** timeline at the beginning of each period and chapter. These timelines provide a chronological overview of key events and processes in that particular section of the book.

> Identify the important forces shaping each period and make connections between chapters in **Understanding AP® Themes**, located at the beginning of each period.

Find your way and focus on important information in each chapter

At the beginning of each chapter, a **chapter outline** indicates what will be covered in the chapter with a list of topics.

CHAPTER 4

Political Transformations

Empires and Encounters

1450–1750

European Empires in the Americas, 204
 The European Advantage, 204
 The Great Dying and the Little Ice Age, 208
 The Columbian Exchange, 211
Comparing Colonial Societies in the Americas, 213
 In the Lands of the Aztecs and the Incas, 214
 Colonies of Sugar, 217
 Settler Colonies in North America, 220

CONNECTING PAST AND PRESENT

"Putin [president of Russia] wants the old Russian Empire back. . . . As Russian tsar, which is how he sees himself, his empire cannot work without Ukraine. He sees us as a colony."[1] This was the view of Ukrainian president Petro Poroshenko in 2018, as he resisted persistent Russian incursions into the affairs of his country. The Russian invasion of Ukraine in early 2022 only enhanced this view of Russia's imperial ambitions. In a similar vein, critics of Turkey's intervention in Libya's civil war in 2020 claimed that Turkey's president Erdogan embraced "expansionist visions of reviving the Ottoman Empire, with—naturally—himself as the supreme sultan."[2] Thus memories of the Russian and Ottoman empires, initially constructed in the early modern era, continue to shape understandings of

Connecting Past and Present chapter-opening vignettes encourage you to examine the links between the past and present.

Finding the Main Point questions following each main heading in the narrative help you focus on the key concepts of each section. They are repeated in the Chapter Review for extra practice.

Empire Building in Russia and China

Finding the Main Point: What were the unique strategies and the larger impact of the expanding Russian and Chinese empires during this period?

Even as Western Europeans were building their empires in the Americas, other imperial projects were likewise under way in Asia, the Middle East, and Africa. Unlike Europe's overseas empires, all of them were contiguous land-based territories. The

Read the **Conclusions and Reflections** essays at the end of each chapter for examples on how to use your developing historical thinking skills to answer provocative questions about the unfolding of the human story.

CONCLUSIONS AND REFLECTIONS

Comparing Empires

Finding the Main Point: What were similarities and differences between the strategies and consequences of imperial expansions between 1450 and 1750?

Comparison is an essential feature of world history. We see more clearly when we juxtapose related events or processes against one another. The empires of the early modern era offer many opportunities for this kind of seeing.

At one level, these empires had much in common. Like almost all empires both earlier and later, they were the product of bloody conquest against substantial resistance. And all of them, with the exception of Songhay, were created and sustained by gunpowder weapons, which were just beginning to take hold across the world. No wonder they are sometimes called the "gunpowder empires."

These conquests caused enormous human suffering everywhere. A Christian eyewitness to the Ottoman conquest of Constantinople wrote of his beloved city:

CHAPTER REVIEW

AP Key Terms

Hernán Cortés, 207
Great Dying, 210
Little Ice Age, 210
General Crisis, 210
Columbian exchange, 212
mercantilism, 213
mestizo, 215
mulattoes, 219
settler colonies, 222
Russian Empire, 223
yasak, 224

Ming dynasty, 226
Qing expansion, 228
Ottoman Empire, 230
devshirme, 233
Safavid Empire, 235
Mughal Empire, 235
zamindars, 235
Akbar, 236
Aurangzeb, 237
Songhay Empire, 237
Pueblo Revolt, 239

Use the list of **key terms** at the end of each chapter to check your grasp of the material. Definitions for the key terms from each chapter as well as for useful academic terms can be found at the back of the book in the **Glossary/Glosario.**

Dig into the details with fascinating chapter features

ZOOMING IN

THEN AND NOW

CONTROVERSIES

The **Zooming In** features link specific people, places, and events to big themes in world history. **Then and Now** features examine engaging themes in both historical and contemporary settings. **Controversies** essays highlight debates about key historical issues, giving you great examples of how to use historical evidence and make historical arguments.

Mapping History exercises invite you to read maps carefully and to interpret their implications.

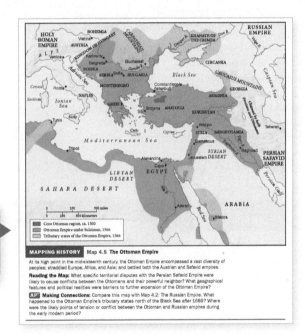

MAPPING HISTORY Map 4.5 **The Ottoman Empire**

At its high point in the mid-sixteenth century, the Ottoman Empire encompassed a vast diversity of peoples; straddled Europe, Africa, and Asia; and battled both the Austrian and Safavid empires.

Reading the Map: What specific territorial disputes with the Persian Safavid Empire were likely to cause conflicts between the Ottomans and their powerful neighbor? What geographical features and political realities were barriers to further expansion of the Ottoman Empire?

AP Making Connections: Compare this map with Map 4.2: The Russian Empire. What happened to the Ottoman Empire's tributary states north of the Black Sea after 1689? Where were the likely points of tension or conflict between the Ottoman and Russian empires during the early modern period?

Look for **Snapshot** boxes that offer practice in working with charts, graphs, and tables — all types of secondary sources common on the AP® Exam.

SNAPSHOT Ethnic Composition of Colonial Societies in Latin America (1825)

AP
COMPARISON
How did ethnic composition differ within Latin America?

	Highland Spanish America	Portuguese America (Brazil)
Europeans	18.2 percent	23.4 percent
Multiracial	28.3 percent	17.8 percent
Africans	11.9 percent	49.8 percent
Native Americans	41.7 percent	9.1 percent

Source: Data from Thomas E. Skidmore and Peter H. Smith, *Modern Latin America* (New York: Oxford University Press, 2001), 25.

xxix

Build and develop your AP® skills for success on the AP® World History Exam

AP® Skills Questions throughout the book give you constant practice in AP® Historical Thinking Skills and Reasoning Processes.

Read and take notes on the **AP® Exam Tips** to learn important concepts and identify skills that will help you succeed on the AP® Exam.

▲ AP
CAUSATION
What political and economic factors explain the pattern of Russian expansion shown in Map 4.2?

AP EXAM TIP
The AP® Exam frequently includes questions about empire building throughout world history. Note this example of how the Russian Empire developed.

Map 4.2 The Russian Empire
From its beginnings as a small principality under Mongol control, Moscow became the center of a vast Russian Empire during the early modern era.

migrants to these new eastern lands, the empire offered "economic and social improvements over what they had known at home—from more and better land to fewer lords and officials."[18] Political leaders and educated Russians generally defined the empire in grander terms: defending Russian frontiers; enhancing the power of the Russian state; and bringing Christianity, civilization, and enlightenment to savages. But what did that empire mean to those on its receiving end?

First, of course, empire meant conquest. Although resistance was frequent, in the long run Russian military might, based in modern weaponry and the organizational capacity of a state, brought both the steppes and Siberia under Russian control. Everywhere Russian authorities demanded an oath of allegiance by which native peoples swore "eternal submission to the grand tsar," the monarch of the Russian Empire. They also demanded *yasak*, or "tribute," paid in cash or in kind. In Siberia, this meant enormous quantities of furs, especially the extremely

---

AP SKILLS WORKSHOP

Contextualization

In this workshop, you will learn about contextualization, a historical reasoning skill that you can also apply to your everyday life. You may have heard people complain that their words were taken out of context, or that context is important to understand a current event. In this workshop, we'll look specifically at the role that context plays in the study of history.

UNDERSTANDING CONTEXTUALIZATION

So what is context, and how will you use the skill of contextualization in the AP® course as you build your skills as a historian? First, let's think about what "contextualization" means.

> **Contextualization: Considering the historical situation surrounding an event or process**

That means that a historian looks at an event in terms of the cultural norms, political structures, religious beliefs, geographic and environmental factors, and other contexts that might have affected how the event occurred or how people responded to it. Context helps a historian see an event through the eyes of those who experienced it and take into account all of the surrounding factors. While something might seem unusual from our perspective or context, a good historian understands the historical context and moves beyond making judgments.

Contextualization is an important part of understanding why something happened. But be careful: contextualization is not causation! When we contextualize, we are not looking for the thing that started an event, but rather the situation or setting in which the event occurred. Often, contextualization is used to lay the groundwork for a claim or thesis. Let's see how the authors of this book do it. In the following paragraph excerpt, the authors use contextualization to set the stage for their claim:

Contextualization —

> For many centuries, the Chinese had interacted with the nomadic peoples who inhabited the dry and lightly populated regions now known as Mongolia, Xinjiang, and Tibet. Trade, tribute, and warfare ensured that these ecologically and culturally different worlds were well known to the Chinese, quite unlike the New World "discoveries" of the Europeans. Chinese authority in these regions had been intermittent and actively resisted. Then,

From sourcing a primary document to developing a continuity and change argument, the **AP® Skills Workshops** introduce, and help you develop, essential AP® skills in context. There is a workshop for each of the AP® Historical Thinking Skills and Reasoning Processes in the College Board's Course and Exam Description.

AP® LOOKING AGAIN

Louis XIV on "Spectacle" as an Aid to Royal Rule

During the early modern era, Europe was divided into many competitive states that focused their resources on the twin projects of imperial expansion abroad and political integration at home. Perhaps the most well-known example of these European state-building efforts is that of France under the rule of Louis XIV (r. 1643–1715), who governed from the spectacular Palace of Versailles just outside of Paris. Louis, like many other European monarchs, claimed to rule through "divine right" granted by God and thus claimed sole and uncontested authority in his realm.

Around 1670, Louis composed a *memoir* for his son offering practical advice about how to rule France. Wide-ranging and full of examples from Louis's own experiences, his memoir offers insight into how an early modern European ruler understood the powers of a king and how he sought to bolster his authority and secure the support of his subjects. The passage that follows focuses on the importance of spectacle and public display in solidifying the exalted role of the monarch.

1 A FIRST LOOK

Because Louis composed his memoir as an instruction book or guide for his son, let's start by reading this passage to discover what Louis wanted his son to know about the role of spectacle in solidifying or strengthening royal rule. While reading, answer the following:

1. Which specific audiences for royal spectacle does Louis XIV identify?

2. According to Louis XIV, what is the purpose of spectacle in the functioning of the French state? Does its purpose vary by audience?

3. What is Louis XIV's point of view? How does he assume that his subjects and foreign observers think about him?

LOUIS XIV | *Memoirs* | 1670

The society of pleasures [shared public activities], which gives to people of the Court [powerful aristocrats who interacted with Louis] a moral closeness with us, touches and charms them more than one can express. The common people, on the other hand, delight in the spectacle, by which in the end we always seek to please them. . . . By this, we hold their minds and their hearts, sometimes more tightly maybe than through rewards and charitable gestures. With regards to foreigners, in a state seen as otherwise flourishing and well-ordered, whatever is consumed in these expenses potentially viewed as superfluous, makes on them a very favorable impression of magnificence, power, riches, and greatness. . . .

AP® HISTORIANS' VOICES

Early Modern Rulers

The following two voices provide recent descriptions of how early modern rulers defined and displayed their authority and power. In Voice 4.1, Charles Parker compares Emperor Kangxi of China and Louis XIV of France and finds them "cut from the same cloth." In Voice 4.2, John Darwin examines the many cultural influences that shaped the royal government of the Mughal emperor Akbar.

VOICE 4.1

Charles Parker on Emperor Kangxi of China and Louis XIV of France | 2010

For Europe's most powerful monarch [Louis XIV], the Qing dynasty under Kangxi emperor (r. 1661–1722) represented an ideal political order. The emperor wielded absolute power and enjoyed divine blessing; he employed an army of civil servants to govern his dominions; he possessed authority over a vast domain stretching from the eastern coastline to Outer Mongolia and Tibet; and he resided in a magnificent palace that exuded majestic order and power. In many respects Louis's reign (1643–1715) also embodied these characteristics, though on a less grand scale. Casting himself in the image of Apollo (the Greek god of light and sun), Louis promoted himself as the Sun King and he professed to rule by divine right; he dominated Europe and pushed France's borders to the farthest point; and he too presided over an elaborate court life at Versailles that reflected his prestige and authority. The

legacy as "world conquerors." Mughal court ritual—especially Akbar's daily appearance on an elevated platform—emphasized the *padshah*'s [an elevated Persian royal title referring to the monarch] supreme authority over even the greatest and wealthiest of his subjects. The court was the centre of lavish literary patronage. It promoted the study of the Muslim "rational sciences" and the writing of poetry, the main literary medium of the Islamic world. But Mughal court culture looked to Persian or Central Asian models for its art and literature. Persian was the language of intellectual life as well as of government. The life and landscape of Iran (not that of India) inspired the Mughal poets, who evoked a world far away "from the polluting influences of the subject peoples." . . . Akbar's regime was cosmopolitan and eclectic, a tribute to Central Asia's influence as a great cultural entrepôt. It is even possible that his abortive attempt to impose a more centralized government in the 1570s and '80s (which led to the great revolt of 1580–82) was remotely inspired by the Chinese system of meritocratic bureaucracy. . . . Famously, Akbar rejected the classic Islamic distinction between the Muslim faithful (the *umma*) and the unbelievers. He abolished the *jizya* (poll-tax on non-Muslims) in 1579, and flirted with propagating a new religious synthesis of Islam and Hinduism.

Source: John Darwin, *After Tamerlane: The Rise and Fall of Global Empires 1400–2000* (London: Bloomsbury, 2008), 85–86.

AP® WORKING WITH EVIDENCE

State Building in the Early Modern Era

Imperial states—Mughal India, the Ottoman Empire, France, the Inca Empire, and Ming dynasty China—were invariably headed by kings or emperors who were the ultimate political authority in their lands. Those rulers sought to govern societies divided by religion, region, ethnicity, or class. During the three centuries between 1450 and 1750, all of these states, and a number of nonimperial states as well, moved toward greater political integration through more assertive monarchs and more effective central bureaucracies, which curtailed, though never eliminated, entrenched local interests. The growth of empire accompanied this process of political integration, and perhaps helped cause it. The documents that follow allow us to catch a glimpse of this state-building effort in several distinct settings.

LOOKING AHEAD As you read through the documents in this collection, consider **AP® DBQ PRACTICE** what actions rulers take, or intentionally do not take, to increase their control over the territories they rule.

DOCUMENT 1 An Outsider's View of the Inca Empire

Pedro de Cieza de León (1520–1554), a Spanish chronicler of the Inca Empire of the early sixteenth century, took part as a soldier in a number of expeditions that established Spanish rule in various parts of South America. Along the way, he collected a great deal of information, especially about the Inca Empire, which he began to publish on his return to Spain in 1550. Despite a very limited education, Cieza wrote a series of works that have become a major source for historians about the workings of the Inca Empire and about the Spanish conquest of that land. The selection that follows focuses on the techniques that the Incas used to govern their huge empire.

Source: Spanish conquistador Pedro de Cieza de León on Incan rulers, from *Chronicles of the Incas*, ca. 1550.

One of the things most to be envied in these rulers is how well they knew to conquer such vast lands. . . .

[T]hey entered many lands without war, and the soldiers who accompanied the Inca were ordered to do no damage or harm, robbery or violence. If there was a shortage of food in the province, he ordered supplies brought in from other regions so that those newly won to his

xxxi

Practice for the AP® Exam at the end of each chapter, the end of each period, and the end of the book

CHAPTER 6 AP® EXAM PRACTICE

Multiple-Choice Questions Choose the correct answer for each question.

Questions 1–3 refer to this map.

The Global Silver Trade

1. Which of the following was a significant change in long-distance trade networks in the era ca. 1450–ca. 1750?
   a. Trade networks expanded to cover the globe for the first time.
   b. The Indian Ocean became the world's most significant trade network for the first time.
   c. The Silk Roads expanded to connect Asia and Europe for the first time.
   d. Overall commercial activity expanded for the first time.

Short-Answer Questions Read each question carefully and write a short response. Use complete sentences.

1. **Use this passage and your knowledge of world history to answer all parts of the question that follows.**

   All of the residents of these United Provinces shall be allowed to participate in this Company and to do so with as little or as great an amount of money as they choose. Should it occur that there are more moneys offered than are needed for the voyage, those who have more than 30,000 guilders in the Company will have to decrease their capital pro rata in order to make place for others....
   As soon as 5% of a return cargo has been cashed shall it be distributed to the participants.

   — Charter of the Dutch East India Company, granted by the States General of the United Netherlands, 1602

> Test yourself at the end of each chapter with **AP®-style Multiple-Choice Questions** and **Short-Answer Questions**.

> Test yourself at the end of each period with an **AP®-style Document-Based Question** and **Long Essay Questions**.

PERIOD 2 AP® Exam Practice

Document-Based Question Using these sources and your knowledge of world history, develop an argument in response to the prompt.

1. Evaluate the extent to which rulers of the early modern era differed in their methods of establishing authority.

Document 1

Source: Letter from Ogier Ghiselin de Busbecq, Flemish nobleman and Austrian ambassador to the Ottoman Empire. Austria was under threat of an Ottoman invasion, 1555–1562.

The Sultan's hall was crowded with people, among whom were several officers of high rank. Besides these there were all the troopers of the Imperial guard and a large force of Janissaries; but there was not in all that great assembly a single man who owed his position to aught save his valor and his merit. No distinction is attached to birth among the Turks.... In making his appointments the Sultan pays no regard to any pretensions on the score of wealth or rank, nor does he take into consideration recommendations or popularity.... It is by merit that men rise in the service, a system which ensures that posts should only be assigned to the competent.

Long Essay Questions Using your knowledge of world history, develop an argument in response to one of the following questions.

2. In the period 1450–1750, transoceanic voyages connected the Eastern and Western hemispheres and had a significant economic, cultural, social, and demographic impact on the world.

   Develop an argument that evaluates how one or more societies were affected by the new global connections created through trade in this time period.

3. In the period 1450–1750, agriculture, labor systems, and social structures changed as new states and empires developed around the world.

   Develop an argument that evaluates how labor and/or social systems were transformed in this time period.

> Bring your knowledge and skills together to test your readiness for the exam with the **full-length AP® Practice Exam** at the end of the book.

AP® Practice Exam

Multiple-Choice Questions

Questions 1–2 refer to this map.

Read, study, and practice with our robust digital platform, which includes all the resources you need in one convenient place

The **interactive e-book** allows you to read, highlight, and take notes on any device, online or offline.

Test your knowledge with **online quizzing** and activities. Your results will automatically sync to your teacher's gradebook.

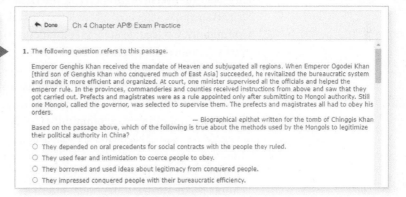

Explore alternate primary and secondary source sets for each chapter with **Thinking Through Sources**, the companion reader to *Ways of the World*. This collection of sources is also available in the digital platform for the main title.

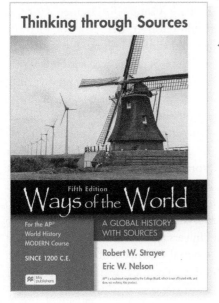

Acknowledgments

We are grateful to the community of fellow historians who contributed their expertise to this revision. We especially thank our colleagues Bryan Brinkman, Tonia E. Tinsley, and John F. Chuchiak IV for their translations for our primary source features. We also thank the following reviewers of this edition: Dorian Borbonus, University of Dayton; Matthew Conn, Eastern Michigan University; Adrianna L. Ernstberger, Marian University; Andrei Gandila, University of Alabama at Huntsville; MayaLisa Holzman, Oregon State University; Toby Huff, Harvard University; Jeremy LaBuff, Northern Arizona University; Susan Maneck, Jackson State University; Dean Pavlakis, Carroll College; Charles V. Reed, Elizabeth City State University; Kimberly B. Sherman, Cape Fear Community College; Ira Spar, Ramapo College of New Jersey; Bianka Rhodes Stumpf, Central Carolina Community College; Jeanne M. Vloyanetes, Brookdale Community College; Erin Warford, Hilbert College; and Tara S. Wood, Ball State University.

We also offer our gratitude to reviewers of earlier editions: Andreas Agocs, University of the Pacific; Tonio Andrade, Emory University; Maria S. Arbelaez, University of Nebraska–Omaha; Monty Armstrong, Cerritos High School; Melanie Bailey, Piedmont Virginia Community College; Djene Bajalan, Missouri State University; Veronica L. Bale, Mira Costa College; Anthony Barbieri-Low, University of California, Santa Barbara; Christopher Bellitto, Kean University; Christine Bond, Edmond Memorial High School; Monica Bord-Lamberty, Northwood High School; Mike Burns, Concordia International School, Hanoi; Stanley Burstein, California State University–Los Angeles; Elizabeth Campbell, Daemen College; Theodore Cohen, Lindenwood University; Ralph Croizier, University of Victoria; Gregory Cushman, the University of Kansas; Edward Dandrow, University of Central Florida; Bradley Davis, Eastern Connecticut State University; Peter L. de Rosa, Bridgewater State University; Carter Findley, Ohio State University; Amy Forss, Metropolitan Community College; Denis Gainty, Georgia State University; Duane Galloway, Rowan-Cabarrus Community College; Steven A. Glazer, Graceland University; Sue Gronewald, Kean University; Andrew Hamilton, Viterbo University; J. Laurence Hare, University of Arkansas; Jay Harmon, Houston Christian High School; Michael Hinckley, Northern Kentucky University; Bram Hubbell, Friends Seminary; Ronald Huch, Eastern Kentucky University; Michael Hunt, University of North Carolina at Chapel Hill; Elizabeth Hyde, Kean University; Mark Lentz, University of Louisiana–Lafayette; Ane Lintvedt, McDonogh School; Aran MacKinnon, Georgia College and State University; Harold Marcuse, University of California, Santa Barbara; Kate McGrath, Central Connecticut State University; Merritt McKinney, Volunteer State Community College; C. Brid Nicholson, Kean

University; Erin O'Donnell, East Stroudsburg University; Sarah Panzer, Missouri State University; Donna Patch, Westside High School; Charmayne Patterson, Clark Atlanta University; Dean Pavlakis, Carroll College; Chris Peek, Bellaire High School; Tracie Provost, Middle Georgia State University; Masako Racel, Kennesaw State University; Jonathan T. Reynolds, Northern Kentucky University; James Sabathne, Hononegah High School; Christopher Sleeper, Mira Costa College; Ira Spar, Ramapo College and Metropolitan Museum of Art; Kristen Strobel, Lexington High School; Eddie Supratman, Arkansas State University–Beebe; Michael Vann, Sacramento State University; Peter Winn, Tufts University; and Judith Zinsser, Miami University of Ohio.

Prologue

From Cosmic History to Human History

History books in general, and world history textbooks in particular, have something in common with those Russian nested dolls in which a series of carved figures fit inside one another. In much the same fashion, all historical accounts take place within some larger context, as stories within stories unfold. Individual biographies and histories of local communities, particularly modern ones, occur within the context of one nation or another. Nations often find a place in some more encompassing civilization, such as the Islamic world or the West, or in a regional or continental context such as Southeast Asia, Latin America, or Africa. And those civilizational or regional histories in turn take on richer meaning when they are understood within the even broader story of world history, which embraces humankind as a whole.

In recent decades, some world historians have begun to situate that remarkable story of the human journey in the much larger framework of both cosmic and planetary history, an approach that has come to be called "big history." It is really the "history of everything" from the big bang to the present, and it extends over the enormous, almost unimaginable timescale of some 13.8 billion years, the current rough estimate of the age of the universe.[1]

The History of the Universe

To make this vast expanse of time even remotely comprehensible, some scholars have depicted the history of the cosmos as if it were a single calendar year (see Snapshot). On that cosmic calendar, most of the action took place in the first few milliseconds of January 1. As astronomers, physicists, and chemists tell it, the universe that we know began in an eruption of inconceivable power and heat. Out of that explosion of creation emerged matter, energy, gravity, electromagnetism, and the "strong" and "weak" forces that govern the behavior of atomic nuclei. As gravity pulled the rapidly expanding cosmic gases into increasingly dense masses, stars formed, with the first ones lighting up around 600 million years after the big bang or toward the end of January on the cosmic calendar.

Hundreds of billions of stars followed, each with its own history, though following common patterns. They emerged, flourished for a time, and then collapsed and died. In their final stages, they sometimes generated supernovae, black holes, and pulsars—phenomena at least as fantastic as the most exotic of earlier creation stories. Within the stars, enormous nuclear reactions gave rise to the elements that are reflected in the periodic table known to all students of chemistry. Over eons, these stars came together in galaxies, such as our own Milky Way, which probably

SNAPSHOT The History of the Universe as a Cosmic Calendar

Big bang	January 1	13.8 billion years ago
Stars and galaxies begin to form	End of January	13.2? billion years ago
Milky Way galaxy forms	March / early April	10 billion years ago
Origin of the solar system and earth	September 9	4.5 billion years ago
Earliest life on earth	Late September	3.8 billion years ago
Oxygen forms on earth	December 1	1.3 billion years ago
First worms	December 16	658 million years ago
First fish, first vertebrates	December 19	534 million years ago
First reptiles, first trees	December 23	370 million years ago
Age of dinosaurs	December 24–28	66 to 240 million years ago
First human-like creatures	December 31 (late evening)	2.7 million years ago
First agriculture	December 31: 11:59:35	12,000 years ago
Birth of the Buddha / Greek civilization	December 31: 11:59:55	2,500 years ago
Birth of Jesus	December 31: 11:59:56	2,000 years ago

Information from Carl Sagan, *The Dragons of Eden* (New York: Random House, 1977), 13–17; David Christian, *Origin Story: A Big History of Everything* (New York: Little, Brown, 2018), 13–14.

emerged in March or early April, and in even larger structures called groups, clusters, and superclusters. Adding to the strangeness of our picture of the cosmos is the recent and controversial notion that perhaps 90 percent or more of the total mass of the universe is invisible to us, consisting of a mysterious and mathematically predicted substance known to scholars only as "dark matter."

The contemplation of cosmic history has prompted profound religious or philosophical questions about the meaning of human life. For some, it has engendered a sense of great insignificance in the face of cosmic vastness. In disputing the earth- and human-centered view of the cosmos, long held by the Catholic Church, the eighteenth-century French thinker Voltaire wrote: "This little globe, nothing more than a point, rolls in space like so many other globes; we are lost in this immensity."[2] Nonetheless, human consciousness and our awareness of the mystery of this immeasurable universe render us unique and generate for many people feelings of awe, gratitude, and humility that are almost religious. As tiny but knowing observers of this majestic cosmos, we have found ourselves living in a grander home than ever we knew before.

The History of a Planet

For most of us, one star, our own sun, is far more important than all the others, despite its quite ordinary standing among the billions of stars in the universe and its somewhat remote location on the outer edge of the Milky Way galaxy. Circling that star is a series of planets, formed of leftover materials from the sun's birth. One of those planets, the third from the sun and the fifth largest, is home to all of us. Human history—our history—takes place not only on the earth but also as part of the planet's history.

That history began with the emergence of the entire solar system, including the earth, about two-thirds of the way through the history of the universe, some 4.5 billion years ago, or early September on the cosmic calendar. Geologists have learned a great deal about the history of the earth: the formation of its rocks and atmosphere; the movement of its continents; the collision of the tectonic plates that make up its crust; and the constant changes of its landscape as mountains formed, volcanoes erupted, and erosion transformed the surface of the planet. All of this has been happening for more than 4 billion years and continues still.

The most remarkable feature of the earth's history—and so far as we know unrepeated elsewhere—was the emergence of life from the chemical soup of the early planet. It happened rather quickly, only about 700 million years after the earth itself took shape, or late September on the cosmic calendar. Then for some 3 billion years, life remained at the level of microscopic single-celled organisms. According to biologists, the many species of larger multicelled creatures—all of the flowers, shrubs, and trees as well as all of the animals of land, sea, and air—have evolved in an explosive proliferation of life-forms over the past 600 million years, or since mid-December on the cosmic calendar. The history of life on earth has, however, been periodically punctuated by massive die-offs, at least five of them, in which very large numbers of animal or plant species have perished. The most widespread of these "extinction events," known to scholars as the Permian mass extinction, occurred around 250 million years ago and eliminated some 90 percent of living species on the planet. That catastrophic diminution of life-forms on the earth has been associated with massive volcanic eruptions, the release of huge quantities of carbon dioxide and methane into the atmosphere, and a degree of global warming that came close to extinguishing all life on the planet. Much later, around 66 million years ago, another such extinction event decimated about 75 percent of plant and animal species, including what was left of the dinosaurs. Most scientists now believe that it was caused primarily by the impact of a huge asteroid that landed near the Yucatán Peninsula off the coast of southern Mexico, generating enormous earthquakes, tsunamis, fireballs, and a cloud of toxic dust and debris. Many scholars believe we are currently in the midst of a sixth extinction event, driven, like the others, by major climate change, but which, unlike the others, is the product of human actions.

So life on earth has been and remains both fragile and resilient. Within these conditions, every species has had a history as its members struggled to find resources, cope with changing environments, and deal with competitors. Egocentric creatures that we are, however, human beings have usually focused their history books and history courses entirely on a single species—our own, *Homo sapiens*, humankind. On the cosmic calendar, *Homo sapiens* is an upstart primate whose entire history occurred in the last few minutes of December 31. Almost all of what we normally study in history courses—agriculture, writing, civilizations, empires, industrialization—took place in the very last minute of that cosmic year. The entire history of the United States occurred in the last second.

Yet during that very brief time, humankind has had a career more remarkable and arguably more consequential for the planet than any other species. At the heart of human uniqueness lies our amazing capacity for accumulating knowledge and skills. Other animals learn, of course, but for the most part they learn the same things over and over again. Twenty-first-century chimpanzees in the wild master much the same set of skills as their ancestors did a million years ago. But the exceptional communication abilities provided by human language allow us to learn from one another, to express that learning in abstract symbols, and then to pass it on, cumulatively, to future generations. Thus we have moved from stone axes to lasers, from spears to nuclear weapons, from "talking drums" to the Internet, from grass huts to the pyramids of Egypt, the Taj Mahal of India, and the skyscrapers of modern cities.

This extraordinary ability has translated into a human impact on the earth that is unprecedented among all living species.[3] Human populations have multiplied far more extensively and have come to occupy a far greater range of environments than has any other large animal. Through our ingenious technologies, we have appropriated for ourselves, according to recent calculations, some 25 to 40 percent of the solar energy that enters the food chain. We have recently gained access to the stored solar energy of coal, gas, and oil, all of which have been many millions of years in the making, and we have the capacity to deplete these resources in a few hundred or a few thousand years. Other forms of life have felt the impact of human activity, as numerous extinct or threatened species testify. Human beings have even affected the atmosphere and the oceans as carbon dioxide and other emissions of the industrial age have warmed the climate of the planet in ways that broadly resemble the conditions that triggered earlier extinction events. Thus human history has been, and remains, of great significance, not for ourselves alone, but also for the earth itself and for the many other living creatures with which we share it.

The History of the Human Species . . . in a Single Paragraph

The history of our species has occurred during roughly the last 250,000–350,000 years, conventionally divided into three major phases, based on the kind of technology that was most widely practiced. The enormously long Paleolithic age, with its gathering and hunting way of life, accounts for 95 percent or more of the time that humans have occupied the planet. People utilizing a stone-age Paleolithic technology initially settled every major landmass on the earth and constructed the first human societies (see Chapter 1). Then beginning about 12,000 years ago with the first Agricultural Revolution, the domestication of plants and animals increasingly became the primary means of sustaining human life and societies. In giving rise to agricultural villages and chiefdoms, to pastoral communities depending on their herds of animals, and to state- and city-based civilizations, this agrarian way of life changed virtually everything and fundamentally reshaped human societies and their relationship to the natural order. Finally, around 1750 a quite sudden spurt in the rate of technological change, which we know as the Industrial Revolution, began to take hold. That vast increase in productivity, wealth, and human control over nature once again transformed almost every aspect of human life and gave rise to new kinds of societies that we call "modern."

Here then, in a single paragraph, is the history of humankind—the Paleolithic era, the agricultural era, and, most recently and briefly, the modern industrial era. Clearly this is a big-picture perspective, based on the notion that the human species as a whole has a history that transcends any of its particular and distinctive cultures. That perspective—known variously as planetary, global, or world history—has become increasingly prominent among those who study the past. Why should this be so?

Why World History?

Not long ago—in the mid-twentieth century, for example—virtually all college-level history courses were organized in terms of particular civilizations or nations. In the United States, courses such as Western Civilization or some version of American History served to introduce students to the study of the past. Since then, however, a set of profound changes has pushed much of the historical profession in a different direction.

The world wars of the twentieth century, revealing as they did the horrendous consequences of unchecked nationalism, persuaded some historians that a broader view of the past might contribute to a sense of global citizenship. Economic and cultural globalization has highlighted both the interdependence of the world's peoples and their very unequal positions within that world. Moreover, we are aware as never before that our problems—whether they involve economic well-being, global warming, disease, or terrorism—respect no national boundaries. To many thoughtful people, a global present seemed to call for a global past. Furthermore, as colonial empires shrank and new nations asserted themselves on the world stage, these peoples also insisted that their histories be accorded equivalent treatment with those of Europe and North America. An explosion of new knowledge about the histories of Asia, Africa, and pre-Columbian America erupted from the research of scholars around the world. All of this has generated a "world history movement," reflected in college and high school curricula, in numerous conferences and specialized studies, and in a proliferation of textbooks, of which this is one.

This world history movement has attempted to create a global understanding of the human past that highlights broad patterns cutting across particular civilizations and countries, while acknowledging in an inclusive fashion the distinctive histories of its many peoples. This is, to put it mildly, a tall order. How is it possible to encompass within a single book or course the separate stories of the world's various peoples? Surely it must be something more than just recounting the history of one civilization or culture after another. How can we distill a common history of humankind as a whole from the distinct trajectories of particular peoples? Because no world history book or course can cover everything, what criteria should we use for deciding what to include and what to leave out? Such questions have ensured no end of controversy among students, teachers, and scholars of world history, making it one of the most exciting fields of historical inquiry.

Context, Change, Comparison, and Connection: The Four Cs of World History

Despite much debate and argument, most scholars and teachers of world history would probably agree on four major emphases of this remarkable field of study. The first lies in the observation that in world history, nothing stands alone. Every event, every historical figure, every culture, society, or civilization gains significance from its inclusion in some larger framework. This means that **context** is central to world history and that contextual thinking is the essential skill that world history teaches. And so we ask the same question about every particular occurrence: where does it fit in the larger scheme of things?

A second common theme in world history involves **change** over time. Most often, it is the "big-picture" changes—those that affect large segments of humankind—that are of greatest interest. How did the transition from a gathering and hunting economy to one based on agriculture take place? How did cities, empires, and civilizations take shape in various parts of the world? What impact did the growing prominence of Europe have on the rest of the world in recent centuries? A focus on change provides an antidote to a persistent tendency of human thinking that historians call "essentialism." A more common term is "stereotyping." It refers to our inclination to define particular groups of people with an unchanging or essential set of characteristics. Women are nurturing; peasants are conservative; Americans are aggressive; Hindus are religious. Serious students of history soon become aware that every significant category of people contains endless variations and conflicts and that those human communities are constantly in flux. Peasants may often accept the status quo, except of course when they rebel, as they frequently have. Americans have experienced periods of isolationism and withdrawal from the world as well as times of aggressive engagement with it. Things change.

But some things persist, even if they also change. We should not allow an emphasis on change to blind us to the continuities of human experience. A recognizably Chinese state has operated for more than 2,000 years. Slavery and patriarchy persisted as human institutions for thousands of years until they were challenged in recent centuries, and in various forms they exist still. The teachings of Buddhism, Christianity, and Islam have endured for centuries, though with endless variations and transformations.

A third element that operates constantly in world history books and courses is that of **comparison**. Whatever else it may be, world history is a comparative discipline, seeking to identify similarities and differences in the experience of the world's peoples. What is the difference between the development of agriculture in the Middle East and in Mesoamerica? Was the experience of women largely the same in all patriarchal societies? Why did the Industrial Revolution and a modern way of life evolve first in Western Europe rather than somewhere else? What distinguished the

French, Russian, and Chinese revolutions from one another? Describing and, if possible, explaining such similarities and differences are among the major tasks of world history. Comparison has proven an effective tool in efforts to counteract Eurocentrism, the notion that Europeans or people of European descent have long been the primary movers and shakers of the historical process. That notion arose in recent centuries when Europeans were in fact the major source of innovation in the world and did for a time exercise something close to world domination. But comparative world history sets this recent European prominence in a global and historical context, helping us to sort out what was distinctive about the development of Europe and what similarities it bore to other major regions of the world. Puncturing the pretensions of Eurocentrism has been high on the agenda of world history.

A fourth emphasis within world history, and in this book, involves the interactions, encounters, and **connections** among different and often distant peoples. Focusing on cross-cultural connections — whether those of conflict or more peaceful exchange — represents an effort to counteract a habit of thinking about particular peoples, states, or cultures as self-contained or isolated communities. Despite the historical emergence of many separate and distinct societies, none of them developed alone. Each was embedded in a network of relationships with both near and more distant peoples.

Moreover, these cross-cultural connections did not begin with Columbus. The Chinese, for example, interacted continuously with the nomadic peoples on their northern border; generated technologies that diffused across all of Eurasia; transmitted elements of their culture to Japan, Korea, and Vietnam; and assimilated a foreign religious tradition, Buddhism, that had originated in India. Though clearly distinctive, China was not a self-contained or isolated civilization. Thus world history remains always alert to the networks, webs, and encounters in which particular civilizations or peoples were enmeshed.

Context, change, comparison, and connection — all of them operating on a global scale — represent various ways of bringing some coherence to the multiple and complex stories of world history. They will recur repeatedly in the pages that follow.

A final observation about this account of world history: *Ways of the World*, like all other world history textbooks, is radically unbalanced in terms of coverage. Chapter 1, for example, takes on some 95 percent of the human story, well over 200,000 years of our history. By contrast, the last century alone occupies four entire chapters. In fact, the four major sections of the book deal with progressively shorter time periods, in progressively greater detail. This imbalance owes much to the relative scarcity of information about earlier periods of our history. But it also reflects a certain "present-mindedness," for we look to history, always, to make sense of our current needs and circumstances. And in doing so, we often assume that more recent events have a greater significance for our own lives in the here and now than those that occurred in more distant times. Whether you agree with this assumption or not, you will have occasion to ponder it as you consider the many and various "ways of the world" that have emerged in the course of the human journey and as you contemplate their relevance for your own journey.

Ways of the World

A Brief Global History with Sources

FOR THE AP® WORLD HISTORY: MODERN COURSE

SINCE 1200 C.E.

Diversity and Interaction in the World of 1200–1450

THE BIG PICTURE

1200: Jumping into the Stream of World History

Like all storytellers, historians have to decide where to begin their accounts. Starting the AP® World History Modern course around 1200 raises important historical questions. What significance does 1200 have in the story of humankind as a whole? Clearly, it is different from, say, 1492, when the voyages of Columbus began an enduring interaction between the Eastern and Western hemispheres, a process that had a global impact. By contrast, no single event marks 1200 as a year of global significance. Nonetheless, the centuries between 1200 and 1450 mark important changes in many parts of the world. New and larger states or empires emerged in Asia (the Mongol Empire), in Africa (the Kingdom

2

TEACHING IDEA

Bell Ringer

You can use material in "The Big Picture" features to introduce and highlight the most important concepts in the chapters ahead. Point out to students that these essays summarize the "must know" events in AP® World History: Modern. Encourage students to keep a record of the events and trends found in "The Big Picture" to guide chapter reading and note taking.

TEACHING IDEA

Class Discussion

It could be interesting to discuss with students some of the historical questions that emerge when the starting point of this course is 1200. *You can find some suggestions for discussion on pages 2 and 3 and also bring in other ideas. These ideas should lead to a good discussion of chronology and periodization, both of which are important to the AP® World History: Modern course.*

of Mali), in the Americas (the Inca Empire), and in Europe and the Middle East (France and the Ottoman Empire). New or revived patterns of international commerce linked distant lands and peoples across oceans, deserts, and continents. Established cultural or religious traditions, Islam for example, were spreading to new regions and were being transformed in the process.

Other questions arise in defining this AP® course as "modern" world history. What distinguishes the "modern" era from all that preceded it? Some have linked it to the Industrial Revolution of the nineteenth century, while others have dated it to the creation of a linked Atlantic world following European colonization of the Americas and the transatlantic slave system. But some historians have found sprouts of modernity even earlier. Song dynasty China (960–1279), for example, witnessed substantial population increase, urbanization, and technological innovation, all of which have been widely regarded as features of "modern" life.

More practical questions confront students, teachers, and textbook writers alike: since history is a seamless flow of events and processes, how can we simply jump into this ongoing stream of the human story in 1200? Certainly, topics introduced in the 1200–1450 time period will need to refer back to prior threads of historical development. Thus the chapters of Period 1 will frequently provide some context or background from well before 1200.

In this version of *Ways of the World*, the three chapters of Period 1 deal with this starting point of 1200 in various ways. The first chapter identifies some of the major patterns of world history prior to 1200, such as the enormously long

Paleolithic era, the Agricultural Revolution, the emergence of those more complex societies that we call "civilizations," and the development of the world's larger religious or cultural traditions. Thus Chapter 1 corresponds to what some AP® World History teachers have called Unit Zero, providing a "big picture" perspective on the world before 1200. Then Chapter 2 examines the global tapestry of major civilizations across the world as they appeared during the centuries between 1200 and 1450. It also addresses the themes of Unit 1 of the AP® World History: Modern course. These two chapters highlight the theme of diversity, emphasizing the various kinds of human communities and traditions that had become established by 1450.

Chapter 3, aligned with Unit 2 of the AP® World History course, turns the historical spotlight on the interactions, encounters, and connections that linked the various peoples of the world, such as long-distance trade, empire and conquest, and the spread of religion, especially Islam.

FIRST REFLECTIONS

1. **Questioning Chronology** How do the authors propose to address the challenges of beginning their history of the world midstream in 1200 c.e.?

2. **Assessing Diversity** What major processes and patterns of world history produced the great diversity of human communities and traditions across the globe in 1450? What forces brought this global tapestry of societies into contact with one another?

3. **Thinking like a World Historian** What events or processes have historians identified as critical to the emergence of the "modern" era? What do you think separates the modern era from what came before?

PERIOD 1

BUILDING AP® SKILLS

Developments and Processes

The title for this course is "AP® World History: Modern." Ask students exactly what the term "modern" means to them. Then ask them what the term "modern" means to the study of history. Have them read the explanation for "modern" world history on this page and then ask why providing context would be important for the study of "modern" world history. *Answers will vary.*

TEACHING IDEA

Class Discussion

After having students read pages 2 and 3, consider breaking them into small groups to answer the "First Reflections" questions found on page 3. After the small groups have had time to discuss their answers, bring the conversation to the entire class and have the class discuss the questions. *Answers will vary.*

Contextualization

Have students look at "Landmarks in World History (Before 1450)" on pages 4 and 5. Then ask the following questions to help students explain the ways in which the historical events prior to 1450 can be organized into discrete, different, and definable historical periods.

■ What events began before the period started? *Answers will vary. Some examples include the Upanishads, emergence of Christianity, and the Maya civilization.*

■ What events continued after the period ended? *Answers will vary. Some examples include Melaka as a commercial center, African contact with the Portuguese, and the Aztec and Inca empires.*

■ Why might these events still be included in this time period? *These events are included in this time period because they followed the patterns of the time period or because their impact was felt in the time period.*

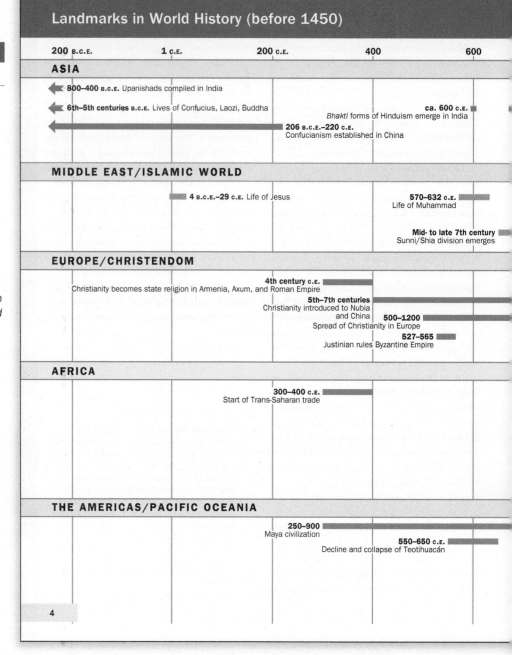

Landmarks in World History (before 1450)

200 B.C.E.	1 C.E.	200 C.E.	400	600

ASIA

800–400 B.C.E. Upanishads compiled in India

6th–5th centuries B.C.E. Lives of Confucius, Laozi, Buddha

ca. 600 C.E. *Bhakti* forms of Hinduism emerge in India

206 B.C.E.–220 C.E. Confucianism established in China

MIDDLE EAST/ISLAMIC WORLD

4 B.C.E.–29 C.E. Life of Jesus

570–632 C.E. Life of Muhammad

Mid- to late 7th century Sunni/Shia division emerges

EUROPE/CHRISTENDOM

4th century C.E. Christianity becomes state religion in Armenia, Axum, and Roman Empire

5th–7th centuries Christianity introduced to Nubia and China

500–1200 Spread of Christianity in Europe

527–565 Justinian rules Byzantine Empire

AFRICA

300–400 C.E. Start of Trans-Saharan trade

THE AMERICAS/PACIFIC OCEANIA

250–900 Maya civilization

550–650 C.E. Decline and collapse of Teotihuacán

4

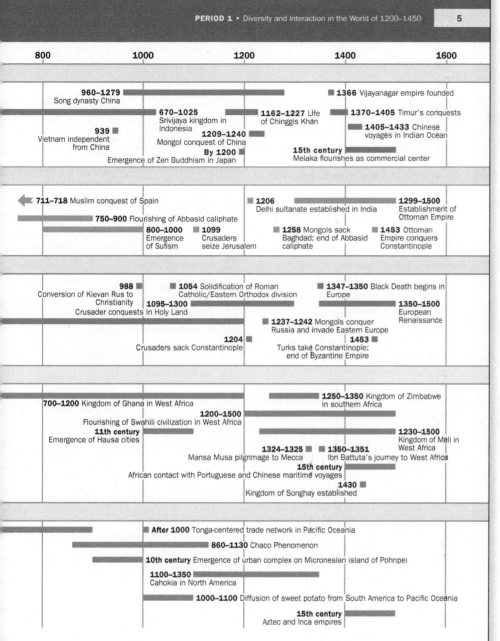

800	1000	1200	1400	1600

960–1279 Song dynasty China

1366 Vijayanagar empire founded

670–1025 Srivijaya kingdom in Indonesia

1162–1227 Life of Chinggis Khan

1370–1405 Timur's conquests

939 Vietnam independent from China

1209–1240 Mongol conquest of China

1405–1433 Chinese voyages in Indian Ocean

By 1200 Emergence of Zen Buddhism in Japan

15th century Melaka flourishes as commercial center

711–718 Muslim conquest of Spain

1206 Delhi sultanate established in India

1299–1500 Establishment of Ottoman Empire

750–900 Flourishing of Abbasid caliphate

800–1000 Emergence of Sufism

1099 Crusaders seize Jerusalem

1258 Mongols sack Baghdad; end of Abbasid caliphate

1453 Ottoman Empire conquers Constantinople

988 Conversion of Kievan Rus to Christianity

1054 Solidification of Roman Catholic/Eastern Orthodox division

1347–1350 Black Death begins in Europe

1095–1300 Crusader conquests in Holy Land

1350–1500 European Renaissance

1237–1242 Mongols conquer Russia and invade Eastern Europe

1204 Crusaders sack Constantinople

1453 Turks take Constantinople; end of Byzantine Empire

700–1200 Kingdom of Ghana in West Africa

1250–1350 Kingdom of Zimbabwe in southern Africa

1200–1500 Flourishing of Swahili civilization in West Africa

11th century Emergence of Hausa cities

1230–1500 Kingdom of Mali in West Africa

1324–1325 Mansa Musa pilgrimage to Mecca

1350–1351 Ibn Battuta's journey to West Africa

15th century African contact with Portuguese and Chinese maritime voyages

1430 Kingdom of Songhay established

After 1000 Tonga-centered trade network in Pacific Oceania

860–1130 Chaco Phenomenon

10th century Emergence of urban complex on Micronesian island of Pohnpei

1100–1350 Cahokia in North America

1000–1100 Diffusion of sweet potato from South America to Pacific Oceania

15th century Aztec and Inca empires

EXPLORING AP® THEMES

Cultural Developments and Interactions (CDI)

The spread of religions is a critical part of global history. To understand the extent of religious spread and the overlap of religions, you could show students the Business Insider video of an animated map of the spread of religion, which can be found on YouTube. As students watch the animated map, have them answer the following questions:

■ Which religion expanded first? *Hinduism expanded first.*

■ Which religion expanded most recently? *Islam expanded most recently.*

■ Which religion expanded the fastest? *Islam expanded the fastest.*

■ What interesting expansion fact did you notice about Buddhism? *Buddhism expanded throughout India, then moved to East Asia while it receded from India.*

■ What did you notice about Judaism? *It did not have much of a presence on the map for a time. When the state of Israel was created, it reappeared.*

■ What was most influential in the expansion of Christianity? *The Age of Exploration was most influential in the expansion of Christianity.*

■ How did the partition of Africa influence religion? *The partition of Africa by the Europeans helped to spread Christianity.*

■ Why do you think there is a pocket of Hinduism in the Suriname area of South America? *There was a South Asian diaspora as a result of the demand for sugar.*

Regional and Interregional Interactions

Period 1 encompasses the first major time period of the AP® World History Modern course (ca. 1200 C.E. to 1450 C.E.) as well as some earlier background and context for these several centuries. AP® World History students often struggle with how to make sense of all of the historical content of this course. Being able to organize historical information by theme will make it easier to understand difficult historical concepts and help you make connections across time periods and regions. There are six major themes you should focus on as you go through this course. Humans and the Environment looks at how humans shape the environment, but also how the environment has impacted humans and how humans have adapted to it. Cultural Developments and Interactions looks at various cultures around the world and, more importantly, how they impact one another (think about how religions like Islam or Buddhism spread across long-distance trade routes and interacted with local religions). Governance is about how states form and stay in power over time, keeping control with bureaucracies, taxation, or military power. Economic Systems is about more than just money; it is about how goods are produced and traded inside societies and among other societies; for example, it compares goods traded on the Silk Roads versus goods on the Indian Ocean. Social Interactions and Organization looks at how various peoples have organized their societies and the impact of those patterns on government and economic systems. Technology and Innovation focuses

on the tools humans use, such as the plow and horse saddle, and their wider outcomes. Use these six themes as lenses through which you can observe world history, but also pay attention to how the themes impact one another.

ENVIRONMENT	CULTURES
Pastoralism's impact on the environment	Continuing spread of Buddhism in Asia
Long-distance commerce, such as on the Silk Roads, creates exchanges of plants and animals	Monumental architecture in Maya region
	Rise of Islam
Environmental consequences of interactions between China and northern pastoralists	Christianity ■ Contraction in Asia and Africa ■ Expansion in Europe and Russia ■ Conflicts between Roman Catholic Church and Eastern Orthodoxy
Arab agricultural revolution	Islamic "golden age"
Environmental impact of dense Maya population, and resulting collapse	Buddhism persecuted in China
Feudal crop systems change environments in Europe	Growing prominence of Neo-Confucianism in East Asia
Deforestation in Europe and China accelerates as population grows	Hindu Angkor Wat complex built in Southeast Asia
Increased trade connections in Afro-Eurasia facilitate the spread of the Black Death across the region	Synthesis of faith and reason in European Christianity
	Crusades in Southwest Asia bring cultural exchanges
	Rise of Zen Buddhism in Japan
	Effects of cultural exchanges with Mongols
	Perceptions of Mongols in conquered regions
	Travels of Ibn Battuta and Marco Polo

ca. 1200–1450

6

GOVERNANCE	ECONOMIES	SOCIAL STRUCTURES	TECHNOLOGY
Development of Southeast Asian states and the Byzantine state	Silk Road trading networks continue	Gender roles in pastoral societies	Chinese *junks*, Indian/Arab *dhows* used in Indian Ocean trade
Rise and fragmentation of Islamic empires	Indian Ocean trading networks continue	Slavery in West African civilizations and the trans-Saharan slave trade	Chinese technological innovations: paper money, woodblock printing
Development of West African empires	Dar al-Islam's exchange networks continue	Patriarchal civilizations	Arab "agricultural revolution" introduces new crops to Central and Southwest Asia
State building in Korea, Vietnam, and Japan	Commercial networks in the Americas expand	Women's roles in Christianity	Muslim travelers introduce Chinese papermaking into the Middle East
Charlemagne's European empire	Trans-Saharan trading networks established	Continued caste system in South Asia	Introduction of three-field system of crop rotation and wheeled plow in Western Europe
Rise of Kievan Rus	Decline of European cities as trade centers after collapse of western Roman Empire	Social status of men and women in early Islam	Indian, Arab, Chinese technologies begin to arrive in Europe, including "Arabic" numbering system
Development of Malay Srivijaya kingdom	China's economic revolution	Continuity and change in gender roles in Song China	
Decline of Maya civilization	Urban and commercial growth in Europe	Beginning of foot binding as a sign of status in Song China	Mongols introduce gunpowder and printing along the Silk Roads
Peak of Abbasid caliphate	Swahili trading communities thrive	Feudalism reshapes social system in Europe	Beginnings of *chinampas* system in Mexico
Song dynasty in China	Crusades increase contacts between Europe and Southwest Asia/Middle East	Changing social roles in medieval European cities	Asian astrolabe, compass, and lateen sail influence European maritime technology
Flowering of Swahili city-states in East Africa		Black Death reorients societies across Afro-Eurasia	
European states sponsor Crusades to Southwest Asia	Mongol Empire as a Eurasian economic network		China sends Zheng He on voyages
Nomadic Jin rule northern China	Mansa Musa's pilgrimage to Mecca affects economies (1324–1325)		
The Mongol conquests: comparing China, Persia, and Russia	*Pochteca* merchants in the Americas		
Delhi sultanate in South Asia			
Post-Mongol Chinese, European, Islamic world			
Aztec and Inca empires rise and flourish			

EXPLORING AP® THEMES

Cultural Developments and Interactions (CDI)

Ask students to list some specific ways that cultures interacted during this period. *They interacted through trade and spread silk-making technology, food crops, crystallized sugar, numbers, cotton textile technology, corn, and diseases such as the Black Death.*

BUILDING AP® SKILLS

Developments and Processes

A good way to have students practice looking at the thematic "big picture" of each time period is to have them write a summary statement for each theme on what's happening during the time period. Ask students to look at the events for each theme and write a general statement about the patterns they see for the period. *(Suggested answers are provided in italics.)*

■ **Environment:** *Humans are interacting with the environment by learning how to adapt to variations and using the variations to their advantage.*

■ **Cultures:** *The spread of religion dominates the cultures theme, but other forms of cultural exchange also emerge.*

■ **Governance:** *The rise of new states prevails, as does the spread of state organizations to new places.*

■ **Economies:** *Large, multiregional trade networks dominate developments in economies.*

■ **Social Structures:** *The main patterns in social structures involve relationships between men and women, relationships between social classes, and relationships between pastoral and sedentary peoples.*

■ **Technology:** *Improved transportation technologies help increase trade on both land-based and maritime trade routes, while increased trade helps spread new technologies between societies.*

Before 1200: Patterns in World History

AP® Overview for Chapter 1

Chapter 1 corresponds to portions of Unit 1: The Global Tapestry that predate ca. 1200 C.E. While the AP® World History: Modern course begins officially in ca. 1200 C.E., it is important to contextualize what was happening in the world before 1200 C.E., particularly with regard to the major belief systems that shaped so much of world history.

This course is often a high school student's first exposure to college-level material and the deeper skills involved in historical inquiry. The material in this chapter works as a good introduction to some of the historical skills they will need to be successful in the course, along with easing them into the broader context of world history. Chapter 1 takes a brief look at the beginning of human societies, the Neolithic Revolution and its impacts, and the rise of complex civilizations and empires, before taking a deeper dive into the history of major religious and cultural traditions. The final sections on these cultural traditions are especially important with helping students "set the stage" for the ca. 1200 C.E. start of the course.

It is imperative that you move through Chapter 1 with some haste. Remember, the exam will not directly cover material from this chapter, but it is essential to helping students contextualize their study of global history.

Chapter 1 Essential Activity

To help students create a "big picture" view of a major topic of this chapter, ask students to create an annotated map of the emergence and spread of the major Eurasian religions and philosophies. Students should include the following elements on their annotated map:

- Label the origins of the major religions and philosophies on the map, along with their founding dates
- Show the spread of the religions and philosophies across Afro-Eurasia during the classical era
- List the basic doctrines and beliefs of the religions and philosophies next to their location on the map
- Create the following charts on the sides or the back of the annotated map: Contextualization for the beginning of the religion or philosophy, Impact of the religion or philosophy on political structures, Impact of the religion or philosophy on social structures

Differentiation

If you need to scaffold work with your classes, following a "Must Do, Should Do, Strive For" scaffold (adapted from the Modern Classrooms Project at modernclassrooms.org) can help students build the skills needed to be successful not only on the assignment but also in the larger AP® World History: Modern course.

- Must Do = the bare minimum of what students need to know to grasp the basics of the skill or topic

- Should Do = extend the skills or topics by connecting them to new information or connecting to another topic (like connecting different themes to one another)
- Strive For = students should be able to apply what they have learned to another skill (such as writing an SAQ or LEQ)

If you want to differentiate the Chapter 1 Essential Activity, follow the "Must Do, Should Do, Strive For" model below.

- Must Do: Students should know the origins of the belief systems (location and date), the basic doctrines of the belief systems, and where the belief systems spread throughout the world.

- Should Do: Students should be able to contextualize the belief systems and explain how belief systems impacted political structures and social structures in different societies.

- Strive For: Students should answer the following SAQ prompt.

  Answer all parts of the question that follows.
  A. Identify ONE way in which Hinduism and Buddhism were <u>different</u> in their beliefs.
  B. Explain ONE way in which Hinduism and Buddhism were <u>similar</u> in their beliefs.
  C. Explain ONE way in which the beliefs of Buddhism helped the philosophy spread out of South Asia.

  TRM Map 1A: Europe, Asia, and Africa

Chapter 1 Resources

The following resources can be found in the Resources section of the book's digital platform or by clicking on the linked TRM buttons in the Teacher's Edition e-book.

TRM AP® Skills Workshop Activity Handout: Developments and Processes

TRM Chapter 1 DBQ Activity Handout

TRM Chapter 1 Guided Reading

TRM Chapter 1 Lecture Presentation Slides

TRM Chapter 1 Outline

TRM Chapter 1 Suggested Responses to Questions

TRM Eric's Activity 1: Thinking about Chronology

TRM Handout 1.1: SIO Comparison Graphic Organizer for India and China

TRM Handout 1.2: OPTIC Chart for Caste in India

TRM Handout 1.3: Chart for Levels of Inequality in Confucian Relationships

TRM Handout 1.4: KWL Chart for Confucius

TRM Handout 1.5: Comparison Graphic Organizer for Daoism and Confucianism

TRM Handout 1.6: Comparison Graphic Organizer for Sunni and Shi'a Islam

TRM Map 1A: Europe, Asia, and Africa

TRM Map 1B: The World

Pacing Guide

Below is a pacing guide for the AP® World History: Modern course beginning in ca. 1200 C.E. This pacing guide is based on a schedule with 120 sessions of 50 minutes each before the AP® Exam. It is meant as a place to start. If you have a different number of sessions before the exam, you can modify the pacing to suit your needs.

Day	Pages Assigned	AP® Theme	Suggested Assignments	Coverage Notes
1	Read pages 9–26 to "Civilizations and Cultural Traditions"	ENV GOV SIO TEC	Teaching Idea: AP® Exam Strategies on page 11 Building AP® Skills: Claims and Evidence in Sources on page 13 Eric's Activity 1: Thinking about Chronology on page 16	The beginning of Chapter 1 can be a short introduction to world history prior to 1200 C.E. Students will need contextualization for what they will be learning in this course, and these pages can help quickly set the stage for them before they dive into world history in 1200 C.E.
2	Read pages 26–32 from "Civilizations and Cultural Traditions" to "Chinese Cultural Traditions: Confucianism"	CDI	Chapter 1 Essential Activity Building AP® Skills: Claims and Evidence in Sources on page 27 Teaching Idea: Incorporating Outside Resources on page 29	While learning about the origins of global belief systems are not explicitly mentioned in the new Course Framework, the College Board expects students to have this background knowledge as they begin Unit 1. Students need to learn about the different religions and ideologies from throughout world history to help them contextualize and understand later historical topics.
3	Read pages 32–35 from "Chinese Cultural Traditions: Confucianism" to "Middle Eastern Cultural Traditions: Judaism and Christianity"	CDI	Chapter 1 Essential Activity Building AP® Skills: Claims and Evidence in Sources on page 33 Building AP® Skills: Making Connections: Comparison on page 34	See above.
4	Read pages 35–46 from "Middle Eastern Cultural Traditions: Judaism and Christianity" through "Conclusions and Reflections"	CDI	Chapter 1 Essential Activity Apply the Tip activity on page 37 Building AP® Skills: Argumentation on page 40	See above.

Bell Ringer

The following activity should take no more than 5 to 10 minutes of your class period and can offer an effective and engaging way to begin your lessons.

As an introduction to the beginning of human history, ask students: What could cause early humans to migrate to new areas? *Answers may include: Need to find a new food source; searching for warmer climate; pushed out by aggressive groups; change in animal migration patterns.*

BUILDING AP® SKILLS

Claims and Evidence in Sources

Knowing how to analyze a painting or image is an important skill that will help students prepare for multiple-choice questions, stimulus-based SAQs, and the DBQ on the AP® Exam. Ask students to discuss the painting on page 8 with a partner. Make sure to draw their attention to the caption. As a class, compile a list of observations about the image. *Observations could include the variety of people, the different animals, and the celebratory atmosphere of what might appear to be a military expedition. The men seem to come from diverse ethnic backgrounds.*

Muslim Pilgrims on the Way to Mecca The most enduring legacies of ancient civilizations lay in their religious or cultural traditions. Islam is among the most recent of those traditions. The pilgrimage to Mecca, known as the *hajj*, has long been a central religious ritual in the Muslim world. It also reflects the cosmopolitan character of Islam, as pilgrims from all over the vast Islamic realm assemble in the city where the faith was born. This painting, dating to 1237, shows a group of joyful pilgrims, led by a band, on their way to Mecca. (Bibliothèque Nationale de France, Paris, France/© BnF, Dist. RMN–Grand Palais/Art Resource, NY)

8

Before 1200: Patterns in World History

◀ **AP**
**CLAIMS AND
EVIDENCE IN SOURCES**
What clues does this image provide
about the Islamic practice of
pilgrimage?

**CONNECTING
PAST AND
PRESENT**

In September of 2009, Kong Dejun returned to China
from her home in Great Britain. The occasion was a birthday celebration for her ancient ancestor Kong Fuzi, or
Confucius, born 2,560 years earlier. Together with some
10,000 other people—descendants, scholars, government officials, and foreign representatives—Kong Dejun attended ceremonies at the Confucian Temple in Qufu, the hometown of China's famous sage. "I was touched to see my
ancestor being revered by people from different countries and nations," she
said.[1] What made this celebration remarkable was that it took place in a country still ruled by the Communist Party, which had long devoted enormous efforts
to discrediting Confucius and his teachings. In the communist outlook, Confucianism was associated with class inequality, patriarchy, feudalism, superstition, and all things old and backward. But the country's ancient teacher and
philosopher had apparently outlasted modern communism. Since the 1990s
the Communist Party has claimed Confucius as a national treasure and has
established over 300 Confucian Institutes to study his writings. He appears
in TV shows and movies, and many anxious parents offer prayers at Confucian
temples when their children are taking the national college entrance exams.
Buddhism and Daoism (DOW-i'zm) have also experienced something of a revival
in China, as thousands of temples, destroyed during the heyday of communism,
have been repaired and reopened. Christianity too has grown rapidly in China
since the 1970s. ■

H ere are reminders, in a Chinese context, of the continuing appeal
of cultural traditions forged long ago. Those ancient traditions and
the civilizations in which they were born provide a link between
the world of 1200–1450 and all that came before it. This chapter seeks to
ease us into the stream of world history after 1200 by looking briefly at
several major turning points in the human story that preceded 1200. These

9

TRM **Chapter 1 Guided Reading**
You can find a guided reading handout
for this chapter in the Teacher's Resource
Materials.

TRM **Chapter 1 Lecture Slides**
You can find curated lecture slides for this
chapter in the Teacher's Resource Materials.

TRM **Chapter 1 Outline**
You can find a chapter outline to model good
note-taking for this chapter in the Teacher's
Resource Materials.

TRM **Suggested Responses to Questions**
You can find suggested responses to all of
the AP® margin questions in this chapter in
the Teacher's Resource Materials.

EXPLORING AP® THEMES

Humans and the Environment (ENV)

Students can struggle with basic geography
(being able to locate and label countries,
identify major geographic features, etc.)
when they begin the AP® World History:
Modern course. This problem can lead to
future struggles on multiple-choice questions
and essays. Before you dive into the content
of the course (either the first or second day
of the year), have students go through a
quick geography review session. You can do
this by either providing students with a list of
locations to identify on **Map 1B: The World**
or by turning it into a bit of competition by
having them label as much information as
they can on the map from memory.

TRM **Map 1B: The World**

include the transition to agriculture, the rise of distinctive societies called civilizations, the making of the major cultural or religious traditions that accompanied those civilizations, and the broad patterns of interaction among the peoples of the ancient world.

From the Paleolithic Era to the Age of Agriculture

| **Finding the Main Point:** In what ways did the Agricultural Revolution transform human life?

Homo sapiens, human beings essentially similar to ourselves, first emerged around 350,000 to 260,000 years ago, most likely in the highlands of East Africa. Then, somewhere between 100,000 and 60,000 years ago, our species began a remarkable migration out of Africa that, over tens of thousands of years, led to the "peopling" of almost every inhabitable landmass on the planet. While critical to the success of humankind, from the viewpoint of the many species of plants and animals that were affected, it was a process of violent colonization. The last phase of that epic journey came to an end around 1200 C.E., when the first humans occupied what is now New Zealand. By then, every major landmass, except Antarctica, had acquired a human presence.

With the exception of those who settled the islands of Pacific Oceania, all of this grand process had been undertaken by people practicing a gathering and hunting way of life and assisted only by stone tools. Thus human history begins with what scholars call the **Paleolithic era** or the Old Stone Age, which represents over 95 percent of the time that humans have occupied the planet (see Controversies: Debating the Timescales of History, page 12). During these many centuries and millennia, humankind sustained itself by foraging: gathering wild foods, scavenging dead animals, hunting live animals, and fishing.

AP
CAUSATION
In what ways did a gathering and hunting economy shape other aspects of Paleolithic societies?

In their long journeys across the earth, Paleolithic people created a multitude of separate and distinct societies, each with its own history, culture, language, identity, stories, and rituals. Some were small, nomadic, and egalitarian societies, organized as bands of perhaps twenty-five to fifty people in which all relationships were intensely personal and normally understood in terms of kinship. Others lived in permanent settlements with somewhat larger populations that generated clear differences of wealth and status among their people. A few of these gathering and hunting societies practiced slavery or constructed large-scale monuments. Cultural creativity was much in evidence, reflected in numerous technological innovations (bone needles, sickles, baskets, nets, and pottery, for example), in sophisticated oral traditions such as the Dreamtime stories of the Aboriginal peoples of Australia, and in remarkable cave paintings and sculptures found in many places around the world.

What followed was the most fundamental transformation in all of human history, the transition to an agricultural economy. Between 10,000 and 2000 B.C.E. (12,000 to 4,000 years ago), this momentous process unfolded separately in fifteen to twenty

Cultural Landmarks before 1200

| 600 B.C.E. | 300 B.C.E. | 1 C.E. | 300 C.E. | 600 C.E. | 900 C.E. | 1200 C.E. | 1500 C.E. |

THE EAST ASIAN WORLD: CONFUCIANISM AND DAOISM

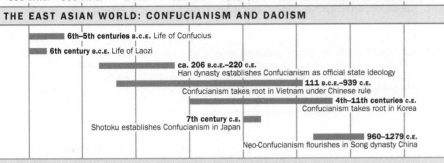

6th–5th centuries B.C.E. Life of Confucius

6th century B.C.E. Life of Laozi

ca. 206 B.C.E.**–220** C.E. Han dynasty establishes Confucianism as official state ideology

111 B.C.E.**–939** C.E. Confucianism takes root in Vietnam under Chinese rule

4th–11th centuries C.E. Confucianism takes root in Korea

7th century C.E. Shotoku establishes Confucianism in Japan

960–1279 C.E. Neo-Confucianism flourishes in Song dynasty China

THE SOUTH ASIAN WORLD: HINDUISM AND BUDDHISM

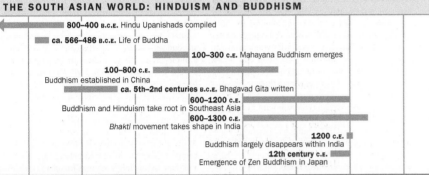

800–400 B.C.E. Hindu Upanishads compiled

ca. 566–486 B.C.E. Life of Buddha

100–300 C.E. Mahayana Buddhism emerges

100–800 C.E. Buddhism established in China

ca. 5th–2nd centuries B.C.E. Bhagavad Gita written

600–1200 C.E. Buddhism and Hinduism take root in Southeast Asia

600–1300 C.E. *Bhakti* movement takes shape in India

1200 C.E. Buddhism largely disappears within India

12th century C.E. Emergence of Zen Buddhism in Japan

THE MIDDLE EASTERN WORLD

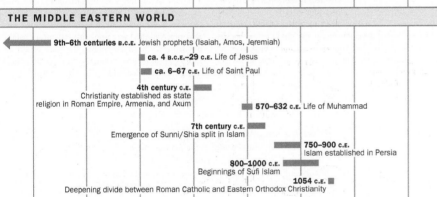

9th–6th centuries B.C.E. Jewish prophets (Isaiah, Amos, Jeremiah)

ca. 4 B.C.E.**–29** C.E. Life of Jesus

ca. 6–67 C.E. Life of Saint Paul

4th century C.E. Christianity established as state religion in Roman Empire, Armenia, and Axum

570–632 C.E. Life of Muhammad

7th century C.E. Emergence of Sunni/Shia split in Islam

750–900 C.E. Islam established in Persia

800–1000 C.E. Beginnings of Sufi Islam

1054 C.E. Deepening divide between Roman Catholic and Eastern Orthodox Christianity

11

TEACHING IDEA

Class Discussion

As you will be covering this topic early in the school year, having students have an actual debate over the idea of when history begins may be difficult; however, this activity can be a good start to getting students participating in class. Assign students "Debating the Timescales of History" found on pages 12–13. Divide your class into groups with no more than six students per group, and then split each group into two halves and assign each half one of the following opinions on the timescales of history.

■ History encompasses all societies on earth.

■ History only begins with writing.

Each side will research to find evidence that supports their assigned stance. Students should be able to get most of their evidence from this article and Chapter 1. Either have the students conduct research as homework or give them no more than 20 minutes of class time to research. Rather than having a large class debate, have the groups debate each other. Give each side 3 minutes to present their case and then 2 minutes for rebuttal and questions. Have students take notes on the opposing side's argument as they debate. After the debate is over, have the students discuss as a class the Questions to Consider found at the end of this activity on page 13. (Hint: If your class doesn't want to participate, consider pulling names out of a cup to get students to actively engage in this discussion.)

CONTROVERSIES Debating the Timescales of History

So when does history begin? And does it matter? If "history" refers to the story of humankind, professional historians until recently were largely in agreement that history began with writing, for as one book published in 1898 put it, "No documents, no history."[2] While humans clearly existed before writing—for hundreds of thousands of years, in fact—historians viewed their pasts as almost completely unrecoverable from the few physical remains that survived. They described these earlier peoples as prehistoric or "before history" and left their study to archeology and what was later called paleoanthropology. But writing emerged only about 5,500 years ago, and even then was limited to a few places. Furthermore, until the last several centuries writing was confined largely to elites, who wrote primarily about "the wars they fought, the literature they wrote, and the gods they worshipped."[3] Thus an understanding of the human journey based only on written records was massively skewed and incomplete.

From the mid-twentieth century onward, increasingly accurate and affordable scientific techniques—including radio-carbon dating, DNA testing, and advances in linguistics and archeology—allowed scholars to date artifacts and the movements of human populations that occurred tens or even hundreds of thousands of years ago. A much clearer understanding of early human history emerged as scholars were able to trace chronologically such crucial developments as the spread of our species across the planet and the dissemination of bronze-working technologies. The world before writing no longer seemed so unrecoverable, and many scholars—historians, archeologists, and others—broadened the definition of "history" to incorporate peoples of the distant past who had left no written record. While large gaps in our knowledge persisted, the new techniques opened up windows into the past that had been mostly shut before.

Even as historians debated the extent to which the "prehistory" of our species should or could be incorporated into historical accounts, a related question emerged about how—or whether—to locate all of human history within some greater context. Over the past several decades, some historians have begun to integrate the human story into the much larger frameworks of planetary and cosmic evolution, an approach that has come to be called "big history." Remarkable advances in the natural sciences—astronomy, geology, and evolutionary biology—suggest that the cosmos as a whole has a history, as do the stars, the solar system, the planets, including the earth, and life itself. They have a history because they have changed over time, for change is the fundamental feature of all historical accounts.

Such understandings have caused some to conclude that human history can be fully understood only if contextualized in the changing patterns of the cosmos. As the historian William McNeill has written, "Human beings, it appears, do indeed belong to the universe and share its unstable, evolving character . . . what happens among human beings and what happens among the stars looks to be part of a grand, evolving story."[4] Supporters of this view assert that big history "offers a powerful way of understanding the place of our own species, *Homo sapiens*, within the universe. By doing so it helps us to understand better what human history is all about."[5]

---

places spread across Asia, Africa, and the Americas alike. It meant the deliberate cultivation of particular plants as well as the taming and breeding of particular animals. Thus a new way of life gradually supplemented and eventually replaced the earlier practices of gathering and hunting in most parts of the world, so that by the early twenty-first century only minuscule groups of people followed that ancient way of living.

But the transition to agriculture took place over many centuries and millennia, hesitantly and experimentally, and in some places was temporarily reversed. Some gathering and hunting peoples deliberately rejected farming, even if they

But not all historians agree with this perspective. Some critics of "big history" argue that its almost unimaginable timescales, measured in billions or many millions of years, leave too little room for the human story, reducing it to insignificance. The types of problems or questions that have long occupied professional historians, such as the legacies of the Chinese warring states period or the Great Depression of the 1930s, are worthy of little more than a mention in big history timescales. Others complain that the careful reading and analysis of documents have been replaced by scientific forms of inquiry. Is "big history," they ask, really history at all?

Whatever one may think of these debates, big history represents the latest chapter in a remarkable rethinking of when world history begins. At the turn of the twentieth century few historians could conceive of history beginning more than 6,000 years ago, but by the early twenty-first century some began to argue that the human story finds its most appropriate place in a process that began over 13 billion years earlier.

Clearly the timescales of human history matter, because they shape the questions we ask and the techniques of inquiry that we employ. If we seek to understand the ups and downs of civilizations over the past five millennia, written records are essential. Without them, we would know little about the evolution of Buddhism, the rise and fall of empires, the Industrial Revolution, and much more. But if we want to know something of the process by which humans came to occupy almost every environmental niche on the earth, then written records are of little help, because almost all of that process took place long before writing was invented anywhere.

So we must rely on DNA analysis, carbon dating, and linguistics.

Finally, when historians turn to the cosmic or "big history" timescale, they are motivated by still other concerns. For David Christian, one of the leading practitioners of "big history," that grand scale of things offers a "creation myth" for our times, a coherent and scientifically informed explanation of the origins and evolution of our universe and the place of humankind within it.[6] For those more philosophically or spiritually inclined, the "big history" outlook raises profound questions about the relationship of human history to the larger narrative of cosmic and planetary evolution. Does the human experiment represent the story of just one more species thrown up by the ceaseless transformations of the web of life on this planet? Or is human consciousness distinctive, representing perhaps the cosmos becoming aware of itself? In these perspectives the human story is solidly anchored within the unfolding of the universe, the geological transformations of the planet, and the evolution of life on the earth.

QUESTIONS TO CONSIDER

1. How might your understanding of world history change if you subscribed to the idea that history began with writing, began with the emergence of our species, or began at the start of the universe?

2. In what specific ways have advancements in science affected how historians understand world history?

knew about it from their agricultural neighbors, preferring their freedom of movement over the necessary regimentation of growing crops. But in the long run of our history, agriculture triumphed, profoundly transforming human life all across the planet. Thus that process deserves to be called the **Agricultural Revolution**. It provided the foundation for much that followed: growing populations, settled farming villages, animal-borne diseases, an explosion of technological innovation, cities, states, empires, civilizations, writing, literature, and much more (see Snapshot: Continental Populations in World History, 400 B.C.E.–2017, page 14).

CHAPTER 1

BUILDING AP® SKILLS

Claims and Evidence in Sources

Analyzing arguments in secondary sources is one of the AP® Historical Thinking Skills. One of the specific skills is to identify and describe a claim and/or argument in a text-based source. Have students work in pairs to identify and describe the claims made in "Debating the Timescales of History." After students identify the claims, have them discover the evidence used in this source to support the claim. After about 15 minutes, bring the class back together and have students discuss the claims and evidence they found.

TEACHING IDEA

Class Discussion

Ask students what they think when they hear the word "revolution." Most students are going to mention rebellion, war for independence, civil war, and so on. This is a good opportunity to discuss how the term "revolution" can mean something completely different.

APPLY THE TIP

Partner students up and have them study the "Snapshot: Continental Populations in World History: 400 B.C.E.–2017" chart. While they study the chart, have them take notes on the demographic shifts they observe; they should think about population growth over time and shifts in demography due to migration. Then ask students: What accounts for the demographic shifts that occurred throughout world history? *Answers will vary, but may include: The Agricultural Revolution led to increased food supply, which led to population growth; Better technology and medicine in the twentieth century allowed more people to survive previously deadly diseases; There was significant population growth in the Americas after the European "discovery" of the continents.*

TEACHING IDEA

Incorporating Outside Resources

Understanding the Agricultural Revolution is important to understanding the development of the early river valley societies. Now would be a good time to show students *The Agricultural Revolution: Crash Course World History 1.* You can find the video on YouTube by searching for Crash Course World History. Either assign the video as homework or show it in class. Then ask students the following questions:

■ What are the advantages and disadvantages of agriculture (farming)? *Advantage: controllable food supply, grow food surplus, can be practiced all over the world; Disadvantage: changing environment of the planet, farming is hard.*

■ What are some of the theories for the occurrence of the Agricultural Revolution? *Population pressure may have necessitated it; People had the leisure to experiment with domestication; Planting might have been a fertility rite; People needed to domesticate grains to produce more alcohol.*

■ What are some of the ways in which humans have had an impact on the environment? *Building dams, clearing forests, and drilling for oil.*

AP
CONTINUITY AND CHANGE
How does this chart show continuities and/or changes over time in the distribution of population across the world?

AP EXAM TIP
Be able to define and describe the processes of demographic change throughout world history.

AP
CAUSATION
How did the Agricultural Revolution make these new forms of human society possible?

SNAPSHOT Continental Populations in World History, 400 B.C.E.–2017

Human numbers matter! This chart shows population variations among the major continental landmasses and their changes over long periods of time. (Note: Population figures for such early times are merely estimates and are often controversial among scholars. Percentages do not always total 100 percent due to rounding.)

	Eurasia	Africa	North America	Central/ South America	Australia/ Oceania	Total World
Area (in square miles and as percentage of world total)						
	21,049,000 (41%)	11,608,000 (22%)	9,365,000 (18%)	6,880,000 (13%)	2,968,000 (6%)	51,870,000
Population (in millions and as percentage of world total)						
400 B.C.E.	127 (83%)	17 (11%)	1 (0.7%)	7 (5%)	1 (0.7%)	153
10 C.E.	213 (85%)	26 (10%)	2 (0.8%)	10 (4%)	1 (0.4%)	252
200 C.E.	215 (84%)	30 (12%)	2 (0.8%)	9 (4%)	1 (0.4%)	257
600 C.E.	167 (80%)	24 (12%)	2 (1%)	14 (7%)	1 (0.5%)	208
1000 C.E.	195 (77%)	39 (15%)	2 (0.8%)	16 (6%)	1 (0.4%)	253
1500	329 (69%)	113 (24%)	4.5 (0.9%)	53 (11%)	3 (0.6%)	477
1750	646 (83%)	104 (13%)	3 (0.4%)	15 (1.9%)	3 (0.4%)	771
2017	5,246 (69.5%)	1,256 (16.6%)	361 (4.8%)	646 (8.6%)	40 (0.5%)	7,549

Source: Data for the population figures through 1750 are from Paul Adams et al., *Experiencing World History* (New York: New York University Press, 2000), 334; data for the 2017 figures are from "World Population by Region," Worldometers, http://www.worldometers.info/world-population/#region. Accessed December 8, 2017.

The resources generated by the Agricultural Revolution opened up vast new possibilities for the construction of human societies, but they led to no single or common outcome. Rather, various distinct kinds of societies emerged as agriculture took hold, all of which have endured into modern times.

In areas where farming was difficult or impossible—arctic tundra, certain grasslands, and deserts—some people came to depend far more extensively on their domesticated animals, such as sheep, goats, cattle, horses, camels, or reindeer. Those animals could turn grass or waste products into meat, fiber, hides, and milk; they were useful for transport and warfare; and they could walk to market. People who depended on such animals—known as herders, nomads, or **pastoral societies**—emerged most prominently in Central Asia, the Arabian Peninsula, the Sahara, and parts of eastern and southern Africa. What they had in common was mobility, for they moved seasonally as they followed the changing patterns of the vegetation that their animals needed to eat. Except for a few small pockets of the Andes where domesticated llamas and alpacas made pastoral life possible, no such societies emerged in the Americas because most animals able to be domesticated simply did not exist in the Western Hemisphere.

The relationship between nomadic herders and their farming neighbors has been one of the enduring themes of Afro-Eurasian history. Frequently, it was a relationship of conflict, as pastoral peoples, unable to produce their own agricultural products, were attracted to the wealth and sophistication of agrarian societies and sought access to their richer grazing lands as well as their food crops and manufactured products. But not all was conflict between pastoral and farming peoples. The more peaceful exchange of technologies, ideas, products, and people between pastoral and agricultural societies also enriched and changed both sides. Much later, in the thirteenth century, this kind of relationship between pastoral and agricultural societies found a dramatic expression in the making of the Mongol Empire, described in Chapter 3.

Another kind of society to emerge from the Agricultural Revolution was that of permanently settled farming villages. Many such societies retained much of the social and gender equality of gathering and hunting communities, as they continued to live without kings, chiefs, bureaucrats, or aristocracies. Such village-based agricultural societies flourished well into the modern era in Eurasia, Africa, and the Americas, usually organizing themselves in terms of kinship groups or lineages, which incorporated large numbers of people well beyond the immediate or extended family. Some were linked into larger regional complexes through ties of culture and commerce. Given the frequent oppressiveness of organized political power in human history, agricultural village societies represent an intriguing alternative to the states, kingdoms, and empires so often highlighted in the historical record. They pioneered the human settlement of vast areas; adapted to a variety of environments; maintained a substantial degree of social and gender equality; created numerous cultural, artistic, and religious traditions; and interacted continuously with their neighbors.

In some places, agricultural village societies created inherited positions of power and privilege that introduced a more distinct element of inequality and political

Contemporary Gathering and Hunting Peoples: The San of Southern Africa A very small number of gathering and hunting peoples have maintained their ancient way of life into the twenty-first century. Here two young men from the Jul'hoan !Kung San of southern Africa set a trap for small animals in 2009. (robertharding/Alamy)

▲ **AP**
CLAIMS AND EVIDENCE IN SOURCES
How does this image provide evidence for the gender roles that might have existed in Paleolithic societies?

AP
COMPARISON
What kinds of relationships developed between pastoral and agricultural peoples?

AP
COMPARISON
How did the various kinds of societies that emerged out of the Agricultural Revolution differ from one another?

TEACHING IDEA

Class Discussion

Chiefdoms were an alternate form of agricultural society. Ask students the following questions:

■ What are the characteristics of chiefdoms? *Chiefdoms had inherited positions of power, often claiming a legendary ancestor; The leader often had religious and political power.*

■ How did chiefdoms differ from agricultural village societies? *Chiefdoms were more unequal socially than agricultural village societies; They had a warrior class.*

■ What are some examples of chiefdom societies? *Traditional Pacific islander societies and eastern woodlands societies of North America.*

authority. Sometimes called chiefs or "big men," these leaders could seldom use force to compel the obedience of their subjects. Instead, they relied on their generosity or gift giving, their ritual status, or their personal charisma to persuade their followers. Such societies emerged in all parts of the world, with the earliest ones appearing in the Tigris-Euphrates river valley (present-day Iraq) sometime after 6000 B.C.E. More recent societies of this kind have been much studied by anthropologists. They flourished everywhere in the Pacific islands, which had been colonized by agricultural Polynesian peoples. There, "chiefs" usually derived from a senior lineage, tracing their descent to the first son of an imagined ancestor. With both religious and secular functions, they led important rituals and ceremonies, organized the community for warfare, directed its economic life, and sought to resolve internal conflicts. They collected tribute from commoners in the form of food, manufactured goods, and raw materials. These items in turn were redistributed to warriors, craftsmen, religious specialists, and other subordinates, while rulers kept enough to maintain their prestigious positions and imposing lifestyle. In North America as well, a remarkable series of partially agricultural societies emerged between 200 B.C.E. and 1200 C.E. in the eastern woodlands, where an extensive array of large earthen mounds testifies to their organizational capacity. Thus these various kinds of agricultural or pastoral societies existed alongside their gathering and hunting neighbors for many thousands of years.

AP®
CAUSATION
What was the historical impact or significance of the Agricultural Revolution?

Civilizations

Finding the Main Point: What is distinctive about civilizations compared to other forms of human society? How did particular civilizations differ from one another?

AP®
CONTEXTUALIZATION
What environmental factors could have helped or hindered the rise of civilizations?

Among the most significant outcomes of the Agricultural Revolution was yet another distinctive type of society that we know as civilization. The earliest civilizations emerged in Mesopotamia (what is now Iraq), in Egypt, and along the central coast of Peru between 3500 and 3000 B.C.E. At the time, these First Civilizations were small islands of innovation in a sea of people living in much older ways. But over the next 4,000 years, this way of living spread globally, taking hold all across the planet—in India and China; in Western, Central, and Southeast Asia; in various parts of Europe; in the highlands of Ethiopia, along the East African coast, and in the West African interior; in Mesoamerica; and in the Andes Mountains. Over many centuries, particular civilizations rose, expanded, changed, and sometimes collapsed and disappeared. But as a style of human life, civilization persisted and became a global phenomenon. By 1200, a considerable majority of humankind lived in one or another of these civilizations (see Map 1.1).

AP®
CONTEXTUALIZATION
What was the role of cities in the early civilizations?

What these civilizations shared was the size and concentration of their populations. Their largest settlements, which we know as cities, numbered initially in the tens of thousands of people and later the hundreds of thousands. As historians normally use the term, "civilization" refers to societies based in cities, even though

ERIC'S ACTIVITY **1** Thinking about Chronology

Skill: Making Connections

Many of my students find the scale and scope of world history daunting and need to reconsider their own preconceptions about how history is organized before they can engage with more global perspectives. I like to challenge their preconceptions of how history is organized and the role of chronology in the study of history by asking students to explore how this chapter on the emergence of First Civilizations is organized and to then identify how their perspective might change if the material were organized differently. A handout for this activity is available in the Teacher's Resource Materials.

TRM Eric's Activity 1: Thinking about Chronology

most people in those civilizations remained in the rural areas. Such cities served as political and administrative capitals; they functioned as cultural hubs, generating works of art, architecture, literature, ritual, and ceremony; they acted as marketplaces for both local and long-distance trade; and they housed major manufacturing enterprises. In the ancient Mesopotamian poem called the *Epic of Gilgamesh*, dating to about 2000 B.C.E., cities were places where the hustle and bustle of urban life meant that "even the great gods are kept from sleeping at night."[7]

Civilizations were the outcome of a highly productive agricultural economy, which could support substantial numbers of people who did not produce their own food. Thus an altogether new degree of occupational specialization emerged as scholars, merchants, priests, officials, scribes, soldiers, servants, entertainers, and artisans of all kinds appeared. All of these people were supported by the work of peasant farmers and herders, who represented the overwhelming majority of the population in all civilizations. Civilizations also generated impressive artistic, scientific, and technological innovations. Chinese civilization, for example, virtually invented bureaucracy and pioneered silk production, papermaking, printing, and gunpowder. Islamic civilization generated major advances in mathematics, medicine, astronomy, metallurgy, water management, and more. Later European movements, particularly the Scientific and Industrial Revolutions (1600–1900 C.E.), likewise reflected this innovative capacity of civilizations. And civilizations everywhere generated remarkable works of art and architecture that continue to awe and inspire us to this day. In addition, the written literatures of civilizations—poetry, stories, history, philosophy, sacred texts—have expressed distinctive outlooks on the world.

A Mesopotamian Ziggurat Among the features of civilizations were monumental architectural structures. This massive ziggurat or temple to the Mesopotamian moon god Nanna was built around 2100 B.C.E. in the city of Ur. The solitary figure standing atop the staircase illustrates the size of this huge building. (© Richard Ashworth/Robert Harding)

▲ **AP**

CONTEXTUALIZATION
How could monumental architecture reinforce a government's legitimacy?

AP EXAM TIP

Societies' expectations for gender roles are an important theme throughout the course.

Civilizations and the Environment

Like all human communities, civilizations have been shaped by the environments in which they developed. It is no accident that many of the early civilizations, such as Mesopotamia, Egypt, Peru, India, and China, grew up in river valleys that offered rich possibilities for productive agriculture. The mountainous terrain of Greece favored the development of rival city-states rather than a single unified empire. The narrow bottleneck of Panama, largely covered by dense rain forests, inhibited contact between the civilizations of Mesoamerica and those of the Andes. And oceans long separated the Afro-Eurasian world from that of the Western Hemisphere.

AP EXAM TIP

The relationship between humans and the environment is a key theme throughout the course.

BUILDING AP® SKILLS

Making Connections: Continuity and Change

Ask students the following questions:

■ In what ways did cities mark a significant departure from the agricultural villages where many sedentary people lived? *Answers should include the scale of the cities, the existence of monumental architecture, the large walls protecting the cities, and the level of noise.*

■ In what ways did cities and city-dwellers continue patterns of living established earlier in villages? *Like villages, cities depended on agricultural workers to provide the food necessary to sustain the population.*

TEACHING IDEA

Class Discussion

Many of the early civilizations had huge monumental architecture. Ask students how building these structures could solidify the legitimacy of a ruler and the government. *Answers will vary but should include that the structures required planning and a strong centralized bureaucracy to build and also showed the power of the ruler to all subjects.*

You can also extend the discussion by asking students what other evidence could be used to show the legitimacy of a ruler and the government. *Answers will vary but should include legal codes like Hammurabi's code.*

Another extension is to use several laws from Hammurabi's code to show students how legal codes could help control social classes and reinforce gender roles. Completing a Google search should give you several examples of Hammurabi's code to use for this activity extension. You can also use the excerpt from SAQ 2 on page 67.

BUILDING AP® SKILLS

Making Connections: Comparison

Display Map 1.1 for students. Use Map 1.1 to begin practicing the AP® Reasoning Process of Comparison by asking students the following question: Why do you think there are fewer civilizations in the Americas than there are in Afro-Eurasia? *Answers may include: There were more rivers located in temperate zones in Afro-Eurasia, which allowed for the establishment of more farming communities; Isolation of the Americas from other groups due to geography (mountains, deserts, oceans) limited the exchange of technology that helped the growth of civilizations; Access to more large domesticated animals helped the growth of Afro-Eurasian civilizations.*

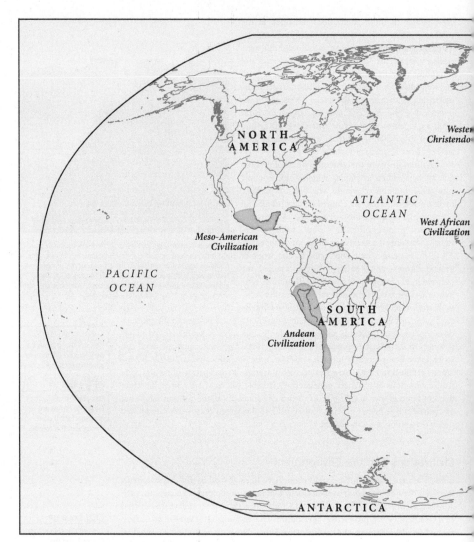

Map 1.1 Major World Civilizations, 500–1450
In the thousand years or so before 1450, growing numbers of people lived in civilizations, while many others continued to dwell in hunting and gathering societies, agricultural village communities, or pastoral societies. This map shows the location of the major civilizations of that era.

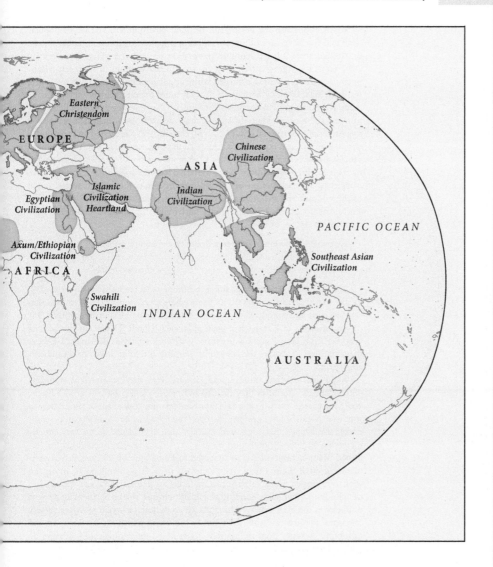

CHAPTER 1

EXPLORING AP® THEMES

Humans and the Environment (ENV)

Continue to display Map 1.1 for the class to see. Ask students: What explains the emergence and growth of these civilizations around the world? *Answers should include: Location near fertile lands and rivers and water sources enabled agriculture; Location along trade routes encouraged the growth of merchant societies; Civilizations expanded through migration or conquest.*

AP® Exam Strategies

Reading for historical information is an important test-taking skill for AP® World History: Modern because the multiple-choice questions are all stimulus-based. This activity can introduce students to reading and gathering information from what they read to answer questions.

Have students read the first three paragraphs on page 20 (either in small groups or on their own) and take notes on all of the examples of interactions between humans and the environment that appear in them. After students have finished, have them share the examples they found with the class. Possible examples:

■ Irrigation in southern Mesopotamia led to soil salinization and caused farmers to switch to growing barley.

■ Growth of civilizations led to deforestation and soil erosion, such as with the growth of China toward the Yangzi River valley and the expansion of civilizations in Europe.

■ The growth of farming led to drained swamps, deforestation, and terracing.

■ The pressure the Maya civilization placed on their surrounding environment contributed to the decline and possibly to the collapse of this civilization.

Then ask students: Why do you think the relationship between humans and the environment is such a major theme in world history? Answers will vary.

Incorporating Outside Resources

In the "Water and Classical Civilizations" episode of Crash Course World History 2, John Green discusses the importance of water and resources to classical civilizations such as the Maya in Central America and the Khmer civilization. The video can be found on YouTube. Either assign the video as homework or show it in class. Then ask students the following questions:

■ Why was access to water important to civilizations? It was necessary for the survival of the people living in the civilizations and to raise plants and animals; It also held religious significance for some civilizations, such as the Indus Valley civilization, and in dry regions, the access to and ability to control water were symbolic of wealth and power.

Civilizations also left an imprint on their environment. The larger populations and intensive agriculture of civilizations had a far more substantial impact on the landscape than Paleolithic, pastoral, or agricultural village societies. By 2000 B.C.E. the rigorous irrigation that supported farming in southern Mesopotamia generated soils that turned white as salt accumulated. As a result, wheat was largely replaced by barley, which is far more tolerant of salty conditions. In many places the growth of civilizations was accompanied by extensive deforestation and soil erosion. Plato declared that the area around Athens had become "a mere relic of the original country. . . . All the rich soil has melted away, leaving a country of skin and bone."[8] As Chinese civilization expanded southward toward the Yangzi River valley after 200 C.E., that movement of people, accompanied by their intensive agriculture, set in motion a vast environmental transformation marked by the destruction of the old-growth forests that once covered much of the country and the retreat of the elephants that had inhabited those lands. Around 800 C.E., the Chinese official and writer Liu Zongyuan lamented the devastation that followed:

> A tumbled confusion of lumber as flames on the hillside crackle
> Not even the last remaining shrubs are safeguarded from destruction
> Where once mountain torrents leapt—nothing but rutted gullies.[9]

Something similar was happening in Europe as its civilization was expanding in the several centuries after 1000. Everywhere trees were felled at tremendous rates to clear agricultural land and to use as fuel or building material. By 1300, the forest cover of Europe had been reduced to about 20 percent of the land area. Far from lamenting this situation, one German abbot declared: "I believe that the forest . . . covers the land to no purpose and hold this to be an unbearable harm."[10]

As agricultural civilizations spread, farmers everywhere stamped the landscape with a human imprint as they drained swamps, leveled forests, terraced hillsides, and constructed cities, roads, irrigation ditches, and canals. Maya civilization in southern Mexico, for example, has been described as an "almost totally engineered landscape" that supported a flourishing agriculture and a very rapidly increasing and dense population by 750 C.E.[11] But that very success also undermined Maya civilization and contributed to its collapse by 900 C.E. Rapid population growth pushed total Maya numbers to perhaps 5 million or more and soon outstripped available resources, resulting in deforestation and the erosion of hillsides. Under such conditions, climate change in the form of prolonged droughts in the 800s may well have placed an unbearable strain on Maya society. It was not the first case, and would not be the last, in which the demographic and economic pressures from civilizations undermined the ecological foundation on which those civilizations rested.

(continued)

■ Why was the Yucatán Peninsula not an "ideal" place for the Maya to build their civilization? The soils in the area are poor and the water table is too low to be able to dig wells to use; There also aren't a lot of rivers in the region and rainfall is seasonal, with downpours during an unpredictable wet season followed by a long dry season.

■ How were the Maya able to overcome the environmental and water challenges of their region to create a thriving civilization? In some city-states, they built reservoirs to provide water to the people who lived there; In others, they built cisterns to capture rainwater and canals to connect the reservoirs to the city; In the lowlands, cities built aqueducts and dams and drains to control flooding and manage the water supply.

Comparing Civilizations

While civilizations shared a number of common features, they were hardly carbon copies of one another. Some civilizations—Mesopotamian, Egyptian, Chinese, and Maya, for example—developed written languages and used them to record substantial bodies of literature; others, such as West African and the Andean civilizations in the Americas, did not. Furthermore, a number of early civilizations—in the Indus River valley in what is now Pakistan, along the Niger River in West Africa, and along the coast of Peru—show little sign of sharp class divisions, oppressive patriarchy, frequent warfare, or authoritarian state structures. Eventually, however, almost all civilizations came to embody these features. The ancient Hebrew prophet Samuel forewarned his people about what was coming if they chose the "way of the king":

> He will take your sons and make them serve with his chariots and horses. . . . He will take your daughters to be perfumers and cooks and bakers. He will take the best of your fields and vineyards and olive groves. . . . Your male and female servants and the best of your cattle and donkeys he will take for his own use. He will take a tenth of your flocks, and you yourselves will become his slaves.[12]

But even among those civilizations that followed the "way of the king," they differed sharply in how their societies were structured and stratified. Consider the difference between China and India. China gave the highest ranking to an elite bureaucracy of government officials, drawn largely from the landlord class and selected by their performance on a set of examinations. They were supported by a vast mass of peasant farmers who were required to pay taxes to the government and rent to their landlords. Although honored as the hardworking and productive backbone of the country by their social superiors, Chinese peasants were oppressed and exploited and periodically erupted in large-scale rebellions.

India's social organization shared certain broad features with that of China. In both civilizations, birth determined social status for most people; little social mobility was available for the vast majority; sharp distinctions and great inequalities characterized social life; and religious or cultural traditions defined these inequalities as natural, eternal, and ordained by the gods. But India's social system was distinctive. It gave priority to religious status and ritual purity, for the priestly caste known as Brahmins held the highest rank, whereas China elevated political officials to the most prominent of elite positions. The caste system divided Indian society into vast numbers of distinct social groups based on occupation and perceived ritual purity; China had fewer, but broader, categories of society—scholar-gentry, landlords, peasants, and merchants. Finally, India's caste society defined social groups far more rigidly than in China, forbidding members of different castes to marry or eat together. This meant even less opportunity for social mobility than in China, where

AP®

COMPARISON
In what respects did the political and social structures of various civilizations of the pre-1200 world differ from one another? What common features did they share?

TEACHING IDEA

Class Discussion

Even though the material in this chapter is not tested on the AP® World History: Modern Exam, it is still important for students to understand because it provides contextualization for the test material. Talk to students about what they think makes a civilization. Use the information on pages 16–21 to discuss what makes societies different from each other. *Answers will vary, but students should understand the difference between sedentary, pastoral, and nomadic societies.*

BUILDING AP® SKILLS

Making Connections: Comparison

Students should practice the skills of the AP® World History: Modern course on a continuous basis. Use this quick activity to have students better understand the AP® Theme of Social Interactions and Organization (understanding this theme is difficult because many students view SIO and CDI as identical). Ask the students to create a Venn diagram comparing the social structure of India with the social structure of China using the information on this page. When they finish, lead them in a discussion on what they found when creating their diagrams.

TRM Handout 1.1: SIO Comparison Graphic Organizer for India and China

Economic Systems (ECN) and Social Interactions and Organization (SIO)

For many students, the only exposure to slavery they have had is through their U.S. history classes. Students often don't realize that slavery is part of the Economic Systems (ECN) AP® Theme as well as the Social Interactions and Organizations (SIO) AP® Theme. To help students understand the development of slavery throughout human history, share the following information with them:

■ Slavery was already established in human societies before the emergence of civilizations, as there is evidence of slavery in hunting and gathering societies.

■ Enslaved people in early civilizations and classical civilizations were typically prisoners of war, criminals, or debtors and were mainly women.

■ In early civilizations, enslaved people were not commonly used for agricultural labor, but during the Roman Empire enslaved people worked on large plantations known as latifundias.

■ Enslaved people could hold a variety of jobs in these early and classical civilizations, including important jobs in government bureaucracies, though none in the military.

■ Enslaved people could be emancipated and were sometimes even allowed to purchase their own freedom.

■ Children born to an enslaved mother were not automatically considered enslaved persons in some societies.

After sharing the information, ask students: How was the practice of slavery in early civilizations different from the practice of slavery you've learned about in U.S. history? *Answers will vary, but may include: They were different because in early civilizations enslaved people were mainly women, while later in the United States they were predominantly men because of the hard labor demanded on plantations; They were different because in early civilizations enslaved people could gain or even buy their freedom; They were different because children born to enslaved mothers in some early civilizations were not automatically considered enslaved; Slavery was similar in the Roman Empire and the United States because enslaved people were used as laborers on large plantations.*

Caste in India This 1947 photograph from *Life* magazine illustrates the "purity and pollution" thinking that has long been central to the ideology of caste. It shows a high-caste landowner carefully dropping wages wrapped in a leaf into the outstretched hands of his low-caste workers. By avoiding direct physical contact with them, he escapes ritual pollution. (Margaret Bourke-White/Getty Images)

▲ AP®
CLAIMS AND EVIDENCE IN SOURCES
How does this image show the distinctions created between castes?

the examination system offered a route to social promotion to a few among the common people.

At the bottom of the social hierarchy in all civilizations were enslaved or owned people, often debtors or prisoners of war, with few if any rights in the larger society. But the extent of slavery varied considerably. Persian, Chinese, Indian, and West African civilizations certainly practiced slavery, but it was not central to their societies. In Greek and Roman civilizations, however, it was. The Athens of Socrates, Plato, and Aristotle was home to some 60,000 enslaved persons, about one-third of the total population. On an even larger scale, slavery was a defining element of Roman society. The Italian heartland of the Roman Empire contained some 2 to 3 million enslaved people, representing 33 to 40 percent of the population.

Patriarchy, or male dominance, was common to the social life of all civilizations, but it too varied from place to place and changed over time. (See Then and Now: Patriarchy, page 24.) Generally, patriarchies were less restrictive for women in the early years of a civilization's development and during times of upheaval, when established patterns of life were disrupted. Chinese patriarchy, for example, loosened somewhat, especially for elite women, when northern China was disrupted by the incursion of pastoral and nomadic peoples, whose women were far less restricted than those of China itself. Even within the small world of ancient Greek city-states, the patriarchy of a semidemocratic Athens was far more confining for women than in a highly militaristic Sparta, where women competed in sports with men, could divorce with ease, and owned substantial landed estates. However, elite women everywhere both enjoyed privileges and suffered the restrictions of seclusion in the home to a much greater extent than their lower-class counterparts, whose economic circumstances required them to operate in the larger social arena.

Finally, civilizations differed in the range and extent of their influence. Roman civilization dominated the Mediterranean basin for much of the millennium between 500 B.C.E. and 500 C.E. (see Map 1.2), while Chinese civilization has directly shaped the cultural history of much of eastern Asia and indirectly influenced economic life all across Eurasia for much longer. Between roughly 650 and 1450, Islamic civilization represented the most expansive, influential, and pervasive presence throughout the entire Afro-Eurasian world (see Map 2.3 in Chapter 2).

Sourcing and Situation

Ask students to fill out an OPTIC chart like the one below for "Caste in India." (Answers are provided in italics.)

Overview	*This photograph is showing the relationship between different castes in 1947 India.*
Parts	*There is a high-caste landowner on the left side of the photograph; opposite the landowner is a group of low-caste workers; the landowner is paying his workers without touching them, and the landowner and workers are standing in front of what appears to be a nice building, possibly the landowner's own home.*
Title	*The title of this photograph could be "Caste in India" (as written in the caption under the photograph). The title helps show the unequal social structure that existed in India for millennia.*

Map 1.2 The Roman Empire
At its height in the second century C.E., the Roman Empire incorporated the entire region surrounding the Mediterranean Sea, including the less developed region of Western Europe, the heartland of Greek civilization, and the ancient civilization of Egypt.

▲ **AP**

CAUSATION
Based on Map 1.2, what geographic realities might have challenged the political unity of the Roman Empire?

AP **EXAM TIP**

Knowledge of maps throughout world history is critical. Be sure you know how to read maps and understand what they convey.

Large-scale empires in West Africa, such as Mali and Songhay, as well as the huge Inca Empire in South America, also encompassed vast territories.

Other civilizations had a much more limited range in the world before 1450. The civilization of Axum (100–700 C.E.) was largely limited to what is now Ethiopia and Eritrea, and Swahili civilization (800–1500 C.E.), embodied in a set of competing city states, was restricted to the coastal region of eastern Africa. Maya civilization, flourishing between 250 and 900, was a phenomenon of southern Mexico and Central America. As Western European civilization crystallized after 1000 C.E., it too was a regional civilization with nothing like the reach of Chinese or Islamic civilizations. In the five centuries after 1450, however, Western Europe

EXPLORING AP® THEMES
Humans and the Environment (ENV)

Show students Map 1.2, "The Roman Empire," and ask the following question: What benefits do you see that Rome gained from its location? *Answers will vary but should include: It was centered around the Mediterranean, which allowed the empire to control trade as well as protect its boundaries.*

As an extension to the question, have students locate maps of other early empires in the Mediterranean (Persia and Alexander the Great's empire) to compare the similarities and differences in regards to the extent of the Roman Empire. *Answers will vary but should include: Rome did not extend into Southwest Asia or parts of India like the Persian Empire or Alexander's empire, but it did control Anatolia and Egypt like the two previous empires; The Roman Empire had access to more major bodies of water; The Romans established a road system like the Persian royal road to help facilitate transportation and communication across the empire.*

CHAPTER 1

(continued)

Interrelationships	The distance between the landowner and his workers was meant to show their social separation due to their differing castes, while his refusal to touch them to give them their pay shows the discrimination against the lower castes.
Conclusion	This photograph is trying to demonstrate how the caste system drove interactions between people in India, even as the state was gaining independence and had political leaders calling for an end to the caste system.

TRM Handout 1.2: OPTIC Chart for Caste in India

Making Connections: Continuity and Change

Understanding Continuity and Change can be difficult. Use the Think-Pair-Share teaching strategy to help students make connections with continuity and change. This technique allows individual thinking, collaboration, and presentation in the same class period. To begin this lesson, ask students to write down what the word "patriarchy" means in the twenty-first century. Give students about 1 to 3 minutes to write down their definition. Most students will know that it means a male-dominated society, but students probably will not understand how different patriarchy is in different societies. After students write their answer down, have them get into pairs (you can assign partners or let students choose their own) to discuss what they wrote down. Then have the partners read "Then and Now: Patriarchy" on pages 24–25. As they read the information, have them take notes on how patriarchy has changed from the earliest civilizations to the twenty-first century. This portion of the activity should take about 10 minutes. After the partners have read the material and taken some notes, bring the class together and have the partners share what they learned from reading the selection.

THEN AND NOW   Patriarchy

Civilization and patriarchy have long gone hand in hand. A rigid patriarchy appeared in early Mesopotamian civilization, and something broadly similar has been apparent in every civilization that followed over the next 5,500 years. Patriarchy became so inscribed in the texture of civilization that until quite recently it was widely assumed to be natural.

The term means the "rule of the father," suggesting a pervasive male dominance and female subordination in almost every dimension of private and public life. It found expression almost everywhere. An ancient Indian text called the Laws of Manu declared, "In childhood a female must be subject to her father, in youth to her husband, and when her lord is dead, to her sons; a woman must never be independent."[13] In China, Confucian-based texts asserted that "men go out; women stay in," thus highlighting the public roles of men in contrast to the private domain of women.[14] The Christian New Testament declared that "wives should submit to their husbands in everything." And the Quran asserted that "men have authority over women because Allah has made the one superior to the other."

Ancient patriarchies were often more nuanced than these formulations might suggest. Men were often urged to behave kindly toward women and to offer protection to the "weaker sex." Furthermore, a few women rose to prominence in political or cultural life, and women on occasion pushed back against particular restrictions on their lives. But few if any wholesale critiques or direct challenges to patriarchy as a social system arose.

In the past several centuries, however, fundamental challenges to male dominance have in fact arisen. That is the chief difference between patriarchy then and now. In the European Enlightenment of the eighteenth century, the French philosopher Condorcet looked forward to the "complete destruction of the prejudices which have established an inequality of rights between the two sexes."[15] During the French Revolution, a small group of women campaigned for women's rights, arguing that "everywhere, the laws favor men at the expense of women, because all the power is in your [men's] hands."[16] In the second half of the nineteenth century a substantial feminist movement emerged in Europe and North America that focused especially on securing the right to vote as an important step toward securing a wider equality between the sexes. Communist regimes in Russia and China during the twentieth century rejected many patriarchal traditions by encouraging women to work outside the home and by treating marriage and divorce as civil contracts between equal partners. And since the 1960s, feminism has both globalized and radicalized as new expressions of the movement have attacked patriarchy on a wide range of issues: access to education, health care, birth control, and abortion; workplace discrimination and wage inequality; women in politics; rape, domestic violence, and sexual harassment; lesbian rights and gay marriage; and prostitution and pornography. By the early twenty-first century, some 183 out of 193 nations had signed a United Nations Convention on the Elimination of All Forms of Discrimination against Women. By then, patriarchy was clearly on the defensive, even if it persisted in every society.

By any measure, the scope and speed of this challenge to patriarchy were astonishing. In little more than two centuries, a deeply rooted and rarely noticed institution had been widely discussed, dramatically challenged, and in many places substantially eroded.

Politically, women have gained the right to vote in every country in the world and have achieved the highest office in some fifty-six countries since the mid-1960s. Educationally, the gender gap in rates of literacy decreased sharply from the 1970s on, and by 2018 some 83 percent of the world's adult women were literate. And after centuries of being denied entry to universities, in 2018 women outnumbered men in university enrollment globally. In the largely Muslim country of Malaysia, women represented 64 percent of university students in 2018, while in Britain nearly 57 percent of undergraduates were women.

In economic life, women in the twentieth century entered the paid workforce in large numbers. In the United States, some 47 percent of the labor force was female in 2000, and two-earner families were common. Many professions have recently opened to women. Furthermore, women's personal freedom enlarged as birth control pills became widely available, as abortion became a legal option, and as access to jobs allowed some single women to be financially independent. Liberalized divorce laws in many countries have allowed women to

In 2018 Saudi Arabia became the last country in the world to allow women to drive. (Amer Hilabi/AFP/Getty Images)

leave abusive or unhappy marriages. In the United States, where some 50 percent of marriages end in divorce, women have initiated 70 percent of those divorces.

But if patriarchy has been challenged and eroded, it has also been stubbornly persistent. The gains made for women have varied widely around the world and have often been more available for urban and well-educated women than for their rural and uneducated sisters. Child marriages, which clearly restrict the freedom of girls, remain prevalent, particularly in South Asia. The rise of Islamic "fundamentalism" has often been associated with a reassertion of decisive male control over women, including required veiling, the segregation of women, and their exclusion from educational opportunities. The Catholic Church remains an all-male hierarchy at its highest levels, with women still barred from the priesthood. The percentage of women in the legislative bodies of the world in 2016 ranged from a high of 61 percent in Rwanda, to 25 percent in China, 23.6 percent in the United States, 12 percent in India, and 5.4 percent in Thailand.

Furthermore, the very erosion of patriarchy has spurred a backlash against feminism among those who felt that its agenda undermined family life, the proper relationship of men and women, and civilization generally. To Phyllis Schlafly, a prominent American critic of feminism, it was a "disease" that brought in its wake "fear, sickness, pain, anger, hatred, danger, violence, and all manner of ugliness."[17] Many African governments defined feminism of any kind as "un-African" and an unwelcome Western intrusion.

So is the glass half empty or half full? Clearly the differences between ancient patriarchies and contemporary social life are substantial, and the changes in the lives of many women since the mid-twentieth century have been enormous. Nonetheless, the cultural legacy of patriarchy, deeply embedded in many institutions and individuals, still persists. The balance of gains or losses lies in the eye of the beholder.

QUESTIONS

Why do you think that patriarchy persisted for so long largely unchallenged? In what ways has patriarchy been challenged over the last two centuries? In what ways has it persisted into modern times? Do you think that the recent erosion of patriarchy in many places reflects a permanent break with the past, or might patriarchy reassert itself in the future?

Bell Ringer

The following activity should take no more than 5 to 10 minutes of your class period and offers an effective and engaging way to begin your lessons.

Ask students the following question: "Why would early human societies develop religion?" *Answers may include: To explain the unexplainable; to understand natural phenomena; to create moral and social order as societies grew in population.*

Ask students to define the following terms related to Hinduism. (Answers are provided in italics.)

■ Brahman: *The world soul, the final and ultimate reality.*

■ Moksha: *Literally, "liberation," which refers to the final goal of humankind—uniting with Brahman and ending the human perception of a separate existence.*

■ Samsara: *Rebirth or reincarnation, during which human souls migrate from body to body over many lifetimes, waiting to achieve moksha.*

Ask students to create a T-chart to take notes on the impact of the caste system on India's political and social structures. The paragraphs on pages 21–22 of this chapter will help students create their chart, though they may need to do some outside research to complete it.

---

followed in the tradition of these more expansive civilizations, as it achieved genuinely global power and approached world domination by 1900.

Civilizations and Cultural Traditions

Finding the Main Point: What similarities and differences can you identify among the major religious traditions that emerged in the Afro-Eurasian world before 1200 C.E.?

Civilizations also differed in their cultural or religious traditions. These traditions provided a common identity for millions of individuals and for entire civilizations, even as divisions within them generated great social conflicts. Cultural traditions also made the inequalities of civilizations legitimate, providing moral justification for established elites and oppressive states. But religion was a doubled-edged sword, for it sometimes stimulated movements that challenged those in power. It also enabled millions of ordinary people to endure their sufferings, shaping the meanings that they attached to the world they inhabited and providing moral guidance for living a good life or making a good society. (See Working with Evidence: The "Good Life" in Asian Cultural Traditions, page 53.)

By 1200, the major cultural traditions of the Afro-Eurasian world had been long established. Hinduism and Buddhism; Confucianism and Daoism; Judaism, Christianity, and Islam—all of them had taken shape in the centuries between 600 B.C.E. and 700 C.E. Since they will recur often in the chapters that follow, some attention to their origins and development is appropriate.

South Asian Cultural Traditions: Hinduism

Few cultures were as fundamentally religious as that of India, where sages and philosophers embraced the Divine and all things spiritual with enthusiasm and generated elaborate philosophical visions about the nature of ultimate reality. **Hinduism**, the oldest, largest, and most prominent religious tradition in India, had no historical founder, unlike Islam, Christianity, and another later Indian tradition, Buddhism. Instead it grew up over many centuries as an integral part of Indian civilization. Although it later spread into Southeast Asia, Hinduism was not a missionary religion seeking converts, but was, like Judaism, associated with a particular people and territory.

In fact, "Hinduism" was never a single tradition at all, and the term itself derived from outsiders—Greeks, Muslims, and later the British—who sought to reduce the infinite variety of Indian cultural patterns into a recognizable system. From the inside, however, Hinduism contained a vast diversity of gods, spirits, beliefs, practices, rituals, and philosophies. This endlessly variegated Hinduism served to incorporate into Indian civilization the many diverse peoples who migrated into or invaded the South Asian peninsula over many centuries.

At one level, this emerging Hindu religious tradition was emphatically polytheistic, embracing a vast diversity of gods and goddesses, each of whom had various consorts and appeared in a variety of forms. A priestly caste known as Brahmins presided over the sacrifices, offerings, and rituals that these deities required. But at another more philosophical level, Indian thinkers argued for a more unified understanding of reality. This point of view found expression in the **Upanishads** (oo-PAHN-ee-shahds), a collection of sacred texts composed by largely anonymous thinkers between 800 and 400 B.C.E. These texts elaborated the idea of Brahman, the World Soul, the final and ultimate reality. Beyond the multiplicity of material objects and individual persons, and beyond even the various gods themselves, lay this primal unitary energy or divine reality infusing all things. This alone was real; the immense diversity of existence that human beings perceived with their senses was but an illusion. One contemporary Hindu monk summarized the essence of the Hindu outlook by saying, "there is no multiplicity."

The fundamental assertion of this philosophical Hinduism was that the individual human soul, or *atman*, was in fact a part of Brahman. The chief goal of humankind then lay in the effort to achieve union with Brahman, putting an end to our illusory perception of a separate existence. This was *moksha* (MOHK-shuh), or liberation, compared sometimes to a bubble in a glass of water breaking through the surface and becoming one with the surrounding atmosphere.

Achieving this exalted state was held to involve many lifetimes, and the notion of *samsara*, or rebirth or reincarnation, became a central feature of Hindu thinking. Human souls migrated from body to body over many lifetimes, depending on the actions of individuals. This was the law of *karma*. Pure actions, appropriate to one's station in life, resulted in rebirth in a higher social position or caste. Thus the caste system of distinct and ranked groups, each with its own duties, became a measure of spiritual progress.

Various paths to this final release, appropriate for people of different temperaments, were spelled out in Hindu teachings. Some might achieve moksha through knowledge or study; others by doing their ordinary work without regard to consequences; still others through passionate devotion to some deity or through extended meditation practice. Such ideas became widely known throughout India—carried

Hindu Ascetics In the final stage of life, Hinduism called for devotees, mostly but not always men, to leave ordinary ways of living and withdraw into the forests to seek spiritual liberation, or moksha. Here, in an illustration from an early-thirteenth-century Indian manuscript, a holy man explores a text with three male disciples in a secluded rural setting. (Musée des Arts Asiatiques-Guimet, Paris, France/© RMN-Grand Palais/Art Resource, NY)

▲ **AP®**
CLAIMS AND EVIDENCE IN SOURCES
What evidence can you find in this image to support the importance of asceticism in Hindu religious practices?

by Brahmin priests and wandering ascetics or holy men, who had withdrawn from ordinary life to pursue their spiritual development.

South Asian Cultural Traditions: Buddhism

About the same time as philosophical Hinduism was emerging, another movement took shape in South Asia that soon became a distinct and separate religious tradition—Buddhism. Unlike Hinduism, this new faith had a historical founder, **Siddhartha Gautama** (ca. 566–ca. 486 B.C.E.), a prince from a small kingdom in north India or southern Nepal. According to Buddhist tradition, the prince had enjoyed a sheltered and delightful youth until he encountered human suffering in the form of an old man, a sick person, and a corpse. Shattered by these revelations of aging, illness, and death, Siddhartha determined to find the cause of such sufferings and a remedy for them. And so, at the age of twenty-nine, the young prince left his luxurious life as well as his wife and child, shed his royal jewels, cut off his hair, and set off on a quest for enlightenment that ended with an indescribable experience of spiritual realization. Now he was the **Buddha**, the man who had awakened. For the next forty years, he taught what he had learned, setting in motion the cultural tradition of Buddhism.

To the Buddha, suffering or sorrow—experiencing life as imperfect, impermanent, and unsatisfactory—was the central and universal feature of human life. This kind of suffering derived from desire or craving for individual fulfillment, from attachment to that which inevitably changes, particularly to the notion of a core self or ego that is uniquely and solidly "me." He spelled out a cure for this "dis-ease" in his famous "eightfold path," which emphasized a modest and moral lifestyle, mental concentration practices, including meditation, and wisdom or understanding of reality as it is. Those who followed the Buddhist path most fully could expect to achieve enlightenment, or *nirvana*, an almost indescribable state in which individual identity would be "extinguished" along with all greed, hatred, and delusion. With the pain of unnecessary suffering finally ended, the enlightened person would experience an overwhelming serenity, even in the midst of difficulty, as well as an immense loving-kindness, or compassion, for all beings. It was a simple message, elaborated endlessly and in various forms by those who followed the Buddha.

Much of the Buddha's teaching reflected the Hindu traditions from which it sprang. The idea that ordinary life is an illusion, the concepts of karma and rebirth, the goal of overcoming the incessant demands of the ego, the practice of meditation, the hope for final release from the cycle of rebirth—all of these Hindu elements found their way into Buddhist teaching. In this respect, Buddhism was a simplified and more accessible version of Hinduism.

Other elements of Buddhist teaching, however, sharply challenged prevailing Hindu thinking. Rejecting the religious authority of the Brahmins, the Buddha ridiculed their rituals and sacrifices as irrelevant to the hard work of dealing with one's suffering. Nor was he much interested in abstract speculation about the creation of

---

EXPLORING AP® THEMES

Cultural Developments and Interactions (CDI)

Ask students the following questions:

■ Why is Buddhism universally appealing? *Answers include the egalitarian nature of Buddhism, which appeals to women and people in lower castes.*

■ How did the appeal of Buddhism contribute to its spread to East Asia? Answer: *When Buddhist ideas moved with people along trade and missionary routes, Buddhism's message was easily received by women and people with lower social status in East and Southeast Asia.*

APPLY THE TIP

Ask students: How did Buddhism challenge the Hindu political system? *Buddhism encouraged egalitarianism, which is counter to the rigid caste system of Hinduism.*

AP®
COMPARISON
To what extent were Buddhist teachings similar to Hindu beliefs? Provide a similarity or difference to justify your answer.

AP® EXAM TIP
You should know the basic differences and similarities between Hinduism and Buddhism.

AP®
COMPARISON
What is the difference between the Theravada and Mahayana expressions of Buddhism?

the world or the existence of God, for such questions, he declared, "are not useful in the quest for holiness; they do not lead to peace and to the direct knowledge of *nirvana*." Individuals had to take responsibility for their own spiritual development with no help from human authorities or supernatural beings. It was a path of intense self-effort, based on personal experience. The Buddha also challenged the inequalities of a Hindu-based caste system, arguing that neither caste position nor gender was a barrier to enlightenment. At least in principle, the possibility of "awakening" was available to all.

As Buddhism spread across the trade routes of Central Asia to China, Japan, and Southeast Asia, differences in understanding soon emerged. An early version of the new religion, known as **Theravada Buddhism** (Teaching of the Elders), portrayed the Buddha as an immensely wise teacher and model, but certainly not divine. The gods, though never completely denied, played little role in assisting believers in achieving enlightenment. But as the message of the Buddha gained a mass following and spread across much of Asia, some of its early features—rigorous and time-consuming meditation practice, a focus on monks and nuns withdrawn from ordinary life, the absence of accessible supernatural figures able to provide help and comfort—proved difficult for many converts. And so the religion adapted. A new form of the faith, **Mahayana Buddhism**, developed in the early centuries of the Common Era and offered greater accessibility, a spiritual path available to a much wider range of people beyond monks and ascetics, who were the core group in early Buddhism.

In most expressions of Mahayana Buddhism, enlightenment (or becoming a Buddha) was available to everyone; it was possible within the context of ordinary life, rather than a monastery; and it might occur within a single lifetime rather than over the course of many lives. While Buddhism had originally put a premium on spiritual wisdom or insight, Mahayana expressions of the faith emphasized compassion—the ability to feel the sorrows of other people as if they were one's own. This compassionate religious ideal found expression in the notion of bodhisattvas, fully enlightened beings who postponed their own final liberation in order to assist a suffering humanity. They were spiritual beings on their way to "Buddhahood." Furthermore, the historical Buddha himself became something of a god, and both earlier and future Buddhas were available to offer help. Elaborate descriptions and artistic representations of these

▼**AP**
ARGUMENTATION
How does this visual representation of the Buddha differ from the description of the prince in the beginning of this section? What could account for this difference?

The Buddha's Enlightenment Dating from the late eighth century in Korea, this monumental and beautifully proportioned sculpture portrays the Buddha at the moment of his enlightenment, symbolized by his right hand touching the earth. Seated on a lotus pedestal, this image of the Buddha also shows the *ushnisha*, the raised area at the top of his head, which represents his spiritual attainment, and the dot in the center of his forehead indicating wisdom. (Copyright © Cultural Heritage Administration of Korea, Courtesy of the Academy of Korean Studies, South Korea)

BUILDING AP® SKILLS
Sourcing and Situation

Show students examples of bodhisattvas found at the Metropolitan Museum's website. Then ask students: How did the bodhisattvas allow individuals to extend their personal relationship with the Divine? *The Divine feels inaccessible, but the bodhisattvas are human-like connections to the Divine that feel more familiar and make the deity seem more accessible.*

TEACHING IDEA
Incorporating Outside Resources

Since we are still in the nontested material in the AP® World History: Modern course, you should be moving rather quickly. Sometimes it is easy to use videos like those found in Crash Course World History. In the episode *Buddha and Ashoka: Crash Course World History 6*, John Green offers a quick history of India after the Indus Valley civilization. Topics covered include Hinduism, Buddhism, and the reign of Buddhist emperor Ashoka. The video can be found on YouTube. Either assign this as homework or show it in class. Then ask students the following questions:

■ What are the eight parts of this video? *The Vedas; The Caste System; Dharma; Moksha and Karma; Buddhism; Totally Tangential; Ashoka; The Big Finish.*

■ When did the beginnings of Buddhism occur, and who was Siddhartha Gautama? *Sixth century B.C.E. Gautama was a prince who felt there might be more to life than his lavish lifestyle. He went on a journey and found enlightenment along the way.*

■ What do you think are the five most important terms that Green refers to? *Answers will vary.*

EXPLORING AP® THEMES

Cultural Developments and Interactions (CDI)

Display Map 1.3 for students to study and ask: Based on the map, what could have helped the spread of Christianity and Buddhism throughout the Eastern Hemisphere? *Answers may include: Missionaries had access to water routes (seas and rivers) to travel along; Trade routes made cultural diffusion easier at this time, allowing for the spread of religions.*

⬅	Spread of Buddhism
⬅	Spread of Christianity
—	Silk Roads
—	Indian Ocean trade routes

MAPPING HISTORY   Map 1.3 **The Spread of Early Buddhism and Christianity**

In the five centuries after the birth of Jesus, Christianity found converts from Spain to Northeast Africa, the Middle East, Central Asia, and India. In the Roman Empire, Axum, and Armenia, the new religion enjoyed state support as well. Subsequently, Christianity took root solidly in Europe and after 1000 C.E. in Russia. Meanwhile, Buddhism was spreading from its South Asian homeland to various parts of Asia, even as it was weakening in India itself.

Reading the Map: From its start on the eastern shore of the Mediterranean Sea, in which directions did Christianity spread the farthest?

AP® Making Connections: What political or economic factors could facilitate the spread of a religious tradition like the ones seen on the map?

AP® EXAM TIP

Be able to give examples of factors that attract people to particular belief systems or religious traditions.

supernatural beings, together with various levels of Heavens and Hells, transformed Buddhism into a popular religion of salvation. Furthermore, religious merit, leading to salvation, might now be earned by acts of piety and devotion, such as contributing to the support of a monastery, and that merit might be transferred to others. In many forms and variations, Mahayana Buddhism took root in Central Asia, China, Japan, Korea, Southeast Asia, and elsewhere. Buddhism thus became the first major tradition to spread widely outside its homeland (see Map 1.3).

In Tibet, a distinctive form of Buddhism began to take shape during the seventh century C.E. This Tibetan Buddhism gave special authority to learned teachers,

---

TEACHING IDEA

AP® Exam Strategies

If you want to have students practice working with an AP®-style stimulus-based question, have them partner up and work on answering the three stimulus-based multiple-choice questions that accompany this map. The questions can be found on pages 63–64.

known as Lamas, and emphasized an awareness of and preparation for death. Its many spiritual practices included multiple prostrations (repeatedly lying stretched out on the ground), visualizing or imagining various bodhisattvas or deities, complex meditations, ceremonies associated with numerous heavenly beings both peaceful and violent, and the frequent use of art and music. Incorporating various elements from native Tibetan traditions and from Hinduism, Tibetan Buddhism was expressed in a set of distinctive texts compiled during the fourteenth century. A section of these texts became famous in the West as *The Tibetan Book of the Dead*, which vividly describes the various stages of transition from life to death to rebirth.

But by 1200 Buddhism had largely disappeared in India, the land of its birth, even as it was expanding in other parts of Asia. Its decline in India owed something to the mounting wealth of monasteries as the economic interests of leading Buddhist figures separated them from ordinary people. Hostility of the Brahmin priests and competition from Islam after 1000 C.E. also played a role. But the most important reason for the waning of Buddhism in India was the growth during the first millennium C.E. of a new kind of popular Hinduism.

That path took shape in what is known as the **bhakti movement**, which involved devotion to one or another of India's many gods and goddesses. Beginning in south India and moving northward between 600 and 1300 C.E., it featured the intense adoration of and identification with a particular deity through songs, prayers, and rituals. By far the most popular deities were Vishnu, the protector and preserver of creation who was associated with mercy and goodness, and Shiva, a god representing the Divine in its destructive aspect, but many others also had their followers. This form of Hindu expression sometimes pushed against the rigid caste and gender hierarchies of Indian society by inviting all to an adoration of the Divine. In a famous section of the long Indian epic *Mahabharata*, the Hindu deity Krishna declares that "those who take shelter in Me, though they be of lower birth—women, vaishyas [merchants] and shudras [workers]—can attain the supreme destination."

Bhakti practice was more accessible to ordinary people than the elaborate sacrifices of the Brahmins or the philosophical speculations of intellectuals. Through good deeds, simple living, and emotionally fulfilling rituals of devotion, individuals could find salvation without a complex institutional structure, orthodox doctrine, or prescribed meditation practices. Bhakti spirituality also had a rich poetic tradition that flourished especially in the centuries after 1200. One ninth-century poet illustrated the intense emotional impact of bhakti devotion:

> He [God] grabbed me lest I go astray/Wax before an unspent fire, mind
> melted, body trembled./I bowed, I wept, danced, and cried aloud/I sang, and
> I praised him. . . ./I left shame behind, took as an ornament the mockery of
> local folk.[18]

The proliferation of gods and goddesses, and of their bhakti followers, occasioned very little friction or serious religious conflict. "Hinduism," writes a leading

AP
COMPARISON
How did the evolution of cultural traditions in India and China differ from one another?

AP EXAM TIP
Major belief systems are often divided and subdivided across time and place. One example is the development of Theravada and Mahayana Buddhism. Be able to provide other examples through world history.

AP EXAM TIP
Be able to provide examples of the expansion and contraction of major religions over time.

AP
CAUSATION
How did changes in Hinduism contribute to the decline of Buddhism in India?

EXPLORING AP® THEMES

Cultural Developments and Interactions (CDI)

Ask students the following questions:

■ What characterized bhakti? *Bhakti worship was devotion to a single god or goddess in the Hindu pantheon. Bhakti worship involved song, prayer, and other rituals.*

■ Why did this form of worship threaten the caste system and traditional religious practices? *Bhakti cults were more egalitarian.*

APPLY THE TIP

The annotated map from Chapter 1's Essential Activity can help students understand the expansion of belief systems and religions over time.

EXPLORING AP® THEMES

Social Interactions and Organization (SIO)

Ask students to create a chart of the levels of inequality in four of the five Confucian relationships, like the chart shown below. (Answers are provided in italics.)

Position	Direct Subordinate
Ruler	*Subject*
Husband	*Wife*
Father	*Son*
Elder brother	*Younger brother*

After students have completed the chart, ask the following questions:

■ What is the fifth Confucian relationship, and how does it rank in the hierarchy of subordination? *The fifth Confucian relationship is friendship, and it is the only one of the five that stresses equality.*

■ How do these relationships reinforce order in society? *Order may be maintained if people in a dominant position ensure the safety and well-being of those in a subservient position and people in a subservient position work in the service of those in the dominant position.*

■ What are some of the drawbacks of the Confucian ideal? *Answers will vary.*

TRM Handout 1.3: Chart for Levels of Inequality in Confucian Relationships

TEACHING IDEA

Incorporating Outside Resources

Use the short NTDTV documentary *Discovering China: Confucius* on YouTube and a "KWL" chart like the one shown below to help students learn more about Confucius. Before playing the video, ask students to fill in the K portion of a KWL chart about Confucius based on their readings and activities in class so far. Next, students should note in the W portion what more they want to learn about him and his ideas. Then play the video; you'll want to stop the video at 5:26 to just watch the section on Confucius. After the video concludes, ask students to complete the L portion of the chart and to reflect on whether the questions they raised in the W portion were answered. If not, ask students to do further research. A reproducible version of this chart is available in the Teacher's Resource Materials.

---

scholar, "is essentially tolerant, and would rather assimilate than rigidly exclude."[19] This capacity for assimilation extended to an already declining Buddhism, which for many people had become yet another religious tradition worshipping yet another god. The Buddha in fact was incorporated into the Hindu pantheon as the ninth incarnation of Vishnu.

Chinese Cultural Traditions: Confucianism

AP®
ARGUMENTATION
In what ways can Confucianism be defined as a secular or "humanistic" philosophy rather than a supernatural religion?

At the far eastern end of the Eurasian continent, Chinese civilization gave birth to two major cultural traditions that have persisted into the modern era, Confucianism and Daoism. Compared to Hindu, Christian, and Islamic traditions, these Chinese outlooks were less overtly religious; were expressed in more philosophical, humanistic, or rational terms; and were oriented toward life in this world. They emerged in what the Chinese remember sadly as "the age of warring states" (ca. 500–221 B.C.E.), dreadful centuries of disorder and turmoil. At that time some Chinese thinkers began to consider how order might be restored, how the imagined tranquility of an earlier time could be realized again. From their reflections emerged the classical cultural traditions of Chinese civilization.

One of these traditions was derived from the thinking of Confucius (551–479 B.C.E.), a learned and ambitious aristocrat who believed that he had uncovered a path back to social and political harmony. He attracted a group of followers, who compiled his writings into a short book called *The Analects*, and later scholars elaborated and commented endlessly on his ideas, creating a body of thought known as **Confucianism**. By the time of the **Han dynasty**, around 200 B.C.E., those ideas became the official ideology of the Chinese state and remained so into the early twentieth century.

The Confucian answer to the problem of China's disorder was rooted not in force, law, and punishment, but in the power of moral behavior. For Confucius, human society consisted primarily of unequal relationships: the father and son; husband and wife; the older brother and younger brother; ruler and subject. If the superior party in each of these relationships behaved with sincerity, benevolence, and genuine concern for the other, then the inferior party would be motivated to respond with deference and obedience. Harmony would then prevail. In Confucian thinking, the family became a model for political life, a kind of miniature state. Filial piety, the honoring of one's ancestors and parents, was both valuable in itself and a training ground for the reverence due to the emperor and state officials.

For Confucius, the key to nurturing these moral qualities was education, particularly an immersion in language, literature, history, philosophy, and ethics, all applied to the practical problems of government. Ritual and ceremonies were also important, for they conveyed the rules of appropriate behavior in the many and varying circumstances of life. For the "superior person," or "gentleman" in Confucian terms, serious personal reflection and a willingness to strive continuously to perfect his moral character were essential.

(continued)

K	
What do you know?	
W	
What do you want to know?	
L	
What did you learn?	

TRM Handout 1.4: KWL Chart for Confucius

Such ideas had a pervasive influence in Chinese life, as Confucianism became almost synonymous with Chinese elite culture. As China's bureaucracy took shape during and after the Han dynasty (206 B.C.E.–220 C.E.), Confucianism became the central element of the educational system, which prepared students for the examinations required to gain official positions. Thus generation after generation of China's male elite was steeped in the ideas and values of Confucianism.

Confucianism also placed great importance on history, for the ideal good society lay in the past. Those ideas also injected a certain meritocratic element into Chinese elite culture, for the great sage had emphasized that "superior men" and potential government officials were those of outstanding moral character and intellectual achievement, not simply those of aristocratic background. Usually only young men from wealthy families could afford the education necessary for passing examinations, but on occasion villagers could find the resources to sponsor one of their bright sons, potentially propelling him into the stratosphere of the Chinese elite while bringing honor and benefit to the village itself.

Confucian ideas were clearly used to legitimate the many inequalities of Chinese society, but they also established certain expectations for the superior parties in China's social hierarchy. Thus emperors should keep taxes low, administer justice, and provide for the material needs of the people. Those who failed to govern by these moral norms forfeited what the Chinese called the Mandate of Heaven, which granted legitimacy to the ruler. Under such conditions, natural disaster, famine, or rebellion followed, leading to political upheaval and a new dynasty. Likewise, at the level of the family, husbands should deal kindly with their wives and children, lest they provoke conflict and disharmony.

Finally, Confucianism marked Chinese elite culture by its secular, or nonreligious, character. Confucius did not deny the reality of gods and spirits. In fact, he advised people to participate in family and state rituals "as if the spirits were present," and he believed that the universe had a moral character with which human beings should align themselves. But the thrust of Confucian teaching was distinctly this-worldly and practical, concerned with human relationships, effective government, and social harmony. Members of the Chinese elite generally acknowledged that magic, the gods, and spirits were perhaps necessary for the lower orders of

The Chinese Examination System The Chinese imperial government selected officials through an elaborate system of civil service exams. This Song dynasty painting shows candidates taking the highest level of these tests, known as the palace exams, at the imperial capital Kaifeng. Success opened the way to prestigious appointments at the top levels of the Chinese government. (Pictures from History/Bridgeman Images)

▲ **AP®**

CLAIMS AND EVIDENCE IN SOURCES
How could this image be used to support an argument that the Chinese examination system led to a more fluid social structure?

BUILDING AP® SKILLS

Claims and Evidence in Sources

To help students practice their analysis skills and their skill at understanding differing perspectives on a topic, have them read Document 2 from "The 'Good Life' in Asian Cultural Traditions" found on pages 54–55. After reading this document, students can begin to practice skills for writing by answering the questions at the end of the document.

EXPLORING AP® THEMES

Social Interactions and Organization (SIO)

Ask students: How would a woman be able to gain a position as an official in the Chinese court if only men could participate in the civil service exam? What obstacles might she face in reaching that position? *Answer may include: It would be an advantage to have a connected family that were willing to educate her and knew how to position her within the court or to have a family that could use their influence to bypass the exam system to get her a position; Other court officials might try to stop her from gaining a position at court, or the government-sponsored Confucian schools might refuse to accept her as a student.*

BUILDING AP® SKILLS

Making Connections: Comparison

Ask students to create a Venn diagram comparing the beliefs of Daoism and Confucianism. Answers may include:

■ Similarities—*Both believed that certain actions and behaviors would bring stability to China; Both believed family life was central to society; Both incorporated the traditional Chinese practice of ancestor veneration.*

■ Differences—*While Confucianism focused on the importance of human relationships, Daoism focused on understanding the way of nature; Daoism believed that withdrawal from the world into nature was important, whereas Confucianism emphasized a specific role for everyone in society; Confucianism emphasized the importance of education, while Daoism believed that education could actually make a situation worse.*

After students complete the Venn diagram, ask them: *Despite their differences, why did some Chinese scholars believe the two philosophies could live in harmony? Answers may vary but could include how the concept of yin and yang existed in both philosophies and the idea that Confucianism could guide daily, public activities while Daoism could guide private interactions.*

TRM Handout 1.5: Comparison Graphic Organizer for Daoism and Confucianism

BUILDING AP® SKILLS

Contextualization

Now is a good time to practice some contextualization skills by helping students situate the East Asian and South Asian religions in a broader regional context. Ask students to compare Buddhism as a response to Hinduism with Daoism as a response to Confucianism. *Buddhism was accepted as a rejection of the excess that existed within mainstream South Asian (Hindu) society. According to Buddhists, these excesses caused suffering, and the only way to eliminate this suffering was to eliminate desires for material items. Similarly, Daoists saw the political state in East Asia as excessive and unnecessary and rejected it to live in harmony with nature.*

---

society, but educated people, they argued, would find them of little help in striving for moral improvement and in establishing a harmonious society.

In various forms Chinese Confucianism proved attractive to elites elsewhere in East Asia, such as Korea, Vietnam, and Japan. Those distinct civilizations drew heavily on the culture of their giant and highly prestigious neighbor. When an early Japanese state emerged in the seventh century C.E., its founder, Shotoku, issued the Seventeen Article Constitution, proclaiming the Japanese ruler a Chinese-style emperor and encouraging both Buddhism and Confucianism. In good Confucian fashion, that document emphasized the moral quality of rulers as a foundation for social harmony.

Chinese Cultural Traditions: Daoism

As Confucian thinking became generally known in China, a quite different school of thought also took shape. Known as **Daoism**, it was associated with the legendary figure Laozi, who, according to tradition, was a sixth-century-B.C.E. archivist. He is said to have penned a short poetic volume, the *Daodejing* (dau-duh-jing) (*The Way and Its Power*), before vanishing in the wilderness to the west of China on his water buffalo.

COMPARISON
How did the Daoist outlook on society differ from that of Confucianism?

In many ways, Daoist thinking ran counter to that of Confucius, who had emphasized the importance of education and earnest striving for moral improvement and good government. The Daoists ridiculed such efforts as artificial and useless, claiming that they generally made things worse. In the face of China's disorder and chaos, Daoists urged withdrawal into the world of nature and encouraged behavior that was spontaneous, individualistic, and natural. The central concept of Daoist thinking is *dao*, an elusive notion that refers to the way of nature, the underlying and unchanging principle that governs the endless transformation of all things. Whereas Confucius focused on the world of human relationships, the Daoists turned the spotlight on the immense realm of nature and its mysterious unfolding patterns in which the "ten thousand things" appeared, changed, and vanished. "Confucius roams within society," the Chinese have often said. "Laozi wanders beyond."

CONTEXTUALIZATION
How does the yin yang symbol reflect Chinese attitudes toward differing philosophies?

The Yin Yang Symbol

Applied to human life, Daoism invited people to withdraw from the world of political and social activism, to disengage from the public life so important to Confucius, and to align themselves with the way of nature. It meant simplicity in living, small self-sufficient communities, limited government, and the abandonment of education and active efforts at self-improvement. "Give up learning," declares the *Daodejing*, "and put an end to your troubles."

Despite its various differences with the ideas of Confucianism, the Daoist perspective was widely regarded by elite Chinese as complementing rather than contradicting Confucian values. Such an outlook was facilitated by the ancient Chinese concept of *yin* (female) and *yang* (male), which expressed a belief in the unity or complementarity of opposites. Thus a scholar-official might pursue the Confucian project of "government by goodness" during the day, but upon returning home in the evening or following his retirement, he might well behave in a more Daoist fashion—pursuing the simple life, reading Daoist philosophy, practicing meditation or breathing exercises, retreating to mountain settings, or enjoying painting, poetry, or calligraphy.

Daoism also shaped the culture of ordinary people as it became a part of Chinese popular religion. This kind of Daoism sought to tap the power of the dao for practical uses and came to include magic, fortune-telling, and the search for immortality. Sometimes it also provided an ideology for peasant uprisings, such as the Yellow Turban Rebellion (184–204 C.E.), which imagined a utopian society without the oppression of governments and landlords. In its many and varied forms, Daoism, like Confucianism, became an enduring element of the Chinese cultural tradition.

Middle Eastern Cultural Traditions: Judaism and Christianity

From the southeastern coast of the Mediterranean Sea, now home to Israelis and Palestinians, through the lands of the Arabian Peninsula, emerged three religious traditions—Judaism, Christianity, and Islam—often known as Abrahamic faiths because all of them revered the biblical character called Abraham. Amid the proliferation of gods and spirits that had long characterized religious life throughout the ancient Middle East, Jews, Christians, and Muslims alike affirmed a distinctly monotheistic faith. This idea of a single supreme deity or Divine Presence, the sole source of all life and being, was a radical cultural innovation in the region. This monotheistic tradition began with Judaism and Jews, while its Christian and Muslim expressions created the possibility of a universal religion, open to all of humankind.

The earliest of these traditions to emerge was **Judaism**, born among one of the region's less numerous and, at the time, less politically significant peoples—the Hebrews, much later known also as Jews. Unlike the peoples of ancient Mesopotamia, India, Greece, Rome, and elsewhere—all of whom populated the invisible

Chinese Landscape Painting Focused largely on mountains and water, Chinese landscape paintings were much influenced by the Daoist search for harmony with nature. Thus human figures and buildings were usually eclipsed by towering peaks, waterfalls, clouds, mists, and trees. This thirteenth-century ink-on-silk painting illustrates that sensibility. The poem at the top reads: "Night rains cleansed the capital's suburban farms, / Morning sun brightens the emperor's city; / People work happily in a good year, / Dancing and singing they cross a path in the field." (Art Collection 2/Alamy)

APPLY THE TIP

Ask students to compare and contrast social relationships within the belief system traditions of the eastern Mediterranean and Asia. *Religions of the eastern Mediterranean and Asia were organized around monotheism, and practitioners worshipped both communally and individually. Christians sought to proselytize, thus expanding their numbers. Hindus typically believed in a polytheistic view and developed shrines within their homes. Buddhists and Daoists largely removed themselves from society and focused on their inner lives.*

AP® EXAM TIP

You should be able to point out the similarities and differences between the monotheistic religions in this section and the other major belief systems discussed in the chapter.

AP® EXAM TIP

You should be able to describe the basic outlooks of the major world religions and their relationship to political and social life.

AP®

ARGUMENTATION

What was distinctive about the Jewish religious tradition as compared to the other religions discussed in this chapter?

AP®

COMPARISON

How would you compare the teachings of Jesus and the Buddha? In what different ways did the two religions evolve after the deaths of their founders?

AP®

CONTINUITY AND CHANGE

In what ways was Christianity transformed in the five centuries following the death of Jesus?

realm with numerous gods and goddesses—Jews found in their God, whose name they were reluctant to pronounce because of its sacredness, a powerful and jealous deity, who demanded their exclusive loyalty. "Thou shalt have no other gods before me"—this was the first of the Ten Commandments.

Over time, this God evolved into a lofty, transcendent deity of utter holiness and purity. But the Jews also experienced their God as a divine person, accessible and available to his people, not remote or far away. Furthermore, for some, he was transformed from a god of war, who ordered his people to "utterly destroy" the original inhabitants of the Promised Land, to a god of social justice and compassion for the poor and the marginalized, especially in the passionate pronouncements of Jewish prophets, such as Isaiah, Amos, and Jeremiah. Here was a distinctive conception of the Divine—singular, transcendent, personal, revealed in the natural order, engaged in history, and demanding social justice and moral righteousness above sacrifices and rituals. In terms of world history, the chief significance of Jewish religious thought lay in the foundation it provided for those later and far more widespread Abrahamic faiths of Christianity and Islam.

Christianity began in a distinctly Jewish cultural setting. In the remote province of Judaea, which was incorporated into the Roman Empire in 63 B.C.E., a young Jewish craftsman or builder called **Jesus of Nazareth** (ca. 4 B.C.E.–29 C.E.) began a brief career of teaching and healing before he got in trouble with local authorities and was executed. In one of history's most unlikely stories, the life and teachings of that obscure man, barely noted in the historical records of the time, became the basis of the world's most widely practiced religion.

In his short public life, Jesus was a "wisdom teacher," challenging the conventional values of his time, urging the renunciation of wealth and self-seeking, and emphasizing the supreme importance of love or compassion as the basis for a moral life. In his famous Sermon on the Mount, Jesus told his followers to "love your enemies and pray for those who persecute you." Jesus inherited from his Jewish tradition an intense devotion to a single personal deity with whom he was on intimate terms, referring to him as Abba ("father"). And he gained a reputation as a healer and miracle worker. Furthermore, Jesus' teachings had a sharp social and political edge, as he spoke clearly on behalf of the poor and the oppressed, directly criticized the hypocrisies of the powerful, and deliberately associated with lepers, adulterous women, and tax collectors, all of whom were regarded as "impure." His teachings galvanized many of his followers into a social movement that so antagonized and threatened both Jewish and Roman authorities that he was crucified as a political rebel.

Jesus had not intended to establish a new religion, but rather to revitalize his Jewish tradition. Nonetheless, Christianity soon emerged as a separate faith. Its transformation from a small Jewish sect to a world religion began with **Saint Paul** (ca. 6–67 C.E.), an early convert whose missionary journeys in the eastern Roman Empire led to the founding of small Christian communities that included non-Jews. The Good News of Jesus, Paul argued, was for everyone, Jews and non-Jews alike.

BUILDING AP® SKILLS

Making Connections: Comparison

It's important to have students practice writing skills throughout the year, even without writing a full essay. Have students write a one-paragraph argument answering one of the following questions:

■ In what ways was the development of Buddhism similar to the development of Christianity?

■ Compare the impact of Buddhism and Christianity on Eurasian societies.

■ Compare the factors that led to the spread of Christianity and Buddhism in the classical era.

This is an easy assignment and can involve an argument (topic sentence) and three pieces of evidence in a paragraph.

This inclusive message was one of the attractions of the new faith as it spread very gradually within the Roman Empire during the several centuries after Jesus's death. In the Roman world, the strangest and most offensive feature of the new faith was its exclusive monotheism and its antagonism to all other supernatural powers, particularly the cult of the emperors. Christians' denial of these other gods caused them to be tagged as "atheists" and was one reason behind the empire's intermittent persecution of Christians during the first three centuries of the Common Era (see the discussion of **Perpetua** in Zooming In: Perpetua, Christian Martyr, page 38). All of that ended with Emperor Constantine's conversion in the early fourth century C.E. and the proclamation of Christianity as the state religion in 380 C.E. About the same time the new faith also gained official status in Armenia, located in the south Caucasus region east of Turkey, and in Axum, an African state in what is now Ethiopia and Eritrea. In fact, during the first six centuries of the Christian era, most followers of Jesus lived in the Middle East and in northern and northeastern Africa, with small communities in India and China as well (see Map 1.3).

As Christianity spread within the Roman Empire and beyond, it developed an elaborate hierarchical organization, with patriarchs, bishops, and priests—all men—replacing the house churches of the early years, in which women played a more prominent part. The emerging Christian movement was, however, anything but unified. Its immense geographic reach, accompanied by inevitable differences in language, culture, and political regime, ensured that a single focus for Christian belief and practice was difficult to achieve. Eventually, separate church organizations emerged in the eastern and western regions of the Roman Empire as well as in Egypt, Syria, Persia, Armenia, Ethiopia, and southern India, some of which were accompanied by sharp differences in doctrine. The bishop of Rome gradually emerged as the dominant leader, or pope, of the church in the western half of the empire, but his authority was sharply contested in the East. This division contributed to the later split between the Latin, or Roman Catholic, and the Greek, or Eastern Orthodox, branches of Christendom, a division that continues to the present. Thus by 1200 or so, the Christian world was not only geographically extensive but also politically and theologically very diverse and highly fragmented.

The Legacy of Axumite Christianity A distinctive form of Christianity in what is now Ethiopia began in the fourth century and endures to this day. This late-fourteenth- or early-fifteenth-century depiction of the ascension of Jesus, with his disciples pointing upwards, illustrates that legacy. (Rogers Fund, 1998 [1998.66]/The Metropolitan Museum of Art, New York, NY, USA/Image copyright © The Metropolitan Museum of Art/Image source: Art Resource, NY)

AP EXAM TIP
You should know the factors that led to divisions within major belief systems.

AP EXAM TIP
Be ready to provide examples of how power was used to promote religion, and vice versa.

EXPLORING AP® THEMES

Cultural Developments and Interactions (CDI)

Ask students: What does the Roman response to Christianity's denial of other gods tell us about Romans' polytheism and comparative toleration? *The power of the cult of the emperor was inextricably tied to social, political, and religious control. However, by the third century C.E., Constantine and his successor were making political decisions to incorporate Christianity, which eventually became a state religion supplanting the polytheism of the previous Roman Empire.*

APPLY THE TIP

After students have read all of the religion sections in Chapter 1, have them list how each of the major belief systems was promoted by political powers and how it supported political systems. This could help them fill out part of the "Should Do" section in the Chapter 1 Essential Activity. Possible answers are provided in italics.

■ Buddhism: *Ashoka promoted Buddhism as the main belief system of India during his rule, which also facilitated its spread to other regions in Asia.*

■ Confucianism: *The Han dynasty adopted Confucianism as their official ruling philosophy. Confucianism was used by later Chinese dynasties to justify their power and to provide bureaucrats for the government through the use of Confucian knowledge in the civil service examination system.*

■ Christianity: *While at first the Roman Empire persecuted Christians, it later adopted Christianity, which helped Christianity spread. After the fall of the Roman Empire, rulers in Western Europe used Christianity to legitimize and justify their rule.*

■ Islam: *Muhammad was both the religious and political leader of the early Islamic community. Later leaders in Islam also promoted their power by claiming to be the religious successors of Muhammad.*

EXPLORING AP® THEMES

Social Interactions and Organization (SIO)

While famous women are scattered throughout world history, students are not always exposed to the lives of more "everyday" women. To allow students to see this different perspective, have them read "Zooming In: Perpetua, Christian Martyr" and use the questions at the end of the passage to guide a class discussion. These questions will also help students practice their sourcing and situation skills.

TEACHING IDEA

Incorporating Outside Resources

To introduce Dar al-Islam, consider having your students watch *Islam, the Quran, and the Five Pillars: Crash Course World History 13*. This roughly 14-minute video found on YouTube provides a good basic overview of the origins of Islam as well as the beginnings of the Islamic empire, all of which provides excellent contextualization for Topic 1.2: Developments in Dar al-Islam in Unit 1. This video can be assigned as homework using your LMS and a quiz.

ZOOMING IN   Perpetua, Christian Martyr

"The blood of the martyrs," declared the Christian writer Tertullian, "is the seed of the church." Few of those martyrs, whose stories so inspired the persecuted converts of the early Christian centuries, could match that of Perpetua, a young woman whose prison diary provides a highly personal account of her arrest and trial.[20]

Born in 181 C.E. in the North African city of Carthage, Perpetua hailed from an upper-class Roman family and was quite well educated, literate in Latin and probably Greek, and acquainted with Roman philosophical writings. By the time she entered the historical record at age twenty-two, she had given birth to a son, had lost her husband to either death or abandonment, and had recently begun to study Christianity, becoming part of a small but growing group of educated people who were turning toward the new faith. Coinciding with her conversion was a wave of persecutions ordered by the Roman emperor Septimus Severus, also of North African descent and a devotee of the Egyptian cult of Isis and Osiris. Severus sought to forbid new conversions rather than punish long-established Christians. In line with this policy, in 203 C.E., the hard-line governor of the region ordered the arrest of Perpetua along with four others—two free men and two enslaved people, including

a woman named Felicitas who was eight months pregnant. Before she was taken to the prison, however, Perpetua decisively confirmed her commitment to Christianity by accepting baptism.

Once in the "dark hole" of the prison, Perpetua was terrified. It was crowded and stiflingly hot, and she was consumed with anxiety for her child. Several fellow Christians managed to bribe the prison guards to permit Perpetua to nurse her baby son. Reunited with her child, she found that "my prison had suddenly become a palace, so that I wanted to be there rather than anywhere else."

A few days later, Perpetua's deeply distressed non-Christian father arrived for a visit, hoping to persuade his only daughter to recant her faith and save her life and the family's honor. It was a heartbreaking encounter. "Daughter," he said, "have pity on my grey head.... Do not abandon me to be the reproach of men. Think of your brothers, think of your mother and your aunt, think of your child, who will not be able to live once you are gone. Give up your pride! You will destroy all of us!" Firm in her faith, Perpetua refused his entreaties, and she reported that "he left me in great sorrow."

On the day of her trial, with her distraught father in attendance, the governor Hilarianus also begged

Middle Eastern Cultural Traditions: Islam

The world historical significance of Islam, the third religion in the Abrahamic family of faiths, has been enormous. It thrust the previously marginal and largely nomadic Arabs into a central role in world history, for it was among them and in their language that the newest of the world's major religions was born during the seventh century C.E. Its emergence was accompanied by the rapid creation of a huge empire that stretched from Spain to India, but the religion of Islam reached beyond that empire, to both East and West Africa, to India, and to Central and Southeast Asia. Within the Arab Empire and beyond it, a new and innovative civilization took shape, drawing on Arab, Persian, Turkic, Greco-Roman, South Asian, and African cultures. It was known as the Dar al-Islam, the house or the abode of Islam.

Perpetua.

Perpetua to consider her family and renounce her faith by offering a sacrifice to the emperor. Again she refused and together with her four companions was "condemned to the beasts," a humiliating form of execution normally reserved for the lower classes. Although she was now permanently separated from her child, she wrote, "We returned to the prison in high spirits." During her last days in the prison, Perpetua and the others were treated "more humanely" and were allowed to visit with family and friends, as the head of the jail was himself a Christian.

But then, on the birthday of the emperor, this small band of Christians was marched to the amphitheater, "joyfully as though they were going to heaven," according to an eyewitness account. After the prisoners strenuously and successfully resisted dressing in the robes of pagan priests, the three men were sent into the arena to contend with a boar, a bear, and a leopard. Then it was the turn of the women, Perpetua and Felicitas, who had given birth only two days earlier. When a mad cow failed to kill them, a soldier was sent to finish the work. As he approached Perpetua, he apparently hesitated, but as an eyewitness account put it, "she took the trembling hand of the young gladiator and guided it to her throat." Appended to her diary was this comment from an unknown observer: "It was as though so great a woman, feared as she was by the unclean spirit, could not be dispatched unless she herself were willing."

QUESTIONS

How might a historian understand the actions and attitudes of Perpetua toward religion? How would modern-day scholars understand her experiences in the context of the era she lived in?

The Arabian Peninsula from which Islam emerged was a land of pastoral people, herders of sheep and camels, but it also contained some regions of settled agricultural communities and sophisticated commercial cities such as Mecca that were linked to long-distance trading routes. Religiously, these people recognized and venerated a variety of gods, goddesses, ancestors, and nature spirits. Arabia was located on the periphery of two established and rival civilizations of that time—the Byzantine Empire, heir to the Roman world, and the Sassanid Empire, heir to the imperial traditions of Persia. Many Jews, Christians, and Zoroastrians lived among the Arabs, and their monotheistic ideas became widely known.

The catalyst for the emergence of Islam was a single individual, **Muhammad** Ibn Abdullah (570–632 C.E.), a trader from Mecca. A highly reflective man who

AP°

CAUSATION

Explain how Muhammad's profession as a merchant may have influenced the early years of Islam.

BUILDING AP® SKILLS

Making Connections: Comparison

To work on building the skill of Comparison, have students discuss the following questions with a partner. After they've had some time to talk with a partner, bring the class back together and have students share what they discussed.

▪ According to the text, how were the Buddha, Jesus, and Muhammad similar? *All three men had powerful religious experiences that convinced them to lead a religious movement.*

▪ Do you think that noting the similarities of such prominent religious figures diminishes their uniqueness? *Answers will vary. Some students may feel that comparing the three diminishes the divinity of Jesus. Many may feel that the comparison doesn't diminish the importance of each leader.*

BUILDING AP® SKILLS

Argumentation

Help students learn how to defend an argument using specific pieces of evidence. Provide students with the following claim and ask them to develop evidence that would support it: "Islam was a revolutionary force religiously and politically for the Arabian Peninsula." They can find evidence in the second, third, and fourth paragraphs on this page. *Possible pieces of evidence include:*

▪ *The belief in Allah as the sole divine being challenged the polytheistic religion of the Arabs.*

▪ *The Quran's teachings challenged the widespread practices of Mecca, such as hoarding wealth, exploiting the poor, charging high interest rates on loans, abusing women, and neglecting widows and orphans.*

▪ *Politically, Islam challenged the tribal and clan structure of Arab society, uniting the formerly separate tribes politically.*

▪ *Tribal, ethnic, and racial identities, which contributed to the fractured nature of the tribes, were replaced with the unifying idea of the umma, the community of all believers in Islam.*

▪ *Women were granted certain legal protections by the Quran.*

Differentiation

Since 60 percent of the AP® World History: Modern Exam score comes from the SAQs, LEQ, and DBQ, it's important to work on writing skills from the start of the course. If you want to start building essay argumentation skills, consider using the "Must Do, Should Do, Strive For" structure:

was deeply troubled by the corruption and social inequalities of Mecca, he often undertook periods of withdrawal and meditation in the arid mountains outside the city. There, Muhammad had a powerful, overwhelming religious experience that left him convinced, albeit reluctantly, that he was Allah's messenger to the Arabs, commissioned to bring to them a scripture in their own language. According to Muslim tradition, the revelations began in 610 and continued periodically over the next twenty-two years. Those revelations, recorded in the **Quran**, became the sacred scriptures of Islam, which to this day most Muslims regard as the very words of God and the core of their faith.

It was a revolutionary message that Muhammad conveyed. Religiously, it presented Allah, the Arabic word for God, as the sole divine being, the all-powerful Creator, thus challenging the highly polytheistic religion of the Arabs. In its exalted conception of Deity, Muhammad's revelations drew heavily on traditions of Jewish and Christian monotheism. As "the Messenger of God," Muhammad presented himself in the line of earlier prophets—Abraham, Moses, Jesus, and many others. He was the last, "the seal of the prophets," bearing God's final revelation to humankind. Islam was socially revolutionary as well. Over and over again the Quran denounced the prevailing social practices of an increasingly prosperous Mecca: the hoarding of wealth, the exploitation of the poor, the charging of high rates of interest on loans, corrupt business deals, the abuse of women, and the neglect of widows and orphans. Like the Jewish prophets of the Hebrew scriptures, the Quran demanded social justice and laid out a prescription for its implementation.

Finally, Islam was politically revolutionary because the Quran challenged the entire tribal and clan structure of Arab society, which was prone to war, feuding, and violence. The just and moral society of Islam was the **umma** (OOM-mah), the community of all believers, which replaced tribal, ethnic, or racial identities. In this community, women too had an honored and spiritually equal place. "The believers, men and women, are protectors of one another," declared the Quran. The umma, then, was to be a new and just community, bound by common belief rather than by territory, language, or tribe.

Like Jesus, Muhammad was threatening to the established authorities in Mecca, and he was forced to leave. But unlike Jesus, he was in a position to resist, for there was no overwhelming force such as the Roman Empire to contend with. So he gathered an army, and by 630 c.e. he had largely unified Arabia under the banner of Islam. Thus Islam began its history as a new state, while Christianity was at odds with the Roman state for over three centuries.

That state soon became a huge empire as Arab armies took the offensive after Muhammad's death in 632 c.e. (see Map 1.4). In many places, conversion to Islam soon followed. In Persia, for example, some 80 percent of the population had made a transition to a Muslim religious identity by 900, and Persian culture became highly prestigious and influential within the Islamic world. One of the early rulers of this Arab Empire observed: "The Persians ruled for a thousand years and did not

AP®
COMPARISON
How could the teachings of the Quran regarding social justice and the poor be seen as attractive to people in lower social classes? How do these teachings compare to those of Buddhism and Christianity?

AP®
COMPARISON
Explain the similarities and differences in the spread of Islam and Christianity.

(continued)

▪ Must Do: Create a bullet point list of evidence that could be used to support the claim "Islam was a revolutionary force religiously and politically for the Arabian Peninsula."

▪ Should Do: Turn the bullet points of evidence into complete sentences to create a simple body paragraph (claim or topic sentence followed by supporting evidence).

▪ Strive For: Extend the body paragraph by analyzing the evidence: How does the evidence show or prove that Islam was a revolutionary force?

TEACHING IDEA

Class Discussion

In what specific ways did Islam differ from Christianity? *Answers should include: Christianity developed independently of political rule; a separate church and state structure evolved. As Islam evolved, however, the political and religious structures grew simultaneously and were held by the same person. Thus there was no difference between religious law and civic law, as there was in the Christian West. One law, the sharia, regulated every aspect of life.*

Map 1.4 The Arab Empire and the Initial Expansion of Islam, 622–900 C.E.
Far more so than with Buddhism or Christianity, the initial spread of Islam was both rapid and extensive. And unlike the other two world religions, Islam quickly gave rise to a huge empire, ruled by Muslim Arabs, that encompassed many of the older civilizations of the region.

▲ **AP**
CAUSATION
How might this map help to explain the rapid spread of Islam?

need us Arabs even for a day. We have been ruling them for one or two centuries and cannot do without them for an hour."[21]

But the idea of a unified Muslim community, so important to Muhammad, proved difficult to realize as conquest and conversion vastly enlarged the Islamic world. Political conflict over who should succeed Muhammad led to civil war and to an enduring division between what became known as the Sunni and Shia branches of Islam. It began as a purely political conflict but acquired over time a deeper significance. For much of early Islamic history, Shia Muslims saw themselves as the minority opposition within Islam. They felt that history had taken a wrong turn and that they were "the defenders of the oppressed, the critics and opponents of privilege and power," while the Sunnis were the advocates of the established order.[22] Other conflicts arose among Arab clans or factions, between Arabs and non-Arabs, and between privileged and wealthy rulers and their less fortunate

EXPLORING AP® THEMES

Humans and the Environment (ENV)

Ask students to study Map 1.4, "The Arab Empire and the Initial Expansion of Islam, 622–900 C.E." Then ask: Where did Islam spread in the centuries after the death of Muhammad? *Islam spread throughout the Arabian Peninsula and into parts of Southwest and Central Asia, North Africa, and the Iberian Peninsula.*

If you want to take the discussion a little further, ask students: How did geography influence the spread of Islam? *Answers may include: The deserts of Southwest Asia and North Africa hindered the spread of Islam; Access to trade routes (Mediterranean Sea, Indian Ocean, Silk Roads, Trans-Saharan network) made it easier for Islam to spread.*

EXPLORING AP® THEMES

Governance (GOV)

To continue getting students to think about the connection between belief systems and politics, you can try asking students: Why did the Islamic empire struggle with maintaining unity as it grew? *After Muhammad's death, an argument erupted over who would succeed him, which led to a civil war between the factions that would become the Sunni and Shi'a. This political conflict later became a religious divide between two branches of Islam, which continued to make it difficult for Islamic leaders to unify their state.*

BUILDING AP® SKILLS

Making Connections: Comparison

It can be helpful to do quick check-ins with students to assess their understanding of the material and quickly practice needed skills. To help students practice comparisons and check their understanding of Christianity and Islam, you could ask them to explain why divisions emerged within Christianity and Islam, leading to different branches of these religions. *In Christianity, there was a disagreement over who was the leader of the church, either the pope or the Byzantine emperor, which led to the creation of Roman Catholic Christianity and Eastern Orthodox Christianity. Islam also had a disagreement over who would lead the community after Muhammad's death, causing division into the Sunni and Shi'a branches of Islam.*

subjects. After 900 or so, any political unity that Islamic civilization had earlier enjoyed had vanished.

And yet, there was much that bound the Islamic world together, culturally if not politically. The rise of Islam had generated a transcontinental civilization, embracing at least parts of virtually every other civilization in the Afro-Eurasian hemisphere. The Quran, universal respect for Muhammad, common religious texts, a ritual prayer five times a day, and the required pilgrimage to Mecca—all of this was common to the many peoples of the Islamic world.

AP® EXAM TIP
Compare features of leadership in major religions, using the ulama in Islam as one example.

No group was more important in the transmission of those beliefs and practices than the **ulama**. These learned scholars served as judges, interpreters, administrators, prayer leaders, and reciters of the Quran, but especially as preservers and teachers of the **sharia** or Islamic law. In their homes, mosques, shrines, and Quranic schools, the ulama passed on the core teachings of the faith. Beginning in the eleventh century, formal colleges called **madrassas** offered more advanced instruction in the Quran and the sayings of Muhammad; grammar and rhetoric; sometimes philosophy, theology, mathematics, and medicine; and, above all else, law. Teaching was informal, mostly oral, and involved much memorization of

▶ **AP®**
CLAIMS AND EVIDENCE IN SOURCES
How could this image be used to explain cultural connections between Islamic, Jewish, and Christian traditions?

The Dome of the Rock, Jerusalem The Dome of the Rock was constructed on the site from which Muslims believe that Muhammad ascended into the presence of Allah during his Night Journey, referred to in the Quran. Centered on its great golden dome, it was the first large-scale building project in the Islamic world. Its placement on the Temple Mount in the heart of Jerusalem, a site that is also sacred to Jews and Christians, offers a physical reminder of the close relationship between these three monotheistic faiths. (Pictures from History/Andrew Shiva/Bridgeman Images)

APPLY THE TIP

This is a good place to have a quick discussion using the exam tip; you can even use it to jump into the skill-building idea below. Ask students to explain the role the ulama played in Islam. *These were learned scholars who served as judges, administrators, and prayer leaders, who recited the Quran, and who taught the sharia.*

Then ask: How was the role of the ulama as leaders in Islam different from the role of leaders in other major religions? *Answers will vary.*

BUILDING AP® SKILLS

Claims and Evidence in Sources

To practice the skill of finding an author's argument and supporting evidence, ask students to list the specific evidence the authors use on pages 42 and 43 to support their thesis that many factors united Dar al-Islam (the larger Islamic community). (Answers are provided in italics.)

■ Ulama: *The ulama were learned scholars of Islam who preserved and taught the sharia.*

■ Madrassas: *These Quranic schools offered teachings in law, grammar, rhetoric, philosophy, theology, mathematics, and medicine.*

■ Internationalism: *The ulama lived in all parts of the empire and served as an international elite that traveled long distances to confer with one another.*

texts. It was also largely conservative, seeking to preserve an established body of Islamic learning.

The ulama were an "international elite," and the system of education they created bound together an immense and diverse civilization. Common texts were shared widely across the world of Islam. Students and teachers alike traveled great distances in search of the most learned scholars. From Indonesia to West Africa, educated Muslims inhabited a widely shared tradition.

Paralleling the educational network of the ulama were the emerging religious orders of the Sufis, who had a quite different understanding of Islam, for they viewed the worldly success of Islamic civilization as a distraction and deviation from the purer spirituality of Muhammad's time. Emerging strongly by 1000, Sufis represented Islam's mystical dimension, in that they sought a direct and personal experience of the Divine. Through renunciation of the material world, meditation on the words of the Quran, chanting of the names of God, the use of music and dance, and the veneration of Muhammad and various "saints," adherents of **Sufism** pursued an interior life, seeking to tame the ego and achieve spiritual union with Allah.

This mystical tendency in Islamic practice, which became widely popular by the ninth and tenth centuries, was at times sharply critical of the more scholarly and legalistic practitioners of the sharia. To Sufis, establishment teachings about the law and correct behavior, while useful for daily living, did little to bring the believer into the presence of God. Furthermore, Sufis felt that many of the ulama had been compromised by their association with worldly and corrupt governments. Sufis therefore often charted their own course to God, implicitly challenging the religious authority of the ulama. For many centuries, roughly 1100 to 1800, Sufism was central to mainstream Islam, and many, perhaps most, Muslims affiliated with one or another Sufi organization, making use of its spiritual practices. Nonetheless, differences in emphasis about the essential meaning of Islam remained an element of tension and sometimes discord within the Muslim world.

In the twelfth and thirteenth centuries, Sufis began to organize in a variety of larger associations, some limited to particular regions and others with chapters throughout the Islamic world. Sufi orders were especially significant in the frontier regions of Islam because they followed conquering armies or traders into Central and Southeast Asia, India, Anatolia, parts of Africa, and elsewhere. Their devotional teachings, modest ways of living, and reputation for supernatural powers gained a hearing for the new faith. Their emphasis on personal experience of the Divine, rather than on the law, allowed the Sufis to accommodate elements of local belief and practice and encouraged the growth of a popular or blended Islam. The veneration of deceased Sufi "saints," or "friends of God," particularly at their tombs, created sacred spaces that enabled Islam to take root in many places despite its foreign origins. But that flexibility also often earned Sufi practitioners the enmity of the ulama, who were sharply critical of any deviations from the sharia.

BUILDING AP® SKILLS

Making Connections: Comparison

Have students create a Venn diagram to compare the beliefs and practices of Sufism with the other two branches of Islam (Sunni and Shi'a). Students should make at least two to four points of comparison in each part of their diagram using the information found on pages 40–43. For this activity, the Teacher's Resource Materials include a reproducible diagram.

TRM **Handout 1.6: Comparison Graphic Organizer for Sunni and Shi'a Islam**

EXPLORING AP® THEMES

Cultural Developments and Interactions (CDI)

Students don't always think about the role Sufis played in the spread of Islam. The last two paragraphs on this page are a good place to ask students about that role: By 1000 c.e., a new aspect of Islam known as Sufism emerged, representing Islam's mystical element. What role did the Sufis play in the spread and organization of Islam after 1000 c.e.?

Answers may include: Sufis challenged the authority of the ulama and offered a more personal religious experience, which allowed the Sufis to accommodate local beliefs and encouraged the growth of Islam; Many Muslims made use of Sufi religious practices, and they became central to mainstream Islam; Sufi orders' teachings, way of living, and reputation for supernatural powers helped gain followers for Islam in the frontier regions.

Interactions and Encounters

Finding the Main Point: How did cultural and religious traditions spread across regions before 1200 C.E.?

AP®
CAUSATION
In what ways did cross-cultural interactions drive change in the pre-1200 world?

AP® EXAM TIP
Have a map in your head of where major religions began and where they spread to. Make sure you know how they spread as well (such as through conquest or trade).

AP® EXAM TIP
Be sure to know the similarities and differences among major trade routes over time.

Long before the globalized world of the twentieth century and well before the voyages of Columbus connected the Eastern and Western hemispheres, interactions across the boundaries of these civilizations and cultural traditions had transformed human societies, for better and for worse. Thus world history is less about what happened within particular civilizations or cultures than about the interactions and encounters among them. Focusing on cross-cultural connections counteracts a habit of thinking about particular peoples or civilizations as self-contained or isolated communities. To varying degrees, each of them was embedded in a network of relationships with both neighboring and more distant peoples. And broadly speaking, those cross-cultural connections grew more dense and complex over time. Various kinds of interactions and encounters had emerged long before 1200, many of which persisted and accelerated in the centuries that followed.

One setting in which culturally different societies encountered one another was that of empire, for those large states often incorporated a vast range of peoples and provided opportunity for communication and borrowing among them. Empires also served as arenas of exchange, as products, foods, ideas, religions, and disease circulated among the many peoples of imperial states. For example, various non-Roman cultural traditions—such as the cult of the Persian god Mithra or the compassionate Egyptian goddess Isis, and, most extensively, the Jewish-derived religion of Christianity—spread throughout the Roman Empire during the early centuries of the Common Era. In the tenth century and after, a state-sponsored adoption of Christianity occurred in the emerging Russian state, later leading to the eastern spread of Christianity across much of northern Asia in an expanding Russian Empire. An Arab Empire, expanding rapidly in the several centuries after the death of Muhammad in 632 C.E., encompassed all or part of Egyptian, Persian, Mesopotamian, Roman, and Indian civilizations. Both within and beyond that empire the new religion of Islam spread quite rapidly, generating a major cultural transformation across much of the Afro-Eurasian world.

Yet another mechanism for the interaction of distant peoples lay in commercial exchange. Premodern commerce moved along a chain of separate transactions in which goods traveled farther than individual merchants. Networks of exchange and communication extending all across the Afro-Eurasian world, and separately in parts of the Americas and Oceania as well, slowly came into being. Such long-distance trade was a powerful motor of historical change. It altered habits of consumption, changed the working lives of many people, enabled class distinctions, stimulated and sustained the creation of states, and fostered the diffusion of religion, technology, and disease.

The most famous of these early commercial networks is widely known as the **Silk Roads**, a reference to their most famous product. Beginning around 200 B.C.E., the Silk Road trading complex operated to varying degrees for over 1,500 years, linking China and the Mediterranean world as well as many places in between. Paralleling the land-based routes of the Silk Roads and flourishing at roughly the same time were sea-based networks—the **Sea Roads**—that traversed the Indian Ocean and the South China Sea, linking the diverse peoples living between southern China and East Africa. Yet another important pattern of long-distance trade—this one across the vast reaches of the Sahara in a series of **Sand Roads** (also called the trans-Saharan trade routes)—linked North Africa and the Mediterranean world with the land and peoples of interior West Africa. Finally, in the Americas, direct connections among various civilizations and cultures were less densely woven than in the Afro-Eurasian region. Nonetheless, scholars have discerned a variety of cultural and commercial linkages that operated throughout the Americas.[23] (See Chapter 3 for more on this topic.)

All of this exchange began well before 1200 and persisted well after it. The chapters that follow will continue the story of these diverse civilizations and societies, the movement of their cultural traditions, and their multiple interactions with one another.

CONCLUSIONS AND REFLECTIONS

Religion and Historians

Finding the Main Point: What problems or tensions can arise when historians study the religious experiences of humans around the world?

Chapter 1 provides a big picture context for this AP® World History Modern course by looking at major turning points in the human journey before 1200. It reminds us that most of that story—perhaps 250,000 years—took place while humankind sustained itself with a gathering and hunting economy. But beginning around 12,000 years ago, the Agricultural Revolution created wholly new ways of living that gradually spread around the world. Then about 5,500 years ago, productive agricultural economies began to generate "civilizations" with their characteristic cities, states, and massive social and gender inequalities. Those civilizations subsequently gave rise to cultural traditions, often expressed in religious terms, that gave meaning and structure to the growing numbers of people living in them. However, historians' efforts to understand the cultural or religious dimension of human life have generated various tensions and misunderstandings between scholars and believers.

One of these tensions involves the question of change. Most religions present themselves as timeless revelations from the beyond that partake of eternity or at least reflect ancient practice. In the eyes of historians, however, the religious aspect of human life changes as much as any other. Buddhism became more conventionally religious, with an emphasis on the supernatural, as it evolved from Theravada to Mahayana forms. A male-dominated hierarchical Christian Church, with

TEACHING IDEA

Exit Slip

As a quick way to gauge student understanding of the different religions and philosophies in Chapter 1, you might try asking students to write a quick response to the following question: Of the various belief systems described in Chapter 1, which one do you think is the most effective in helping maintain political and social order? Defend your answer with specific pieces of evidence. *Answers will vary.* Have students give you their answers as they leave the room.

EXPLORING AP® THEMES

Cultural Developments and Interactions (CDI)

The spread of religions is a critical part of early world history and helps with contextualization in later periods of global history. To help students understand how religions spread and overlapped, you could show students the *Business Insider* video's animated map of the spread of religion, which can be found on YouTube. As students watch the animated map, have them answer the following questions:

■ Which religion expanded first? *Hinduism expanded first.*

■ Which religion expanded most recently? *Islam expanded most recently.*

■ Which religion expanded the fastest? *Islam expanded the fastest.*

■ What interesting expansion fact did you notice about Buddhism? *Buddhism expanded throughout India, then moved to East Asia while it receded from India.*

■ What did you notice about Judaism? *It did not have much of a presence on the map for a time. When the state of Israel was created, it reappeared.*

■ What was most influential in the expansion of Christianity? *The age of exploration was most influential in the expansion of Christianity.*

■ How did the partition of Africa influence religion? *The partition of Africa spread Christianity.*

■ Why do you think there is a pocket of Hinduism in the Suriname area of South America? *There was a South Asian diaspora as a result of the demand for sugar.*

TEACHING IDEA

Class Discussion

If you want students to dig into challenges historians face while studying history and to think about how that knowledge might affect them while studying world history, have them read the last four paragraphs on page 46. Then ask: What challenges do historians face when studying global belief systems? *Possible answers include: Historians might be uncomfortable with the claims of believers that they have experienced a divine reality or that God or gods shape human history; Historians might have to resist the urge to "take sides" in debates about religious beliefs and traditions and about what the "real" beliefs are (like the Catholic-Protestant debate or Sunni-Shi'a debate); Historians might struggle with the fact that belief systems are used to justify social and political inequalities for some groups while also providing sources of comfort and hope to others.*

You could then follow up with this question: How does knowing about these challenges historians face affect or influence how you'll study material in world history? *Answers will vary.*

If you are uncomfortable discussing this topic with a full class, you could ask students to silently reflect on it through writing.

its patriarchs, popes, bishops, priests, and state support, was very different from the small house churches that suffered persecution by imperial authorities in the early Christian centuries. Islam evolved both legalistic and more mystical practices. The implication—that religions are largely a human phenomenon—has been troublesome to some believers.

Historians, on the other hand, have sometimes been uncomfortable in the face of claims by believers that they have actually experienced a divine reality or that God or the gods have shaped human history. Certainly, modern scholars, dependent on evidence in this world, are in no position to validate or refute the spiritual claims of religious leaders and their many followers. But historians need to take those ideas seriously. Although we will never know precisely what happened to the Buddha as he sat in meditation in northern India or what transpired when Jesus spent forty days in the wilderness, clearly those experiences changed the two men and motivated their subsequent actions. Millions of their followers have also acted on the basis of what they perceived to be a compelling encounter with an unseen realm. This interior dimension of human experience, though difficult to grasp with any precision and impossible to verify, has been a significant mover and shaper of the historical process.

Yet a third problem arises from debates within particular religious traditions about which group most accurately represents the "real" or authentic version of the faith. Historians usually refuse to take sides in such disputes. They simply notice with interest that most human cultural traditions generate conflicting views, some of which become the basis for serious conflict in societies. The differences between Roman Catholic, Eastern Orthodox, and later Protestant Christians, as well as between Sunni and Shia Muslims, illustrate the point.

Reconciling personal religious convictions with the perspectives of modern historical scholarship is no easy task. At the very least, all of us can appreciate the immense human effort that has gone into the making of cultural or religious traditions, and we can acknowledge their enormous significance in the unfolding of the human story.

These religious traditions have been used to justify the vast social inequalities and oppressive governments of human civilizations by persuading millions that their lot in life was fixed by ancient tradition or divine decree. But religions have also enabled human beings to find comfort and hope amid the multiple sufferings that attend human life. Furthermore, religions have often been critical of established social patterns and on occasion have stimulated reform and rebellion. Jewish prophets railed against the injustices of their societies; Jesus and Muhammad alike attacked elite corruption and hypocrisy. Both the Buddha and bhakti Hindus pushed back against the restrictions of India's caste system. And popular forms of Daoism inspired resistance and rebellion in a number of peasant-based upheavals in China. Finally, religious traditions have shaped the meanings that billions of people over thousands of years have attached to the world they inhabit. In doing so, they have guided much of humankind in its endless efforts to penetrate the mysteries of the world beyond and of the world within.

CHAPTER REVIEW

AP° Key Terms

Paleolithic era, 10

Agricultural Revolution, 13

pastoral society, 14

patriarchy, 22

Hinduism, 26

Upanishads, 27

Siddhartha Gautama (the Buddha), 28

Theravada Buddhism, 29

Mahayana Buddhism, 29

bhakti movement, 31

Confucianism, 32

Han dynasty, 32

Daoism, 34

Judaism, 35

Jesus of Nazareth, 36

Saint Paul, 36

Perpetua, 37

Muhammad, 39

Quran, 40

umma, 40

ulama, 42

sharia, 42

madrassas, 42

Sufism, 43

Silk Roads, 44

Sea Roads, 45

Sand Roads, 45

Finding the Main Point

1. In what ways did the Agricultural Revolution transform human life?

2. What is distinctive about civilizations compared to other forms of human society? How did particular civilizations differ from one another?

3. What similarities and differences can you identify among the major religious traditions that emerged in the Afro-Eurasian world before 1200 c.e.?

4. How did cultural and religious traditions spread across regions before 1200 c.e.?

5. What problems or tensions can arise when historians study the religious experiences of humans around the world?

AP° Big Picture Questions

1. What different types of societies emerged out of the Agricultural Revolution?

2. In what ways might the advent of "civilization" have marked a revolutionary change in the human condition? And in what ways did it carry on earlier patterns from the past?

3. In what ways did religion support political authorities and social elites? How did it challenge them?

4. Why have human cultural traditions, such as religions, generally changed less over time than the political systems in which they were born?

TRM Suggested Responses to Questions

You can find suggested responses to the Chapter Review questions in the Teacher's Resource Materials.

BUILDING AP® SKILLS

Developments and Processes

This is a good section to have your class read through to get an introduction to the skill of Developments and Processes. To help them practice this skill, assign students major events, developments, people, or processes from Chapter 1 and have them write out the three steps (identify, describe, explain) for their assigned topic as demonstrated in this section. Suggested topics: civilizations; development of patriarchy; Hinduism; Buddhism; Confucianism; Daoism; Judaism; Christianity; Islam; Sufism.

Developments and Processes

In this workshop, you will learn about developments and processes, an AP® skill that is foundational to any history course. You will need to know developments and processes before you can apply more complex historical thinking skills and reasoning processes.

UNDERSTANDING DEVELOPMENTS AND PROCESSES

When learning about world history, it is essential to be able to identify and explain historical events. This skill is the jumping-off point that allows for all other historical reasoning skills to occur. History is a collection of events, developments, and processes. As a student of history, your first job is to IDENTIFY a certain historical concept, development, or process, DESCRIBE its characteristics, and then EXPLAIN its importance. From there, you can begin to discuss causation, compare it to other events, and analyze what changed or stayed the same over time. You will need to identify, describe, and explain the significance of historical events, developments, people, and processes from 1200 to the present on the AP® Exam. Let's go over the steps you should go through when thinking about developments and processes:

Identify: Name a historical process, development, or event.

> The passage is discussing the Agricultural Revolution.

Describe: Make something clear by describing or defining it in detail.

> This was a time period when the people in different places around the world began using agriculture to grow food.

Explain: Discuss why this concept, development, or process is important or significant to world history.

> This is significant because the Agricultural Revolution changed how societies organized themselves from hunters and gatherers to people in permanent farming settlements. Agriculture also led to the creation of social classes, an increase in patriarchy, and a worldwide population increase.

When discussing and writing about a historical event, we want to follow these steps: IDENTIFY the event, DESCRIBE the event, and then EXPLAIN why it is significant. We do this naturally all the time when we are discussing our day-to-day lives. Think about it. When someone asks you what you did last weekend, you first IDENTIFY what happened: "I went to the beach on Saturday." Then you DESCRIBE the event with more detail: "I went with Chloe and Sophia to celebrate Chloe's sixteenth birthday. We swam all day, played beach volleyball, and had pizza until the sun went down." And then finally, you EXPLAIN why it was significant: "The sunset was one of the most beautiful

I have seen in a long time, and I could tell it meant a lot to Chloe that we were all there to celebrate her special day."

It is the same with history. First you IDENTIFY a historical concept, development, or process that is being referred to in a document: "This passage discussing the proper roles of husbands and fathers in East Asia is illustrating Confucianism." Then you DESCRIBE the historical concept, development, or process you identified: "Confucianism was an ideology created by Kong Fuzi during the warring states period that sought to promote societal harmony by creating and enforcing proper roles for everyone in society." And then you EXPLAIN why this event was significant to world history: "This is an important development because Confucianism became the main political and social institution in China. Aspects of Confucianism such as filial piety spread to other East Asian nations like Korea, Japan, and Vietnam."

DEVELOPMENTS AND PROCESSES ON THE AP® WORLD HISTORY EXAM

You will use this skill on the AP® World History Exam with the Multiple-Choice Questions, Short-Answer Questions, the Document-Based Question, and the Long Essay Question. These questions will assess your ability to identify and explain historical documents. If you don't have a good understanding of the course content—of the empires, processes, and events of world history—it will be difficult to answer any of the questions on the exam.

On Multiple-Choice Questions, you may be asked to read a passage or look at an image and then pick a historical development that best illustrates what is being discussed in the passage or image. In this situation, you are learning what is happening in the reading and then IDENTIFYING the historical process that is occurring. On Short-Answer Questions, you may be asked to IDENTIFY a historical process associated with an image and then EXPLAIN its significance. On a Document-Based Question, you may be asked to EXPLAIN how and why a historical concept, development, or process emerged. On a Long Essay Question, you may be asked to DESCRIBE the characteristics of a historical process and EXPLAIN its significance.

BUILDING AP® SKILLS

1. **Activity: Identifying Developments and Processes.** Identify ONE way Buddhism was diffused across Asia.

2. **Activity: Identifying Developments and Processes.** Explain ONE way in which Islam changed the societies in which it took root as it spread across Afro-Eurasia.

3. **Activity: Identifying Developments and Processes.** Look at the image "The Chinese Examination System" on page 33 and do a quickwrite identifying the historical development, describing it, and explaining its significance.

TRM Suggested Responses to Questions
You can find suggested responses to the Building AP® Skills questions in the Teacher's Resource Materials.

BUILDING AP® SKILLS

Argumentation

You can extend the Developments and Processes activity from page 48 by asking students to practice writing a Short-Answer Question (SAQ) response based on what they learned. Since this is the first time students are diving into the material and are starting to practice their writing skills, use the prompt from Activity 1 on page 49 to introduce SAQ writing to them. Once students have written their response, you can have them share what they wrote with a partner or ask for volunteers to share with the entire class to give feedback.

49

Islamic Practice in West Africa through the Eyes of a Foreign Traveler

TRM Suggested Responses to Questions

You can find suggested responses to the AP® Looking Again questions in the Teacher's Resource Materials.

BUILDING AP® SKILLS

Sourcing and Situation

Sourcing a document (explaining how or why a document's point of view, purpose, historical situation, and/or audience is relevant to an argument) is one of the most difficult points to achieve on the Document-Based Question essay. Practicing this skill throughout the year is the best way to help students learn it and build confidence in being able to do it. If you want to start working on this skill with students early, the Ibn Battuta document on pages 50 and 51 is a great place to start. Have the students read the excerpt and answer the two questions in the "First Look" (it might be a good idea to have the excerpt and questions on a separate sheet of paper so they don't read ahead). The questions will guide the students on how to analyze a document to prepare to write a sourcing statement. Once the students have read and answered the questions, ask them to share what they found with the class.

To reconstruct the past, historians rely on primary sources—that is, evidence from the period being studied. While sources come in many forms, written accounts by eyewitnesses provide one rich type of source for historical research. But eyewitness accounts, like all written sources, must be handled with care because they are filtered through the perspectives of their creators and are frequently produced with a specific purpose or intended audience in mind. Thus, when analyzing a source, the historian must place it in its historical situation—what is commonly referred to as "sourcing a document." No source simply recounts "what happened" without a perspective, although some are more heavily influenced by the creator's perspective and purpose than others.

To explore how an awareness of a source's perspective, purpose, and intended audience can shape how a historian interprets a source, let's examine one of the few surviving descriptions of fourteenth-century Islamic West African civilization. It was composed by the North African Ibn Battuta (1304–1368) shortly after his return from a journey to the kingdom of Mali in 1354. His account offers a wide-ranging description of this West African society. The passage reproduced here offers a detailed account of how men and women interacted in the region.

1 A FIRST LOOK

While reading, consider the following:

1. How would you describe the tone of Ibn Battuta's account? Is his description neutral, positive, negative, or perhaps a mixture of the three?

2. Can you identify specific passages where he passes judgment on what he sees? What criteria does he use to make these judgments? What can these judgments reveal about Ibn Battuta's perspective?

IBN BATTUTA | *Travels in Asia and Africa* | 1354

Men and Women in Iwalatan

Thus we reached the town of Iwalatan after a journey . . . [across the Sahara Desert] of two months to a day. Iwalatan is the northernmost province of the blacks. . . .

Their women are of surpassing beauty, and are shown more respect than the men. The state of affairs amongst these people is indeed extraordinary. Their men show no signs of jealousy whatever; no one claims descent from his father, but on the contrary from his mother's brother. A person's heirs are his sister's sons, not his own sons. This is a thing which I have seen nowhere in the world except among the Indians of Malabar. But those are heathens; these people are Muslims, punctilious in observing the hours of prayer, studying books of law, and memorizing the Koran [Quran]. Yet their women show no bashfulness before men and do not veil themselves, though they are assiduous in attending the prayers.

The women there have "friends" and "companions" amongst the men outside their own families, and the men in the same way have "companions" amongst the women of other families. A man may go into his house and find his wife entertaining her "companion," but he takes no objection to it. One day at Iwalatan I went into the qadi's [an Islamic judge] house, after asking his permission to enter, and found with him a young woman of remarkable beauty. When I saw her I was shocked and turned to go out, but she laughed at me, instead of being overcome by shame, and the qadi said to me "Why are you going out? She is my companion." I was amazed at their conduct, for he was a theologian and a pilgrim [to Mecca] to boot. . . .

Source: Ibn Battuta, *Travels in Asia and Africa, 1325–1354*, translated and edited by H. A. R. Gibb (London: Broadway House, 1929), 319–34.

---

2 A SECOND LOOK

Now that you have read his account, let's consider what we know about Ibn Battuta himself. He was a well-educated Muslim legal scholar from Morocco in North Africa who came from a family of Islamic legal scholars. Thus he considered himself a representative of traditional orthodox Islam. When he trekked across the Sahara to West Africa at the age of fifty, he was surely one of the most widely traveled people of his age. He had already journeyed more than 50,000 miles and visited almost every corner of the Islamic world, including the Arab heartland with its holy cities of Mecca and Medina, the vast steppes of Central Asia, the states of northern India, the Indian Ocean basin from East Africa to Southeast Asia, and even the small Muslim trading community in China. Along the way, he encountered many non-Muslim communities as well. Journeying at different times as a pilgrim, a Sufi religious seeker, or a legal scholar, he often traveled in the company of Muslim merchants and frequently served for a time as an Islamic judge in the places he visited. Thus, by the time that Battuta arrived in West Africa, he was a seasoned traveler with considerable experience encountering new and unfamiliar cultures and societies.

1. How might Ibn Battuta's extensive travels have influenced his description of West Africa? Can you find any direct evidence of his earlier travels in his account of the relationship between women and men in Iwalatan?

3 A THIRD LOOK

Shortly after returning from West Africa, a local ruler in Ibn Battuta's home region arranged for a young scholar to work with the intrepid traveler in recording his remarkable journeys across Asia and Africa in a form of Arabic literature known as rihla, a journey in search of knowledge. Over the next several years, the two created what became known as A Gift to Those Who Contemplate the Wonders of Cities and the Marvels of Traveling, commonly referred to simply as The Rihla. Thus Battuta's description of relations between women and men in Iwalatan was created at the behest of a powerful

---

BUILDING AP® SKILLS
Sourcing and Situation

If you feel that your students are ready to take the next step with practicing sourcing or if you'd like to challenge them, have them read through the "Second Look" and "Third Look" sections on pages 51 and 52 and answer the questions. This would also be a good place to have a class discussion on their observations of Ibn Battuta and how their ideas are changing after taking another look or two at him.

patron, written primarily for an elite Islamic audience in his home region, and part of a much larger account of his many journeys over several decades.

1. How might the experiences and cultural norms of his intended audience have influenced how Ibn Battuta described West African civilization?

2. Can you identify any specific passages where Ibn Battuta judges West African civilization with reference to the cultural norms of his home region, including such practices as the strict limitation of interactions between men and women who were not from the same family, modest dress for both sexes that covered the body, and family lineages defined primarily through the male line?

3. What might make Ibn Battuta's account more accessible to his intended audience of well-educated fourteenth-century Muslim North Africans than it is to you?

AP® ACTIVITY WRITING A SOURCING STATEMENT

When using evidence like Ibn Battuta's description of West Africa, historians introduce the source by creating a sourcing statement that helps a reader know where the evidence comes from and what to take into account when evaluating it. This usually takes the form of a sentence or two introducing the creator of the source and the source itself and typically precedes the first use of the source.

1. Take on the role of a historian by writing a sourcing statement for Ibn Battuta's description of the relationship between men and women in Iwalatan with a fellow student in mind. What do you think is essential for your classmate to know before reading the account? Be sure to consider the perspective of the author and the historical situation in which his account was written.

FURTHER ACTIVITY

Travelers' accounts also often inadvertently reveal much about the author and the society that the author came from. What does Ibn Battuta's description of his visit to Mali reveal about his own attitudes and his image of himself?

TEACHING IDEA

Class Discussion

It can be fun for students to connect what they are learning to their own lives, while also building the skills needed to be successful in AP® World History: Modern. To start a class discussion on how your personal history and attitudes can influence how you perceive other groups and history, use the prompt about Ibn Battuta under the "Further Activity" section on page 52, "What does Ibn Battuta's description of his visit to Mali reveal about his own attitudes and his image of himself?" *Possible answers include: Ibn Battuta came from a more patriarchal society and was shocked by the "extraordinary" way the Malian people ran their society; He followed a stricter practice of Islam regarding the roles of men and women; He might have seen himself as a "better" Muslim than the Malians because of the way Malian men and women interacted.*

After students have discussed their observations, ask, "Has there been a time when your view of another group, country, or culture was shaped by your attitudes and image of yourself? Make sure to be respectful in your answer." *Answers will vary.*

AP® WORKING WITH EVIDENCE

The "Good Life" in Asian Cultural Traditions

Many wisdom traditions that emerged in Asia before 1200 were fundamentally religious, focusing on human interaction with an unseen realm. Sometimes they expressed this realm as a world of divine beings, God or gods, as in Judaism, Christianity, and some forms of Hinduism and Buddhism. Alternatively, the more mystical expressions of these faiths, as well as Chinese Daoism, at times articulated the unseen realm in less personal ways, as a sustaining or pervasive Presence, located variously above, beyond, beneath, or within the human and visible realm. Some of these traditions—Chinese Confucianism and Greek rationalism, for example—were less overtly religious, expressed in more philosophical, humanistic, or rational terms. But what they all shared was an impulse to address the moral and social implications of their understandings of the cosmos, probing the nature of a "good life" for an individual person or a "good society" for a community of people. How should we live in this world? This was among the central questions that have occupied human beings since the beginning of conscious thought. And that question certainly played a major role in the emerging cultural traditions of civilizations all across Eurasia. The sources that follow present a sample of this thinking drawn from Chinese, Indian, and Middle Eastern traditions.

LOOKING AHEAD

AP® DBQ PRACTICE

As you read the documents in this collection, consider what they reveal about belief systems in Eurasia. Think also about the effects these traditions had on social hierarchies.

DOCUMENT 1 **Reflections from Confucius**

No one was more central to the making of Chinese civilization than Confucius (551–479 B.C.E.). In the several generations following their master's death, his disciples recalled his teachings and his conversations, recording them in a small book called the *Analects*. This text became a touchstone for all educated people in China and across much of East Asia as well. Over the centuries, extensive commentaries and interpretations of Confucius's teachings gave rise to a body of literature known generally as Confucianism, though these ideas encompassed the thinking of many others as well.

In the translation from the *Analects* that follows, the word "virtue" refers to the qualities of a complete or realized human being, sometimes rendered in Confucian literature as a "gentleman" or a "virtuous man."

TRM **Suggested Responses to Questions**
You can find suggested responses to the AP® Working with Evidence questions in the Teacher's Resource Materials.

BUILDING AP® SKILLS

Claims and Evidence in Sources

Analyzing text-based as well as non-text-based sources is an important skill for AP® World History students. If you have the time, have students learn more about how different belief systems viewed the "good life" by using the evidence in "The 'Good Life' in Asian Cultural Traditions" beginning on page 53. Consider having students analyze one or more of the sources found on pages 53–59. Check for understanding by:

■ Using the questions at the end of each source as a discussion starting point.

■ Pairing students to identify and describe the author or creator's point of view, purpose, historical situation, and audience.

■ Assigning a source to a group of three to four students and having them present an overview of the source along with the sourcing to the rest of the class.

■ Having students present an overview of the source. Then have them discuss how they might use it to develop an argument in response to Question 1 under Doing History (page 60).

53

The Master said, "He who exercises government by means of his virtue may be compared to the north polar star, which keeps its place and all the stars turn toward it." . . .

Chi K'ang asked how to cause the people to reverence their ruler, to be faithful to him. The Master said, "Let him preside over them with gravity; then they will reverence him. Let him be filial and kind to all; then they will be faithful to him. Let him advance the good and teach the incompetent; then they will eagerly seek to be virtuous."

The Master said, "If the will be set on virtue, there will be no practice of wickedness." . . .

The Master said, "Of all people, girls and servants are the most difficult to behave to. If you are familiar with them, they lose their humility. If you maintain a reserve toward them, they are discontented."

Question to Consider: How do "virtue," "filial piety," and "learning" relate to the larger task of creating good government and a harmonious society?

AP Analyzing Sources: What was going on before and during Confucius's life that motivated his writings?

DOCUMENT 2 | A Daoist Perspective on the Good Life

Chinese thinking about the good life was not limited to the Confucian tradition. An alternative or perhaps a complement to it took shape in the writings of the mysterious figure of Laozi, who, it is said, chose to pursue the Way (*dao*) beyond the confines of Chinese civilization. The tradition that arose from Laozi and those who expanded on his ideas became known as Daoism. Here are brief selections from Laozi's famous work, the *Daodejing* (The Way and Its Power), which emerged around 400 B.C.E.

1. Do not exalt the worthy, so that the people shall not compete. Do not value goods that are hard to get, so that the people shall not steal. Do not display objects of desire, so that the people's hearts shall not be disturbed. Therefore in the government of the sage, he keeps their hearts vacuous, fills their bellies, weakens their ambitions, and strengthens their bones. He always causes his people to be without knowledge or desire, and the crafty to be afraid to act. By acting without action, all things will be in order. . . .

8. The best man is like water. Water is good; it benefits all things and does not compete with them. It dwells in lowly places that all disdain. This is why it is so near to the Dao. The best man in his dwelling loves the earth. In his heart, he loves what is profound. In his associations, he loves humanity. In his words, he loves faithfulness. In government, he loves order. In handling affairs, he loves competence. In his activities, he loves timeliness. . . .

17. The best rulers are those whose existence is merely known by the people. The next best are those who are loved and praised. The next are those who are feared. And the next are those who are despised. It is only when one does not have enough faith in others that others will have no faith in him.

Question to Consider: How does Laozi's prescription for a good life differ from that of Confucius?

AP® **Analyzing Sources:** How does the point of view of Lao Tzu impact how he views the role of government?

DOCUMENT 3 **Reflections from the Hindu Scriptures**

The flavor of Indian thinking about the good life and the good society is quite different from that of Confucius and Laozi. This distinctive outlook is reflected in these selections from the Bhagavad Gita (The Song of the Lord), perhaps the most treasured of Hindu writings. Its dating is highly uncertain, although most scholars put it somewhere between the fifth and second centuries B.C.E. The Bhagavad Gita itself is an episode within the *Mahabharata*, one of the huge epic poems of India's classical tradition that describes the struggle for power between two branches of the same family. The Bhagavad Gita takes place on the eve of a great battle, when the fearless warrior Arjuna is overcome with the realization that in this battle he will be required to kill some of his own kinsmen. In his distress, he turns for advice to his charioteer, Lord Krishna, who is an incarnation of the great god Vishnu. Krishna's response to Arjuna's anguished questions, a part of which is reproduced here, conveys the essence of Hindu thinking about life and action in this world. A central question in the Bhagavad Gita is how a person can achieve spiritual fulfillment while remaining active in the world.

Source: From the Bhagavad Gita (The Song of the Lord), a Hindu epic poem, ca. 5th–2nd centuries B.C.E.

Every man intent on his own respective duties obtains perfection. Listen, now, how one intent on one's own duty obtains perfection. Worshipping, by the performance of his own duty, him from whom all things proceed, and by whom all this is permeated, a man obtains perfection. One's duty, though defective, is better than another's duty well performed. Performing the duty prescribed by nature, one does not incur sin. O son of Kunti! one should not abandon a natural duty though tainted with evil; for all actions are enveloped by evil, as fire by smoke.

55

One who is self-restrained, whose understanding is unattached everywhere, from whom affections have departed, obtains the supreme perfection of freedom from action by renunciation. Learn from me, only in brief, O son of Kunti! how one who has obtained perfection attains the Brahman, which is the highest culmination of knowledge. A man possessed of a pure understanding, controlling his self by courage, discarding sound and other objects of sense, casting off affection and aversion, who frequents clean places, who eats little, whose speech, body, and mind are restrained, who is always intent on meditation and mental abstraction, and has recourse to unconcern, who, abandoning egoism, stubbornness, arrogance, desire, anger, and all belongings, has no thought that this or that is mine, and who is tranquil, becomes fit for assimilation with the Brahman.

Tashinath Trimbak Teland, trans., The Bhagavad Gita, in *The Sacred Books of the East*, edited by Max Mueller (Oxford: Clarendon Press, 1879–1910).

Question to Consider: How does this text differ from the *Analects* of Confucius and the *Daodejing*? Are these texts asking the same questions?

AP **Analyzing Sources:** How might the message of the Bhagavad Gita be used to explain and justify the caste system?

DOCUMENT 4 **Filial Piety Illustrated**

Central to the Confucian understanding of a good life and a good society was the notion of "filial piety." This concept defined relationships between social inferiors and superiors, beginning in the family and extending to the larger arena of state and society. *The Classic of Filial Piety*, composed around 200 B.C.E., gave this fundamental Chinese value an enduring expression. "Our body, skin, and hair are all received from our parents," the text declared. "We dare not injure them. This is the first priority in filial duty. To establish oneself in the world and practice the Way; to uphold one's good name for posterity and give glory to one's father and mother — this is the completion of filial duty. Thus filiality begins with service to parents, continues in service to the ruler, and ends with establishing oneself in the world [and becoming an exemplary person]."[24]

Reissued many times over many centuries, the text of *The Classic of Filial Piety* was accompanied by images illustrating the concept. Document 4 is an example of one such image, showing a good son and his wife honoring the son's parents, while two children at the bottom right observe the scene.

Source: Illustration of children honoring parents that would have appeared alongside *The Classic of Filial Piety*, ca. 200 B.C.E.

Question to Consider: How is the son expressing filial piety?

AP Analyzing Sources: To what audience was this image likely directed?

DOCUMENT 5 Reflections from Jesus

Like Confucius, Jesus apparently never wrote anything himself. His sayings and his actions were recorded in the gospels by his followers. The Gospel of Matthew, from which this selection is taken, was composed around 80–85 C.E. For Christian people, this passage, known as the Sermon on the Mount, has long been among the most beloved of biblical texts, regarded as a guide for effective living and the core of Jesus's ethical and moral teachings. In this selection, Jesus contrasts the "broad road" of conventional understanding and values with the "narrow road that leads to life."

57

Source: "The Sermon on the Mount" from the Gospel of Matthew, Chapters 5–7, a book in the New Testament of the Bible, ca. 80–85 C.E.

Now when he [Jesus] saw the crowds, he went up on a mountainside and sat down. His disciples came to him, and he began to teach them saying:

"Blessed are the poor in spirit, for theirs is the kingdom of heaven.
"Blessed are those who mourn, for they will be comforted.
"Blessed are the meek, for they will inherit the earth.
"Blessed are those who hunger and thirst for righteousness, for they will be filled.
"Blessed are the merciful, for they will be shown mercy.
"Blessed are the pure in heart, for they will see God.
"Blessed are the peacemakers, for they will be called sons of God.
"Blessed are those who are persecuted because of righteousness, for theirs is the kingdom of heaven.

"You are the salt of the earth. But if the salt loses its saltiness, how can it be made salty again? It is no longer good for anything, except to be thrown out and trampled by men.
"You are the light of the world. A city on a hill cannot be hidden. Neither do people light a lamp and put it under a bowl. Instead they put it on its stand, and it gives light to everyone in the house. In the same way, let your light shine before men, that they may see your good deeds and praise your Father in heaven."

Question to Consider: How would you summarize "the good life" as Jesus might have defined it?

AP **Analyzing Sources:** What audience would likely be most receptive to Jesus' words?

DOCUMENT 6 **Toward "Mature Manhood"**

An important element of early Christian teaching about a good life involved avoiding sin and resisting temptation. This emphasis found expression in an instructional book for monks, composed in the sixth or early seventh century C.E. by Saint John Climacus and known as the *Ladder of Divine Ascent.* Written by an ascetic monk with a reputation for great piety and wisdom, the book advised monks to renounce the world, with its many temptations and vices; to nurture the corresponding virtues; and to ascend step-by-step toward union with God. A twelfth-century Byzantine painting or icon was added much later to illustrate the book. In this illustration, monks are climbing the ladder of the spiritual journey toward God but are beset by winged demons representing various sins—lust, anger, pride, lying, gluttony, avarice, slander, talkativeness, and bearing grudges, among others—described in Climacus's book. Some have fallen off the ladder into the mouth of a dragon, which represents Hell. Repentance, or the "unbroken remembrance of one's slightest sins," is the precondition for cultivating the virtues of meekness, forgiveness, selflessness, humility, discernment, and simplicity, among others. But the journey toward "mature manhood" is difficult. "Truly perilous," Climacus wrote, "is the sea that we humble monks are crossing."

Source: Illuminated manuscript illustrating the *Ladder of Divine Ascent,* 12th century c.e.

Paul Fearn/Alamy

Question to Consider: Does this image support or challenge Jesus's Sermon on the Mount in describing the journey toward human fulfilment and a good life?

AP **Analyzing Sources:** What purpose might have motivated the author of this image?

AP DOING HISTORY

1. **DBQ Practice:** Evaluate the extent to which belief systems impacted social hierarchies in Eurasia before 1200 C.E.

2. **Contextualization:** In what ways were these sources reacting against the conventional wisdom of their times? How was each shaped by the social and political circumstances in which it was composed?

3. **Causation:** How might religious belief impact relationships between individuals? How did it also impact relationships between people and government?

4. **Developments and Processes:** How does each of these sources characterize the fulfilled person or the fully realized human being? How does it define personal virtue?

5. **Making Connections:** What views about social hierarchies were consistent in the documents? What differences were apparent?

The Historical Jesus

Beginning with the publication in 1906 of Albert Schweitzer's *Quest for the Historical Jesus*, the past century has witnessed periodic efforts to uncover what limited historical records allow scholars to say about the man called Jesus of Nazareth. One problem in using these materials, which are mostly found in the New Testament of the Christian Bible, is that they were composed 40 to 100 years or more after Jesus's death. Furthermore, these studies are undertaken by researchers operating within the standards of historical scholarship. This means that they view Jesus as a fully human person shaped by the culture of his times rather than as a divine figure with supernatural powers. Thus historical study of religious teachers such as Jesus is different from the religious study of those teachers undertaken by committed believers.

Here two recent scholars offer their view of the man whose life and teachings established the Christian tradition. Voice 1.1, by the Iranian-born historian of religion Reza Aslan, presents Jesus as a political revolutionary or zealot whose later followers sought to play down his radicalism. In Voice 1.2, Marcus Borg, a leading figure in the Jesus Seminar of major biblical scholars, views Jesus in somewhat broader terms and emphasizes his deep spirituality.

VOICE 1.1

Reza Aslan on Jesus as Zealot | 2013

In the end there are only two hard historical facts about Jesus of Nazareth upon which we can confidently rely: the first is that Jesus was a Jew who led a popular Jewish movement in Palestine at the beginning of the first century c.e.; the second is that Rome crucified him for doing so. . . .

[T]he Jesus that emerges from this historical exercise—a zealous revolutionary swept up, as all Jews of the era were, in the religious and political turmoil of first-century Palestine—bears little resemblance to the image of the gentle shepherd cultivated by the early Christian community.

Consider this: Crucifixion was a punishment that Rome reserved almost exclusively for the crime of sedition [rebellion against established political authority]. . . . The notion that the leader of a popular messianic movement calling for the imposition of the "kingdom of God"—a term that would have been understood by Jew and gentile alike as implying revolt against Rome—could have remained uninvolved in the revolutionary fervor that had gripped nearly every Jew in Judea is simply ridiculous. . . .

Jesus was crucified by Rome because his messianic aspirations threatened the [Roman] occupation of Palestine, and his zealotry endangered the [Jewish] temple authorities.

Source: Reza Aslan, *Zealot: The Life and Times of Jesus of Nazareth* (New York: Random House, 2013), xxvii–xxix, 79.

VOICE 1.2

Marcus Borg on Jesus as Spirit Person | 1995

The historical Jesus was a *spirit person*, one of those figures in human history with an experiential awareness of the reality of God. . . . He had visions. . . . he prayed for hours at a time. . . . Jesus was perceived . . . as an exorcist who cast demons out of people and as a healer of diseases. . . .

Jesus was a *teacher of wisdom* who regularly used the classic forms of wisdom speech (parable, and memorable short sayings known as aphorisms) to teach a subversive and alternative wisdom. . . . He directly attacked the central values of his social world's conventional wisdom: family, wealth, honor, purity, and religiosity. . . .

Jesus was a *social prophet*, similar to the classical prophets of ancient Israel. As such he criticized the elites (economic, political, and religious) of his time, was an advocate of an alternative social vision, and was often in conflict with authorities.

BUILDING AP® SKILLS

Making Connections: Comparison

Interpreting secondary sources is an important skill for AP® World History: Modern students. Consider having students read both of the sources found on page 61 and answer Question 1 on page 62. You could follow this up by having students discuss what they think as a class. This activity can help students practice the comparison skills necessary for writing good AP® World History essays.

If you want to take this activity further, you can use Question 2 on page 62 to start a discussion on how primary sources and secondary sources (from historians) help support or contradict each other. This discussion should give students practice in comparing primary sources to secondary sources.

61

TRM **Suggested Responses to Questions**
You can find suggested responses to the AP®
Analyzing Secondary Sources questions in the
Teacher's Resource Materials.

Jesus was a *movement founder* who brought into being a Jewish renewal or revitalization movement that challenged and shattered the social boundaries of his day, a movement that eventually became the early Christian church. . . . Within the [Jesus] movement itself, the sharp boundaries of the social world were subverted and an alternative vision affirmed and embodied. It was a "discipleship of equals". . . .

He [Jesus] was a spirit person, subversive sage, social prophet, and movement founder who invited his followers and hearers into a transforming relationship with the same Spirit that he himself knew, and into a community whose social vision was shaped by the core value of compassion.

Source: Marcus Borg, *Meeting Jesus Again for the First Time* (New York: Harper Collins, 1995), 29–30, 35–36, 57, 81, 119.

AP **Analyzing Secondary Sources**

1. How do these two depictions of Jesus differ from each other? What areas of overlap or agreement can you observe?

2. **Integrating Primary and Secondary Sources:** Consider Working with Evidence Document 5, taken from Jesus's Sermon on the Mount, in light of these two accounts from recent historians. To what extent does it support or challenge the outlooks of Aslan and Borg?

Multiple-Choice Questions Choose the correct answer for each question.

Questions 1–3 refer to this map.

The Spread of Early Buddhism and Christianity

Legend:
← Spread of Buddhism
← Spread of Christianity
— Silk Roads
— Indian Ocean trade routes

1. Which of the following best describes the pattern shown on this map?
   a. Independent development of religion
   b. Differentiation of religious concepts
   c. Gradual diffusion of religion
   d. Variations of beliefs within a religion

2. Which of the following is an accurate comparison of Christianity and Buddhism by ca. 500 c.e.?
   a. Both challenged the predominant religion in their places of origin.
   b. No changes were made in either religion's teachings as they spread.
   c. Both had one recognized earthly leader who defended the faith of the founding deity.
   d. Neither used violent force to add converts to the faith.

TRM Suggested Responses to Questions
You can find suggested responses to the Chapter 1 AP® Exam Practice questions in the Teacher's Resource Materials.

TEACHING IDEA

AP® Exam Strategies

Teaching students how to answer stimulus-based multiple-choice questions early in the semester gives them the best chance possible to be successful on the AP® Exam. When students practice test-taking skills on a regular basis, their reasoning abilities will improve as they learn the skills and tips needed to answer stimulus-based MCQs. It can be helpful to watch the Heimler's History video *How to Answer STIMULUS-BASED Multiple Choice Questions*. You can find the video by searching for it on YouTube. Copy the stimulus-based MCQs found on pages 63 to 64 and give them to students as a practice quiz after covering the material in this chapter, encouraging them to use the skills and tips from the Heimler's History video.

63

3. As Christianity and Buddhism spread throughout Eurasia, which of these social influences did they both have?

   a. Christianity and Buddhism favored the elites of society in their teachings on achieving a good afterlife.

   b. Christianity and Buddhism offered women an escape from traditional gender roles through monastic living.

   c. Christianity and Buddhism promoted the violent upheaval of traditional social structures.

   d. Buddhism and Christianity encouraged women to challenge the spiritual authority of their husbands and fathers.

Questions 4–5 refer to this passage.

> The Master said, "If the people be led by laws, and uniformity sought to be given them by punishments, they will try to avoid the punishment, but have no sense of shame. If they be led by virtue, and uniformity sought to be given them by the rules of propriety, they will have the sense of shame, and moreover will become good."
>
> — Confucius, *The Analects*, ca. 479–221 B.C.E.

4. The sentiments expressed in the excerpt above are best illustrated by which of the following tenets of Confucianism?

   a. Strict laws and governments are the way to achieve social order.

   b. Order in society and government comes from looking toward the relationship between humans and nature.

   c. The only way to achieve social order is through the elimination of desire.

   d. Order in society and government comes from the promotion of proper rituals and behavior.

5. Which of the following describes the rise of Confucianism as the dominant political philosophy in classical China?

   a. Confucianism's promise of a joyful afterlife attracted many political elites.

   b. A series of peasant rebellions were led by Confucius.

   c. The Mandate of Heaven required that Confucianism be accepted by political elites.

   d. The Han emperor made Confucianism the official state philosophy.

64

Short-Answer Questions

Read each question carefully and write a short response. Use complete sentences.

1. Use the following two images and your knowledge of world history to answer all parts of the question that follows.

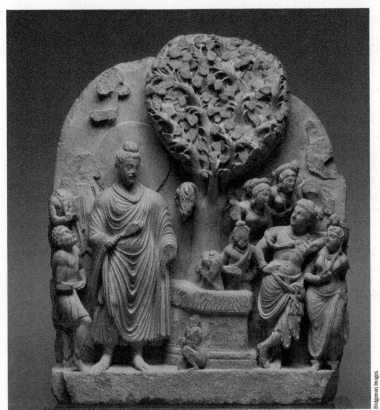

Gandharan relief of temptation of the Buddha, reflecting Greco-Roman influence, 2nd or 3rd century C.E.

Bridgeman Images

Argumentation

Just like with practicing multiple-choice test-taking skills, it's important for students to practice writing skills regularly. The Short-Answer Question is a good place to start teaching writing skills. To help students begin practicing this skill, choose one of the three SAQs on pages 65–67 to have students write individually. These SAQs can also be used to check for understanding after covering the material in Chapter 1.

65

The Maitreya Buddha, or Buddha of the Future, in the Chinese style as the "laughing Buddha," said to be modeled after a Chinese monk, Feilai Feng caves, 10th–14th centuries c.ε.

A. Identify ONE common historical process that is reflected in both images.

B. Explain ONE way in which images such as these can be seen as examples of the changes that occurred in Buddhism as it spread from its place of origin.

C. Explain ONE change that occurred in the beliefs and teachings of Buddhism as it spread from its origins in India into East Asia.

2. **Use this passage and your knowledge of world history to answer all parts of the question that follows. The passage has been edited for clarity.**

> If anyone steals an animal from a leader in the court, the thief shall pay back thirty times the animal's value. If it belongs to a free man of the king, the thief will repay ten times the value. If the thief cannot pay, he shall be put to death. If a man puts out the eye of a free man, he shall pay back in gold. If he puts out the eye of a slave, he shall pay one half the value. If a man strikes a man of higher rank, he shall receive sixty lashes with a whip in public.
>
> — From the Code of Hammurabi, Mesopotamian laws, ca. 1800 B.C.E.

A. Identify and explain one SIMILARITY between a concept found in these Mesopotamian laws and those from another civilization discussed in this chapter.

B. Explain ANOTHER similarity between a concept found in these Mesopotamian laws and those from another civilization discussed in this chapter.

C. Explain one DIFFERENCE between a concept in these Mesopotamian laws and those from another civilization discussed in this chapter.

3. **Use your knowledge of world history to answer all parts of the question that follows.**

A. Identify ONE way in which humans adapted to their environment in the era before ca. 1200 C.E.

B. Explain ONE economic effect of a change to their environment in the era before ca. 1200 C.E.

C. Compare ONE effect of a change to their environment made by two civilizations before ca. 1200 C.E.

67

2 States and Civilizations
A Global Tapestry, 1200–1450

AP® Overview for Chapter 2

Chapter 2 corresponds with Unit 1: The Global Tapestry, ca. 1200 to ca. 1450, and covers Asia, Europe, and the Americas, officially beginning the material tested for AP® World History: Modern. This course is typically a high school student's first exposure to these regions prior to 1450. The material in this chapter is rich with historical information and images that will expose students to the civilizations that developed during this time period in Asia, Europe, and the Americas. Students should begin to use their AP® World History: Modern skills to compare the civilizations in this chapter. Examining the religious, economic, political, and social aspects of these civilizations will allow students to go deeper into the skills that the AP® World History: Modern course seeks to develop.

Chapter 2 Essential Activity

It's important for students to know the regions of the world and which states, empires, and kingdoms belong to those regions in order to be successful on the exam. Essay prompts and short-answer questions frequently ask students to discuss regions as well as specific states. Creating annotated maps can be a helpful way of getting students to know what states belong to a region and to learn the characteristics of those states. Give students two blank maps: one of Eurasia (including the Mediterranean region, the Middle East, and the Indian Ocean) and one of the Americas. To help with geography, ask students to identify the civilizations of the Global Tapestry (look at the Unit 1 section of the AP® World History: Modern Course and Exam Description to create a list of civilizations), as well as regions, continents, and important geographic features. After they have labeled their maps, have the students create note boxes on their map that connect to each of the civilizations on the map. In each box, they should take notes on the following AP® Themes:

- Governance
- Social Interactions and Organization
- Cultural Developments and Interactions
- Technology and Innovation
- Economic Systems
- Humans and the Environment

These annotated maps will be used throughout Chapter 2 as students learn about each civilization. For blank maps that you can use with this activity, download **Map 2A: Europe, Asia, and Africa** and **Map 2B: The Americas** from the Resources section of the book's digital platform or click on the linked TRM buttons in the Teacher's Edition e-book.

Differentiation

If you want to differentiate the Chapter 2 Essential Activity and have students practice presentation skills, follow the "Must Do, Should Do, Strive For" model below.

- Must Do: Students should label their maps so that they know the civilizations and geography of different regions of the world, and they should be able to identify the political structures, social hierarchies and gender roles, cultures, innovations and technologies, economic structures, and interactions with the environment for at least one of the civilizations in their notes (you may want to assign the civilizations if you choose to do the "Must Do, Should Do, Strive For" with your class).

- Should Do: Students should be able to, either on their own or in a group of three to four people, create a short presentation on one of the civilizations from the annotated map. Presentations can be created digitally (Google Slides, PowerPoint, Prezi, etc.) or on a poster. Students should be able to present the main ideas of the civilization to the class and include pictures and images to help illustrate the information. To help students access information for all of the civilizations, post the presentations online to your school's LMS.

- Strive For: For students comfortable with presenting in front of their peers, give them 4 to 6 minutes to present their slides or poster to their classmates to teach them about their assigned civilization.

TRM Map 2A: Europe, Asia, and Africa

TRM Map 2B: The Americas

Chapter 2 Resources

- **TRM** AP® Skills Workshop Activity Handout: Claims
- **TRM** Chapter 2 DBQ Activity Handout
- **TRM** Chapter 2 Guided Reading
- **TRM** Chapter 2 Lecture Presentation Slides
- **TRM** Chapter 2 Outline
- **TRM** Chapter 2 Suggested Responses to Questions
- **TRM** Eric's Activity 2: Interpreting Visual Sources
- **TRM** Handout 2.1: Comparison Chart for China and Islamic World Politics and Technology
- **TRM** Handout 2.2: Chart for Economic, Cultural, and Political Characteristics of Ottoman Empire
- **TRM** Handout 2.3: Continuity and Change Chart for the Islamic World
- **TRM** Handout 2.4: Causation Chart for Religious Toleration in al-Andalus
- **TRM** Handout 2.5: Thematic Chart for Swahili City-States
- **TRM** Handout 2.6: Comparison Chart for Pre-Renaissance and Renaissance Art
- **TRM** Handout 2.7: Comparison Chart for the Aztec and Inca
- **TRM** Map 2A: Europe, Asia, and Africa
- **TRM** Map 2B: The Americas
- **TRM** Note-Taking Tips Lecture Slides
- **TRM** Writing Organizer for LEQ Practice

Pacing Guide

Below is a pacing guide for the AP® World History: Modern course beginning in ca. 1200 C.E. This pacing guide is based on a schedule with 120 sessions of 50 minutes each before the AP® Exam. It is meant as a place to start. If you have a different number of sessions before the exam, you can modify the pacing to suit your needs.

Day	Pages Assigned	AP® Topic	AP® Theme	Suggested Assignments	Coverage Notes
1	Read pages 69–73 to the third paragraph about China's economic revolution	1.1	CDI GOV	Chapter 2 Essential Activity Teaching Idea: AP® Exam Strategies on page 69 Eric's Activity 2: Interpreting Visual Sources on page 70 Building AP® Skills: Making Connections: Comparison on pages 72 and 73	While the first two days of this chapter focus on the Song dynasty, students will need to know a little bit about the Sui and Tang dynasties to contextualize the Song and to show continuity and change in government practices. Consider giving students a short homework assignment on those dynasties to help them.
2	Read pages 73–75 starting at the third paragraph about China's economic revolution	1.1	CDI ECN SIO	Chapter 2 Essential Activity AP® Working with Evidence: Social Patterns in Tang and Song China Apply the Tip on page 74	This part of the chapter focuses heavily on Song China's economic developments, role in trade, and the innovations happening in China. These are all important concepts to teach about Song China.
3	Read pages 76–79 to "The Worlds of Southeast Asia"	1.1	CDI GOV ECN SIO	Chapter 2 Essential Activity Apply the Tip on page 76 Building AP® Skills: Making Connections: Comparison on page 79	It's more important to focus on the impact China had on Korea and Japan than on the specifics of these societies. It may be helpful to incorporate the impact China had on these countries into your lesson on their characteristics.
4	Read pages 79–81 starting from "The Worlds of Southeast Asia"	1.1 1.3	CDI GOV ECN SIO	Chapter 2 Essential Activity Building AP® Skills: Making Connections: Comparison on page 80 Exploring AP® Themes: ECN and GOV on page 80	With the section on Vietnam, it's important to focus more on the impact China had on society and what elements Vietnam borrowed from China. The second part of this section looks at Southeast Asian states that were influenced by trade on the Indian Ocean. It may be good to revisit these states when teaching about the Indian Ocean trade network in Unit 2.

Day	Pages Assigned	AP® Topic	AP® Theme	Suggested Assignments	Coverage Notes
5	Read pages 82–85	1.2	CDI GOV	Chapter 2 Essential Activity Exploring AP® Themes: ENV on page 83 Building AP® Skills: Making Connections: Comparison on page 84	This section of the chapter discusses the Abbasid and Ottoman Empires; you will need to go more in depth into the Abbasid Empire at this time. You may also want to revisit the rise of Islam as a new state from Chapter 1 and briefly discuss the Umayyad Empire to help contextualize the Abbasids.
6	Read pages 86–88 to "Emerging Civilizations in Africa"	1.2	CDI GOV TEC	Chapter 2 Essential Activity Apply the Tip on page 86 Building AP® Skills: Making Connections: Causation on page 87 Building AP® Skills: Making Connections: Comparison on page 88	The expansion of Islamic rule and cultural transfers are important topics to study for Dar al-Islam. This is a good overview of these topics and could be a good way to jump into a larger discussion of the expansion of Islam.
7	Read pages 88–92 from "Emerging Civilizations in Africa" to "The Worlds of Christendom"	1.5	CDI GOV ECN SIO	Chapter 2 Essential Activity Exploring AP® Themes: ECN on page 89 Apply the Tip on page 90 Teaching Idea: Class Discussion on page 91	When starting African civilizations, it might be good to spend a little time discussing why the class is focusing on only a few West and East African civilizations in this period of history (for example, lack of written language in most of the continent). Also, as with the Southeast Asian states, it may be good to revisit these African states when teaching about the Indian Ocean trade network and the trans-Saharan trade network in Unit 2 so that you can discuss how trade helped these states rise.
8	Read pages 92–99 from "The Worlds of Christendom" to "Society, Economy, and Culture in the West"	1.6	CDI GOV SIO	Chapter 2 Essential Activity Exploring AP® Themes: CDI on page 95 Exploring AP® Themes: GOV on page 96 AP® Classroom: AP® Topic Questions on page 98	While the Byzantine Empire and Kievan Rus are not technically part of the Course Framework, it's still important for students to at least get a basic understanding of them. This knowledge will help them contextualize the rest of Europe in this time period. However, the biggest topics to focus on in this section are the development of feudalism, manorialism, and decentralization in Europe.
9	Read pages 99–104 from "Society, Economy, and Culture in the West" to "Civilizations of the Americas"	1.6	CDI ECN SIO TEC	Chapter 2 Essential Activity Apply the Tip on page 99 Building AP® Skills: Making Connections: Comparison on page 101	This section looks at the development of Europe leading up to ca. 1450 C.E. and is important for setting Europe up politically, economically, and culturally for the post-1450 eras.
10	Read pages 104–112 from "Civilizations of the Americas" to Chapter Review	1.4	CDI GOV	Chapter 2 Essential Activity AP® Classroom: AP® Daily Videos on page 104 Building AP® Skills: Making Connections: Comparison on page 110 Building AP® Skills: Sourcing and Situation on page 111	Students need to understand the states and empires that existed in the Americas prior to the arrival of Europeans. If you are running short on time, it may be helpful to focus primarily on the government structures of these states.

NOTES

Bell Ringer

To start off this chapter and Unit 1: The Global Tapestry, ask students to write down three things they remember from Chapter 1 about hunter-forager societies and early agricultural societies. When they are done, either have students share their items with a neighbor or call for volunteers to share their answers. As with all bell ringers, keep this exercise brief. *Students should recall that gatherers and foragers were more gender equal, lived in smaller groups, and were nomadic. Neolithic Agricultural Revolution societies were settled, consisted of larger groups, and were less gender equal.*

Lady Murasaki Shikibu Lady Murasaki Shikibu drew on her experience as a lady-in-waiting at the imperial court of Japan to craft her famous novel, *The Tale of Genji*, which describes aristocratic life. She allegedly began to write the novel in 1004 at a Buddhist temple under the inspiration of a full moon, as depicted in this eighteenth-century woodblock print. Both the novel and this image raise questions about the place of elite women in the patriarchal civilizations of the world before 1200. (Pictures from History/Bridgeman Images)

68

BUILDING AP® SKILLS

Making Connections: Comparison

It's good to have students begin comparing civilizations and themes early in the course to help them practice the skill of comparison and to start to see the continuity and change in certain topics throughout world history. Have students study the picture of Lady Murasaki Shikibu on page 68 and read the accompanying caption. Then ask them to compare the lives of women in Japan in this time period to the lives of women from Chapter 1. It can be helpful to have them write down their thoughts before sharing with the class. *Answers may include: Elite women in Japan at this time were well educated while elite women in earlier societies had limited education; Elite women in Japan participated in creating aspects of culture while in earlier societies men were the creators of culture; Japan at this time seems to be less patriarchal than other societies because of how Lady Murasaki Shikibu is represented in the painting (the focus on a woman and her ability to write a novel).*

CHAPTER 2

States and Civilizations

A Global Tapestry

1200–1450

◀ **AP®**

CLAIMS AND EVIDENCE IN SOURCES
Based on the evidence in this image, what can
you infer about the lives of elite women in
Japan in this period?

CONNECTING PAST AND PRESENT

"Sometimes the weight of civilization can be overwhelming. The fast pace, the burdens of relationships, the political strife, the technological complexity—it's enough to make you dream of escaping to a simpler life more in touch with nature."[1] This expression of discontent with modernity, written in 2019, reflects an urge to "escape from civilization" that has long been a feature of modern life. Nor has this impulse been limited to recent societies and the Western world. The ancient Chinese teachers of Daoism likewise urged their followers to abandon the structured and demanding world of urban and civilized life and to immerse themselves in the eternal patterns of the natural order. It is a strange paradox that we count the creation of civilizations among the major achievements of humankind and yet people within them have often sought to escape the constraints, artificiality, hierarchies, and other discontents of civilized living. ∎

Despite these discontents, by 1200 civilizations with their substantial cities, stratified societies, and powerful states had long been home to most of the world's peoples, extending their reach through time at the expense of those who lived in gathering and hunting societies, independent farming villages, or pastoral communities. This chapter presents a kind of global tour of the world's civilizations during the several centuries after 1200. Many of them had begun long before 1200, and all of them were constantly evolving, spreading, or shrinking.

In East Asia, an ancient Chinese civilization continued to thrive even as newer civilizations in Korea, Japan, and Vietnam borrowed from it as they created distinctive civilizations of

69

TRM Chapter 2 Guided Reading
You can find a guided reading handout for this chapter in the Teacher's Resource Materials.

TRM Chapter 2 Lecture Slides
You can find curated lecture slides for this chapter in the Teacher's Resource Materials.

TRM Chapter 2 Outline
You can find a chapter outline to model good note-taking for this chapter in the Teacher's Resource Materials.

TRM Suggested Responses to Questions
You can find suggested responses to all of the AP® margin questions in this chapter in the Teacher's Resource Materials.

TEACHING IDEA

Class Discussion

Chapter 2 aligns with Unit 1 of the AP® World History: Modern course. Having students examine the topics in Chapter 2 could be an interesting way to get them to think about the importance of the Global Tapestry in setting the "foundation" for the course. To start the discussion, ask students to study the topics and subtopics for the chapter on the left-hand side of this page. Then ask: What are the "big ideas" of this chapter? *Answers may include: Emergence of new civilizations; diffusion of culture; impact of trade on some civilizations; growth and consolidation of civilizations; overview of states and civilizations from around the world.* You can take the discussion further by asking: How can these topics help you understand the importance of the Global Tapestry unit? *Answers will vary, but could include: Helps give us background on each of these states and civilizations so we can see how they change over time; Introduces us to different types of governments and cultures around the world.*

TEACHING IDEA

AP® Exam Strategies

This could be the first AP® course that many of your students will take, or at least the first AP® history course they take. Effectively taking notes as they read is an important skill to help them build early in the semester. Many students may find it easy to use the outline method to take notes. Point out that history textbooks help them

structure those outline notes with the topics and subtopics in each chapter (like the ones seen on the left-hand side of this page). You can find a quick lecture slide lesson on how to take reading notes in the Teacher's Resource Materials.

TRM Note-Taking Tips Lecture Slides

their own. The heartland of a politically fragmented Islamic civilization stretched from the Atlantic Ocean across North Africa and the Middle East to India, while its frontiers extended to sub-Saharan Africa and Central and Southeast Asia, where new civilizations were emerging. In the worlds of Christendom, Byzantium was in a state of terminal decline, even as other Christian civilizations were emerging in Russia and Western Europe. Meanwhile, in the Western Hemisphere new civilizations flourished in Mesoamerica and the Andes that were completely separated from those of Afro-Eurasia.

The Worlds of East Asia: China and Its Neighbors

Finding the Main Point: What accounts for China's political and economic vitality in this era? What impact did China have on its neighbors?

Around 1200, East Asia was among the most sophisticated and dynamic regions of the world. At its core was the enormous Chinese civilization, which for centuries had experienced a powerful and relatively stable state, cultural, and intellectual flowering, and remarkable technological innovation and economic growth. East Asian civilization was also expanding elsewhere. Between roughly 600 and 1600, the new states and civilizations of Korea, Japan, and Vietnam had emerged along China's borders. Proximity to their giant Chinese neighbor decisively shaped the histories of these new East Asian civilizations, for all of them borrowed major elements of Chinese culture and entered, at least for a time, into tributary relationships with China. But none were fully incorporated into the Chinese state or society. Instead they created new distinct forms of East Asian civilization.

China before the Mongol Takeover

AP®

CONTINUITY AND CHANGE

Why are the centuries of the Song dynasty in China sometimes regarded as a high point in Chinese history?

In 1200 the **Song dynasty** (960–1279) ruled over large parts of an ancient Chinese civilization that could trace its origins back thousands of years (see Map 2.1). Since the late seventh century, China had experienced, with a few exceptions, a period of relatively stable political rule. Successive dynasties drew on much older cultural and political traditions that in turn outlasted even the Song, enduring into the twentieth century. Culturally, the Song dynasty was a "golden age" of arts and literature, setting standards of excellence in poetry, landscape painting, and ceramics, even as its scholars debated new forms of Confucian philosophy.

Politically, the Song dynasty built on earlier precedents to create an elaborate bureaucratic state structure that endured into the twentieth century. To staff this bureaucracy, an examination system first established by the Han dynasty (206 B.C.E.–220 C.E.) was revived and made more elaborate, facilitated by the ability to print

---

TEACHING IDEA

Class Discussion

To get students thinking about cultural diffusion and interactions between societies (a major theme in Units 1 and 2 of AP® World History: Modern), have students read the introductory paragraph to "The Worlds of East Asia: China and Its Neighbors." Then ask students: What are some reasons that certain East Asian civilizations would not copy all of China's philosophical and government innovations? *A possible answer is: While most of the other civilizations in East Asia borrowed certain elements of the Chinese civilization they found appealing, most preferred to rule themselves rather than be controlled by China.*

ERIC'S ACTIVITY ②   **Interpreting Visual Sources**

Skill: Analyzing Evidence

The visual sources in "AP® Working with Evidence: Social Patterns in Tang and Song China," starting on page 119, offer a rich window into China's elite class. They also provide a useful set of images with which to explore the strengths and weaknesses of visual sources in answering historical questions. I use this feature to examine how sources shape the types of questions historians ask. Find the complete activity in the Teacher's Resource Materials.

TRM Eric's Activity 2: Interpreting Visual Sources

Landmarks for Chapter 2

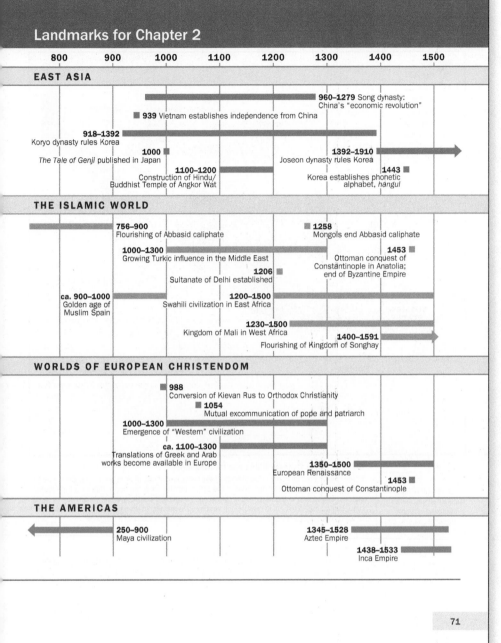

EAST ASIA

800 | 900 | 1000 | 1100 | 1200 | 1300 | 1400 | 1500

960–1279 Song dynasty: China's "economic revolution"

939 Vietnam establishes independence from China

918–1392 Koryo dynasty rules Korea

1000 *The Tale of Genji* published in Japan

1100–1200 Construction of Hindu/Buddhist Temple of Angkor Wat

1392–1910 Joseon dynasty rules Korea

1443 Korea establishes phonetic alphabet, *hangul*

THE ISLAMIC WORLD

756–900 Flourishing of Abbasid caliphate

1258 Mongols end Abbasid caliphate

1000–1300 Growing Turkic influence in the Middle East

1453 Ottoman conquest of Constantinople in Anatolia; end of Byzantine Empire

1206 Sultanate of Delhi established

ca. 900–1000 Golden age of Muslim Spain

1200–1500 Swahili civilization in East Africa

1230–1500 Kingdom of Mali in West Africa

1400–1591 Flourishing of Kingdom of Songhay

WORLDS OF EUROPEAN CHRISTENDOM

988 Conversion of Kievan Rus to Orthodox Christianity

1054 Mutual excommunication of pope and patriarch

1000–1300 Emergence of "Western" civilization

ca. 1100–1300 Translations of Greek and Arab works become available in Europe

1350–1500 European Renaissance

1453 Ottoman conquest of Constantinople

THE AMERICAS

250–900 Maya civilization

1345–1528 Aztec Empire

1438–1533 Inca Empire

BUILDING AP® SKILLS

Making Connections: Continuity and Change

Using the "Landmarks for Chapter 2," you might try having students practice the skill of Continuity and Change by tracking what political and cultural continuities and changes from 1200 to 1450 they see on the timeline. It might be good to mention that while the timeline stretches from 800 C.E. to 1500 C.E., Unit 1 is marked from 1200 to 1450. Ask students to create their own lists and then compare what they found with a classmate.

- Political Changes: *End of Koryo dynasty and beginning of Joseon dynasty in Korea; Fall of Abbasid caliphate; Ottomans conquered Constantinople and ended the Byzantine Empire; Beginning of Sultanate of Delhi; Flourishing of Songhay; Beginning of Aztec and Inca Empires.*

- Political Continuities: *Joseon dynasty ruled Korea; Swahili civilization flourished in East Africa; Mali ruled in West Africa.*

- Cultural Changes: *Construction of Angkor Wat completed; Korea established hangul alphabet; Emergence of "Western" civilization in Europe; Translations of Greek and Arab works became available in Europe; European Renaissance.*

- Cultural Continuities: *Continued importance of Islam in the Middle East and Africa; Continued importance of Christianity in Europe.*

EXPLORING AP® THEMES

Humans and the Environment (ENV)

Studying maps to draw evidence from them is a good skill to practice throughout the year. Display Map 2.1, "Song Dynasty China and Its Neighbors," for students to study, and then ask: Based on what you see on the map, what would building the Great Wall and the Grand Canal accomplish for China? *The Great Wall could keep out invaders and help maintain safety for the Chinese, and the Grand Canal could allow faster transportation within China.*

BUILDING AP® SKILLS

Making Connections: Comparison

The recommended AP® skill of Unit 1 is Comparison, specifically being able to compare the civilizations and states of the unit (Topic 1.7 in the CED). It might be easiest to compare the political characteristics and technology of China and the Islamic world during this time period. To help students practice this skill and prepare for an LEQ practice prompt, you might try having them create a comparison chart of the two groups. While students will begin the chart here, they will revisit it throughout the chapter to continue filling it in. For this activity, the Teacher's Resource Materials include a reproducible chart and an LEQ practice.

Students can use the information on pages 72 and 73 to fill in the section on China's political characteristics.

TRM Handout 2.1: Comparison Chart for China and Islamic World Politics and Technology

TRM Writing Organizer for LEQ Practice

Map 2.1 Song Dynasty China and Its Neighbors

In the twelfth century nomadic Jurchen peoples conquered much of northern China, giving rise to two states—the native Chinese Song in the south and the Jin in the north. Rulers of both states claimed to be heirs to the earlier Tang dynasty and thus the true emperors of China. At the same time, distinct new East Asian civilizations continued to develop in Korea, Japan, and Vietnam, all of which were decisively shaped by their proximity to their giant Chinese neighbor.

▲ **AP**®
CONTEXTUALIZATION
What does this map suggest about China's relationship with the nomadic peoples to the north?

books for the first time in world history. Schools proliferated to prepare candidates for the rigorous exams, which allowed entry into the high elite for upper-class men. While candidates from privileged backgrounds were better able to access the education needed to pass exams, village communities or a local landowner sometimes sponsored the education of a bright young man from a commoner background, enabling him to enter the charmed circle of officialdom while also bringing prestige and perhaps more concrete benefits to those who sponsored him. Thus the examination system provided a modest measure of social mobility in an otherwise quite hierarchical society.

Underlying these cultural and political achievements was **China's economic revolution**, which made Song dynasty China "by far the richest, most skilled, and most populous country on earth."[2] The most obvious sign of China's prosperity was its rapid growth in population, which jumped from about 50 million or 60 million in the ninth century to 120 million by 1200. Behind this doubling of the population were remarkable achievements in agricultural production, particularly the adoption from Vietnam of a fast-ripening and drought-resistant strain of rice, known as Champa rice.

As many people found their way to the cities, China became the most urbanized country in the world. Dozens of Chinese cities numbered over 100,000, while the Song dynasty capital of **Hangzhou** was home to more than a million people. For the thirteenth-century Italian visitor Marco Polo, Hangzhou was "beyond dispute the finest and noblest [city] in the world."[3] (See Working with Evidence, Chapter 3, page 178, for a fuller description of Marco Polo's impressions of Hangzhou.)

Industrial production likewise soared. In both large-scale enterprises employing hundreds of workers and in smaller backyard furnaces, China's metallurgy industry increased its output dramatically. By the eleventh century, it was providing the government with 32,000 suits of armor and 16 million iron arrowheads annually, in addition to supplying metal for coins, tools, construction, and bells in Buddhist monasteries. This industrial growth was fueled almost entirely by coal, which also came to provide most of the energy for heating homes and cooking, and no doubt generated considerable air pollution. Technological innovation in other fields also flourished. Inventions in printing, both woodblock and movable type, led to the world's first printed books, and by 1000 relatively cheap books had become widely available in China. Chinese navigational and shipbuilding technologies led the world, and the Chinese invention of gunpowder created, within a few centuries, a revolution in military affairs that had global dimensions.

These innovations occurred within the world's most highly commercialized society, in which producing for the market, rather than for local consumption, became a very widespread phenomenon. An immense network of internal waterways (canals, rivers, and lakes), described by one scholar as "an engineering feat without parallel in the world of its time," stretched around 30,000 miles, including a Grand Canal of over 1,000 miles linking the Yellow River in the north to the Yangzi River in the south.[4] (See Map 2.1.) These waterways facilitated the cheap

AP
CONTINUITY AND CHANGE
What did the Song dynasty borrow from previous dynasties to build an enduring state?

AP EXAM TIP
You should know that for much of history China has had the world's highest population and the greatest number of urban areas with large populations.

AP EXAM TIP
Understand the uses and spread of gunpowder after 1200.

APPLY THE TIP

To compare the size of China's cities with that of others in this era, have students search the Internet for city populations throughout history. A good place to start is "Largest Cities through History" by Matt T. Rosenberg, which you can find on the ThoughtCo.com website. After students read the article, ask the following questions:

■ What do you notice about the population of China's cities in comparison to that of other cities during the time period? *Answers will vary depending on the cities and years chosen. However, China's cities will have larger populations than almost all others.*

■ What do you think led to the vast differences in population? *The advances in agriculture dramatically increased food production, which provided enough surplus food to support a growing population. In addition, many people moved to the cities in China, probably because of the increasing number of opportunities for employment.*

BUILDING AP® SKILLS

Making Connections: Comparison

If you are having students complete the comparison chart on China and the Islamic world from the note on page 72, have them pause here and use the information in the last two paragraphs on page 73 and the first paragraph on page 74 to complete China's technology section of the chart.

EXPLORING AP® THEMES

Humans and the Environment (ENV)

To get a discussion going about the relationship between population and food, ask students: What explains China's rapid population growth in this era? *Changes in agriculture provided more food to feed a growing population. Fast-ripening rice as well as a strain of drought-resistant rice, both imported from Vietnam into southern China, allowed for multiple harvests each year, which, in turn, allowed for a more reliable food supply.*

Then ask: How is this population increase similar to other major booms in population in world history, like during the Neolithic era? *When there's more food available, the population can grow. When societies and civilizations are able to produce a surplus of food, they usually see an increase in population (more food = more people).*

BUILDING AP® SKILLS

Claims and Evidence in Sources

This would be a good place for students to practice image analysis. Ask students to work on their own or with a partner to examine the picture of Chinese cities and answer the following questions:

▪ What similarities do you see between the image on page 74 and the description of cities in China on page 73? *The picture matches the description well. They both include many people walking around the streets and on the bridge, vendors selling their wares, carts moving items, people of all ages interacting, open buildings, few trees, and people talking to one another.*

▪ What similarities do you see between the city in the image and modern cities? *Then and now, cities are the center of activity and trade. They offer food, entertainment, lodgings, and opportunities. They are crowded and noisy.*

APPLY THE TIP

It might surprise some students to learn that China had the world's leading economy and was a major leader in innovations during 1200–1450. China developed innovations in this time period to further its economic growth, including paper money and a network of canals. To help students make the connections between these innovations and economic growth, ask the following questions:

▪ How would an extensive network of canals help the economy of a state like Song China? *Answers may include: Canals would allow crops grown in the southern part of China to be transported to the population-heavy north; Canals allow internal trade to take place; Canals can help move goods within major cities, such as Hangzhou.*

▪ How would paper money promote economic growth in a state like Song China? *Carrying large amounts of paper money would be easier for merchants than carrying large amounts of coins, facilitating trade and economic growth.*

▲ **AP**
CAUSATION
What developments in China led to the intense urbanization depicted in this image?

AP **EXAM TIP**
China had the world's leading economy around 1200, and you should know its features, such as paper money.

AP
CONTINUITY AND CHANGE
In what ways did women's lives change during the Song dynasty?

Chinese Cities This detail comes from a huge watercolor scroll, titled *Along the River during the Qingming Festival*, originally painted during the Song dynasty. It illustrates the urban sophistication of Chinese cities at that time and has been frequently imitated and copied since then. (Werner Forman/Getty Images)

movement of goods, allowing peasants to grow specialized crops for sale while they purchased rice or other staples on the market. In addition, government demands for taxes paid in cash rather than in goods required peasants to sell something—their products or their labor—in order to meet their obligations. The growing use of paper money, which the Chinese pioneered, as well as financial instruments such as letters of credit and promissory notes, further contributed to the commercialization of society. Two prominent scholars have described the outcome: "Output increased, population grew, skills multiplied, and a burst of inventiveness made Song China far wealthier than ever before—or than any of its contemporaries."[5]

However, the "golden age" of Song dynasty China was perhaps less than "golden" for many of its women. Confucian writers emphasized the subordination of women to men and the need to keep males and females separate in every domain of life. The Song dynasty historian and scholar Sima Guang (1019–1086) summed up the prevailing view: "The boy leads the girl, the girl follows the boy; the duty of husbands to be resolute and wives to be docile begins with this."[6] For elite men, masculinity came to be defined less in terms of horseback riding, athleticism, and warrior values and more in terms of the refined pursuits of calligraphy, scholarship, painting, and poetry. Corresponding views of feminine qualities emphasized women's weakness, reticence, and delicacy.

Furthermore, a rapidly commercializing economy undermined the position of women in the textile industry. Urban workshops and state factories, run by men, increasingly took over the skilled tasks of weaving textiles, especially silk, which had previously been the work of rural women in their homes. Although these women continued to tend silkworms and spin silk thread, they had lost the more lucrative income-generating work of weaving silk fabrics.

The most compelling expression of a tightening patriarchy among elite women lay in **foot binding**. Apparently beginning among dancers and courtesans in the tenth or eleventh century C.E., this practice involved the tight wrapping of young girls' feet, usually breaking the bones of the foot and causing intense pain. During and after the Song dynasty, foot binding found general acceptance among elite families and later became even more widespread in Chinese society. It was associated with new images of female beauty and eroticism that emphasized small size, frailty, and deference and served to keep women restricted to the "inner quarters," where Confucian tradition asserted that they belonged. For many women, it became a rite of passage, and their tiny feet and the beautiful slippers that encased them became a source of some pride, even a topic of poetry for some literate women.

In other ways, though, there were more positive trends in the lives of women during the Song dynasty. Their property rights expanded, allowing women to control their own dowries and to inherit property from their families. "Neither in earlier nor in later periods," writes one scholar, "did as much property pass through women's hands" as during the Song dynasty.[7] Furthermore, lower-ranking but ambitious officials strongly urged the education of women, so that they might more effectively raise their sons and increase the family's fortune. Song dynasty China, in short, offered a mixture of tightening restrictions and new opportunities to its women.

> **AP**
> CONTEXTUALIZATION
> How does the Chinese practice of foot binding illustrate social and gender changes during the Song dynasty?

Foot Binding While the practice of foot binding painfully deformed the feet of young girls and women, it was also associated aesthetically with feminine beauty, particularly in the delicate and elaborately decorated shoes that encased their bound feet. (foot: MARK RALSTON/AFP/Getty Images; shoe: ClassicStock/Masterfile)

TEACHING IDEA

Incorporating Outside Resources

For more insights into ideals of feminine appearance and behavior in this era, it could be good to ask students to research the "Four Beauties" of China in this time period, including Xi Shi. They might begin with the short video *The Four Most Beautiful Chinese Women Ever*, on Off the Great Wall's YouTube channel. To focus students as they research, ask them to answer this question: What changes occurred in Chinese ideas about the beauty of women, and how did these changes affect women's role in society? *Women were valued for their natural beauty, but over time they were expected to alter their appearance to meet new standards. The alterations often limited their ability to move and restricted their lives even further. Additionally, women had more rights in China in earlier periods, but over time their rights became more limited.*

EXPLORING AP® THEMES

Social Interactions and Organization (SIO)

While patriarchy was dominant in almost all societies in this period of world history, there were sometimes positive changes in women's lives during the Song dynasty. To help students think about these changes, have them read the last paragraph on page 75 and ask: What were some of the positive trends in the lives of women in Song China? *Women were permitted more property rights, education focused on bettering their ability to raise sons to benefit the family, and they experienced fewer restrictions in general. In the cities, they participated in commercial life.*

TEACHING IDEA

Bell Ringer

Before starting the sections on Japan, Korea, and Vietnam, ask students: What influences from China do you see in other societies today? *Answers will vary.*

APPLY THE TIP

Cultural diffusion, especially between major empires and their neighbors, is a constant theme in world history, and it's good for students to be able to identify examples of diffusion throughout the course. Ask students to re-create the chart below in their notes to give examples of cultural diffusion between China, Korea, and Japan as they read pages 76–79.

Chinese Influence on Korea	Chinese Influence on Japan

BUILDING AP® SKILLS

Making Connections: Continuity and Change

You can continue to reinforce the skill of Continuity and Change by having students find examples of it in the chapter. Ask students to read page 76 and write down the different examples of how Korea changed culturally and socially due to Chinese influence. (Suggested answers are provided in italics.)

■ Cultural: *Students were sent to China to study Confucianism as well as Chinese science and art; Buddhist monks brought in popular forms of Chinese Buddhism, which quickly took root; Korea established schools to study Confucianism.*

■ Social: *Among the elite, Chinese models of family life and female behavior replaced the more flexible Korean patterns; The previous practice of a woman raising her children in her parents' home was strongly discouraged; The practice of plural marriage for men was eroded; Korean restrictions on elite women, influenced by Confucianism, exceeded the restrictions on women in China.*

Continuity is the more difficult part of this skill because it's not as easy to identify as Change. If you want students to practice Continuity, have them answer this question as they read page 76 or use it to start a

(continued)

class discussion: What allowed Korea to maintain cultural independence? *Chinese influence affected the Korean aristocracy more than it did the rest of the nation. The examination system did not predominate in Korea as it did in China. Most importantly, the development of a popular phonetic Korean alphabet, hangul, allowed people to retain a Korean language identity.*

AP® EXAM TIP
Be aware of the interactions between major empires and the states near them, such as China with Korea and Japan.

AP®
COMPARISON
Evaluate the similarities and differences in the influence China had on Korea and Japan. In what ways was that influence resisted?

AP®
CONTINUITY AND CHANGE
What cultural changes occurred in Korea in response to Chinese influence?

Korea and Japan: Creating New Civilizations

Immediately adjacent to northeastern China, the Korean people have long lived in close proximity to their much larger neighbor. Under a succession of dynasties—the Unified Silla (688–900), Koryo (918–1392), and Joseon (1392–1910)—Korea generally maintained its political independence while participating in a tributary relationship with China. During regular missions to the Chinese imperial court, Korean emissaries acknowledged China's preeminent position in East Asia by presenting tribute—products of value produced in Korea—and performing rituals of submission that included *kowtowing* or prostration before the emperor while touching the ground with their heads. In return Chinese emperors gave their Korean visitors gifts or "bestowals" to take back to Korea, reaffirmed peaceful relations, and allowed both official and personal trade.

Chinese culture had a pervasive influence on Korean political and cultural life in many ways (see "Religion and the Silk Roads" in Chapter 3). For instance, efforts to plant Confucian values and Chinese culture in Korea had what one scholar has called an "overwhelmingly negative" impact on Korean women, particularly after 1300.[8] Early Chinese observers noticed, and strongly disapproved of, free choice marriages in Korea, as well as the practice of women singing and dancing together late at night. With the support of the Korean court, Chinese models of family life and female behavior based on the Confucian concept of filial piety gradually replaced the more flexible Korean patterns, especially among the elite. Korean customs—women giving birth and raising their young children in their parents' home, funeral rites in which a husband was buried in the sacred plot of his wife's family, the remarriage of widowed or divorced women, and female inheritance of property—eroded under the pressure of Confucian orthodoxy. Korean restrictions on elite women, especially widows, came to exceed even those in China itself.

Still, Korea remained Korean. Despite periodic threats, after 688 the country largely maintained its political independence from China. Chinese cultural influence, except for Buddhism, had little impact beyond the aristocracy and certainly did not penetrate the lives of Korea's serf-like peasants. Nor did it register among Korea's many enslaved people, who amounted to about one-third of the country's population by 1100. A Chinese-style examination system to recruit government officials, though encouraged by some Korean rulers, never assumed the prominence that it gained in Song dynasty China. Korea's aristocratic class was able to maintain an even stronger monopoly on bureaucratic office than its Chinese counterpart did. And in the mid-1400s, Korea moved toward greater cultural independence by developing a phonetic alphabet, known as **hangul** (HAHN-gool), for writing the Korean language. Although resisted by conservative male elites, who were long accustomed to using the more prestigious Chinese characters to write Korean, this new form of writing gradually took hold, especially in private correspondence, in popular fiction, and among women. Clearly part of the Chinese world order, Korea nonetheless retained a distinctive culture as well as a separate political existence.

◄ **AP**

CLAIMS AND EVIDENCE IN SOURCES

Using this image as evidence, describe where the Chinese placed themselves in the tributary relationship with other states. What was the role of tribute in Chinese relations with outside powers?

The Tribute System This eighteenth-century Korean painting depicts a Korean diplomatic mission to Qing China approaching the city of Sanhaegwan on its way to offer tribute to the emperor in Beijing, 190 miles away. Such tribute missions offered opportunities for the Korean delegation to see something of China. According to diaries of Korean envoys, they categorized sites along the route to Beijing under such titles as historical, curiosity, or spectacle. (© Copyright The Korean Christian Museum at Soongsil University)

Unlike Korea, the Japanese islands were physically separated from China by 100 miles or more of ocean and were never successfully invaded or conquered by their giant mainland neighbor. Thus Japan's very extensive borrowing from Chinese civilization was wholly voluntary, rather than occurring under conditions of direct military threat or outright occupation. The high point of that borrowing took place during the seventh to the ninth centuries C.E., as the first more or less unified Japanese state began to emerge from dozens of small clan-based aristocratic chiefdoms. That state found much that was useful in China and set out, deliberately and systematically, to transform Japan into a centralized bureaucratic state on the Chinese model. Chinese culture, no less than its political practices, also found favor in Japan. Various schools of Chinese Buddhism took root, first among the educated and literate classes and later more broadly in Japanese society. Buddhism deeply affected Japanese art, architecture, education, medicine, views of the afterlife, and attitudes toward suffering and the impermanence of life. The Chinese writing system—and with it an interest in historical writing, calligraphy, and poetry—likewise proved attractive among the elite.

But the absence of any compelling threat from China made it possible for the Japanese to be selective in their borrowing. By the tenth century, deliberate efforts to

AP **EXAM TIP**

Note the differences between the ways Chinese culture was introduced into Japan compared to Korea.

BUILDING AP® SKILLS

Contextualization

Since 60 percent of the exam score for AP® World History: Modern is based on writing, it's good to begin practicing specific writing skills early in the year to give students time to build those skills. You can teach smaller parts of essays to help students become comfortable with them before attempting a larger essay. The image of the tribute system on this page is a possible place to practice contextualization, which involves understanding the historical context of the historical development or process seen in a source. Have students study the image and read the caption. Then ask the following questions to help contextualize the image:

■ What was tribute? *Tribute was payment, in the form of money or goods, to the Chinese emperor.*

■ What was the role of tribute in Chinese relations with outside powers? *Tribute was often given by foreigners in exchange for permission to trade within China.*

■ How does this information help you understand what is happening in the image? *Answers will vary.*

EXPLORING AP® THEMES

Humans and the Environment (ENV) and Governance (GOV)

Themes affect and influence one another throughout world history, and this paragraph on page 77 is a good place to get students to think about the impact the environment can have on government. Have students read the paragraph and then ask: What role did geography play in the expansion of China into Japan? *Japan's distance from China's mainland allowed Japan to keep most of its own culture and to pick and choose, to a degree, what it wanted to import from Chinese culture.*

TEACHING IDEA

Incorporating Outside Resources

If you have time or if some students are particularly interested in samurai and Japanese feudalism, it could be fun to have students investigate a good primary source on the code of bushido. Written in the late seventeenth century, *Code of the Samurai: A Modern Translation of the Bushido Shoshinshu of Taira Shigesuke,* translated by Thomas Cleary (Tuttle Publishing, 1999), is the best available study of the code of bushido in Japan. Students especially interested in the subject matter could be given the option to create a short presentation for the class on the rules of samurai life.

The Samurai of Japan This thirteenth-century suit of armor with horned helmet is typical of that worn by samurai, the professional warrior class of Japan. Comprising hundreds of small metal plates laced together in an overlapping pattern, samurai armor was strong but still flexible enough to allow a warrior to fight on horseback. The prominence of martial values in Japanese culture was one of the ways in which Japan differed from its Chinese neighbor, despite much borrowing. (Pictures from History/Bridgeman Images)

▲ **AP®**

CLAIMS AND EVIDENCE IN SOURCES
What does this image tell us about the social status of warriors in Japan?

AP®

COMPARISON
In what different ways did Japanese and Korean women experience the pressures of traditional Confucian teachings?

absorb additional elements of Chinese culture diminished, and formal tribute missions to China stopped, although private traders and Buddhist monks continued to make the difficult journey to the mainland. Over many centuries, the Japanese combined what they had assimilated from China with elements of their own tradition into a distinctive Japanese civilization.

In the political realm, for example, the Japanese never succeeded in creating an effective centralized and bureaucratic state to match that of China. Although the court and the emperor retained an important ceremonial and cultural role, their real political authority over the country gradually diminished in favor of competing aristocratic families, both at court and in the provinces. As political power became increasingly decentralized, local authorities developed their own military forces, the famous *samurai* warrior class of Japanese society (see AP® Looking Again: Japanese Samurai Culture, page 116). Bearing their exquisite curved swords, the samurai developed a distinctive set of values featuring bravery, loyalty, endurance, honor, great skill in martial arts, and a preference for death over surrender. This was *bushido* (boo-shee-doh), the way of the warrior. Japan's celebration of the samurai and of military virtues contrasted sharply with China's emphasis on intellectual achievements and political office holding, which were accorded higher prestige than bearing arms. "The educated men of the land," wrote a Chinese minister in the eleventh century, "regard the carrying of arms as a disgrace."[9] The Japanese, clearly, did not agree.

Religiously as well, Japan remained distinctive. Although Buddhism in many forms took hold in the country, it never completely replaced the native beliefs and practices, which focused attention on numerous *kami*, sacred spirits associated with human ancestors and various natural phenomena. Much later referred to as Shinto, this tradition provided legitimacy to the imperial family, based on claims of descent from the sun goddess. Because veneration of the kami lacked an elaborate philosophy or ritual, it conflicted very little with Buddhism. In fact, numerous kami were assimilated into Japanese Buddhism as local expressions of Buddhist deities or principles.

Japanese literary and artistic culture likewise evolved in distinctive ways, despite much borrowing from China. As in Korea, a unique writing system emerged that combined Chinese characters with a series of phonetic symbols. A highly refined aesthetic culture found expression at the imperial court, even as the court's real political authority melted away. Court aristocrats and their ladies lived in splendor, composed poems, arranged flowers, and conducted their love affairs. "What counted," wrote one scholar, "was the proper costume, the right ceremonial act, the successful turn of phrase in a poem, and the appropriate expression of refined taste."[10] *The Tale of Genji,* a Japanese novel written by the author Murasaki Shikibu,

BUILDING AP® SKILLS

Contextualization

To continue practicing the skill of Contextualization and have students study a primary source, you might try asking students to research *The Tale of Genji,* one of the most elaborate works of literature from Japan. Summaries of the story can be found online. After students have read about the story, ask: What is special about *The Tale of Genji,* and why is it an important record of court life at the time? *It is written in beautiful language. The book was written by a woman in Japanese script, not Chinese, which helped Japan to maintain its own unique written language despite Chinese influence. It also showed Japanese women having more freedoms in society than in Chinese society.*

BUILDING AP® SKILLS

Making Connections: Comparison

If you had the students complete the Chinese influence on Korea and Japan chart from page 76, you could assess student understanding by dividing the class into groups to create a Venn diagram. Divide the class up into groups of three to four students. Have each group create a Venn diagram comparing the influence of China on Korea and Japan. Once all the groups are finished, have them share what they created to see how their thoughts compared. *Answers will vary.*

a lady-in-waiting at the imperial court around 1000, provides an intimate picture of the intrigues and romances of court life.

At this level of society, Japanese women, unlike Korean women, largely escaped the more oppressive features of Chinese Confucian culture, such as the prohibition of remarriage for widows and seclusion within the home. Japanese women continued to inherit property; Japanese married couples often lived apart or with the wife's family; and marriages were made and broken easily. None of this corresponded to Confucian values. When Japanese women did begin to lose status in the twelfth century and later, it had less to do with Confucian pressures than with the rise of a warrior culture.

The Worlds of Southeast Asia

Finding the Main Point: What were the cultural and political effects of Southeast Asia's encounters with other civilizations?

As a geographical and cultural region, Southeast Asia is often divided into two parts. Mainland Southeast Asia encompasses the modern countries of Vietnam, Cambodia, Laos, Thailand, and Myanmar. Maritime Southeast Asia refers to the Philippine and Indonesian islands as well as New Guinea. During the centuries between 600 and 1500, this linguistically diverse region gave rise to a series of cities and states or kingdoms, all of them connected in various ways to the growing commercial network of the Indian Ocean (see Chapter 3). At the same time, the traders and sailors of that network introduced three major religious traditions to the region—Buddhism, Hinduism, and later, Islam. Located between the major civilizations of China and India, the new civilizations of Southeast Asia were shaped by their interactions with both of them.

Vietnam: Living in the Shadow of China

At the southeastern fringe of the Chinese cultural world, the people who eventually came to be called Vietnamese were shaped by their historical encounter with China. As in Korea, the elite culture of Vietnam borrowed heavily from China—adopting Confucianism, Daoism, Buddhism, administrative techniques, the examination system, and artistic and literary styles—even as its popular culture remained distinctive. And, like Korea, Vietnam achieved political independence while participating fully in the **tribute system** as a vassal state.

Unlike Korea, however, the cultural heartland of Vietnam in the Red River valley had been fully incorporated into the Chinese state for more than a thousand years (111 B.C.E.–939 C.E.). Even in 1200, centuries after securing their independence, Vietnamese rulers carefully maintained Vietnam's tributary role, sending repeated missions to do homage at the Chinese court.

Successive Vietnamese dynasties found the Chinese approach to government useful, styling their rulers as emperors, claiming the Mandate of Heaven, and making use of Chinese court rituals. More so than in Korea, a Chinese-based examination system in Vietnam functioned to undermine an established aristocracy, to provide some measure of social mobility for commoners, and to create a merit-based scholar-gentry class to staff the bureaucracy. Furthermore, members of the Vietnamese elite class remained

AP

COMPARISON
Compare China's influence on Vietnam with its influence on Korea and Japan.

BUILDING AP® SKILLS

Claims and Evidence in Sources

This image on Chinese influence in Vietnam is good for helping students explain the historical context of a work. Ask students the following questions:

■ What aspects of this image show Chinese influence? *The style of painting, clothing, hairstyles, instruments, and symbols all show Chinese influence.*

■ Based on the chapter text on Vietnam and the image, why is the Chinese influence seen in this image significant? *The Chinese had direct control over the Vietnamese for a thousand years, and this image helps emphasize that influence. Vietnam adopted many Chinese ideas, like the civil service exam as seen in the image, and created a merit-based bureaucracy. Although eventually Vietnam did overthrow Chinese rule, its culture continued to reflect Chinese influence.*

BUILDING AP® SKILLS

Making Connections: Comparison

It's important for students to be able to compare different states and civilizations. You could have students review what they've just learned about Korea and Japan and compare that to Vietnam (after having them read pages 79 and 80). To guide students in making a comparison, ask: How was the relationship with China similar for Korea, Vietnam, and Japan? *All three retained distinct identities, but they also borrowed major elements of Chinese culture.*

Chinese Influence in Vietnam This painted scroll in the Chinese style was created in Vietnam and dates from the fourteenth or fifteenth centuries. It depicts the triumphant return of a government official to his native village after passing his civil service exams. He rides atop an elephant, while people gather to play instruments to welcome him. Both the painting's style and its subject, the passing of civil service exams, reflect the deep influence of Chinese cultural and political traditions on Vietnamese society.
(Werner Forman Archive/Bridgeman Images)

▲ AP®
CLAIMS AND EVIDENCE IN SOURCES
How does this image reflect the political influence of China on Vietnam?

deeply committed to Chinese culture, viewing their own country less as a separate nation than as a southern extension of a universal civilization, the only one they knew.

Beyond the elite, however, there remained much that was uniquely Vietnamese, such as a distinctive language, a fondness for cockfighting, and the habit of chewing betel nuts. More importantly, Vietnam long retained a greater role for women in social and economic life, despite heavy Chinese influence. In the third century C.E., Lady Triêu led an anti-Chinese resistance movement, declaring: "I want to drive away the enemy to save our people. I will not resign myself to the usual lot of women who bow their heads and become concubines." Female nature deities and a "female Buddha" continued to be part of Vietnamese popular religion, even as Confucian-based ideas took root among the elite.

In the centuries following independence from China, as Vietnam expanded to the south, northern officials tried in vain to impose more orthodox Confucian gender practices in place of local customs that allowed women to choose their own husbands and married men to live in the households of their wives. So persistent were these practices that a seventeenth-century Chinese visitor commented, with disgust, that Vietnamese preferred the birth of a girl to that of a boy. These features of Vietnamese life reflected larger patterns of Southeast Asian culture that distinguished it from China. And like the Koreans and the Japanese, the Vietnamese developed a variation of Chinese writing called **chu nom** ("southern script"), which provided the basis for an independent national literature and a vehicle for the writing of most educated women.

Maritime Southeast Asia: Commerce, Religion, and State Building

While Chinese culture shaped Vietnam, Indian cultural influences—both Hindu and Buddhist—were more prominent in the islands of Southeast Asia (see Map 2.2). In a region shaped by Indian Ocean trade, the case of **Srivijaya** (SREE-vih-juh-yuh) provides an early example of the connection between commerce, state building, and religious change. When Malay sailors, long active in the waters around Southeast Asia, opened an all-sea route between India and China through the Strait of Melaka, the many small ports along the Malay Peninsula and the coast of Sumatra began to compete intensely to attract the growing number of traders and travelers making their way through the strait. From this competition emerged the Malay kingdom of

EXPLORING AP® THEMES

Economic Systems (ECN) and Governance (GOV)

This is another good place to have students think about the connections between themes in world history. You can facilitate a quick class discussion on the connection between economics and government by first having the students read about Srivijaya at the end of page 80 and the beginning of page 81. Then ask: What are some connections between commerce and state building?

In Srivijaya, there was access to highly desired resources such as gold and spices. In addition, taxes could be levied on ships passing through the Strait of Melaka. These taxes provided the funding necessary to support a state government. In addition, trade attracted people to the area, and these residents supported the protection that a military and naval force provided.

Srivijaya, which dominated this critical choke point of Indian Ocean trade from 670 to 1025. A number of factors—Srivijaya's plentiful supply of gold; its access to the source of highly sought-after spices, such as cloves, nutmeg, and mace; and the taxes levied on passing ships—provided resources to attract supporters, to fund an embryonic bureaucracy, and to create the military and naval forces that brought some security to the area.

Srivijayan monarchs employed Indians as advisers, clerks, or officials and assigned Sanskrit titles to their subordinates. The capital city of Palembang was a cosmopolitan place, where even the parrots were said to speak four languages. While these rulers continued to draw on indigenous beliefs that chiefs possessed magical powers and were responsible for the prosperity of their people, they also made use of imported Indian political ideas and Buddhist religious concepts, which provided a "higher level of magic" for rulers as well as the prestige of association with Indian civilization.[11] They also sponsored the creation of images of the Buddha and of various bodhisattvas whose faces resembled those of deceased kings and were inscribed with traditional curses against anyone who would destroy them. Srivijaya grew into a major center of Buddhist observance and teaching, attracting thousands of monks and students from throughout the Buddhist world.

Elsewhere as well, elements of Indian culture took hold in maritime Southeast Asia. On the island of Java a number of states emerged, heavily influenced by Hindu religious ideas, giving rise to a distinctive Hindu-Javanese cultural blend. Among the largest of these states was the kingdom of **Madjapahit**, which at the peak of its power in the mid-1300s dominated much of what is now Indonesia and Malaya. In 1365, a local poet extravagantly praised its ruler, Hayam Wuruk: "His retinue, treasures, chariots, elephants, horses are (immeasurable) like the sea. The island of Java is becoming more and more famous for its blessed state throughout the world."[12] Indian cultural influences found further expression in what is now Indonesia through widely popular shadow puppet performances based on Hindu epics such as the *Ramayana*, though mixed with local material as well. Hinduism was also well established by 1000 in the Champa kingdom in what is now southern Vietnam, where Shiva was worshiped, cows were honored, and phallic imagery was prominent. A little later it took root further inland, where during the twelfth century, the prosperous and powerful Khmer kingdom of Angkor constructed the most stunning architectural expression of Hinduism in the temple complex known as **Angkor Wat**. The largest religious structure in the world of its time, it sought to express a Hindu understanding of the cosmos centered on a mythical Mount Meru, the home of the gods. Later, it was used by Buddhists as well, with little sense of contradiction.

Map 2.2 Southeast Asia, ca. 1200 c.e.
Both mainland and island Southeast Asia were centrally involved in the commerce of the Indian Ocean basin, and both were transformed by that experience.

AP **EXAM TIP**
Angkor Wat and the temple of Borobudur are examples of architecture influenced by religion.

EXPLORING AP® THEMES
Humans and the Environment (ENV)

Along with being able to analyze images, it's important for students to be able to study a map and pull information and evidence from it. Students can practice this skill by studying Map 2.2, "Southeast Asia, ca. 1200 c.e." After studying the map, ask students the following questions:

■ What are important geographic features in Southeast Asia? *The Strait of Melaka and the South China Sea.*

■ Why are these geographic features significant? *Whoever controls these areas has the potential to control trade throughout the region, thereby gaining wealth and power.*

APPLY THE TIP

One way to provide a challenge to students is to have them compare two pieces of architecture, like Angkor Wat and Borobudur, both UNESCO World Heritage Sites. To help them make comparisons, ask students to research the similarities and differences between Angkor Wat and Borobudur using information found about the sites on the UNESCO website. As students research the two sites, have them consider the following questions:

■ Why was Borobudur designed as a single structure and Angkor Wat as many structures? *Answers will vary.*

■ What does the architecture of each site indicate about the society that built it? *Answers will vary.*

Borobudur This huge Buddhist monument in Java, constructed probably in the ninth century C.E., was later abandoned and covered with layers of volcanic ash and vegetation as Java came under Islamic influence. A mountain-shaped structure, it contained a three-mile walkway portraying the spiritual journey from ignorance to enlightenment and represented the grounding of Buddhism in a distinctively Javanese form. (robertharding/Alamy)

TEACHING IDEA

Class Discussion

A quick way to get students to look at and think about monumental architecture (an important part of the theme of Cultural Developments and Interactions) is have them look at the image of Borobudur on this page. Give students a sense of the scale of Borobudur by pointing out that the tiny figures near the left edge of the picture are people. After giving them time to study the image, start a class discussion by asking the following questions:

■ What function does monumental architecture like Borobudur serve in a civilization? *Monumental architecture displays the power of the ruler and the elite. Monumental architecture is typically so large it can be seen from far away.*

■ What does Borobudur reflect about the civilization in which it was built? *Borobudur shows both the power of the civilization and its Indian heritage.*

The Worlds of Islam: Fragmented and Expanding

Finding the Main Point: What political and intellectual transformations took place in Islamic civilization as it spread?

By around 1200, what Muslims called the Dar al-Islam or the House of Islam was firmly established along a vast and continuous expanse of Afro-Eurasia, stretching from Spain and Morocco in the west to northern India in the east, with its heartland in the Middle East and Egypt. Many of these territories had been incorporated into the Islamic world through the construction of the Arab Empire in the century and a half following Muhammad's death in 632, even if wide-scale conversion of subject peoples to the faith took considerably longer (see Chapter 1). From around 1000, a second major expansion by conquest brought India, Anatolia, and a little later the Balkans into the world of Islam, spearheaded by Turkic-speaking groups who had recently converted to the Muslim faith. By 1200, Islam was also spreading far beyond these regions of conquest into Southeast and Central Asia and sub-Saharan Africa through the activities of Muslim merchants and missionaries (see Map 2.3; see Chapter 3). Between 1200 and 1450, the Islamic world was politically fragmented, but Islamic culture and religion remained vibrant in the Middle

APPLY THE TIP

Since the Global Tapestry "drops" students into the middle of many postclassical civilizations, it can be helpful to point out how the introductions to sections can provide context. To find context for the Islamic world, have students read the first paragraph in the section "The Worlds of Islam: Fragmented and Expanding." Ask students to list the areas that Islam spread to after Muhammad's death in 632. *Spain, northern Africa, northern India, Anatolia, the Balkans, Central Asia, Southeast Asia, sub-Saharan Africa.*

MAPPING HISTORY Map 2.3 **The Growing World of Islam, 900–1500**

Islam as a religion, a civilization, and an arena of commerce continued to grow even as the Arab Empire fragmented. The journeys made during the fourteenth century by Ibn Battuta, an Arab scholar, merchant, and public official, reveal how long-distance trade routes linked the Islamic heartland in southwest Asia, North Africa, and Spain to its frontiers and regions beyond.

Reading the Map: To what extent did Ibn Battuta rely upon established long-distance trade routes during his travels? At what point in his journeys did he travel far beyond the borders of the worlds of Islam?

AP **Making Connections:** Between 900 and 1500, Islam primarily spread along trade routes. To what extent does the map support this statement?

EXPLORING AP® THEMES

Humans and the Environment (ENV)

Students can continue to practice analysis by studying Map 2.3, "The Growing World of Islam, 900–1500." After studying the map, ask students the following questions:

■ What are some major geographic features in the world of Islam? *Deserts such as the Sahara and Arabian deserts; Major waterways such as the Mediterranean Sea, Red Sea, Arabian Sea, and Indian Ocean; Mountains like the Himalayas.*

■ How could geography influence the spread of Islam? *Waterways would make it easier for missionaries to move and spread the religion; Easy access to trade routes would also make it easy for the religion to spread; Deserts could be a barrier to spread, but Muslims were able to cross the deserts; Mountains could have stopped the spread to certain areas.*

East, while the continuing spread of the faith gave rise to cultural encounters with Hindu, Christian, and African civilizations.

The Islamic Heartland

In 1200, the **Abbasid caliphate**, an Arab dynasty that had ruled the Islamic world in theory if not practice since 750, was a shadow of its former self. At the start of their rule, the Abbasids built a splendid new capital in Baghdad, from which the

AP®
CONTINUITY AND CHANGE
How did the rise of Islam affect the role of the pastoral Turkic peoples in world history?

BUILDING AP® SKILLS

Making Connections: Comparison

If you are having students complete the comparison chart on China and the Islamic world, have them pause here and use the information on pages 84 to 87 to complete the Islamic world's political section of the chart.

APPLY THE TIP

The Ottoman Empire is an incredibly influential empire in Unit 3, so it can be good to introduce the empire here and help students see how it was a part of the wider Islamic world in the 1200–1450 time period. Have students create a chart like the one below to take notes on the Ottoman Empire's economic, cultural, and political significance using information from the last paragraph on page 84 and the first paragraph on page 85. Note that students may need to do additional research to find all of the information. (Answers are provided in italics in the chart.)

Economic	Cultural	Political
The economy was largely agricultural, and trade tended to be domestic. The Ottomans sought to control the export and import of precious metals, cotton, and wheat, in contrast to European mercantilism. Strong artisan trade groups developed in major Ottoman cities. Trading partners included some of the Italian city-states.	*Ottoman culture was Islamic but incorporated people of many different backgrounds. Foreign traders of Christian or Jewish origin were tolerated. Greek, Persian, and Arab customs and art were cultural influences. The decorative arts flourished in the Ottoman court.*	*The Ottomans were a great military power and controlled a huge empire that included many different people. They sought to unify the Islamic world, and their seizure of Constantinople marked the end of Christian Byzantium. The Ottomans continued to press westward into Central Europe. Religious scholars and experts in Islamic law served in positions of authority.*

TRM Handout 2.2: Chart for Economic, Cultural, and Political Characteristics of Ottoman Empire

AP® EXAM TIP
Be aware of the Ottoman Empire's economic, cultural, and political significance.

▼ AP®
CAUSATION
What does this tile reveal about Turkish culture after settlement in Anatolia?

Seljuk Tiles Among the artistic achievements of Turkic Muslims were lovely ceramic tiles used to decorate mosques, minarets, palaces, and other public spaces. They contained intricate geometric designs, images of trees and birds, and inscriptions from the Quran. This one, dating from the thirteenth century, was used in a Seljuk palace, built as a summer residence for the sultan in the city of Konya in what is now central Turkey. (Images & Stories/Alamy)

dynasty presided over a flourishing and prosperous Islamic civilization. But for all its accomplishments, the Abbasid dynasty's political grip on the vast Arab Empire slipped away quickly. Beginning in the mid-ninth century, many local governors or military commanders asserted the autonomy of their regions, while still giving formal allegiance to the caliph in Baghdad.

A major turning point in both the political and cultural history of the Islamic Middle East was the arrival, starting around 1000, of Turkic-speaking pastoralists from the steppes of Central Asia into the fragmenting political landscape of the Abbasid Empire. At first, they served as slave soldiers within the Abbasid caliphate, and then, as the caliphate declined, they increasingly took political and military power themselves. In the **Seljuk Turkic Empire** of the eleventh and twelfth centuries, for instance, rulers began to claim the Muslim title of *sultan* (ruler) rather than the Turkic *kaghan* as they became major players in the Islamic Middle East. Even as their political power grew, the Turks were themselves experiencing a major turning point in their history as ever more groups of Turkic-speaking warriors converted to Islam between the tenth and fourteenth centuries. This extended process represented a significant expansion of the faith and launched the Turks into a new role as a major sustainer of Islam and carrier of the faith to new regions.

By 1200, the Islamic heartland had fractured politically into a series of "sultanates," many ruled by Persian or Turkish military dynasties. In the thirteenth century, the Mongols, another pastoral people, invaded the region, put an official end to the Abbasid caliphate in 1258, and ruled much of Persia for a time. In the long run, though, it was the **Ottoman Empire**, a creation of one of the many Turkic warrior groups that had migrated into Anatolia (what is now Turkey), that brought greater long-term political unity to the Islamic Middle East and North Africa. By the mid-fifteenth century, the Ottoman Turks had already carved out a state that encompassed much of the Anatolian peninsula and had pushed deep into southeastern Europe (the Balkans), acquiring in the process a substantial Christian population and a capital city in **Constantinople**. (See Zooming In: 1453 in Constantinople.) During the sixteenth century, the Ottoman Empire extended its control to much of the Middle East, Egypt, coastal North Africa, the lands surrounding the Black Sea, and even

BUILDING AP® SKILLS

Making Connections: Continuity and Change

While Comparison is the recommended skill for Unit 1, it's still a good idea to have students work with the other reasoning processes of Causation and Continuity and Change. The second paragraph on this page provides a good place for students to work on Continuity and Change. Have students fill in a chart like the one here to show the continuities and changes for pastoralists as they interacted with Islam. A reproducible version of this chart is available in the Teacher's Resource Materials. (Possible answers are provided in italics.) ●

farther into Eastern Europe. This impressive and enduring new empire lasted in one form or another from the fourteenth to the early twentieth century.

The Ottoman Empire was a state of enormous significance in the world of the fifteenth century and beyond. In its huge territory, long duration, incorporation of many diverse peoples, and economic and cultural sophistication, it was one of the great empires of world history. In the fifteenth century, only Ming dynasty China and the Incas matched it in terms of wealth, power, and splendor. That empire represented the emergence of the Turks as the dominant people of the Islamic world, ruling now over many Arabs, who had initiated this new faith more than 800 years before. In adding "caliph" (successor to the Prophet) to their other titles, Ottoman sultans claimed the legacy of the earlier Abbasid Empire. They sought to bring a renewed unity to the Islamic world, while also serving as protector of the faith, the "strong sword of Islam." Along with the Safavid dynasty that emerged to the east in Persia in the sixteenth century, the Ottomans brought to the Islamic Middle East a greater measure of political coherence, military power, economic prosperity, and cultural brilliance than it had known since the early centuries of Islam. (See "In the Islamic Heartland: The Ottoman and Persian Safavid Empires" in Chapter 4.)

▼ **AP®**
COMPARISON
What does this image reveal about the characteristics of the Ottoman Janissaries as a military force?

Ottoman Janissaries Originating in the fourteenth century, the Janissaries became the elite infantry force of the Ottoman Empire. Complete with uniforms, cash salaries, and marching music, they were the first standing army in the region since the days of the Roman Empire. When gunpowder technology became available, Janissary forces soon were armed with muskets, grenades, and handheld cannons. This Turkish miniature painting dates from the sixteenth century. (Topkapi Palace Museum, Istanbul, Turkey/Album/Art Resource, NY)

BUILDING AP® SKILLS

Making Connections: Comparison

You can continue to build on the skill of Comparison by having students investigate the Janissaries and note their similarities and differences with soldiers of other cultures. Use the image as a starting point, though students will probably need to do outside research as well. (Answers are provided in italics.)

■ *Janissaries were usually Christian. Given the possibilities for advancement, some poor Muslim parents gave their sons to Christian families, hoping the boys would become Janissaries. This would not have usually occurred in other cultures.*

■ *Janissaries were taken for military training as young children, like Spartan soldiers were.*

■ *Janissaries experienced opportunities for advancement in the government, like the men who passed the Chinese civil service exam.*

■ *Janissaries were fearsome fighters. Some towns and cities surrendered to the Ottomans simply because people saw the Janissaries, just as others had surrendered upon the appearance of Chinggis Khan and his warriors.*

(continued)

Changes	Continuities
■ *Introduction of Islam*	■ *Allied against common enemies*
■ *Transmission of Islam into new areas*	■ *Traded with existing settled peoples*
■ *Transformation to sedentary farming*	■ *Extorted tribute payments*
■ *Turkic peoples settled and formed new states*	

TRM Handout 2.3: Continuity and Change Chart for the Islamic World

APPLY THE TIP

To help students understand the information referenced in this AP® Exam Tip, you can display Map 2.4, "The Sultanate of Delhi and Vijayanagar Empire," and note that the Delhi sultanate was mainly located in northern India. Then ask students: Why was the Delhi sultanate able to control northern India politically but not culturally? (They can use the information in the first two paragraphs of this page to help them answer the question.) *Many Hindus were willing to cooperate politically with the Muslim leaders of the Delhi sultanate; however, Hindu culture was not seriously challenged by the Muslim culture.*

EXPLORING AP® THEMES

Cultural Developments and Interactions (CDI)

In the Islam section of Chapter 1, students learned about Sufis and the role they play in the religion. This is a good place for students to practice drawing on their prior knowledge. Ask students: What role did Sufi missionaries play in integrating Islam into the Hindu and Buddhist culture of the region? *Sufis were particularly important in facilitating conversion, for India had always valued "god-filled men" who were detached from worldly affairs. Sufis also offered a more personal religious experience, which allowed them to accommodate local beliefs and encouraged the growth of Islam.*

AP EXAM TIP

Understand the political and cultural features of states such as the Delhi sultanate.

On the Peripheries of the Islamic World: India and Spain

Even as Turkish political and cultural influence increased in the Islamic heartland, Turkic-speaking warrior groups were also spreading the Muslim faith into India, initiating an enduring encounter with an ancient Hindu civilization. Beginning around 1000, those conquests gave rise to a series of Islamic regimes that governed much of India into the nineteenth century. The early centuries of this encounter were violent indeed, as the invaders smashed Hindu and Buddhist temples and carried off vast quantities of Indian treasure. With the establishment of the Sultanate of Delhi in 1206 (see Map 2.4), Turkic rule became more systematic, although the Turks' small numbers and internal conflicts allowed only a very modest penetration of Indian society.

In the centuries that followed, substantial Muslim communities emerged in northern India, particularly in regions less tightly integrated into the dominant Hindu culture. Aside from the spiritual attractions of the faith, the egalitarian aspects of Islam attracted some disillusioned Buddhists, low-caste Hindus, and untouchables (people considered beneath even the lowest caste), along with those just beginning to make the transition to settled agriculture. Others benefited from converting to Islam by avoiding the *jizya*, a tax imposed on non-Muslims. Muslim holy men, known as Sufis, were particularly important in facilitating conversion, for India had always valued "god-filled men" who were detached from worldly affairs.

Map 2.4 The Sultanate of Delhi and Vijayanagar Empire
Between 1206 and 1526, a number of Muslim dynasties ruled northern India as the Delhi sultanate, while an explicitly Hindu kingdom of Vijayanagar arose in the south in 1336. It drew on north Indian Muslim architectural features and made use of Muslim mercenaries for its military forces.

Unlike the earlier experience of Islam in the Middle East and North Africa, where it rapidly became the dominant faith, in India it was never able to claim more than 20 to 25 percent of the total population. Furthermore, Muslim communities were especially concentrated in the Punjab and Sind regions of northwestern India and in Bengal to the east. The core regions of Hindu culture in the northern Indian plain were not seriously challenged by the new faith, despite centuries of Muslim rule. Muslims usually lived quite separately, remaining a distinctive minority within an ancient Indian civilization, which they now largely governed but which they proved unable to completely transform. However, these religious and cultural boundaries proved permeable in at least some contexts. Many prominent Hindus, for instance, willingly served in the political and military structures of a Muslim-ruled India.

Further south, well beyond the boundaries of the Delhi sultanate and its successors, several Hindu states flourished. Perhaps the most impressive was the powerful Vijayanagar empire (1336–1646), which at its height controlled nearly all of southern India from a thriving capital city of perhaps half a million people, described by one sixteenth-century European visitor as "the best provided city in the world . . . as large as Rome and very beautiful to the sight."[13] Formed in part to resist Muslim incursions from the north, the Vijayanagar empire was also a site of sustained and more peaceful Hindu-Muslim encounters. Muslim merchants were a prominent presence in many trading ports, and a scholar has recently described a Muslim district of the capital as being "as vibrant as the Hindu precincts of the city."[14] As in northern India, the Hindu faith predominated, but a permanent Muslim presence in the south fostered an ongoing encounter between the two faiths and cultures.

In the far west of the Islamic world, Spain, called **al-Andalus** by Muslims, was also the site of a sustained cross-cultural encounter, this time with Christian Western Europe. Muslims, Christians, and Jews mixed more freely in Spain than Muslims and Hindus did in India, though there were still waves of religious persecution. Conquered by Muslim forces in the early eighth century during the first wave of Islamic expansion, Muslim Spain became a vibrant civilization by the 900s. Its agricultural economy was the most prosperous in Europe during this time, and its capital of Córdoba was among the largest and most splendid cities in the world. Muslims, Christians, and Jews alike contributed to a brilliant high culture in which astronomy, medicine, the arts, architecture, and literature flourished. Furthermore, social relationships among upper-class members of different faiths were easy and frequent. By 1000, perhaps 75 percent of the population had converted to Islam. Many of the remaining Christians learned Arabic, veiled their women, stopped eating pork, appreciated Arabic music and poetry, and sometimes married Muslims. During the reign of Abd al-Rahman III (r. 912–961), freedom of worship was declared, as well as the opportunity for all to rise in the state bureaucracy.

But this so-called "golden age" of Muslim Spain was both limited and brief. Even assimilated or Arabized Christians remained religious infidels and second-class citizens in the eyes of their Muslim counterparts, and by the late tenth century toleration began to erode. The Córdoba-based Muslim regime fragmented into numerous rival states. Warfare with the remaining Christian kingdoms in northern Spain picked up in the tenth and eleventh centuries, and more puritanical and rigid forms of Islam entered Spain from North Africa. Tolerance turned to overt persecution against Christians and Jews. Social life also changed. Devout Muslims increasingly avoided contact with members of other faiths, and Arabized Christians were permitted to live only in particular places. Thus, writes

AP

COMPARISON

How did the experience of Islam in India and Spain differ? In what ways was it similar?

▼ **AP**

CLAIMS AND EVIDENCE IN SOURCES

What can one learn about the transmission of knowledge in the Muslim world from this image?

Islamic Scholars at Work Islamic learning flourished in Spain, where, after 1000, it was increasingly transmitted to Christian Western Europe. This twelfth-century miniature depicts scholars listening intently to the figure reading from a book, while numerous texts lie stacked on shelves in the background. It was environments like this where learning was preserved and disseminated throughout the Islamic world. (De Agostini Picture Library/Bridgeman Images)

BUILDING AP® SKILLS

Making Connections: Causation

This section on al-Andalus is a good place to introduce the skill of Causation if you want to have your students practice it. To help students understand the short-term and long-term effects of historical events on religious tolerance, ask them to fill out a cause-and-effect chart as they read this section. Give students the three causes listed in the chart below and ask them to list various effects using pages 87 and 88 to find information. A reproducible version of this chart is available in the Teacher's Resource Materials. (Answers are provided in italics.)

Cause	Effect
Prosperous Muslim Spain	*The city of Córdoba was large and splendid. It developed a cultural tolerance. This toleration contributed to innovations in astronomy, medicine, art, literature, and architecture. Frequent interactions occurred between Christians and Muslims.*
Warfare and fragmentation of Córdoba	*A more puritanical form of Islam came to predominate. Muslims plundered churches and persecuted Christians.*
Reconquista	*Spain was unified under the Catholic monarchs. Jews and then Muslims were expelled. Muslim mosques became Christian churches.*

TRM Handout 2.4: Causation Chart for Religious Toleration in al-Andalus

TEACHING IDEA

Incorporating Outside Resources

The section on the Islamic world in Chapter 2 hints at the scientific and intellectual innovations that happened throughout Dar al-Islam in this time period, but it doesn't go into a lot of detail. Watching the Crash Course video *The Medieval Islamicate World* would be a good way to help students learn about these achievements of the Islamic world. You can find the video by searching for it on YouTube. While students watch the video, have them answer the following questions:

■ What is an Islamicate scholar? *These were people influenced by Islamic civilization, regardless of their religious views.*

■ What was the House of Wisdom? *This was a library that became an international center for translation and research in Baghdad. Scholars from different regions of Eurasia brought in texts to the House of Wisdom, where they were translated.*

■ What was the translation movement? *This movement lasted from 750 to 950 and focused on translating texts from Greek, Chinese, Sanskrit, Persian, and Syriac into Arabic.*

■ What new ideas and technologies were developed during this period of Islamic history? *Scholars proposed heliocentric models of the solar system, calculated the circumference of the earth, invented the astrolabe, developed algebra and trigonometry, improved hydraulic engineering and agricultural science, and even invented the earliest programmable machine.*

BUILDING AP® SKILLS

Making Connections: Comparison

If you are having students complete the comparison chart on China and the Islamic world, have them pause here and use the information on pages 87 and 88 to complete the Islamic world's technology section of the chart. If students watched the Crash Course *The Medieval Islamicate World*, they can also use what they learned from the video to fill in this section.

Differentiation

Once students have completed their comparison chart of China and the Islamic world, you could provide more of a challenge by having them use what they have learned to answer the LEQ prompt below.

■ In the period 1200–1450, states in Afro-Eurasia demonstrated continuity, innovation, and diversity in how they formed and developed.
Develop an argument that evaluates the extent to which Song China and at least one Islamic state differed in how they developed their governments.

Since it's early in the year, you can have students work through the following "Must Do, Should Do, and Strive For" model below to practice writing skills.

■ Must Do: Students should use what they have learned from their comparison chart to write a thesis statement that answers the prompt.

■ Should Do: Students should write down at least three pieces of evidence, in bullet point format, that would help support their prompt.

■ Strive For: Students should choose one argument from their thesis and write a full body paragraph for it (topic sentence, at least two pieces of evidence, and analysis of the evidence).

AP® EXAM TIP
The ways that dominant cultures treat outsiders or "others" are frequent topics on the AP® Exam.

AP®
ARGUMENTATION
"Islam had a revolutionary impact on every society that it touched." What evidence might support this statement, and what might challenge it?

---

one scholar, "the era of harmonious interaction between Muslim and Christian in Spain came to an end, replaced by intolerance, prejudice, and mutual suspicion."[15]

That intolerance intensified as the Christian reconquest of Spain gained ground after 1200. The end came in 1492, when Ferdinand and Isabella, the Catholic monarchs of a unified Spain, took Granada, the last Muslim stronghold on the Iberian Peninsula. Despite initial promises to maintain the freedom of Muslims to worship, in the opening decades of the sixteenth century the Spanish monarchy issued a series of edicts outlawing Islam in its various territories, forcing Muslims to choose between conversion or exile. Many Muslims were thus required to emigrate, often to North Africa or the Ottoman Empire, along with some 200,000 Jews expelled from Spain because they too refused to convert. In the early seventeenth century, Muslim converts to Christianity were also banished from Spain. And yet cultural interchange persisted for a time. The translation of Arab texts into Latin continued under Christian rule, while Muslim palaces and mosques were often converted to Christian uses and new Christian buildings incorporated Islamic artistic and architectural features.

Thus Spain, unlike most other regions incorporated into the Islamic world, experienced a religious reversal between 1200 and 1450 as Christian rule was reestablished and Islam was painfully eradicated from the Iberian Peninsula. In world historical terms, perhaps the chief significance of Muslim Spain was its role in making the rich heritage of Islamic learning available to Christian Europe. As a cross-cultural encounter, it was largely a one-way street. European scholars wanted the secular knowledge—Greek as well as Arab—that had accumulated in the Islamic world, and they flocked to Spain to acquire it. That knowledge of philosophy, mathematics, medicine, optics, astronomy, botany, and more played a major role in the making of a new European civilization in the thirteenth century and beyond. Muslim Spain remained only as a memory (see "Society, Economy, and Culture in the West.")

Emerging Civilizations in Africa

> **Finding the Main Point:** How might you compare the emerging civilizations of East and West Africa?

Africa too was a significant arena of the Islamic world. North Africa had been incorporated into the early Arab Empire during the seventh century C.E., and conversion to Islam was widespread in the centuries that followed. After 1000, Islam likewise took hold in parts of sub-Saharan Africa, even as new states and civilizations emerged in these regions.

The Making of an East African Civilization

One of these, known as **Swahili civilization**, emerged in the eighth century C.E. as a set of commercial city-states stretching all along the East African coast, from present-day Somalia to Mozambique. The earlier ancestors of the Swahili lived in small farming and fishing communities, spoke African Bantu languages, and traded with the Arabian, Greek, and Roman merchants who occasionally visited the coast in ancient times. But what stimulated the development of Swahili civilization was

---

AP® CLASSROOM

AP® Topic Questions

AP® Classroom has great resources for teachers, from Daily Videos that cover the unit topics to practice MCQs, SAQs, LEQs, and DBQs. You can assign Topic Questions and Personal Progress Checks to help students practice their test-taking skills or writing skills. A good Topic Question to assign as a wrap-up to the Worlds of Islam is the Nizam al-Muk SAQ. You can find this SAQ by logging

into AP® Classroom, clicking on Unit 1 under Classroom Resources, and then selecting Topic Questions.

When you assign the Topic Questions or Personal Progress Checks, it can be a good idea to put a timer on the question(s) so students can practice the skill in a timed setting like the AP® Exam.

the region's growing involvement with the world of Indian Ocean trade. Local people and aspiring rulers found opportunity for wealth and power in the growing demand for East African products that were associated with an expanding Indian Ocean commerce. Gold, ivory, quartz, leopard skins, and sometimes enslaved people acquired from interior societies, as well as iron and processed timber manufactured along the coast, found a ready market in Arabia, Persia, India, and beyond. And so an African merchant class developed, villages turned into sizable towns, and clan chiefs became kings.

By 1200, the Swahili civilization was flourishing along the coast, and it was a very different kind of society from the farming and pastoral cultures of the East African interior. It was thoroughly urban, centered in cities of 15,000 to 18,000 people, such as Lamu, Mombasa, Kilwa, Sofala, and many others. (See the map The Swahili Coast of East Africa.) These cities were commercial centers that accumulated goods from the interior and exchanged them for the products of distant civilizations, such as Chinese porcelain and silk, Persian rugs, and Indian cottons. While the transoceanic journeys occurred largely in Arab vessels, Swahili craft navigated the coastal waterways, concentrating goods for shipment abroad.

Like the city-states of ancient Greece, each Swahili city was politically independent, was generally governed by its own king, and was in sharp competition with other cities. No imperial system or larger territorial states unified the world of Swahili civilization. But like all civilizations, it featured class-stratified urban societies with sharp distinctions between a mercantile elite and commoners.

Culturally as well as economically, Swahili civilization participated in the interacting Indian Ocean world. Arab, Indian, and Persian merchants were welcome visitors, and some settled permanently as diasporic communities, much as Chinese merchants did in Southeast Asian commercial cities. Certainly, many ruling families of Swahili cities claimed Arab or Persian origins as a way of bolstering their prestige, even while they dined from Chinese porcelain and dressed in Indian cottons. The Swahili language, widely spoken in East Africa today, was grammatically an African tongue within the larger Bantu family of languages, but it was written in Arabic script and contained a number of Arabic loan words.

Furthermore, Swahili civilization rapidly became Islamic. Introduced by Arab traders, Islam was voluntarily and widely adopted within the Swahili world. Like Buddhism in Southeast Asia, Islam linked Swahili cities to the larger Indian Ocean world, and these East African cities were soon dotted with substantial mosques. When Ibn Battuta (IH-buhn ba-TOO-tuh), a widely traveled Arab scholar, merchant, and public official, visited the Swahili coast in the early fourteenth century, he found Muslim societies in which religious leaders often spoke Arabic, and all were eager to welcome a learned Islamic visitor. But these were African Muslims, not colonies of transplanted Arabs. As one prominent historian commented, "The rulers, scholars, officials, and big merchants as well as the port workers, farmers, craftsmen, and slaves, were dark-skinned people speaking African tongues in everyday life."[16]

The Swahili Coast of East Africa

AP®
CONTINUITY AND CHANGE
What changes did trans-Saharan trade bring to West Africa?

BUILDING AP® SKILLS

Claims and Evidence in Sources

This would be a good place to pause to have students investigate a primary source from Leo Africanus, a Moroccan diplomat who traveled throughout North and West Africa. You can find an excerpt on the city of Timbuktu from his *Description of Africa* by searching for it on Fordham University's Internet History Sourcebooks Project. Use the questions below to facilitate a class discussion on what students have learned about Timbuktu and West Africa from the excerpt as an introduction to African civilizations.

■ What does the excerpt tell us about government and state formation in West Africa?

■ What does the excerpt tell us about the importance of learning in Timbuktu?

APPLY THE TIP

As with the Swahili civilization, the West African kingdoms of Ghana, Mali, and Songhay are not directly mentioned in Unit 1 of the CED. However, it is still helpful for students to be able to identify the thematic characteristics of states, and these three states offer a good opportunity for a quick practice. You can have students create a thematic chart like the one below in their reading notes to identify the characteristics of the West African kingdoms. (Answers are provided in italics.)

Cultural	*Muslim elite; predominately Muslim, though lower classes continued to follow local beliefs*
Political	*Monarchies*
Economic	*Wealth gained from taxing merchants*
Social	*Highly stratified class system*

MAPPING HISTORY   Map 2.5 **The Sand Roads**

For a thousand years or more, the Sahara was an ocean of sand that linked the interior of West Africa with the world of North Africa and the Mediterranean but separated them as well.

Reading the Map: Which cities were built at points where the Sand Road trade routes arrived at the Niger River?

AP Making Connections: The Kingdom of Mali was much larger than the earlier Kingdom of Ghana. What might you infer from the map about the motives for Mali's westward expansion?

AP EXAM TIP

Features of West African kingdoms such as Ghana and Mali are important information for the AP® Exam.

The Making of a West African Civilization

On the other side of the continent, a West African civilization also emerged, likewise driven by commercial exchange and the penetration of Islam. Stretching from the Atlantic coast to Lake Chad, this new **West African civilization** included the large states or empires of Ghana (ca. 700–1200), Mali (ca. 1230–1500), Songhay (1430–1591), and Kanem-Bornu (at its height 1571–1603), as well as numerous towns and cities within them, such as Kumbi Saleh, Jenne, Timbuktu, and Gao (see Map 2.5). In contrast to these large territorial empires, the Hausa-speaking people of what is now northern Nigeria created a substantial number of independent city-states—among them Kano, Katsina, and Gobir—that broadly resembled the Swahili city-states of the East African coast. Beginning in the eleventh century, these Hausa cities created a flourishing urban and commercial culture and acted as middlemen in West African commerce, obtaining kola nuts, for example, from the forest region and sending them north into the trans-Saharan trade. In the fourteenth and fifteenth centuries, one of those states, Kano, had become famous for the production of beautifully dyed cotton textiles, which entered the circuits of West African and trans-Saharan trade.

All of these states were monarchies with an elaborate court life and varying degrees of administrative complexity and military forces at their disposal. All drew on the wealth of trans-Saharan trade, taxing the merchants who conducted it. In the wider world, these states soon acquired a reputation for great riches. An Arab traveler in the tenth century c.e. described the ruler of Ghana as "the wealthiest king on the face of the earth because of his treasures and stocks of gold."[17] At its high point in the fourteenth century, the rulers of **Mali** monopolized the import of strategic goods such as horses and metals; levied duties on salt, copper, and other merchandise; and reserved large nuggets of gold for themselves while permitting the free export of gold dust. (See Working with

Evidence, Chapter 3, Document 5, for an early sixteenth-century account of Timbuktu in Mali.)

This growing integration with the world of international commerce generated the social complexity and hierarchy characteristic of all civilizations. Royal families and elite classes, mercantile and artisan groups, military and religious officials, free peasants and enslaved people—all of these were represented in this emerging West African civilization. So too were gender hierarchies, although without the rigidity of more established Eurasian civilizations. Rulers, merchants, and public officials were almost always male, and by 1200 earlier matrilineal descent patterns had been largely replaced by those tracing descent through the male line. Male bards, the repositories for their communities' history, often viewed powerful women as dangerous, not to be trusted, and a seductive distraction for men. But ordinary women were central to agricultural production and weaving; royal women played important political roles in many places; and oral traditions and mythologies frequently portrayed a complementary rather than hierarchal relationship between the sexes. According to a recent scholar:

> Men [in West African civilization] derive[d] their power and authority by releasing and accumulating *nyama* [a pervasive vital power] through acts of transforming one thing into another—making a living animal dead in hunting, making a lump of metal into a fine bracelet at the smithy. Women derive[d] their power from similar acts of transformation—turning clay into pots or turning the bodily fluids of sex into a baby.[18]

Certainly, the famous Muslim traveler Ibn Battuta, visiting Mali in the mid-fourteenth century, was surprised, and appalled, at the casual intimacy of unmarried men and women, despite their evident commitment to Islam (see AP® Looking Again: Islamic Practice in West Africa through the Eyes of a Foreign Traveler, page 50).

As in all civilizations, slavery found a place in West Africa. Early on, most enslaved people had been women, working as domestic servants and concubines. As West African civilization crystallized, however, enslaved men were put to work as state officials, porters, craftsmen, miners harvesting salt from desert deposits, and especially agricultural laborers producing for the royal granaries on large estates or plantations. Most came from non-Islamic and stateless societies farther south, which were raided during the dry season by cavalry-based forces of West African states. A song in honor of one eleventh-century ruler of Kanem-Bornu boasted of his slave-raiding achievements: "The best you took (and sent home) as the first fruits of battle. The children crying on their mothers you snatched away from their mothers. You took the slave wife from a slave, and set them in lands far removed from one another."[19] Most of these enslaved people were used within this emerging West African civilization, but a **trans-Saharan slave trade** also developed. Between 1100 and 1400, perhaps 5,500 enslaved people per year made the perilous trek across the desert, where most were put to work in the homes of the wealthy in Islamic North Africa.

The states of this West African civilization developed substantial urban and commercial centers where traders congregated and goods were exchanged. Some of these cities also became centers of manufacturing, creating finely wrought beads, iron tools,

TEACHING IDEA

Incorporating Outside Resources

Crash Course World History videos are a good way to get a big picture view of a historical topic to the students and can be fun to watch. In the episode *Mansa Musa and Islam in Africa* of Crash Course World History, John Green teaches about sub-Saharan Africa. In addition to Mansa Musa and his empire of Mali, topics covered include trade, conversion to Islam, visits from Ibn Battuta, architecture, the empire of Ghana, and the East African city-states. You can find the video on YouTube. After showing the video, ask the following questions:

- What problems did Mansa Musa cause in the places he traveled? *He spread so much gold around that it was devalued for decades, harming the economy.*

- How did the empires of West Africa convert to Islam? *They came into contact with the Berbers of North Africa, who were early converts to Islam.*

- What do the writings of Ibn Battuta tell us about cross-cultural interactions and how culture and religion become transformed when brought to new places? *As Islam spread to new areas, it absorbed many of the local cultural traditions.*

- What linked the peoples of East Africa? *Islam and trade linked the peoples of East Africa.*

TEACHING IDEA

Class Discussion

As was mentioned in Chapter 1, often the only exposure students have to slavery is through U.S. history classes. They may not realize that slavery existed in Africa prior to the transatlantic slave trade. You might try facilitating a class discussion to address this learning gap by first asking students to define slavery in their own words. Write their answers on the board, and then ask the class to create a working definition of slavery using the various definitions they have provided. Compare the definition created in their own words to a dictionary definition of slavery. After checking for understanding on the definition of slavery, ask students: What changed in the practice of slavery in West Africa? *Early on, most enslaved people were women. As West African civilization grew, enslaved males were used as state officials, craftsmen, miners, and agricultural laborers.*

Humans and the Environment (ENV)

You can refer back to the questions with Map 2.3 about geography and the spread of Islam by asking students to think more specifically about how the Sahara Desert impacted Islam. Ask students: How did the Sahara Desert serve as both a carrier and a conduit for Islam? *The desert prevented easy interaction between Islamized North Africa and sub-Saharan West Africa. The trans-Saharan trade routes allowed Islamic merchants to interact with sub-Saharan West African merchants, thus introducing them to Islam.*

To help students understand the spread of Christianity over time, you can provide **Map 2A: Europe, Asia, and Africa** and ask them to annotate it by indicating the spread of Christianity from its origin to 1450. Students should mark where Christianity originated, the areas into which it spread, and any major centers of Christianity that emerged as it spread, such as Rome and Constantinople. Students should take notes about how Christianity spread to these new areas. Students can use Map 1.3, "The Spread of Early Buddhism and Christianity," on page 30 in Chapter 1. Another good resource is Business Insider's video *Animated Map Shows How Religion Spread Around the World*, found on YouTube. This video covers the spread of religions from their origins to the current day. Students may need to watch the video a couple of times to get the information they need. After students complete their annotated map, ask the following questions:

■ Where had Christianity spread by 1450? *By 1450, Christianity had spread to Western Europe, parts of Southwest Asia, parts of Africa, parts of India, parts of China, and along the Silk Roads in Central Asia.*

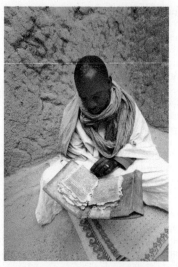

Manuscripts of Timbuktu The West African city of Timbuktu, a terminus of the Sand Road commercial network, became an intellectual center of Islamic learning—both scientific and religious. Its libraries were stocked with books and manuscripts, often transported across the Sahara from the heartland of Islam. Many of these have been preserved and are now being studied once again. (Alex Dissanayake/Getty Images)

or cotton textiles, some of which entered the circuits of commerce. Visitors described them as cosmopolitan places where court officials, artisans, scholars, students, and local and foreign merchants all rubbed elbows. One of the major trading cities, **Timbuktu**, was described in 1525 by a North African traveler:

> Here are great numbers of [Muslim] religious teachers, judges, scholars, and other learned persons who are bountifully maintained at the king's expense. Here too are brought various manuscripts or written books from Barbary [North Africa] which are sold for more money than any other merchandise. . . . Here are very rich merchants and to here journey continually large numbers of negroes who purchase here cloth from Barbary and Europe. . . . It is a wonder to see the quality of merchandise that is daily brought here and how costly and sumptuous everything is.[20]

Like the trade of the Indian Ocean basin, this trans-Saharan commerce was also facilitated by diasporic communities (see AP® Looking Again: Islamic Practice in West Africa through the Eyes of a Foreign Traveler, page 50). By the mid-fourteenth century and no doubt much earlier, settled communities of North African merchants lived in the kingdom of Mali. And Hausa merchants established permanent settlements in many parts of the West African commercial network. Thus the growth of long-distance trade had stimulated the development of a West African civilization, which was linked to the wider networks of exchange in the Eastern Hemisphere.

The Worlds of Christendom

Finding the Main Point: What role did Christianity play in the development of states and civilization in both Eastern and Western Europe?

Much like the worlds of Islam, between 1200 and 1450 the worlds of Christendom were both spreading and contracting. Since 600 C.E. the Christian faith had expanded dramatically in Europe even as it contracted sharply in Asia and Africa, where many had converted to Islam. The **Byzantine Empire**, or Byzantium (bihz-ANN-tee-hum), which for centuries had been the most sophisticated and powerful Christian empire and civilization, entered a state of terminal decline around 1200. But even as this ancient Christian state disappeared, its religious, political, and cultural traditions profoundly influenced Rus, an emerging civilization in Eastern Europe. Meanwhile, the trajectory of civilization in Western Europe traced an opposite path to that of Byzantium, for by 1200 that region was emerging as an especially dynamic, expansive, and innovative

(continued)

■ What do you think may have helped Christianity spread to those regions? *Missionaries, merchants traveling along major trade routes, and migrants moving to new areas all spread Christianity. When people move, they take their culture with them.*

TRM **Map 2A: Europe, Asia, and Africa**

civilization, combining elements of its Greco-Roman-Christian past with the culture of Germanic and Celtic peoples to produce a distinctive hybrid or blended civilization.

The Eastern Orthodox World: A Declining Byzantium and an Emerging Rus

For most people, the Byzantine Empire was simply a continuation of the Roman Empire, and they viewed themselves as "Romans." It initially encompassed large parts of the eastern Roman Empire, including Egypt, Greece, Syria, and Anatolia. Much that was late Roman—its roads, taxation system, military structures, centralized administration, imperial court, laws, Christian Church—persisted in Byzantium for many centuries as the empire consciously sought to preserve the legacy of classical Greco-Roman civilization. Despite major territorial losses to the Arab Islamic Empire, until roughly 1200, a more compact and resilient Byzantine Empire remained a major force in the eastern Mediterranean, controlling Greece, much of the Balkans (Southeastern Europe), and Anatolia (see Map 2.6). From that territorial base, the empire's naval and merchant vessels were active in both the Mediterranean and Black seas.

AP
CONTINUITY AND CHANGE
How did belief systems change as they took root in different areas? Pay particular attention to the changing role of Christianity in both Eastern and Western Europe.

▼ **AP**
CLAIMS AND EVIDENCE IN SOURCES
What does this map suggest about the motivation for Justinian's conquests?

Map 2.6 The Byzantine Empire
The Byzantine Empire reached its greatest extent under Emperor Justinian in the mid-sixth century c.e. It later lost considerable territory to various Christian European powers as well as to Muslim Arab and Turkic invaders.

BUILDING AP® SKILLS

Making Connections: Continuity and Change

Asking the following question can be a good way to introduce the Byzantine Empire and quickly practice the skill of Continuity and Change. Ask students: Why would the Byzantine Empire refer to Constantinople as the "New Rome"? *Constantinople was referred to as the "New Rome" because the Byzantine Empire worked to preserve the legacy of classical Greco-Roman civilization and the Roman Empire.*

TEACHING IDEA

Incorporating Outside Resources

If you have the time in class, this could be a fun place to pause and watch the Crash Course World History video on the Byzantine Empire to give students a brief overview of the empire's history and to practice comparison skills. In the episode *Fall of the Roman Empire . . . in the 15th Century* of Crash Course World History, John Green provides an overview of the Byzantine Empire. He describes how the Roman Empire survived the collapse of the western half of the empire and continued as the Byzantine Empire for another 1,000 years. The video can be found on YouTube. If you don't have time to show it in class, you could also assign the video as homework. Then ask students the following questions:

■ What were the political and economic similarities and differences between the western Roman Empire and the Byzantine Empire?

   ■ Political similarities: *Each empire was ruled by a single man who wielded absolute military power. Both followed Roman law.*

   ■ Economic similarities: *Each empire was exceptionally rich due to trade and valuable agricultural land.*

   ■ Political differences: *The Byzantine Empire was more compact than the western Roman Empire, making it easier to administer. The Byzantines practiced the idea of caesaropapism, meaning that the emperor had absolute control over the empire and the Christian Church.*

   ■ Economic differences: *The Byzantine Empire was more involved in trade.*

■ What were the contributions of the emperor Justinian and his wife Theodora to the Byzantine Empire? *Justinian codified the different Roman laws into one legal code that existed throughout the empire, reconquered old Roman lands, and built one of the great churches of the age, Hagia Sophia. Theodora acted as an adviser to Justinian; at one point she convinced him not to flee the city during a major riot. She also fought to expand the rights of women in divorce and property ownership, and she advocated the passing of a law that prevented adulterous women from being executed.*

BUILDING AP® SKILLS

Developments and Processes

The fall of Constantinople in 1453 is a major turning point in world history because it marked the end of the Byzantine Empire and the rise of the Ottoman Empire. You could try something a little different here with students by asking them to write a firsthand news story or blog entry (including pictures) describing the fall of Constantinople to the Ottoman sultan Mehmed II. Have students read "Zooming In: 1453 in Constantinople" to get an introduction to the event and do further research on the fall to prepare for their news story or blog entry.

ZOOMING IN **1453 in Constantinople**

On May 29, 1453, forces of the Muslim Ottoman sultan Mehmed II seized control of the great Christian city of Constantinople, an event that marked the final end of the Roman/Byzantine Empire and the ascendancy of the Ottoman Empire. In retrospect, this event acquired a certain air of inevitability about it, for the Byzantine Empire had been retreating for almost two centuries before the steady advance of the Ottomans. By 1453, that

Ottoman Turks storm the walls of Constantinople in 1453.

once-great empire, heir to all things Roman, had shrunk to little more than the city itself, with only some 50,000 inhabitants and 8,000 active defenders compared to a vast Ottoman army of 60,000 soldiers. Little was left of the fabled wealth of the city. But what later observers see as inevitable generally occurs only with great human effort and amid vast uncertainty about the outcome. So it was in Constantinople in 1453.

Constantine XI, the last Byzantine emperor, was well aware of the odds he faced. Yet his great city, protected by water on two sides and a great wall on a third, had repeatedly withstood many attacks and sieges. Furthermore, until

the very end, he had hoped for assistance from Western Christians, even promising union with the Roman Church to obtain it. But no such help arrived, at least not in sufficient quantities to make a difference, though rumors of a fleet from Venice persisted. The internal problems of the Western powers as well as the long-standing hostility between Eastern Orthodoxy and Roman Catholicism ensured that Constantinople would meet its end alone.

On the Ottoman side, enormous effort was expended with no assurance of success. In 1451, a new sultan came to the throne of the Ottoman Empire, Mehmed II, only nineteen years old and widely regarded as not very promising. Furthermore, some among the court officials had reservations about an attack on Constantinople. But the young sultan seemed determined to gain the honor promised in Islamic prophesies, going back to Muhammad himself, to the one who conquered the city. Doing so could also rid him of a potential rival to the Ottoman throne, who had taken refuge in Constantinople.

AP®

CAUSATION

How did links to Byzantium contribute to the development of the new civilization in Kievan Rus?

But destabilizing civil wars and incursions by aggressive Western Europeans and Turks continued to shrink Byzantine territory. The end came in 1453 in the **Ottoman seizure of Constantinople**, when the Turkic Ottoman Empire finally took the capital city, and an empire that had survived over 1,000 years passed into history. (See Zooming In: 1453 in Constantinople.)

But the heritage of the Byzantine Empire persisted among the Rus, Slavic peoples of what is now Ukraine and western Russia. In this culturally diverse region, which also included Finnic and Baltic peoples as well as Viking traders, a modest state known as **Kievan Rus** (KEE-yehv-ihn ROOS)—named after

And so preparations began for an assault on the once-great city. The Ottomans assembled a huge fleet, gathered men and materials, and constructed a fortress to control access to Constantinople by water. In late 1452, Mehmed secured the services of a Hungarian master cannon builder named Orban, who constructed a number of huge cannons, one of which could hurl a 600-pound stone ball over a mile. These weapons later had a devastating effect on the walls surrounding Constantinople. Interestingly enough, Orban had first offered his services to the Byzantine emperor, who simply could not afford to pay for this very expensive project.

In early April of 1453, the siege began, and it lasted for fifty-seven days. As required by Islamic law, Mehmed offered three times to spare the emperor and his people if they surrendered. Constantine apparently considered the offer seriously, but he finally refused, declaring, "We have all decided to die with our own free will." After weeks of furious bombardment, an ominous silence descended on May 28. Mehmed had declared a day of rest and prayer before the final assault the next day. That evening, the Byzantine emperor ordered a procession of icons and relics about the city and then entered the ancient Christian church of Hagia Sophia, seeking forgiveness for his sins and receiving Holy Communion.

And then, early the next day, the final assault began as Ottoman forces breached the walls of Constantinople and took the city. The Christians bravely defended their most prominent city, and Constantine discarded his royal regalia and died fighting like a common soldier. A later legend suggested that angels turned Constantine into marble and buried him in a nearby cave from which he would eventually reappear to retake the city for Christendom.

Islamic law required that soldiers be permitted three days of plundering the spoils, but Mehmed was reluctant, eager to spare the city he longed for as his capital. So he limited plundering to one day. Even so, the aftermath was terrible. According to a Christian eyewitness, "The enraged Turkish soldiers . . . gave no quarter. When they had massacred and there was no longer any resistance, they were intent on pillage and roamed through the town stealing, disrobing, pillaging, killing, raping, taking captive men, women, children, monks, priests."[21] When Mehmed himself entered the city, praying at the Christian altar of Hagia Sophia, he reportedly wept at seeing the destruction that had occurred.

Constantinople was now a Muslim city, capital of the Ottoman Empire, and Hagia Sophia became a mosque. The long and often contentious relationship between the world of Islam and that of Christendom had entered a new phase.

QUESTIONS

What factors contributed to Mehmed's victory? Under what circumstances might a different outcome have been possible?

the most prominent city, Kiev—emerged in the ninth century. Loosely led by various princes, Rus was a society of freemen and enslaved peoples, privileged people and commoners, dominant men and subordinate women. This stratification marked it as a civilization in the making. In 988, a decisive turning point occurred. The growing interaction of Rus with the larger world prompted Prince Vladimir of Kiev to affiliate with the **Eastern Orthodox Christianity** of the Byzantine Empire. The prince was searching for a religion that would unify the diverse peoples of his region while linking Rus into wider networks of communication and exchange.

EXPLORING AP® THEMES

Cultural Developments and Interactions (CDI)

A recurring theme in Chapter 2, outside of politics, is the spread of culture and how it influenced other societies. One way to draw students back into this theme is to ask them to read the sections on Kievan Rus on pages 94 to 96 and discuss the following questions:

■ What cultural ideas and traditions did Rus borrow from the Byzantine Empire? *From the Byzantine Empire, Rus adopted Orthodox Christianity, Byzantine architectural styles, the Cyrillic alphabet, the use of icons, a monastic tradition stressing prayer and service, and political ideals of imperial control of the Church.*

■ What impact did these borrowings have on the development of Russia? *These cultural borrowings brought Russia firmly into the world of Orthodox Christianity, separating it from the realms of Islam and the Catholic West. Orthodoxy also provided a more unified identity for the Russian peoples, religious legitimacy for Russia's rulers, and a cultural connection between Russia and the Byzantine Empire.*

EXPLORING AP® THEMES

EXPLORING AP® THEMES

Humans and the Environment (ENV) and Governance (GOV)

As noted in earlier parts of Chapter 2, geography and the environment can affect the development of states and politics. The first paragraph under "The Roman Catholic World: A Fragmented Political Landscape" is a good place to revisit this idea and show how geography can be a dividing force. Pose the following question to students: The first paragraph of this section claims that "Western Europe's geography made political unity difficult." What evidence do the authors provide to back up that claim? *Population centers were divided by mountains and dense forests, and five major peninsulas and two large islands made it difficult to politically unify the region.*

EXPLORING AP® THEMES

Governance (GOV)

It's important to try to take a moment with students to let them know that unlike a majority of the other civilizations and states in Chapter 2, European civilization was fragmented and decentralized in this time period. This decentralization led to feudalism, which can be a difficult concept for students to grasp. To help them understand feudalism, ask students to describe how feudalism functioned in Western Europe during the Middle Ages. (The first paragraph on this page can be helpful with this topic.) *Feudalism developed as a political and social structure in the fragmented and decentralized society of Western Europe. In the thousands of independent, self-sufficient, and largely isolated estates, a warrior elite of landowning lords exercised social, political, and economic power. Lesser lords and knights swore allegiance to the greater lords or kings, becoming their vassals and frequently receiving lands and wealth in return for military service. At the bottom of the feudal structure were serfs, who were bound to the land of a manor and worked for the lord of the manor in exchange for a small farm and protection.*

Another way to help students understand how feudalism functioned is to do a quick class simulation to visualize the feudal structure. You'll need rulers or markers for the simulation. Stand in the center of the room and invite the students to circle their desks around you. Explain that you are the monarch of all of the land in your room, but

The Conversion of the Kievan Rus The conversion of Prince Vladimir of Kiev in 988 had profound long-term implications for Russian history, for it brought this fledgling civilization firmly into the world of Eastern Orthodox Christianity. This image from a fifteenth-century chronicle depicts the baptism of Vladimir, the ceremony that officially made him a member of the Church. (Heritage Images/Getty Images)

▲ **AP®**

CLAIMS AND EVIDENCE IN SOURCES
What does this image tell us about the relationship between politics and religion in Russian civilization?

AP®

COMPARISON
How was Christian civilization in Western Europe different from that in Eastern Europe?

As elsewhere in Europe, the coming of Christianity to Rus was a top-down development in which ordinary people followed their rulers into the church. It was a slow process with elements of traditional religious sensibility (ancestral spirits, household deities, nature gods) lingering among those who defined themselves as Christian. Nonetheless, it was a fateful choice with long-term implications for Russian history, for it brought this fledgling civilization firmly into the world of Orthodox Christianity, separating it from both the realm of Islam and the Roman Catholic West. Like many new civilizations, Rus borrowed extensively from its older and more sophisticated Byzantine neighbor. Among these borrowings were Byzantine architectural styles, the Cyrillic alphabet based on its Greek counterpart, the extensive use of religious images known as icons, a monastic tradition stressing prayer and service, and political ideals of imperial control of the church, all of which became part of a transformed Rus. Orthodoxy also provided a more unified identity for this emerging civilization and religious legitimacy for its rulers.

The Roman Catholic World: A Fragmented Political Landscape

The western half of the European Christian world followed a rather different path from that of the Byzantine Empire. Unlike Byzantium, which sat at the crossroads of several long-distance trade networks, **Western Christendom** was distinctly on the margins of world history until around 1000 C.E. Its geographic location at the far western end of the Eurasian landmass was at a distance from the growing routes of world trade—by sea in the Indian Ocean and by land across the Silk Roads to China and the Sand Roads to West Africa (see Chapter 3). Internally, Western Europe's geography made political unity difficult, for population centers were divided by mountain ranges and dense forests as well as by five major peninsulas and two large islands (Britain and Ireland). However, its extensive coastlines and interior river systems facilitated exchange, while a moderate climate, plentiful rainfall, and fertile soils enabled a productive agriculture that could support a growing population.

Unlike the large centralized states of Byzantium, the Islamic world, and China, this new European civilization never achieved political unity. In the political chaos of the ninth and tenth centuries, a highly fragmented and decentralized society

(continued)

that you need help controlling the land and collecting taxes. Reach out with a ruler and give each student you can touch with your ruler a ruler of their own, explaining that they are lords or nobles who will swear allegiance to you in exchange for land and wealth from you (the monarch). Then have those students reach out with their rulers and give each student they can touch a marker; explain that these students are the knights who swear to fight for the lords for land and wealth. Then have the second group of

students reach out with their markers and see which other students they can touch; this final group of students are the serfs who are bound to the land of the lord and work it in exchange for protection. This activity is inspired by Kendra Garrett (Flower Mound High School, Texas).

emerged in a variety of local expressions and persisted in some regions into the fifteenth century. In a practice widely known as **feudalism**, lesser lords and knights swore allegiance to greater lords or kings and thus became their vassals, frequently receiving lands and plunder in return for military service. Meanwhile, on thousands of independent, self-sufficient, and largely isolated landed estates or manors, power—political, economic, and social—was exercised by landowning lords in a system known as manorialism.

Within feudal Europe, Roman-style slavery gradually gave way to serfdom. Unlike enslaved people, serfs were not the personal property of their masters, could not be arbitrarily thrown off their land, and were allowed to live in families. However, they were bound to their masters' estates as peasant laborers and owed various payments and services to the lord of the manor. In return, the serf family received a small farm and such protection as the lord could provide. In a violent and insecure world, the only security available to many individuals or families lay in these communities, where the ties to kin, manor, lord, and church constituted the primary human loyalties.

But after 1000, European political life began to crystallize into a system of competing states that has persisted into the twenty-first century. In many regions of Western Europe during the eleventh through the thirteenth centuries, monarchs gradually and painfully began to consolidate their authority, and the outlines of French, English, Spanish, Scandinavian, and other states began to appear, each with its own distinct language and culture. Royal courts and fledgling bureaucracies were established, and groups of professional administrators appeared. More effective institutions of government increasingly commanded the loyalty, or at least the obedience, of their subjects. In other regions, smaller states predominated. In Italy, for instance, city-states flourished as urban areas grew wealthy and powerful, while the Germans also remained divided among numerous small principalities within the Holy Roman Empire (see Map 2.7). Europe's multicentered political system shaped the emerging civilization of the West in many ways. It gave rise to frequent wars that brought death, destruction, and disruption to many communities. These same conflicts enhanced the role and status of military men, and thus European elite society and values were far more militarized than in China, which gave greater prominence to scholars and bureaucrats. Intense interstate rivalry, combined with a willingness to borrow, also stimulated European technological development. By 1450, Europeans had gone a long way toward catching up with their more advanced Asian counterparts. Gunpowder, for instance, was invented in China; but Europeans were probably the first to use it in cannons, in the early fourteenth century, and by 1500 they had the most advanced arsenals in the world. Advances in shipbuilding and navigational techniques provided the foundation for European mastery of the seas. These included the magnetic compass and sternpost rudder from China and adaptations of the Mediterranean or Arab lateen sail, which enabled vessels to sail against the wind.

AP EXAM TIP

Be able to identify periods of political unity and those of division in the history of the European/Mediterranean world.

AP

COMPARISON

Why was Europe unable to achieve the same level of political unity that China experienced in this era?

(continued)

■ Where these reunification attempts successful? Why or why not? *Answers may include: Both Charlemagne's and Otto's unified kingdoms disintegrated over time and were not successful in reunifying Europe in the long term; Charlemagne's empire was divided among his later successors, according to the custom of the time; The Holy Roman Empire struggled with the quarreling principalities under its rule, which caused divisions within the empire; After 1000, Western Europe began to permanently solidify into a system of competing political states, and monarchs began to consolidate their power in their states.*

EXPLORING AP® THEMES

Technology and Innovation (TEC)

It's important for students to understand the impact of technology on civilizations and states throughout world history. The last paragraph on page 97 is a good place to pause and have them investigate the impact of technology on Western Europe, especially since this region was behind compared to other civilizations like Song China and Dar al-Islam. Ask students to list examples of technology throughout history that caused dramatic changes in civilizations. *Among the many examples of technology that have caused dramatic changes in civilizations were irrigation systems, the water-driven mill, and steam-powered engines.* Use the following prompts to discuss new technologies introduced to Europe toward the end of the Middle Ages:

■ What was the impact of new energy sources such as the windmill and water mill on Europe in the High Middle Ages? *Europeans were able to grind grain, sieve flour, tan hides, make beer, saw wood, manufacture iron, and make paper with the power generated by windmills and water mills. Overall, these technologies allowed Europeans to revolutionize production in a number of industries and to break away from old sources of energy—animal and human.*

■ What impact did the introduction of gunpowder and advances in maritime technology have on Europe? *Gunpowder revolutionized warfare in Europe because it allowed Europeans to create gunpowder weapons. Advances in maritime technology like the magnetic compass, the lateen sail, and the sternpost rudder enabled Europeans to begin long-distance maritime expeditions.*

APPLY THE TIP

Even though Western Europe spent a majority of the postclassical period politically fragmented, it's good for students to know that there were attempts to reunify the region. You could ask students the follow questions:

■ Were any attempts made to reunify Western Europe after the collapse of the Roman Empire? Give specific examples. *Charlemagne, ruler of the Carolingian Empire, worked to unify the modern-day territories of France, Belgium, the Netherlands, and part of Germany under his rule. He began to act as an imperial ruler, creating an imperial bureaucracy and standardizing weights and measures, and was crowned as a new Roman emperor by the pope in 800. Otto I of Saxony unified much of modern-day Germany under his rule, seeing himself as renewing Roman rule in the region. Like Charlemagne, Otto was crowned by the pope as emperor of what would be known as the Holy Roman Empire.* ➲

TEACHING IDEA

Bell Ringer

A bell ringer, or quick check for understanding with students, is a good way to practice skills frequently throughout the year, like map analysis. Show students Map 2.7, "Europe in 1500," and ask: What is the significance of the location of the Holy Roman Empire? *The central location of the Holy Roman Empire means it can control access to most of Europe.*

BUILDING AP® SKILLS

Making Connections: Comparison

This is a good place to practice with a comparison LEQ prompt. Since it's early in the year, it would be better to have the students create a timed outline of an essay rather than writing a full essay. Timed outlines allow students to practice drawing on their prior knowledge to put together the elements of an LEQ without the pressure of writing a full essay. Essay outlines should include a couple of bullet points for ideas on contextualization, a full thesis statement, ideas for at least two arguments, and bullet points for evidence to support their arguments. You can find a reproducible version of an LEQ outline in the Teacher's Resource Materials. Give students 15 minutes to create an essay outline using the following prompt.

■ Evaluate the extent to which the political institutions of medieval Western Europe differed from the political institutions of the Islamic world or China.

TRM **Writing Organizer for LEQ Practice**

▲ **AP²**

CAUSATION
Based on this map, what factors account for the relative political and social fragmentation of Europe?

Map 2.7 Europe in 1500
By the end of the fifteenth century, Christian Europe had assumed its early modern political shape as a system of competing states threatened by an expanding Muslim Ottoman Empire.

European rulers generally were weaker than their counterparts in Asian civilizations, for they had to contend with competing sources of power such as the nobility and the church. By 1450, nearly all of Western Europe had embraced a distinctive version of Christianity referred to as Roman Catholic to distinguish it from Eastern Orthodoxy and other Christian traditions, and the **Roman Catholic Church** had become the one organization that linked the entire region. Its hierarchical organization of popes, bishops, priests, and monasteries meant that the church had a representative in nearly every community in Europe, and Latin provided a shared language among churchmen, even as it gave way to various vernacular languages in common speech. Over the centuries, the church grew quite wealthy, possessing large amounts of land, the proceeds of which gave it great power and influence within states and funded its many religious, charitable, and educational initiatives.

AP® CLASSROOM

AP® Topic Questions

This would be a good place to pause for some multiple-choice question practice. You can find a set of questions about European feudalism by logging into AP® Classroom, clicking on Unit 1 under Classroom Resources, and then selecting Topic Questions. Look for the questions labeled "Countess of Bearn."

You can either assign the questions to the students to complete individually or allow them to partner up to work through the set together.

The wealth also funded the lavish lifestyles and political aspirations of many leading churchmen, causing reformers to accuse it of forgetting its spiritual mission.

Church authorities, rulers, and nobles often competed against each other, for they were rival centers of power, but they also reinforced each other. Rulers, for instance, provided protection for the papacy and strong encouragement for the faith. In return, the church offered religious legitimacy for the powerful and the prosperous. "It is the will of the Creator," declared the teaching of the church, "that the higher shall always rule over the lower. Each individual and class should stay in its place [and] perform its tasks."[22]

The relative weakness of European rulers provided room for urban-based merchants in Europe to achieve an unusual independence from political authority. Many cities, where wealthy merchants exercised local power, won the right to make and enforce their own laws and appoint their own officials. Some of them—Venice, Genoa, Florence, and Milan, for example—became almost completely independent city-states. Elsewhere, kings, often in search of allies and resources for their struggles with aristocrats and the church, granted charters that allowed cities to have their own courts, laws, and governments, while paying their own kind of taxes to the king. By contrast, Chinese cities, which were far larger than those of Europe, were simply part of the empire and enjoyed few special privileges. Although commerce was far more extensive in China than in the emerging European civilization, the powerful Chinese state favored the landowners over merchants and actively controlled and limited merchant activity far more than the new and weaker royal authorities of Europe were able to do.

According to some historians, the greater freedom of Europe's merchants opened the way to a more thorough development of capitalism in later centuries. In Spain, Portugal, France, and England, it also led to the creation of representative institutions or parliaments from the late twelfth through the early fourteenth centuries. Intended to strengthen royal authority by consulting with major social groups, these embryonic parliaments did not represent the "people" or the "nation" but instead embodied the three great "estates of the realm"—the clergy (the first estate), the landowning nobility (the second estate), and urban merchants (the third estate).

Society, Economy, and Culture in the West

In the several centuries after 1000, a favorable climate, along with greater security and stability, initiated what is commonly called the European High Middle Ages (1000–1300). An acceleration in the tempo of economic and social change in Western and Central Europe represented the making of a new Western civilization.

The population of this civilization grew from perhaps 35 million in 1000 to about 80 million in 1340. Great lords, bishops, and religious orders organized new villages on what had recently been forest, marshes, or wasteland. As expansion brought new opportunities for settlement, many peasants were able to loosen the shackles of serfdom, a trend facilitated by greater stability and the power of states over local lords. This trend accelerated after 1350, as the terrible loss of life caused by the Black Death (the plague) created shortages of labor across much of Europe and those who were still alive could demand lower rents and better wages and conditions.

AP® EXAM TIP

Note the similarities and differences in the functions of cities in various civilizations of Eurasia.

AP®

CONTINUITY AND CHANGE
In what ways did European civilization change after 1000?

APPLY THE TIP

If you feel that it's too early for students to attempt an LEQ outline, another good way to get them to compare Western Europe and other Eurasian civilizations is to have a class discussion on the similarities and differences. Ask students to list the differences between Western European cities and Chinese cities during the postclassical period. Suggest that they focus on the relationship between the cities and the government. *Some European cities won the right to make and enforce their own laws and choose their own officials, while others (like the Italian city-states) became almost completely independent. In contrast, Chinese cities, while larger than European cities, were a part of the larger Chinese empire and did not enjoy the same level of independence European cities did. Chinese cities also enjoyed fewer special privileges from the government. Chinese merchants living in cities experienced more restrictions because of the centralized nature of the Chinese government. The weakness of Europe's rulers allowed merchants living in cities more leeway.*

EXPLORING AP® THEMES

Humans and the Environment (ENV)

As a way to get students to think about turning points in world history, you could ask students why climate change could help bring about a new phase in the development of European civilization. *Warmer climates can bring about more favorable growing seasons, leading to population increase, which can lead to economic growth.*

EXPLORING AP® THEMES

Technology and Innovation (TEC) and Humans and the Environment (ENV)

Technological breakthroughs in Europe influenced the development of agriculture. To explore this subject, you could ask students the following questions. Have students think about their answers on their own and then share their thoughts with a partner.

■ What agricultural breakthroughs did Europe experience during the Middle Ages? *Europeans developed the heavy wheeled plow that could handle the dense soils of Northern Europe. They also began to rely more on horses to pull the plows and developed iron horseshoes and a more efficient collar to help horses pull the plow. Finally, Europeans developed a new three-field system of crop rotation, which allowed more land to be planted at one time.*

■ What was the impact of these breakthroughs on Europe's population and on urban development? *These agricultural breakthroughs meant a more productive agriculture that could support the growing European population, especially in its urban centers.*

TEACHING IDEA

Class Discussion

As mentioned earlier, Western Europe was technologically behind other major civilizations during 1200–1450. The Snapshot chart on page 100 is a great way to help students see what technologies Europe borrowed during this time period and where those technologies originally came from. Display "Snapshot: European Borrowing" for students to see and lead a class discussion on the technologies Europe borrowed from other societies around Afro-Eurasia. Ask students if they are surprised by any of the ideas or technologies that Europeans borrowed.

Technological breakthroughs in agriculture underpinned this expansion as Europeans brought new lands under cultivation. They developed a heavy wheeled plow that could handle the dense soils of Northern Europe. They also began to rely increasingly on horses rather than oxen to pull the plow and to use iron horseshoes and a more efficient collar, which probably originated in China or Central Asia (see Snapshot: European Borrowing). In addition, Europeans developed a new three-field system of crop rotation, which allowed considerably more land to be planted at any one time. These were the technological foundations for a more productive agriculture that could support the growing population of European civilization, especially in its urban centers, far more securely than before. But these developments also took a heavy toll on the environment. For instance, deforestation and the tilling of fields, overfishing, human waste, and the proliferation of new water mills and their associated ponds damaged freshwater ecosystems in many places. Lamenting the declining availability of fish, the French king Philip IV declared in 1289: "Today each and every river and waterside of our realm, large and small, yields nothing."[23]

SNAPSHOT European Borrowing

Like people in other emerging civilizations, Europeans borrowed extensively from their near and more distant counterparts. They adapted these imports, both technological and cultural, to their own circumstances and generated distinctive innovations as well.

Borrowing	Source	Significance
Horse collar	China / Central Asia via Tunisia	Enabled heavy plowing and contributed to European agricultural development
Stirrup	India/Afghanistan	Revolutionized warfare by enhancing cavalry forces
Gunpowder	China	Enhanced the destructiveness of warfare
Paper	China	Enabled bureaucracy; fostered literacy; prerequisite for printing
Spinning wheel	India	Sped up production of yarn, usually by women at home
Wheelbarrow	China	Laborsaving device for farm and construction work
Aristotle	Byzantium / Islamic Spain	Recovery of classical Greek thought
Medical knowledge/ treatments	Islamic world	Sedatives, antiseptics, surgical techniques, optics, and knowledge of contagious diseases enriched European medicine
Christian mysticism	Muslim Spain	Mutual influence of Sufi, Jewish, and Christian mysticism
Music/poetry	Muslim Spain	Contributed to tradition of troubadour poetry about chivalry and courtly love
Mathematics	India / Islamic world	Foundation for European algebra
Chess	India/Persia	A game of prestige associated with European nobility

After 1000, Europeans also began to tap mechanical sources of energy in a major way, revolutionizing production in many industries and breaking with the ancient tradition of depending almost wholly on animal or human muscle as sources of energy. Devices such as cranks, flywheels, camshafts, and complex gearing mechanisms, when combined with windmills and especially water mills, provided power for grinding grain, sieving flour, tanning hides, making beer, sawing wood, manufacturing iron, and producing paper. The increased production associated with agricultural expansion and new sources of energy stimulated a considerable growth in long-distance trade, both within Europe and with the more established civilizations of Byzantium and Islam. Thus the self-sufficient communities of earlier centuries increasingly forged commercial bonds among themselves and with more distant peoples.

The population of towns and cities likewise grew. In the early 1300s, London had about 40,000 people, Paris had approximately 80,000, and Venice by the end of the fourteenth century could boast perhaps 150,000. To keep these figures in perspective, Constantinople housed some 400,000 people in 1000, Córdoba in Muslim Spain about 500,000 at about the same time, and the Song dynasty capital of Hangzhou more than 1 million in the thirteenth century. European towns gave rise to and attracted new groups of people, particularly merchants, bankers, artisans, and university-trained professionals such as lawyers, doctors, and scholars. Thus, from the rural social order of lord and peasant, a new, more productive, and complex division of labor took shape in European society.

These changes, which together represented the making of a new civilization, had implications for the lives of countless women and men. Economic growth and urbanization initially offered European women substantial new opportunities. Women were active in a number of urban professions, such as weaving, brewing, milling grain, midwifery, small-scale retailing, laundering, spinning, and prostitution. However, much as economic and technological change in China had eroded female silk production during the Song dynasty, so too in Europe were women increasingly restricted or banned from working in many trades by the fifteenth century.

The church had long offered some women an alternative to home, marriage, family, and rural life. Substantial numbers of women, particularly from aristocratic families, were attracted to the secluded monastic life of poverty, chastity, and obedience within a convent, in part for the relative freedom from male control that it offered. Here was one of the few places where women might exercise authority as leaders in their orders and obtain a measure of education. But by 1300, much of the independence that such abbesses and their nuns had enjoyed was curtailed, and male control tightened as older ideas of women's intellectual inferiority, the

European Technology Europeans' fascination with technology and their religious motivation for investigating the world are apparent in this thirteenth-century portrayal of God as a divine engineer, laying out the world with a huge compass. (Oesterreichische Nationalbibliothek, Vienna, Austria/Erich Lessing/Art Resource, NY)

▲ AP
CONTEXTUALIZATION
How does this image of God using a compass to lay out the world reflect Western European understandings of science and religion in the thirteenth century?

AP
COMPARISON
How was the development of technologies in Western Europe similar to that in Song China?

AP EXAM TIP
Be prepared for questions about cultural borrowing in world history.

(continued)

■ Social: *Serfs began to move away from the manors to cities, looking for new types of work. As towns rose up, they attracted new groups of people, such as merchants, bankers, artisans, lawyers, doctors, and scholars, who helped with the development and growth of cities during the High Middle Ages.*

■ Economic: *Technological breakthroughs led to a more productive agriculture that could support a growing population. These advancements in agriculture stimulated a considerable growth in long-distance trade.*

■ Environmental: *During the late Middle Ages, Western Europe began to experience a warmer climate, which allowed people to expand agriculture. Farmers began to clear forests to create more land for cultivation, which added to the expansion of agriculture. This expansion of agriculture allowed for the growth of a larger population and helped stimulate long-distance trade.*

EXPLORING AP® THEMES

Social Interactions and Organization (SIO)

You can continue to reinforce the themes in the course by asking questions during class. Students struggle with the AP® Theme of Social Interactions and Organization (SIO). Use these questions to discuss this theme with your students.

■ How did urbanization cause changes in the role of women during the Middle Ages? *Urbanization and the economic growth that accompanied it initially offered women more opportunities. Women became active in a number of urban professions, such as weaving, milling grain, midwifery, small-scale retailing, and laundering. Women became a larger part of the urban workforce and were entitled to train female apprentices in some occupations. Widows of great merchants were allowed to continue their husbands' businesses.*

■ How had women's roles changed by the fifteenth century? *By the fifteenth century, artisan opportunities for women in Europe were declining, and women were being restricted or banned from joining guilds or being apprenticed in an occupation. Men began to take on the more lucrative tasks women had performed prior to the fifteenth century, such as weaving.*

BUILDING AP® SKILLS

Making Connections: Comparison

As the recommended AP® skill of Unit 1 is Comparison, specifically being able to compare the civilizations and states of the unit (Topic 1.7 in the CED), it is a good idea to continue practicing comparison with your students. Divide the class into four groups and assign each group one of the following themes: political, social, economic, or environmental. Ask each group to describe the role of its assigned theme in European urban growth in this era. Then ask each group to share its description with the class. Students should note any overlapping factors. (Answers are provided in italics.)

■ Political: *The population growth in Europe during the High Middle Ages opened up new land for cultivation and expansion. Great lords, bishops, and religious orders organized new villages on the newly cultivated land; these villages would continue to grow due to the relative peace and expanding population of Europe.* ➡

A European Urban Market This image from a fourteenth-century Italian illuminated manuscript depicts a market scene in an urban setting. It illustrates two major elements of an emerging Western European civilization—urbanization and commercialization.
(Mondadori Portfolio/Electa/Paolo Manusardi/Bridgeman Images)

BUILDING AP® SKILLS

Making Connections: Causation

Understanding Causation is an important AP® skill for this course. By 1000 C.E. European intellectual life had dramatically changed, and there was a growing interest in rational thought. Ask students: What impact did this interest in rational thought have on European intellectual life? *European interest in rational thought led to the development of a new field of study known as "natural philosophy." In the twelfth and thirteenth centuries, the translations of Greek and Arabic works became more widely available and continued to boost the studies of new subject areas.*

BUILDING AP® SKILLS

Making Connections: Comparison

Since the AP® skill of Comparison is central to Unit 1, you should continue to practice it with your students. Ask students to research examples of pre-Renaissance art and Renaissance art, and compare the changes they can visualize. You can find the examples below by searching on the Internet.

- Medieval examples might include the following:
  - Paintings by Duccio
  - Paintings by Giotto
  - Paintings by Cimabue
  - Jamb statues from the west portal of Chartres Cathedral
- Renaissance examples might include the following:
  - Masaccio, *The Holy Trinity with the Virgin* — one of the first examples of the use of perspective in painting
  - Statues of David by Michelangelo or Donatello
  - Botticelli, *The Birth of Venus*

Use the categories shown in the table. A reproducible version of this chart is available in the Teacher's Resource Materials. (Answers are provided in italics.)

▶ **AP®**
CLAIMS AND EVIDENCE IN SOURCES
What does this image illustrate about commercial life and gender roles in Western European urban centers?

AP®
CAUSATION
In what ways did the rediscovery of Greek philosophy and science affect European Christianity?

impurity of menstruation, and their role as sexual temptresses were mobilized to explain why women must operate under male control.

Intellectual life in Europe also changed dramatically in the several centuries after 1000, amid a rising population, a quickening commercial life, emerging towns and cities, and contact with Islamic learning. A legal system developed during the period that provided a measure of independence for a variety of institutions—towns and cities, guilds, professional associations, and especially universities. An outgrowth of earlier cathedral schools, these European universities—in Paris, Bologna, Oxford, Cambridge, Salamanca—became "zones of intellectual autonomy" in which scholars could pursue their studies with some freedom from the dictates of religious or political authorities, although that freedom was never complete and was frequently contested.[24]

This was the setting in which a small group of literate churchmen began to emphasize the ability of human reason to penetrate divine mysteries and to grasp the operation of the natural order. The new interest in rational thought was applied first to theology, the "queen of the sciences" to European thinkers. Logic, philosophy, and rationality would operate in service to Christ. Through time, European intellectuals also applied their newly discovered confidence in human reason to law, medicine, and the world of nature, exploring optics, magnetism, astronomy, and alchemy. Slowly and never completely, the scientific study of nature, known as "natural philosophy," began to separate itself from theology. This mounting enthusiasm for rational inquiry

(continued)

	Pre-Renaissance Art	**Renaissance Art**
Financing	*Mainly the Church and some elites, though even the art paid for by the Church had to meet the Church's standards*	*Wealthy elites*
Perspective	*No; blue or gold backgrounds, with the size of figures shown according to their theological importance*	*Yes*
Nudity	*Not acceptable*	*Acceptable for Greek and Roman gods and goddesses and Old Testament figures*
Subject Matter	*Religious*	*Both religious and secular subjects; many portraits of elites*

TRM Handout 2.6: Comparison Chart for Pre-Renaissance and Renaissance Art stimulated European scholars to seek out original Greek texts, particularly those of Aristotle. They found them in the Greek-speaking world of Byzantium and in the Islamic world, where they had long ago been translated into Arabic. In the twelfth and thirteenth centuries, an explosion of translations from Greek and Arabic into Latin, many of them undertaken in Spain, gave European scholars direct access to the works of ancient Greeks and to the remarkable results of Arab scholarship in astronomy, optics, medicine, pharmacology, and more. One of these translators, Adelard of Bath (1080–1142), remarked that he had learned, "under the guidance of reason from Arabic teachers," not to trust established authority.[25]

Beginning in the vibrant commercial cities of Italy between roughly 1350 and 1500, the **European Renaissance** also turned to the ancient past for inspiration. But its agenda reflected the belief of the wealthy male elite that they were living in a wholly new era, far removed from the confined religious world of feudal Europe. First in the cities of Italy and later across much of Europe, educated citizens sought inspiration in the art and literature of ancient Greece and Rome; they were "returning to the sources," as they put it. Their purpose was not so much to reconcile these works with the ideas of Christianity but to use them as a cultural standard to imitate and then to surpass. The elite patronized great Renaissance artists such as Leonardo da Vinci, Michelangelo, and Raphael, whose paintings and sculptures

European University Life in the Middle Ages This fourteenth-century manuscript painting shows a classroom scene from the University of Bologna in Italy. Notice the sleeping and disruptive students. Some things apparently never change. (bpk Bildagentur/Kupferstichkabinett, Staatliche Museen, Berlin, Germany/Photo: Joerg P. Anders/Art Resource, NY)

◀ **AP**
COMPARISON
What comparisons can you make between this image and the image of Muslim scholars on page 87?

BUILDING AP® SKILLS

Claims and Evidence in Sources

Looking for claims and evidence in sources is an important AP® skill throughout the course. Thomas Aquinas was a famous theologian and philosopher from the thirteenth century who integrated rational thought into his theological writings. His most influential work was the *Summa Theologica*. This would be a good time to practice document analysis skills by having students analyze the *Summa Theologica*. Ask students to work with a partner to read Article II and Article III of the *Summa Theologica*, which can be found in Fordham University's Internet Medieval Sourcebook (instruct students to scroll down to Question 2 to find Article II and Article III). Students should list examples of rational thought and the influence of Greek philosophy that they find in the documents. After each pair has finished creating a list, ask students to share their findings. (*Answers will vary.*)

BUILDING AP® SKILLS

Making Connections: Comparison

This can be a fun and light-hearted activity to practice the AP® skill of Comparison. Take a picture of your classroom with your students and project it alongside the image on page 103. Ask students to look at the image of the classroom in the fourteenth century and ask: What is different and what is similar about the medieval classroom and your classroom today? *Answers will vary.*

Bell Ringer

The following activity takes no more than 5 to 10 minutes of your class period and offers an effective and engaging way to begin your lesson.

Before starting the section on the civilizations of the Americas, ask students: What could cause the civilizations in the Americas to develop differently from civilizations in Afro-Eurasia? *Answers may include: Geographic features in the Americas made it difficult for groups to interact with each other; A lack of long-distance trade routes; A lack of large domesticated animals.*

Use this tip to continue practicing the AP® skill of Comparison. Ask students to list and discuss the environmental differences between Afro-Eurasia and the Americas in this era. *Differences include the lack of domesticated animals in the Americas, the rugged mountains in the Americas, greater ecological and coastal environments, and rain forests. The geography of the Americas prevented the easy contact among civilizations that Afro-Eurasia experienced. Geographic isolation in the Americas encouraged linguistic and ethnic diversity and the development of many distinct and competing entities.*

AP® Daily Videos

Consider using the AP® Classroom site to enrich your course and help you cover the enormous amount of material in AP® World History: Modern. Show your students **1.4 Daily Video**, which looks at the political structures in the Americas prior to 1450. Watching this video will reinforce the idea of state building, which can be confusing to students. This video will also give them practice identifying evidence in a text that would support an argument or claim.

were far more naturalistic, particularly in portraying the human body, than those of their medieval counterparts. Although religious themes remained prominent, Renaissance artists now included portraits and busts of well-known contemporary figures and scenes from ancient mythology.

In its focus on the affairs of this world, Renaissance culture reflected the urban bustle and commercial preoccupations of Italian cities. Its secular elements challenged the otherworldliness of Christian culture, and its individualism signaled the dawning of a more capitalist economy of private entrepreneurs. By 1450, a new Europe was in the making, one very different from its own recent past.

Civilizations of the Americas

Finding the Main Point: What were the political and cultural differences in states that developed in the Americas between 1200 and 1450?

AP® EXAM TIP
Pay close attention to these explanations of differences between the rise of civilizations in Afro-Eurasia and the Americas.

Separated from Afro-Eurasia by the Pacific and Atlantic oceans lay the altogether separate world, later known as the Americas, that housed two major and long-established centers of civilization in this era—Mesoamerica and the Andes. Together, they were home to a majority of the population of the Americas by 1200. But unlike the civilizations of Africa and Eurasia, Mesoamerica and the Andes had little if any direct contact with each other. They shared, however, a rugged mountainous terrain with an enormous range of microclimates as well as great ecological and biological diversity. Arid coastal environments, steamy lowland rain forests, cold and windy highland plateaus cut by numerous mountains and valleys—all of this was often encompassed in a relatively small area. Such conditions contributed to substantial linguistic and ethnic diversity. By 1200, both regions had witnessed the rise and decline of a series of increasingly sophisticated states, a trend that culminated in the fifteenth century with the emergence of the Aztec and Inca empires. Both were the work of previously marginal peoples who had forcibly taken over and absorbed older cultures, thus gaining new energy. Both were also decimated in the sixteenth century at the hands of Spanish conquistadores and their diseases (see Map 2.8).

The Emergence of the Aztecs in Mesoamerica

The Aztec Empire inherited an ancient set of cultural, religious, and political traditions associated with civilizations centered on a region stretching from central Mexico to northern Central America. Despite its environmental and ethnic diversity, Mesoamerica was also a distinct region, bound together by a common culture. Its many peoples shared an intensive agricultural technology devoted to raising maize, beans, chili peppers, and squash and based their economies on market exchange. They practiced religions featuring a similar pantheon of male and female deities, understood time as a cosmic cycle of creation and destruction, practiced human sacrifice, and constructed monumental ceremonial centers. Furthermore, they employed a common ritual calendar and hieroglyphic writing.

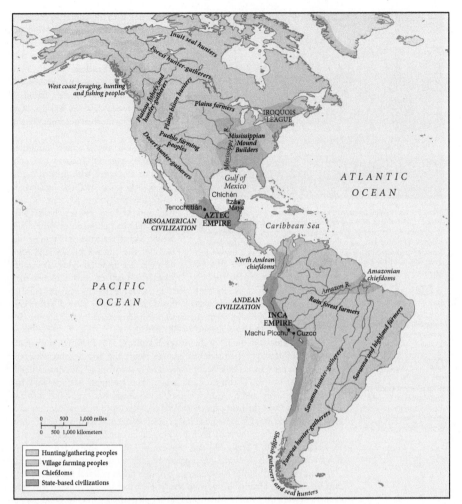

EXPLORING AP® THEMES

Humans and the Environment (ENV)

Ask students: What accounts for the shape of the Inca Empire? *The Andes prevented eastward expansion. Instead the Incas expanded north and south along the coast.*

Map 2.8 The Americas in the Fifteenth Century

The Aztec and Inca empires dominated two civilizational zones in the Americas during the century before Columbus's voyage in 1492 brought these two "old worlds" into contact with one another. But the Aztec and Inca states had little, if any, direct contact with each other.

BUILDING AP® SKILLS

Making Connections: Comparison

Ask students: What features of Maya civilization distinguish it from other American cultures in this and earlier periods? *Distinguishing features include a written language, monumental architecture, and the ability to do advanced mathematical calculations.*

Aztec Double-Headed Serpent Sixteen inches long and composed of around 2,000 pieces of blue-green turquoise for the body and rare red and white shells for its nostrils, gums, and terrifying fangs, this remarkable sculpture of a snake with one body and two heads was likely for ritual use. The important Aztec god Quetzalcóatl is often depicted as a serpent, and some scholars have argued that this sculpture represents him. (Werner Forman/Getty Images)

▲ **AP®**

MAKING CONNECTIONS
How does this work of art suggest the importance of religion in Aztec society?

AP®

CAUSATION
What different kinds of societies inhabited the Americas in the fifteenth century? How might you explain their distribution?

EXPLORING AP® THEMES

Governance (GOV)

Ask students the following question: What made the Aztec Empire different from the Chinese empire? *The Aztecs were a loose confederation of tribute states, while the Chinese empire had a strong central government with a professional bureaucracy.*

Starting with the Olmec around 1200 B.C.E., civilizations regularly emerged, flourished, and declined in the region. None has attracted more attention than the **Maya civilization**, which dominated a region centered on modern-day Guatemala and the Yucatán region of Mexico between 250 and 900 C.E. Maya artistic and intellectual accomplishments were impressive. Builders and artists created substantial urban centers dominated by temples, pyramids, palaces, and public plazas, all graced with painted murals and endless stone carvings. Intellectuals developed the most elaborate writing system in the Americas, which used both pictographs and phonetic or syllabic elements, and a mathematical system that included the concept of zero and place notation that made complex calculations possible. Organized into a highly fragmented political system of city-states, local lords, and regional kingdoms with no central authority and frequent warfare, this dynamic culture thrived before collapsing by around 900 with a completeness and finality rare in world history. (See "Civilizations and the Environment" in Chapter 1.)

The state known to history as the **Aztec Empire** (1345–1528) was the last and largest of the Mesoamerican states to emerge before the Spanish conquered the region in the early sixteenth century. It was largely the work of the Mexica (meh-SHEEH-kah) people, a semi-nomadic group from northern Mexico who had migrated southward and by 1325 had established themselves on a small island in Lake Texcoco. Over the next century, the Mexica developed their military capacity, served as mercenaries for more powerful people, negotiated elite marriage alliances with those people, and built up their own capital city of Tenochtitlán (te-nawch-tee-tlahn). In 1428, a Triple Alliance between the Mexica and two nearby city-states launched a highly aggressive program of military conquest that in less than 100 years brought more of Mesoamerica within a single political framework than ever before. Aztec authorities, eager to shed their rather undistinguished past, now claimed descent from earlier Mesoamerican peoples, emphasizing the continuity of Mesoamerican civilization.

With a core population recently estimated at 5 to 6 million people, the Aztec Empire was a loosely structured and unstable conquest state that witnessed frequent rebellions by its subject peoples. Conquered peoples and cities were required to provide labor for Aztec projects and to regularly deliver goods to their Aztec rulers, such as impressive quantities of textiles and clothing, military supplies, jewelry and other luxuries, various foodstuffs, animal products, building materials, rubber balls, paper, and more. The process was overseen by local imperial tribute collectors, who sent the required goods on to Tenochtitlán, a metropolis of 150,000 to 200,000 people, where they were meticulously recorded.

That city featured numerous canals, dikes, causeways, and bridges. A central walled area of palaces and temples included a pyramid almost 200 feet high. Surrounding the city were *chinampas* or "floating gardens," artificial islands of fertile soil created from swamplands that supported a highly productive agriculture. Vast marketplaces reflected the commercialization of the economy. A young Spanish soldier who beheld the city in 1519 declared, "Gazing on such wonderful sights, we did not know what to say, or whether what appeared before us was real."[26]

Enslaved people, especially those captured in war, played a prominent role in Aztec society, for they were often destined for sacrifice in the bloody rituals so central to Aztec religious life. Long a part of Mesoamerican and many other world cultures, human sacrifice assumed an unusually prominent role in Aztec public life and thought during the fifteenth century. Tlacaelel (1398–1480), who was for more than half a century a prominent official of the Aztec Empire, is often credited with crystallizing the ideology of state that gave human sacrifice such great importance.

In the Aztecs' understanding of the world, the sun, central to all life and identified with the Aztec patron deity Huitzilopochtli (wee-tsee-loh-pockt-lee), tended to lose its energy in a constant battle against encroaching darkness. Thus the Aztec world hovered always on the edge of catastrophe. To replenish its energy and thus postpone the descent into endless darkness, the sun required the life-giving force found in human blood. Because the gods had shed their blood ages ago in creating humankind, it was wholly proper for people to offer their own blood to nourish the gods in the present. The high calling of the Aztec state was to supply this blood, largely through its wars of expansion. Enslaved prisoners of war were "those who have died for the god." The growth of the Aztec Empire therefore became the means for maintaining cosmic order and avoiding utter catastrophe. This ideology also shaped the techniques of Aztec warfare, which put a premium on capturing prisoners rather than on killing the enemy. As the empire grew, priests and rulers became mutually dependent, and "human sacrifices were carried out in the service of politics."[27] Massive sacrificial rituals, together with a display of great wealth, impressed enemies, allies, and subjects with the immense power of the Aztecs and their gods.

The Emergence of the Incas in the Andes

Yet another and quite separate center of civilization in the Americas lay in the dramatic landscape of the Andes. Bleak deserts along the coast supported human habitation only because they were cut by dozens of rivers flowing down from the mountains, offering the possibility of irrigation and cultivation. The offshore waters

TEACHING IDEA

Incorporating Outside Resources

Videos can help explain many concepts that students have a hard time visualizing. In Episode 3 of "The Aztecs" of *Engineering an Empire* from the History channel (available online), host Peter Weller discusses Aztec religious practices as well as chinampa agriculture. After students watch the video, ask the following questions:

- What was a chinampa? *Chinampas were small rectangular areas of land built up on shallow lake beds. They were used in agriculture in Mesoamerica.*

- How did chinampas influence Aztec society? *They greatly increased food production. Surplus food made a large military possible, which made conquest possible.*

- How was the Aztec emphasis on the military related to Aztec religious practices? *Prisoners of war were needed for religious sacrifices.*

EXPLORING AP® THEMES

Governance (GOV)

Students should understand the causes and outcomes of wars. Ask students: How did Aztec beliefs make their style of warfare different from that of other societies? *Aztecs, unlike many other societies, were not trying to kill enemies to ensure victory and gain territory. Rather, their religion called for the sacrifice of humans. They needed prisoners of war to avert catastrophe; they believed that the sun required the life-giving force found in human blood to replenish its energy and thus postpone the descent into endless darkness.*

BUILDING AP® SKILLS

Making Connections: Comparison

This chapter is full of comparisons, and this is an AP® skill that you should practice throughout Unit 1. Project or draw a Venn diagram and ask students to provide social, political, economic, and cultural (SPEC) evidence for the Aztecs and Incas. After discussion with the Venn diagram, project maps of the postclassical Americas to refresh the location of these states with students.

EXPLORING AP® THEMES

Governance (GOV)

Have students read the last paragraph on page 108 and the first paragraph on page 109. As students read, have them list the methods that the Incas used to integrate the conquered into their empire. *Learn Quechua, sons taken to the capital to learn Inca culture and language, acknowledge Inca deities, mita.*

of the Pacific Ocean also provided an enormously rich marine environment with an endless supply of seabirds and fish. The Andes themselves, a towering mountain chain with many highland valleys, afforded numerous distinct ecological niches, depending on altitude. Andean societies generally sought access to the resources of these various environments through colonization, conquest, or trade—seafood from the coastal regions; maize and cotton from lower-altitude valleys; potatoes, quinoa, and pastureland for their llamas from the high plains; tropical fruits and coca leaves from the moist eastern slope of the Andes.

Over thousands of years, many small civilizations had flourished in the Andes region. But in the early 1400s, a relatively small community of Quechua-speaking people, known to us as the Incas, built a huge empire along almost the entire spine of the Andes Mountains. Much as the Aztecs drew on the traditions of the earlier Mesoamerican societies, the Incas incorporated the lands and cultures of earlier Andean civilizations. The **Inca Empire** (1438–1533), however, was much larger than the Aztec state; it stretched some 2,500 miles along the Andes and contained perhaps 10 million subjects during its short life in the fifteenth and early sixteenth centuries.

COMPARISON
What distinguished the Aztec and Inca empires from each other?

Both the Aztec and Inca empires represent rags-to-riches stories in which quite modest and remotely located people very quickly created by military conquest the largest states ever witnessed in their respective regions, but the empires themselves were quite different. In the Aztec realm, the Mexica rulers largely left their conquered people alone if the required tribute was forthcoming. The Incas, on the other hand, erected a more bureaucratic and intrusive empire. At the top reigned the emperor, an absolute ruler regarded as divine, a descendant of the creator god Viracocha and the son of the sun god Inti. Each of the some eighty provinces in the empire had an Inca governor. In theory, the state owned all land and resources, though in practice state lands, known as "lands of the sun," existed alongside properties owned by temples, elites, and traditional communities. At least in the central regions of the empire, local officials were incorporated into the Inca administration, supervised by an Inca governor or the emperor. A separate set of "inspectors" provided the imperial center with an independent check on these provincial officials.

COMPARISON
How does the Inca employment of bureaucrats compare to that of other societies, such as China?

Births, deaths, marriages, and other population data were carefully recorded on *quipus*, the knotted cords that served as an accounting device. A resettlement program moved one-quarter or more of the population to new locations, in part to disperse conquered and no doubt resentful people and sometimes to reward loyal followers with promising opportunities. Efforts at cultural integration required the leaders of conquered peoples to learn Quechua (keh-choo-wah). Their sons were removed to the capital of Cuzco for instruction in Inca culture and language. While the Incas required their subject peoples to acknowledge major Inca deities, these peoples were then largely free to carry on their own religious traditions. Thus the Inca Empire was a fluid system that varied greatly from place to place and over time.

◀ **AP®**

CAUSATION

What can you infer from this image about how the massive building projects of the Inca Empire reflected the power of the state?

Machu Picchu Machu Picchu, high in the Andes Mountains, was constructed by the Incas in the fifteenth century on a spot long held sacred by local people. Its 200 buildings stand at some 8,000 feet above sea level, making it a "city in the sky." It was probably a royal retreat or religious center, rather than a location serving administrative, commercial, or military purposes. The outside world became aware of Machu Picchu only in 1911, when it was popularized by a Yale University archeologist. (fStop/Superstock)

Inca demands on their conquered people were expressed, not so much in terms of tribute, as in the Aztec realms, but as labor service, known as *mita*, which was required periodically of every household. What people produced at home usually stayed at home, but almost everyone also had to work for the state. Some labored on large state farms or on "sun farms," which supported temples and religious institutions; others herded, mined, served in the military, or toiled on state-directed construction projects.

Those with particular skills were put to work manufacturing textiles, metal goods, ceramics, and stonework. The most well known of these specialists were the "chosen women," who were removed from their homes as young girls, trained in Inca ideology, and set to producing corn beer and cloth at state centers. Later they were given as wives to men of distinction or sent to serve as priestesses in various temples, where they were known as "wives of the Sun." In return for such labor services, Inca ideology, expressed in terms of family relationships, required the state to arrange elaborate feasts at which large quantities of food and drink were consumed and to provide food and other necessities when disaster struck. Thus the authority of the state penetrated and directed Inca society and economy far more than did that of the Aztecs. (See AP® Working with Evidence, Chapter 4, Document 1, page 247, for an early Spanish account of Inca governing practices.)

AP® EXAM TIP

Know the meaning and significance of the *mita* (or *mit'a*) system.

AP® EXAM TIP

The AP® Exam frequently includes questions about the Inca economic system.

AP®

COMPARISON

How do gender relations in Aztec society compare to gender relations in Inca society?

TEACHING IDEA

Incorporating Outside Resources

Machu Picchu is an amazing look at Inca architecture and culture. Ask students to take a virtual tour of Machu Picchu using Google Arts and Culture. This activity can help provide more understanding of the important Inca sites.

BUILDING AP® SKILLS

Claims and Evidence in Sources

Have students read the last paragraph on page 109 and examine the image on page 110. Ask students what they can tell you about gender roles in the Inca Empire. *Gender roles appear to be more equal than in some societies.*

EXPLORING AP® THEMES

Social Interactions and Organization (SIO)

This activity can help students who are struggling with the AP® theme of Social Interactions and Organization (SIO). Ask students: What is gender parallelism? *Gender parallelism describes a social arrangement in which men and women operate in separate spheres but are considered equal in the eyes of society.*

BUILDING AP® SKILLS

Making Connections: Comparison

Continuing with the AP® skill of Comparison, the focus of Unit 1, have students create a chart like the one here to compare the Aztecs and the Incas. Charts like this one are valuable to students to help them organize evidence to write SAQs or LEQs. A reproducible version of this chart is available in the Teacher's Resource Materials. (Answers are provided in italics.)

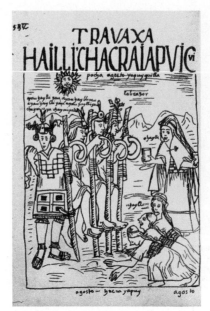

Inca Agricultural Practice This sixteenth-century drawing by Felipe Guaman Poma, an Inca nobleman, illustrates the cooperation of Inca men and women in agriculture. The men are loosening the soil with a "foot-plow," while the women plant the seeds. (Werner Forman/Getty Images)

▲ **AP®**
CLAIMS AND EVIDENCE IN SOURCES
How does this image portray the respective roles of men and women in Inca agricultural life?

If the Inca and Aztec civilizations differed sharply in their political and economic arrangements, they resembled each other more closely in their gender systems. Both societies practiced what scholars call "gender parallelism," in which "women and men operate in two separate but equivalent spheres, each gender enjoying autonomy in its own sphere."[28] In both Mesoamerican and Andean societies, such systems had emerged long before their incorporation into the Aztec and Inca empires. In the Andes, men reckoned their descent from their fathers and women from their mothers, while Mesoamericans had long viewed children as belonging equally to their mothers and fathers. Parallel religious cults for women and men likewise flourished in both societies. Inca men venerated the sun, while women worshipped the moon, with matching religious officials. In Aztec temples, both male and female priests presided over rituals dedicated to deities of both sexes. Particularly among the Incas, parallel hierarchies of male and female political officials governed the empire, while in Aztec society, women officials exercised local authority under a title that meant "female person in charge of people." Social roles were clearly defined and different for men and women, but the domestic concerns of women—childbirth, cooking, weaving, cleaning—were not regarded as inferior to the activities of men. Among the Aztecs, for example, sweeping was a powerful and sacred act with symbolic significance as "an act of purification and a preventative against evil elements penetrating the center of the Aztec universe, the home."[29] In the Andes, men broke the ground, women sowed, and both took part in the harvest.

CONCLUSIONS AND REFLECTIONS

"Civilization": What's in a Word?

Finding the Main Point: What problems arise in defining the word "civilization"?

By 1200, most of the world's population lived in civilizations, which had over the centuries incorporated many of the gathering and hunting peoples of the world as well as independent agricultural village communities and pastoral societies. These civilizations shared a number of common features: cities, states, sharp class inequalities, patriarchy, and writing.

	Aztec	Inca
Founding	*Small migrant tribe expanding to a large land empire*	*Small migrant tribe expanding to a large land empire*
Government	*Loose tributary state, male rulers*	*Large, complex bureaucracy, much more government control, joint king and queen rule*
Religion	*Polytheistic with emphasis on mass human sacrifice to keep the world from chaos and destruction*	*Polytheistic with limited human sacrifice, often of children raised specifically for that purpose*
	Men and women worshipped the same gods	*Intended to prevent natural disasters such as earthquakes and floods*
		Men and women worshipped different gods
Land Ownership	*Individuals could own land*	*In theory, the state (the Ince, or king) owned all the land*
Patrilineal or Matrilineal	*Parents had equal claim on children*	*Men traced lineage from fathers, women from mothers*
Economy	*Women had limited involvement*	*Women were very involved*

TRM **Handout 2.7: Comparison Chart for the Aztec and Inca**

But they also differed in many ways. Some of these civilizations, such as Chinese, Indian, and Byzantine civilizations, had their origins in ancient times. Others were more recent, such as those in Japan, Korea, Southeast Asia, East and West Africa, Russia, and Western Europe. The Aztec and Inca civilizations in the Americas, which emerged in the fifteenth century, built upon much earlier Mesoamerican and Andean precedents.

The size and influence among civilizations likewise differed greatly. China was a huge East Asian civilization with an extensive impact in Korea, Japan, Vietnam, and elsewhere. Islamic civilization began in the seventh century in Arabia and soon encompassed many other civilizations in the Middle East, Africa, and Asia. Southeast Asian and East African civilizations, by contrast, had a smaller cultural footprint.

Politically, too, civilizations varied. Large empires prevailed in Chinese, Inca, West African, and, for a time, Islamic civilizations. In contrast, Hausa and Swahili civilizations were organized in a series of small city-states, and a fragmented Western European civilization found expression primarily in an emerging system of rival kingdoms.

In examining civilizations, we are worlds away from life in agricultural villages or gathering and hunting societies. Historians have been somewhat uncertain as to how to refer to these more complex forms of society, despite their central and ever-growing place in the human story. Following common practice, we have called them "civilizations," but scholars have reservations about the term for two reasons. The first is its implication of superiority. In popular usage, "civilization" suggests refined behavior, a "higher" form of society, something unreservedly positive. The opposite of "civilized"—"barbarian," "savage," or "uncivilized"—is normally understood as an insult implying inferiority. That, of course, is precisely how the inhabitants of many civilizations have viewed outsiders, particularly those neighboring peoples living without the alleged benefit of cities and states.

Modern assessments of earlier civilizations reveal a profound ambiguity about these new, larger, and more complex societies. On the one hand, these civilizations have given us inspiring art, profound reflections on the meaning of life, more productive technologies, increased control over nature, and the art of writing—all of which have been cause for celebration. On the other hand, as anthropologist Marvin Harris noted, "human beings learned for the first time how to bow, grovel, kneel, and kowtow."[30] Massive inequalities, state oppression, slavery, large-scale warfare, the subordination of women, and epidemic disease also accompanied the rise of civilization, generating discontent, rebellion, and sometimes the urge to escape.

A second reservation about using the term "civilization" derives from its implication of solidity—the idea that civilizations represent distinct and widely shared identities with clear boundaries that mark them off from other such units. It is unlikely, however, that many people living in China, the Islamic world, or Latin Christendom felt themselves primarily part of these larger units. Local identities defined by occupation, clan affiliation, village, city, or region were surely more important for most people than those of some larger civilization. At best, members

AP

COMPARISON

What is the main disagreement in point of view among historians regarding the word "civilization"?

CHAPTER 2

BUILDING AP® SKILLS

Sourcing and Situation

This is an excellent opportunity to introduce students to "point of view," one of the AP® skills included in Sourcing and Situation. Students should be able to recognize the differing points of view on what it means to be a civilization. Suggest that they consider the "Conclusions and Reflections" essay paragraph by paragraph and think of it as a "battle of the historians." Ask students: What is the main disagreement in point of view among the historians? *In the fifth paragraph, we read that some historians are opposed to using the term "civilization" because it suggests cultural superiority. Civilization might be more barbaric than the barbarians. In the seventh paragraph, we read that some historians are concerned about the implied solidity, that the term implies a shared culture and a specific border, neither of which was true for the premodern civilizations.*

TEACHING IDEA

Incorporating Outside Resources

For an extension activity for "'Civilization': What's in a Word?" consider showing students *Rethinking Civilization: Crash Course World History 201* found on YouTube. This is the first episode in Crash Course World History 2, and it deals with the idea of civilization, some of the traditional hallmarks of civilizations, and why some people choose to live outside the traditional civilization model. This video would be good for your visual and auditory learners.

of an educated upper class who shared a common literary tradition may have felt themselves part of some more inclusive civilization, but that left out most of the population. Moreover, unlike modern nations, none of the earlier civilizations had definite borders. Any identification with a civilization surely faded as distance from its core region increased. Finally, the line between civilizations and other kinds of societies is not always clear. Just when does a village or town become a city? At what point does a chiefdom become a state?

Despite these reservations, this book continues to use the term "civilization," both because it is so deeply embedded in our way of thinking about the world and because no alternative concept has achieved widespread acceptance. For historians, however, "civilization" is a purely descriptive term, referring to a distinctive type of human society—one with cities and states—without consciously implying any judgment or assessment, any sense of superiority or inferiority. You may want to assess whether we have been successful in this effort or not.

CHAPTER REVIEW

AP Key Terms

Song dynasty, 70
China's economic revolution, 73
Hangzhou, 73
foot binding, 75
hangul, 76
bushido, 78
tribute system, 79
chu nom, 80
Srivijaya, 80
Madjapahit, 81
Angkor Wat, 81
Abbasid caliphate, 83
Seljuk Turkic Empire, 84
Ottoman Empire, 84
Constantinople, 84
jizya, 86
al-Andalus, 87

Swahili civilization, 88
West African civilization, 90
Mali, 90
trans-Saharan slave trade, 91
Timbuktu, 92
Byzantine Empire, 92
Ottoman seizure of Constantinople, 94
Kievan Rus, 94
Eastern Orthodox Christianity, 95
Western Christendom, 96
feudalism, 97
Roman Catholic Church, 98
European Renaissance, 103
Maya civilization, 106
Aztec Empire, 106
Inca Empire, 108

Finding the Main Point

1. What accounts for China's political and economic vitality in this era? What impact did China have on its neighbors?
2. What were the cultural and political effects of Southeast Asia's encounters with other civilizations?
3. What political and intellectual transformations took place in Islamic civilization as it spread?
4. How might you compare the emerging civilizations of East and West Africa?
5. What role did Christianity play in the development of states in both Eastern and Western Europe?
6. What were the political and cultural differences in states that developed in the Americas between 1200 and 1450?
7. What problems arise in defining the word "civilization"?

AP Big Picture Questions

1. What similarities and differences can you identify between the civilizations examined in this chapter?
2. What distinguishes the civilizations of the Americas from those of Afro-Eurasia?
3. In what different ways were civilizations spreading beyond their traditional heartlands between 1200 and 1450?
4. AP Making Connections: Considering Chapters 1 and 2 together, what major political and social changes occurred between 500 and 1450?

TRM Suggested Responses to Questions
You can find suggested responses to the Chapter Review questions in the Teacher's Resource Materials.

CHAPTER 2

TRM AP® Skills Workshop Activity Handout: Claims

BUILDING AP® SKILLS

Argumentation

Being able to recognize effective arguments is an important skill not only for AP® World History: Modern but for other areas as well. Being able to identify effective arguments can help students once they begin to create their own arguments. Divide the class into groups of three or four and assign each group a section of the chapter. Each group is responsible for finding three claims or arguments in their section. Have students share their examples and discuss as a class if it is a claim or not.

Claims

A significant skill in the AP® World History course is the ability to create a historical argument based on a claim and supported by evidence. In this workshop, we'll talk about the first part of that process, the claim. Before you can create your own historical claims, it's helpful to get comfortable finding the claims in other people's arguments. Once you can easily identify the claim, the next step is to evaluate the effectiveness of the claim: Does it set up an argument or state the obvious? Is it broad, or focused?

UNDERSTANDING CLAIMS

So, what is a claim, and how is it used to help build a historical argument? A claim is the argument's main idea. It is the idea that gets developed into the thesis of an essay.

Claim: The main idea of an argument

Historians formulate claims by applying reasoning skills to historical information, for instance, by making a comparison, thinking about causes and effects, or tracing changes and continuities across time. An effective claim takes a stance on an issue. Let's look at an example of an effective claim found on page 73 of this chapter.

> As many people found their way to the cities, China became the most urbanized country in the world.

This claim is effective for three reasons. First, this statement is *evaluative*, meaning it makes a judgment on the issue. A good claim cannot just state an obvious fact or give a list of causes or factors; it has to take a stance that is debatable. For instance, "Cause A is more important than Cause B" is a good claim. "Cause A and Cause B are both important" is not, because it does not take a stance on the relative importance of the two causes. In this case, the authors are telling the reader that they will be proving that China became the most urbanized country in the world. Second, this claim is *specific*. It's not claiming any other aspects of China as being more than any other country at this point. The claim narrows in on the process known as urbanization, making for a manageable argument. Last, the claim is a statement that can be supported by specific evidence; it is *historically defensible*. From reading this claim, the reader can anticipate that the authors will draw on specific examples to demonstrate how China became the "most urbanized" country before 1200.

CLAIMS ON THE AP® WORLD HISTORY EXAM

Why do you need to learn how to identify and create claims? As a historian in training, you will be expected to write your own historical arguments. On the AP® Exam, you

114

will need to use a claim to build an effective essay. Your claim must address the question in the exam prompt by "answering" it in your own words, as well as create a roadmap for your essay by providing unity to the evidence you will include. Your claim should also set up your argument by being provable. As such, it needs to be strong, succinct, and in direct response to the prompt, while also being broad enough to unify the information you will include in the essay. To do this well, you should read historians' claims. Then, you need to practice writing your own claims. As with so many things, practice makes perfect!

In addition to creating your own claims, you will be expected to describe and explain the claims of others. This is actually fairly simple once you have written enough claims yourself. Sometimes, this skill will be tested on a Short-Answer Question. Other times, you may encounter claims in the stimulus-based Multiple-Choice Questions. In either case, you will need to refer to an excerpt from a historian and then choose the answer that best represents the historian's claim. In your own writing, knowing how to work with claims is part of the Argumentation skill, which is the foundation of the Document-Based Question and the Long Essay Questions; these collectively account for 40 percent of your score on the exam. Both of these essays require that you make a strong claim (stated in a thesis) and summon evidence to support it in order to get full credit.

BUILDING AP® SKILLS

1. **Activity: Identifying a Claim.** Let's begin working with claims by rereading a paragraph from "The Emergence of the Aztecs in Mesoamerica" (page 106). Do you agree or disagree that the following is the main claim made by the historian in the paragraph? Explain.

   With a core population recently estimated at 5 to 6 million people, the Aztec Empire was a loosely structured and unstable conquest state that witnessed frequent rebellions by its subject peoples.

2. **Activity: Identifying a Claim.** Now, read AP® Historians' Voices 2.1 later in this chapter (page 127), and see if you can determine the claim in that paragraph.

3. **Activity: Creating a Claim.** Now that you have had some practice identifying professional historians' claims, let's see if you can create your own. To make it easier, you will have an AP®-style prompt to answer:

   Using the information in the section "Emerging Civilizations in Africa" from pages 88 to 92, evaluate the extent to which the culture of East Africa transformed through trade with Asia.

   Remember to create a claim that answers the prompt, takes a stance on the issue that could be debatable, and goes beyond a simple listing of factors or causes so that it ties the evidence together.

115

TRM Suggested Responses to Questions
You can find suggested responses to the Building AP® Skills questions in the Teacher's Resource Materials.

BUILDING AP® SKILLS

Argumentation

Writing a historically defensible claim is an important part of the AP® skill of Argumentation. After students have practiced finding effective claims in the activity on page 114, continue with the group activity of having students write an effective claim. You can use the prompt found in Activity 3 on this page or create one of your own. Each group can critique the other groups' claims. This group activity will help prepare students for individual writing later on.

Japanese Samurai Culture

From the twelfth to the mid-nineteenth century, a distinctive feature of Japanese civilization emerged in the celebration of martial virtues and the warrior class—the samurai—that embodied those values. Public life and government in Japan were dominated by the samurai, while their culture and values, known as bushido, expressed the highest ideals of political leadership and of personal conduct. At least in the West, the samurai are perhaps best known for preferring death over dishonor, a posture expressed in seppuku (ritual suicide). But there was much more to bushido, for the samurai served not only as warriors but also as bureaucrats—magistrates, land managers, and provincial governors—acting on behalf of their lords (daimyo) or in service to military rulers, the shoguns. Furthermore, although bushido remained a distinctively Japanese cultural expression, it absorbed both Confucian and Buddhist values as well as those of the indigenous Shinto tradition.

To understand an emerging bushido culture, historians rely on a variety of sources, but especially the writings of prominent samurai. One such source takes the form of a highly critical letter composed by Imagawa Ryoshun (1325–1420), addressed to his wayward adopted son (who was also his younger brother). A famous poet, military commander, and devout Buddhist, Imagawa closely approximated in his own life the ideal of a cultivated warrior, and his letter became hugely influential among the warrior class in Japan. It was published and republished hundreds of times and used for centuries as a primer or school text for the instruction of young samurai.

But his letter requires careful analysis and evaluation by historians, for it is not just a straightforward statement of the ideal beliefs and behavior of a samurai. Instead, his letter is expressed in specific criticisms of his son's life. Thus you must read "between the lines"—by which historians mean reading for information not explicitly stated in the source—to identify what Imagawa understood as the key elements of bushido culture and correct behavior for a samurai. In doing so, you will be following in the steps of generations of young samurai who through these criticisms sought guidance on how to become an honorable member of their society.

1 A FIRST LOOK

It makes sense to read the source several times, focusing on different elements of your analysis in stages. In your first reading, you will want to get a sense of what modern historians might call Imagawa's main thesis, argument, or claim.

1. Can you identify a passage or passages that express his criticism of his son's behavior in general terms?

2. Why, according to Imagawa, is his son destined to fail? You might pay particular attention to the first line of the passage.

116

TRM Suggested Responses to Questions

You can find suggested responses to the AP® Looking Again questions in the Teacher's Resource Materials.

BUILDING AP® SKILLS

Sourcing and Situation

It is never too soon in the course to work on sourcing documents. This is one of the most important AP® skills to learn for the DBQ. Sourcing describes the point of view, purpose, historical situation, and/or audience of a source. *The Imagawa Letter* on page 117, written in 1412, would be a good practice for sourcing skills. Have students read the background material as well as the documents and answer the questions under "A First Look" on page 116. These questions will help guide students in learning how to analyze a document in preparation for writing a sourcing statement. Once students have answered the questions, have them share with the class.

As you do not understand the Arts of Peace [literary skills such as poetry, history, philosophy, and ritual] your skill in the Arts of War [horsemanship, archery, swordsmanship] will not, in the end, achieve victory.

You like to roam about, hawking and cormorant fishing, relishing the purposelessness of taking life.

You live in luxury by fleecing the people and plundering the shrines.

To build your own dwelling you razed the pagoda and other buildings of the memorial temple of our ancestors.

You do not distinguish between good and bad behavior of your retainers, but reward or punish them without justice.

You permit yourself to forget the kindness that our lord and father showed us; thus you destroy the principles of loyalty and filial piety.

You do not understand the difference in status between yourself and others; sometimes you make too much of other people, sometimes too little.

You disregard other people's viewpoints; you bully them and rely on force.

You excel at drinking bouts, amusements, and gambling, but you forget the business of our clan.

You provide yourself lavishly with clothes and weapons, but your retainers are poorly equipped.

You ought to show utmost respect to Buddhist monks and priests and carry out ceremonies properly.

You impede the flow of travelers by erecting barriers everywhere in your territory.

Whether you are in charge of anything—such as a province or a district—or not, it will be difficult to put your abilities to any use if you have not won the sympathy and respect of ordinary people.

Just as the Buddhist scriptures tell us that the Buddha incessantly strives to save mankind, in the same way you should exert your mind to the utmost in all your activities, be they civil or military, and never fall into negligence.

It should be regarded as dangerous if the ruler of the people in a province is deficient even in a single [one] of the cardinal virtues of human-heartedness, righteousness, propriety, wisdom, and good faith.

You were born to be a warrior, but you mismanage your territory, do not maintain the army, and are not ashamed although people laugh at you. It is, indeed, a mortifying situation for you and our whole clan.

Source: Carl Steenstrup, trans., "The Imagawa Letter," *Monumenta Nipponica* 28, no. 3 (1973), 295–316.

---

2 **A SECOND LOOK**

Once you have identified the general thrust of Imagawa's letter, return to the text to more specifically identify what different kinds or categories of criticism Imagawa is making.

1. Do some criticisms fall into multiple categories?

2. What do your categories reveal about a samurai's values, responsibilities, and activities?

3 A THIRD LOOK

Finally, return to the letter a third time to consider the specific examples cited by Imagawa when criticizing his son.

1. What examples does he use to support his criticisms?

2. Do these examples suggest that Imagawa was more concerned with some types of behavior than others?

AP® ACTIVITY IDENTIFYING AN ARGUMENT

1. In a sentence or two, explain why Imagawa believes that his son is destined to fail.

2. Which of his specific criticisms do you find most compelling in support of his argument?

FURTHER ACTIVITY

Take on the persona of Imagawa Ryoshun and write a short follow-up letter to your son more explicitly describing an ideal samurai.

Social Patterns in Tang and Song China

During the Tang and Song dynasties, China experienced an age of economic and cultural flowering. Scholar-officials solidified their place at the top of the Chinese social hierarchy, even as urban entrepreneurs—especially those active in manufacturing and trade—grew in wealth and sought a place among China's established land- and office-holding elites. But the benefits of these developments were not equally experienced by all parts of society. Few among the vast numbers of peasant farmers were able to participate in China's cultural flowering or enjoy an equivalent share of the proceeds from the country's growing overall wealth. The sources that follow offer a series of windows into the complex social world of Tang and Song dynasty China.

LOOKING AHEAD As you read the documents in this collection, consider the effect of Confucian values on Chinese society during China's "golden age."

AP® DBQ PRACTICE

DOCUMENT 1 Family and Society

Since ancient times, Chinese thinkers had used the family as a model for how society as a whole should be structured. Confucius viewed both families and the social order as consisting primarily of unequal relationships: the father was superior to the son; the husband to the wife; the ruler to the subject. Benevolence and sincere concern for others displayed by the superior party motivated subordinates to respond with deference and obedience. These Confucian principles remained hugely influential during China's long history, with many commentators linking well-ordered families to a tranquil and prosperous society.

Document 1 offers practical guidance about how to oversee a well-ordered family. Its author, Yan Zhitui (531–591), a member of a distinguished clan of scholar-officials, composed this tract during the period of disorder and political turmoil shortly before the Sui and then Tang dynasties reunited China. While he wrote his instructions specifically for his family, his thinking reflects well-established principles in Chinese society.

TRM Suggested Responses to Questions
You can find suggested responses to the AP® Working with Evidence questions in the Teacher's Resource Materials.

BUILDING AP® SKILLS

Claims and Evidence in Sources

Analyzing text-based as well as visual sources is an important skill for AP® World History: Modern students. If time is available, have students learn more about China's social hierarchy and traditions by using the evidence in "Social Patterns in Tang and Song China" beginning on page 119. (The AP® Theme of Social Interactions and Organization, or SIO, is one that students struggle with throughout the course, so extra practice is helpful.) Consider having students analyze one or more of the sources found on pages 119–125. Check for understanding by:

■ Using questions at the end of each source as a discussion starting point.

■ Pairing students to analyze (identify and describe) the author or creator's point of view, purpose, historical situation, and/or audience.

■ Assigning a source to a group of three to four students and having them present an overview of the source along with the sourcing to the rest of the class.

■ Having students present an overview of the source. Then have them discuss how they might use it to develop an argument in response to Question 1 under AP® Doing History (page 126).

119

Source: Chinese scholar-official Yan Zhitui, from *Family Instructions for the Yen Clan*, 6th century.

[A]s soon as a baby can recognize facial expressions and understand approval and disapproval, training should be begun in doing what he is told and stopping when so ordered. For several years punishment with the bamboo rod should be avoided. Parental strictness and dignity mingled with tenderness will usually lead boys and girls to a feeling of respect and carefulness and so arouse filial piety. . . .

Relations between parents and children should be dignified without familiarity; in the love between blood-relations there should be no rudeness. If there is rudeness, affection and fidelity cannot unite; if there is familiarity, carelessness and disrespect will grow. . . .

Manners and breeding are transmitted from the upper to the lower classes and bequeathed by earlier to later generations. So if a father is not kind, the son will not be filial; if an elder brother is not friendly, the younger will not be respectful; if a husband is not just, the wife will not be obedient. When a father is kind but the son refractory [stubborn or resistant], when an elder brother is friendly but the younger arrogant, when a husband is just but a wife cruel, then indeed they are the bad people of the world; they must be controlled by punishments; teaching and guidance will not change them. . . .

In the state, women should not be allowed to participate in politics; in the family, they should not be permitted to meddle in others' affairs. If they are wise, talented and versed in the ancient and modern writings, they ought to help their husbands by supplementing the latter's deficiency. No hen should herald the dawn lest misfortune follow.

Question to Consider: How does family life impact societal structures?

AP **Analyzing Sources:** What elements of Confucian thinking can you identify in this text?

DOCUMENT 2 On War, Soldiers, and Society

In this document, the poet Du Fu (712–770), who lived during a period of frequent wars and disorder, reflects on the personal suffering and disruption in the wider rural society that was caused by government policies, especially military conscription.

Source: Chinese poet Du Fu, "A Song of War Chariots," 8th century.

The war-chariots rattle,
The war-horses whinny;
Each man of you has a bow and a quiver at his belt. . . .
Father, mother, son, wife, stare at you going,
Till dust shall have buried the bridge beyond Haienyang.
We trot with them and cry and catch at their long sleeves,
But the sound of our crying goes up to the clouds;
For every time a bystander asks the men a question,
The men can only answer us that they have to go. . . .
Some of them, at fifteen sent north to guard the river.
. . .
At the front where the blood of men spills like the sea —
And still the heart of Emperor Wu is lifted up for war.
Do you know that, east of the mountain, in two hundred districts
And in thousands of villages, only weeds grow
And though strong women plough, the rows are all broken? . . .
Soldiers of Ch'in can face arduous battle,
But their officers drive them like chickens and dogs. . . .
We have learned now that to have a boy is bad luck —
And having a girl is very much better,
Who marries and lives in the house of a neighbor,
While under the sod we bury our boys. . . .

Du Fu, "A Song of War Chariots," in The Bookman (New York: George H. Doran, 1921), 568.

Question to Consider: What specific demands of war are placed on rural communities?

AP° Analyzing Sources: Consider the broader Confucian and Chinese ideas about gender. How does the content of this poem compare to those ideologies? Why?

DOCUMENT 3 Becoming a Scholar-Official

At the top of the social hierarchy during this period were the scholar-officials, who represented only a tiny fraction of the country's huge population. These were men who had passed the highest levels of the civil service examinations, which often required years of study and extensive practice writing literary compositions. Po Chu-I (772–846), a prominent government official and renowned poet, composed several poems reflecting on the importance of exams in the lives of ambitious young men, including himself, who aspired to scholar elite status. In "Escorting Candidates to the Examination Hall," he writes from the perspective of a retired official.

121

Source: Chinese poet and government official, Po Chu-I, "Escorting Candidates to the Examination Hall," 805.

At dawn I rode to escort the Doctors of Art;
In the eastern quarter the sky was still grey.
I said to myself, "You have started far too soon,"
But horses and coaches already thronged the road.
High and low the riders' torches bobbed;
Muffled or loud, the watchman's drum beat.
Riders when I see you prick
To your early levee, pity fills my heart.
When the sun rises and the hot dust flies
And the creatures of earth resume their great strife,
You, with your striving what shall you each seek?
Profit and fame, for that is all you care.
But I, you courtiers, rise from my bed at noon.
And live idly in the city of Ch'ang-an.
Spring is deep and my term of office spent;
Day by day my thoughts go back to the hills.

Arthur Waley, trans., *More Translations from the Chinese* (New York: Knopf, 1919).

Question to Consider: What message does this poem convey about the importance of the examination system?

AP **Analyzing Sources:** What is the author's tone in the passage? What could explain the tone?

DOCUMENT 4 Life in the Fields

Unlike the tiny number of elite scholar-officials who constituted the highest echelon of society, the vast majority of commoners worked on the land, enduring lives of hard physical labor. While long respected in Confucian thinking as the primary creators of society's wealth, this massive class of rural workers was heavily exploited by its social superiors through taxes, rents, forced labor, and more. The voices of these largely illiterate rural workers have left few traces in the historical record, with one of the best sources provided by the poetry of elites, who sometimes described the daily lives and challenges of commoners. Written by Po Chu-I, this poem describes the intense communal labor in rural communities at harvest time.

Source: Chinese poet and government official, Po Chu-I, "Watching the Reapers," 806.

Tillers of the soil have few idle months;
In the fifth month their toil is double-fold.
A south-wind visits the fields at night:
Suddenly the hill is covered with yellow corn.
Wives and daughters shoulder baskets of rice;
Youths and boys carry the flasks of wine.
Following after they bring a wage of meat,
To the strong reapers toiling on the southern hill,
Whose feet are burned by the hot earth they tread,
Whose backs are scorched by flames of the shining sky.
Tired they toil, caring nothing for the heat,
Grudging the shortness of the long summer day.
A poor woman follows at the reapers' side
With an infant child carried close at her breast.
With her right hand she gleans the fallen grain;*
In her left arm a broken basket hangs.
And I to-day . . . by virtue of what right
Have I never once tended field or tree?
My government-pay is three hundred tons;
At the year's end I have still grain in hand.
Thinking of this, secretly I grew ashamed;
And all day the thought lingered in my head.

*The poor were traditionally allowed to glean, that is, to gather any grain left behind in the fields after the harvest.
Arthur Waley, trans., *More Translations from the Chinese* (New York: Knopf, 1919), 41.

Question to Consider: What challenges did farming communities face?

AP **Analyzing Sources:** What do you notice about the author's tone? What aspects of Chinese society could help explain that tone?

DOCUMENT 5 Scholar-Officials and the Emperor

The close association of China's scholar class with the country's political life is reflected in Document 5, which shows a group of scholar-officials drinking tea and wine together with the emperor, who is presiding at the left. The painting is usually attributed to the emperor Huizong (1082–1135), who was himself a noted painter, poet, calligrapher, and collector. This emperor's great attention to the arts rather than to affairs of state gained him a reputation as a negligent and dissolute ruler. His reign ended in disgrace as China suffered a humiliating defeat at the hands of the northern nomadic Jin people, who took the emperor captive.

123

Question to Consider: What does the image say about the relationship between the emperor and the scholar-officials? Using the source description as well, how is social status depicted in the image?

AP **Analyzing Sources:** Why do you think it is important to know that the emperor painted this document? How can that detail impact the way the original audience looked at the painting?

DOCUMENT 6 City Life in Art

During China's Tang and Song dynasties, cities grew and prospered as centers of commerce, manufacturing, government administration, and more. Scores of large cities—with a few topping a million inhabitants—provided many opportunities for economic and social advancement and access to amenities unheard of in the countryside. For scholar-elites in the imperial government, cities were a potential source of social disorder and moral decadence, requiring careful oversight.

Merchants, who seemed to produce nothing while growing rich from commerce, were viewed as selfish and willing to undermine society for profit. Despite these misgivings among government officials, merchants and urban centers prospered during these centuries.

Document 6 is an urban scene painted by the artist Zhang Zeduan in the twelfth century. Just one section of a much larger scroll (for another section, see the image on page 74), it depicts a busy crossroads in an unidentified city and captures something of the dynamism of urban life during the period.

Source: Chinese artist Zhang Zeduan, from the painting *Along the River during the Qingming Festival*, 12th century.

Werner Forman/Getty Images

Question to Consider: What activities can you identify in this image? Can you find different commercial activities? Cultural activities?

AP **Analyzing Sources:** What view of Chinese urban life might the painter have wanted to convey? Was he celebrating or criticizing city living?

AP **DOING HISTORY**

1. **DBQ Practice:** Evaluate the extent to which Confucian values were practiced or violated within the golden age of China.

2. **Contextualization:** What is the broader role of the Confucian tradition in Chinese history?

3. **Developments and Processes:** What broader processes in Chinese historical development are reflected in these sources?

4. **Making Connections:** How can you use the information from one source to corroborate or modify the outlook of another source? Think about Documents 1 and 2 and their messages about gender. What other documents can be used together in such a way?

Economy and Society in Golden Age China

The growth in long-distance trade and the rapidly commercializing economy of Tang and Song dynasty China had profound social implications, which the two voices that follow explore from different angles. In Voice 2.1, Morris Rossabi, a specialist in Chinese history, examines the growing and evolving place of merchants in society during the Southern Song period (1127–1279). Then, in Voice 2.2, Valerie Hansen, a specialist on Eurasian long-distance trade, explores the wide-ranging social implications of China's commercializing economy.

VOICE 2.1

Morris Rossabi on the Place of Merchants in Chinese Society | 2014

Merchants were no longer limited to the capitals of specific counties and thus traded in small towns and villages as well. Although government officials continued to supervise markets, merchants faced fewer restrictions in trade. Enclosed markets became rarer, allowing merchants to trade in neighborhoods that had earlier had restricted commercial areas. . . .

Commercialization created a prosperous merchant class but . . . despite their wealth, merchants did not have commensurate political power. A strong state that valued agriculture above all other economic pursuits did not permit much leverage to merchants and suppressed any assertions of merchant independence. The state itself participated in trade and officials clambered on to foreign ships before the entry of individual merchants and garnered some of the most precious goods. Then and only then would merchants be permitted to trade for the rest of the foreign merchandise. In addition, wealthy merchants would, on occasion, buy land as a possible first step toward their families' eventual acceptance as part of the gentry. They also would aspire to have sons who passed the civil-service examinations.

Source: Morris Rossabi, *A History of China* (Oxford: Wiley Blackwell, 2014), 202–3.

VOICE 2.2

Valerie Hansen on the Social Implications of the Commercializing Economy | 2020

China's international contacts were so extensive that they affected people at all social levels—not just the residents of Chinese port cities but also those living deep in the hinterland. The Chinese weren't experiencing a preparatory phase for globalization. They lived in a globalized world, pure and simple. . . .

The prosperity of Quanzhou and other nearby ports spilled over to the entire province of Fujian, enabling the province's residents to shift away from subsistence farming so that they could produce goods for commercial markets. . . . They stopped growing their own food. They discovered that they could make more money if they cultivated cash crops . . . or if they grew local textile fibers. . . . They came to purchase food for their families at local markets. . . . Many gave up agriculture altogether. . . .

The ceramics industry absorbed the largest share of the labor force. Entrepreneurs built dragon kilns. . . . [P]roducing between 10,000 and 30,000 vessels in a single firing, such kilns employed hundreds, if not thousands, of laborers. . . . We don't think of these kilns as industrial simply because they didn't use steam or electric power . . . but these enterprises were just as large and complex as the first factories of the Industrial Revolution. . . . [S]ome 375,000 people were involved in making export ceramics in the twelfth and thirteenth centuries.

Source: Valerie Hansen, *The Year 1000: When Explorers Connected the World—and Globalization Began* (New York: Scribner, 2020), 199, 216.

AP Analyzing Secondary Sources

1. According to Rossabi, how did the influence of merchants increase during this period, and how were their growing wealth and prominence limited?

2. As described by Hansen, how did commercialization change the social and economic lives of commoners?

3. **Integrating Primary and Secondary Sources:** How do these voices add to the picture of society during Tang and Song China as portrayed by the sources in AP® Working with Evidence?

BUILDING AP® SKILLS

Making Connections: Comparison

Continuing with Comparison as the AP® skill central to Unit 1, have students practice interpreting secondary sources and comparing them. This practice will help students master the stimulus-based multiple-choice questions. Consider having students read both of the sources found on page 127 and answer Question 1 on page 127. Take this activity farther by using Question 2 on page 127 to get a discussion started on the roles of the economy and society during the golden age of Song China.

TRM Suggested Responses to Questions

You can find suggested responses to the AP® Analyzing Secondary Sources questions in the Teacher's Resource Materials.

Multiple-Choice Questions Choose the correct answer for each question.

Questions 1–3 refer to this map.

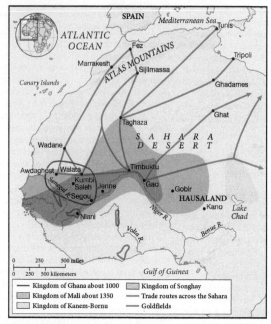

The Sand Roads

1. Which of the following most directly led to the expansion and intensification of the commercial routes depicted in the map above?
   a. Growing contacts among cultures resulting from the Crusades
   b. The discovery by Europeans of diamonds in West Africa
   c. The use of pack animals to overcome harsh environments
   d. Northern military expansion of African empires

128

TRM **Suggested Responses to Questions**
You can find suggested responses to the Chapter 2 AP® Exam Practice questions in the Teacher's Resource Materials.

TEACHING IDEA

AP® Exam Strategies

Continue having students practice test-taking skills so they are comfortable with the type of multiple-choice questions they will encounter as well as the time limit. Copy the MCQs found on pages 128 and 129. Give students the questions as a practice quiz prior to the unit or chapter test. Have students discuss why their answer choice was correct or incorrect.

AP® CLASSROOM

AP® Personal Progress Check

You can extend the AP® Exam Strategies activity above by logging into your AP® Classroom account and using the questions in the Progress Check for Unit 1 as more practice for your students. AP® Classroom allows you to set the quiz up digitally or print out a copy for each student. After students take the Progress Check for Unit 1, you can discuss the answers as a class.

2. The economic and political transformations evident in the map would best be understood in the context of

   a. continuities in techniques of state building.

   b. the rise and diffusion of a new belief system.

   c. the widening practice of state-issued currencies.

   d. the Mongol conquests and their consequences.

3. Which of the following developments was a direct result of new patterns of trans-Saharan trade?

   a. A desire on the part of African monarchs to discover maritime routes to markets in Europe and Asia

   b. The decentralization of political power in sub-Saharan African states

   c. A dramatic increase in the use of gold currency across the Mediterranean region

   d. A decrease in the social complexity of urban areas

Use your knowledge of world history and the document below to answer questions 4 and 5.

> I received permission from the Governor to go to a village of which we had heard, which was a hundred leagues away on the sea-coast, in a town called Pachacamac. It took us twenty-two days to reach it. The road over the mountains is a thing worth seeing, because, though the ground is so rugged, such beautiful roads could not in truth be found throughout Christendom. The greater part of them is paved. There is a bridge of stone or wood over every stream. We found bridges of network over a very large and powerful river, which we crossed twice, which was a marvelous thing to see. The horses crossed over by them. At each passage they have two bridges, the one by which the common people go over, and the other for the lords of the land and their captains. The approaches are always kept closed, with Indians to guard them. These Indians exact transit dues from all passengers. The chiefs and people of the mountains are more intelligent than those of the coast. The country is populous. There are mines in many parts of it. It is a cold climate, it snows, and there is much rain.
>
> — Excerpt from Hernando Pizarro's description of the conquest of Peru, 1533

4. The tone of the document is most consistent with which of the following statements?

   a. State building in the Americas created less developed governments than state building in Afro-Eurasia.

   b. Some civilizations in the Americas enjoyed wealth on a par with many in Afro-Eurasia.

   c. European visitors approached the Americas with a desire to build mutually beneficial relationships.

   d. The Incas were a mostly violent people, prone to war and conquest, who paid little attention to the development of infrastructure.

5. In what ways had the Incas adapted their civilization to the environment by the sixteenth century?

   a. The Incas built up large floating islands of soil to grow crops in their many lakes.

   b. The Incas hunted and gathered using horses they bought from Europeans.

   c. The Incas built roads and bridges to facilitate networks of exchange in mountainous areas.

   d. The Incas imported potatoes and wheat from far distant trading partners to supplement their diet.

129

Argumentation

The old adage "practice makes perfect" works for writing skills in the AP® World History: Modern course. Writing skills should be practiced on a regular basis. Have students answer the SAQs on pages 130 and 131 at the end of class as an "exit ticket" to check for understanding. The three SAQs can be spread across several days. If you think that your students are not ready to write an SAQ this early in the course, consider having students write the SAQs with a partner. This practice can help students feel more confident about their AP® World History: Modern writing skills.

Short-Answer Questions

Read each question carefully and write a short response. Use complete sentences.

1. **Use this image and your knowledge of world history to answer all parts of the question that follows.**

The baptism of Vladimir of Kievan Rus to Orthodox Christianity. From *The Tale of Bygone Years*, a political history that traces the origin of the Slavic people to the biblical story of Noah and the Ark, ca. 1113.

A. Identify ONE motive for the creation of the work depicted above.

B. Explain ONE way in which the political strategies of Song China were different from those of Kievan Rus.

C. Explain ONE way in which another civilization adopted policies similar to those depicted in the source above.

2. **Use this passage and your knowledge of world history to answer all parts of the question that follows.**

> The Middle Ages constituted a period in which the relationship of human societies to nature varied greatly in parts of the world distant from one another. . . . Patterns of increasing economic activity and growth were sporadically interrupted by stress and decline. At times ecosystems suffered from overuse; at other times they recovered and flourished. Human societies, too, alternately burgeoned and faced disasters against which they often had no effective defenses. They worked with what they had, and demonstrated creativity in ways of dealing with the natural world. Important new discoveries occurred in technology, exploration, education, government, and agriculture. Their success or failure often depended on the degree to which they understood and were able to adapt to ecosystems.

> — Johnson Donald Hughes, *An Environmental History of the World: Humankind's Changing Role in the Community of Life*, 2002

130

A. Identify ONE piece of evidence that supports the author's claim that patterns of economic activity and growth in this time period were interrupted by stress and decline.

B. Explain ONE example of a way humans adapted to the natural world during this time period.

C. Explain WHY the author might have written in the early twenty-first century about these patterns of human interaction with the environment.

3. **Use your knowledge of world history to answer all parts of the question that follows.**

A. Identify ONE new technology adopted by Europeans between 1200 and 1450.

B. Explain ONE social or economic consequence of Europe's use of new technologies between 1200 and 1450.

C. Explain how Europe's interaction with other civilizations after 1200 led to cultural transformations.

3 Connections and Interactions

Networks of Exchange, 1200–1450

AP® Overview for Chapter 3

Chapter 3 corresponds with AP® Unit 2: Networks of Exchange, ca. 1200 to ca. 1450. It focuses on the trade and cultural networks that developed in the first chronological period of AP® World History. *Ways of the World* describes a variety of these global systems together, which works well with the themes and key concepts of the course. Students should be able to outline the major trade systems described in the chapter: Eurasian Silk Roads, Indian Ocean Sea Roads, trans-Saharan Sand Roads, and the network of commerce in the Americas. Students should also know that the Mongols were major players in the Afro-Eurasian networks of exchange, through the creation of their massive empire, the rule of their khanates, and their support of transregional trade. As students read through the chapter, they should also be able to recognize the states and empires that emerged and interacted with one another from 1200 to 1450, along with the cultural and environmental exchanges happening along these networks of exchange.

Chapter 3 Essential Activity

Chapter 3 covers Unit 2 for AP® World History. Because trade and other interactions play an important role in the period this chapter covers, students will benefit from creating an annotated map that shows connections and exchanges. You can find the activity handout in the Resources section of the book's digital platform or by clicking on the linked TRM button in the Teacher's Edition e-book.

TRM Essential Activity: Annotated Commerce and Culture Map

Chapter 3 Resources

TRM AP® Skills Workshop Activity Handout: Evidence

TRM Chapter 3 DBQ Activity Handout

TRM Chapter 3 Guided Reading

TRM Chapter 3 Lecture Presentation Slides

TRM Chapter 3 Outline

TRM Chapter 3 Suggested Responses to Questions

TRM Eric's Activity 3: What Makes Something Valuable?

TRM Essential Activity: Annotated Commerce and Culture Map

TRM Handout 3.1: Causation Chart for East and Southeast Asian Buddhism

TRM Handout 3.2: Writing Organizer for Spread of Buddhism DBQ

TRM Handout 3.3: Comparison Chart for Mongol Rule in China and Persia

TRM Handout 3.4: Thematic Chart for the Mongol Conquest

TRM Handout 3.5: Causation Chart for the Black Death

TRM Map 3A: The Americas

TRM Writing Organizer for DBQ Practice

TRM Writing Organizer for LEQ Practice

Pacing Guide

Below is a pacing guide for the AP® World History: Modern course beginning in ca. 1200 C.E. This pacing guide is based on a schedule with 120 sessions of 50 minutes each before the AP® Exam. It is meant as a place to start. If you have a different number of sessions before the exam, you can modify the pacing to suit your needs.

Day	Pages Assigned	AP® Topic	AP® Theme	Suggested Assignments	Coverage Notes
1	Read pages 132–137 to "Religion and the Silk Roads"	2.1	ECN CDI	Chapter 3 Essential Activity Eric's Activity 3: What Makes Something Valuable? on page 135 Exploring AP® Themes: ENV on page 136	Trade routes in world history provide an excellent subject to help students practice and build their Comparison and Continuity and Change skills. A few good topics to focus on are technologies, innovation, cultural diffusion, and economic impact.
2	Read pages 137–140 from "Religion and the Silk Roads" to "Connections across Eurasia: The Mongol Network"	2.1	ECN CDI	Chapter 3 Essential Activity Exploring AP® Themes: CDI on page 138 Building AP® Skills: Developments and Processes on page 139	See above.
3	Read pages 140–144 from "Connections across Eurasia: The Mongol Network" to "Encountering the Mongols: Russia, China, and Persia"	2.2	GOV CDI	Chapter 3 Essential Activity Exploring AP® Themes: GOV on page 141 Teaching Idea: AP® Exam Strategies on page 142	The Mongols used unique empire-building tactics. Have students examine how the Mongols built their empire and compare that process to other states and empires they learned about in Chapters 1 and 2.
4	Read pages 144–148 from "Encountering the Mongols: Russia, China, and Persia" to "The Plague: An Afro-Eurasian Pandemic"	2.2	GOV ECN CDI	Chapter 3 Essential Activity Building AP® Skills: Making Connections: Comparison on page 145 AP® Classroom: AP® Topic Questions on page 146	This section includes a great comparison of Mongol rule in different regions of Eurasia. It would be a good place to have students practice their comparison skills while studying the impact of the Mongols on different regions.
5	Read pages 148–150 from "The Plague: An Afro-Eurasian Pandemic" to "Connections across the Indian Ocean: The Sea Roads"	2.6	ENV	Chapter 3 Essential Activity Apply the Tip on page 149	This section highlights the environmental role of the bubonic plague in the fourteenth century. This is a good place to discuss the effect of natural disasters on human societies.
6	Read pages 150–155 from "Connections across the Indian Ocean: The Sea Roads" to "Chinese Maritime Voyages in the Indian Ocean World"	2.3	ECN CDI	Chapter 3 Essential Activity Teaching Idea: Incorporating Outside Resources on page 150 Exploring AP® Themes: ENV on page 153	Trade routes in world history provide an excellent subject to help students practice and build their Comparison and Continuity and Change skills. A few good topics to focus on are technologies, innovation, cultural diffusion, and economic impact.
7	Read pages 155–156 from "Chinese Maritime Voyages in the Indian Ocean World" to "Connections across the Sahara: The Sand Roads"	2.3	ECN CDI	Chapter 3 Essential Activity Building AP® Skills: Claims and Evidence in Sources on page 154 Teaching Idea: Class Discussion on page 155	Zheng He's voyages are a good way to close out the Indian ocean trade network for the ca. 1200 to ca. 1450 time period, especially because they help set the stage for the changes that will occur in Units 3 and 4.
8	Read pages 156–160 from "Connections across the Sahara: The Sand Roads" to "Connections across the Islamic World"	2.4	ECN CDI	Chapter 3 Essential Activity Building AP® Skills: Claims and Evidence in Sources on page 157 Teaching Idea: Incorporating Outside Resources on page 158	Remind students of what they have already learned about African history before starting on the Sand Roads.

Day	Pages Assigned	AP® Topic	AP® Theme	Suggested Assignments	Coverage Notes
9	Read pages 160–163 from "Connections across the Islamic World" to "Encounter: The Islamic World and Christendom"	2.5 2.7	ECN CDI	Chapter 3 Essential Activity Building AP® Skills: Claims and Evidence in Sources on page 161 Exploring AP® Themes: CDI on page 162	While cultural diffusion along trade routes is woven throughout the chapter, this section offers a more specific case study with the Islamic world. This is a good place to really dive into cultural diffusion with students and ties back to Dar al-Islam from Unit 1.
10	Read pages 163–166 from "Encounter: The Islamic World and Christendom" to "Connections across the Americas"	2.5 2.6 2.7	ECN CDI ENV	Chapter 3 Essential Activity Building AP® Skills: Making Connections: Causation on page 162 Exploring AP® Themes: ENV on page 165	The Crusades are not included in the Course Framework but are important for contextualization in Unit 1. If you are short on time, you can skip this section.
11	Read pages 166–169 beginning with "Connections across the Americas"	2.5 2.6 2.7	ECN CDI ENV	Apply the Tip on page 166 Exploring AP® Themes: ENV on page 167 Exploring AP® Themes: ECN and GOV on page 169	The American trade networks are not required in the Course Framework but would be helpful for students to know. However, if you are short on time, skip the section on the Americas.
12	Read pages 170–171 "Globalization—Ancient and Modern"	2.5 2.6 2.7	ECN CDI ENV	Building AP® Skills: Making Connections: Comparison on page 170 Building AP® Skills: Making Connections: Causation on page 171	This section can provide an excellent wrap-up for Units 1 and 2.

NOTES

Bell Ringer

Bell ringers should take no more than 5 to 10 minutes of your class period and offer an effective and engaging way to begin your lessons.

Typically, students do not understand all the interactions and connections along the various trade routes. As a quick activity to get the thinking process started, ask them to do a "tag check" to see where their shoes, shirts, and backpacks were manufactured. By a show of hands, how many items are from China? From the United States? Other nations? Afterwards, discuss the global nature of trade as an introduction to the main idea of this chapter—exchange across distance.

Claims and Evidence in Sources

Students should understand that many things, including physical goods and other intangibles, are spread along trade routes. Examine the ceramic figurine in the photo. Then ask students the following questions:

- Can you identify the instrument the man on the left is playing? *He is playing a lute.*

- What else do you see in this figurine? *The proud stance of the camel.*

- Why do you think the camel plays a central part in this figurine? *Camels were an important pack animal on both the Silk Roads and trans-Saharan routes. They can walk easily on shifting sands, can carry up to 500 pounds of goods, can go long periods without water, and can be used for food.*

- What is the significance of the fact that this figurine shows Chinese and Central Asian merchants together on the camel? *It suggests that the cultures have important interactions with each other.*

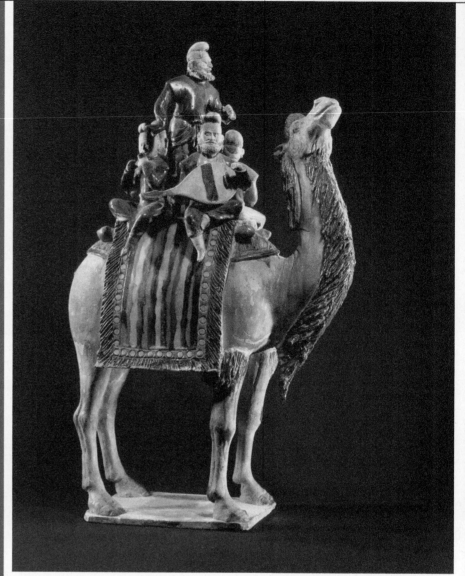

Travels on the Silk Roads This ancient Chinese ceramic figurine shows a group of musicians riding on a camel along the famous Silk Road commercial network that long linked the civilizations of western and eastern Eurasia. The bearded figures represent Central Asian merchants, while the others depict Chinese. (Martha Avery/Getty Images)

132

◀ **AP**

MAKING CONNECTIONS
What does this image suggest about the relationship between the Chinese and the nomadic people of Central Asia?

Connections and Interactions

Networks of Exchange

1200–1450

CONNECTING PAST AND PRESENT

In late 2013, Chinese president Xi Jinping announced a massive and massively expensive project, known as the Belt and Road Initiative, that was intended to link the economies of Asia, Africa, and Europe and spur economic development. If fully implemented, it would consist of a "belt" of overland connections—highways, railroads, energy pipelines, power grids—and a "road" of sea-based ports and shipping lanes. To its Chinese proponents it would "enhance regional connectivity and embrace a brighter future."[1] Its critics worried that it could become a vehicle for Chinese global dominance. Very quickly, the project was dubbed a twenty-first-century Silk Road, evoking the ancient commercial network that long spanned much of Eurasia. ∎

That reference provides a useful reminder that the various peoples, societies, and civilizations of earlier times were never wholly self-contained or isolated communities. To varying degrees, each of them was embedded in a network of relationships with both neighboring and more distant peoples. Modern globalization, in short, has an ancient legacy. World historians have an abiding interest in such connections, viewing them as a major motor of change and transformation. Much as diversity and variation were the central themes of Chapters 1 and 2, connection and interaction provide the primary focus for Chapter 3.

Nothing has been more important in fostering relationships among distant peoples than commerce or the urge to trade. The exchange of goods among communities occupying different ecological zones has long been a prominent feature of human history. Coastlands and highlands, steppes and farmlands, islands and

TRM **Chapter 3 Guided Reading**
You can find a guided reading handout for this chapter in the Teacher's Resource Materials.

TRM **Chapter 3 Lecture Slides**
You can find curated lecture slides for this chapter in the Teacher's Resource Materials.

TRM **Chapter 3 Outline**
You can find a chapter outline to model good note-taking for this chapter in the Teacher's Resource Materials.

TRM **Suggested Responses to Questions**
You can find suggested responses to all of the AP® margin questions in this chapter in the Teacher's Resource Materials.

BUILDING AP® SKILLS

Developments and Processes

To build connections between different topics in world history, ask students: What are examples of people, societies, and civilizations interacting with the groups around them that you learned about in Chapters 1 and 2? Answers may include:

■ *The spread of religions from their place of origin—for example, the spread of Buddhism to China and the spread of Christianity throughout the Roman Empire*

■ *The spread of Chinese influence and traditions into Korea, Vietnam, and Japan*

■ *The connections created by Dar al-Islam between different regions and the sharing of technologies and ideas*

■ *Song China's increasing role in the Indian Ocean trade network*

■ *European borrowing of knowledge and technologies from the Islamic and Chinese worlds*

133

Ask students: How did trade routes or networks of exchange affect politics, social structures, and economies? *States could tax the trade routes and gain money for their treasuries. The merchant class could gain power and wealth. The luxury goods exchanged over the trade routes acted as a visible sign of wealth and status for the elite. The ability to trade opened up economic opportunities for manufacturers of luxury goods.* After students have shared their answers, have them compare their answers to the discussion on pages 133 and 134.

Ask students the following questions:

■ How might the exchange of goods affect Eurasian cultures? *The contact among different cultures that occurred with trade led to the spread of religion and technology. It linked different civilizations and created the conditions for cultural diffusion.*

■ What goods, ideas, technologies, and people traveled on the Silk Roads? (Answers are provided in italics.)

　■ Goods: *silk, cotton, porcelain, paper, horses, hides, copper, spices, dried fruit, dyes, precious stones, glassware, jewelry, perfume, olive oil.*

　■ Ideas: *Buddhism, Christianity, Islam*

　■ Technologies: *papermaking, compass, saddles, stirrups, bridles for camels and horses*

　■ People: *Central Asian nomads, Europeans, Chinese, Muslims*

AP° EXAM TIP
You must know the economic, social, and political effects of networks of exchange.

mainlands, valleys and mountains, deserts and forests—each has generated different products. Furthermore, some societies have been able to monopolize, at least temporarily, the production of particular goods—such as silk in China, certain spices in Southeast Asia, and incense in southern Arabia—that others have found valuable. This uneven distribution of goods and resources has long motivated exchange, not only within particular civilizations or regions but among them as well.

Such long-distance commerce shaped the daily life of many millions. It altered habits of consumption as goods from afar became available, some of which, such as silk or jade, enabled elites to distinguish themselves from commoners. Trade also affected the working lives of many people, encouraging them to specialize in producing particular products for sale in distant markets rather than for use in their own communities. Merchants often became a distinct social group, sometimes viewed with suspicion by others because of their ability to accumulate wealth without actually producing anything themselves. Trade also had the capacity to transform political life. The wealth available from controlling and taxing trade motivated the creation of states in various parts of the world and sustained those states once they had been constructed. Moreover, trade became a vehicle for the spread of religious ideas, technological innovations, disease-bearing germs, and plants and animals to regions far from their places of origin. All of this long-distance trade began long before 1200 and increased dramatically in the centuries after 1450.

In addition to international commerce, other processes likewise facilitated the networks of interaction that developed among distinct societies. The growth of large states, such as the Ottoman or Inca empires, brought a variety of distinct peoples into contact with one another, often violently. The clash of these empires or civilizations also represented an important form of interaction, as in the enduring rivalry between the Islamic world and the Christian world. Geographical proximity fostered interaction, such as the long relationship between the agricultural Chinese and the pastoral peoples living north of the Great Wall. The journeys of missionaries or travelers like Ibn Battuta and Marco Polo likewise promoted awareness of a larger world. So did the spread of religions, such as Buddhism, Christianity, and Islam, well beyond their places of origin. And finally, migrations brought culturally different peoples into contact with one another, as in the movement of Turkic-speaking peoples from Central Asia into the Middle East. However they occurred, encounters and interactions across cultural boundaries have long been potent sources of transformation in human history.

AP° EXAM TIP
Understanding the goods, ideas, technology, and peoples that traveled the Silk Roads, and their impact on Eurasian cultures, is key for success on the AP° Exam.

Connections across Eurasia: The Silk Roads

Finding the Main Point: What was the economic and cultural impact of the Silk Road trading network?

The most famous of those networks of exchange, widely known now as the **Silk Roads** after their most famous product, linked the various peoples and civilizations of the Eurasian landmass from China to Europe by the early centuries of the Common

Landmarks for Chapter 3

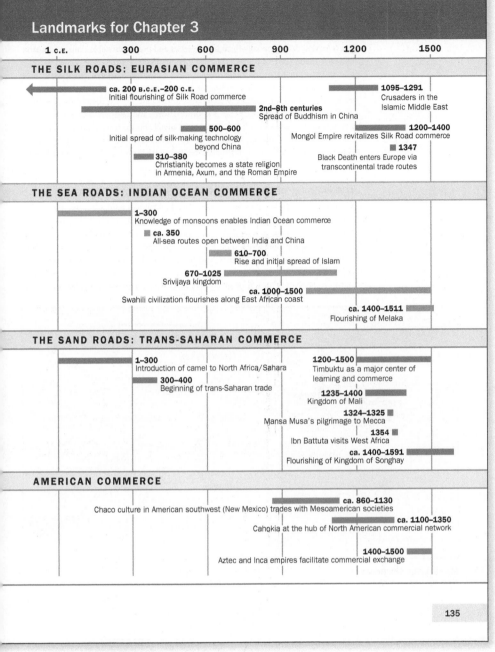

1 C.E. — 300 — 600 — 900 — 1200 — 1500

THE SILK ROADS: EURASIAN COMMERCE

ca. 200 B.C.E.–200 C.E.
Initial flourishing of Silk Road commerce

2nd–8th centuries
Spread of Buddhism in China

500–600
Initial spread of silk-making technology beyond China

310–380
Christianity becomes a state religion in Armenia, Axum, and the Roman Empire

1095–1291
Crusaders in the Islamic Middle East

1200–1400
Mongol Empire revitalizes Silk Road commerce

1347
Black Death enters Europe via transcontinental trade routes

THE SEA ROADS: INDIAN OCEAN COMMERCE

1–300
Knowledge of monsoons enables Indian Ocean commerce

ca. 350
All-sea routes open between India and China

610–700
Rise and initial spread of Islam

670–1025
Srivijaya kingdom

ca. 1000–1500
Swahili civilization flourishes along East African coast

ca. 1400–1511
Flourishing of Melaka

THE SAND ROADS: TRANS-SAHARAN COMMERCE

1–300
Introduction of camel to North Africa/Sahara

300–400
Beginning of trans-Saharan trade

1200–1500
Timbuktu as a major center of learning and commerce

1235–1400
Kingdom of Mali

1324–1325
Mansa Musa's pilgrimage to Mecca

1354
Ibn Battuta visits West Africa

ca. 1400–1591
Flourishing of Kingdom of Songhay

AMERICAN COMMERCE

ca. 860–1130
Chaco culture in American southwest (New Mexico) trades with Mesoamerican societies

ca. 1100–1350
Cahokia at the hub of North American commercial network

1400–1500
Aztec and Inca empires facilitate commercial exchange

135

BUILDING AP® SKILLS

Making Connections: Causation

Help students explain the long- or short-term causes and effects of a historical development with the following exercise. After you review "Landmarks for Chapter 3" with students, ask them to work with a partner to discuss events from Chapters 1 and 2 that may have caused events on the timeline. Then go through the timeline as a class and compile a list. This activity can help students understand that many events have a profound effect on events in a future time frame. *Answers may include: Song China's governmental support of long-distance trade by land and sea, the spread of Islam under the Umayyads and Abbasids, the Bantu migrations in sub-Saharan Africa.*

CHAPTER 3

ERIC'S ACTIVITY 3 What Makes Something Valuable?

Theme 4: Economic Systems

What makes something valuable? Students are often puzzled that shells or cocoa beans could serve as currencies, yet they have never examined exactly why they think that gold, silver, and diamonds are valuable. I have found that helping students explore the question "What makes something valuable?" can help them understand the dynamics of long-distance trade during the third-wave period. The complete activity can be found in the Teacher's Resource Materials.

TRM Eric's Activity 3: What Makes Something Valuable?

Era (see Map 3.1). Especially during prosperous and politically stable times, a vast array of goods made their way across the Silk Roads, often carried in large camel caravans that traversed the harsh and dangerous steppes, deserts, and oases of Central Asia. Those caravans stopped at inns or guesthouses, known as caravanserai, located all along the trade routes from the eastern Mediterranean to China. There merchants could rest, exchange goods with local people and other traders, and resupply their animals. Such places became centers of cultural exchange as merchants from many religious and cultural traditions met and mingled. Some of the caravanserai developed into major Central Asian commercial cities such as Bukhara, Samarkand, Khotan, Kashgar, and **Dunhuang**.

The Making of the Silk Roads

Most of the goods that made their way across this Eurasian network of exchange were luxury products destined for an elite and wealthy market, rather than staple goods, for only readily moved commodities of great value could compensate for the high costs of transportation across such long and forbidding distances. Silk was the most prominent of those luxury goods. China had long held a monopoly on its production, but by the sixth century C.E., the knowledge and technology for producing raw silk had spread beyond China to Korea, Japan, India, Persia, and the Byzantine Empire. As

▼ **AP**

CAUSATION
According to this map, what geographic or environmental obstacles did Silk Road traders have to contend with? How did traders overcome these obstacles?

Map 3.1 The Silk Roads
For 2,000 years, goods, ideas, technologies, and diseases made their way across Eurasia on the several routes of the Silk Roads.

EXPLORING AP® THEMES

Humans and the Environment (ENV)

Discussion of the Silk Roads should emphasize the importance of the study of geography in history. Show students Map 3.1, "The Silk Roads." Then ask: What are some of the geographic features that made the Silk Roads difficult to travel? *Geographic features that made the Silk Roads difficult to travel include mountains, deserts, and extreme temperature changes.*

TEACHING IDEA

Class Discussion

Ask students if they are aware that the Silk Roads were not one long route, but multiple routes connecting China with regions to the west. Use the following questions to help students understand how the short segments making up the Silk Roads allowed for more diffusion of goods, ideas, technology, and peoples:

■ How did trade occur on the Silk Roads? *Merchants traveled along short segments, stopping at towns along the way to trade goods. As they traded goods, they also facilitated the spread of technology, culture, and disease.*

■ Why wouldn't merchants have traveled the entire length of the Silk Roads? *The route was too long to travel the entire length. Merchants would not have been able to make a profit if they traveled the entire length.*

■ Why did the short segments of the Silk Roads create more diffusion of goods, ideas, technology, and peoples? *The network of shorter segments made travel more manageable. More people traveled to trade, and merchants came into contact with more people. This facilitated the spread of ideas, technology, and culture.*

the supply of silk increased, its many varieties circulated even more extensively across Afro-Eurasian trade routes. In Central Asia, silk was used as currency and as a means of accumulating wealth. In both China and the Byzantine Empire, silk became a symbol of high status, and governments passed laws that restricted silk clothing to members of the elite. Furthermore, silk became associated with the sacred in the expanding world religions of Buddhism and Christianity. Chinese Buddhist pilgrims who traveled to India seeking religious texts and relics took large quantities of silk with them as gifts to the monasteries they visited. In the world of Christendom, silk wall hangings, altar covers, and priest's robes became highly prestigious signs of devotion and piety. By the twelfth century, the West African king of Ghana was wearing silk, and silk circulated in Egypt, Ethiopia, and along the East African coast as well.

Over many centuries, various technological innovations, such as yokes, saddles, and stirrups, made the use of camels, horses, and oxen more effective means of transportation across the vast distances of the Silk Roads. A "frame and mattress" saddle, most likely an Arab invention, allowed camels to carry much heavier loads in a stable fashion. New forms of credit and economic exchange also facilitated the operation of the Silk Road network. Paper money, initially a Chinese innovation called "flying cash" because of its tendency to fly away in the wind, made it unnecessary to carry heavy metal coins. European traders introduced "bills of exchange," a kind of contract promising payment. And novel banking practices allowed urban-based banking houses to offer credit to merchants.

Compared to global commerce today, the volume of trade on the Silk Roads was modest, and its focus on luxury goods limited its direct impact on most people. Nonetheless, it had important economic and social consequences. Peasants in the Yangzi River delta of southern China sometimes gave up the cultivation of food crops, choosing to focus instead on producing silk, paper, porcelain, lacquerware, or iron tools, many of which were destined for the markets of the Silk Roads. In this way, the impact of long-distance trade trickled down to affect the lives of ordinary farmers. Furthermore, merchants could benefit immensely from their involvement in long-distance trade. One such individual, a twelfth-century Persian trader named Ramisht whose ships traversed the Indian Ocean and Red Sea, made a personal fortune with which he commissioned an enormously expensive covering made of Chinese silk for the Kaaba, the central shrine of Islam in Mecca.

Religion and the Silk Roads

More important even than the economic impact of the Silk Roads was their role as a conduit of culture. Buddhism, for example, a product of Indian civilization, spread widely throughout Central and East Asia as Indian traders and Buddhist monks brought the new religion to the trans-Eurasian trade routes of the Silk Roads. There it took root especially in the oasis cities of Central Asia, such as Merv, Samarkand, Khotan, and Dunhuang. Conversion to Buddhism in such places was voluntary, without the pressure of conquest or foreign rule. Dependent on long-distance trade, the inhabitants

AP EXAM TIP
Be able to explain the relationships between governments and trade routes across time and place.

AP
CAUSATION
What lay behind the emergence of Silk Road commerce, and what kept it going for so many centuries?

AP EXAM TIP
Understanding that Buddhism, like other major religions, spread along trade routes is fundamental to success on the AP* Exam.

TEACHING IDEA
Incorporating Outside Resources

In the episode *The Silk Road and Ancient Trade* of Crash Course World History, John Green discusses the Silk Road, a network of trade routes where goods were exchanged across the ancient world, from China to the West. Things like disease and ideas made the trip in addition to consumer goods. Green connects the Silk Road to modern life and how we acquire our possessions. This video can be found on YouTube. You can upload it to your LMS and attach a quiz to make it a homework assignment or watch the video in class. After watching the video in class, ask students the following questions.

■ If the Silk Road wasn't a road, what was it, and why was it called the Silk Road? *It was a network of small trade routes, and silk was the most desired good that was traded. All of the routes together made up the Silk Road.*

■ Why would nomadic people be important along the Silk Road? *Answers may include: Nomads traveled the Silk Road continuously and provided pack animals and security for merchants.*

■ Why did the new cities developed by nomads become important? Name one example and explain. *New cities were on the trade routes and soon become areas of exchange. One example is Palmyra, a town located on an oasis north of Damascus. All the silk and incense that went to Rome had to travel through Palmyra.*

APPLY THE TIP

If you had students complete the Essential Activity in Chapters 1 (annotated map of belief systems) and 3 (annotated map of trade networks), have them study their annotated maps and ask: Do you see any connections between the spread of religions and how trade networks connected different regions to one another? Give specific examples of your observations. *Answers will vary.*

and rulers of those sophisticated and prosperous cities found in Buddhism both a rich spiritual tradition and a link to the larger, wealthy, and prestigious civilization of India.

As Buddhism spread across the Silk Roads from India to Central Asia, China, and beyond, it also changed. The original faith had shunned the material world, but Buddhist monasteries in the rich oasis towns of the Silk Roads found themselves very much involved in secular affairs. Some of them became prosperous, receiving gifts from well-to-do merchants, artisans, and local rulers. The begging bowls of the monks became a symbol rather than part of a daily activity. Sculptures and murals in the monasteries depicted musicians and acrobats, women applying makeup, and even drinking parties, all of which suggested a wealthier and more worldly style of living, far removed from traditions of Buddhist asceticism.

Religious practice changed as well. It was the more devotional Mahayana form of Buddhism—featuring the Buddha as a deity, numerous bodhisattvas (fully enlightened beings who assisted a suffering humanity), an emphasis on compassion, and the possibility of earning merit—that flourished on the Silk Roads, rather than the more austere psychological teachings of the historical Buddha. Moreover, Buddhism picked up elements of other cultures while in transit on the Silk Roads. In the Sogdian city of Samarkand, the use of Zoroastrian fire rituals apparently became a part of Buddhist practice. In a similar way, the gods of many peoples along the Silk Roads were incorporated into Buddhist practice as bodhisattvas.

APPLY THE TIP

To help students develop their essay-planning skills and understand the spread of Buddhism throughout Asia, ask them to create a cause-and-effect chart on the spread of Buddhism into East and Southeast Asia. Once they complete the chart, you could also ask students to compare how these causes and effects played out in the different regions.

TRM Handout 3.1: Causation Chart for East and Southeast Asian Buddhism

EXPLORING AP® THEMES

Cultural Developments and Interactions (CDI)

Dunhuang was a critical junction on the Silk Roads as well as a center of Buddhist learning, painting, and sculpture. This mixture of sculpture and painted images provides an excellent visual example of how Buddhism changed and adapted as the religion spread into China. Use the following questions to discuss some of the cultural syncretism that appears in the painting.

■ Why would merchants have wanted to pay to create the art inside the caves in Dunhuang? *Merchants may have wished to earn religious merit by supporting the monks. In turn, the monks provided resting places for the merchants traveling back and forth to Dunhuang.*

■ Why did Dunhuang and other towns on the Silk Roads become centers of learning? *Dunhuang grew because of traffic along the Silk Roads; monasteries were built. As more monks arrived, the area became a center of learning.*

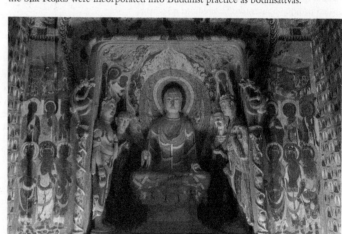

Dunhuang Located in western China at a critical junction of the Silk Road trading network, Dunhuang was also a center of Buddhist learning, painting, and sculpture as that religion made its way from India to China and beyond. In some 492 caves, carved out of the rock between about 400 and 1400 c.e., a remarkable gallery of Buddhist art has been preserved. In this mixture of sculpture and painted images, the Buddha is surrounded by other enlightened beings or bodhisattvas. (Zhang Peng/Getty Images)

Buddhism initially entered China via the Silk Road trading network during the first and second centuries C.E. and by the eighth century C.E. had become widely accepted, particularly in its broader Mahayana form. One of the most popular expressions of Buddhism in China was the Pure Land school, in which faithfully repeating the name of an earlier Buddha, the Amitabha, ensured rebirth in a beautifully described heavenly realm, the Pure Land. In its emphasis on salvation by faith, without arduous study or intensive meditation, Pure Land Buddhism became a highly popular and authentically Chinese version of the Indian faith.

The impressive growth of Chinese Buddhism, however, was accompanied by a persistent undercurrent of resistance and criticism. In 819, Han Yu, a leading figure in the Confucian counterattack on Buddhism, gave expression to this hostility:

> Now the Buddha was of barbarian origin. His language differed from Chinese speech; his clothes were of a different cut; his mouth did not pronounce the prescribed words of the Former Kings. . . . He did not recognize the relationship between prince and subject, nor the sentiments of father and son.[2]

Several decades later, the Chinese state took direct action against the Buddhist establishment and against other foreign religions. A series of imperial decrees between 841 and 845 ordered some 260,000 monks and nuns to return to normal life as tax-paying citizens. Thousands of monasteries, temples, and shrines were either destroyed or turned to public use, while the state confiscated the lands, money, metals, and serfs belonging to monasteries. Buddhists were now forbidden to use gold, silver, copper, iron, and gems in constructing their images. These actions dealt a serious blow to Chinese Buddhism. Its scholars and monks were scattered, its creativity was diminished, and its institutions came even more firmly under state control.

Despite this persecution, Buddhism did not vanish from China. The Chan school of Chinese Buddhism, which drew heavily on Daoist outlooks and emphasized strict meditation practice, became dominant during the Song dynasty and was favored by court officials and scholars. At the level of elite culture, Buddhist philosophical ideas played a role in a reformulation of Confucian thinking called Neo-Confucianism that took place during the Song dynasty. Focused on the study and interpretation of classical Confucian texts, this outlook rejected the religious aspects of both Buddhism and Daoism but appreciated the high moral standards of Buddhist teachings, which were understood as aligning with Confucian values. At the village level, Buddhism became one element of Chinese popular religion, which also included the veneration of ancestors, the honoring of Confucius, and Daoist shrines and rituals. Temples frequently included statues of Confucius, Laozi, and the Buddha, with little sense of any incompatibility among them. "Every black-haired son of Han," the Chinese have long said, "wears a Confucian thinking cap, a Daoist robe, and Buddhist sandals." Unlike in Europe, where the new religion of Christianity triumphed over and excluded all other faiths, Buddhism in China became assimilated into Chinese culture alongside its other traditions (see AP® Looking Again: Chinese Cultural Traditions, page 175).

AP®
CAUSATION
What facilitated the initial acceptance and spread of Buddhism in China?

Making Connections: Continuity and Change

Ask students to read through the first two paragraphs on page 140 and write down the different examples of how Korea and Japan changed culturally due to Chinese influence.

■ Korea: *Students were sent to China to study Confucianism as well as Chinese science and art; Buddhist monks brought in popular forms of Chinese Buddhism, which quickly took root; Korea established schools to study Confucianism.*

■ Japan: *The Chinese Chan school of Buddhism became Zen Buddhism and was very popular among the samurai warrior class; Neo-Confucian teachings became popular with the Japanese elite.*

Bell Ringer

Ask students to create a list of characteristics and skills that nomadic people would need to survive. *Answers will vary.*

Ask students to consider what advantages nomadic people had in the larger economy. *Answers will vary.*

Confucian Education This eighteenth-century image of a Korean Confucian classroom reflects the long-enduring role of Confucius in education across much of East Asia, where mastery of his teachings became an important mark of elite status and a means for social advancement. (National Museum, Seoul, Korea/Bridgeman Images)

AP®

CONTINUITY AND CHANGE

What cultural changes occurred in Korea and Japan in response to Chinese influence?

AP® EXAM TIP

The cultural, economic, and political impacts of the Mongol Empire are important issues for the AP® Exam.

Meanwhile, many of China's own traditions spread to nearby societies such as Korea, Japan, and Vietnam, which actively borrowed cultural features from their giant and highly prestigious neighbor. Korea, for example, sent tribute missions to China, which gave legitimacy for Korean rulers and offered models of court life and administrative techniques that they sought to replicate back home. A new capital city of Kumsong was modeled directly on the Chinese capital of Chang'an (chahng-ahn). Tribute missions also enabled both official and private trade, mostly in luxury goods such as ceremonial clothing, silks, fancy teas, Confucian and Buddhist texts, and artwork. All of this enriched the lives of a Korean aristocracy that was becoming increasingly Chinese in culture. Thousands of Korean students were sent to China, where they studied primarily Confucianism but also the sciences and the arts. Buddhist monks visited centers of learning and pilgrimage in China and brought back popular forms of Chinese Buddhism, which quickly took root in Korea. Schools for the study of Confucianism, using texts in the Chinese language, were established in Korea. In these ways, Korea became a part of the expanding world of Chinese culture.

Chinese culture also found favor in Japan. Various schools of Chinese Buddhism took root, first among the educated and literate classes and later more broadly in Japanese society. By 1200, the Chinese Chan school of Buddhism had become Zen in Japan, where it was highly popular among the samurai warrior class. Chinese Neo-Confucian teachings arrived in Japan around 1240 and proved highly influential among intellectuals. By the seventeenth century Neo-Confucianism had become the official ideology of the Japanese Tokugawa regime. The Chinese writing system—and with it an interest in historical writing, calligraphy, and poetry—likewise proved attractive among the elite.

Connections across Eurasia: The Mongol Network

Finding the Main Point: What was the significance of the Mongol Empire in world history?

Silk Road trading networks prospered most when large and powerful states provided relative security for merchants and travelers across long distances. In the several centuries after 1200, the Mongols conquered a region from the Pacific coast of Asia to Eastern Europe that incorporated almost the entire Silk Road network into the largest land-based empire in human history (see Map 3.2). The stability that this empire provided gave a renewed vitality to long-distance trade, fostered cultural and religious exchange, and facilitated the spread of diseases such as the Black Death. The Mongols' conquests joined the pastoral peoples of the inner Eurasian steppes with the settled agricultural civilizations of outer Eurasia more extensively and more intimately than ever before. Mongol rule also brought the major civilizations of Eurasia—Europe, China, and the Islamic world—into far more direct contact than in earlier times. Both the enormous destructiveness of the process and the networks of exchange and communication that it spawned were the work of the Mongols, numbering only about 700,000 people. It was one of history's most unlikely stories.

AP®

CAUSATION
What were the primary influences on the process of Mongol state building?

MAPPING HISTORY   Map 3.2 The Mongol Empire

Encompassing much of Eurasia, the Mongol Empire was divided into four khanates after the death of Chinggis Khan.

Reading the Map: Which of the four khanates included the traditional Mongol homeland?

AP® Making Connections: What does a comparison of this map with Map 3.1: The Silk Roads suggest about the limits of Mongol expansion? Look closely at the geographic features shown in Map 3.1.

CHAPTER 3

EXPLORING AP® THEMES

Governance (GOV)

Show students Map 3.2, "The Mongol Empire." Ask them to predict the challenges the Mongols might have faced in governing this vast area. *Challenges included communication across large areas of land, the many khanates within the empire, and the possibility that local people might challenge a ruler who was far away.*

TEACHING IDEA

Incorporating Outside Resources

In the TED-Ed *History vs. Genghis Khan*, Alex Gendler looks at the controversy surrounding the place of Chinggis Khan in history and asks if he was a vicious barbarian or a "unifier who paved the way for the modern world." Find the video by searching for it on the TED-Ed website. After students watch the video, ask them to discuss the following question:

■ Can a leader's historical or cultural significance outweigh the deaths he caused along the way? *Answers will vary.*

For all of its size and fearsome reputation, the Mongol Empire left a surprisingly modest cultural imprint on the world it had briefly governed, for by 1450 it was gone. Unlike the pastoral Arabs or Turks, whose languages and culture flourish today in many places, Mongol culture remains confined largely to Mongolia. The Mongol Empire proved to be "the last, spectacular bloom of pastoral power in Inner Eurasia."[3] With the disintegration of the Mongol Empire, the tide turned against the pastoralists of inner Eurasia, who were increasingly swallowed up in the expanding Russian or Chinese empires. Nonetheless, while it lasted, the Mongol Empire made an enormous impact throughout the entire Eurasian world.

The Making of the Mongol Empire

The creation of this enormous empire owed much to a single individual—**Temujin** (TEM-oo-chin) (1162–1227), later known as **Chinggis Khan** (universal ruler). Born into an impoverished family, Temujin's personal magnetism and courage, and his inclination to rely on trusted friends rather than relatives, allowed him to build up a small following and to ally with a more powerful tribal leader. This alliance received a boost from Chinese patrons, always eager to keep the pastoralists divided. Amid shifting alliances and betrayals, Temujin achieved a mounting string of military victories, and in 1206, a Mongol tribal assembly recognized him as Chinggis Khan, supreme leader of a now unified Great Mongol Nation. It was a remarkable achievement.

Within a few years, Chinggis Khan launched a major attack on China, long a source of great wealth for pastoral peoples. Thus was set in motion half a century of a **Mongol world war**, a series of military campaigns, massive killing, and empire building without precedent in world history. In the process, Chinggis Khan, followed by his sons and grandsons (Ogodei, Mongke, and Khubilai), constructed an empire that encompassed China, Central Asia, Russia, much of the Islamic Middle East, and parts of Eastern Europe (see Map 3.2, page 141).

The Mongol realm grew of its own momentum without any grand scheme or blueprint for world conquest. Each fresh victory brought new resources for making war and new threats or insecurities that seemed to require further expansion. But by the end of his life, Chinggis Khan had come to see his career in terms of a universal mission. "I have accomplished a great work," he declared, "uniting the whole world in one empire."[4]

What made this "great work" possible? In part it was the luck of good timing, for China was divided,

Mongol Warriors Horseback-riding skills, honed in herding animals and adapted to military purposes, were central to Mongol conquests, as illustrated in this fourteenth-century Persian manuscript image of Mongol mounted warriors fighting with bows and swords. (De Agostini Picture Library/M. Seemuller/Bridgeman Images)

AP® Exam Strategies

It is important to work on writing skills throughout the year with students. After students learn about the Mongol Empire is a good point to have them practice writing a Short-Answer Question (SAQ) response to answer the following:

1. A. Identify ONE way in which the Mongols affected the culture of Eurasia.

   B. Explain ONE way in which the Mongol Empire impacted established political powers throughout Eurasia.

   C. Explain ONE way in which the Mongol Empire affected economics in Eurasia.

with the Song dynasty having already lost control of its northern territory to the pastoral Jurchen people, while the decrepit Abbasid caliphate, once the center of the Islamic world, had shrunk to a fraction of its earlier size. But the key to the Mongols' success lay in their army. According to one scholar, "Mongol armies were simply better led, organized, and disciplined than those of their opponents."[5] In an effort to diminish a divisive tribalism, Chinggis Khan reorganized the entire social structure of the Mongols into military units of 10, 100, 1,000, and 10,000 warriors, an arrangement that allowed for effective command and control. Thus the Mongols achieved a kind of internal unity they had never known before.

An impressive discipline and loyalty to their leaders made possible the elaborate tactics of encirclement, retreat, and deception that proved decisive in many a battle. To compensate for their own small population, the Mongols incorporated huge numbers of conquered peoples into their military forces. "People who lived in felt tents"—mostly Mongol and Turkic pastoralists—were conscripted en masse into the cavalry units of the Mongol army, while settled agricultural peoples supplied the infantry and artillery forces. Mongols also demanded that their conquered people serve as laborers, building roads and bridges and ferrying supplies over long distances. Artisans, craftsmen, and skilled people generally were carefully identified, spared from massacre, and often sent to distant regions of the empire where their services were required. And the flow of wealth from conquered civilizations provided enormous resources for the Mongols. They were also willing to borrow and quickly acquired Chinese techniques and technology of siege warfare.

Also contributing to Mongol military effectiveness was a growing reputation for ruthless brutality and destructiveness. City after city was utterly destroyed. Chinggis Khan's policy was clear: "Whoever submits shall be spared, but those who resist, they shall be destroyed with their wives, children and dependents . . . so that the others who hear and see should fear and not act the same."[6]

The Mongols likewise demonstrated an impressive ability to mobilize both the human and material resources of their growing empire. Elaborate census-taking enabled the systematic taxation of conquered people. An effective system of relay stations, about a day's ride apart, provided rapid communication across the empire and fostered trade as well. The beginnings of a centralized bureaucracy with various specialized offices took shape in the new capital of Karakorum. There scribes translated official decrees into the various languages of the empire, such as Persian, Uighur, Chinese, and Tibetan.

Other policies appealed to various groups among the conquered peoples of the empire. Interested in fostering commerce, Mongol rulers often offered merchants 10 percent or more above their asking price and allowed them the free use of the relay stations for transporting their goods. In administering the conquered regions, Mongols held the highest decision-making posts, but Chinese and Muslim officials held many advisory and lower-level positions in China and Persia, respectively. In religious matters, the Mongols welcomed and supported many religious traditions—Buddhist, Christian, Muslim, Daoist—as long as they

AP® EXAM TIP

It is important to know how empires used military forces, as well as diplomacy, to gain and maintain control.

AP® EXAM TIP

Be able to compare Mongol techniques of imperial management with those of other empires in this period and later.

AP®

CAUSATION

What accounts for the political and military success of the Mongols?

APPLY THE TIP

Divide students into groups of three or four each and assign them one of the following empires to compare to the Mongol Empire: Islamic empires (divide into the Umayyad and Abbasid), Tang dynasty, and Song dynasty. Students should research what techniques of imperial management their assigned empire and the Mongols used to govern their territories. After they are done researching, students will create a Venn diagram to compare the two empires to each other.

BUILDING AP® SKILLS

Sourcing and Situation

Show students the painting of Mongol Russia. Ask them how the difference in time between the event (1237) and the painting (sixteenth century) might have influenced the veracity of the portrayed event. Answers should note that the image shows the Mongols (on horseback) in a more negative light than may have been warranted by actual events, it shows buildings that may not have existed during the thirteenth century, and it shows that peasants are being burned, which highlights the perception that Mongols were barbarians.

Mongol Russia This sixteenth-century painting depicts the Mongol burning of the Russian city of Ryazan in 1237. Similar destruction awaited many Russian towns that resisted the invaders. (akg-images/Universal Images Group/Sovfoto)

▲ **AP**

CLAIMS AND EVIDENCE IN SOURCING
What does this image seek to convey about the Mongol attack on Ryazan?

AP

COMPARISON
How did Russians experience Mongol rule?

AP

CONTINUITY AND CHANGE
How did Mongol rule change China? How did Mongol rulers continue using Chinese traditions to govern?

did not become the focus of political opposition. Such policies provided some benefits and a place within the empire—albeit subordinate—for many of its conquered peoples.

Encountering the Mongols: Russia, China, and Persia

The Mongol moment in world history represented an enormous cultural encounter between pastoralists and the settled civilizations of Eurasia, such as Russia, China, and Persia. What those civilizations shared was the experience of devastating military defeat. Russian chroniclers, for example, reported mass slaughter of "men, women, and children, monks, nuns and priests" and the violation of "good women and girls in the presence of their mothers and sisters."[7] The sacking of Baghdad in 1258, which put an end to the Islamic Abbasid caliphate, was accompanied by the massacre of more than 200,000 people, according to the Mongol commander himself.

But these encounters varied considerably from place to place. The Mongols occupied and administered China and Persia directly while making use of their established bureaucratic systems. In Russia, however, there were no garrisoned cities, permanently stationed administrators, or Mongol settlers. From the Mongol point of view, Russia as a new and less developed civilization was simply not worth the expense of occupying. They could dominate and exploit Russia while maintaining their preferred pastoral way of life on the nearby steppe lands. This absence of direct rule had implications for the Mongols themselves, for they were far less influenced by or assimilated within Russian culture when compared to their counterparts who conquered China and Persia. But required tribute payments, heavy taxes, and enslavement created a very heavy burden, especially on the Russian peasantry. The city of Moscow, however, benefited as it became the primary collector of tribute for the Mongols. As Mongol domination receded in the fifteenth century, the princes of Moscow used these resources to become the nucleus of a renewed Russian state and later of a huge Russian Empire.

In China, by contrast, the occupying Mongols had turned themselves into a Chinese dynasty, the Yuan, suggesting a new beginning in Chinese history. For many, their conquest of the region had unified a divided China, a treasured ideal among educated Chinese. **Khubilai Khan** (koo-buh-l'eye kahn), the grandson of Chinggis Khan and China's Mongol ruler from 1271 to 1294, sought to rule as a benevolent Confucian-inspired Chinese emperor.

But the Mongols did not become Chinese. Few Mongols learned Chinese, and Mongol law discriminated against the Chinese. In social life, the Mongols forbade intermarriage and prohibited Chinese scholars from learning the Mongol script. Mongol women never adopted foot binding and scandalized the Chinese by mixing freely with men at official gatherings and riding to the hunt with their husbands. And to ordinary Chinese, Mongol rule was often harsh, exploitative, foreign, and resented. Marco Polo, who was in China at the time, reported that some Mongol officials or their intermediaries treated Chinese "just like slaves," demanding bribes for services, ordering arbitrary executions, and seizing women at will—all of which generated outrage and hostility.

But Mongol rule in China was relatively brief, lasting little more than a century. By the mid-fourteenth century, intense factionalism among the Mongols, rapidly rising prices, furious epidemics of the plague, and growing peasant rebellions combined to force the Mongols out of China. By 1368, rebel forces had triumphed, and thousands of Mongols returned to their homeland in the steppes. For several centuries, they remained a periodic threat to China, but during the **Ming dynasty** that followed, the memory of their often brutal and alien rule stimulated a renewed commitment to Confucian values and restrictive gender practices and an effort to wipe out all traces of the Mongols' impact.

Persia's encounter with the Mongols differed from that of China in several ways. The in-migration of pastoral Mongols, together with their immense herds of sheep and goats, turned much agricultural land into pasture and sometimes into desert. As a result, a fragile system of underground water channels that provided irrigation to the fields was neglected, and much good agricultural land was reduced to waste. Furthermore, the Mongols who conquered Persia became Muslims, following the lead of its Mongol ruler Ghazan, who converted to Islam in 1295. No such widespread conversion to the culture of the conquered occurred in China or in Christian Russia. Members of the court and Mongol elites learned at least some Persian, unlike most of their counterparts in China. A number of Mongols also turned to farming, abandoning their pastoral ways, while some married local people.

When the Mongol dynasty in Persia collapsed in the 1330s for lack of a suitable heir, the Mongols were not driven out of Persia as they had been from China. Rather, they and their Turkic allies simply disappeared, assimilated into Persian society. From a Persian point of view, the barbarians had been civilized, and Persians had successfully resisted cultural influence from their uncivilized conquerors.

Khubilai Khan This famous portrait of Khubilai Khan was probably painted by Aniko (1244–1306), a Nepalese artist and architect who designed a number of buildings for China's Mongol ruler. (Science History Images/Alamy)

▲ **AP®**
SOURCING AND SITUATION
Why might Mongol rulers have commissioned artists from among their conquered peoples to paint their portraits?

AP®
COMPARISON
How was Mongol rule in Persia different from that in China? How was it similar?

AP® EXAM TIP
Look for patterns in the decline of empires in world history, such as peasant rebellions, diseases, and a poor economy.

BUILDING AP® SKILLS

Making Connections: Comparison

As in Unit 1, the focused AP® skill for Unit 2 is Comparison. Continue practicing comparison skills with your students by having them create a chart like the one shown below to compare Mongol interactions with the Indigenous Chinese and with the Persians. A reproducible version of this chart is available in the Teacher's Resource Materials. (Answers are provided in italics.)

Chinese	Persians
■ *Mongols did not kill large numbers of Chinese people*	■ *Mongols killed at least 200,000 at sacking of Baghdad*
■ *Taxes were regulated during bad harvests*	■ *Taxes were heavy*
■ *Torture was limited*	■ *Torture was used*
■ *Although animals grazed in cities, there was no widespread destruction of soil*	■ *Mongols pushed peasants off the land, and overgrazing turned agricultural land to desert*
■ *Industry continued*	■ *Wine production increased*
■ *Mongols used the Chinese government bureaucracy but replaced top officials with Mongols or foreign bureaucrats*	■ *Silk production increased and improved*
■ *There was no widespread adoption of Chinese ideology*	■ *The Mongols retained the sophisticated Persian government bureaucracy*
■ *Few Mongols learned Chinese; Chinese were forbidden to learn Mongol script*	■ *Persians adopted Islam*
■ *Intermarriage was forbidden*	■ *Mongols in Persia learned some Persian*
	■ *Some Mongols married Persians*

TRM Handout 3.3: Comparison Chart for Mongol Rule in China and Persia

---

APPLY THE TIP

As students read through the sections on Mongol rule in China, Persia, and Russia, have them create a chart, like the example below, on the reasons for the decline of the Mongols in each of those regions. (Answers provided in italics.)

Mongol Decline in China	Mongol Decline in Persia	Mongol Decline in Russia
■ *Intense factionalism among Mongols*	■ *Lack of a suitable heir*	■ *Divisions among the Mongols*
■ *Rising prices of goods*	■ *Assimilated into Persian society*	■ *Disruptive influence of the plague*
■ *Plague epidemics*		■ *Growing strength of Russian state, centered in Moscow*
■ *Growing peasant rebellions*		

AP® CLASSROOM

AP® Topic Questions

Assign students the Topic Questions for Topic 2.2: The Mongol Empire and the Making of the Modern World. This is a set of three multiple-choice questions on the Mongols and will provide a good opportunity for students to practice test-taking skills. The questions can be found in your AP® Classroom account under Unit 2 resources.

The Mongols and Islam in Persia This image from the first half of the fourteenth century depicts a Mongol prince studying the Quran in what is likely a mosque tent. The arch at the left marks the *mihrab*, which points toward Mecca and indicates the direction that worshippers should face during ritual prayers. Above it is an inscription reading "Allah is the Ruler." The conversion of the Mongols in Persia to Islam was a crucial development in their rule over the region. (bpk Bildagentur/Staatsbibliothek zu Berlin, Stiftung Preussicher Kulturbesitz/Photo: Ellwardt/Art Resource, NY)

▲ **AP®**

CLAIMS AND EVIDENCE IN SOURCES
Based on your knowledge of world history and the evidence in this image, compare how the Mongols adopted local customs to govern in China and Persia.

AP®

CAUSATION
How did the Mongol Empire lead to cross-cultural interactions?

The Mongol Empire as a Eurasian Network

Beyond these particular encounters, the Mongol Empire, during the thirteenth and fourteenth centuries, brought all of these regions into a single interacting network, enabling the circulation of goods, information, disease, and styles of warfare all across Eurasia. Economically, the Mongols themselves did not produce much of value for distant markets, nor were they active traders. Nonetheless, they consistently promoted international commerce, largely so that they could tax it and thus extract wealth from more developed civilizations. In providing a relatively secure environment for merchants making the long and arduous journey across Central Asia between Europe and China, the Mongol Empire brought the two ends of the Eurasian world into closer contact than ever before and launched a new phase in the history of the Silk Roads. Marco Polo was only the most famous of many European merchants, mostly from Italian cities, who traveled along the Silk Roads to Mongol-controlled China. They returned with tales of rich lands and prosperous commercial opportunities, but what they described were long-established trading networks of which Europeans had been largely ignorant. Furthermore, China was then the fulcrum of a vast system, connecting the overland route through the Mongol Empire with the oceanic routes through the South China Sea and Indian Ocean (see Map 3.3).

The Mongol Empire also prompted diplomatic relationships from one end of Eurasia to the other. Fearful of Mongol intentions, both the pope and European rulers dispatched delegations to the Mongol capital, mostly led by Franciscan friars. They hoped to learn something about Mongol intentions, to secure Mongol aid in the Christian crusade against Islam, and, if possible, to convert Mongols to Christianity. Within the Mongol Empire itself, close relationships developed between the courts of Persia and China. They regularly exchanged ambassadors, shared intelligence information, fostered trade between their regions, and sent skilled workers back and forth. Thus, more than ever before, political authorities all across Eurasia engaged in diplomatic relationships with one another.

Accompanying these transcontinental economic and political relationships was a substantial exchange of peoples and cultures. Mongol policy forcibly transferred many thousands of skilled craftsmen and educated people from their homelands to distant parts of the empire, while the Mongols' religious tolerance and support of merchants drew missionaries and traders from afar. The Mongol capital at Karakorum was a cosmopolitan city with places of worship for Buddhists, Daoists, Muslims, and Christians. Chinggis Khan and several other Mongol rulers married Christian women. Actors and musicians from China, wrestlers from Persia, and a

MAPPING HISTORY　Map 3.3 **Trade and Disease in the Fourteenth Century**

The Mongol Empire played a major role in the commercial integration of the Eurasian world as well as in the spread of the plague across this vast area.

Reading the Map: Which circuits of trade played the greatest role in the spread of the plague?

AP **Making Connections:** What does the map suggest about the regions—temperate, tropical (along the equator), subarctic—in which the plague spread most widely?

jester from Byzantium provided entertainment for the Mongol court. Persian and Arab doctors and administrators were sent to China, while Chinese physicians and engineers found their skills in demand in the Islamic world.

This movement of people facilitated the exchange of ideas and techniques, a process actively encouraged by Mongol authorities. A great deal of Chinese technology and artistic conventions—such as painting, printing, gunpowder weapons, compass navigation, high-temperature furnaces, and medical techniques—flowed westward. Muslim astronomers brought their skills and knowledge to China because Mongol authorities wanted "second opinions on the reading of heavenly signs and portents" and assistance in constructing accurate calendars.[8] Plants and crops likewise circulated within the Mongol domain. Lemons and carrots from the Middle East found a welcome reception

AP **EXAM TIP**

Religious tolerance was one of the Mongols' practical approaches to statecraft. Consider how religious tolerance could help any empire govern a foreign population.

EXPLORING AP® THEMES

Economic Systems (ECN)

Ask students to consider the many items that would have traversed the Silk Roads, and then identify the top three items in order of importance in terms of their impact on the world's population. Students should be able to explain why they chose these items. *Items that had the greatest impact on the world's population included ideas (ideologies, numerals, scientific method), commodities (silk, spices, porcelain), diseases (plague), and people (voluntary and involuntary migration).*

APPLY THE TIP

Students sometimes have a difficult time recognizing that any method a government uses for control is political. The Mongol's use of religious tolerance was useful to help them govern a large foreign population. Ask the following questions:

■ If a government uses religion to control its people, is that political or religious control? *Any method the government uses for control, including religion, is considered political control.*

■ In what way was China's "Mandate of Heaven" an unusual form of political control? *The Mandate of Heaven was unusual because even though the emperor was seen as quasi-divine (the Son of Heaven), if his rule was judged to be poor or he was weak and came to be overthrown, it was understood that he no longer held the Mandate of Heaven and a new dynasty was accepted.*

■ How could religious tolerance help an empire legitimize and maintain its boundaries? *Religious tolerance would allow the conquered to feel that they were accepted, and the resulting lack of protest against the conquerors would promote the idea of legitimacy.*

EXPLORING AP® THEMES

Social Interactions and Organization (SIO)

Students have a difficult time understanding that cultures and social hierarchies are different themes. They often want to lump everything under an umbrella of culture. Use the image on page 148 to start a discussion on how Mongol women were treated differently than women in other societies. You should point out that patriarchy was well established in most of the other postclassical societies and that Mongol women had more responsibilities and privileges than women in sedentary societies. Mongol women were in charge of everything while the men were away conquering territory.

APPLY THE TIP

Ask students to combine their notes on the various regions of Mongol conquest into a single thematic chart like the one shown in **Handout 3.4: Thematic Chart for the Mongol Conquest**. If you are short on time, consider dividing the class into small groups and have each group be responsible for one section of the thematic chart. Students can then share the information gathered with a gallery walk.

TRM Handout 3.4: Thematic Chart for the Mongol Conquest

▶ **AP**
COMPARISON
How were the roles of Mongol women as shown in this image different from the roles of women in most other settled societies during this era? What accounts for the differences?

Mongol Rulers and Their Women The wives of Mongol rulers exercised considerable influence at court. This fourteenth-century painting shows Chinggis Khan's fourth son, Tului, the ruler of the Mongol heartland after his father's death, with his Christian wife Sorgaqtani. After her husband's early death from alcoholism, she maneuvered her children, including Khubilai Khan, into powerful positions and strongly encouraged them in the direction of religious toleration. (akg-images)

AP **EXAM TIP**
You should know the economic and political impact of the Mongols as well as the cultural and technological transfers they initiated.

in China, while the Mongol ruler of Persia, Ghazan, sent envoys to India, China, and elsewhere to seek "seeds of things which are unique in that land."[9]

Europeans arguably gained more than most from these exchanges, for they had long been cut off from the fruitful interchange with Asia, and in comparison to the Islamic and Chinese worlds, they were less technologically developed. Now they could reap the benefits of new technology, new crops, and new knowledge of a wider world without having suffered the devastating consequences of Mongol conquest. In these circumstances, some historians have argued, lay the roots of Europe's remarkable rise to global prominence in the centuries that followed.

The Plague: An Afro-Eurasian Pandemic

Any benefits derived from participation in Mongol networks of communication and exchange must be measured alongside the hemispheric catastrophe known as the "plague" or the "pestilence" and later called the **Black Death**. Originating most likely in China, the bacteria responsible for the disease, known as *Yersinia pestis*, spread across the trade routes of the vast Mongol Empire in the early fourteenth century (see Map 3.3, page 147). Carried by rodents and transmitted by fleas to humans, the plague erupted initially in 1331 in modern northeastern China and had reached the Middle East and Western Europe by 1347. Some genetic evidence suggests that it penetrated sub-Saharan Africa as well.

In the densely populated civilizations of China, the Islamic world, and Europe, as well as in the steppe lands of the pastoralists, the plague claimed enormous numbers of human victims, causing a sharp contraction in Eurasian population for a century or more. A fifteenth-century Egyptian historian reported that within a month of the plague's arrival in 1349, "Cairo had become an abandoned desert. . . . Everywhere one heard lamentations and one could not pass by any house without being overwhelmed by the howling."[10] Other contemporary chroniclers reported death rates that ranged from 50 to 90 percent of the affected population, depending on the time and place. While no modern estimates exist for China, recent scholarship suggests that by the early fifteenth century the Middle East generally had lost perhaps one-third of its population and by the 1370s Europe's population had declined by half.[11]

In those places where it struck hardest, the plague left thoughtful people grasping for language with which to describe a horror of such unprecedented dimensions. One Italian man, who had buried all five of his children with his own hands, wrote in 1348 that "so many have died that everyone believes it is the end of the world."[12] In the Islamic world, the famous historian Ibn Khaldun declared that the plague "devastated nations and caused populations to vanish. It swallowed up many of the good things of civilization and wiped them out."[13]

The plague also had larger consequences. Ironically, that human disaster, born of the Mongol network, was a primary reason for the demise of that network in the fourteenth and fifteenth centuries. Population contracted, cities declined, and the volume of trade diminished all across the Mongol world. By 1350, the Mongol Empire itself was in disarray, and within a century the Mongols had lost control of Chinese, Persian, and Russian civilizations. The Central Asian trade route, so critical to the entire Afro-Eurasian world economy, largely closed. The Mongol moment in world history was over.

This disruption of the Mongol-based land routes to the East, coupled with a desire to avoid Muslim intermediaries, provided incentives for Europeans to take to the sea in their continuing efforts to reach the riches of Asia. Their naval technology gave them military advantages on the seas, much as the Mongols' skill with the bow and their mobility on horseback gave these pastoralists a decisive edge in land battles. As Europeans penetrated Asian and Atlantic waters in the sixteenth century, they took on, in some ways, the role of the Mongols in organizing and fostering world trade and in creating a network of communication and exchange over an

AP® EXAM TIP

You need to know the long-term demographic (population), economic, and political effects of the bubonic plague on Afro-Eurasia.

▼AP®

CAUSATION
Based on your knowledge of world history and the evidence in this image, what were the social effects of the plague in Western Europe?

The Plague Produced just a few years after the event, this image from a medical text depicts the townspeople of Tournai in modern Belgium burying their dead during an outbreak of the plague in 1349. Cities often resorted to mass graves as the numbers of dead mounted. (Bibliothèque Royale de Belgique, Brussels, Belgium/Bridgeman Images)

APPLY THE TIP

Ask students to create a chart, similar to the one below, examining the demographic, economic, and political effects of the Black Death on Afro-Eurasia. A reproducible version of this chart is available in the Teacher's Resource Materials. (Suggested answers in italics.)

Demographic Effects	Economic Effects	Political Effects
■ *50% to 90% of Eurasia died from the plague* ■ *The Middle East lost about one-third of its population by the early fifteenth century* ■ *Europe may have lost about 50% of its population during the initial outbreak of the plague*	■ *Europe saw labor shortages after the plague* ■ *Labor shortage in Europe led workers to seek higher wages and gave women more employment opportunities* ■ *Trade diminished in the Mongol world* ■ *The Central Asian trade route was mostly closed due to the plague*	■ *Helped lead to the end of feudalism in Western Europe* ■ *A series of peasant revolts broke out in Western Europe due to issues with the labor shortage* ■ *Mongols lost control of China, Persia, and Russia by the fifteenth century* ■ *Sparked European voyages of exploration for trade routes to Asia, which led to future European colonization*

TRM **Handout 3.5: Causation Chart for the Black Death**

CHAPTER 3

even larger area. Like the Mongols, Europeans were people on the periphery of the major established civilizations; they too were economically less developed in comparison to Chinese and Islamic civilizations. Both Mongols and Europeans forcibly plundered the wealthier civilizations they encountered, and European empire building in the Americas, like that of the Mongols in Eurasia, brought devastating disease and catastrophic population decline in its wake.[14] Europeans, of course, brought far more of their own culture and many more of their own people to the societies they conquered, as Christianity, European languages, settler societies, and Western science and technology took root within their empires. Although their imperial presence lasted far longer and operated on a much larger scale, European actions at the beginning of their global expansion bore some resemblance to those of their Mongol predecessors. Perhaps they were, as one historian put it, "the Mongols of the seas."[15]

Connections across the Indian Ocean: The Sea Roads

Finding the Main Point: In what ways did the Sea Roads network generate political, economic, and cultural changes in the region?

If the Silk Roads linked Eurasian societies by land, sea-based trade routes likewise connected distant peoples all across the Indian Ocean basin and the South China Sea. Until the creation of a genuinely global oceanic system of trade after 1500, the Indian Ocean represented the world's largest sea-based network of communication and exchange, stretching from southern China to eastern Africa (see Map 3.4).

The Making of the Sea Roads

Like the Silk Roads, these transoceanic trade routes—the **Sea Roads**—grew out of the environmental and cultural diversities of the region. The desire for various goods not available at home—such as porcelain from China, spices from the islands of Southeast Asia (present-day Indonesia), cotton goods and pepper from India, ivory and gold from the East African coast, incense from southern Arabia—provided incentives for Indian Ocean commerce. Transportation costs were lower on the Sea Roads than on the Silk Roads because ships could accommodate larger and heavier cargoes than camels. Thus the Sea Roads eventually carried more bulk goods and products destined for a mass market—textiles, pepper, timber, rice, sugar, wheat—than the Silk Roads, which were limited largely to luxury goods for the few.

What made Indian Ocean commerce possible was the monsoons, alternating wind currents that blew predictably northeast during the summer months and southwest during the winter (see Map 3.4). By the early centuries of the Common Era, an understanding of monsoons and a gradually accumulating technology of shipbuilding and oceanic navigation enabled the construction of "an interlocked human world joined by the common highway of the Indian Ocean."[16]

This network of exchange drew on the ingenuity of many peoples—Chinese, Malays, Indians, Arabs, Persians, Swahilis, and others. Various technological innovations

---

In the episode *International Commerce, Snorkeling Camels, and the Indian Ocean Trade* of Crash Course World History, John Green teaches the history of Indian Ocean trade. He includes a tale of swashbuckling adventure, along with information on advancements in seafaring technology and how the monsoon winds work. Watch the video on YouTube. After showing the video, ask students the following questions:

▪ How did the Mongols contribute to the decline of trading by sea? *With the pax Mongolica, the Mongols kept the Silk Roads safe. This safety made land trade more desirable.*

▪ What made Muslim merchants successful enough to be key players in Indian Ocean trading? *Muslim merchants had the money to build ships. Shipping allowed merchants to trade bulk items produced for a mass market.*

▪ Why isn't trade the best strategy for building an empire? How can it lead to the downfall of a city-state? *Reliance on trade can bring wealth, but it can also bring about decline if other cities offer lower taxes or other more desirable features and people decide to move.*

Divide students up into small groups (no more than three or four) or have them work on their own to complete this activity. Give students the following list of technological developments that facilitated Indian Ocean trade to create a short slideshow presentation or poster on the technologies. The presentation or poster should focus on explaining what each of the technologies did, explain how they aided Indian Ocean trade, and include a picture of the technology.

Technological developments: compass, astrolabe, dhow, junk, lateen sail, use of monsoon winds

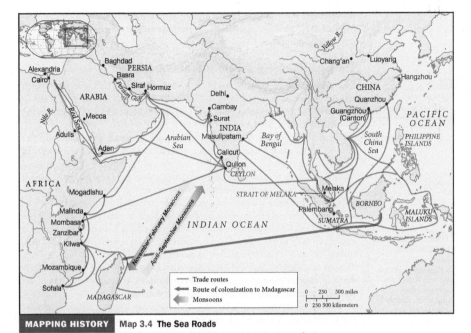

MAPPING HISTORY   Map 3.4 **The Sea Roads**

Paralleling the Silk Road trading network, a sea-based commerce in the Indian Ocean basin connected the many peoples between China and East Africa.

Reading the Map: If a captain wanted to sail from Malindi on the east coast of Africa to Calicut in southern India, what months in the monsoon season would give favorable winds?

AP **Making Connections:** Compare this map with Map 3.1: The Silk Roads. Where do the Silk and Sea roads intersect? What different geographical obstacles might travelers or traders confront on these two routes?

also facilitated Indian Ocean trade—improvements in sails, new kinds of ships such as Chinese *junks* and Indian or Arab *dhows*, new means of calculating latitude such as the astrolabe, and evolving versions of the magnetic needle or compass. In the centuries following 1000, China's remarkable economic growth further stimulated Indian Ocean commerce. A massive outflow of Chinese products entered the circuits of Indian Ocean trade, even as the thriving Chinese economy attracted goods from India and Southeast Asia.

Also enabling the Sea Roads network was the spread of Islam, a religion distinctly friendly to trade and traders. After all, the Prophet Muhammad himself had been a merchant. The creation of an Islamic Arab Empire, stretching from the Atlantic Ocean through the Mediterranean basin and all the way to India, provided a vast arena for the energies of Muslim traders. And widespread conversion to Islam

BUILDING AP® SKILLS

Contextualization

Show students Map 3.4, "The Sea Roads." Ask: Where might piracy be a problem? With reference to the map, where might you choose to operate if you were a pirate? *The islands of Indonesia provided a good location for piracy because of the narrow passages between them. The Strait of Melaka funneled merchant vessels into confined shipping lanes. The region also had the advantage of lying between India and China, two major trading regions in the network. The Persian Gulf and Red Sea, where shipping was relatively constrained and therefore vulnerable, also provided good locations for piracy.*

BUILDING AP® SKILLS

Making Connections: Causation

Ask students what they remember about monsoon winds from World Geography. Fill in any blanks in their memory, and then ask the class to make a list of the effects of the monsoon winds on trade in the Indian Ocean.

■ *The spread of goods, ideas, and technology occurred much faster than it did on the Silk Roads because there were more interconnections between more people on the Indian ocean routes. The predictable monsoon winds made this travel possible.*

created an element of trust among culturally different merchants. All of this contributed to "a maritime Silk Road . . . a commercial and informational network of unparalleled proportions."[17]

The Sea Roads as a Catalyst for Change

COMPARISON
To what extent did the Silk Roads and the Sea Roads operate in a similar fashion? How did they differ?

Like the Silk Roads, the commercial network of the Indian Ocean region fostered substantial change, both politically and culturally. Chapter 2 highlighted the rise of new states and civilizations in both Southeast Asia and East Africa as commerce and state building went hand in hand. Ambitious rulers used the wealth derived from commerce to construct larger and more centrally governed states or cities. (See Chapter 2.) Yet another example of this process lay in southeastern Africa, where the impact of Indian Ocean trade extended well into the African interior, though Islam did not. Hundreds of miles inland, between the Zambezi and Limpopo rivers, lay rich sources of gold, much in demand on the Swahili coast. The emergence of a powerful state, known as **Great Zimbabwe**, seems clearly connected to the growing trade in gold to the coast and to the wealth from its large herds of cattle. At its peak between 1250 and 1350, Great Zimbabwe had the resources and the labor power to construct huge stone enclosures entirely without mortar, with walls sixteen feet thick and thirty-two feet tall. "[It] must have been an astonishing sight," writes a recent historian, "for the subordinate chiefs and kings who would have come there to seek favors at court."[18] Here in the interior of southeastern Africa lay yet another example of the reach and transforming power of Indian Ocean commerce.

ARGUMENTATION
Based on the evidence in this map, why might the cities from Kilwa to Mogadishu have developed an Islamic culture while Great Zimbabwe did not?

Indian Ocean voyaging also had an ecological impact in Africa because it enabled the spread of the banana, which was originally domesticated in Southeast Asia. Just when and how the banana reached Africa is unclear. Many scholars have credited its spread to Malagasy-speaking sailors from Indonesia who crossed the Indian Ocean and arrived with the banana on the island of Madagascar or the East African coast in the early centuries of the Common Era. From there, banana production spread inland, where it enhanced agricultural productivity, enabled population growth, and laid the economic foundation for the growth of chiefdoms and states in various parts of the continent. For example, during the fifteenth through the seventeenth centuries the extensive cultivation of bananas supported the rise of the powerful kingdoms of Bunyoro and Buganda in the interior of East Africa.

East African States, ca. 1250–1450

The Sea Roads commercial network also catalyzed profound cultural changes. Proximity to China ensured that Vietnam was heavily influenced by Chinese cultural traditions, particularly at the level of elite culture. More broadly in Southeast Asia, it was Indian cultural traditions that accompanied the growth of seaborne trade. Indian alphabets such as Sanskrit and Pallava were used to write a number of Southeast Asian languages. Indian artistic forms provided models for Southeast Asian sculpture and architecture, while the Indian epic *Ramayana* became widely popular across the region. Both Hinduism and Buddhism took hold across Southeast Asia, as described in Chapter 2.

This extensive Indian influence in Southeast Asia has led some scholars to speak of the "Indianization" of the region, but this cultural change was not imposed from outside. Rather, it was a matter of voluntary borrowing by independent societies that found Indian traditions and practices useful and that were free to adapt those ideas to their own needs and cultures. Traditional religious practices mixed with the imported faiths or existed alongside them with little conflict. And much that was distinctively Southeast Asian persisted despite influences from afar. In family life, for example, most Southeast Asian societies traced an individual's ancestry from both the mother's and father's line, in contrast to India and China, where patrilineal descent was practiced. Furthermore, Southeast Asian women had fewer restrictions and a greater role in public life than women in the more patriarchal civilizations of China and India. They were generally able to own property together with their husbands and to initiate divorce. A Chinese visitor to Angkor observed, "The local people who know how to trade are all women."[19] Women in Angkor also served as gladiators, warriors, members of the palace staff, and as poets, artists, and religious teachers.

An Arab Dhow Painted by the thirteenth-century Arab artist Al-Wasiti, this image shows an oceangoing vessel of Indian or Arab origin known as a *dhow*, which was central to the commerce of the Sea Roads. In use in the Red Sea and Indian Ocean since at least the early centuries of the Common Era, dhows used triangular sails and were constructed without nails by sewing or stitching the boards of the hull together with fibers, cords, or thongs. (Pictures from History/Bridgeman Images)

▲ **AP®**

CAUSATION
How could technological developments, such as this dhow ship, help transform the culture of the Indian Ocean region?

Islam too rode the commercial currents of the Indian Ocean, drawing many Southeast Asian peoples into the wider world of Islam by 1400. By embracing the new religion, rulers of Southeast Asian states hoped to attract Muslim traders from Persia, Arabia, and India. Frequently, Islam blended easily with Hindu, Buddhist, or traditional shamanistic practices.

The city of **Melaka**, located on the southeastern edge of the Malay Peninsula, illustrates the growing role of Islam in Southeast Asia, the connection between commerce and state building, and the cosmopolitan quality of the Indian Ocean network (see Map 3.5). Established in the early fourteenth century by a prince from neighboring Sumatra, it was quickly transformed from a small fishing village to a major port city that became the capital of a Malay Muslim sultanate until it was conquered by the Portuguese in 1511. Its strategic location on the Strait of Melaka gave it a central role in the trade of the entire Indian Ocean basin.

By the later fifteenth century, Melaka had a population of perhaps 100,000 people and was thus the largest city in Southeast Asia. Attracted by the city's stable government, low customs duties, and openness to all merchants, some 15,000 foreign merchants established themselves in Melaka, speaking dozens of languages and hailing from China, Japan, Java, Vietnam, India, the Philippine Islands, Egypt, East Africa, and elsewhere. Many of these diasporic communities had their own neighborhoods in the city. The sultan of Melaka appointed four merchants from the major settlements to oversee the trade, resolve disputes, and act as intermediaries between his government and the foreign merchant communities. Some of these merchants also served as officials in the sultan's government.

EXPLORING AP® THEMES

Humans and the Environment (ENV)

Have students look at Map 3.4 on page 151. Ask students the following questions:

■ What are important geographic features in Southeast Asia? *The Strait of Melaka and the South China Sea.*

■ Why are these geographic features significant? *These geographic features are significant because whoever controls these areas has the potential to control trade throughout the region, thereby gaining wealth and power.*

AP® CLASSROOM

AP® Daily Video

Assign students the Topic 2.3 Daily Video, which examines trade patterns in the Indian Ocean. The lesson will also highlight the comparison between the Indian Ocean and the Silk Roads. The video can be found in your AP® Classroom account under Unit 2 resources.

Map 3.5 Asia in the Fifteenth Century: Ming Maritime Voyages
The fifteenth century in Asia witnessed the massive Ming dynasty voyages into the Indian Ocean, the last major eruption of pastoral power in Timur's empire, and the flourishing of the maritime city of Melaka.

▲ AP

CLAIMS AND EVIDENCE IN SOURCES
What factors would have encouraged Ming expeditions to the port cities on this map?

AP EXAM TIP
Compare the discoveries and transfers of knowledge of Zheng He's expeditions with those of European expeditions in the fifteenth century.

A Portuguese visitor in 1512 described Melaka as "a city that was made for merchandise, fitter than any other in the world. Commerce between different nations for a thousand leagues on every hand must come to Melaka."[20] No wonder some have called Melaka one the world's first globalized cities. Its many shops sold books from the Islamic Middle East, textiles from India, spices from the Spice Islands, carpets from Java, silk and porcelain from China, sugar from the Philippines, and more. Gold was so readily available, it was said, that children used it in their games. During the fifteenth century, this commercial city created a loose imperial control over neighboring regions of coastal Malaya and eastern Sumatra. Melaka also fostered a distinctive Malay ethnic identity, for it was during the fifteenth century that the people of the city began referring to themselves as Malay.

The rise of Melaka as a commercial city owed much to its relationship with China, the major economic and political power in the region. Melaka sent tribute missions to China, where its envoys received "seals . . . and suits of colored silk," and Melaka served as a base for Chinese naval expeditions into the Indian Ocean world. Many Chinese trading ships anchored in the city's harbor every year. Particularly profitable for merchants of Melaka was pepper. Grown in Sumatra and southern Thailand, much of it passed through

---

BUILDING AP® SKILLS

Claims and Evidence in Sources

To help students practice their primary source analysis and gain a new perspective on the voyages of Zheng He, ask them to analyze and discuss "Working with Evidence, Document 4: A Chinese Maritime Explorer in India," located on page 182. In this document, students will read about Zheng He's voyages and the places Zheng He visited around the Indian Ocean basin from the perspective of Ma Huan, who sailed with Zheng He. Use the questions that accompany the passage to guide a class discussion, or assign them as homework.

AP® CLASSROOM

AP® Topic Question

To wrap up looking at the Indian Ocean trade, have students write a response to the SAQ titled "Abd-al-Razzak Samarqandi Travel Embassy" found in the Topic Questions for Unit 2 in AP® Classroom. This will provide students with practice writing an SAQ response with a stimulus. Make certain that you time this assignment so students can practice writing within the time framework of the AP® Exam.

Melaka on its way to China, where it was in great demand and could be sold for three times what it cost in Melaka.

Melaka also became a springboard for the spread of Islam throughout the region. In the eclectic style of Southeast Asian religious history, the Islam of Melaka demonstrated much blending with local, as well as Hindu and Buddhist, traditions, while the city itself, like many port towns, had a reputation for "rough behavior." An Arab Muslim pilot in the 1480s commented critically: "They have no culture at all. . . . You do not know whether they are Muslim or not."[21] Nonetheless, Melaka became a center for Islamic learning, and students from elsewhere in Southeast Asia were studying there in the fifteenth century.

Melaka's experience was part of an expansion of Islam that gave rise to an international maritime culture by 1200, shared by individuals living in the widely separated port cities around the Indian Ocean. The attractiveness of the faith and the immense prestige, power, and prosperity of the Islamic world stimulated widespread conversion, which in turn facilitated commercial transactions. Even those who did not convert to Islam, such as Buddhist rulers in Burma, nonetheless regarded it as commercially useful to assume Muslim names. After 1200, the culture of this sea-based network of exchange was increasingly Islamic.

Chinese Maritime Voyages in the Indian Ocean World

Nothing more effectively illustrates the connections operating in the Indian Ocean basin than a series of massive Chinese maritime expeditions that took place during the early fifteenth century. Since about 1000 C.E., Chinese sailors and traders had been a major presence in the South China Sea and in Southeast Asian port cities, with much of this activity in private hands. But then, after decades of preparation, an enormous fleet, commissioned by the Chinese emperor Yongle of the Ming dynasty, was launched in 1405, followed over the next twenty-eight years by six more such expeditions. On board more than 300 ships of the first voyage was a crew of some 27,000, including 180 physicians, hundreds of government officials, 5 astrologers, 7 high-ranking or grand eunuchs, carpenters, tailors, accountants, merchants, translators, cooks, and thousands of soldiers and sailors. Visiting many ports in Southeast Asia, Indonesia, India, Arabia, and East Africa, these fleets, captained by the Muslim eunuch **Zheng He** (JUHNG-huh), sought to enroll distant peoples and states in the Chinese tribute system (see Map 3.5 and AP® Working with Evidence, Document 4). Dozens of rulers accompanied the fleets back to China, where they presented tribute, performed the required rituals of submission, and received in return abundant gifts, titles, and trading opportunities. Officially described as "bringing order to the world," Zheng He's expeditions established Chinese power and prestige in the Indian Ocean and exerted Chinese control over foreign trade in the region. The Chinese, however, did not seek to conquer new territories, establish Chinese settlements, or spread their culture, though they did intervene in a number of local disputes.

The most surprising feature of these voyages was how abruptly and deliberately they were ended. After 1433, Chinese authorities simply stopped such expeditions and allowed this enormous and expensive fleet to deteriorate in port. "In less than a hundred years," wrote a recent historian of these voyages, "the greatest navy the world had ever known had ordered itself into extinction."[22]

Part of the reason involved the death of the emperor Yongle, who had been the chief patron of the enterprise. Many high-ranking officials had long seen the expeditions as a waste of resources because China, they believed, was the self-sufficient "middle kingdom," the center of the civilized world, requiring little from beyond its borders. Chinese were very much aware of their own antiquity, believed strongly in the absolute superiority of their culture, and felt with good reason that, should they desire something from abroad, others would bring it to them. In their eyes, the real danger to China came from the north, where nomadic people, whom the Chinese called "barbarians," constantly threatened. Finally, they viewed the voyages as the project of the court eunuchs, whom these officials despised.

Even as these voices of Chinese officialdom prevailed, private Chinese merchants and craftsmen continued to settle and trade in Japan, the Philippines, Taiwan, and Southeast Asia, but they did so without the support of their government. The Chinese state quite deliberately turned its back on what was surely within its reach—a large-scale maritime empire in the Indian Ocean basin.

The consequences of this action were important. Since the voyages led to no lasting outcome, they were long neglected in China's historical memory, revived only in the early twenty-first century in the context of China's reentry on the global stage. At the time, however, the Chinese withdrawal from the Indian Ocean actually facilitated the European entry. It cleared the way for the Portuguese to penetrate the region, where they faced only the eventual naval power of the Ottoman Empire. Had Vasco da Gama encountered Zheng He's massive fleet as his four small ships sailed into Asian waters in 1498, world history may well have taken a different turn.

Connections across the Sahara: The Sand Roads

Finding the Main Point: How did the Sand Roads contribute to the spread of Islam in West Africa?

AP CONTINUITY AND CHANGE
What changes did trans-Saharan trade bring to West Africa?

In addition to the Silk Roads and the Sea Roads, another important pattern of long-distance trade—this one across the vast reaches of the Sahara in a series of **Sand Roads**—linked North Africa and the Mediterranean world with the land and peoples of interior West Africa (see Map 2.5, page 90). Like the others, these Sand Road commercial networks had a transforming impact, stimulating and enriching West African civilization well before the European slave system linked West Africa to a larger Atlantic network of exchange.

The Making of the Sand Roads

Trans-African trade, like the commerce of the Silk Roads and the Sea Roads, was rooted in environmental variation. The North African coastal regions, long part of Roman or later Arab empires, generated cloth, glassware, weapons, books, and other manufactured goods. The great Sahara held deposits of copper and especially salt, and its oases produced sweet and nutritious dates. While the sparse populations of

AP® CLASSROOM
AP® Daily Video

Assign students the Topic 2.4 Daily Video 1, which will examine the ways that empires and new technology furthered the expansion of trade along the trans-Saharan trade routes. This video will also focus on the skill of identifying a historical process.

AP® CLASSROOM
AP® Daily Video

Continue with Topic 2.4 by assigning the Daily Video 2. This video uses the knowledge of the trans-Saharan trade routes gained in Video 1 to focus on the skill of describing a historical process.

the desert were largely pastoral and nomadic, farther south lived agricultural peoples who grew a variety of crops, produced their own textiles and metal products, and mined a considerable amount of gold. These agricultural regions of sub-Saharan Africa are normally divided into two ecological zones: the savanna grasslands immediately south of the Sahara, which produced grain crops such as millet and sorghum, and the forest areas farther south, where root and tree crops such as yams and kola nuts predominated. These varied environments provided the economic incentive for the exchange of goods.

A major turning point in African commercial life occurred with the introduction of the **Arabian camel** to North Africa and the Sahara in the early centuries of the Common Era. This remarkable animal, which could go for ten days without water, finally made possible the long trek across the Sahara. Camel-owning dwellers of desert oases initiated regular trans-Saharan commerce by 300 to 400 C.E. Several centuries later, North African Arabs, now bearing the new religion of Islam, also organized caravans across the desert.

What these Arab merchants sought, above all else, was gold, which was found in some abundance in the border areas straddling the grasslands and the forests of West Africa. African ivory, kola nuts, and enslaved people were likewise in considerable demand in the desert, the Mediterranean basin, and beyond. In return, the peoples of West African civilization south of the desert received horses, cloth, dates, various manufactured goods, and especially salt from the rich deposits in the Sahara.

Thus the Sahara was no longer simply a barrier to commerce and cross-cultural interaction; for a thousand years, it was a major international trade route that fostered new relationships among distant peoples. As in Southeast Asia and East Africa, this trans-Saharan trade provided both incentives and resources for building new and larger political structures. The West African peoples living in the savannah grasslands between the forests and the desert were in the best position to take advantage of these new opportunities. The result was the sophisticated West African civilizations described in Chapter 2.

Islam in West Africa

As in East Africa, Islam accompanied trade and after 1000 became an important element in the urban culture of West Africa. Its gradual acceptance was largely peaceful and voluntary, lacking the incentives associated elsewhere with foreign conquest. For African merchant communities, Islam provided an

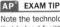

AP EXAM TIP

Note the technologies that helped facilitate trade across the Sahara Desert.

AP EXAM TIP

Understand the significance of the introduction of the camel into Africa from Southwest Asia.

The Arabian Camel From 500 to 1500, the camel was the chief means of transportation between the interior of West Africa and the Mediterranean region. This image, derived from an Arab painting created about 1240, also illustrates the distinctive saddle that enabled the camel to carry heavy loads. The commerce that camels facilitated stimulated the construction of states and empires in West Africa even as it introduced Islam to the region. (BnF, Dist. RMN – Grand Palais/Art Resource, NY)

APPLY THE TIP

Ask students: What was the significance of the introduction of the camel into Africa? *Camels can go without water for almost two weeks and can carry very large loads. They provide milk, meat, and hides for clothing and shelter. Camels therefore supported a population in the Sahara and allowed it to develop trans-Saharan commerce.*

BUILDING AP® SKILLS

Claims and Evidence in Sources

This is a good time to use "Working with Evidence, Document 5: A Moroccan Diplomat in West Africa," on page 183. Base a class discussion on the Question to Consider, or you can assign it as homework.

TEACHING IDEA

Incorporating Outside Resources

In the episode *Mansa Musa and Islam in Africa* of Crash Course World History, John Green teaches about sub-Saharan Africa. In addition to Mansa Musa and his empire of Mali, topics covered include trade, conversion to Islam, visits from Ibn Battuta, architecture, the empire of Ghana, and the East African city-states. You can find the video on YouTube. After showing the video, ask the following questions:

■ What problems did Mansa Musa cause in the places he traveled? *He spread so much gold around that it was devalued for decades, harming the economy.*

■ How did the empires of West Africa convert to Islam? *They came into contact with the Berbers of North Africa, who were early converts to Islam.*

■ What do the writings of Ibn Battuta tell us about cross-cultural interactions and how culture and religion become transformed when brought to new places? *As Islam spread to new areas, it absorbed many of the local cultural traditions.*

■ What linked the peoples of East Africa? *Islam and trade linked the peoples of East Africa.*

TEACHING IDEA

Class Discussion

West African kingdoms, such as Ghana and Mali, gained great wealth and influence due to their location along the trans-Saharan trade network. This wealth and influence also drew in Muslim merchants, leading to the expansion of Islam into the kingdom of Mali. To show students the wealth and influence enjoyed by Mali, ask them to read "Zooming In: Mansa Musa, West African Monarch and Muslim Pilgrim." Use the questions at the end of the Zooming In to guide a discussion on the significance of Mansa Musa's pilgrimage.

ZOOMING **Mansa Musa, West African Monarch and Muslim Pilgrim**

Mansa Musa.

In 1324, Mansa Musa, the ruler or *mansa* of the Kingdom of Mali, set out on an arduous journey from his West African homeland to the holy city of Mecca. His kingdom stretched from the Atlantic coast a thousand miles or more to the fabled inland city of Timbuktu and beyond, and his pilgrimage to Mecca reflected the growing penetration of Islam in this emerging West African civilization. Mansa Musa was a pious Muslim, fluent in Arabic, an avid builder of mosques, and on occasion he freed a few of the enslaved people in his kingdom.

In the fourteenth century, Mali was an expanding empire. According to Musa, one of his immediate predecessors had launched a substantial maritime expedition into "the furthest limits of the Atlantic Ocean." The voyagers never returned, and no other record of the expedition exists, but it is intriguing to consider that Africans and Europeans alike may have been exploring the Atlantic at roughly the same time. Mansa Musa, however, was more inclined to expand on land as he sought access to the goldfields to the south and the trans-Saharan trade network to the north. Control of this lucrative commercial complex enriched Mansa Musa's empire, enabled a major building program of mosques and palaces, and turned the city of Timbuktu into a thriving center of trade, religion, and intellectual life. Merchants and scholars from across West and North Africa flocked to the city.

Mansa Musa's journey to Mecca fascinated observers then and still fascinates us now. Such a pilgrimage has long been one of the duties—and privileges—of all Muslims. It also added the prestigious title of *hajji* to their names. For rulers in particular, it conveyed a spiritual power known as *baraka* that helped legitimate their rule.

When Mansa Musa began his journey in 1324, he was accompanied by an enormous entourage, with thousands of fellow pilgrims, some 500 enslaved servants, his wife and other women, hundreds of camels, and a huge quantity

important link to Muslim trading partners, much as Buddhism and later Islam had done in Southeast Asia. For the monarchs and their courts, it offered a source of literate officials to assist in state administration as well as religious legitimacy, particularly for those who gained the prestige conferred by a pilgrimage to Mecca. The most prominent such pilgrim was Mansa Musa, the ruler of Mali, who in 1324 undertook the hajj accompanied by a huge entourage and enormous quantities of gold. (See Zooming In: Mansa Musa, West African Monarch and Muslim Pilgrim.) As a world religion with a single universal Creator-God, Islam had a religious appeal for societies that were now participating in a wider world.

By the sixteenth century, a number of West African cities had become major centers of Islamic religious and intellectual life. Timbuktu became a renowned center of learning, boasting more than 150 lower-level Quranic schools and several major centers of higher education and attracting thousands of students from all

AP
CAUSATION
How did the expansion of Islam lead to the spread of learning?

of gold. It was the gold that attracted the most attention, as he distributed it lavishly along his journey. Egyptian sources reported that the value of gold in their country was depressed for years after his visit. On his return trip, Mansa Musa apparently had exhausted his supply and had to borrow money from Egyptian merchants at high interest rates. Those merchants also profited greatly from Musa's pilgrims, who, unsophisticated in big-city shopping, were made to pay far more than their purchases were worth. Europeans also became aware of Mansa Musa, featuring him holding a large nugget of gold in a famous map from 1375 with a caption referring to him as "the richest and most noble king in all the land."

In Cairo, Mansa Musa displayed both his pride and his ignorance of Islamic law. Invited to see the sultan of Egypt, he was initially reluctant because of a protocol requirement to kiss the ground and the sultan's hand. He consented only when he was persuaded that he was really prostrating before God, not the sultan. And in conversation with learned clerics, Mansa Musa was surprised to learn that Muslim rulers were not allowed to take the beautiful unmarried women of their realm as concubines. He quickly committed himself to abandoning the practice.

In Mecca, Mansa Musa completed the requirements of the hajj, dressing in the common garb of all pilgrims, repeatedly circling the Kaaba, performing ritual prayers,

and visiting various sites associated with Muhammad's life, including a side trip to the Prophet's tomb in Medina. He also sought to recruit a number of sharifs, prestigious descendants of Muhammad's family, to add Islamic luster to his kingdom. After considerable difficulty and expense, he found four men who were willing to return with him to what Arabs understood to be the remote frontier of the Islamic world. Some reports suggested that they were simply formerly enslaved individuals, hoping for better lives.

In the end, perhaps Mansa Musa's goals for the pilgrimage were achieved. On a personal level, one source reported that he was so moved by the pilgrimage that he actually considered abandoning his throne altogether and returning to Mecca so that he might live near the sacred sanctuary of the Kaaba. His visit certainly elevated Mali's status in the Islamic world. Some 200 years after that visit, one account of his pilgrimage placed the sultan of Mali as one of four major rulers in the Islamic world, equal to those of Baghdad and Egypt. Mansa Musa would have been pleased.

QUESTIONS

What significance did Mansa Musa likely attach to his pilgrimage? How might Egyptians, Arabians, and Europeans have viewed it?

over West Africa and beyond. Libraries held tens of thousands of books and scholarly manuscripts. (See the photo "Manuscripts of Timbuktu" on page 92.) Monarchs subsidized the construction of mosques as West Africa became an integral part of a larger Islamic world. Arabic became an important language of religion, education, administration, and trade, but it did not become the dominant language of daily life. Nor did West Africa experience the massive migration of Arab peoples that had promoted the Arabization of North Africa and the Middle East.

Islam remained the culture of urban elites and spread little into the rural areas of West Africa until the nineteenth century. Although many rulers adopted Islam, they governed people who steadfastly practiced African religions and whose sensibilities they had to respect if social peace were to prevail. Thus they made few efforts to impose the new religion on their rural subjects or to govern in strict accordance with Islamic law. During his mid-fourteenth-century travels in West Africa, the north African visitor Ibn Battuta

TEACHING IDEA

Incorporating Outside Resources

A fun activity to get a good conversation going in class is to talk about who is the "wealthiest" person in history. Mansa Musa is always at the top of the list. To help students understand the significance of Mansa Musa in West African history, show students the TED-Ed *Mansa Musa, One of the Wealthiest People Who Ever Lived*. The video is available on YouTube and on the TED-Ed website.

The Great Mosque at Jenne This mosque in the city of Jenne, initially constructed in the thirteenth century, illustrates the assimilation of Islam into West African civilization. (Antonello Lanzellotto/AGE Fotostock)

was appalled that practicing Muslims in Mali permitted their women to appear in public almost naked and to mingle freely with unrelated men. "The association of women with men is agreeable to us," he was told, "and a part of good conduct to which no suspicion attaches. They are not like the women of your country." [23] (See AP® Looking Again: Islamic Practice in West Africa through the Eyes of a Foreign Traveler, Chapter 1, page 50.) Sonni Ali, a fifteenth-century ruler of Songhay, observed Ramadan and built mosques, but he also consulted traditional diviners and performed customary sacrifices. In such ways, Islam became Africanized even as parts of West Africa became Islamized.

▲ AP®

ARGUMENTATION
Explain how this mosque in West Africa is an example of cultural diffusion.

AP®

CAUSATION
What was the relationship between long-distance trade networks and the religion of Islam?

AP® EXAM TIP
You are expected to be able to give examples of religions and cultures that spread through long-distance trade routes.

Connections across the Islamic World

Finding the Main Point: In what ways was the Islamic world an arena of cross-cultural interaction?

Alongside the Silk, Sea, and Sand roads, and intersecting with them, was yet another arena of Afro-Eurasian interaction and exchange—the transcontinental Islamic world, stretching from Spain and West Africa across the Middle East to India and Southeast Asia. Within that vast realm and despite many variations, conflicts, and religious differences, millions of people shared elements of a common faith, and many of them spoke Arabic.

Well before 1200, the Islamic world had also become a huge trading zone of hemispheric dimensions. Commerce was valued positively within Islamic teaching, and laws regulating it figured prominently in the sharia, creating a predictable framework for exchange across many cultures. The pilgrimage to Mecca, as well as the urbanization that accompanied the growth of Islamic civilization, likewise fostered commerce, as the appetite of urban elites for luxury goods stimulated both craft production and the desire for foreign products.

Thus Muslim merchants, especially Arabs and Persians, quickly became prominent and sometimes dominant players in all the major Afro-Eurasian trade routes—in the Mediterranean Sea, along the Silk Roads, across the Sahara, and throughout the Indian Ocean basin. As early as the eighth century, Arab and Persian traders had established a commercial colony in Canton in southern China, thus linking the Islamic heartland with Asia's other giant and flourishing economy. Various forms of banking, partnerships, business contracts, and instruments for granting credit facilitated these long-distance economic relationships and generated a prosperous, sophisticated, and highly commercialized economy that spanned the Eastern Hemisphere.

Patterns of Exchange in the Islamic World

The transcontinental expanse of Islamic civilization stimulated many kinds of exchange. Agricultural products and practices, for example, spread from one region to another. Among the food crops that circulated within and beyond the Islamic world were different varieties of sugarcane, rice, apricots, artichokes, eggplants, lemons, oranges, almonds, figs, and bananas. Equally significant were water-management practices, so important to the arid or semi-arid environments of many parts of the Islamic world. Persian-style reservoirs and irrigation technologies spread as far as Tunisia and Morocco, the northern fringes of the Sahara, Spain, and Yemen. All of this contributed to an "Islamic Green Revolution" that was well under way by 1200. It gave rise to increased food production, as well as population growth, urbanization, and industrial development across the Islamic world.

Technology too diffused widely within the realm of Islam. Muslim technicians made improvements on rockets, first developed in China, by developing one that carried a small warhead and another that was used to attack ships. Papermaking techniques entered the Abbasid Empire from China in the eighth century or earlier, and paper mills soon operated in Persia, Iraq, and Egypt. This revolutionary technology, which strengthened bureaucratic governments, passed from the Middle East into India and Europe over the following centuries. Everywhere it spurred the emergence of books and written culture at the expense of earlier orally based cultural expressions.

Ideas likewise circulated across the Islamic world. The religion itself drew heavily and quite openly on Jewish and Christian precedents. Persia also contributed much in the way of bureaucratic practice, court ritual, and poetry, and Persian became a major literary language in elite circles. Scientific, medical, and philosophical texts, especially from ancient Greece, the Hellenistic world, and India, were systematically translated into Arabic, providing an enormous boost to Islamic scholarship and science for several centuries. In 830, the Abbasid caliph al-Mamun, himself a poet and scholar with a passion for foreign learning, established the **House of Wisdom** in Baghdad as an academic center for this research and translation. Stimulated by Greek texts, a school of Islamic thinkers known as Mutazalites ("those who stand apart") argued that reason, rather than revelation, was the best way to the truth. In the long run,

AP® EXAM TIP

The spread of technology and science across long-distance trade routes is very important.

▼ **AP®**

CLAIMS AND EVIDENCE IN SOURCES

What scientific or technological achievements are reflected in this image?

A Muslim Astronomical Observatory Drawing initially on Greek, Indian, and Persian astronomy, the Islamic world after 1000 developed its own distinctive tradition of astronomical observation and prediction, reflected in this sixteenth-century Turkish observatory. Muslim astronomy later exercised considerable influence in both China and Europe. (Bridgeman Images)

APPLY THE TIP

Ask students to trace the diffusion of the following technical innovations. (Answers are provided in italics.)

■ Reservoirs: *From Persia to Tunisia, Morocco, northern fringes of the Sahara, Spain, and Yemen*

■ Rockets: *From China to the Muslim heartland, where technicians developed one that carried a warhead and another that could attack ships*

■ Papermaking: *From China to Persia, Iraq, and Egypt, and then to India and Europe*

BUILDING AP® SKILLS

Claims and Evidence in Sources

Using the image and information on page 161 to help get a discussion started, ask students: What were scientific achievements of the Islamic world? *Algebra, which used Indian numbers (which came to be known as Arabic numbers), was a key mathematical achievement. There were also achievements in astronomy and optics. In medicine, doctors in the Islamic world diagnosed hay fever, measles, smallpox, diphtheria, rabies, and diabetes. The first hospitals, clinics, and examinations for physicians were developed.*

however, the philosophers' emphasis on logic, rationality, and the laws of nature was subject to increasing criticism by those who held that only the Quran, the sayings of the Prophet, or mystical experience represented a genuine path to God.

But the realm of Islam was much more than a museum of ancient achievements from the civilizations that it encompassed. Those traditions mixed and blended to generate a distinctive Islamic civilization with many new contributions to the world of learning. (See Snapshot: Key Achievements in Islamic Science and Scholarship.) Using Indian numerical notation, for example, Arab scholars developed algebra as a novel mathematical discipline. They also undertook much original work in astronomy and optics. They built on earlier Greek and Indian practice to create a remarkable tradition in medicine and pharmacology. Arab physicians such as al-Razi and Ibn Sina accurately diagnosed many diseases, such as hay fever, measles, smallpox, diphtheria, rabies, and diabetes. In addition, treatments such as using a mercury ointment for scabies, conducting cataract and hernia operations, and filling teeth with gold were pioneered by Arab doctors. The first hospitals, traveling clinics, and examinations for physicians and pharmacologists were also developed within the Islamic world. In the eleventh and twelfth centuries, this enormous body of Arab medical scholarship entered Europe via Spain, and it remained at the core of European medical practice for many centuries.

SNAPSHOT   Key Achievements in Islamic Science and Scholarship

Person/Dates	Achievement
al-Khwarazim (790–840)	Mathematician; spread use of Arabic numerals in Islamic world; wrote first book on algebra
al-Razi (865–925)	Discovered sulfuric acid; wrote a vast encyclopedia of medicine, drawing on Greek, Syrian, Indian, and Persian work and his own clinical observation
al-Biruni (973–1048)	Mathematician, astronomer, cartographer; calculated the radius of the earth with great accuracy; worked out numerous mathematical innovations; developed a technique for displaying a hemisphere on a plane
Ibn Sina (Avicenna) (980–1037)	Prolific writer in almost all fields of science and philosophy; especially known for *Canon of Medicine*, a fourteen-volume work that set standards for medical practice in Islamic and Christian worlds for centuries
Omar Khayyam (1048–1131)	Mathematician; critic of Euclid's geometry; measured the solar year with great accuracy; Sufi poet; author of *The Rubaiyat*
Ibn Rushd (Averroës) (1126–1198)	Translated and commented widely on Aristotle; rationalist philosopher; made major contributions in law, mathematics, and medicine
Nasir al-Din Tusi (1201–1274)	Founder of the famous Maragha observatory in Persia (data from Maragha probably influenced Copernicus); mapped the motion of stars and planets
Ibn Khaldun (1332–1406)	Greatest Arab historian; identified trends and structures in world history over long periods of time

A final pattern of exchange occurred within the Islamic religious tradition itself. Various understandings of Islamic law (*sharia*) were generated within the *madrassas* or colleges of the Islamic educational system. There learned scholars, known as *ulema*, attracted eager students, many of whom traveled long distances to study with the most renowned teachers. Likewise Sufi masters, operating from within their brotherhoods (*tariqa*), offered a variety of mystical teachings and practices to spiritual seekers, who also sought out the most well-known or favored teachers. Both the colleges and Sufi orders were international institutions, and their texts were exchanged and debated across the Islamic world.

Encounter: The Islamic World and Christendom

In addition to these patterns of exchange within the larger Islamic world, a growing Islamic civilization bumped up against Chinese, Persian, Hindu, Central and Southeast Asian, and African peoples, sometimes peacefully and at other times more violently. The encounter between the world of Islam and that of Christendom was surely among the most significant of these interactions, with a long history that continues into the present.

The earliest phase of that encounter began in the seventh and eighth centuries C.E. as a rapidly expanding Arab Empire captured the southern territories of the Christian Byzantine Empire—Syria and Egypt, for example—and twice laid siege to its capital city of Constantinople, though unsuccessfully. Arab armies likewise overran Christian North Africa and Spain by the early eighth century. One Arab poet described the outcome: "The Arabs became rich, numerous and spread over the land which they had taken from the Byzantines and which was delivered to pillage....The Christians were in despair; some of them said 'why does God allow this to happen?'"[24]

Several centuries later, a reviving Christian Western European civilization took the initiative in the encounter with Islam in a series of "holy wars" known as the **Crusades**. From the viewpoint of the Islamic world, they represented naked and brutal aggression. Many Christians, however, saw them as defensive, a response to the earlier Arab Muslim invasion of Christian lands and to the recent threat of Turkic Muslim incursions against the Byzantine Empire. Either way, they were an episode in a much longer encounter between Christian and Islamic civilizations.

The Crusades began in 1095 and occurred intermittently for the next two centuries. In European thinking and practice, the Crusades were wars undertaken at God's command and authorized by the pope as Christ's representative on earth. Any number of political, economic, and social motives underlay the Crusades, but at their core they were religious wars. Within Europe, the amazing support for the Crusades reflected an understanding of them "as providing security against mortal [Muslim] enemies threatening the spiritual health of all Christendom and all Christians."[25] Crusading drew on both Christian piety and the warrior values of the elite, with little sense of contradiction between these impulses.

TEACHING IDEA

Incorporating Outside Resources

For good background information on the Crusades, consider having students watch *The Crusades: Pilgrimage or Holy War?* of Crash Course World History. John Green discusses the Crusades in the twelfth and thirteenth centuries. This video will help students understand Europeans' motivations for joining the Crusades. The video can be found on YouTube. Either assign the video as homework to watch on your LMS with a quiz, or show it in class. Then ask students the following questions:

■ How did the Seljuk Turks differ from the Umayyads and Abbasids in their attitudes toward Christianity? *The Umayyads and the Abbasids permitted Christians to live among them, as long as they paid a tax. The Seljuk Turks were not willing to coexist with Christians. They sacked holy cities and made it difficult for Christians to go on pilgrimages.*

■ Why is the Third Crusade the most famous? *The Third Crusade was a European response to the emergence of a new Islamic power out of Egypt. While the crusade failed in its ultimate goal, which was to take Jerusalem, it changed the direction of the Crusades by making Egypt a target.*

■ What happened to Constantinople in 1204 during the Fourth Crusade? *When Alexius did not pay the European Crusaders after they helped him take the throne, they sacked Constantinople.*

■ Why were the Crusades ultimately a failure for Christians? *The Crusades failed to establish long-term Christian kingdoms in the Holy Land, and they were a large drain on Europe's resources.*

(continued)

■ Article on History.com about the Crusades

After the presentations, ask students to discuss the influence of each motivation on the Crusaders and determine as a class which motivation had the greatest impact. Guide the discussion by asking students what might motivate them to go on a crusade. Ask students to imagine that they have never traveled beyond the town of their birth. What could motivate them to travel thousands of miles away

from home to fight against an enemy they know little about? *(Answers will vary.)*

Differentiation

If you want to differentiate this activity and have students practice presentation skills, follow the "Must Do, Should Do, Strive For" model below.

■ Must Do: Students should understand the assigned motivation for fighting in a

crusade and be able to create a presentation on the motivation.

■ Should Do: Students should be able to explain why their assigned motivation had the greatest impact, using specific examples of evidence within their presentation.

■ Strive For: Students should be able to present their assigned motivation for fighting in a crusade to the class while trying to convince their classmates that their motivation had the greatest impact.

BUILDING AP® SKILLS

Sourcing and Situation

Students should understand alternative views of historical events. When the Crusaders took over Jerusalem in the First Crusade, they committed multiple atrocities against the Muslim and Jewish communities in the city. Ask students to analyze the following quote from a Jewish resident of Jerusalem during the First Crusade and answer the accompanying questions: "And Satan—the Pope of evil Rome—also came and proclaimed to all the nations believing in that stock of adultery that they should assemble and ascend to Jerusalem so as to conquer the city and journey at the tomb of the superstition whom they call their God. Satan came and mingled with the nations, and they gathered as one man to fulfill the command, coming in great numbers like the grains of sand upon the seashore, the noise of them clamorous as a whirlwind and a storm. When the drops of the bucket had assembled, they looked in anger at us. . . . [T]hey said (about us): 'Why should we concern ourselves with going to war against the Ishmaelites dwelling about Jerusalem, when here, in the midst, is a people who disrespect our god—indeed, their ancestors are those who crucified him. Why should we let them live and tolerate their dwelling among us?' (they asked) . . . [T]his is the persecution of our community." — *The Solomon bar Simson Chronicle*, ca. 1140, from *Readings in Medieval History*, vol. 2, *The Later Middle Ages*, edited by Patrick J. Geary

■ According to the excerpt from the *Solomon bar Simson Chronicle*, how did the Crusaders view the Jewish population of Jerusalem? *The Crusaders saw the Jewish population as the real threat in Jerusalem because of the Jews' perceived disrespect for the Christian God and the crucifixion of Christ by the Jewish leadership.*

■ How did the Jewish people living in Jerusalem view the Crusaders and their behavior during the First Crusade? *The Jewish people viewed the Crusaders as an evil ("Satan") and destructive force that had come to Jerusalem to persecute the Jewish community.*

The Crusades This fourteenth-century painting depicts Crusaders using a catapult to batter a city's defenses, while Muslim defenders fire arrows and hurl projectiles at the attackers. During the First Crusade, Christian forces seized Jerusalem after a lengthy siege that was followed by a bloody massacre of its Muslim and Jewish inhabitants. (Bibliothèque Nationale, Paris, France/Bridgeman Images)

▲ **AP®**
ARGUMENTATION
How could the weapons technology shown in this picture impact warfare?

The most famous Crusades were those aimed at wresting Jerusalem and the holy places associated with the life of Jesus from Islamic control and returning them to Christendom (see Map 3.6). Beginning in 1095, wave after wave of Crusaders from all walks of life and many countries flocked to the eastern Mediterranean, where they temporarily carved out four small Christian states, the last of which was recaptured by Muslim forces in 1291. Led or supported by an assortment of kings, popes, bishops, monks, lords, nobles, and merchants, the Crusades demonstrated a growing European capacity for organization, finance, transportation, and recruitment, made all the more impressive by the absence of any centralized direction for the project.

They also demonstrated considerable cruelty. The seizure of Jerusalem in 1099, for instance, was accompanied by the slaughter of many Muslims and Jews. "If you had been there you would have seen our feet colored to our ankles with the blood of the slain," reported one Christian eyewitness. "But what more shall I relate? None of them were left alive; neither women nor children were spared."[26]

Well before the Crusades, Muslim impressions of the Christians of Western Europe, whom they called Franks, were stereotypical and negative. In their view, Europeans were uncivilized barbarians—personally dirty, sexually promiscuous, and allowing their women altogether too much independence. According to one Arab writer of the twelfth century, Europeans were "animals, possessing the virtues of courage and fighting, nothing else."[27] The Crusades hardened and supplemented such perceptions.

Beyond the trauma of invasion and military defeat during the First Crusade, the very presence of the Christians defiled the sacred spaces of Islam. Particularly offensive was the placing of a Christian cross atop the beloved Muslim shrine known as the Dome of the Rock. Widely associated with filth, disease, and contamination, the Crusaders were also seen as a threat to the sanctity of Muslim women. Moreover, as Muslims became aware of the fundamentally religious impulses that motivated the Crusaders, their perception of the differences between Islam and Christianity sharpened.

Surprisingly perhaps, the Crusades had little lasting impact, either politically or religiously, in the Islamic world. European power was not sufficiently strong or long-lasting to induce much conversion, and the small European footholds there had returned to Muslim control by 1300. Mongol invasions of Islamic Persia were far more threatening

MAPPING HISTORY   Map 3.6 **The Crusades**

Western Europe's crusading tradition reflected the expansive energy and religious impulses of an emerging civilization. It was directed against Muslims in the Middle East, Sicily, and Spain as well as the Eastern Orthodox Christians of the Byzantine Empire. The Crusades also involved attacks on Jewish communities, probably the first organized mass pogroms against Jews in Europe's history.

Reading the Map: Which of the first four Crusades ended in Constantinople? From the information provided on this map, how would you describe the role of Constantinople in the first four Crusades?

AP® Making Connections: How might this map be used to support the thesis that the Crusades were about much more than just securing the Christian holy sites in Jerusalem?

EXPLORING AP® THEMES

Humans and the Environment (ENV)

As you study Map 3.6, "The Crusades," ask the following questions:

■ What major city did the majority of the Crusader routes travel through? *The majority of the Crusader routes traveled through Constantinople.*

■ Why was Constantinople a major crossroads on the Crusader routes? *Constantinople was on the trade routes leading to the Holy Land, and the Crusaders originally became involved in the recovery of the Holy Land at the request of the Byzantine emperor.*

to the Islamic world generally than the incursions of the Crusaders. Furthermore, even during the Crusades, trade between Muslims and Christians persisted, and they rented property to one another. Friendships and even marriages developed across religious boundaries, and some Crusaders assimilated to the local culture.

In Europe, however, the Crusades had very significant long-term consequences. Tens of thousands of Europeans came into personal contact with the Islamic world, from which they picked up a taste for the many luxury products available there, stimulating a demand for Asian goods. They learned techniques for producing

AP®

CAUSATION

What were the major political and cultural effects of the Crusades?

The effect of the Crusades on the Islamic world and on Western Europe differed. Use the following prompts to discuss the long-term consequences of the Crusades on these two regions:

■ What effects did the Crusades have on the Islamic world? *The Crusades had little lasting impact on the Islamic world. European power at the time was neither strong enough nor lasting enough to stimulate conversion in the Islamic world, and any territory Europeans had won in the Crusades was under Muslim control by 1300.*

■ What cultural effects did the Crusades have on Western Europe? *The Crusades brought Spain, Sicily, and the Baltic region permanently into the world of Western Christendom. Muslim scholarship, combined with Greek learning, flowed into Europe as a result of the Crusades and the long-distance trade the Crusades sparked. The rift between the Eastern Orthodox and Roman Catholic Churches deepened further, and Christian anti-Semitism was exacerbated by the Crusades.*

■ What economic effects did the Crusades have on Western Europe? *During the Crusades, tens of thousands of Europeans came into personal contact with the Islamic world, where they picked up a taste for luxury items and stimulated a demand for more trade to gain access to Asian goods. Europeans learned the techniques for producing sugar on large plantations, setting the stage for later economic development with cash crops.*

After the class discussion, ask students to use evidence from the text and class discussion to write a one-paragraph response to the following prompt:

■ Which region was more affected by the events of the Crusades? *Europe was affected the most by the events of the Crusades because contact with the Islamic world introduced Europe to new luxury goods, helped reintroduce long-distance trade in Europe, and prompted the flow of Muslim scholarship into Europe, which helped stimulate a new age of learning.*

sugar on large plantations using enslaved labor, a process that had incalculable consequences in later centuries as Europeans transferred the plantation system to the Americas. Muslim scholarship, together with the ancient Greek learning that it incorporated, flowed into Europe, largely through Spain and Sicily.

Even more enduring outcomes of the Crusades are also apparent. In European thinking, the Christian conquest of Muslim Spain, completed by 1492, was the work of Crusaders. Compared to just two centuries of Crusader presence in the Middle East, Muslim Spain was brought permanently into the world of Christendom. Furthermore, European empire building, especially in the Western Hemisphere, continued the crusading notion that "God wills it," and the Americas remain largely within the Christian world today. Finally, over the past two centuries, as the world of the Christian West and that of Islam have collided, both sides have found many occasions for which images of the Crusades, however distorted, have proven politically popular or ideologically useful.

Yet another turn in the long interaction between the Islamic and Christian worlds began with the rise of the Turkish Ottoman Empire around 1300. Over the next several centuries, the Ottomans conquered what remained of the Christian Byzantine Empire, capturing its capital city of Constantinople in 1453 and sending large numbers of Turkic Muslims to settle in the Byzantine heartland of Anatolia. Furthermore, Ottoman armies seized much of southeastern Europe and in 1529 laid siege to Vienna in the very heart of Central Europe. From a Christian European viewpoint, the Ottoman invasions represented both a political/military and a religious threat. The English playwright Christopher Marlowe expressed this sense of profound foreboding when he wrote in 1587: "Now shalt thou feel the force of Turkish arms, which lately made all Europe quake for fear."[28] (See Chapter 4 for a more complete treatment of the Ottoman Empire and its impact on European Christendom.)

Connections across the Americas

> **Finding the Main Point:** What kinds of cross-cultural interactions took shape in the Americas?

Before the voyages of Columbus, the world of the Americas developed quite separately from that of Afro-Eurasia. But if the Silk, Sea, and Sand roads linked the diverse peoples of the Eastern Hemisphere, did a similar network of interaction join and transform the various societies of the Western Hemisphere?

Clearly, direct connections among the various civilizations and cultures of the Americas were less densely woven than in the Afro-Eurasian region. The llama and the potato, both domesticated in the Andes, never reached Mesoamerica; nor did the writing system of the Maya diffuse to Andean civilizations. The Aztecs and the Incas, contemporary civilizations in the fifteenth century, had little if any direct contact with each other. Thus nothing equivalent to the long-distance

AP® EXAM TIP

Take notes on the ways that the American trade network was similar to and different from the Sand, Sea, and Silk roads.

As in Unit 1, the recommended thinking skill of Unit 2 is Comparison. This is a good place to practice that skill along with working on argumentation. After learning about all the global trade networks, have students work as a class to brainstorm similarities and differences between the American trade networks, the Sand Roads, the Sea Roads, and the Silk Roads. After the students have

finished brainstorming, have them write a quick LEQ-style paragraph (topic sentence, at least two pieces of evidence, and explanations for how the evidence supports the topic sentence) in response to the following prompt:

■ Evaluate the extent to which the American trade networks were similar to Afro-Eurasian trade networks during 1200–1450.

trade of the Silk, Sea, or Sand roads of the Eastern Hemisphere arose in the Americas, even though local and regional commerce flourished in many places. Nor did distinct cultural traditions spread widely to integrate distant peoples, as Buddhism, Christianity, and Islam did in the Afro-Eurasian world.

The limits of these interactions owed something to the absence of horses, donkeys, camels, wheeled vehicles, and large oceangoing vessels, all of which facilitated long-distance trade and travel in Afro-Eurasia. Geographic or environmental differences added further obstacles. The narrow bottleneck of Panama, largely covered by dense rain forests, surely inhibited contact between South and North America. Furthermore, the north/south orientation of the Americas—which required agricultural practices to move through, and adapt to, quite distinct climatic and vegetation zones—slowed the spread of agricultural products.

Nonetheless, scholars have discerned "a loosely interactive web stretching from the North American Great Lakes and upper Mississippi south to the Andes."[29] Partly, it was a matter of slowly spreading crops and cultural elements. Maize, for instance, gradually diffused from its Mesoamerican place of origin to the southwestern United States and then on to eastern North America as well as to much of South America in the other direction. And a game played with rubber balls on an outdoor court has left traces in the Caribbean, Mexico, and northern South America. The spread of particular pottery styles and architectural conventions likewise suggests at least indirect contact over wide distances.

Commerce too played an important role in the making of this **American web**. In the centuries between 1000 and 1500, four distinct nodes of commercial activity and wider connections emerged in the Americas: at Cahokia, Chaco Canyon, Mesoamerica, and the Inca Empire in the Andes (see Map 3.7).

Between about 1100 and 1350 in the eastern woodlands, a North

▼ **AP®**

COMPARISON

Using this map, compare the patterns of trade in the Americas with the patterns of trade in Eurasia. What are the reasons for the differences?

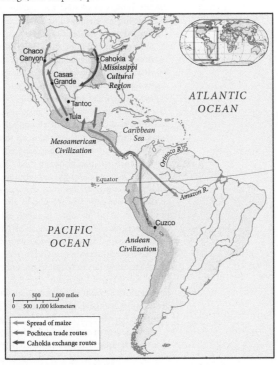

Map 3.7 The American Web
Transcontinental interactions within the American web were more modest than those of the Afro-Eurasian hemisphere. The most intense areas of exchange and communication occurred at Cahokia in the Mississippi valley, at Chaco Canyon, in Mesoamerica, and in the Andean region.

EXPLORING AP® THEMES

Humans and the Environment (ENV)

It's good for students to understand why networks of exchange in the Americas in this time period were different from ones in Afro-Eurasia. You can give students a map of the Americas and ask them to draw in the trade routes (Map 3.7 on page 167 can help). If you assigned the Chapter 3 Essential Activity, you may suggest that students use the same map for this exercise. After they complete the map, ask students: Why do you think exchange networks in the Americas didn't develop to the extent that they developed in Afro-Eurasia? *The north-south orientation of the Americas created a diverse geography that hindered the movement of people. The lack of large domesticated animals, like camels and oxen, meant that humans had to be the primary "pack animals" for trade in the Americas, limiting the amount of goods they could take and the distance they could travel. A lack of wheeled vehicles or large oceangoing vessels also meant that merchants had to trade less and travel shorter distances, limiting trade. A reproducible version of this map is available in the Teacher's Resource Materials.*

TRM Map 3A: The Americas

TEACHING IDEA

Class Discussion

Students might be tempted to "dismiss" the American civilizations as not experiencing cultural diffusion the way Afro-Eurasian civilizations did because the Americas lacked major trade networks like the Silk Roads. One way to challenge that idea or belief is to ask students to read the third paragraph about the American web on page 167 and have them list the different examples of cultural diffusion discussed there. Have students share what they have found with the class when they are done making their lists. *The use of maize, which spread out of Mesoamerica, became a major part of the culture of groups in the Southwest. The Caribbean, Mexico, and northern South America had evidence of a similar game played with rubber balls on an outdoor court. Evidence of particular pottery styles and architectural conventions also suggests contact between groups.*

EXPLORING AP® THEMES

Economic Systems (ECN)

If you had students do the discussion on the American web on page 167, you could extend that discussion to include the theme of economics by asking: What were some of the goods traded in the American web? *Goods traded included shells from the Atlantic coast, buffalo hides from the Great Plains, copper from the area around Lake Superior, obsidian from the Rocky Mountains, and mica.*

EXPLORING AP® THEMES

Economic Systems (ECN)

You might try extending the map from page 167 where students drew in the American trade networks. Have students build on it by identifying the four major commercial nodes of the Americas on the map (see pages 168 and 169): Cahokia, Chaco Canyon, Mesoamerica, and the Inca Empire. Then ask them to take notes on the sides of the map on each of these civilizations or regions, focusing on their economic characteristics.

TRM **Map 3A: The Americas**

American chiefdom at Cahokia, near present-day St. Louis, lay at the center of a widespread trading network. This network brought to Cahokia shells from the Atlantic coast, copper from the Lake Superior region, buffalo hides from the Great Plains, obsidian from the Rocky Mountains, and mica from the southern Appalachian Mountains. Sturdy dugout canoes plied the rivers of the eastern woodlands, loosely connecting the diverse societies of this Mississippi culture.

Cahokia is perhaps most well known for its huge terraced pyramid of four levels, measuring 1,000 feet long by 700 feet wide, rising more than 100 feet above the ground, and occupying fifteen acres. It was the largest structure north of Mexico and the focal point of a community numbering 10,000 or more people. Evidence from burials and from later Spanish observers suggests that Cahokia and other centers of this Mississippi culture were stratified societies with a clear elite and with rulers able to mobilize the labor required to build such enormous structures. One high-status male was buried on a platform of 20,000 shell beads, accompanied by 800 arrowheads, sheets of copper and mica, and a number of sacrificed men and women nearby.[30]

A second commercial node in this American web took shape in Chaco Canyon in what is now northwestern New Mexico. There, between 860 and 1130 C.E., five major settlements or pueblos emerged. This **Chaco Phenomenon** encompassed 25,000 square miles and linked some 150 outlying settlements to the main centers. The largest of these towns, or "great houses," Pueblo Bonito, stood five stories high and contained more than 600 rooms and many kivas, pits used for ceremonial purposes. Hundreds of miles of roads, up to forty feet wide, radiated out from Chaco, prompting much debate among scholars. Without wheeled carts or large domesticated animals, such an elaborate road system seems unnecessary for ordinary trade or travel. Did the roads represent, as some scholars speculate, a ceremonial or sacred landscape leading perhaps to an entrance to the underworld?

By the eleventh century, Chaco also had become a dominant center for the production of turquoise ornaments, which became a major item of regional commerce, extending as far south as Mesoamerica. In return many items from Mesoamerica—copper bells, macaw feathers, tons of shells—traveled to Chaco and have been found in the Chaco region. Residents of Chaco also drank liquid chocolate, using jars of Maya origin and cacao beans imported from Mesoamerica, where the practice began. An extended period of drought in the half century following 1130 brought this flourishing culture to a rather abrupt end. By 1200, the great houses had been abandoned and their inhabitants scattered in small communities that later became the Pueblo peoples of more recent times.

A third node of commercial activity developed in Mesoamerica. During the flourishing of Mesoamerican civilization (200–900 C.E.), both the Maya cities in the Yucatán area of Mexico and Guatemala and the huge city-state of Teotihuacán in central Mexico maintained commercial relationships with one another and throughout the region. In addition to this land-based trade, the Maya conducted a seaborne commerce, using large dugout canoes holding forty to fifty people, along both the Atlantic and Pacific coasts. Among the Aztecs of the fifteenth century, professional merchants known as **pochteca** (pohch-TEH-cah) undertook large-scale trading expeditions both within and well beyond the borders of their empire, sometimes as agents for the state or for members of the nobility, but more often acting on their own as private businessmen. Although they were legally commoners, their wealth, often exceeding that of the nobility, allowed them to rise in society and become "magnates of the land."

Beyond tribute from conquered peoples, ordinary trade (both local and long-distance) permeated Aztec domains. The extent of the Aztec Empire and its rapid population growth stimulated the development of markets and the production of craft goods, particularly in the fifteenth century. Virtually every settlement, from the capital city to the smallest village, had a marketplace that hummed with activity during weekly market days. The largest was that of Tlatelolco, near the capital city, which stunned the Spanish with its huge size, its good order, and the immense range of available goods. Hernán Cortés, the Spanish conquistador who defeated the Aztecs, wrote that "every kind of merchandise such as can be met with in every land is for sale there, whether of food and victuals, or ornaments of gold and silver, or lead, brass, copper, tin, precious stones, bones, shells, snails and feathers."[31]

A final node in the American web lay in the vast domains of the Inca Empire, stretching all along the Andes Mountains. Unlike in the Aztec Empire, where private traders largely handled the distribution of goods, economic exchange in the Inca realm during the fifteenth century was a state-run operation, and no merchant group similar to the Aztec pochteca emerged there. Instead, great state storehouses bulged with immense quantities of food, clothing, military supplies, blankets, construction materials, and more, all carefully recorded on *quipus* (knotted cords used to record numerical data) by a highly trained class of accountants. From these state centers, goods were transported as needed by caravans of human porters and llamas across the numerous roads and bridges of the empire. Totaling some 20,000 miles, Inca roads traversed the coastal plain and the high Andes in a north/south direction, while lateral roads linked these diverse environments and extended into the eastern rain forests and plains as well. Despite the general absence of private trade, local exchange took place at highland fairs and along the borders of the empire with groups outside the Inca state.

Inca Roads Used for transporting goods by pack animal or sending messages by foot, the Inca road network included some 2,000 inns where travelers might find food and shelter. Messengers, operating in relay, could cover as many as 150 miles a day. Here contemporary hikers still make use of an old Inca trail road. (William H. Mullins/Science Source)

▲ **AP**

CAUSATION
Explain how the roads pictured here strengthened Inca civilization.

EXPLORING AP® THEMES

Economic Systems (ECN) and Governance (GOV)

One of the few regions in the Americas to have a supported trade network was Mesoamerica, with civilizations such as the Maya and the Aztecs. Ask students the following question to help them think about the connection between government and economics: How did the Aztecs support trade and exchange in the territories they controlled? *Professional Aztec merchants known as pochteca went on large-scale trading expeditions both within the Aztec Empire and beyond its borders. While pochteca most often were acting in their own interests, they sometimes undertook trade expeditions as agents of the state. The growth of the Aztec Empire also stimulated the development of markets and the production of goods for trade.*

BUILDING AP® SKILLS

Making Connections: Comparison

The picture of the Inca roads on this page is a good place to check in with students and have them do a quick comparison practice. Show students the photo of the Inca road. Ask students: What other societies also had a well-developed system of roads? *Answers may include: Persia, Rome.* How do road systems help governments rule their territory? *Messages can be quickly sent across the territory, and soldiers can move quickly to new areas. Roads also make it easier to move supplies around the state.*

AP® Daily Videos

The final unit topic Daily Video in AP®
Classroom can help wrap up a unit
with students and also show how the
recommended thinking skill plays into the
unit. Consider showing students Daily Video
2.7: Comparison of Economic Exchange,
which looks at the similarities and differences
in the networks of exchange from 1200 to
1450. This video will also help with practice in
developing and supporting an argument using
evidence.

BUILDING AP® SKILLS

Making Connections: Comparison

Another way you could wrap up a chapter is
to ask students to read "Conclusions and
Reflections: Globalization—Ancient and
Modern." Then ask them to respond to the
following prompt with a response that's no
more than one to two paragraphs. (If you want
to practice timed writing with them, set a timer
for 10 minutes to respond to the prompt.)

■ What are the differences between the
postclassical trade networks and the trade
networks of the twenty-first century? *In
postclassical trade networks, most goods were
produced for consumption rather than market,
most trade was in luxury goods, trade patterns
were not truly global, and trade relationships
were more balanced than in future centuries.
In twenty-first-century trade networks, most
goods are produced for market rather than
consumption, trade is in luxury goods as well as
necessary goods, trade patterns are global, and
trading patterns are not equal.*

CONCLUSIONS AND REFLECTIONS

Globalization—Ancient and Modern

Finding the Main Point: What are the major continuities and changes seen in long-distance trade throughout world history?

"Encounters with strangers," wrote the famous world historian William McNeill, "were the main drive wheel of social change" in world history.[32] The cross-cultural commercial exchanges that were well established by 1200 and subsequently accelerated illustrate McNeill's point. For some, economic life changed substantially. Peasants in parts of China—men and women alike—came to focus on producing silk and other products that entered the Silk Road trading networks, a shift that required them to purchase food in the growing marketplaces of an increasingly commercialized economy. Most people, however, continued to produce necessities for themselves or their local landlords.

Long-distance commerce also generated social changes as mercantile elites, such as the Aztec pochteca, emerged as more distinct and prominent groups. An international merchant culture accompanied the growth of Indian Ocean commerce, and permanent communities of both Indian and Chinese merchants established themselves in Southeast Asia. Elite groups in many places used products from distant sources—silk, ceramics, gold, ivory, and incense, for example—to signify and reinforce their status.

Political life also changed as aspiring rulers used the resources derived from long-distance trade to create and sustain new states. The kingdoms of Srivijaya and Madjapahit in Southeast Asia, the Swahili city-states and Great Zimbabwe of East Africa, and the large imperial states of West Africa illustrate this link between commerce and state building.

Among the most significant changes associated with international commerce involved the spread of cultural traditions. Commercial networks enabled the extension of Buddhism across Asia, of Hinduism into parts of Southeast Asia, and of Islam to both East and West Africa.

These widespread networks of exchange in the centuries before 1450 remind us that alongside the separate histories of particular civilizations and societies, there lies another history—that of connections, interactions, and encounters across cultural boundaries—which we have recently come to call globalization. In several ways, this ancient "globalization" broadly resembles that of recent centuries. In both eras, ties of commerce and culture linked distant peoples; states and their rulers drew support from the resources made available by long-distance trade; and social status was marked by the possession of prestigious goods from far away.

But the differences are surely more striking. The entangled webs of modern times, linked by networks of roads, railroads, pipelines, shipping lanes, flight patterns, fiber-optic cables, and the Internet, have created a far more densely connected world than the modest relationships generated by the Silk Roads, Sea Roads, and

Sand Roads before 1450. And the speed of modern commercial transactions hardly compares to the slow journeys of camel caravans and wind-driven ships.

Furthermore, most people in these earlier times still produced primarily for their own consumption rather than for the market, and a much smaller range of goods was exchanged in the marketplaces of the world. Far fewer people then sold their own labor for wages, an almost universal practice in modern economies. Because of transportation costs and technological limitations, most trade was in luxury goods rather than in necessities. In addition, the circuits of commerce were rather more limited than the truly global patterns of exchange that emerged after 1500.

Finally, the world economy of the modern era increasingly had a single center—industrialized Western European countries—that came to dominate much of the world both economically and politically during the nineteenth century. Though never completely equal, the economic relationships of earlier times occurred among much more equivalent units. For example, no one region dominated the complex pattern of Indian Ocean exchange, although India and China generally offered manufactured goods, while Southeast Asia and East Africa mostly contributed agricultural products or raw materials. And with the exception of the brief Mongol control of the Silk Roads and the Inca domination of the Andes for a century, no single power exercised political control over the major networks of world commerce.

Economic relationships among earlier civilizations, in short, were more balanced and multicentered than those of the modern era. Although massive inequalities occurred within particular regions or societies, interaction among the major civilizations operated on a rather more equal basis than in the globalized world of the past several centuries. With the rise of China, India, Turkey, and Brazil as major players in the world economy of the twenty-first century, are we perhaps witnessing a return to that earlier pattern? Globalization, like everything else, has a history.

CHAPTER REVIEW

AP® Key Terms

Silk Roads, 134	Melaka, 153
Dunhuang, 136	Zheng He, 155
Temujin/Chinggis Khan, 142	Sand Roads, 156
Mongol world war, 142	Arabian camel, 157
Khubilai Khan, 144	House of Wisdom, 161
Ming dynasty, 145	Crusades, 163
Black Death, 148	American web, 167
Sea Roads, 150	Chaco Phenomenon, 168
Great Zimbabwe, 152	*pochteca*, 169

BUILDING AP® SKILLS

Making Connections: Causation

If you want students to practice their writing skills, have them write a timed LEQ using the following prompt. Give them 40 minutes to write the essay.

■ In the period 600–1450, the expansion of trade and communication networks facilitated the spread of culture, technology, and disease around the Eastern Hemisphere.
Develop an argument that evaluates the extent to which the increased spread of culture, technology, and/or disease impacted societies in Afro-Eurasia during this period.

Differentiation

To provide support for students who are struggling with writing LEQs or to just work on building skills with all students, follow the "Must Do, Should Do, Strive For" model below.

■ Must Do: Students will complete an LEQ outline to preplan their essay. You can find a reproducible version of an LEQ outline in the Teacher's Resource Materials.

■ Should Do: Students will use their LEQ outline to write a timed essay. Give them 40 minutes to write the essay.

■ Strive For: Students will peer-grade one another's essays. Give each student a generic LEQ rubric (which can be found on the College Board® website) and one of their peer's essays. You'll need to walk them through each point as they peer-grade, but this will help students better understand the rubric and how they need to write an essay.

TRM Writing Organizer for LEQ Practice

TRM **Suggested Responses to Questions**
You can find suggested responses to the Chapter Review questions in the Teacher's Resource Materials.

AP® CLASSROOM

AP® Personal Progress Check

This is a good place to pause and assign the Personal Progress Check for Unit 2 as more multiple-choice practice for your students. AP® Classroom allows you to set the quiz up digitally or print out a copy for each student. After students take the Progress Check for Unit 2, you can discuss the answers as a class.

Finding the Main Point

1. What was the economic and cultural impact of the Silk Road trading network?
2. What was the significance of the Mongol Empire in world history?
3. In what ways did the Sea Roads network generate political, economic, and cultural changes in the region?
4. How did the Sand Roads contribute to the spread of Islam in West Africa?
5. In what ways was the Islamic world an arena of cross-cultural interaction?
6. What kinds of cross-cultural interactions took shape in the Americas?
7. What are the major continuities and changes seen in long-distance trade throughout world history?

AP Big Picture Questions

1. What motivated and sustained the long-distance commerce of the Silk Roads, Sea Roads, and Sand Roads?
2. Why did the peoples of the Eastern Hemisphere develop long-distance trade more extensively than did those of the Western Hemisphere?
3. How did commerce change political, social, and economic life?
4. In what ways was Afro-Eurasia a single interacting zone, and in what respects was it a vast region of separate cultures and civilizations?
5. **AP** **Making Connections:** Based on Chapters 2 and 3, do developments between 1200 and 1450 represent a continuation of earlier patterns or a sharp break from them?

Evidence

One of the most significant skills in the AP® World History course is the ability to support a historical argument with evidence. In this workshop, we'll take a look at how professional historians use evidence to support their claim, and how you can too.

UNDERSTANDING EVIDENCE

A historical claim must always be backed up with evidence. Through this combination of a claim supported by evidence, a historian creates a cohesive, fact-based argument. So what counts as evidence?

Evidence: Facts from primary and secondary sources that are historically accurate and relevant

Primary source evidence is gathered directly from the people who were living at the time of a historical event. In addition to written documents, it can come in the form of images, cartoons, photographs, artifacts, works of art, historical maps, and more. Secondary source evidence includes texts written by historians, economists, art historians, and other experts, but it also includes data sets, maps, graphs, and charts. Another type of evidence that is a bit harder to pin down is "facts." A fact is a piece of well-known information that does not necessarily need to be taken directly from a primary or secondary source. Some common facts include historical events, names, dates, and other verifiable information. Let's look at how the authors of this book establish an evaluative claim and then use evidence to support it (page 169):

Beyond tribute from conquered peoples, ordinary trade (both local and long-distance) permeated Aztec domains. The extent of the Aztec Empire and its rapid population growth stimulated the development of markets and the production of craft goods, particularly in the fifteenth century. Virtually every settlement, from the capital city to the smallest village, had a marketplace that hummed with activity during weekly market days. The largest was that of Tlatelolco, near the capital city, which stunned the Spanish with its huge size, its good order, and the immense range of available goods. Hernán Cortés, the Spanish conquistador who defeated the Aztecs, wrote that "every kind of merchandise such as can be met with in every land is for sale there, whether of food and victuals, or ornaments of gold and silver, or lead, brass, copper, tin, precious stones, bones, shells, snails and feathers."[31]

Claim

Factual evidence

Factual evidence

Factual evidence

Primary source evidence

TRM AP® Skills Workshop Activity
Handout: Evidence

BUILDING AP® SKILLS

Claims and Evidence in Sources

Students need to be able to understand evidence in two major ways for the AP® Exam: being able to find evidence in an author's argument and being able to use evidence to support an argument the student has created. It could be helpful to have students read through the overview of evidence from the AP® Skills Workshop on pages 173 and 174 first and then have them practice finding evidence in a source using Activity 1 on page 174.

173

So, the claim that commerce permeated the Aztec Empire is backed up with evidence—from facts derived from primary sources and secondary sources.

EVIDENCE ON THE AP® WORLD HISTORY EXAM

Why do you need to learn how to use evidence effectively? As a historian in training, you will need to know how claims and evidence work in tandem to create an effective argument. You will be expected to write your own arguments on the AP® exam. This means you will need to be able to use appropriate evidence to support your claim, whether that means facts that you remember, or primary sources given to you as part of the exam. You will also be expected to describe and explain the claim of a secondary source and the evidence used to support it. You may also encounter claims in the Multiple-Choice Questions, where you are referred to an excerpt from a historian and asked to choose the answer that best represents the historian's claim. Finally, knowing how to work with claims and evidence is the foundation of the Document-Based Question and the Long Essay Question, which account for 40 percent of your score on the exam. Both of these essays require that you make a strong claim (stated in a thesis) and summon evidence to support it in order to get full credit. On the Document-Based Question, you will work with the primary sources given to you, while on the Long Essay Question you will need to use facts as your evidence.

BUILDING AP® SKILLS

1. **Activity: Identifying Evidence.** In AP® Historians' Voices 3.1 (page 185), John Larner argues against claims that Marco Polo never traveled to China. Identify two pieces of evidence Larner offers to support the claim that Marco Polo visited the Yuan dynasty in China.

2. **Activity: Working with Evidence.** In AP® Historians' Voices 3.2 (page 185), Natalie Zemon Davis discusses two audiences Leo Africanus wrote for, claiming his primary audience was Italy. What evidence does Davis provide in this excerpt to prove this?

3. **Activity: Working with Claims and Evidence.** Using the information you have learned in this chapter about the Mongols, read the claim below and then answer the questions that follow.

Claim: The Mongols were responsible for significant technological and cultural transfers in Eurasia between 1200 and 1400 C.E.

a. Identify three pieces of evidence that support this claim.
b. Explain how the evidence provided substantiates the claim.

TRM Suggested Responses to Questions
You can find suggested responses to the Building AP® Skills questions in the Teacher's Resource Materials.

BUILDING AP® SKILLS

Argumentation

To help students work on using evidence to support an argument, have them work through Activity 3 on this page to develop evidence for an argument about the Mongols. Before they start, you should tell students that evidence cannot simply be a "name-drop" in their argument. They have to be able to explain the evidence within the argument (ex. "The Mongols helped the spread of gunpowder" vs. "The Mongols' use of gunpowder in their conquests helped the technology spread throughout Eurasia").

AP® LOOKING AGAIN

Chinese Cultural Traditions: The Relationship between Confucianism, Daoism, and Buddhism

For many centuries, three major cultural traditions have circulated and interacted within China. Two of them, Confucianism and Daoism, were homegrown, arising in China itself around the sixth century B.C.E. A third one, Buddhism, was born in India and arrived in China via the Silk Road commercial network in the early centuries of the Common Era. Much later the Chinese artist Wang Shugu (1649–1730) painted a hanging scroll that expressed his impression of the relationship among these three traditions. For scholars interested in the cultural history of China, this painting provides a visual source about that relationship.

WANG SHUGU | *China's Cultural Traditions*

The Art Archive/Shutterstock

175

TRM **Suggested Responses to Questions**
You can find suggested responses to the AP® Looking Again questions in the Teacher's Resource Materials.

BUILDING AP® SKILLS

Claims and Evidence in Sources

Students need to be able to interpret images to help them answer multiple-choice questions and to find evidence for the DBQ on the AP® Exam. The biggest struggle some of them will face is being able to "look" beyond just what the image is showing to understand the message of the image. You can use Wang Shugu's painting of China's cultural traditions to help students build this skill. Start by displaying the image for the students to see, and ask them what they think is going on in the image. *Answers will vary.*

Then have students read through the information under "A First Look" on page 176 and answer the accompanying questions. This will help them start to interpret Wang's painting by explaining who each figure is and will get them looking deeper into the image.

1 A FIRST LOOK

Let's start by taking a closer look at this Chinese painting by Wang Shugu (1649–1730) to better understand what it depicts.

First have a careful look at the figure to the left. What distinguishing features catch your attention? Wang's contemporaries in China would have focused on his bald spot, beard, and earring, all common visual cues used by Chinese painters to depict Laozi, the legendary founder of Daoism.

Now consider the figure to the right. What visual cues draw your eye? For Wang's intended audience, the figure's beard, distinctive head covering, and scholar's robes make him easily recognizable as the great Chinese philosopher Confucius whose ideas became the official state ideology of China.

Finally, have a careful look at the baby that Confucius holds. Do you think that the child is simply a prop for Confucius or distinctive figure in his own right? Among Wang's intended audience, the tuft of hair on the child's forehead is an unmistakable sign that this baby is the Buddha, the founder of the Buddhist tradition.

Through such visual clues, Wang would have expected his audience to easily identify the three figures, all of them very well known in the China of 1200. Historians working with visual sources of the past must be aware of these symbolic languages that artists rely upon to communicate with their intended audiences.

1. What action is depicted in the scene?

2. How might you describe the tone or feeling of the painting and the relationship among its three figures?

2 A SECOND LOOK

We know little about the context of this painting—when it was painted, for instance, or whether a patron commissioned it. Nonetheless, elements of the painting itself—the figures, their interactions, its overall tone—provide hints as to its possible purpose, meaning, or point of view. Have another careful look at the painting.

1. What do you think that Wang intended to convey? What specific features of the painting support your answer?

2. Buddhism assimilated into Chinese society centuries after Daoism and Confucianism had taken root. Does the image in any way represent this difference? How might the dress of the three figures and their relative ages convey the deeper roots of Confucianism and Daoism in Chinese society?

BUILDING AP® SKILLS

Claims and Evidence in Sources

If you would like your students to dig deeper into Wang Shugu's painting, have them read through the "Second Look" and "Third Look" sections on pages 176 and 177 and answer the questions. This would be a good place to have either a small group (three or four students) or a class discussion on what they believe the message of the painting was and what it says about Chinese cultural traditions.

3 A THIRD LOOK

In Chinese painting, Laozi, Confucius, and the Buddha frequently stood in as personifications (figurative representations) of their respective cultural traditions.

1. Could Wang be using personification in this image? If so, how might this purpose affect how you describe the scene?

2. What overall relationship between the three cultural traditions do you think that Wang wished to convey? What do you make of the baby Buddha's outstretched arms? Does Wang's image depict the three faith traditions as essentially equal, or might the image imply that some traditions are more central or important in Chinese society?

AP° ACTIVITY IDENTIFYING INTENTION

In a brief paragraph, describe Wang's point of view or purpose in depicting China's three major cultural traditions.

FURTHER ACTIVITY

When Wang painted this image in the late seventeenth or early eighteenth centuries, Daoism, Confucianism, and Buddhism had been long established in China. To what extent does his image match the reality of Buddhism's arrival and integration into Chinese society? What elements of the Buddhist experience are downplayed or missing?

BUILDING AP® SKILLS

Sourcing and Situation

Since sourcing is one of the hardest points to earn on the DBQ essay, it's good to have students work on this skill throughout the year. You can have students practice sourcing by asking them to respond to the prompt under "AP® Activity: Identifying Intention" on this page.

177

You can find suggested responses to the AP® Working with Evidence questions in the Teacher's Resource Materials.

BUILDING AP® SKILLS

Claims and Evidence in Sources

Interpreting text-based as well as non-text-based sources is an important skill for AP® World History students. If time is available, have students learn more about travelers on the trade routes by reading "Travelers' Tales and Observations" beginning on page 178. Consider having students analyze one or more of the sources found on pages 178–183. Check for understanding by:

- Using the questions at the end of each source as a discussion starting point.

- Pairing students up to analyze (identify and describe) the author or creator's point of view, purpose, historical situation, and/or audience.

- Assigning a source to a group of three to four students and having them present an overview of the source along with the sourcing to the rest of the class.

- Having students practice document analysis skills by focusing on Documents 1, 4, and 5 to learn more about the men who wrote them.

A good discussion can begin with questions such as:

- "What motivated these men to travel so far from home?"

- "What do their differing perspectives tell us about their views of the places they traveled to?"

- "How did they integrate with the societies they visited?"

Travelers' Tales and Observations

As long-distance trade flourished and large transregional empires grew, opportunities increased for individuals to travel far beyond their homelands. Their accounts have provided historians with invaluable information about particular regions and cultures, as well as about interactions among disparate peoples. The authors of these accounts, perhaps inadvertently, also reveal much about themselves and about the perceptions and misperceptions generated by cross-cultural encounters. The sources that follow offer examples of how intrepid long-distance travelers described distant lands and how artists and mapmakers depicted faraway regions for those who stayed at home.

LOOKING AHEAD

AP® DBQ PRACTICE

As you read the documents in this collection, consider what they reveal about how networks of human interaction developed. Think also about the cultural and political consequences of these interactions.

DOCUMENT 1 A European Christian in China

Of all the travelers along the Silk Road network, the best known and most celebrated, at least in the West, was Marco Polo (1254–1324). Born and raised in the prosperous commercial city-state of Venice in northern Italy, he was a member of a family engaged in the long-distance trade of the Mediterranean and Black Sea regions. At the age of seventeen, Marco accompanied his father and an uncle on an epic journey across Eurasia that, by 1275, brought the Polos to China, recently conquered by the Mongols. It was, in fact, the relative peace that the Mongols had created in their huge transcontinental empire that facilitated the Polos' journey (see Map 3.2). For the next seventeen years, they lived in China, where they were employed in minor administrative positions by Khubilai Khan, the country's Mongol ruler. During these years, Marco Polo apparently traveled widely within China, where he gathered material for a book about his travels, which he dictated to a friend after returning home in 1295. The selection that follows conveys Marco Polo's description of Hangzhou — one of the largest cities in the world at the time — which he refers to as Kinsay. Polo tells his reader that he constructed this description from both his visit to Hangzhou and a written account of the city sent to the Mongol khan in the hopes of sparing the city from destruction following its conquest.

Source: Marco Polo, Venetian traveler along the Silk Road, describing the Chinese city of Hangzhou, from *The Book of Ser Marco Polo, the Venetian, Concerning the Kingdoms and Marvels of the East,* 1295.

The city is beyond dispute the finest and the noblest in the world. . . . First and foremost, then, the document stated the city of Kinsay to be so great that it hath a hundred miles of compass. And there are in it 12,000 bridges of stone. . . .

[T]here were in this city twelve guilds of the different crafts, and each guild had 12,000 houses in the occupation of its workmen. Each of these houses contains at least twelve men, whilst some contain twenty and some forty. . . . And yet all these craftsmen had full occupation, for many other cities of the kingdom are supplied from this city with what they require.

[T]he number and wealth of the merchants, and the amount of goods that passed through their hands, were so enormous that no man could form a just estimate thereof. . . . [T]hose masters of the different crafts. . . . neither they nor their wives ever touch a piece of work with their own hands, but live as nicely and delicately as if they were kings and queens. . . .

Inside the city there is a Lake. . . . and all round it are erected beautiful palaces and mansions, of the richest and most exquisite structure that you can imagine, belonging to the nobles of the city. There are also on its shores many abbeys and churches of the Idolaters [Buddhists]. In the middle of the Lake are two Islands, on each of which stands a rich, beautiful, and spacious edifice, furnished in such style as to seem fit for the palace of an Emperor. And when any one of the citizens desired to hold a marriage feast, or to give any other entertainment, it used to be done at one of these palaces. And everything would be found there ready to order, such as silver plates, trenchers, and dishes, napkins and table-clothes, and whatever else was needful.

Question to Consider: What evidence in this section reveals that Marco Polo viewed China from the vantage point of an outsider?

AP **Analyzing Sources:** Analyze the author's purpose. What impact did he hope to have on European readers?

DOCUMENT 2 A Korean World Map

Created in Korea in 1402, the Kangnido map by the Confucian scholar Kwŏn Kŭn is the oldest world map from East Asia of which copies survive. It provides an East Asian perspective on the world in the early fifteenth century, a period immediately following the collapse of the Mongol Empire, which had put distant regions of the Afro-Eurasian world into more sustained contact than ever before. The Kangnido map drew upon earlier maps from China, Korea, Japan, and the Islamic world. While Korea features prominently, appearing larger than Africa, China is understood as the center of the world, as Kwŏn Kŭn makes clear in the preface: "The world is very wide. We do not know how many tens of thousands of *li* there are from China in the center to the four seas in the outer limits." (A *li* is a Chinese unit of distance, about a third of a mile.) The map includes hundreds of place names for even the most remote regions of Eurasia. Most of those for North Africa and Europe incorporate Arabic or

179

Persian roots, revealing the influence of Islamic maps and mapmakers brought to East Asia by the Mongols. Regional labels not original to the map have been added to help you orient yourself. Note that the Mediterranean Sea is clearly outlined between Africa and Europe but is not colored in. Also note that much of the center of Africa is shaded in, indicating either a large body of water or perhaps the Sahara Desert.

Source: *The Honkoji Copy of the Kangnido Map, Korea*, from Confucian scholar Kwŏn Kŭn, depicting an East Asian perspective of the 15th-century world, 1402.

Pictures from History/Bridgeman Images

Question to Consider: What can a map like this tell us about East Asian knowledge of Eurasia and Africa around 1400?

AP **Analyzing Sources:** Analyze the ways in which this map provides evidence of Korea's relationship to the outside world.

DOCUMENT 3   A European Artist Depicts Asia

While Marco Polo's account is largely devoid of the wondrous monsters and races of humans that peopled many earlier European accounts of the East, his book did not immediately overturn these more fanciful ideas about distant lands. Document 3, an image that was created to illustrate an elaborate manuscript copy of Polo's book, provides a revealing window into the persistence of older ideas. Drawn around 1400, it depicts three mythical creatures—a blemmyae or headless man, a sciopod or single-footed man, and a cyclops or one-eyed monster—none of which are mentioned in Polo's text.

Source: Image depicting "The Marvelous Races of the East" that accompanied a manuscript of Marco Polo's travels, ca. 1410–1412.

Bridgeman Images

Question to Consider: What does this source add to our understanding of how Europeans viewed East Asia in the early fifteenth century?

AP **Analyzing Sources:** Why might the artist have depicted East Asians this way even though Marco Polo's text makes no mention of other species of humans?

181

DOCUMENT 4 A Chinese Maritime Explorer in India

Around 1380, Ma Huan was born in the coastal region of southern China, almost certainly into a family of modest means. Little is known about his life, except that he accompanied Zheng He, the great Ming dynasty Chinese admiral, on three of his seven expeditions into the Indian Ocean, the last in 1433, and in 1451 published an account of his experiences entitled *Ying-Yai Sheng-Lan: The Overall Survey of the Ocean's Shores* (see "Chinese Maritime Voyages in the Indian Ocean World"). Entries in the *Overall Survey* chronicle the fleet's journeys and offer succinct but vivid descriptions of places it visited. The extracts reproduced here focus on a mission to the south Indian kingdom of Cochin and especially its major trading port of Calicut—the same port that the Portuguese explorer Vasco da Gama would visit in the 1490s when he became the first European to sail directly to India. While Ma Huan's text is primarily descriptive, largely avoiding overt judgments of the societies that he visited, it was written for a Chinese audience and with an eye to providing a guide for later visitors. Ma Huan's writing had little impact on his contemporaries because, by the time of its publication, Chinese naval expeditions had ended and the focus of the Chinese government had shifted away from expanding its influence in the Indian Ocean. Nonetheless, his account provides a fascinating perspective of the Indian Ocean world during a period when China was unusually interested in discovering more about the lands to its west.

Source: Ma Huan, who accompanied Chinese admiral Zheng He on his Indian Ocean expeditions, from *Ying-Yai Sheng-Lan: The Overall Survey of the Ocean's Shores,* 1451.

In the fifth year of the Yung-lo [period] the court ordered the principal envoy the grand eunuch Cheng Ho [Zheng He] and others to deliver an imperial mandate to the king of this country [Cochin] and to bestow on him a patent conferring a title of honour, and the grant of a silver seal, [also] to promote all the chiefs and award them hats and girdles of various grades.

[So Zheng He] went there in command of a large fleet of treasure-ships, and he erected a tablet with a pavilion over it and set up a stone which said "Though the journey from this country to the Central Country [China] is more than a hundred thousand *li*, yet the people are very similar, happy and prosperous, with identical customs. We have engraved a stone, a perpetual declaration for ten thousand ages."

Ma Huan, *Ying-Yai Sheng-Lan: The Overall Survey of the Ocean's Shores 1433*, translated by Ch'eng Chun (London: The Hakluyt Society, 1970), pp. 138, 140–41, 143, 145.

Question to Consider: What does this section reveal about the relationship between the Chinese emperor and the Cochin king?

AP **Analyzing Sources:** Analyze the impact on the potential audience. Why do you think Chinese readers might have been interested in knowing about this?

DOCUMENT 5 A Moroccan Diplomat in West Africa

Known to the world by his European-derived nickname of Leo Africanus, this widely traveled Arabic-speaking Muslim was actually born as al-Hassan Ibn Muhammad al Wazzan in Granada, Spain, during the late fifteenth century, just as Islam was being pushed out of that country. His family moved to Fez in Morocco, where he was educated in Islamic law. Later, he served the sultan of Morocco as a diplomat and commercial agent, traveling widely in North Africa, the Middle East, Italy, and West Africa. On one of these journeys, he was captured by pirates and wound up in Rome, where he came to the attention of Pope Leo X. There he apparently converted to Christianity, at least for a time, though he later chose to live in Muslim North Africa and likely returned to his original Muslim faith. It was during his stay in Italy that he completed in 1526 the book for which he is most clearly remembered, *The History and Description of Africa*, based on observations and knowledge picked up during his travels. Later published in many languages, it became a major source of European knowledge of the African Islamic world, much as Marco Polo's writings introduced Europeans to China. In the following excerpts from that book, Leo Africanus describes Timbuktu, one of the major cities of West African civilization.

> Source: Moroccan diplomat Leo Africanus describing Timbuktu, from *The History and Description of Africa*, 1526.
>
> All its houses are. . . . cottages, built of mud and covered with thatch. However, there is a most stately mosque to be seen, whose walls are made of stone and lime, and a princely palace also constructed by the highly skilled craftsmen of Granada. Here there are many shops of artisans and merchants, especially of those who weave linen and cotton, and here Barbary [Muslim North African] merchants bring European cloth. The inhabitants, and especially resident aliens, are exceedingly rich, since the present king married both of his daughters to rich merchants. There are many wells, containing sweet water. Whenever the Niger River overflows, they carry the water into town by means of sluices. This region yields great quantities of grain, cattle, milk, and butter, but salt is very scarce here, for it is brought here by land from Tegaza, which is five hundred miles away.
>
> The rich king of Timbuktu has many plates and scepters of gold, some of which weigh 1,300 pounds, and he keeps a magnificent and well-furnished court. When he travels anywhere, he rides upon a camel, which is led by some of his noblemen. . . .
>
> Here are great numbers of [Islamic] religious teachers, judges, scholars and other learned persons, who are bountifully maintained at the king's expense. Here too are brought various [Arabic] manuscripts or written books from Barbary, which are sold for more money than any other merchandise.

Question to Consider: What evidence does the author present about life in Timbuktu and the city's interaction with global markets?

AP Analyzing Sources: Analyze West Africa's relationship to broader networks of exchange.

1. **DBQ Practice:** Develop an argument in which you evaluate the extent to which global commerce led to cultural interactions during this period.

2. **Sourcing and Situation:** All of these sources were created by outsiders to the peoples or societies they described. What different postures toward these foreign cultures are evident in the sources? How did the travelers' various religions shape their perception of the places they visited?

3. **Sourcing and Situation:** What can we learn from Documents 1, 4, and 5 about the men who wrote them? What motivated them to travel so far from home? How did they define themselves in relationship to the societies they observed?

4. **Argumentation:** What information in these sources would be most valuable for historians? What about these sources might be viewed with the most skepticism? You will want to consider the creators' purposes and their intended audiences.

5. **Sourcing and Situation:** What are the advantages and limitations for historians of drawing on the observations of foreign observers?

AP® HISTORIANS' VOICES

On Travel Writers

Travel accounts provide rich and often unique sources for historians, but they must be handled with care. The two selections that follow consider issues that historians confront when studying travelers' accounts. In Voice 3.1, John Larner, an expert on Marco Polo, examines the suspicion put forward by some that Polo never traveled to China. In Voice 3.2, Natalie Zemon Davis, a prominent historian of the early modern period, explores the audiences for which Leo Africanus wrote his book.

VOICE 3.1

John Larner on Whether Polo Really Traveled to China | 1999

From the eighteenth century, as a result above all of Marco's silence about many things in the China of his own time, the suspicion has been aroused in some readers that we are faced here with a fiction, the nagging doubt that the whole of Marco's story of having been to China is untrue. Why does he never mention the Great Wall? Why is there nothing about what, in the fourteenth century, Odoric da Pordenone [another traveler] was to notice: fishing with cormorants, or the binding up of young girls' feet? Why nothing on printing, Chinese script, acupuncture, tea or tea-houses? Why no mention of Confucianism or Taoism? Had he actually *seen* China . . . ? It is not too difficult to offer answers to most of these points. The myth of the Great Wall, for instance, obscures . . . the fact that much of it had fallen down by the thirteenth century. Almost everything the tourist is normally shown today was built in the sixteenth century. Referred to as the "sensi" or "sensin," Taoist monks are in fact briefly mentioned in chapter LXXV. Foot binding was at this period limited to upper class ladies who were confined to their houses, and would be rarely observed by anyone outside their family. Tea-culture at that time had not reached North and Central China where Marco mostly resided. . . . [I]t can also easily be thought that Marco identified himself so strongly with Mongol rulers that he was indifferent to the mass of the population over whom they rule.

Source: John Larner, *Marco Polo and the Discovery of the World* (New Haven, CT: Yale University Press, 1999), 59.

VOICE 3.2

Natalie Zemon Davis on Leo Africanus's Audiences | 2006

He [Leo Africanus] was keeping notes throughout his travels and consulting manuscripts whenever he could; he may have had an initial plan for a book and partial drafts of some sections in Arabic on his person when he was kidnapped. However that may be, it was in Italy that he became an author, and the final version [of his book] bears the stamp of his stay there. . . .

In a sense, though, [Leo Africanus] wrote his book with two audiences in mind. His primary audience was in Italy. For his Italian readers he searched for equivalents in weights, measures, coinages, foods, and material objects. For them, he sought Italian translations for words with no perfect equivalent. . . . For them, he struggled valiantly to transcribe Arabic words, names, and place names. . . . For Italian readers, too, he included only those animals "not found in Europe or that were in some ways different from those in Europe."

Yet [he] also had African or at least North African readers and listeners in part of his mind as he composed. He must have imagined at least a few of them as possible readers of this Italian manuscript, and many of them as potential readers of a much revised Arabic version.

Source: Natalie Zemon Davis, *Trickster Travels: A Sixteenth-Century Muslim between Worlds* (New York: Hill and Wang, 2006), 105–7.

AP® Analyzing Secondary Sources

1. Why have scholars questioned whether Marco Polo actually traveled to China?

2. How might Leo Africanus have altered his account for a North African rather than Italian audience?

3. **Integrating Primary and Secondary Sources:** How do these two voices influence your reading of the Polo and Africanus selections in the source feature?

BUILDING AP® SKILLS

Argumentation

Interpreting secondary sources is an important skill for AP® World History: Modern students. Consider having students read one or both of the sources found on page 185. Ask students to practice argumentation skills by having them identify the claims in one or both selections and the evidence used to support those claims. This activity can help them practice the skills necessary for writing good DBQs and LEQs. If students are struggling with the format of an argument, it might be helpful for them to go back and look at the model provided in the AP® Skills Workshop: Evidence on page 173.

TRM Suggested Responses to Questions
You can find suggested responses to the AP® Analyzing Secondary Sources questions in the Teacher's Resource Materials.

185

TRM Suggested Responses to Questions
You can find suggested responses to the
Chapter 3 AP® Exam Practice questions in the
Teacher's Resource Materials.

TEACHING IDEA

AP® Exam Strategies

Continue having students practice test-taking
skills. Copy the multiple-choice questions
found on pages 186 to 189. Give students the
questions as a practice quiz prior to the unit
or chapter test. Have students discuss with a
partner why their answer choice was correct or
incorrect.

CHAPTER 3 (AP®) EXAM PRACTICE

Multiple-Choice Questions Choose the correct answer for each question.

Questions 1–3 refer to this map.

The Crusades

1. The First through Fourth Crusades (1095–1204) involved the Byzantine Empire, Muslim states,
   and Western Europe in a series of conflicts over what world region?
   a. Southwest Asia
   b. East Africa
   c. Southeast Asia
   d. Northwest Africa

2. Which of the following comparisons between the Byzantine Empire and other empires is most
   historically accurate?
   a. Like the Russian Empire, the Byzantine Empire was short-lived.
   b. As in the Abbasid caliphate, religious leaders in the Byzantine Empire were polytheistic.
   c. Like the Song dynasty, the Byzantine Empire built on the legacy of an earlier empire.
   d. Like the Ottoman Empire, the Byzantine Empire declined and fell quickly.

186

3. Based on the map above and your knowledge of world history, which of the following was true by the thirteenth century?

   a. Catholic Christianity was expanding in Western Europe.

   b. The Holy Roman Empire controlled all of Catholic Europe.

   c. The Seljuk Turks controlled most of the Muslim world.

   d. Europe saw a decreasing amount of trade with the Muslim world.

Questions 4–6 refer to this map.

The Sea Roads

4. Which of the following most directly led to the expansion and intensification before 1450 of the commercial routes depicted in the map above?

   a. Growing contacts among cultures resulting from the voyages of Zheng He

   b. The discovery by Europeans of spices in Southeast Asia

   c. New technologies and knowledge of monsoon wind patterns

   d. Northern military expansion of Southeast Asian empires

187

5. The economic and political transformations evident in the map would best be understood in the context of
   a. continuities in techniques of state building.
   b. the rise of trading cities on the Indian Ocean coast.
   c. the widening practice of state-issued currencies.
   d. the Mongol conquests and their consequences.

6. Which of the following developments was a direct result of new patterns of Indian Ocean trade?
   a. A desire on the part of African monarchs to discover maritime routes to markets in Europe and Asia
   b. The decentralization of political power in Southeast Asian states
   c. The spread of Islam across the region
   d. A decrease in the social complexity of urban areas

Questions 7–9 refer to these passages.

> Inside the city . . . there are many abbeys and churches of the Idolaters. . . . Both men and women clothe themselves in silk, so vast is the supply of the material. . . . The crowd of people . . . is so vast that no one would believe it possible to [feed them all]. . . . All the squares are crammed with traders who have brought in stores . . . by land or water. . . . And [they are] free from all jealousy or suspicion of the conduct of their women. These they treat with the greatest respect.
>
> — Marco Polo describing a Chinese city in *The Book of Ser Marco Polo, the Venetian,*
> *Concerning the Kingdoms and Marvels of the East*

> The garments of the town's inhabitants are made of fine Egyptian fabrics. . . . [T]heir women show no bashfulness before men and do not veil themselves, though they are [faithful] in attending the prayers. . . . A traveler in this country carries no provisions, [not] food or seasonings, neither gold nor silver. When he comes to a village the women bring out millet, milk, chickens, plump lotus fruit, rice and . . . pounded haricot beans.
>
> — Ibn Battuta describing a West African city in *Travels in Asia and Africa 1325–1354*

7. Which of the following is the most likely reason for similarities between Marco Polo's and Ibn Battuta's accounts of their travels in the thirteenth and fourteenth centuries?
   a. Historians believe they may have met each other on their journeys and compared observations.
   b. Both the areas observed participated in significant long-distance trade.
   c. Both the areas observed were highly influenced by Confucian teachings.
   d. The travelers had the same religious background and prejudices.

8. Which of these statements accurately describes the political status of China in Marco Polo's time?
   a. China was under foreign influence by European commercial interests.
   b. China was experiencing a series of civil wars led by regional warlords.
   c. China was under the control of Mongol rulers.
   d. China was controlled by religious leaders who chose the emperor.

9. Which of these statements best accounts for the observations made by these travelers about the status of women in China and West Africa in this era?

   a. Religious syncretism had lowered the status of women dramatically in the areas visited by Polo and Battuta.

   b. Both observers assumed that most of the readers of their accounts would be women, so their observations complimented women.

   c. Both observed the societies they visited through the lens of their own cultural values.

   d. Ibn Battuta was writing as a Muslim in a Muslim land, while Polo was a Christian in a Confucian land, so Battuta's observations are less subjective.

Short-Answer Questions

Read each question carefully and write a short response. Use complete sentences.

1. **Use the passage below and your knowledge of world history to answer all parts of the question that follows.**

   [The Crusades have] been variously interpreted. [They have] been presented as warfare to defend a beleaguered Faith or the ultimate expression of secular piety. Alternatively, some have regarded [them] as . . . a defining commitment of the church to accommodate the spiritual aspirations of the laity. [C]rusading is portrayed as an agent as well as a symbol of religious, cultural, or ethnic identity or even superiority; a vehicle for personal or communal [gain], commercial expansion, or political conquest. . . . Conflicting assessments of the Crusades have described them as manifestations of religious love, by Christians for fellow believers and by God for his people; an experiment in European colonialism; an excuse for religious persecution, ethnic cleansing, and acts of barbarism; or a noble cause. — Christopher Tyermann, *Fighting for Christendom: Holy War and the Crusades*

   A. Identify ONE specific example that supports an interpretation of the Crusades referenced in the excerpt above.

   B. Identify ANOTHER specific example that supports an interpretation of the Crusades referenced in the excerpt above.

   C. Explain ONE effect of the Crusades not mentioned in the excerpt above.

BUILDING AP® SKILLS

Argumentation

Writing skills should be practiced on a regular basis, and SAQs are a good way for students to quickly work on those needed skills. Choose one of the SAQs on pages 189 and 190 for students to write at the end of class as an "exit ticket" to check for understanding.

189

2. Use the map below and your knowledge of world history to answer all parts of the question that follows.

The American Web

A. Identify and explain ONE similarity between Aztec and Inca trading systems.

B. Identify and explain ONE difference between Aztec and Inca trading systems.

C. Explain WHY exchanges between North and South America occurred on a significantly smaller scale than across Afro-Eurasia.

3. Use your knowledge of world history to answer all parts of the question that follows.

A. Identify ONE technology that helped merchants overcome environmental barriers to trade between 1200 and 1450 c.e.

B. Explain ONE way in which the rise of an organized state facilitated Eurasian trade routes between 1200 and 1450 c.e.

C. Explain ONE way in which commercial contacts facilitated state building between 1200 and 1450 c.e.

PERIOD 1 | AP® Exam Practice

Document-Based Question
Using these sources and your knowledge of world history, develop an argument in response to the prompt.

1. Evaluate the extent to which religious belief systems impacted governance in Afro-Eurasia from 1200 to 1550.

Document 1

Source: *The Chronicle of Novgorod*, a Russian account of the 13th-century Mongol invasion of Russia, written in the 13th century.

In 1238, the Mongols came in countless numbers, like locusts, into our land. They sent messengers to our princes demanding one-tenth of everything. And the princes said, "Only when none of us remain will all be yours."

But it was too late to oppose the wrath of God on us. God took our strength and put us into perplexity and thunder and dread because of our sins. And then the pagan foreigners surrounded us ... and killed the princes, men, women, children, nuns and priests. But God saved the Bishop, for he had departed the morning the Mongols invaded.

Document 2

Source: Mongol emperor Möngke Khan speaking to Christian traveler William Rubruck, 1255.

We Mongols believe in one God, by Whom we live and die. Just as God gave different fingers to the hand so has He given different ways to men. To you God has given the Scriptures and you Christians do not observe them. Tell your [Christian] leaders I will offer my cooperation, but, if you bring an army against us—we know what we can do.

Document 3

Source: Court official and member of Japan's imperial family, Kitabatake Chikafusa, on the uniqueness of Japan; from *The Chronicle of the Direct Descent of Gods and Sovereigns*, 1339.

Japan is the divine country. The heavenly ancestor it was who first laid its foundations, and the Sun Goddess left her descendants to reign over it forever and ever. This is true only of our country, and nothing similar may be found in foreign lands. That is why it is called the divine country.

In China, nothing positive is stated concerning the creation of the world, even though China is a country which accords special importance to the keeping of records....

China is also a country of notorious disorders. Even in ancient times, when life was simple and conduct was proper, the throne was offered to wise men, and no single lineage was established. Later, in times of disorder, men fought for control of the country.

Only in our country has the succession remained inviolate from the beginning of heaven and earth to the present. It has been maintained within a single lineage, and even when, as inevitably has happened, the succession has been transmitted collaterally, it has returned to the true line. This is due to the ever-renewed Divine Oath and makes Japan unlike all other countries....

191

TRM Suggested Responses to Questions
You can find suggested responses to the Period 1 AP® Exam Practice questions in the Teacher's Resource Materials.

BUILDING AP® SKILLS

Argumentation

The Document-Based Question (DBQ) is an important part of the AP® World History: Modern Exam because it is 25 percent of the overall score on the exam. Since the topic of this DBQ is near the beginning of the material tested on the AP® Exam, have students analyze the documents and then write an "outline" DBQ where they will write a contextualization, a thesis, two to three arguments, at least two documents to defend each argument, and sourcing for at least three documents. You can find a reproducible version of a DBQ outline in the Teacher's Resource Materials.

TRM Writing Organizer for DBQ Practice

Document 4

Source: Painting of Charlemagne, king of the Franks, being crowned by Pope Leo III in the 9th century; painting from the 14th century.

Document 5

Source: A Christian witness to the sacking of Constantinople, 1453.

The enraged Turkish soldiers gave no quarter. When they had massacred and there was no longer any resistance, they roamed through the town stealing, pillaging, killing, and taking captive men, women, children, monks and priests. Saints' altars, torn from their foundations, were overturned. All the most holy hiding places were violated and broken in order to get out the holy treasures which they contained. . . .

When [Muslim leader] Mehmed saw the ravages, the destruction and the deserted houses and all that had perished and become ruins, then a great sadness took possession of him and he repented the pillage and all the destruction. Tears came to his eyes and sobbing, he expressed his sadness.

Document 6

Source: Queen Isabella of Spain, *Royal Edict of Expulsion*, which expelled all Muslims from Spain, 1502.

And because Our Lord has helped us in our time to throw out from that kingdom our ancient enemies, who have for so long and so many years fought against our Faith, and against the Kings, our ancestors, and against our kingdoms, so it is with good reason that we are grateful for this, and for the other great benefits we have received from His Divine Majesty. Now, let us cast out of our kingdoms the enemies of his most Holy Name, and let us no longer allow that there be in our kingdoms people who follow the reprobate laws of the infidels.

Document 7

Source: Leo Africanus, high-ranking Muslim official from Morocco, from his book *The History and Description of Africa*, 16th century.

"The Kingdom of Borno": They embrace no religion at all, being neither Christian, Muslim nor Jew, but living in a brutish manner, having wives and children in common. Their king is most powerful, and the people are not forced to pay many taxes, except on their grain. Most revenue for the government comes from spoils taken from his enemies by frequent invasions.

"The City of Timbuktu": The rich king of Timbuktu has many plates of gold, some of which weigh 1300 pounds. Here are great numbers of Islamic religious teachers, judges and other learned persons, who are bountifully maintained at the king's expense. The inhabitants are gentle and cheerful and spend a great part of the night in singing and dancing throughout the city streets.

Long Essay Questions

Using your knowledge of world history, develop an argument in response to one of the following questions.

2. In the era ca. 1200–ca. 1450, empires continued to maintain their power.

   Evaluate the extent to which Islamic civilizations and American civilizations were similar in the methods they used to maintain their power.

3. At its peak, the Mongol Empire stretched from East Asia to Eastern Europe and into Southwest Asia.

   Evaluate the extent to which the Mongols affected Eurasian trade networks beginning in the thirteenth century.

4. In the era ca. 1200–ca. 1450, the Silk, Sand, and Sea roads were the dominant trade networks in Afro-Eurasia.

   Evaluate the extent to which products and cultural exchanges were similar between the Silk Roads and the Indian Ocean trade network.

BUILDING AP® SKILLS

Argumentation

The Long Essay Question (LEQ) is the last writing part of the AP® World History: Modern Exam and is 15 percent of the overall score on the exam. Some of the skills students have learned from the DBQ and SAQs can be transferred over to the LEQ, like contextualization, developing an argument, and using evidence to support an argument, so it's okay if you choose to teach the LEQ after the other two writing styles. Students will be able to pick from one of three prompts listed on the exam, so you can have students practice choosing which prompt works best for them from the three listed on page 193. Since the topics of these LEQs are near the beginning of the material tested on the AP® Exam, have students write an "outline" LEQ where they will write a contextualization, a thesis, two to three arguments, and at least two pieces of evidence to defend their arguments. You can find a reproducible version of an LEQ outline in the Teacher's Resource Materials.

TRM **Writing Organizer for LEQ Practice**

Prior AP® World History Exam questions are available on the AP® World History: Modern course website. While older DBQs and FRQs are excellent practice for building writing skills in AP® students, it is important to keep in mind that the essay format changed slightly in the 2019–2020 school year. The following questions are relevant to this part of the text. Questions marked with an asterisk (*) are available on the AP® World History: Modern course website or in AP® Classroom in a modified version, compatible with the 2011 revisions to the Course Framework, but they may need further revision to fit the 2019–2020 model.

Document-Based Questions

■ 2006, Question 1: Evaluate the extent to which the global flow of silver affected economic and/or social structures around the world in the mid-sixteenth to the eighteenth century. (Revised prompt)

■ 2002, Question 1: Evaluate the extent to which the attitudes of Christianity and Islam toward trade differed from their origins through the sixteenth century. (Revised prompt)

■ 2017, Question 1: Evaluate the extent to which religious and political attitudes toward wealth accumulation were similar from ca. 600 B.C.E. to 1500 C.E. (Revised prompt)

■ 2019, Question 1: Evaluate the extent to which the Portuguese transformed maritime trade in the Indian Ocean in the sixteenth century.

Long Essay Questions

■ 2008, Question 2: Develop an argument that evaluates the extent to which commerce in the Indian Ocean transformed in the period 650 to 1750.* (Revised prompt)

■ 2003, Question 2: Develop an argument that evaluates the extent to which Islam influenced culture, economics, and/or politics in Afro-Eurasia from 1000 to 1750.* (Revised prompt)

■ 2005, Question 2: Develop an argument that evaluates the extent to which contacts with Afro-Eurasia led to social and/or economic transformations in the Americas from 1492 to 1750.* (Revised prompt)

■ 2014, Question 2: Develop an argument that evaluates the extent to which the various ways states/groups around the world participated in interregional trade changed from 1500 to 1750. (Revised prompt)

■ 2007, Question 3: Develop an argument that evaluates the extent to which the methods of empire building differed between two or more empires in the period 1450 to 1750. (Revised prompt)

PERIOD 2

The Early Modern World
1450–1750

Chapter 4 Political Transformations: Empires and Encounters, 1450–1750

Chapter 5 Cultural Transformations: Religion and Science, 1450–1750

Chapter 6 Economic Transformations: Commerce and Consequence, 1450–1750

THE BIG PICTURE

Toward Modernity . . . or Not?

For the sake of clarity and coherence, historians often characterize a particular period of time in a brief phrase such as "the age of First Civilizations" or "the era of revolutions." Though useful and even necessary, such capsule descriptions vastly oversimplify what actually happened. Historical reality is always more messy, more complicated, and more uncertain than any shorthand label can convey. Such is surely the case when we examine the three centuries spanning the years from roughly 1450 to 1750, commonly labeled the "early modern era."

194

■ 2012, Question 3: Develop an argument that evaluates the extent to which the Columbian exchange contributed to demographic changes around the world from 1492 to 1750. (Revised prompt)

■ 2017, Question 2: Develop an argument that evaluates the extent to which labor migration contributed to cultural and/or social changes in the period 1450 to 1750. (Revised prompt)

■ 2018, Question 3: Develop an argument that evaluates the extent to which the Columbian exchange affected peoples in the Americas in the period 1450–1750. (Revised prompt)

■ 2021, Question 3: In the period circa 1450–1750, European expansion affected the development of numerous East Asian and South Asian states. Develop an argument that evaluates the extent to which the economies of East and/or South Asian states in this time period changed in response to European expansion.

■ 2022, Question 3: In the period circa 1450–1750, the global increase in transregional contacts led to both expansion and contraction of existing religions as well as the development of new religious practices. Develop an argument that evaluates the extent to which military conflict or conquest was the main cause of religious change in this period.

Sprouts of Modernity?

In defining those centuries as "the early modern era," historians are suggesting that during this period of time we can find some initial signs, markers, or sprouts of what became the modern world. Such indicators of a new era in human history include the beginnings of genuine globalization; new demographic, economic, and intellectual patterns; and a growing European presence in world affairs.

The most obvious expression of globalization lay in the oceanic journeys of European explorers, the European conquest and colonial settlement of the Americas, and all that followed from these events. The Atlantic slave trade linked Africa permanently to Europe and the Western Hemisphere, while the global silver trade allowed Europeans to buy their way into ancient Asian markets. The massive exchange of plants, animals, diseases, and people, known to historians as the Columbian exchange, created wholly new networks of interaction across both the Atlantic and Pacific oceans, with enormous global implications. Furthermore, missionaries carried Christianity far beyond Europe, making it a genuinely global religion with a presence in the Americas, China, Japan, the Philippine Islands, Siberia, and south-central Africa.

But Western Europeans were not alone in weaving this emerging global web. Russians marched across Siberia to the Pacific, creating the world's largest territorial state. China expanded deep into Inner Asia, bringing Mongolia, Xinjiang, and Tibet into a much enlarged Chinese empire. The Turkish Ottoman Empire brought much of the Middle East, North Africa, and southeastern Europe into the Islamic world's largest and most powerful state. Japanese merchants moved aggressively to open up commercial opportunities in Southeast Asia even as Indian traders penetrated the markets of Central Asia, Persia, and Russia.

Scattered signs of what later generations thought of as "modern life" likewise appeared in various places around the world. The most obviously modern cultural development took place in Europe, where the Scientific Revolution transformed, at least for a few people, their view of the world, their approach to seeking knowledge, and their understanding of traditional Christianity. Subsequently, a scientific outlook spread globally, becoming perhaps the most potent marker of modern life.

Demographically, China, Japan, India, and Europe experienced the beginnings of modern population growth. Human numbers more than doubled between 1400 and 1800 (from about 374 million to 968 million), even as the globalization of disease produced a demographic catastrophe in the Americas and the slave trade limited African population growth.

Yet another indication of modern life lay in more highly commercialized economies centered in large cities that developed in various parts of Eurasia and the Americas. By the early eighteenth century, for example, Japan was one of the most urbanized societies in the world. In China, Southeast Asia, India, and across the Atlantic basin, more and more people found themselves, sometimes willingly and at other times involuntarily, producing for distant markets rather than for the use of their local communities.

BUILDING AP® SKILLS

Developments and Processes

To get students thinking about how historians have titled this era of history, you can have them read "Sprouts of Modernity?" on pages 195 and 196. Then ask students: What is this period called, and why? *The period is called the early modern era because of the increased globalization seen in the transatlantic slave trade, the silver trade, and the Columbian exchange and the creation of more highly commercialized economies. It also saw the development and spread of new scientific ideas during the Scientific Revolution, which became a marker of modernity.*

EXPLORING AP® THEMES

Humans and the Environment (ENV)

Point out to students the global population change mentioned in the third paragraph of the second column. Ask students: Why do you think the world's population increased during this time period? *Answers may vary, but can include: Eurasia had recovered from the Black Death and the impact of the Mongol wars; In Afro-Eurasia, American foods like corn and potatoes helped feed more people.*

BUILDING AP® SKILLS

Developments and Processes

The AP® World History: Modern Course Framework dates this era from 1450 to 1750. It can be interesting for students to look at the chapter topics and predict what they might learn about in this era. Consider asking students: Looking at the chapter titles, what are some of the patterns of the period?

Patterns include political transformations as a result of encounters as empires expanded; consequences of economic transformations such as expanded commerce; and transformations of cultures as religion expanded into new areas and as scientific thought expanded.

Making Connections: Continuity and Change

This is a good place to mention to students that European states started to become dominant around the world during the period 1450–1750. After reading "Sprouts of Modernity?," ask students to think about some of the changes European states experienced: In what ways did the global power of European countries change? In what ways did their power continue from the previous period? *European countries controlled the seas and the Americas. Their power was strictly limited in many ways. Natives in Africa controlled the slave trade. China and Japan controlled European missionaries. Europe, China, and India had about equal manufacturing power.*

Making Connections: Continuity and Change

Continuity and Change is the recommended skill for Unit 4, so it's good to have students practice it where they can throughout Period 2. You can try a practice here by asking students: Is the pattern described in the third paragraph in "Continuing Older Patterns?" one of continuity or one of change? Support your answer with evidence from the text. *Continuity. The paragraph describes the ways in which society did not change, such as the fact that animal and human muscles, wind, and water still provided almost all the energy that powered human economies. Handicraft techniques of manufacturing had nowhere been displaced by factory-based production or steam power. Long-established elites, not middle-class upstarts, everywhere provided leadership and enjoyed the greatest privileges, while rural peasants, not urban workers, represented the primary social group in the lower classes. Kings and nobles, not parliaments and parties, governed. Female subordination was assumed to be natural almost everywhere.*

Stronger and more cohesive states represented yet another modern global pattern as they incorporated various local societies into larger units while actively promoting trade, manufacturing, and a common culture within their borders. France, the Dutch Republic, Russia, Morocco, the Mughal Empire, Vietnam, Burma, Siam, and Japan all represent this kind of state. Their military power likewise soared as the "gunpowder revolution" kicked in around the world. Thus large-scale empires proliferated across Asia and the Middle East, while various European powers carved out new domains in the Americas. Within these empires, human pressures on the land intensified as forests were felled, marshes were drained, and the hunting grounds of foragers and the grazing lands of pastoralists were confiscated for farming or ranching.

Continuing Older Patterns?

But all of this may be misleading if it suggests that European world domination and more fully modern societies were a sure thing, an inevitable outgrowth of early modern developments. In fact, that future was far from clear in 1750. Although Europeans ruled the Americas and controlled the world's sea routes, their political and military power in mainland Asia and Africa was very limited, and they certainly did not hold all the leading roles in the global drama of these three centuries.

Furthermore, Islam, not Christianity, was the most rapidly spreading faith in much of Asia and Africa. And in 1750 Europe, India, and China were roughly comparable in their manufacturing output. It was not obvious that Europeans would soon dominate the planet. Moreover, populations and economies had surged at various points in the past, only to fall back again in a cyclical pattern. Nothing guaranteed that the early modern surge would be any more lasting than the others.

Nor was there much to suggest that anything approaching modern industrial society was on the horizon. Animal and human muscles, wind, wood, and water still provided almost all of the energy that powered human economies. Handicraft techniques of manufacturing had nowhere been displaced by factory-based production, steam power, or electricity. Long-established elites, not middle-class upstarts, everywhere provided leadership and enjoyed the greatest privileges, while rural peasants, not urban workers, represented the primary social group in the lower classes. Kings and nobles, not parliaments and parties, governed. Female subordination was assumed to be natural almost everywhere, for nowhere had ideas of gender equality taken root.

Thus modern society, with its promise of liberation from ancient inequalities and from mass poverty, hardly seemed around the corner. Kings ruled most of Europe, and male landowning aristocrats remained at the top of the social hierarchy. Another change in ruling dynasties occurred in China, where that huge country affirmed Confucian values and a social structure that privileged landowning and office-holding elites, all of them men. Most Indians practiced some form of Hinduism and owed their most fundamental loyalty to local castes. The realm of Islam maintained its central role in the Eastern Hemisphere as the Ottoman Empire revived the political fortunes of Islam, and the religion sustained its long-term expansion into Africa and Southeast Asia. In short, for the majority of people, the three centuries between 1450 and 1750 marked less an entry into the modern era than the continuation of older patterns.

From this mixture of what was new and what was old during the early modern era, the three chapters that follow highlight the changes. Chapter 4 aligns with AP® World History Unit 3 and turns the spotlight on the new empires of those three centuries — European, Middle Eastern, and Asian. New cultural trends — both within the major religious traditions of the world and in the emergence of modern science — come together in Chapter 5. New global patterns of long-distance commerce in spices, sugar, silver, fur, and slaves represent the

themes of Chapter 6. Chapters 5 and 6 cover Unit 4 of the AP® World History course. With the benefit of hindsight, we may see various "sprouts of modernity" as harbingers of things to come, but from the viewpoint of 1700 or so, the future was open and uncertain, as it almost always is.

FIRST REFLECTIONS

1. **Questioning Chronology** How might you support the authors' decision to describe the centuries from 1450 to 1750 as an "early modern era"? How might you criticize that decision?

2. **Questioning a Concept** The idea of an "early modern era" has sometimes been criticized as Eurocentric. How do the authors seek to avoid this criticism while continuing to use the term?

3. **Thinking Like a Historian** The authors say that they chose to emphasize what was new during these three centuries rather than what persisted from earlier times. What is potentially lost in making this choice?

TEACHING IDEA

Class Discussion

If you want to extend the Argumentation activity from above, consider placing students into small groups and have them discuss Question 2 or 3 from "First Reflections." After giving them time to discuss in small groups, bring the class back together and have one student from each group share what they discussed.

TRM Suggested Responses to Questions

You can find suggested responses to the First Reflections questions in the Teacher's Resource Materials.

BUILDING AP® SKILLS

Argumentation

Students need to be able to identify an author's argument and supporting evidence to be successful on the AP® Exam. Consider asking students after they read "The Big Picture": Do the authors describe this as a period of early modernity or late agrarian empires? Justify your answer.

In European, Islamic, and Chinese societies alike, some people urged a return to earlier ways of living and thinking rather than embracing what was new and untried. Although Europeans were increasingly prominent on the world stage, they certainly did not hold all the leading roles in the global drama of these three centuries. Most of the world's peoples, in fact, continued to live in long-established ways, and their societies operated according to traditional principles. Kings ruled most of Europe, and male landowning aristocrats remained at the top of the social hierarchy. Another change in ruling dynasties occurred in China, while that huge country affirmed Confucian values and a social structure that privileged landowning and office-holding elites, all of them men. Most Indians practiced some form of Hinduism and owed their most fundamental loyalty to local castes, even as South Asia continued its centuries-long incorporation into the Islamic world.

Contextualization can be a hard skill for students to understand and successfully use. To help students work with this skill, show them the timeline "Landmarks in World History (ca. 1450–ca. 1750)." Then ask: What events began before the period started? What events continued after the period ended? Why might these events still be included in this time period? *The only events that began before the period are the ones with an arrow pointing to the left: "The Renaissance" and "Islam established in Southeast Asia." Because the interactions of religions and cultures are important components of this time period, the events need to be included. Events whose dates go beyond 1750 continued after the period. These include "Wars of Islamic renewal in West Africa" and the "Wahhabi movement of Islamic reform in Arabia." These events are included in this time period because they followed the patterns of the time period, which included some people urging a return to earlier ways of living and thinking rather than embracing what was new and untried.*

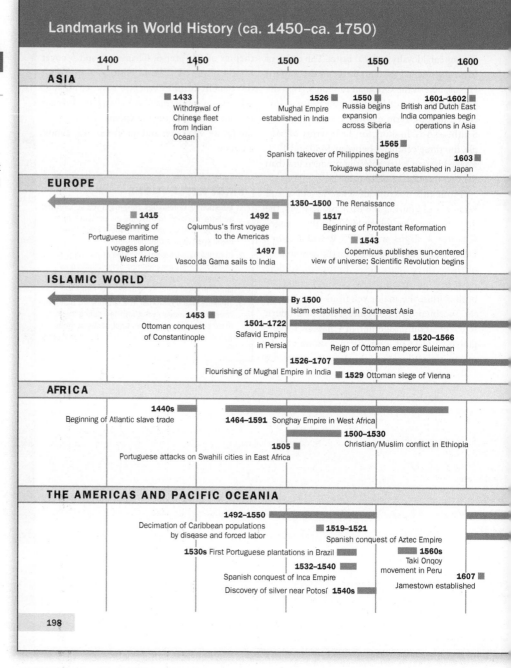

Landmarks in World History (ca. 1450–ca. 1750)

ASIA

1433 Withdrawal of Chinese fleet from Indian Ocean

1526 Mughal Empire established in India

1550 Russia begins expansion across Siberia

1601–1602 British and Dutch East India companies begin operations in Asia

1565 Spanish takeover of Philippines begins

1603 Tokugawa shogunate established in Japan

EUROPE

1350–1500 The Renaissance

1415 Beginning of Portuguese maritime voyages along West Africa

1492 Columbus's first voyage to the Americas

1497 Vasco da Gama sails to India

1517 Beginning of Protestant Reformation

1543 Copernicus publishes sun-centered view of universe; Scientific Revolution begins

ISLAMIC WORLD

By 1500 Islam established in Southeast Asia

1453 Ottoman conquest of Constantinople

1501–1722 Safavid Empire in Persia

1520–1566 Reign of Ottoman emperor Suleiman

1526–1707 Flourishing of Mughal Empire in India

1529 Ottoman siege of Vienna

AFRICA

1440s Beginning of Atlantic slave trade

1464–1591 Songhay Empire in West Africa

1500–1530 Christian/Muslim conflict in Ethiopia

1505 Portuguese attacks on Swahili cities in East Africa

THE AMERICAS AND PACIFIC OCEANIA

1492–1550 Decimation of Caribbean populations by disease and forced labor

1519–1521 Spanish conquest of Aztec Empire

1530s First Portuguese plantations in Brazil

1560s Taki Onqoy movement in Peru

1532–1540 Spanish conquest of Inca Empire

Discovery of silver near Potosí 1540s

1607 Jamestown established

198

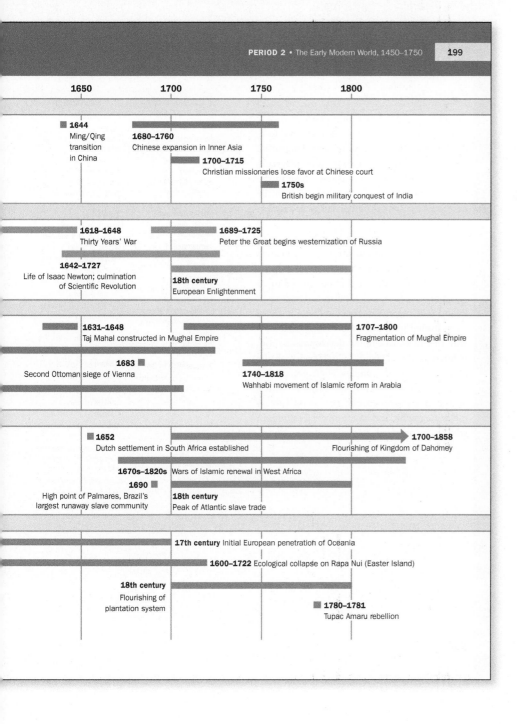

1650   1700   1750   1800

1644
Ming/Qing transition in China

1680–1760
Chinese expansion in Inner Asia

1700–1715
Christian missionaries lose favor at Chinese court

1750s
British begin military conquest of India

1618–1648
Thirty Years' War

1689–1725
Peter the Great begins westernization of Russia

1642–1727
Life of Isaac Newton; culmination of Scientific Revolution

18th century
European Enlightenment

1631–1648
Taj Mahal constructed in Mughal Empire

1707–1800
Fragmentation of Mughal Empire

1683
Second Ottoman siege of Vienna

1740–1818
Wahhabi movement of Islamic reform in Arabia

1652
Dutch settlement in South Africa established

1700–1858
Flourishing of Kingdom of Dahomey

1670s–1820s Wars of Islamic renewal in West Africa

1690

High point of Palmares, Brazil's largest runaway slave community

18th century
Peak of Atlantic slave trade

17th century Initial European penetration of Oceania

1600–1722 Ecological collapse on Rapa Nui (Easter Island)

18th century
Flourishing of plantation system

1780–1781
Tupac Amaru rebellion

UNDERSTANDING AP® THEMES IN PERIOD 2

Global Interactions

Encompassing the three centuries between 1450 and 1750, this part is commonly referred to as the "early modern era." While this designation remains controversial among some historians, these centuries represent a new phase in the human journey because for the first time the interactions among distinct cultures and societies occurred on a genuinely global scale. Now the Americas became permanently linked into a network of communication and exchange with the Afro-Eurasian world, and sub-Saharan Africa was more thoroughly connected to an emerging world system. The three chapters of Period 2 are organized thematically, with Chapter 4 dealing with empire building; Chapter 5 with transregional cultural developments, both religious and secular; and Chapter 6 with the making of a global economy. These processes in turn had major effects on the social evolution of human cultures around the world and on the demographic and environmental settings in which they operated.

ca. 1450–1750

ENVIRONMENT	CULTURES
The Little Ice Age: global cooling and its consequences	Muslim/Christian encounters in Ottoman realm
The Columbian exchange: global biological transformations	Continued Islamic expansion in Southeast Asia
Global population growth and environmental change due to Columbian exchange	Continued Muslim/Hindu encounters in India
Demographic history of slave trade: migration and change over time	Neo-Confucianism, *kaozheng*, and popular culture in China
Disease and demographic collapse: the Americas and Siberia	Popularization of *bhakti* tradition in India
Environmental effects of silver mining in Bolivia	Protestant Reformation
Species depletion due to the fur trade (Russia and North America)	Emergence of Sikhism in India
Reforestation in Japan	Emergence of modern science in Europe
Deforestation in China	Christianity in - Philippines - Siberia - Spanish America - Russia - China - Japan
	African religious cultures in the Americas
	Responses to European science: China, Japan, and the Islamic world
	European Enlightenment
	Islamic renewal: the Wahhabi example

200

GOVERNANCE	ECONOMIES	SOCIAL STRUCTURES	TECHNOLOGY
The making of a Russian Empire	Continuation of Asian commercial networks in Asia	Class and gender in the early modern era	Terrace farming in Andes
The Ottoman Empire: Muslim state building in the Middle East and Southeast Europe	The Atlantic slave trade: • Origins • Operations • Outcomes	Importance of female merchants in Southeast Asia	Gunpowder technology improves
Early modern state building: primary sources from Asia, the Middle East, Europe, and the Americas	The spice trade: empires of European commerce in Asia	Women in Mughal and Ottoman empires	Improved maritime technology allows empires to expand
European conquest and empire building in the Americas	Global silver trade: effects on • Spanish America • Japan • China • Europe	Multiculturalism in China	Aztec Chinampas farming techniques
African state building and state disintegration in the slave-trade era	Plantation economies begin in the Americas	Erosion of pastoralism in Russian and Chinese empires	Portuguese develop new maritime technologies
The Mughals: a Muslim empire in India	Forced labor and the hacienda system	Emergence of mestizo/mulatto classes in the Americas	Development of new ships: caravel, carrack, fluyt
A Spanish colonial state in the Philippines	The fur trade: North America and Russia compared	Gender and social change in Africa as a result of the slave trade	Introduction of Afro-Eurasian technologies to the Americas
Japan and China: limiting European incursions	Settler economies in the Americas	Women in American colonial societies	Telescope as a technology of scientific inquiry
The Tokugawa state in Japan	Erosion of hunting and herding economies in Russian Empire	The fur trade's effect on gender roles in North America	
Spread of Chinese empire into Central Asia	Growth of silver-mining economy: Potosí	Comparing colonial social structures in North and South America	
Peter the Great and Russia's "catching up" efforts		Erosion of women's roles in the colonial Philippines	
		Women in the Scientific Revolution and the Enlightenment	

EXPLORING AP® THEMES

Previewing the time period students are about to study can help them get an idea of the major concepts they need to keep an eye out for as they work through Units 3 and 4. You can ask students to study the events on the thematic chart on pages 200 and 201 and then write a general statement about the patterns they see for each theme in the period. (Suggested answers are provided in italics.)

■ **Environment:** *The patterns of this period include deforestation, global diseases, and the Columbian exchange.*

■ **Cultures:** *The patterns of this period include the spread of major religions like Christianity and Islam, as well as the rise of scientific thought.*

■ **Governance:** *The patterns of this period include the rise of new empires such as the transoceanic empires of Europe, the movement east of Russia, and the new empires in China and Japan.*

■ **Economies:** *The patterns of this period include the global interconnections of expanding trade, such as in silver and enslaved people.*

■ **Social Structures:** *The patterns of this period include changes in the relationship between men and women, as well as the growing multiculturalism in the social hierarchy.*

■ **Technology:** *The patterns of this period include new maritime technologies that facilitated exploration and expansion, as well as new farming techniques in the Americas.*

PERIOD 2

4 Political Transformations

Empires and Encounters, 1450–1750

AP® Overview for Chapter 4

This chapter corresponds to Unit 3: Land-Based Empires, 1450–1750, and Unit 4: Transoceanic Interconnections, 1450–1750. Although Chapter 4 is titled "Political Transformations," it involves a great deal more than politics; it covers the beginning of the modern world because it reunites the two hemispheres after millennia of their being apart. Thus the chapter also discusses the ecological and biological impact of this global connection by focusing heavily on the Columbian exchange. In addition, the chapter explores the cultural interactions of this increasingly connected world.

Chapter 4 Essential Activity

Units 3 and 4 of AP® World History: Modern examine the major land-based and maritime empires of 1450 to 1750. Since students need to know the characteristics of these empires and be able to compare them, have students create presentations for each empire to decide which empire was the "greatest" for this time period. You will probably want to extend this activity into Chapter 6 because students will also need information from there to create their presentations. To help with extending the activity between the two chapters, have students focus more on the land-based empires (Qing, Ottoman, Safavid, Mughal, Russia) in Chapter 4 and the maritime empires (Portugal, Spain, France, England, and the Netherlands) in Chapter 6. You can find detailed instructions for this activity in the Teacher's Resource Materials.

TRM Essential Activity: Greatest Empire in the World

Chapter 4 Resources

TRM AP® Skills Workshop Activity Handout: Contextualization

TRM Chapter 4 DBQ Activity Handout

TRM Chapter 4 Guided Reading

TRM Chapter 4 Lecture Presentation Slides

TRM Chapter 4 Outline

TRM Chapter 4 Suggested Responses to Questions

TRM Eric's Activity 4: The Columbian Exchange and You

TRM Essential Activity: Greatest Empire in the World

TRM Handout 4.1: SOAPSTone Charts for Meeting between Moctezuma and Cortés

TRM Handout 4.2: Causation Chart for European Exploration

TRM Handout 4.3: Causation Chart for Columbian Exchange

TRM Handout 4.4: Graphic Organizer for Comparing Colonial Societies

TRM Handout 4.5: Comparison Chart for Nonelites in European, Song, and Mongol Empires

TRM Handout 4.6: Graphic Organizer for Slavery in the Americas

TRM Handout 4.7: Comparison Chart for American Colonies

TRM Handout 4.8: Comparison Chart for Asian Empires and European Empires

TRM Handout 4.9: OPTIC Chart for Painting of Machang

TRM Handout 4.10: Thematic Chart of the Ottoman Empire

TRM Handout 4.11: OPTIC Chart for Painting of the Siege of Vienna

TRM Handout 4.12: Chart for Treatment of Religious and Ethnic Groups by Empires

TRM Handout 4.13: Chart for Religious Policies of Empires

TRM Map 4A: The World

Pacing Guide

Below is a pacing guide for the AP® World History: Modern course beginning in ca. 1200 C.E. This pacing guide is based on a schedule with 120 sessions of 50 minutes each before the AP® Exam. It is meant as a place to start. If you have a different number of sessions before the exam, you can modify the pacing to suit your needs.

Day	Pages Assigned	AP® Topic	AP® Theme	Suggested Assignments	Coverage Notes
1	Read pages 222–226 from "Empire Building in Russia and China" to "Into Central Asia: The Making of a Chinese Empire"	3.1 3.2 3.4	GOV ECN	Chapter 4 Essential Activity Apply the Tip on page 225 Building AP® Skills: Making Connections: Comparison on page 225	Chapter 4 lends itself well to comparing maritime and land-based empires and can be a good place to practice comparison with students, while helping students connect their knowledge from Unit 3 to Unit 4.
2	Read pages 226–227 from "Into Central Asia: The Making of a Chinese Empire" to the third paragraph about the Ming voyages	3.1 3.2 3.4	GOV ECN	Chapter 4 Essential Activity Building AP® Skills: Making Connections: Continuity and Change on page 226 Teaching Idea: Class Discussion on page 227	See above.
3	Read pages 227–229 from the fourth paragraph about the Qing takeover to "Empires of the Islamic World"	3.1 3.2 3.4 4.7	GOV ECN SIO	Chapter 4 Essential Activity Building AP® Skills: Sourcing and Situation on page 228 Apply the Tip on page 229	See above.
4	Read pages 229–233 from "Empires of the Islamic World" to the first paragraph on the *devshirme*	3.1 3.2 3.3 3.4 4.7	CUL GOV ECN SIO	Chapter 4 Essential Activity Building AP® Skills: Developments and Processes on page 230 Apply the Tip on page 231 Apply the Tip on page 232	See above. The Ottoman Empire was one of the most powerful empires of the 1450–1750 time period (if not *the* most powerful empire). Make sure students understand the significance of this empire, especially compared to the other land-based and maritime empires of this era.
5	Read pages 233–235 from the second paragraph on Ottoman administration to "On the Frontiers of Islam: The Mughal and Songhay Empires"	3.1 3.2 3.3 3.4	CUL GOV	Chapter 4 Essential Activity AP® Classroom: AP® Topic Questions on page 233 Teaching Idea: Incorporating Outside Resources on page 234	See above.
6	Read pages 235–237 from "On the Frontiers of Islam: The Mughal and Songhay Empires" to the fourth paragraph ending the Mughals	3.1 3.2 3.4 4.7	CUL GOV SIO	Chapter 4 Essential Activity Teaching Idea: Bell Ringer on page 235 Building AP® Skills: Claims and Evidence in Sources on page 237	See above.
7	Read pages 237–240 from the fifth paragraph introducing the Songhay through "Conclusions and Reflections"	3.1 3.2 3.4	CUL GOV ECN	Chapter 4 Essential Activity AP® Classroom: AP® Daily Video on page 238 AP® Classroom: AP® Topic Questions on page 240	See above.

Day	Pages Assigned	AP® Topic	AP® Theme	Suggested Assignments	Coverage Notes
8	Read pages 203–208 to "The Great Dying and the Little Ice Age"	4.1 4.2	ENV TEC	Chapter 4 Essential Activity Building AP® Skills: Claims and Evidence in Sources on page 206 Apply the Tip on page 207	European maritime empires are divided between Chapters 4 and 6. It may be helpful to teach these two sections back to back, while using the Columbian exchange as an introduction. Chapter 4 examines the European colonies of the Americas, while Chapter 6 looks at European colonies in Africa and Asia. If you choose to teach by chapter, you may want to refer to this section when students read more about maritime empires in Chapter 6.
9	Read pages 208–211 from "The Great Dying and the Little Ice Age" to "The Columbian Exchange"	4.1 4.8	TEC	AP® Classroom: AP® Topic Questions on page 210 Teaching Idea: Incorporating Outside Resources on page 210	See above.
10	Read page 211: the first three paragraphs of "The Columbian Exchange"	4.3	ENV	Eric's Activity 4: The Columbian Exchange and You on page 204 Teaching Idea: Bell Ringer on page 211	The Columbian exchange is a major concept in the AP® World History: Modern course, especially its effects on the globe. While the demographic effects are easy for students to see, they may need some guidance on the environmental effects.
11	Read pages 212–213 from the first paragraph about American food crops to "Comparing Colonial Societies in the Americas"	4.3	ENV	Apply the Tip on page 208 Apply the Tip on page 212 Teaching Idea: Incorporating Outside Resources on page 212	See above.
12	Read pages 213–214 from "Comparing Colonial Societies in the Americas" to "In the Lands of the Aztecs and the Incas"	4.2 4.4	GOV ECN	Chapter 4 Essential Activity Building AP® Skills: Making Connections: Comparison on page 214	Chapter 4 lends itself well to comparing maritime and land-based empires and can be a good place to practice comparison skills with students, while helping them connect their knowledge from Unit 3 to Unit 4. The following four days also focus on comparison between the different practices of European colonies in the Americas.
13	Read pages 214–217 from "In the Lands of the Aztecs and the Incas" to "Colonies of Sugar"	4.2 4.4 4.7 4.8	GOV ECN SIO	Chapter 4 Essential Activity Apply the Tip on page 214 Exploring AP® Themes: CDI on page 215	See above.
14	Read pages 217–220 from "Colonies of Sugar" to "Settler Colonies in North America"	4.2 4.4 4.7 4.8	GOV ECN SIO	Chapter 4 Essential Activity Building AP® Skills: Making Connections: Causation on page 218 Apply the Tip on page 220	See above.
15	Read pages 220–222 from "Settler Colonies in North America" to "Empire Building in Russia and China"	4.2	GOV ECN	Chapter 4 Essential Activity Apply the Tip on page 221 Building AP® Skills: Making Connections: Comparison on page 222 AP® Classroom: AP® Daily Video on page 222	See above.

NOTES

Bell Ringer

The AP® World History: Modern Curriculum Framework begins Units 3 and 4 at 1450. As an introduction to this period of study, you could ask students to think about alternative dates that could mark the beginning of this era. What events might signify the beginning of this era? *Two possible events that might signify the beginning of what is known as the "early modern period" are the Ottoman conquest of Constantinople in 1453 and the first voyage of Columbus to the Americas in 1492.*

Cultural Developments and Interactions (CDI) and Social Interactions and Organization (SIO)

Analyzing paintings and other images for how they represent culture, politics, and social interactions in civilizations and empires is a good skill to practice throughout the year. This illustration of the Mughal court is one you could use to practice this skill with students. Have students study the illustration and then ask: Based on this illustration, what can we say about the court of Shah Jahan? *There are only men in the painting, so women may not be welcome at court or may be placed in a separate location. The men seem to be of different ethnicities, so this court is multicultural. But the men seem to be wearing similar clothing, so there seems to be an accepted form of dress at court. Some men are carrying items that appear to be weapons; these may be trusted military men or guards of the emperor. There appears to be food and drink, so people seem to be enjoying themselves. There are books and written documents, which may indicate some value in intellectual pursuits. The men are barefoot, which may indicate the ceremonial nature of the occasion or respect for the court. People are depicted at different levels, with most at the bottom and the emperor on top. All figures face in toward the center plane of the composition, where the emperor is positioned, which may also indicate his elevated status.*

The Mughal Empire Among the most magnificent of the early modern empires was that of the Mughals in India. In this painting by an unknown Mughal artist, the seventeenth-century emperor Shah Jahan is holding a durbar, or ceremonial assembly, in the audience hall of his palace. The material splendor of the setting shows the immense wealth of the court, while the halo around Shah Jahan's head indicates the special spiritual grace or enlightenment associated with emperors. (Royal Collection Trust © Her Majesty Queen Elizabeth II, 2020/Bridgeman Images)

202

CHAPTER 4

Political Transformations

Empires and Encounters

1450–1750

◀ **AP®**

SOURCING AND SITUATION
What might have been the artist's purpose for creating this work of art?

CONNECTING PAST AND PRESENT

"Putin [president of Russia] wants the old Russian Empire back. . . . As Russian tsar, which is how he sees himself, his empire cannot work without Ukraine. He sees us as a colony."[1] This was the view of Ukrainian president Petro Poroshenko in 2018, as he resisted persistent Russian incursions into the affairs of his country. The Russian invasion of Ukraine in early 2022 only enhanced this view of Russia's imperial ambitions. In a similar vein, critics of Turkey's intervention in Libya's civil war in 2020 claimed that Turkey's president Erdogan embraced "expansionist visions of reviving the Ottoman Empire, with—naturally—himself as the supreme sultan."[2] Thus memories of the Russian and Ottoman empires, initially constructed in the early modern era, continue to shape understandings of current events and perhaps to inspire actions in the present as well. ■

Underlying these comments is a sharply critical posture toward any revival of these earlier empires. Indeed, empire building has been largely discredited during the twentieth and twenty-first centuries, and "imperialist" has become a term of insult rather than a source of pride. How very different were the three centuries (1450–1750) of the early modern era, when empire building was a global process! In the Americas, the Aztec and Inca empires flourished before they, along with nearly all of the Western Hemisphere, were incorporated into the rival empires of the Spanish, Portuguese, British, French, and Dutch. Within those European imperial systems, vast transformations took place: old societies were destroyed, and new societies arose as Native Americans, Europeans, and Africans came into sustained contact with one another for the first time in world history. It was an encounter with revolutionary implications that extended far beyond the Americas themselves.

But these empires in the Americas were not alone on the imperial stage of the early modern era. Across the immense expanse of Siberia, the

203

BUILDING AP® SKILLS

Contextualization

Contextualization is an important skill for students to understand and be able to use in AP® World History: Modern for both essays and multiple-choice questions. To help prepare students for writing contextualization in LEQs and DBQs, it would be good to have them practice it by either identifying the context of a written passage or discussing the context for a historical event. You could ask students to turn to a partner and briefly discuss why imperialism is considered an insult today but was a point of pride in 1450–1750, as referenced in the opening of the chapter. How does the context of the time explain this shift? *During this time, creating an empire meant building strength. Today, empire building implies domination and exploitation.*

BUILDING AP® SKILLS

Making Connections: Continuity and Change

The early modern era (1450–1750), which is covered in Units 3 and 4, marks the beginning of Europe's rise to global power. This would be a good place to have students start to think about the changes European states might go through to achieve this rise. Have students list what European empires or states they think will be discussed in the early modern era. *Dutch, French, British, Spanish, and Portuguese.* Then ask: Describe what Europe was like during Unit 1 (1200–1450). How do you think European states will change during this era? *Answers will vary.*

CONTINUITY AND CHANGE
How has the reputation of empire building changed between the period 1450–1750 and the present?

COMPARISON
In what ways did European empires in the Americas resemble their Russian, Chinese, Mughal, and Ottoman counterparts, and in what respects were they different? Do you find the similarities or the differences more significant?

EXAM TIP
Understand the process of European state building in the Americas.

CONTEXTUALIZATION
What historical developments enabled Europeans to carve out huge empires an ocean away from their homelands?

Russians constructed what was then the world's largest territorial empire, making Russia an Asian as well as a European power. Qing (chihng) dynasty China penetrated deep into Inner Asia, doubling the size of the country while incorporating millions of non-Chinese people who practiced Islam, Buddhism, or animistic religions. Within the vast Islamic world, four new imperial states reconfigured the political structure of the region. In the Middle East, the Turkish Ottoman Empire reestablished something of the earlier political unity of heartland Islam and posed a serious military and religious threat to European Christendom. Furthermore, a new expression of the Persian imperial tradition took shape in the Safavid Empire in what is now Iran. On the South Asian peninsula, the Islamic Mughal Empire brought Hindus and Muslims into a closer relationship than ever before, sometimes quite peacefully and at other times with great conflict. And the Muslim-ruled Songhay Empire encompassed a huge territory in West Africa, giving a new shape to that civilization. Thus the early modern era was an age of empire all across the world.

European Empires in the Americas

Finding the Main Point: In what ways did European colonial empires in the Americas set in motion vast historical changes?

Among the early modern empires, those of Western Europe were distinctive because the conquered territories lay an ocean away from the imperial heartland, rather than adjacent to it. Following the breakthrough voyages of Columbus, the Spanish focused their empire-building efforts in the Caribbean and then, in the early sixteenth century, turned to the mainland, making stunning conquests of the powerful but fragile Aztec and Inca empires. Meanwhile, the Portuguese established themselves along the coast of present-day Brazil. In the early seventeenth century, the British, French, and Dutch launched colonial settlements along the eastern coast of North America. From these beginnings, Europeans extended their empires to encompass most of the Americas, at least nominally, by the mid-eighteenth century (see Map 4.1). It was a remarkable achievement. What had made it possible?

The European Advantage

Geography provides a starting point for explaining Europe's American empires. Countries on the Atlantic rim of Europe (Portugal, Spain, Britain, and France) were simply closer to the Americas than were any potential Asian competitors. Moreover, the enormously rich markets of the Indian Ocean world provided little incentive for its Chinese, Indian, or Muslim participants to venture much beyond their own waters. Europeans, however, were powerfully motivated to do so.

After 1200 or so, European elites were increasingly aware of their region's marginal position in the rich world of Eurasian commerce and were determined to gain access to that world. Once the Americas were discovered, windfalls of natural

---

APPLY THE TIP

As students read through the section "European Empires in the Americas," it would be good to have them take notes on the ways that different European states (such as the Spanish, British, and Portuguese) built their empires in the Americas. After they have taken notes, you could have a brief class discussion using the following question: How were European states similar and different in the ways they built their empires in the Americas? *Answers will vary.*

TEACHING IDEA

Incorporating Outside Resources

Thomas More, the greatest humanist of sixteenth-century England, published *Utopia* in 1515. The first "utopian" novel, it takes place in a fictional country in the New World and provides a revealing look at European philosophy and Europeans' attitudes toward the New World. If you have the time or have a class you would like to challenge, consider giving students a summary of the novel and have them research its attitudes about the New World. Then ask them to write a short response on what they've learned about European views of the New World from the book.

ERIC'S ACTIVITY ④   **The Columbian Exchange and You**

Theme: Humans and the Environment

We open this chapter with the Columbian exchange and the Great Dying because, to examine this period, one must understand the implications of the most extensive biological exchange in human history. I like to help my students grasp its long-term importance by exploring how it affects the world and their own lives today. Find the complete activity in the Teacher's Resource Materials.

TRM Eric's Activity 4: The Columbian Exchange and You

Landmarks for Chapter 4

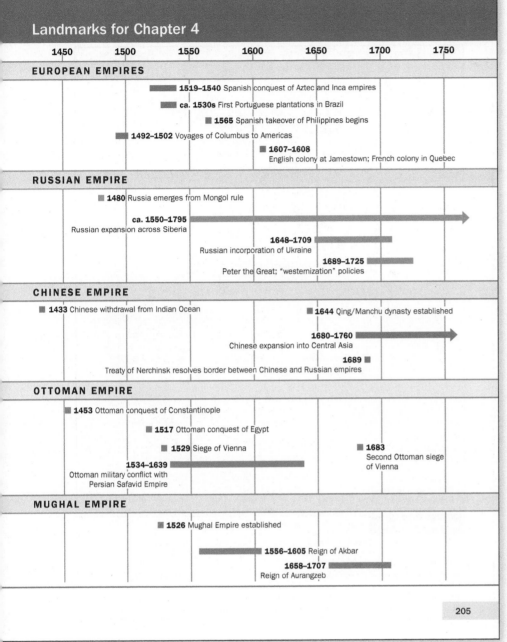

| | 1450 | 1500 | 1550 | 1600 | 1650 | 1700 | 1750 |

EUROPEAN EMPIRES

1519–1540 Spanish conquest of Aztec and Inca empires

ca. 1530s First Portuguese plantations in Brazil

1565 Spanish takeover of Philippines begins

1492–1502 Voyages of Columbus to Americas

1607–1608
English colony at Jamestown; French colony in Quebec

RUSSIAN EMPIRE

1480 Russia emerges from Mongol rule

ca. 1550–1795
Russian expansion across Siberia

1648–1709
Russian incorporation of Ukraine

1689–1725
Peter the Great; "westernization" policies

CHINESE EMPIRE

1433 Chinese withdrawal from Indian Ocean

1644 Qing/Manchu dynasty established

1680–1760
Chinese expansion into Central Asia

1689
Treaty of Nerchinsk resolves border between Chinese and Russian empires

OTTOMAN EMPIRE

1453 Ottoman conquest of Constantinople

1517 Ottoman conquest of Egypt

1529 Siege of Vienna

1683
Second Ottoman siege of Vienna

1534–1639
Ottoman military conflict with Persian Safavid Empire

MUGHAL EMPIRE

1526 Mughal Empire established

1556–1605 Reign of Akbar

1658–1707
Reign of Aurangzeb

205

EXPLORING AP® THEMES

Humans and the Environment (ENV)

It's important for students to know where each of the empires of this time period are located, both to understand their geography and to be able to visualize how empires could interact with one another. Give students an outline map of the world and ask them to plot the locations of the empires listed in the "Landmarks for Chapter 4" on this page. You can find a blank map, **Map 4A: The World**, in the Teacher's Resource Materials.

Differentiation

If you want to take the map activity further, consider having students create a class-annotated map using the empires and events found in the "Landmarks for Chapter 4" and the "Landmarks for Chapter 6" on page 319. Using the "Must Do, Should Do, Strive For" model below for this activity will help students make connections between the political and economic changes that happened in the early modern era.

■ Must Do: Students must label the empires listed in the "Landmarks for Chapter 4" on the class map.

■ Should Do: Divide the class into small groups (three to four students) and assign each group one of the empires from Units 3 and 4. They should research the political and economic characteristics of their assigned empire and record their research on the map. After all groups have finished putting their information on the class-annotated map, give students 15 to 25 minutes to study the map and write down any comparisons they can make between the different empires.

■ Strive For: After students have written down their observations, have a class discussion comparing the politics and economics of the different empires.

TRM Map 4A: The World

BUILDING AP® SKILLS

Making Connections: Causation

"Land = Power" is a phrase that can help students understand European attitudes toward exploration and conquest during the 1450–1750 time period. Map 4.1, "European Colonial Empires in the Americas," could be used to help students visualize this attitude. Ask students to study the map, and then ask: Using evidence from the description and the map, what conclusions can you draw about European rivalries during 1450–1750? *The English and Spanish empires expanded, while the French empire got smaller. Therefore, we can conclude that Spain and England were more powerful than France and could become wealthier because they had larger empires.*

BUILDING AP® SKILLS

Claims and Evidence in Sources

Looking at historical events from multiple perspectives is critical for helping students gain a better understanding of the event, as with the conquest of the Americas. You can find two perspectives of the conquest, through the meeting between Moctezuma and Cortés, on the American Historical Association website (www.historians.org). Search for Bernal Díaz del Castillo's "Cortes Meets Moctezuma" and Fray Bernardino de Sahagún's translation "Mexica Accounts of Moctezuma Meeting Cortes" on the website. You might try dividing the class into groups of four to analyze the different sources. Ask two students in each group to read Díaz's account and fill out a SOAPSTone chart, with the categories shown here. Ask the other two students in each group to do the same with the Mexica account. A reproducible version of this chart is available in the Teacher's Resource Materials.

SOAPSTone Categories

- **Speaker:** The voice that tells the story
- **Occasion:** The time and place; the context that prompted the writing
- **Audience:** The readers to whom the piece is directed
- **Purpose:** The reason behind the text; the motivation for writing the piece
- **Subject:** Paraphrase of the content of the piece
- **Tone:** Attitude of the author

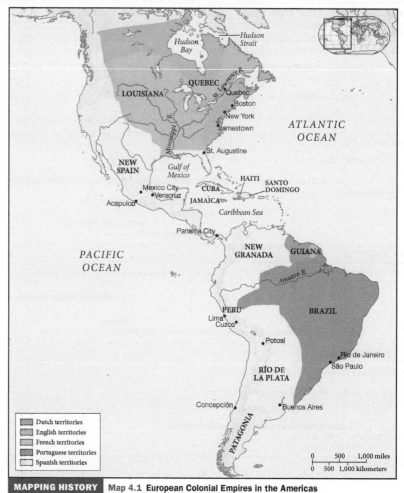

MAPPING HISTORY   Map 4.1 European Colonial Empires in the Americas

By the beginning of the eighteenth century, European powers had laid claim to most of the Western Hemisphere. Their wars and rivalries during that century led to an expansion of Spanish and English claims, at the expense of the French.

Reading the Map: Which European power controlled the most territory in the Americas? Which controlled the least?

AP **Making Connections:** Compare Map 4.1 with Map 7.3. Which European powers lost control of their Central and South American colonies by the 1830s? Which retained theirs? Which did both?

(continued)

When students have completed their charts, they should discuss their findings, first with the other person in their group who read the same article, and then as a larger group of four. To help guide their discussion, ask students to list the similarities in how the meeting is presented in the two accounts. You could also bring the class back together at the end of the activity and invite volunteers to share if they observed any differences in the way the meeting was presented.

Both are personal accounts of the conquest of Mexico, and both describe the wonderful city of Tenochtitlán. Both record "welcome speeches" made by Moctezuma and should counter the notion that either Moctezuma or the Spaniards were viewed as gods.

TRM Handout 4.1: SOAPSTone Charts for Meeting between Moctezuma and Cortés resources, including highly productive agricultural lands, drove further expansion, ultimately underpinning the long-term growth of the European economy into the nineteenth and twentieth centuries. The drive to expand beyond Europe was also motivated by the enduring rivalries of competing European states. At the same time, the growing and relatively independent merchant class sought direct access to Asian wealth to avoid the reliance on Muslim intermediaries that they found so distasteful. In addition, impoverished nobles and commoners alike found opportunity for gaining wealth and status in the colonies. Missionaries and others were inspired by crusading zeal to enlarge the realm of Christendom. Persecuted religious minorities were in search of a new start in life. All of these compelling motives drove the relentlessly expanding imperial frontier in the Americas. Summarizing their intentions, one Spanish conquistador declared: "We came here to serve God and the King, and also to get rich."[3]

In carving out these empires, often against great odds and with great difficulty, Europeans nonetheless had certain advantages, despite their distance from home. Their states and trading companies effectively mobilized both human and material resources. Technological borrowing also enabled European empire building. Gunpowder was invented in China, but by 1500 Europeans had the most advanced arsenals of gunpowder weapons in the world. In 1517, one Chinese official, on first encountering European ships and weapons, remarked with surprise, "The westerners are extremely dangerous because of their artillery. No weapon ever made since memorable antiquity is superior to their cannon."[4] Advances in shipbuilding and navigational techniques—including the magnetic compass and sternpost rudder from China and adaptations of the Mediterranean or Arab lateen sail, which enabled vessels to sail against the wind—provided the foundation for European mastery of the seas.

Another source of advantage was divisions within and between local societies in the Americas, which provided allies for the determined European invaders. (See Chapter 2 for more on the Aztec and Inca empires.) Various subject peoples of the Aztec Empire, for example, resented Mexica domination and willingly joined conquistador **Hernán Cortés** in the Spanish assault on that empire. In the final attack on the Aztec capital of Tenochtitlán, Cortés's forces contained fewer than 1,000 Spaniards and many times that number of Tlaxcalans, former subjects of the Aztecs. After their defeat, tens of thousands of Aztecs themselves joined Cortés as he conquered a Spanish Mesoamerican empire far larger than that of the Aztecs. (See Zooming In: Doña Marina, page 208.) Much of the Inca elite, according to a recent study, "actually welcomed the Spanish invaders as liberators and willingly settled down with them to share rule of Andean farmers and miners."[5] A violent dispute between two rival contenders for the Inca throne, the brothers Atahualpa and Huáscar, certainly helped the European invaders recruit allies to augment their own minimal forces. In short, Spanish military victories were not solely of their own making, but the product of alliances with local peoples, who supplied the bulk of the Europeans' conquering armies.

AP® EXAM TIP

Understand the various motivations for European exploration.

AP® EXAM TIP

Understand the causes and consequences of the Spanish conquest of the Aztec and Inca empires.

APPLY THE TIP

If students have already taken early U.S. history, they're probably able to immediately say that European motivations for exploration were "Gold, God, and Glory." Challenge them to think deeper about what the "3 Gs" stand for by asking them to create a cause-and-effect chart on the motivations for European exploration like the one shown below. A reproducible version of this chart is available in the Teacher's Resource Materials. (Answers are provided in italics.)

Motivations/ Causes	Results/Effects
Desire for natural resources	*Widespread exploration and exploitation of Indigenous workers when valuable natural resources were found*
Desire for agricultural lands	*Confiscation of land from Native Americans*
	Creation of plantations and/or encomiendas
Rivalry between competing states	*Territory explored even slightly was quickly claimed for the glory and power of the conquering state*
	In Spanish and French territories, mission systems were established to help maintain a claim to territory
	Development of towns around the missions
Desire to spread Christianity (crusading spirit)	*Expansion and globalization of Christianity as missionaries and monks worked to convert people*
	Creation of Folk Catholicism in the Americas

TRM Handout 4.2: **Causation Chart for European Exploration**

TEACHING IDEA

Incorporating Outside Resources

It could be interesting to students to investigate the city of Tenochtitlán and the Spanish siege of the city by looking at a map of the city and a close-up of the ships blockading it. The map of Tenochtitlán can be found at the American Historical Association (AHA) site by searching for "A Detailed View of Tenochtitlan." The close-up of the ships can also be found at the AHA site by searching for "Spaniards Besiege Tenochtitlan." If you choose to do this, ask students to analyze the defensive strength and vulnerability of Tenochtitlán using the two images. *The city's strength rested on its location in the middle of a lake with causeway bridges that could be removed. There were also defensive walls around the perimeter of the city. The city was vulnerable once the Spanish were able to control the water around the city; this allowed the Spanish to control access from the city to the surrounding agricultural lands and the water supply. Furthermore, the brigantines could carry cannons and horses, which overwhelmed the defenders of Tenochtitlán.*

APPLY THE TIP

After students learn about the Spanish conquest of the Aztec (Mexica) and Inca empires, you could give an exit ticket using the following question to assess student understanding of the conquest: What factors allowed Spain to conquer the Aztec (Mexica) and Inca empires? *Answers can include: Divisions within local societies provided allies for the Spanish; Infighting among the Incas made it easier for the Spanish to conquer the empire; Diseases brought by Europeans to people who had no previous exposure to them also reduced and weakened Indigenous populations; Better weapons, such as guns, gave the Spanish an advantage over Indigenous warriors.*

CHAPTER 4

EXPLORING AP® THEMES

Social Interactions and Organization (SIO)

Doña Marina is an interesting figure in world history, especially considering how infrequently non-noble women are referenced in historical sources. This could be a good place to pause and have students read the "Zooming In" feature about Doña Marina to learn about her role in the Spanish conquest of the Aztecs (Mexica). You can use the questions at the end of the reading to start a class discussion about Doña Marina and patriarchy.

ZOOMING IN   Doña Marina: Between Two Worlds

In her brief life, she was known variously as Malinal, Doña Marina, and La Malinche. By whatever name, she was a woman who experienced the encounter of the Old World and the New in particularly intimate ways, even as she became a bridge between them. Born around 1505, Malinal was the daughter of an elite and cultured family in the borderlands between the Maya and Aztec cultures in what is now southern Mexico. Two dramatic events decisively shaped her life. The first occurred when her father died and her mother remarried, bearing a son to her new husband. To protect this boy's inheritance, Malinal's family sold her into slavery. Eventually, she came into the possession of a Maya chieftain in Tabasco on the Gulf of Mexico.

Here her second life-changing event took place in March 1519, when the Spanish conquistador Hernán Cortés landed his troops and inflicted a sharp military defeat on Tabasco. In the negotiations that followed, Tabasco authorities gave lavish gifts to the Spanish, including twenty women, one of whom was Malinal.

Doña Marina (left) translating for Cortés.

Described by Bernal Díaz, one of Cortés's associates, as "good-looking, intelligent, and self-assured," the teenage Malinal soon found herself in service to Cortés himself. Since Spanish men were not supposed to touch non-Christian women, these newcomers were distributed among his officers, quickly baptized, and given Christian names. Thus Malinal became Doña Marina.

With a ready ear for languages and already fluent in Mayan and Nahuatl, the language of the Aztecs, Doña Marina soon picked up Spanish and quickly became indispensable to Cortés as an interpreter, cross-cultural broker, and strategist. She accompanied him on his march inland to the Aztec capital, Tenochtitlán, and on several occasions her language skills and cultural awareness allowed her to uncover spies and plots. Díaz reported that "Doña Marina, who understood full well what was happening, told [Cortés] what was going on." In the Aztec capital, where Cortés took the emperor Moctezuma captive, it fell to Doña Marina to persuade him to accept this humiliating

photo: Bridgeman Images

Perhaps the most significant of European advantages lay in their germs and diseases, with which Native Americans had no familiarity. Those diseases decimated society after society, sometimes in advance of the Europeans' actual arrival. In particular regions such as the Caribbean, Virginia, and New England, the rapid buildup of immigrant populations, coupled with the sharply diminished native numbers, allowed Europeans to actually outnumber local peoples within a few decades.

AP® EXAM TIP

The demographic effects of Afro-Eurasian diseases on the Americas are an especially important concept for the AP® Exam.

The Great Dying and the Little Ice Age

However Europeans acquired American empires, their global significance is apparent. Chief among the consequences was the demographic collapse of Native American societies. Although precise figures are debated, scholars generally agree that the pre-Columbian population of the Western Hemisphere was substantial, perhaps

---

APPLY THE TIP

You could use the following prompt to practice the SAQ with students after they have learned about the effects of Columbian exchange. You can assign it either as homework or as a timed writing in class. If you time the SAQ, give students 14 minutes to write their response.

Answer all parts of the question that follows.

A. Identify ONE environmental exchange that happened between the Western and Eastern hemispheres due to the Columbian exchange.

B. Explain ONE way in which demography in the Americas changed as a result of the Columbian exchange.

C. Explain ONE way in which culture in the Americas changed as a result of European exploration.

position and surrender his wealth to the Spanish. Even Cortés, who was never very gracious with his praise for her, acknowledged that "after God, we owe this conquest of New Spain to Doña Marina." Aztecs soon came to see this young woman as the voice of Cortés, referring to her as La Malinche, a Spanish approximation of her original name. So paired did Cortés and La Malinche become in Aztec thinking that Cortés himself was often called Malinche.

More than an interpreter for Cortés, Doña Marina also became his mistress and bore him a son. But after the initial conquest of Mexico was complete and he no longer needed her skills, Cortés married Doña Marina off to another Spanish conquistador, Juan Jaramillo, with whom she lived until her death, probably around 1530. Cortés did provide her with several pieces of land, one of which, ironically, had belonged to Moctezuma. Her son, however, was taken from her and raised in Spain.

In 1523, Doña Marina performed one final service for Cortés, accompanying him on a mission to Honduras to suppress a rebellion. There her personal life seemed to come full circle, for near her hometown she encountered her mother, who had sold her into slavery, and her half-brother. Díaz reported that they "were very much afraid of Doña Marina," thinking that they would surely be put to death by their now-powerful and well-connected relative. But in a replay of the biblical story of Joseph and

his brothers, Doña Marina quickly reassured and forgave them, while granting them "many golden jewels and some clothes."

In the centuries since her death, Doña Marina has been highly controversial. For much of the colonial era, she was viewed positively as an ally of the Spanish. But after independence, some came to see her as a traitor to her own people, shunning her heritage and siding with the invaders. Still others have considered her as the mother of Mexico's multiracial, or mestizo, culture. Should she be understood primarily as a victim, a skillful woman negotiating hard choices under difficult circumstances, or a traitor to her people?

Whatever the judgments of later generations, Doña Marina herself seems to have made a clear choice to cast her lot with the Europeans. Even when Cortés had given her to another man, Doña Marina expressed no regret. According to Díaz, she declared, "Even if they were to make me mistress of all the provinces of New Spain, I would refuse the honor, for I would rather serve my husband and Cortés than anything else in the world."

QUESTIONS

How might you define the significance of Doña Marina's life? In what larger contexts might her life find a place?

---

60 to 80 million. The greatest concentrations of people lived in the Mesoamerican and Andean zones dominated by the Aztec and Inca empires. Long isolation from the Afro-Eurasian world and the lack of most domesticated animals meant the absence of acquired immunities to Old World diseases such as smallpox, measles, typhus, influenza, malaria, and, later, yellow fever.

Therefore, when Native American peoples came into contact with these European and African diseases, they died in appalling numbers, in many cases losing up to 90 percent of the population. The densely settled peoples of Caribbean islands virtually vanished within fifty years of Columbus's arrival. Central Mexico, with a population estimated at some 10 to 20 million before the Spanish conquest, declined to about 1 million by 1650. A native Nahuatl (nah-watl) account depicted the social breakdown that accompanied the smallpox pandemic: "A great many died from this plague, and many others died of hunger. They could not get up to

AP®

CONTINUITY AND CHANGE

What large-scale transformations did European empires generate in the Americas, in Europe, and globally?

BUILDING AP® SKILLS

Claims and Evidence in Sources

It's good to have students working with primary sources throughout the year. You could assign students to read excerpts of primary source documents about death among the Native Americans after the Europeans arrived. These documents can be found on the World History for Us All website under "Big Era Six." Look for Landscape 6.2: "The Columbian Exchange and its consequences" at the bottom of the page to find the primary source in the Lesson 1 section of the lesson PDF. While students read the sources, have them answer the following question: What reasons does this curated group of primary sources give for the rapid decrease in the Native American population? *Reasons for the rapid decrease in the Native American population include brutality and torture, low birthrate, malnourishment, overwork, consumption of crops by cattle, killing off of animals such as the llama, diseases, and accidental or willful destruction of crops.*

AP® Topic Questions

To wrap up the section on the Great Dying, consider assigning students the Topic Questions for Topic 4.3: Columbian Exchange. This is a set of three multiple-choice questions on the Indigenous reactions to the Great Dying and will provide a good opportunity for students to practice test-taking skills. The questions can be found in your AP® Classroom account under Unit 4 resources.

EXPLORING AP® THEMES

Humans and the Environment (ENV)

This would be a great place to pause and have students investigate the ways that climate impacted different societies during the Little Ice Age. You could ask students: How did climate play an important role in shaping human history in the seventeenth century? *Because of the change in climate, China, Europe, and North America experienced record cold winters, and regions near the equator experienced extreme conditions and irregular rainfall. These conditions reduced food production drastically, which led to famines, epidemics, uprisings, and war. The crisis led to the collapse of the Ming dynasty, constant warfare in Europe, and civil war in Mughal India. In the Americas, drought caused the price of maize to rise and left many without water. In the Caribbean, wet weather created ideal breeding conditions for mosquitoes, which led to an outbreak of yellow fever and malaria.*

---

search for food, and everyone else was too sick to care for them, so they starved to death in their beds."[6]

The situation was similar in Dutch and British territories of North America. A Dutch observer in New Netherland (later New York) reported in 1656 that he had been told by local people that disease had "melted down" their numbers by 90 percent since the coming of the Europeans.[7] To Governor Bradford of Plymouth colony (in present-day Massachusetts), such conditions represented the "good hand of God" at work, "sweeping away great multitudes of the natives . . . that he might make room for us."[8] Not until the late seventeenth century did native numbers begin to recuperate somewhat from this catastrophe, and even then, not everywhere.

AP® EXAM TIP
You need to understand the effects of environmental events on human history.

As the **Great Dying** took hold in the Americas, it interacted with another natural phenomenon, this time one of genuinely global proportions. Known as the **Little Ice Age**, it was a period from the thirteenth to nineteenth centuries of unusually cool temperatures that spanned much of the early modern period, most prominently in the Northern Hemisphere. Its causes were complex and multifaceted. Several natural processes contributed to global cooling, including a low point in sunspot activity, slight changes in the earth's orbit around the sun, and an unusually large number of volcanic eruptions in the tropics whose ash and gases blocked the sun's warming energy. But human actions also contributed to climate change. As many millions died, large areas of Native American farmland were deserted and the traditional practice of using burning to manage forests also stopped in many regions. These changes sparked a resurgence of plant life, which in turn took large amounts of carbon dioxide, a greenhouse gas, out of the atmosphere, contributing to global cooling. These factors combined with natural medium- and short-term climate fluctuations to bring shorter growing seasons and less hospitable weather conditions that adversely affected food production across the globe.

AP®
CAUSATION
How did climate fluctuations disrupt social and political stability in seventeenth-century world history?

While the onset, duration, and effects of the Little Ice Age varied from region to region, the impact of a cooler climate reached its peak in many areas in the mid-seventeenth century, helping to spark what scholars term the **General Crisis**. Much of China, Europe, and North America experienced record or near-record cold winters during this period. Regions near the equator in the tropics and Southern Hemisphere also experienced extreme conditions and irregular rainfall, resulting, for instance, in the growth of the Sahara Desert. Wet, cold summers reduced harvests dramatically in Europe, while severe droughts ruined crops in many other regions, especially China, which suffered terrible drought between 1637 and 1641. Difficult weather conditions accentuated other stresses in societies, leading to widespread famines, epidemics, uprisings, and wars in which millions perished. Eurasia did not escape lightly from these stresses: the collapse of the Ming dynasty in China, nearly constant warfare in Europe, and civil war in Mughal India all occurred in the context of the General Crisis, which only fully subsided when more favorable weather patterns took hold starting in the eighteenth century.

Nor were the Americas, already devastated by the Great Dying, spared the suffering that accompanied the Little Ice Age and the General Crisis of the seventeenth century.

TEACHING IDEA

Incorporating Outside Resources

The Crash Course World History series can be a great way to help students learn about specific historical events. In the episode *Climate Change, Chaos, and the Little Ice Age*, John Green describes the Little Ice Age, a cooling of the earth's temperature that affected the world from the thirteenth to the nineteenth century. The video can be found on YouTube. Consider having students watch the video and answer the following questions:

■ What was the most catastrophic result of the Little Ice Age? *Slowing of crop production, which brought on famine.*

■ What were the political effects of this food shortage? *Bread riots, unrest, and crime.*

■ Why does John Green consider the seventeenth century to be a century of crisis? *Because many wars and periods of unrest occurred throughout the world.*

■ How did the economy of the seventeenth century make people more vulnerable to the colder temperatures? *The dependence on agriculture meant that even a slight change in temperatures affected the amount of food available to the population because it reduced the number of days in*

a growing season. Not only was there less food, but there was also less work for a large portion of the population.

■ How did warfare increase the destruction of the Little Ice Age? *Soldiers looted land, and peasants paid large taxes in food to finance the wars.*

■ How are a decrease in population and an increase in food prices related? *When there is less food, women marry at a later age, fewer children survive into adulthood, people are more vulnerable to disease, wars increase the deaths among men, and emigration reduces the population.*

In central Mexico, heartland of the Aztec Empire and the center of Spanish colonial rule in the area, severe drought in the five years after 1639 sent the price of maize skyrocketing, left granaries empty and many people without water, and prompted an unsuccessful plot to declare Mexico's independence from Spain. Continuing drought years in the decades that followed witnessed repeated public processions of the statue of Our Lady of Guadalupe, a Catholic representation of the Virgin Mary, who had gained a reputation for producing rain. The Caribbean region during the 1640s experienced the opposite condition—torrential rains that accompanied more frequent El Niño weather patterns—which provided ideal conditions for the breeding of mosquitoes that carried both yellow fever and malaria. A Maya chronicle for 1648 noted, "There was bloody vomit and we began to die."[9]

Like the Great Dying, the General Crisis reminds us that climate often plays an important role in shaping human history. But it also reminds us that human activity—the importation of deadly diseases to the Americas, in this case—also helped shape the climate, and that this has been true long before our current climate crisis.

The Columbian Exchange

In sharply diminishing the population of the Americas, the Great Dying, together with the impact of the Little Ice Age, created an acute labor shortage and certainly did make room for immigrant newcomers, both colonizing Europeans and enslaved Africans. Over the several centuries of the colonial era and beyond, various combinations of Indigenous, European, and African peoples created entirely new societies in the Americas, largely replacing the many and varied cultures that had flourished before 1492.

To those colonial societies, free Europeans and enslaved Africans brought not only their germs and their people but also their plants and animals. European crops such as wheat, barley, rye, sugarcane, grapes, and many garden vegetables and fruits, as well as numerous weeds, took hold in the Americas, where they transformed the landscape and made possible a recognizably European diet and way of life. African contributions to the diet of the Americas included African varieties of rice, castor beans, black-eyed peas, okra, sesame, watermelons, and yams. Accompanying the introduction of these new food crops was widespread deforestation, as the land was burned, logged, and turned into fields and pastures by Europeans, often using enslaved labor. In what is now the United States, some 90 percent of the old growth forests have been destroyed since 1600.

Even more revolutionary were the newcomers' animals—horses, pigs, cattle, goats, sheep—all of which were new to the Americas and multiplied spectacularly in an environment largely free of natural predators. These domesticated animals made possible the ranching economies and cowboy cultures of both North and South America. Horses also transformed many Native American societies, particularly in the North American West, as settled farming peoples such as the Pawnee abandoned their fields to hunt bison from horseback. As a male-dominated hunting

AP° EXAM TIP

Be sure you understand the definition of the Columbian exchange and its global economic, environmental, and cultural effects.

AP°

CAUSATION

How did the Columbian exchange transform societies in the Americas?

TEACHING IDEA

Bell Ringer

For a fun way to quickly test students' ability to differentiate a New World item from an Old World item, ask them to determine the origins of the following items. You might want to use a website such as Kahoot! or Quizlet Live to make the game electronically interactive, or you can hang signs with the following words around the room and have students write down the origin of each item or post sticky notes.

Turkey: *New World*　　**Tomatoes:** *New World*

Citrus: *Old World*　　**Peppers:** *New World*

Llama: *New World*　　**Peanuts:** *New World*

Pig: *Old World*　　　　**Sweet potatoes:** *New World*

Horse: *Old World*

Guinea pig: *New World*　**Smallpox:** *Old World*

　　　　　　　　　　Broccoli: *Old World*

Potatoes: *New World*　**Cassava:** *New World*

Peas: *Old World*　　　**Coffee:** *Old World*

Beans: *New World*　　**Cocoa:** *New World*

APPLY THE TIP

One common misconception students have is that the Columbian exchange was a trade route. It would be helpful to go over the definition of the Columbian exchange with your students and emphasize that while the exchange happened along a trade network, it was the exchange of *biological* items (such as diseases, plants, animals, and people) between the Old World (Afro-Eurasia) and the New World (the Americas). Then ask students to create a chart to take notes on the economic, environmental, and cultural effects of the Columbian exchange on the world. A reproducible version of this chart is available in the Teacher's Resource Materials.

Economic Effects	Environmental Effects	Cultural Effects
■ The introduction of new domesticated animals to the Americas allowed for the growth of ranching economies ■ Helped provide food for industrial workers in Europe ■ European imperial powers used the wealth from access to raw materials in their colonies to lay the foundation for the Industrial Revolution	■ New crops transformed the environments and landscapes of the Old World and the New World ■ The Americas experienced mass deforestation to make way for agricultural land	■ The introduction of new domesticated animals to the Americas led to the creation of cowboy cultures ■ The mass dying of Native Americans due to the introduction of new diseases made it easier to spread Christianity in the Americas ■ The exchange contributed to Europe's Scientific Revolution

Differentiation

If you want to extend this activity, consider using the "Must Do, Should Do, Strive For" structure below:

■ Must Do: Have students complete the Causation Chart for Columbian Exchange.

■ Should Do: Have a class discussion on which effect of the Columbian exchange was the most important. Each student should participate in the class discussion at least once.

■ Strive For: Have students write an argumentative paragraph of four or five sentences on which effect of the Columbian exchange they believe is the most important. The paragraph should open with a clear claim and have at least two pieces of evidence to support it.

TRM Handout 4.3: Causation Chart for Columbian Exchange

and warrior culture emerged, women lost much of their earlier role as food producers. Both environmentally and socially, these changes were revolutionary.

In the other direction, American food crops such as corn, potatoes, and cassava spread widely in the Eastern Hemisphere, where they provided the nutritional foundation for the population growth that became everywhere a hallmark of the modern era. In Europe, calories derived from corn and potatoes helped push human numbers from some 60 million in 1400 to 390 million in 1900. Those American crops later provided cheap and reasonably nutritious food for millions of industrial workers. Potatoes, especially, allowed Ireland's population to grow enormously and then condemned many of the Irish to starvation or emigration when an airborne fungus, also from the Americas, destroyed the crop in the mid-nineteenth century. In China, corn, peanuts, and especially sweet potatoes supplemented the traditional rice and wheat to sustain China's modern population explosion. By the early twentieth century, food plants of American origin represented about 20 percent of total Chinese food production. In Africa, corn took hold quickly and was used as a cheap food for the enslaved Africans transported and traded across the Atlantic Ocean.

Beyond food crops, American stimulants such as tobacco and chocolate were soon used around the world. By the seventeenth century, how-to manuals instructed Chinese users on smoking techniques, and tobacco had become, in the words of one enamored Chinese poet, "the gentleman's companion, it warms my heart and leaves my mouth feeling like a divine furnace."[10] Tea from China and coffee from the Islamic world also spread globally, contributing to this worldwide biological exchange. Never before in human history had such a large-scale and consequential diffusion of plants and animals operated to remake the biological environment of the planet.

This enormous network of communication, migration, trade, disease, and the transfer of plants and animals, all generated by European colonial empires in the Americas, has been dubbed the **Columbian exchange**. It gave rise to something wholly new in world history: an interacting Atlantic world that permanently connected Europe, Africa, and North and South America. But the long-term benefits of this Atlantic network were very unequally distributed. The peoples of Africa and the Americas experienced social disruption, slavery, disease, and death on an almost unimaginable scale, while Western Europeans reaped the greatest rewards. Mountains of

AP
DEVELOPMENTS AND PROCESSES
In what ways was the Columbian exchange a global phenomenon?

AP **EXAM TIP**
Understand the impact of American plants on places in Africa, Asia, and Europe.

▼ **AP**
CAUSATION
What historical factors made Europeans less susceptible to the disease pictured here than the Indigenous population?

Disease and Death among the Aztecs Smallpox, which accompanied the Spanish to the Americas, devastated native populations. This image, drawn by an Aztec artist and contained in the sixteenth-century Florentine Codex, illustrates the impact of the disease in Mesoamerica. (Peter Newark American Pictures/Bridgeman Images)

APPLY THE TIP

You could ask students to create a specific list in their reading notes on the impact American food crops had on Afro-Eurasian societies. (Answers are provided in italics.)

■ **Europe:** *The calories from corn and potatoes caused population to increase from 60 million in 1400 to 390 million in 1900. These crops also provided cheap food for millions of workers during the Industrial Revolution.*

■ **Ireland:** *Although potatoes helped feed the growing population of Ireland, the Irish people became dependent on them for a steady food supply, which led to disaster when a fungus destroyed the crop in the mid-1800s.*

■ **China:** *China's population grew rapidly after corn, peanuts, and sweet potatoes from the Americas were introduced to the food supply.*

■ **Africa:** *Corn became a staple food in African societies and was used as a cheap food source for the human cargoes in the transatlantic slave trade.*

After students have taken notes, consider checking for understanding by asking: What was the overall impact of American food crops on Afro-Eurasian societies? *The access to new food sources that were high in calories caused the population of Afro-Eurasia to skyrocket.*

TEACHING IDEA

Incorporating Outside Resources

A fun way to look at the impact of the Columbian exchange on today's world is the OER Project's activity, "World Zone Café." This activity asks students to build menus for a new café that represents different world regions both before and after the Columbian exchange. You can find the PDF of the activity and more in-depth instructions in Unit 4 of the World History, AP® section of the OER Project site, at the end of Lesson 4.1, "Columbian Exchange."

new information flooded into Europe, shaking up conventional understandings of the world and contributing to a revolutionary new way of thinking known as the Scientific Revolution. The wealth of the colonies—precious metals, natural resources, new food crops, slave labor, financial profits, colonial markets—provided one of the foundations on which Europe's Industrial Revolution was built. The colonies also provided an outlet for the rapidly growing population of European societies and represented an enormous extension of European civilization. In short, the colonial empires of the Americas greatly facilitated a changing global balance of power, which now thrust the previously marginal Western Europeans into an increasingly central and commanding role on the world stage. "Without a New World to deliver economic balance in the Old," concluded a prominent world historian, "Europe would have remained inferior, as ever, in wealth and power, to the great civilizations of Asia."[11]

> **AP EXAM TIP**
> Understand this explanation of the long-term effects of the Columbian exchange.

Comparing Colonial Societies in the Americas

Finding the Main Point: In what different ways did European colonialism take shape in the Americas?

European colonial empires—Spanish, Portuguese, British, and French alike—did not simply conquer and govern established societies, but rather generated wholly new societies, born of the decimation of Native American populations and the introduction of European and African peoples, cultures, plants, and animals. European colonial strategies were based on an economic theory known as **mercantilism**, which held that governments served their countries' economic interests best by encouraging exports and accumulating bullion (precious metals such as silver and gold). In this scheme of things, colonies provided closed markets for the manufactured goods of the "mother country" and, if they were lucky, supplied great quantities of bullion as well. Such an outlook fueled European wars and colonial rivalries around the world in the early modern era.

Meanwhile, in the colonies themselves, empire took shape in various ways. Some differences derived from the contrasting societies of the colonizing powers, such as a semi-feudal and Catholic Spain and a more rapidly changing Protestant England. The kind of economy established in particular regions—settler-dominated agriculture, plantations based on slave labor, ranching, or mining—likewise influenced the colonies' development. So too did the character of the Native American cultures—the more densely populated and urbanized Mesoamerican and Andean civilizations differed greatly from the more sparsely populated rural villages of North America.

Furthermore, women and men often experienced colonial intrusion in quite distinct ways. Beyond the common burdens of violent conquest, epidemic disease, and coerced labor, both Native American and enslaved African women had to cope with the additional demands made on them as females. Conquest was often accompanied by the transfer of women to the new colonial rulers. Cortés, for example, commanded the Aztec ruler: "You are to deliver women with light skins, corn, chicken, eggs, and tortillas."[12] Soon after conquest, many Spanish men

> **AP EXAM TIP**
> Remember these examples of how Native American women were treated by both native men and Europeans after the European conquest.

Incorporating Outside Resources

To help students understand the long-term effects of the Columbian exchange, consider showing the Crash Course World History episode *The Columbian Exchange*. In this episode, John Green discusses the work of Alfred Crosby on the biological and cultural consequences of the Columbian exchange. You can find the video on YouTube. As students watch the video, have them answer the following questions:

■ How did disease help the Spanish conquer Native American empires? *The death of between 50 and 90 percent of the Indigenous population from European diseases reduced their ability to defend themselves. The death of leaders led to widespread wars. The reduction in population led to a decline in agricultural productivity, and many Native Americans were weakened by malnutrition or died of starvation.*

■ How did New World foods lead to a population increase in Europe? *New World foods had higher calorie values than Old World foods and could be grown in soils that did not support Old World crops. These benefits increased the nutritional value of foods and the amount of food that could be produced; more calories available meant that agricultural production could support a larger population.*

■ What is one long-term effect of the Columbian exchange mentioned in the video? *One long-term effect is the move toward more homogeneity in plants and animals, including humans.*

APPLY THE TIP

For a quick Continuity and Change practice, you could ask students: How were Native American women treated after the European conquest? *At the elite level of Indigenous society, Europeans intermarried with Native American women. Below the elite level, rape and sexual exploitation were not uncommon.*

BUILDING AP® SKILLS

Making Connections: Comparison

When students are learning about the maritime empires of the early modern era, it's important that they know how these empires ruled their colonies, not just how the government was run in the home state. You might try having students create a Venn diagram comparing European colonial rule in the Caribbean and North America to European colonial rule in South America, using the section "Comparing Colonial Societies in the Americas" for research. You can find a reproducible Venn diagram for this activity in the Teacher's Resource Materials.

After they complete their diagrams, have students complete a quickwrite response to the following question: Evaluate the extent to which European colonial rule in the Caribbean and North America differed from European colonial rule in South America. *Answers will vary.*

TRM Handout 4.4: Graphic Organizer for Comparing Colonial Societies

APPLY THE TIP

Students are going to be introduced to different types of coercive labor systems in Chapters 4 and 6, two of which are the mit'a (*repartimiento*) and the *encomienda* in the Spanish colonies. You might try having students discuss the similarities and differences in the two systems with a partner. Students can read about the encomienda system in the second paragraph of "In the Lands of the Aztecs and the Incas." Remind them that they learned about the origins of the mit'a on page 109 in Chapter 2, and they can search the Spanish version of the mit'a (repartimiento) system online for more information. After students are done discussing the systems with their partner, invite volunteers to share what comparisons they made with the class. *Although the Incas started the mit'a system, under the Spanish it evolved into the encomienda system. Under the mit'a system, all Inca males from fifteen to fifty were required to labor for the state, including in military service. It has been estimated that the wealth of the Inca Empire often meant that families needed only about sixty-five days to farm, and the rest of the time was given to the mit'a system. Later the Spanish used this system to get workers for the silver mine at Potosí. The Spanish used the encomienda system to control and regulate*

married elite native women. It was a long-standing practice in Native American societies and was encouraged by both Spanish and Indigenous male authorities as a means of cementing their new relationship. It was also advantageous for some of the women involved. One of Aztec emperor Moctezuma's daughters, who was mistress to Cortés and was eventually married, successively, to several other Spaniards, wound up with the largest landed estate in the Valley of Mexico. Below this elite level of interaction, however, far more women experienced sexual violence and abuse. Rape accompanied conquest in many places, and dependent or enslaved women working under the control of European men frequently found themselves required to perform sexual services. This was a tragedy and humiliation for native and enslaved men as well, for they were unable to protect their mothers, wives, daughters, and sisters from such abuse.

Such variations in culture, policy, economy, and gender generated quite different colonial societies in several major regions of the Americas.

In the Lands of the Aztecs and the Incas

The Spanish conquest of the Aztec and Inca empires in the early sixteenth century gave Spain access to the most wealthy, urbanized, and densely populated regions of the Western Hemisphere. Within a century, and well before the British had even begun their colonizing efforts in North America, the Spanish in Mexico and Peru had established nearly a dozen major cities; several impressive universities; hundreds of cathedrals, churches, and missions; an elaborate administrative bureaucracy; and a network of regulated international commerce.

The economic foundation for this emerging colonial society lay in commercial agriculture, much of it on large rural estates, and in silver and gold mining. In both cases, native peoples, rather than enslaved Africans or European workers, provided most of the labor, despite their much-diminished numbers. Almost everywhere, that labor was coerced, often directly required by colonial authorities under a legal regime known as *encomienda*. It was, in fact, a forced labor system not far removed from slavery. By the seventeenth century, the *hacienda* system had taken shape, by which the private owners of large estates directly employed native workers. With low wages, high taxes, and large debts to the landowners, the *peons* who worked these estates enjoyed little control over their lives or their livelihood.

On this economic base, a distinctive social order grew up, replicating something of Spanish class and gender hierarchies while accommodating the racially and culturally different Native Americans and Africans as well as growing numbers of multiracial people. At the top of this colonial society were the male Spanish settlers, who were politically and economically dominant and seeking to become a landed aristocracy. One Spanish official commented in 1619: "The Spaniards, from the able and rich to the humble and poor, all hold themselves to be lords and will not serve [do manual labor]."[13] Politically, they increasingly saw themselves not as colonials, but as residents of a Spanish kingdom, subject to the Spanish monarch yet separate

AP CONTINUITY AND CHANGE
What was the economic foundation of colonial rule in Mexico and Peru? How did it shape the kinds of societies that developed there?

AP EXAM TIP
Systems of coerced labor are important to know for the AP® Exam.

(continued)

Indigenous labor and behavior. Under the encomienda system, the encomenderos (the conquistadors and wealthy leaders) received a number of Native Americans, from whom they exacted "tribute" in the form of gold or labor. The encomenderos were supposed to convert and protect the Native Americans, but the system was often used to enslave them and take their lands.

and distinct from Spain itself and deserving of a large measure of self-government. Therefore, they chafed under the heavy bureaucratic restrictions imposed by the Crown. "I obey but I do not enforce" was a slogan that reflected local authorities' resistance to orders from Spain.

But the Spanish minority, never more than 20 percent of the population, was itself a divided community. Descendants of the original conquistadores sought to protect their privileges against immigrant newcomers; Spaniards born in the Americas (*creoles*) resented the pretensions to superiority of those born in Spain (*peninsulares*); land-owning Spaniards felt threatened by the growing wealth of commercial and mercantile groups practicing less prestigious occupations. Spanish missionaries and church authorities were often sharply critical of how these settlers treated native peoples.

While Spanish women shared the racial privileges of their husbands, they were clearly subordinate in gender terms, unable to hold public office and viewed as weak and in need of male protection. But they were also regarded as the "bearers of civilization," and through their capacity to produce legitimate children, they were the essential link for transmitting male wealth, honor, and status to future generations. This required strict control of their sexuality and a continuation of the Iberian obsession with "purity of blood." In Spain, that concern had focused on potential liaisons with Jews and Muslims; in the colonies, the alleged threat to female virtue derived from Native American and African men.

From a male viewpoint, the problem with Spanish women was that there were very few of them. This demographic fact led to the most distinctive feature of these new colonial societies in Mexico and Peru—the emergence of a **mestizo** (mehs-TEE-zoh), or multiracial, population, initially the product of unions between Spanish men and Native American women. Rooted in the sexual imbalance among Spanish immigrants (seven men to one woman in early colonial Peru, for example), the emergence of a mestizo population was facilitated by the desire of many surviving Indigenous women for the relative security of life in a Spanish household, where they and their children would not be subject to the abuse and harsh demands made on native peoples. Over the 300 years of the

> ▼ **AP®**
>
> **CLAIMS AND EVIDENCE IN SOURCES**
>
> In what ways would the husband and wife shown in this painting have both benefited from their marriage? What evidence in the painting supports your argument?

Interracial Marriage in Colonial Mexico This eighteenth-century painting by the famous Zapotec artist Miguel Cabrera shows a Spanish man, a *mestiza* woman, and their child, who was labeled as *castiza*. By the twentieth century, such multiracial people represented the majority of the population of Mexico, and cultural blending had become a central feature of the country's identity. (Bridgeman Images)

EXPLORING AP® THEMES

Cultural Developments and Interactions (CDI)

Consider showing students the painting *Human Races* on the Annenberg Learner website. You can find the painting in the "Art through Time: A Global View" section under "Classroom Resources." Look for Unit 1: Converging Cultures and then Section 2 Art: Human Races (Las Castas) to find the painting. You can also watch the accompanying video on the Converging Cultures front page. (Note that the Spanish conquest and castas painting portion of the video begins at minute 7 and lasts about 3 minutes.) After watching the video, ask students: How were castas paintings used to stabilize a society? *Castas paintings were sociological paintings that were used to point people to the rung in society to which they belonged. Because race was really only part of the equation, what people wore and how much wealth they possessed were as important as the color of their skin.*

BUILDING AP® SKILLS

Claims and Evidence in Sources

This is a good place to help students use insights from art history to better understand the historical issues presented by the castas. Ask students to study the photo titled "Interracial Marriage in Colonial Mexico" on page 215 and discuss the following questions with a partner:

■ Based on the painting, what conclusions can you make about race, social status, and wealth? *The woman and child appear to be as well dressed as the man, and he has clearly been able to provide his wife with fine clothes, jewelry, a wardrobe of shoes, and abundant food. The man, wearing a wig and fine jacket, appears to be of high social standing. Despite the differences in their race and Spanish concerns about "purity of blood," they appear to be a family and he looks at her with affection.*

■ Based on your conclusions about race, social status, and wealth, what do you think might have been the young castiza's future? *It seems likely that the girl's father would have provided her with wealth. She might have gone on to marry a Spaniard herself, thus raising her social status further.*

APPLY THE TIP

As mentioned in previous chapters, it's important for students to be able to make connections across time periods. One way to get students to practice this skill is to ask them to create a chart, like the one below, to compare the treatment of nonelites in European empires in Latin America to the treatment of nonelites in the Song dynasty and the Mongol khanates. A reproducible version of this chart is available in the Teacher's Resource Materials.

Treatment of Nonelites in European Empires in Latin America	Treatment of Nonelites in the Song Dynasty	Treatment of Nonelites in the Mongol Khanates
▪ The colonial government divided the mestizo population into dozens of separate groups, or castas, based on their precise racial heritage. ▪ Spaniards looked down on the mestizos as illegitimate and did not allow them to gain political or social power in the colonies, but did recognize them for their economic usefulness. ▪ Indigenous people were placed at the bottom of colonial society in Latin America, were exploited as a labor force by the Spanish empire, and were forcibly relocated to larger settlements.	▪ Under the Confucian social hierarchy, nonelites were farmers and merchants. ▪ Farmers were supposed to be respected because they were considered the "backbone" of Chinese society as major food suppliers. ▪ Merchants were not viewed highly under Confucianism because it was believed that they were "thieves" and did not produce anything of value for the state. ▪ Both farmers and merchants could try to improve their social status by educating sons in Confucianism, with the goal of joining the scholar-gentry, along with accumulating land.	▪ Chinese nonelites were not viewed highly in the Mongol khanates, but other foreign groups were valued by Mongol khans. ▪ Northern Chinese subjects were viewed as lower than southern Chinese subjects under the Yuan Mongol dynasty. ▪ All khanates utilized foreign scholars, merchants, and philosophers as advisers in their courts.

TRM Handout 4.5: Comparison Chart for Nonelites in European, Song, and Mongol Empires

---

colonial era, mestizo numbers grew substantially, becoming the majority of the population in Mexico sometime during the nineteenth century. Such multiracial people were divided into dozens of separate groups known as *castas* (castes), based on their precise racial heritage and skin color.

Mestizos were largely Hispanic in culture, but Spaniards looked down on them during much of the colonial era, regarding them as illegitimate, for many were not born of "proper" marriages. Despite this attitude, their growing numbers and the economic usefulness of their men as artisans, clerks, supervisors of labor gangs, and lower-level officials in both church and state bureaucracies led to their recognition as a distinct social group. *Mestizas*, women of various racial backgrounds, worked as domestic servants or in their husbands' shops, wove cloth, and manufactured candles and cigars, in addition to performing domestic duties. A few became quite wealthy. An illiterate mestiza named Mencia Perez successively married two reasonably well-to-do Spanish men and, upon their deaths, took over their businesses, becoming in her own right a very rich woman by the 1590s. At that point, no one would have referred to her as a mestiza. Particularly in Mexico, mestizo identity blurred the sense of sharp racial difference between Spanish and Native American peoples and became a major element in the identity of modern Mexico. More recently, however, the use of the term "mestizo" has been criticized for being associated with colonialism, for privileging lighter-skinned people, and for distancing individuals from those of African background.

At the bottom of Mexican and Peruvian colonial societies were the Indigenous peoples, known to Europeans as "Indians." Traumatized by the Great Dying, they were subject to gross abuse and exploitation as the primary labor force for the mines and estates of the Spanish Empire and were required to render tribute payments to their Spanish overlords. Their empires dismantled by Spanish conquest, their religions attacked by Spanish missionaries, and their diminished numbers forcibly relocated into larger settlements, many Native Americans gravitated toward the world of their conquerors. Many learned Spanish; converted to Christianity; moved to cities to work for wages; ate the meat of cows, chickens, and pigs; used plows and draft animals rather than traditional digging sticks; and took their many grievances to Spanish courts. Women endured some distinctive conditions because Spanish legal codes generally defined them as minors rather than responsible adults. As those codes took hold, Indigenous women were increasingly excluded from the courts or represented by their menfolk. This made it more difficult to maintain female property rights. In 1804, for example, a Maya legal petition identified eight men and ten women from a particular family as owners of a piece of land, but the Spanish translation omitted the women's names altogether.

But much that was Indigenous persisted. At the local level, Indigenous male authorities retained a measure of autonomy, and traditional markets operated regularly. Both Andean and Maya women continued to leave personal property to their female descendants. Maize, beans, and squash persisted as the major elements of Indigenous diets in Mexico. Christian saints in many places blended easily

AP® EXAM TIP
Look back at other empires in history. How were nonelites treated? Compare these examples from earlier empires to the treatment of nonelites in Latin America.

BUILDING AP® SKILLS

Making Connections: Continuity and Change

One of the recommended reasoning skills for Units 3 and 4 is Continuity and Change. Students can practice that skill here by looking at how Indigenous societies changed after the European conquest. After students have read pages 216 and 217, ask the following questions:

▪ How were the processes of Spanish acculturation and patriarchy linked? *Spanish legal codes generally defined Native American women as minors rather than responsible adults. As these codes took hold, Indigenous women were* increasingly excluded from the courts or represented by their menfolk. This change made it more difficult to maintain female property rights. In 1804, for example, a Maya legal petition identified eight men and ten women from a particular family as owners of a piece of land, but the Spanish translation omitted the women's names altogether.

▪ What did not change about Indigenous culture? Provide specific examples. *At the local level, Indigenous male authorities retained a measure of autonomy, and traditional markets* ➔

with specialized Indigenous gods, while belief in magic, folk medicine, and communion with the dead remained strong. Memories of the past also endured. The Tupac Amaru revolt in Peru during 1780–1781 was made in the name of the last independent Inca emperor. In that revolt, the wife of the leader, Micaela Bastidas, was referred to as La Coya, the female Inca, evoking the parallel hierarchies of male and female officials who had earlier governed the Inca Empire (see "The Emergence of the Incas in the Andes" in Chapter 2).

Thus Spaniards, mestizos, and Native Americans represented the major social categories in the colonial lands of what had been the Inca and Aztec empires, while enslaved Africans and freemen were less numerous than elsewhere in the Americas. Despite the sharp divisions among these groups, some movement was possible. Native Americans who acquired an education, wealth, and some European culture might "pass" as mestizo. Likewise, more fortunate mestizo families might be accepted as Spaniards over time. Colonial Spanish America was a vast laboratory of ethnic variety and cultural change. It was dominated by Europeans, to be sure, but was a rather more fluid and culturally blended society than the racially rigid colonies of British North America.

Colonies of Sugar

Another and quite different kind of colonial society emerged in the lowland areas of Brazil, ruled by Portugal, and in the Spanish, British, French, and Dutch colonies in the Caribbean. These regions lacked the great civilizations of Mexico and Peru. Nor did they provide much mineral wealth until the Brazilian gold rush of the 1690s and the discovery of diamonds a little later. Still, Europeans found a very profitable substitute in sugar, which was much in demand in Europe, where it was used as a medicine, a spice, a sweetener, a preservative, and in sculptured forms as a decoration that indicated high status. Whereas commercial agriculture in the Spanish Empire served a domestic market in its towns and mining camps, these sugar-based colonies produced almost exclusively for export, while importing their food and other necessities.

Large-scale sugar production had been pioneered by Arabs, who had introduced it in the Mediterranean. Europeans learned the technique and transferred it to their Atlantic island possessions and then to the Americas. For a century (1570–1670), Portuguese planters along the northeast coast of Brazil dominated the world market for sugar. Then the British, French, and Dutch turned their Caribbean territories into highly productive sugar-producing colonies, breaking the Portuguese and Brazilian monopoly.

Sugar decisively transformed Brazil and the Caribbean. Its production, which involved both growing the sugarcane and processing it into usable sugar, was very labor-intensive and could most profitably occur in a large-scale, almost industrial setting. It was perhaps the first modern industry in that it produced for an international and mass market, using capital and expertise from Europe, with production facilities located in the Americas. However, its most characteristic feature—the massive use of

AP®
CAUSATION
How did sugar transform Brazil and the Caribbean?

AP®
COMPARISON
How did the plantation societies of Brazil and the Caribbean differ from those of southern colonies in British North America?

EXPLORING AP® THEMES

Social Interactions and Organization (SIO)

If you want to extend the Apply the Tip chart from page 216 and challenge students' understanding of social hierarchies, consider asking students to explain how they could have moved up in the social hierarchy if they had been born as mestizos in colonial Latin America. Students can use the second paragraph on this page to give them some ideas for answering the question. *Answers could include: Native Americans who acquired an education, wealth, and some European culture might "pass" as mestizo. Likewise, more fortunate mestizo families might be accepted as Spaniards over time. Colonial Spanish America was a vast laboratory of ethnic mixing and cultural change. It was dominated by Europeans, to be sure, but had a more fluid and culturally blended society than the racially rigid colonies of British North America.*

(continued)

operated regularly. Both Andean and Maya women continued to leave personal property to their female descendants. Maize, beans, and squash persisted as the major elements of Indigenous diets in Mexico. Christian saints in many places blended easily with specialized Indigenous gods, while belief in magic, folk medicine, and communion with the dead remained strong.

APPLY THE TIP

Students sometimes think that the features and effects of slavery throughout world history are the same as the features and effects of slavery they've learned about in U.S. history. To help students learn about the differences, divide the class up into groups of four. In each group, have two students take notes on the features of the African slave trade and its effects on Africa and the other two students take notes on the features of the African slave trade and its effects on the Americas. The information on pages 218 and 219 can help them with this assignment. After they have finished finding their information, they should share what they found with the rest of their group.

BUILDING AP® SKILLS

Making Connections: Causation

A good way to help students visualize the connection between the production of sugar and the growth of slavery in the Americas is to show them Slate's animated map of the transatlantic slave trade. You can find the map by Googling "Slate: The Atlantic Slave Trade in Two Minutes." Show students the map and let them know that each dot moving on the map represents a slave trade ship. Then ask them: What do you notice about where enslaved peoples are going? *Answers may include: A few ships went to Europe; Not many ships went to North America; A majority of the ships went to the Caribbean and Brazil.*

Then you can ask: What would have caused a majority of the enslaved people to be taken to the Caribbean and Brazil? *Sugar cane plantations led to a large demand for enslaved laborers.*

If any students seem especially interested in the map, you can let them know that if you pause the map and click on a dot, it will display the information available about that particular slave ship.

AP® EXAM TIP

You must understand the demographic features and impact of the transatlantic slave system in both the Americas and Africa.

▼ AP®

SOURCING AND SITUATION

How does the image provide clues about the perspective of the artist? Was the artist more likely for or against the institution of slavery?

slave labor—was an ancient practice. In the absence of a Native American population, which had been almost totally wiped out in the Caribbean or had fled inland in Brazil, European sugarcane planters turned to Africa and the Atlantic slave trade for an alternative workforce. The vast majority of the African captives transported across the Atlantic, some 80 percent or more, ended up in Brazil and the Caribbean. (See "Commerce in People: The Transatlantic Slave System" in Chapter 6.)

Enslaved people worked on sugar-producing estates in horrendous conditions. The heat and fire from the cauldrons, which turned raw sugarcane into crystallized sugar, reminded many visitors of scenes from Hell. These conditions, combined with disease, generated a high death rate, perhaps 5 to 10 percent per year, which required plantation owners to constantly import more enslaved people. A Jesuit observer in 1580 aptly summarized the situation: "The work is great and many die."[14]

More males than females were imported from Africa into the sugar economies of the Americas, leading to major and persistent gender imbalances. Nonetheless, enslaved women did play distinctive roles in these societies. Women made up about half of the field gangs that did the heavy work of planting and harvesting

Plantation Life in the Caribbean This painting from 1823 shows the use of slave labor on a plantation in Antigua, a British-ruled island in the Caribbean. Notice the overseer with a whip supervising the tilling and planting of the field. (© British Library Board. All Rights Reserved/Bridgeman Images)

BUILDING AP® SKILLS

Sourcing and Situation

One of the most difficult points of the DBQ essay is Sourcing: being able to use point of view, purpose, historical situation, and/or audience to explain how or why a document is relevant to an argument. It's good to have students practice this skill throughout the year. The image of "Plantation Life in the Caribbean" and its accompanying margin question could be good to give to students to help them practice Sourcing, especially with thinking about the artist's point of view.

sugarcane. They were subject to the same brutal punishments and received the same rations as their male counterparts, though they were seldom permitted to undertake the more skilled labor inside the sugar mills. Women who worked in urban areas, mostly for white female owners, did domestic chores and were often hired out as laborers in various homes, shops, laundries, inns, and brothels. Discouraged from establishing stable families, women had to endure, often alone, the wrenching separation from their children that occurred when they were sold. Mary Prince, an enslaved Caribbean woman who wrote a brief account of her life, recalled the pain of families torn apart: "The great God above alone knows the thoughts of the poor slave's heart, and the bitter pains which follow such separations as these. All that we love taken away from us—oh, it is sad, sad! and sore to be borne!"[15]

The extensive use of African slave labor gave these plantation colonies a very different ethnic and racial makeup than that of highland Spanish America, as indicated by the Snapshot: Ethnic Composition of Colonial Societies in Latin America (1825). Thus, after three centuries of colonial rule, a substantial majority of Brazil's population was either partially or wholly of African descent. In the French Caribbean colony of Haiti in 1790, the corresponding figure was 93 percent.

As in Spanish America, interracial unions were common in colonial Brazil. Cross-racial unions accounted for only about 10 percent of all marriages, but the use of concubines and informal liaisons among Native Americans, Africans, and Portuguese produced a substantial multiracial population. From their ranks derived much of the urban skilled workforce and many of the supervisors in the sugar industry. As many as forty separate and named groups, each indicating a different racial mixture, emerged in colonial Brazil. The largest group at the time were the product of European-African unions, which the Portuguese called *mulattoes*, a highly derogatory term widely used in the eighteenth century but offensive to many people then and now.

The plantation complex of the Americas, based on African slave labor, extended beyond the Caribbean and Brazil to encompass the southern colonies of British North America, where tobacco, cotton, rice, and indigo were major crops, but the social outcomes of these plantation colonies were quite different from those farther south. Because European women had joined the colonial migration to North America at an

SNAPSHOT Ethnic Composition of Colonial Societies in Latin America (1825)

	Highland Spanish America	Portuguese America (Brazil)
Europeans	18.2 percent	23.4 percent
Multiracial	28.3 percent	17.8 percent
Africans	11.9 percent	49.8 percent
Native Americans	41.7 percent	9.1 percent

Source: Data from Thomas E. Skidmore and Peter H. Smith, *Modern Latin America* (New York: Oxford University Press, 2001), 25.

◀ **AP**
COMPARISON
How did ethnic composition differ within Latin America?

APPLY THE TIP

To help students compare slavery in Latin America and the Caribbean with slavery in British North America, ask them to complete a comparison chart like the one shown here. In addition to the information on pages 219 and 220, students can use information found online on the Trans-Atlantic Slave Trade Database website. Hover over the regions marked on the map on the left-hand side to see the information. A reproducible version of this chart is available in the Teacher's Resource Materials. (Answers are provided in italics.)

Slavery in Latin America and the Caribbean	Similarities	Slavery in British North America
▪ *Sugar plantation workers* ▪ *Women made up about half of the field gangs that planted and harvested sugar* ▪ *Disease and accidents caused a death rate of 5 to 10 percent* ▪ *New Africans were imported every year* ▪ *Enslaved people were discouraged from establishing stable families* ▪ *Multiracial classes common*	▪ *Brutal working and living conditions* ▪ *Primarily plantation agriculture workers* ▪ *Associated with Black people* ▪ *Coerced labor*	▪ *Indigo, cotton, tobacco, and rice plantation workers* ▪ *Racial purity was much more important* ▪ *One-drop rule: if one of your ancestors was enslaved, you were enslaved* ▪ *Enslaved people were not as frequently imported; a majority were children born to enslaved women*

TRM Handout 4.6: Graphic Organizer for Slavery in the Americas

---

early date, these colonies experienced less racial variety and certainly demonstrated less willingness to recognize the offspring of multiracial unions and accord them a place in society. A sharply defined racial system (with Black Africans, "red" Native Americans, and white Europeans) evolved in North America, whereas both Portuguese and Spanish colonies acknowledged a wide variety of multiracial groups.

AP EXAM TIP

Compare slavery in Latin America and the Caribbean with slavery in British North America.

Slavery too was different in North America than in the sugar colonies. By 1750 or so, enslaved people in what became the United States were reproducing at such a rate that by the time of the Civil War almost all enslaved North Americans had been born in the New World. That was never the case in Latin America, where large-scale importation of new enslaved people continued well into the nineteenth century. Nonetheless, many more enslaved people were voluntarily set free by their owners in Brazil than in North America, and free Blacks and biracial or multiracial people in Brazil had more economic opportunities than did their counterparts in the United States. At least a few among them found positions as political leaders, scholars, musicians, writers, and artists. Some were even hired as slave catchers.

Does this mean, then, that racism was absent in colonial Brazil? Certainly not, but it was different from racism in North America. For one thing, in North America, any African ancestry, no matter how small or distant, made a person "Black"; in Brazil, a person of African and non-African ancestry was considered not Black, but some other biracial or multiracial category. Racial prejudice surely persisted, for European characteristics were prized more highly than African features, and people regarded as white had enormously greater privileges and opportunities than others. Nevertheless, skin color in Brazil, and in Latin America generally, was only one criterion of class status, and the perception of color changed with the educational or economic standing of individuals. A light-skinned person of biracial or multiracial background who had acquired some wealth or education might well "pass" as a white. One curious visitor to Brazil was surprised to find a darker-skinned man serving as a local official. "Isn't the governor a mulatto?" inquired the visitor. "He was, but he isn't any more," was the reply. "How can a governor be a mulatto?"[16]

Settler Colonies in North America

AP COMPARISON

What distinguished the British settler colonies of North America from their Spanish or Portuguese counterparts in Latin America?

Yet another distinctive type of colonial society emerged in the northern British colonies of New England, New York, and Pennsylvania. The lands the British acquired were widely regarded in Europe as the unpromising leftovers of the New World, lacking the obvious wealth and sophisticated cultures of the Spanish possessions. Until at least the eighteenth century, these British colonies remained far less prominent on the world stage than those of Spain or Portugal.

The British settlers came from a more rapidly changing society than did those from an ardently Catholic, semi-feudal, authoritarian Spain. When Britain launched its colonial ventures in the seventeenth century, it had already experienced considerable conflict between Catholics and Protestants, the rise of a merchant capitalist class distinct from the nobility, and the emergence of Parliament as a check on the authority of kings. Although they brought much of their English culture

---

BUILDING AP® SKILLS

Making Connections: Causation

Unlike the Latin American colonies, North American colonies did not have a multiracial social hierarchy like the castas. One way to challenge students to think about this difference is to ask: How did racial ideology differ in Latin America and in North America? *In Latin America, there were various racial categories within the castas system. In North America, the racial system was much more clearly defined. A person was Native American, African, or European, and those identities were not fluid in the way they were in Latin America. In Latin America, free Blacks and multiracial people had more economic opportunities and even the possibility of acquiring a higher social position.*

with them, many of the British settlers—Puritans in Massachusetts and Quakers in Pennsylvania, for example—sought to escape aspects of an old European society rather than to re-create it, as was the case for most Spanish and Portuguese colonists. The easy availability of land and the outsider status of many British settlers made it even more difficult to follow the Spanish or Portuguese colonial pattern of sharp class hierarchies, large rural estates, and dependent laborers.

Thus men in Puritan New England became independent heads of family farms, a world away from Old England, where most land was owned by nobles and gentry and worked by servants, tenants, and paid laborers. But if men escaped the class restrictions of the old country, women were less able to avoid its gender limitations. While Puritan Christianity extolled the family and a woman's role as wife and mother, it reinforced largely unlimited male authority. "Since he is thy Husband," declared Boston minister Benjamin Wadsworth in 1712 to the colony's women, "God has made him the Head and set him above thee."[17]

Furthermore, British settlers were far more numerous than their Spanish counterparts, outnumbering them five to one by 1750. By the time of the American Revolution, some 90 percent or more of the population in the New England and middle Atlantic colonies were Europeans. Devastating diseases and a highly aggressive military policy had largely cleared the colonies of Native Americans, and their numbers, which were far smaller to start with, did not rebound in subsequent centuries as they did in the lands of the Aztecs and the Incas. Moreover, slave labor was not needed in an agricultural economy dominated by numerous small-scale

Settler Farms In this eighteenth-century engraving, men work clearing the land for agriculture while a woman in the foreground collects water from a well. Unlike other regions of the Americas, the New England and middle Atlantic colonies were dominated by European immigrants who created small family farms. (Sarin Images/Granger, NYC—All rights reserved)

AP® EXAM TIP

Notice organizational features of this paragraph that can help you improve your essays, such as the many specific examples, the direct comparisons, and the ranking of evidence.

◀ AP®

COMPARISON

How were the organization and class structures of settler communities different from those of sugar colonies? What evidence of those differences do you find in this image?

APPLY THE TIP

A great way to help students understand how to structure or formulate an argument is to have them evaluate the arguments historians make in their books. Make a copy of the last paragraph on this page for each of your students (note that the paragraph extends onto the next page). Have them read the paragraph and highlight or annotate for the following items: claim or assertion of the argument, direct comparisons, specific examples of evidence to back up the argument, and explanation of the evidence. After students finish, consider having them share what they found with a partner and discuss their breakdown of the paragraph.

BUILDING AP® SKILLS

Making Connections: Comparison

Comparison is one of the recommended reasoning skills for students to use in Units 3 and 4, especially comparison of empires. Consider having students fill in a two-column thematic chart to help them see the differences mentioned in the text between Latin American colonies and North American colonies. A reproducible version of this chart is available in the Teacher's Resource Materials.

TRM Handout 4.7: Comparison Chart for American Colonies

BUILDING AP® SKILLS

Making Connections: Comparison

If you had students complete the comparison chart from above, it could be good to have them follow up with a short writing assignment. Ask students to write a 4- to 5-sentence response to the following question: What differences emerged between North American and Latin American colonies during 1450–1750? *Answers may include: Religion and the colonial government were not as closely connected in the North American colonies as they were in the Latin American colonies; British settler colonies had more of a tradition of local self-government than Latin American colonies; Latin American colonies were more culturally diverse than English colonies.*

AP® CLASSROOM

AP® Daily Video

One way to wrap up this section on maritime empires is to show students the Unit 4.4: Daily Video 1 in AP® Classroom. This video examines the process of state building and expansion for maritime empires, as well as giving students practice on analyzing the source of a document.

AP®

COMPARISON

How was the role of religion different in the colonization of Latin America than in the colonization of North America?

---

independent farmers working their own land, although elite families, especially in urban areas, sometimes employed enslaved people as household servants. These were almost entirely European **settler colonies**, for they lacked the substantial presence of Indigenous, African, and multiracial people who were so prominent elsewhere.

Other differences likewise emerged. A largely Protestant England was far less interested in spreading Christianity among the remaining native peoples than were the large and well-funded missionary societies of Catholic Spain. Although religion loomed large in the North American colonies, the church and colonial state were not so intimately connected as they were in Latin America. The Protestant emphasis on reading the Bible for oneself led to a much greater mass literacy than in Latin America, where three centuries of church education still left some 95 percent of the population illiterate at independence. By contrast, well over 75 percent of white males in British North America were literate by the 1770s, although women's literacy rates were somewhat lower. Furthermore, British settler colonies evolved traditions of local self-government more extensively than in Latin America. Preferring to rely on joint stock companies or wealthy individuals operating under a royal charter, Britain had nothing resembling the elaborate imperial bureaucracy that governed Spanish colonies. For much of the seventeenth century, a prolonged power struggle between the English king and Parliament meant that the British government paid little attention to the internal affairs of the colonies. Therefore, elected colonial assemblies, seeing themselves as little parliaments defending "the rights of Englishmen," vigorously contested the prerogatives of royal governors sent to administer their affairs.

The grand irony of the modern history of the Americas lay in the reversal of long-established relationships between the northern and southern continents. For thousands of years, the major centers of wealth, power, commerce, and innovation lay in Mesoamerica and the Andes. That pattern continued for much of the colonial era, as the Spanish and Portuguese colonies seemed far more prosperous and successful than their British or French counterparts in North America. In the nineteenth and twentieth centuries, however, the balance shifted. What had once been the "dregs" of the colonial world became the United States, more politically stable, more democratic, more economically successful, and more internationally powerful than a divided, unstable, and much less prosperous Latin America.

Empire Building in Russia and China

Finding the Main Point: What were the unique strategies and the larger impact of the expanding Russian and Chinese empires during this period?

Even as Western Europeans were building their empires in the Americas, other imperial projects were likewise under way in Asia, the Middle East, and Africa. Unlike Europe's overseas empires, all of them were contiguous land-based territories. The

Russians and Chinese created vast new empires by conquering much of Central and Northern Asia. Meanwhile, after centuries of political fragmentation, much of the Islamic world came together in four major empires—Mughal, Safavid, Ottoman, and Songhay—stretching from South Asia through the Middle East to sub-Saharan West Africa.

None of these empires had the global reach or worldwide impact of Europe's American colonies; they were regional rather than global in scope. Nor did they have the same devastating and transforming impact on their conquered peoples, for those peoples were not being exposed to new diseases. Nonetheless, these expanding Asian and African empires reflected the energies and vitality of their respective civilizations in the early modern era, and they gave rise to profoundly important cross-cultural encounters, with legacies that echoed for many centuries.

The Steppes and Siberia: The Making of a Russian Empire

By 1480, a small Russian state centered on the city of Moscow was emerging from two centuries of Mongol rule. That state soon conquered a number of neighboring Russian-speaking cities and incorporated them into its expanding territory. Located on the remote, cold, and heavily forested eastern fringe of Christendom, it was perhaps an unlikely candidate for constructing one of the great empires of the modern era. And yet, over the next three centuries, it did precisely that, extending Russian domination over the vast tundra, forests, and grasslands of northern Asia that lay to the south and east of Moscow, all the way to the Pacific Ocean. Russians also expanded westward, bringing numerous Poles, Germans, Ukrainians, Belorussians, and Baltic peoples into the **Russian Empire**.

It was security concerns that drew Russian attention to the grasslands south and east of the Russian heartland, where pastoral peoples, like the Mongols before them, frequently raided their agricultural Russian neighbors and sold many into slavery. Across the vast expanse of Siberia, Russian motives were quite different, for the scattered peoples of its endless forests and tundra posed no threat to Russia. Numbering only some 220,000 in the seventeenth century and speaking more than 100 languages, they were mostly hunting, gathering, and herding people, living in small-scale societies and largely without access to gunpowder weapons. What drew the Russians across Siberia was opportunity—primarily the "soft gold" of fur-bearing animals, whose pelts were in great demand on the world market, especially as the world cooled during the Little Ice Age.

Whatever motives drove it, this enormous Russian Empire took shape in the three centuries between 1500 and 1800 (see Map 4.2). A growing line of wooden forts offered protection to frontier towns and trading centers as well as to mounting numbers of Russian farmers. Empire building was an extended process, involving the Russian state and its officials as well as a variety of private interests—merchants, hunters, peasants, churchmen, exiles, criminals, and adventurers. For the Russian

> **AP®**
> CAUSATION
> What motivated Russian expansion?

EXPLORING AP® THEMES

Humans and the Environment (ENV) and Governance (GOV)

As noted in Unit 1, geography and the environment can affect the development of states and politics. Use Map 4.2, "The Russian Empire," to explore this idea with students. Give them time to study the map, and then ask the following questions:

■ Using the scale at the top of the map, estimate the size of the Russian Empire in 1795. *Approximately 8 million square miles.*

■ With reference to the borders—from Europe to Asia—what cultural and political challenges might Russia face with so expansive an empire? *Cultural and political challenges would include ethnic diversity, cultural variations, language differences, and the influence of the centralized government and the capital city, which was far away from much of the empire.*

APPLY THE TIP

To help students think about how the Russian Empire developed, you could ask students: How did Russian leaders view their empire-building efforts during the period 1450–1750? *Empire building was seen as an extended process that included private interest groups as well as the government. Leaders saw building a Russian Empire in multiple ways: it helped defend the frontier, enhanced the power of the state, and brought Christianity, civilization, and enlightenment to "barbarian" groups.*

▲ **AP®**
CAUSATION
What political and economic factors explain the pattern of Russian expansion shown in Map 4.2?

AP® EXAM TIP
The AP® Exam frequently includes questions about empire building throughout world history. Note this example of how the Russian Empire developed.

Map 4.2 The Russian Empire
From its beginnings as a small principality under Mongol control, Moscow became the center of a vast Russian Empire during the early modern era.

migrants to these new eastern lands, the empire offered "economic and social improvements over what they had known at home—from more and better land to fewer lords and officials."[18] Political leaders and educated Russians generally defined the empire in grander terms: defending Russian frontiers; enhancing the power of the Russian state; and bringing Christianity, civilization, and enlightenment to savages. But what did that empire mean to those on its receiving end?

First, of course, empire meant conquest. Although resistance was frequent, in the long run Russian military might, based in modern weaponry and the organizational capacity of a state, brought both the steppes and Siberia under Russian control. Everywhere Russian authorities demanded an oath of allegiance by which native peoples swore "eternal submission to the grand tsar," the monarch of the Russian Empire. They also demanded **yasak**, or "tribute," paid in cash or in kind. In Siberia, this meant enormous quantities of furs, especially the extremely valuable sable, which Siberian peoples were compelled to produce. As in the Americas, devastating epidemics accompanied conquest, particularly in the more remote regions of Siberia, where local people had little immunity to smallpox or measles. Also accompanying conquest was an intermittent pressure to convert to Christianity. Tax breaks, exemptions from paying tribute, and the promise of land or cash provided incentives for conversion, while the destruction of many mosques and the forced resettlement of Muslims added to the pressures. Yet the Russian state did not pursue conversion with the single-minded intensity that Spanish authorities exercised in Latin America, particularly if missionary activity threatened political and social stability. The empress Catherine the Great, for example, established religious tolerance for Muslims in the late eighteenth century and created a state agency to oversee Muslim affairs.

Unlike its expansion to the east, Russia's westward movement occurred in the context of military rivalries with the major powers of the region—the Ottoman Empire, Poland, Sweden, Lithuania, Prussia, and Austria. During the late seventeenth and eighteenth centuries, Russia acquired substantial territories in the Baltic region, Poland, and Ukraine. This contact with Europe also fostered an awareness of Russia's backwardness relative to Europe and prompted an extensive program of westernization, particularly under the leadership of Peter the Great (r. 1689–1725). His massive efforts included vast administrative changes, the enlargement and modernization of Russian military forces, a new educational system for the sons of noblemen, and dozens of manufacturing enterprises. Russian nobles were instructed to dress in European styles and to shave their sacred and much-revered beards. The newly created capital city of St. Petersburg was to be Russia's "window on the West." One of Peter's successors, Catherine the Great (r. 1762–1796), followed up with further efforts to Europeanize Russian cultural and intellectual life, viewing herself as part of the European Enlightenment. Thus Russians were the first of many peoples to measure themselves against the West and to mount major "catch-up" efforts.

The Cossacks In the vanguard of Russian expansion across Siberia were the Cossacks, bands of fiercely independent warriors consisting of peasants who had escaped serfdom as well as criminals and other adventurers. In this eighteenth-century painting, a Cossack is depicted preparing to depart from an encampment and surrounded by the items of everyday Cossack life, including his horse, spear, bow, hunting horn, lyre, and pipe. Note also his red hat hanging from a tree branch. (Bridgeman Images)

AP® EXAM TIP

Remember that all empires levy taxes of some sort and interact with outside societies.

▼ AP®

CONTEXTUALIZATION

Why might the Russian state depend on armies of Cossacks, like the one shown in the image, more on the borders of its empire than near its administrative center?

APPLY THE TIP

One of the historical developments students need to know for Topic 3.2 Empires: Administration is "Rulers used tribute collection, tax farming, and innovative tax-collection systems to generate revenue in order to forward state power and expansion." As students work through this section on land-based empires, it's good to stop and note the types of tribute collection, tax farming, and tax collection each empire used. For Russia, ask students: What was the *yasak*? *The yasak was the tribute or tax payment demanded by the Russian Empire from the Indigenous peoples under its rule. It could be paid in cash or in goods; Siberian peoples used furs to pay the yasak.*

BUILDING AP® SKILLS

Making Connections: Comparison

If you had students work on the Comparison exercise on page 222, you might suggest that they build on their answer by creating a third column for the Russian Empire. This will help them compare the processes the Russians and the Europeans used to build their respective empires. *The Russians created an empire similar to those of Western Europe in terms of conquest, settlement, exploitation, religious conversion, and feelings of superiority. However, the Russians acquired their empire under different circumstances than had the Western Europeans. The British conquered and colonized the New World, an ocean away and wholly unknown to them before 1492. They acquired those empires only after establishing themselves as distinct European states. The Russians, on the other hand, absorbed adjacent territories, and they did so at the same time that a modern Russian state was taking shape. The differences can be summed up by the words of historian Geoffrey Hosking: "The British had an empire. Russia was an empire."*

AP

CONTINUITY AND CHANGE

How did Russia's westward expansion change Russia? What continuities remained despite these changes?

AP

ARGUMENTATION

What evidence from the text might you use to support the claim that Russia was a "society organized for continuous war"?

AP

COMPARISON

Compare the processes by which the Russians and Western Europeans built their empires.

But this European-oriented and Christian state had also become an Asian power, bumping up against China, India, Persia, and the Ottoman Empire. It was on the front lines of the encounter between Christendom and the world of Islam. This straddling of Asia and Europe was the source of a long-standing identity problem that has troubled educated Russians for 300 years. Was Russia a backward European country, destined to follow the lead of more highly developed Western European societies? Or was it different, uniquely Slavic or even Asian, shaped by its Mongol legacy and its status as an Asian power? It is a question that Russians have not completely answered even in the twenty-first century. Either way, the very size of that empire, bordering on virtually all of the great agrarian civilizations of outer Eurasia, turned Russia, like many empires before it, into a highly militarized state, "a society organized for continuous war," according to one scholar.[19] It also reinforced the highly autocratic character of the Russian Empire because such a huge state arguably required a powerful monarchy to hold its vast domains and highly diverse peoples together.

Clearly, the Russians had created an empire, similar to those of Western Europe in terms of conquest, settlement, exploitation, religious conversion, and feelings of superiority. Nonetheless, the Russians had acquired their empire under different circumstances than did the Western Europeans. The Spanish and the British had conquered and colonized the New World, an ocean away and wholly unknown to them before 1492. They acquired those empires only after establishing themselves as distinct European states. The Russians, on the other hand, absorbed adjacent territories, and they did so at the same time that a modern Russian state was taking shape. "The British had an empire," wrote historian Geoffrey Hosking. "Russia *was* an empire."[20] Perhaps this helps explain the unique longevity of the Russian Empire. Whereas the Spanish, Portuguese, and British colonies in the Americas long ago achieved independence, the Russian Empire remained intact until the collapse of the Soviet Union in 1991. So thorough was Russian colonization that Siberia and much of the steppes remain still an integral part of the Russian state.

Into Central Asia: The Making of a Chinese Empire

AP EXAM TIP

As you read this section, compare the expansion of land-based empires such as Russia and China to the expansion of sea-based empires such as Spain in the Americas.

Among the most significant of the expanding civilizations of the early modern era was that of China. That civilization had been greatly disrupted by a century of Mongol rule, and its population had been sharply reduced by the plague. During the **Ming dynasty** (1368–1644), however, China recovered. In the early decades of that dynasty, the Chinese attempted to eliminate all signs of foreign rule, discouraging the use of Mongol names and dress while promoting Confucian learning and traditional gender roles. Emperor Yongle (YAHNG-leh) (r. 1402–1424) sponsored an enormous *Encyclopedia* of some 11,000 volumes that sought to summarize or compile all previous writing on history, geography, philosophy, ethics, government, and more. Yongle also relocated the capital to Beijing, ordered the building of a magnificent imperial residence known as the Forbidden City, and constructed the

---

APPLY THE TIP

As students read through the pages on the Asian empires, think about having them fill in a comparison chart like the one below on the similarities and differences between Asian empires and European empires. A reproducible version of this chart is available in the Teacher's Resource Materials. (Answers are provided in italics.)

Similarities	Differences
Both regions created empires in which religious diversity existed. Both regions created empires in which cross-cultural encounters reverberated for many centuries.	*Asian empires were regional; European empires became global. European empires had a devastating and transforming impact on conquered peoples because of diseases, which led to population collapse. In Asia, conquest led to deaths, but not to the same extent as in the Americas.*

TRM Handout 4.8: Comparison Chart for Asian Empires and European Empires

---

BUILDING AP® SKILLS

Making Connections: Continuity and Change

The Course and Exam Description focuses on the Chinese dynasties and Islamic empires of this time period as the "need to know" land-based empires. An interesting activity to help students understand the rise and expansion of these empires is the OER Project's "CCOT: Networks of Exchange to Land-Based Empires," which has students analyze the continuities and changes in the world from Unit 2 to Unit 3. You can find this activity in the Unit 3 Introduction of the World History: AP® section of the OER Project.

Temple of Heaven, where subsequent rulers performed Confucian-based rituals to ensure the well-being of Chinese society. Two empresses wrote instructions for female behavior, emphasizing traditional expectations after the disruptions of the previous century. Culturally speaking, China was looking to its past.

Politically, the Ming dynasty reestablished the civil service examination system that had been neglected under Mongol rule and went on to create a highly centralized government with power concentrated in the hands of the emperor himself. The state acted vigorously to repair the damage of the Mongol years by restoring millions of acres to cultivation; rebuilding canals, reservoirs, and irrigation works; and planting, according to some estimates, a billion trees in an effort to reforest China. The economy rebounded as rice and other crops were produced commercially on a large scale, both international and domestic trade flourished, and the population grew. Also contributing to the growth of a market economy was a policy established in the early sixteenth century that required the payment of taxes in hard currency, mostly silver, rather than in rice. Taxpayers were thus forced to sell goods or their labor in the market to meet their obligations to the state. Thus China recovered during the fifteenth century to become perhaps the best governed and most prosperous of the world's major civilizations.

During the early Ming dynasty, the Chinese state had launched a series of massive maritime voyages into the Indian Ocean. (See "Chinese Maritime Voyages in the Indian Ocean World" in Chapter 3.) These voyages offered China the possibility of creating a sea-based empire in the Indian Ocean basin. But that possibility was decisively rejected, in part because Chinese authorities feared further incursions from the recently ousted Mongols.

Instead, during the seventeenth and eighteenth centuries China built another kind of empire on its northern and western frontiers that vastly enlarged the territorial size of the country and incorporated a number of non-Chinese peoples, including many nomadic pastoralists. Undertaking this enormous project of imperial expansion was China's Qing, or Manchu, dynasty (1644–1912), which was itself of foreign and nomadic origin, hailing from Manchuria, north of the Great Wall. The violent Manchu takeover of China, part of the General Crisis of the seventeenth century, was facilitated by a widespread famine and peasant rebellions associated with the Little Ice Age. But having conquered China, the Qing rulers sought to maintain their ethnic distinctiveness by forbidding intermarriage between themselves and the Chinese, even as they enforced outward obedience to their rule by requiring Chinese men to adopt the Manchu hairstyle of a long braid or queue. Through time, though, Manchu ruling elites adopted Chinese ways by mastering the Chinese language and Confucian teachings and using Chinese bureaucratic techniques to govern the empire.

For many centuries, the Chinese had interacted with the nomadic peoples who inhabited the dry and lightly populated regions now known as Mongolia, Xinjiang, and Tibet. Trade, tribute, and warfare ensured that these ecologically and culturally different worlds were well known to the Chinese, quite unlike the

---

AP® EXAM TIP

You must know features of the Qing (Manchu) dynasty for success on the AP® Exam.

AP®

CONTINUITY AND CHANGE

What changes took place in the relations between China and other states between 1450 and 1750?

TEACHING IDEA

Class Discussion

China was ruled by two dynasties during the 1450–1750 time period: the Ming and the Qing. Talk to students about how the Ming reestablished ethnically Han Chinese rule after the fall of the Mongol dynasty and how the Manchus established the second (and final) foreign dynasty when they founded the Qing. Considering these differences in the rulers of each dynasty, it could be interesting to have a class discussion on how the two dynasties legitimized their power over China. (Some possible talking points are listed below in italics.)

■ **Ming:** *The Ming tried to eliminate all signs of foreign (Mongol) rule, relocated the capital to Beijing and built an imperial residence known as the Forbidden City, performed Confucian-based rituals at the newly built Temple of Heaven, reestablished the civil service exam system and created a highly centralized government, and worked to repair the agricultural damage of the Mongol years.*

■ **Qing:** *The Manchus established foreign rule over China by adopting Chinese traditions; Manchu ruling elites mastered the Chinese language, followed Confucian teachings, and performed ceremonial Confucian practices to legitimize their rule; they also used Chinese bureaucratic techniques to govern their empire.*

APPLY THE TIP

Consider doing a quick check for understanding after students have learned about how the Qing dynasty ruled China. Ask students to describe how the Qing dynasty governed its empire. *Answers should include creating the Court of Colonial Affairs, using local notables to help govern, and allowing local notables to wear Manchu hairstyles.*

New World "discoveries" of the Europeans. Chinese authority in these regions had been intermittent and actively resisted. Then, in the early modern era, the Qing dynasty undertook an eighty-year military effort (1680–1760) that brought these huge areas solidly under its control. It was largely security concerns, rather than economic need, that motivated this aggressive posture. During the late seventeenth century, the creation of a substantial state among the western Mongols, known as the Zunghars, revived Chinese memories of an earlier Mongol conquest. As in so many other cases, expansion was viewed as a defensive necessity. The eastward movement of the Russian Empire likewise appeared potentially threatening, but after increasing tensions and a number of skirmishes and battles, this danger was resolved diplomatically, rather than militarily, in the Treaty of Nerchinsk (1689), which marked the boundary between Russia and China.

The Qing dynasty campaigns against the Zunghar Mongols marked the evolution of China into a Central Asian empire. The Chinese, however, seldom thought of themselves as an imperial power. Rather, when describing this **Qing expansion**, they spoke of the "unification" of the peoples of central Eurasia within a Chinese state. But although unification was achieved through conquest, it did not involve the assimilation of local people into Chinese culture. Instead, the Qing ruled the conquered area separately from the rest of China through a new office called the Court of Colonial Affairs and showed considerable respect for the Mongolian, Tibetan, and Muslim cultures of

AP®

COMPARISON

What were the distinctive features of Chinese empire building in the early modern era?

▶ **AP®**

CONTINUITY AND CHANGE

What does this image suggest about the process of China's imperial expansion?

Qing Conquests in Central Asia Painted by the Chinese artist Jin Tingbiao in the mid-eighteenth century, this image portrays Machang, a leading warrior involved in the westward extension of the Qing Empire. The painting was commissioned by the emperor himself and served to honor the bravery of Machang. (Pictures from History/CPA Media)

BUILDING AP® SKILLS

Sourcing and Situation

This painting of a Qing warrior is a good place to practice image analysis. Ask students to fill in an OPTIC (Overview, Parts, Title, Interrelationship, Conclusion) chart, like the one below, for the painting. A reproducible version of this chart is available in the Teacher's Resource Materials. (Answers are provided in italics.)

Overview	*A painting of a warrior, commissioned by the emperor.*
Parts	*The warrior Machang, holding bow and arrows as he rides on his horse.*
Title	*The title of this painting could possibly be "The Bravery of Machang" since that was why the emperor commissioned the painting.*
Interrelationship	*The warrior and the horse are one; the warrior doesn't need the reins to guide the horse — they are moving forward at full speed.*
Conclusion	*In this painting, the power and speed of the horse are juxtaposed with the seemingly perfect stillness of the man. Both are completely focused on what is in front of them. Since this painting was commissioned by the emperor, Machang is immortalized not just as a brave soldier but also as the quintessential Qing warrior.*

TRM Handout 4.9: OPTIC Chart for Painting of Machang

the region. People of noble rank, Buddhist monks, and those associated with monasteries were excused from the taxes and labor service required of ordinary people. Nor was the area flooded with Chinese settlers. In parts of Mongolia, for example, Qing authorities sharply restricted the entry of Chinese merchants and other immigrants in an effort to preserve the area as a source of recruitment for the Chinese military. They feared that the "soft" and civilized Chinese ways might erode the fighting spirit of the Mongols.

The long-term significance of this new Qing imperial state was tremendous. It greatly expanded the territory of China and added a small but important minority of non-Chinese people to the empire's vast population (see Map 4.3). The borders of contemporary China are essentially those created during the Qing dynasty. Some of those peoples, particularly those in Tibet and Xinjiang, have retained their older identities and in recent decades have actively sought greater autonomy or even independence from China.

Even more important, Qing conquests, together with the expansion of the Russian Empire, utterly transformed Central Asia. For centuries, that region had been the cosmopolitan crossroads of Eurasia, hosting the Silk Road trading network, welcoming all the major world religions, and generating an enduring encounter between the nomads of the steppes and the farmers of settled agricultural regions. Now under Russian or Qing rule, it became the backward and impoverished region known to nineteenth- and twentieth-century observers. Land-based commerce across Eurasia increasingly took a backseat to oceanic trade. Indebted Mongolian nobles lost their land to Chinese merchants, while nomads, no longer able to herd their animals freely, fled to urban areas, where many were reduced to begging. The incorporation of inner Eurasia into the Russian and Qing empires "eliminated permanently as a major actor on the historical stage the nomadic pastoralists, who had been the strongest alternative to settled agricultural society since the second millennium [B.C.E.]."[21] It was the end of a long era.

Empires of the Islamic World

Finding the Main Point: How did Islamic empires in this period manage their expansion and their interactions with diverse cultures?

Stretching across much of Afro-Eurasia, the enormous domain of Islam experienced remarkable changes during the early modern era. The most notable change lay in the political realm, for an Islamic civilization that had been severely fragmented

Map 4.3 China's Qing Dynasty Empire
After many centuries of intermittent expansion into Central Asia, the Qing dynasty brought this vast region firmly under its control.

▲ **AP**
COMPARISON
Compare the pattern of Qing expansion with that of Russia. What were similarities and differences in how the two empires interacted with conquered people?

AP EXAM TIP
Understand these important effects of Chinese expansion in the era ca. 1450–ca. 1750.

AP
CAUSATION
How did the expansion of Russia and China transform Central Asia?

CHAPTER 4

Map 4.4 Empires of the Islamic World
The most prominent political features of the vast Islamic world in the fifteenth and sixteenth centuries were four large states: the Songhay, Ottoman, Safavid, and Mughal empires.

since at least 900 now crystallized into four major states or empires (see Map 4.4). In the process, the Middle Eastern heartland of the Islamic world was transformed, as were several regions on the frontier of that civilization.

In the Islamic Heartland: The Ottoman and Persian Safavid Empires

The most significant of these new imperial states was the **Ottoman Empire**, the creation of Turkic warrior groups, whose aggressive raiding of agricultural civilizations was sometimes legitimized in Islamic terms as *jihad*, religiously sanctioned warfare against infidels. Beginning around 1300 from a base area in northwestern Anatolia, these Ottoman Turks over the next three centuries swept over much of southeastern Europe, the Middle East, and North Africa to create the Islamic world's most significant empire (see Map 4.5). During those centuries, the Ottoman state was transformed from a small frontier principality to a prosperous, powerful, cosmopolitan empire, heir both to the Byzantine Empire and to leadership within the Islamic world. Its sultan combined the roles of a Turkic warrior prince, a Muslim caliph, and a conquering emperor, bearing the "strong sword of Islam" and serving as chief defender of the faith.

Gaining such an empire transformed Turkish social life as well. The relative independence of Central Asian pastoral women, their open association with men, and their political influence in society all diminished as the Turks adopted Islam, beginning in the tenth century, and later acquired an empire in the heartland of ancient and patriarchal Mediterranean civilizations. Now elite Turkish women found themselves secluded and often veiled; enslaved women from the Caucasus Mountains and the Sudan grew more numerous; official imperial censuses did not count women; and orthodox Muslim reformers sought to restrict women's religious gatherings.

And yet within the new constraints of a settled Islamic empire, Turkish women retained something of the social power they had enjoyed in pastoral societies. From around 1550 to 1650, women of the royal court had such an influence in political matters that their critics referred to the "sultanate of women." Islamic law permitted women important property rights, which enabled some to become quite wealthy, endowing religious and charitable institutions. Many women actively used the Ottoman courts to protect their legal rights in matters of marriage, divorce, and inheritance, sometimes representing themselves or acting as agents for female relatives. In 1717, the wife of an English ambassador to the Ottoman Empire compared the lives of Turkish and European women, declaring, "'Tis very easy to see that they have more liberty than we have."[22]

AP®
COMPARISON
Compare the Ottoman Empire's relations with conquered people with the Spanish Empire's relations with conquered people.

Within the Islamic world, the Ottoman Empire represented the growing prominence of Turkic people, for their empire now incorporated a large number of Arabs, among whom the religion had been born. The responsibility and the prestige of protecting Mecca, Medina, and Jerusalem—the holy cities of Islam—now fell to the Ottoman Empire.

But the Ottoman Empire was also the site of a highly significant cross-cultural encounter in the early modern era, adding yet another chapter to the long-running story of interaction between the Islamic world and Christendom. As the Ottoman Empire expanded across Anatolia, and as the Byzantine state visibly weakened and large numbers of Turks settled in the region, the empire's mostly Christian population converted in large numbers to Islam. By 1500, some 90 percent of Anatolia's inhabitants were Muslims and Turkic speakers. The climax of this Turkic assault on the Christian world of Byzantium occurred in the 1453 conquest of Constantinople, when the city fell to Muslim invaders. (See Zooming In: 1453 in Constantinople, Chapter 2, page 94.) Renamed Istanbul, that splendid Christian city became the capital of the Ottoman Empire. Byzantium, heir to the glory of Rome and the guardian of Orthodox Christianity, was no more.

In the empire's southeastern European domains, known as the Balkans, the Ottoman encounter with Christian peoples unfolded quite differently than it had in Anatolia. In the Balkans, Muslims ruled over a large Christian population, but

AP®   EXAM TIP
Several AP® Exam questions have dealt with the Ottoman Empire's political, social, and economic features. The interactions between Muslims and Christians in the Ottoman Empire are also an important topic.

AP®   EXAM TIP
The Muslim conquest of Constantinople was a major turning point in the political and cultural history of Europe, North Africa, and Southwest Asia.

APPLY THE TIP

The segment "The Fall of Constantinople" from Episode 7 in the series Mankind: The Story of All of Us, which includes reenactments of events and clips of historians, will help students understand the economic significance of Constantinople's transition from a Christian to a Muslim city. The video clip can be found in the Vault on History.com's website on the series, or you can search for the selection on YouTube using "Mankind Fall of Constantinople." After students have watched the video, ask the following questions:

■ How was technology used to conquer Constantinople? *The conquest of Constantinople was achieved through the use of artillery. It rendered city walls useless.*

■ How was the fall of Constantinople linked to Columbus's voyage to America? *When the Turks conquered Constantinople, they disrupted the spice and silk trade from Asia and increased the price of those items. High costs encouraged exploration of other routes and sources.*

APPLY THE TIP

The Ottoman Empire plays an important role in Unit 3 through Unit 7. Creating a thematic chart on the Ottomans from 1450 to 1750 can help students access the evidence needed to answer an essay question about the Ottomans with confidence. A reproducible version of this chart is available in the Teacher's Resource Materials. (Answers are provided in italics.)

Theme	Ottoman Empire
Humans and the Environment (ENV)	■ *High population density in parts of the empire*
Cultural Developments and Interactions (CDI)	■ *Former subjects of the Byzantine Empire converted to Islam after the Ottomans took over* ■ *Ottomans ruled over a large Christian population in the Balkans and were willing to accommodate them* ■ *Christians and Jews had to pay the jizya* ■ *Christian boys from the Balkans were conscripted through the devshirme*
Governance (GOV)	■ *Seen as a threat to European Christendom* ■ *Divided empire into millets to rule over diverse territory*
Economic Systems (ECN)	■ *Located at a crossroads of Eurasian trade* ■ *Acted as middlemen in trade between Europe and East Asia*
Social Interactions and Organization (SIO)	■ *Devshirme offered the possibility of upward mobility* ■ *Jewish and Christian women saw their property rights increase under Islamic law* ■ *Christian elites became part of the Ottoman elite (sometimes without converting to Islam)*
Technology and Innovation (TEC)	■ *Used cannons and gunpowder weapons in their wars of conquest (which helped them capture Constantinople)*

TRM Handout 4.10: Thematic Chart of the Ottoman Empire

BUILDING AP® SKILLS

Sourcing and Situation

This painting of the Ottoman siege of Vienna in 1683 is a good place to discuss how art helps historians understand historical developments. Ask students to fill in an OPTIC (Overview, Parts, Title, Interrelationship, Conclusion) chart, like the one below, for the painting. A reproducible version of this chart is available in the Teacher's Resource Materials. (Answers are provided in italics.)

Overview	*The painting shows the Ottoman siege of Vienna in 1683 (the Ottomans made multiple attempts to conquer Vienna).*
Parts	*The painting shows a heated battle with men on horseback and camels in the foreground. There is a lot of smoke close to the walls of the city, and artillery is being used to try to break through the walls.*
Title	*The title of this painting is probably "The Siege of Vienna" and would be meant to celebrate the Austrian victory over the Ottomans.*
Interrelationship	*The Ottoman army is stationed on the hill above the city, some distance away. The defenders are stationed closer to the city walls. Men are engaged in combat.*
Conclusion	*This appears to be an eyewitness account of the battle. It is difficult to tell from the painting who will eventually win. The painting clearly shows the massive size of the armies, and even though Vienna appears to be small in the painting, it was the capital of the Austrian Empire and viewed as the gateway to Europe by the Ottomans.*

TRM Handout 4.11: OPTIC Chart for Painting of the Siege of Vienna

The Ottoman Siege of Vienna, 1683 This anonymous late-seventeenth-century painting captures the crucial moment in the siege of Vienna when a last Ottoman attack is pushed back by Austrian, French, and Polish forces. The siege marked the end of a serious Muslim threat to Christian Europe. (akg-images/Newscom)

▲ **AP®**

SOURCING AND SITUATION
What is the value of this picture for a historian studying the Siege of Vienna? What are the picture's limitations?

AP® EXAM TIP
Pay close attention to how empires dealt with various religious and ethnic groups in the period 1450–1750.

the scarcity of Turkish settlers and the willingness of the Ottoman authorities to accommodate the region's Christian churches led to far fewer conversions. By the early sixteenth century, only about 19 percent of the area's people were Muslims, and 81 percent were Christians.

Many of these Christians had welcomed Ottoman conquest because taxes were lighter and oppression less pronounced than under their former Christian rulers. Christian communities such as the Eastern Orthodox and Armenian churches were granted considerable autonomy in regulating their internal social, religious, educational, and charitable affairs. Nonetheless, many Christian and Jewish women appealed legal cases dealing with marriage and inheritance to Muslim courts, where their property rights were greater. A substantial number of Christian men—Balkan landlords, Greek merchants, government officials, and high-ranking clergy—became part of the Ottoman elite, sometimes without converting to Islam. Jewish refugees fleeing Christian persecution in a Spain recently "liberated" from Islamic rule likewise found greater opportunity in the Ottoman Empire, where they became prominent in trade and banking circles.

APPLY THE TIP

Understanding how empires deal with various religious and ethnic groups is important when looking at the development of empires between 1450 and 1750. Ask students to create a chart to compare how different empires dealt with these issues in their territories. A reproducible version of this chart is available in the Teacher's Resource Materials.

TRM Handout 4.12: Chart for Treatment of Religious and Ethnic Groups by Empires

In another way, however, Turkish rule bore heavily on Christians. Through a process known as the *devshirme* (devv-shirr-MEH) (the collecting or gathering), Ottoman authorities siphoned off many thousands of young boys from Christian families into the service of the state. Removed from their families and required to learn Turkish, these boys usually converted to Islam and were trained for either the civil administration or service in the elite Ottoman infantry force known as the Janissaries. Although it was a terrible blow for families who lost their children, the devshirme also represented a means of upward mobility within the Ottoman Empire. But this social gain occurred at a high price.

Beyond the devshirme, Ottoman authorities used other techniques for funding and administering their vast domains. Early on, in a system known as *timar*, sultans granted land and tax revenues to individuals in return for military service. Later a system of tax farming was practiced in which the state auctioned off to the highest bidders the right to collect taxes, allowing them to keep a portion of the revenue for their own use.

If Ottoman authorities were relatively tolerant toward Christians within their borders, the empire itself represented an enormous threat to Christendom generally. The seizure of Constantinople, the conquest of the Balkans, Ottoman naval power in the Mediterranean, and the siege of Vienna in 1529 and again in 1683 raised anew "the specter of a Muslim takeover of all of Europe."[23] One European ambassador reported fearfully in 1555 from the court of the Turkish ruler Suleiman: "He tramples the soil of Hungary with 200,000 horses, he is at the very gates of Austria, threatens the rest of Germany, and brings in his train all the nations that extend from our borders to those of Persia."[24] Indeed, the "terror of the Turk" inspired fear across much of Europe and placed Christendom on the defensive, even as Western Europeans were expanding aggressively across the Atlantic and into the Indian Ocean.

But the Ottoman encounter with Christian Europe spawned admiration and cooperation as well as fear and trembling. Italian Renaissance artists sometimes portrayed the splendor of the Islamic world in their paintings. The sixteenth-century French philosopher Jean Bodin praised the religious tolerance of the Ottoman sultan in contrast to Christian intolerance: "The King of the Turks who rules over a great part of Europe safeguards the rites of religion as well as any prince in this world. Yet he constrains no-one, but on the contrary permits everyone to live as his conscience dictates."[25] The French government on occasion found it useful to ally with the Ottoman Empire against its common enemy of Habsburg Austria, while European merchants willingly violated a papal ban on selling firearms to the Turks. Cultural encounter involved more than conflict.

In the neighboring Persian lands to the east of the Ottoman Empire (see Map 4.5), another Islamic state was also taking shape in the late fifteenth and early sixteenth centuries—the Safavid (SAH-fah-vihd) Empire, which had emerged from a Sufi religious order founded several centuries earlier by Safi al-Din (1252–1334). It was the latest expression of a Persian imperial tradition some 2,000 years old. Lasting from 1501 to 1736, the empire was led by an absolute monarch, known as the shah, who

AP
COMPARISON
How did the origins of the Safavid Empire differ from those of the Ottoman Empire?

BUILDING AP® SKILLS

Making Connections: Comparison

This is a good opportunity for students to practice comparison skills. Ask students to compare Map 4.5, "The Ottoman Empire," with Map 2.6, "The Byzantine Empire," on page 93. Ask: What areas did both empires control? *Both areas controlled Anatolia, Eastern Europe, the Levant on the eastern end of the Mediterranean Sea, and parts of North Africa.*

MAPPING HISTORY   Map 4.5 **The Ottoman Empire**

At its high point in the mid-sixteenth century, the Ottoman Empire encompassed a vast diversity of peoples; straddled Europe, Africa, and Asia; and battled both the Austrian and Safavid empires.

Reading the Map: What specific territorial disputes with the Persian Safavid Empire were likely to cause conflicts between the Ottomans and their powerful neighbor? What geographical features and political realities were barriers to further expansion of the Ottoman Empire?

AP Making Connections: Compare this map with Map 4.2: The Russian Empire. What happened to the Ottoman Empire's tributary states north of the Black Sea after 1689? Where were the likely points of tension or conflict between the Ottoman and Russian empires during the early modern period?

legitimized his position by claiming direct descent from Muhammad himself. Its central location in Eurasia allowed it to benefit from transcontinental trade, particularly in silk products such as luxurious Persian carpets. It also witnessed a flourishing culture that made major contributions in art, literature, philosophy, architecture, and formal

TEACHING IDEA

Incorporating Outside Resources

The Safavid Empire has a long and detailed history, but not much of that rich history is explored in the World History: Modern course. If you have time and students seem interested, consider showing the short video *Top Ten Facts About the Safavid Empire* found on YouTube. This video does an excellent job of explaining the origins of the Safavid Empire as well as the important cultural elements that originated with the empire. As students watch the video, have them answer the following questions:

■ Where did the Safavid dynasty have its origins? *Sufism and an Iranian dynasty of Kurdish origin with intermarriage throughout Central Asia.*

■ What modern-day states did the Safavids control at their height of power? *Iran, Azerbaijan Republic, Bahrain, Armenia, eastern Georgia, parts of the North Caucasus, Iraq, Kuwait, and Afghanistan, as well as parts of Turkey, Syria, Pakistan, Turkmenistan, and Uzbekistan.*

■ Why were the Safavids able to establish their own state? *Ability to remain neutral and build a strong following of their own.*

■ How did Abbas I legitimize his rule and create a strong Safavid state? *Made peace with the Ottomans and engaged in a major reform of the army.*

■ What was the cultural legacy of the Safavid dynasty? *Safavid book arts, architecture, and painting.*

gardens, sometimes said to represent an Islamic paradise. Persian culture, especially its poetry, painting, and traditions of imperial splendor, occupied a prominent and prestigious position among elites throughout the eastern Islamic world.

The long-term historical significance of the **Safavid Empire** lay in its decision to forcibly impose a Shia version of Islam as the official religion of the state. This decision led to an astonishing cultural transformation. Persian Islam had previously adhered largely to the Sunni tradition, but over time, Shia Islam gained popular support and came to define the unique identity of Persian (Iranian) culture, which has persisted to the present day. Shia Islam also spread elsewhere in the Middle East.

This transformation introduced a sharp divide into the political and religious life of heartland Islam, for almost all of Persia's neighbors practiced a Sunni form of the faith. For a century (1534–1639), periodic military conflict erupted between the Ottoman and Safavid empires, reflecting both territorial rivalry and sharp religious differences. In 1514, the Ottoman sultan wrote to the Safavid ruler in the most bitter of terms:

> You have denied the sanctity of divine law . . . you have deserted the path of salvation and the sacred commandments . . . you have opened to Muslims the gates of tyranny and oppression . . . you have raised the standard of irreligion and heresy. . . . [Therefore] the *ulama* and our doctors have pronounced a sentence of death against you, perjurer and blasphemer.[26]

A similar rivalry developed with the Mughal Empire of India, where Sunni Islam prevailed, and resulted in a sharp military encounter, the Safavid-Mughal war between 1649 and 1653. This Sunni/Shia hostility has continued to divide the Islamic world into the twenty-first century.

On the Frontiers of Islam: The Mughal and Songhay Empires

If the Ottoman Empire gave rise to a new phase of the encounter between the Islamic world and Christendom, India's **Mughal Empire** represented a further development in the long interaction of Islamic and Hindu cultures in South Asia. That empire was the product of Central Asian warriors who were Muslims in religion and Turkic in culture and who claimed descent from Chinggis Khan and Timur. Their brutal conquests in the sixteenth century provided India with a rare period of relative political unity (1526–1707), as Mughal emperors exercised a fragile control over a diverse and fragmented subcontinent that had long been divided into a bewildering variety of small states, principalities, tribes, castes, sects, and ethno-linguistic groups. Large local landowners known as *zamindars* played a crucial role in extending imperial authority by collecting taxes on behalf of the emperor, while pocketing some of those funds for themselves.

The central division within Mughal India was religious. The ruling dynasty and perhaps 20 percent of the population were Muslims; most of the rest

The Mughal Empire

APPLY THE TIP

Students should understand that the Sunni/Shia split in Islam plays a role within the Islamic world into the present. This is a good time to have a short discussion and review of the history of Islam with your students. Ask students:

■ What caused the Sunni/Shia split? *After the death of Muhammad, no successor was named, and the debate over the successor has never been resolved.*

■ Who do the Sunnis believe is the successor to Muhammad? *The Sunnis believe that the community should choose a pious successor.*

■ Who does the Shia believe is the successor to Muhammad? *The Shia believe that one from the Prophet's bloodline should succeed him.*

TEACHING IDEA

Bell Ringer

Show students the illustration of Shah Jahan and the caption on page 202. Then ask: How does the illustration reflect the social and economic status of the people it depicts? *The material splendor of the clothing, jewelry, vessels, carpets, and palace setting shows the immense wealth of the court and the economic well-being of the men present. The halo around Shah Jahan's head indicates the special spiritual grace or enlightenment associated with emperors.*

AP®

CONTINUITY AND CHANGE

How did Mughal attitudes and policies toward Hindus change from the time of Akbar to that of Aurangzeb?

AP® EXAM TIP

Understand the religious policies of major empires in this chapter.

AP®

COMPARISON

Compare the political, social, and economic aspects of the Mughal and Ottoman empires.

practiced some form of Hinduism. Mughal India's most famous emperor, **Akbar** (r. 1556–1605), clearly recognized this fundamental reality and acted deliberately to accommodate the Hindu majority, much as the Ottomans did with their Christian population in the Balkans. After conquering the warrior-based and Hindu Rajputs of northwestern India, Akbar married several of their princesses but did not require them to convert to Islam. He incorporated a substantial number of Hindus into the political-military elite of the empire and supported the building of Hindu temples as well as mosques, palaces, and forts. But Akbar also softened some Hindu restrictions on women, encouraging the remarriage of widows and discouraging child marriages and *sati* (the practice in which a widow followed her husband to death by throwing herself on his funeral pyre). A few elite women were also able to exercise political power, including Nur Jahan, the twentieth and favorite wife of Akbar's successor, Emperor Jahangir (r. 1605–1627). She was widely regarded as the power behind the throne of her alcohol- and opium-addicted husband, giving audiences to visiting dignitaries, consulting with ministers, and even having a coin issued in her name.

In directly religious matters, Akbar imposed a policy of toleration, deliberately restraining the more militantly Islamic *ulama* (religious scholars) and removing the special tax (*jizya*) on non-Muslims. He constructed a special House of Worship where he presided over intellectual discussion with representatives of many religions—Muslim, Hindu, Christian, Buddhist, Jewish, Jain, and Zoroastrian. Akbar went so far as to create his own state cult, a religious faith aimed at the Mughal elite that drew on Islam, Hinduism, and Zoroastrianism and emphasized loyalty to the emperor himself. The overall style of the Mughal Empire was that of a blended elite culture in which both Hindus and various Muslim groups could feel comfortable. Thus Persian artists and writers were welcomed into the empire, and the Hindu epic *Ramayana* was translated into Persian, while various Persian classics appeared in Hindi and Sanskrit. Mughal architects created mosques, palaces, gardens, and tombs that combined distinctly Muslim themes with elements of Indian, Persian, and Turkic cultures, none more exquisite than the Taj Mahal. Thus Akbar and his immediate successors downplayed a distinctly Islamic identity for the Mughal Empire in favor of a cosmopolitan and hybrid Indian-Persian-Turkic culture.

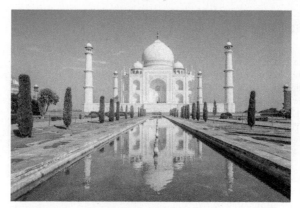

The Taj Mahal Commissioned in 1632 by the Mughal emperor as a tomb for his favorite wife, this monumental white marble mausoleum in the city of Agra in northern India is considered by many the finest single example of Mughal architecture. Its intricately carved decorations created by over 20,000 artisans were inspired by older Indo-Islamic artistic styles. (Mlenny/E+Getty Images)

Such policies fostered sharp opposition among some Muslims. The philosopher Shaykh Ahmad Sirhindi (1564–1624), claiming to be a "renewer" of authentic Islam in his time, strongly objected to this cultural synthesis. The worship of saints, the sacrifice of animals, and support for Hindu religious festivals all represented impure intrusions of Sufi Islam or Hinduism that needed to be rooted out. In Sirhindi's view, it was primarily women who had introduced these deviations: "Because of their utter stupidity [Muslim] women pray to stones and idols and ask for their help. . . . Women participate in the holidays of Hindus and Jews. They celebrate Diwali [a major Hindu festival] and send their sisters and daughters presents similar to those exchanged by the infidels."[27] It was therefore the duty of Muslim rulers to impose the sharia (Islamic law), to enforce the jizya, and to remove non-Muslims from high office.

AP®
CONTINUITY AND CHANGE
What are the continuities and changes in the way women were treated in India over the course of Mughal rule?

This strain of Muslim thinking found a champion in the emperor **Aurangzeb** (ow-rang-ZEHB) (r. 1658–1707), who reversed Akbar's policy of accommodation and sought to impose Islamic supremacy. While Akbar had discouraged the Hindu practice of sati, Aurangzeb forbade it outright. Music and dance were now banned at court, and previously tolerated vices such as gambling, drinking, prostitution, and narcotics were actively suppressed. Dancing girls were ordered to get married or leave the empire altogether. Some Hindu temples were destroyed, and the jizya was reimposed. "Censors of public morals," posted to large cities, enforced Islamic law.

Aurangzeb's religious policies, combined with intolerable demands for taxes to support his many wars of expansion, antagonized Hindus and prompted various movements of opposition to the Mughals. "Your subjects are trampled underfoot," wrote one anonymous protester. "Every province of your empire is impoverished. . . . God is the God of all mankind, not the God of Mussalmans [Muslims] alone."[28] Such sentiments motivated opposition movements, such as the self-consciously Hindu Maratha Confederacy, which battled the Mughal Empire from 1680 to Aurangzeb's death in 1707. These conflicts fatally fractured the Mughal Empire and opened the way for a British takeover in the second half of the eighteenth century.

Thus the Mughal Empire was the site of a highly significant encounter between two of the world's great religious traditions. It began with an experiment in multicultural empire building and ended in growing antagonism between Hindus and Muslims. In the centuries that followed, both elements of the Mughal experience would be repeated.

AP®   EXAM TIP
Remember that an empire that unites South Asia is the exception to the typical organization of South Asian politics.

Completing the quartet of Muslim empires that structured the Islamic world during the early modern era was that of Songhay (song-GAH-ee) in West Africa, named for its dominant ethnic group. Between the 1460s and 1590s, the **Songhay Empire** encompassed a huge region running from the Atlantic coast to what is now northeastern Nigeria, including almost the entire Niger River basin and extending well into the Sahara Desert. It was the largest and the latest of a series of imperial states (Ghana and Mali, for example) that had given a measure of political unity to an emerging West African civilization since at least 1000 C.E. (see Chapter 2).

Like these earlier empires, Songhay relied on trade for much of its wealth because it was well positioned to dominate the Sand Road commerce across the Sahara as well as the river-based trade along the Niger. Gold and salt were major trade items, but horses

BUILDING AP® SKILLS

Claims and Evidence in Sources

This is an excellent time to introduce "Working with Evidence, Document 4: The Memoirs of Emperor Jahangir" on page 250. In this passage, Jahangir describes a conversation with his father, Akbar, about Akbar's policy of religious tolerance. Use the questions at the bottom of page 250 to guide your discussion, or assign them as homework.

AP® CLASSROOM

AP® Topic Questions

Consider assigning students the Topic Questions for Topic 3.1: Empires Expand. This is a set of three multiple-choice questions on the Battle of Panipat and will provide an opportunity for students to practice test-taking skills. The questions can be found in your AP® Classroom account under Unit 3 resources.

When you assign the Topic Questions or Personal Progress Checks, it can be a good idea to put a timer on the question(s) so students can practice the skill in a timed setting like the AP® Exam.

EXAM TIP

Know examples of the variety of states that developed in Africa between 1450 and 1750.

AP®

COMPARISON

Compare the effects of Islam on Songhay with its effects on Mughal India.

imported from further north played a major role in the cavalry forces that enabled the creation of this huge state. A trans-Saharan commerce in enslaved people took thousands of Africans across the desert to new lives in Islamic North Africa. Songhay's major cities of Gao and Timbuktu had populations numbering around 40,000 to 50,000 people and were cosmopolitan centers of both commerce and Islamic learning.

Like the Mughal Empire, Songhay was on the frontier of an expanding Islamic world. North African Muslim merchants and Sufi religious teachers had introduced the new faith to West Africa in the centuries after 1000 C.E. (See "Islam in West Africa" in Chapter 3.) But Islam in Songhay was largely limited to urban elites—rulers, merchants, and scholars—while the majority of the population in the countryside remained loyal to older ways of living and religious practices. Thus conversion in the Songhay and Mughal empires was less widespread than in the Ottoman and Safavid empires.

The modest penetration of Islam created a dilemma for Songhay's rulers. The founder of the empire, Sonni Ali (r. 1464–1492), had to walk a political and cultural tightrope. On the one hand, he had to retain the loyalty of his rural subjects, who regarded him as a magician and warrior king. In this role he took part in traditional religious ceremonies and consulted with traditional religious officials. On the other hand, he needed to accommodate the Muslim merchant class, whose international trading activity was so important for the economy of the empire. And so he declared himself a Muslim, funded the building of mosques, observed Ramadan, and offered prayers, though not always at the prescribed times. But the violence of his conquests and his lukewarm embrace of Islam incurred the hostility of Muslim scholars, who regarded him as tyrannical, cruel, and impious and labeled him an infidel or unbeliever.

Later rulers assumed a more solidly Islamic posture. One of them, Askiya Muhammad, allied closely with the Muslim scholars of Timbuktu. He also made the pilgrimage to Mecca and returned with the prestigious title of "caliph" (successor to the Prophet) granted to him by Egyptian religious officials. Nonetheless, tensions remained between the court and Muslim scholars. When one of the Timbuktu scholars visited the court of Askiya Dawud (r. 1549–1582), he was appalled to find pre-Islamic customs still being practiced.

Despite these tensions, Islam flourished in the major cities of the empire, especially Timbuktu. By 1550, the city housed several large mosques, many libraries holding huge manuscript collections, over 150 Quranic schools, and a major center of higher learning. Teaching focused largely on the Quran and Islamic law but also included medicine, astronomy, mathematics, chemistry, philosophy, the study of languages, and history. Many thousands of students from all over West Africa and beyond flocked to this highly prestigious center of Islamic learning. Writing in 1526, a North African observer commented on Timbuktu: "Here are great numbers of [Islamic] religious teachers, judges, scholars and other learned persons, who are bountifully maintained at the king's expense."[29]

By the early 1590s, the Songhay Empire was weakening. Political instability, succession conflicts, rebellion in outlying regions, and continued tension between Muslims and traditionalists made Songhay vulnerable to external invasion. The end came in 1591, when a Moroccan sultanate, eager to wrest control of the valuable trans-Saharan trade routes, decisively defeated the forces of Songhay, aided by its possession of gunpowder weapons, which the Songhay forces lacked. As the Songhay Empire fragmented into many smaller states, the age of large West African empires was over.

CONCLUSIONS AND REFLECTIONS

Comparing Empires

> **Finding the Main Point:** What were similarities and differences between the strategies and consequences of imperial expansions between 1450 and 1750?

Comparison is an essential feature of world history. We see more clearly when we juxtapose related events or processes against one another. The empires of the early modern era offer many opportunities for this kind of seeing.

At one level, these empires had much in common. Like almost all empires both earlier and later, they were the product of bloody conquest against substantial resistance. And all of them, with the exception of Songhay, were created and sustained by gunpowder weapons, which were just beginning to take hold across the world. No wonder they are sometimes called the "gunpowder empires."

These conquests caused enormous human suffering everywhere. A Christian eyewitness to the Ottoman conquest of Constantinople wrote of his beloved city: "The city deserted, lying lifeless, naked, soundless, without either form or beauty. O city, head of all cities, center of the four corners of the world, pride of the Romans, civilizer of the barbarians. . . . Oh, what a loss!"[30] But while Christian Europe lamented Ottoman conquests, Christian conquests in the Americas also caused great suffering, as expressed in this Aztec poem: "We wander here and there in our desolate poverty. . . . We have seen bloodshed and pain, where once we saw beauty and valor; we are crushed to the ground; we lie in ruins. There is nothing but grief and suffering."[31]

Even after initial conquests, all of these empires experienced revolts or rebellions from their resentful, exploited, or oppressed subjects. Cossacks, fiercely independent warrior communities in southern Russia and Ukraine known for their horsemanship and military prowess, frequently contested the growing power of the Russian Empire even as they assisted Russian conquests in Siberia. The Mughal Empire was rocked by the revolt of the Maratha Confederacy in the late seventeenth century. In the Spanish territory of New Mexico, the **Pueblo Revolt** of 1680 was a response to brutal Spanish policies of conquest, forced labor, and persistent attacks on Pueblo religious beliefs and practices. The rebels killed some 400 Spaniards, drove another 2,000 out of the territory, and destroyed many of the mission churches. Their leader, Po'pay, declared, "The God of the Christians is dead. He was made of rotten wood."[32] For twelve years the area sustained its independence, seeking to revive traditional ways of living, until it was reconquered by Spanish forces in 1692.

AP® CLASSROOM

AP® Daily Video

Topic 3.4 in Unit 3 of AP® World History: Modern is Comparison in Land-Based Empires. The 3.4 Daily Video focuses on using specific examples of historical evidence to practice the skill of argumentation in Unit 3. Have students watch the video and use the prompt in the video to understand how to use historical evidence.

The fragility of empire that these revolts disclosed provided incentives for developing various techniques for maintaining imperial rule beyond the use of force. One was bureaucracy, a more or less coherent system for adjudicating disputes, collecting taxes, and enforcing imperial policy. The Chinese Qing dynasty administered their recently acquired Central Asian territories through a separate Court of Colonial Affairs, which was an extension of the famed Chinese civil service system. At least initially it was staffed only by officials of Manchurian or Mongolian background while incorporating at the local level Mongol aristocrats, Muslim officials, and prominent Buddhists. The Ottoman Empire used the distinctive devshirme system of recruiting young Christian boys into training for military and civilian administrative positions while converting them to Islam. In the Mughal Empire, the imperial court relied on zamindars to collect imperial taxes on the large estates that these elite landowners controlled.

Beyond bureaucracy, imperial rulers sought to legitimate their empires in various ways, many of them religious. European and Russian rulers claimed that they were governing by "divine right." In a similar fashion, Ottoman rulers claimed the title of "caliph," which meant they were the civil and religious successors of Muhammad himself. The rulers of Spain's American empire strongly supported missionary efforts at conversion in the hope of generating a common Christian culture that would link rulers and ruled. The Safavid Empire sought a similar religious unity in Persia by imposing a Shia version of Islam.

In other cases, cultural accommodation rather than cultural uniformity provided a mechanism of imperial integration. Ottoman tolerance for Christians in the Balkans, Mughal willingness to accommodate Hinduism, and the Songhay Empire's refusal to impose Islam on its rural subjects illustrate this kind of practice. Likewise, the Chinese Qing dynasty did not seek to incorporate Central Asian peoples into mainstream Chinese culture.

In terms of their wider impact, the early modern empires differed significantly. The Chinese, Mughal, and Songhay empires continued older patterns of cultural interaction, while those of Europe represented something wholly new in human history—an interacting Atlantic world of Europe, Africa, and the Americas. Furthermore, the European empires had a far greater impact on the peoples they incorporated than did other empires. With the exception of parts of Russian Siberia, nowhere else did empire building generate such a catastrophic population collapse as in the Americas. Nor did Asian empires foster societies based on enslaved labor and a transcontinental trade in enslaved people like that of Europe's American colonies.

Finally, Europe was enriched and transformed by its American possessions far more than China and the Ottomans were by their territorial acquisitions. Europeans gained enormous new biological resources from their empires—corn, potatoes, tomatoes, chocolate, tobacco, timber, furs, and much more—as well as great wealth in the form of gold, silver, and land. The wealth of empire propelled Europe to a dominant position in the world by the nineteenth century. Here again Russia's experience paralleled that of

AP® CLASSROOM

AP® Topic Questions

This is a good point to have students practice writing skills. Rather than writing a full-length essay, consider having students write an outline essay using the prompt in the Topic Question for Topic 3.4. This activity is faster to grade and allows students to practice writing skills. On a 5 by 8 index card, have students write a thesis, provide two arguments with two pieces of evidence for each argument, and show which historical reasoning skill was used.

TEACHING IDEA

Exit Slip

Ask students to compare and contrast the Qing, Mughal, and Ottoman empires with the Spanish Empire. *The Chinese, Mughal, and Ottoman empires continued the patterns of empire building from the previous time period, while the Spanish Empire included the entire Atlantic world in a new form of empire with massive migration and a 95 percent death rate from diseases such as smallpox and measles.*

Western Europe, though to a lesser extent, as its empire enabled the country to emerge as one of the Great Powers of Europe by the eighteenth century.

CHAPTER REVIEW

AP Key Terms

Hernán Cortés, 207	Ming dynasty, 226
Great Dying, 210	Qing expansion, 228
Little Ice Age, 210	Ottoman Empire, 230
General Crisis, 210	*devshirme*, 233
Columbian exchange, 212	Safavid Empire, 235
mercantilism, 213	Mughal Empire, 235
mestizo, 215	*zamindars*, 235
mulattoes, 219	Akbar, 236
settler colonies, 222	Aurangzeb, 237
Russian Empire, 223	Songhay Empire, 237
yasak, 224	Pueblo Revolt, 239

Finding the Main Point

1. In what ways did European colonial empires in the Americas set in motion vast historical changes?
2. In what different ways did European colonialism take shape in the Americas?
3. What were the unique strategies and the larger impact of the expanding Russian and Chinese empires during this period?
4. How did Islamic empires in this period manage their expansion and their interactions with diverse cultures?
5. What were similarities and differences between the strategies and consequences of imperial expansions between 1450 and 1750?

AP Big Picture Questions

1. The experience of empire for conquered peoples was broadly similar whoever their rulers were. Does the material in this chapter support or challenge this idea?
2. In thinking about the similarities and differences among the empires of the early modern era, what categories of comparison might be most useful to consider?
3. In the chapter maps, notice areas of the world not included in a major empire. Pick an area and research what was happening there in the early modern era.
4. In what ways is the legacy of these early modern empires still visible in the early twenty-first century?
5. **Looking Back** What patterns of empire building after 1450 had no precedents in the period between 1200 and 1450?

TRM Suggested Responses to Questions
You can find suggested responses to the Chapter Review questions in the Teacher's Resource Materials.

Contextualization

In this workshop, you will learn about contextualization, a historical reasoning skill that you can also apply to your everyday life. You may have heard people complain that their words were taken out of context, or that context is important to understand a current event. In this workshop, we'll look specifically at the role that context plays in the study of history.

UNDERSTANDING CONTEXTUALIZATION

So what is context, and how will you use the skill of contextualization in the AP® course as you build your skills as a historian? First, let's think about what "contextualization" means.

> **Contextualization: Considering the historical situation surrounding an event or process**

That means that a historian looks at an event in terms of the cultural norms, political structures, religious beliefs, geographic and environmental factors, and other contexts that might have affected how the event occurred or how people responded to it. Context helps a historian see an event through the eyes of those who experienced it and take into account all of the surrounding factors. While something might seem unusual from our perspective or context, a good historian understands the historical context and moves beyond making judgments.

Contextualization is an important part of understanding why something happened. But be careful: contextualization is not causation! When we contextualize, we are not looking for the thing that started an event, but rather the situation or setting in which the event occurred. Often, contextualization is used to lay the groundwork for a claim or thesis. Let's see how the authors of this book do it. In the following paragraph excerpt, the authors use contextualization to set the stage for their claim:

Contextualization — For many centuries, the Chinese had interacted with the nomadic peoples who inhabited the dry and lightly populated regions now known as Mongolia, Xinjiang, and Tibet. Trade, tribute, and warfare ensured that these ecologically and culturally different worlds were well known to the Chinese, quite unlike the New World "discoveries" of the Europeans. Chinese authority in these regions had been intermittent and actively resisted. Then, in the early modern era, the Qing dynasty undertook an eighty-year military effort (1680–1760) that brought these huge areas solidly under its control. **Claim** — It was largely security concerns, rather than economic need, that motivated this aggressive posture. **Evidence** — During the late seventeenth century, the creation of a substantial state among the western Mongols, known as Zunghars, revived Chinese memories of an earlier Mongol conquest.

242

BUILDING AP® SKILLS

Contextualization

Understanding contextualization and using contextualization are important skills to master for AP® World History. Students must be able to analyze broader historical events, developments, or processes that are related to the LEQ and DBQ essays. One of the points on both the LEQ and DBQ rubrics is contextualization. To earn this point, students must learn to use contextualization to set the groundwork for a claim or thesis.

Students often struggle with understanding the difference between contextualization and causation. Take students through the example on page 242 to model contextualization. After discussing what contextualization is and is not, choose one of the Building AP® Skills activities on page 243 to have students practice contextualization.

Notice how the authors use contextualization to paint a full picture of the historical situation they'll be dealing with in their argument. This passage demonstrates three different types of context. The first sentence sets a chronological context by saying that the Chinese had interacted with pastoralists on their periphery over the centuries leading up to this time period. The second sentence sets the context across geography and culture by comparing the Chinese knowledge of the pastoralists' world in Central Asia, and what they could provide to China, to the Europeans' prior lack of knowledge of the New World. The third and fourth sentences describe the immediate setting within which the claim is situated. This is a good example of the moves you'll need to make to be successful writing essays on the AP® Exam.

CONTEXTUALIZATION ON THE AP® WORLD HISTORY EXAM

On the AP® Exam, the historical thinking skill of contextualization will be tested in a variety of ways. A Multiple-Choice Question may test your understanding of the context behind historical events and processes. A Short-Answer Question may require you to accurately explain how the historical context influenced a specific process or development. In the Long Essay Question and Document-Based Question, you will need to use contextualization as the basis of your intro paragraph, setting the stage for your claim by contextualizing the event that the prompt is asking you to write about.

BUILDING AP® SKILLS

1. **Activity: Identifying Contextualization.** Read the opening and second paragraph for the section "Colonies of Sugar" (page 217). What is the international and regional context within which the authors are situating the development of "highly productive sugar-producing colonies" in the New World?

2. **Activity: Identifying Contextualization and Claims.** Read the section "In the Islamic Heartland: The Ottoman and Persian Safavid Empires," which begins on page 230. First, identify the claim in this section, and then explain what context the authors provide, and how this context sets the stage for that claim.

3. **Activity: Working with Contextualization.** Look at the painting of Interracial Marriage in Colonial Mexico and its caption on page 215. Create a contextualizing statement for the claim below:

   Despite the Iberian focus on "purity of blood," the Iberian men who came to Central or South America to work and gain riches increasingly married Indigenous women or women of African descent.

TRM **Suggested Responses to Questions**
You can find suggested responses to the Building AP® Skills questions in the Teacher's Resource Materials.

Louis XIV on "Spectacle" as an Aid to Royal Rule

TRM Suggested Responses to Questions

You can find suggested responses to the AP® Looking Again questions in the Teacher's Resource Materials.

During the early modern era, Europe was divided into many competitive states that focused their resources on the twin projects of imperial expansion abroad and political integration at home. Perhaps the most well-known example of these European state-building efforts is that of France under the rule of Louis XIV (r. 1643–1715), who governed from the spectacular Palace of Versailles just outside of Paris. Louis, like many other European monarchs, claimed to rule through "divine right" granted by God and thus claimed sole and uncontested authority in his realm.

Around 1670, Louis composed a *memoir* for his son offering practical advice about how to rule France. Wide-ranging and full of examples from Louis's own experiences, his memoir offers insight into how an early modern European ruler understood the powers of a king and how he sought to bolster his authority and secure the support of his subjects. The passage that follows focuses on the importance of spectacle and public display in solidifying the exalted role of the monarch.

1 A FIRST LOOK

Because Louis composed his memoir as an instruction book or guide for his son, let's start by reading this passage to discover what Louis wanted his son to know about the role of spectacle in solidifying or strengthening royal rule. While reading, answer the following:

1. Which specific audiences for royal spectacle does Louis XIV identify?

2. According to Louis XIV, what is the purpose of spectacle in the functioning of the French state? Does its purpose vary by audience?

3. What is Louis XIV's point of view? How does he assume that his subjects and foreign observers think about him?

LOUIS XIV | *Memoirs* | 1670

The society of pleasures [shared public activities], which gives to people of the Court [powerful aristocrats who interacted with Louis] a moral closeness with us, touches and charms them more than one can express. The common people, on the other hand, delight in the spectacle, by which in the end we always seek to please them. . . . By this, we hold their minds and their hearts, sometimes more tightly maybe than through rewards and charitable gestures. With regards to foreigners, in a state seen as otherwise flourishing and well-ordered, whatever is consumed in these expenses potentially viewed as superfluous, makes on them a very favorable impression of magnificence, power, riches, and greatness. . . .

BUILDING AP® SKILLS

Sourcing and Situation

Sourcing a document (explaining how or why a document's point of view, purpose, historical situation, and/or audience is relevant to an argument) is one of the most difficult points to achieve on the Document-Based Question essay. Continuing practice on this skill throughout the year is the best way to help students learn it and build confidence in being able to do it. The selection from Louis XIV's Memoirs on pages 244 and 245 is an excellent document for practicing sourcing. Have the students read the excerpt and answer the three questions listed under "A First Look" (it might be a good idea to have the excerpt and questions on a separate sheet of paper so they don't read ahead). The questions will guide the students on how to analyze a document to prepare to write a sourcing statement. Once the students have read and answered the questions, ask them to share what they found with the class.

The carousel [a type of pageant] . . . had only been envisaged as a simple celebration at the beginning, but we discussed it with passion, and it became a sufficiently large and magnificent spectacle, either by the number of movements, or by the novelty of the dress, or from the variety of emblems.

It was from this day that I started to adopt the emblem I have had ever since, and that you see in so many places. I believed that, without stopping at something particular and lesser, it had to represent somehow the duties of a prince, and inspire me personally to fulfill them. We chose as the body, the sun, which is the noblest in all the rules of this art form, and which by its singular quality, by the brilliance surrounding it, by the light that it sends to the other stars making up a sort of Court for it, by the equal and fair sharing of this same light to all the climates of the world that it accomplishes, by the good that it does in all places, incessantly producing from all sides, life, joy, and action, by its endless motion in which it nonetheless seems ever peaceful, by this constant and unchanging path from which it never waivers or wanders, is certainly the brightest and most beautiful image of a great monarch.

Source: *Mémoires de Louis XIV*, edited by Jean Longonon (Paris: "Éditions Jules Tallandier," 1927), 122–24. Translated by Tonia E. Tinsley.

2 A SECOND LOOK

The "carousel" that Louis XIV refers to in this passage was an extravagant pageant held in Paris in June 1662. It featured various exotic animals, princes and nobles arrayed in fantastic costumes representing distant lands, and many equestrian competitions. Unifying this disparate assembly was King Louis himself, dressed as a Roman emperor, while on the shields of the nobles was that grand symbol of the monarchy, the sun, which as Louis explains became his personal symbol after the carousel. Return to the memoir and answer the following:

1. How does Louis's carousel example support his assertions in the opening paragraph about the importance of spectacle? What specific connections can you identify?

3 A THIRD LOOK

The sun symbol that Louis first adopted in 1662 developed over the decades that followed. Louis regularly took on the persona of Apollo, the Roman god of light and the sun, in paintings and court entertainments. And the image stuck. Even today Louis is frequently referred to as the Sun King. But beyond a personal symbol, Louis developed the sun concept to define his role in the French state and society. Return once again to the final paragraph of Louis's memoir, and answer the following:

1. What specific attributes of the sun does Louis associate with kingship?

2. What does the choice of the sun as a royal symbol suggest about Louis's conception of his role in the French state and society?

BUILDING AP® SKILLS

Sourcing and Situation

If you would like to challenge your students, have them read through the "Second Look" and "Third Look" sections on page 245 and answer the questions. This would also be a good place to have a class discussion on what their observations are of Louis XIV.

245

BUILDING AP® SKILLS

Making Connections: Comparison

Making comparisons is an important skill in AP® World History: Modern. Not only do students need to learn to make comparisons thematically, but they should also be able to use both printed and visual sources to make comparisons. Use the selection from Louis XIV Memoirs, the painting of Mughal ruler Shah Jahan on page 202, and the painting depicting a reception at the court of Ottoman sultan Selim III on page 253 to have students compare how rulers use art and symbols to legitimize their rule. Answers will vary but should include: *Louis XIV: the carousel (type of pageant) and the use of the sun as a symbol to represent him; Shah Jahan: wealth of the court on display, halo around Shah Jahan's head shows his divine designation as the ruler; Selim III: surrounded by his advisers, subjects showing their allegiance to him, elaborate headgear used to designate different social or political ranks.*

AP® ACTIVITY **IDENTIFYING AN ARGUMENT**

Louis wrote his memoir specifically to give his son advice about how to rule France. In a few sentences, summarize the lessons that Louis hoped his son would learn from his account of how he used spectacle during his reign.

FURTHER ACTIVITY

Primary sources are often difficult to read because they include words that are no longer commonly used or had a different meaning in the past. They also often incorporate long sentences with unfamiliar or little used grammatical constructions. Louis's memoir is an example of this. In this activity, your job is to update Louis's language. Rewrite one or more of Louis's paragraphs in modern English that would be easy for another student to read and understand. Note any difficulties that you have. Are you concerned that any of your translation might not fully convey what Louis XIV meant?

AP WORKING WITH EVIDENCE

State Building in the Early Modern Era

Imperial states—Mughal India, the Ottoman Empire, France, the Inca Empire, and Ming dynasty China—were invariably headed by kings or emperors who were the ultimate political authority in their lands. Those rulers sought to govern societies divided by religion, region, ethnicity, or class. During the three centuries between 1450 and 1750, all of these states, and a number of nonimperial states as well, moved toward greater political integration through more assertive monarchs and more effective central bureaucracies, which curtailed, though never eliminated, entrenched local interests. The growth of empire accompanied this process of political integration, and perhaps helped cause it. The documents that follow allow us to catch a glimpse of this state-building effort in several distinct settings.

LOOKING AHEAD

AP DBQ PRACTICE

As you read through the documents in this collection, consider what actions rulers take, or intentionally do not take, to increase their control over the territories they rule.

DOCUMENT 1 An Outsider's View of the Inca Empire

Pedro de Cieza de León (1520–1554), a Spanish chronicler of the Inca Empire of the early sixteenth century, took part as a soldier in a number of expeditions that established Spanish rule in various parts of South America. Along the way, he collected a great deal of information, especially about the Inca Empire, which he began to publish on his return to Spain in 1550. Despite a very limited education, Cieza wrote a series of works that have become a major source for historians about the workings of the Inca Empire and about the Spanish conquest of that land. The selection that follows focuses on the techniques that the Incas used to govern their huge empire.

> Source: Spanish conquistador Pedro de Cieza de León on Incan rulers, from *Chronicles of the Incas*, ca. 1550.
>
> One of the things most to be envied in these rulers is how well they knew to conquer such vast lands. . . .
>
> [T]hey entered many lands without war, and the soldiers who accompanied the Inca were ordered to do no damage or harm, robbery or violence. If there was a shortage of food in the province, he ordered supplies brought in from other regions so that those newly won to his service would not find his rule and acquaintance irksome. . . .
>
> In many others, where they entered by war and force of arms, they ordered that the crops and houses of the enemy be spared. . . . But in the end the Incas always came out victorious, and when they had vanquished the others, they did not do them further harm, but released those they had taken prisoner . . . and put them back in possession of their property and

---

TRM Suggested Responses to Questions

You can find suggested responses to the AP® Working with Evidence questions in the Teacher's Resource Materials.

BUILDING AP® SKILLS

Claims and Evidence in Sources

Interpreting text-based as well as non-text-based sources is an important skill for AP® World History: Modern students. If time is available, have students learn more about rulers in the early modern era by using the evidence in "State Building in the Early Modern Era" beginning on page 247. Consider having students analyze one or more of the sources found on pages 247–253. Check for understanding by:

■ Using the questions at the end of each source as a discussion starting point.

■ Pairing students to analyze (identify and describe) using the author/creator's point of view, purpose, historical situation, and/or audience.

■ Assigning a source to a group of three or four students and having them present an overview of the source along with the sourcing to the rest of the class.

■ Then checking for understanding by having students complete any of the activities under "Doing History" on page 254.

rule, exhorting them not to be foolish and try to compete with his royal majesty nor abandon his friendship, but to be his friends as their neighbors were. . . .

[T]hey [the Incas] had their representatives in the capitals of all the provinces. . . . They served as head of the provinces or regions, and from every so many leagues around the tributes were brought to one of these capitals. . . .

When the Incas set out to visit their kingdom, it is told that they traveled with great pomp, riding in rich litters set upon smooth, long poles of the finest wood and adorned with gold and silver.

The Incas of Pedro de Cieza de León, translated by Harriet de Onis (Norman: University of Oklahoma Press, 1959).

Question to Consider: What various methods did the Incas use to conquer and control their territory? How are these methods similar or different from methods used by other rulers in the documents below?

AP **Analyzing Sources:** Consider Cieza's purpose and intended audience for this work. How could these details explain his tone toward the Inca people?

DOCUMENT 2 **Ivan the Terrible's Treatment of Boyars**

Heinrich von Staden was a German man from the province of Westphalia who lived in Moscow in the late 1560s and early 1570s, working as a translator and tavern keeper. Tsar Ivan IV ("the Terrible") seems to have favored Staden, but the German fled Moscow in 1572 when the khan of Crimea attacked the city. The extract that follows is taken from his observations about Russia that Staden presented to the German Holy Roman Emperor Rudolf II in 1578 and focuses on the *oprichnina*, the "state within a state" that Tsar Ivan created between 1565 and 1572 to weaken the Russian nobility.

Source: Heinrich von Staden, a German man who lived in Moscow, reporting on Ivan the Terrible's private court and household (*oprichnina*), from *The Land and Government of Muscovy*, 1578–1579.

The *oprichnina* was [composed of] his people, the *zemschina*, of the ordinary people. The Grand Prince thus began to inspect one city and region after another. And those who, according to the military muster roll, had served [the Grand Prince's] forefathers by fighting the enemy with their *votchiny* were deprived of their estates, which were given to those in the oprichnina.

The princes and boyars who were taken into the *oprichnina* were ranked not according to riches but according to birth. They then took an oath not to have anything to do with any of the *zemskia* people [members of the *zemschina*] or form any friendships with them. Those in the *oprichnina* also had to wear black hats; and in their quivers, where they put their arrows, they carried some kind of brushes or brooms tied on the end of sticks. The *oprichniks* [members of the *oprichnina*] were recognized in this way.

Question to Consider: How does Ivan the Terrible use social status to maintain control in the Russian Empire?

AP® Analyzing Sources: Does it matter that the author is a German living in Russia, not a Russian? Does it matter that his audience is ultimately leaders outside the Russian Empire? Why?

DOCUMENT 3 The Court of Benin

We know little about the life of Pieter de Marees, who was most likely a merchant from the major European trading city of Antwerp. Because of the account he published shortly after his return from a journey, we are certain that he visited West Africa aboard a Dutch ship and that his trip took place between November 1600 and November 1601. In this extract from his account, Marees offers a detailed eyewitness description of the major African city of Benin, which he visited during the journey.

Source: European merchant Pieter de Marees describing the king's court in the West African city of Benin, 1602.

The king's court is very big and has inside it many large, square courtyards surrounded by galleries, in which one always finds guards. I have gone so far into that court that I passed through no less than four such large courtyards. Wherever I looked I saw other places through the gates, and thus I went farther than any Dutchman has been which was into the stables of the best horses, passing through a long corridor, so that it seems that the king has many warriors, as I myself sometimes also saw at court.

   The king also has many noblemen. When a nobleman comes to court, they come on horseback. They sit on their horses as the women do in our country, and on both sides they have a man to whom they hold on. . . .

   The king has very many male and female slaves. . . . The king often sends out presents (of food), which are carried in good order along the street.

Pieter de Marees, *Description and Historical Account of the Gold Kingdom of Guinea (1602)*, trans. and ed. Albert van Dantzig and Adam Jones (Oxford: Oxford University Press, 1987), 226–232.

Question to Consider: What role do wealth and social class play in the king's court? How do these things impact the government's control?

AP® Analyzing Sources: Who do you suspect is the primary intended audience for this piece? Why?

The diverse peoples of India had seldom experienced a political system that encompassed most of the subcontinent. But in the early modern era, the Mughal Empire gave to South Asia a rare period of substantial political unity. Document 4 offers excerpts from the memoirs of Jahangir, who ruled the Mughal state from 1605 to 1627, following the reign of his more famous father, Akbar.

Source: Emperor Jahangir of the Islamic Mughal Empire on his father Emperor Akbar's policy of religious tolerance, from *Memoirs*, 1605–1627.

[H]aving on one occasion asked my father [Akbar] the reason why he had forbidden any one to prevent or interfere with the building of these haunts of idolatry [Hindu temples], his reply was in the following terms: "My dear child," said he, "I find myself a powerful monarch, the shadow of God upon earth. I have seen that he bestows the blessings of his gracious providence upon all his creatures without distinction. Ill should I discharge the duties of my exalted station, were I to withhold my compassion and indulgence from any of those entrusted to my charge. With all of the human race, with all of God's creatures, I am at peace: why then should I permit myself, under any consideration, to be the cause of molestation or aggression to any one? Besides, are not five parts in six of mankind either Hindus or aliens to the faith; and were I to be governed by motives of the kind suggested in your inquiry, what alternative can I have but to put them all to death! I have thought it therefore my wisest plan to let these men alone. Neither is it to be forgotten, that the class of whom we are speaking . . . are usefully engaged, either in the pursuits of science or the arts, or of improvements for the benefit of mankind, and have in numerous instances arrived at the highest distinctions in the state, there being, indeed, to be found in this city men of every description, and of every religion on the face of the earth."

Question to Consider: What reasons did Jahangir's father offer for his commitment to tolerance of non-Muslim citizens?

AP **Analyzing Sources:** Why might Jahangir describe his father's advice instead of discussing his own process for developing a commitment to religious tolerance?

DOCUMENT 5 **French State Building and Louis XIV**

Louis XIV (r. 1643–1715), the king of France, and other European monarchs, such as those in Spain and Russia, operated under a set of assumptions known as absolutism, which held that kings ruled by "divine right" and could legitimately claim sole and uncontested authority in their realms. Louis's famous dictum *"L'état, c'est moi"* ("I am the state") summed up the absolutist ideal.

Document 5 illustrates one way in which Louis attempted to realize this ideal. Written by Louis himself, this document focuses on the importance of "spectacle" and public display in solidifying the exalted role of the monarch. The "carousel" described here was an extravagant pageant held in Paris in June 1662. It featured various exotic animals, princes, and nobles arrayed in fantastic costumes representing distant lands, as well as many equestrian competitions. Unifying this disparate assembly was King Louis himself, dressed as a Roman emperor, while on the shields of the nobles was that grand symbol of the monarchy, the sun.

Source: French King Louis XIV on the importance of spectacle for the common people, from his *Memoirs*, 1670.

The more I moved away from all the excesses towards gentler pursuits, the more I had to preserve and cultivate carefully everything that connected me through affection to my peoples and especially people of noble carriage, without diminishing my authority or the respect that was owed me, to make them see in so doing that it was in no way by aversion to them nor an assumed strictness nor crudeness of spirit, but simply reason and duty that made me in other ways more reserved and exacting towards them. The society of pleasures [shared public activities], which gives to people of the Court [powerful aristocrats who interacted with Louis] a moral closeness with us, touches and charms them more than one can express. The common people, on the other hand, delight in the spectacle, by which in the end we always seek to please them. . . . By this, we hold their minds and their hearts, sometimes more tightly maybe than through rewards and charitable gestures. . . .

The carousel . . . had only been envisaged as a simple celebration at the beginning, but we discussed it with passion, and it became a sufficiently large and magnificent spectacle, either by the number of movements, or by the novelty of the dress, or from the variety of emblems.

Mémoires de Louis XIV, edited by Jean Longonon (Paris: Éditions Jules Tallandier, 1927). Translated by Tonia E. Tinsley.

Question to Consider: What methods does Louis use to control the people of France? How do these methods vary according to social status?

AP **Analyzing Sources:** Consider Louis's attitude toward himself, the elite members of society, and the commoners in France. Is his tone similar or different? Why?

251

The *Sacred Edict* of the Qing dynasty was a set of moral and government instructions enacted by imperial authority, beginning with the Kangxi emperor (r. 1662–1722), for use in local rituals conducted throughout the Qing Empire.

Source: The Kangxi Emperor of Qing dynasty China's *Sacred Edict*, ca. 1670.

1. Esteem most highly filial piety and brotherly submission, in order to give due importance to human moral relations.

3. Cultivate peace and concord in your neighborhoods, in order to prevent quarrels and litigations.

4. Give importance to agriculture and sericulture [production of silk], in order to ensure a sufficiency of clothing and food.

6. Foster colleges and schools, in order to give the training of scholars a proper start.

7. Do away with errant teachings, in order to exalt the correct doctrine.

8. Expound on the laws, in order to warn the ignorant and obstinate.

11. Instruct sons and younger brothers, in order to prevent them from doing what is wrong.

14. Promptly remit your taxes, in order to avoid being pressed for payment.

Question to Consider: How does the edict use social expectations and family structures to maintain order?

AP **Analyzing Sources:** Consider the fact that this edict was compiled by imperial authority over time. Does that strengthen or weaken your argument about the Question to Consider?

DOCUMENT 7 **The Palace of an Ottoman Emperor**

Begun in 1465 and finished in 1478, the Topkapi Palace in Constantinople served for centuries as the main residence of the Ottoman emperors in their capital city. The palace, which was organized around a series of courtyards, housed government offices and a mint, an educational establishment, and the living quarters of the emperor and his harem. At the height of Ottoman power, around 4,000 family members, servants, eunuchs, officials, and soldiers of the imperial entourage resided in the complex.

Topkapi also served as a ceremonial space where important state occasions and religious celebrations took place. This late-eighteenth-century painting depicts the second courtyard and the Felicity Gate, which guarded the entrance to the inner court, where no one aside from the ruler's relatives and closest advisers was granted access. Here, at the principal ceremonial site in the palace, emperors observed religious ceremonies, received foreign ambassadors, celebrated accessions to the throne, and at times of war handed the banner of the Prophet Muhammad to their military leaders. In this image, Sultan Selim III (r. 1789–1807) sits on his throne with his chief advisers around him. Ottoman officials and court dignitaries pay homage to their ruler. Participants are arrayed in hierarchical order according to their relative social or political importance, signaled by their clothing—note their increasingly tall and elaborate headgear—and their proximity to the sultan.

Source: Painting depicting a reception at the court of Ottoman sultan Selim III in the Topkapi Palace in Constantinople, late 18th century.

Bridgeman Images

Question to Consider: How could a ceremony like the one in the image strengthen the sultan's rule?

AP **Analyzing Sources:** Who might be the intended audience of this painting? What details in the image might have special or unique impact on that audience?

AP DOING HISTORY

1. **DBQ Practice:** Evaluate the extent to which imperial states utilized varying methods of control over their territories in the period 1450–1750.

2. **Contextualization:** All these empires have common characteristics. What are they? How do these shared characteristics demonstrate features of the time period 1450–1750?

3. **Outside Evidence:** What methods of control are not mentioned in this collection of documents that were utilized by imperial rulers in the period from 1450 to 1750?

4. **Complex Argumentation:** Write an argument that recognizes both differences and similarities in the methods used by imperial rulers. While evaluating similarities and differences, also evaluate the effectiveness of various methods of control.

Early Modern Rulers

The following two voices provide recent descriptions of how early modern rulers defined and displayed their authority and power. In Voice 4.1, Charles Parker compares Emperor Kangxi of China and Louis XIV of France and finds them "cut from the same cloth." In Voice 4.2, John Darwin examines the many cultural influences that shaped the royal government of the Mughal emperor Akbar.

VOICE 4.1

Charles Parker on Emperor Kangxi of China and Louis XIV of France | 2010

For Europe's most powerful monarch [Louis XIV], the Qing dynasty under Kangxi emperor (r. 1661–1722) represented an ideal political order. The emperor wielded absolute power and enjoyed divine blessing; he employed an army of civil servants to govern his dominions; he possessed authority over a vast domain stretching from the eastern coastline to Outer Mongolia and Tibet; and he resided in a magnificent palace that exuded majestic order and power. In many respects Louis's reign (1643–1715) also embodied these characteristics, though on a less grand scale. Casting himself in the image of Apollo (the Greek god of light and sun), Louis promoted himself as the Sun King and he professed to rule by divine right; he dominated Europe and pushed France's borders to the farthest point; and he too presided over an elaborate court life at Versailles that reflected his prestige and authority. The Kangxi emperor and the Sun King, on opposite ends of Eurasia, were cut from the same cloth.

Source: Charles H. Parker, *Global Interactions in the Early Modern Age, 1400–1800* (Cambridge: Cambridge University Press, 2010), 13–14.

VOICE 4.2

John Darwin on Emperor Akbar's Public Image | 2008

Akbar projected himself not as a Muslim warrior-king, but as the absolute monarch of a diverse subject population. His official genealogy laid claim to descent from both Tamerlane and Genghis Khan, and thus to their

legacy as "world conquerors." Mughal court ritual—especially Akbar's daily appearance on an elevated platform—emphasized the *padshah*'s [an elevated Persian royal title referring to the monarch] supreme authority over even the greatest and wealthiest of his subjects. The court was the centre of lavish literary patronage. It promoted the study of the Muslim "rational sciences" and the writing of poetry, the main literary medium of the Islamic world. But Mughal court culture looked to Persian or Central Asian models for its art and literature. Persian was the language of intellectual life as well as of government. The life and landscape of Iran (not that of India) inspired the Mughal poets, who evoked a world far away "from the polluting influences of the subject peoples." . . . Akbar's regime was cosmopolitan and eclectic, a tribute to Central Asia's influence as a great cultural entrepôt. It is even possible that his abortive attempt to impose a more centralized government in the 1570s and '80s (which led to the great revolt of 1580–82) was remotely inspired by the Chinese system of meritocratic bureaucracy. . . . Famously, Akbar rejected the classic Islamic distinction between the Muslim faithful (the *umma*) and the unbelievers. He abolished the *jizya* (poll-tax on non-Muslims) in 1579, and flirted with propagating a new religious synthesis of Islam and Hinduism.

Source: John Darwin, *After Tamerlane: The Rise and Fall of Global Empires 1400–2000* (London: Bloomsbury, 2008), 85–86.

AP® Analyzing Secondary Sources

1. According to Parker, what attributes of a powerful ruler did Kangxi and Louis XIV share?

2. According to Darwin, what cultural and political traditions did Akbar draw upon to rule over the Mughal Empire? Which did he reject, abandon, or modify?

3. **Integrating Primary and Secondary Sources:** What elements of kingship described by Parker and Darwin are evident in the documents preceding this feature? To what extent are these elements specific to certain rulers or states?

255

TRM Suggested Responses to Questions
You can find suggested responses to the AP® Analyzing Secondary Sources questions in the Teacher's Resource Materials.

Multiple-Choice Questions Choose the correct answer for each question.

Questions 1–3 refer to this table.

NUMBER OF ENSLAVED PEOPLE DELIVERED TO EACH DESTINATION BY YEAR

	Spain / Uruguay	Portugal / Brazil	Great Britain	Netherlands	U.S.A.	France	Denmark / Baltic	Totals
1501–1525	6,363	7,000	0	0	0	0	0	13,363
1526–1550	25,375	25,387	0	0	0	0	0	50,762
1551–1575	28,167	31,089	1,685	0	0	66	0	61,007
1576–1600	60,056	90,715	237	1,365	0	0	0	152,373
1601–1625	83,496	267.519	0	1,829	0	0	0	352,844
1626–1650	44,313	201,609	33,695	31,729	824	1,827	1,053	315,050
1651–1675	12,601	244,793	122,367	100,526	0	7,125	653	488,065
1676–1700	5,860	297,272	272,200	85,847	3,327	29,484	25,685	719,675
1701–1725	0	474,447	410,597	73,816	3,277	120,939	5,833	1,088,909
1726–1750	0	536,696	554,042	83,095	34,004	259,095	4,793	1,471,725
1751–1775	4,239	528,693	832,047	132,330	84,580	325,918	17,508	1,925,315
1776–1800	6,415	673,167	748,612	40,773	67,443	433,061	39,199	2,008,670
1801–1825	168,087	1,160,601	283,959	2,669	109,545	135,815	16,316	1,876,992
1826–1850	400,728	1,299,969	0	357	1,850	68,074	0	1,770,978
1851–1875	215,824	9,309	0	0	478	0	0	225,609
Totals	1,061,524	5,848,266	3,259,441	554,336	305,326	1,381,404	111,040	12,521,337

Source: Data from http://www.slavevoyages.org/assessment/estimates.

1. Which of the following is the most significant cause for the varied distribution of enslaved people in the areas listed above?
   a. During the eighteenth century the British and Dutch successfully abolished the slave trade.
   b. Relations weakened between British and Dutch merchants and leaders of West Africa who cooperated in the slave trade.
   c. Spain and Portugal had extensive sugar production in the American colonies.
   d. Enslaved people in North America engaged in more strenuous work and were more likely to lead shorter lives.

2. A historian would most likely use the data above to support which of the following conclusions?
   a. The rivalry between the Spanish and the Dutch to acquire enslaved people from West Africa was most intense at the beginning of the period shown in the table.
   b. The British introduced intensive agriculture in their colonies before the French did.

256

   c. Racial integration varied widely across regions in the Americas.

   d. There was a shift away from dependence on cash crops at the very end of the date range shown in the table.

3. Which of the following best compares the impact of the slave trade on colonial societies in North America and Latin America?

   a. In Latin America, slavery contributed to a class system based on race, while in North America there were fewer enslaved people and less racial integration.

   b. In North America, a large percentage of the enslaved population converted to Christianity, while in Latin America there were few attempts to convert enslaved people.

   c. In Latin America enslaved families were more likely to be kept intact; in North America plantation work required only male labor, creating a gender imbalance.

   d. There was a greater degree of religious syncretism between African religions and Christianity in North American societies than in Latin American societies.

Questions 4–6 refer to this image.

DEA PICTURE LIBRARY/Getty Images

Mughal miniature painting depicting Emperor Akbar having discussions with leaders of other religions.

257

AP® CLASSROOM

AP® Personal Progress Check

You can extend the AP® Exam Strategies activity on page 256 by logging into your AP® Classroom account and using the questions in the Progress Check for Unit 3 as more practice for your students. AP® Classroom allows you to set the quiz up digitally or print out a copy for each student. After students take the Progress Check for Unit 3, you can discuss the answers as a class.

When you assign the Topic Questions or Personal Progress Checks, it can be a good idea to put a timer on the question(s) so students can practice the skill in a timed setting like the AP® Exam.

4. Which of the following features of civilizations between 1450 and 1750 provides the best context for understanding this painting?

    a. Conservative leaders frequently resisted the process of cultural syncretism.

    b. Empires had to manage diversity as they expanded.

    c. A process of decentralization distributed political power to smaller regions.

    d. Most empires sponsored missionary efforts to disseminate their belief systems.

5. Which of the following characteristics of the Mughal Empire is supported by this image?

    a. Its peaceful attempts to convert adherents of other religions to Islam

    b. Its competition with the Ottoman Empire for being the defender of Sunni Islam

    c. Its repeated attempts to obtain cooperation with its Shia Safavid neighbors

    d. Its desire to promote cultural tolerance among its populations

6. This image best reflects which of the following continuities in world history?

    a. The contact of various cultures through expanding networks of trade

    b. The use of painting to establish doctrinal purity in religion

    c. The use of art to serve the political agendas of rulers

    d. The support for the arts by a thriving merchant class

Short-Answer Questions

Read each question carefully and write a short response. Use complete sentences.

1. **Use this passage and your knowledge of world history to answer all parts of the question that follows.**

> Regardless of the economic, political, and religious motives that inspired Spaniards to colonize and control the Americas, their ability, as that of any empire, to impose their policies was inextricably connected with the imperial center's ability to establish workable relations with two groups of people: the indigenous people who were colonized, and the non-elite Spanish people who lived in the Americas as colonists. The social integration and willing involvement of both groups was essential to the maintenance of empire, and necessarily involved negotiation between the ideological constructs that organized the social imperial effort, and the requirements and demands of people in local settings.
>
> — Kathleen Deagan, "Dynamics of Imperial Adjustment in Spanish America: Ideology and Social Integration,"
> in *Empires: Perspectives from Archeology and History*, ed. Susan E. Alcock et al.

A. Identify ONE way in which the strategies of the Spanish Empire, as described above, were different from the colonial strategies of other Europeans in North America.

B. Explain ONE strategy adopted by the Spanish in their quest to achieve the social integration described above.

C. Explain a strategy for social integration, as described above, of ANOTHER empire in Afro-Eurasia during the period 1450–1750.

2. Use this image and your knowledge of world history to answer all parts of the question that follows.

Planting the Tree of the State of Russia, 1668. The trunk begins in the Kremlin, the seat of the Russian government, and branches out to well-known political and religious figures.

A. Identify how the painting above reflects a continuity in world history.

B. Explain how ONE aspect of the painting above would have served the Russian state.

C. Explain how the strategy of empire building illustrated in the painting above was used by ANOTHER empire in the period 1450–1750.

3. Use your knowledge of world history to answer all parts of the question below.

A. Identify ONE way in which the European empires were different from the empires of Asia during the period 1450–1750.

B. Explain ONE motive for European empire building in the period 1450–1750.

C. Explain ONE long-term consequence of European empire building in the period 1450–1750.

259

5 Cultural Transformations
Religion and Science, 1450–1750

AP® Overview for Chapter 5

Chapter 5 corresponds most closely with Topic 3.3 Empires: Belief Systems in AP® Unit 3 and Topic 5.1 The Enlightenment in AP® Unit 5. It also covers Topic 4.7 Changing Social Hierarchies 1450 to 1750 in AP® Unit 4. This chapter picks up the religious theme again as a primary focus. Several of the world religions that students studied earlier in the year, such as Islam, Christianity, Confucianism, and Hinduism, are viewed through the prism of the changes of the early modern period. Other cultural transformations, including the Protestant Reformation, the Scientific Revolution, and the Enlightenment, also emerged during this period.

Chapter 5 Essential Activity

Ask students to search the Internet for maps showing the global spread of religions throughout history. One good example can be found by searching for "Animated map shows how religion spread around the world" by Business Insider on YouTube. Next, ask students to create a chart that summarizes the continuity and change in Christianity, Islam, Confucianism, and Hinduism from 1450 to 1750. The maps on pages 267 and 268–269 will also be helpful. A student version of this chart and an answer key are available in the Teacher's Resource Materials.

> **TRM** Essential Activity 5: Continuity and Change in Religion from 1450 to 1750

Chapter 5 Resources

> **TRM** AP® Skills Workshop Activity Handout: Causation
> **TRM** Chapter 5 DBQ Activity Handout
> **TRM** Chapter 5 Guided Reading
> **TRM** Chapter 5 Lecture Presentation Slides
> **TRM** Chapter 5 Outline
> **TRM** Chapter 5 Suggested Responses to Questions
> **TRM** Eric's Activity 5: Christianity Becomes a World Religion

> **TRM** Essential Activity 5: Continuity and Change in Religion from 1450 to 1750
> **TRM** Handout 5.1: Graphic Organizer for the Spread of Christianity
> **TRM** Handout 5.2: Chart for Scientists and Their Contributions
> **TRM** Handout 5.3: Chart for Nineteenth- and Twentieth-Century Scientific Thinkers

Pacing Guide

Below is a pacing guide for the AP® World History: Modern course beginning in ca. 1200 C.E. This pacing guide is based on a schedule with 120 sessions of 50 minutes each before the AP® Exam. It is meant as a place to start. If you have a different number of sessions before the exam, you can modify the pacing to suit your needs.

Day	Pages Assigned	AP® Topic	AP® Theme	Suggested Assignments	Coverage Notes
1	Read pages 261–269	3.3	CDI	Chapter 5 Essential Activity Building AP® Skills: Developments and Processes on page 263 Exploring AP® Themes: Cultural Developments and Interactions (CDI) on page 265 Eric's Activity 5: Christianity Becomes a World Religion on page 294	It may be helpful to break this chapter up into two parts; we've recommended sessions and days to help wrap up Units 3 and 4 as well as to introduce Unit 5. This section on the globalization of Christianity is a good place to practice the Causation skill with students, especially focusing on the causes and effects of the Protestant Reformation.
2	Read pages 274–279 from "Persistence and Change in Afro-Asian Cultural Traditions" to "A New Way of Thinking: The Birth of Modern Science"	3.3 4.5	CDI	Apply the Tip on page 275 Apply the Tip on page 276 Building AP® Skills: Making Connections: Comparison on page 277	Students need to understand that religious changes were not just exclusive to Europe in this time period. This section gives a good overview of the changes in the Islamic world and China, as well as the emergence of Sikhism.
3	Read pages 270–274 from "Christianity Outward Bound" to "Persistence and Change in Afro-Asian Cultural Traditions"	4.5	CDI	Building AP® Skills: Making Connections: Comparison on page 270 Exploring AP® Themes: Cultural Developments and Interactions (CDI) on page 272 Apply the Tip on page 273	Students need to understand that religious changes are not just exclusive to Europe in this time period. This section gives a good explanation of cultural synthesis with Christianity in the Americas.
4	Read pages 279–286 from "A New Way of Thinking: The Birth of Modern Science" to "Science and Enlightenment"; pages 289–295 from "European Science beyond the West" through "Conclusions and Reflections"	5.1	CDI	Apply the Tip on page 280 Exploring AP® Themes: Cultural Developments and Interactions (CDI) on page 283 Exploring AP® Themes: Cultural Developments and Interactions (CDI) on page 291	While the new framework does not reference the Scientific Revolution, it is still important for students to know because of how it contributes to the age of reason and the Enlightenment. The Scientific Revolution can also help show the intellectual shift from China and the Islamic world toward the West. Move quickly through this section if you are short on time.
5	Read pages 286–289 from "Science and Enlightenment" to "European Science beyond the West"	5.1	CDI SIO	Apply the Tip on page 286 Building AP® Skills: Sourcing and Situation on page 288 Exploring AP® Themes: Cultural Developments and Interactions (CDI) on page 289	The Enlightenment helps set the stage for the Revolutions unit. Make sure students understand Enlightenment ideals and how they led to the eighteenth- and nineteenth-century revolutions.

Have students brainstorm ways in which major belief systems, such as Christianity, Confucianism, Buddhism, and Islam, changed from their founding to the sixteenth and seventeenth centuries. After brainstorming changes, ask students to share what they came up with. *Answers will vary.*

Have students look at the painting and read the caption that goes with it. Ask students: What do you notice in the painting? *Some of the salient features of the painting include two women on the sides, the shields with an eagle and a lion (possibly symbolizing Mexico and Spain), cherubs, and Mary in Mexican clothing and adornments.*

Then ask students: What does the painting of the virgin of Guadalupe say about the diffusion of Christianity? *Christianity incorporated aspects of local beliefs to meet the needs of the people and possibly assist with conversion efforts.*

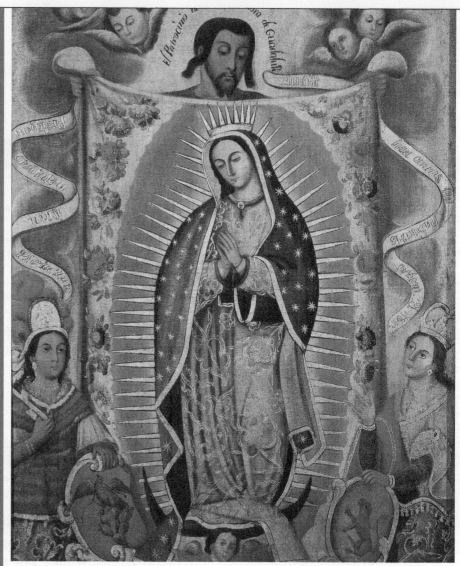

The Virgin of Guadalupe According to Mexican tradition, a dark-skinned Virgin Mary appeared to an Indigenous peasant named Juan Diego in 1531, an apparition reflected in this Mexican painting from 1720. Belief in the Virgin of Guadalupe represented the incorporation of European Catholicism into the emerging culture and identity of Mexico. (Gianni Dagli Orti/Shutterstock)

260

CHAPTER

5

Cultural Transformations

Religion and Science

1450–1750

◀ **AP**

DEVELOPMENTS AND PROCESSES
Explain how this Mexican painting is
an example of cultural syncretism.
What specific elements in the
painting support your answer?

CONNECTING PAST AND PRESENT — "Britain brought the gospel to us in the past. Now, by God's providence we are here when Christianity is very much challenged and the UK churches are really declining."[1] This was the view expressed in 2017 by Girma Bishaw, a London-based Ethiopian-British pastor, referring to a growing movement among African Christian organizations who sought to bring the Gospel back to an increasingly secular West. These "reverse missionaries" represented a remarkable shift from earlier efforts by European and North American missionaries to bring Christianity to Africa and Asia, beginning in the early modern era. One reason for the empty churches in the West lay in another cultural change—the spread of modern scientific and secular thinking, which for some people undermined religious belief. That enormous transformation likewise took shape in the early modern era. ■

And so, alongside new empires, the early modern centuries also witnessed novel cultural and religious transformations that likewise connected distant peoples. Riding the currents of European empire building and commercial expansion, Christianity was established solidly in the Americas and the Philippines and, though far more modestly, in Siberia, China, Japan, and India. A cultural tradition largely limited to Europe in 1500 was now becoming a genuine world religion, spawning a multitude of cultural encounters—though it spread hardly at all within the vast and still-growing domains of Islam. This globalization of Christianity persisted in the nineteenth and twentieth centuries. But while Christianity was spreading globally, a new understanding of the universe and a new approach to knowledge were taking shape among European thinkers of the Scientific Revolution, giving rise to another kind of cultural encounter—that between science and religion. Science was a new

261

BUILDING AP® SKILLS

Contextualization

Use a quick discussion to set up
contextualization for the topic in Chapter 5.
Ask students: What modern scientific ideas
might have challenged and threatened the
Church in this period, and given what you
know from earlier chapters, how might the
Church have responded? *Ideas that might
have threatened the Church's teachings
included new ideas about the universe such
as the position of the sun relative to the
planets, competing worldviews, and ideas
about the natural world that challenged the
authority of God. The Church was likely to
attempt to suppress the new ideas or limit the
information that was published. The Church
might have supported the diffusion of some
new scientific ideas as long as they did not
interfere with or challenge church teachings.*

BUILDING AP® SKILLS

Making Connections: Continuity and Change

Ask students to explain how cultural transformations during the early modern period were to some degree the result of interactions between cultures and not solely the result of European domination. *The interaction of Indigenous peoples with Europeans and Christianity determined how and what would be accepted, rejected, or transformed as it spread. Science emerged in an international context. Christianity began to rival Islam as a world religion, even as Islam continued to spread. Buddhism and Hinduism continued in South Asia, East Asia, and Southeast Asia. Smaller, traditional religions continued in Africa. Europeans were affected by these new worlds and new religions.*

APPLY THE TIP

The Chapter 5 Essential Activity can help students understand the expansion of major religions in this time period. If you want to add in a new element to the activity, ask students to add another column to their Continuity and Change chart for notes on syncretic belief systems that emerged because of increased cross-cultural interactions.

AP
CAUSATION
To what extent did the cultural changes of the early modern world derive from cross-cultural interactions rather than from developments within societies and civilizations?

AP   EXAM TIP
Understand how major religions spread through world history. In addition, be able to identify examples of cultural diffusion and syncretism.

AP
CAUSATION
To what extent were cultural transformations during the early modern period the result of interactions within or among non-Western cultures and not solely the result of European domination?

AP
CAUSATION
What were the long-term and short-term causes of the Protestant Reformation?

---

and competing worldview, and for some it became almost a new religion. In time, it grew into a defining feature of global modernity, achieving a worldwide acceptance that exceeded that of Christianity or any other religious tradition.

Although Europeans were central players in the globalization of Christianity and the emergence of modern science, they were not alone in shaping the cultural transformations of the early modern era. Asian, African, and Native American peoples largely determined how Christianity would be accepted, rejected, or transformed as it entered new cultural environments. Science emerged within an international and not simply a European context, and it met varying receptions in different parts of the world. Islam continued a long pattern of religious expansion and renewal, even as Christianity began to compete with it as a world religion. Buddhism maintained its hold in much of East Asia, as did Hinduism in South Asia and numerous smaller-scale religious traditions in Africa. And Europeans themselves were certainly affected by the many "new worlds" that they now encountered. The cultural interactions of the early modern era, in short, did not take place on a one-way street.

The Globalization of Christianity

Finding the Main Point: In what different ways did Europe, Latin America, and China experience religious or cultural change in the early modern era?

Despite its Middle Eastern origins and its earlier presence in many parts of the Afro-Asian world, Christianity was largely limited to Europe at the beginning of the early modern era. In 1500, the world of Christendom stretched from the Iberian Peninsula in the west to Russia in the east, with small and beleaguered communities of various kinds in Egypt, Ethiopia, southern India, and Central Asia. Internally, the Christian world was seriously divided between the Roman Catholics of Western and Central Europe and the Eastern Orthodox of Eastern Europe and Russia. Externally, it was very much on the defensive against an expansive Islam. Muslims had ousted Christian Crusaders from their toeholds in the Holy Land by 1300, and with the Ottoman seizure of Constantinople in 1453, they had captured the prestigious capital of Eastern Orthodoxy. The Ottoman siege of Vienna in 1529, and again in 1683, marked a Muslim advance into the heart of Central Europe. Except in Spain and Sicily, which had recently been reclaimed for Christendom after centuries of Muslim rule, the future, it must have seemed, lay with Islam rather than Christianity.

Western Christendom Fragmented: The Protestant Reformation

As if these were not troubles enough, in the early sixteenth century the **Protestant Reformation** shattered the unity of Roman Catholic Christianity, which for the

Landmarks for Chapter 5

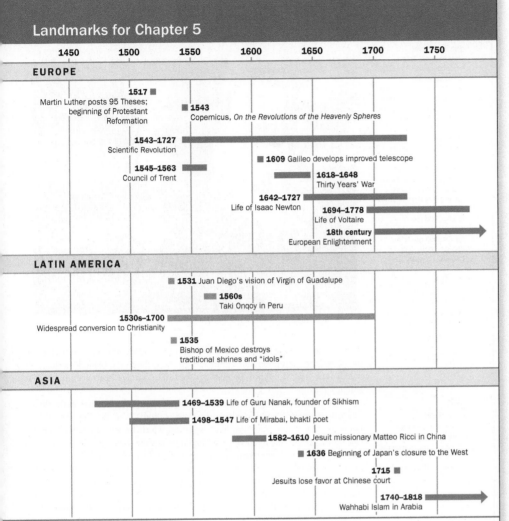

EUROPE

| 1450 | 1500 | 1550 | 1600 | 1650 | 1700 | 1750 |

1517 Martin Luther posts 95 Theses; beginning of Protestant Reformation

1543 Copernicus, *On the Revolutions of the Heavenly Spheres*

1543–1727 Scientific Revolution

1545–1563 Council of Trent

1609 Galileo develops improved telescope

1618–1648 Thirty Years' War

1642–1727 Life of Isaac Newton

1694–1778 Life of Voltaire

18th century European Enlightenment

LATIN AMERICA

1531 Juan Diego's vision of Virgin of Guadalupe

1560s Taki Onqoy in Peru

1530s–1700 Widespread conversion to Christianity

1535 Bishop of Mexico destroys traditional shrines and "idols"

ASIA

1469–1539 Life of Guru Nanak, founder of Sikhism

1498–1547 Life of Mirabai, bhakti poet

1582–1610 Jesuit missionary Matteo Ricci in China

1636 Beginning of Japan's closure to the West

1715 Jesuits lose favor at Chinese court

1740–1818 Wahhabi Islam in Arabia

previous 1,000 years had provided the cultural and organizational foundation of an emerging Western European civilization. The Reformation began in 1517 when a German priest, **Martin Luther** (1483–1546), publicly invited debate about various abuses within the Roman Catholic Church by issuing a document, known as the Ninety-Five Theses, allegedly nailing it to the door of a church in Wittenberg. In

263

TEACHING IDEA

Incorporating Outside Resources

The sixteenth century in early modern Europe is a century full of upheaval and conflict. Now might be a good time to show *Crash Course World History: Luther and the Protestant Reformation.* In this episode, John Green talks about all the changes brought about by the Protestant Reformation. You can find the video by searching for it on YouTube. While students watch the video, have them answer the following questions:

■ Why is the study of religions important to world history? *It helps students of global history understand the lenses through which people have viewed their lives and communities.*

■ How did the Protestant Reformation change Christianity in Europe? *Roman Catholicism no longer dominated Christianity in Europe. Many more denominations such as Lutherans, Presbyterians, and Anglicans emerged. The Reformation also led to more literacy and more people thinking for themselves, and governments were forced to allow religious freedom.*

■ Why did Luther dislike the sale of indulgences? *He believed in salvation by faith, and the sale of indulgences allowed people to purchase their salvation.*

■ How did Martin Luther's ideas spread so fast? *The printing press spread his ideas.*

■ Why did all of the new religious ideas cause mayhem? *People began interpreting the Bible for themselves, clergy preached the new ideas, and governments resisted the changes.*

■ Why would breaking with the Catholic Church be appealing to rulers in the German states? *They were able to keep more wealth and power for themselves.*

■ What themes in world history other than culture did the Protestant Reformation influence? *Social interactions and organization, and Governance.*

The Protestant Reformation This woodcut by the Protestant artist Lucas Cranach the Younger, entitled *The True and False Churches*, depicts Martin Luther at its center preaching the pure word of God from his pulpit. On the left and below Luther, Cranach depicts an orderly and godly Protestant congregation at worship. To the right the open flaming mouth of a demon consumes bishops, monks, and the pope, who physically embody for Cranach the false and disorderly Catholic Church. (akg-images/Newscom)

▶ **AP**

SOURCING AND SITUATION

How would you describe Lucas Cranach the Younger's point of view?

AP

CAUSATION

How might Luther's understanding of salvation have challenged the Catholic Church of the sixteenth century?

AP

CONTINUITY AND CHANGE

In what ways did the Protestant Reformation transform European society, culture, and politics?

itself, this was nothing new, for many had long been critical of the luxurious life of the popes, the corruption and immorality of some clergy, the Church's selling of indulgences (said to remove the penalties for sin), and other aspects of church life and practice.

What made Luther's protest potentially revolutionary, however, was its theological basis. A troubled and brooding man anxious about his relationship with God, Luther came to a new understanding of salvation, which, he believed, came through faith alone. Neither the good works of the sinner nor the sacraments of the Church had any bearing on the eternal destiny of the soul. To Luther, the source of these beliefs, and of religious authority in general, was not the teaching of the Church, but the Bible alone, interpreted according to the individual's conscience. All of this challenged the authority of the Church and called into question the special position of the clerical hierarchy and the pope. In sixteenth-century Europe, this was the stuff of revolution. (See Snapshot: Catholic/Protestant Differences in the Sixteenth Century, page 265.)

Contrary to Luther's original intentions, his ideas provoked a massive schism within the world of Catholic Christendom, for they came to express a variety of political, economic, and social tensions as well as religious differences. Some kings and princes, many of whom had long disputed the political authority of the pope, found in these ideas a justification for their own independence and an opportunity

BUILDING AP® SKILLS

Making Connections: Causation

Ask students to read "This Day in History: Martin Luther Posts 95 Theses" found on the History channel website. After students have examined this material, ask the following questions:

■ What led Luther to speak out against church practices? *Frustration over the practice of selling indulgences led Luther to write and post the Ninety-Five Theses.*

■ What is the origin of the term "Protestant"? *The term "Protestant" refers to the protest of Luther's supporters, who declared that their allegiance to God should take precedence over their support of the emperor.*

SNAPSHOT Catholic/Protestant Differences in the Sixteenth Century

	Catholic	Protestant
Religious authority	The Bible and church tradition as defined by pope and church councils	The Bible alone
Role of the pope	Leader of church	Authority of the pope denied
Ordination of clergy	Apostolic succession: direct line between original apostles and all subsequently ordained clergy	Apostolic succession denied; ordination by individual congregations or denominations
Role of clergy	Priests are generally celibate; sharp distinction between priests and laypeople; priests are mediators between God and humankind	Ministers may marry; priesthood of all believers; clergy have different functions (to preach, administer sacraments) but no distinct spiritual status
Salvation	Importance of church sacraments as channels of God's grace	Importance of faith alone; God's grace is freely and directly granted to believers
Status of Mary	Highly prominent, ranking just below Jesus; provides constant intercession for believers	Less prominent; Mary's intercession on behalf of the faithful denied
Role of saints	Prominent spiritual exemplars and intermediaries between God and humankind	Generally disdained as a source of idolatry; saints refer to all Christians
Prayer	To God, but often through or with Mary and saints	To God alone; no role for Mary and saints

◀ **AP®**
CAUSATION
Using the information from this chart, what might be the causes for the appeal of Martin Luther's ideas among many Europeans?

to gain the lands and revenues previously held by the Church. In the Protestant idea that all vocations were of equal merit, middle-class urban dwellers found a new religious legitimacy for their growing role in society. For common people, who were offended by the corruption and luxurious living of some churchmen, the new religious ideas expressed their opposition to the entire social order, particularly in a series of German peasant revolts in the 1520s.

Although large numbers of women were attracted to Protestantism, Reformation teachings and practices did not offer them a substantially greater role in the Church or society. Protestant opposition to celibacy and monastic life closed the convents, which had offered some women an alternative to marriage. Nor were Protestants (except the Quakers) any more willing than Catholics to offer women an official role within their churches. The importance that Protestants gave to reading the Bible for oneself stimulated education and literacy for women, but given the emphasis on women as wives and mothers subject to male supervision, they had little opportunity to use that education outside of the family.

AP® EXAM TIP
Understand how the Protestant Reformation represented a major change within the world of Western Christianity.

EXPLORING AP® THEMES

Cultural Developments and Interactions (CDI)

Have students look at "Snapshot: Catholic/Protestant Differences in the Sixteenth Century" and use the following questions to have students participate in a "Think, Pair, Share" activity. Once students have finished the activity, continue on with a class discussion of the main themes of this chapter.

■ What impact did Protestant beliefs have on the power of kings in Europe? *Protestant beliefs gave kings more power, further decreasing the power of the Catholic Church.*

■ As seen in this chart, which differences between the Catholic and Protestant churches are most significant? *According to Protestant beliefs, the Bible is the authority, not the pope. Apostolic succession is denied. Faith alone leads to grace. The status of Mary is less prominent. People must pray to God alone. Transubstantiation is denied. Ministers may marry. Saints are disdained as a source of idolatry.*

EXPLORING AP® THEMES

Social Interactions and Organization (SIO)

Ask students to describe why many women were attracted to Protestantism. *Women were attracted to Protestantism, although they did not truly have a larger role in the Church. The role of Mary, along with the veneration of both male and female saints, diminished and ended. Opposition to celibacy and monastic life caused monasteries in predominantly Protestant regions to close, which in turn restricted opportunities for women. Protestantism did, however, allow for some education of women in reading and writing since it encouraged reading and interpreting the Bible for oneself, but women's opportunities to use this education outside the home were limited.*

Ask students: Given that Europe was already sharply divided between the Catholic and Eastern Orthodox churches, how might the addition of Protestantism have added to this division and further affected the Catholic Church? *The addition of Protestantism further weakened the power and prestige of the Catholic Church in Europe. As regional monarchs converted to Protestantism and took over the Catholic Church's landholdings, the Church's lands decreased and its tax revenues were depleted.*

APPLY THE TIP

Ask students: What are some of the political and social factors that divided Europe? *Political and social factors that divided Europe included sharp class divisions, fractured political systems, and religious differences between and within states.*

AP® CONTEXTUALIZATION How did the printing press impact the spread of Protestantism and the divisions within it?

AP® EXAM TIP Understand how some conflicts can have both religious and secular causes.

Reformation thinking spread quickly both within and beyond Germany, thanks in large measure to the recent invention of the printing press. Luther's many pamphlets and his translation of the New Testament into German were soon widely available. "God has appointed the [printing] Press to preach, whose voice the pope is never able to stop," declared the English Protestant writer John Foxe in 1563.[2] As the movement spread to France, Switzerland, England, and elsewhere, it also divided, amoeba-like, into a variety of competing Protestant churches—Lutheran, Calvinist, Anglican, Quaker, Anabaptist—many of which subsequently subdivided, producing a bewildering array of Protestant denominations. Each was distinctive, but none gave allegiance to Rome or the pope. The French theologian John Calvin, for example, built on Luther's doctrine of justification by faith alone. He emphasized the absolute sovereignty of God, who "freely and unchangeably ordained whatsoever comes to pass." Applied to human salvation, this emphasis generated the doctrine of predestination, which argued that God alone chooses those who will be saved and those who will be damned. These religious ideas also spread throughout Europe, giving rise to what is often called the Reformed tradition within Protestant Christianity.

Thus to the sharp class divisions and the fractured political system of Europe was now added the potent brew of religious difference, operating both within and between states (see Map 5.1). For more than thirty years (1562–1598), French society was torn by violence between Catholics and the Protestant minority known as Huguenots (HYOO-guh-noh). The culmination of European religious conflict took shape in the **Thirty Years' War** (1618–1648), a Catholic–Protestant struggle that began in the Holy Roman Empire but eventually engulfed most of Europe. It was a horrendously destructive war, during which, scholars estimate, between 15 and 30 percent of the German population perished from violence, famine, or disease. Finally, the Peace of Westphalia (1648) brought the conflict to an end, with some reshuffling of boundaries and an agreement that each state was sovereign, authorized to control religious affairs within its own territory. Whatever religious unity Catholic Europe had once enjoyed was now permanently splintered.

The Protestant breakaway, combined with reformist tendencies within the Catholic Church itself, provoked a Catholic Reformation, or **Counter-Reformation**. In the Council of Trent (1545–1563), Catholics clarified and reaffirmed their unique doctrines, sacraments, and practices, such as the authority of the pope, priestly celibacy, the veneration of saints and relics, and the importance of Church tradition and good works, all of which Protestants had rejected. Moreover, they set about correcting the abuses and corruption that had stimulated the Protestant movement by placing a new emphasis on the education of priests and their supervision by bishops. New religious orders, such as the Society of Jesus (Jesuits), provided a dedicated brotherhood of priests committed to the revival of the Catholic Church and its extension abroad. Renewed efforts to foster individual spirituality and personal piety were accompanied by crackdowns on dissidents and the censorship of books.

Although the Reformation was profoundly religious, it encouraged a skeptical attitude toward authority and tradition, for it had, after all, successfully challenged the immense prestige and power of the established Church. Protestant reformers

Protestant dominant
Some Protestant influence
Catholic
Eastern Orthodox Christian
Boundary of the Holy Roman Empire

MAPPING HISTORY Map 5.1 **Reformation Europe in the Sixteenth Century**

The rise of Protestantism added yet another set of religious divisions, both within and between states, to the world of Christendom, which was already sharply divided between the Roman Catholic Church and the Eastern Orthodox Church. Note that France and much of Eastern Europe returned firmly to the Catholic faith during the seventeenth century.

Reading the Map: What parts of Western Europe were predominantly Protestant by the end of the sixteenth century? Which regions remained predominantly Catholic? How would you describe the religious situation in the Holy Roman Empire?

AP **Making Connections:** Compare this map with Map 5.2: The Globalization of Christianity. Did Catholic or Protestant states control the largest overseas colonies?

EXPLORING AP® THEMES

Cultural Developments and Interactions (CDI)

Have students look at Map 5.1, "Reformation Europe in the Sixteenth Century." Ask students: Which areas and countries show mixed religious allegiances? *France, Ireland, the Swiss Confederation, and Saxony appear to have both Catholic and Protestant allegiances.*

BUILDING AP® SKILLS

Making Connections: Causation

Have students look at Map 5.2, "The Globalization of Christianity." Ask them to identify and analyze the emerging patterns in the spread of Christianity. *All the areas shown on the map were accessible to overseas trade, travel, and exploration. Christianity spread to areas where European nations sought to increase their overseas influence.*

▶ AP®

CONTEXTUALIZATION
Examine the areas on this map that had not converted to Christianity by 1700. Why would these areas not have adopted Christianity?

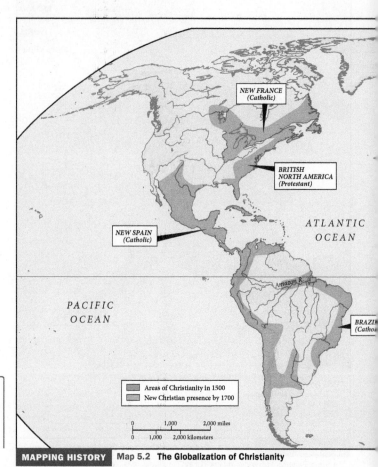

NEW FRANCE
(Catholic)

BRITISH
NORTH AMERICA
(Protestant)

NEW SPAIN
(Catholic)

ATLANTIC
OCEAN

Amazon R.

PACIFIC
OCEAN

BRAZIL
(Catholic)

Areas of Christianity in 1500
New Christian presence by 1700

0   1,000   2,000 miles
0   1,000   2,000 kilometers

MAPPING HISTORY   Map 5.2   **The Globalization of Christianity**

The growing Christian presence in Asia, Africa, and especially the Americas, combined with older centers of that faith, gave the religion derived from Jesus a global dimension during the early modern era.

Reading the Map: Where did Protestants establish overseas colonies?

AP® **Making Connections:** Did the Catholic, Protestant, or Russian Orthodox Church have the most success in establishing itself as a global faith during the early modern period? How might you explain the variations among them?

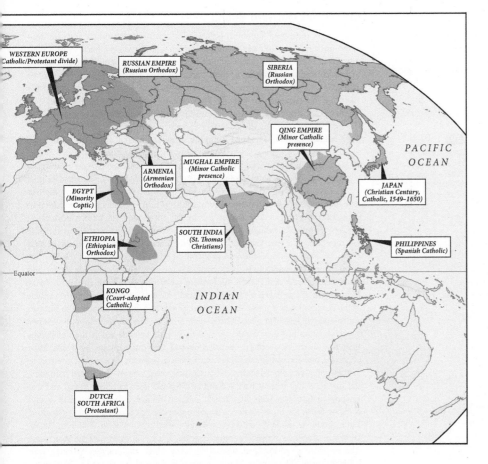

WESTERN EUROPE
(Catholic/Protestant divide)

RUSSIAN EMPIRE
(Russian Orthodox)

SIBERIA
(Russian Orthodox)

QING EMPIRE
(Minor Catholic presence)

PACIFIC OCEAN

MUGHAL EMPIRE
(Minor Catholic presence)

ARMENIA
(Armenian Orthodox)

EGYPT
(Minority Coptic)

JAPAN
(Christian Century, Catholic, 1549–1650)

SOUTH INDIA
(St. Thomas Christians)

ETHIOPIA
(Ethiopian Orthodox)

PHILIPPINES
(Spanish Catholic)

Equator

KONGO
(Court-adopted Catholic)

INDIAN OCEAN

DUTCH SOUTH AFRICA
(Protestant)

BUILDING AP® SKILLS

Making Connections: Continuity and Change

Have students continue looking at Map 5.2, "The Globalization of Christianity." Then ask: Why do you think Christianity did not gain many followers in Africa or most of Asia? *These regions had long-standing belief systems already in place that met the needs of their people. Throughout the modern era, peoples solidly rooted in Confucian, Buddhist, Hindu, or Islamic traditions proved far more resistant to the Christian message than those who practiced more localized, small-scale, orally based religions.*

fostered religious individualism, as people now read and interpreted the scriptures for themselves and sought salvation without the mediation of the Church. In the centuries that followed, some people turned that skepticism and the habit of thinking independently against all conventional religion. Thus the Protestant Reformation opened some space for new directions in European intellectual life.

In short, it was a more highly fragmented but also a renewed and revitalized Christianity that established itself around the world in the several centuries after 1500 (see Map 5.2).

BUILDING AP® SKILLS

Making Connections: Causation

Ask students: What motivated European political and economic expansion in the late fifteenth century? *Christianity and the long crusading tradition, particularly under the Spanish and Portuguese, helped to motivate expansion during this period.*

Christianity Outward Bound

Christianity motivated European political and economic expansion and also benefited from it. The resolutely Catholic Spanish and Portuguese both viewed their movement overseas as a continuation of a long crusading tradition that only recently had completed the liberation of their countries from Muslim control. When Vasco da Gama's small fleet landed in India in 1498, local authorities understandably asked, "What brought you hither?" The travelers replied that they had come "in search of Christians and of spices,"[3] with no sense of contradiction or hypocrisy in this blending of religious and material concerns.

If religion drove and justified European ventures abroad, it is difficult to imagine the globalization of Christianity (see Map 5.2) without the support of empire. Colonial settlers and traders, of course, brought their faith with them and sought to replicate it in their newly conquered homelands. New England Puritans, for example, planted a distinctive Protestant version of Christianity in North America, with an emphasis on education, moral purity, personal conversion, civic responsibility, and little tolerance for competing expressions of the faith. They did not show much interest in converting native peoples but sought rather to push them out of their ancestral territories. It was missionaries, mostly Catholic, who actively spread the Christian message beyond European communities. Organized primarily in religious orders such as the Dominicans, Franciscans, and Jesuits, Portuguese missionaries took the lead in Africa and Asia, while Spanish and French missionaries were most prominent in the Americas. Missionaries of the Russian Orthodox Church likewise accompanied the expansion of the Russian Empire across Siberia, where priests and monks ministered to Russian settlers and trappers, who often donated their first sable furs to a church or monastery.

Missionaries had their greatest success in Spanish America and in the Philippines, areas that shared two critical elements beyond their colonization by Spain. Most important, perhaps, was an overwhelming European presence, experienced variously as military conquest, colonial settlement, missionary activity, forced labor, social disruption, and disease. Surely it must have seemed as if the old gods had been bested and that any possible future lay with the powerful religion of the European invaders. A second common factor was the absence of a literate universalizing religion in these two regions. Throughout the modern era, peoples solidly rooted in Confucian, Buddhist, Hindu, or Islamic traditions proved far more resistant to the Christian message than those who practiced more localized, small-scale, orally based religions. (See Working with Evidence, page 302, for primary sources illustrating the global spread of Christianity.) Spanish America and China illustrate the difference between those societies in which Christianity became widely practiced and those that largely rejected it.

Conversion and Adaptation in Spanish America

The decisive conquest of the Aztec and Inca empires and all that followed from it—disease, population collapse, loss of land to Europeans, forced labor, resettlement—created a setting in which the religion of the victors took hold in Spanish American colonies. Europeans saw their political and military success as a demonstration of the power of

---

Making Connections: Comparison

Ask students: What was the difference between Protestant and Catholic conversion efforts during expansion? *Protestants tended to settle and push Indigenous peoples out of their ancestral homelands. Catholics worked to convert native peoples to expand Catholicism beyond the European communities.*

Making Connections: Comparison

Comparison continues to be an important skill in AP® World History: Modern. One way to have students practice this skill is to have them complete a comparison chart like the one below that compares the spread of Christianity in the Americas to the spread of Christianity in Asia and Africa. A reproducible version of this chart is available in the Teacher's Resource Materials.

Spread of Christianity in the Americas	Similarities	Spread of Christianity in Africa and Asia
■ Conversion was often forced, along with the adoption of European dress and political and social systems.	■ Christianity spread throughout the world with European missionaries.	■ Conversion was less accepted because people already had long-standing belief systems. ■ In Africa, Christianity was competing with Islam for converts, and people still participated in traditional belief systems.

TRM Handout 5.1: Graphic Organizer for the Spread of Christianity the Christian God. Native American peoples generally agreed, and by 1700 or earlier the vast majority had been baptized and saw themselves in some respects as Christians. After all, other conquerors such as the Aztecs and the Incas had always imposed their gods in some fashion on defeated peoples. So it made sense, both practically and spiritually, for many millions of Indigenous people to accept baptism, contribute to the construction of village churches, attend services, and embrace images of saints.

Despite the prominence of the Virgin Mary as a religious figure across Latin America, the cost of conversion was high, especially for women. Many women who had long served as priests, shamans, or ritual specialists had no corresponding role in a Catholic Church, led by an all-male clergy. And convent life, which had provided some outlet for female authority and education in Catholic Europe, was reserved largely for Spanish women in the Americas.

Earlier conquerors had made no attempt to eradicate local deities and religious practices. The flexibility and inclusiveness of Mesoamerican and Andean religions had made it possible for subject people to accommodate the gods of their new rulers while maintaining their own traditions. But Europeans were different. They claimed an exclusive religious truth and sought the utter destruction of local gods and everything associated with them. Operating within a Spanish colonial regime that actively encouraged conversion, missionaries often proceeded by persuasion and patient teaching. At times, though, their frustration with the persistence of "idolatry, superstition, and error" boiled over into violent campaigns designed to uproot old religions once and for all. In 1535, the bishop of Mexico proudly claimed that he had destroyed 500 pagan shrines and 20,000 idols. During the seventeenth and early eighteenth centuries, Church authorities in the Andean region periodically launched movements of "extirpation," designed to fatally undermine native religion. They destroyed religious images and ritual objects, publicly urinated on native "idols," desecrated the remains of ancestors, flogged "idolaters," and held religious trials and "processions of shame" aimed at humiliating offenders.

Such aggressive action generated resistance. Writing around 1600, the native Peruvian nobleman Guaman Poma de Ayala commented on the posture of native women toward Christianity: "They do not confess . . . nor do they go to mass. . . . And resuming their ancient customs and idolatry, they do not want to serve God or the crown."[4] Occasionally, overt resistance erupted. One such example was the religious revivalist movement in central Peru in the 1560s, known as

AP®
CAUSATION
What was the impact of European Christianity on the Native American cultures of Latin America?

▼ **AP®**
COMPARISON
How does this image show both similarities and differences between European and Latin American Christianity?

Andean Christianity Religious syncretism in the Andes emerged during the early modern era and continues to play an important role in the religious life of the region today. This modern image shows Peruvians, at an altitude of 16,000 feet, participating in a pilgrimage that combines ancient Andean celebrations of the approaching harvest and new year with a Catholic festival. (Hughes Hervé/AGE Fotostock)

EXPLORING AP® THEMES

Governance (GOV)

Ask students: What were the advantages of allowing conquered people to keep their own religion? *When conquered people were not forced to change their beliefs and traditions, they were more compliant and easier to control.*

BUILDING AP® SKILLS

Developments and Processes

Have students look at the image titled "Andean Christianity." Then ask: How do local traditions combine with Christianity in the picture to represent the blending of European Christianity and New World conversions? *The picture shows Peruvians participating in a Catholic religious procession that has elements of Inca celebrations of the approaching harvest and new year combined with a Catholic festival. This picture shows a practice that was familiar and therefore appealing to local people.*

APPLY THE TIP

Previous AP® World History Exams have asked questions about various types of forced conversions. Ask students to describe forced conversions in Latin America. *Destroying pagan shrines, images, objects, and idols symbolically destroyed the Indigenous gods and caused people to more readily accept Christianity. Desecrating the remains of ancestors to whom Indigenous people prayed for guidance removed their power. Flogging "idolaters" who refused to convert and who continued to worship the native gods set the precedent that those who refused to convert would be beaten and possibly killed. Religious trials and "processions of shame" to humiliate those who refused to convert could be devastating enough to the offenders that they would convert.*

EXPLORING AP® THEMES

Cultural Developments and Interactions (CDI)

Ask students: In what ways were Christian practices assimilated into an Andean framework? *Some people took the names of Christian saints, seeking to appropriate for themselves the religious power of Christian figures. Within Andean Christian communities, women might offer the blood of a llama to strengthen a village church or use the same material to make a cloth covering for the Virgin Mary and a shirt for an image of a huaca.*

Continue the discussion by asking students to describe how Mexican Christians incorporated aspects of pre-Christian religious beliefs into Christian practices. *In areas of daily life not specifically addressed by Christian practices, Mexican Christians used incantations, sacrifices, offerings, hallucinogenic drugs, and other means to assist themselves spiritually.*

AP EXAM TIP

You should know examples of resistance to state expansion and forced cultural conversions.

AP EXAM TIP

Past AP® Exams have asked questions about syncretic belief systems that developed after Christianity was introduced in Latin America.

Taki Onqoy (dancing sickness). Possessed by the spirits of local gods, or *huacas*, traveling dancers and teachers predicted that an alliance of Andean deities would soon overcome the Christian God, inflict the intruding Europeans with the same diseases that they had brought to the Americas, and restore the world of the Andes to an imagined earlier harmony. "The world has turned about," one member declared, "and this time God and the Spaniards [will be] defeated and all the Spaniards killed and their cities drowned . . . so that there will remain no memory of them."[5]

Even some Spanish missionaries opposed the atrocities committed against Native Americans. Most notably, Bartolomé de las Casas strongly denounced Spanish behavior, which "inhumanely and barbarously butchered and harassed [Native Americans] with several kinds of Torments, never before known." For much of his life, de las Casas sought to persuade the Spanish court to pursue a more humane approach to colonial rule on the grounds that Indigenous peoples were fully human and deserved better treatment.

More common than frontal attacks on Christianity, which colonial authorities smashed, were efforts at blending religious traditions by reinterpreting Christian practices within an Andean framework and incorporating local elements into an emerging Andean Christianity. Women, for instance, might offer the blood of a llama to strengthen a village church or make a cloth covering for the Virgin Mary and a shirt for an image of a huaca with the same material. Some Andeans continued to venerate local huacas even as they engaged with Christian missionaries who sought to destroy images and holy sites. "Father, are you tired of taking our idols from us?" asked one resilient Andean resident of a Jesuit missionary. "Take away that mountain if you can, since that is the God I worship."[6]

In Mexico as well, an immigrant Christianity was assimilated into patterns of local culture. Churches built on or near the sites of old temples became the focus of community identity. *Cofradias*, church-based associations of laypeople, organized community processions and festivals and made provisions for proper funerals and burials for their members. Central to an emerging Mexican Christianity were the saints who closely paralleled the functions of precolonial gods. Saints were imagined as parents of the local community and the true owners of its land, and their images were paraded through the streets on the occasion of great feasts and were collected by individual households. Mexico's Virgin of Guadalupe neatly combined both Mesoamerican and Spanish notions of Divine Motherhood (see the chapter-opening painting and Historians' Voices 5.1, page 311). Although parish priests were almost always Spanish, the *fiscal*, or leader of the church staff, was a native Christian of great local prestige who carried on the traditions and role of earlier religious specialists.

Throughout the colonial period and beyond, many Mexican Christians also took part in rituals derived from the past, with little sense of incompatibility with Christian practice. Incantations to various gods for good fortune in hunting, farming, or healing and sacrifices involving self-bleeding provided spiritual assistance in those areas of everyday life not directly addressed by Christian rites. Conversely, these practices also showed signs of Christian influence. Wax candles, normally used in Christian services, might now appear in front of a stone image of a precolonial god. The anger of a neglected saint, rather than that of a traditional god, might explain someone's illness and require offerings, celebration, or a new covering to regain his or her favor. In such ways did Christianity take root in the new cultural environments of Spanish America, but it was a distinctly Andean or Mexican Christianity, not merely a copy of the Spanish version.

An Asian Comparison: China and the Jesuits

The Chinese encounter with Christianity was very different from that of Native Americans in Spain's New World empire. At no point was China's political independence or cultural integrity threatened by the handful of European missionaries and traders working there during the early modern period. A strong, independent, confident China required a different missionary strategy, for Europeans needed the permission of Chinese authorities to operate in the country. Whereas Spanish missionaries working in a colonial setting sought to convert the masses, the **Jesuits in China**, the leading missionary order there, took deliberate aim at the official Chinese elite. Following the example of their most famous missionary, Matteo Ricci (in China 1582–1610), many Jesuits learned Chinese, became thoroughly acquainted with classical Confucian texts, and dressed like Chinese scholars. Initially, they downplayed their mission to convert and instead emphasized their interest in exchanging ideas and learning from China's ancient culture. For a time in the seventeenth and early eighteenth centuries, the Jesuits found favor at the Chinese imperial court. Their Western mathematical, astronomical, technological, and mapmaking skills rendered them useful, and the emperor appointed a series of Jesuits to head the Chinese Bureau of Astronomy.

In presenting Christian teachings, Jesuits were at pains to be respectful of Chinese culture, pointing out parallels between Confucianism and Christianity rather than portraying Christianity as something new and foreign. They chose to define Chinese rituals honoring the emperor or venerating ancestors as secular or civil observances rather than as religious practices that had to be abandoned. Such efforts to accommodate Chinese culture contrast sharply with the frontal attacks on Native American religions in the Spanish Empire.

The religious and cultural outcomes of the missionary enterprise likewise differed greatly in the two regions. Nothing approaching mass conversion to Christianity took place in China, as it had in Latin America. During the sixteenth and seventeenth centuries, a modest number of Chinese scholars and officials did become Christians, attracted by the personal lives of the missionaries, by their interest in Western science, and by the moral certainty that Christianity offered. Among ordinary people, Christianity spread very modestly amid tales of miracles attributed to the Christian God, while missionary teachings about "eternal life" sounded to some like Daoist prescriptions for immortality. At most, though, missionary efforts over the course of some 250 years (1550–1800) resulted in 200,000 to 300,000 converts, a minuscule number in a Chinese population approaching 300 million by 1800. What explains the very limited acceptance of Christianity in early modern China?

Fundamentally, the missionaries offered little that the Chinese really wanted. Confucianism for the elites and Buddhism, Daoism, and a multitude of Chinese gods and spirits

AP®
COMPARISON
In what different ways did Chinese authorities respond to Christian missionaries?

AP® EXAM TIP
You should be able to describe the significance of the Jesuit missionary effort in China.

AP®
CONTEXTUALIZATION
Why were missionary efforts to spread Christianity less successful in China than in Latin America?

Cultural Developments and Interactions (CDI)

Have students look at the image titled "Jesuits in China." Ask: What elements of cultural or religious syncretism can be seen in the image? *Jesuit missionaries are wearing the traditional robes and headgear of Confucian scholars, and scriptures are written in Chinese on the Christian altar.*

Bell Ringer

Blending was common as religious traditions spread. Ask students to read the introductory paragraph on page 274 under "Persistence and Change in Afro-Asian Cultural Traditions," and ask them if they have heard of any of these blended traditions. *Answers will vary.*

Jesuits in China In this seventeenth-century engraving, two Jesuit missionaries stand before a Christian altar in China dressed in the clothing of imperial officials. The Jesuits were initially welcomed among the educated elite of the country because of their Western learning, particularly in the fields of astronomy and mapmaking, even if their Christian missionary endeavors were less warmly received. (Bridgeman Art Library/Image Partner/Getty Images)

▲ **AP®**
MAKING CONNECTIONS
What evidence of cultural or religious syncretism can be seen in the painting?

at the local level adequately supplied the spiritual needs of most Chinese. Furthermore, it became increasingly clear that Christianity was an all-or-nothing faith that required converts to abandon much of traditional Chinese culture. Christian monogamy, for example, seemed to require Chinese men to put away their concubines. What would happen to these deserted women? Finally, despite all their efforts, Christian missionaries remained outsiders in China. From the mid-seventeenth century on, this status was only reinforced in the minds of many Chinese elites by the growing numbers of Europeans in East Asia, most of whom did not try to assimilate into Chinese culture, and the Jesuits' willingness to work under what many saw as the foreign and uncivilized Manchus after the Qing dynasty seized power in 1644. (For more on Ming and Qing dynasty China, see "Into Central Asia: The Making of a Chinese Empire" in Chapter 4.)

By the early eighteenth century, the papacy and competing missionary orders came to oppose the Jesuit policy of accommodation. The pope claimed authority over Chinese Christians and declared that sacrifices to Confucius and the veneration of ancestors were "idolatry" and thus forbidden to Christians (see Working with Evidence, Document 6). The pope's pronouncements represented an unacceptable challenge to the authority of the emperor and an affront to Chinese culture. In 1715, an outraged Emperor Kangxi prohibited Westerners from spreading Christian doctrine in his kingdom. This represented a major turning point in the relationship between Christian missionaries and Chinese society. Many were subsequently expelled, and missionaries lost favor at court.

Persistence and Change in Afro-Asian Cultural Traditions

Finding the Main Point: In what ways did Afro-Asian religions change in the early modern era?

Although Europeans were central players in the globalization of Christianity, theirs was not the only expanding or transformed culture of the early modern era. African religious ideas and practices, for example, accompanied enslaved people to the Americas. Common African forms of religious revelation—divination, dream interpretation, visions, spirit possession—found a place in the Africanized versions of Christianity that emerged in the New World. Europeans frequently perceived these practices as evidence of sorcery, witchcraft, or even devil worship and tried to suppress them. Nonetheless, syncretic (blended) religions such as Vodou in Haiti, Santeria in Cuba, and Candomblé and Macumba in Brazil persisted. They derived from various West African traditions and featured drumming, ritual dancing, animal sacrifice, and spirit possession. Over time, they incorporated Christian beliefs and practices such as church attendance, the search for salvation, and the use of candles and crucifixes and often identified their various spirits or deities with Catholic saints.

Expansion and Renewal in the Islamic World

In 1500 Islamic civilization was far more widespread than that of Christendom. From its beginning during the life of the Prophet Muhammad (570–632), Islam had become rooted in its Middle Eastern heartland. It had also established itself in Central, South, and Southeast Asia, in both East and West Africa, and in southeastern Europe. The early modern era witnessed the continuation of this "long march of Islam" across the Afro-Asian world as the expansion of the Islamic frontier, a process already a thousand years in the making, extended farther still.

Conversion to Islam generally did not mean a sudden abandonment of old religious practices in favor of the new. Rather, it was more often a matter of "assimilating Islamic rituals, cosmologies, and literatures into . . . local religious systems."[7] Continued Islamization was not usually the product of conquering armies and expanding empires. It depended instead on wandering Muslim holy men or Sufis, Islamic scholars, and itinerant traders, none of whom posed a threat to local rulers. In fact, such people often were useful to those rulers and their communities. They offered literacy in Arabic, established informal schools, provided protective charms containing passages from the Quran, served as advisers to local authorities and healers to the sick, often intermarried with local people, and generally did not insist that new converts give up their older practices. What they offered, in short, was connection to the wider, prestigious, prosperous world of Islam. Islamization extended modestly even to the Americas, particularly in Brazil, where Muslims led a number of slave revolts in the early nineteenth century.

The islands of Southeast Asia illustrate the diversity of belief and practice that accompanied the spread of Islam in the early modern era. During the seventeenth century in Aceh, a Muslim sultanate on the northern tip of Sumatra, authorities sought to enforce the dietary codes and almsgiving practices of Islamic law. After four successive women ruled the area in the late seventeenth century, women were forbidden from exercising political power. On Muslim Java, however, numerous women served in royal courts, and women throughout Indonesia continued their longtime role as buyers and sellers in local markets. Among ordinary Javanese, traditional animistic practices of spirit worship coexisted easily with a tolerant and accommodating Islam, while merchants often embraced a more orthodox version of the religion in line with Middle Eastern traditions.

AP® EXAM TIP

Be able to identify examples of syncretic belief systems, but more importantly, understand how these syncretic practices emerged.

AP®

CONTINUITY AND CHANGE

What new departures in cultural life are apparent in the Islamic world, China, and India during the early modern era?

AP®

CONTINUITY AND CHANGE

What accounts for the continued spread of Islam in the early modern era and for the emergence of reform or renewal movements within the Islamic world?

APPLY THE TIP

Divide your class into small groups and have them research one of the syncretic religions mentioned in the text on page 275 or another of their choosing. Questions to consider include the following:

■ Where was the religion practiced?

■ Is it still practiced today?

■ What are the characteristics of the religion?

■ How is it a blended (syncretic) religion?

■ How did nonpractitioners react to the religion?

After students have completed their research, have them share their information with the class. *Answers will vary.*

To check for understanding, have students practice their writing skills by writing an LEQ-style body paragraph answering the following prompt:

■ Evaluate the extent to which the syncretic forms of Afro-Asian Christianity <u>differed</u> from the syncretic forms of Latin American Christianity.

Differentiation

If you want to differentiate this activity, follow the "Must Do, Should Do, Strive For" model below.

■ Must Do: Students research the material with their group.

■ Should Do: Students need to participate at least once during the class discussion.

■ Strive For: Students will use what they have learned from this research to write the LEQ paragraph above.

TEACHING IDEA

Class Discussion

Ask students: What did Islam offer converts that allowed it to spread so easily? *It offered literacy and education in general as well as access to the prosperous world of Islam.*

One of the most visible and well known of the changes in religions in the early modern era was the Wahhabi movement in Arabia. Have students read about Wahhabism on page 276 and ask the following question: What was the impact of the Wahhabi movement on Arabia? *The Wahhabi movement led to the formation of a centralized state in central Arabia that removed aspects of Islam that did not adhere to absolute monotheism. It eliminated anything the movement felt was not authorized by the religious teachings of Islam.*

EXPLORING AP® THEMES

Social Interactions and Organization (SIO)

Ask students to describe how the role of women changed under the Wahhabi movement. *The Wahhabi movement allowed for more rights for women, which had been embedded in Islamic law, such as the right to consent to and stipulate conditions for marriage, control their dowry, divorce, and engage in commerce. It did not force head-to-toe covering in public and allowed the mixing of unrelated men and women for business or medical purposes.*

AP®
CONTINUITY AND CHANGE
How did Islam change as the religion spread to new regions?

AP®
CAUSATION
What local cultural or religious traditions account for the rise of Islamic reform or renewal movements?

AP® EXAM TIP
You will run across many examples of how religious traditions change over time and region. Be able to compare and contrast those changes across religions and time periods.

To such orthodox Muslims, religious syncretism, which accompanied Islamization almost everywhere, became increasingly offensive, even heretical. Such sentiments played an important role in movements of religious renewal and reform that emerged throughout the vast Islamic world of the eighteenth century. The leaders of such movements sharply criticized those practices that departed from earlier patterns established by Muhammad and from the authority of the Quran. For example, in India, governed by the Muslim Mughal Empire, religious resistance to official policies that accommodated Hindus found concrete expression during the reign of the emperor Aurangzeb (r. 1658–1707) (see "On the Frontiers of Islam: The Mughal and Songhay Empires" in Chapter 4). A series of religious wars in West Africa during the eighteenth and early nineteenth centuries took aim at corrupt Islamic practices and the rulers, Muslim and non-Muslim alike, who permitted them. In Southeast and Central Asia, tension grew between practitioners of localized and blended versions of Islam and those who sought to purify such practices in the name of a more authentic and universal faith.

The most well-known and widely visible of these Islamic renewal movements took place during the mid-eighteenth century in Arabia, the original homeland of the faith, where they found expression in the teachings of the Islamic scholar Muhammad Ibn Abd al-Wahhab (1703–1792). The growing difficulties of the Islamic world, such as the weakening of the Ottoman Empire, were directly related, he argued, to deviations from the pure faith of early Islam. Al-Wahhab was particularly upset by common religious practices in central Arabia that seemed to him idolatry—the widespread veneration of Sufi saints and their tombs, the adoration of natural sites, and even the respect paid to Muhammad's tomb at Medina. In the view of Al-Wahhab, all of this was a dilution of the absolute monotheism of authentic Islam.

The Wahhabi movement took a new turn in the 1740s when it received the political backing of Muhammad Ibn Saud, a local ruler who found al-Wahhab's ideas compelling. With Ibn Saud's support, the religious movement became an expansive state in central Arabia. Within that state, offending tombs were razed; "idols" were eliminated; books on logic were destroyed; the use of tobacco, hashish, and musical instruments was forbidden; and certain taxes not authorized by religious teaching were abolished.

Although **Wahhabi Islam** has long been identified with sharp restrictions on women, al-Wahhab himself generally emphasized the rights of women within a patriarchal Islamic framework. These included a woman's right to consent to and stipulate conditions for a marriage, to control her dowry, to divorce, and to engage in commerce. Such rights, long embedded in Islamic law, had apparently been forgotten or ignored in eighteenth-century Arabia. Furthermore, al-Wahhab did not insist on head-to-toe covering of women in public and allowed for the mixing of unrelated men and women for business or medical purposes.

By the early nineteenth century, this new reformist state encompassed much of central Arabia, with Mecca itself coming under Wahhabi control in 1803 (see Map 5.3). Although an Egyptian army broke the power of the Wahhabis in 1818, the movement's influence continued to spread across the Islamic world. Together with the ongoing expansion of the religion, these movements of reform and renewal signaled the continuing cultural vitality of the Islamic world even as the European presence on the world stage assumed larger dimensions.

China: New Directions in an Old Tradition

Neither China nor India experienced cultural or religious change as dramatic as that of the Reformation in Europe or the Wahhabi movement in Arabia. Nor did Confucian or Hindu cultures during the early modern era spread widely, as did Christianity and Islam. Nonetheless, neither of these traditions remained static. As in Christian Europe, challenges to established orthodoxies in China and India emerged as commercial and urban life, as well as political change, fostered new thinking.

China during the Ming and Qing dynasties continued to operate broadly within a Confucian framework, enriched now by the insights of Buddhism and Daoism to generate a system of thought called Neo-Confucianism. Chinese Ming dynasty rulers, in their aversion to the despised Mongols, embraced and actively supported this native Confucian tradition and expanded its famous civil service system. So too did the foreign Qing rulers in an effort to woo Chinese intellectuals to support the new dynasty. Within this context, a considerable amount of controversy, debate, and new thinking emerged during the early modern era.

During late Ming times, for example, the influential thinker **Wang Yangming** (1472–1529) argued that "intuitive moral knowledge exists in people . . . even robbers know that they should not rob."[8] Thus anyone could achieve a virtuous life by introspection and contemplation, without the extended education, study of classical texts, and constant striving for improvement that traditional Confucianism prescribed for an elite class of "gentlemen." Such ideas figured prominently among Confucian scholars of the sixteenth century, although critics contended that such thinking promoted an excessive individualism. Critics also argued that Wang Yangming's ideas had undermined the Ming dynasty and contributed to China's conquest by the foreign Qing. Some Chinese Buddhists as well sought to make their religion more accessible to ordinary people by suggesting that laypeople at home could undertake practices

Map 5.3 The Expansion of Wahhabi Islam
From its base in central Arabia, the Wahhabi movement represented a challenge to the Ottoman Empire, while its ideas subsequently spread widely within the Islamic world.

▲ AP®

CAUSATION

How did the spread of the Wahhabi movement displayed in the map influence the practice of Islam in Arabia?

AP®

CONTINUITY AND CHANGE

What kinds of cultural changes occurred in China during the early modern era? What would account for those changes?

AP®

COMPARISON

How did Neo-Confucianism differ from traditional Confucianism?

BUILDING AP® SKILLS

Making Connections: Continuity and Change

Ask students: Why did some accuse Neo-Confucianism of promoting individualism? *Neo-Confucians believed that "intuitive moral knowledge" exists in all people, whatever their rank or education. Any individual could achieve a virtuous life through individual contemplation.*

BUILDING AP® SKILLS

Making Connections: Comparison

Students can often get traditional Confucian teachings confused with Neo-Confucian teaching. Ask students: How did Neo-Confucianism differ from traditional Confucianism? *Neo-Confucianism contained aspects of Buddhism and Daoism and promoted ideas that did not require the study of Confucian texts to raise one's social position. Traditional Confucianism required the study of Confucian texts and did not promote Buddhism or Daoism.*

Dream of the Red Chamber This mid-eighteenth-century image depicts a garden scene from *The Dream of the Red Chamber*, a wildly popular epic novel that found a wide readership in Qing China and is now considered one of China's "Four Great Classical Novels." (Pictures from History/Bridgeman Images)

▲ **AP**

CONTINUITY AND CHANGE
What does this image suggest about the roles of elite women in China?

AP **EXAM TIP**
Understand the attempts to connect Hindu and Muslim beliefs in South Asia in this era.

AP
CAUSATION
What caused the cultural changes that took place in India during the early modern period?

similar to those performed by monks in monasteries. Withdrawal from the world was not necessary for enlightenment. This kind of moral or religious individualism bore some similarity to the thinking of Martin Luther, who argued that individuals could seek salvation by "faith alone," without the assistance of a priestly hierarchy.

While such matters occupied the intellectual elite of China, in the cities a lively popular culture emerged among the less educated. For city-dwellers, plays, paintings, short stories, and especially novels provided diversion and entertainment that were a step up from what could be found in teahouses and wineshops. Numerous "how-to" painting manuals allowed a larger public to participate in this favorite Chinese art form. Even though Confucian scholars disdained popular fiction, a vigorous printing industry responded to the growing demand for exciting novels. The most famous was Cao Xueqin's mid-eighteenth-century novel **The Dream of the Red Chamber**, a huge book that contained 120 chapters and some 400 characters, most of them women. It explored the social life of an eighteenth-century elite family with connections to the Chinese court.

India: Bridging the Hindu/Muslim Divide

In a largely Hindu India, ruled by the Muslim Mughal Empire, several significant cultural departures took shape in the early modern era that brought Hindus and Muslims together in new forms of religious expression. At the level of elite culture, the Mughal ruler Akbar formulated a state cult that combined elements of Islam, Hinduism, and Zoroastrianism (see "On the Frontiers of Islam: The Mughal and Songhay Empires" in Chapter 4). The Mughal court also embraced Renaissance Christian art, and soon murals featuring Jesus, Mary, and Christian saints appeared on the walls of palaces, garden pavilions, and harems. Muslim political and religious authorities likewise sought to incorporate Hindu-based yoga postures and breathing exercises into Sufi practice. (See Looking Again: Religious Interaction in Indian Art, page 299.)

Within popular culture, the flourishing of a devotional form of Hinduism known as *bhakti* also bridged the gulf separating Hindu and Muslim. Through songs, prayers, dances, poetry, and rituals, devotees sought to achieve union with one or another of India's many deities. Appealing especially to women, the bhakti movement provided an avenue for social criticism. Its practitioners often set aside caste distinctions and disregarded the detailed rituals of the Brahmin priests in favor of personal religious experience. Among the most beloved of bhakti poets was **Mirabai** (1498–1547), a high-caste woman from northern India who upon her husband's death abandoned her upper-class family and conventional Hindu practice. Much of her poetry deals with her yearning for union with Krishna, a Hindu deity she regarded as her husband, lover, and lord. This mystical dimension of the bhakti movement had much in common with Sufi forms of Islam, which also emphasized direct experience of the Divine. Such similarities helped blur the distinction between Hinduism and Islam in India, as both bhaktis and Sufis honored spiritual sages and all those seeking after God.

Yet another major cultural change that blended Islam and Hinduism emerged with the growth of **Sikhism** as a new and distinctive religious tradition in the Punjab region of northern India. Its founder, Guru Nanak (1469–1539), had been involved in the bhakti movement but came to believe that "there is no Hindu; there is no Muslim; only God." His teachings and those of subsequent gurus also generally ignored caste distinctions and untouchability and ended the seclusion of women, while proclaiming the "brotherhood of all mankind" as well as the essential equality of men and women. Drawing converts from Punjabi peasants and merchants, both Muslim and Hindu, the Sikhs gradually became a separate religious community. They developed their own sacred book, known as the Guru Granth (teacher book); created a central place of worship and pilgrimage in the Golden Temple of Amritsar; and prescribed certain dress requirements for men, including keeping hair and beards uncut, wearing a turban, and carrying a short sword. During the seventeenth century, Sikhs encountered hostility from both the Mughal Empire and some of their Hindu neighbors. In response, Sikhism evolved from a peaceful religious movement, blending Hindu and Muslim elements, into a militant community whose military skills were highly valued by the British when they took over India in the late eighteenth century.

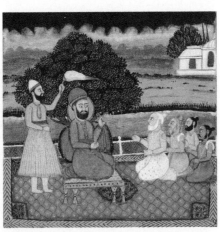

Guru Nanak This painting shows a seated Guru Nanak, the founder of Sikhism, disputing with four kneeling Hindu holy men. (© British Library Board. All Rights Reserved /Bridgeman Images)

▲ **AP**
COMPARISON
How was the role of Guru Nanak, as depicted in this painting, similar to the role Martin Luther played in the Reformation?

AP
COMPARISON
In what ways did religious changes in Asia and the Middle East parallel those in Europe, and in what ways were they different?

A New Way of Thinking: The Birth of Modern Science

Finding the Main Point: What were the main causes and long-term effects of the Scientific Revolution?

While some Europeans were actively attempting to spread the Christian faith to distant corners of the world, others were developing an understanding of the cosmos at least partially at odds with Christian teaching. These were the makers of the

AP® EXAM TIP
Understand the causes, as well as the long-term effects, of the Scientific Revolution.

AP®
CAUSATION
What conflicts did the Scientific Revolution cause in Europe?

AP®
CAUSATION
What factors help to explain the birth of modern science in Europe?

AP®
COMPARISON
Why did the Scientific Revolution occur in Europe rather than in China or the Islamic world?

Scientific Revolution, a vast intellectual and cultural transformation that took place between the mid-sixteenth and early eighteenth centuries. These new scientists no longer relied on the external authority of the Bible, the Church, the speculations of ancient philosophers, or the received wisdom of cultural tradition. For them, knowledge was acquired through rational inquiry based on evidence, the product of human minds alone. Many who created this revolution saw themselves as departing radically from older ways of thinking. "The old rubbish must be thrown away," wrote a seventeenth-century English scientist. "These are the days that must lay a new Foundation of a more magnificent Philosophy."[9]

The long-term significance of the Scientific Revolution was enormous. Within European elite circles, it fundamentally altered ideas about the place of humankind within the cosmos and sharply challenged both the teachings and the authority of the Church. When applied to the affairs of human society, scientific ways of thinking challenged ancient social hierarchies and political systems and played a role in the revolutionary upheavals of the modern era. But scientific inquiry was also used to legitimize existing gender and racial inequalities, giving new support to old ideas about the natural inferiority of women and enslaved people. When married to the technological innovations of the Industrial Revolution, science fostered both the marvels of modern production and the horrors of modern means of destruction. By the twentieth century, science had become so widespread that it largely lost its association with European culture and became the chief marker of global modernity. Like Buddhism, Christianity, and Islam, modern science became a universal worldview, open to all who could accept its premises and its techniques. Over the past several centuries, it has substantially eroded religious belief and practice, particularly among the well educated in the West.

The Question of Origins

Why did Europeans take a leading role in the Scientific Revolution, and why did it occur during the early modern period? One critical factor was Europe's ability to draw on technological and scientific advances made elsewhere in Afro-Eurasia. China's technological accomplishments, based on practical knowledge of the natural world, were unmatched anywhere in the several centuries after 1000, and many of its innovations flowed to Europe in the centuries before the Scientific Revolution. There they inspired further practical discoveries. Speaking of the development of printing, gunpowder, and the magnetic compass, a prominent seventeenth-century English scientist, Francis Bacon, declared that "no empire, no sect, no star, seems to have exerted greater power and influence in human affairs than these mechanical discoveries."[10] While Bacon described the origins of these technologies as "obscure and inglorious," we now know that all three appeared first in China.

From the realm of Islam, Europeans accessed both ancient Greek learning and the remarkable achievements of Muslim scholars. After 1000 or so, this learning entered Christian Europe in an explosion of translations from Greek and

Arabic into Latin, primarily accomplished in regions of southern Spain and Sicily where Christian states came to rule over formerly Muslim territories. The prolific Aristotle, with his logical approach and "scientific temperament," made the deepest impression, helping to fuel a growing interest in rational thought and confidence in human reason. But European thinkers also learned from scholars in the Islamic world. Muslim thinkers had brought together ancient Greek and Persian learning, Indian mathematics, and the Muslim belief in a single all-powerful creator God to achieve significant breakthroughs in optics, astronomy, medicine, pharmacology, and much more. Muslim scholars pioneered new approaches to systematic observation, experimental science, and the application of mathematics to the study of the natural world, all of which were similar to approaches later taken up by European scientists.

Then, starting in the fifteenth century, Europeans found themselves at the center of a massive new exchange of information created by their expanding overseas empires, commercial networks, and missionary initiatives. As they became aware of lands, peoples, plants, animals, societies, and religions from around the world, this unprecedented tidal wave of new knowledge, uniquely available to Europeans, shook up older ways of thinking. It also stoked curiosity, fueled discoveries and inventions, and sparked the development of new tools to manage knowledge, including natural history collections, botanical gardens, and classification systems. The sixteenth-century Italian doctor, mathematician, and writer Girolamo Cardano (1501–1576) expressed a sense of wonderment at these developments: "The most unusual [circumstance of my life] is that I was born in this century in which the whole world became known; whereas the ancients were familiar with but a little more than a third part of it." He worried, however, that amid this explosion of knowledge, "certainties will be exchanged for uncertainties."[11] It was precisely those uncertainties—skepticism about established views—that provided such a fertile cultural ground for the emergence of modern science. The Reformation too contributed to that cultural climate in its challenge to authority, its encouragement of mass literacy, and its affirmation of secular professions.

The needs of new overseas empires and commerce also drove scientific and technological advances. Europeans focused considerable resources on improving navigation, cartography, and shipbuilding to facilitate their long-distance voyages; ballistics and artillery to maintain their superiority in naval warfare; and mining techniques to produce the precious metals that they used to trade in Asian markets. Some innovations occurred overseas. In the Spanish Empire, shipbuilders discovered new types of timber and tree resins in the forests of the Americas and the Philippines, while entrepreneurs developed new processes for extracting silver from low-grade ores in the mining centers of the Andes and Mexico.

Across the globe, Europeans drew on the knowledge of Indigenous peoples as they sought local products, technologies, and natural resources that possessed economic or other potential value. For his botanical catalog of local plants, for instance, one French trading company official in India relied on Hindu holy men and healers with "a lot of wisdom" to identify and describe the uses of native plants.[12] He also

AP® EXAM TIP
Be able to explain how previous cross-cultural exchanges contributed to the Scientific Revolution.

AP® EXAM TIP
This paragraph is a good example of how cross-cultural interactions create change.

AP®
DEVELOPMENTS AND PROCESSES
In what ways did the Scientific Revolution emerge from a global context, not just a European framework?

APPLY THE TIP

Have students read the first full paragraph on page 281 about the cross-cultural interactions between Europe and the Islamic world. Then ask: What changes came about because of the interactions between Europe and the Islamic world in this time period? *The new knowledge coming in from the Islamic world shook up the older ways of thinking in Europe and led the way to new conceptions of the world. Arab medical texts, astronomical research, and translations of Greek classics led to the creation of European natural philosophy (what later became science).*

EXPLORING AP® THEMES

Cultural Developments and Interactions (CDI)

This is a good place to point out that just as China and the Islamic world had an impact on Western Europe, Western Europe also had an impact on the Islamic world and other areas. Ask students: What was the impact of Western European interaction with the Islamic world and other areas during the early modern period? *New knowledge in the form of ancient texts as well as technology from the Islamic world allowed Western Europe to advance and led to the development of modern science.*

employed local artists who drew hundreds of scientifically exact images and Indigenous gardeners who traveled sometimes hundreds of miles to secure live specimens.

If growing contact with other regions of the world provided critical impetus for Europe's Scientific Revolution, its historical development as a reinvigorated and fragmented civilization also gave rise to conditions particularly favorable to the scientific enterprise. By the twelfth and thirteenth centuries, Europeans had evolved a legal system that guaranteed a measure of independence for a variety of institutions—the Church, towns and cities, guilds, professional associations, and universities. This legal revolution was based on the idea of the "corporation," a collective group of people that was treated as a unit, a legal person, with certain rights to regulate and control its own members. Most important for the development of science was the emergence of universities as corporations with legal privileges that allowed scholars to pursue their studies in relative freedom from the dictates of Church or state authorities. Within them, the study of the natural world began slowly to separate itself from philosophy and theology and to gain a distinct identity. Their curricula featured "a core of readings and lectures that were basically scientific," drawing heavily on the writings of Aristotle, which had only recently become available to Western Europeans.[13] Most of the major European figures in the Scientific Revolution were trained in universities, and after the mid-seventeenth century another type of corporation, the scientific academy, emerged in which science was also disseminated and discussed.

Science as Cultural Revolution

While knowledge flowing along new global networks transformed European understandings of the natural world, it was breakthroughs in the study of the heavens that most directly challenged traditional Christian understandings of the universe. Before the Scientific Revolution, educated Europeans held to an ancient view of the world in which the earth was stationary and at the center of the universe, and around it revolved the sun, moon, and stars embedded in ten spheres of transparent crystal. This understanding coincided well with the religious outlook of the Catholic Church because the attention of the entire universe was centered on the earth and its human inhabitants, among whom God's plan for salvation unfolded. It was a universe of divine purpose, with angels guiding the hierarchically arranged heavenly bodies along their way while God watched over the whole from his realm beyond the spheres. The Scientific Revolution was revolutionary because it fundamentally challenged this understanding of the cosmos.

The initial breakthrough came from the Polish mathematician and astronomer Nicolaus **Copernicus**, whose famous book *On the Revolutions of the Heavenly Spheres* was published in the year of his death, 1543. Its essential argument was that "at the middle of all things lies the sun" and that the earth, like the other planets, revolved around it. Thus, the earth was no longer unique or at the obvious center of God's attention.

AP
CAUSATION
Explain how the rise of universities contributed to the Scientific Revolution.

AP EXAM TIP
Here's another example of the roles played by cities in world history: the rise of universities in major European towns.

AP
CONTINUITY AND CHANGE
What was revolutionary about the Scientific Revolution and all that followed from it?

AP EXAM TIP
The Scientific Revolution marked a major turning point in the way Westerners saw the world around them. As you continue studying topics in the modern era, like the Enlightenment, keep in mind how the Scientific Revolution led to these new developments.

APPLY THE TIP

Ask students to describe how the rise of universities reflected the role of cities in world history. *As cities grew and more people began to separate church teachings and scientific inquiry, cities became the safe place to do research. Universities, usually located in cities, became safe places to pursue scientific investigations. Major cities began to represent the ability of intellectuals to pursue their studies without fear of persecution from the Church or the state, including the study of the natural order as it began to gain a distinct identity.*

APPLY THE TIP

The Scientific Revolution changed the way that people looked at the world around them. Ask students: How did the new world outlook affect the culture of Europe at the time? *The Scientific Revolution led people to question church teachings, which further caused the separation between church and state. This occurred at a time when the Catholic Church was struggling to justify its importance.*

But it took more than a century for numerous astronomers, natural philosophers, and mathematicians to empirically prove that Copernicus was correct and to overturn other aspects of the traditional earth-centered cosmos. In the early seventeenth century Johannes Kepler, a German mathematician, showed that the planets followed elliptical orbits, undermining the ancient belief that they moved in perfect circles. In 1609 the Italian **Galileo** (gal-uh-LAY-oh) developed an improved telescope, with which he made many observations that undermined established understandings of celestial bodies (see Zooming In: Galileo and the Telescope: Reflecting on Science and Religion, page 284). Some thinkers began to discuss the notion of an unlimited universe in which humankind occupied a mere speck of dust in an unimaginable vastness. The seventeenth-century French mathematician and philosopher Blaise Pascal perhaps spoke for many when he wrote, "The eternal silence of these infinite spaces frightens me."[14]

The culmination of this new science of the heavens came in the work of Sir Isaac **Newton** (1642–1727), the Englishman who formulated the modern laws of motion and mechanics, which remained unchallenged until the twentieth century. At the core of Newton's thinking was the concept of universal gravitation. "All bodies whatsoever," Newton declared, "are endowed with a principle of mutual gravitation."[15] Here was the grand unifying idea of early modern astronomy and physics. The radical implication of this view was that the heavens and the earth, long regarded as separate and distinct spheres, were not so different after all, for the motion of a cannonball or the falling of an apple obeyed the same natural laws that governed the orbiting planets. While often portrayed as a solitary genius, Newton tested and sometimes revised his thinking in light of data gathered across the globe on such natural phenomena as the motion of pendulums near the equator, tides in Southeast Asia, and the stars of the southern sky.

By the time Newton died, a revolutionary new understanding of the physical universe had emerged among educated Europeans: the universe was no longer propelled by supernatural forces but functioned on its own according to scientific principles that could be described mathematically. Articulating this view, Kepler wrote, "The machine of the universe is not similar to a divine animated being but similar to a clock."[16] Furthermore, it was a machine that regulated itself, requiring neither God nor angels to account for its normal operation.

▼ **AP**
CONTEXTUALIZATION
What does the development of the telescope show about European cultural and economic development?

The Telescope Johannes Hevelius, an astronomer of German Lutheran background living in what is now Poland, constructed extraordinarily long telescopes in the mid-seventeenth century with which he observed sunspots, charted the surface of the moon, and discovered several comets. Such telescopes played a central role in transforming understandings of the universe during the Scientific Revolution. (World History Archive/Alamy)

EXPLORING AP® THEMES

Cultural Developments and Interactions (CDI)

Many scientists contributed to the Scientific Revolution; however, there are some that students need to know. Ask students to create a chart like the one here of scientists and their contributions. Include a column that describes the impact of the contributions. A reproducible version of this chart is available in the Teacher's Resource Materials. (Answers are provided in italics.)

Scientist	Contribution(s)	Impact
Johannes Kepler (German mathematician)	*Discovered the elliptical orbit of planets*	*Changed accepted beliefs of planetary movement*
Nicolaus Copernicus (Polish astronomer and mathematician)	*Determined that the sun, not the earth, is the center of the solar system*	*Influenced Galileo's studies*
Galileo Galilei (Italian philosopher, mathematician, and astronomer)	*Improved the telescope, discovered some of the moons of Jupiter, supported the Copernican worldview*	*Allowed for the observation of the cosmos, undermined accepted beliefs*
Isaac Newton (English mathematician and scientist)	*Discovered the laws of motion, gravity, and mechanics*	*Laid the foundation for modern physics*

TRM **Handout 5.2: Chart for Scientists and Their Contributions**

ZOOMING **IN** ## Galileo and the Telescope: Reflecting on Science and Religion

Galileo on trial.

The Scientific Revolution was predicated on the idea that knowledge of how the universe worked was acquired through a combination of careful observations, controlled experiments, and the formulation of general laws, expressed in mathematical terms. Perhaps no single invention enabled the Scientific Revolution more than telescopes, the first of which were produced in the early seventeenth century by Dutch eyeglass makers.

The impact of new instruments depended on how scientists employed them. In the case of the telescope, it was the brilliant Italian mathematician and astronomer Galileo Galilei (1564–1642) who unlocked its potential when he used it to observe the night sky. Within months of creating his own telescope, which improved on earlier designs, Galileo made a series of discoveries that called into question well-established understandings of the cosmos. He observed craters on the moon and sunspots, or blemishes, moving across the face of the sun, which challenged the traditional notion that no imperfection or change marred the heavenly bodies. Moreover, his discovery of the moons of Jupiter and many new stars suggested a cosmos far larger than the finite universe of traditional astronomy. In 1610, Galileo published his remarkable findings in a book titled *The Starry Messenger*, where he emphasized time and again that his precise observations provided irrefutable evidence of a cosmos unlike that described by traditional authorities. "With the aid of the telescope," he argued, "this has been scrutinized so directly and with such ocular certainty that all the disputes which have vexed the philosophers through so many ages have been resolved, and we are at last freed from wordy debates about it."[17]

Galileo's empirical evidence transformed the debate over the nature of the cosmos. His dramatic and unexpected discoveries were readily grasped, and with the aid of a telescope anyone could confirm their veracity. His

photo: Bridgeman Images

AP®
COMPARISON
How was Kepler's idea that "the machine of the universe is not similar to a divine animated being but similar to a clock" different from the Catholic Church's understanding of the universe?

Knowledge of that universe could be obtained through human reason alone—by observation, deduction, and experimentation—without the aid of ancient authorities or divine revelation.

Like the physical universe, the human body also lost some of its mystery. The careful dissections of cadavers and animals enabled doctors and scientists to describe the human body with much greater accuracy and to understand the circulation of the blood throughout the body. The heart was no longer the mysterious center of the body's heat and the seat of its passions; instead it was just another machine, a complex muscle that functioned as a pump.

Much of this scientific thinking developed in the face of strenuous opposition from the Catholic Church, for both its teachings and its authority were under attack. The Italian philosopher Giordano Bruno, proclaiming an infinite universe and many worlds, was burned at the stake in 1600, and Galileo was compelled by initial findings were heralded by many in the scientific community, including Christoph Clavius, the Church's leading astronomer in Rome. Galileo's findings led him to conclude that Copernicus (1473–1543), an earlier astronomer and mathematician, had been correct when he had advanced the theory that the sun rather than the earth was at the center of the solar system. But Galileo's evidence could not definitively prove Copernicus's theory to the satisfaction of critics, leading Galileo to study other phenomena, such as the tides, that could provide further evidence that the earth was in motion.

When the Church condemned Copernicus's theory in 1616, it remained silent on Galileo's astronomical observations, instead warning him to refrain from teaching or promoting Copernicus's ideas. Ultimately, though, Galileo came into conflict with Church authorities when in 1629 he published, with what he thought was the consent of the Church, the *Dialogue Concerning the Two Chief World Systems*, a work sympathetic to Copernicus's sun-centric system. In 1632, Galileo was tried by the Roman Inquisition, an ecclesiastical court charged with maintaining orthodoxy, and convicted of teaching doctrines against the express orders of the Church. He recanted his beliefs and at the age of sixty-nine was sentenced to house arrest.

Although Galileo was formally convicted of disobeying the Church's order to remain silent on the issue of Copernicus's theory, the question most fundamentally at stake in the trial was "What does it mean, 'to know something'?"[18] This question of the relationship between scientific knowledge, primarily concerned with how the universe works, and other forms of "knowledge," derived from divine revelation or mystical experience, has persisted in the West. Over 350 years after the trial, Pope John Paul II spoke of Galileo's conviction in a public speech in 1992, declaring it a "sad misunderstanding" that belongs to the past, but one with ongoing resonance because "the underlying problems of this case concern both the nature of science and the message of faith." Then the pope declared scientific and religious knowledge to be compatible: "There exist two realms of knowledge, one which has its source in Revelation and one which reason can discover by its own power. . . . The distinction between the two realms of knowledge ought not to be understood as opposition. . . . The methodologies proper to each make it possible to bring out different aspects of reality."[19]

Galileo himself had expressed something similar centuries earlier. "Nor is God," he wrote, "any less excellently revealed in Nature's actions than in the sacred statements of the Bible."[20] Finding a place for new scientific knowledge in a constellation of older wisdom traditions proved a fraught but highly significant development in the emergence of the modern world.

QUESTION

What can Galileo's discoveries with his telescope and his conviction by the Inquisition tell us about the Scientific Revolution?

---

the Church to publicly renounce his belief that the earth orbited around the sun and rotated on its axis.

But scholars have sometimes exaggerated the conflict of science and religion, casting it in military terms as an almost unbroken war. Many of the leaders of the early movement saw themselves as natural philosophers studying natural theology, the idea that God could be known through the study of his creation. Newton, a serious biblical scholar, proclaimed, "This most beautiful system of the sun, planets, and comets could only proceed from the counsel and dominion of an intelligent Being."[21] In such ways the scientists sought to accommodate religion. Over time, scientists and Church leaders learned to coexist through a kind of compartmentalization. Science might prevail in its limited sphere of describing the physical universe, but religion was still the arbiter of truth about those ultimate questions concerning human salvation, righteous behavior, and the larger purposes of life.

AP® EXAM TIP

Compare the cooperation and conflict between science and religion in Christian Europe to the cooperation and conflict between science and religion in the Islamic world.

CHAPTER 5

BUILDING AP® SKILLS

Making Connections: Causation

Ask students to read the last two paragraphs of "Zooming In: Galileo and the Telescope: Reflecting on Science and Religion." Then ask; Why did it take more than 300 years for the Church to acknowledge the compatibility of science and religion, which Galileo had written about centuries earlier? *The idea that science and religion could be compatible threatened the Church's authority. The idea that knowledge derived solely from divine revelation persisted for hundreds of years. At the time, there was no clear division between scientific knowledge and faith. Today, this idea is widely accepted.*

APPLY THE TIP

This is a good place for some writing practice. Ask students to look back at "Snapshot: Key Achievements in Islamic Science and Scholarship" on page 162 and the discussion of scholarship in mathematics and science under Islamic rulers on pages 162 and 163. Then ask them to write a paragraph comparing cooperation and conflict between science and religion in Europe and in the Islamic world. *Answers should note that Islam in the earlier period encouraged scientific observation and inquiry, whereas the Church in Europe did not.*

Science and Enlightenment

Initially limited to a small handful of scholars, the ideas of the Scientific Revolution spread to a wider European public during the eighteenth century, aided by novel techniques of printing and bookmaking, by a popular press, by growing literacy, and by a host of scientific societies. Moreover, the new approach to knowledge—rooted in human reason, skeptical of authority, expressed in natural laws—was now applied to human affairs, not just to the physical universe. The Scottish professor Adam Smith (1723–1790), for example, formulated laws that accounted for the operation of the economy and that, if followed, he believed, would generate inevitably favorable results for society. Growing numbers of people believed that the long-term outcome of scientific development would be "enlightenment," a term that has come to define the eighteenth century in European history. If human reason could discover the laws that governed the universe, surely it could uncover ways in which humankind might govern itself more effectively.

"What is Enlightenment?" asked the prominent German intellectual Immanuel Kant (1724–1804). "It is man's emergence from his self-imposed . . . inability to use one's own understanding without another's guidance. . . . Dare to know! 'Have the courage to use your own understanding' is therefore the motto of the enlightenment."[22] Although they often disagreed sharply with one another, **European Enlightenment** thinkers shared this belief in the power of knowledge to transform human society. They also shared a satirical, critical style, a commitment to open-mindedness and inquiry, and in various degrees a hostility to established political and religious authority. Many took aim at arbitrary governments, the "divine right of kings," and the aristocratic privileges of European society. The English philosopher John Locke (1632–1704) offered principles for constructing a constitutional government, a contract between rulers and ruled that was created by human ingenuity rather than divine prescription.

Much of Enlightenment thinking was directed against the superstition, ignorance, and corruption of established religion. In his *Treatise on Toleration*, the French writer **Voltaire** (1694–1778) reflected the outlook of the Scientific Revolution as he commented sarcastically on religious intolerance:

> This little globe, nothing more than a point, rolls in space like so many other globes; we are lost in its immensity. Man, some five feet tall, is surely a very small part of the universe. One of these imperceptible beings says to some of his neighbors in Arabia or Africa: "Listen to me, for the God of all these worlds has enlightened me; there are nine hundred million little ants like us on the earth, but only my anthill is beloved of God; He will hold all others in horror through all eternity."[23]

Voltaire's own faith, like that of many others among the "enlightened," was deism. Deists believed in a rather abstract and remote deity, sometimes compared to a clockmaker, who had created the world and set it in motion, but not in a personal God who intervened in history or tampered with natural law. Others became *pantheists*,

---

The Philosophers of the Enlightenment This painting shows the French philosopher Voltaire with a group of intellectual luminaries at the summer palace of the Prussian king Frederick II. Such literary gatherings, sometimes called salons, were places of lively conversation among mostly male participants and came to be seen as emblematic of the European Enlightenment. (Balfore Archive Images/Alamy)

◀ AP

CONTEXTUALIZATION
According to this painting, what social class did Enlightenment thinkers belong to? How can you tell?

who believed that God and nature were identical. Here were conceptions of religion shaped by the outlook of science. Sometimes called "natural religion," this outlook was devoid of mystery, revelation, ritual, and spiritual practice, while proclaiming a God that could be "proven" by human rationality, logic, and the techniques of scientific inquiry. In this view, all else was superstition. Among the most radical of such thinkers were the several Dutchmen who wrote the *Treatise of Three Imposters*, which claimed that Moses, Jesus, and Muhammad were fraudulent deceivers who based their teachings on "the ignorance of Peoples [and] resolved to keep them in it."[24]

Prominent among the debates spawned by the Enlightenment was the question of women's nature, their role in society, and the education most appropriate for them. Although well-to-do Parisian women hosted many gatherings of the largely male Enlightenment figures in their elegant salons, most of those men were anything but ardent feminists. The male editors of the famous *Encyclopédie*, a vast compendium of Enlightenment thought, included very few essays by women. One of the male authors expressed a common view: "[Women] constitute the principal ornament of the world.... May they, through submissive discretion and ... artless

AP EXAM TIP
Understand how the Enlightenment led to new ideas about women's roles in Western society.

EXPLORING AP® THEMES

Social Interactions and Organization (SIO)

Ask students: What was the purpose of salons in Enlightenment Europe? *Salons were mainly places for men to gather and discuss ideas. Many women sponsored these gatherings and supported the discussion of ideas that occurred, thus giving themselves opportunities to participate in the discussion and further Enlightenment thought.*

APPLY THE TIP

This would be a good place to have students practice writing skills. Ask students to read the last paragraph on page 287 and the first paragraph on page 288 discussing the views of different Enlightenment thinkers on the role of women. After they have read the paragraphs, ask them to write a paragraph on whether the Enlightenment caused a shift in the view of women's roles in society or not. *Answers will vary.*

cleverness, spur us [men] on to virtue."[25] In his treatise *Emile*, Jean-Jacques Rousseau described women as fundamentally different from and inferior to men and urged that "the whole education of women ought to be relative to men."[26]

Such views were sharply contested by any number of other Enlightenment figures—men and women alike. The *Journal des Dames* (Ladies Journal), founded in Paris in 1759, aggressively defended women. "If we have not been raised up in the sciences as you have," declared Madame Beaulmer, the *Journal*'s first editor, "it is you [men] who are the guilty ones; for have you not always abused . . . the bodily strength that nature has given you?"[27] The French philosopher Marquis de **Condorcet** (1743–1794) looked forward to the "complete destruction of those prejudices that have established an inequality of rights between the sexes."[28] And in 1792, the British writer Mary Wollstonecraft directly confronted Rousseau's view of women and their education: "What nonsense! . . . till women are more rationally educated, the progress of human virtue and improvement in knowledge must receive continual checks."[29] Thus was initiated a debate that echoed throughout the centuries that followed.

Though solidly rooted in Europe, Enlightenment thought was influenced by the growing global awareness of its major thinkers. Voltaire, for example, idealized China as an empire governed by an elite of secular scholars selected for their talent, which stood in sharp contrast to continental Europe, where aristocratic birth and military prowess were far more important. The example of Confucianism—supposedly secular, moral, rational, and tolerant—encouraged Enlightenment thinkers to imagine a future for European civilization without the kind of supernatural religion that they found so offensive in the Christian West.

The central theme of the Enlightenment—and what made it potentially revolutionary—was the idea of progress. Human society was no longer fixed by tradition or divine command but could be changed, and improved, by human action guided by reason. Such views had political implications. The French Enlightenment philosopher Montesquieu, for instance, advocated for the separation of powers or "checks and balances" in a central government as a means of preventing the tyranny of a single ruler. No one expressed this soaring confidence in human possibility more clearly than Condorcet, who boldly declared that "the perfectibility of humanity is indefinite." Belief in progress was a sharp departure from much of premodern social thinking, and it inspired those who later made the great revolutions of the modern era in the Americas, France, Russia, China, and elsewhere. Born of the Scientific Revolution, that was the faith of the Enlightenment. For some, it was virtually a new religion.

The age of the Enlightenment, however, also witnessed a reaction against too much reliance on human reason. Jean-Jacques Rousseau (1712–1778) minimized the importance of book learning for the education of children and prescribed instead an immersion in nature, which taught self-reliance and generosity rather than the greed and envy fostered by "civilization." The Romantic movement in art and literature appealed to emotion, intuition, passion, and imagination rather than cold reason and scientific learning. Religious awakenings—complete with fiery sermons, public repentance, and intense personal experience of sin and redemption—shook Protestant Europe and North America in the eighteenth and early nineteenth centuries. The Methodist

---

BUILDING AP® SKILLS

Sourcing and Situation

Ask students to read the quote from Mary Wollstonecraft in the first paragraph on page 288. Then ask: What did Wollstonecraft mean when she said, "Till women are more rationally educated, the progress of human virtue and improvement in knowledge must receive continual checks"? *Until women are educated as men are, progress in human goodness and advances in knowledge will be held back.*

APPLY THE TIP

Students need to understand how the Enlightenment ideas led to the political and social reforms in Unit 5. Ask students to list the long-term causes that led to the major political and social reforms during the eighteenth and nineteenth centuries. *The Enlightened philosophes used the new ideas of the Scientific Revolution to try to explain human behavior. This new outlook led to many of the political and social reforms that emerged during the eighteenth and nineteenth centuries.*

AP® EXAM TIP

It's important to note the long-term causes that led to the Enlightenment, which then led to major political and social reforms during the eighteenth and nineteenth centuries.

movement—with its emphasis on Bible study, confession of sins, fasting, enthusiastic preaching, and resistance to worldly pleasures—was a case in point.

Various forms of "enlightened religion" also arose in the early modern centuries, reflecting the influence of Enlightenment thinking. Quakers, for example, emphasized tolerance, an absence of hierarchy and ostentation, a benevolent God, and an "inner light" available to all people. Unitarians denied the Trinity, original sin, predestination, and the divinity of Jesus, but honored him as a great teacher and a moral prophet. Later, in the nineteenth century, proponents of the "social gospel" saw the essence of Christianity not in personal salvation but in ethical behavior. Science and the Enlightenment surely challenged religion, and for some they eroded religious belief and practice. Just as surely, though, religion persisted, adapted, and revived for many others.

European Science beyond the West

In the long run, the achievements of the Scientific Revolution spread globally, becoming the most widely sought-after product of European culture and far more desired than Christianity, democracy, socialism, or Western literature. In the early modern era, however, interest in European scientific thinking within major Asian societies was both modest and selective.

In the seventeenth century, Chinese scholars developed their own sophisticated approach to studying the natural world known as *kaozheng*, or "research based on evidence." Intended to "seek truth from facts," kaozheng was critical of the unfounded speculation of conventional Confucian philosophy and instead emphasized the importance of verification, precision, accuracy, and rigorous analysis in all fields of inquiry. It was a genuinely scientific approach to knowledge, but one that was applied more to the study of the past and to practical applications of learning in medicine, farming, and industry than to fields like astronomy, physics, or anatomy, which were more prominent in Europe.

European scientific learning arrived in China at about the same time that kaozheng was taking root, and Chinese elites took interest in some aspects of it. Imperial officials, for instance, were impressed by European techniques for predicting eclipses, reforming the calendar, and making accurate maps of the empire. European mathematics was also of particular interest to Chinese scholars who were exploring the history of Chinese mathematics. To convince their skeptical colleagues that the Europeans, whom they viewed as barbarians, had something to offer in this field, some Chinese scholars argued that European mathematics had in fact grown out of much earlier Chinese ideas and could therefore be adopted with comfort. European medicine, however, had little impact on Chinese physicians before the nineteenth century. In such ways, early modern Chinese thinkers selectively assimilated Western science into their own studies of history and the natural world on their own terms.

Although Japanese authorities largely closed their country off from the West in the early seventeenth century (see "Asians and Asian Commerce" in Chapter 6), one window remained open. Alone among Europeans, the Dutch were permitted to

AP
CONTEXTUALIZATION
How was European science received in the major civilizations of Asia in the early modern era?

EXPLORING AP® THEMES

Cultural Developments and Interactions (CDI)

The Enlightenment also led to many changes in religion. Ask students to identify the changes that took place in Christianity during the early modern era. *The Methodist movement emphasized the study of the Bible, confession of sins, fasting, preaching, and resistance to worldly pleasures. Quakers emphasized tolerance, absence of hierarchy and ostentation, a benevolent God, and an "inner light" available to all people. Unitarians denied the Trinity, original sin, predestination, and the divinity of Jesus; however, they honored Jesus as a great teacher and moral prophet. Proponents of the "social gospel" said that the essence of Christianity was ethical behavior.*

EXPLORING AP® THEMES

Cultural Developments and Interactions (CDI)

This is a good place to remind students that prior to the Scientific Revolution in Europe, China and the Islamic world were the intellectual and technological leaders of the world. To get students to think about how these older intellectual powers reacted to the rise of European intellectualism, ask: How did the Chinese respond to European science? *Chinese scholars were interested in European astronomical and mapmaking techniques. They were also interested in European mathematics; to persuade their more skeptical colleagues to adopt it, some scholars argued that it had grown out of earlier Chinese ideas. However, the scholars were not interested in European medicine until the nineteenth century.*

BUILDING AP® SKILLS

Making Connections: Comparison

Consider having students partner up to read the section "European Science beyond the West" on pages 289–290 and discuss the following question after reading it: What similarities and differences may be seen in the reactions of China, Japan, and the Ottoman Empire to the European Scientific Revolution? *Answers may include: All three saw no need to fully embrace European ideas and so selectively chose what ideas they wanted to adopt; All three were more interested in practical sciences like mapmaking and calendars, while theoretical science faced more difficulty due to conservative ideas; All three resisted wholesale adoption of European ideas until the nineteenth century; the Japanese were impressed with European anatomical studies, while China and the Ottomans were not interested in European medical studies; Japanese scholars seemed more interested in translating European texts than Chinese or Ottoman scholars.*

BUILDING AP® SKILLS

Argumentation

This might be a good place to pause and practice writing skills. Ask students to write a paragraph responding to the following prompt:

■ Evaluate the extent to which cultural borrowing changed societies in the time period 1450–1750.

Their paragraph should include a topic sentence to introduce their argument, have at least two pieces of evidence, and explain how or why their evidence supports their argument.

 EXAM TIP

Be able to give other examples of cultural borrowing like the ones in this section.

AP®
CAUSATION
What effect did Dutch learning have on Japan?

trade in Japan at a single location near Nagasaki, but not until 1720 did the Japanese lift the ban on importing Western books. Then a number of European texts in medicine, astronomy, geography, mathematics, and other disciplines were translated and studied by a small group of Japanese scholars. They were especially impressed with Western anatomical studies, for in Japan dissection was work fit only for outcasts. Returning from an autopsy conducted by Dutch physicians in the mid-eighteenth century, several Japanese observers reflected on their experience: "We remarked to each other how amazing the autopsy had been, and how inexcusable it had been for us to be ignorant of the anatomical structure of the human body."[30] Nonetheless, this small center of "Dutch learning," as it was called, remained isolated amid a pervasive Confucian-based culture. Not until the mid-nineteenth century, when Japan was forcibly opened to Western penetration, would European-style science assume a prominent place in Japanese culture.

Like China and Japan, the Ottoman Empire in the sixteenth and seventeenth centuries was an independent, powerful, successful society whose intellectual elites saw no need for a wholesale embrace of things European. Ottoman scholars were certainly conscious of the rich tradition of Muslim astronomy and chose not to translate the works of major European scientists such as Copernicus, Kepler, or Newton, although they were broadly aware of European scientific achievements by 1650. They valued astronomy mainly for its practical usefulness in making maps and calendars rather than for its larger philosophical implications. In any event, the notion of a sun-centered solar system did not cause the kind of upset in the Ottoman Empire that it did in Europe. As in Japan, the systematic embrace of Western science would have to await the nineteenth century, when the Ottoman Empire was under far more intense pressure from Europeans and reform seemed more necessary.

Looking Ahead: Science in the Nineteenth Century and Beyond

In Europe itself, the impetus of the Scientific Revolution continued to unfold. Modern science, it turned out, was a cumulative and self-critical enterprise, which in the nineteenth century and later was applied to new domains of human inquiry in ways that undermined some of the assumptions of the Enlightenment. This remarkable phenomenon justifies a brief look ahead at several scientific developments in the nineteenth and twentieth centuries. (See Then and Now: Science, page 292.)

In the realm of biology, for example, Charles Darwin (1809–1882) laid out a complex argument that all life was in constant change, that an endless and competitive struggle for survival over millions of years constantly generated new species of plants and animals, while casting others into extinction. Human beings were not excluded from this vast process, for they too were the work of evolution operating through natural selection. Darwin's famous books *The Origin of Species* (1859) and *The Descent of Man* (1871) were threatening to many traditional Christian believers, perhaps more so than Copernicus's ideas about a sun-centered universe had been several centuries earlier.

CONTINUITY AND CHANGE
How did nineteenth- and twentieth-century developments in the sciences challenge Enlightenment ideas and principles?

At the same time, Karl Marx (1818–1883) articulated a view of human history that likewise emphasized change and struggle. Conflicting social classes—enslaved people and their owners, peasants and nobles, workers and capitalists—successively drove the process of historical transformation. Although he was describing the evolution of human civilization, Marx saw himself as a scientist. He based his theories on extensive historical research; like Newton and Darwin, he sought to formulate general laws that would explain events in a rational way. Nor did he believe in heavenly intervention, chance, or the divinely endowed powers of kings. In Marx's view, the coming of socialism—a society without classes or class conflict—was not simply a good idea; it was inevitable, inscribed in the laws of historical development. (See "Social Protest" in Chapter 8.) Like the intellectuals of the Enlightenment, Darwin and Marx believed strongly in progress, but in their thinking, conflict and struggle rather than reason and education were the motors of progress. The Enlightenment image of the thoughtful, rational, and independent individual was fading. Individuals—plant, animal, and human alike—were now viewed as enmeshed in vast systems of biological, economic, or social conflict.

The work of the Viennese doctor Sigmund Freud (1856–1939) applied scientific techniques to the operation of the human mind and emotions and in doing so cast further doubt on Enlightenment conceptions of human rationality. While some of his theories have come into question, Freud argued that at the core of each person lay primal impulses toward sexuality and aggression, which were only barely held in check by the thin veneer of social conscience derived from civilization. Our neuroses arose from the ceaseless struggle between our irrational drives and the claims of conscience and society. This too was a far cry from the Enlightenment conception of the human condition.

And in the twentieth century, developments in physics, such as relativity and quantum theory, called into question some of the established verities of the Newtonian view of the world, particularly at the subatomic level and at speeds approaching that of light. In this new physics, time is relative to the position of the observer; space can warp and light can bend; matter and energy are equivalent; black holes and dark matter abound; and probability, not certain prediction, is the best that scientists can hope for. None of this was even on the horizon of those who made the original Scientific Revolution in the early modern era.

CONCLUSIONS AND REFLECTIONS

What's New?

Finding the Main Point: What major cultural and religious continuities and changes are visible in early modern world history (1450–1750)?

"What's new?" It is a common greeting, but it is also a profound historical question, especially when applied to human culture, religion, and ways of thinking about the world. Yet the answers are not always obvious or clear-cut.

TEACHING IDEA

Class Discussion

It's always good to try to get students to connect what they are learning to the contemporary world. After finishing the Scientific Revolution, start a class discussion by asking students to describe the long-term impact of cultural borrowing in world history. *Answers will vary, but may include: Cultural borrowing throughout history has been a source of frequent conflicts and in many cases has led to deep resentment of Western or foreign interference and domination. Many of these conflicts left scars that still directly or indirectly affect diplomatic relations today (conflict between India and Pakistan; China's resistance to many Western ideas; divisions in Africa, etc.).*

EXPLORING AP® THEMES

Cultural Developments and Interactions (CDI)

As the world moved into the nineteenth and twentieth centuries, science became a symbol of modernity for many Western states, showing the continuing influence of the Scientific Revolution. The section "Looking Ahead: Science in the Nineteenth Century and Beyond" covers some of the major thinkers of those centuries. You could ask students to create a chart in their reading notes to look at the developments and scientific ideas created by the following figures: Charles Darwin, Karl Marx, and Sigmund Freud. A reproducible version of this chart is available in the Teacher's Resource Materials.

Charles Darwin	Argued that all life was constantly changing and that new species of plants and animals (including human beings) were being created due to an endless and competitive struggle for survival over millions of years. He argued that this same struggle also led to the extinction of plants and animals.
Karl Marx	Focused on a social science argument about human history claiming that conflicting social classes (like workers and capitalists) drove the process of historical transformation. He believed that the coming of socialism would be good (and was inevitable due to the laws of historical development) because it would lead to a society without classes or class conflict.
Sigmund Freud	Applied scientific technique to the operation of the human mind and emotions; claimed that human neuroses came from the ceaseless struggle between our irrational drives (focusing on primal impulses) and the claims of conscience and society. These ideas cast doubt on the Enlightenment belief in human rationality.

TRM Handout 5.3: Chart for Nineteenth- and Twentieth-Century Scientific Thinkers

Consider using "Then and Now: Science" on pages 292 and 293 to start a class discussion on how views of science have changed throughout world history. Ask students to read the section and then use the questions on page 293 to start the class discussion. If you want a different way of doing a class discussion, you could do a silent discussion, posting questions or prompts on poster paper and having students write down their responses to them. A silent discussion can cause students to be more reflective in their answers and may make it easier for your more introverted students to fully participate in the discussion.

TEACHING IDEA

Incorporating Outside Resources

Crash Course videos are always a good way to introduce or wrap up a topic, and students usually enjoy watching them. In the Crash Course European History episode *Scientific Revolution*, John Green looks at the huge advances that came out of the European scientific community in the seventeenth century. You can find the video by searching for it on YouTube. While students watch the video, have them answer the following questions:

■ What was one of the first breaks in scientific knowledge between the Catholic Church and Renaissance scientists? *The change in the belief that the earth was the center of the universe (supported by the Church) to the heliocentric theory of the universe (determined by Nicolaus Copernicus).*

■ What were some of Galileo's scientific discoveries? How did the Catholic Church react to his work on the nature of the universe? *Galileo invented many tools, like an early thermometer and his own telescope. He was the first person to observe the moons of Jupiter, he was the first to understand that the Milky Way was a collection of stars, and he used the telescope to show irregular spots on the sun. The Catholic Church did not like his teachings on the heliocentric theory of the universe and found him guilty of heresy.*

■ List the achievements of the following scientific thinkers.

■ Johannes Kepler: *developed the laws of planetary motion that showed that planets moved in an elliptical orbit*

■ William Harvey: *challenged medical thought by describing the heart as a "piece of machinery" that worked according to natural laws*

THEN AND NOW   Science

"Science is not now what it was at its start," reflected the Nobel Prize–winning physicist Steven Weinberg in 2015.[31] Each new discovery since the Scientific Revolution has raised further questions and problems, making final answers elusive, tentative, and always open to revision. Moreover, in our own time, science—and the technologies derived from it—shape nearly every aspect of our lives, making our "scientific age" very different from that of the "scientific revolution" now more than four centuries in the past.

Nonetheless, contemporary science still has much in common with the outlook of Copernicus, Galileo, and Newton. Scientists then and now share a method or technique that embraces careful observation, controlled repeatable experiments, and application of evidence to formulate theories or laws. Weinberg observed that science is a method "well tuned to nature" that was "waiting for people to discover it."[32] Strikingly similar in his thinking, Galileo asserted almost four centuries earlier that the universe was like a great book lying open before us, if we could just "understand the language. . . that it was written in."[33] This shared way of thinking and practice links today's scientists to their earliest predecessors.

But over the centuries science has also changed in important ways. Today, the scope of the physical sciences has expanded substantially from the fields of astronomy and physics, where early breakthroughs were made, into fields like chemistry, electromagnetism, and the atomic and subatomic structures of matter. Moreover, whole new fields of science have emerged. Our understanding of living things—cell structures, ecosystems, evolution, and more—has been transformed by the natural sciences and especially by the science of biology. Meanwhile, earth sciences, such as geology, oceanography, and meteorology, have unlocked the secrets of our planet's history, including its changing climate and the movements of its tectonic plates.

The methods of science have also been applied to the study of human societies. Social scientists—sociologists, political scientists, anthropologists, economists—use scientific principles to examine how human societies are structured and evolve. Psychologists too have used scientific techniques to examine the operation of the human mind and emotions. Some historians have embraced "scientific history," including Karl Marx, who formulated general laws of human development. Thus the continuing process of scientific investigation has expanded the scope of inquiry into the mysteries of the physical universe, of life, and of humankind.

As the scope of science has expanded and scientific learning has evolved, modern scientists have challenged and even overturned some of the most important understandings and perspectives of their early modern predecessors. Newton viewed his concept of "universal gravitation" as applicable everywhere, but today contemporary scientists have come to understand that very different laws apply at quantum and subatomic scales. And twentieth- and twenty-first-century scientists have disclosed amazing features of the universe—such as black holes, dark matter, and dark energy—of which Newton and his contemporaries were wholly unaware.

Early modern scientists focused on the earth and its place in the solar system. Their modern counterparts, however, have ventured far beyond this limited sphere, disclosing an ever-expanding universe with billions of galaxies containing an uncountable number of stars, some of which contain planetary systems. In line with the religious thinking of his time, Newton believed that the earth was created about 4000 B.C.E. Modern scientists have dated its formation to about 4.5 billion years ago.

Modern scientists have also replaced the certainty that Newton's laws provided with a sense of the limitations of what science can know—especially at the quantum or subatomic level. It turns out that knowing the precise position of a particle makes it impossible to know its precise velocity at the same time. All of this reminds us that science—like the study of history—is a continuing process of discovery, revision, and the formulation of new questions.

In undertaking their work, current scientists have many advantages. They receive enormous financial support from governments and corporations, while their early modern

---

(continued)

■ Francis Bacon: *developed the scientific method, where he sought to use reason to understand the natural world, creating his own observations and experiments, and encouraged others to do the same*

■ Isaac Newton: *developed new methodology for his own findings in his universal laws of motion; quantified the major constructs of mass, inertia, force, velocity, and acceleration and produced the law of gravitation*

■ Garcia da Orta: *traveled with explorers and learned from local healers in the areas he traveled to; helped bring what became quinine back to Europe*

■ How did governments get involved in the Scientific Revolution? *Governments gave scientists stipends to support their work and labeled them "court mathematicians." Rulers sponsored the creation of academies and theaters of anatomy, as when Louis XIV started the Royal Academy of Sciences.*

counterparts funded their own work or received support from wealthy patrons. And scientists today have at their disposal an enormous array of technological aids—particle accelerators and powerful computers, for example—while Galileo and Newton were assisted only by modest telescopes.

In the sixteenth and seventeenth centuries, the study of science was almost exclusively an elite European phenomenon, and, aside from medicine, its discoveries were largely theoretical in nature with few practical applications. In contrast, today's

Galileo could not have imagined the telescopes available to modern scientists.
(EUROPEAN SOUTHERN OBSERVATORY/Science Source)

science is a global phenomenon, an important driver of technological innovation, and for many a defining feature of modernity. It has also transformed almost every part of the world economy—medicine, manufacturing, communication, transportation, and the military. Thus science plays a much greater role in the everyday lives of people today. This accelerating pace of scientific breakthroughs has encouraged many to view science as a powerful source of human progress.

Others, however, have pushed back against science. Religious teachings on occasion continue to elicit opposition to science as they did in the early modern period, when the Church felt challenged by scientific views that left little place for God. Some Christians, for instance, still reject Darwin's theory of evolution because it contradicts their literal understanding of biblical teachings about the creation of life. According to a 2013 poll, substantial majorities of people in some Islamic countries such as Iraq, Indonesia, and Afghanistan also continue to reject evolution, viewing it in opposition to their religious beliefs, though most Muslims generally do not find a conflict between religion and science.

Much modern criticism of science focuses on the horrendous outcomes that it has generated: nuclear weapons, capable of obliterating a sizable city in an instant, and environmental devastation, including an emerging climate crisis, deriving from industrialization. While generating much human progress, some have argued, science has also given us the means of our own destruction.

Still others have criticized the use by authoritarian governments of scientifically based technologies, from surveillance cameras to artificial intelligence, to control or oppress their citizens. Social critics abhor the references to alleged scientific findings to perpetuate racism and ideas of female inferiority. And significant numbers of people outside of the scientific community have rejected the scientific consensus about the human causes of global warming, in part because they associate those ideas with a political ideology they find offensive. Thus, while science has triumphed as an essential element of modern life, it has also provoked controversy in both its earlier and its more recent expressions.

QUESTIONS

In what ways is science today similar to science in the sixteenth and seventeenth centuries? In what ways is it different? How does modern science shape your understanding of the Scientific Revolution?

TEACHING IDEA

Incorporating Outside Resources

If you want to give students a different view of the Scientific Revolution and dive into historiography, consider showing the Crash Course History of Science episode *The Scientific Revolution*. In this episode, Hank Green examines what a scientific revolution is and how historians mark the beginning and ending of things through time. You can find the video on YouTube. After students watch the video, use the following questions to drive a class discussion:

■ According to the video, when do different sciences undergo a "revolution"? *The sciences can undergo a "revolution" when scientists collect enough data that they can't explain using their current paradigm (understanding or worldview) of how the universe works.*

■ What arguments could be made against starting the Scientific Revolution with the publishing of Nicolaus Copernicus's heliocentric theory? *Answers can include: Copernicus was not the first scientific thinker to propose heliocentrism and was really just continuing the ideas of earlier astronomers; Nicole Oresme argued for the heliocentric theory over 100 years before Copernicus did; A Greek astronomer, Aristarchus of Samos, first proposed heliocentrism in 310 B.C.E.; Copernicus's ideas were not widely known or supported when they were first published.*

■ Why did historians choose to begin the Scientific Revolution with Copernicus and his ideas? *In the nineteenth century, historians looked back to when scientific thought really began to change and noted a major change starting in the middle of the 1500s.*

■ What are arguments for and against the Scientific Revolution actually being revolutionary? *For: Major inventions and scientific theories were developed during the 1500s, 1600s, and 1700s: Galileo proved the heliocentric theory and discovered moons around Jupiter, Newton invented calculus, and other scientific thinkers were sharing ideas and arguing through journals. Against: Not that many people were involved in the revolution, nonscholars weren't involved in debating and learning the new ideas, and daily life for most people did not change because of the new discoveries being made.*

At one level, the early modern era, culturally speaking, witnessed much that was new. The Protestant Reformation was a new departure within the Christian tradition, as was the spread of Christianity to the Americas, the Philippine Islands, and Siberia. The emergence of the bhakti tradition within Hinduism and of the separate religious tradition of Sikhism likewise represented something new in South Asian cultural life. In China, *kaozheng* and the growing popularity of novels were also recent developments. For leading scientists and churchmen of Europe, the ideas of the Scientific Revolution were certainly novel and for some immensely threatening.

And yet some cultural transformations that appeared new within particular times and places were part of longer-term historical processes. As Islam increasingly took hold in Southeast Asia and parts of Africa, it was certainly something new to recent converts. But the "long march of Islam" across the Afro-Eurasian world had been in the making for 1,000 years. And while Luther's formal break with the Catholic Church marked a decisive change in Latin Christendom, it drew on long-standing criticisms of the wealth of popes, clerical immorality, and the selling of indulgences. What is "new" in one context may be "old" in another.

Furthermore, what appears as an innovation was often the product of cultural borrowing and the blending of old and new. Conversion to Christianity or Islam, for example, did not usually mean the wholesale abandonment of established religions, but the assimilation of new elements within older patterns of belief and practice. Thus as Latin American Christianity evolved, it was not a mere copy of what European missionaries sought to impose. Haitian Vodou and Brazilian Candomblé incorporated both European Christian and traditional West African elements. Sikhism in north India drew on both Islam and Hinduism. Even the Scientific Revolution, so apparently a Western innovation, was facilitated by European access to ancient Greek learning, Islamic science, Indian mathematics, and the knowledge of Indigenous peoples.

So cultural borrowing was often selective rather than wholesale. Many peoples who adopted Christianity or Islam in the Americas, sub-Saharan Africa, and Southeast Asia certainly did not accept the rigid exclusivity and ardent monotheism of more orthodox versions of those faiths. Elite Chinese were far more interested in European mapmaking and mathematics than in Western medicine, while Japanese scholars became fascinated with the anatomical work of the Dutch. Neither, however, adopted Christianity in a widespread manner.

Cultural borrowing was also frequently contested. Some objected to much borrowing at all. Thus members of the Taki Onqoy movement in Peru sought to wipe out Spanish influence and control, while Chinese and Japanese authorities clamped down firmly on European missionaries, even as they maintained some interest in European technological and scientific skills. European missionaries in Latin America and Muslim reformers in Wahhabi Arabia both objected strenuously to cultural borrowing from other traditions, which they understood as "idolatry" and the dilution of the pure faith.

To ease the tensions of cultural borrowing, efforts to "domesticate" foreign ideas and practices proliferated. Thus the Jesuits in China tried to point out similarities between Christianity and Confucianism, and Native American converts identified Christian saints with their own gods and spirits. Various Europeans, including

---

ERIC'S ACTIVITY 5   **Christianity Becomes a World Religion**

Theme 2: Cultural Developments and Interactions

What does it mean to be a Christian in the early modern period? I use this question to explore the varieties of Christianity that emerged as the faith became a world religion. In doing so, I help my students understand how beliefs evolve within and disseminate across cultures. I encourage them to deepen their understanding by comparing the development of Christianity with that of Islam and Buddhism. Find the complete activity in the Teacher's Resource Materials.

TRM Eric's Activity 5: Christianity Becomes a World Religion

Galileo, Newton, deists, Quakers, and Unitarians, sought to accommodate the perspectives of modern science while retaining a religious outlook on life. Such efforts did not always succeed. For instance, some in Europe denied discoveries such as a sun-centered universe and biological evolution, at least for a time.

Cultural borrowing complicates our understanding of "what's new" in history. How much of what appears "new" in human cultural evolution is altogether novel? And how much is a rearrangement of existing patterns, a gradual change over time, or a blending of borrowed elements?

CHAPTER REVIEW

AP Key Terms

Protestant Reformation, 262
Martin Luther, 263
Thirty Years' War, 266
Counter-Reformation, 266
Taki Onqoy, 272
Jesuits in China, 273
Wahhabi Islam, 276
Wang Yangming, 277
The Dream of the Red Chamber, 278
Mirabai, 279

Sikhism, 279
Scientific Revolution, 280
Copernicus, 282
Galileo, 283
Newton, 283
European Enlightenment, 286
Voltaire, 286
Condorcet, 288
kaozheng, 289

Finding the Main Point

1. In what different ways did Europe, Latin America, and China experience religious or cultural change in the early modern era?
2. In what ways did Afro-Asian religions change in the early modern era?
3. What were the main causes and long-term effects of the Scientific Revolution?
4. What major cultural and religious continuities and changes are visible in early modern world history (1450–1750)?

AP Big Picture Questions

1. What factors drive cultural change?
2. Which of the cultural changes described in this chapter seemed to affect small elite groups, and which had a wider impact? Does this difference affect your judgment about their historical significance?
3. In what ways were the cultural changes of the early modern era associated with sharp social or political conflicts?
4. **Looking Back** Based on Chapters 4 and 5, how might you challenge a Eurocentric understanding of the early modern era while acknowledging the growing role of Europeans on the global stage?

TRM Suggested Responses to Questions
You can find suggested responses to the Chapter Review questions in the Teacher's Resource Materials.

Causation

TRM AP® Skills Workshop Activity Handout: Causation

BUILDING AP® SKILLS

Making Connections: Causation

The early modern era (1450–1750) began a wave of causes and effects that stretched into the twentieth century. It's important for students to continue to work on identifying the causation surrounding historical events, especially since they have connections to the contemporary era. Depending on your students' skill level, you could assign either Activity 1 on page 297 or Activity 3 on page 298 to help them develop this skill. Activity 1 is good for students still struggling with identifying causes and effects of historical events. Activity 3 is good for students who can identify causation and are ready for the challenge of writing a historical argument about it.

Causation is a historical reasoning skill that you will encounter repeatedly. You might have encountered it in other courses as "cause and effect." It's how historians think about not just what happened, but why it happened and what impact it had.

UNDERSTANDING CAUSATION

Let's begin by defining what we mean by causation in the study of world history.

Causation: Identifying the causes and effects of historical events or processes

Generally, this reasoning skill is used when a historian needs to pinpoint the reason(s) for or effect(s) of a particular event, pattern, or trend. As you might imagine, this is one of the more important and challenging tasks for a historian. In many cases, a historical event has multiple causes, and historians work to create an argument that explains which causes are the most significant and how they interact with one another. A historian might also differentiate between long-term and short-term effects, as well as direct and indirect causes. Causes can also be grouped into thematic categories. For example, a historian might focus specifically on the economic causes of long-distance trade and then discuss the environmental or cultural effects.

It's very important as you work with causation not to oversimplify. Just because you think something is the primary cause or effect doesn't mean that it was the only cause or effect. Acknowledging other causes or effects doesn't weaken your position, but ignoring them most certainly does. Let's look at how the authors of this book use causation. In this example from pages 262–264, the authors discuss the short-term and long-term causes and then offer two effects born from the Protestant Reformation.

Contextualization — In the early sixteenth century the Protestant Reformation shattered the unity of Roman Catholic Christianity, which for the previous 1,000 years had provided the cultural and organizational foundation of an emerging Western European civilization.

Cause 1 — The Reformation began in 1517 when a German priest, Martin Luther (1483–1546), publicly invited debate about various abuses within the Roman Catholic Church by issuing a document, known as the Ninety-Five Theses, allegedly nailing it to the door of a church in Wittenberg. In itself, this was nothing new, for many had long been

Cause 2 — critical of the luxurious life of the popes, the corruption and immorality of some

Cause 3 —

Cause 4 — clergy, the Church's selling of indulgences (said to remove the penalties for sin), and other aspects of church life and practice.

What made Luther's protest potentially revolutionary, however, was its theological basis. A troubled and brooding man anxious about his relationship with God, Luther came to a new understanding of salvation, which, he believed, came through faith alone. Neither the good works of the sinner nor the sacraments of the Church had any bearing on the eternal destiny of the soul. To Luther, the source of these beliefs, and of religious authority in general, was not the teaching of the Church, but the Bible alone, interpreted according to the individual's conscience. All of this challenged the authority of the Church and called into question the special position of the clerical hierarchy and the pope. In sixteenth-century Europe, this was the stuff of revolution.

Cause 5

Effect 1

Effect 2

In this excerpt, the authors begin with context and then propose a variety of short-term and long-term causes of the Protestant Reformation. They then offer two significant effects of the Protestant Reformation (it challenged the authority of the Roman Catholic Church and questioned the power of the pope). Causation can move in the other direction as well, beginning with effects and then connecting them to causes.

CAUSATION ON THE AP® WORLD HISTORY EXAM

On the AP® Exam, causation is a favorite on the Multiple-Choice section, where you have to identify a cause in one question and an effect in a different question. Similarly, in a Short-Answer Question you might be asked to explain a primary cause in one part of the question, a secondary cause in the next part, and then a long-term effect. Causation can also be used to score the contextualization point on the Long Essay Question (LEQ) or Document-Based Question by discussing relevant events that led up to or occurred as a result of the historical event or process addressed in the prompt. The analysis and reasoning point on the LEQ is another way that effective use of causation can help you succeed on the AP® Exam. In order to score this point, you must correctly use a historical reasoning skill (e.g., comparison, causation, continuity and change) to frame or structure an argument that addresses the prompt.

BUILDING AP® SKILLS

1. **Activity: Identifying Causation.** Read the feature Then and Now: Science on pages 292–293. Then identify a few effects of the Scientific Revolution and explain why these effects are considered significant in world history.

2. **Activity: Working with Causation.** Read Historians' Voices 5.1: Merry Wiesner-Hanks on the Virgin of Guadalupe on page 311. In this passage, Wiesner-Hanks offers a claim of causation regarding the creation of the story of the Virgin of Guadalupe. Identify the claim of causation that is expressed in the passage, and identify what evidence is provided to support that claim.

TRM **Suggested Responses to Questions**
You can find suggested responses to the Building AP® Skills questions in the Teacher's Resource Materials.

297

3. Activity: Creating a Causation Statement. Using information from this chapter, write a causation paragraph that answers the prompt below:

Analyze the causes and effects of the Enlightenment in Europe from 1450 to 1750.

Follow these steps:

1. Identify and describe the Enlightenment.
2. Identify possible causes and explain how they connect to the Enlightenment.
3. Identify possible effects and explain how they connect to the Enlightenment.

Religious Interaction in Indian Art

When examining a work of art as a primary source, historians must place it in its historical situation—what is commonly referred to as sourcing the piece of art. Did a patron commission the work of art, and if so, why? Who created it and when? Who was the intended audience, and where was the piece of art displayed? What do we know about how viewers reacted to it?

Sourcing information can be particularly revealing for historians interested in understanding how cultural traditions mix in a specific time or place. India under the Mughal Empire provides a compelling example of this kind of cultural encounter. The vast majority of the population practiced some form of Hinduism, while the empire's rulers and a distinct minority of its people were Muslims. Sikhism had recently emerged as a separate religious tradition even as Christian religious art, introduced by Portuguese missionaries, found favor at the Mughal court. (See "On the Frontiers of Islam: The Mughal and Songhay Empires" in Chapter 4 and "India: Bridging the Hindu/Muslim Divide" in this chapter.) The image reproduced here illustrates this blending of cultural traditions. It was created around 1600 by an anonymous Hindu artist working at the court of the Muslim Mughal emperor Akbar (r. 1556–1605) in northern India.

1 A FIRST LOOK

Carefully examine the image by answering the following:

1. What do you think the figure in the illustration is doing? What specific elements of the image inform your answer?

2. The Persian writing above and below the image contains instructions about a particular form of breathing exercise. What does this suggest about the illustration?

3. What else would you like to know about the illustration to better understand what it depicts?

TRM Suggested Responses to Questions
You can find suggested responses to the AP® Looking Again questions in the Teacher's Resource Materials.

BUILDING AP® SKILLS

Claims and Evidence in Sources

It can be difficult for students to find evidence in pieces of art as primary sources, so any practice in this skill is helpful. Consider assigning the "*Kumbhaka* (breathing exercises)" illustration on page 300 to students to explain religious interactions in India; the questions under "A First Look" on page 299 will guide them in their analysis.

299

Kumbhaka (breathing exercises) | ca. 1600

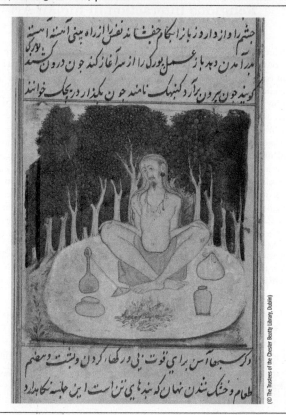

2 **A SECOND LOOK**

Now that you are familiar with the illustration, let's explore the historical situation in which it was created. We know that it was commissioned by the Muslim Mughal prince Salim, who later became Emperor Jahangir. He commissioned the illustration during the reign of his father, Akbar, who as emperor regularly presided over what we might now call interfaith gatherings of Muslims, Hindus, Christians, Buddhists, and others. Akbar created and promoted a blended religious cult for Mughal elites that combined elements of several faiths. We also know that Prince Salim commissioned this image as part of a series to illustrate a book entitled *The Ocean of Life* by Muhammad Gwaliyari.

300

A Muslim Sufi mystic who was closely connected to the Mughal court, Gwaliyari compiled in his book descriptions of twenty-two yoga postures that he hoped to incorporate into Muslim Sufi religious practice. The illustration depicts one of these postures, and the accompanying text describes a particular breathing practice. Gwaliyari's book reflected a growing interest among the Muslim Mughal elite in the ancient Hindu mind-body practice known as yoga, especially the idea that yoga postures and practices conveyed great power.

1. How does this sourcing information affect your understanding of the image?

2. Why might Muslim rulers and Sufi masters want to incorporate Hindu-based yoga techniques into their own practices?

3. What does this sourcing information reveal about the mixing or blending of cultural traditions in Mughal India around 1600?

3 A THIRD LOOK

Now let's consider what we know about the painter who created the illustration. The name of the artist is unknown, but from the techniques and styles that he used we can be sure that he was part of a Hindu community of artists patronized by Mughal elites. Experts in Indian art have also established that the artist who created our image was influenced by European artistic traditions that were much admired at Akbar's court and regularly imitated by local Hindu artists. Specifically, the yogi's face in this illustration resembles that of Jesus as depicted in European religious art then circulating at the Mughal court.

1. What does this information about the artist and the artistic styles that influenced his illustration add to your understanding of cultural mixing in Mughal India?

2. What does the painting of a yoga practitioner with the face of Christ suggest about Indian views of Jesus?

3. What other sourcing information would you like to know about the painter or the image? Why?

AP° ACTIVITY WRITING A SOURCING STATEMENT

In a couple of sentences, write a sourcing statement that emphasizes the various ways that this illustration of a yoga posture reflects the remarkable cultural blending occurring at the Mughal court around 1600.

FURTHER ACTIVITY

Both the illustration in this activity and the painting by Wang Shugu in the AP® Looking Again activity for Chapter 3 offer evidence of cultural mixing. In your own words, explain how each image illustrates cultural mixing. What similarities and differences can you identify?

301

BUILDING AP® SKILLS

Claims and Evidence in Sources

If you would like your students to dig deeper into the Indian illustration of breathing exercises to practice sourcing skills, have them read through the "Second Look" and "Third Look" sections on pages 300 and 301 and answer the questions. This would be a good place to have either a small group (three or four students) or a class discussion on what they believe the illustration says about the attitudes toward the interactions of different religions in the Mughal Empire in this time period.

TEACHING IDEA

AP® Exam Strategies

Since sourcing is one of the hardest points to earn on the DBQ essay, it's good to have students work on this skill throughout the year. You can have students practice sourcing by asking them to respond to the prompt under "AP® Activity: Writing a Sourcing Statement" at the bottom of this page.

AP® WORKING WITH EVIDENCE

Christianity: Becoming a Global Religion

During the early modern centuries, missionaries—mostly Roman Catholic—rode the tide of European expansion to establish Christianity in the Americas and parts of Africa and Asia. In those places, native converts sometimes imitated European patterns and at other times adapted the new religion to their own cultural traditions. Thus the Christian world of the early modern era was far more globalized than before 1500. The sources that follow illustrate the variety of receptions that Christianity received in different places and the cultural blending or mixing that occurred when new peoples embraced the faith.

LOOKING AHEAD

AP® DBQ PRACTICE

Analyze the reasons for syncretism and the various forms it took during the period 1450–1750.

DOCUMENT 1 | **European Influence in Kongo**

The Kingdom of Kongo, centered in what is now northern Angola, had welcomed Portuguese traders as early as the 1480s, for its rulers imagined that an alliance with Portugal could strengthen their regime. The royal family converted to Christianity and encouraged the importation of European guns, cattle, and horses. Several Kongolese were sent to Portugal for education, while Portuguese priests, artisans, merchants, and soldiers found a place in the kingdom. None of this worked as planned, however, and by the early sixteenth century Kongo was in disarray and the authority of its ruler greatly undermined, as the kingdom became heavily involved in the Atlantic slave trade. This was the context in which its monarch Nzinga Mbemba, whose Christian name was Afonso I, wrote a series of letters to King João of Portugal in 1526, extracts of which are presented here.

> **Source:** Kongo monarch Nzinga Mbemba (Afonso I), from his letters to the King of Portugal, 1526.
>
> [W]e cannot reckon how great the damage is, since the mentioned [Portuguese] merchants are taking every day our natives, sons of the land and the sons of our noblemen and vassals and our relatives, because the thieves and men of bad conscience grab them wishing to have the things and wares of this Kingdom which they are ambitious of; they grab them and get them to be sold; and so great, Sir, is the corruption and licentiousness that our country is being completely depopulated, and Your Highness should not agree with this nor accept it as in your service. And to avoid it we need from those [your] Kingdoms no more than some priests and a few people to teach in schools, and no other goods except wine and flour for the holy sacrament. That is why we beg of Your Highness to help and assist us in this matter,

302

commanding your factors that they should not send here either merchants or wares, because it is our will that in these Kingdoms there should not be any trade of slaves nor outlet for them. . . .

Moreover, Sir, in our Kingdoms there is another great inconvenience which is of little service to God, and this is that many of our people, keenly desirous as they are of the wares and things of your Kingdoms, which are brought here by your people, and in order to satisfy their voracious appetite, seize many of our people, freed and exempt men, and very often it happens that they kidnap even noblemen and the sons of noblemen, and our relatives, and take them to be sold to the white men who are in our Kingdoms; and for this purpose they have concealed them; and others are brought during the night so that they might not be recognized.

Basil Davidson, trans., *The African Past* (London: Curtis Brown, 1964), 54–57.

Question to Consider: What were the major grievances that motivated Mbemba's letter? What does the letter reveal about Mbemba's interest in Christianity?

AP **Analyzing Sources:** How might you explain the deferential tone of Mbemba's letter to the King of Portugal?

DOCUMENT 2 Christian Missionaries in India

During this period, the Society of Jesus was among the most aggressive European missionary organizations. The Jesuits sent members across the globe establishing missions in the Americas, Africa, and Asia, and these missionaries regularly wrote letters addressed to their leaders back in Europe detailing their activities. The most famous of the early Jesuit missionaries was Francis Xavier (1506–1552), who worked in India and Japan and inspired later generations of missionaries by his example. He was later made a saint by the Catholic Church for his work spreading the faith. In the letter that follows, Xavier writes of his successes and optimism regarding his work in India. This passage describes a reliance on local children to teach the Christian message, thus exhibiting a European perspective on the role of Indigenous populations in the spread of Christianity.

Source: Saint Francis Xavier, letter from India to the Society of Jesus in Rome, 1543.

As I could not go myself, I sent round children whom I could trust in my place. They went to the sick persons, assembled their families and neighbours, recited the Creed with them, and encouraged the sufferers to conceive a certain and well-founded confidence of their restoration. Then after all this, they recited the prayers of the Church. To make my tale short, God was moved by the faith and piety of these children and of the others, and restored to a great number of sick persons health both of body and soul. How good He was to them! He made the very disease of their bodies the occasion of calling them to salvation, and drew them to the Christian faith almost by force!

303

I have also charged these children to teach the rudiments of Christian doctrine to the ignorant in private houses, in the streets, and the crossways. As soon as I see that this has been well started in one village, I go on to another and give the same instructions and the same commission to the children, and so I go through in order the whole number of their villages. When I have done this and am going away, I leave in each place a copy of the Christian doctrine, and tell all those who know how to write to copy it out, and all the others are to learn it by heart and to recite it from memory every day.

Henry James Coleridge, ed., *The Life and Letters of St. Francis Xavier*, 2d ed. (London: Burns and Oates, 1890), 2:67–75.

Question to Consider: Why would Xavier make children the focus of his outreach in India?

AP **Analyzing Sources:** What historical context would explain the expanding activities of missionary organizations such as the Society of Jesus?

DOCUMENT 3 Christianity as a Threat to Japan

Portuguese traders and missionaries arrived in Japan in the mid-sixteenth century at a time when the country was deeply divided among a series of local warrior lords. Soon some 300,000 people had converted to Christianity, and a Japanese church organization flourished. By the late sixteenth century, however, as Japanese authorities unified the country, they also turned sharply against Christianity as a foreign religion. In a letter to the Portuguese Viceroy of the Indies, the Japanese ruler Toyotomi Hideyoshi, who had unified the country, sought to explain why Christian missionaries were no longer welcome.

Source: Japanese ruler Toyotomi Hideyoshi, *Letter to the Viceroy of the Indies*, 1591.

Ours is the land of the Gods, and God is mind. . . . God is the root and source of all existence. This God is spoken of by Buddhism in India, Confucianism in China, and Shinto in Japan. To know Shinto is to know Buddhism as well as Confucianism.

If you are interested in the profound philosophy of God and Buddha, request an explanation and it will be given to you. In your land one doctrine is taught to the exclusion of others, and you are not yet informed of the [Confucian] philosophy of Humanity and Righteousness. Thus there is no respect for God and Buddha and no distinction between sovereign and ministers. Through heresies you intend to destroy the righteous law. Hereafter, do not expound, in ignorance of right and wrong, unreasonable and wanton doctrines. A few years ago the so-called Fathers came to my country seeking to bewitch our men and women, both of the laity and clergy. At that time punishment was administered to them, and it will be repeated if they should return to our domain to propagate their faith. It will not matter what sect or denomination they represent—they shall be destroyed.

Ryosaku Tsunoda, Wm. Theodore de Bary, and Donald Keene, eds, *Sources of Japanese Tradition* (New York: Columbia University Press, 1965), 325–27.

Question to Consider: On what grounds does Hideyoshi oppose the presence of missionaries in Japan? What are Hideyoshi's reasons for his opposition?

AP **Analyzing Sources:** What can you infer about the Japanese approach to religion from this letter? How might it differ from that of the Portuguese Christians?

DOCUMENT 4   Conversion of the Mohawks

In the 1660s the Jesuits, with the support of the French government, established for the first time a mission among the Indigenous Iroquois in parts of modern Canada that France claimed for its empire. Long bitter enemies of the French, some Iroquois, including the Mohawk community, decided to make peace with France in 1667. Peace, in turn, provided an opportunity for Jesuit missionaries to dwell in native communities for extended periods. One such Jesuit was Father Jean Pierron, who recounted his experiences in a letter to his superiors back in Europe. He also intended the letter to be circulated among the Jesuit order and published for an even wider audience. In this extract, Father Pierron threatens to abandon the community he was living in. While he frames his threat in terms of the failure of the Mohawks to adopt Christian teachings, the Mohawks would have understood that his abandonment of their community would likely bring a breach with France and a possible invasion by French forces at a time when the Mohawks were particularly vulnerable.

Source: Jesuit Father Jean Pierron describing his address to the Mohawks in a letter to French Jesuits, 1669–1670.

You wish me to remain here with you, in order to maintain the peace, and to keep me, you often allege to me that you are now one, in body and soul, with the governor of the French and with me. Have you any reason to say this, you who have neither the same sentiments, the same inclinations, nor the same behavior as us? How could my soul be yours when I am convinced that mine is a pure spirit, immortal, and like to the master of your lives, while you believe that yours is either a bear, a wolf, a serpent, a fish, a bird, or some other kind of animal that you have seen in a dream? Moreover, your soul and mine have very opposite

305

sentiments. You think that the master of life is a demon, who you call Agreskoue, whereas I say that your Agreskoue is a slave whom God, who is the master of our lives, keeps chained in Hell as a proud and wicked spirit. You believe in an infinite number of fables as so many truths, and I regard them as so many lies. If, then, our souls have such opposite tendencies, how can there be any firm and true peace between the soul of the French and the soul of the Mohawks?

Allan Greer, ed., *The Jesuit Relations: Natives and Missionaries in Seventeenth-Century North America*, 2nd ed. (Boston: Bedford/St. Martin's, 2019).

Question to Consider: How did Pierron view the Mohawks?

AP **Analyzing Sources:** How did the intended audience for the letter in Europe impact Pierron's writing?

DOCUMENT 5 **Christianity through Maya Eyes**

European missionaries, clergy, inquisitors, and government officials wrote most of the surviving sources about the conversion of Mesoamerica, but the *Books of the Chilam Balam* offer a rare Indigenous perspective. Written in the seventeenth and eighteenth centuries, their Maya authors recorded local rituals, medical knowledge, history, myths, prophecies, and Christian instruction in the Yucatec Mayan language using the European Latin alphabet. The passages that follow come from the *Chilam Balam of Chumayel*, a town on the Yucatán Peninsula of modern Mexico. They reveal how Christian concepts were integrated into an existing Maya worldview and cosmology.

Source: On the coming of Christianity and prophecy on the End Times from the Mayan *Book of Chilam Balam of Chumayel*, 17th to 18th centuries.

Then with the true God, the true Dios [God], came the beginning of our misery. It was the beginning of tribute, the beginning of church dues, the beginning of strife with purse-snatching, the beginning of strife with blow-guns, the beginning of strife by trampling on the people, the beginning of robbery with violence, the beginning of forced debts. . . . This was the origin of service to the Spaniards and priests, of service to the local chiefs. . . . It was by Antichrist on earth, the kinkajous [a small rain forest mammal] of the towns, the foxes of the towns, the blood-sucking insects of the town, those who drained the poverty of the working people [who made working people poor]. But it shall still come to pass that tears shall come to the eyes of our Lord God. The justice of our Lord God shall descend upon every part of the world, straight from God upon . . . the avaricious hagglers of the world.

Then [in the End Times] they shall come forth from the forests and from among the rocks and live like men; then towns shall be established [again]. There shall be no fox to bite them. . . . Five years shall run until the end of my prophecy, and then shall come the time for the tribute to come down. Then there shall be an end to the paying for the wars which our fathers raised [against the Spaniards]. You shall not call the *katun* [a twenty-year period] which is to come a hostile one, when Jesus Christ, the guardian of our souls shall come. Just as [we are saved] here on earth, so shall he bear our souls to his holy heaven also. You are sons of the true God. Amen.

Question to Consider: How is the exploitation of the Maya in the Spanish colonial system reflected in these passages?

AP **Analyzing Sources:** How might the point of view of the author(s) have impacted these documents?

DOCUMENT 6 The Chinese Rites Controversy

Religious syncretism on occasion provoked heated debate, as the Chinese rites controversy illustrates. European opponents of the Jesuits raised objections to Jesuit acceptance of some Chinese customs, including the honoring of ancestors (what their critics called ancestor worship) and devotion to Confucius. The Jesuits viewed ancestor reverence as compatible with Christianity and Confucian ceremonies as civil rites rather than religious observances, but many European opponents understood these Chinese practices as religious in nature and therefore incompatible with orthodox Christian teachings. Ultimately the Jesuits lost this debate when Pope Clement XI issued a decree banning these "Chinese rites" in 1715. Document 6 is the pope's decree.

Source: Pope Clement XI, *Decree Banning Chinese Rites*, 1715.

I. The West calls *Deus* [God] the creator of Heaven, Earth, and everything in the universe. Since the word *Deus* does not sound right in the Chinese language, the Westerners in China and Chinese converts to Catholicism have used the term "Heavenly Lord" for many years. From now on such terms as "Heaven" and "Shangti" should not be used: *Deus* should be addressed as the Lord of Heaven, Earth, and everything in the universe. . . .

II. The spring and autumn worship of Confucius, together with the worship of ancestors, is not allowed among Catholic converts. It is not allowed even though the converts appear in

307

the ritual as bystanders, because to be a bystander in this ritual is as pagan as to participate in it actively.

III. Chinese officials and successful candidates in the metropolitan, provincial, or prefectural examinations, if they have been converted to Roman Catholicism, are not allowed to worship in Confucian temples on the first and fifteenth days of each month. . . .

IV. No Chinese Catholics are allowed to worship ancestors in their familial temples.

V. Whether at home, in the cemetery, or during the time of a funeral, a Chinese Catholic is not allowed to perform the ritual of ancestor worship. . . .

Despite the above decisions, I have made it clear that other Chinese customs and traditions that can in no way be interpreted as heathen in nature should be allowed to continue among Chinese converts. The way the Chinese manage their households or govern their country should by no means be interfered with.

Dun J. Li, *China in Transition, 1517–1911* (New York: Van Nostrand Reinhold, 1969), 22–24.

Question to Consider: What specific practices did Clement prohibit, and what reasons did he offer for his ban?

AP **Analyzing Sources:** What was the purpose of Clement's decree?

DOCUMENT 7 Cultural Blending in Andean Christianity

Throughout Latin America, Christianity was established in the context of European conquest and colonial rule. As the new faith took hold across the region, it incorporated much that was of European origin, as the construction of many large and ornate churches illustrates. But local communities also sought to blend this European Catholic Christianity with religious symbols and concepts drawn from their own traditions in a process that historians call syncretism. In the Andes, for example, Inca religion featured a supreme creator god (Viracocha); a sun god (Inti), regarded as the creator of the Inca people; a moon goddess (Killa), who was the wife of Inti; and an earth mother goddess (Pachamama), associated with mountain peaks and fertility. Those religious figures found their way into Andean understanding of Christianity, as Document 7 illustrates.

Painted around 1740 by an unknown artist, this striking image shows the Virgin Mary placed within the "rich mountain" of Potosí in Bolivia, from which the Spanish had extracted so much silver. Thus Christianity was visually expressed in an Andean tradition that viewed mountains as the embodiment of the gods. Native miners whose labor enriched their colonial rulers are depicted as smaller figures on the mountainside. A somewhat larger figure at the bottom of the mountain is an Inca ruler dressed in royal garb receiving tribute from his people. At the bottom left are the pope and a cardinal, while on the right stand the Habsburg emperor Charles V and perhaps his wife.

Source: *La Virgen del Cerro* (Virgin Mary of the Mountains), ca. 1740.

Museo de la Casa de la Moneda, Potosí, Bolivia/Gilles Mermet/akg-images

Question to Consider: What marks this painting as an example of syncretism?

AP Analyzing Sources: Analyze the historical context for the source. What events of the period influenced the artist of the painting?

309

AP DOING HISTORY

1. **DBQ Practice:** Evaluate the extent to which the spread of Christianity to Asia and the Americas led to cultural consequences.

2. **Comparison:** What common Christian elements can you identify in these sources? What differences in the expression of Christianity can you define?

3. **Causation:** Consider the reasons for the development of syncretic forms of Christianity.

4. **Sourcing and Situation:** What are the strengths and limitations of the visual source in this collection, as opposed to the texts, for historians seeking to understand the globalization of Christianity in the early modern era?

310

Missions in Mesoamerica and China

Missionary efforts to win new converts and strengthen the devotion of new Christians took many different forms during the early modern period. These voices examine specific missionary efforts in sixteenth-century Mesoamerica and seventeenth- and eighteenth-century China. In Voice 5.1, Merry Wiesner-Hanks explores two alternative foundation narratives for the Virgin of Guadalupe shrine in Mexico (see the image at the beginning of this chapter). In Voice 5.2, Diarmaid MacCulloch describes Jesuit missionary strategies in China.

mother of the most powerful Aztec God Huitzilopochtli, and that aspects of the veneration of the Virgin of Guadalupe were also part of honoring Coatlicue or other Aztec mother goddesses. In their view, the colonial Catholic Church had simply invented the story as part of its efforts to strip Aztec Holy sites of their original meaning.

Source: Merry E. Wiesner-Hanks, *A Concise History of the World* (Cambridge: Cambridge University Press, 2015), 267.

VOICE 5.1

Merry Wiesner-Hanks on the Virgin of Guadalupe | 2015

[T]he Virgin of Guadalupe can serve as a good example [of syncretism]. . . . In the seventeenth century, published texts in Spanish and Nahuatl [an indigenous Mexican language] told of the appearance of the Virgin Mary in 1531 to Juan Diego Cuauhtlatoatzin, an indigenous farmer and Christian convert, on a hill near Tenochtitlan (now within Mexico City). Speaking in Nahuatl, the apparition told Juan Diego that a church should be built at the site, and her image miraculously appeared on his cloak. Shortly afterward a church dedicated to the Virgin of Guadalupe was begun. . . . Preachers and teachers interpreted her appearance as a sign of the Virgin's special protection of indigenous people and those of mixed ancestry . . . , and pilgrims from all over Mexico began to make the trek to her shrine. . . .

In the twentieth century, however, many scholars, including some members of the Mexican clergy, came to doubt whether the apparition had ever happened or Juan Diego himself had even existed. They pointed out that written accounts were not published until over a century later, and that church officials and missionaries active in central Mexico in 1531 made no mention of the event. . . . Specialists in Nahuatl culture note that the hill where the apparition was reported was originally the site of a shrine to Coatlicue, the

VOICE 5.2

Diarmaid MacCulloch on Jesuit Missionary Strategies in China | 2009

The Jesuits quickly decided that missionaries must adapt themselves to Chinese customs. This involved much rapid self-education. Their first great missionary, the Italian Matteo Ricci, on his arrival in 1582 adopted the dress of a Buddhist monk (*bonze*), without realizing that *bonzes* were despised by the people who mattered. When his mistake was pointed out, he and his fellow Jesuits began dressing as Confucian scholars, complete with long beards; they were determined to show that their learning was worthy of respect in a culture with a deep reverence for scholarship. . . . The Chinese upper class was indeed impressed by the Jesuits' knowledge of mathematics, astronomy and geography, and the Society gained an honoured place at the emperor's court through its specialist use of these skills. . . .

The Jesuit emphasis on their honoured place at Court was always something of a diversion from the real reasons for the growth of adherents, who were very different in their social profile from the exalted figures around the emperor. At the peak of the Chinese mission's success at the end of the seventeenth century, it was serving perhaps around a quarter of a million people. . . . Yet at that time there were only seventy-five priests to serve this

311

BUILDING AP® SKILLS

Claims and Evidence in Sources

Interpreting secondary sources is an important skill for AP® World History: Modern students. Consider having students read both of the sources found on page 311 and answer Questions 1–3 on page 312. Then you could discuss the questions as a class. This activity can help students practice reading and interpreting secondary sources, which are found on the Multiple-Choice and SAQ sections of the exam.

Differentiation

If you want to differentiate this activity, follow the "Must Do, Should Do, Strive For" model below.

■ Must Do: Students need to read the two sources and answer Questions 1–3 on page 312 on a separate sheet of paper.

■ Should Do: Students need to participate at least once during a class discussion on the sources and accompanying questions.

■ Strive For: Students will use what they have learned from these secondary sources to contextualize the Working with Evidence sources on pages 302–309 (Question 4 on page 312).

number, laboring under enormous difficulties with language. . . . What the Jesuits did very effectively in this situation was to inspire a local leadership which was not clerical, both catechists [teachers of the basic tenets of the faith] and a particular Chinese phenomenon . . . , "Chinese virgins": laywomen consecrated to singleness but still living with their families, teaching women and children.

Source: Diarmaid MacCulloch, *Christianity: The First Three Thousand Years* (New York: Penguin, 2009), 706–7.

AP Analyzing Secondary Sources

1. How does your understanding of the Virgin of Guadalupe shrine and the way that Mexico was Christianized change depending on which interpretation of its foundation you accept?

2. What challenges did the Jesuit mission in China face, and how did the Jesuits seek to overcome them?

3. What strategies for strengthening the devotion of new converts are highlighted in these two voices?

4. **Integrating Primary and Secondary Sources:** How do these voices help you to better understand the Working with Evidence sources?

CHAPTER 5 AP® EXAM PRACTICE

Multiple-Choice Questions Choose the correct answer for each question.

Questions 1–3 refer to this passage.

> But the more we learn of the Kirishitan [Christian] doctrines the greater becomes our conviction that they are evil. We were taught that, unless a person committing a sin confesses it to a padre and secures his pardon, he shall not be saved in the world beyond. In that way the people were led into believing in padres. All that was for the purpose of taking lands of others. Hereafter we shall not harbor any thought of the Kirishitan in our heart.
>
> — Statement to the Magistrate by former Japanese converts, renouncing the Kirishitan [Christian] faith, 1645

1. Which of the following groups had a similar reaction to the spread of Christianity as the Japanese?
   a. The Native Americans in the New World
   b. The people of the Philippines
   c. The Ming Chinese
   d. The Catholics in Spain

2. Which of the following caused the ideas expressed in the edict?
   a. The intensification of connections within hemispheres
   b. The development of Sikhism
   c. The rejection of Islam in the Middle East
   d. The desire to develop a syncretic belief system in Japan

3. Which of the following serves as the larger context for the source?
   a. The spread of Buddhism into China
   b. The creation of Islam
   c. The creation of Sikhism
   d. The missionary outreach of Christian Europe

Questions 4 and 5 refer to this passage.

> Thus they bartered, like idiots, cotton and gold for fragments of bows, glasses, bottles, and jars; which I forbad as being unjust, and myself gave them many beautiful and acceptable articles which I had brought with me, taking nothing from them in return; I did this in order that I might the more easily conciliate them, that they might be led to become Christians.
>
> — Christopher Columbus, letter to Ferdinand and Isabella, 1493

4. Which of the following was one of the effects of the situation described in the letter?
   a. The development of a blended religious culture in the Americas
   b. The widespread violent rejection of the Christian faith among many Native Americans
   c. The rise of Native American women in the Catholic Church in the Americas
   d. Native Americans' rejection of their native culture in favor of European culture

5. Which of the following aided the Europeans in fulfilling the goals described in the letter?
   a. The presence of Muslim Sufis in the Americas
   b. The exchange of domesticated foods and plants
   c. The spread of smallpox to the Native Americans
   d. The failure of the Jesuits

313

TRM Suggested Responses to Questions

You can find suggested responses to the Chapter 5 AP® Exam Practice questions in the Teacher's Resource Materials.

TEACHING IDEA

AP® Exam Strategies

Continue having students practice test-taking skills. Copy the multiple-choice questions found on page 313. Give students the questions as a practice quiz prior to the unit or chapter test. Have students discuss with a partner why their answer choice was correct or incorrect.

AP® CLASSROOM

AP® Topic Questions

You can extend the AP® Exam Strategies activity on this page by logging into your AP® Classroom account and using the MCQ AP® Topic Questions under Topic 3.3, "Luther on War against the Turks," as more practice for your students. AP® Classroom allows you to set the questions up digitally or print out a copy for each student. Consider having students partner up and discuss the questions together to come to the correct answer.

When you assign the Topic Questions or Personal Progress Checks, it can be a good idea to put a timer on the question(s) so students can practice the skill in a timed setting like the AP® Exam.

Argumentation

AP® World History writing skills should be practiced on a regular basis. You can use the SAQs on pages 314 and 315 for students to write an "exit ticket" at the end of class to check for understanding and to practice their writing skills. The three SAQs can be spread across several days or as practice for the AP® Exam by writing them all at once. If you choose to make this exercise a timed writing, make certain that students have the correct amount of time for it. On exam day, students will have a total of 40 minutes to write three SAQs.

Short-Answer Questions

Read each question carefully and write a short response. Use complete sentences.

1. **Use this text and your knowledge of world history to answer all parts of the question that follows.**

> No religion is static, and over its two millennia of existence the Roman Catholic Church has transformed itself several times. In medieval Europe, ordinary laypeople knew little church doctrine. They received no formal religious instruction, and their pastors rarely preached. Such ignorance did not matter greatly in a world where everyone was by default Catholic.
>
> — Benjamin J. Kaplan, *European Faiths and States*, 2017

A. Explain ONE piece of historical evidence that would support Kaplan's argument that the Roman Catholic Church transformed itself during the early modern era.

B. Explain ONE piece of historical evidence that would contradict Kaplan's argument that the Roman Catholic Church transformed itself during the early modern era.

C. Explain ONE cause of the transformation described by Kaplan.

2. **Use these images and your knowledge of world history to answer all parts of the question that follows.**

Figure A: Skeleton drawings, 1300s

Figure B: Woodcut of a skeleton, 1543

314

A. Identify ONE change in Western Europe that accounts for the differences in the above images.

B. Identify ANOTHER change in Western Europe that accounts for the differences in the above images.

C. Explain ONE effect of the change depicted in these images.

3. **Use your knowledge of world history to answer all parts of the question that follows.**

A. Explain ONE specific similarity between Catholicism and Protestantism.

B. Explain ONE specific difference between Catholicism and Protestantism.

C. Explain the role of women in EITHER Catholicism or Protestantism.

315

6 Economic Transformations
Commerce and Consequence, 1450–1750

AP® Overview for Chapter 6

Chapter 6 corresponds with AP® Unit 4: Transoceanic Interconnections, 1450–1750. Trade and commerce form a critical part of the study of world history through all the major periods of the course. In the period between 1450 and 1750, expanding trade networks became truly global for the first time. In this early modern period, Western Europe emerged as a major player in international trade. In setting the stage for this era, trade was driven by the newly found wealth of Western Europe and the desire for global commodities such as silk, tea, porcelain, silver, fur, and even enslaved people. As Europeans moved into the Indian Ocean to trade and took control of the New World, networks of exchange developed that shaped the human interactions of this early modern period. The driving forces behind the desire for global commodities helped lay the foundation for the role that Western Europe would play on the world stage in the future.

Chapter 6 Essential Activity

This is a good place in the course to review the basics of writing the DBQ essay and to practice with the released Question 1 from the 2006 exam. Be aware that this prompt does not match the current essay format, but it is still good practice for the students. This DBQ asks students to analyze the social and economic effects of the global flow of silver from the mid-sixteenth century to the early eighteenth century. Find the essay question on the AP® World History page at AP® Central.

In order to bring Question 1 from the 2006 exam into alignment with the current DBQ requirements, consider removing Documents 1 and 5. Replace Document 1 with Map 6.2, located on page 328 in Chapter 6. You can also change the prompt to: Evaluate the extent to which the global flow of silver affected economic and/or social structures around the world in the mid-sixteenth to the eighteenth centuries.

Differentiation

If you want to differentiate the Chapter 6 Essential Activity and give students more practice with building their writing skills, follow the "Must Do, Should Do, Strive For" model below for a DBQ poster. You'll want to create groups of three to four students for the DBQ poster. More specific instructions for this assignment can be found in the Teacher's Resource Materials.

- Must Do: In their groups, students must analyze the documents and decide what two or three arguments they can create out of them. On their provided butcher paper (to create their poster), they need to name their arguments, glue the supporting documents under the corresponding argument, and write a quick analysis next to each document. Finally, students need to create a thesis statement that answers the prompt and write it at the bottom of their poster.

- Should Do: In their groups, students need to write one or two sourcing statements for each argument (ending with a total of at least three sourcing statements) and a contextualization (which should go above the thesis) on their poster. Once all the groups have completed their DBQ poster, have students hang them up and do a gallery walk to see how other groups put together this DBQ. As they look at each poster, ask students to leave "I wonder . . ." and "I like . . ." statements.

- Strive For: For students who want or need a writing challenge, have them choose one of their arguments from their DBQ poster and write a full argument paragraph on it.

TRM Essential Activity 6: DBQ Poster

Chapter 6 Resources

- **TRM** AP® Skills Workshop Activity Handout: Making Connections: Continuity and Change
- **TRM** Chapter 6 DBQ Activity Handout
- **TRM** Chapter 6 Guided Reading
- **TRM** Chapter 6 Lecture Presentation Slides
- **TRM** Chapter 6 Outline

- **TRM** Chapter 6 Suggested Responses to Questions
- **TRM** Eric's Activity 6: Commodities Change the World
- **TRM** Essential Activity 6: DBQ Poster
- **TRM** Handout 6.1: Graphic Organizer for European Interactions in Trade Networks
- **TRM** Handout 6.2: Dutch East India Company Questions

TRM Handout 6.3: Continuity and Change Chart for European Trade in the Indian Ocean

TRM Handout 6.4: Comparison Chart for Role of Silver in Spain and Japan

TRM Handout 6.5: Graphic Organizer for Atlantic World Debate

TRM Handout 6.6: Comparison Chart for Features and Effects of Slavery in Historical Eras

TRM Handout 6.7: Comparison Chart for Women in West Africa

TRM Handout 6.8: Comparison Chart for Role in the Slave Trade

TRM Map 6A: The Eastern Hemisphere

TRM Map 6B: The Western Hemisphere

TRM Map 6C: The World

TRM Writing Organizer for LEQ

Pacing Guide

Below is a pacing guide for the AP® World History: Modern course beginning in ca. 1200 C.E. This pacing guide is based on a schedule with 120 sessions of 50 minutes each before the AP® Exam. It is meant as a place to start. If you have a different number of sessions before the exam, you can modify the pacing to suit your needs.

Day	Pages Assigned	AP® Topic	AP® Theme	Suggested Assignments	Coverage Notes
1	Read pages 317–320 to "A Portuguese Empire of Commerce"	4.1 4.2 4.4 4.5 4.8	GOV ECN TEC	Teaching Idea: Class Discussion on page 317 Eric's Activity: Commodities Change the World on page 318 AP® Classroom: AP® Daily Videos on page 320	The beginning of Chapter 6 examines European involvement in already existing trade networks, such as the Indian Ocean network. It also looks at the development of European maritime empires in Afro-Eurasia, which would be good to link back to the discussion on maritime empires in the Americas in Chapter 4.
2	Read pages 320–323 from "A Portuguese Empire of Commerce" to "Spain and the Philippines"	4.2 4.4 4.5 4.8	GOV ECN	Building AP® Skills: Making Connections: Comparison on page 321 Apply the Tip on page 322 Teaching Idea: AP® Exam Strategies on page 322	See above.
3	Read pages 323–324 from "Spain and the Philippines" to "The East India Companies"	4.2 4.4 4.5 4.8	GOV ECN	Apply the Tip on page 323	See above.
4	Read pages 324–325 from "The East India Companies" to "Asians and Asian Commerce"	4.4 4.5	GOV ECN	Exploring AP® Themes: ECN on page 324 Apply the Tip on page 324 Apply the Tip on page 325	This section looks at the role that joint stock companies played in European involvement in global trade. You can compare the tactics of the East India Companies to the economic tactics used by Portugal and Spain in this chapter.
5	Read pages 325–327 from "Asians and Asian Commerce" to "Silver and Global Commerce"	4.4 4.8	ECN	Exploring AP® Themes: CDI on page 326 Building AP® Skills: Making Connections: Continuity and Change on page 327	While it's easy to focus on the actions of European states in Eurasian trade in this time period, it's important to also examine the role that Asian states played in this trade. It may be helpful to have students examine how Asian states' role in trade stayed the same and changed as Europeans became more involved in it.
6	Read pages 327–330 from "Silver and Global Commerce" through the second paragraph about the role of silver in Spain	4.5	ECN	Building AP® Skills: Claims and Evidence in Sources on page 328 Teaching Idea: Incorporating Outside Resources on page 328 Building AP® Skills: Argumentation on page 329	The global silver trade had major economic and political effects during the 1450–1750 era. Make sure to go over those with students.

Day	Pages Assigned	AP® Topic	AP® Theme	Suggested Assignments	Coverage Notes
7	Read pages 330–331 from the third paragraph about the role of silver in Japan to "'The World Hunt': Fur in Global Commerce"	4.5	ECN	Chapter 6 Essential Activity Building AP® Skills: Making Connections: Comparison on page 330	See above.
8	Read pages 331–335 from "'The World Hunt': Fur in Global Commerce" to "Commerce in People: The Transatlantic Slave System"	4.5	ECN	Teaching Idea: Class Discussion on page 331 Building AP® Skills: Making Connections: Causation and Making Connections: Comparison on page 332 Building AP® Skills: Making Connections: Comparison on page 335	Students can use this section to compare the impact of the fur trade on North America and Siberia.
9	Read pages 335–341 from "Commerce in People: The Transatlantic Slave System" to "The Slave Trade in Practice"	4.4 4.8	ECN SIO	Teaching Idea: Class Discussion on page 336 Exploring AP® Themes: ECN on page 337 Exploring AP® Themes: ECN on page 340	You should start off teaching about the transatlantic slave system by reviewing the features of slavery in earlier periods of world history and show the changes that happened with the introduction of the transatlantic slave trade.
10	Read pages 341–344 from "The Slave Trade in Practice" to "Consequences: The Impact of the Slave Trade in Africa"	4.4 4.5 4.6 4.8	ECN SIO	Teaching Idea: Incorporating Outside Resources on page 341 Teaching Idea: Incorporating Outside Resources on page 342 Apply the Tip on page 343 AP® Classroom: AP® Topic Questions on page 344	See above.
11	Read pages 344–348 from "Consequences: The Impact of the Slave Trade in Africa" to "Commerce and Social Change"	4.4 4.5 4.8	GOV ECN SIO	Building AP® Skills: Contextualization on page 344 Exploring AP® Themes: SIO on page 346 Building AP® Skills: Claims and Evidence in Sources on page 347	See above.
12	Read pages 348–352 from "Commerce and Social Change" through "Conclusions and Reflections"	4.5 4.7 4.8	ECN SIO	Apply the Tip on page 349 AP® Classroom: AP® Daily Videos on page 349 Apply the Tip on page 352	See above. A good culminating activity to bring together what students have learned about the slave trade during 1450–1750 would be to have them compare the features and effects of the slave trade in the Old World to its features and effects in the New World.

NOTES

Bell Ringer

A good knowledge of geography and map-reading skills are essential for success on the AP® World History: Modern Exam. Essay prompts often ask students to discuss regions as well as specific countries. To start off Chapter 6, give students two blank maps: one of the Eastern Hemisphere (including the Atlantic and Indian oceans and Pacific Oceania) and one of the Western Hemisphere (including the Atlantic and Pacific oceans). Ask students to identify and label the regions, continents, and important bodies of water. These maps will be used throughout Chapter 6. For blank maps that you can use with this activity, see the Teacher's Resource Materials.

TRM Map 6A: The Eastern Hemisphere

TRM Map 6B: The Western Hemisphere

BUILDING AP® SKILLS

Claims and Evidence in Sources

Consider having students work with a partner to analyze the illustration on this page of a sale of enslaved Africans to a European merchant. After they have had time to examine the image and discuss it with their partner, ask the following questions:

■ What emotions are expressed in the illustration? *The expressions on the faces of the people being sold are sad, even forlorn. The African selling the enslaved men seems casual and unconcerned.*

■ Do any other features surprise you? *Answers may vary, but could include: The image of an African involved in trade negotiations for enslaved people is surprising.*

The Atlantic Slave Trade This eighteenth-century French engraving shows the sale of enslaved Africans at Gorée, a major slave-trading port in what is now Dakar in Senegal. A European merchant and an African authority figure negotiate the arrangement, while the shackled victims wait for their fate to be decided. (Archives Charmet/Bridgeman Images)

316

Economic Transformations

Commerce and Consequence

1450–1750

◀ **AP®**

CLAIMS AND EVIDENCE IN SOURCES

What does this image tell historians about the relationship between Europeans and Africans in the Atlantic slave trade?

CONNECTING PAST AND PRESENT

"In the bowels of the Cape Coast Castle in Ghana, there's a dungeon built beneath the church chapel, where kidnapped and enslaved Africans could hear the devils above worshipping their god, while those below languished in misery until the slave ships arrived. I stood there, in that place, and inhaled deeply, swallowing mouthfuls of last breaths, and I almost choked. I could taste every bead of sweat and pain and blood and loss. I ran my fingers across the jagged walls and could feel their scarred flesh and bowed spines."[1] Such were the reflections of a young African American man, one of hundreds who journeyed to Ghana in 2019 as a part of the Year of Return, marking the 400th anniversary of the arrival in Virginia of the first enslaved Africans. ■

This visitor's emotional encounter with the legacy of the transatlantic slave system reminds us of the enormous significance of this commerce in human beings for the early modern world and of its continuing resonance even in the twenty-first century. Commerce in enslaved people, however, was only one component of those international networks of exchange that shaped human interactions during the centuries between 1450 and 1750. Europeans now smashed their way into the ancient spice trade of the Indian Ocean, developing new relationships with Asian societies. Silver, obtained from mines in Spanish America, enriched Western Europe, even as much of it made its way to China, where it allowed Europeans to participate more fully in the rich commerce of East Asia. Furs from North America and Siberia found a ready market in Europe and China, while the hunting and trapping of those fur-bearing animals transformed both natural environments and human societies. And despite their growing prominence in long-distance exchange, Europeans were far from the only actors in early modern commerce. Southeast Asians, Chinese, Indians, Armenians, Arabs,

317

TRM **Chapter 6 Guided Reading**
You can find a guided reading handout for this chapter in the Teacher's Resource Materials.

TRM **Chapter 6 Lecture Slides**
You can find curated lecture slides for this chapter in the Teacher's Resource Materials.

TRM **Chapter 6 Outline**
You can find a chapter outline to model good note-taking for this chapter in the Teacher's Resource Materials.

TRM **Suggested Responses to Questions**
You can find suggested responses to all of the AP® margin questions in this chapter in the Teacher's Resource Materials.

TEACHING IDEA

Class Discussion

To get students thinking about the major economic changes they are going to learn about in Chapter 6, you could ask them to define "globalization." After getting their definitions, explain that globalization has been happening since civilizations and states first began interacting with one another, though the definition of what the "globe" is has changed as groups expanded their understanding of the world around them. The first age of a truly interconnected world is 1450–1750. Then ask students to read the introduction to Chapter 6 with a partner and list the indicators of a truly global network of exchange they see in it. After students have done this, bring the class together to share what they have found. *Indicators of a global network of exchange include the African slave trade in the Americas, Europeans forcing their way into the Indian Ocean trade, new relationships with Asian societies, the emergence of silver as a global commodity, and animal hunting and trapping in North America for fur to be sold across the ocean.*

AP®
CONTINUITY AND CHANGE
In what different ways did global commerce transform human societies and the lives of individuals during the early modern era?

Africans, and Native Americans likewise played major roles in the making of the world economy during the early modern era.

Thus commerce joined empire and the spread of major cultural traditions as the joint creators of interlocking global networks during these centuries. Together they gave rise to new relationships, disrupted older ways of living, brought distant peoples into contact with one another, enriched some, and impoverished or enslaved others. What was gained and what was lost in the transformations born of global commerce have been the subject of great controversy ever since.

Europeans and Asian Commerce

Finding the Main Point: How did the strategies of different European states in the Indian Ocean region compare, and what effects did their involvement have on Asian commerce?

European empires in the Western Hemisphere grew out of an accident—Columbus's unknowing encounter with the Americas. In Asia, it was a very different story. The voyage (1497–1499) of the Portuguese mariner Vasco da Gama, in which Europeans sailed to India for the first time, was certainly no accident. It was the outcome of a deliberate, systematic, century-long Portuguese effort to explore a sea route to the East. Aided by the development of a small and agile sailing ship known as a caravel, the Portuguese during the fifteenth century crept slowly down the West African coast, around the tip of South Africa, up the East African coast, and finally crossed the Indian Ocean to India. There Europeans encountered an ancient and rich network of commerce that stretched from East Africa to China. They were certainly aware of the wealth of that commercial network, but largely ignorant of its workings.

AP®
CAUSATION
What drove European involvement in the world of Asian commerce?

The most immediate motivation for this massive effort was the desire for tropical spices—cinnamon, nutmeg, mace, cloves, and, above all, pepper—which were widely used as condiments, preservatives, medicines, and aphrodisiacs. A fifteenth-century English book declared: "Pepper [from Java] is black and has a good smack, And every man doth buy it."[2] Other products of the East, such as Chinese silk, Indian cottons, rhubarb for medicinal purposes, emeralds, rubies, and sapphires, were also in great demand.

AP®
CONTEXTUALIZATION
Why was Europe just beginning to participate in global commerce during the sixteenth century?

Underlying this growing interest in Asia was the more general recovery of European civilization following the disaster of the Black Death in the early fourteenth century. During the fifteenth century, Europe's population was growing again, and its national monarchies—in Spain, Portugal, England, and France—were learning how to tax their subjects more effectively and to build substantial military forces equipped with gunpowder weapons. Its cities were growing too. Some of them—in England, the Netherlands, and northern Italy, for example—were becoming centers of international commerce, giving birth to economies based on market exchange, private ownership, and the accumulation of capital for further investment.

Landmarks for Chapter 6

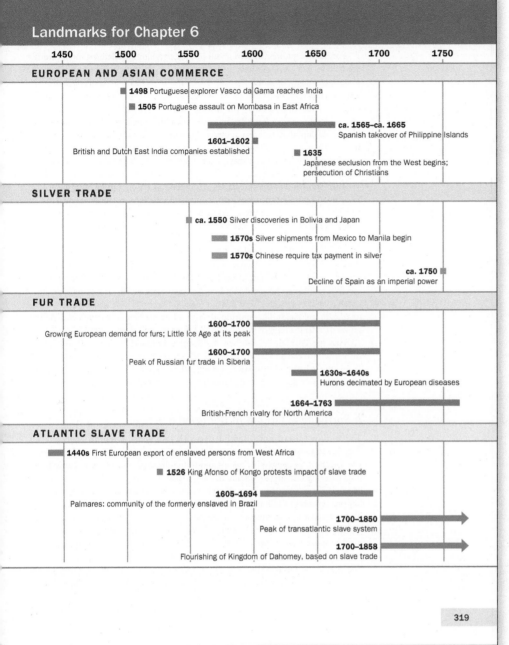

	1450	1500	1550	1600	1650	1700	1750

EUROPEAN AND ASIAN COMMERCE

1498 Portuguese explorer Vasco da Gama reaches India

1505 Portuguese assault on Mombasa in East Africa

ca. 1565–ca. 1665 Spanish takeover of Philippine Islands

1601–1602 British and Dutch East India companies established

1635 Japanese seclusion from the West begins; persecution of Christians

SILVER TRADE

ca. 1550 Silver discoveries in Bolivia and Japan

1570s Silver shipments from Mexico to Manila begin

1570s Chinese require tax payment in silver

ca. 1750 Decline of Spain as an imperial power

FUR TRADE

1600–1700 Growing European demand for furs; Little Ice Age at its peak

1600–1700 Peak of Russian fur trade in Siberia

1630s–1640s Hurons decimated by European diseases

1664–1763 British-French rivalry for North America

ATLANTIC SLAVE TRADE

1440s First European export of enslaved persons from West Africa

1526 King Afonso of Kongo protests impact of slave trade

1605–1694 Palmares: community of the formerly enslaved in Brazil

1700–1850 Peak of transatlantic slave system

1700–1858 Flourishing of Kingdom of Dahomey, based on slave trade

319

EXPLORING AP® THEMES

Governance (GOV) and Economic Systems (ECN)

It's good for students to know that politics and economics were closely intertwined during the early modern era. Have students look at "Landmarks for Chapter 6" and ask if it is possible to differentiate events that reflect global commerce and events that are political. *Because there is a close relationship between trade and politics, it is hard to distinguish these two influences as separate. Conquests in this period were often made to enhance global trade. Monarchs financed exploration voyages and helped trading companies such as the British and Dutch East India companies get established.*

Differentiation

If you would like to help students work on taking these connections further, use the "Must Do, Should Do, Strive For" model below:

■ Must Do: Students must be able to explain if it's possible to differentiate events that reflect global commerce and events that are political.

■ Should Do: Students should be able to examine the "Landmarks for Chapter 4," found on page 205, and make connections from the information about political changes on page 205 to the economic changes seen in "Landmarks for Chapter 6."

■ Strive For: Students can write an argument (one or two paragraphs) on whether they think the political changes or the economic changes from this time period had a greater impact on the world, using evidence they've gathered from Must Do and Should Do.

BUILDING AP® SKILLS

Contextualization

The early modern era is the first time Russia has emerged as a major player on the global stage for students. To help them situate the development of Russia's role on the global stage, ask: Why was Russia just now beginning to participate in global commerce? *Russia had to reorganize politically after the Mongol threat was over, and part of its political reorganization involved conquering Siberia. In this period, Russian monarchs wanted to expand their territory and become involved in the wealth available by participating in global commerce.*

TEACHING IDEA

Bell Ringer

Before students start learning about how the Portuguese built up their trading-post empire in the Indian Ocean, consider asking them to brainstorm reasons for how Portugal, and later on other European states, were able to become a controlling force in Indian Ocean trade. After a few minutes, ask them to share their thoughts with the class. Then ask them to read the introductory paragraph to "A Portuguese Empire of Commerce" on this page and compare what they've read to their brainstormed ideas. *Answers will vary, but may include: Brainstorming: The Portuguese had better and more advanced technology than groups in the Indian Ocean; Europeans "tricked" their way into Indian Ocean trade and then forced the already existing groups out. Comparison: Non-European ships in the Indian Ocean were not heavily armed like Portuguese ships (which had cannons); the withdrawal of the Chinese fleet from the Indian Ocean in the mid-1400s left the Ottoman Empire as the only group in a position to challenge the incoming Europeans, and the Portuguese were able to defeat the Ottomans after a series of military conflicts.*

For many centuries, Eastern goods had trickled into the Mediterranean through the Middle East from the Indian Ocean commercial network. From the viewpoint of an increasingly dynamic Europe, several major problems accompanied this pattern of trade. First, of course, the source of supply for these much-desired goods lay solidly in Muslim hands, most immediately in Egypt. The Italian commercial city of Venice largely monopolized the European trade in Eastern goods, annually sending convoys of ships to Alexandria in Egypt. Venetians resented the Muslim monopoly on Indian Ocean trade, and other European powers disliked relying on Venice as well as on Muslims. Circumventing these monopolies provided both religious and political motivations for the Portuguese to attempt a sea route to India that bypassed both Venetian and Muslim intermediaries. In addition, many Europeans were persuaded that a mysterious Christian monarch, known as Prester John, ruled somewhere in Asia or Africa. Joining with his mythical kingdom to continue the Crusades and combat a common Islamic enemy was likewise a goal of the Portuguese voyages.

A further problem for Europeans lay in paying for Eastern goods. Few products of an economically less developed Europe were attractive in Eastern markets. Thus Europeans were required to pay cash—gold or silver—for Asian spices or textiles. This persistent trade deficit contributed much to the intense desire for precious metals that attracted early modern European explorers, traders, and conquerors. Portuguese voyages along the West African coast, for example, were seeking direct access to African goldfields. The enormously rich silver deposits of Mexico and Bolivia provided at least a temporary solution to this persistent European problem.

First the Portuguese and then the Spanish, French, Dutch, and British found their way into the ancient Asian world of Indian Ocean commerce (see Map 6.1). How they behaved in that world and what they created there differed considerably, but collectively they contributed much to the new regime of globalized trade.

A Portuguese Empire of Commerce

The **Indian Ocean commercial network** into which Vasco da Gama and his Portuguese successors sailed was a world away from anything they had known. It was vast, both in geographic extent and in the diversity of those who participated in it. East Africans, Arabs, Persians, Indians, Malays, Chinese, and others traded freely. Most of them were Muslims, though hailing from many separate communities, but practitioners of Hinduism, Buddhism, Christianity, Judaism, and Confucianism likewise had a role in this commercial network. Had the Portuguese sought simply to participate in peaceful trading, they certainly could have done so, but it was quickly apparent that European trade goods were crude and unattractive in Asian markets and that Europeans would be unable to compete effectively. Moreover, the Portuguese soon learned that most Indian Ocean merchant ships were not heavily armed and certainly lacked the onboard cannons that Portuguese ships carried. Since the withdrawal of the Chinese fleet from the Indian Ocean early in the fifteenth century, only the Muslim Ottoman Empire was in a position to challenge

AP®
DEVELOPMENTS AND PROCESSES
To what extent did the Portuguese realize their goals in the Indian Ocean?

MAPPING HISTORY | Map 6.1 **Europeans in Asia in the Early Modern Era**

The early modern era witnessed only very limited territorial control by Europeans in Asia. Trade, rather than empire, was the chief concern of the Western newcomers, who were not, in any event, a serious military threat to major Asian states.

Reading the Map: Where were Dutch-controlled territories concentrated? Where were Portuguese territories concentrated?

AP® Making Connections: Compare this map with Map 10.1: Colonial Asia in the Early Twentieth Century. What distinguished the European empires of the early modern period from those of the early twentieth century? What remained similar?

the intruding Portuguese. A series of military confrontations during the sixteenth century ended in a decisive victory for the Portuguese, whose ships outgunned and outmaneuvered both Ottoman and other competing naval forces, while their onboard cannons devastated coastal fortifications.

Although their overall economy lagged behind that of Asian producers, this military advantage enabled the Portuguese to quickly establish fortified bases at several key locations within the Indian Ocean world—Mombasa in East Africa, Hormuz at the entrance to the Persian Gulf, Goa on the west coast of India, Melaka in Southeast Asia, and Macao on the south coast of China. With the exception of Macao, which had been obtained through bribery and negotiations with Chinese authorities, these Portuguese bases were obtained forcibly against small and weak states. In Mombasa, for example, the commander of a Portuguese fleet responded

---

BUILDING AP® SKILLS

Making Connections: Comparison

It's good for students to be able to explain why Europeans' colonial holdings in the Eastern Hemisphere were different from their holdings in the Western Hemisphere. Display Map 6.1, "Europeans in Asia in the Early Modern Era," and Map 4.1, "European Colonial Empires in the Americas" (found on page 206) for students to study. Ask students:

■ Which parts of Asia were Europeans able to control? *In Asia, Europeans were able to control port cities along the African coastline, Malaysia, and the Philippines.*

■ Why do you think Europeans controlled less territory in the Indian Ocean basin than in the Americas? *Answers will vary, but may include: Europeans had better technology than people in the Americas, making it easier to take over large areas, while they would have been more evenly matched with groups in the Indian Ocean; Europeans might have had a harder time establishing their presence in the Indian Ocean basin because of the already existing strong states there; The Indian Ocean might have been more difficult to control for Europeans than the lands of the Americas.*

The text in "A Portuguese Empire of Commerce" will help students understand the difference between European holdings in the two regions if students struggle with answering the second question.

EXPLORING AP® THEMES

Humans and the Environment (ENV)

Students should know at least one port city on each of the western, northern, and eastern edges of the Indian Ocean in case they need to reference it as evidence in an essay. Ask students to name the cities controlled by the Portuguese, the Dutch, and the Spanish. (Answers are provided in italics.)

■ **Portuguese:** *Luanda, Mombasa, Zanzibar, Mozambique, Sofala, and Delagoa Bay*

■ **Dutch:** *Gallo, Melaka, and Batavia*

■ **Spanish:** *Manila*

If you used the Bell Ringer activity on page 316 involving blank maps, suggest that students label these port cities on their Eastern Hemisphere maps. For a blank map that you can use with this activity, see the Teacher's Resource Materials.

TRM Map 6A: The Eastern Hemisphere

to local resistance in 1505 by burning and sacking the city, killing some 1,500 people, and seizing large quantities of cotton and silk textiles and carpets. The king of Mombasa wrote a warning to a neighboring city:

> This is to inform you that a great lord has passed through the town, burning it and laying it waste. He came to the town in such strength and was of such a cruelty that he spared neither man nor woman, or old nor young—nay, not even the smallest child. . . . Nor can I ascertain nor estimate what wealth they have taken from the town.[3]

What the Portuguese created in the Indian Ocean is commonly known as a **trading post empire**, for they aimed to control commerce, not large territories or populations, and to do so by force of arms rather than by economic competition. Seeking to monopolize the spice trade, the Portuguese king grandly titled himself "Lord of the Conquest, Navigation, and Commerce of Ethiopia, Arabia, Persia, and India." Portuguese authorities in the East tried to require all merchant vessels to purchase a *cartaz*, or pass, and to pay duties of 6 to 10 percent on their cargoes. They partially blocked the traditional Red Sea route to the Mediterranean and for a century or so monopolized the highly profitable route around Africa to Europe. Even so, they never succeeded in controlling much more than half of the spice trade to Europe, and from the mid-sixteenth into the eighteenth century older routes by both land and sea through the Ottoman Empire into the Mediterranean revived and even prospered.

Failing to dominate Indian Ocean commerce as they had hoped, the Portuguese gradually assimilated themselves to its ancient patterns. They became heavily involved in the "carrying trade," transporting Asian goods to Asian ports, thus selling their shipping services because they were largely unable to sell their goods. Even in their major settlements, the Portuguese were outnumbered by Asian traders, and

The Spice Trade For thousands of years, spices were a major trade item in the Indian Ocean commercial network, as this fifteenth-century French depiction of the gathering of pepper in southern India illustrates. In the early modern era, Europeans gained direct access to this ancient network for the first time. (Archives Charmet/Bridgeman Images)

---

many married Asian women. Hundreds of Portuguese escaped the control of their government altogether and settled in Asian or African ports, where they learned local languages, sometimes converted to Islam, and became simply one more group in the diverse trading culture of the East.

By 1600, the Portuguese trading post empire was in steep decline. This small European country was overextended, and rising Asian states such as Japan, Burma, Mughal India, Persia, and the sultanate of Oman actively resisted Portuguese commercial control. Unwilling to accept a dominant Portuguese role in the Indian Ocean, other European countries also gradually contested Portugal's efforts to monopolize the rich spice trade to Europe.

Spain and the Philippines

The Spanish were the first to challenge Portugal's position as they established themselves on what became the Philippine Islands, named after the Spanish king Philip II. There they found an archipelago of islands, thousands of them, occupied by culturally diverse peoples and organized in small and highly competitive chiefdoms. One of the local chiefs later told the Spanish: "There is no king and no sole authority in this land; but everyone holds his own view and opinion, and does as he prefers."[4] Some of these chiefdoms were involved in tribute trade with China, and a small number of Chinese settlers lived in the port towns. Nonetheless, the region was of little interest to the governments of China and Japan, the major powers in the area.

These conditions—proximity to China and the Spice Islands, small and militarily weak societies, the absence of competing claims—facilitated the Spanish in establishing outright colonial rule on the islands of the **Philippines**, rather than imitating a Portuguese-style trading post empire. Accomplished largely from Spanish Mexico, conquest and colonization involved small-scale military operations, gunpowder weapons, local alliances, gifts and favors to chiefs, and the pageantry of Catholic ritual, all of which contributed to a relatively easy and often bloodless Spanish takeover of the islands in the century or so after 1565. Accompanying Spanish rule was a major missionary effort that turned Filipino society into the only major outpost of Christianity in Asia. That effort also opened up a new front in the long encounter of Christendom and Islam, for on the southern island of Mindanao, Islam was gaining strength and provided an ideology of resistance to Spanish encroachment for 300 years. Indeed, Mindanao remains a contested part of the Philippines into the twenty-first century.

Beyond the missionary enterprise, other features of Spanish colonial practice in the Americas found expression in the Philippines. People living in scattered settlements were persuaded or forced to relocate into more concentrated Christian communities. Tribute, taxes, and forced labor became part of ordinary life. Large landed estates emerged, owned by Spanish settlers, Catholic religious orders, or prominent Filipinos. Women who had played major roles as ritual specialists, healers, and midwives were now displaced by male Spanish priests, and the ceremonial instruments of these women were deliberately defiled and disgraced. Short-lived revolts and flight to interior mountains were among the Filipino responses to colonial oppression.

AP EXAM TIP
Note the factors that led to Portugal's decline as a power in the Indian Ocean trade network.

AP EXAM TIP
Understand Spain's reasons for taking over the Philippines.

AP
COMPARISON
How did the Portuguese, Spanish, Dutch, and British initiatives in Asia differ from one another?

APPLY THE TIP

After students have learned about the Portuguese trading-post empire, have a quick class discussion on why they declined as a power in the Indian Ocean trade network. *The Portuguese economy was overextended, and Asian states such as Japan, Mughal India, and the Sultanate of Oman actively resisted Portuguese commercial control. Other European states, such as Spain, France, the Netherlands, and England, actively contested Portugal's attempts to monopolize the spice trade.*

APPLY THE TIP

It can be helpful for students to look into why individual European states were motivated to conquer the areas they did. Ask students: Why did Spain take over the Philippines? *Spain took over the Philippines because of their proximity to China. The Philippines had no clear political centralization, which made it easy for Spain to exert control through bribery, gunpowder weapons, and alliances. Spain used the Philippines as an outpost in the Pacific to handle the silver coming from the Americas into Asia.*

EXPLORING AP® THEMES

Cultural Developments and Interactions (CDI)

Students are often familiar with the cultural influence that European empires had on American societies, but they are less familiar with their influence in the Indian Ocean and Asia. You can start a brief class discussion by asking students to explain how the Spanish changed the culture of the Philippines by turning the Philippines into the only major outpost of Christianity in Asia. *Local practices declined as the population was forced to live in more concentrated Christian communities. Women who had been ritual specialists, healers, and midwives were replaced by male Spanish priests, and their former practices were disgraced.*

EXPLORING AP® THEMES

Economic Systems (ECN)

Understanding the terms "capitalism" and "mercantilism" is important from this point on in AP® World History: Modern. Knowing how to use these terms correctly can help students understand economic events on a global basis. Ask students to work with a partner using "Think, Pair, Share" to define "capitalism" and "mercantilism" in their own words. Discuss their definitions as a class, and then give students a working definition of both terms as they apply to this chapter. *The Oxford English Dictionary defines capitalism as "an economic and political system in which a country's trade and industry are controlled by private owners for profit, rather than by the state." Its definition for mercantilism is "the economic theory that trade generates wealth and is stimulated by the accumulation of profitable balances, which a government should encourage by means of protectionism."*

APPLY THE TIP

In the episode *Capitalism and the Dutch East India Company* of Crash Course World History, John Green talks about the Vereenigde Oostindische Compagnie (VOC) doing business as the Dutch East India Company. In the sixteenth and seventeenth centuries, the Netherlands dominated world trade through the innovative use of corporations and finance. Watching this video can help students understand the meaning of joint stock corporation, maritime insurance, and futures trading. The video can be found on YouTube. You can either assign the video as homework or show it in class. A list of questions for use with the video can be found in the Teacher's Resource Materials.

TRM Handout 6.2: Dutch East India Company Questions

Yet others fled to **Manila**, the new capital of the colonial Philippines. By 1600, it had become a flourishing and culturally diverse city of more than 40,000 inhabitants and was home to many Spanish settlers and officials and growing numbers of Filipino migrants. Its rising prosperity also attracted some 3,000 Japanese and more than 20,000 Chinese. Serving as traders, artisans, and sailors, the Chinese in particular became an essential element in the Spanish colony's growing economic relationship with China; however, their economic prominence and their resistance to conversion earned them Spanish hostility and clearly discriminatory treatment. Periodic Chinese revolts, followed by expulsions and massacres, were the result. On one occasion in 1603, the Spanish killed about 20,000 people, nearly the entire Chinese population of the island.

The East India Companies

Far more important than the Spanish as European competitors for the spice trade were the Dutch and English, both of whom entered Indian Ocean commerce in the early seventeenth century. Together these rising North European powers quickly overtook and displaced the Portuguese, often by force, even as they competed vigorously with each other as well. During the sixteenth century, the Dutch had become a highly commercialized and urbanized society, and their business skills and maritime shipping operations were the envy of Europe. Around 1600, both the British and the Dutch, unlike the Portuguese, organized their Indian Ocean ventures through private companies. Both the **British East India Company** and the **Dutch East India Company** were joint stock companies, a novel form of corporate finance that pooled money from investors who purchased shares, or units, in the company. This form of corporate finance, so central to global capitalism today, allowed investors to benefit from the company's success through distributions of profits and rising share prices, while limiting their losses to the amount invested. Both companies were granted charters by their governments that gave great latitude to their investors and employees, allowing them to form their own armies, make war, govern conquered peoples, and print their own money. In this way, they established their own

A European View of Asian Commerce The various East India companies (British, French, and Dutch) represented the major vehicle for European commerce in Asia during the early modern era. This wall painting, dating from 1778 and titled *The East Offering Its Riches to Britannia*, hung in the main offices of the British East India Company. (© British Library Board. All Rights Reserved/Bridgeman Images)

BUILDING AP® SKILLS

Claims and Evidence in Sources

You should try to have students practice the skill of analyzing all types of sources for evidence throughout the year, since this practice will help them on multiple parts of the AP® Exam. Ask students to look at the painting titled *The East Offering Its Riches to Britannia* (captioned "A European View of Asian Commerce" on this page). Then ask students to read the full caption and write a paragraph that describes the European view toward non-Europeans reflected in the painting.

Answers may vary, but can include: The painting uses symbolism from the European Greek and Roman past; The Europeans are portrayed as Roman gods and goddesses and therefore appear to be superior to all others; The Indigenous population appears to be a supplicant and seems to be offering goods, probably spices, to the gods in return for good treatment and peace; The Indigenous population is viewed as subservient to the Europeans.

parallel and competing trading post empires, with the Dutch focused on the islands of Indonesia and the English on India. A similar French company also established a presence in the Indian Ocean basin, beginning in 1664.

Operating in a region of fragmented and weak political authority, the Dutch acted to control not only the shipping of cloves, cinnamon, nutmeg, and mace but also their production. With much bloodshed, the Dutch seized control of a number of small spice-producing islands, forcing their people to sell only to the Dutch and destroying the crops of those who refused. One Indonesian sultan asked a Dutch commander, "Do you believe that God has preserved for your trade alone islands which lie so far from your homeland?"[5] Apparently the Dutch did. And for a time in the seventeenth century, they were able to monopolize the trade in nutmeg, mace, and cloves. Using a combination of *fluyts* (large, innovative, and relatively inexpensive cargo ships) for regional trade and hardier, more heavily armed ships for transoceanic voyages, the Dutch transported these spices to ports across Eurasia, selling them at fourteen to seventeen times the price they paid in Indonesia.[6] While Dutch profits soared, the local economy of the Spice Islands was shattered and their people were impoverished.

The British East India Company operated differently from its Dutch counterpart. Less well financed and less commercially sophisticated, the British were largely excluded from the rich Spice Islands by the Dutch monopoly. Thus they fell back on India, where they established three major trading settlements during the seventeenth century: Bombay (now Mumbai) on India's west coast, and Calcutta (now Kolkata) and Madras (now Chennai) on the east coast. Although British naval forces soon gained control of the Arabian Sea and the Persian Gulf, largely replacing the Portuguese, on land they were no match for the powerful Mughal Empire, which ruled most of the Indian subcontinent.

Therefore, the British were unable to practice "trade by warfare," as the Dutch did in Indonesia.[7] Rather, they secured their trading bases with the permission of Mughal authorities or local rulers, with substantial payments and bribes as the price of admission to the Indian market. When some independent English traders plundered a Mughal ship in 1636, local authorities detained British East India Company officials for two months and forced them to pay a whopping fine.

Like the Portuguese before them, both the Dutch and English became heavily involved in trade within Asia. The profits from this "carrying trade" enabled them to purchase Asian goods without paying for them in gold or silver from Europe. Dutch and English traders also began to deal in bulk goods for a mass market—pepper, textiles, and later, tea and coffee—rather than just luxury goods for an elite market. In the second half of the eighteenth century, both the Dutch and British trading post empires slowly evolved into a more conventional form of colonial domination, in which the British came to rule India and the Dutch controlled Indonesia.

Asians and Asian Commerce

The European presence was far less significant in Asia than it was in the Americas or Africa during these centuries. European political control was limited to the Philippines, parts of Java, and a few of the Spice Islands. The small Southeast Asian state of Siam

---

AP®

CONTINUITY AND CHANGE
To what extent did the British and Dutch trading companies change the societies they encountered in Asia?

AP®

COMPARISON
What was similar and what was different in how the Dutch and British behaved in the Indian Ocean world?

AP® EXAM TIP
Understand how European trade in the Indian Ocean evolved over time in the era 1450–1750.

AP®

CONTINUITY AND CHANGE
What role did Asian political authorities and merchants play in Indian Ocean commerce in the face of European intrusion?

AP® CLASSROOM

AP® Question Bank

A good set of multiple-choice questions that go along with this section on the Dutch East India Company can be found in the Question Bank in AP® Classroom. You can find the three questions by searching for "Differences in clove prices and imperialism," "Dutch monopoly on clove trade," and "Price fluctuations of cloves and causes of" in the Question Bank. Students could either work through the questions on their own as a quick check for knowledge or discuss them with a partner.

APPLY THE TIP

If you had students write the 2019 released DBQ from page 322, you could have them look at how other European states impacted trade in the Indian Ocean by creating a continuity and change chart like the one below. Ask students to work with a partner to examine the evolution of European trade in the Indian Ocean between 1450 and 1750 and record their findings in the chart. A reproducible version of this chart is available in the Teacher's Resource Materials. (Answers are provided in italics.)

European Trade in the Indian Ocean, ca. 1450	European Trade in the Indian Ocean, ca. 1750
▪ *The Portuguese began voyages of exploration into the Indian Ocean; they saw the wealth from the commerce and wanted to insert themselves into these long-established trade routes.* ▪ *The Portuguese established themselves by creating a trading-post empire in the Indian Ocean.* ▪ *The Portuguese attempted to control the Indian Ocean trade.*	▪ *Portugal was no longer the primary European power in the Indian Ocean.* ▪ *The Netherlands took control of the spice trade in Indonesia.* ▪ *The British were slowly taking control of India as well as the port cities.* ▪ *Both the Dutch and British took part in the "carrying trade," or trade within Asia, which allowed them to purchase Asian goods without gold or silver.* ▪ *Dutch and British traders began dealing in bulk goods for a mass market rather than just luxury goods for the elite.*

TRM Handout 6.3: Continuity and Change Chart for European Trade in the Indian Ocean was able to expel the French in 1688, outraged by their aggressive religious efforts at conversion and their plotting to extend French influence. To the great powers of Asia—Mughal India, China, and Japan—Europeans represented no real military threat and played minor roles in their large and prosperous economies. Japan provides a fascinating case study in the ability of major Asian powers to control the European intruders.

When Portuguese traders and missionaries first arrived in that island nation in the mid-sixteenth century, soon followed by Spanish, Dutch, and English merchants, Japan was plagued by endemic conflict among numerous feudal lords, known as *daimyo*, each with his own cadre of *samurai* warriors. In these circumstances, the European newcomers found a hospitable welcome; their military technology, shipbuilding skills, geographic knowledge, commercial opportunities, and even religious ideas proved useful or attractive to various elements in Japan's fractious and competitive society. The second half of the sixteenth century, for example, witnessed the growth of a substantial Christian movement, with some 300,000 converts and a Japanese-led church organization.

AP EXAM TIP
Understand the roles of the samurai and the daimyo during the Tokugawa shogunate, as well as the interactions between Japan and European traders in this era.

By the early seventeenth century, however, a series of remarkable military figures had unified Japan politically under the leadership of a supreme military commander known as the *shogun*, who hailed from the Tokugawa clan. With the end of Japan's civil wars, many samurai warriors gradually became salaried bureaucrats or administrators, even as they maintained a distinctive status in society, expressed in the unique permission granted them to wear their exquisite swords. Furthermore, successive shoguns came to view Europeans as a threat to the country's newly established unity rather than as an opportunity. They therefore expelled Christian missionaries and violently suppressed the practice of Christianity. This policy included the execution, often under torture, of some sixty-two missionaries and thousands of Japanese converts. In Japan's Closed Country Edict of 1635, shogunate authorities also forbade Japanese from traveling abroad and banned most European traders altogether. Thus, for two centuries (1650–1850), Japanese authorities of the Tokugawa shogunate pursued isolationist trade policies, largely closing their country off from the emerging world of European commerce. Alone among Europeans, the Dutch, regarded as less interested in spreading Christianity, were permitted to trade from the small artificial island of Dejima in the port of Nagasaki. That connection gave Japan a limited exposure to advances in European technology and medicine. This "Dutch learning" may have contributed something to Japan's rapid modernization in the later nineteenth century.

But Japan retained its trading ties with China, Korea, and Southeast Asia. In the early seventeenth century, a large number of Japanese traders began to operate in Southeast Asia, where they behaved much like the newly arriving Europeans, frequently using force in support of their commercial interests. But unlike European states, the Japanese government of the Tokugawa shogunate explicitly disavowed any responsibility for or connection with these Japanese merchants. In one of many letters to rulers of Southeast Asian states, the Tokugawa shogun wrote to officials in Cambodia in 1610:

> Merchants from my country [Japan] go to several places in your country [Cambodia] as well as Cochinchina and Champa [Vietnam]. There they become cruel and ferocious. . . . These men cause terrible damage. . . . They

APPLY THE TIP

The Tokugawa shogunate is an important part of the development of East Asia in this period because it gives context for Japan's growth on the global stage during the Meiji Restoration in the 1860s. You could ask students to review the history of Japan from Chapter 2 with a partner. Give the class 3 minutes to write down everything they remember about Japan. Then discuss the facts that students remember and fill in the gaps. (Answers are provided in italics.)

■ *Japanese rulers adopted many items from the Chinese government, including Chinese-style court rituals, court rankings for officials, the Chinese calendar, and tax and legal codes.*

■ *Although Japan borrowed heavily from Chinese culture, the influence diminished by the tenth century and a very distinctive Japanese culture began to develop.*

■ *Political power became decentralized and the emperor began to have only a ceremonial role. Warlords in the provinces had their own armies made up of samurai warriors and often fought for political control.*

Then ask: Why was the unification of Japan under the Tokugawa shogun significant in the history of East Asia? *Ending the civil wars allowed the Japanese economy to grow. Because European merchants and missionaries were expelled from Japan after initially being welcomed, Japanese culture was less influenced by Europeans than cultures in other parts of Asia.*

EXPLORING AP® THEMES

Cultural Developments and Interactions (CDI)

Cultural diffusion due to trade is a concept that constantly pops up throughout world history. You can get students to think about how cultural diffusion in Tokugawa Japan was different from other examples of cultural diffusion by asking: How did European traders and the Japanese interact in the early modern period? *At first the Portuguese and other Europeans were welcomed. Missionaries spread Christianity throughout Japan. The Tokugawa used European military technology to unite Japan politically. By the end of the early modern period, Japan had expelled all Europeans and isolated itself from European contact except for a few Dutch merchants. Christianity was viewed as harmful to Japanese culture, and missionaries were also expelled.*

commit crimes and cause suffering. . . . Their offenses are extremely serious. Please punish them immediately according to the laws of your country. It is not necessary to have any reservations in this regard.[8]

Thus Japanese merchants lacked the kind of support from their government that European merchants consistently received, but they did not refrain from trading in Southeast Asia.

Nor did other Asian merchants disappear from the Indian Ocean, despite European naval dominance. Arab, Indian, Japanese, Chinese, Javanese, Malay, Vietnamese, and other traders benefited from the upsurge in seaborne commerce. Despite an official Ming dynasty policy sharply restricting private maritime trading, a long-term movement of Chinese merchants into Southeast Asian port cities continued in the early modern era, enabling the Chinese to dominate the growing spice trade between that region and China. Southeast Asian merchants, many of them women, continued a long tradition of involvement in international trade. Malay proverbs from the sixteenth century, for example, encouraged "teaching daughters how to calculate and make a profit."[9] Overland trade within Asia remained wholly in Asian hands and grew considerably. Based in New Julfa near the capital of the Safavid Empire, Christian merchants originally from Armenia were particularly active in the commerce linking Europe, the Middle East, Central Asia, and India, with a few traveling as far as the Philippines and Mexico in pursuit of trading opportunities. Tens of thousands of Indian merchants and moneylenders, mostly Hindus representing sophisticated family firms, lived throughout Central Asia, Persia, and Russia, thus connecting this vast region to markets in India. These international Asian commercial networks, equivalent in their commercial sophistication to those of Europe, continued to operate successfully even as Europeans militarized the seaborne commerce of the Indian Ocean.

Within India, large and wealthy family firms, such as the one headed by Virji Vora during the seventeenth century, were able to monopolize the buying and selling of particular products, such as pepper or coral, and thus dictate terms and prices to the European trading companies. "He knoweth that wee must sell," complained one English trader about Vora, "and so beats us downe till we come to his owne rates." Furthermore, Vora was often the only source of loans for the cash-strapped Europeans, forcing them to pay interest rates as high as 12 to 18 percent annually. Despite their resentments, Europeans had little choice, because "none but Virji Vora hath moneye to lend or will lend."[10]

Silver and Global Commerce

Finding the Main Point: What was the significance of the silver trade in the global history of the early modern era?

Even more than the spice trade of Eurasia, it was the silver trade that gave birth to a genuinely global network of exchange (see Map 6.2). As one historian put it, silver "went round the world and made the world go round."[11] The mid-sixteenth-century discovery of enormously rich silver deposits in Bolivia, and simultaneously in Japan, suddenly

BUILDING AP® SKILLS

Claims and Evidence in Sources

You should try to have students practice analyzing maps, graphs, and images for evidence or to create arguments frequently throughout the year. You can show students Map 6.2, "The Global Silver Trade," and then ask the following questions:

■ How might you describe the flow of silver around the world, based on your observations of the map? *The Viceroyalty of Peru and Japan had a net outflow; India and Qing China had a net inflow; and New Spain, Spain, Arabia, and the Netherlands appear to have both imported and exported silver.*

■ Where did most of the silver end up after it left Spain? What was the reason for its ultimate destination? *Most of it seems to have ended up in either India or China. Spain was using much of the silver it gained to purchase exotic goods such as silk and porcelain from India and China.*

TEACHING IDEA

Incorporating Outside Resources

The Crash Course World History video *The Spanish Empire, Silver, and Runaway Inflation* is a great way for students to learn about the impact of the global silver trade during 1450–1750. In this episode, John Green examines how Spanish exploitation of the New World enabled Spain to become one of the most powerful empires on earth in a very short time. John Green goes on to explain how Spain destroyed both the Aztec and Inca empires in the Americas. The video can be found on YouTube. Either assign the video as homework or show it in class. Then ask students the following questions:

■ Describe the political structure of the Aztecs. *The Aztec state was very hierarchical, with the emperor at the top and nobles beneath him. A powerful priest class kept order.*

■ Why did the Spanish rely on Indigenous people as a labor source instead of importing enslaved people from Africa? *Enslaved Africans did not have experience working at high altitudes. In addition, enslaved people were expensive, and mine work was very dangerous. High death rates and the need for frequent replacement of enslaved workers would have made the use of enslaved labor too costly.*

■ Why did the Spanish economy begin to decline despite the influx of silver? *The influx*

▲ AP® DEVELOPMENTS AND PROCESSES
Based on the map, what role did silver play in global trade? Why did a majority of silver end up in Spain and China?

AP® CONTEXTUALIZATION
What was the significance of the silver trade in the early modern era of world history?

Map 6.2 The Global Silver Trade
Silver was one of the first major commodities to be exchanged on a genuinely global scale.

provided a vastly increased supply of that precious metal. Spanish America alone produced perhaps 85 percent of the world's silver during the early modern era. Spain's sole Asian colony, the Philippines, provided a critical link in this emerging network of global commerce, with Manila, the colonial capital of the Philippines, as the destination of annual Spanish shipments of silver. Drawn primarily from the rich mines of Bolivia, transported initially to Acapulco in Mexico, this silver was shipped across the Pacific to the Philippines aboard large and heavily armed ships called Manila galleons. This trade was the first direct and sustained link between the Americas and Asia, and it initiated a web of trans-Pacific commerce that grew steadily over the centuries.

At the heart of that Pacific web, and of early modern global commerce generally, was China's huge economy, especially its growing demand for silver. In the 1570s, Chinese authorities consolidated a variety of tax levies into a single tax, which its huge population was now required to pay in silver. This sudden new demand for the white metal caused its value to skyrocket. It meant that foreigners with silver could now purchase far more of China's silks and porcelains than before.

This demand set silver in motion around the world, with the bulk of the world's silver supply winding up in China and much of the rest elsewhere in Asia. The routes by which this **"silver drain"** operated were numerous. Chinese, Portuguese, and Dutch traders flocked to Manila to sell Chinese goods in exchange for silver. European ships carried Japanese silver to China. Much of the silver shipped across the Atlantic to Spain was spent in Europe generally and then used to pay for the Asian goods that the French,

(continued)

of silver caused massive inflation. The Spanish never set tax rates to account for inflation. They restricted economic development and spent a huge amount on warfare.

■ How could silver be described as the first truly global market? *China and Spain experienced inflation, which weakened both countries' economies and governments. Everyone, even India and Japan, was involved in the silver trade.*

◄ **AP®**
CLAIMS AND EVIDENCE
IN SOURCES
What does the image
show about the labor
system used at the
silver mine of Potosí?

A Silver Mine of Potosí This colonial-era painting shows the enormously rich silver mines of Potosí, then a major global source of the precious metal and the largest city in the Americas. Brutally hard work and poisonous exposure to the mercury used in the refining process led to the deaths of many thousands of workers, even as the silver transformed the world economy in the early modern era. (Granger – Historical Picture Archive)

British, and Dutch so greatly desired. Silver paid for some enslaved Africans and for spices in Southeast Asia. The standard Spanish silver coin, known as a **piece of eight**, was used by merchants in North America, Europe, India, Russia, and West Africa as a medium of exchange. By 1600, it circulated widely in southern China. A Portuguese merchant in 1621 noted that silver "wanders throughout all the world . . . before flocking to China, where it remains as if at its natural center."[12]

In its global journeys, silver transformed much that it touched. At the world's largest silver mine in what is now Bolivia, the city of **Potosí** arose from a barren landscape high in the Andes, ten weeks' journey by mule from Lima. "New people arrive by the hour, attracted by the smell of silver," commented a Spanish observer in the 1570s.[13] With 160,000 people, Potosí became the largest city in the Americas and equivalent in size to London, Amsterdam, or Seville. Its wealthy European elite lived in luxury, with all the goods of Europe and Asia at their disposal. Meanwhile, the city's Native American miners worked in conditions so horrendous that some families held funeral services for men drafted to work in the mines. A Spanish priest observed, "Once inside they spend the whole week in there without emerging. . . . If 20 healthy Indians enter on Monday, half may emerge crippled on Saturday."[14] The environment too suffered, as highly intensive mining techniques caused severe deforestation, soil erosion, and flooding.

TEACHING IDEA

Incorporating Outside Resources

Students may be surprised to discover that the mine at Potosí, where the Spanish mined for silver in the sixteenth century, is still an active mine today. The short video *City of Potosí* is an interesting look at Potosí, a large industrial complex controlled by Spain in the sixteenth century. The extraction of silver from the mountain was a complex process that relied on both technology and forced Indigenous labor. The video can be found by searching "city of Potosí" on the UNESCO World Heritage site and clicking on the "Video" tab of the city's page. You can either assign the video as homework or show it in class. Then ask students the following questions:

■ How much of the world's silver during the sixteenth century was extracted from Potosí? *Over 50 percent of the world's silver during the sixteenth century was extracted from Potosí.*

■ Why was Potosí referred to as the "El Dorado of the Andes"? *Almost everything used in the churches was produced in silver. Wealth was very obvious throughout the city.*

■ What do modern-day miners have to purchase to mine the little amounts of tin that remain? *Miners need to purchase everything from food and water to dynamite and safety supplies.*

■ What role does the coca leaf play in the mining process? *Miners chew the leaves to help them deal with the conditions in the mine.*

BUILDING AP® SKILLS

Argumentation

For a quick writing practice and to get students to connect what they have learned about the labor system at Potosí to labor systems discussed in Chapter 4, you could ask students to write an LEQ-style argument paragraph responding to the prompt below. The paragraph should include a topic sentence that introduces their argument, at least two pieces of evidence, and an explanation of how and why the evidence supports their argument.

■ Explain how the labor system used by the Spanish at Potosí was similar to or different from the encomienda system used by the Spanish in the Viceroyalty of New Spain. *Answers will vary.*

BUILDING AP® SKILLS

Making Connections: Comparison

The two major producers of silver during the early modern era were Spain and Japan. You could have students work on comparison skills by asking them to create a chart comparing the role of silver in Spain and Japan, like the one shown here. A reproducible version of this chart is available in the Teacher's Resource Materials. (Answers are provided in italics.)

	Spain	**Japan**
Political	*Silver allowed Spain to conquer a large part of the Americas and politically dominate Europe for almost a century.*	*The Tokugawa shoguns used the profits from silver to defeat their rival warlords and politically unify Japan.*
Economic	*The Spanish economy was very restrictive, which prevented economic growth even with the influx of silver. When the price of silver dropped, the Spanish economy did not fare well, resulting in Spain's loss of dominance in Europe.*	*The Tokugawa shoguns allied themselves with the domestic merchant class to develop a market-based economy as well as to invest in agriculture and industry.*
Social	*The inflation that occurred as a result of Spain's economic mistakes led to financial ruin for many of the elite, and peasants rebelled against the Crown.*	*The Japanese took steps to have fewer children by practicing late marriage, contraception, abortion, and infanticide. This practice slowed population growth.*

But the silver-fueled economy of Potosí also offered opportunity, not least to women. Spanish women might rent out buildings they owned for commercial purposes or send their often enslaved servants into the streets as small-scale traders, earning a few pesos for the household. Those less well-to-do often ran stores, pawnshops, bakeries, and taverns. Native American and *mestiza* women likewise opened businesses that provided the city with beverages, food, clothing, and credit.

In Spain itself, which was the initial destination for much of Latin America's silver, the precious metal vastly enriched the Crown, making Spain the envy of its European rivals during the sixteenth century. Spanish rulers could now pursue military and political ambitions in both Europe and the Americas far beyond the country's own resource base. "New World mines," concluded several prominent historians, "supported the Spanish empire."[15] Nonetheless, this vast infusion of wealth did not fundamentally transform the Spanish economy, because it generated inflation of prices more than real economic growth. A rigid economy laced with monopolies and regulations, an aristocratic class that preferred leisure to enterprise, and a crusading insistence on religious uniformity all prevented the Spanish from using their silver windfall in a productive fashion. When the value of silver dropped in the early seventeenth century, Spain lost its earlier position as the dominant Western European power. More generally, the flood of American silver that circulated in Europe drove prices higher, further impoverished many, stimulated uprisings across the continent, and, together with the Little Ice Age of global cooling, contributed to what historians sometimes call a General Crisis of upheaval and instability in the seventeenth century. (See "The Great Dying and the Little Ice Age" in Chapter 4.)

Japan, another major source of silver production in the sixteenth century, did better. Its military rulers, the Tokugawa shoguns, used silver-generated profits to defeat hundreds of rival feudal lords and unify the country. Unlike their Spanish counterparts, the shoguns allied with the country's vigorous domestic merchant class to develop a market-based economy and to invest heavily in agricultural and industrial enterprises. Japanese state and local authorities alike acted vigorously to protect and renew Japan's dwindling forests, while millions of families in the eighteenth century took steps to have fewer children by practicing late marriages, contraception, abortion, and infanticide. The outcome was the dramatic slowing of Japan's population growth, the easing of an impending ecological crisis, and a flourishing, highly commercialized economy. These were the foundations for Japan's remarkable nineteenth-century Industrial Revolution.

In China, silver deepened the already substantial commercialization of the country's economy. Thus the Chinese economy became more regionally specialized and oriented toward production for the market. Particularly in southern China, this surging economic growth resulted in the loss of about half the area's forest cover as more and more land was devoted to cash crops. No Japanese-style conservation program emerged to address this growing problem. An eighteenth-century Chinese poet, Wang Dayue, gave voice to the fears that this ecological transformation generated, writing that "the hills resembled heads shaven clean of hair."[16]

China's role in the silver trade is a useful reminder of Asian centrality in the world economy of the early modern era. Its large and prosperous population, increasingly

AP®
COMPARISON
How were the effects of the silver trade different for Japan and Spain?

AP®
COMPARISON
Why were the environmental consequences of the silver trade different in Japan than they were in Spanish America?

AP®
COMPARISON
How did the impact of silver on China differ from its impact on Japan and Spain?

(continued)

Differentiation

If you want to differentiate the chart and add in the role that silver played in China, the biggest importer of silver, follow the "Must Do, Should Do, Strive For" model shown here.

■ Must Do: Students complete the comparison chart on Spain and Japan.

■ Should Do: Students create and fill in a third column on their chart to examine the role that silver played in China.

■ Strive For: To practice writing skills, students can write a short response to the following prompt using what they have learned from the chart: "Explain why Japan and/or China benefited from the silver trade more than Spain did." *Answers should note the points listed in the chart.*

TRM Handout 6.4: Comparison Chart for Role of Silver in Spain and Japan operating within a silver-based economy, fueled global commerce, vastly increasing the quantity of goods exchanged and the geographic range of world trade. Despite their obvious physical presence in the Americas, Africa, and Asia, economically speaking Europeans were essentially middlemen, funneling American silver to Asia and competing with one another for a place in the rich markets of the East. The productivity of the Chinese economy was evident in Spanish America, where cheap and well-made Chinese goods easily outsold those of Spain. In 1594, the Spanish viceroy of Peru observed that "a man can clothe his wife in Chinese silks for [25 pesos], whereas he could not provide her with clothing of Spanish silks with 200 pesos."[17] Indian cotton textiles likewise outsold European woolen or linen textiles in the seventeenth century to such an extent that French laws in 1717 prohibited the wearing of Indian cotton or Chinese silk clothing as a means of protecting French industry.

"The World Hunt": Fur in Global Commerce

Finding the Main Point: What was the significance of the fur trade in the global history of the early modern era?

In the early modern era, furs joined silver, textiles, and spices as major items of global commerce.[18] Harvesting those furs had an important environmental impact as well as serious implications for the human societies that generated and consumed them. Furs, of course, had long provided warmth and conveyed status in colder regions of the world, but the integration of North America and of northern Asia (Siberia) into a larger world economy vastly increased their significance in global trade.

By 1500, European population growth and agricultural expansion had sharply diminished the supply of fur-bearing animals, such as beaver, rabbits, sable, marten, and deer. Furthermore, much of the early modern era witnessed a period of cooling temperatures and harsh winters, known as the Little Ice Age, which may well have increased the demand for furs. "The weather is bitterly cold and everyone is in furs although we are almost in July," observed a surprised visitor from Venice while in London in 1604.[19] These conditions pushed prices higher, providing strong economic incentives for European traders to tap the immense wealth of fur-bearing animals found in North America.

The **fur trade** was a highly competitive enterprise. The French were most prominent in the St. Lawrence valley, around the Great Lakes, and later along the Mississippi River; British traders pushed into the Hudson Bay region; and the Dutch focused their attention along the Hudson River in what is now New York. They were frequently rivals for the great prize of North American furs. In the southern colonies of British North America, deerskins by the hundreds of thousands found a ready market in England's leather industry (see Map 6.3).

Only a few Europeans directly engaged in commercial trapping or hunting. They usually waited for Native Americans to bring the furs or skins initially to their coastal settlements and later to their fortified trading posts in the interior of North America. European merchants paid for the furs with a variety of trade goods, including guns,

---

TEACHING IDEA

Class Discussion

If you showed the Crash Course World History video *Climate Change, Chaos, and the Little Ice Age* in Chapter 4 (page 210), you can refer to that video when starting the section "'The World Hunt': Fur in Global Commerce." If you didn't show it in Chapter 4, consider pausing here and having students watch it. Then have a quick class discussion on how this event could have influenced the emerging global fur trade. *Answers will vary, but may include: Fur became a global commodity because of the warmth it provided during the Little Ice Age, when temperatures were cooling; Population growth in Europe had diminished fur-bearing animals on the European continent as there was a growing demand for warm furs; Fur became popular because it was a sign of wealth.*

BUILDING AP® SKILLS

Making Connections: Causation and
Making Connections: Comparison

During the early modern era, commercial connections between places increased significantly. Consider having students complete visual notes on a blank map of the world as they investigate commercial connections related to the fur trade. Give students the following instructions:

■ Using Map 6.3, "The North American Fur Trade," on page 332 as your guide, label Hudson Bay, the St. Lawrence River, the Gulf of Mexico, and the Great Lakes. Using different colors, indicate the fur-trading regions of France, England, and Russia. Use arrows to indicate where furs were sent.

■ Using the text on pages 331–335, annotate your map with at least three reasons why the fur trade was so successful, including five impacts (positive and negative) of this trade on North American society.

■ Using Map 4.2, "The Russian Empire," on page 224, and the text on pages 223–226 and 331–335 as your guide, map the fur trade across Siberia. On the map, label Siberia and draw an arrow moving across Siberia from Moscow to Okhotsk and an arrow indicating where furs were sold. Next, label the people who moved from west to east across Siberia. Annotate your map with a phrase describing the reasons for this movement of people and furs, including five impacts, both positive and negative, of this trade. When students have completed their maps, ask them to compare the effects of the fur trade in Russia and in North America. (Answers are provided in italics.)

■ **Similarities:** *In both locations, fur traders worked with local populations as intermediaries. In both places, the trade produced increased conflict between and among local populations, as well as the spread of disease to local inhabitants and the wide-scale destruction of fur-bearing animal populations. Both regions also experienced large-scale migrations that were due in part to the fur-trading network. The demand for furs in both locations was due in large part to the Little Ice Age and European fashion. Both Native Americans and Siberians increasingly became dependent on the European- and Russian-made goods that were part of the exchange. Christianity also spread alongside the trade, resulting in the conversions of local and Indigenous peoples to varying degrees.*

■ **Differences:** *The North American trade included competitors from at least three European nations, which caused more conflict but also initially meant higher prices*

MAPPING HISTORY Map 6.3 **The North American Fur Trade**

North America, as well as Russian Siberia, funneled an apparently endless supply of furs into the circuits of global trade during the early modern era.

Reading the Map: To which overseas markets were American furs shipped? Did the trading networks originally established by the French and English remain completely separate, or did they interact with each other in some regions to funnel furs to overseas markets?

AP **Making Connections:** How might waterways have facilitated the movement of furs from the interior of the Americas to overseas markets?

(continued)

for Indigenous trappers. In Russia, the government extracted a tribute in furs from Siberian men between the ages of eighteen and fifty.

For a blank map that you can use with this activity, see the Teacher's Resource Materials.

TRM **Map 6C: The World**

blankets, metal tools, rum, and brandy, amid much ceremony, haggling over prices, and ritualized gift giving. Native Americans represented a cheap labor force in this international commercial effort, but they were not a directly coerced labor force.

Over the three centuries of the early modern era, enormous quantities of furs and deerskins found their way to Europe, where they considerably enhanced the standard of living in those cold climates. The environmental price was paid in the Americas, and it was high. A consistent demand for beaver hats led to the near extinction of that industrious animal in much of North America by the early nineteenth century and with it the degradation or loss of many wetland habitats. By the 1760s, hunters in southeastern British colonies took about 500,000 deer every year, seriously diminishing the deer population of the region. As early as 1642, Miantonomo, a chief of the New England Narragansett people, spoke of the environmental consequences of English colonialism:

> You know our fathers had plenty of deer and skins and our plains were full
> of game and turkeys, and our coves and rivers were full of fish. But, brothers,
> since these Englishmen have seized our country, they have cut down the grass
> with scythes, and the trees with axes. Their cows and horses eat up the grass,
> and their hogs spoil our bed of clams; and finally we shall all starve to death.[20]

For the Native American peoples who hunted, trapped, processed, and transported these products, the fur trade bore various benefits, particularly at the beginning. One Native American trapper told a French missionary, "The beaver does everything perfectly well. It makes kettles, hatchets, swords, knives, bread; and, in short, it makes everything."[21] The Hurons, who lived on the northern shores of Lakes Erie and Ontario in the early seventeenth century, annually exchanged some 20,000 to 30,000 pelts, mostly beaver, for trade items, some of which they used to strengthen their relationships with neighboring peoples. These goods also enhanced the authority of Huron chiefs by providing them with gifts to distribute among their followers. At least initially, competition among Europeans ensured that Native American leaders could negotiate reasonable prices for their goods. Furthermore, their important role in the lucrative fur trade protected them for a time from the kind of extermination, enslavement, or displacement that was the fate of native peoples in Portuguese Brazil.

Nothing, however, protected them against the diseases carried by Europeans. In the 1630s and 1640s, to cite only one example of many, about half of the Hurons perished from influenza, smallpox, and other European-borne diseases. Furthermore, the fur trade generated warfare beyond anything previously known. Competition among Native American societies became more intense as the economic stakes grew higher. Catastrophic population declines owing to disease stimulated "mourning wars," designed to capture people who could be assimilated into much-diminished societies. A century of French-British rivalry for North America (1664–1763) forced Native American societies to take sides, to fight, and to die in these European imperial conflicts. Firearms, of course, made warfare far more deadly than before.

Beyond the fur trade, many Native American peoples actively sought to take advantage of the new commercial economy now impinging upon them. The Iroquois,

AP
CONTEXTUALIZATION
Describe Miantonomo's concerns about European colonization, and explain how his concerns reflect his background.

AP
CAUSATION
What impact did the fur trade have on the Indigenous peoples of North America?

BUILDING AP® SKILLS

Claims and Evidence in Sources

To practice skills needed to write a Document-Based Question essay, you can ask students to read Miantonomo's statement with a partner. Then ask each pair to explain Miantonomo's concerns and to describe his point of view. *Miantonomo is concerned about the disappearance of food and changes in the environment. Miantonomo is speaking to his people about his concerns regarding the Englishmen. He is concerned that the changes brought by the English may cause hardships for his people.*

TEACHING IDEA

Class Discussion

If you have time in class, it could be interesting to have a mini class debate on whether the fur trade was more helpful or harmful to Native Americans. Divide the class into two groups (pro and con) or into subgroups if you have a larger class. Give each side at least 20 to 30 minutes to research the impact of the fur trade on native peoples, using the paragraphs on Native Americans and the fur trade on pages 333 and 334 as a starting point, and to work together to build their main arguments before starting the debate. It may help to have a guiding statement to drive the debate, such as "Overall, the North American fur trade helped Indigenous groups more than it harmed them."

CHAPTER 6

for example, began to sell new products such as ginseng root, much in demand in China as a medicine. They also rented land to Europeans, worked for wages in various European enterprises, and started to use currency when barter was ineffective. But as they became enmeshed in these commercial relationships, Native Americans grew dependent on European trade goods. Among the Algonquians, for example, iron tools and cooking pots replaced those of stone, wood, or bone; gunpowder weapons took the place of bows and arrows; European textiles proved more attractive than traditional beaver and deerskin clothing; and flint and steel were found to be more effective for starting fires than wooden drills. A wide range of traditional crafts were thus lost, while the native peoples did not gain a corresponding ability to manufacture the new items for themselves. Enthusiasm for these imported goods and continued European demands for furs and skins frequently eroded the customary restraint that characterized traditional hunting practices, resulting in the depletion of many species. One European observer wrote of the Creek Indians: "[They] wage eternal war against deer and bear . . . which is indeed carried to an unreasonable and perhaps criminal excess, since the white people have dazzled their senses with foreign superfluities."[22]

Alongside germs and guns, yet another highly destructive European import was alcohol—rum and brandy, in particular. Whiskey, a locally produced grain-based alcohol, only added to the problem. With little prior experience of alcohol and little time to adjust to its easy availability, these drinks "hit Indian societies with explosive force."[23] Binge drinking, violence among young men, promiscuity, and addiction followed in many places. In 1753, Iroquois leaders complained bitterly to European authorities in Pennsylvania: "These wicked Whiskey Sellers, when they have once got the Indians in liquor, make them sell their very clothes from their backs. . . . If this practice be continued, we must be inevitably ruined."[24] In short, it was not so much the fur trade itself that decimated Native American societies, but all that accompanied it—disease, dependence, guns, alcohol, and the growing encroachment of European colonial empires.

All of this had particular implications for women. A substantial number of native women married European traders according to the "custom of the country"—with no sanction from civil or church authorities. Such marriages eased the difficulties of this cross-cultural exchange, providing traders with guides, interpreters, and negotiators. But sometimes these women were left abandoned when their husbands returned to Europe. More generally, the fur trade enhanced the position of men in their societies because hunting or trapping animals was normally a male occupation. Among the Ojibwa, a gathering and hunting people in the northern Great Lakes region, women had traditionally acquired economic power by creating food, utensils, clothing, and decorations from the hides and flesh of the animals that their husbands caught. With the fur trade in full operation, women spent more time processing those furs for sale than in producing household items, some of which were now available for purchase from Europeans. And so, as one scholar put it, "women lost authority and prestige." At the same time, however, women generated and controlled the trade in wild rice and maple syrup, both essential to the livelihood of European traders.[25] Thus the fur trade offered women a mix of opportunities and liabilities.

BUILDING AP® SKILLS
Making Connections: Causation

To help students evaluate the impact of European culture on the New World, ask them the following questions:

■ In addition to germs and guns, what other destructive imports did Europeans bring to the New World? *Alcohol, including brandy, rum, and whiskey, was another destructive European import.*

■ Why was alcohol so destructive? *Indigenous people had little or no experience with alcohol, and exposure led to binge drinking, violence, promiscuity, and addiction.*

EXPLORING AP® THEMES
Social Organization and Interactions (SIO)

Women and the impact that historical events have on them can be easy to overlook in the larger picture of world history. Consider having students pause here and discuss with a partner or small group (three or four students) how the global fur trade impacted Indigenous women in North America. *Answers should include: Native women married European traders, which helped ease the difficulties of cross-cultural exchange that traders experienced, but some of these women were abandoned when their husbands returned to Europe; The fur trade enhanced men's positions at the expense of women's economic power in some societies like the Ojibwa because hunting and trapping animals was a male occupation; Women lost economic power because they had to spend more time processing the furs of the animals their husbands caught than creating household items; Women in some groups began to control the trade in wild rice and maple syrup, which were needed by European traders.*

BUILDING AP® SKILLS
Claims and Evidence in Sources

You could challenge students by asking them to analyze the engraving of the Siberian fur hunter on page 335 to find evidence that would support the following claim: "The fur tribute from Siberia demanded by the Russian Empire led to changes in the lives of Siberians." *Answers will vary, but may include: Since Russia required all able-bodied Siberian males to pay tribute in furs, the tribute system could have led to a severe decline in the population of fur-bearing animals and affected Siberian lifestyles; The Siberian in the engraving is wearing fur clothing, but with the high demand for furs for trade, Siberians might have had to change what types of clothes they wore; Local economies in Siberia could become dependent on the fur trade, which means they could experience severe economic problems if the animal population declined too much.*

Paralleling the North American fur trade was the one simultaneously taking shape within a rapidly expanding Russian Empire, which became a major source of furs for Western Europe, China, and the Ottoman Empire. The profitability of that trade in furs was the chief incentive for Russia's rapid expansion during the sixteenth and seventeenth centuries across Siberia, where the **"soft gold"** of fur-bearing animals was abundant. The international sale of furs greatly enriched the Russian state as well as many private merchants, trappers, and hunters. Here the silver trade and the fur trade intersected, as Europeans paid for Russian furs largely with American gold and silver. The consequences for native Siberians were similar to those in North America, as disease took its toll, as indigenous people became dependent on Russian goods, as the settler frontier encroached on native lands, and as many species of fur-bearing mammals were seriously depleted.

In several ways, however, the Russian fur trade was unique. Whereas several European nations competed in North America and generally obtained their furs through commercial negotiations with Native American societies, no such competition accompanied Russian expansion across Siberia. Russian authorities imposed a tax or tribute, payable in furs, on every able-bodied Siberian male between eighteen and fifty years of age. To enforce the payment, they took hostages from Siberian societies, with death as a possible outcome if the required furs were not forthcoming. A further difference lay in the large-scale presence of private Russian hunters and trappers, who competed directly with their Siberian counterparts.

The Fur Trade in Russia Russian authorities demanded tribute paid in furs from every able-bodied native Siberian male between eighteen and fifty years of age. This early-eighteenth-century engraving depicts a fur-clad Siberian holding in one hand his hunting bow and trident and in the other two mink or ermine. The thick, soft fur of both these animals was much in demand on world markets. (Science & Society Picture Library/Getty Images)

▲ **AP®**
ARGUMENTATION
How would a historian use this image to explain the expansion of the Russian Empire?

AP®
COMPARISON
How did the North American and Siberian trade systems differ from each other? What did they have in common?

AP®
COMPARISON
What differences can you identify in the operation and impact of the spice, silver, and fur trades?

Commerce in People: The Transatlantic Slave System

Finding the Main Point: What transcontinental relationships did the Atlantic slave system generate? What was its impact on Europe, Africa, and the Americas?

Of all the commercial ties that linked the early modern world into a global network of exchange, none had more profound or enduring human consequences than the **transatlantic slave system**. (See Controversies: Debating the Atlantic World, page 336.) Between 1500 and 1866, this trade in human beings took an

---

(continued)

reproducible version of an LEQ outline in the Teacher's Resource Materials.

■ Evaluate the extent to which the social and environmental effects of the spice trade in Asia differed from the social and environmental effects of the fur trade in North America.

■ Strive For: For students who want practice with writing a full essay, have them use their completed essay outline to write a full LEQ essay. Students should be given no more than 40 minutes to write their essay. *Answers should include the following points:*

Spice Trade

■ **Social:** *Established hierarchies changed with the involvement of the Dutch and Portuguese. The arrival of Christianity changed the gender roles of women.*

■ **Environmental:** *Native populations were forced to grow cash crops for the Europeans. Nutrients in the soil were no longer enough to keep the soil fertile. Cutting down forests for plantation crops caused environmental problems.*

Fur Trade

■ **Social:** *Established hierarchies changed with the arrival of European fur traders. Gender roles changed as Indigenous populations became dependent on European goods received as payment for fur.*

■ **Environmental:** *Fur-bearing animal populations across North America were decimated. Several species were hunted almost to extinction. Loss of indigenous animal populations changed the environmental landscape. Europeans brought their own animals to the New World.*

TRM Writing Organizer for LEQ

BUILDING AP® SKILLS

Making Connections: Comparison

As a wrap-up to this section on the fur trade, you could ask students to compare the operation and impact of the spice, silver, and fur trades. *The fur trade had a greater ecological impact than the spice or silver trades. Willing Indigenous people who were not forced to trap animals drove the fur trade in North America. The silver trade drove the commercialization of China to a greater extent than did the other two trades. All except the Siberian fur trade relied on new European sea trade routes.*

Differentiation

If you want to extend this comparison and have students practice their writing skills, follow the "Must Do, Should Do, Strive For" model below:

■ Must Do: Students must discuss or write down comparisons of the operation and impact of the spice, silver, and fur trades.

■ Should Do: Students should create an outline for a Comparison essay using the following prompt. You can find a ➡

TEACHING IDEA

Class Discussion

Assign students "Controversies: Debating the Atlantic World" found on pages 336–337. Divide your class into groups with no more than six students per group, and then split each group into two halves for a debate activity. Assign each half one of the following stances on the Atlantic world concept:

■ The Atlantic world has had a positive impact on the modern world.

■ The Atlantic world has had a negative impact on the modern world.

Each side will research to find evidence that supports their assigned stance. Students should be able to get most of their evidence from Chapters 4 and 6. Either have the students conduct research as homework or give them no more than 20 minutes of class time to research. You could have the smaller groups debate one another rather than conduct a large class debate. Give each side 3 minutes to present their case and then 2 minutes for rebuttal and questions. Have the students take notes on the opposing side's argument as they debate. After the debate is over, have the students complete a quickwrite on the following prompt:

■ In your opinion, did the "Atlantic world" concept help or hurt humanity? Defend your answer with specific pieces of evidence.

Differentiation

You could break down this activity by following the "Must Do, Should Do, Strive For" model below:

■ Must Do: Students will create a Venn diagram to examine the negative and positive effects of the Atlantic world concept. A reproducible version of this chart is available in the Teacher's Resource Materials.

■ Should Do: Divide the students into groups and have them compare the information in their Venn diagrams. Then assign each group one of the stances on the Atlantic world concept listed above and have them do a little more research to prepare for the debate. Once research time is over, conduct the debate.

■ Strive For: To practice writing skills, students can write a quick response to the prompt above.

TRM Handout 6.5: Graphic Organizer for Atlantic World Debate

CONTROVERSIES   Debating the Atlantic World

Beginning in the 1970s, the notion of an "Atlantic world" increasingly swept the historical profession like a storm. It referred to the creation of a network of communication, interaction, and exchange all around the Atlantic basin among the peoples of Europe, Africa, and North and South America, often known as the Columbian exchange. This Atlantic world sensibility reflected the international politics of the post–World War II era, in which the North Atlantic Treaty Organization (NATO), an anticommunist alliance of North American and Western European states, played an important role. Studies of the Atlantic world in earlier centuries resonated with this transatlantic Cold War–era political partnership.

For historians, the "Atlantic world" idea held many attractions. It helped to free historical study from the rigid framework of the nation-state, allowing scholars and students to examine "flows" or "circulations"—such as the Columbian exchange—that operated beyond particular states and within larger spaces. In this respect, Atlantic world thinking paralleled historical investigation of the Mediterranean world or the Indian Ocean world, other sea-based zones of interaction.

The "Atlantic world" idea also encouraged comparison, particularly attractive to world historians. How similar or different were the various European empires—Spanish, Portuguese, British, French, Dutch—constructed in the Americas? Students in the United States are often surprised to learn that fewer than 5 percent of the enslaved Africans transported across the Atlantic wound up in North America and that the vast majority landed in Brazil or the Caribbean region.

Moreover, the Atlantic world provided a larger context in which to situate the history of particular societies or nations. The modern history of the Caribbean region, for example, is inexplicable without some grasp of its connection to Africa, the source of enslaved people; to Europe, the source of settlers, disease, and empires; and to North America, the source of valuable trade.

For some historians, however, the Atlantic world idea distorted our understanding of the early modern era. There never was a single cohesive Atlantic world, some have argued. Instead there were British, Spanish, French, and Dutch Atlantic worlds, each different and often in conflict. There were Catholic, Protestant, Islamic, and Jewish Atlantic worlds, and a Black Atlantic world as well.

Furthermore, the Atlantic region was never a self-contained unit, but interacted with other regions of the world. Asian tea was dumped in Boston harbor during the American "tea party." Silver from the Americas fueled trade with Asia, with some 75 percent of it winding up in China. Textiles from India and cowrie shells from the Maldives, a group of islands in the Indian Ocean, served as currency in the transatlantic slave trade. And in the mid-eighteenth century, the value of British and Dutch imports from Asia was greater than the value of those from the Americas.

Critics also argued that an overly enthusiastic or exclusive focus on the Atlantic world exaggerates its significance in early modern world history. But placing the Atlantic world in a larger global framework corrects any such exaggeration and raises many fascinating questions. Why were Europeans able to construct major empires in the Americas but not in Africa or Asia? Why did European empires in the Americas feature large-scale European settlement, while the Chinese and Ottoman empires in Asia and the Middle East did not involve much Chinese or Turkish migration? How does the transatlantic slave system look when it is compared to the trans-Saharan and Indian Ocean slave trades, both of which were much older? And how does the transatlantic commerce in the early modern era compare with earlier Afro-Eurasian patterns of long-distance trade that had a much longer history? In short, the Atlantic world becomes a more meaningful concept when it is framed in genuinely global contexts.

estimated 12.5 million people from African societies, shipped them across the Atlantic in the infamous Middle Passage, and deposited some 10.7 million of them in the Americas, where they lived out their often brief lives as enslaved people. About 1.8 million (14.4 percent) died during the transatlantic crossing, while countless others perished in the process of capture and transport to the African

---

TEACHING IDEA

Bell Ringer

This chapter is all about commerce and the European role in global commerce in the early modern era of world history. One of the most profitable types of commerce in the early modern world was the slave trade, also known as human trafficking. Ask students to define the word "commerce" and compare their definitions to a dictionary definition. Once the class has a working definition of the word, ask students to write a few sentences to describe commerce as it pertained to the Atlantic slave trade, taking into account that this was commerce in human beings. *Commerce along the triangular trade routes of the Atlantic Ocean included goods and resources from the American colonies to Europe, goods such as weapons from Europe to Africa, and finally Africans to the New World to provide labor for the cash crops grown in the Americas.*

Beyond these controversies about the usefulness and limitations of the Atlantic world concept, historians have also debated the operation of this transoceanic network, with particular focus on questions of "agency" and "impact." "Agency" refers to the ability of individuals or groups to take action, to make things happen, and to affect the outcome of historical processes. So who created the Atlantic world? The earliest and most obvious answer to this question claimed that the Atlantic world was the product of European rulers, explorers, armies, settlers, merchants, and missionaries. But taking a closer look, historians have discovered agency in other places as well. Unknown to their European carriers, pathogens "acted" independently to generate the Great Dying in the Americas, largely beyond the intention or control of any human agent. Many Indigenous rulers, acting in their own interests, joined their larger military forces to the small armies of the Spanish conquistadores to defeat the powerful Aztec and Inca empires. African rulers and commercial elites violently procured the human cargoes of the slave trade and sold them to European merchants waiting on Africa's western coast.

Agency was also expressed in numerous acts of resistance against Europeans, such as the great Pueblo Revolt of 1680, the creation of runaway slave communities in Brazil, and the Haitian Revolution, all of which shaped the contours of the Atlantic world. Culturally too, conquered and enslaved people retained their human capacity to act and create, even in enormously repressive conditions. For example, they adapted Christianity to their own needs, often blending it with elements of traditional beliefs and practices. A famous book about slavery in the American south by Eugene Genovese bore the pointed subtitle *The World the Slaves Made*. Agency, in short, was not limited to Europeans, and the Atlantic world was not wholly a European creation.

The multiple interactions of the Atlantic world have also stimulated debate about "impact" or the consequences of inclusion in this transoceanic network. For millions of enslaved individuals and millions more who perished in the Great Dying, the impact was tragic and painful almost beyond description. About this there is little debate. More controversial questions arise about the impact of Atlantic world encounters on broader regions and their peoples. Were Indigenous societies of the Western Hemisphere destroyed or decimated by conquest, disease, labor demands, and loss of land? Or were they, as historian John Kicze describes them, remarkably "resilient cultures"? How did the demand for enslaved people affect African population growth, economic development, the role of women, and state formation? Did the wealth derived from the Atlantic world of empire, commerce, and slavery enable Britain's Industrial Revolution, or was it only a minor factor?

Finally, the intersection of questions about agency and impact in the Atlantic world has raised contentious issues about moral responsibility. If Europeans or Euro-Americans were the primary agents of the slave trade, the Great Dying, and the exploitation of native peoples, do they owe an apology and compensation to the descendants of their victims? How does the alliance of Spanish and Native American forces in the conquest of Mexico or the well-documented role of African political and economic elites in the transatlantic slave system complicate our thinking about such issues?

About all of this, debate continues.

QUESTIONS TO CONSIDER

1. With what questions about the Atlantic world do you feel most engaged? Why?

2. What makes the Atlantic world a compelling concept for historians?

3. How does the treatment of early modern empires in Chapter 4 and commerce in Chapter 6 respond to the questions raised in this essay?

coast.[26] (See Map 6.4.) Despite the language of commerce and exchange with which it is often described, this transatlantic slave system was steeped in violence, coercion, and brutality. It involved forcible capture and repeated sale, beatings and brandings, chains and imprisonment, rebellions and escapes, lives of enforced and unpaid labor, broken families, and humans treated as property.

EXPLORING AP® THEMES

Economic Systems (ECN)

Slavery has been around since the earliest farming societies emerged; however, in the early modern era, slavery was viewed differently and the transatlantic slave trade began to give Europeans the cheap labor they needed for their cash crops in the New World. Now would be a good time to have students research the history of slavery. Many students believe that slavery began with the transatlantic slave trade, but students should understand that slavery has been around for millennia and that there are different forms of slavery. Students should be able to situate slavery within a broader global and historical context.

Ask students to review their notes about slavery from Chapters 1, 2, and 4. Then ask them to complete a chart like the one here to compare the features and effects of slavery in the classical, postclassical, and early modern eras. A reproducible version of this chart is available in the Teacher's Resource Materials. (Answers are provided in italics.)

	Features	Effects
Classical slavery	*Enslaved people were usually prisoners of war and women. Often enslaved people were highly educated and treated as members of the family. In the Roman Empire, enslaved people were used on the latifundia to grow and harvest the cash crops that fed the empire.*	*Both Greece and Rome depended on slave labor.*
Postclassical slavery	*There was little slavery in Europe, but there was a dependence on serf labor within manorialism. In the Islamic world, enslaved people from Africa were used for domestic work.*	*Serfs were not enslaved, and after the bubonic plague, serfdom declined in Western Europe. In the Islamic world, many enslaved people converted to Islam and gained freedom.*
Early modern slavery	*A high volume of slave trafficking was conducted. Slavery was central to the economic system of the colonial Americas, and it was prominent in plantation agriculture.*	*Atlantic slavery came to be identified with Africa. Enslaved people were treated as dehumanized property, without any rights and at the mercy of owners. Enslaved status was inherited, which gave people little hope of freedom.*

TRM Handout 6.6: Comparison Chart for Features and Effects of Slavery in Historical Eras

EXPLORING AP® THEMES

Humans and the Environment (ENV)

Consider having students practice their map-reading skills by showing them Map 6.4, "The Transatlantic Slave System." Use the following questions to guide their analysis:

■ Which parts in the Americas were the main areas of importation of enslaved people? *The main areas of importation included southeast North America, Cuba, Jamaica, Haiti, Puerto Rico, Guiana, Brazil, Ecuador, Buenos Aires, and Venezuela.*

■ Comparing the trans-Saharan, Red Sea, and East African slave trades with the Atlantic slave trade, which one involved a higher volume of people enslaved? Why? *The Atlantic slave trade involved many more people enslaved than the Red Sea, trans-Saharan, and East African slave trades because enslaved people sent over the Atlantic were used mostly for large-scale agriculture, whereas enslaved people sent to the Mediterranean, the Middle East, and farther east were used in more limited roles, as household enslaved people or soldiers.*

APPLY THE TIP

If you showed Slate's animated map of the transatlantic slave trade in Chapter 4 (page 218), this is a great place to refer to it and have students compare what they remember to Map 6.4, "The Transatlantic Slave System." If you didn't show Slate's animated map, consider showing it here. Then ask the following questions:

■ Where, in addition to the Americas, were enslaved people taken? *Enslaved people were taken to Europe, to the Arabian Peninsula and on to Damascus and Baghdad, and to India and Southeast Asia.*

■ What might have been the demographic effects of the slave trade in both Africa and the Americas? *In Africa, the population declined, primarily the population of young men. In the Americas, a new race of people, primarily men, was added.*

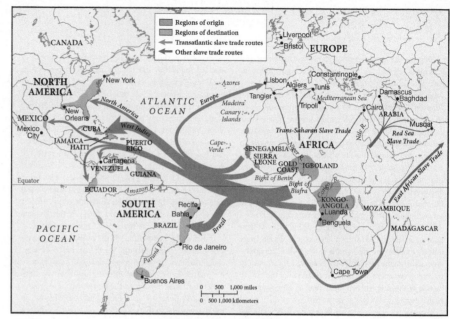

Map 6.4 The Transatlantic Slave System
Stimulated by the plantation complex of the Americas, the transatlantic slave system represented an enormous extension of the ancient practice of people owning and selling other people.

▲ **AP**
MAKING CONNECTIONS
What economic developments best explain the changes illustrated in the map?

▲ **AP EXAM TIP**
Look at the map and take note of the origins and destinations of the African slave trade in this era, as they may appear on the AP® Exam. Understand the demographic effects of the African slave trade on both sides of the Atlantic.

Beyond the multitude of individual tragedies that it spawned, the transatlantic slave system transformed entire societies. Within Africa itself, that commerce thoroughly disrupted some societies, strengthened others, and corrupted many. Elites often enriched themselves, while the enslaved Africans, of course, were victimized almost beyond imagination.

In the Americas, this transatlantic network added a substantial African presence to the mix of European and Native American peoples. This **African diaspora** (the global spread of African peoples) injected into these new societies issues of race that endure still in the twenty-first century. It also introduced elements of African culture, such as religious ideas, musical and artistic traditions, and cuisine, into the making of American cultures. The profits from the slave trade and the labor of enslaved Africans certainly enriched European and Euro-American societies, even as the practice of slavery contributed to European racial stereotypes of other peoples. Finally, slavery became a metaphor for many kinds of social oppression, quite different from plantation slavery, in the centuries that followed. Workers protested the "slavery" of wage labor, colonized people rejected the slavery of imperial domination, and feminists sometimes defined patriarchy as a form of slavery.

The Slave Trade in Context

The transatlantic slave system represented the most recent large-scale expression of a very ancient and widespread practice—the owning and exchange of human beings. Before 1500, the Mediterranean and Indian Ocean basins were the major arenas of Old World slave systems, and southern Russia was a major source of its victims. Many African societies likewise both practiced slavery themselves and sold enslaved people into these international commercial networks. A trans-Saharan slave trade had long funneled African captives into Mediterranean slavery, and an East African slave trade from at least the seventh century C.E. brought Africans into the Middle East and the Indian Ocean basin. Both operated largely within the Islamic world and initiated the movement of African peoples beyond the continent itself.

Furthermore, slavery came in many forms. In the Indian Ocean world, for example, enslaved Africans were often assimilated into the societies of their owners and lost the sense of a distinctive identity that was so prominent in North America. In some places, children inherited the enslaved status of their parents; elsewhere those children were free persons. Within the Islamic world, where most enslaved people worked in domestic settings, the preference was for enslaved women and girls by a two-to-one margin, while the later transatlantic slave system, which funneled captives into plantation labor, favored males by a similar margin. Not all enslaved people, however, occupied degraded positions. Some in the Islamic world acquired prominent military or political status. Most enslaved people in the premodern world worked in their owners' households, farms, or shops, with smaller numbers laboring in large-scale agricultural or industrial enterprises.

The slave system that emerged in the Americas was distinctive in several ways. One was simply the immense size of that system and its centrality to the economies of colonial America, which featured a great deal of plantation agriculture. Furthermore, slave status throughout the Americas was inherited across generations, and there was little hope of eventual freedom for the vast majority. Nowhere else, with the possible exception of ancient Greece, was the contradiction between slavery and the social values affirming human freedom and equality quite so sharp. Perhaps

Slavery in the Islamic World This eighteenth-century image of an enslaved woman accompanying her upper-class Turkish owner to the public baths highlights the slave trade in the Ottoman and Indian Ocean worlds and serves as a reminder that slavery was not limited to the Atlantic world in the early modern era. Unlike in the Americas, most enslaved people in North Africa and Southwest Asia served as domestic servants, with enslaved women generally preferred to males. (Bridgeman Images)

▲ **AP**
COMPARISON
Based on the image, how did slavery in the Islamic world differ from Atlantic slavery?

AP
COMPARISON
What was distinctive about the Atlantic slave trade as compared to other systems of forced labor? What did it share with other patterns of slave owning and slave trading?

APPLY THE TIP

This is a good place to have students practice contextualization of a historical event. Have students read through the first two paragraphs on this page and then ask: What were the characteristics of slavery in the Mediterranean before the Atlantic slave trade began? (Students could share their thoughts with a partner or in small groups.) *Slavery has always been a feature of human societies, though the scale of the Atlantic slave trade was unprecedented. The practice was linked to warfare and capture. An African slave trade existed among African societies and in the Islamic world. However, before the Atlantic slave trade, the majority of enslaved people working on Mediterranean plantations to produce sugar were Slavic people from the Black Sea area. In the early fifteenth century, this source of enslaved people was cut off by the Ottoman Turks. At about the same time, Portuguese explorers looking for gold in West Africa encountered enslaved people for sale. This encounter marked the beginning of the Atlantic slave trade.*

EXPLORING AP® THEMES

Economic Systems (ECN)

In Chapter 4, students learned about the Great Dying in the Americas and how that led European colonists to search for new sources of labor. This section can help students understand why Europeans turned toward Africa as their source of enslaved laborers. Have students answer the following question either in their notes or as part of a class discussion on the origins of the transatlantic slave system: Why did Africa become the chief source of enslaved labor for the plantation economies of the Americas? *The pope granted the kings of Portugal and Spain permission to seek, capture, and subjugate anyone considered pagan. The Native American population was decimated. Marginal Europeans were Christian, and indentured servants were too expensive and temporary. Africans were experienced farmers, were immune to tropical and European diseases, were not Christian, and were readily available through the established slave trade in Africa.*

AP **CONTEXTUALIZATION**
In what larger contexts can the Atlantic slave system be understood?

AP **CAUSATION**
What explains the rise of the Atlantic slave trade?

AP **EXAM TIP**
Note the characteristics of slavery in the Mediterranean before the Atlantic slave trade began.

most distinctive was the racial dimension: Atlantic slavery came to be identified wholly with Africa and with "blackness."

The origins of Atlantic slavery clearly lie in the Mediterranean world and with that now-common sweetener known as sugar. Until the Crusades, Europeans knew nothing of sugar and relied on honey and fruits to sweeten their bland diets. However, as they learned from the Arabs about sugarcane and the laborious techniques for producing usable sugar, Europeans established sugar-producing plantations within the Mediterranean and later on various islands off the coast of West Africa. It was a "modern" industry, perhaps the first one, in that it required huge capital investment, substantial technology, an almost factory-like discipline among workers, and a mass market of consumers. The immense difficulty and danger of the work and the general absence of wageworkers made slave labor an attractive option for producers of sugar.

Initially, Slavic-speaking communities from the Black Sea region furnished the bulk of the enslaved people for Mediterranean plantations, so much so that "Slav" became the basis for the word "slave" in many European languages. In 1453, however, when the Ottoman Turks seized Constantinople, the supply of Slavs was effectively cut off. At the same time, Portuguese mariners were exploring the coast of West Africa; they were looking primarily for gold, but they also found there an alternative source of enslaved people available for sale. Thus, when sugar, and later tobacco and cotton, plantations took hold in the Americas, Europeans had already established links to a West African source of supply. They also now had religious justification for their actions, for in 1452 the pope formally granted to the kings of Spain and Portugal "full and free permission to invade, search out, capture, and subjugate the Saracens [Muslims] and pagans and any other unbelievers . . . and to reduce their persons into perpetual slavery."[27]

Largely through a process of elimination, Africa became the primary source of slave labor for the plantation economies of the Americas. Slavic peoples were no longer available; Native Americans quickly perished from European diseases; even marginal Europeans such as poor people and criminals were Christians and therefore supposedly exempt from slavery; and European indentured servants, who agreed to work for a fixed period in return for transportation, food, and shelter, were expensive and temporary. Africans, on the other hand, were skilled farmers; they had some immunity to both tropical and European diseases; they were not Christians; they were, relatively speaking, close at hand; and they were readily available in substantial numbers through African-operated commercial networks.

Moreover, Africans were Black. The precise relationship between slavery and European racism has long been a much-debated subject. Historian David Brion Davis has suggested the controversial view that "racial stereotypes were transmitted, along with black slavery itself, from Muslims to Christians."[28] For many centuries, Muslims had drawn on sub-Saharan Africa as one source of enslaved people and in the process had developed a form of racism. The fourteenth-century Tunisian scholar Ibn Khaldun wrote that Black people were "submissive to slavery, because Negroes have little that is essentially human and have attributes that are quite similar to those of dumb animals."[29]

Other scholars find the origins of racism within European culture itself. For the English, argues historian Audrey Smedley, the process of conquering Ireland had generated by the sixteenth century a view of the Irish as "rude, beastly, ignorant, cruel, and unruly infidels," perceptions that were then transferred to Africans enslaved on English sugar plantations of the West Indies.[30] Whether Europeans borrowed such images of Africans from their Muslim neighbors or developed them independently, slavery and racism soon went hand in hand. "Europeans were better able to tolerate their brutal exploitation of Africans," writes a prominent world historian, "by imagining that these Africans were an inferior race, or better still, not even human."[31]

The Slave Trade in Practice

The European demand for enslaved people was clearly the chief cause of this tragic commerce, and from the point of sale on the African coast to the massive use of slave labor on American plantations, the entire enterprise was in European hands. Within Africa itself, however, a different picture emerges, for over the four centuries of the Atlantic slave trade, European demand elicited an African supply. The slave trade quickly came to operate largely with Europeans waiting on the coast, either on their ships or in fortified settlements, to purchase enslaved people from African merchants and political elites. Certainly, Europeans tried to exploit African rivalries to obtain enslaved people at the lowest possible cost, and the firearms they funneled into West Africa may well have increased the warfare from which so many enslaved people were derived. But from the point of initial capture to sale on the coast, the entire enterprise was normally in African hands. Almost nowhere did Europeans attempt outright military conquest; instead they generally dealt as equals with local African authorities.

An arrogant agent of the British Royal Africa Company in the 1680s learned the hard way who was in control when he spoke improperly to the king of Niumi, a small state in what is now Gambia. The company's records describe what happened next:

> One of the grandees [of the king], by name Sambalama, taught him better manners by reaching him a box on the ears, which beat off his hat, and a few thumps on the back, and seizing him . . . and several others, who together with the agent were taken and put into the king's pound and stayed there three or four days till their ransom was brought, value five hundred bars.[32]

In exchange for enslaved persons, African sellers sought both European and Indian textiles, cowrie shells (widely used as money in West Africa), European metal goods, firearms and gunpowder, tobacco and alcohol, and various decorative items such as beads. Europeans purchased some of these items—cowrie shells and Indian textiles, for example—with silver mined in the Americas. Thus the transatlantic slave system connected with commerce in silver and textiles as it became part of an emerging worldwide network of exchange. Issues about the precise mix of goods that African authorities desired, about the number and quality of enslaved people to be purchased, and always about the price of everything were settled in endless negotiation. Most of the time, a leading historian concluded, the slave trade took place "not unlike international trade anywhere in the world of the period."[33]

AP® EXAM TIP

Pay attention to this discussion of important factors in the development of the Atlantic slave trade.

AP®

CONTEXTUALIZATION
What roles did Europeans and Africans play in the unfolding of the Atlantic slave trade?

APPLY THE TIP

You can use this tip to help students practice the AP® skills of Contextualization and Causation. Ask students to create a list of the important factors in the development of the Atlantic slave trade. *European demand for enslaved workers was clearly the chief cause of the trade. From the point of sale on the African coast to the massive use of slave labor on American plantations, the entire enterprise was in European hands. Europeans tried to exploit African rivalries to obtain enslaved people at the lowest possible cost, and the firearms they funneled into West Africa may well have increased the warfare that supplied so many enslaved people. From the point of initial capture to the sale on the coast, the slave trade was normally in African hands. African elites and merchants secured enslaved people and brought them to the coast for sale to Europeans waiting on ships or in fortified settlements. Africans who were transported as enslaved workers also played a critical, if unwilling and tragic, role in the trade.*

TEACHING IDEA

Incorporating Outside Resources

In the Crash Course World History episode *The Atlantic Slave Trade*, John Green covers one of the most difficult subjects in the study of history: slavery. He describes when and where slavery was instituted and how slavery changed over the centuries. He examines how Europeans and colonists in the Americas arrived at the idea that people could own other people based on skin color. The video can be found on YouTube. You can either assign the video as homework or show it in class. Then ask students the following questions:

■ What two areas in the Americas received the most enslaved people from Africa? *The Caribbean received 48 percent and Brazil received 41 percent.*

■ What three main agricultural products were produced by enslaved workers? *Sugar, tobacco, and coffee.*

■ Slavery as defined by sociologist Orlando Patterson is "the permanent, violent, and personal domination of naturally alienated and generally dishonored persons." Explain this statement in your own words. *Answers will vary.*

■ Which two groups helped define the attitudes that characterized the Atlantic slave trade? *The Portuguese and Spanish were most influential in defining the attitudes that characterized the Atlantic slave trade.*

BUILDING AP® SKILLS

Claims and Evidence in Sources

A quick way to practice using evidence from images to back up an argument is to have students study the illustration "The Middle Passage" on this page and use what they see to write a one-paragraph description of the conditions on the slave ships. *Answers will vary, but should include points such as: The deplorable conditions included small, close quarters; darkness and lack of fresh air; lack of adequate sanitation; constantly being chained; and insufficient food.*

TEACHING IDEA

Incorporating Outside Resources

The OER Project has a fantastic activity for students to analyze first-person accounts of the transatlantic slave trade and practice sourcing. This would be a good place to pause and have students work through this activity, either on their own or with a partner. You can find the activity, "Quick Sourcing — First Person Accounts of the Transatlantic Slave Trade," in Unit 4.2 Transoceanic Empires: Expansion and Resistance of the AP® World History: Modern section of the OER Project.

▶ **AP®**

CLAIMS AND EVIDENCE IN SOURCES
How would a historian use this image to describe the conditions on slave ships sailing on the Middle Passage? What conditions on those ships does this image NOT reveal?

The Middle Passage   This nineteenth-century painting of enslaved people held below decks illustrates the horrendous crowded conditions and the use of chains to restrain the enslaved during the transatlantic voyage, a journey experienced by many millions of captured Africans. (DEA/G. DAGLI ORTI/Getty Images)

For the enslaved individuals themselves—seized in the interior, often sold several times on the harrowing journey to the coast, sometimes branded, and held in squalid dungeons while awaiting transportation to the New World—it was anything but a normal commercial transaction. One European engaged in the trade noted that "the negroes are so willful and loath to leave their own country, that they have often leap'd out of the canoes, boat, and ship, into the sea, and kept under water till they were drowned, to avoid being taken up and saved by our boats."[34]

Over the four centuries of the slave trade, millions of Africans underwent such experiences, but their numbers varied considerably over time. During the sixteenth century, slave exports from Africa averaged fewer than 3,000 annually. In those years, the Portuguese were at least as much interested in African gold, spices, and textiles. Furthermore, as in Asia, the Portuguese became involved in transporting African goods, including enslaved people, from one African port to another, thus becoming the "truck drivers" of coastal West African commerce.[35] In the seventeenth century, the pace picked up as the slave trade became highly competitive, with the British, Dutch, and French contesting the earlier Portuguese monopoly. The century and a half between 1700 and 1850 marked the high point of the slave trade as the plantation economies of the Americas boomed. (See Snapshot: The Slave Trade in Numbers, page 343.)

Geographically, the slave system drew mainly on the societies of West and South-Central Africa, from present-day Mauritania in the north to Angola in the south. Initially focused on the coastal regions, the slave raiding progressively penetrated

SNAPSHOT The Slave Trade in Numbers (1501–1866)

THE RISE AND DECLINE OF THE SLAVE TRADE

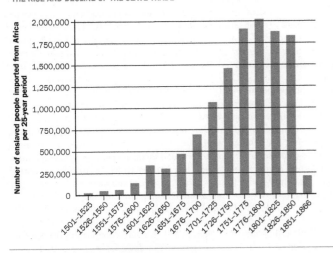

THE DESTINATION OF ENSLAVED PEOPLE

Numbers of enslaved people brought to each country

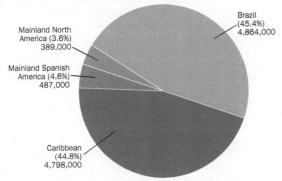

Mainland North America (3.6%) 389,000

Mainland Spanish America (4.6%) 487,000

Caribbean (44.8%) 4,798,000

Brazil (45.4%) 4,864,000

Source: Data from Trans-Atlantic Slave Trade Database, accessed December 26, 2017, http://www.slavevoyages.org/assessment/estimates.

◀ **AP**

CAUSATION

What best explains the rapid growth in the slave trade leading up to 1800? What explains the steep drop in the slave trade after 1850? According to the pie chart, in which two regions did a vast majority of enslaved Africans end up? What best explains this trend?

◀ **AP** **EXAM TIP**

Charts and graphs frequently show up on the AP® Exam, so develop your skills in "reading" all parts of these documents for information such as trends over time.

APPLY THE TIP

This activity can help students practice analyzing charts and graphs for evidence. Charts and graphs can be found in both the multiple-choice and short-answer sections of the AP® World History: Modern Exam. Using the two-part Snapshot, have students answer the following questions and then discuss them as a class.

1. What length of time does each column on the bar graph represent? *Twenty-five years*

2. How long did it take for the slave trade to reach its height of 2 million people trafficked from Africa? *300 years*

3. After the British abolition of the slave trade in 1807, how long did it take for there to be a noticeable effect and why? *It took fifty years (until the 1850s and after), because many nations, including Brazil, did not ban the slave trade until much later; even for those nations that did ban the trade, there continued to be a considerable amount of illegal trade.*

4. What does the bottom graph show? What conclusions can you make based on your reading of this graph? *The bottom graph depicts the numbers and percentages of enslaved people who survived the voyage and where they disembarked. A total of 90.2 percent of all enslaved people landed in either the Caribbean or Brazil. Less than 4 percent disembarked in mainland North America.*

into the interior as the demand for enslaved people picked up. Socially, these enslaved people were mostly drawn from various marginal groups in African societies—prisoners of war, criminals, debtors, people who had been "pawned" during times of difficulty. Thus Africans did not generally sell "their own people" into slavery. Divided into hundreds of separate, usually small-scale, and often rival communities—cities, kingdoms, microstates, clans, and villages—the various peoples of West Africa had no concept of an "African" identity. Those whom they captured and sold were normally outsiders, vulnerable people who lacked the protection of membership in an established community. When short-term economic or political advantage could be gained, such people were sold. In this respect, the transatlantic slave system was little different from the experience of enslavement elsewhere in the world.

The destination of enslaved Africans, half a world away in the Americas, however, made the transatlantic system very different. The vast majority wound up in Brazil or the Caribbean, where the labor demands of the plantation economy were most intense. Smaller numbers found themselves in North America, mainland Spanish America, or Europe. Their journey across the Atlantic was horrendous, with the Middle Passage having an overall mortality rate of more than 14 percent. (See AP® Looking Again: Describing the Middle Passage, page 357, for more on the Middle Passage.) Enslaved Africans frequently resisted their fates in a variety of ways. About 10 percent of the transatlantic voyages experienced a major rebellion by desperate captives, and resistance continued in the Americas, taking a range of forms from surreptitious slowdowns of work to outright rebellion. Throughout the Americas, slave rebellions were frequent, most of them local, small scale, and crushed with great brutality. Hundreds of such rebellions have been identified in North America alone and many others in Latin America and the Caribbean. It was only with the Haitian Revolution of the 1790s that a full-scale slave revolt brought lasting freedom for its participants. (See "The Haitian Revolution, 1791–1804" in Chapter 7.) One common form of resistance was to flee. Many who escaped joined free communities of formerly enslaved people known as **maroon societies**, which were founded in remote regions, especially in South America and the Caribbean. The largest such settlement was **Palmares** in Brazil, which endured for most of the seventeenth century, housing 10,000 or more people, mostly of African descent but also including Native Americans, mestizos, and renegade whites.

Consequences: The Impact of the Slave Trade in Africa

From the viewpoint of world history, the chief outcome of the transatlantic slave system lay in the new global linkages that it generated as Africa became a permanent part of an interacting Atlantic world. Millions of its people were now compelled to make their lives in the Americas, where they made an enormous impact both demographically and economically. Until the nineteenth century, they outnumbered European immigrants to the Americas by three or four to one, and West African societies were increasingly connected to an emerging European-centered

---

AP® Topic Questions

After students have read the last section of "The Slave Trade in Practice" on page 344, you could have them complete the British Treaty with Jamaican Maroons MCQ Topic Questions in AP® Classroom for practice. You can find these MCQs to assign by logging into AP® Classroom, clicking on Unit 4 under Classroom Resources, and then selecting Topic Questions. When students have completed the questions, consider displaying them on a screen and reviewing them as a class.

Contextualization

While the AP® skill of Contextualization is difficult, consistently practicing this skill will allow students to master it. Ask students to describe the changes and continuities in global trade between the early modern era and the present. *Trade will always be an important part of the globalization of the world. Natural resources as well as manufactured goods will remain important, but now the world has added technology to the mixture. Technology will increase the speed of communication and transportation.*

world economy. These vast processes set in motion a chain of consequences that transformed the lives and societies of people on both sides of the Atlantic.

Although the slave trade from Africa did not result in the kind of population collapse that occurred in the Americas, it certainly slowed Africa's growth at a time when Europe, China, and other regions were expanding demographically. Beyond the loss of millions of people over four centuries, the demand for enslaved Africans produced economic stagnation and social disruption. Economically, the slave trade stimulated little positive change in Africa because those Africans who benefited most from the traffic in people were not investing in the productive capacities of their societies. Although European imports generally did not displace traditional artisan manufacturing, no technological breakthroughs in agriculture or industry increased the wealth available to these societies. Maize and manioc (cassava), introduced from the Americas, added a new source of calories to African diets, but the international demand was for Africa's people, not its agricultural products.

Socially too, the slave trade shaped African societies. It surely fostered moral corruption, particularly as judicial proceedings were manipulated to generate victims for export. A West African legend tells of cowrie shells, a major currency of the slave trade, growing on corpses of decomposing enslaved people, a symbolic recognition of the corrupting effects of this commerce in human beings.

African women felt the impact of the slave trade in various ways, beyond those who numbered among its transatlantic victims. Since far more men than women were shipped to the Americas, the labor demands on those women who remained increased substantially, compounded by the growing use of cassava, a labor-intensive import from the New World. Unbalanced sex ratios also meant that far more men than before could marry multiple women. Furthermore, the use of enslaved women and girls within West African societies grew as the export trade in enslaved men expanded. Retaining women and girls for their own use allowed warriors and nobles in the Senegambia region to distinguish themselves more clearly from ordinary peasants. In the Kongo, enslaved women provided a source of dependent laborers for the plantations that sustained the lifestyle of urban elites. A European merchant on the Gold Coast in the late eighteenth century observed that every free man owned at least one or two enslaved people.

For much smaller numbers of women, the slave trade provided an opportunity to exercise power and accumulate wealth. In the Senegambia region, where women had long been involved in politics and commerce, marriage to European traders

AP
CONTINUITY AND CHANGE
What changes did the Atlantic slave system bring to African societies?

▼ **AP**
CLAIMS AND EVIDENCE IN SOURCES
Use evidence from this image to explain how signares expressed their wealth and power.

A Signare of Senegal While many women suffered greatly because of the Atlantic slave trade, a few grew quite wealthy and powerful. Known as *signares*, they married European merchants and built their own trading networks. The signare in this eighteenth-century French image is shown at the slave port of Saint Louis Island in Senegal. She is dressed in the fashionable and imported textiles that display her status. (Florilegius/Alamy Stock Photo)

EXPLORING AP® THEMES

Social Interactions and Organization (SIO)

The subject of the impact of the slave trade on Africa is a good place to examine the role of women. Ask students: How did the departure of so many men affect African society? *The shortage of men led to an increased demand for labor from women, unbalanced male-to-female ratios, and an increase in the use of enslaved females from West African societies. For smaller numbers of women, the shortage of men created an opportunity for power and wealth.*

BUILDING AP® SKILLS

Claims and Evidence in Sources

You can introduce the idea of different roles for women in Africa by having students look at the image on page 345. Explain to students how the *signares* developed, and then have students use evidence from the image to explain how the signares expressed wealth and power. *The signare in this image expressed her wealth and power through luxurious, imported textiles.*

BUILDING AP® SKILLS

Claims and Evidence in Sources

Have students look at the portrait of Ayuba Suleiman Diallo. Ask students: Does anything in the painting show him to be a member of an elite class? *His elaborate turban, his clothing, the medallion around his neck, and his confident posture and expression all give him the appearance of being a member of an elite class.*

EXPLORING AP® THEMES

Social Interactions and Organization (SIO)

This is a good place to focus on the changes in social and gender roles in Africa during the Atlantic slave trade by considering opportunities for women in the state-building enterprises that often accompanied the slave trade in West Africa. Using the information found on page 345–347, ask students to create a chart like the one below showing how women in West Africa gained important political roles during the Atlantic slave trade era. A reproducible version of this chart is available in the Teacher's Resource Materials. (Answers are provided in italics.)

ZOOMING IN Ayuba Suleiman Diallo: To Slavery and Back

Ayuba Suleiman Diallo.

February 1730 found Ayuba Suleiman Diallo, less than thirty years of age, living between the Gambia and Senegal rivers in West Africa among the Fulbe-speaking people.[36] Like his father, a prominent Islamic scholar and teacher, Ayuba was a Muslim who was literate in Arabic, a prayer leader in the local mosque, and a *hafiz*, someone who had memorized the entire Quran. He was also husband to two wives and father to four children. Now his father sent the young man on an errand. He was to take several of their many enslaved people to a location some 200 miles away, where an English trading ship had anchored, and exchange them for paper and other goods. The paper was especially important, for his father's income depended on inscribing passages from the Quran on small slips of paper and selling them as protective charms.

To put it mildly, things did not go as planned. Unable to reach an agreement with the English merchant Captain Stephen Pike, Ayuba traveled to the lands of the Mandinka, where he traded the people that his father had entrusted him with for a number of cows. Well beyond the safety of his own country, he was in dangerous territory. As he and his companions stopped to rest on the journey home, they were seized, their heads were shaved, and they were sold to the very same Captain Pike. Although Ayuba was able to send a message to his father asking to be ransomed, the ship sailed before a reply was received. And so Ayuba, along with 168 others, both men and women, headed for the British American colony of Maryland, where 150 of them arrived alive.

Sold to a local planter, Ayuba was immediately sent to the tobacco fields, but when he became ill from this heavy and unaccustomed work, his owner assigned him the less arduous and more familiar task of tending cattle. Alone

photo: Photo © Christie's Images/Bridgeman Images

offered advantage to both partners. For European male merchants, as for fur traders in North America, such marriages afforded access to African-operated commercial networks as well as the comforts of domestic life. Some of the women involved in these cross-cultural marriages, known as *signares*, became quite wealthy, operating their own trading empires, employing large numbers of enslaved women, and acquiring elaborate houses, jewelry, and fashionable clothing.

Furthermore, the state-building enterprises that often accompanied the sale of enslaved people in West Africa offered yet other opportunities to a few women. As the Kingdom of **Dahomey** (deh-HOH-mee) expanded during the eighteenth century, the royal palace, housing thousands of women and presided over by a powerful Queen Mother, served to integrate the diverse regions of the state. Each lineage was required to send a daughter to the palace even as well-to-do families sent additional girls to increase their influence at court. In the Kingdom of Kongo, women held lower-level administrative positions, the head wife of a nobleman exercised authority over hundreds of junior wives and enslaved people, and women served on the council

Women in West Africa

Dahomey	Kongo	Matamba
■ *Thousands of women were housed at the royal palace.* ■ *Each lineage was required to send a daughter to the palace for education.* ■ *Well-to-do families often sent more girls to have additional influence at court.*	■ *Women held lower-level administrative positions.* ■ *The head wife of a nobleman had authority over hundreds of junior wives and enslaved people.* ■ *Women served on the council that advised the monarch.*	■ *The religion was known for female rulers, for example, Queen Nzinga.* ■ *Queen Nzinga resisted Portuguese imperialism.*

TRM Handout 6.7: Comparison Chart for Women in West Africa with the cattle, Ayuba was able to withdraw into a nearby forest to pray, but he was spotted by a young white boy who mocked him and threw dirt in his face. Sometime later, no doubt in despair, Ayuba ran away, but he was soon captured and housed in the county jail, located in the back room of a tavern. There he became something of a local curiosity and attracted the attention of a lawyer named Thomas Bluett. When Ayuba refused wine, wrote a few lines in Arabic, and mentioned "Allah" and "Muhammad," Bluett realized that he was "no common slave." Bluett became fascinated by Ayuba's story, and he initiated a process that took both of them to England in 1733, where philanthropists purchased Ayuba's freedom.

Ayuba's reception in England was amazing. Now fluent in English, Ayuba was received by the English royal family and various members of the nobility, hosted by leading scholars, and entertained by wealthy merchants, eager to tap his knowledge of economic conditions in West Africa. The prominent artist William Hoare painted his portrait, complete with a small Quran hanging from his neck.

In 1734, he finally set off for home, loaded with gifts from his English friends. There he encountered, quite by chance, the same Mandinka men who had sold him only a few years before. Francis Moore, a European trader accompanying Ayuba, wrote that he "fell into a most terrible passion and was for killing them" and was restrained from doing so only with difficulty. He arrived in his hometown to find that his father had recently died. His wives and children, however, were all alive and welcomed him warmly. One of his wives had remarried, believing him gone forever, but her new husband readily gave way, and Ayuba resumed his place of prominence in his own community until his death in 1773.

He also resumed his life as a slave owner. Selling some of the gifts he had acquired in England, he purchased an enslaved woman and two horses soon after his arrival back in West Africa. According to Moore, he "spoke always very handsomely of the English," and he continued his association with the Royal African Company, the primary English slave-trading firm in West Africa, in its rivalry with French traders.[37] The last mention of Ayuba in the records of that company noted that he was seeking compensation for the loss of two enslaved people and a watch, probably the one given him in England by Queen Caroline.

QUESTIONS

What might you infer about Ayuba's own view of slavery and the slave trade? What insights or questions about the slave trade does his remarkable story suggest?

---

that advised the monarch. The neighboring kingdoms of Ndongo and Matamba in what is now Angola were known for their female rulers, who guided these states amid the complexities and intrigues of various European and African rivalries. The powerful Queen Ana Nzinga (1624–1663), for instance, gained a reputation for her resistance to Portuguese imperialism.

Within particular African societies, the impact of the transatlantic slave system differed considerably from place to place and over time. Many small-scale kinship-based societies, lacking the protection of a strong state, were thoroughly disrupted by raids from more powerful neighbors, and insecurity was pervasive. Oral traditions in southern Ghana, for example, reported that "there was no rest in the land," that people went about in groups rather than alone, and that mothers kept their children inside when European ships appeared.[38] Some larger kingdoms such as Kongo and Oyo slowly disintegrated as access to trading opportunities and firearms enabled outlying regions to establish their independence. (For an account of one young man's journey to slavery and back, see Zooming In: Ayuba Suleiman Diallo, page 346.)

BUILDING AP® SKILLS
Claims and Evidence in Sources

Ask students to read "Zooming In: Ayuba Suleiman Diallo: To Slavery and Back" with a partner. Ask partners to create a sequential list of the events in Ayuba's journey as an enslaved person. (Answers are provided in italics.)

■ *Ayuba took several of his family's enslaved persons to trade for European goods, including highly prized paper.*

■ *Ayuba did not reach agreement with the English captain, so he traveled farther and traded enslaved people for cows in Mandinka.*

■ *Ayuba was captured and sold as an enslaved person to the English captain with whom he had originally bargained.*

■ *Ayuba headed to Maryland and was sold to a local planter.*

■ *Ayuba became ill in the plantation tobacco field and was assigned to tend cattle.*

■ *Ayuba ran away but was captured and then housed in the back of a local tavern.*

■ *A local lawyer named Thomas Bluett recognized that Ayuba was not a "common slave" and arranged for philanthropists to purchase his freedom.*

■ *Ayuba returned home to his family and once again became an owner of enslaved people.*

Bell Ringer

A good way to have students quickly practice their writing skills at the start of class is to post a prompt and give students 5 minutes to write a thesis statement for it. Ask students to write a thesis statement for the following prompt:

■ In the period 1450–1750, transoceanic voyaging made the interconnection between the Eastern and Western hemispheres possible and led to significant economic, cultural, and demographic changes around the world.

Develop an argument that evaluates how the new interconnections between the Eastern and Western hemispheres impacted global economic structures in this time period.

Thesis statements should include at least one of the following elements:

■ *Continual commerce throughout Afro-Eurasia*

■ *Continual trade in luxury items (silk, spices, porcelain, cotton textiles)*

■ *Changes in trade routes (addition of the transatlantic routes)*

■ *Changes in trade goods (silver, fur, enslaved people)*

However, African authorities also sought to take advantage of the new commercial opportunities and to manage the slave trade in their own interests. The Kingdom of **Benin**, in the forest area of present-day Nigeria, successfully avoided a deep involvement in the trade while diversifying the exports with which it purchased European firearms and other goods. As early as 1516, its ruler began to restrict the slave trade and soon forbade the export of enslaved men altogether, a ban that lasted until the early eighteenth century. By then, the ruler's authority over outlying areas had declined, and the country's major exports of pepper and cotton cloth had lost out to Asian and then European competition. In these circumstances, Benin felt compelled to resume limited participation in the slave trade. The neighboring Kingdom of Dahomey, on the other hand, turned to a vigorous involvement in the slave trade in the early eighteenth century under strict royal control. The army conducted annual slave raids, and the government soon came to depend on the trade for its essential revenues. The slave trade in Dahomey became the chief business of the state and remained so until well into the nineteenth century.

Commerce and Social Change

Finding the Main Point: How did commerce transform societies and increase social tensions in Europe, Asia, and across the colonial world?

Commerce has a very long history. Over the course of the human journey, buying and selling in a market, rather than producing and consuming within one's immediate family or community, has become an increasingly prominent feature of economic life. The new transoceanic trade routes established during the early modern period hastened and intensified, albeit unevenly, the scale and scope of commerce across the globe. In doing so, they strengthened and deepened a process, often referred to as commercialization, that was already under way in a few regions, especially China and the Indian Ocean basin, in earlier centuries. (See Chapter 3 for earlier examples of commercialization.) This acceleration of commercialization only intensified in the centuries since 1750, so that by the early twenty-first century almost all economic activity occurred within market-based networks of production and exchange. In short, today nearly everything is for sale.

That was decidedly not the case at the start of the early modern era. Then most people in most places continued to work in subsistence agriculture producing most of what they consumed with their own hands. Specialist artisans in small workshops were the chief manufacturers of products for sale. They generally specialized in items that subsistence farmers could not make at home, such as metal tools, and their production was mostly consumed locally. Economic life in these communities was primarily shaped by custom, tradition, or the commands of social superiors rather than by the demands and opportunities of the market. Nonetheless, commercialization variously reshaped the lives of individuals and the structure of societies as the early modern era unfolded.

Beyond the particular outcomes of trade in spices, silver, furs, and enslaved people, more general patterns of social change accompanied commercialization during the early modern era. One of them involved merchants, people who buy and sell for their own profit commodities that others produce. It is hardly surprising that more commerce meant growing numbers of such merchants—international traders and local shopkeepers alike—and in some places their increasing social prominence.

Examples abound. Jews and Christian Armenians, both of them frequently persecuted religious minorities, found an outlet in trade as commercialization swept across parts of Eurasia. Growing numbers of Jewish traders operated in Central and Eastern Europe, the Middle East, and the Atlantic world, and their networks served as important commercial conduits for trade across cultural boundaries, especially the boundary between Christian and Muslim civilizations. More broadly, all across the Atlantic world the immense volume of transoceanic commerce gave rise to growing merchant communities in the Americas, Europe, and Africa. In the Netherlands of the seventeenth century, clearly the most highly commercialized European state, a mercantile elite exercised an unusual degree of social and political power compared to aristocratic dominance elsewhere on the continent. In Western Europe's major trading cities, merchants drew on credit, speculated in markets, accumulated capital, and sought profits to reinvest rather than hoard or spend—embracing what later historians have labeled commercial capitalism. A new commercial class whose members derived much of their wealth from transoceanic trade had taken root by 1750.

Sometimes the growing wealth of merchant families enabled them to cross previously sharp social barriers, leading to tension with other elites. Some Chinese merchants, for example, became wealthy enough to work their way into the scholar-gentry class, despite their low status in the traditional hierarchy of Chinese society. Stereotyped as greedy, luxury loving, and materialistic, upwardly mobile merchants stirred resentments among established bureaucratic and landowning families, who viewed themselves as frugal, altruistic, and cultured. In Europe too, money talked, as wealthy merchants or their heirs often abandoned commerce to "live nobly," using their resources to buy land, marry into established aristocratic families, and purchase noble titles from rulers. The aspirations of these merchants frequently elicited loud complaints from established aristocrats who argued that these new families lacked the pedigree of old nobility who had secured their status through military service. Likewise in an increasingly commercialized Japan, prosperous merchant families sometimes loaned money to impoverished but high-status samurai, much to the latter's embarrassment and resentment. These merchants also came in for sharp criticism for dressing themselves and their wives in fine and expensive clothes, which led to a series of laws seeking to ensure that people dressed according to their prescribed station in Japanese society.

Another important social change associated with commercialization occurred in rural areas where families abandoned, partially or entirely, their subsistence farming practices in favor of producing crops or other products for sale on the market. In the highly commercialized economy of Ming dynasty China, substantial

AP® EXAM TIP

The AP® Exam frequently asks students to analyze the reasons for social change.

AP®

CAUSATION

How did commerce blur the divisions in traditional social structures?

APPLY THE TIP

This is a good place to reinforce the AP® theme of Social Interactions and Organization (SIO). Many students confuse this theme with Cultural Developments and Interactions (CDI), and constant practice with the differences in the themes helps students remember that these themes are not the same. Ask students to use the information on page 349 to examine the reasons for social change. *The wealth that merchants gained allowed them to have more social and political power. By 1750, a new commercial class existed. The Netherlands was the most commercialized state in the seventeenth century, and many merchants achieved political power. In China, many merchants were able to work their way into the scholar-gentry class. Social change also occurred in rural areas when families switched from subsistence farming to producing crops or other products for sale on the market. Peasants found new ways of earning money and improving their social status. In some areas, forced labor became a standard practice, such as the "encomienda" system in the Americas and the African slave trade. Wage labor became more important in urban areas, and many peasants migrated to find work.*

AP® CLASSROOM

AP® Daily Videos

A good way to help students understand the changing social hierarchies and their impact in the early modern era is to have them watch the AP® Daily Video 4.7. This video examines how previous hierarchies changed and how racial hierarchies were created in the Americas to justify European dominance. This video can be found in your AP® Classroom account under Unit 4 Resources.

numbers of Chinese peasants produced cash crops for sale (rice, tea, fruits, mulberry trees) on family farms and as workers on large-scale plantations. Communities that devoted themselves to growing mulberry trees, for example, on which silkworms fed, had to buy their rice from other regions. Similarly, merchants of the British East India Company came to focus heavily on Indian cotton textiles, which were becoming widely popular in England and its American colonies. In response, hundreds of villages in the interior of southern India became specialized producers for this British market. In Europe as well, textile production took root in some rural regions. In the "putting-out system," peasant farmers and their families spun thread and weaved cloth for merchants who provided the raw materials. In this way merchants benefited from cheaper labor in the countryside, while peasant farmers found opportunities for earning money, especially during quiet times in the agricultural year. Thus Chinese, Indian, and European villagers alike were responding to market opportunities.

In many places, however, commercialization went hand in hand with forced rather than voluntary labor. In Spanish America and the Philippines, the *encomienda* system virtually required that native peoples provide their labor on large estates producing cash crops and livestock. On the Banda Islands in what is now Indonesia, the authorities of the Dutch East India Company killed, enslaved, or left to starve virtually the entire population of some 15,000 people. They then replaced them with Dutch planters, using a slave labor force, mostly from other parts of Asia, to produce the highly profitable nutmeg crop. And in the Americas the market demand in Europe for sugar, cotton, and tobacco gave rise to plantation agriculture worked by millions of enslaved Africans, who were themselves treated as commodities, their labor stolen and forced rather than offered freely.

In yet another pattern of social change associated with commercialization, people sold their labor power to employers in return for wages. Hired labor, of course, was nothing new, but in the early modern world, it encompassed growing numbers of people. Wage labor was, broadly speaking, a market-based transaction that occurred most prominently in urban areas. In India, China, Japan, the Ottoman Empire, colonial Brazil, and Western Europe, urban populations grew substantially during the early modern era and more and more people began working for wages, though it was not until the nineteenth and twentieth centuries that massive urbanization, driven by industrialization, really took off.

Japan was among the most rapidly urbanizing regions of the world, with some 16 to 17 percent of the population living in towns or cities by 1700 and the city of Edo (Tokyo) having grown to over 1 million inhabitants. In these cities, populated substantially by migrants from impoverished rural areas, wage labor became common. Servants, previously limited to samurai households, now grew in number and worked in the homes of merchants, artisans, and businessmen, often under various forms of contracts. Casual laborers, needed for large-scale construction projects, also worked for wages, which marked a major change from the earlier practice of *corvée* or unpaid labor required of commoners by their social superiors.[39] Changing

AP®

CONTINUITY AND CHANGE

What changes occurred in traditional forms of labor as a result of increased commercial activity?

BUILDING AP® SKILLS

Making Connections: Continuity and Change

The AP® Continuity and Change margin question on this page would be a great guiding question for a class discussion on the changes that occurred in traditional forms of labor as the result of increased commercial activity. You can find suggested responses to this question in the Teacher's Resource Materials.

market conditions now shaped the lives of these workers rather than customary obligations to political or social elites.

In Western Europe a rising population, stagnant crop yields, the loss of access to common lands, and poor growing conditions linked to the Little Ice Age meant that by the mid-seventeenth century most farmers were unable to feed their families from their own land. To make ends meet, they and their families worked for wages on larger farms or spun and weaved for textile merchants. Those who possessed no land of their own became completely reliant on wage labor to survive.

Many migrated to cities or moved from region to region in search of work. Migrants often received a hostile reception from locals, who feared that these outsiders brought crime, disease, and social disorder to their communities even as they overwhelmed charitable institutions. European authorities passed laws to control, punish, or confine vagrants without roots in the community, effectively making being poor a crime. Defined as the "undeserving poor," they were denied both public and private charity. "In giving alms one does more harm than good," explained one charitable institution in Toulouse, France, "because it seems . . . that one thereby maintains a network of weaklings, tavern haunters, fornicators, villains, robbers, and thieves, in short, a network of vice."[40]

In these various ways, commerce had social consequences in early modern world history, as it always has.

CONCLUSIONS AND REFLECTIONS

Global Trade and Moral Complexity

Finding the Main Point: What historical or moral questions arise as we consider early modern global commerce?

"Trade Makes the World Go Round" was the title of an article in the *Wall Street Journal* in 2005. It was certainly an appropriate description for the commercially entangled world of the early twenty-first century. But long-distance or transregional trade has long propelled human societies, though at various speeds and in various directions. For millennia the Silk Road commerce across northern Eurasia and the Sea Road trade in the Indian Ocean basin generated substantial change in the societies that they linked, as did the Sand Road exchange across the Sahara Desert that emerged after 300 C.E. (See Chapter 3.)

In the early modern era, however, major changes in patterns of world trade made the world go round even faster. One was the growing prominence of Western Europeans. Previously marginal players in global commerce, now they established a major presence in the ancient exchange networks of the Indian Ocean, initially through a Portuguese "trading post empire" and later through the British and Dutch East India companies. By far the most significant European initiative was the creation of economic networks of trade in furs, silver, sugar, enslaved people, and more across both the Atlantic and Pacific oceans.

AP EXAM TIP
Make a brief list of continuities and changes in global commerce from this era to the early twenty-first century.

AP® CLASSROOM

AP® Topic Questions

A good wrap-up to this section is to assign the multiple-choice questions for Topic 4.7 on tolerance in the Ottoman Empire. You can find these multiple-choice questions by logging into AP® Classroom, clicking on Unit 4 under Classroom Resources, and then selecting Topic Questions.

When you assign the Topic Questions or Personal Progress Checks, it can be a good idea to put a timer on the question(s) so students can practice the skill in a timed setting like the AP® Exam.

APPLY THE TIP

This tip is a good way to examine this section. Ask students to brainstorm the continuities and changes in global commerce from the early modern era to today. *In the early modern era, long-distance trade involved long-distance travel and a large amount of time. Communication took a long time as well. However, in this era the world first saw truly global trade and a global currency. Western Europe slowly became the dominant power in the world. Economic life was still preindustrial. Today travel and communication are considerably faster. Many of the goods produced are in the technological field.*

These new and unprecedented patterns of world trade were enormously consequential. They permanently linked the Eastern and Western hemispheres for the first time in human history, thus laying the foundations of the genuinely global economy of modern times. Exploring this complex historical process raises an endlessly debated question about trade: Who benefits? Answering that question raises still other issues: Was the trade genuinely voluntary or coerced? What differences in political or military power existed among the participants? How equivalent were the economies of the trading partners? Who produced the goods that were exchanged, and in what circumstances? And how were traded products distributed within the receiving societies?

In the Dutch trade with the Spice Islands, military power enabled merchants to control both production and shipping, thus generating enormous profits while reducing native growers to slavery, poverty, or starvation. By contrast, British merchants in India had to operate under the control of the powerful Mughal Empire and were often dependent on wealthy Indian lenders. Meanwhile, British demand for highly popular cotton textiles transformed many Indian villagers into specialized producers for the European market.

The silver trade enabled many Europeans to purchase valued Chinese goods and also enabled Spain to become a major power for a time. But the miners who produced silver in colonial Potosí were subjected to horrendous conditions that made their lives miserable and brief, while their wealthy Spanish rulers lived in luxury.

The North American fur trade obviously benefited those Europeans who were able to purchase warm clothing. And the Indigenous North American peoples who generated those furs gained access to useful European products and were not directly coerced. However, the fur trade decimated many Native American societies as it introduced devastating diseases, alcoholic beverages, and firearms. And many animal species, such as beaver and deer, also paid the price for this trade.

The commerce in enslaved Africans raises an even more complex moral equation. Clearly African, American, and European merchants benefited economically from this commerce, as did their rulers. So too did American plantation owners and all those who now had access to cheap sugar, cotton, tobacco, and other goods produced by enslaved people. The enslaved Africans themselves, however, deported from their homeland and treated as commodities, were subject to abuse and exploitation almost beyond description. Who is most responsible for what we now see as a moral calamity—African sellers, European buyers, or perhaps all those who purchased commodities produced by enslaved people and the products made from them? And to complicate matters even further, commerce in enslaved persons was widespread and considered "natural" in early modern times in many parts of the world, including Africa. To what extent should prevailing cultural norms at the time shape our assessment?

To put it mildly, the costs and benefits of early modern global trade were not borne equally by its many participants. The question of "who benefits?" is both complex and sometimes morally ambiguous. Such are the unsettling issues that arise as we contemplate how "trade made the world go round."

Role in the Slave Trade

Africans	Europeans	European Colonists in the Americas
■ *Merchant and political elites from certain areas captured other Africans to sell to Europeans.* ■ *West Africa may have increased warfare to capture more enslaved people.* ■ *Slave trade within Africa was entirely in their hands, rather than under European control.*	■ *European demand for enslaved people led to African groups supplying them.* ■ *Bought enslaved people from groups on both the west and east coasts of Africa and then transported them to Europe or the American colonies.* ■ *Provided firearms and manufactured goods in exchange for enslaved people.*	■ *Increase in plantations led to higher demand for enslaved people in the colonies.* ■ *Because of the harsh labor needed on sugarcane plantations in Brazil and the Caribbean, a large number of enslaved people were brought to these regions.*

TRM Handout 6.8: Comparison Chart for Role in the Slave Trade

CHAPTER REVIEW

AP Key Terms

Indian Ocean commercial network, 320

trading post empire, 322

Philippines, 323

Manila, 324

British East India Company, 324

Dutch East India Company, 324

"silver drain," 328

piece of eight, 329

Potosí, 329

fur trade, 331

"soft gold," 335

transatlantic slave system, 335

African diaspora, 338

maroon societies / Palmares, 344

signares, 346

Dahomey, 346

Benin, 348

Finding the Main Point

1. How did the strategies of different European states in the Indian Ocean region compare, and what effects did their involvement have on Asian commerce?
2. What was the significance of the silver trade in the global history of the early modern era?
3. What was the significance of the fur trade in the global history of the early modern era?
4. What transcontinental relationships did the Atlantic slave system generate? What was its impact on Europe, Africa, and the Americas?
5. How did commerce transform societies and increase social tensions in Europe, Asia, and across the colonial world?
6. What historical or moral questions arise as we consider early modern global commerce?

AP Big Picture Questions

1. To what extent did Europeans transform earlier patterns of commerce, and in what ways did they assimilate into those older patterns?
2. What lasting legacies of early modern trading networks are evident today? And what aspects of those networks are no longer in operation?
3. Who should be assigned the moral responsibility for the transatlantic slave system? Is this an appropriate task for historians?
4. **Looking Back** Asians, Africans, and Native Americans interacted with early modern European expansion in quite different ways. Based on Chapters 4, 5, and 6, how might you describe and explain those differences? In what ways were they active agents in the historical process rather than simply victims of European actions?

TRM Suggested Responses to Questions

You can find suggested responses to the Chapter Review questions in the Teacher's Resource Materials.

BUILDING AP® SKILLS

Making Connections: Continuity and Change

The early modern era (1450–1750) examines the continuities and changes of historical events that will stretch into the twentieth century. This is an important skill to master for AP® World History: Modern as students must be able to deal with details without losing sight of the big picture.

Depending on your students' skill level, you could assign either Activity 1 or Activity 3 on page 356 to help them develop this skill. Activity 1 is good for students still struggling with identifying continuities and changes in historical events. Activity 3 is good for students who can identify continuity and change and are ready for the challenge of writing a historical argument about it.

Making Connections: Continuity and Change

As historical processes and events unfold, some things change and some things persist. Analyzing how these changes and continuities shape history is a key part of a historian's work. In this workshop, we are going to learn about the skill of tracking those changes and continuities over time.

UNDERSTANDING CONTINUITY AND CHANGE

Let's start by defining what the terms "continuity" and "change" mean:

Continuity and Change: Analyzing the historical patterns of change over a period of time, while also recognizing what stayed the same

In the AP® World History course, this means learning how to deal with the particular without losing sight of the big picture. To track changes, you will need to **establish how things were at some point in the past**, and then look at the historical details to **identify how things changed over time**, *step by step*. You are looking for patterns and trying to establish a clear timeline—first this, then that, then that. When looking for continuities, you are tracking what remained unchanged, continued, or persisted in a slightly different form.

This is one of the *trickiest* skills in the AP® course because it seemingly overlaps with others. If we're looking at how things changed or remained the same across different time periods, isn't that a comparison? Yes, in a sense it is. A comparison in this course is usually from place to place (for instance, comparing the social effects of the spice trade in Asia with the social effects of the fur trade in North America), while continuity and change over time is usually a comparison of one time to another time (tracing how the merchant societies of the Indian Ocean commercial network both endured and changed after European arrival). What's important to keep in mind is that tracing continuity and change should be done **step by step** and should always discuss **both** what changed and what stayed the same.

If we are tracking what changed over time, isn't it important to say **why** things changed? If so, isn't this really causation? Causation is a closely related skill, certainly, but it's important to focus specifically on what you're being asked to do. When you're tracing continuity and change over time, you're being asked to lay out the various stages of change and/or continuity. Weaving in causation can add some depth to an extended argument, but it's important not to lose sight of your primary goal, which is to trace continuity and change step by step.

Let's see what this looks like in context by reading a description of the changes and continuities that resulted from the European fur trade in North America between the early seventeenth century and the late nineteenth century (page 334).

354

[The North American fur trade] had particular implications for women. A substantial number of native women married European traders according to the "custom of the country"—with no sanction from civil or church authorities. Such marriages eased the   *Change*

difficulties of this cross-cultural exchange, providing traders with guides, interpreters, and negotiators. But sometimes these women were left abandoned when their husbands returned to Europe. More generally, the fur trade enhanced the position of men in their societies because hunting or trapping animals was normally a male occupation.   *Continuity*

Among the Ojibwa, a gathering and hunting people in the northern Great Lakes region, women had traditionally acquired economic power by creating food, utensils, clothing, and decorations from the hides and flesh of the animals that their husbands caught. With the fur trade in full operation, women spent more time processing those furs for sale than in producing household items, some of which were now available for purchase from Europeans. And so, as one scholar put it, "women lost authority and prestige."   *Change*

At the same time, however, women generated and controlled the trade in wild rice and maple syrup, both essential to the livelihood of European traders.[25] Thus the fur trade   *Continuity and change*

offered women a mix of opportunities and liabilities.

In this example, you can see that the focus of the passage is on the social and economic changes women experienced during the European fur trade in North America, but it also notes some economic continuities in regards to men and women. This paragraph is a classic example of the intermingling of continuity and change.

CONTINUITY AND CHANGE ON THE AP® WORLD HISTORY EXAM

On the AP® Exam, the reasoning process of continuity and change is likely to come up repeatedly on the Multiple-Choice Questions of the exam, where you will be asked to track either changes or continuities in a stimulus item. It is guaranteed to appear on the Short-Answer Questions and will be found either in a stand-alone question or in association with a primary source. Most importantly, the skill of continuity and change is one of the three reasoning processes you can use to answer the Long Essay Question and the Document-Based Question.

There are a couple of common pitfalls for students encountering continuity and change questions on the Long Essay or Document-Based Questions of the AP® Exam. The first is that they slip into a comparison of two time periods, rather than tracing step by step the process of change and seeing the continuities. **Remember to go step by step.** The other pitfall is that students sometimes concentrate on just the obvious part

355

of this paired skill—the change—and forget to discuss the continuities. We'll talk more about writing a continuity and change argument in a later workshop.

BUILDING AP® SKILLS

1. **Activity: Identifying Continuity and Change.** Read the following sentences from this chapter, identifying each one as a statement of either continuity or change. Make note of the words and evidence that indicate continuity or change.

   a. Thus, for two centuries (1650–1850), Japanese authorities of the Tokugawa shogunate pursued isolationist trade policies, largely closing their country off from the emerging world of European commerce. . . . But Japan retained its trading ties with China, Korea, and Southeast Asia. (page 326)

   b. In the second half of the eighteenth century, both the Dutch and British trading post empires slowly evolved into a more conventional form of colonial domination, in which the British came to rule India and the Dutch controlled Indonesia. (page 325)

   c. Nor did other Asian merchants disappear from the Indian Ocean, despite European naval dominance. Arab, Indian, Japanese, Chinese, Javanese, Malay, Vietnamese, and other traders benefited from the upsurge in seaborne commerce. (page 327)

   d. Even more than the spice trade of Eurasia, it was the silver trade that gave birth to a genuinely global network of exchange. (page 327)

   e. Stimulated by the plantation complex of the Americas, the transatlantic slave system represented an enormous extension of the ancient practice of people owning and selling other people. (page 338)

2. **Activity: Working with Continuity and Change.** Based on the information in the section "Commerce and Social Change," which begins on page 348, create a chart like the one shown here to track the continuities and changes discussed.

Continuities	Changes

3. **Activity: Creating a Continuity and Change Paragraph.** Now that you understand the skill of tracing continuity and change over time, read the section "Consequences: The Impact of the Slave Trade in Africa" on page 344 and create a paragraph in response to the following prompt:

   To what extent did the Atlantic slave system change African societies over time?

   Make sure that you create a claim that clearly conveys both changes and continuities, while emphasizing which you believe is most significant. In addition, use evidence from the text to support your claim.

356

Describing the Middle Passage:
Comparing the Accounts of Two Historians

The questions and intentions that historians bring to their work as well as the sources they use can lead to accounts of the same event or process that differ significantly in tone or emphasis. In this activity you will consider two descriptions by modern historians of the Middle Passage—the harrowing sea journey across the Atlantic taken by millions of enslaved Africans. Each is based on analysis of primary sources and offers a coherent account of these harrowing voyages, but their tones and emphases are different. Your purpose is to define and perhaps account for those differences.

1 A FIRST LOOK

First read this passage written by the historian Lisa Lindsay on the conditions below decks during the Middle Passage. While reading, answer the following questions:

1. What is Lindsay's chief purpose in writing this passage? Although she does not explicitly state her thesis, how would you summarize her argument and conclusions?

2. What specific types of primary source evidence does Lindsay rely upon to sustain her argument? How do these sources affect the tone of her description?

Lisa Lindsay on Conditions above and below Deck during the Middle Passage | 2008

Between the large numbers of people crammed into unventilated spaces and the intestinal diseases that ravaged them, the holds of slave vessels became filthy cesspools. "The close-ness of the place, and the heat of the climate," Equiano [an enslaved African who survived the passage] wrote, "added to the number in the ship, which was so crowded that each had scarcely room to turn himself, almost suffocated us. This produced copious perspirations, so that the air soon became unfit for respiration, from a variety of loathsome smells, and brought on a sickness among the slaves, of which many died." The French slave trader Jean Barbot noted that sometimes the heat and lack of oxygen on the lower decks of slave ships were so intense that "the surgeons would faint away and the candles would not burn." . . . Below decks, the muck and stench from blood, sweat, urine, feces, and vomit overwhelmed any attempts at cleanliness. Crews were ordered to mop up the mess, scrub down the ship, and clear the air below decks with vinegar, whitewash or tar. . . .

Women and children frequently were allowed to move freely on deck, but slave traders brought out adult men only at specific times, including for exercise. With the prodding of a whip and occasionally a drum, accordion, or fiddle for accompaniment, they forced slaves to "dance" on deck. . . . Sometimes ships' crews took sadistic delight in such spectacles. In

357

TRM Suggested Responses to Questions
You can find suggested responses to the AP® Looking Again questions in the Teacher's Resource Materials.

BUILDING AP® SKILLS
Sourcing and Situation

Sourcing a document (explaining how or why a document's point of view, purpose, historical situation, and/or audience is relevant to an argument) is one of the most difficult points to achieve on the Document-Based Question essay. Continuing practice on this skill throughout the year is the best way to help students learn it and build confidence in being able to do it. The two accounts of the Middle Passage will help students practice sourcing and comparison skills. Have the students read the first excerpt and answer the two questions listed above it in the "First Look" (it might be a good idea to have the excerpt and questions on a separate sheet of paper so they don't read ahead). The questions will guide the students on how to analyze a document to prepare to write a sourcing statement. Once the students have read and answered the questions, ask them to share what they found with the class.

1792, for instance, Capitan John Kimber was tried in the British Court of Admiralty over the death of a 15-year-old female slave. . . . According to the prosecution, Kimber tortured the young woman to death because she had refused to dance naked on the deck of his ship. He was ultimately acquitted. . . .

Source: Lisa A. Lindsay, *Captives as Commodities: The Transatlantic Slave Trade* (Upper Saddle River, NJ: Pearson /Prentice Hall, 2008), 91–92.

2 A SECOND LOOK

Now read Johannes Postma's assessment of mortality rates among enslaved people during the Middle Passage. While reading, answer the following questions:

1. What is Postma's chief purpose in writing this passage? Although he does not explicitly state his thesis, how would you summarize his argument and conclusions?

2. What specific types of primary source evidence does Postma rely upon to sustain his argument? How do these sources affect the tone of his description?

Johannes Postma on Mortality during the Middle Passage | 2003

One of the much debated issues concerning the Atlantic slave trade is the death rate for slaves during the Middle Passage. . . . Abolitionists cited extremely high mortality figures for slaves and sailors, and used them to denounce the slave trade as both immoral and wasteful. Because slaves were valuable investment property, ship captains kept careful records in logbooks and mortality lists of the dates and causes of death, as well as the gender and age of the deceased. These records survive for about one-fifth of the documented slave voyages and are now accessible through the Cambridge University Press Database. They show that on average 12 percent of the enslaved did not survive the ocean crossing, though there was considerable variation from one transport to another. Before 1700, death rates tended to be higher, averaging more than 22 percent. They decreased to about 10 percent by the end of the eighteenth century, but rose again to nearly 12 percent during the years of illegal trading in the mid-nineteenth century. . . .

High mortality rates during the Middle Passage were usually blamed on conditions aboard the slave ships, and there is no doubt that crowding spread contagious diseases quickly. Intestinal disorders such as dysentery were the most common killers, often appearing in epidemic proportions. These ailments, along with tropical diseases such as malaria and yellow fever were responsible for about 70 percent of the casualties. Smallpox and scurvy also killed slaves, particularly before the mid-eighteenth century. Respiratory illnesses, heart attacks, suicide (jumping overboard or refusing to eat), revolts, storms, shipwrecks, attacks by pirates, and fights among slaves were also listed as causes of death.

Source: Johannes Postma, *The Atlantic Slave Trade* (Westport, CT: Greenwood Press, 2003), 43–45.

---

3 A THIRD LOOK

Now let's consider these two descriptions together. Consider the following:

1. How do the two accounts differ in tone and coverage?

2. Do these accounts contradict or complement each other? What does each voice add to your understanding of the Middle Passage?

3. How do the types of primary sources that these historians use affect the tone and content of their accounts?

AP® ACTIVITY SUMMARIZING ARGUMENTS

Summarize Lindsay's and Postma's arguments in a couple of sentences each. Note the primary sources that they rely upon and the tone of their description. Then in a few sentences compare the two accounts, assessing their relative strengths and what each adds to your understanding of the Middle Passage.

FURTHER ACTIVITY

Write a brief description of the Middle Passage that integrates the perspectives of both sources. How would you describe the tone and emphasis of your account as compared to those of Lindsay and Postma?

BUILDING AP® SKILLS

Sourcing and Situation

Continue working with the Middle Passage documents and use the three questions in the "Third Look" to help students compare the two documents and understand how the documents differ in tone and coverage.

You can end the activity by having students practice their writing skills by following the instructions in the "Further Activity."

359

TRM Suggested Responses to Questions
You can find suggested responses to the
AP® Working with Evidence questions in the
Teacher's Resource Materials.

BUILDING AP® SKILLS

Claims and Evidence in Sources

Interpreting text-based as well as non-text-based sources is an important skill of AP® World History: Modern students. If time is available, have students learn more about the consumption of goods and cultural exchanges in global commerce during the early modern era by using the evidence in "Consumption and Culture in the Early Modern World" beginning on page 360. Consider having students analyze one or more of the sources found on pages 360–367. Check for understanding by:

- Using the questions at the end of each source as a discussion starting point.

- Pairing students to analyze (identify and describe) using author/creator's point of view, purpose, historical situation, and/or audience. This activity can continue to reinforce sourcing.

- Assigning a source to a group of three or four students and having them present an overview of the source along with the sourcing to the rest of the class.

- Having students present an overview of the source, and then having students practice Contextualization skills using Question 2 under Doing History on page 368.

Consumption and Culture in the Early Modern World

One significant impact of the Columbian exchange was that growing numbers of people around the world gained increased access to goods from far away, and some of these products—sugar, pepper, tobacco, tea, and cotton textiles, for example—gradually dropped in price, becoming more widely available. Widespread consumption of these formerly exclusive goods brought cultural change because it threatened their use as signifiers of elite status, and profits generated by their trade created commercial classes of traders and merchants who were often more wealthy than traditional elites. The consumption of some products, including tea, coffee, chocolate, and tobacco, also created new arenas for social interaction.

LOOKING AHEAD

AP® DBQ PRACTICE

As you read through the documents in this collection, consider how they illustrate the relationship between consumption and culture during the several centuries after 1500, using clothing, tea, porcelain, and coffee as examples.

DOCUMENT 1 Regulating Dress in Europe

Moralists and government authorities everywhere worried that the growing availability of what had been rare and expensive textiles and furs might undermine the social order by allowing people to dress beyond their station. In Europe many governments sought to maintain social distinctions in dress by promulgating laws strictly limiting what could be worn by different groups. Document 1 is taken from the 1582 clothing ordinance issued by the town council of Augsburg, a wealthy and important trading city in southern Germany. The extracts concern the dress of the wives and daughters of men who were members of the Merchants' Room, one of four recognized groups of elite townsmen.

Source: Town Council of Augsburg, *Clothing Ordinance*, 1582.

An Honorable Council of this laudable city of Augsburg would like nothing better than to see each of the citizens and residents here behaving in accordance with their estate [social status] when it comes to clothing and adornments, and avoiding unnecessary expenses. However, the council has noted for some time now that luxury in clothing and adornments among some people has so taken the upper hand that one can hardly tell one estate from another. . . . Therefore, [the council] has composed the following ordinance. . . .

The honorable ladies and maidens of the Merchants' Room are not allowed to use watered silk or anything better for their capes, but only double taffeta [a type of plain woven silk], or something of lower value, without embroidery. And they are allowed no better lining than marten underbelly fur. . . .

On the other hand, [women of this estate] are permitted and allowed to wear gold rings of the value established by the wedding ordinance or less; a belt decorated with silver that does not cost more than 8 gulden. . . . But otherwise they should no longer wear golden bonnets, strings of pearls . . . nor belts made entirely of silver chains.

B. Ann Tlusty, *Augsburg during the Reformation Era: An Anthology of Sources* (Indianapolis, IN: Hackett, 2012), 70–72.

Question to Consider: How has the increasing affordability of clothing impacted the social structures of Augsburg?

AP Analyzing Sources: What reasons do the Augsburg authorities give for issuing their law? Do the reasons appear completely valid? Why or why not?

DOCUMENT 2 A Critical View of Coffeehouses in the Ottoman Empire

During the early modern period, coffee, like tea, became a popular beverage for the first time in many regions around the globe. As coffee entered the Ottoman Empire in the sixteenth century from its place of origin in Ethiopia and Yemen, it encountered considerable opposition, partly because it was consumed in the new social arena of the coffeehouse. Authorities suspected, sometimes quite rightly, that coffeehouses were places of moral decadence and political intrigue. Moralists in the Islamic world labeled the coffeehouse a "refuge of Satan" that drew people away from the mosques even as it brought together all different classes. In Document 2, Mustafa bin Ahmed (1541–1600), an Ottoman official and writer better known by his pen name Mustafa Ali, offers his assessment of Cairo's coffeehouses in his description of a visit to the city in 1599.

361

Also [remarkable] is the multitude of coffee-houses in the city of Cairo, the concentration of coffee-houses at every step, and of perfect places where people can assemble. Early rising worshippers and pious men get up and go [there], drink a cup of coffee adding life to their life. They feel, in a way, that its slight exhilaration strengthens them for their religious observance and worship. From that point of view their coffee-houses are commended and praised. But if one considers the ignorant people that assemble in them it is questionable whether they deserve praise. . . .

    To make it short, the coffee-houses of Egypt are filled mostly with dissolute persons and opium-eaters. Many are occupied by veteran soldiers, aged officers. When they arrive early in the morning rags and rush mats are spread out, and they stay until evening. . . . [These former military men] are a bunch of parasites . . . whose work consists of presiding over the coffeehouse, of drinking coffee on credit, talking of frugality, when the matter comes up, and, having told certain matters with all sorts of distortions. . . . In other words, their talk is mostly lies, their nonsensical speeches are either gossip and backbiting or slander and calumny. . . .

Mustafa Ali, *Mustafa Ali's Description of Cairo of 1599*, translated by Andreas Tietze (Vienna:Verlag der Österreichischen Akademie Der Wissenschaften, 1975), 37.

Question to Consider: How does Ali feel the coffeehouses are impacting the Islamic focus of Ottoman society?

AP Analyzing Sources: Is Ali's tone more supportive or critical? What do you know about Ali that might explain his tone?

DOCUMENT 3 Tobacco Smoking in Eurasia

Tobacco, like coffee, soon found a growing range of consumers all across Eurasia in the sixteenth and seventeenth centuries. Originating in the Americas, tobacco smoking spread quickly to Europe and Asia. Typically "lower sorts"—sailors, soldiers, laborers—brought tobacco to new regions, and almost everywhere elites criticized smoking upon its first arrival. The rulers of England, China, the Ottoman Empire—and with greater effect Russia—published promulgations or laws against the production and consumption of tobacco. In Document 3, King James I of England offers his reasons for opposing tobacco in his treatise *A Counterblaste to Tobacco*, published in 1604. His arguments were designed to counter common reasons for using tobacco at the opening of the seventeenth century, providing a window into the debate raging in Europe just as tobacco was becoming increasingly available.

Source: England's King James I, *A Counterblaste to Tobacco*, 1604.

For *Tobacco* being a common herb, which . . . grows almost every where, was first found out by some of the barbarous Indians, to be a Preservative, or Antidote against the Pox. . . . [S]o from them likewise was brought this use of *Tobacco*. . . . Why do we not as well imitate them in walking naked as they do? In preferring glasses, feathers and such toys, to gold and precious stones, as they do? yea why do we not deny God and adore the Devil as they do?

[H]erein is not only a great vanity but a great contempt for God's good gifts, that the sweetness of man's breath, being a good gift of God, should be willfully corrupted by this stinking smoke. . . . A custom loathsome to the eye, hateful to the Nose, harmful to the brain, dangerous to the Lungs. . . .

Question to Consider: What are King James's critiques of tobacco?

AP **Analyzing Sources:** What might explain King James's disdain for Indigenous Americans or his comment that they "adore the Devil"?

DOCUMENT 4 Coffeehouse Culture in England

Coffee spread from the Ottoman Empire to Europe, where authorities worried that coffee and coffeehouses encouraged both laziness and disorder, as King Charles II of England proclaimed in a short-lived effort to ban coffeehouses in his kingdom. But European authorities had even less success than their Ottoman counterparts in restraining coffee consumption and suppressing coffeehouse culture. "News from the Coffee-house," a song published in 1667 by the actor and poet Thomas Jordan, conveys the types of conversation that one might expect at a coffeehouse in seventeenth-century London.

363

Source: English poet Thomas Jordan, "News from the Coffee-house," 1667.

You that delight in Wit and Mirth,
And long to hear such News,
As comes from all parts of the Earth,
Dutch, Danes, and Turks and Jews,
I'll send you a Rendezvous,
Where it is smoking new;
Go hear it at a *Coffee-house*;
It cannot but be true.

There battles and sea-fights are fought,
And bloody plots displayed;
They know more things that ere was thought,
Or ever was betrayed:
No money in the Minting-house
Is half so bright and new;
And coming from the coffee-house,
It cannot but be true. . . .

You shall know there what fashions are,
How periwiggs are curl'd,
And for a penny you shall heare
All novells in the world;
Both old and young, and great and small,
And rich and poore, you'll see;
Therefore let's to the coffee all,
Come all away with me.

R. Chambers, ed., *The Book of Days: A Miscellany of Popular Antiquities in Connection with the Calendar* (London: W. & R. Chambers, 1879), 1:172–73.

Question to Consider: According to the song, who gathers at the coffeehouse?

AP **Analyzing Sources:** Consider Jordan's audience. How could his audience impact his lyrics and tone?

DOCUMENT 5 · Regulating Dress in Japan

In Japan, the emergence of a vibrant urban culture based on commerce and consumption challenged traditional distinctions between social classes and caused the government to issue ever more detailed laws regulating dress. Document 5 is taken from *The Japanese Family Storehouse* (1688), a book about how merchants made and squandered their fortunes in the seventeenth century. It was written by Ihara Saikaku, a prominent poet and novelist.

Source: Japanese poet Ihara Saikaku, from *The Japanese Family Storehouse*, 1688

Fashions have changed from those of the past and have become increasingly ostentatious. In everything people have a liking for finery above their station. Women's clothes in particular go to extremes. Because they forget their proper place, extravagant women should be in fear of divine punishment. Even the robes of the awesome high-ranking families used to be of nothing finer than Kyoto habutae [a smooth, strong silk]. . . . But in recent years, certain shrewd Kyoto [the imperial capital of Japan] people have started to lavish every manner of magnificence on men's and women's clothes and to put out design books in color.

Such behavior by wives and the marriages of daughters have drained the household finances and impaired the family business of countless merchants. . . .

It is distressing to see a merchant wearing good silks. Pongee suits him better and looks better on him. But fine clothes are essential to a samurai's status, and therefore even a samurai who is without attendants should not dress like an ordinary person.

Donald Shively, "Sumptuary Regulation and Status in Early Tokugawa Japan," *Harvard Journal of Asiatic Studies* 25 (1964–1965): 124–25.

Question to Consider: How has the increasing affordability of clothing impacted the social structures in Japan?

AP° Analyzing Sources: Does Ihara seem supportive or critical of the government? What aspects of his background may explain his position?

DOCUMENT 6 · Tea and Porcelain in Europe

This German painting from the early eighteenth century illustrates the growing popularity of tea as a beverage of choice in Europe, as well as the popularity of Chinese porcelain teacups. Initially, tea was extremely expensive and limited to the very wealthy, but the price dropped as the supply increased, and by the eighteenth century it was widely consumed in Europe by all classes of people. By the seventeenth century, the demand for Chinese porcelain in Europe was so large that Chinese artisans created styles and

365

patterns specifically for a European market. Unlike tea, fine Chinese porcelain remained an expensive luxury item and sign of status, but the widespread demand for teacups caused European manufacturers to mass-produce cheaper alternatives that often mimicked Chinese porcelain. The teacups sitting on the table in the foreground of the image are of the finest quality and were manufactured in China between 1662 and 1722. The image also depicts the practice of pouring the tea into the saucer to cool it.

Source: *Tea Drinking and Chinese Porcelain Cups*, 18th century.

Staatliche Schloesser und Gaerten, Karlsruhe; Germany/Erich Lessing//Art Resource, NY

Question to Consider: What are the symbols of status and culture shown in this image?

AP Analyzing Sources: Look at the actual cups and note the European house on the teacup at the bottom left. What does this indicate about the willingness of the Chinese to cater to European tastes?

DOCUMENT 7 **Chinese Poems about Smoking**

Laws against the production and consumption of tobacco were largely ineffective, and tobacco use quickly spread to all levels of society across Eurasia. As one seventeenth-century observer in China put it: "Among those throughout the realm who enjoy smoking there is no distinction of high and low, or of male and female."[41] This enthusiasm for tobacco was expressed in the verses in Document 7, written by elite Chinese poets and compiled in Cheng Cong's *Tobacco Manual* in 1805.

Source: Poems from Cheng Cong's *Tobacco Manual*, 17th and 18th centuries.

[1]

Soul-summoning fragrance rises from the tobacco
All over the country all the time the plant is being picked.
I laugh to think that in days of yore people had only ordinary leaves
As I watch a world of smoke and cloud pour out of you.

[2]

Through my pipe I draw the fiery vapour,
From out of my chest I spew white clouds.
The attendant takes away the ash.
Brings wine to amplify the intoxication.
I apply the flame to know the taste,
Letting it burn in the elephant's tusk.

[3]

The tobacco box is casually produced for my arriving guest,
A gentleman who has known all the matters of my heart for a decade.
Poetic blossoms have sprung from his brush since childhood,
And now *The Tobacco Manual* emerges from our clouds of smoke.

Timothy Brook, *Vermeer's Hat: The Seventeenth Century and the Dawn of the Global World* (London: Bloomsbury, 2008), 144 [1], 143 [2], 144–45 [3].

Question to Consider: Think about terms like "gentleman" as used in Chinese society. What is the concept of a gentleman in the third poem?

AP Analyzing Sources: Think about the importance of poetry in Chinese society. What is suggested by the fact that the author is writing poems about tobacco instead of politics, education, or family?

AP® DOING HISTORY

1. **DBQ Practice:** Evaluate the extent to which the increasing availability of goods facilitated societal changes in the period 1450–1750.

2. **Contextualization:** Many of the goods in these sources moved from one place to another through maritime trade. How can that fact help develop context for these documents?

3. **Outside Evidence:** Look at the claims you have developed in response to the DBQ Practice prompt. What additional information helps you prove those claims?

4. **Complex Argumentation:** Many of the sources address the same goods (tea, coffee, tobacco); how do those sources support, modify, or even refute one another?

368

On Consumer Culture in the Early Modern World

Here two historians assess the development of consumer culture during the early modern period. Frank Trentmann, a leading expert on the emergence of modern consumer culture, examines in Voice 6.1 what made the cultures of consumption in the Netherlands and Britain during the seventeenth and eighteenth centuries distinct from earlier consumer cultures in Renaissance Europe and Ming China. In Voice 6.2, Anne Gerritsen, a professor of Chinese history, and Giorgio Riello, a historian of global history and culture, assess the varied impacts of increased global exchange on the production and consumption of goods across the globe in the early modern period.

VOICE 6.1

Frank Trentmann on Consumer Culture in the Netherlands and Britain | 2016

It was in the north-west of Europe, in the Netherlands and Britain, that a more dynamic, innovative culture of consumption came to take hold in the seventeenth and eighteenth centuries. The growth in shops, markets and personal belongings was well under way in Renaissance Europe and Ming China, but their further expansion in the Netherlands and Britain was only in part a continuation of this earlier trend. For the two countries separated by the North Sea changed after 1600 in ways that, together, created a new kind of consumer culture. The exponential rise in [the amount of] stuff went hand in hand with a rise in novelty, variety and availability, and this was connected to a more general openness to the world of goods and its contribution to the individual self [individual identity and well-being], to social order and economic development. What distinguished the basket of goods in the eighteenth century was the combination of novelty, variety and the speed of change. Tobacco, tea and porcelain were new things that spawned new forms of consuming, socializing and self-representation. Equally important was the jump in variety. The manufacturer Matthew Boulton, who sold tea kettles, buckles, buttons and toothpick cases, had 1,500 designs on his books.

Source: Frank Trentmann, *Empire of Things: How We Became a World of Consumers, from the Fifteenth Century to the Twenty-First* (New York: Harper, 2016), 53.

VOICE 6.2

Anne Gerritsen and Giorgio Riello on the Impacts of Global Consumption and Exchange | 2018

Between 1500 and 1800 the exchange of goods became global, and European consumers could buy goods from all over the world. At the beginning of the period, goods from Asia were seen as exotic luxuries for kings and noblemen; by the end of the period silks and porcelains had come within the reach of orphans in Amsterdam or the descendants of slaves in New Spain. The impact of this development was huge: the African slave trade and the sugar and cotton plantations throughout the Americas were closely related to the almost insatiable desire for global goods. In early modern Europe, the demand for Asian goods vastly outstripped supply, and new commodities were manufactured to make up for this shortfall. Arguably the textile manufacturers and potteries of Central and Northern England that drove the Industrial Revolution did so because of the competition with Asian goods. In sum, global goods transformed the early modern world.

Source: Beat Kümin, ed., *The European World 1500–1800: An Introduction to Early Modern History*, 3rd ed. (London: Routledge, 2018), 212–13.

AP Analyzing Secondary Sources

1. According to Trentmann, what specific factors made the culture of consumption distinctly dynamic and innovative in the Netherlands and Britain during the early modern period?

2. In what ways did consumption spurred by global exchange transform the early modern world according to Gerritsen and Riello?

3. **Integrating Primary and Secondary Sources:** How might you construct an essay about early modern consumer culture using the two voices and the various sources in this feature?

BUILDING AP® SKILLS

Claims and Evidence in Sources

Interpreting secondary sources is an important skill for AP® World History: Modern students. Consider having students read both of the sources here and answer Questions 1–3 on page 369. Then you could discuss the questions as a class. This activity can help students practice reading and interpreting secondary sources, as found on the Multiple-Choice and SAQ sections of the exam.

Differentiation

If you want to differentiate this activity, follow the "Must Do, Should Do, Strive For" model below.

- Must Do: Students need to read the two sources and answer Questions 1–3 on page 369 on a separate sheet of paper.

- Should Do: Students need to participate at least once during a class discussion on the sources and the accompanying questions.

- Strive For: Students will use what they have learned from these secondary sources to contextualize the Working with Evidence sources on pages 360–367 (Question 3 on page 369).

TRM **Suggested Responses to Questions**
You can find suggested responses to the AP® Analyzing Secondary Sources questions in the Teacher's Resource Materials.

TEACHING IDEA

AP® Exam Strategies

Continue having students practice test-taking skills. Copy the multiple-choice questions found on pages 370–372. Give students the questions as a practice quiz prior to the unit or chapter test. Have students discuss with a partner why their answer choice was correct or incorrect.

AP® CLASSROOM

AP® Personal Progress Check

You can extend the AP® Exam Strategies activity on this page by logging into your AP® Classroom account and using the MCQ AP® Personal Progress Check under Unit 4, as more practice for your students. AP® Classroom allows you to set the questions up digitally or print out a copy for each student. Consider having students partner up and discuss the questions together to come to the correct answer.

When you assign the Personal Progress Checks, it can be a good idea to put a timer on the question(s) so students can practice the skill in a timed setting like the AP® Exam.

Multiple-Choice Questions Choose the correct answer for each question.

Questions 1–3 refer to this map.

The Global Silver Trade

1. Which of the following was a significant change in long-distance trade networks in the era ca. 1450–ca. 1750?
   a. Trade networks expanded to cover the globe for the first time.
   b. The Indian Ocean became the world's most significant trade network for the first time.
   c. The Silk Roads expanded to connect Asia and Europe for the first time.
   d. Overall commercial activity expanded for the first time.

2. Which of the following statements is most accurate for the era ca. 1450–ca. 1750?
   a. The use of silver as a trading commodity declined.
   b. The Spanish became the only European state with trade markets in the Americas and Asia.
   c. Native American empires began to trade directly with Asian markets.
   d. The amount of trade goods exported from China to Europe and the Americas increased dramatically.

3. What economic effects did the increased flow of silver into Spain have on its economy?
   a. It caused commercial activity within Europe to decline after the discovery of the New World.
   b. It caused significant price inflation in Spain that eventually led to the kingdom's near bankruptcy.
   c. It caused the Spanish government to begin generous social programs for all Spaniards.
   d. It caused Spain's economy to remain stable for over a century.

370

Questions 4–6 refer to these tables.

TABLE 1 CHANGING PATTERNS IN THE TRADE OF ENSLAVED PERSONS

Century	Total Taken from Africa	Total Landed at Destination	% Died during Middle Passage	Avg. Days in Middle Passage	Avg. % Enslaved Persons = Children	Avg. % Enslaved Persons = Male
1501–1600	227,506	199,285	12.0	—	0	58
1601–1700	1,875,631	1,522,677	23.3	76.1	11.6	58.4
1701–1800	6,494,619	5,609,869	11.9	70	18.4	64.2
1801–1866	3,873,580	3,370,825	10.3	45.9	29.4	67.6
TOTAL or AVERAGE	12,521,336 (Total)	10,702,656 (Total)	11.9 (Avg.)	60 (Avg.)	20.9 (Avg.)	64.7 (Avg.)

Source: Voyages: The Trans-Atlantic Slave Trade Database, 2009, accessed June 8, 2015, http://www.slavevoyages.org.

TABLE 2 PERCENTAGE OF ARRIVALS OF ENSLAVED PERSONS BY DESTINATION

Century	Europe	North America	Caribbean	Spanish American Mainland	Brazil	Africa	Other
1502–1600	1.1	—	8	66.7	1.9	0.3	22
1601–1700	0.6	1.5	56.4	22.7	17	0.1	1.6
1701–1800	0.1	5.2	64.4	1.2	29	0.1	0.1
1801–1866	—	2.0	31.9	0.9	60	4.8	0
Average of Total	0.1	3.8	51.9	3.3	38.9	1.8	0.3

Source: Voyages: The Trans-Atlantic Slave Trade Database, 2009, accessed June 8, 2015, http://www.slavevoyages.org.

4. A historian could use Table 1 to argue which of the following?

   a. The worsening conditions on ships during the Middle Passage led to an increase in deaths after 1700.

   b. An increase in the forced movement of male enslaved persons from West Africa led to changing gender roles in the region.

   c. The slave trade increased trade of many goods between West Africa and Europe.

   d. The decrease in African enslaved persons after 1800 was a result of the unification of West African societies into one state.

5. Which of the following best explains the percentage of enslaved persons transported to the Caribbean and Brazil as seen in Table 2?

   a. The high death toll of African enslaved persons due to disease

   b. The high number of runaway enslaved persons

   c. The stabilization of the demand for enslaved persons in North America

   d. The increased need for cheap labor on the sugarcane plantations

6. The transatlantic slave trade developed because
   a. there was a shortage of labor in the Americas because of harsh working conditions on plantations and the spread of disease.
   b. Europeans and Indigenous Americans formed partnerships to import Africans to work on the plantations.
   c. competition for enslaved persons from Asia into the Americas lowered the purchase price of African enslaved persons.
   d. European kings forced plantation owners in the Americas to trade exclusively in African enslaved persons.

Short-Answer Questions
Read each question carefully and write a short response. Use complete sentences.

1. **Use this passage and your knowledge of world history to answer all parts of the question that follows.**

   > All of the residents of these United Provinces shall be allowed to participate in this Company and to do so with as little or as great an amount of money as they choose. Should it occur that there are more moneys offered than are needed for the voyage, those who have more than 30,000 guilders in the Company will have to decrease their capital pro rata in order to make place for others....
   > As soon as 5% of a return cargo has been cashed shall it be distributed to the participants.
   >
   > — Charter of the Dutch East India Company, granted by the States General of the United Netherlands, 1602

   A. Identify ONE common economic process in the early modern era that is reflected in the passage.
   B. Explain ONE way in which passages such as this one can be seen as examples of how a government could use economic power to establish its authority.
   C. Explain ONE example of another economic system used by governments prior to 1750 to establish their authority.

2. **Use this passage and your knowledge of world history to answer all parts of the question that follows.**

   > It is only with the New World that one can explain the European demand for large numbers of slaves. As the Spanish and Portuguese conquistadores strode across the Americas, they expropriated wealth and shipped it home until there was little left to seize. Soon enough, they found that they would have to satisfy their thirst for wealth by going beyond expropriation: they would have to produce wealth. But since these conquistadores had no intention of performing the work themselves, their desire to produce entailed the creation of a labor force under their control. Such a labor force would have to be both productive and cheap, for otherwise the cost of production and transportation would prevent the resulting goods from being sold on the distant markets of Europe, and no profit would be realized.
   >
   > — Patrick Manning, *Slavery and African Life: Occidental, Oriental, and African Slave Trades*, 1990

AP® World History writing skills should be practiced on a regular basis. You can use the SAQs on pages 372 and 373 for students to write an "exit ticket" at the end of class to check for understanding and to practice their writing skills. The three SAQs can be spread across several days or as practice for the AP® Exam by writing them all at once. If you choose to make them a timed writing, make certain that students have the correct amount of time for this exercise. On exam day, students will have a total of 40 minutes to write three SAQs.

A. Identify ONE piece of evidence the author uses to support a commonly held belief about European motivations for exploration prior to 1750.

B. Explain ONE reason why enslaving the Native American population in the New World was not a continually viable option for the conquistadores.

C. Explain ONE example of a motivation for the transatlantic slave trade that is reflected in the passage above.

3. **Answer all parts of the question that follows.**

A. Identify ONE way in which the discovery of silver at Potosí in the sixteenth century changed global trade.

B. Explain ONE way in which interregional trade systems changed after the inclusion of the Americas in the global economy.

C. Explain ONE way in which interregional trade systems stayed the same after the inclusion of the Americas in the global economy.

TEACHING IDEA

AP® Exam Strategies

The Document-Based Question (DBQ) is
an important part of the AP® World History:
Modern Exam because it is 25 percent of the
overall score on the exam. It also requires
practice to master the skills required on the
DBQ. Have students write a full-length DBQ
using this Document-Based Question found on
pages 374–376.

   If you are running short on time, you can
have students work in groups to create a
DBQ poster. Create groups of three or four
students. Give each group a copy of the
DBQ. Use butcher paper for posters and
have each group cut the documents up. Have
each group write a thesis, two arguments
(paste documents used in the argument
to the butcher paper), analysis for each
document, and sourcing for three of the seven
documents. Exercises like this are good
practice for the writing skills that need to be
mastered for the AP® World History: Modern
Exam.

Document-Based Question Using these sources and your knowledge of world history, develop an argument in response to the prompt.

1. Evaluate the extent to which rulers of the early modern era differed in their methods of establishing authority.

Document 1

Source: Letter from Ogier Ghiselin de Busbecq, Flemish nobleman and Austrian ambassador to the Ottoman Empire. Austria was under threat of an Ottoman invasion, 1555–1562.

The Sultan's hall was crowded with people, among whom were several officers of high rank. Besides these there were all the troopers of the Imperial guard and a large force of Janissaries; but there was not in all that great assembly a single man who owed his position to aught save his valor and his merit. No distinction is attached to birth among the Turks. . . . In making his appointments the Sultan pays no regard to any pretensions on the score of wealth or rank, nor does he take into consideration recommendations or popularity. . . . It is by merit that men rise in the service, a system which ensures that posts should only be assigned to the competent.

Document 2

Source: Pedro de Cieza de León's *Chronicles of the Incas*, which described the Inca Empire and the Spanish conquest of the Incas, ca. 1550. De León was a conquistador and descendant of Jewish *conversos* who participated in various expeditions in South America. (*Conversos* were Jews who converted to Roman Catholicism in the 14th and 15th centuries.)

One of the things most to be envied in these rulers is how well they knew to conquer such vast lands. . . . [They] entered many lands without war, and the soldiers who accompanied the Inca were ordered to do no damage or harm, robbery or violence. If there was a shortage of food in the province, he ordered supplies brought in from other regions so that these newly won to his service would not find his rule and acquaintance irksome.

374

Document 3

Source: *The Memoirs of the Emperor Jahangir*, an account of his reign of the Mughal Empire depicting major political and cultural events in his life, 1605–1627.

[H]aving on one occasion asked my father [Akbar] the reason why he had forbidden any one to prevent or interfere with the building of these haunts of idolatry [Hindu temples], his reply was in the following terms: ". . . Ill should I discharge the duties of my exalted station, were I to withhold my compassion and indulgence from any of those entrusted to my charge. With all of the human race, with all of God's creatures, I am at peace: why then should I permit myself, under any consideration, to be the cause of molestation or aggression to any one? Besides, are not five parts in six of mankind either Hindus or aliens to the faith; and were I to be governed by motives of the kind suggested to your inquiry, what alternative can I have but to put them all to death! I have thought it therefore my wisest plan to let these men alone."

Document 4

Source: Excerpt from James I's speech to the English Parliament, 1610.

The state of monarchy is the supremest thing upon earth, for kings are not only God's lieutenants upon earth and sit upon God's throne, but even by God himself they are called gods. There be three principal [comparisons] that illustrate the state of monarchy: one taken out of the word of God, and the two other out of the grounds of policy and philosophy. In the Scriptures kings are called gods, and so their power after a certain relation compared to the Divine power. Kings are also compared to fathers of families; for a king is truly parens patriae [parent of the country], the political father of his people. And lastly, kings are compared to the head of this microcosm of the body of man.

Document 5

Source: The *Talloq Chronicle*, official court histories written to preserve the deeds of the kings of Talloq, a state in Indonesia, ca. 1660.

The King was called an expert, a brave person, a renowned person, a wise person. . . . He often read holy books, never neglected [prayer] times once he became a Muslim. . . . It was he who first made gold coins, ordered tin coins made. It was this king who first forged muskets and swivel guns, first armed soldiers with small firearms. It was with him that Makassarese became adept at forging swords. . . . It was he who conquered Bulukumba twice, marched on and battled in Meru.

Document 6

Source: Etching of the Palace of Versailles by Israel Silvestre, a French draftsman who worked for the court of Louis XIV, 1682.

The Metropolitan Museum of Art, New York. Brisbane Dick Fund, 1930

Document 7

Source: Excerpt from the *Sacred Edict* of the Qing dynasty, a set of moral and government instructions enacted by imperial authority, beginning with the Kangxi emperor (r. 1662–1722), for use in local rituals conducted throughout the Qing Empire.

1. Esteem most highly filial piety and brotherly submission, in order to give due importance to human moral relations.
3. Cultivate peace and concord in your neighborhoods, in order to prevent quarrels and litigations.
4. Give importance to agriculture and sericulture, in order to ensure a sufficiency of clothing and food.
6. Foster colleges and schools, in order to give the training of scholars a proper start.
7. Do away with errant teachings, in order to exalt the correct doctrine.
8. Expound on the laws, in order to warn the ignorant and obstinate.
11. Instruct sons and younger brothers, in order to prevent them from doing what is wrong.
14. Promptly remit your taxes, in order to avoid being pressed for payment.

Long Essay Questions

Using your knowledge of world history, develop an argument in response to one of the following questions.

2. In the period 1450–1750, transoceanic voyages connected the Eastern and Western hemispheres and had a significant economic, cultural, social, and demographic impact on the world.

   Develop an argument that evaluates how one or more societies were affected by the new global connections created through trade in this time period.

3. In the period 1450–1750, agriculture, labor systems, and social structures changed as new states and empires developed around the world.

   Develop an argument that evaluates how labor and/or social systems were transformed in this time period.

4. In the period 1450–1750, as empires expanded globally, new challenges emerged in managing and incorporating a diverse population.

   Develop an argument that evaluates the methods rulers used to legitimize and consolidate their power.

BUILDING AP® SKILLS

Argumentation

The Long Essay Question (LEQ) is an important part of the AP® World History: Modern Exam. The LEQ is 15 percent of the overall score on the exam. Students will pick from one of three prompts. Consider giving students all three prompts and allowing them to choose the prompt they wish to write on. This will mimic the exam layout and give them practice. Students should have 40 minutes to write the LEQ.

Differentiation

If you want to differentiate this activity, follow the "Must Do, Should Do, Strive For" model below.

■ Must Do: Students write a contextualization and a thesis for the prompt.

■ Should Do: Students write two arguments (Claims) for the prompt with three pieces of evidence to defend their argument.

■ Strive For: Students write a full-length LEQ in 40 minutes.

Argumentation

The early modern era has a wealth of essay prompts for you to use as practice with your students. Prior AP® World History Exam questions are available on the AP® World History course website. Remember that while older DBQs and FRQs are excellent practice for building writing skills in AP® students, it is important to note that the essay format changed in the 2017–2018 school year. You may want to visit the AP® World History course website to review the changes to the essay format before working on writing with your students. The following questions are relevant for this part of the text. Questions marked with an asterisk (*) are available on the AP® World History course website in a modified version, compatible with the 2011 revisions to the AP® Course Framework, but they may need further revision to fit the 2017–2018 model.

Document-Based Questions

■ 2003, Question 1: Analyze the causes and consequences of indentured servitude as part of global economic changes in the nineteenth and twentieth centuries.

■ 2009, Question 1: Analyze African actions and reactions to the European scramble for Africa.

■ 2010, Question 1: Analyze similarities and differences in the mechanization of the cotton industry in Japan and India from the 1880s to the 1930s.

■ 2013, Question 1: Analyze connections between regional issues and European struggles for global power in the mid-eighteenth century.

■ 2018, Question 1: Evaluate the extent to which railroads affected the process of empire building in Afro-Eurasia between 1860 and 1918.

■ 2022, Question 1: Evaluate the extent to which European imperialism affected economies in Africa and/or Asia in the nineteenth and early twentieth centuries.

Long Essay Questions

■ 2004, Question 2: Analyze changes and continuities in labor systems in one of several areas between 1750 and 1914.*

■ 2011, Question 2: Analyze changes and continuities in the long-distance migrations in the period from 1700 to 1900.

■ 2015, Question 2: Analyze changes and continuities in labor systems in one of several areas between 1450 and 1900.

■ 2002, Question 3: Analyze and compare the responses of China and Japan to Western penetration in the nineteenth century.*

(continued)

■ 2003, Question 3: Compare and contrast the role of women in two regions during 1750 to 1914.*

■ 2009, Question 3: Compare North American racial ideologies and their effects on society with Latin American and Caribbean racial ideologies and their effects on society from 1500 to 1830.

■ 2016, Question 3: Analyze similarities and differences in the causes of two of the following revolutions: American Revolution, French Revolution, Haitian Revolution.

PERIOD 3

The European Moment in World History

1750–1900

Chapter 7 Atlantic Revolutions, Global Echoes, 1750–1900

Chapter 8 Revolutions of Industrialization, 1750–1900

Chapter 9 Empires in Collision: Europe, the Middle East, and East Asia, 1800–1900

Chapter 10 Colonial Encounters in Asia, Africa, and Oceania, 1750–1950

THE BIG PICTURE

European Centrality and the Problem of Eurocentrism

During the century and a half between 1750 and 1900, sometimes referred to as the "long nineteenth century," two new and related phenomena held center stage in the global history of humankind and represent the major themes of the four chapters that follow. The first of these, explored in Chapters 7 and 8, was the creation of a new kind of human society, commonly called "modern," emerging from the intersection of the Scientific, French, and Industrial Revolutions, all of which took shape initially in Western Europe. These chapters align closely with the topics of AP® Unit 5 in the AP® Course Description. The second theme of this long nineteenth century, which is addressed

378

TEACHING IDEA

Class Discussion

The AP® World History Course Framework dates this era from 1750 to 1900. Ask students: Looking at the chapter titles, what are some of the patterns of the period? *Patterns include Atlantic revolutions, the Industrial Revolution, and imperialism in Africa, Asia, the Middle East, East Asia — specifically the Ottoman Empire and the Qing Empire — and Oceania. One broad pattern would be a great increase in global interactions from previous periods.*

in Chapters 9 and 10, was the growing ability of these modern societies to exercise enormous power and influence over the rest of humankind through their empires, economic penetration, military intervention, diplomatic pressure, and missionary activity. These issues correspond to the major topics of the AP® Unit 6.

These developments marked a significant turning point in world history in several ways. Western Europeans and their North American offspring now assumed a new and far more prominent role in the world than ever before. Furthermore, this "European moment" in world history established a new phase of human connectedness or entanglement that later generations labeled as "globalization." Finally, Europeans were also leading a human intervention in the natural order of unprecedented dimensions, largely the product of industrialization. Thus the long nineteenth century represents the starting point of the Anthropocene era, or the "age of man," a concept that points to the many ways in which humankind itself has become an active agent of change in the physical and biological evolution of the planet. It marks an epic transformation in the relationship of humanity to the earth, equivalent perhaps to the early stages of the Agricultural Revolution.

Europe's global centrality during the nineteenth century generated among Europeans understandings of both geography and history that centered the entire human story on Europe. Thus flat maps placed Europe at the center of the world, while dividing Asia in half. Europe was granted continental status, even though it was more accurately only the western peninsula of Asia, much as India was its southern peninsula. Other regions of the world, such as the Far East or the Near (Middle) East, were defined in terms of their distance from Europe. History textbooks often portrayed people of European extraction at the center of human progress. Other peoples and civilizations, by contrast, were long believed to be static or stagnant, thus largely lacking any real history. Most Europeans assumed that these "backward" peoples and regions must either imitate the Western model or face further decline and possible extinction. Until the mid-twentieth century, such ideas went largely unchallenged in the Western world.

The rise of the academic discipline of world history in the decades following World War II represented a sharp challenge to such Eurocentric understandings of the human past. But in dealing with recent centuries, historians have confronted a distinct problem: how to avoid Eurocentrism when considering a phase of world history in which Europeans were in fact central.

At least five responses to this dilemma are reflected in the chapters that follow. First, the "European moment" has been recent and perhaps brief. Other peoples too had times of "cultural flowering" that granted them a period of primacy or influence — for example, the Arabs (600–1000), Chinese (1000–1500), Mongols (1200–1350), and Incas and Aztecs (fifteenth century) — but all of these were limited to particular regions of Afro-Eurasia or the Americas.[1] Even though the European moment operated on a genuinely global scale, Western peoples enjoyed their worldwide primacy for two centuries at most. The events of the late twentieth

Contextualization

This is a good place to practice contextualization skills. Ask students: What international contexts allowed Europe to dominate in the long nineteenth century? *China withdrew its naval fleet from the Indian Ocean. The lack of immunity among Native Americans helped Europeans take over the Western Hemisphere, where they benefited from the natural resources and a new market in which to sell goods. Although Europeans controlled much territory, they needed the help of local elites to administer it.*

Argumentation

Students often have a problem understanding that the long nineteenth century is not all about Europeans. This is a good point to explain this concept to your students. Then ask: How can historians create an accurate portrayal of the long nineteenth century without being Eurocentric, given that Europe was at the center of power during this period? *It is important to place the long nineteenth century in context; it is only about 150-200 years in 10,000 years of human history. For most of that time, Europeans were not at the center of the action. We can also note that the rise of Europe occurred in an international context. Europe achieved its position in the face of great opposition, which caused it, in some cases, to change and adapt to local conditions at least to some degree. Local peoples also made active use of Europeans and European ideas for their own purposes, seeking to gain advantage over rivals or to benefit themselves in light of new conditions. A fifth and final antidote to Eurocentrism in an age of European centrality lies in the recognition that although Europeans gained an unprecedented prominence on the world stage, they were not the only actors on the world stage, nor were they the sole preoccupation of Asian, African, and Middle Eastern peoples.*

and early twenty-first centuries — the dissolution of colonial empires, the rise of India and especially China, and the assertion of Islam — suggest the end, or at least the erosion, of the age of European predominance.

Second, we need to remember that the rise of Europe occurred within an international context. It was the withdrawal of the Chinese naval fleet that allowed Europeans to enter the Indian Ocean in the sixteenth century, while Native Americans' lack of immunity to European diseases and their own divisions and conflicts greatly assisted the European takeover of the Western Hemisphere. The Industrial Revolution, explored in Chapter 8, benefited from New World resources and markets and from the stimulus of superior Asian textile and pottery production. Chapters 9 and 10 make clear that European control of other regions everywhere depended on the cooperation of local elites. Europeans, like everyone else, were embedded in a web of relationships that shaped their own histories.

A third reminder is that the rise of Europe to a position of global dominance was not an easy or automatic process. Frequently it occurred in the face of ferocious resistance and rebellion, which often required Europeans to modify their policies and practices. The so-called Indian mutiny in mid-nineteenth-century South Asia, a massive uprising against British colonial rule, did not end British control, but it substantially transformed the character of the colonial experience. Even when Europeans exercised political power, they could not do precisely as they pleased. Empire, formal and informal alike, was always in some ways a negotiated arrangement.

Fourth, peoples the world over made active use of Europeans and European ideas for their own purposes, seeking to gain advantage over local rivals or to benefit themselves in light of new conditions. During the Haitian Revolution, examined in Chapter 7, enslaved Africans made use of radical French ideas about "the rights of man" in ways that most Europeans never intended. Later in Southeast Asia, a number of highland minority groups, long oppressed by the dominant lowland Vietnamese, viewed the French invaders as liberators and assisted in their takeover of Vietnam. Recognizing that Asian and African peoples remained active agents, pursuing their own interests even in oppressive conditions, is another way of countering residual Eurocentrism.

Moreover, what was borrowed from Europe was always adapted to local circumstances. Thus Japanese or Russian industrial development did not wholly follow the pattern of England's Industrial Revolution. The Christianity that took root in the Americas or later in Africa evolved in culturally distinctive ways. Ideas of nationalism, born in Europe, were used to oppose European imperialism throughout Asia and Africa. The most interesting stories of modern world history are not simply those of European triumph or the imposition of Western ideas and practices but those of encounters, though highly unequal, among culturally different peoples.

Finally, despite Europeans' unprecedented prominence on the world stage, they were not the only game in town, nor were they the sole preoccupation of Asian, African, and Middle Eastern peoples. While China confronted Western aggression in the nineteenth century, it was also absorbing a huge population increase and experiencing massive peasant rebellions that grew out of distinctly Chinese conditions. Furthermore, cultural influence moved in many directions as European and American intellectuals began to absorb the spiritual traditions of India and as Japanese art became highly fashionable in the West.

None of this diminishes the significance of the European moment in world history, but it sets that moment in a longer historical perspective and highlights the significance of interaction and exchange among culturally different peoples.

FIRST REFLECTIONS

1. **Questioning Chronology** What marks 1750–1900 as a distinct period of world history?

2. **Applying Historical Perspective** As the authors note, other civilizations have also experienced periods of primacy or greater influence in the past. How does this fact shape your understanding of growing European dominance in world affairs between 1750 and 1900?

3. **Thinking about Bias** How do the authors seek to avoid Eurocentrism while acknowledging the growing prominence of Europeans on the world stage during this period of time (1750–1900)?

4. **Considering Alternative Perspectives** How might historians from Asia, Africa, or the Islamic world view these centuries differently from historians in the Western world?

TEACHING IDEA

Class Discussion

To continue with the idea on page 380 that Europe was not the center of the long nineteenth century, consider asking students: How did events in Asian, African, and Middle Eastern states show that Europe was not the sole preoccupation of their worlds?

In China, a burgeoning population led to massive peasant rebellions because of the lack of land. In Europe and the United States, intellectuals began to absorb the spiritual traditions of India, and Japanese art became highly fashionable in the West.

Making Connections: Continuity and Change

Periodization skills continue to elude history students. This is an important skill that students struggle with over the entire course. Use the Landmarks in World History (ca. 1750–ca. 1900) on pages 382–383 to reinforce these periodization skills. Have students look at the timeline, and ask the following questions:

■ What events began before the period started? *The fragmentation of the Mughal Empire and the Wahhabi movement of Islamic renewal in Arabia.*

■ What event continued after the period ended? *The only event with a right-pointing arrow is the rapid industrialization in the United States.*

■ Why might these events still be included in this time period? *The Wahhabi movement is included because the mixing of various religions is an important component of this time period, while the fragmentation of the Mughal Empire helps contextualize the rise of the British Empire in India. The rapid industrialization in the United States is included because industrialization is a major theme of this time period.*

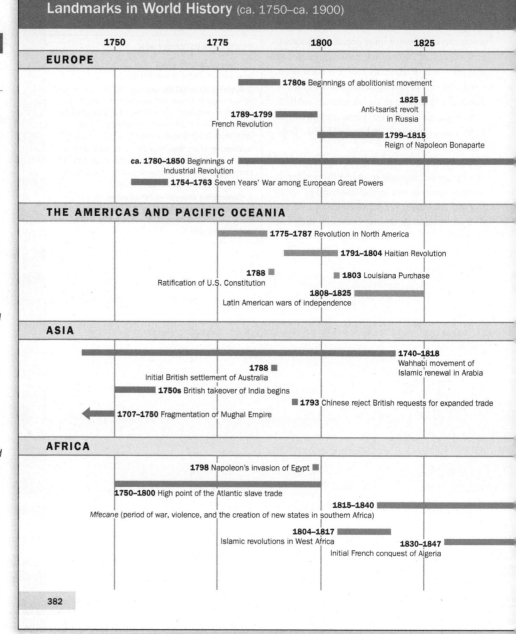

Landmarks in World History (ca. 1750–ca. 1900)

1750   1775   1800   1825

EUROPE

1780s Beginnings of abolitionist movement

1825 Anti-tsarist revolt in Russia

1789–1799 French Revolution

1799–1815 Reign of Napoleon Bonaparte

ca. 1780–1850 Beginnings of Industrial Revolution

1754–1763 Seven Years' War among European Great Powers

THE AMERICAS AND PACIFIC OCEANIA

1775–1787 Revolution in North America

1791–1804 Haitian Revolution

1788 Ratification of U.S. Constitution

1803 Louisiana Purchase

1808–1825 Latin American wars of independence

ASIA

1740–1818 Wahhabi movement of Islamic renewal in Arabia

1788 Initial British settlement of Australia

1750s British takeover of India begins

1793 Chinese reject British requests for expanded trade

1707–1750 Fragmentation of Mughal Empire

AFRICA

1798 Napoleon's invasion of Egypt

1750–1800 High point of the Atlantic slave trade

Mfecane (period of war, violence, and the creation of new states in southern Africa)

1815–1840

1804–1817 Islamic revolutions in West Africa

1830–1847 Initial French conquest of Algeria

382

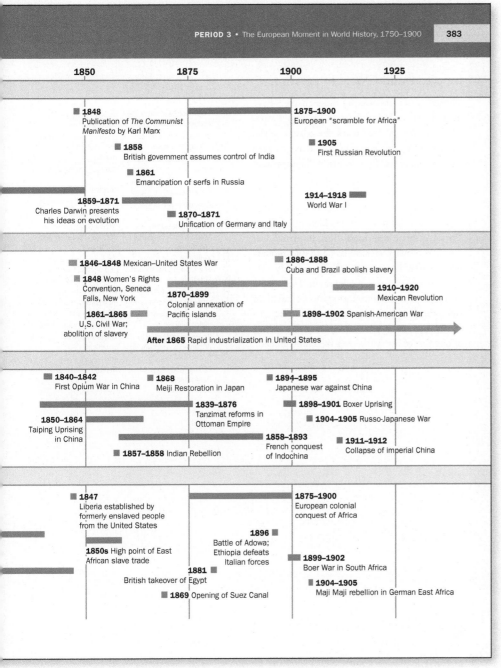

1850   1875   1900   1925

1848
Publication of *The Communist Manifesto* by Karl Marx

1858
British government assumes control of India

1861
Emancipation of serfs in Russia

1859–1871
Charles Darwin presents his ideas on evolution

1870–1871
Unification of Germany and Italy

1875–1900
European "scramble for Africa"

1905
First Russian Revolution

1914–1918
World War I

1846–1848 Mexican–United States War

1848 Women's Rights Convention, Seneca Falls, New York

1861–1865
U.S. Civil War; abolition of slavery

1870–1899
Colonial annexation of Pacific islands

After 1865 Rapid industrialization in United States

1886–1888
Cuba and Brazil abolish slavery

1910–1920
Mexican Revolution

1898–1902 Spanish-American War

1840–1842
First Opium War in China

1868
Meiji Restoration in Japan

1850–1864
Taiping Uprising in China

1839–1876
Tanzimat reforms in Ottoman Empire

1857–1858 Indian Rebellion

1858–1893
French conquest of Indochina

1894–1895
Japanese war against China

1898–1901 Boxer Uprising

1904–1905 Russo-Japanese War

1911–1912
Collapse of imperial China

1847
Liberia established by formerly enslaved people from the United States

1850s High point of East African slave trade

1881
British takeover of Egypt

1869 Opening of Suez Canal

1875–1900
European colonial conquest of Africa

1896
Battle of Adowa; Ethiopia defeats Italian forces

1899–1902
Boer War in South Africa

1904–1905
Maji Maji rebellion in German East Africa

TEACHING IDEA

Class Discussion

To continue with the periodization skill practice from page 382, ask students: In general, are the events in this timeline long-lasting or fairly short? *There seem to be many more short-term events on this timeline than on earlier ones. Many events seem to last two years or less.*

UNDERSTANDING AP® THEMES IN PERIOD 3

Industrial and Global Integration

The 150 years addressed in these chapters have great historical significance in many ways. Environmentally, they mark the advent of the Anthropocene era, when human activity began to affect the planet in ways that will be apparent for centuries to come. Much of this activity was occasioned by the Industrial Revolution (IR), a thorough transformation of economic life that began in Europe but grew to global dimensions. That economic transformation, in turn, lay at the heart of what we have come to call "modernity," as new kinds of social life and new cultural outlooks began to take shape. In political terms, all of this led to a growing influence of European peoples and countries, amounting to an unprecedented, albeit temporary, dominance of one part of the world over the entire globe.

ENVIRONMENT	CULTURES
Industrial Revolution (IR) and population growth	Cultural expressions of nationalism
IR as beginning of the Anthropocene era	Enlightenment ideas and revolution in the Atlantic world
Environmental effects of IR	Ottoman ideologies: Islamic modernism, secularism, nationalism
Ecological windfall from the Americas	Ideologies of imperialism
Disease in the colonial world	Colonial racism and racial identity
Changing roles of agriculture in industrial economies	Colonial education and westernization
American food crops and Chinese population growth	Hinduism: emergence of a distinct tradition in India and its spread to the West
Romantic poets and early environmentalism	Marxist socialism as an idea and a movement
Coal replaces wood as major fuel	Japanese westernization
Environmental effects of cash-crop agriculture: Burma and Vietnam	Africanization of Christianity
Ecological damage of Bantustan policy in South Africa	Missionaries and "female circumcision"
	"Tribalism" and pan-Africanism

1750–1900

GOVERNANCE	ECONOMIES	SOCIAL STRUCTURES	TECHNOLOGY
Conquest and colonial states in Asia and Africa	Settler economies	Class in colonial North America	Cotton gin
Contraction and reform in Ottoman Empire	Colonial economies compared:	New and old elites in colonial regimes	Spinning jenny
Revolutions compared and connected: North American, French, Haitian, Latin American, Decembrist	▪ Forced labor systems ▪ Cash-crop production ▪ Mining economies ▪ Settler economies	Patterns of migration: European, Asian, African	Steam engine
		Women in Atlantic revolutions	Guillotine
			Indoor plumbing
	Industrial Revolutions compared: British, French, American, Russian, Japanese, Latin American	Class and gender outcomes of French Revolution	Threshing machine
Post-independence state building in U.S., Haiti, Latin America		Class, race, and social upheaval in Haiti	Telegraph
U.S. "informal empire" in Latin America	Limitations of colonial industrialization	Early feminism	Bicycle
		Abolition of slavery	Battery
European empires and the IR	Destruction of plantation economy in Haiti	Class and IR: aristocracy, middle classes, artisans, workers	Luddites and hostility to technology
Opium Wars (1840–1842 and 1856–1858)	Post-slavery labor regimes in the Americas	Gender and IR: domesticity and return to the workforce	Sewing machine
Taiping Uprising in China (1850–1864)	Opium trade and its outcomes	Absence of social change in Latin American revolutions	McCormick Reaper
Meiji Restoration in Japan	Failure of Chinese industrialization	Tokugawa society and social change after Meiji Restoration	Rifle
Japan as an imperial power	"Dependent development": Latin America in the world economy	Social policies of Taiping rebels in China	Interchangeable parts and mass production
The end of imperial China		End of serfdom in Russia (1861)	Typewriter
	Taiping Uprising and the devastation of China's economy (1850–1864)	Women and reform in Meiji Japan	Electric light
		African women and colonial economies	Telephone
			Washing machine
			Automobile
			Maxim gun

BUILDING AP® SKILLS

Developments and Processes

A good way to have students practice looking at the thematic "big picture" of each time period is to have them write a summary statement for each theme on what's happening during the time period. Ask students to look at the events for each theme and write a general statement about the patterns they see for the period. (Suggested answers are provided in italics.)

▪ Environment: *The patterns of this period include the effects of the Industrial Revolution and the beginning of the Anthropocene.*

▪ Cultures: *The patterns of this period include the spread of imperialism, colonial racism, nationalism and Enlightenment ideas, westernization, and tribalism.*

▪ Governance: *The patterns of this period include the rise of European empires based on the power derived from the Industrial Revolution, the political revolutions in the Atlantic world, and the rise of Meiji Japan.*

▪ Economies: *The patterns of this period include the global interconnections of expanding trade and coercive labor systems, even when slavery ended. The Industrial Revolution also dominates.*

▪ Social Structures: *The patterns of this period include the beginnings of feminism and the continuing clashes between classes — especially with regard to the Industrial Revolution and imperialism.*

▪ Technology: *The patterns of this period include the beginnings of industrial technology, along with the rapid increase in new technologies.*

7

Atlantic Revolutions, Global Echoes

1750–1900

AP® Overview for Chapter 7

This chapter corresponds to AP® Unit 5: Revolutions, 1750–1900. The revolutionary movements of the eighteenth century form the most significant part of this chapter. Examine these movements as a clear break in the way that historians organize the chronological periods of history. The chapter explores the global consequences of the diffusion of Enlightenment thought (discussed in Chapter 5) by focusing on examples of how Enlightenment thought influenced revolutions in the Caribbean and Europe and how it affected labor systems and national identity.

Chapter 7 Essential Activity

For a fun and creative essential activity, consider having students complete the "Causation: Recipe for a Revolution" activity from the OER Project. Not only will students have fun and enjoy the creativity of the assignment, but they will also practice the AP® World History: Modern skill of Causation. In this activity, students will create a recipe that explains the causes for an assigned political revolution.

Revolutions are often violent, messy, and chaotic, so looking at the causes in detail will allow students to expand their understanding of how causation helps to explain historical processes and how historians focus on particular causes to shape people's understanding of those events. You can find the detailed instructions on the OER Project's World History: AP® curriculum in Unit 5.

Chapter 7 Resources

- **TRM** AP® Skills Workshop Activity Handout: Making Connections: Comparison
- **TRM** Chapter 7 DBQ Activity Handout
- **TRM** Chapter 7 Guided Reading
- **TRM** Chapter 7 Lecture Presentation Slides
- **TRM** Chapter 7 Outline
- **TRM** Chapter 7 Suggested Responses to Questions
- **TRM** Eric's Activity 7: Causation and the Atlantic Revolutions
- **TRM** Handout 7.1: Comparison Chart for Atlantic Revolutions

- **TRM** Handout 7.2: OPTIC Chart for Engraving of the Haitian Revolution
- **TRM** Handout 7.3: Chart for Promotion of Nationalism
- **TRM** Handout 7.4: Chart for Feminist Movements and Leaders
- **TRM** Handout 7.5: OPTIC Chart for Painting of Nationalism in Poland
- **TRM** Handout 7.6: Comparison Chart for Outcomes of Revolutions

Pacing Guide

Below is a pacing guide for the AP® World History: Modern course beginning in ca. 1200 C.E. This pacing guide is based on a schedule with 120 sessions of 50 minutes each before the AP® Exam. It is meant as a place to start. If you have a different number of sessions before the exam, you can modify the pacing to suit your needs.

Day	Pages Assigned	AP® Topic	AP® Theme	Suggested Assignments	Coverage Notes
1	Read pages 387–391 to "The North American Revolution, 1775–1787"	5.2	GOV	Chapter 7 Essential Activity Eric's Activity 7: Causation and the Atlantic Revolutions on page 389 Apply the Tip on page 390	The first half of Chapter 7 lends itself well to practice the causation skill by looking at the causes and outcomes of the Atlantic revolutions. It's also a great section to practice comparing the different revolutions.
2	Read pages 391–394 from "The North American Revolution, 1775–1787" to "The French Revolution, 1789–1815"	5.2	GOV	AP® Classroom AP® Daily Videos on page 391 Building AP® Skills: Making Connections: Comparison on page 391 Exploring AP® Themes: GOV on page 393	Students will likely be familiar with the American Revolution from earlier classes on U.S. history, but they will need help understanding it from a global perspective.
3	Read pages 394–399 from "The French Revolution, 1789–1815" to the end of that section	5.2	GOV	Apply the Tip on page 394 Exploring AP® Themes: SIO on page 397 Teaching Idea: Incorporating Outside Resources on page 398	While the French Revolution is not listed in the framework, the French Declaration of the Rights of Man and Citizen is, and students will need to know about the revolution to give context to that document and the Haitian Revolution.
4	Read pages 400–402 to "Latin American Revolutions, 1808–1825"	5.2	GOV	Apply the Tip on page 400 Teaching Idea: Class Discussion on page 401 Building AP® Skills: Sourcing and Situation on page 401	See above (Day 1).
5	Read pages 402–405 from "Latin American Revolutions, 1808–1825" to "Echoes of Revolution"	5.2	GOV	Apply the Tip on page 402 Exploring AP® Themes: ENV on page 403 Building AP® Skills: Argumentation on page 404	See above.
6	Read pages 405–409 from "Echoes of Revolution" to "Nations and Nationalism"	5.2	SIO	Building AP® Skills: Argumentation on page 405 Exploring AP® Themes: ECN on page 407 Building AP® Skills Making Connections: Comparison on page 408	Like the American Revolution, students are likely familiar with the abolition movement from U.S. history. Make sure they understand the global context of the movement and how it took place outside of the United States.
7	Read pages 409–412 from "Nations and Nationalism" to "Feminist Beginnings"	5.1 5.2	CDI GOV	Teaching Idea: Incorporating Outside Resources on page 409 Apply the Tip on page 410 AP® Classroom: AP® Topic Questions on page 412	Nationalism helps give context for many of the major topics and issues in world history in the nineteenth and twentieth centuries. Students will need to have a firm grasp of this concept to help them understand these future topics in the course.
8	Read pages 412–419 from "Feminist Beginnings" through "Conclusions and Reflections"	5.1	CDI SIO	Apply the Tip on page 412 AP® Classroom: AP® Exam Questions on page 417 Teaching Idea: Exit Ticket on page 419	It may be helpful to study the women's suffrage movement in the context of the different Atlantic revolutions and nationalist movements. Consider having students weave this topic into their overall study of revolutions.

Students often do not understand that words can have multiple meanings. "Revolution" is one of those words that can confuse students. Ask students: What does the term "revolution" mean? *On one hand, revolution means turning. It also means the overthrow of an existing government or a radical change in the way people live or think.*

After you talk about the definition of revolution with your students, ask them to write down three things they know about revolutions. Give them a few minutes to jot down their answers, and either have students share their items with a neighbor or call for volunteers to share their answers. As with all bell ringers, keep this exercise brief. *Answers will vary.*

BUILDING AP® SKILLS

Claims and Evidence in Sources

Project or have students look at the image of Jean-Baptiste Belley-Mars. Have students read the information below the image, and then ask students: Why would a formerly enslaved person go to war and help fight for independence in not one but two revolutions, the American Revolution and the French Revolution? *Answers will vary, but should include some mention of Enlightenment beliefs.*

Revolutionaries Few participants in the Atlantic revolutions were more active than Jean-Baptiste Belley-Mars (ca. 1746–1805). Kidnapped from West Africa, he was sold into slavery on Saint Domingue (modern Haiti). After purchasing his freedom, he fought in the American Revolution. During the French Revolution he helped persuade the revolutionary parliament to outlaw slavery. As a French officer sent to crush the Haitian Revolution, he opposed the brutal tactics used and was imprisoned. Here Belley-Mars is depicted next to a bust of Guillaume Raynal, an ardent opponent of slavery and colonialism. (Photo Josse/Leemage/Getty Images)

386

CHAPTER

7

Atlantic Revolutions, Global Echoes

1750–1900

CONNECTING PAST AND PRESENT

"Two hundred and thirty years after it first erupted, the French Revolution hovers over current events in France."[1] So wrote one analyst of the widespread protests and riots that exploded in France in late 2018 and continued intermittently into 2020, until COVID-inspired lockdowns put an end to public demonstrations, at least temporarily. These protests began with popular opposition to a projected rise in fuel prices and came to encompass a range of other issues, including police brutality, economic insecurity and inequality, and widespread distrust of the government and the "establishment." Dubbed the Yellow Vest Movement for the bright yellow vests they wore, the protesters lacked a clear hierarchical organization, but they marched, most often peacefully, sometimes blocked roads and public spaces, and on occasion set fires and engaged in violence. Their demands evoked the values of fairness and equality that have figured prominently in French public life since the French Revolution of 1789. ∎

◀ **AP**

MAKING CONNECTIONS
How does the life of Jean-Baptiste Belley-Mars illustrate connections across the major Atlantic revolutions?

That upheaval was the centerpiece of a much larger set of revolutions that shook both sides of the Atlantic world between 1775 and 1825. It was preceded by the American Revolution, which gained independence for thirteen British colonies along the eastern coast of North America. And it was followed by a massive slave rebellion in Haiti that ended both slavery and French colonialism in that country even as it helped to shape the revolutions in Latin America that threw off Spanish and Portuguese colonial rule. These four closely related upheavals reflected the new connections among Europe, Africa, North America, and South America that took shape in the wake of Columbus's voyages and the subsequent European conquests. Together, they launched a new chapter in the history of the Atlantic world, while the echoes of those revolutions reverberated in the larger world, as chattel slavery was attacked, nationalism was nurtured, and feminism found its first major public expression.

387

TRM **Chapter 7 Guided Reading**
You can find a guided reading handout for this chapter in the Teacher's Resource Materials.

TRM **Chapter 7 Lecture Slides**
You can find curated lecture slides for this chapter in the Teacher's Resource Materials.

TRM **Chapter 7 Outline**
You can find a chapter outline to model good note-taking for this chapter in the Teacher's Resource Materials.

TRM **Suggested Responses to Questions**
You can find suggested responses to all of the AP® margin questions in this chapter in the Teacher's Resource Materials.

TEACHING IDEA

Class Discussion

Continue looking at the image of Jean-Baptiste Belley-Mars on page 386. Use the Making Connections margin question to have students think and hypothesize about the connections across the major Atlantic revolutions. Answers can be found in the Teacher's Resource Materials.

Contextualization

Contextualization can be difficult for students to master, and they must constantly practice this skill. Use the first sentence in the first paragraph on page 388 and point out that Voltaire called the late eighteenth century "the century of revolutions." Ask students: What examples does the text include to explain the broader context for Voltaire's comment? *Rebellious activity occurred in multiple regions around the world. These rebellious activities included the mfecane, the Pugachev rebellion, the Wahhabi movement, and peasant uprisings in Russia.*

AP®
CONTINUITY AND CHANGE
To what extent did the Atlantic revolutions generate significant transformation during the long nineteenth century?

AP®
CAUSATION
What were the most important primary and secondary causes of the Atlantic revolutions?

AP® EXAM TIP
Note that the era ca. 1750–ca. 1900 is full of political, social, and technological revolutions. Understanding these revolutions is vital for the AP® Exam.

Atlantic Revolutions in a Global Context

Finding the Main Point: What was distinctive about the Atlantic revolutions in comparison to other upheavals during the long nineteenth century?

Writing to a friend in 1772, before any of the Atlantic revolutions had occurred, the French intellectual Voltaire asked, "My dear philosopher, doesn't this appear to you to be the century of revolutions?"[2] He was certainly on target, and not only for Europe. From the early eighteenth century to the mid-nineteenth, many parts of the world witnessed political and social upheaval, leading some historians to think in terms of a "world crisis" or "converging revolutions." By the 1730s, the Safavid dynasty that had ruled Persia (now Iran) for several centuries had completely collapsed, even as the powerful Mughal Empire governing India also fragmented. About the same time, the Wahhabi movement in Arabia seriously threatened the Ottoman Empire, and its religious ideals informed major political upheavals in Central Asia and elsewhere (see "Expansion and Renewal in the Islamic World" in Chapter 5). The Russian Empire under Catherine the Great experienced a series of peasant uprisings, most notably one led by the Cossack commander Pugachev in 1773–1774 that briefly proclaimed the end of serfdom before that rebellion was crushed. China too in the late eighteenth and early nineteenth centuries hosted a number of popular though unsuccessful rebellions, a prelude perhaps to the huge Taiping revolution of 1850–1864. Beginning in the early nineteenth century, a new wave of Islamic revolutions shook West Africa, while in southern Africa a series of wars and migrations known as the *mfecane* (the breaking or crushing) involved widespread and violent disruptions as well as the creation of new states and societies.

Thus the Atlantic revolutions in North America, France, Haiti, and Latin America took place within a larger global framework. Like many of the other upheavals, they too occurred in the context of expensive wars, weakening states, and destabilizing processes of commercialization. But compared to upheavals elsewhere, the Atlantic revolutions were distinctive. The costly wars that strained European imperial states—Britain, France, and Spain in particular—were global rather than regional. In the so-called Seven Years' War (1754–1763), Britain and France joined battle in North America, the Caribbean, West Africa, and South Asia. The expenses of those conflicts prompted the British to levy additional taxes on their North American colonies and the French monarchy to seek new revenue from its landowners. These actions contributed to the launching of the North American and French revolutions, respectively.

Furthermore, the Atlantic revolutions were distinctive in that they were closely connected to one another. The American revolutionary leader Thomas Jefferson was the U.S. ambassador to France on the eve of the French Revolution, providing advice and encouragement to French reformers and revolutionaries. Simón Bolívar, a leading figure in Spanish American struggles for independence, twice visited Haiti, where he received military aid from the first Black government in the Americas.

Landmarks for Chapter 7

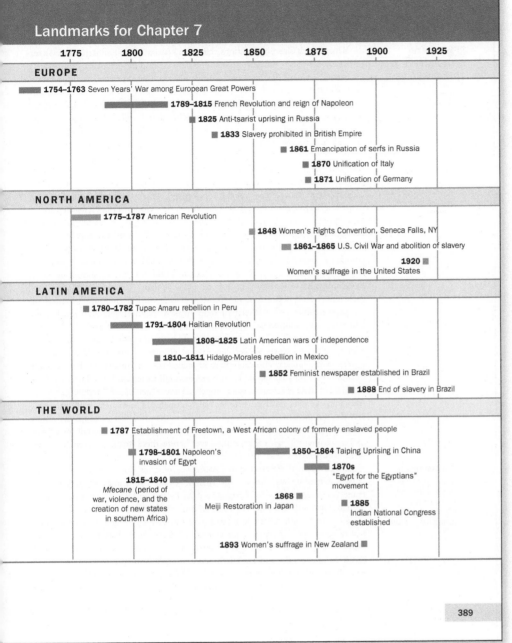

	1775	1800	1825	1850	1875	1900	1925

EUROPE

■ **1754–1763** Seven Years' War among European Great Powers

■ **1789–1815** French Revolution and reign of Napoleon

■ **1825** Anti-tsarist uprising in Russia

■ **1833** Slavery prohibited in British Empire

■ **1861** Emancipation of serfs in Russia

■ **1870** Unification of Italy

■ **1871** Unification of Germany

NORTH AMERICA

■ **1775–1787** American Revolution

■ **1848** Women's Rights Convention, Seneca Falls, NY

■ **1861–1865** U.S. Civil War and abolition of slavery

1920 ■
Women's suffrage in the United States

LATIN AMERICA

■ **1780–1782** Tupac Amaru rebellion in Peru

■ **1791–1804** Haitian Revolution

■ **1808–1825** Latin American wars of independence

■ **1810–1811** Hidalgo-Morales rebellion in Mexico

■ **1852** Feminist newspaper established in Brazil

■ **1888** End of slavery in Brazil

THE WORLD

■ **1787** Establishment of Freetown, a West African colony of formerly enslaved people

■ **1798–1801** Napoleon's invasion of Egypt

■ **1850–1864** Taiping Uprising in China

■ **1870s** "Egypt for the Egyptians" movement

■ **1815–1840** *Mfecane* (period of war, violence, and the creation of new states in southern Africa)

1868 ■
Meiji Restoration in Japan

■ **1885** Indian National Congress established

1893 Women's suffrage in New Zealand ■

389

BUILDING AP® SKILLS

Making Connections: Causation

It's always a good idea to practice periodization skills. Have students look at the Landmarks for Chapter 7. Ask students to answer the following questions:

■ Which revolution occurred first? *The American Revolution occurred first.*

■ How are the French and Haitian revolutions connected in time? *The Haitian Revolution began during the French Revolution and ended after Napoleon took control of France.*

■ Why would women gaining the right to vote, which is outside the time period of 1750–1900, be included in the timeline? *Women's right to vote is included in the timeline because Seneca Falls is included. Also, emancipation of enslaved people and serfs is included, and one could argue that women were "emancipated" as a result of receiving the right to vote.*

ERIC'S ACTIVITY ⑦ **Causation and the Atlantic Revolutions**

This is a great place to focus on the AP® skill of Causation. You can guide students to see how a change in thinking can bring out immense changes politically, socially, and economically by having them examine the basic principles that inspired the Atlantic revolutions. Find the complete activity in the Teacher's Resource Materials.

TRM Eric's Activity 7: Causation and the Atlantic Revolutions

Beyond such direct connections, the various Atlantic revolutionaries shared a set of common ideas, as the Atlantic basin became a world of intellectual and cultural exchange. The ideas that animated the Atlantic revolutions derived from the European Enlightenment and were shared across the ocean in newspapers, books, and pamphlets. (See "Science and Enlightenment" in Chapter 5.) At the heart of these ideas was the radical notion that human political and social arrangements could be engineered, and improved, by human action. Thus conventional and long-established ways of living and thinking—the divine right of kings, state control of trade, aristocratic privilege, the authority of a single church—were no longer sacrosanct and came under repeated attack. New ideas of liberty, equality, free trade, religious tolerance, republicanism, and human rationality were in the air. Politically, the core notion was "popular sovereignty," which meant that the authority to govern derived from the people rather than from God or from established tradition. As the Englishman John Locke (1632–1704) had argued, the "social contract" between ruler and ruled should last only as long as it served the people well. In short, it was both possible and desirable to start over in the construction of human communities. In the late eighteenth and early nineteenth centuries, these ideas were largely limited to the Atlantic world. While all of the Atlantic revolutions involved the elimination of monarchs, at least temporarily, across Asia and the Middle East such republican political systems (those operating with elected representatives of the people rather than a monarch) were virtually inconceivable until much later. There the only solution to a bad monarch was a new and better one.

In the world of the Atlantic revolutions, ideas born of the Enlightenment generated endless controversy. Were liberty and equality compatible? What kind of government—unitary and centralized or federal and decentralized—best ensured freedom? And how far should liberty be extended? Except in Haiti, the chief beneficiaries of these revolutions were propertied white men of the "middling classes." Although women, enslaved people, Native Americans, and men without property did not gain much from these revolutions, the ideas that accompanied those upheavals gave them ammunition for the future. Because their overall thrust was to extend political rights further than ever before, these Atlantic movements have often been referred to as "democratic revolutions."

A final distinctive feature of the Atlantic revolutions was their immense global impact, extending well beyond the Atlantic world. The armies of revolutionary France, for example, invaded Egypt, Germany, Poland, and Russia, carrying seeds of change. The ideals that animated these Atlantic revolutions inspired efforts in many countries to abolish slavery, to extend the right to vote, to develop constitutions, and to secure greater equality for women. Nationalism, perhaps the most potent ideology of the modern era, was nurtured in the Atlantic revolutions and shaped much of nineteenth- and twentieth-century world history. The ideas of human equality articulated in these revolutions later found expression in feminist, socialist, and communist movements. The Universal Declaration of Human Rights, adopted by the United Nations in 1948, echoed and amplified those principles while providing the basis for any number of subsequent protests against oppression, tyranny, and deprivation. In 1989, a number of Chinese students, fleeing the suppression of a democracy movement in their own country, marched at the head of a huge parade in Paris, celebrating the bicentennial of the French Revolution. And in 2011, the Middle Eastern uprisings known as the Arab Spring initially prompted numerous comparisons with the French Revolution. The Atlantic revolutions had a long reach.

Despite their common political vocabulary and a broadly democratic character, the Atlantic revolutions differed substantially from one another. They were triggered by different circumstances, expressed quite different social and political tensions, and varied considerably in their outcomes. Liberty, noted Simón Bolívar, "is a succulent morsel, but one difficult to digest."[3] Liberty was "digested" in quite distinct ways in the various sites of the Atlantic revolutions.

The North American Revolution, 1775–1787

Finding the Main Point: What were the major causes and effects of the American Revolution?

Every schoolchild in the United States learns early that the **American Revolution** was a struggle for independence from oppressive British rule. That struggle began in 1775 and was formalized by the Declaration of Independence in 1776. It resulted in an unlikely military victory by 1781 and generated a federal constitution in 1787, joining thirteen formerly separate colonies into a new nation (see Map 7.1). It was the first in a series of upheavals that rocked the Atlantic world and beyond in the century that followed. But was it a genuine revolution? What, precisely, did it change?

By making a break with Britain, the American Revolution marked a decisive political change, but in other ways it was, strangely enough, a conservative movement because it originated in an effort to preserve the existing liberties of the colonies rather than to create new ones. For much of the seventeenth and eighteenth centuries, the British colonies in North America enjoyed a considerable degree of local autonomy, as the British government was embroiled in its own internal conflicts and various European wars. Furthermore, Britain's West Indian colonies seemed more profitable and of greater significance than those of North America. In these circumstances, local elected assemblies in North America, dominated by the wealthier property-owning settlers, achieved something close to self-government. Colonists came to regard such autonomy as a birthright and part of their English heritage. Thus, until the mid-eighteenth century, almost no one in the colonies thought of breaking away from England because participation in the British Empire provided many advantages—protection in war, access to British

AP
CONTINUITY AND CHANGE
What was revolutionary about the American Revolution, and what was not?

AP
COMPARISON
What similarities and differences can be seen in the social structure of Britain and the North American colonies?

AP® CLASSROOM

AP® Daily Videos

As you begin studying the Atlantic revolutions in detail, now might be a good time to have students watch AP® Daily Video 5.1. This video takes a look at the revolutions in the Americas that had ties to Enlightenment ideas; it can also give students practice in comparing two sources.

BUILDING AP® SKILLS

Making Connections: Comparison

In preparation for having students write an LEQ later in this chapter on the goals of revolutionary leaders and the outcomes of the revolutions, ask students to fill out a comparison chart like the one shown below as they read information on each revolution. Put students into groups that they will remain with as the class studies the Atlantic revolutions. For every revolution covered, the groups can work together on putting the pertinent information into the chart. They should begin in this section of the text with the American Revolution. A reproducible version of this chart is available in the Teacher's Resource Materials. (Answers are provided in italics.)

Comparative Revolutions Chart

	Goals	Short-Term Outcomes	Long-Term Outcomes
American	*The goals were to preserve the rights given to Englishmen under the English Bill of Rights, specifically, no taxation without representation in Parliament, and eventual independence from Great Britain.*	*Thirteen colonies gained nominal independence but saw themselves as thirteen sovereign states rather than one nation. Accelerated democratic tendencies. Power remained in the hands of the elite.*	*Property requirements were lowered and more men of modest means participated in government. The American Revolution was a model for other revolutions. The U.S. is seen as the most democratic country in the world. The Constitution created a nation.*
French			
Haitian			
Latin American			

TRM Handout 7.1: Comparison Chart for Atlantic Revolutions

EXPLORING AP® THEMES

Humans and the Environment (ENV)

Have students look at Map 7.1, "The United States after the American Revolution." How has this portion of the map changed since 1788? *Maine is no longer part of Massachusetts, but a separate state. The disputed area between New York and New Hampshire is now the state of Vermont. Virginia, North Carolina, and Georgia had more western territory in 1788 than they do now.*

Map 7.1 The United States after the American Revolution

The union of the thirteen British colonies in North America created the embryonic United States, shown here in 1788. Over the past two centuries, which have seen large numbers of former colonies achieve independence, it remains the only example of separate colonies joining together after independence to form a larger and enduring nation, but at the time it was no sure thing.

▲ **AP®**

CAUSATION

How did the organization of the colonies affect the later establishment of the United States?

markets, and confirmation of the settlers' identity as "Englishmen"—and few drawbacks.

There were, however, real differences between Englishmen in England and those in the North American colonies. Within the colonies, English settlers had developed societies described by a leading historian as "the most radical in the contemporary Western world." Certainly class distinctions were real and visible, and a small class of wealthy "gentlemen"—the Adamses, Washingtons, Jeffersons, and Hancocks—wore powdered wigs, imitated the latest European styles, were prominent in political life, and were generally accorded deference by ordinary people. But the ready availability of land following the dispossession of Native Americans, the scarcity of people, and the absence of both a titled nobility and a single established church meant that social life was far more open than in Europe. No legal distinctions differentiated clergy, aristocracy, and commoners, as they did in France. All free men enjoyed the same status before the law, but this excluded enslaved people, numbering about 20 percent of the population in 1776, and, in some ways, white women as well. For white families, these conditions made for less poverty, more economic opportunity, fewer social differences, and easier relationships among the classes than in Europe. The famous economist Adam Smith observed that British colonists were "republican in their manners . . . and their government" well before their independence from England.[4]

Thus the American Revolution grew not from social tensions within the colonies, but from a rather sudden and unexpected effort by the British government to tighten its control over the colonies and to extract more revenue from them. As Britain's global struggle with France drained its treasury and ran up its national debt, British authorities, beginning in the 1760s, looked to America to make good these losses. Abandoning its neglectful oversight of the colonies, Britain began to act like a genuine imperial power, imposing a variety of new taxes and tariffs on the colonies without their consent, for they were not represented in the British Parliament. Many of the colonists were infuriated, because such measures challenged their economic interests, their established traditions of local autonomy, and their identity as true Englishmen. Armed with the ideas of the Enlightenment—popular sovereignty, natural rights, the consent of the governed—they went to war, and by 1781 they had prevailed, with considerable aid from the French, who were only too pleased to harm the interests of their British rivals.

What was revolutionary about the American experience was not so much the revolution itself but the kind of society that had already emerged within the

Patriots and Loyalists This English engraving dating from 1775 depicts a club-wielding mob of "Liberty Men" forcing a Virginian loyalist (someone committed to continued British rule) to sign a document, probably endorsing independence for the colonies. The threat of violence toward the loyalist is apparent in the armed crowd, the barrel of tar being used as a table in the foreground, and the sack of feathers hanging from the gallows in the background. Patriots frequently tarred and feathered recalcitrant loyalists during the lead-up to the American Revolution.

▲ AP
CLAIMS AND EVIDENCE IN SOURCES
Based on the image here, how were the American colonists viewed in England?

AP EXAM TIP
Make sure you can connect the American Revolution to broader aspects of global politics.

EXPLORING AP® THEMES
Governance (GOV)

Ask students the following questions:

■ In what ways did the United States continue the political patterns established under British rule? *Political authority remained largely in the hands of the existing elites who had led the revolution.*

■ In what ways did the United States expand on earlier political patterns? *Because property requirements for voters were lowered, political participation widened to include larger numbers of white males. This change gradually eroded the power of the traditional gentlemen, especially in the North.*

APPLY THE TIP

How did the ideas of the Enlightenment influence the American Revolution as well as other Atlantic revolutions? *Answers will include: The Enlightenment ideas of natural rights and equality became popular after the success of the American Revolution.*

Have students look at the **Handout 7.1: Comparison Chart for Atlantic Revolutions** from page 391 that they are filling out in preparation for writing an LEQ over the goals of revolutionary leaders and outcomes of the revolutions later in this chapter. This chart can help students understand the outcomes of both the American and Latin American revolutions.

TRM Handout 7.1: Comparison Chart for Atlantic Revolutions

This is a good place to remind students that many of the classical and postclassical empires declined and collapsed for the same reasons that the French Empire did. Ask students to brainstorm causes of the collapse of the postclassical empires. After students brainstorm, ask them if those causes are the same for the Atlantic revolutions. Students should be able to see the comparisons easily.

AP EXAM TIP
Be able to compare the outcomes of the American Revolution with those of later Latin American revolutions.

AP EXAM TIP
Pay attention to these recurring factors in the decline of empires throughout history: government mismanagement and angry lower classes.

colonies. Independence from Britain was not accompanied by any wholesale social transformation. Rather, the revolution accelerated the established democratic tendencies of the colonial societies. Political authority remained largely in the hands of the existing elites who had led the revolution, although property requirements for voting were lowered and more white men of modest means, such as small farmers and urban artisans, were elected to state legislatures.

This widening of political participation gradually eroded the power of traditional gentlemen, but no women or people of color shared in these gains. Land was not seized from its owners, except in the case of pro-British loyalists who had fled the country. Although slavery was gradually abolished in the northern states, where it counted for little, it remained firmly entrenched in the southern states, where it counted for much. Chief Justice John Marshall later gave voice to this conservative understanding of the American Revolution: "All contracts and rights, respecting property, remained unchanged by the Revolution."[5] In the century that followed independence, the United States did become the world's most democratic country, but this development was less the direct product of the revolution and more the outcome of the gradual reforms that reflected the principles of equality announced in the Declaration of Independence.

Nonetheless, many American patriots felt passionately that they were creating "a new order for the ages." James Madison in the *Federalist Papers* made the point clearly: "We pursued a new and more noble course . . . and accomplished a revolution that has no parallel in the annals of human society." Supporters abroad agreed. On the eve of the French Revolution, a Paris newspaper proclaimed that the United States was "the hope and model of the human race."[6] In both cases, they were referring primarily to the political ideas and practices of the new country. The American Revolution, after all, initiated the political dismantling of Europe's New World empires. The "right to revolution," proclaimed in the Declaration of Independence and made effective only in a great struggle, inspired revolutionaries and nationalists from Simón Bolívar in nineteenth-century Latin America to Ho Chi Minh in twentieth-century Vietnam. Moreover, the new U.S. Constitution—with its Bill of Rights, checks and balances, separation of church and state, and federalism—was one of the first sustained efforts to put the political ideas of the Enlightenment into practice. That document, and the ideas that it embraced, echoed repeatedly in the political upheavals of the century that followed.

The French Revolution, 1789–1815

Finding the Main Point: In what ways was the French Revolution a more profound and transformative upheaval than its North American counterpart?

Act Two in the drama of the Atlantic revolutions took place in France, beginning in 1789, although it was closely connected to Act One in North America. Thousands of French soldiers had provided assistance to the American colonists

BUILDING AP® SKILLS

Making Connections: Comparison

If you have assigned the **Comparison Chart for Atlantic Revolutions** (Handout 7.1) on page 391, ask students to fill in the information for the French Revolution as they read this section of the chapter. For a completed chart with sample answers, see the Teacher's Resource Materials.

and now returned home full of republican enthusiasm. Thomas Jefferson, the U.S. ambassador in Paris, reported that France "has been awakened by our revolution."[7] More immediately, the French government, which had generously aided the Americans in an effort to undermine its British rival, was teetering on the brink of bankruptcy and had long sought reforms that would modernize the tax system and make it more equitable. In a desperate effort to raise taxes against the opposition of the privileged classes, the French king, Louis XVI, had called into session an ancient representative body, the Estates General. It consisted of male representatives of the three "estates," or legal orders, of prerevolutionary France: the clergy, the nobility, and the commoners. The first two estates comprised about 2 percent of the population, and the Third Estate included everyone else. When that body convened in 1789, representatives of the Third Estate soon organized themselves as the National Assembly, claiming the sole authority to make laws for the country. A few weeks later, they forthrightly claimed in the **Declaration of the Rights of Man and Citizen** that "men are born and remain free and equal in rights," and this declaration later became the preamble of the 1791 French Constitution. These actions, unprecedented and illegal in the *ancien régime* (old regime), launched the **French Revolution** and radicalized many of the participants in the National Assembly.

The French Revolution was quite different from its North American predecessor. Whereas the American Revolution expressed the tensions of a colonial relationship with a distant imperial power, the French insurrection was driven by sharp conflicts within French society. Members of the titled nobility—privileged, prestigious, and wealthy—resented and resisted the monarchy's efforts to subject them to new taxes. Educated middle-class men such as doctors, lawyers, lower-level officials, and merchants were growing in numbers and sometimes in wealth and were offended by the remaining privileges of the aristocracy, from which they were excluded. Ordinary urban men and women, many of whose incomes had declined for a generation, were hit particularly hard in the late 1780s by the rapidly rising price of bread and widespread unemployment. Peasants in the countryside, though largely free of serfdom, were subject to hated dues imposed by their landlords, taxes from the state, obligations to the Church, and the requirement to work without pay on public roads. As Enlightenment ideas penetrated French society, more and more people, mostly in the Third Estate but also including some priests and nobles, found a language with which to articulate these grievances. The famous French writer Jean-Jacques Rousseau had told them that it was "manifestly contrary to the law of nature . . . that a handful of people should gorge themselves with superfluities while the hungry multitude goes in want of necessities."[8]

These social conflicts gave the French Revolution, especially during its first five years, a much more violent, far-reaching, and radical character than its American counterpart. It was a profound social upheaval, more comparable to the revolutions of Russia and China in the twentieth century than to the earlier American Revolution. Initial efforts to establish a constitutional monarchy and promote harmony

AP CAUSATION
How did Louis XVI's desire to keep France solvent contribute to the French Revolution?

AP EXAM TIP
Take notes on the causes of the French Revolution to compare it with other Atlantic revolutions and the later Russian and Chinese revolutions of the twentieth century.

APPLY THE TIP

Ask students: According to the text, what caused the French Revolution to become much more radical than the American Revolution? *Internal resistance and foreign opposition produced a fear that the French Revolution might be overturned. To counter this possibility, urban crowds organized insurrections that led to much more radicalism than did the American Revolution, where the status quo prevailed.*

After a short class discussion, ask students to take notes on the radical phase of the French Revolution, which they can use when studying the twentieth-century Russian and Chinese revolutions.

Comparative Revolutions Chart

	Goals	Short-Term Outcomes	Long-Term Outcomes
American	See page 391.	See page 391.	See page 391.
French	Educated members of the third estate wanted equality in voting rights. Members of the first two estates did not want the king to raise taxes further. The poor wanted a reduction in taxes and fees as well as stable and affordable food prices.	The government became a constitutional monarchy. The National Assembly decreed the end of all legal privileges and eliminated what remained of feudalism in France. Slavery was briefly abolished. Church lands were sold to raise revenue, and priests were put under government authority. Mass executions targeted anyone deemed an enemy to the revolution. An army of citizens was established.	The French Revolution influenced many areas as Napoleon began his conquest of Europe. Napoleon ruled as a dictator and therefore did not maintain the revolution's political goals. However, he preserved some social aspects of the revolution, including civil equality, a secular law code, religious freedom, and promotion by merit.
Haitian			
Latin American			

TRM Handout 7.1: Comparison Chart for Atlantic Revolutions

among the classes gave way to more radical measures, as internal resistance and foreign opposition produced a fear that the revolution might be overturned. In the process, urban crowds organized insurrections. Some peasants attacked the residences of their lords, burning the documents that recorded their dues and payments. The National Assembly decreed the end of all legal privileges and eliminated what remained of feudalism in France. Even slavery was abolished, albeit briefly. Church lands were sold to raise revenue, and priests were put under government authority.

In 1793, King Louis XVI and his queen, Marie Antoinette, were executed, an act of regicide that shocked traditionalists all across Europe and marked a new stage in revolutionary violence. What followed was the Terror of 1793–1794. Under the leadership of Maximilien **Robespierre** (ROHBS-pee-air) and his Committee of Public Safety, thousands deemed enemies of the revolution lost their lives on the guillotine. Shortly thereafter, Robespierre himself was arrested and guillotined, accused of leading France into tyranny and dictatorship. "The revolution," remarked one of its victims, "was devouring its own children."

Accompanying attacks on the old order were efforts to create a wholly new society, symbolized by a new calendar with the Year 1 in 1792, marking a fresh start for France. Unlike the Americans, who sought to restore or build on earlier freedoms, French revolutionaries perceived themselves to be starting from scratch and looked to the future. For the first time in its history, the country became a republic and briefly passed universal male suffrage, although it was never implemented. The old administrative system was rationalized into eighty-three territorial departments, each with a new name. As revolutionary France prepared for war against its threatened and threatening neighbors, it created the world's largest army, with some 800,000 men, and all adult males were required to serve. Led by officers from the middle and even lower classes, this was an army of citizens representing the nation.

In terms of gender roles, the French Revolution did not create a new society, but it did raise the question of female political equality far more explicitly than the American Revolution had done. Partly this was because French women were active in the major events of the revolution. In July 1789, they took part in the famous storming

▼ **AP®**
CONTEXTUALIZATION
How would the mass executions of the Terror have impacted the way that people outside of France interpreted the French Revolution?

The Execution of Louis XVI The regicide of Louis XVI in January 1793 marked an important moment in the radicalization of the French Revolution and shocked many observers across Europe. In this nineteenth-century engraving of the dramatic event, a large crowd looks on as Louis receives last rites from a priest and his executioners prepare the guillotine. (Private Collection/Photo © The Holborn Archive/Bridgeman Images)

of the Bastille, a large fortress, prison, and armory that had come to symbolize the oppressive old regime. In October of that year, some 7,000 Parisian women, desperate about the shortage of bread, marched on the palace at Versailles, stormed through the royal apartments searching for the despised Queen Marie Antoinette, and forced the royal family to return with them to Paris.

Backed by a few male supporters, women also made serious political demands. They signed petitions detailing their complaints: lack of education, male competition in female trades, the prevalence of prostitution, the rapidly rising price of bread and soap. One petition, reflecting the intersection of class and gender, referred to women as the "Third Estate of the Third Estate." Another demanded the right to bear arms in defense of the revolution. Over sixty women's clubs were established throughout the country. A small group called the *Cercle Social* (Social Circle) campaigned for women's rights, noting that "the laws favor men at the expense of women, because everywhere power is in your [men's] hands."[9] The French playwright and journalist Olympe de Gouges appropriated the language of the Declaration of Rights to insist that "woman is born free and lives equal to man in her rights."

But the assertion of French women in the early years of the revolution seemed wildly inappropriate and threatening to most men, uniting conservatives and revolutionaries alike in defense of male privileges. And so in late 1793, the country's all-male legislative body voted to ban all women's clubs. "Women are ill-suited for elevated thoughts and serious meditation," declared one of the male representatives. "A woman should not leave her family to meddle in affairs of government." Here was a conception of gender that defined masculinity in terms of exercising political power. Women who aspired to do so were, in the words of one revolutionary orator, "denatured *viragos*" (unnatural domineering women), in short, not really women at all.[10] Thus French revolutionaries were distinctly unwilling to offer any political rights to women, even though they had eliminated class restrictions, at least in theory; granted religious freedom to Jews and Protestants; and abolished slavery. Nonetheless, according to a leading historian, "the French Revolution, more than any other event of its time, opened up the question of women's rights for consideration" and thus laid the foundations for modern feminism.[11]

The Women's March on Versailles In the autumn of 1789 rising bread prices and fears of an aristocratic plot to starve the poor caused market women in Paris to lead a march to the royal palace of Versailles. After a tense standoff, Louis XVI agreed to return to Paris escorted by thousands of revolutionaries. This contemporary depiction shows women on their way to Versailles armed with a variety of makeshift weapons and a cannon. (Leemage/Getty Images)

AP

CAUSATION

In what ways did the French Revolution impact various social groups in French society?

AP **EXAM TIP**

The growing demands for women's rights that grew out of the Atlantic revolutions are important information for the AP® Exam.

AP

CAUSATION

What caused the French Revolution to become much more radical than the American Revolution?

APPLY THE TIP

Ask students to discuss the following questions in pairs:

■ How did the French Revolution inspire women? *Women participated in the events of the revolution, from storming the Bastille to aiding in the forced return of the monarchs to Paris. Women also participated politically, signing petitions that explained their demands and listing their grievances.*

■ What was the revolution's ultimate effect on women's rights? *Ultimately, men decided that women were not supposed to play a part in the political life of the state, so many of the rights women hoped for were not given to them. However, the French Revolution introduced the question of women's rights and laid the foundation for the feminist movement of the twentieth century.*

EXPLORING AP® THEMES

Social Interactions and Organization (SIO)

Most students think that revolutions are only about political change and do not realize that social or cultural change is very often an outcome of a revolution. Ask students to list some specific changes that occurred as a result of the French Revolution and some specific aspects of society that did not change. *The revolutionary government changed the calendar. All citizens were expected to serve in the army, with officers from the middle and even lower classes. Streets were renamed, and titles vanished. The state took over duties that had previously been handled by the Catholic Church. Although women played an active role in the revolution and demanded political and even social equality, their status remained more or less the same despite the revolution.*

Incorporating Outside Resources

In the episode *The French Revolution* of Crash Course World History, John Green examines the French Revolution and compares it to the American Revolution. Find the video on YouTube. After students watch the video, ask: What evidence does John Green provide to support his claim that the ideas of the French Revolution changed human history more than did those of the American Revolution? *The Declaration of the Rights of Man and Citizen gave liberty, equality, and security to all men — at least in theory. It also insisted that laws apply equally to all and that all men — whether directly or through their representatives — become involved in making laws. The idea that laws come from citizens and not from kings or from God, and that they should apply to everyone equally, was radical because the French had been ruled by a hereditary Crown whose divine right to govern had never before been challenged.*

Ask students to look at their revolution comparison chart and highlight the similarities between the French and American revolutions. The differences will remain un-highlighted.

If not in terms of gender, the immediate impact of the revolution was felt in many other ways. Streets got new names; monuments to the royal family were destroyed; titles vanished; people referred to one another as "citizen so-and-so." Real politics in the public sphere emerged for the first time as many people joined political clubs, took part in marches and demonstrations, served on local committees, and ran for public office. Ordinary men and women, who had identified primarily with their local communities, now began to think of themselves as belonging to a nation. The state replaced the Catholic Church as the place for registering births, marriages, and deaths, and revolutionary festivals substituted for church holidays.

More radical revolutionary leaders deliberately sought to convey a sense of new beginnings and endless possibilities. At a Festival of Unity held in 1793 to mark the first anniversary of the end of monarchy, participants burned the crowns and scepters of the royal family in a huge bonfire while releasing a cloud of 3,000 white doves. The Cathedral of Notre Dame was temporarily turned into the Temple of Reason, while a "Hymn to Liberty" combined traditional church music with the explicit message of the Enlightenment:

> Oh Liberty, sacred Liberty / Goddess of an enlightened people
> Rule today within these walls. / Through you this temple is purified.
> Liberty! Before you reason chases out deception, / Error flees, fanaticism is
>   beaten down.
> Our gospel is nature / And our cult is virtue.
> To love one's country and one's brothers, / To serve the Sovereign People
> These are the sacred tenets / And pledge of a Republican.[12]

Elsewhere too the French Revolution evoked images of starting over. Witnessing that revolution in 1790, the young William Wordsworth, later a famous British Romantic poet, imagined "human nature seeming born again." "Bliss it was in that dawn to be alive," he wrote. "But to be young was very heaven."

The French Revolution also differed from the American Revolution in the way its influence spread. At least until the United States became a world power at the end of the nineteenth century, what inspired others was primarily the example of its revolution and its constitution. French influence, by contrast, spread through conquest, largely under the leadership of **Napoleon Bonaparte** (r. 1799–1815). A highly successful general who seized power in 1799, Napoleon is often credited with taming the revolution in the face of growing disenchantment with its more radical features and with the social conflicts it generated. He preserved many of its more moderate elements, such as civil equality, a secular law code, religious freedom, and promotion by merit, while reconciling with the Catholic Church and suppressing the revolution's more democratic elements in a military dictatorship. In short, Napoleon kept the revolution's emphasis on social equality for men but dispensed with liberty.

Like many of the revolution's ardent supporters, Napoleon was intent on spreading its benefits far and wide. In a series of brilliant military campaigns, his forces subdued

AP EXAM TIP

If you haven't already done so, now is a good time to make a chart of political, economic, and social similarities and differences between the French and American revolutions.

most of Europe, thus creating the continent's largest empire since the days of the Romans (see Map 7.2). Within that empire, Napoleon imposed such revolutionary practices as ending feudalism, proclaiming equality of rights, insisting on religious toleration, codifying the laws, and rationalizing government administration. In many places, these reforms were welcomed, and seeds of further change were planted. But French domination was also resented and resisted, stimulating national consciousness throughout Europe. That too was a seed that bore fruit in the century that followed. More immediately, national resistance, particularly from Russia and Britain, brought down Napoleon and his amazing empire by 1815 and marked an end to the era of the French Revolution, though not to the potency of its ideas.

▼ **AP**

CAUSATION

Based on the evidence in this map, how did the rise of Napoleon facilitate the spread of Enlightenment ideals across the European continent?

Map 7.2 Napoleon's European Empire
The French Revolution spawned a French Empire, under Napoleon's leadership, that encompassed most of Europe and served to spread the principles of the revolution.

EXPLORING AP® THEMES

Humans and the Environment (ENV)

Have students look at Map 7.2, "Napoleon's European Empire," and then have them examine the states or regions that belonged to the French Empire, those that were allied with Napoleon, those that were dependent states, and those that remained at war with France. Then ask: Is there a connection between a state's distance from Paris and the degree to which it was allied with France? *Yes, there is a relationship. Nations closer to France, and not separated from it by water, were more tightly woven into the fabric of the French Empire.*

The Haitian Revolution, 1791–1804

Finding the Main Point: What were the goals of the main groups fighting in the Haitian Revolution?

Nowhere did the example of the French Revolution echo more loudly than in the French Caribbean colony of Saint Domingue, later renamed Haiti (see Map 7.3, page 403). Widely regarded as the richest colony in the world, Saint Domingue boasted 8,000 plantations, which in the late eighteenth century produced some 40 percent of the world's sugar and perhaps half of its coffee. The French had established in Haiti a three-tiered social class structure based primarily on race, but also on wealth and land ownership. Whites, numbering only about 40,000 people, were a small but sharply divided minority of the population. The *grands blancs*, very well-to-do white plantation owners, merchants, and lawyers, were the privileged elite class and had the right to vote in the French National Assembly. The poor whites of the colony, called the *petits blancs*, lacked political power because they did not meet minimum property ownership requirements to gain representation in the National Assembly. A second social group, intermediate between Blacks and whites, consisted of some 30,000 *gens de couleur libres* (free people of color), many of them of multiracial background. Their social status depended on landholdings as well as the number of enslaved people that they owned. Fierce competition existed between the *petits blancs* and the *gens de couleur*. At the lowest level of colonial society, representing the vast majority of the colony's population, were some 500,000 enslaved people. Given its enormous inequalities and its rampant exploitation, this Caribbean colony was primed for explosion.

In such a volatile setting, the ideas and example of the French Revolution lit several fuses and set in motion a spiral of violence that engulfed the colony for more than a decade. The principles of the revolution, however, meant different things to different people. To the *grands blancs*—the rich white landowners—it suggested greater autonomy for the colony and fewer economic restrictions on trade, but they resented the demands of the *petits blancs*, who sought equality of citizenship for all whites. Both white groups were adamantly opposed to the insistence of free people of color that the "rights of man" meant equal treatment for all free people regardless of race. To the enslaved, the promise of the French Revolution was a personal freedom that challenged the entire slave labor system. In a massive revolt beginning in 1791, triggered by rumors that the French king had already declared an end to slavery, enslaved people burned 1,000 plantations and killed hundreds of whites as well as multiracial people.

Soon warring factions of the enslaved, whites, and free people of color battled one another. Spanish and British forces, seeking to enlarge their own empires at the expense of the French, only added to the turmoil. Amid the confusion, brutality, and massacres of the 1790s, power gravitated toward the enslaved population, now led by the astute Toussaint Louverture, who had formerly been enslaved himself. He and his successor overcame internal resistance, outmaneuvered the foreign powers, and even defeated an attempt by Napoleon to reestablish French control.

Comparative Revolutions Chart

	Goals	Short-Term Outcomes	Long-Term Outcomes
American	See page 391.	See page 391.	See page 391.
French	See pages 394–395.	See pages 394–395.	See pages 394–395.
Haitian	Rich white landowners wanted greater autonomy and fewer economic restrictions on trade. Poor whites sought equality of citizenship for all whites. Free people of color wanted equal treatment for all free people regardless of race. Enslaved people believed that the revolution guaranteed an end to slavery.	The French were defeated. British and Spanish forces, which tried to benefit from the French defeat, retreated. Toussaint Louverture and his successor overcame internal resistance, outmaneuvered the foreign powers, and even defeated an attempt by Napoleon to reestablish French control. The country changed its name from Saint Domingue to Haiti. All people were proclaimed equal.	The destructiveness of the Haitian Revolution, its bitter internal divisions of race and class, and continuing external opposition contributed to Haiti's poverty as well as to its authoritarian and unstable politics. France forced Haiti to pay a crippling independence debt. "Freedom" came to mean the end of slavery rather than establishment of political rights for all.
Latin American			

TRM Handout 7.1: Comparison Chart for Atlantic Revolutions

When the dust settled in the early years of the nineteenth century, it was clear that something remarkable and unprecedented had taken place, a revolution unique in the Atlantic world and in world history. Socially, the last had become first. In the only completely successful slave revolt in world history, "the lowest order of the society—slaves—became equal, free, and independent citizens."[13] Politically, they had thrown off French colonial rule, creating the second independent republic in the Americas and the first non-European state to emerge from Western colonialism. They renamed their country Haiti, a term meaning "mountainous" or "rugged" in the language of the original Taino people. It was a symbolic break with Europe and represented an effort to connect with the long-deceased native inhabitants of the land. Some, in fact, referred to themselves as "Incas." At the formal declaration of Haiti's independence on January 1, 1804, Jean-Jacques Dessalines, the new country's first head of state, declared: "I have given the French cannibals blood for blood; I have avenged America."[14] In defining all Haitian citizens as Black and legally equal regardless of color or class, Haiti directly confronted elite preferences for lighter skin even as it disallowed citizenship for most whites. Economically, the country's plantation system, oriented wholly toward the export of sugar and coffee, had been largely destroyed. As whites fled or were killed, both private and state lands were redistributed among formerly enslaved people and free Blacks, and Haiti became a nation of small-scale farmers producing mostly for their own needs, with a much smaller export sector.

The destructiveness of the **Haitian Revolution**, its bitter internal divisions of race and class, and continuing external opposition contributed much to Haiti's abiding poverty as well as to its authoritarian and unstable politics. So too did the enormous "independence debt" that the French forced on the fledgling republic in 1825, a financial burden that endured for well over a century. "Freedom" in Haiti came to mean primarily the end of slavery rather than the establishment of political rights for all. In the early nineteenth century, however, Haiti was a source of enormous hope and of great fear. Within weeks of the Haitian slave uprising in 1791, enslaved people in Jamaica had composed songs in its honor, and it was not long before plantation owners in the Caribbean and North America observed a new "insolence" among those that they had enslaved. Certainly, its example inspired other slave rebellions, gave a boost to the dawning abolitionist movement, and has been a source of pride for people of African descent ever since.

AP®
CAUSATION
Describe the effects of the Haitian Revolution on the United States, Latin America, the Caribbean, and France.

AP®
COMPARISON
In what ways can Enlightenment thought be seen as a cause of the French and Haitian revolutions?

▼**AP®**
CLAIMS AND EVIDENCE IN SOURCES
What aspects of the Haitian Revolution does this image emphasize?

The Haitian Revolution This early nineteenth-century engraving, titled *Revenge Taken by the Black Army*, shows Black Haitian soldiers hanging a large number of French soldiers, thus illustrating both the violence and the racial dimension of the upheaval in Haiti. (Bridgeman Images)

TEACHING IDEA

Class Discussion

Have a quick class discussion by asking students: Which of the Atlantic revolutions do you feel was the most revolutionary? Explain why using the themes of the course. Governance: *The American Revolution began a new form of government, and Latin American colonies gained independence from Spain.* Economic: *The Haitian Revolution was a slave rebellion and the beginnings of the abolitionist movement.* Social: *France ended the monarchy and the estate system that had legally divided France into social classes.*

BUILDING AP® SKILLS

Sourcing and Situation

Students need to be able to analyze images in preparation for the exam. One way to have students practice image analysis is to use images in the textbook. Ask students to fill out an OPTIC chart like the one below for the engraving of the Haitian Revolution. A reproducible version of this chart is available in the Teacher's Resource Materials.

Overview	The illustration depicts the victory of the Haitian army over the French army.
Parts	The foreground shows a hanging in progress in which a prisoner is being hauled up by his neck. In the background, it appears that many more hangings are in various stages.
Title	The engraving is called "Revenge Taken by the Black Army," and it seems to be documenting the end of the battle and the revenge that the Haitian army took on the French army.
Interrelationships	The mountain terrain seems to hide the numerous hangings. The figures in the foreground seem to relish the hangings. The figures in the background make it clear that numerous hangings are happening simultaneously.
Conclusion	Revenge is clearly widespread and complete.

TRM Handout 7.2: OPTIC Chart for Engraving of the Haitian Revolution

To whites throughout the hemisphere, the cautionary saying "Remember Haiti" reflected a sense of horror at what had occurred there and a determination not to allow political change to reproduce that fearful outcome again. Particularly in Latin America, the events in Haiti injected a deep caution and social conservatism in the elites who led their countries to independence in the early nineteenth century. Ironically, though, the Haitian Revolution also led to a temporary expansion of slavery elsewhere. Cuban plantations and their enslaved workers considerably increased their production of sugar as that of Haiti declined. Moreover, Napoleon's defeat in Haiti persuaded him to sell to the United States the French territories known as the Louisiana Purchase, from which a number of "slave states" were carved out. Nor did the example of Haiti lead to successful independence struggles in the rest of the thirty or so Caribbean colonies. Unlike mainland North and South America, Caribbean decolonization had to await the twentieth century. In such contradictory ways did the echoes of the Haitian Revolution reverberate in the Atlantic world.

Latin American Revolutions, 1808–1825

Finding the Main Point: In what ways did the Latin American revolutions differ from their North American counterpart?

AP° EXAM TIP
Understand the political and social power of the creole elites in Latin American history.

AP°
CAUSATION
In what ways did the spread of Enlightenment philosophy affect independence movements in Latin America?

The final act in a half century of Atlantic revolutionary upheaval took place in the Spanish and Portuguese colonies of mainland Latin America (see Map 7.3). These **Latin American revolutions** were shaped by preceding events in North America, France, and Haiti as well as by their own distinctive societies and historical experiences. As in British North America, native-born elites (known as *creoles*) in the Spanish colonies were offended and insulted by the Spanish monarchy's efforts during the eighteenth century to exercise greater power over its colonies and to subject them to heavier taxes and tariffs. Creole intellectuals had also become familiar with ideas of popular sovereignty, republican government, and personal liberty derived from the European Enlightenment. But these conditions, similar to those in North America, led initially only to scattered and uncoordinated protests rather than to outrage, declarations of independence, war, and unity, as had occurred in the British colonies. Why did Spanish colonies win their independence almost fifty years later than those of British North America?

Spanish colonies had long been governed in a rather more authoritarian fashion than their British counterparts and were more sharply divided by class. In addition, whites throughout Latin America were vastly outnumbered by Native Americans, people of African ancestry, and those of biracial and multiracial backgrounds. All of this inhibited the growth of a movement for independence, notwithstanding the example of North America and similar provocations.

Despite their growing disenchantment with Spanish rule, creole elites did not so much generate a revolution as have one thrust upon them by events in Europe.

APPLY THE TIP

Ask students to think back to the Spanish colonies in the Americas and ask. "What political and social power did the creole elites in the Spanish colonies have?" Answers should include: *land ownership, wealth, education in Europe for males, privileges that others did not have.*

BUILDING AP° SKILLS

Making Connections: Comparison

If you have assigned the **Comparison Chart for Atlantic Revolutions** on page 391, ask students to fill in the information for the Latin American revolutions as they read this section of the chapter. For a completed chart with sample answers, see the Teacher's Resource Materials.

Comparative Revolutions Chart

	Goals	Short-Term Outcomes	Long-Term Outcomes
American	See page 391.	See page 391.	See page 391.
French	See pages 394–395.	See pages 394–395.	See pages 394–395.
Haitian	See page 400.	See page 400.	See page 400.
Latin American	Creoles were offended by the Spanish monarchy's efforts during the eighteenth century to exercise more power over its colonies, to impose heavier taxes and tariffs. Creole intellectuals familiar with European Enlightenment ideas of popular sovereignty, republican government, and personal liberty wanted to implement them.	Lower classes, Native Americans, and enslaved people benefited little from independence, despite a concerted effort by creoles to define all races as "American." Efforts to unite all the Spanish colonies into one country failed despite numerous attempts to do so.	In the nineteenth century, newly independent countries in Latin America were relatively underdeveloped, impoverished, undemocratic, politically unstable, and dependent on foreign technology and investment.

TRM Handout 7.1: Comparison Chart for Atlantic Revolutions

In 1808, Napoleon invaded Spain and Portugal, deposing the Spanish king Ferdinand VII and forcing the Portuguese royal family into exile in Brazil. With legitimate royal authority now in disarray, Latin Americans were forced to take action. The outcome, ultimately, was independence for the various states of Latin America, established almost everywhere by 1826. But the way in which independence occurred and the kind of societies it generated differed greatly from the experience of both North America and Haiti.

The process lasted more than twice as long as it did in North America, partly because Latin American societies were so divided by class, race, and region. (See "In the Lands of the Aztecs and the Incas" in Chapter 4 for the social structure of Latin American colonies.) In North America, violence was directed almost entirely against the British and seldom spilled over into domestic disputes, except for some bloody skirmishes with loyalists. In Mexico, by contrast, the move toward independence began in 1810–1811 in a peasant insurrection, driven by hunger for land and by high food prices and led successively by two priests, Miguel Hidalgo and José Morelos. Alarmed by the social radicalism of the **Hidalgo-Morelos rebellion**, creole landowners, with the support of the Church, raised an army and crushed the insurgency. Later that alliance of clergy and creole elites brought Mexico to a more socially controlled independence in 1821. Such violent conflict among Latin Americans, along lines of race, class, and ideology, accompanied the struggle against Spain in many places.

The entire independence movement in Latin America took place under the shadow of a great fear—the dread of social rebellion from below—that had little counterpart in North America. The extensive violence of the French and Haitian revolutions was a lesson to Latin American elites that political change could easily get out of hand and was fraught with danger to themselves. An abortive and

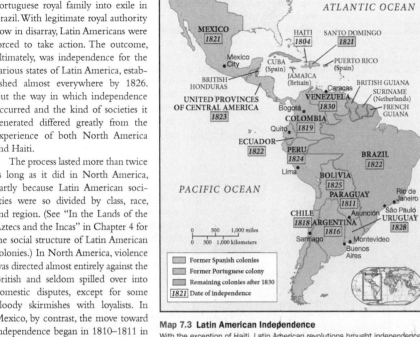

Map 7.3 Latin American Independence
With the exception of Haiti, Latin American revolutions brought independence to new states but offered little social change or political opportunity for the vast majority of people.

AP®
CONTEXTUALIZATION
How were the Spanish American revolutions shaped by the American, French, and Haitian revolutions?

Class Discussion

Ask students: Why did it take so much longer for Spanish American colonies to gain independence than it did for the North American colonies? *Spanish colonies had long been governed in a more authoritarian fashion than their British counterparts and were more sharply divided by class. In addition, whites throughout Latin America were vastly outnumbered by Native Americans, people of African ancestry, and multiracial people. Both of these factors inhibited the growth of a movement for independence.*

Humans and the Environment (ENV)

Show students Map 7.3, "Latin American Independence." Then ask the following questions:

■ After Haiti, when did the first Latin American colony gain independence? *Paraguay gained independence in 1811.*

■ How long did it take for the last country on the map to gain independence? *Venezuela gained independence in 1830, nineteen years after Paraguay.*

■ Which colonies did not gain independence? *Cuba, Jamaica, Puerto Rico, British Guiana, Suriname, and French Guiana — these were colonies of nations other than Spain.*

■ Why did these areas not gain independence as quickly as the others? *They were sugar-producing areas that were very valuable.*

ultimately unsuccessful rebellion of Native Americans in Peru in the early 1780s, led by **Tupac Amaru**, a man who claimed direct descent from the last Inca emperor, reminded whites that they sat atop a potentially explosive society, most of whose members were exploited and oppressed people of color. So too did the Hidalgo-Morelos rebellion in Mexico.

And yet the creole sponsors of independence movements, both regional military leaders such as Simón Bolívar and José de San Martín and their civilian counterparts, required the support of "the people," or at least some of them, if they were to prevail against Spanish forces. The answer to this dilemma was found in nativism, which cast all of those born in the Americas—creoles, Native Americans, multiracial people, free Blacks—as Americanos, while the enemy was defined as those born in Spain or Portugal. This was no easy task, because many creole whites and mestizos saw themselves as Spanish and because great differences of race, culture, and wealth divided the Americanos. Nonetheless, nationalist leaders made efforts to mobilize people of color into the struggle with promises of freedom, the end of legal restrictions, and social advancement. Many of these leaders were genuine liberals who had been influenced by the ideals of the Enlightenment, the French Revolution, and Spanish liberalism. In the long run, however, few of those promises were kept. Certainly, the lower classes, Native Americans, and enslaved people benefited little from independence. "The imperial state was destroyed in Spanish America," concluded one historian, "but colonial society was preserved."[15]

Nor did women as a group gain much from the independence struggle, though they had participated in it in various ways. Upper-class or wealthy women gave and raised money for the cause and provided safe havens for revolutionary meetings. In Mexico, some women disguised themselves as men to join the struggle, while numerous working-class and peasant women served as cooks and carriers of supplies in a "women's brigade." A considerable number of women were severely punished for their disloyalty to the Crown, with some forty-eight executed in Colombia. Yet, after independence, few social gains rewarded these efforts. General

Simón Bolívar Among the heroic figures of Spanish American independence movements, none was more significant than Simón Bolívar, shown here in a moment of triumph entering his hometown of Caracas in present-day Venezuela. But Bolívar was immensely disappointed in the outcomes of independence, as his dream of a unified South America perished amid the rivalries of separate countries. (*Bolívar's Victory Parade in Caracas*, chalk lithograph by R. Weibezahl/Sammlung Archiv für Kunst und Geschichte, Berlin, Germany/akg-images)

BUILDING AP® SKILLS

Claims and Evidence in Sources

Many students struggle with interpreting images. A quick way for students to practice this skill is to have them study the image of Simón Bolívar. Point out the framing of Bolívar (center) with different racial groups on both sides and on the balcony. Also point out the church in the background. Then ask: What does this framing, this contextualization, represent? *The framing indicates that Bolívar has the support of the Church as well as the support of the poor and the elite.*

BUILDING AP® SKILLS

Argumentation

While students need to write full-length essays, writing body paragraphs is also a useful tool to sharpen writing skills. As practice for writing full-length essays, ask students to write an LEQ-style body paragraph on the following prompt:

■ Evaluate the extent to which opportunities for women and nonelites changed during the era of revolutions in Latin America in 1800–1850.

The paragraph should include a topic sentence that introduces their argument, at least two pieces of evidence, and an explanation of how or why the evidence supports their argument.

Answers should note that women did not gain much, though they participated in the cause. Upper-class women gave and raised money and provided safe havens. Some women disguised themselves as men to join the struggle, while many working-class and peasant women served as cooks and supply carriers. About forty women were executed by the Spanish Crown in Colombia. Women gained some access to better educational opportunities and got some level of national recognition for their revolutionary efforts. In general, however, women continued to be excluded from political life and remained under the firm control of men.

San Martín of Argentina accorded national recognition to a number of women, and modest improvement in educational opportunities for women appeared. But Latin American women continued to be wholly excluded from political life and remained under firm legal control of the men in their families.

A further difference in the Latin American situation lay in the apparent impossibility of uniting the various Spanish colonies, so much larger than the small British territories of North America, despite several failed efforts to do so. Thus no United States of Latin America emerged. Distances among the colonies and geographic obstacles to effective communication were certainly greater than in the Eastern Seaboard colonies of North America, and their longer colonial experience had given rise to distinct and deeply rooted regional identities. Shortly before his death in 1830, the prominent independence leader Simón Bolívar, who so admired George Washington and had so ardently hoped for greater unity, wrote in despair to a friend: "[Latin] America is ungovernable. Those who serve the revolution plough the sea."[16]

The aftermath of independence in Latin America marked a reversal in the earlier relationship of the two American continents. The United States, which began its history as the leftover "dregs" of the New World, grew increasingly wealthy, industrialized, democratic, internationally influential, and generally stable, with the major exception of the Civil War. The Spanish colonies, which took shape in the wealthiest areas and among the most sophisticated cultures of the Americas, were widely regarded as the more promising region compared to England's North American territories, which had a backwater reputation. But in the nineteenth century, as newly independent countries in both regions launched a new phase of their histories, those in Latin America became relatively underdeveloped, impoverished, undemocratic, politically unstable, and dependent on foreign technology and investment. Begun in broadly similar circumstances, the Latin American and North American revolutions occurred in very different societies and gave rise to very different historical trajectories.

Echoes of Revolution

Finding the Main Point: In what ways did the experience and values of the Atlantic revolutions stimulate major change in the world of the nineteenth century?

The repercussions of the Atlantic revolutions reverberated far beyond their places of origin and persisted long after those upheavals had been concluded. Britain's loss of its North American colonies, for example, fueled its growing interest and interventions in Asia, contributing to British colonial rule in India and the Opium Wars in China. Napoleon's brief conquest of Egypt (1798–1801) opened the way for a modernizing regime to emerge in that ancient land and stimulated westernizing reforms in the Ottoman Empire (see "The Ottoman Empire and the West in the Nineteenth Century" in Chapter 9). During the nineteenth century, the idea of a "constitution" found advocates in Poland, Russia, the Spanish-ruled Philippines, China, the Ottoman Empire, and British-governed India.

Within Europe, which was generally dominated by conservative governments following Napoleon's final defeat, smaller revolutionary eruptions occurred in 1830,

AP EXAM TIP
You should understand the role of Simón Bolívar and his "Letter from Jamaica" in leading Latin American revolutions.

AP CONTEXTUALIZATION
What opportunities and barriers existed for women and nonelites in the era of revolutions in Latin America in 1800–1850?

AP COMPARISON
Compare the North American, French, Haitian, and Spanish American revolutions. What are the most significant similarities and differences?

AP EXAM TIP
If you haven't already done so, now is a good time to make a chart of political, economic, and social similarities and differences between the North American, French, Haitian, and Spanish American revolutions.

AP EXAM TIP
Be sure to understand the role of Enlightenment thought in political revolutions, but also in other changes of the eighteenth and nineteenth centuries mentioned in this chapter.

BUILDING AP® SKILLS

Argumentation

As a wrap-up to studying the Atlantic revolutions, you could have students write a full-length, timed LEQ using a revised prompt of the 2006 Comparison Essay. If students have been working on the **Comparison Chart for Atlantic Revolutions** throughout this chapter, they should have plenty of background knowledge to write this essay.

■ Revised prompt: Develop an argument that evaluates the extent to which the Atlantic revolutions contributed to political and social changes in the period 1750 to 1900.

Differentiation

If you want to differentiate this LEQ and give students more practice with building their writing skills, follow the "Must Do, Should Do, Strive For" model below for an LEQ poster. You'll want to create groups of three to four students for the LEQ poster.

■ Must Do: In their groups, students must create two arguments to answer the question. On their provided butcher paper (to create their poster), they will need to name their arguments and provide at least three pieces of evidence to support their arguments. Students will also need to create a thesis statement that answers the prompt and write it at the bottom of their poster.

■ Should Do: In their groups, students should write contextualization (which should go above the thesis) on their poster. Once all groups have completed their LEQ poster, have students hang them up and do a gallery walk to see how other groups put together the LEQ. As they look at each poster, ask students to leave "I wonder . . ." and "I like . . ." statements on sticky notes you provided.

■ Strive For: For students who want or need a writing challenge, have them choose one of the arguments from their LEQ poster and write a full argument paragraph on it.

APPLY THE TIP

Now that you have covered the political revolutions in the eighteenth and nineteenth centuries, it is time to move on to other changes. Ask students: What role does the Enlightenment play in the abolition of slavery, nationalism, and the beginnings of feminism? *Answers will vary but should include the idea that slavery is a violation of natural rights, nationalism was a modern idea since science had weakened the sway of religion on many people and revolutions had weakened the power of monarchs, and since women had participated in many of the revolutionary events they felt that the ideas of liberty and equality should include women.*

more widely in 1848, and in Paris in 1870. They reflected ideas of republicanism, greater social equality, and national liberation from foreign rule. Such ideas and social pressures pushed the major states of Western Europe, the United States, and Argentina to enlarge their voting publics, generally granting universal male suffrage by 1914. An abortive attempt to establish a constitutional regime even broke out in autocratic Russia in 1825, led by aristocratic military officers influenced by French revolutionary ideas. While it quickly failed, it marked the beginning of a revolutionary tradition in Russia that came to fruition only in 1917. More generally, the American and French revolutions led sympathetic elites in Central Europe and elsewhere to feel that they had fallen behind, that their countries were "sleeping." As early as 1791, a Hungarian poet gave voice to such sentiments: "O you still in the slave's collar. . . . And you too! Holy consecrated kings . . . turn your eyes to Paris! Let France set out the fate of both king and shackled slave."[17]

Beyond these echoes of the Atlantic revolutions, three major movements arose to challenge continuing patterns of oppression or exclusion. Abolitionists sought the end of slavery; nationalists hoped to foster unity and independence from foreign rule; and feminists challenged male dominance. Each of these movements bore the marks of the Atlantic revolutions, and although they took root first in Europe and the Americas, each came to have a global significance in the centuries that followed.

The Abolition of Slavery

In little more than a century, from roughly 1780 to 1890, a remarkable transformation occurred in human affairs as slavery, widely practiced and little condemned since at least the beginning of civilization, lost its legitimacy and was largely ended. In this amazing process, the ideas and practices of the Atlantic revolutions played an important role.

Enlightenment thinkers in eighteenth-century Europe had become increasingly critical of slavery as a violation of the natural rights of every person, and the public pronouncements of the American and French revolutions about liberty and equality likewise focused attention on this obvious breach of those principles. To this secular antislavery thinking was added an increasingly vociferous religious voice, expressed first by Quakers and then by Protestant evangelicals in Britain and the United States. To them, slavery was "repugnant to our religion" and a "crime in the sight of God."[18]

What made these moral arguments more widely acceptable was the growing belief that, contrary to much earlier thinking, slavery was not essential for economic progress. After all, England and New England were among the most prosperous regions of the Western world in the early nineteenth century, and both were based on free labor. Slavery in this view was out of date, unnecessary in the new era of industrial technology and capitalism. Thus moral virtue and economic success were joined. It was an attractive argument.

The actions of enslaved people themselves likewise hastened the end of slavery. The dramatically successful Haitian Revolution was followed by three major rebellions in the British West Indies, all of which were harshly crushed, in the early nineteenth century. The **Great Jamaica Revolt** of 1831–1832, in which perhaps

---

AP®
CAUSATION
In what ways did the Atlantic revolutions contribute to the abolitionist, nationalist, and feminist movements of the nineteenth century?

AP® EXAM TIP
The abolition of slavery in the Atlantic world is considered one of the greatest political and social achievements of the nineteenth century. This is an important turning point to take note of.

60,000 enslaved people attacked several hundred plantations, was particularly important in prompting Britain to abolish slavery throughout its empire in 1833. These revolts demonstrated clearly that enslaved people were hardly "contented," and the brutality with which they were suppressed appalled British public opinion. Growing numbers of the British public came to believe that slavery was "not only morally wrong and economically inefficient, but also politically unwise."[19]

These various strands of thinking—secular, religious, economic, and political—came together in an **abolitionist movement**, most powerfully in Britain, which brought growing pressure on governments to close down the trade in enslaved people and then to ban slavery itself. In the late eighteenth century, such a movement gained wide support among middle- and working-class people in Britain. Its techniques included pamphlets with heartrending descriptions of slavery, numerous petitions to Parliament, lawsuits, and boycotts of sugar produced using enslaved labor. Frequent public meetings dramatically featured the testimony of Africans who had experienced the horrors of slavery firsthand. In 1807, Britain forbade the sale of enslaved people within its empire and in 1834 emancipated those who remained enslaved. Over the next half century, other nations followed suit, responding to growing international pressure, particularly from Britain, then the world's leading economic and military power. British naval vessels patrolled the Atlantic, intercepted illegal slave ships, and freed their human cargoes in a small West African settlement called Freetown, in present-day Sierra Leone. Following their independence, most Latin American countries abolished slavery by the 1850s. Brazil, in 1888, was the last to do so, bringing more than four centuries of Atlantic slavery to an end. A roughly similar set of conditions—fear of rebellion, economic inefficiency, and moral concerns—persuaded the Russian tsar (zahr) to free the many serfs of that huge country in 1861, although there it occurred by fiat from above rather than from growing public pressure.

None of this happened easily. Even after slavery was outlawed by Britain, it continued to find a place in the British world. Cotton produced by enslaved people in the southern United States supplied Britain's crucial textile industry. And imperial officials often turned a blind eye to the illegal traffic of women and girls into the sex trade in British Southeast Asia. Slave economies continued to flourish well into the nineteenth century, and plantation owners vigorously resisted the onslaught of abolitionists. So did slave traders, both European and African, who together shipped millions of additional captives, mostly to

AP
CONTINUITY AND CHANGE
What accounts for the end of Atlantic slavery during the nineteenth century?

▼ **AP**
SOURCING AND SITUATION
How could resistance by the enslaved, such as the Great Jamaica Revolt, impact how the artist portrayed the enslaved person in this picture?

Abolitionism This unusual late eighteenth-century abolitionist image depicts an enslaved African in chains holding a knife on the deck of a ship. Unlike most abolitionist representations of Africans, which show their subjects kneeling, praying, or pleading, the subject of this engraving strikes a defiant pose as he seemingly contemplates suicide, or perhaps resistance, rather than captivity. (*The Dying Negro ...* by T. Day and J. Bicknell, Second Edition, with additions [London: John Stockdale, 1793], http://access.bl.uk/item/viewer/ark:/81055/vdc_000000028740)

EXPLORING AP® THEMES

Economic Systems (ECN)

Ask students: What were the economic reasons for ending slavery and serfdom? *Slavery and serfdom became economically inefficient for a number of reasons. Free workers worked harder than enslaved workers and cost less in wages than purchasing and maintaining enslaved workers. Slave-produced sugar was boycotted in Great Britain. The interception of slave ships drove up the cost of enslaved workers.*

BUILDING AP® SKILLS

Sourcing and Situation

Since students always need practice with images, consider using the AP® Sourcing and Situation margin question to begin a class discussion for some practice. Suggested answers can be found in the Teacher's Resource Materials.

APPLY THE TIP

Ask students: "Why do you think that indentured servitude gained popularity after the end of slavery?" Answers should include: *it was a cheap form of labor for labor-intensive work, and indentured servants were still considered property.*

BUILDING AP® SKILLS

Making Connections: Comparison

Ask students to compare political and economic lives for ex-enslaved people and ex-serfs in the United States and in Russia in the latter half of the nineteenth century. To get information on Russian serfs, see pages 463–466 in Chapter 8. *The economic well-being of former enslaved people did not change much because, except in Haiti, they did not gain access to land. In the United States, sharecropping kept formerly enslaved workers on their masters' land without providing much better economic circumstances. Serfs did get access to land but had to pay for it, which meant years of having to pay dues. Enslaved people gained freedom but very little political power. In some cases, whites ensured continued political power by using harsh violence and by rewriting laws. Russian serfs retained their local autonomy when they were freed, as long as they stayed in their villages and paid for land. However, because Russia was a more authoritarian society, very limited political rights existed for all but the nobility.*

AP® EXAM TIP

It's important to know that even with the abolition of slavery, other forms of coerced labor continued, like indentured servitude in the Caribbean sugar plantations.

AP®

CONTINUITY AND CHANGE
To what extent did the end of slavery transform the lives of formerly enslaved people?

AP®

COMPARISON
Compare the social conditions for formerly enslaved people in the United States with those for former serfs in Russia in the latter half of the nineteenth century.

Cuba and Brazil, long after the British had declared the trade illegal. Osei Bonsu, the powerful king of the West African state of Asante, was puzzled as to why the British would no longer purchase enslaved people from him. "If they think it bad now," he asked a local British representative in 1820, "why did they think it good before?"[20] Nowhere was the persistence of slavery more evident and resistance to abolition more intense than in the southern states of the United States. It was the only slave-holding society in which the end of slavery occurred through a bitter, prolonged, and highly destructive civil war (1861–1865).

The end of Atlantic slavery during the nineteenth century surely marked a major and quite rapid turn in the world's social history and in the moral thinking of humankind. Nonetheless, the outcomes of that process were often surprising and far from the expectations of abolitionists or the formerly enslaved. In most cases, the economic lives of the enslaved people did not improve dramatically upon emancipation. Nowhere in the Atlantic world, except Haiti, did a redistribution of land follow the end of slavery. But freedmen everywhere desperately sought economic autonomy on their own land, and in parts of the Caribbean such as Jamaica, where unoccupied land was available, independent peasant agriculture proved possible for some. Elsewhere, as in the southern United States, various forms of legally free but highly dependent labor, such as sharecropping, emerged to replace slavery and to provide low-paid and often indebted workers for planters.

The understandable reluctance of the formerly enslaved to continue working in plantation agriculture created labor shortages and set in motion a huge new wave of global migration in the form of indentured servitude. Men, women, and sometimes children who were unable to afford passage to the Americas signed contracts to serve for four to seven years in exchange for transportation and basic needs. Once the terms of the contract had been met, servants were allowed to leave the service of their masters. Nevertheless, in the terms of contract, indentured servants were considered the personal property of their master, and the contract could even be sold or inherited. Large numbers of indentured servants from India and China were imported into the Caribbean, Peru, South Africa, Hawaii, Malaya, and elsewhere to work in mines, on plantations, and in construction projects. There they often toiled in conditions not far removed from slavery itself.

Newly freed people did not achieve anything close to political equality, except in Haiti. White planters, farmers, and mine owners retained local authority in the Caribbean, where colonial rule persisted until well into the twentieth century. In the southern United States, a brief period of "radical reconstruction," during which newly freed Blacks did enjoy full political rights and some power, was followed by harsh segregation laws, denial of voting rights, a wave of lynchings, and a virulent racism that lasted well into the twentieth century. For most formerly enslaved people, emancipation usually meant "nothing but freedom."[21] Unlike the situation in the Americas, the end of serfdom in Russia transferred to the peasants a considerable portion of the nobles' land, but the need to pay for this land with "redemption dues" and the rapid growth of Russia's rural population ensured that most peasants remained impoverished and politically volatile. In both West and East Africa, the closing of the external slave trade decreased the price of enslaved people and increased their use within African societies to produce the export crops that the world economy now sought. Thus, as Europeans imposed colonial rule on Africa in the late nineteenth century, they loudly proclaimed their commitment to ending slavery in a continent from which they had extracted enslaved people for more than four centuries. This was surely among the more ironic outcomes of the abolitionist process.

In the Islamic world, where slavery had long been practiced and elaborately regulated, the freeing of enslaved people, though not required, was strongly recommended as a mark of piety. Some nineteenth-century Muslim authorities opposed slavery altogether on the grounds that it violated the Quran's ideals of freedom and equality. But unlike Europe and North America, the Islamic world generated no popular grassroots antislavery movements. There slavery was outlawed gradually only in the twentieth century under the pressure of international opinion.

AP®
COMPARISON
Compare the end of slavery in North America to the end of slavery in the Muslim world.

Nations and Nationalism

In addition to contributing to the end of slavery, the Atlantic revolutions also gave new prominence to a relatively recent kind of human community—the nation. By the end of the twentieth century, the idea that humankind was divided into separate nations, each with a distinct culture and territory and deserving an independent political life, was so widespread as to seem natural and timeless. And yet for most of human experience, states did not usually coincide with the culture of a particular people, for all the great empires and many smaller states governed culturally diverse societies. Few people considered rule by foreigners itself a terrible offense because the most important identities and loyalties were local, limited to clan, village, or region, with only modest connection to the larger state or empire that governed them. People might on occasion consider themselves part of larger religious communities (such as Christians or Muslims) or ethno-linguistic groupings such as Greek, Arab, or Maya, but such identities rarely provided the basis for enduring states.

All of that began to change during the era of Atlantic revolutions. Independence movements in both North and South America were made in the name of new nations. The French Revolution declared that sovereignty lay with "the people," and its leaders mobilized this people to defend the "French nation" against its external enemies. In 1793, the revolutionary government of France declared a mass conscription (*levée en masse*) with a stirring call to service:

AP®
CONTEXTUALIZATION
What accounts for the growth of nationalism as a powerful political and personal identity in the nineteenth century?

> Henceforth, until the enemies have been driven from the territory of the Republic, all the French are in permanent requisition for army service. The young men shall go to battle; the married men shall forge arms and transport provisions; the women shall make tents and clothes, and shall serve in the hospitals; the children shall turn old linen into lint; the old men shall repair to the public places, to stimulate the courage of the warriors and preach the unity of the Republic and the hatred of kings.[22]

TEACHING IDEA

Incorporating Outside Resources

In the episode *Samurai, Daimyo, Matthew Perry, and Nationalism* of Crash Course World History, John Green explains how nationalist leaders changed the way people thought of themselves and the places they lived by reinventing education, military service, and the relationship between government and governed. He looks at Japan's transformation into a modern nation-state. You can find the video on YouTube. After students watch the video, ask them to answer the following questions:

■ What regions experienced the power of nationalism in the late nineteenth century? *Germany; Italy; Turkey; Egypt; Greece; Christian Balkan states such as Bulgaria, Serbia, and Romania; the United States; British dominions such as Canada, Australia, and New Zealand; India; and China all experienced the power of nationalism in the late nineteenth century.*

■ What is the definition of the modern nation-state? *The modern nation-state is a centralized government that rules over a linguistically and culturally unified area.*

■ How did nationalism manifest in Japan? *External pressure from the United States bolstered internal calls to have a unified power ruling over a defined area. The emperor served the role of a mythical figure whose presence could be used to create a modern nation-state. As did other nation-states, Japan created a bureaucracy, a conscript army, compulsory education for all children, and infrastructure that facilitated communication and interaction. Japan also spent a lot of time expanding its territory, thus proving that nationalism thrives on conflict.*

APPLY THE TIP

Have students create a chart in their notes to keep track of the ways nationalism was promoted by political and cultural leaders. A reproducible version of this chart is available in the Teacher's Resource Materials. (Answers are provided in italics.)

AP EXAM TIP

Take notes on all the ways nationalism was promoted by political and cultural leaders.

Napoleon's conquests likewise stimulated national resistance in many parts of Europe. European states had long competed and fought with one another, but increasingly in the nineteenth century, those states were inhabited by people who felt themselves to be citizens of a nation, deeply bound to their fellows by ties of blood, culture, or common experience, not simply common subjects of a ruling dynasty. It was a novel form of political loyalty.

The rise of **nationalism** was also facilitated by Europe's modern transformation, as older identities and loyalties eroded. Science weakened the hold of religion on some. Migration to industrial cities or abroad diminished allegiance to local communities. At the same time, printing and the publishing industry standardized a variety of dialects into a smaller number of European languages, a process that allowed a growing reading public to think of themselves as members of a common linguistic group or nation. All of this encouraged political and cultural leaders to articulate appealing ideas of their particular nations and ensured a growing circle of people receptive to such ideas. Thus the idea of the "nation" was constructed or even invented, but it was often imagined and presented as a reawakening of older linguistic or cultural identities, and it certainly drew on the songs, dances, folktales, historical experiences, and collective memories of earlier cultures (see Map 7.4).

Whatever its precise origins, nationalism proved to be an infinitely flexible and enormously powerful idea in nineteenth-century Europe and beyond. It inspired the political unification of both Italy (1870) and Germany (1871), gathering their previously fragmented peoples into new states. It encouraged Greeks, Serbs, and Bulgarians to assert their independence from the Ottoman Empire; Czechs and Hungarians to demand more autonomy within the Austrian Empire; Poles and Ukrainians to become more aware of their oppression within the Russian Empire; and the Irish to seek "home rule" and separation from Great Britain. By the end of the nineteenth century, a small Zionist movement, seeking a homeland in Palestine, had emerged among Europe's frequently persecuted Jews.

Popular nationalism made the normal rivalry among European states even more acute and fueled a highly competitive drive for colonies in Asia and Africa. The immensity of the suffering and sacrifice that nationalism generated in Europe was vividly disclosed during the horrors of World War I. Furthermore, nationalism fueled rivalries among the various European-derived states in the Americas, reflected, for example, in the Mexican–United States War of 1846–1848 and the devastating conflict between Paraguay and the Triple Alliance of Argentina, Brazil, and Uruguay between 1864 and 1870, in which about half of Paraguay's population perished.

Governments throughout the Western world now claimed to act on behalf of their nations and deliberately sought to instill national loyalties in their citizens through schools, public rituals, the mass media, and military service. Russian authorities, for example, imposed the use of the Russian language, even in parts of the country where it was not widely spoken. They succeeded, however, only in producing a greater awareness of Ukrainian, Polish, and Finnish nationalism.

Promotion of Nationalism

Leader Name	Country	How Nationalism Was Promoted
Otto von Bismarck	Germany	*Policy of realpolitik, combining military power with diplomacy*
Count Camillo Cavour	Italy	*Diplomacy and Romanticized history of the Roman Empire*
Theodoros Kolokotronis	Greece	*War supported by Britain, France, and Russia to gain independence from Ottoman Empire*
Theodor Herzl	Zionism	*Desire for a homeland for Jews in Palestine to escape anti-Semitism in Europe*
Father Miguel Hidalgo	Mexico	*Peasant rebellion put down by Spanish and creoles. Creoles eventually took up the fight for independence.*

TRM Handout 7.3: Chart for Promotion of Nationalism

MAPPING HISTORY   Map 7.4 **The Nations and Empires of Europe, ca. 1880**

By the end of the nineteenth century, the national principle had substantially reshaped the map of Europe, especially in the unification of Germany and Italy. However, several major empires remained, each with numerous subject peoples who likewise sought national independence.

Reading the Map: In which regions of Europe were empires most prominent? Where did nation-states predominate? How might one generalize about the distribution of empires and nation-states in Europe around 1880?

AP **Making Connections:** Compare this map with Map 7.2: Napoleon's European Empire. What changed on the political map of Europe after the collapse of Napoleon's empire? What stayed the same?

EXPLORING AP® THEMES

Humans and the Environment (ENV)

Maps are a wonderful way to start a discussion about events that have occurred in history. Show students Map 7.4, "The Nations and Empires of Europe, ca. 1880." Then ask: Where in Europe are the nation-states? Where are the empires? *The nation-states are in Western Europe, and the multinational empires are in Eastern Europe.*

Continue using Map 7.4, "The Nations and Empires of Europe, ca. 1880," to discuss political changes with students. Ask students: How might geography have contributed to the push for more autonomy within the large empires? To answer the question, they should review pages 409–412 and use the map. *Ideas diffuse across borders, and the idea of nationalism was no exception. As educated elites in the Russian, Ottoman, and Austro-Hungarian empires became aware of these ideals, they pushed for more autonomy in their regions. The relatively short distance between the emerging European nation-states and the empires explains the quick diffusion of these ideas.*

As it became more prominent in the nineteenth century, nationalism took on a variety of political ideologies. Some supporters of liberal democracy and representative government, as in France or the United States, saw nationalism, with its emphasis on "the people," as an aid to their aspirations toward wider involvement in political life. Often called civic nationalism, such a view identified the nation with a particular territory and maintained that people of various cultural backgrounds could assimilate into the dominant culture, as in the process of "becoming American." Other versions of nationalism, in Germany, for example, sometimes defined the nation in racial terms that excluded those who did not share an imagined common ancestry, such as Jews. In the hands of conservatives, nationalism could be used to combat socialism and feminism, for those movements allegedly divided the nation along class or gender lines. Thus nationalism generated endless controversy because it provided no clear answer to the questions of who belonged to the nation or who should speak for it.

Nor was nationalism limited to the Euro-American world in the nineteenth century. An "Egypt for the Egyptians" movement arose in the 1870s as British and French intervention in Egyptian affairs deepened. When Japan likewise confronted European aggression in the second half of the nineteenth century, its long sense of itself as a distinct culture was readily transformed into an assertive modern nationalism. In British-ruled India, small groups of Western-educated men began to think of their enormously diverse country as a single nation. The Indian National Congress, established in 1885, gave expression to this idea. The notion of the Ottoman Empire as a Turkish national state rather than a Muslim or dynastic empire took hold among a few people. By the end of the nineteenth century, some Chinese intellectuals began to think in terms of a Chinese nation beset both by a foreign ruling dynasty and by predatory Europeans. Along the West African coast, the idea of an "African nation" stirred among a handful of formerly enslaved and missionary-educated men. And among the various Indigenous peoples in British-ruled New Zealand, a sense of Maori nationalism began to emerge from the 1850s on, assisted by Maori-language newspapers and expressed in the creation of a Maori king and a Maori parliament. These were early stirrings of what became in the twentieth century the powerful movements of Afro-Asian nationalisms.

Feminist Beginnings

A third echo of the Atlantic revolutions lay in the emergence of a feminist movement. Although scattered voices had earlier challenged patriarchy, never before had an organized and substantial group of women called into question this most fundamental and accepted feature of all preindustrial civilizations—the subordination of women to men. But in the century following the French Revolution, such a challenge took shape, especially in Europe and North America. Then, in the twentieth century all across the world, feminist thinking transformed "the way in which women and men work, play, think, dress, worship, vote, reproduce, make love and make war."[23] How did this extraordinary process get launched in the nineteenth century?

Nineteenth-Century Feminist Leaders and Groups	Actions and Achievements
Mary Wollstonecraft	*Vindication of the Rights of Woman, earliest expression of feminist consciousness*
Elizabeth Cady Stanton	*Women's Rights Convention in Seneca Falls, NY: the first organized expression of feminism*
Western feminists	*Focused on suffrage in the earliest years of their movement*
Women and the world before World War I	*By World War I, French feminists numbered around 100,000, and there were over 2 million members in the National American Woman Suffrage Association (a peaceful organization advocating for the right to vote for women)*
Women's Social and Political Union	*British organization that organized a campaign of violence to try to bring attention to the suffragist movement*

TRM Handout 7.4: Chart for Feminist Movements and Leaders

Nationalism in Poland In the eighteenth century, Poland had been divided among Prussia, Austria, and Russia and disappeared as a separate and independent state. Polish nationalism found expression in the nineteenth century in a series of revolts against Poland's Russian occupiers. This painting shows Russian officers surrendering their standards to Polish insurgents during the November Uprising of 1830. The revolt was subsequently crushed, and Poland regained its independence as a nation-state only in 1918 at the end of World War I. (ullstein bild/Granger, NYC—All rights reserved)

▲ AP®

CLAIMS AND EVIDENCE IN SOURCING

How were images, such as the one shown here, used to promote nationalism?

Thinkers of the European Enlightenment had challenged many ancient traditions, including on occasion that of women's intrinsic inferiority (see "Science and Enlightenment" in Chapter 5). The French writer Condorcet, for example, called for "the complete destruction of those prejudices that have established an inequality of rights between the sexes." The French Revolution then raised the possibility of re-creating human societies on new foundations. Many women participated in these events, and a few insisted, unsuccessfully, that the revolutionary ideals of liberty and equality must include women. In neighboring England, the French Revolution stimulated the writer Mary Wollstonecraft to pen her famous *Vindication of the Rights of Woman* in 1792, one of the earliest expressions of a feminist consciousness. "Who made man the exclusive judge," she asked, "if woman partake with him of the gift of reason?"

TEACHING IDEA

Incorporating Outside Resources

For a different look at the women's rights movement and how it was a part of modern life in Europe, you can show students the Crash Course European History episode *Modern Life*. In this episode, John Green discusses what life was like in the rapidly growing urban centers of Europe, how new access to information influenced how people saw their leaders and neighbors, and how the women's rights movement made strides toward equality. You can find the video by searching for it on YouTube. Ask students to answer the following questions, either as they watch the video or after they watch it.

■ What contributed to Europe's population growth in the nineteenth century? *Breakthroughs like pasteurization and a better understanding of germs led to lower childhood mortality and increased life spans, and better sanitation made it less likely for people to die of diseases like cholera.*

■ How did women start to leave the household (and their traditional positions in society) during this time? *Laboring-class women were working in factories while middle-class women also began to take jobs in the service sector as secretaries, telegram operators, teachers, and nurses.*

■ What changes did women demand from society in the nineteenth century? *Women wanted legal ownership of their wages and other property, access to higher education, the right to divorce and have custody of their children after divorce, the abolition of slavery, improved working conditions in factories, support for the temperance movement, and civil rights for prostitutes.*

■ Why shouldn't the women's rights movement be considered an entirely middle-class movement? *Working-class women also participated in the movement by advocating for labor unions or social democratic parties to do more for women.*

■ When did women start to gain the right to vote around the world? *New Zealand granted women the right to vote in 1897, Australia granted the right in 1902, Finland in 1906 (the first European state to do so), and Norway in 1913. Women in the United States and Great Britain did not gain the right to vote until after World War I.*

AP®
CONTINUITY AND CHANGE
What were the achievements and limitations of nineteenth-century feminism?

AP® EXAM TIP
Be aware that the nineteenth-century women's suffrage movement became a transatlantic movement.

Within the growing middle classes of industrializing societies, more women found both educational opportunities and some freedom from household drudgery. Such women increasingly took part in temperance movements, charities, abolitionism, and missionary work, as well as socialist and pacifist organizations. Some of their working-class sisters became active trade unionists. On both sides of the Atlantic, small numbers of these women began to develop a feminist consciousness that viewed women as individuals with rights equal to those of men. The first organized expression of this new feminism took place at the Women's Rights Convention in Seneca Falls, New York, in 1848. At that meeting, **Elizabeth Cady Stanton** drafted a statement that began by paraphrasing the Declaration of Independence: "We hold these truths to be self-evident, that all men and women are created equal."

From the beginning, feminism became a transatlantic movement in which European and American women attended the same conferences, corresponded regularly, and read one another's work. Access to schools, universities, and the professions were among their major concerns as growing numbers of women sought these previously unavailable opportunities. The more radical among them refused to take their husbands' surname or wore trousers under their skirts. Elizabeth Cady Stanton published a Women's Bible, excising the parts she found offensive. As heirs to the French Revolution, feminists ardently believed in progress and insisted that it must now include a radical transformation of the position of women.

By the 1870s, feminist movements in the West were focusing primarily on the issue of suffrage and were gaining a growing constituency. Now many ordinary middle-class housewives and working-class mothers joined their better-educated sisters in the movement. By 1914, some 100,000 women took part in French feminist organizations, while the National American Woman Suffrage Association claimed 2 million members. Most operated through peaceful protest and persuasion, but the British Women's Social and Political Union organized a campaign of violence that included blowing up railroad stations, slashing works of art, and smashing department store windows. One British activist, Emily Davison, threw herself in front of the king's horse during a race in Britain in 1913 and was trampled to death. By the beginning of the twentieth century in the most highly industrialized countries of the West, the women's movement had become a mass movement.

That movement had some effect. By 1900, upper- and middle-class women had gained entrance to universities, though in small numbers, and women's literacy rates were growing steadily. In the United States, a number of states passed legislation allowing women to manage and control their own property and wages, separate from their husbands. Divorce laws were liberalized in some places. Professions such as medicine opened to a few, and teaching beckoned to many more. In Britain, Florence Nightingale professionalized nursing and attracted thousands of women into it, while Jane Addams in the United States virtually invented "social work," which also became a female-dominated profession. Progress was slower in the political domain. In 1893, New Zealand became the first country to give the vote to all adult women; Finland followed in 1906. Elsewhere widespread voting rights for women in national elections

---

APPLY THE TIP

Consider having a quick class discussion on how the nineteenth-century women's suffrage movement was a transatlantic movement and how social classes influenced who participated in the movement. You could make this a whole-class discussion or break the class up into smaller groups (four or five students) to discuss the questions. If you break the class up into smaller groups, bring the class back together at the end to share what they discussed.

■ What evidence supports the idea that the nineteenth-century women's suffrage movement was a transatlantic movement? *European and American women attended the same conferences, corresponded with one another frequently to share ideas, and read one another's work.*

■ How did social class influence who participated in the women's suffrage movement? *The movement was made up of mostly upper- and middle-class women because they had the time to attend rallies and protest as well as the opportunity to get an education.*

were not achieved until after World War I, in 1920 in the United States, and in France not until 1945.

Beyond these concrete accomplishments, the movement prompted an unprecedented discussion about the role of women in modern society. In Henrik Ibsen's play *A Doll's House* (1879), the heroine, Nora, finding herself in a loveless and oppressive marriage, leaves both her husband and her children. European audiences were riveted, and many were outraged. Writers, doctors, and journalists addressed previously taboo sexual topics, including homosexuality and birth control. Socialists too found themselves divided about women's issues. Did the women's movement distract from the class solidarity that Marxism proclaimed, or did it provide added energy to the workers' cause? Feminists themselves disagreed about the proper basis for women's rights. Some took their stand on the modern idea of human equality: "Whatever is right for a man is right for a woman." Others, particularly in France, based their claims more on the distinctive role of women as mothers. "It is above all this holy function of motherhood," wrote one advocate of **maternal feminism**, "which requires that women watch over the futures of their children and gives women the right to intervene not only in all acts of civil life, but also in all acts of political life."[24]

Not surprisingly, feminism provoked bitter opposition. Some academic and medical experts argued that the strains of education and life outside the home would cause serious reproductive damage and as a consequence depopulate the nation. Thus feminists were viewed as selfish, willing to sacrifice the family or even the nation while pursuing their individual goals. Some saw suffragists as "a foreign body in our national life," much as they viewed Jews and socialists. Never before in any society had such a passionate and public debate about the position of women erupted. It was a novel feature of Western historical experience in the aftermath of the Atlantic revolutions.

Like nationalism, a concern with women's rights spread beyond Western Europe and North America, though less widely. An overtly feminist newspaper was established in Brazil in 1852, and an independent school for girls was founded in Mexico in 1869. A handful of Japanese women and men, including the empress Haruko, raised issues about marriage, family planning, and especially education as the country began its modernizing process after 1868, but the state soon cracked

Women's Suffrage Suffragists in Britain frequently faced arrest while promoting their cause. This photograph taken in 1914 documents the arrest of Emmeline Pankhurst, leader of the British suffragists, outside Buckingham Palace in London when she tried to deliver a petition to King George V. Some imprisoned suffragists went on hunger strikes to force the authorities to respond to their demands and were met with brutal efforts at forcible feeding by prison officials. (IWM/Getty Images)

▲ **AP®**
SOURCING AND SITUATION
Identify a possible purpose for the publication of this picture in 1914.

AP® EXAM TIP
It's important to recognize that, as with all major movements promoting social change, feminism had opposition.

TEACHING IDEA
Incorporating Outside Resources

If you want to do a fun little activity with students that also has a nostalgia element, think about showing students the song "Sister Suffragette" from the film *Mary Poppins*. Play the song for students, either by showing it on Disney+ or by listening to it on a streaming service like Spotify, and have them list all of the ideas and people they've learned about from the "Feminist Beginnings" section that they hear in the song. You can also point out that the Mrs. Pankhurst mentioned in the song is the same woman in the image on page 415.

APPLY THE TIP

Students need to be able to identify counter arguments on the AP® Exam, such as a question about the feminist movement. To help students with this task, ask them to use the information on this page to describe the opposition to feminism in the nineteenth century. *Medical experts argued that the strains of education and life in the outside world would cause reproductive damage. Feminists were viewed as selfish women who were willing to sacrifice the family or even the nation while pursuing their individual goals. Others saw suffragists as a "foreign body in our national life."*

EXPLORING AP® THEMES

Social Interactions and Organization (SIO)

As students read through the last paragraph on page 414, have them make a list in their notes of the specific demands that women in the nineteenth-century feminist movement succeeded in getting. *Women secured access to universities, management and control of property and wages, liberalization of divorce laws, the ability to work outside the home (especially in education, nursing, and social work), and the right to vote. Female literacy also grew.*

ZOOMING IN   Kartini: Feminism and Nationalism in Java

The ideas of the European Enlightenment and the Atlantic revolutions resonated deeply in the life of a remarkable young Javanese woman named Kartini during the late nineteenth century, when her country was part of the Dutch East Indies (now Indonesia).[25] Born in 1879 into a large aristocratic Javanese family, young Kartini attended a Dutch elementary school, where she learned the Dutch language and observed the relative freedom of her European classmates, in sharp contrast to the constraints and ritualized interactions of her own family. At the age of twelve, in keeping with Javanese Muslim custom, Kartini was abruptly removed from her school. For the next four years, she never left her home.

Through her father, a high official in the Dutch colonial administration who much admired Western education, Kartini still had access to Dutch books, and later she was tutored by several Europeans, including one woman with strong socialist and feminist leanings. She also read widely on her own and began an extensive correspondence, largely with Dutch friends in the Netherlands, that lasted until her death. By the time she was twenty, Kartini had acquired an impressive Western education and a network of relationships with prominent Europeans both in the Netherlands and in Java.

From her letters, we learn something of Kartini's thinking. In light of her exposure to Europeans and European thought, she found the absolute subordination of Javanese women completely unacceptable. The seclusion of girls, the total separation of the sexes, the absence of educational opportunities—all of this drove her almost to despair. "Are fine women of no use to civilization?" she asked. But it was the prospect of a traditional high-class Javanese marriage that she found most appalling. Her husband would be "a stranger, an unknown man, whom my parents would choose for me . . . without my knowledge." During the wedding ceremony, she would be expected to prostrate herself before the bridegroom and kiss his feet as a sign of her future submission. Even then, she would be only one of several wives. "Do you understand now," she wrote to a Dutch confidant, "the deep aversion I have for marriage?"

Kartini was equally outraged by particular features of Dutch colonial rule, especially its racism. Conscious of her membership in a "despised brown race," she deplored the need for "creeping in the dust" before Europeans. Javanese generally were not supposed to speak Dutch with their colonial masters, as if "Dutch is too beautiful to be spoken by a brown mouth." And yet, for Kartini, it was Dutch education and its universal Enlightenment values—"freedom, equality, fraternity," as she put it, echoing the slogan of the French Revolution—that would lead to Javanese emancipation from both Dutch and Javanese oppression. "Europe will teach us to be truly free," she wrote.

APPLY THE TIP

It's important for students to know that the feminist movement was not just limited to Western Europe and the United States. Have students work in groups of three to four to create a list of countries where feminism spread and the specific ways feminism manifested itself in those places. (Answers are provided in italics.)

■ *Brazil: A feminist newspaper was established.*

■ *Mexico: A school for girls was founded.*

■ *Japan: Women, including the empress, raised issues about marriage, family planning, and especially education, but the state quickly cracked down on women's rights.*

■ *Russia: Women helped target the tsarist regime.*

■ *Islamic world and China: Some modernists believed that a higher status for women would be important for strengthening the independence movements.*

AP® EXAM TIP
Pay attention to these examples of nineteenth-century feminism beyond the West.

down firmly, forbidding women from joining political parties or even attending political meetings. In Russia, the most radical feminist activists operated within socialist or anarchist circles, targeting the oppressive tsarist regime. Within the Islamic world and in China, some modernists came to believe that education and a higher status for women strengthened the nation in its struggles for development and independence and therefore deserved support. (See Zooming In: Kartini, for an example from the Dutch East Indies.) Huda Sharawi, founder of the first feminist organization in Egypt, returned to Cairo in 1923 from an international conference in Italy and threw her veil into the sea. Many upper-class Egyptian women soon followed her example.

Nowhere did nineteenth-century feminism have thoroughly revolutionary consequences. But as an outgrowth of the French and Industrial revolutions, it raised issues that echoed repeatedly and more loudly in the century that followed.

Nonetheless, Kartini openly embraced much of her own culture—its art, music, and poetry; its regard for the dead; its hospitality to the poor; its spiritual depth—and she certainly did not seek to transform Javanese into "half-Europeans." But she did believe that "contact with another civilization" and modern European education in particular would enable Javanese "to develop the fine qualities that are peculiar to their race." "Emancipation is in the air," she declared in early 1901.

Kartini's fondest hope was to contribute to that emancipation by studying in the Netherlands and then opening a school for girls in Java. But these grand dreams were thwarted by opposition from her own family, from Javanese officials, and from much of the Dutch colonial bureaucracy. Java's leading newspaper denounced her intentions as "outrageous," and local gossip had it that she simply wanted to marry a European and become a Europeanized woman. A backup plan to study in the colonial capital of Batavia likewise came to naught with a sudden announcement

photo: Royal Tropical Institute

Kartini.

in mid-1903 that her father had arranged for her to be married to a much older and polygamous man of her social class. Kartini was devastated. "My crown has fallen from my head. My golden illusions of purity and chastity lie shattered in the dust.... Now I am nothing more than all the rest."[26]

Although Kartini felt that she was "done with all personal happiness," she determined to make her marriage a model for the future, actually meeting her husband before the wedding and extracting from him a written promise that she could continue with her plans to create a school for girls. But she soon became pregnant, and four days after the birth of her son in 1904, she died at the age of twenty-five. As her writings subsequently became known in Indonesia, Kartini came to be regarded as a pioneer of both feminist and nationalist thinking, and a number of "Kartini schools" were established in her memory.

QUESTION

In what ways was Kartini's life shaped by living at the intersection of Javanese and European worlds?

AP® CLASSROOM

AP® Exam Questions

The Question Bank in AP® Classroom has a great set of questions about Kartini and feminism in Java for students to use as multiple-choice practice. You could have students read the "Zooming In" on Kartini on pages 416 and 417 to prepare to answer those questions. Then give them the question set to answer either in AP® Classroom or printed out on paper. You can find the three questions in the set by searching for "Kartini" in the Question Bank.

CONCLUSIONS AND REFLECTIONS

Pondering the Outcomes of Revolutions

Finding the Main Point: What political or moral issues arise as historians consider the Atlantic revolutions?

Revolutions change things, but not always the same things and not always quickly or permanently. Political life, for example, changed in each of the four locations of the Atlantic revolutions. In the United States, Haiti, and Latin America, political ties to a colonial power were broken, while in France the execution of Louis XVI ended the monarchy. Furthermore, all of these revolutions nurtured nationalist sentiments and loyalties both within and outside those nations. In the Americas, struggles against British, French, Spanish, or Portuguese rule emphasized the distinctive features of

AP® EXAM TIP

On the AP® Exam, you may be asked the extent to which a revolution was truly revolutionary or instead part of a gradual process.

APPLY THE TIP

Consider having students watch the short video *Really a Revolution* from the History channel. This video deals with misconceptions about the American Revolution and can help students understand the difference between a true revolution and a gradual process. You can find the video by searching for it on the History channel website.

After students watch the video, you could also have a class discussion or debate on the major revolutions in this chapter and on whether they were really revolutionary based on the video's definition.

Students should be able to recognize that the revolutions did not have the support of every person and also understand why different groups of people supported or opposed the revolutions. You can help them think about the reasoning of these different groups by asking students:

■ What benefits did the revolutionaries see in fighting the Atlantic revolutions? *The revolutions represented an opening to new worlds of human possibility, while sweeping away old worlds of oppression, exploitation, and privilege. Modern revolutionaries acted on the basis of Enlightenment ideas, believing that the structure of human societies was not forever ordained by God or tradition and that it was both possible and necessary to reconstruct these societies. They saw themselves as correcting ancient and enduring injustices.*

■ Why would some people choose to oppose the revolutions? *Opponents of revolutions used numerous arguments to explain why they didn't support the revolutions. For example, conservatives generally viewed human societies not as machines whose parts could be easily rearranged but as organisms that evolved slowly. Efforts at radical and sudden change only invited disaster, as seen in the French and Haitian revolutions, and worried some about what could happen to their country if a revolution occurred. Critics also charged that revolutions were largely unnecessary since societies were changing before the revolutions started. Thus, they argued that slavery would have ended in Haiti, and the brutal rebellion caused more economic and social harm in the long run than allowing slavery to end "naturally" would have.*

A good way to wrap up the Atlantic revolutions is to ask students to create a simple chart comparing the outcomes of the revolutions, like the one below. You can find a reproducible version of this chart in the Teacher's Resource Materials.

particular colonized peoples as they emerged into independent nationhood. The French Revolution roused its people to defend the French nation against its enemies, while French aggression under Napoleon stimulated national resistance in many countries.

The social outcomes of revolution were more varied. French revolutionaries ended what legal privileges remained to the aristocracy, opening opportunities to men of talent from the lower classes. In Haiti a successful slave revolt completely upended the social order, as the last became first. In North and Latin America, however, no such dramatic social changes occurred, although in the United States, the gradual extension of democracy allowed some white men to rise in political and social life.

Almost everywhere, the aftermath of revolutions produced disappointment as they generated unfulfilled expectations. Women were surely among the most disappointed, for nowhere did they benefit substantially from these revolutions. But the ideas of the revolutions—freedom and equality—percolated in society and inspired later feminist movements, which did begin to alter the social life of women. Even the right to vote, however, had to await the twentieth century for most women.

Except in Haiti, these revolutions also bitterly disappointed enslaved people who expected to gain their freedom as a result of these upheavals. The abolitionist movement that drew on the revolutions' ideas of freedom and equality faced fierce opposition from slaveholders. In the United States a bitter and bloody civil war finally put an end to slavery in that country, but most formerly enslaved people remained impoverished, and their descendants long suffered from a deeply rooted racism. Poverty, dependence, and political instability persisted long after the revolution in Haiti as well, which surely led to some disappointment among its people.

In France, revolutionaries expecting the complete eradication of the monarchy were disappointed when Napoleon declared himself "emperor" in 1802. He was just the first in a series of emperors who ruled France on and off until 1870. In Latin America the failure to unite its various regions as the British colonies of North America did was among the chief disappointments.

Were the benefits of revolution worth the cost in blood, treasure, and disruption? Opinions obviously differed. Many revolutionaries acted on the basis of Enlightenment ideas, believing that the structure of human societies was not forever ordained by God or tradition and that it was both possible and necessary to reconstruct those societies. They saw themselves as correcting ancient and enduring injustices. To those who complained about the violence of revolutions, supporters pointed to the violence that maintained the status quo and the unwillingness of favored classes to accommodate changes that threatened those unjust privileges. It was persistent injustice that made revolution necessary and perhaps inevitable.

To their victims, critics, and opponents, revolutions appeared in a quite different light. Conservatives generally viewed human societies not as machines whose parts could be easily rearranged but as organisms that evolved slowly. Efforts at radical and sudden change only invited disaster, as the unrestrained violence of the French Revolution at its height demonstrated. The brutality and bitterness of the Haitian Revolution arguably contributed to the unhappy future of that country. Furthermore, critics charged that revolutions were largely unnecessary because societies were in fact changing. France

AP®
MAKING CONNECTIONS
How did those opposed to revolutionary activity use events of the period to justify their position?

	Similarities	Differences
Political Outcomes	■ Political ties to a colonial power or a monarchy were broken by the revolutions. ■ Revolutions supported nationalist sentiments and loyalties both within and outside the new nations. ■ New governments based on Enlightenment ideals were established in all of the new nations.	■ The United States, Haiti, and Latin America emphasized the unique features of their particular colonial peoples as they became independent nations. ■ France had to struggle to defend the new nation against its enemies after the revolution and saw a return to monarchy when Napoleon declared himself "emperor" in 1802. ■ Latin America struggled to unify its various regions like the United States did following their revolution.
Social Outcomes	■ Women in all of the new nations did not benefit substantially from the revolutions. ■ Enslaved people did not gain freedom from the revolutions, except in Haiti.	■ No dramatic social change happened in the United States or Latin America, while France and Haiti dramatically changed their social orders. ■ Unlike Latin America, the United States did gradually extend democracy to allow some white men to rise in political and social life.

TRM Handout 7.6: Comparison Chart for Outcomes of Revolutions was becoming a modern society, and feudalism was largely gone well before the revolution exploded. Slavery was ended peacefully in many places, nonviolent protest made many gains for women, and democratic reform proceeded gradually throughout the nineteenth century. Was this not a preferable alternative to revolutionary upheaval?

Such debates persisted into the twentieth century and beyond as revolutions in Mexico, Russia, China, Vietnam, Cuba, and elsewhere raised many of the same questions.

CHAPTER REVIEW

AP Key Terms

American Revolution, 391

Declaration of the Rights of Man and Citizen, 395

French Revolution, 395

Robespierre, 396

Napoleon Bonaparte, 398

Haitian Revolution, 401

Latin American revolutions, 402

Hidalgo-Morelos rebellion, 403

Tupac Amaru, 404

Great Jamaica Revolt, 406

abolitionist movement, 407

nationalism, 410

Vindication of the Rights of Woman, 413

Elizabeth Cady Stanton, 414

maternal feminism, 415

Finding the Main Point

1. What was distinctive about the Atlantic revolutions in comparison to other upheavals during the long nineteenth century?
2. What were the major causes and effects of the American Revolution?
3. In what ways was the French Revolution a more profound and transformative upheaval than its North American counterpart?
4. What were the goals of the main groups fighting in the Haitian Revolution?
5. In what ways did the Latin American revolutions differ from their North American counterpart?
6. In what ways did the experience and values of the Atlantic revolutions stimulate major change in the world of the nineteenth century?
7. What political or moral issues arise as historians consider the Atlantic revolutions?

AP Big Picture Questions

1. What was the role of oppression and injustice, the weakening of political authorities, new ideas, or the activities of small groups of determined activists in fomenting the Atlantic revolutions?
2. "The influence of revolutions endured long after they ended and far beyond where they started." To what extent does this chapter support or undermine this idea?
3. Did the Atlantic revolutions fulfill or betray the goals of those who made them? Consider this question in both short- and long-term perspectives.
4. **Looking Back** To what extent did the Atlantic revolutions reflect the influence of early modern historical developments (1450–1750)?

TRM Suggested Responses to Questions
You can find suggested responses to the Chapter Review questions in the Teacher's Resource Materials.

TEACHING IDEA

Exit Ticket

An easy way to check for understanding is to ask students to write down one concept that stood out to them from each of the following revolutions. Have students turn in their answers as they leave class. (Sample answers are provided in italics.)

■ **American Revolution:** *First successful war for independence. Only example of colonies uniting into a country. First application of Enlightenment ideals.*

■ **French Revolution:** *Influence reverberated worldwide. In the radical phase, revolutionaries sought to expunge the legacy of nobility and church power. Under Napoleon, the concept of a citizen army was applied as he expanded the French territory into an empire.*

■ **Haitian Revolution:** *Direct descendant of the French Revolution. Became a violent rebellion of enslaved people and as such horrified the Latin American and American elite. Eventually led to the end of slavery, as the price of slavery was seen as much greater than the benefits.*

■ **Latin American revolutions:** *Leaders had to walk a fine line between empowering the lower classes and ensuring that there would not be a large-scale revolt as in Haiti. Simón Bolívar hoped to follow in American footsteps by creating the country of Gran Colombia, but this dream did not materialize.*

Making Connections: Comparison

Considering the incredible breadth of world history in terms of civilizations, cultures, environments, and traditions, it is no wonder that comparison is a key skill for understanding the history of our world. How better to draw connections, while acknowledging differences? In this workshop, we will learn how to create an effective comparison and work toward creating a specific type of historical argument: the comparative argument.

BUILDING AP® SKILLS

Making Connections: Comparison

The skill of Comparison might be the easiest skill for students to work with throughout the year, but students can still struggle with applying it to what they have learned or to AP® Exam questions. The AP® Skills Workshop on pages 420 to 422 has a good overview of how historians use comparison in their writing and how students can mimic that use in their own writing. You can have students read through "Understanding Comparison" and then complete Activity 1 on page 421 to work on identifying how historians indicate comparisons in their writing.

Differentiation

If your students have a good grasp of the skill of comparison, consider using the "Must Do, Should Do, Strive For" model below to help them use those skills in their own writing.

■ Must Do: Students complete the chart for Activity 1: Identifying a Comparison.

■ Should Do: Students complete Activity 2 to practice thesis writing skills. They can either use the template provided to write their thesis or use their own method to write their thesis.

■ Strive For: Students write an LEQ-style paragraph using the prompt in Activity 3.

UNDERSTANDING COMPARISON

You are probably very familiar with the skill of comparison, but let's start by defining it:

Comparison: Identifying similarities and differences in two or more things

Notice that the definition mentions both similarities and differences. In AP® World History, contrasting things is also part of the comparison process. This often means comparing two civilizations or sources, in which case your job will be to discuss how they are similar or different, and why the similarities and differences are significant to our understanding of history.

When encountering a comparison question, students sometimes have a tendency to list the aspects of Thing A in one paragraph and then list the aspects of Thing B in another. While the commonalities and differences might be obvious based on those two lists, that isn't a comparison. It is your job as the historian to analyze those two sets of information, point out the commonalities and differences for your audience, and talk about why they're interesting or important. If you don't discuss similarities and differences, it's not an effective comparison.

Here is how the authors of this book compare the effects of the Atlantic revolutions between 1750 and 1900:

Claim of comparison / Evidence supporting comparison - difference / Claim of comparison / Evidence supporting comparison - similarity

Revolutions change things, but not always the same things and not always quickly or permanently. Political life, for example, changed in each of the four locations of the Atlantic revolutions. In the United States, Haiti, and Latin America, political ties to a colonial power were broken, while in France the execution of Louis XVI ended the monarchy. Furthermore, all of these revolutions nurtured nationalist sentiments and loyalties both within and outside those nations. In the Americas, struggles against British, French, Spanish, or Portuguese rule emphasized the distinctive features of particular colonized peoples as they emerged into independent nationhood. The French Revolution roused its people to defend the French nation against its enemies, while French aggression under Napoleon stimulated national resistance in many countries.

420

The social outcomes of revolution were more varied. French revolutionaries ended what legal privileges remained to the aristocracy, opening opportunities to men of talent from the lower classes. In Haiti a successful slave revolt completely upended the social order, as the last became first. In North and Latin America, however, no such dramatic social changes occurred, although in the United States, the gradual extension of democracy allowed some white men to rise in political and social life.

Claim of Comparison

Evidence supporting comparison - difference

As you can see, the point of a comparison is to explain similarities and differences. The authors do not simply list similarities and differences but organize them thematically. First, they compare political effects and then the social effects of the Atlantic revolutions. You should organize your writing in a similar way.

COMPARISON ON THE AP® WORLD HISTORY EXAM

On the AP® Exam, the historical thinking skill of comparison will be tested in a variety of ways. A set of Multiple-Choice Questions could ask you to compare two stimulus items (such as maps or artifacts), and you would need to indicate how they are similar or different. For a Short-Answer Question, you could be given a set of data or other information to compare. Last, and most important, you could be asked to create your own comparative argument on the Long Essay Question or the Document-Based Question.

BUILDING AP® SKILLS

1. **Activity: Identifying a Comparison.** Reread the paragraph below, found on page 405. What are the key words or phrases in these sentences that tell you it is a comparison? Then, use a chart like the one below to record which words indicate that the authors are using comparison in order to understand the similarities and differences in the development of North and South America after their respective independence movements:

   The aftermath of independence in Latin America marked a reversal in the earlier relationship of the two American continents. The United States, which began its history as the leftover "dregs" of the New World, grew increasingly wealthy, industrialized, democratic, internationally influential, and generally stable, with the major exception of the Civil War. The Spanish colonies, which took shape in the wealthiest areas and among the most sophisticated cultures of the Americas, were widely regarded as the more promising region compared to England's North American territories, which had a backwater reputation. But in the nineteenth century, as newly independent countries in both regions launched a new phase of their histories, those in Latin America became relatively underdeveloped, impoverished, undemocratic, politically unstable, and dependent on foreign technology and investment.

Phrases indicating similarities	Phrases indicating differences

TRM **Suggested Responses to Questions**

You can find suggested responses to the Building AP® Skills questions in the Teacher's Resource Materials.

421

2. **Activity: Comparison Thesis.** Read through the "Nations and Nationalism" section (pages 409–412) and create a thesis using the template below for the following prompt:

Compare the effects of nationalist movements in two European states between 1750 and 1900.

Template: Although the effects of nationalist movements between 1750 and 1900 in _____ and _____ were similar in that they both _____, they differed in that the nationalist movement in _____ led to _____ while the nationalist movement in _____ led to _____.

3. **Activity: Creating a Comparison.** Using the information from the chapter, write a comparative paragraph in response to the following prompt:

To what extent were the causes of the political revolutions in North America, France, Haiti, and/or Latin America similar or different?

Make sure that you create an evaluative claim that clearly conveys both similarities and differences, while emphasizing which you believe is most significant. Try to organize your comparisons thematically using political, economic, and/or social themes.

Defining Rights in the United States and France

In this activity, you will compare two of the most famous, influential, and wide-ranging expressions of the fundamental rights of citizens created during the Atlantic revolutions—the U.S. Bill of Rights and the French Declaration of the Rights of Man and Citizen. The Bill of Rights was drawn up in 1789 as a series of amendments to safeguard in law the rights of American citizens vis-à-vis their new government, whose structure and powers had been recently established by the ratification of the U.S. Constitution. Also emerging in 1789 was the Declaration of the Rights of Man and Citizen, composed in the French National Assembly during the opening weeks of the French Revolution. In 1791 it became the preamble of the French Constitution, which set out the powers and structures of a new government for France. While comparing how these two documents define the universal liberties enjoyed by citizens, pay particular attention to the different approaches that their authors take to expressing these fundamental rights.

1 A FIRST LOOK

To start, read these extracts from the U.S. Bill of Rights and answer the following questions:

1. According to the preamble, why was the Bill of Rights created?

2. What specific rights are protected by Amendments I and IV?

3. How exactly are these rights expressed? Note the use of negative wording like "no" and "shall not" in these articles. Why do you think that the drafters of the Bill of Rights chose to express the rights of citizens in this way?

U.S. Bill of Rights | 1789

Preamble

The Conventions of a number of the States, having at the time of their adopting the Constitution, expressed a desire, in order to prevent misconstruction or abuse of its powers, that further declaratory and restrictive clauses should be added: And as extending the ground of public confidence in the Government, will best ensure the beneficent ends of its institution.

Amendment I

Congress shall make no law respecting an establishment of religion, or prohibiting the free exercise thereof; or abridging the freedom of speech, or of the press; or the right of the people peaceably to assemble, and to petition the Government for a redress of grievances.

Amendment IV

The right of the people to be secure in their persons, houses, papers, and effects, against unreasonable searches and seizures, shall not be violated, and no Warrants shall issue, but

TRM Suggested Responses to Questions
You can find suggested responses to the AP® Looking Again questions in the Teacher's Resource Materials.

BUILDING AP® SKILLS

Claims and Evidence in Sources

Students are probably familiar with most of the rights granted to them by the Bill of Rights in the U.S. Constitution. It could be interesting to have them compare the rights given to citizens in the U.S. Bill of Rights to the rights given in the French Declaration of the Rights of Man and Citizen using the "AP® Looking Again" activity on pages 423 to 425. Have students read through the excerpts from the U.S. Bill of Rights and the French Declaration of the Rights of Man and Citizen and answer the questions under "A First Look" on page 423 and "A Second Look" on page 424 on their own. Once they are finished, partner the students up and have them work together to answer the questions under "A Third Look" on page 425.

423

upon probable cause, supported by Oath or affirmation, and particularly describing the place to be searched, and the persons or things to be seized.

2 A SECOND LOOK

Now read these extracts from the Declaration of the Rights of Man and Citizen and answer the following:

1. According to the preamble, why did the French National Assembly compose the declaration?

2. What specific rights does the declaration define?

Declaration of the Rights of Man and Citizen | 1789

Preamble

The representatives of the French people, constituted as a National Assembly, and considering that ignorance, neglect, or contempt of the rights of man are the sole causes of public misfortunes and governmental corruption, have resolved to set forth in a solemn declaration the natural, inalienable and sacred rights of man. . . .

1. Men are born and remain free and equal in rights. Social distinctions may be based only on common utility.

2. The purpose of all political association is the preservation of the natural and imprescriptible rights of man. These rights are liberty, property, security, and resistance to oppression.

4. Liberty consists in the ability to do whatever does not harm another; hence the exercise of the natural rights of each man has no other limits than those which assure to other members of society the enjoyment of the same rights. These limits can only be determined by the law.

5. The law only has the right to prohibit those actions which are injurious to society. No hindrance should be put in the way of anything not prohibited by the law, nor may any one be forced to do what the law does not require.

10. No one should be disturbed for his opinions, even in religion, provided that their manifestation does not trouble public order as established by law.

11. The free communication of thoughts and opinions is one of the most precious of the rights of man. Every citizen may therefore speak, write, and print freely, if he accepts his own responsibility for any abuse of this liberty in the cases set by the law.

17. Property being an inviolable and sacred right, no one may be deprived of it except when public necessity, certified by law, obviously requires it, and on the condition of a just compensation in advance.

Source: *The French Revolution and Human Rights: A Brief Documentary History*, edited, translated, and with an Introduction by Lynn Hunt (Boston: Bedford/St. Martin's, 1996).

3 A THIRD LOOK

Now let's compare these two efforts to articulate and claim the "rights of man" by considering these questions:

1. What particular rights do the two documents share?

2. From what sources do they see threats to these rights?

3. In what different ways do these sources frame or express their concern about rights?

AP° ACTIVITY CONTEXTUALIZING PRIMARY SOURCES

In understanding primary sources, historians pay close attention to the historical circumstances in which those sources were created. The Bill of Rights and the Declaration of the Rights of Man and Citizen arose in different contexts. The Bill of Rights was drafted after the American revolutionaries had prevailed over the British and the American Constitution had been drafted and ratified by the states. The Declaration of the Rights of Man and Citizen was drafted at the opening of the French Revolution before a new government was established. In a paragraph or two, describe how these different contexts are reflected in how rights were expressed in the two documents. You may want to refer back to "The North American Revolution" and "The French Revolution" sections of the chapter when constructing your answer.

FURTHER ACTIVITY

In their attempts to explain the past, scholars often make use of historical imagination or empathy—that is, the conscious and sympathetic effort to grasp how people in earlier times thought and made decisions. How might such an approach help you to understand why large parts of the population in the United States, France, and France's empire, including women, enslaved people, and most free people of color, were deprived in practice of the "universal" rights expressed in the Bill of Rights and the Declaration of the Rights of Man and Citizen? How might the drafters of these two documents explain these exclusions from the universal rights laid out in their documents? Does the failure to fully include these groups under the umbrella of universal rights represent a denial of their citizenship, their humanity, or both? From the viewpoint of the present, is it possible to empathize with such exclusions, or is criticism of those views the more appropriate posture?

BUILDING AP® SKILLS

Contextualization

As mentioned previously, contextualization is one of the hardest skills for students to master, especially on essays. If your students need contextualization practice, the "AP® Activity: Contextualizing Primary Sources" gives them a good activity to practice writing contextualization for the U.S. Bill of Rights and the French Declaration of the Rights of Man and Citizen.

TEACHING IDEA

Class Discussion

If you want to extend students' thinking about the rights granted in the U.S. Bill of Rights and the French Declaration of the Rights of Man and Citizen and practice sourcing, use the questions in "Further Activity" on this page to drive a class discussion or debate. These questions ask students to place themselves in the "shoes" of the men who wrote these documents and to also look at the documents from a modern perspective.

425

BUILDING AP® SKILLS

Claims and Evidence in Sources

Interpreting text-based as well as non-text-based sources is an important skill for AP® World History: Modern students. If time is available, have students investigate the idea of "rights" during the Atlantic revolutions by using the evidence in "Claiming Rights" beginning on page 426. Consider having students analyze one or more of the sources found on pages 426 to 433. You can check for understanding by:

■ Using the questions at the end of each source as a discussion starting point.

■ Pairing students to analyze (identify and describe) using author or creator's point of view, purpose, historical situation, and audience. This activity can continue to reinforce sourcing.

■ Assigning a source to a group of three to four students and having them present an overview of the source along with the sourcing to the rest of the class.

■ Having students present an overview of the source, and then having them practice AP® Comparison skills using Question 3 under AP® Doing History on page 433.

AP® WORKING WITH EVIDENCE

Claiming Rights

In the discourse of the age of Atlantic revolutions, no idea had a more enduring resonance than that of "rights"— natural rights, political and civic rights, and "the rights of man," or, in a more recent expression, "human rights." However these rights were defined, they were understood as both natural and universal. They were considered inherent in the human condition, rather than granted by some authority, and they were envisioned as being the same for everyone rather than depending on a person's birth, rank, or status in society. Growing out of the European Enlightenment, this understanding of "rights" was genuinely revolutionary, challenging almost all notions of government and society prior to the late eighteenth century. But even among supporters, the idea of human rights was highly controversial. What precisely were these rights? Did they support or contradict one another? Did they apply equally to women and slaves? How should they be established and maintained? Such questions were central to this age of revolution and have informed much of the world's political history ever since.

LOOKING AHEAD Consider the cultural and political impacts of the Enlightenment during the period 1750–1900.

AP® DBQ PRACTICE

DOCUMENT 1 **The French Revolution and the "Rights of Man"**

The most prominent example of the language of rights found expression during the French Revolution in the Declaration of the Rights of Man and Citizen. This document was hammered out in the French National Assembly early in that revolutionary upheaval and adopted at the end of August 1789. It has long been viewed as the philosophical core of the French Revolution. Later it became the preamble of the 1791 French Constitution.

The French document bore clear similarities to the language of the U.S. Declaration of Independence, as both drew on the ideas of the European Enlightenment. Furthermore, Thomas Jefferson, who largely wrote the U.S. declaration, served as the ambassador to France at this time and was in close contact with Marquis de Lafayette, the principal author of the French declaration. Lafayette, in turn, had earlier served with the American revolutionary forces seeking independence from England.

Source: Declaration of the Rights of Man and Citizen, 1789.

The representatives of the French people, constituted as a National Assembly, and considering that ignorance, neglect, or contempt of the rights of man are the sole causes of public misfortunes and governmental corruption, have resolved to set forth in a solemn declaration the natural, inalienable and sacred rights of man. . . .

1. Men are born and remain free and equal in rights. Social distinctions may be based only on common utility.

426

4. Liberty consists in the ability to do whatever does not harm another; hence the exercise of the natural rights of each man has no other limits than those which assure to other members of society the enjoyment of the same rights. These limits can only be determined by the law.

6. The law is the expression of the general will. All citizens have the right to take part, in person or by their representatives, in its formation. It must be the same for everyone whether it protects or penalizes. All citizens being equal in its eyes are equally admissible to all public dignities, offices, and employments, according to their ability, and with no other distinction than that of their virtues and talents.

9. Every man being presumed innocent until judged guilty, if it is deemed indispensable to arrest him, all rigor unnecessary to securing his person should be severely repressed by the law.

10. No one should be disturbed for his opinions, even in religion, provided that their manifestation does not trouble public order as established by law.

Question to Consider: What specific rights are spelled out in this document? What rights does it omit?

AP Analyzing Sources: How do the events of the French Revolution contextualize the document?

DOCUMENT 2 A British Conservative's Critique of the Universal Rights of Man

Edmund Burke (1729–1797), a member of the British Parliament and statesman from Ireland, was one of the first and most influential critics of the principles on which the French Revolution was based. In his *Reflections on the Revolution in France*, first published in 1790, Burke accepts that political change can and should occur but argues that successful political reform must happen incrementally and be based on existing political structures and traditions. Political systems founded on statements of universal rights were fatally flawed in Burke's view because they encouraged excessive individualism, selfishness, and personal ambition. At the root of all political communities, Burke identified the sacrifice of natural or universal rights as a positive trade-off that allowed individuals to live in peaceful civil societies. In some ways, Burke's more cautious approach reflected the experiences of his native Britain, which in the previous century had experienced two revolutionary upheavals, one of which included a prolonged and violent civil war that culminated in the execution of the king. Burke, however, was not an opponent of all revolutions. He had supported the American revolutionaries, whom he saw as working within British political traditions rather than abandoning them.

In Document 2, Burke rejects the idea that French revolutionaries could found a successful new state based on the principles espoused in the Declaration of the Rights of Man and Citizen. Burke published these objections before war, violence, and the Terror radicalized the French Revolution, so his arguments focus on those principles on which the Atlantic revolutions were based rather than on revulsion with the disorder and violence that often accompanied the overthrow of political regimes.

> **Source:** Edmund Burke, British Parliament member, from the political pamphlet *Reflections on the Revolution in France*, 1790.
>
> [I]t is in vain to talk to them [revolutionaries] of the practice of their ancestors, the fundamental laws of their country, the fixed form of a constitution. . . . They despise experience as the wisdom of unlettered men; and as for the rest, they have wrought underground a mine that will blow up at one grand explosion all examples of antiquity, all precedents, charters, and acts of parliament. They have "the rights of men." Against these there can be no prescription; against these no agreement is binding: these admit no temperament, and no compromise: any thing withheld from their full demand is so much of fraud and injustice. . . .
>
> Society requires not only that the passions of individuals should be subjected, but that even in the mass and body, as well as in the individuals, the inclinations of men should frequently be thwarted, their will controlled, and their passions brought into subjection. This can only be done by a power out[side] of themselves; and not . . . subject to that will and to those passions which is its office to bridle and subdue. In this sense the restraints on men, as well as their liberties, are to be reckoned among their rights. But as the liberties and the restrictions vary with times and circumstances, and admit of infinite modifications, they cannot be settled upon any abstract rule; and nothing is so foolish as to discuss them upon that principle.

Question to Consider: What is Burke's understanding of universal human rights and their place in government?

AP **Analyzing Sources:** How does Edmund Burke's background impact his point of view in the document?

DOCUMENT 3 The French National Assembly and Slavery

Victory in 1789 left revolutionaries in control of France and faced with the task of reconciling their idealistic slogans and principles with the competing demands of government. Few debates were more contentious than that surrounding the status of free men of color and enslaved people in the French colonies and especially the sugar islands of the Caribbean. Some revolutionary voices pressed for the outlawing of slavery as incompatible with a new state based on universal rights and liberties. Others pressed for free men of color to be embraced as full citizens while maintaining slavery, which, they argued, was too important for the colonial and French economies to be abandoned. Meanwhile, many white plantation owners and people in France whose livelihoods depended on colonial trade argued forcefully against granting any rights to peoples of color because this could lead to the emancipation of enslaved people in the future. In 1791 the lawmaking body in France known as the National Assembly opted for a compromise, rejecting freedom for enslaved people while granting citizenship to free men of color. Document 3 reproduces the text of this decree and an explanation offered by the Assembly for its decision. The law of 1791 set the stage for the Haitian Revolution. Only after a successful uprising by the enslaved population of Haiti did the French revolutionary government finally pass a law abolishing slavery in 1794. But this law was short-lived; Napoleon rescinded it in 1802.

Source: *Decree and Explanation of the French National Assembly*, May 15 and 29, 1791.

Decree of May 15. The National Assembly decrees that the legislature will never deliberate on the political status of people of color who were not born of free fathers and mothers without the previous free, and unprompted request of the colonies; that the presently existing Colonial Assemblies will admit the people of color born of free fathers and mothers if they otherwise have the required status.

Explanation of May 29. The National Assembly, attentive to all means of assuring prosperity in the colonies, to ensure that the citizens living there enjoy the advantages of the constitution . . . , recognizes that local circumstances and the kind of agriculture that brings colonial prosperity appear to require introducing into the colonial constitution several exceptions to the [French Revolution's] general principles.

. . . [On March 28, 1790] The National Assembly declared that the legislature would discuss the status of nonfree persons only on the unprompted request of the Colonial Assemblies.

The National Assembly was able to make this commitment because it only involved individuals [this paragraph refers to enslaved people] of a foreign land who, by their profound ignorance, the misfortune of their exile, the consideration of their own interest, and the urgent law of necessity, can only hope that in time the progress of public opinion and enlightenment will produce a change of conditions that, in the present state of things, would be contrary to the general good and might become equally dangerous for them.

Question to Consider: What does the decision to grant the rights of citizenship to free men of color but not to enslaved people tell us about the reasoning of the Assembly?

AP® Analyzing Sources: What events of the period show the historical significance of the source?

DOCUMENT 4 The Rights of Women: Depicting a Revolutionary Woman

Did the "rights of man" include women? During the French Revolution, the question of women's rights was sharply debated. As the revolution unfolded, many women became actively involved, taking part in street demonstrations, establishing dozens of women's clubs, and petitioning legislative bodies on behalf of women. Nevertheless, most men—even ardent revolutionaries—agreed with the French lawyer Jean-Denis Lanjuinais that "the physique of women, their goal in life [marriage and motherhood], and their position distance them from the exercise of a great number of political rights and duties."[27] In late 1793, all women's clubs were officially prohibited. But in the same year, the posture of these increasingly assertive women found expression in an

429

anonymous engraving titled "Frenchwomen Freed." The woman's cap displays the tri-color cockade that came to symbolize the revolution; she carries a pike inscribed with the slogan "liberty or death"; the medal on her waistband reads: "Liberty, armed with a pike, is victorious, July 14 [Bastille Day]." The prayer to the Roman goddess of war Bellona below the image extols the martial prowess of French women:

> And we [women], too, know how to fight and conquer. We know how to handle other weapons than the needle and the spindle. O Bellona! companion of Mars [the Roman god of war], to your example, all women should they not march in front and with a step equal with the men? Goddess of strength and courage! at least you will no longer have to blush for these French women.

Source: Anonymous engraving entitled "Frenchwomen Freed," 1793.

Question to Consider: How does the woman's physical stance and facial expression contribute to this message?

AP Analyzing Sources: What about the French Revolution might contextualize why a source like this, directed toward women, existed?

DOCUMENT 5 Rights and National Independence

If the "rights of man" could be mobilized on behalf of individuals against an oppressive class system as in France, those rights also came to be applied to oppressed peoples, nations, and colonial subjects, as in the United States, Haiti, Latin America, and later all across Asia and Africa. In a well-known letter written in 1815, Simón Bolívar, a prominent political and military leader in the struggle against Spanish rule in Latin America, made the case for the independence of his continent, arguing that Latin Americans' collective "rights," derived from Europe itself, had been massively violated.

Source: Simón Bolívar, "The Jamaica Letter," 1815.

These laws favor, almost exclusively, the natives of the country who are of Spanish extraction. Thus those born in America have been despoiled of their constitutional rights. . . .

The American provinces are fighting for their freedom, and they will ultimately succeed. . . . It is a grandiose idea to think of consolidating the New World into a single nation, united by pacts into a single bond. It is reasoned that, as these parts have a common origin, language, customs, and religion, they ought to have a single government to permit the newly formed states to unite in a confederation. But this is not possible. Actually, America is separated by climatic differences, geographic diversity, conflicting interests, and dissimilar characteristics. . . . This type of organization may come to pass in some happier period of our regeneration. . . .

As soon as we are strong and under the guidance of a liberal nation which will lend us her protection, we will achieve accord in cultivating the virtues and talents that lead to glory. Then will we march majestically toward that great prosperity for which South America is destined. Then will those sciences and arts which, born in the East, have enlightened Europe, wing their way to a free Colombia, which will cordially bid them welcome.

Question to Consider: What understanding of "rights" informed Bolívar's demand for independence?

AP **Analyzing Sources:** How does the audience for the document impact what Bolívar wrote in the letter?

DOCUMENT 6 Rights and Slavery: An African American Voice

In the United States, the language of the Declaration of Independence, with its affirmation that "all men are created equal," stood in glaring contrast to the brutal realities of slavery. In a famous speech, Frederick Douglass forcefully highlighted that great contradiction in the new American nation. Born into slavery in 1818, Douglass had escaped from bondage to become a leading abolitionist, writer, newspaper publisher, and African American spokesperson. The extract that follows is drawn from his address to an antislavery meeting in Rochester, New York, on July 5, 1852.

431

What, to the American slave, is your 4th of July? I answer: a day that reveals to him, more than all other days in the year, the gross injustice and cruelty to which he is the constant victim. To him, your celebration is a sham; your boasted liberty, an unholy license; your national greatness, swelling vanity; your sounds of rejoicing are empty and heartless; your denunciations of tyrants, brass-fronted impudence; your shouts of liberty and equality, hollow mockery; your prayers and hymns, your sermons and thanksgivings, with all your religious parade, and solemnity, are, to him, mere bombast, fraud, deception, impiety, and hypocrisy—a thin veil to cover up crimes which would disgrace a nation of savages. There is not a nation on the earth guilty of practices, more shocking and bloody, than are the people of these United States, at this very hour. . . .

Question to Consider: What failures in Enlightenment ideals is Douglass drawing attention to?

AP® Analyzing Sources: How does Douglass's point of view impact how we view the document?

DOCUMENT 7 The Rights of Women: An American Feminist Voice

Throughout the nineteenth century, debates about the rights of women echoed loudly across Europe, North America, and beyond. One of the most well-known and eloquent appeals for these rights came from the American feminist leader Elizabeth Cady Stanton (1815–1902) in an 1892 address to a U.S. congressional committee. Stanton was urging then, as she had for decades, an amendment to the Constitution giving women the right to vote. That effort was finally successful in 1920, almost two decades after Stanton died.

Source: Elizabeth Cady Stanton, "The Solitude of Self," address delivered before the Committee of the Judiciary of the United States Congress, January 18, 1892.

The strongest reason for giving woman all the opportunities for higher education, for the full development of her faculties. . . ; for giving her the most enlarged freedom of thought and action; a complete emancipation from all forms of bondage, of custom, dependence, superstition; from all the crippling influences of fear, is the solitude and personal responsibility of her own individual life. The strongest reason why we ask for woman a voice in the government under which she lives; in the religion she is asked to believe; equality in social life, where she is the chief factor; a place in the trades and professions, where she may earn her bread, is because of her birthright to self-sovereignty; because, as an individual, she must rely on herself. No matter how much women prefer to lean, to be protected and supported, nor how much men desire to have them do so, they must make the voyage of life alone. . . . It matters not whether the solitary voyager is man or woman. . . . Alike amid the greatest triumphs and darkest tragedies of life we walk alone. . . .

In [old] age, when the pleasures of youth are passed, children grown up, married and gone, the hurry and hustle of life in a measure over, when the hands are weary of active service, when the old armchair and the fireside are the chosen resorts, then men and women alike must fall back on their own resources. . . .

If from a lifelong participation in public affairs a woman feels responsible for the laws regulating our system of education, the discipline of our jails and prisons, the sanitary conditions of our private homes, public buildings, and thoroughfares, an interest in commerce, finance, our foreign relations, in any or all of these questions, her solitude will at least be respectable.

Question to Consider: How might you summarize in your own words Stanton's argument as to why women should have such rights?

AP Analyzing Sources: What is the purpose of Stanton's address to Congress?

AP DOING HISTORY

1. **DBQ Practice:** Evaluate the extent to which the Enlightenment impacted culture and politics during the period 1750–1900.

2. **Contextualization:** What specific historical contexts or conditions shaped the understanding of "rights" expressed in each of these sources?

3. **Comparison:** Which sources speak more about individual rights, and which focus on collective rights? What common understandings can you identify?

4. **Claims and Evidence in Sources:** How might the creators of these sources have responded to one another? What points of agreement might they share? What differences might arise in a conversation among them?

5. **Sourcing and Situation:** In what respects did each of these sources derive from the French Revolution?

TRM Chapter 7 DBQ Activity Handout

Origins and Echoes of the American Revolution

Many historians, including the two voices that follow, have sought to contextualize the American Revolution by examining its intellectual, social, and cultural origins and its long-term echoes in such developments as abolitionism, nationalism, feminism, and European imperialism. In Voice 7.1, Dorinda Outram, who specializes in the European Enlightenment, explores the impact of that movement's ideas on the American Revolution. In Voice 7.2, Carl Guarneri, a specialist in American history, explores how the American Revolution redirected British imperial ambitions on three continents.

face the French twenty years later, which was the impossibility of constructing a political order based on equality of rights without recasting the unequal social order. . . . This contradiction between support for supposedly universal rights, and the actual exclusion of large numbers of human beings from the enjoyment of those rights is central to, and characteristic of Enlightenment thought.

Source: Dorinda Outram, *The Enlightenment* (Cambridge: Cambridge University Press, 1995), 121–22.

BUILDING AP® SKILLS

Claims and Evidence in Sources

You can use "AP® Historians' Voices: Origins and Echoes of the American Revolution" to help students work on improving skills with understanding and interpreting secondary sources. Have students read both of the sources found on pages 434–435 and answer Questions 1 and 2 on page 435. After students have answered the questions on their own, have them discuss their responses as a class. This activity can help students practice reading and interpreting secondary sources, which are found on the MCQ and SAQ sections of the exam.

VOICE 7.1

Dorinda Outram on Enlightenment Ideas in the American Revolution | 1995

[T]he American Revolution has often been seen as the place where Enlightenment ideas and a violent change of government can best be seen in conjunction. . . .

But the ideology that filled this conflict had many different sources. Puritan religious ideas of man's essential sinfulness sat uneasily with Enlightenment ideas of progress, optimism and faith in man's rationality. . . . Other elements in American ideology also antedated the Enlightenment, especially the Republicanism which originated with classical Greco-Roman models. . . . The American interpretation of Republicanism emphasized the virtue of a simple society of autonomous citizens committed to the common good and emphasized the independence of each individual. . . . However, Americans also believed that citizen and government should be united by contract, an idea very strong in John Locke's *Two Treatises of Civil Government*. . . . This idea of contract itself ran into several difficulties in the American situation. . . . Locke's idea of contract presupposed a society whose members were equal. Could it really be applied in the American colonies, which were underpinned by the labor of slaves? . . . Maybe in the end the American revolutionaries found themselves faced with the same problem as was to

VOICE 7.2

Carl Guarneri on British Expansion Redirected | 2007

Some historians have called the American Revolution "England's Vietnam." Faced with a popular revolt in a distant land where unfamiliar terrain and irregular warfare made conquest impossible, the British, like the Americans 200 years later in southeast Asia, were forced to withdraw. But if the analogy is meant to imply imperial decline, it is off the mark. The British were galled by the colonists' victory, but prompt settlement of new territories compensated for their loss.

The American Revolution indirectly helped to develop three British colonies that eventually became new nations. Thousands of loyalist families fled the thirteen colonies for Canada, where the provinces of New Brunswick and Upper Canada (later Ontario) were organized to accommodate the influx and which their descendants transformed into a thriving British colony. Britain's West African colony of Sierra Leone was another indirect product of the American revolt. Four hundred African American refugees who had been freed and sent to London were settled there in 1787 . . . and were joined by 1200 black loyalists from the Nova Scotia settlement. Finally, when Georgia and other American colonies no longer accepted prisoners sentenced to exile for crimes committed in England,

434

British officials turned to Australia, which Captain James Cook had claimed for the Crown in 1770, as their dumping ground. Far from dampening British ambitions, the American Revolution stimulated British expansion elsewhere. Casting about for additional trade and territory in Africa, Asia, the Pacific, and the Middle East, Britain continued to build its empire. Its heyday was still a century ahead.

Source: Carl Guarneri, *America in the World: The United States in Global Context* (Boston: McGraw-Hill, 2007), 103.

AP **Analyzing Secondary Sources**

1. According to Outram, in what ways did the American Revolution reveal contradictions in Enlightenment thinking?

2. According to Guarneri, what impact did defeat by the American revolutionaries have on the British Empire?

3. **Integrating Primary and Secondary Sources:** Assess the legacy of the American Revolution using Voice 7.2 and AP® Working with Evidence, Documents 6 and 7, pages 431–433.

TRM **Suggested Responses to Questions**
You can find suggested responses to the AP® Analyzing Secondary Sources questions in the Teacher's Resource Materials.

435

Multiple-Choice Questions Choose the correct answer for each question.

Questions 1–3 refer to this image.

Illustration of the Womens' March on Versailles.

1. Based on this image, which of the following best represents a social change in Europe resulting from the French Revolution?
   a. The reordering of social hierarchies in French society
   b. An increase in inclusion of women in the French political system
   c. The beginning of the movement for women's suffrage in France
   d. The encouragement by the Church that women join convents

2. Which of these ideas most significantly influenced the Atlantic revolutions?
   a. The belief that people should give up their individual rights for safety
   b. The idea that inhumane punishments by governments should be abolished
   c. The existence of a social contract between citizens and their government
   d. The concept of universal suffrage to encourage more involvement by citizens in politics

3. The French Revolution differed from other Atlantic revolutions in which of these ways?
   a. Unlike the French Revolution, the other Atlantic revolutions achieved widespread social equality.
   b. Unlike the other Atlantic revolutions, the French Revolution led to the execution of the king.
   c. Unlike in the other Atlantic revolutions, women received equal political rights to men in France.
   d. Unlike the French Revolution, the other Atlantic revolutions were followed by frequent periods of unrest.

436

Questions 4–6 refer to this passage.

The point I wish plainly to bring before you on this occasion is the individuality of each human soul. . . . In discussing the rights of woman, we are to consider, first, what belongs to her as an individual, in a world of her own. . . .

The strongest reason for giving woman opportunities for higher education, for the full development of her faculties . . . is the solitude and personal responsibility of her own individual life. The strongest reason why we ask for woman a voice in the government under which she lives; . . . a place in the trades and professions, where she may earn her bread, is because of her birthright to self-sovereignty; because, as an individual, she must rely on herself.

— Elizabeth Cady Stanton, "The Solitude of Self," 1892

4. In the passage above, Elizabeth Cady Stanton is advocating
   a. against women having a public role in the political and economic world.
   b. for workplace protections for women in industrialized factories.
   c. for more public participation of women in the political and economic world.
   d. against the education of women, but for women's suffrage.

5. Elizabeth Cady Stanton's argument in the passage above is most closely connected to ideas from
   a. the Protestant Reformation.
   b. Enlightenment thinkers.
   c. the Scientific Revolution.
   d. socialist revolutionaries.

6. Which of the following statements best describes the suffrage movement in the Western world in the nineteenth and early twentieth centuries?
   a. Men gradually gained the right to vote throughout the nineteenth century, while women gained the right to vote after World War I.
   b. Universal suffrage had been passed in most of the Western world by the end of the nineteenth century.
   c. International conferences in the late nineteenth century guaranteed that all Western nations would allow women to vote by the year 1900.
   d. Both men and women had to show ownership of property to vote in most of the Western world.

437

AP® CLASSROOM

AP® Topic Questions

If you want to give students more practice with multiple-choice questions, you can log in to your AP® Classroom account and assign the AP® Topic Questions under Topic 5.2, "St Maurice and Kersaint." AP® Classroom allows you to set the questions up digitally or print out a copy for each student. Consider dividing the class into groups of three to four students to discuss the questions together and come to the correct answer.

When you assign the Topic Questions or Personal Progress Checks, it can be a good idea to put a timer on the question(s) so students can practice the skill in a timed setting like the AP® Exam.

BUILDING AP® SKILLS

Argumentation

Students need to practice their writing skills for the AP® Exam on a regular basis too. You could use the SAQs on pages 438 and 439 for students to write as an "exit ticket" at the end of class to check for understanding. You can also spread the three SAQs across several days or have students write them all at once to practice timing for the AP® Exam. If you choose to have students write them all at once, make certain that students have the correct amount of time for this exercise. On exam day, students will have a total of 40 minutes to write three SAQs.

If you want to try something different with the SAQs, partner the students up and have them write the SAQs together by having one student write the claim or topic sentence for an SAQ and the other student write the supporting evidence for the claim.

Short-Answer Questions

Read each question carefully and write a short response. Use complete sentences.

1. **Use this passage and your knowledge of world history to answer all parts of the question that follows.**

> The existence of revolutionary waves is a well-known feature of history. This study contends that revolutionary waves are best understood as systemic phenomena occurring during periods of rapid world-cultural expansion. Rapid expansion and deeper penetration of cultural linkages is theorized to generate contradiction between idealized models and local political practices, empower oppositions, and fracture elites, resulting in waves of revolution.... Results suggest that the occurrence of revolutionary waves is positively associated with relatively rapid world-cultural growth and hegemonic decline, as indicated by periods of hegemonic warfare.
> — Colin J. Beck, *The World-Cultural Origins of Revolutionary Waves*

A. Identify ONE Atlantic revolution that supports the author's argument concerning empowered groups.

B. Explain how ONE Atlantic revolution supports the author's argument concerning political practices.

C. Explain ONE cause of an Atlantic revolution that supports the author's viewpoint that cultural connections encouraged revolution.

2. **Use this image and your knowledge of world history to answer all parts of the question that follows.**

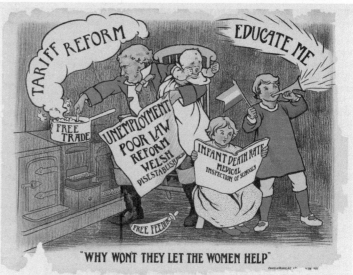

Late nineteenth-century women's suffrage poster, showing John Bull (personification of England) as a mother tending to the pressing issues of the time.

A. Explain how the above image reflects the effect of Enlightenment ideals during the late nineteenth century.

B. Explain how the above image is a response to Atlantic revolutions of the eighteenth and nineteenth centuries.

C. Identify ONE important aspect of the feminist movement outside of Western Europe and the United States.

3. **Answer all parts of the question that follows.**

A. Identify ONE economic cause of the Haitian Revolution.

B. Explain ONE social cause of the Haitian Revolution.

C. Explain ONE global effect of the Haitian Revolution.

439

Revolutions of Industrialization

8

1750–1900

AP® Overview for Chapter 8

Chapter 8 corresponds to AP® Unit 5: Revolutions, 1750–1900 and Topics 6.6 and 6.7 from Unit 6: Consequences of Industrialization. The transformations of the Industrial Revolution restructured the entire global economic and social order. Its repercussions are felt even today. Many different world history themes are linked to industrialism, ranging from the political reach of imperialism to the shifting notion of labor systems, and from the expanding systems of trade to the formation of an entirely new class structure.

Chapter 8 Essential Activity

Students should practice DBQ essay writing skills throughout the year, and sometimes it can be helpful if students work together to practice these skills. The 2002 AP® European History DBQ (Question 1) asks students to identify the issues raised by the growth of Manchester after industrialization in the nineteenth century and the reactions to those issues. The prompt and accompanying documents can be found on the College Board website, in the AP® European History Past Exam Questions section. In this exercise, students (in groups or as individuals) will use this DBQ to create a DBQ poster. Students will need two sets of the DBQ documents, scissors, glue or tape, markers or pens, and a piece of butcher paper. Give the class a 10-minute reading period to read through all the DBQ documents. Then allow students 40–50 minutes to create their DBQ posters using the following directions:

- Write the DBQ question at the top of your poster. Later you will write your thesis at the bottom of the poster (large enough to read), so be sure to leave enough space.
- Cut out one set of the documents.
- Separate the documents into two to three arguments that help you answer the question. Tape or paste the documents onto your poster in groups. Name the arguments and write the name above each grouping of documents.
- Write a quick analysis next to each document (you can do this on a sticky note).
- Write at least three sourcing statements for the whole poster (about one or two documents in each argument).
- Write at least one piece of outside evidence on the poster.
- Discuss the question and come up with a thesis statement that answers the question. Write the thesis at the bottom of the poster.

After students finish creating their posters, have them hang the posters up and do a gallery walk to see how other students put together this DBQ. Have students write an "I wonder . . ." statement (asking questions about the setup of a particular poster) and an "I like . . ." statement (complimenting a poster) for each poster as they go through the gallery walk. Once all the students are finished, have them share their "I wonder . . ." and "I like . . ." statements. This sharing can lead to a discussion among students about how to improve certain DBQ writing skills. To bring this question into alignment with the new DBQ requirements, remove four documents (we recommend cutting Documents 1, 4, 8, and 9, but choose whatever documents will be best for your students). The following prompt could be used to match the updated DBQ format: Evaluate the extent to which the challenges created by industrialization led to various reactions in Manchester from 1750 to 1900.

Differentiation

If you want to differentiate the Chapter 8 Essential Activity and give students more practice with building their writing skills, follow the "Must Do, Should Do, Strive For" model below for the DBQ poster.

- Must Do: In their groups, students must analyze the documents and decide what two or three arguments they can create out of them. On their provided butcher paper (to create their poster), they need to name their arguments, glue the supporting documents under the corresponding argument, and write a quick analysis next to each document. Finally, students need to create a thesis statement that answers the prompt and write it at the bottom of their poster.

- Should Do: In their groups, students need to write one or two sourcing statements for each argument (ending with a total of three sourcing statements) and contextualization (which should go above the thesis) on their poster. Once all the groups have completed their DBQ poster, have students hang them up and do a gallery walk to see how other groups put together this DBQ. As they look at each poster, ask students to leave "I wonder . . ." and "I like . . ." statements.

- Strive For: For students who want or need a writing challenge, have them choose one of their arguments from their DBQ poster and write a full argument paragraph on it.

Chapter 8 Resources

TRM AP® Skills Workshop Activity Handout: Sourcing and Situation in Primary and Secondary Sources

TRM Chapter 8 DBQ Activity Handout

TRM Chapter 8 Guided Reading

TRM Chapter 8 Lecture Presentation Slides

TRM Chapter 8 Outline

TRM Chapter 8 Suggested Responses to Questions

TRM Eric's Activity 8: Living the Industrial Revolution

TRM Handout 7.1: Comparison Chart for Atlantic Revolutions

TRM Handout 8.1: Comparison Chart for Industrial Revolutions

TRM Handout 8.2: Causation Chart for the Industrial Revolution in Britain

TRM Handout 8.3: Comparison Chart for Social Classes in Great Britain

TRM Handout 8.4: Comparison Chart for the Lives of Middle-Class and Laboring-Class Women

TRM Handout 8.5: Chart for Marxism, Capitalism, and Changes in Western Europe

TRM Handout 8.6: Comparison and Causation Chart of Migration in the United States and Russia

TRM Handout 8.7: Comparison Chart for Reactions to Working Conditions in the United States and Europe

TRM Handout 8.8: Comparison Chart for Political, Social, and Economic Characteristics of the United States and Russia

TRM LEQ Outline Handout

TRM Map 8A: The World

Pacing Guide

Below is a pacing guide for the AP® World History: Modern course beginning in ca. 1200 C.E. This pacing guide is based on a schedule with 120 sessions of 50 minutes each before the AP® Exam. It is meant as a place to start. If you have a different number of sessions before the exam, you can modify the pacing to suit your needs.

Day	Pages Assigned	AP® Topic	AP® Theme	Suggested Assignments	Coverage Notes
1	Read pages 441–447 to "The First Industrial Society"	5.3 5.5	ENV TEC	Exploring AP® Themes: ECN on page 441 Teaching Idea: Incorporating Outside Resources on page 442 Teaching Idea: Class Discussion on page 444	The feature "Controversies: Debating 'Why Europe?'" is helpful to introduce the Industrial Revolution, its significance, and why the revolution started in Europe. It also gives context to students before they begin studying the changes that came about because of the Industrial Revolution.
2	Read pages 447–449 from "The First Industrial Society" to "The British Aristocracy"	5.3 5.4 5.5	ENV ECN SIO TEC	Building AP® Skills: Making Connections: Causation on page 447 Exploring AP® Themes: ENV on page 448 Apply the Tip on page 449	While the early phase of the Industrial Revolution in Chapter 8 focuses on Great Britain, it's a good model for students to understand the changes brought about because of industrialization. This is also a good section to start a comparison practice on industrialization and its results on different regions in the world.
3	Read pages 449–451 from "The British Aristocracy" to "The Laboring Classes"	5.8 5.9	SIO	Exploring AP® Themes: SIO on page 450 Teaching Idea: Incorporating Outside Resources on page 450	If you are having students work on building their comparison skills, Days 3 and 4 provide a good foundation on how industrialization affected different social classes in Great Britain.
4	Read pages 451–453 from "The Laboring Classes" to "Social Protest"	5.8 5.9	SIO	Chapter 8 Essential Activity Apply the Tip on page 451 Exploring AP® Themes: SIO on page 452 Building AP® Skills: Making Connections: Comparison on page 453	See above.

➡

Day	Pages Assigned	AP® Topic	AP® Theme	Suggested Assignments	Coverage Notes
5	Read pages 453–457 from "Social Protest" to "Europeans in Motion"	5.7 5.8	GOV ECN SIO	Chapter 8 Essential Activity Apply the Tip on page 453 Teaching Idea: Class Discussion on page 456	Students will need some guidance on how socialism and communism are reactions to industrialization. They may not always have a working understanding of these economic ideologies, so you may need to spend some time defining them before having students study them.
6	Read pages 457–459 from "Europeans in Motion" to "Variations on a Theme: Industrialization in the United States and Russia"	6.6 6.7	ENV ECN SIO	Teaching Idea: Bell Ringer on page 457 Building AP® Skills: Argumentation on page 458	While this is a short section in Chapter 8, migration in the nineteenth century is a major concept for the course. You may want to combine this section with the migrations discussed in Chapter 10.
7	Read pages 459–463 from "Variations on a Theme: Industrialization in the United States and Russia" to "Russia: Industrialization and Revolution"	5.4 5.5 5.6 5.7 5.8 5.9	GOV ECN SIO TEC	Building AP® Skills: Making Connections: Comparison and Causation on page 460 Exploring AP® Themes: ENV on page 461 Building AP® Skills: Making Connections: Comparison on page 462	If you are having students work on their comparison skills, consider having them compare the Industrial Revolution in Great Britain to the ones that took place in the United States and Russia. There are several activities in this chapter to help with this assignment.
8	Read pages 463–466 from "Russia: Industrialization and Revolution" to "The Industrial Revolution and Latin America in the Nineteenth Century"	5.4 5.5 5.6 5.7 5.8 5.9	GOV ECN SIO TEC	Building AP® Skills: Making Connections: Comparison on page 463 Apply the Tip on page 464 Building AP® Skills: Argumentation on page 466	See above.
9	Read pages 466–469 through "The Industrial Revolution and Latin America in the Nineteenth Century"	5.4 5.7	ENV GOV ECN SIO	Apply the Tip on page 466 Building AP® Skills: Claims and Evidence in Sources on page 467 Teaching Idea: Class Discussion on page 468	The beginning of this section is a continuation of the Latin American revolutions discussed in Chapter 7. Spend some time reviewing those revolutions before looking at what occurs after them in this chapter. This section also has a good discussion on how the Industrial Revolution impacted nonindustrialized states in the changing global economy.
10	Read pages 470–474 through "Conclusions and Reflections"	5.4 5.7 5.8 5.9	GOV ECN SIO	Building AP® Skills: Making Connections: Comparison on page 470 Apply the Tip on page 471 Eric's Activity 8: Living the Industrial Revolution on page 474	See above.

NOTES

BUILDING AP® SKILLS

Claims and Evidence in Sources

Students need to continually practice with their nonwritten source analysis skills throughout the year, whether it's an image, map, graph, or chart. To guide students on this type of analysis, you can show them the image of the copper foundry in Wales and ask the following questions:

■ How is the Industrial Revolution reflected in this image? *We see a large number of factories close together, a railroad cutting through the city, crowded living conditions (buildings are very close together), and smoke from factories filling the sky.*

■ What mood was the artist trying to display in the image? What elements from the image lead you to that conclusion? *The artist is depicting a gloomy mood: the colors are muted, the sky is filled with smoke, the humans are dwarfed by the buildings around them, and the river is still and appears lifeless; it contains only the reflections of the smokestacks.*

TEACHING IDEA

Bell Ringer

Before starting the Industrial Revolution, ask students to think back to the early modern era (1450–1750) and what happened to European states in that time period. Then let them know that the Industrial Revolution started in Great Britain and ask: Why did the Industrial Revolution begin in Great Britain? *Answers may include: Great Britain had a stable and open government that encouraged innovation and trade; Great Britain had a powerful middle class that could become the innovators and factory owners of the Industrial Revolution and had an early capitalist economy; Britain had abundant natural resources like coal and iron ore, which would help drive the Industrial Revolution.*

Industrial Britain To the modern eye this engraving of one of the first and largest copper works in Wales vividly conveys a sense of the dirt, smoke, and pollution of early industrial societies. However, at the time of its publication in 1862, many viewers would have seen in this image a celebration of "progress" as modern industry, centered on factories, enhanced humankind's growing productivity. (Gianni Dagli Orti/Shutterstock)

440

EXPLORING AP® THEMES

Economic Systems (ECN)

To help students understand the spread of the Industrial Revolution and the changes to transregional trade, ask them to create an annotated map of the Industrial Revolution and the changes it caused. Students should begin the assignment early in the chapter and continue it throughout their study of the Industrial Revolution. Students may need to conduct additional research to complete the annotated map. On a blank map of the world, ask students to identify where the Industrial Revolution began and the

countries to which it had spread by 1900. To help show the changes in transregional trade, students should indicate the trade items exported from Latin America, Africa, South Asia, Southeast Asia, and East Asia, as well as the trade items exported from Europe, the United States, and other industrialized nations. Then students should indicate on the map the trade items imported by these different regions. After students have completed their maps, ask: What changes occurred in transregional trade due to the Industrial

Revolution? *Europe, the United States, and other industrialized nations became the centers of transregional trade by 1900, as the primary exporters of manufactured goods. Many other areas of the world once exported primarily finished goods but instead began to export more raw materials, and former trade centers such as China and the Islamic world began to decline in their importance in transregional trade.* For a blank map that you can use with this activity, see the Teacher's Resource Materials.

➡

CHAPTER

8

Revolutions of Industrialization

1750–1900

◀ **AP®**

SOURCING AND SITUATION
How is the Industrial Revolution
represented in this image? What
mood was the artist trying to
display? How might this image
illustrate common criticisms of
industrialization? How might it be
interpreted as a positive view of
industrialization?

CONNECTING PAST AND PRESENT

In mid-2017, Erik Solheim, the Norwegian head of the UN Environment Program, argued that "humanity's advancement in science, technology and industrialization [is] harming the planet, hence the need to reverse course."[1] At the same time, Dr. Lloyd G. Adu Amoah, a prominent professor at the University of Ghana in West Africa, declared: "We [Africans] need to industrialize, because if we don't, we are not adding value to what the African continent has."[2] ■

Taken together, these two statements—from a European and an African—represent perhaps the most compelling dilemma facing humankind in the twenty-first century. How can we embrace the wealth and improvement in human life universally associated with industrialization, while coping with the terrible environmental threat to our fragile planet that industrialized economies have generated? That profound dilemma has its origins in the Industrial Revolution, which took place initially in Europe during the century and a half between 1750 and 1900. And so alongside the political upheavals of the Atlantic revolutions and their aftermath, an even more profound transformation was unfolding. Not since the Agricultural Revolution some 12,000 years ago have human ways of living and our relationship to the natural world been so fundamentally altered. And this transformation has unfolded far more rapidly than the earlier transition to agriculture.

Industrialization started in Britain, but it spread quickly during the nineteenth century to continental Western Europe, the United States, Russia, and Japan. Everywhere it took root, the Industrial Revolution transformed economies and created distinctive industrial societies with new working environments, social classes, values, conflict, protests, and patterns of migration. It also had profound effects on regions like Latin

441

TRM **Chapter 8 Guided Reading**
You can find a guided reading handout
for this chapter in the Teacher's Resource
Materials.

TRM **Chapter 8 Lecture Slides**
You can find curated lecture slides for this
chapter in the Teacher's Resource Materials.

TRM **Chapter 8 Outline**
You can find a chapter outline to model good
note-taking for this chapter in the Teacher's
Resource Materials.

TRM **Suggested Responses to Questions**
You can find suggested responses to all of
the AP® margin questions in this chapter in
the Teacher's Resource Materials.

Differentiation

You can guide students in this understanding of the changes to global trade in the nineteenth century by following the scaffolding in the "Must Do, Should Do, Strive For" model below:

■ Must Do: Students must identify the origin location of the Industrial Revolution and mark where it had spread to by 1900. Students must also indicate what trade items were exported from Latin America, Africa, South Asia, Southeast Asia, and East Asia, along with the items exported from industrialized nations such as European nations and the United States.

■ Should Do: Students should draw arrows on the map to show what trade items were imported by the different regions (e.g., rubber from Southeast Asia going to European nations and cotton textiles from Great Britain going to Latin America). Then ask students to study the following trade maps from Chapters 3 and 6: Map 3.1 (page 136), Map 3.4 (page 151), and Map 6.2 (page 328). If you completed the Essential Activity for Chapter 3, you could also ask students to study the annotated map they made for that activity. Then ask: What changes

occurred in transregional trade due to the Industrial Revolution?

■ Strive For: Working either on their own or with a partner, students can extend their thinking from the question in the Should Do section to write an argument paragraph for the following prompt: Evaluate the extent to which the Industrial Revolution led to changes in the global economy in the time period 1750 to 1900.

TRM **Map 8A: The World**

AP®
MAKING CONNECTIONS
How revolutionary was the Industrial Revolution?

AP®
CONTINUITY AND CHANGE
In what ways did the Industrial Revolution mark a sharp break with the past? In what ways did it continue earlier patterns?

AP® EXAM TIP
Pay close attention to this explanation of the significance of the Industrial Revolution.

AP® EXAM TIP
Remember that human interactions with the environment are always important subjects in this course and are fair game for AP® Exam questions.

America that did not industrialize but increasingly supplied the insatiable demands of industrialized economies for raw materials and markets. By 1900 a global transformation was well under way.

In any long-term reckoning, the history of industrialization is very much an unfinished story. Are we at the beginning of a movement leading to worldwide industrialization, stuck in the middle of a world permanently divided into rich and poor countries, or approaching the end of an environmentally unsustainable industrial era? Whatever the future holds, this chapter focuses on the early stages of an immense transformation in the global condition of humankind.

Industrialization: The Global Context

Finding the Main Point: What were the environmental, demographic, and economic consequences of industrial methods of production?

The epic economic transformation of the Industrial Revolution took shape as a very substantial increase in human numbers unfolded—from about 375 million people in 1400 to about 1 billion in the early nineteenth century. Accompanying this growth in population was an emerging energy crisis, most pronounced in Western Europe, China, and Japan, as wood and charcoal, the major industrial fuels, became more scarce and more costly. In short, "global energy demands began to push against the existing local and regional ecological limits."[3] In broad terms, the Industrial Revolution marked a human response to those limits. It was a twofold revolution—drawing on new sources of energy and new technologies—that combined to utterly transform economic and social life on the planet.

In terms of energy, the Industrial Revolution came to rely on fossil fuels such as coal, oil, and natural gas, which supplemented and largely replaced the earlier energy sources of wind, water, wood, and the muscle power of people and animals that had long sustained humankind. It was a breakthrough of unprecedented proportions that made available for human use, at least temporarily, immensely greater quantities of energy. During the nineteenth century, yet another fuel became widely available as Europeans learned to exploit guano, or seabird excrement, found on the islands off the coast of Peru. Used as a potent fertilizer, guano enabled highly productive input-intensive farming practices. In much of Western Europe, North America, Australia, and New Zealand, it sustained the production of crops that fed both the draft animals and the growing human populations of the industrializing world.[4]

The technological dimension of the Industrial Revolution has been equally significant. Early signs of the technological creativity that spawned the Industrial Revolution appeared in eighteenth-century Britain, where a variety of innovations transformed cotton textile production. It was only in the nineteenth century, though, that Europeans in general and the British in particular clearly forged ahead of the rest of the world. (See Controversies: Debating "Why Europe?") The great breakthrough was the coal-fired **steam engine**, which provided an inanimate and almost

Landmarks for Chapter 8

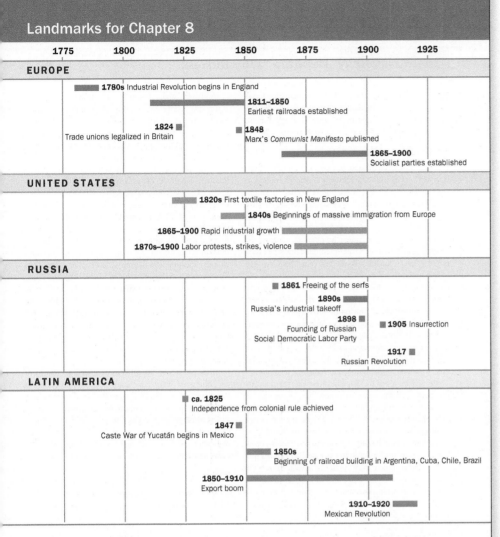

EUROPE

1780s Industrial Revolution begins in England

1811–1850 Earliest railroads established

1824 Trade unions legalized in Britain

1848 Marx's *Communist Manifesto* published

1865–1900 Socialist parties established

UNITED STATES

1820s First textile factories in New England

1840s Beginnings of massive immigration from Europe

1865–1900 Rapid industrial growth

1870s–1900 Labor protests, strikes, violence

RUSSIA

1861 Freeing of the serfs

1890s Russia's industrial takeoff

1898 Founding of Russian Social Democratic Labor Party

1905 Insurrection

1917 Russian Revolution

LATIN AMERICA

ca. 1825 Independence from colonial rule achieved

1847 Caste War of Yucatán begins in Mexico

1850s Beginning of railroad building in Argentina, Cuba, Chile, Brazil

1850–1910 Export boom

1910–1920 Mexican Revolution

limitless source of power that could be used to drive any number of machines as well as locomotives and oceangoing ships. Soon the Industrial Revolution spread beyond the textile industry to iron and steel production, railroads and steamships, food processing, and construction. Later in the nineteenth century, a so-called second Industrial Revolution focused on chemicals, electricity, precision machinery, the telegraph and telephone, rubber, printing, and much more.

AP® EXAM TIP

Look closely at these Landmarks and notice connections between the Industrial Revolution and political revolutions of this era.

Technological innovations, such as the spinning jenny, power loom, steam engine, and cotton gin, helped fuel the Industrial Revolution. Consider dividing the class into groups of three to four students and assign each group to research and prepare a 3- to 6-minute presentation to teach their classmates about one of the following inventions:

- Seed drill
- Mechanical reaper
- Water frame
- Spinning jenny
- Power loom
- Steam engine
- Cotton gin
- Steam locomotive

Either assign the research as homework or give students a day in class to prepare and present the following class day. Students should answer the following questions in their presentation:

- What was the purpose of the invention?
- How was it used during the Industrial Revolution?
- What impact did the invention have on industrial development?

APPLY THE TIP

It's important for students to be able to make connections between topics and time periods. This is a good place to have students reflect on and write down the big ideas of what they learned about the eighteenth- and nineteenth-century political revolutions in Chapter 7. Then ask them to show the connections between five events they've chosen from "Landmarks for Chapter 8" and the political revolutions of 1750–1900. (Suggested answers are provided in italics.)

- *The beginning of the British Industrial Revolution occurred as the American Revolution was ending, which affected British industrialization, as the factories no longer had easy access to cotton from the southern United States.*

- *The end of the independence movements in Latin America led to the beginning of railroad building in Argentina, Cuba, Chile, and Brazil as the newly independent states began to build up their infrastructure and industry.*

Class Discussion

The question of why the Industrial Revolution started in Europe is a major area of debate among historians. It could be fun for students to participate in this debate. Divide the class into three groups and assign each group one school of thought about the Industrial Revolution found in the three sections of "Controversies: Debating 'Why Europe?'": A "European Miracle," The "Great Divergence," and Trade and Empire. Have the groups read through their particular section of the "Controversies" and then prepare to argue why their school of thought is the correct one when studying the beginning of the Industrial Revolution. You may want to consider a "Three then Me" rule for talking during the debate to make sure that one or two students don't dominate it; this is where students have to wait for at least three other classmates to talk before they can contribute to the debate again.

Making Connections: Causation

If you don't have time to do a full class debate, you can still get students to think about why the Industrial Revolution started in Europe with a more "laid back" class discussion. You can use the Contextualization question at the bottom of this page to get students to discuss why Europe was considered an unlikely place for the Industrial Revolution to begin. After students have had time to talk, discuss the reasons why it did in fact occur in Europe first. To guide the discussion, ask the following questions:

■ How did the political structure of Europe foster innovation that led to the Industrial Revolution? *The high number of small, competitive states that had developed in Europe generated economic and technological advancements. These states competed against one another, helping stimulate innovation.*

■ How did the relationship between European governments and merchants help contribute to the start of the Industrial Revolution? *Monarchs needed revenue, which led to an unusual alliance with their merchant class. Merchants might be granted special privileges, monopolies, or tax-collecting responsibilities in exchange for loans or payments to the state. This relationship led governments to actively encourage commerce and innovation and allowed merchants and other innovators*

CONTROVERSIES **Debating "Why Europe?"**

The Industrial Revolution marked a dramatic change in the trajectory of human history. But why did that breakthrough occur first in Europe? This question has long been a source of great controversy among scholars.

A "European Miracle"

Does the answer lie in some unique or "miraculous" feature of European history, culture, or society? Perhaps, as one scholar recently suggested, Europeans have been distinguished for several thousand years by a restless, creative, and freedom-loving culture with its roots in the aristocratic warlike societies of early Indo-European invaders, which rendered them uniquely open to change and development.[5] But critics have questioned both the claims to European cultural uniqueness and causal links between industrialization and developments of the distant past.

Or should we focus more narrowly on the period between about 1400 and 1800 for the origins of this "European miracle"?[6] During those centuries distinctive new forms of landowning and farming practices emerged, especially in Britain, that made land and labor available for capitalist agriculture and enabled the accumulation of wealth in the hands of a few. Was this "agricultural revolution" a prelude to the subsequent "industrial revolution"?

Or perhaps it was the Scientific Revolution, a distinctly European event that generated a new view of the cosmos, that stimulated industrialization. It turns out, however, that early industrial technologies derived from the workshops of artisans and craftsmen rather than from the laboratories of scientists. And so by the early twenty-first century, many historians were thinking in terms of a broader cultural pattern, an eighteenth-century "Industrial Enlightenment" in which scientific methods and a general belief in an ordered universe mixed with commitment to the ideas of "progress" and human improvement to foster technological innovation.

And what about Europe's many relatively small and highly competitive states? Perhaps their rivalries stimulated innovation and provided an "insurance against economic and technological stagnation," which the larger Chinese, Ottoman, or Mughal empires lacked. In their struggles with other states, European governments desperately needed revenue, and to get it, European authorities developed an unusual alliance with their merchant classes. Merchant capitalists were granted special privileges, monopolies, or even tax-collecting responsibilities in exchange for much-needed loans or payments to the state. Governments granted charters and monopolies to private trading companies, and states founded scientific societies and offered prizes to promote innovation. European merchants and other innovators after the fifteenth century became more independent from state control and enjoyed a higher social status than their counterparts in more established civilizations. Such internally competitive semi-capitalist economies, coupled with a highly competitive system of rival states, arguably fostered innovation in the new civilization taking shape in Western Europe. But at the same time, nearly constant war and the destruction that accompanied it also served as a long-term drain on European resources.

Britain especially benefited from several advantages of the "European miracle," including a spirit of innovation, a lot of easily accessible coal, a growing consumer market, plentiful cheap capital accumulated in agriculture and trade, and its island geography, which frequently shielded it from the worst effects of Europe's wars. It also had a relatively high-wage workforce, which gave British businesses an extraordinary incentive to invent laborsaving technologies.

The "Great Divergence"

But was Europe alone destined to lead the way to modern economic life? To many world historians, such views

CONTEXTUALIZATION
Drawing on your prior knowledge about Europe, explain why historians might consider Europe an unlikely place for the Industrial Revolution to have begun.

Agriculture too was affected as mechanical reapers, chemical fertilizers, pesticides, and refrigeration transformed this most ancient of industries. Sustaining this explosion of technological innovation was a novel "culture of innovation," a widespread and almost obsessive belief that things could be endlessly improved.

Together, these new sources of energy and new technologies gave rise to an enormously increased output of goods and services. In Britain, where the Industrial Revolution began, industrial output increased some fiftyfold between 1750

(continued)

from the fifteenth century onward to gain an unusual amount of freedom from state control and a higher social status. By the eighteenth century, major Western European societies were highly commercialized and governed by states that were generally supportive of private commerce; these societies were on their way to becoming capitalist economies. The internally competitive economies, combined with the competitive state structure, helped foster the innovation that led to industrialization.

■ How did the economic structure of Europe help lead to the Industrial Revolution? *European monarchs' need for revenue led to an unusual relationship with their merchant class. This relationship led governments to actively encourage commerce and innovation and eventually led Western European societies to become highly commercialized, setting the stage for capitalist economies that fostered industrialization.*

are both Eurocentric and deterministic; they also fly in the face of much recent research. Historians now know that India, the Islamic world, and especially China had experienced times of great technological and scientific flourishing. For reasons much debated, all of these flowerings of creativity had slowed down considerably or stagnated by the early modern era, when the pace of technological change in Europe began to pick up. But these earlier achievements certainly suggest that Europe was not alone in its capacity for technological innovation.

Nor did Europe enjoy any overall economic advantage as late as 1750. Recent scholars have found rather "a world of surprising resemblances" among major Eurasian societies during the eighteenth century. Economic indicators such as life expectancies, patterns of consumption and nutrition, wage levels, general living standards, widespread free markets, and prosperous merchant communities suggest "a global economic parity" across the major civilizations of Europe and Asia.[7] Thus Europe had no obvious economic lead, even on the eve of the Industrial Revolution. So much for the "European miracle"!

Trade and Empire

But if there was little that was economically distinctive within Europe itself, perhaps it was the spoils of empire and the benefits of global trade after 1500 that allowed Europeans to accumulate the wealth that funded industrial enterprises back home. Far more than their early modern counterparts, European empires provided access to an abundance of raw materials—timber, fish, maize, potatoes—along with products like sugar and cotton produced by enslaved labor. Moreover, these empires generated a global economy that funneled the trade of the world through Europe. Demand for Asian goods, including porcelain and especially cotton cloth, spurred manufacturers

in Europe to produce similar items, while production for overseas markets further sparked industry in Europe. The new wealth spawned a growing middle class in Europe whose members bought the products of the Industrial Revolution. As one scholar has put it, "The industrial revolution . . . emerged from the exploitive advantages Europe was already gaining in the world's markets."[8] So rather than something distinctive about European society, perhaps it was Europe's increasing engagement with the wider world that sparked industrialization.

Many or most of these factors likely played some role in Europe's industrialization. But in considering the "Why Europe?" question, historians confront the relative importance of internal and external factors in explaining historical change. Was industrialization primarily spurred by some special combination of elements peculiar to Western Europe, or were broader global relationships of greater significance? Arguments giving great weight to internal features of European life seem to congratulate Europeans on their good fortune or wisdom, while those that contextualize it globally and point to the unique character of European imperial trade and exploitation are rather more critical. Furthermore, the former seem to imply a certain long-term inevitability to European prominence, while the latter see the Industrial Revolution as more of a surprise, the outcome of a unique conjuncture of events . . . in short, luck.

QUESTIONS TO CONSIDER

1. How might your understanding of the Industrial Revolution change if you subscribed to the "European miracle," the "Great Divergence," or the "Trade and Empire" school of thought?

2. How does this overview of the "Why Europe?" debate shape your understanding of the Industrial Revolution?

and 1900. It was a wholly unprecedented and previously unimaginable jump in the capacity of human societies to produce wealth, to extend life expectancies, and to increase human numbers. Furthermore, industrialization soon spread beyond Britain to continental Western Europe and then in the second half of the nineteenth century to the United States, Russia, and Japan. In the twentieth century it became a genuinely global process. More than anything else, industrialization marks the past 250 years as a distinct phase of human history.

AP® EXAM TIP
Understand the differences between the first and second Industrial Revolutions.

APPLY THE TIP

Students might be surprised to learn that there was more than one Industrial Revolution in the 1750–1900 time period and that they were vastly different in what they focused on. To help students understand the differences between the first and second Industrial Revolutions, ask them to create a chart, like the one seen below, to take notes on the two revolutions. After they have completed the chart, have them work with a partner to develop an argument paragraph for the following question: Evaluate the extent to which the first Industrial Revolution <u>differed</u> from the second Industrial Revolution in the period 1750–1900.

Highlights of the First Industrial Revolution	Highlights of the Second Industrial Revolution
The first Industrial Revolution began in the eighteenth century with a variety of innovations that transformed cotton textile production. In the nineteenth century, the great breakthrough was the invention of the coal-fired steam engine, which was powerful enough to drive machines, locomotives, and ships. With this new source of power, the Industrial Revolution spread beyond textiles to the production of iron and steel and to railroads and steamships, food processing, and construction.	The second Industrial Revolution began later in the nineteenth century and focused on chemicals, electricity, precision machinery, the telegraph and telephone, printing, the production of rubber, and more. Agriculture was also transformed as mechanical reapers, chemical fertilizers, pesticides, and refrigeration were introduced.

TRM Handout 8.1: Comparison Chart for Industrial Revolutions

Making Connections: Causation

The Industrial Revolution dramatically changed the economies, societies, and environments of states that participated in it. While later sections of Chapter 8 go into more detail on these effects, this is a good place to have students start thinking about them. Ask students: What were the environmental and economic effects of the Industrial Revolution? (Answers are provided in italics.)

■ **Environmental effects:** *The extraction of raw materials altered the landscape of many areas; sewers and industrial waste emptied into rivers; smoke from coal-fueled factories, domestic use, and locomotives polluted the air.*

■ **Economic effects:** *New sources of energy gave rise to a greatly increased output of goods and services; increased output of goods and services led to increased wealth in nations.*

If you are having students complete the annotated map assignment from page 441, have them add a chart to their map on the social, economic, political, and environmental consequences of the Industrial Revolution in Europe, the United States, Russia, and Latin America. The information on page 446 and the first paragraph on page 447 can help them get started.

Producing Gas from Coal Coal was central to the Industrial Revolution. An early industrial process in Britain involved the burning of coal to produce "coal gas," used for public lighting. This image from 1822 shows that process in action at one such production facility in London. Those who stoked the furnaces often developed various lung diseases and died early. (Print Collector/Getty Images)

▲ **AP**

CLAIMS AND EVIDENCE IN SOURCES

How does the image illustrate the social and economic changes that took place during the Industrial Revolution?

AP EXAM TIP

As always in world history, when a process "goes global" like the Industrial Revolution, pay attention to the social, economic, and political consequences.

In the long run, the Industrial Revolution unarguably improved the material conditions of life for much of humankind. But it also unarguably wrought a mounting impact on the environment. At first the worst effects were primarily local or regional, concentrated in places where mines or factories were located. The extraction of raw materials—coal, iron ore, petroleum—altered landscapes and polluted local groundwater. The factory waste and human sewage generated by industrial towns emptied into rivers, turning them into poisonous cesspools. In 1858 the Thames River running through London smelled so bad that the British House of Commons had to suspend its session. Smoke from coal-fired industries and domestic use polluted the air in urban areas and sharply increased the incidence of respiratory illness. The British novelist Charles Dickens, who witnessed the impact of industrialization firsthand, described a typical factory town in one of his novels:

> It was a town of red brick, or of brick that would have been red if the smoke and ashes had allowed it; . . . It was a town of machinery and tall chimneys, out of which interminable serpents of smoke trailed themselves for ever and ever, and never got uncoiled. It had a black canal in it, and a river that ran purple with ill-smelling dye.[9]

As the Industrial Revolution grew and spread, pollution and environmental degradation became increasingly global in scale. In 1900 the world consumed fifty-five times as much coal per year as it had in 1800. This growing use of fossil fuels began a gradual increase in greenhouse gas levels in the atmosphere, a trend that sharply accelerated only in the second half of the twentieth century, when its impact on climate change became increasingly well known. In the early industrial era, however, only a few scientists even suspected such a connection.

The Industrial Revolution also allowed humankind to reengineer ever-larger parts of the planet that in the past had been only lightly populated and exploited. Beginning in the 1850s, grasslands in relatively arid regions across the globe, from Argentina and Australia to the steppes of Central Asia and the Great Plains of North America, were put under the plow for the first time. This enormous expansion of tilled lands was made possible by innovations in farm machinery, irrigation pumps, and especially the railroads and steamships that brought fertilizer from distant lands and transported crops grown in remote, often landlocked regions to world markets.

These new agricultural lands—alongside new pasturelands as well—fed a growing population that was also living longer thanks to advances in public health and medicine, setting in motion a historic rise in the human population. World population doubled between 1800 and 1900 and then quadrupled in the twentieth century.

Thus for many historians, the Industrial Revolution marked a new era in both human history and the history of the planet that scientists increasingly call the Anthropocene era, or the "age of man." More and more, human industrial activity left a mark not only on human society but also on the ecological, atmospheric, and geological history of the earth, with enormous implications for all life.

The First Industrial Society

Finding the Main Point: How were traditional social and gender structures transformed during the Industrial Revolution?

Wherever it took hold, the Industrial Revolution generated, within a century or less, an economic miracle, at least in comparison with earlier technologies. Nowhere were the revolutionary dimensions of industrialization more apparent than in Great Britain, the world's first industrial society. The **British textile industry**, which used 52 million pounds of cotton in 1800, consumed 588 million pounds in 1850, as multiple technological innovations and factory-based production vastly increased output. Britain's production of coal likewise soared from 5.23 million tons in 1750 to 68.4 million tons a century later.[10] Railroads crisscrossed Britain and much of Europe like a giant spider web (see Map 8.1). Most of this dramatic increase in production occurred in mining, manufacturing, and services. Thus agriculture, for millennia the overwhelmingly dominant economic sector in every civilization, shrank in relative importance. In Britain, for example, agriculture generated only 8 percent of national income in 1891 and employed fewer than 8 percent of working Britons in 1914.

Accompanying this vast economic change was an epic transformation of social and intellectual life. "In two centuries," wrote one prominent historian, "daily life changed more than it had in the 7,000 years before."[11] And a new set of ideas, now known as "classical liberalism," provided the ideological underpinnings of industrial capitalism. First articulated by British thinkers such as Adam Smith and John Stuart Mill, this novel outlook asserted that individuals, unencumbered by the state, should have the liberty to do with their wealth and their lives as they please. From the ceaseless competition of individuals, operating within a free market system, the collective good of society would automatically emerge. Or so they believed.

The social transformation of the Industrial Revolution both destroyed and created. Referring to the impact of the Industrial Revolution on British society, historian Eric Hobsbawm wrote: "In its initial stages it destroyed their old ways of living and left them free to discover or make for themselves new ones, if they could and knew how. But it rarely told them how to set about it."[12] For many people, it was an enormously painful, even traumatic process, full of social conflict, insecurity, and

BUILDING AP® SKILLS

Making Connections: Causation

Within Europe, Great Britain was the starting point of the Industrial Revolution in the eighteenth century and was an industrial leader in the nineteenth century. You can have students evaluate the relative significance of the different causes that contributed to Britain being the starting point of the Industrial Revolution by asking them to create a causation chart listing economic, social, political, and geographic factors. **Handout 8.2: Causation Chart for the Industrial Revolution in Britain** contains a completed chart with answers and a blank version for students to complete. You can find the handout in the Teacher's Resource Materials.

Economic	Social	Political	Geographic
Britain was the most highly commercialized of Europe's larger states.	Britain had a relatively fluid society that allowed adjustments in the face of social changes without revolution, unlike other European states.	British political life encouraged commercialization and economic innovation.	Britain had a ready supply of coal and iron ore, often located close to each other and within easy reach of major industrial centers.
The enclosure movement pushed smaller farmers off the land and allowed larger farmers to produce for the market, which led to lower food prices.		A policy of religious tolerance welcomed people with technical skills regardless of their faith and therefore encouraged talented immigrants who came from places where they were persecuted.	The nation's island location protected it from the invasions suffered by many other European states during the Napoleonic era.
Guilds had largely disappeared, which allowed employers to run their manufacturing enterprises as they saw fit.		The government favored businessmen with a number of measures and laws, including tariffs that kept out cheap Indian textiles, laws that made it easy to form companies, laws that prohibited the formation of worker's unions, patent laws that protected the interests of inventors, and construction of roads and canals that helped the internal market.	
Economic change, including the availability of workers no longer employed in agriculture, ensured a ready supply of industrial workers.			
Unlike their European counterparts, some British aristocrats took part in the new mining and manufacturing enterprises.		The checks placed on the monarchy provided a freer arena for private enterprise.	
British commerce spread around the world; the merchant fleet was protected by the Royal Navy.			

TRM Handout 8.2: Causation Chart for the Industrial Revolution in Britain

EXPLORING AP® THEMES

Humans and the Environment (ENV)

You can work with students on their map analysis skills by showing them Map 8.1, "The Early Phase of Europe's Industrial Revolution." Give them the questions below to consider as they study the map. After they've had time to study the map, ask students to share their answers to the questions.

■ Based on your observations, what is the relationship between areas of natural resources and the growth of industrial centers? *Industrial centers developed near sources of coal and iron, which were important elements of the Industrial Revolution.*

■ How does this map help explain Great Britain's prominent role in the Industrial Revolution? *Great Britain had an abundance of coal to use in its factories and easy access from its industrial areas to the sea to ship manufactured goods to other regions.*

MAPPING HISTORY   **Map 8.1 The Early Phase of Europe's Industrial Revolution**

From its beginning in Great Britain, industrialization had spread by 1850 across Western Europe to include parts of France, Germany, Belgium, Bohemia, and Italy.

Reading the Map: How would you describe the relationship between the major industrialized areas of Great Britain and deposits of coal and iron? How do railways impact your description? Do all the early major industrialized regions of Europe share a similar relationship with sources of raw materials?

AP **Making Connections:** Identify potential sites for further industrialization. Why did you choose these sites? Where might the building of further railway lines facilitate the growth of already established major industrial areas?

Railroads This 1830s image celebrates the opening of a railway line in Scotland linking the industrial center of Garnkirk (pictured in the background) with the major city of Glasgow about six miles away. The large crowd of spectators reflects the fascination of the public with this new technology. (Private Collection/Photo © Christie's Images/Bridgeman Images)

◀ **AP**
CONTEXTUALIZATION
Why were railroads considered a powerful symbol of the Industrial Revolution?

false starts even as it offered new opportunities, an eventually higher standard of living, and greater participation in public life. The human gains and losses associated with the Industrial Revolution have been debated ever since. Amid the arguments, however, one thing is clear: not everyone was affected in the same way.

The British Aristocracy

Individual landowning aristocrats, long the dominant class in Britain, suffered little in material terms from the Industrial Revolution. In the mid-nineteenth century, a few thousand families still owned more than half of the cultivated land in Britain, most of it leased to tenant farmers, who in turn employed agricultural wage laborers to work it. A rapidly growing population and urbanization sustained demand for food products grown on that land. For most of the nineteenth century, landowners continued to dominate the British Parliament.

As a class, however, the British aristocracy declined as the Industrial Revolution unfolded, as did large landowners in every industrial society. As urban wealth became more important, landed aristocrats had to make way for the up-and-coming businessmen, manufacturers, and bankers, newly enriched by the Industrial Revolution. By the end of the century, landownership had largely ceased to be the basis of great wealth, and businessmen, rather than aristocrats, led the major political parties. Even so, the titled nobility of dukes, earls, viscounts, and barons retained great social prestige and considerable personal wealth. Many among them found an outlet for their energies and opportunities for status and enrichment in the vast domains of the British Empire, where they went as colonial administrators or settlers. Famously described as a "system of outdoor relief for the aristocracy," the empire provided a cushion for a declining class.

AP **EXAM TIP**
Pay attention to changes in British society due to the Industrial Revolution, because they will also occur throughout the industrialized world.

AP
CONTINUITY AND CHANGE
How did industrial production transform the social position of England's aristocratic class?

APPLY THE TIP

As students start to learn about how industrialization changed British society, consider having them recall what they learned about social and economic transformations in "Industrialization: The Global Context." This exercise will also help students practice the recommended skill for Unit 5, Continuity and Change. Ask students: What economic and social transformations occurred as a result of the Industrial Revolution? *Economic transformations included a dramatic increase in production in mining, manufacturing, and services. Agriculture, which had been the dominant economic sector in Britain, shrank in importance. Social transformations included the creation of new social classes, which led to social conflict, insecurity, and false starts as well as new opportunities, a high standard of living, and greater participation in public life.*

TEACHING IDEA
Incorporating Outside Resources

In the episode *The Railroad Journey and the Industrial Revolution* of Crash Course World History, John Green discusses railroad building during the Industrial Revolution and some of the ways in which railroads changed the world. This video will help students understand the impact of railroads on the nineteenth-century world and how the railroads represented the changes of industrialization on a smaller scale. You can find the video on YouTube. Ask students to answer the following questions as they watch the video, either as homework or in class.

■ How did railroads destroy traditional relationships humans had with nature? *Humans modified nature in order to build the railroads; they cut tunnels through hills and graded depressions to make the railroad lines as straight as possible.*

■ How did railroads change time? *Railroads sped up travel times, which shrank the world. Railroad timetables used Greenwich Mean Time, which created standardized timekeeping.*

■ What arguments does the video make for how railroads changed the way people looked at the world and the way people behaved? *Railroads changed the perception of time and power and also changed how people viewed the world. When they traveled on trains, people saw the changing views as something new and exciting. As people began to travel on trains, usually for a shorter period of time than on a stagecoach, they began to read books and other literature on the trains. This was a way for upper-class passengers to avoid talking to one another, a change from the rapport built on stagecoach journeys. Fear and anxiety about railway journeys and accidents also began to be reflected in new ideas about psychology.*

■ Why were the changes brought about by the Industrial Revolution and railroads different from those brought about by previous inventions? *Industrialization and railroads were different because they had a profound effect on large numbers of people in a very short time, and the changes continued to happen at a rapid pace.*

The Middle Classes

Those who benefited most conspicuously from industrialization were members of that amorphous group known as the middle class. At its upper levels, this middle class contained extremely wealthy factory and mine owners, bankers, and merchants. Such rising businessmen readily assimilated into aristocratic life, buying country houses, obtaining seats in Parliament, sending their sons to Oxford or Cambridge University, and gratefully accepting titles of nobility from Queen Victoria.

Far more numerous were the smaller businessmen, doctors, lawyers, engineers, teachers, journalists, scientists, and other professionals required in any industrial society. Such people set the tone for a distinctly **middle-class society** with its own values and outlooks. Politically they were liberals, favoring constitutional and limited government, private property, free trade, and social reform within limits. Their agitation resulted in the Reform Bill of 1832, which broadened the right to vote to many men of the middle class, but not to middle-class women. Ideas of thrift and hard work, a rigid morality, "respectability," and cleanliness characterized middle-class culture. According to Samuel Smiles's famous book *Self-Help*, an enterprising spirit was what distinguished the prosperous middle class from Britain's poor. The misery of the poorer classes was "voluntary and self-imposed—the results of idleness, thriftlessness, intemperance, and misconduct."[13]

Women in such middle-class families were increasingly cast as homemakers, wives, and mothers, charged with creating an emotional haven for their men and a refuge from a heartless and cutthroat capitalist world. They were also expected to be the moral centers of family life, the educators of "respectability," and the managers of household consumption as "shopping"—a new concept in eighteenth-century Britain—became a central activity for the middle classes. An **ideology of domesticity** defined homemaking, child rearing, charitable endeavors, and "refined" activities such as embroidery and music as the proper sphere for women, while paid employment and the public sphere of life outside the home beckoned to men.

Male elites in many civilizations had long established their status by detaching women from productive labor. The new wealth of the Industrial Revolution now allowed larger numbers of families to aspire to a special kind of status. With her husband as "provider," a woman was now a "lady." "She must not work for profit," wrote the Englishwoman Margaretta Greg in 1853, "or engage in any occupation that money can command."[14] Employing even one servant became a proud marker of such middle-class status. But the withdrawal of middle-class women from the labor force turned out to be only a temporary phenomenon. By the late nineteenth century, some middle-class women began to enter the teaching, clerical, and nursing professions, and in the second half of the twentieth century, many more flooded into the labor force. By contrast, the withdrawal of children from productive labor into schools has proved a more enduring phenomenon as industrial economies increasingly required a more educated workforce.

As Britain's industrial economy matured, it also gave rise to a sizable **lower middle class**, which included people employed in the growing service sector as

TEACHING IDEA

Incorporating Outside Resources

The OER Project has an interesting activity on practicing claim-testing skills and the changing gender roles of the modern era, including changes that happened due to industrialization. After students finish Chapter 8, you could have them complete this activity to review how women's roles changed throughout the modern era and to practice their argumentation skills. You can find the PDF of the activity and more detailed instructions in Unit 5 of the World History: AP® section of the OER Project site, in the middle of Lesson 5.6: "Social Transformation."

EXPLORING AP® THEMES

Social Interactions and Organization (SIO)

New social classes, including the middle class and the laboring class, appeared as a result of the Industrial Revolution in Great Britain. You can have students create a comparison chart that lists characteristics of the three major social classes of nineteenth-century Great Britain: the aristocracy, the middle class, and the laboring class. A reproducible chart is available in the Teacher's Resource Materials.

Aristocracy	Middle Class	Laboring Class
▪ *Individual landowners continued to own large tracts of land and dominated the British Parliament.*	▪ *The newly formed middle class benefited the most from the Industrial Revolution. In the upper middle class, extremely wealthy factory and mine owners, bankers, and merchants readily assimilated into aristocratic life.*	▪ *The laboring class made up the overwhelming majority of Britain's nineteenth-century population: 70 percent or more.*
▪ *By the 1840s the aristocracy began to experience declining political clout, and by the end of the century businessmen led the major political parties.*	▪ *Smaller businessmen, doctors, lawyers, engineers, teachers, journalists, scientists, and other professionals made up the majority of the middle class; these groups set the tone for a distinctly middle-class society with its own values and outlooks.*	▪ *The laboring class included workers in mines, ports, factories, construction sites, workshops, and farms.*
▪ *The aristocracy retained great social prestige and personal wealth. Many found an outlet for their energies and new opportunities in the domains of the British Empire.*	▪ *Ideas of thrift and hard work, rigid morality, and cleanliness characterized middle-class culture.*	▪ *The laboring class suffered the most and benefited the least from the transformations of the Industrial Revolution.*
	▪ *A sizable lower middle class began to emerge as Britain's industrial economy matured; this group consisted of clerks, salespeople, bank tellers, hotel staff, secretaries, telephone operators, and police. Type of employment distinguished the middle class and working class.*	▪ *The lives of the laboring class were shaped primarily by the new working conditions of the industrial era: people lived in crowded, polluted cities and worked long hours for low wages.*

TRM Handout 8.3: Comparison Chart for Social Classes in Great Britain

The Industrial Middle Class This late nineteenth-century painting shows a prosperous French middle-class family, attended by a servant. (Bridgeman Images)

◀ **AP®**
CONTINUITY AND CHANGE
In what ways does this painting reflect changes to society and gender brought about by industrialization? What features in the painting help illustrate the newfound prosperity of middle-class families?

clerks, salespeople, bank tellers, hotel staff, secretaries, telephone operators, police officers, and the like. By the end of the nineteenth century, this growing segment of the middle class represented about 20 percent of Britain's population and provided new employment opportunities for women as well as men. In just twenty years (1881–1901), the number of female secretaries in Britain rose from 7,000 to 90,000. Almost all were single and expected to return to the home after marriage. For both men and women, such employment represented a claim on membership in the larger middle class and a means of distinguishing themselves clearly from a working class tainted by manual labor. The mounting ability of these middle classes to consume all manner of material goods—and their appetite for doing so—were among the factors that sustained the continuing growth of the industrializing process.

The Laboring Classes

The overwhelming majority of Britain's nineteenth-century population—some 70 percent or more—were neither aristocrats nor members of the middle classes. They were manual workers in the mines, ports, factories, construction sites, workshops, and farms of an industrializing Britain. Although their conditions varied considerably and changed over time, it was the **laboring classes** who suffered most and benefited least from the epic transformations of the Industrial Revolution. Their efforts to accommodate, resist, protest, and change those conditions contributed much to the texture of the first industrial society.

AP® EXAM TIP
How the Industrial Revolution affected the lower classes—for better and worse—is a very important topic in AP® World History.

Making Connections: Comparison

As Britain's industrial economy grew, a new section of the middle class, the lower middle class, began to emerge and grow. Have students read through the last paragraph of "The Middle Classes" (starting on the bottom of page 450) and answer the question: What do you think distinguished the lower middle class from the upper middle class and the laboring class? *The jobs performed by the members of the lower middle class gave them a claim to membership in the middle class, but also distinguished them from the upper middle class and the laboring class. The lower middle class was employed in the growing service sector, rather than in the manual labor performed by the laboring class.*

The Industrial Revolution probably had the largest impact on the laboring classes, and students should be able to identify those effects. You can ask students to make a list of the effects of the Industrial Revolution on the lower classes as they read through this section. After they have made their list, have them divide the effects into positives and negatives and answer the following question: Was the Industrial Revolution more harmful or more beneficial to the laboring and lower classes? *Answers will vary.*

Bell Ringer

An interesting way to start class when students are learning about the effects of industrialization could be to display the British political cartoon "The Silent Highwayman." A copy of this image can be found by searching for it on the Wikimedia Commons website.

Ask students: What side effect of the Industrial Revolution is this political cartoon showing? *The cartoon is showing the pollution, especially water pollution, caused by industrialization and the health problems caused by pollution. The cartoon depicts the figure of Death rowing a boat down the polluted Thames River while dead animals float by.*

EXPLORING AP® THEMES

Social Interactions and Organization (SIO)

As industrialization increased throughout Britain, urban centers developed around the factories and grew as the new laboring class flooded into the cities looking for work. Cities grew dramatically during the nineteenth century and struggled to keep up with their growing populations. Consider asking students to read "Life in Industrial Towns" by C. N. Truman, found by searching for the article on the History Learning website. Have students answer the following questions in class, or assign them as homework:

▪ Why did many people move to industrial cities during the Industrial Revolution? *People moved because the enclosure movement and technical developments in agriculture reduced the need for people to work on farmland.*

▪ How did builders deal with the high demand for housing as people flooded into cities during the nineteenth century? *There were very few building regulations at this time. Builders put up houses quickly and cheaply, which led to the creation of back-to-back terrace housing.*

▪ What were living conditions like in the new housing arrangements in urban areas? *Homes were built cheaply, without indoor plumbing. Waste was thrown into the courtyard between houses, which contributed to major epidemics. Toilets were cesspits that were not drained regularly, and freshwater was difficult to access. Crowded living conditions added to the sanitation problems.*

▪ Why was so little done to improve living conditions in cities? *The poor of the cities did not have much political or social influence. The wealthy, who had the most political and social influence, were not motivated to help improve conditions because they saw no personal benefit from such efforts.*

The lives of the laboring classes were shaped primarily by the rapid urbanization of the industrial era. Liverpool's population alone grew from 77,000 to 400,000 in the first half of the nineteenth century. By 1851, a majority of Britain's population lived in towns and cities, an enormous change from the overwhelmingly rural life of almost all previous civilizations.

These cities were vastly overcrowded and smoky, with wholly insufficient sanitation, periodic epidemics, few public services or open spaces, and inadequate and often-polluted water supplies. This was the environment in which most urban workers lived in the first half of the nineteenth century. By 1850, the average life expectancy in England was only 39.5 years, less than it had been some three centuries earlier. Nor was there much personal contact between the rich and the poor of industrial cities. Benjamin Disraeli's novel *Sybil*, published in 1845, described these two ends of the social spectrum as "two nations between whom there is no intercourse and no sympathy; who are ignorant of each other's habits, thoughts and feelings, as if they were dwellers in different zones or inhabitants of different planets."[15]

The industrial factories to which growing numbers of desperate people looked for employment offered a work environment far different from the artisan's shop or the tenant's farm. Long hours, low wages, and child labor were nothing new for the poor, but the routine and monotony of work, dictated by the factory whistle and the needs of machines, imposed novel and highly unwelcome conditions of labor. Also objectionable were the direct and constant supervision and the rules and fines aimed at enforcing work discipline. In addition, the ups and downs of a capitalist economy made industrial work insecure as well as onerous.

In the early decades of the nineteenth century, Britain's industrialists favored girls and young unmarried women as employees in the textile mills, for they were often willing to accept lower wages, while male owners believed them to be both docile and more suitable for repetitive tasks such as tending machines. A gendered hierarchy of labor emerged in these factories, with men in supervisory and more skilled positions, while women occupied the less skilled and "lighter" jobs that offered little opportunity

DEATH'S DISPENSARY.
OPEN TO THE POOR, GRATIS, BY PERMISSION OF THE PARISH.

The Urban Poor of Industrial Britain This 1866 political cartoon shows an impoverished urban family forced to draw its drinking water from a polluted public well, while a figure of Death operates the pump. (Sarin Images/Granger, NYC – All rights reserved)

Incorporating Outside Resources

To further illustrate how pollution from industrialization caused health problems for urban dwellers and sometimes sparked epidemics, you can show the clip "Cholera" from *Mankind: The Story of All of Us* about the cholera epidemic in nineteenth-century London. The video clip can be found by searching for it on History.com's website.

for advancement. Nor were women welcome in the unions that eventually offered men some ability to shape the conditions under which they labored.

Thus, unlike their middle-class counterparts, many girls and young women of the laboring classes engaged in industrial work or found jobs as domestic servants for upper- and middle-class families to supplement meager family incomes. But after marriage, they too usually left outside paid employment because a man who could not support his wife was widely considered a failure. Within the home, however, many working-class women continued to earn money by taking in boarders, doing laundry, or sewing clothes in addition to the domestic and child-rearing responsibilities long assigned to women.

Social Protest

For workers of the laboring classes, industrial life "was a stony desert, which they had to make habitable by their own efforts."[16] Such efforts took many forms. By 1815, about 1 million workers, mostly artisans, had created a variety of "friendly societies." With dues contributed by members, these working-class self-help groups provided insurance against sickness, a decent funeral, and an opportunity for social life in an otherwise bleak environment. Other skilled artisans who had been displaced by machine-produced goods and forbidden to organize in legal unions sometimes wrecked the offending machinery and burned the mills that had taken their jobs. (See Zooming In: The English Luddites and Machine Breaking, page 454.) The class consciousness of working people was such that one police informer reported that "most every creature of the lower order both in town and country are on their side."[17]

Others acted within the political arena by joining movements aimed at obtaining the vote for working-class men, a goal that was gradually achieved in the second half of the nineteenth century. When trade unions were legalized in 1824, growing numbers of factory workers joined these associations in their efforts to achieve better wages and working conditions. Initially their strikes, attempts at nationwide organization, and threat of violence made them fearful indeed to the upper classes. One British newspaper in 1834 described unions as "the most dangerous institutions that were ever permitted to take root, under shelter of law, in any country,"[18] although they later became rather more "respectable" organizations.

Socialist ideas of various kinds gradually spread within the working class, challenging the assumptions of a capitalist society. Robert Owen (1771–1858), a wealthy British cotton textile manufacturer, urged the creation of small industrial communities where workers and their families would be well treated. He established one such community, with a ten-hour workday, spacious housing, decent wages, and education for children, at his mill in New Lanark in Scotland.

Of more lasting significance was the socialism of **Karl Marx** (1818–1883). German by birth, Marx spent much of his life in England, where he witnessed the brutal conditions of Britain's Industrial Revolution and wrote voluminously about history and economics. His probing analysis led him to conclude that industrial

AP EXAM TIP
Understand how the condition of the laboring classes led to political reforms and the development of economic ideologies.

AP EXAM TIP
You may see AP® Exam questions on Marx's economic theories and their application in later world history.

APPLY THE TIP

As students read through "Social Protest," ask them to create a list in their reading notes of how the laboring class reacted to the Industrial Revolution with new social, political, and economic ideas. (Answers provided in italics.)

- **Social:** *Working-class people began to create a variety of "friendly societies" to help support one another. These working-class self-help groups provided insurance against sickness, a decent funeral, and an opportunity for social life. Some workers, forbidden from creating unions and displaced by machine-made goods, wrecked the machinery and factories that had taken their jobs.*

- **Political:** *Some workers joined movements aimed at gaining the vote for working-class men; when trade unions became legal in 1824, factory workers joined them to achieve better wages and working conditions. Union strikes, attempts at nationwide organization, and threat of violence scared the upper classes.*

- **Economic:** *New economic ideas and ideologies, like socialism and Marxism, began to emerge as a challenge to capitalist society.*

BUILDING AP® SKILLS

Making Connections: Comparison

The lives of women were changing during the nineteenth century, but these changes depended on social class. It would be good for students to be able to compare the changes that happened in the lives of middle-class women and laboring-class women. Ask students to use the information on pages 450–453 to create a chart comparing the lives of women in different social classes. A reproducible version of this chart can be found in the Teacher's Resource Materials.

Middle-Class Women	Laboring-Class Women
■ *During the early nineteenth century middle-class women were pushed out of the workforce, but by the end of the century some women began to join the workforce.*	■ *Girls and young unmarried women from the laboring class were favored by industrialists as employees in the textile mills because they were often willing to accept lower wages and were seen as more docile and more suitable for the repetitive task of tending machines.*
■ *Middle-class women could hire servants, which was a sign of prosperity.*	■ *Laboring-class women found work as domestic servants for upper- and middle-class families.*
■ *Middle-class women were cast as homemakers, wives, and mothers and were expected to create an emotional haven and refuge for their men.*	■ *Laboring-class women made money in their homes by taking in boarders, doing laundry, or sewing clothes in addition to fulfilling their domestic and child-rearing responsibilities.*
■ *Middle-class women were expected to be the moral centers of their homes and to follow the "ideology of domesticity," while educating their children in respectability.*	

TRM Handout 8.4: Comparison Chart for the Lives of Middle-Class and Laboring-Class Women

TEACHING IDEA

Incorporating Outside Resources

Students sometimes struggle with understanding the new economic ideologies of the industrial era. The Crash Course World History episode *Capitalism and Socialism* discusses how the Industrial Revolution led to the rise of capitalism and socialism. This video will help students understand the ideals behind capitalism and socialism in the context of industrialization and will help them compare the two systems. You can find the video by searching for it on YouTube. After students finish the video, ask them the following questions to drive a discussion on new economic ideologies:

■ What is the difference between mercantile capitalism and industrial capitalism? *In mercantile capitalism, merchants borrowed money in order to buy goods that they would then resell at a profit, using the profits to pay back their original loan. Industrial capitalism relied on the investment of capital in machines and technology that increased the production of goods that entrepreneurs and companies could sell at a profit.*

■ What were some of the problems created by industrial capitalism in the nineteenth century? How did workers and society respond to these problems? *Working conditions were terrible and pay was low; workdays were long, difficult, and monotonous; workers lived in crowded, polluted cities. Workers created labor unions to negotiate for better conditions, and new economic theories like socialism developed.*

■ Why were Karl Marx's ideas on socialism more popular than the earlier types of socialism (utopian and revolutionary)? *He believed that workers would be able to work together to overthrow the bourgeoisie oppressors on their own and establish an egalitarian society. His ideas empowered workers.*

ZOOMING (IN)   **The English Luddites and Machine Breaking**

If you do Not Cause those Dressing Machines to be Remov'd Within the Bounds of Seven Days . . . your factory and all that it Contains Will and Shall Surely Be Set on fire . . . it is Not our Desire to Do you the Least Injury, But We are fully Determin'd to Destroy Both Dressing Machines and Steam Looms.[19]

Luddites smashing a loom.

Between 1811 and 1813, this kind of warning was sent to hundreds of English workshops in the woolen and cotton industry, where more efficient machines, some of them steam-powered, threatened the jobs and livelihoods of workers. Over and over, that threat was carried out as well-organized bands of skilled artisans destroyed the offending machines, burned buildings, and on occasion attacked employers. These were the Luddites, taking their name from a mythical Robin Hood–like figure, Ned Ludd. A song called "General Ludd's Triumph" expressed their sentiments: "These Engines of mischief were sentenced to die / By unanimous vote of the Trade / And Ludd who can all opposition defy / Was the Grand executioner made."

So widespread and serious was this Luddite uprising that the British government sent 12,000 troops to suppress it, more than it was then devoting to the struggle against Napoleon in continental Europe. And a new law, rushed through Parliament as an "emergency measure" in 1812, made those who destroyed mechanized looms subject to the death penalty. Some sixty to seventy alleged Luddites were in fact hanged, and sometimes beheaded as well, for machine breaking.

In the governing circles of England, Luddism was widely regarded as blind protest, an outrageous, unthinking, and futile resistance to progress. It has remained in more recent times a term of insult applied to those who resist or reject technological innovation. And yet, a closer look suggests that the Luddites deserve some sympathy as an understandable response to a painful transformation of social life when few alternatives for expressing grievances were available.

At the time of the Luddite uprising, England was involved in an increasingly unpopular war with Napoleon's France, and mutual blockades substantially reduced trade and

photo: Chronicle/Alamy

AP®

CONTEXTUALIZATION
In what situations would the ideas of Karl Marx have the most appeal among the lower classes?

capitalism was an inherently unstable system, doomed to collapse in a revolutionary upheaval that would give birth to a classless socialist society, thus ending forever the ancient conflict between rich and poor. (See AP® Working with Evidence, Document 2, "Socialism According to Marx and Engels," page 484.)

In Marx's writings, the combined impact of Europe's industrial, political, and scientific revolutions found expression. Industrialization created both the social conditions against which Marx protested so bitterly and the enormous wealth he felt would make socialism possible. The French Revolution, still a living memory in Marx's youth, provided evidence that grand upheavals, giving rise to new societies,

---

BUILDING AP® SKILLS

Claims and Evidence in Sources

To help students better understand how socialism developed in different areas during the Industrial Revolution, you can ask students to analyze and discuss "Working with Evidence, Document 2: Socialism According to Marx and Engels," on pages 484–485. In this document, students will learn about the ideas Karl Marx and Friedrich Engels discussed in *The Communist Manifesto*. Use the questions on page 485 to guide your discussion, or assign them as homework.

hurt the textile industry. The country was also in the early phase of an Industrial Revolution in which mechanized production was replacing skilled artisan labor. All of this, plus some bad weather and poor harvests, combined to generate real economic hardship, unemployment, and hunger. Bread riots and various protests against high prices proliferated.

Furthermore, English elites were embracing new laissez-faire, or free market, economic principles, which eroded customary protections for the poor and working classes. Over the previous several decades, many laws that had regulated wages and apprenticeships and prohibited certain laborsaving machines had been repealed, despite repeated workers' appeals to Parliament to maintain some minimal protections for their older way of life. A further act of Parliament in 1799 had forbidden trade unions and collective bargaining. In these circumstances, some form of direct action is hardly surprising.

At one level, the Luddite machine-breaking movement represented "collective bargaining by riot," a way of pressuring employers when legal negotiations with them had been outlawed. And the issues involved more than laborsaving machines. Luddites also argued for price reductions, minimum wages, and prohibitions on the flooding of their industry by unapprenticed workers. They wanted to return to a time when "full fashioned work at the old fashioned price is established by custom and law," according to one of their songs. More generally, Luddites sought to preserve elements of an older way of life in which industry existed to provide a livelihood for workers, in which men could take pride in their craft, in

which government and employers felt some paternalistic responsibility to the lower classes, and in which journeymen workers felt some bonds of attachment to a larger social and moral order. All of this was rapidly eroding in the new era of capitalist industrialization. In these ways, the Luddite movement looked backward to idealized memories of an earlier time.

And yet in other ways, the rebels anticipated the future with their demands for a minimum wage and an end to child labor, their concern about inferior-quality products produced by machines, and their desire to organize trade unions. At the height of the Luddite movement, some among them began to move beyond local industrial action toward a "general insurrection" that might bring real political change to the entire country. In one letter from a Luddite in 1812, the writer expressed "hope for assistance from the French emperor [Napoleon] in shaking off the yoke of the rottenest, wickedest, and most tyranious government that ever existed." He continued, "Then we will be governed by a just republic."

After 1813, the organized Luddite movement faded away. But it serves as a cautionary reminder that what is hailed as progress claims victims as well as beneficiaries.

QUESTIONS

To what extent did the concerns of the Luddites come to pass as the Industrial Revolution unfolded? How does your understanding of the Luddites affect your posture toward technological change in our time?

had in fact taken place and could do so again. Moreover, Marx regarded himself as a scientist, discovering the laws of social development in much the same fashion as Newton discovered the laws of motion. His was therefore a "scientific socialism," embedded in these laws of historical change; revolution was a certainty and the socialist future was inevitable.

It was a grand, compelling, prophetic, utopian vision of human freedom and community — and it inspired socialist movements of workers and intellectuals amid the grim harshness of Europe's industrialization in the second half of the nineteenth century. Socialists established political parties in most European states and

AP
CAUSATION
How did Karl Marx's ideas about the Industrial Revolution affect the industrializing world in the nineteenth century?

BUILDING AP® SKILLS
Claims and Evidence in Sources

Consider showing students the image titled "The Pyramid of the Capitalist System" (Document 7 on page 489 in "AP® Working with Evidence") to help them practice their image analysis skills. Then ask: Based on what can be seen in the poster, how did the artist view the capitalist society developing in Europe in the nineteenth century? *The upper classes of capitalist society — the bourgeoisie, the police and militia, religious figures, and state officials — were supported by the lower, working class. The artist appears to think that the upper classes did not care about what was happening to the lower classes as long as their good life continued.*

This would be a good place to pause and ask students to create a chart describing Karl Marx's ideas on capitalism, his suggestions to reform capitalism, and changes in Western Europe that made Marxism less appealing. **Handout 8.5: Chart for Marxism, Capitalism, and Changes in Western Europe** contains a completed chart with answers and a blank version for students to complete. You can find the handout in the Teacher's Resource Materials.

TRM Handout 8.5: Chart for Marxism, Capitalism, and Changes in Western Europe

TEACHING IDEA

Class Discussion

It could be interesting to have students take on the personas of different groups from the Industrial Revolution to debate some of the major ideas and issues of the era. Divide the class into three groups for the debate: factory owners, factory workers, and a neutral group such as members of Parliament. Groups should research wages in industrial factories, working conditions, unionism, capitalism, and socialism. Factory owners and factory workers should prepare position statements on each topic from the point of view of their assigned role. The neutral group should prepare questions to ask each group. The goal of the factory owners' group and the factory workers' group during the debate is to get members of the neutral group to agree with their position on the different topics.

Give students one class period for debate research and preparation, or assign these tasks for homework the night before the debate. On the day of the debate, have the room set up into three groups of desks; factory owners sit on one side of the room, factory workers sit on the opposite side of the room, and the neutral group sits in the middle of the room. Give groups 5 to 10 minutes to select a representative and prepare a statement. One representative of the factory owners and one representative of the factory workers will make an opening statement to begin the debate. After the opening statements, each group can make a rebuttal. Then allow the neutral group to take turns asking questions of the other two groups. At the end of the debate, take a vote in the neutral group to see who made the most persuasive case.

Differentiation

If you want to scaffold the debate to help students prepare for it and give them the opportunity to further research a topic they are

linked them together in international organizations as well. These parties recruited members, contested elections as they gained the right to vote, agitated for reforms, and in some cases plotted revolution.

AP EXAM TIP
Understand how governments in Western Europe responded to Marx's ideas.

In the later decades of the nineteenth century, such ideas echoed among more radical trade unionists and some middle-class intellectuals in Britain, and even more so in a rapidly industrializing Germany and elsewhere. By then, however, the British working-class movement was not overtly revolutionary. When a working-class political party, the **Labour Party**, was established in the 1890s, it advocated a reformist program and a peaceful democratic transition to socialism, largely rejecting the class struggle and revolutionary emphasis of classical Marxism. Generally known as "social democracy," this approach to socialism was especially prominent in Germany during the late nineteenth century and spread more widely in the twentieth century, when it came into conflict with the more violent and revolutionary movements calling themselves "communist."

▼ AP
CAUSATION
What developments drove people to the kinds of actions seen in this painting?

Improving material conditions during the second half of the nineteenth century helped move the working-class movement in Britain, Germany, and elsewhere away from a revolutionary posture. Marx had expected industrial capitalist societies to polarize into a small wealthy class and a huge and increasingly impoverished proletariat. However, standing between "the captains of industry" and the workers was a sizable middle and lower middle class, constituting perhaps 30 percent of the population, most of whom were not wealthy but were immensely proud that they were not manual laborers. Marx had not foreseen the development of this intermediate social group, nor had he imagined that workers could better their standard of living within a capitalist framework. But they did. Wages rose under pressure from unions; cheap imported food improved working-class diets; infant mortality rates fell; and shops and chain stores catering to working-class families multiplied. As English male workers gradually obtained the right to vote, politicians had an incentive to legislate in their favor, by abolishing child labor, regulating factory conditions, and even, in 1911, inaugurating a system of relief for the unemployed. Sanitary reform considerably cleaned up the "filth and stink" of early nineteenth-century cities, and urban parks made a modest appearance. Contrary to Marx's expectations, capitalist societies demonstrated some capacity for reform.

Socialist Art Dating from 1901, this iconic painting entitled "The Fourth Estate" (the working classes) by the Italian artist Giuseppe Pellizza da Volpedo depicts striking workers peacefully marching toward a better future. It has become a symbol and rallying point for many socialists, who find inspiration in the sense of determination, unity, and humanity conveyed by the workers in the image. (Museo del Novecento, Milan, Italy/Photo © A. Dagli Orti/De Agostini Picture Library/Bridgeman Images)

Further eroding working-class radicalism was a growing sense of nationalism, which

(continued)

interested in, consider following the "Must Do, Should Do, Strive For" model below:

■ Must Do: Students must research and record their research for the following topics: wages in industrial factories, working conditions, unionism, capitalism, socialism, living conditions in cities, and industrial pollution. Working with their group, they should create position statements for each topic from the point of view of their assigned role.

■ Should Do: Students should participate in the class debate, either by asking questions or providing evidence to support their side's point of view on a given topic.

■ Strive For: Students can choose to complete further research on the new ideas of the Industrial Revolution. Topics can include population theories such as Malthus's theory, capitalism, Marxism, utilitarianism, the Chartist movement, public education, public health care, universal suffrage, and socialism. Students should present their findings in a 1- to 2-page paper.

bound workers to their middle-class employers, offsetting to some extent the economic and social antagonism between them. When World War I broke out, the "workers of the world," far from uniting against their bourgeois enemies as socialist leaders had urged, instead set off to slaughter one another in enormous numbers on the battlefields of Europe. National loyalty had trumped class loyalty.

Nonetheless, as the twentieth century dawned, industrial Britain was hardly a stable or contented society. Immense inequalities still separated the classes. Some 40 percent of the working class continued to live in conditions then described as "poverty." A mounting wave of strikes from 1910 to 1913 testified to the intensity of class conflict. The Labour Party was becoming a major force in Parliament. Some socialists and some feminists were becoming radicalized. "Wisps of violence hung in the English air," wrote Eric Hobsbawm, "symptoms of a crisis in economy and society, which the [country's] self-confident opulence . . . could not quite conceal."[20] The world's first industrial society remained dissatisfied and conflicted.

It was also a society in economic decline relative to industrial newcomers such as Germany and the United States. Britain paid a price for its early lead, for its businessmen became committed to machinery that became obsolete as the century progressed. Latecomers invested in more modern equipment and in various ways had surpassed the British by the early twentieth century.

Europeans in Motion

Finding the Main Point: What were the effects of European migrations on the South Pacific, North and South America, and Russia?

Europe's Industrial Revolution prompted a massive migratory process that uprooted many millions, setting them in motion both internally and around the globe. Within Europe itself, by the mid-nineteenth century half or more of the region's people had relocated from the countryside to the cities. Equally significant was the exodus between 1815 and 1939 of fully 20 percent of Europe's population, some 50 to 55 million people, who left home for the Americas, Australia, New Zealand, South Africa, and elsewhere (see Map 8.2). They were pushed by poverty, a rapidly growing population, and the displacement of peasant farming and artisan manufacturing. And they were pulled abroad by the enormous demand for labor overseas, the ready availability of land in some places, and the relatively cheap transportation of railroads and steamships. But not all found a satisfactory life in their new homes, and perhaps 7 million returned to Europe.[21]

This huge process had a transformative global impact, temporarily increasing Europe's share of the world's population and scattering Europeans around the world. In 1800, less than 1 percent of the total world population consisted of overseas Europeans and their descendants; by 1930, they represented 11 percent.[22] In some regions, the impact was profound. Australia and New Zealand became settler

AP CONTEXTUALIZATION
How could nationalism lessen the potential for socialist revolutions in some countries?

AP EXAM TIP
Understand the different patterns of migrations initiated by the Industrial Revolution.

AP CAUSATION
What aspects of the Industrial Revolution facilitated the migration of Europeans to other parts of the world?

CHAPTER 8

BUILDING AP® SKILLS

Making Connections: Continuity and Change

You could do a quick Continuity and Change skill practice here with an exit ticket for students. This exercise will also allow you to check student understanding of the changes that happened due to industrialization. Ask students to write a response to the following question and turn it in as they leave class: What did British society and industrialization look like at the start of the twentieth century? (Answers are provided in italics.)

■ **Society:** *Immense inequalities still separated the social classes. Forty percent of the working class lived in poverty. Class conflict was evident in the wave of strikes that occurred from 1910 to 1913. The Labour Party was becoming a major force in Parliament. Some socialists and feminists were becoming radicalized.*

■ **Industrialization:** *Britain was in economic decline by the start of the twentieth century relative to industrial newcomers such as Germany and the United States. Businessmen who got an early start in industrialization became committed to machinery that became obsolete as the century progressed.*

TEACHING IDEA

Bell Ringer

To introduce migration in the nineteenth century, you can ask students: What are "push" and "pull" factors in migration? *Push factors are forces that act to drive people away from a place. Pull factors are forces that act to draw people to a new location.*

Then ask students to create their own lists of possible push and pull factors for migration in the nineteenth century and share the lists with their classmates. (Possible answers are provided in italics.)

■ **Push factors:** *Poverty, a rapidly growing population, and the displacement of peasant farming and artisan manufacturing.*

■ **Pull factors:** *Large demand for labor overseas, the ready availability of land in some places, and the relatively cheap transportation of railroads and steamships, which made it easy to move to new places.*

EXPLORING AP® THEMES

Humans and the Environment (ENV)

While Europeans migrated in large numbers during the nineteenth century, people from other regions of the world also migrated to new places. To compare European migration to migration from other regions during this period, you could have students research and study a map of all migrations taking place from 1750 to 1900. You can find a good migrations map on Freeman-pedia's website, in the Modern Period section of the AP® World: Modern area of the site. After students study the map, ask the following questions:

■ What regions of the world, outside of Europe, saw large numbers of migrants moving away from 1750 to 1900? *Migrants left Africa, India, China, and Japan.*

■ Where did these migrants move? *These migrants moved to the Americas, Africa, and Southeast Asia.*

■ Why do you think these migrants moved to new regions? *While there was some involuntary migration, many migrants moved to new regions in search of work.*

BUILDING AP® SKILLS

Argumentation

To help students understand the reasons people migrated during the modern era and the labor systems that existed in this period, consider assigning the documents from the 2003 released DBQ Question 1. This question asks students to analyze the causes and consequences of the system of indentured servitude that developed in the nineteenth century. The question and accompanying documents can be found on the College Board website, in the AP® World History: Modern Past Exam Questions section. Have students write evidence statements for each of the documents on how they help answer the prompt to practice their DBQ writing skills. If you want to give students extra DBQ writing practice, have them pick one document to practice writing a sourcing statement.

The prompt will need to be updated to match the current format of the AP® Exam. You can change the prompt to the following: Evaluate the extent to which the changes to the global economy transformed the system of indentured servitude in the nineteenth and early twentieth centuries.

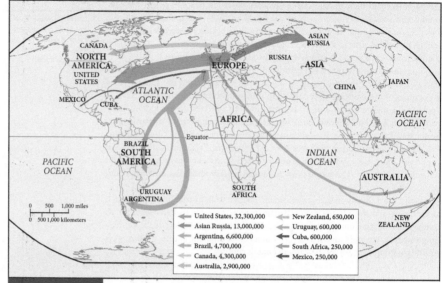

MAPPING HISTORY   **Map 8.2 European Migration in the Industrial Age**

The Industrial Revolution not only transformed European society but also scattered millions of Europeans to the far corners of the world.

Reading the Map: Which continent received the fewest European migrants?

AP® Making Connections: Which regions of the world were most affected by European emigration? Which regions were little affected? How might you explain the variations?

colonies, outposts of European civilization in the South Pacific that overwhelmed their native populations through conquest, acquisition of their lands, and disease. Smaller numbers of Europeans found their way to South Africa, Kenya, Rhodesia (now Zimbabwe), Algeria, and elsewhere, where they injected a sharp racial divide into those colonized territories.

But it was the Americas that felt the brunt of this huge movement of people. Latin America received about 20 percent of the European migratory stream, mostly from Italy, Spain, and Portugal, with Argentina and Brazil accounting for some 80 percent of those immigrants. Considered "white," they enhanced the social weight of the European element in those countries and thus enjoyed economic advantages over the multiracial, Indian, and African populations.

In several ways the immigrant experience in the United States was distinctive. It was far larger and more diverse than elsewhere, with some 32 million newcomers arriving from all over Europe between 1820 and 1930. Furthermore, the United States offered affordable land to many and industrial jobs to many more, neither of which were widely available in Latin America. And the United States was unique in turning the immigrant experience into a national myth—that of the melting pot. Despite this ideology of assimilation, the earlier immigrants, mostly Protestants from Britain and Germany, were anything but welcoming to Catholics and Jews from Ireland and Southern and Eastern Europe who arrived later. The newcomers were seen as distinctly inferior, even "un-American," and blamed for crime, labor unrest, and socialist ideas. Nonetheless, this surge of immigration contributed much to the westward expansion of the United States, to the establishment of a European-derived culture in a vast area of North America, and to the displacement of the native peoples of the region.

In the vast domains of the Russian Empire, a parallel process of European migration likewise unfolded. After the freeing of the serfs in 1861, some 13 million Russians and Ukrainians migrated to Siberia, where they overwhelmed the native population of the region, while millions more settled in Central Asia. The availability of land, the prospect of greater freedom from tsarist restrictions and from the exploitation of aristocratic landowners, and the construction of the trans-Siberian railroad—all of this facilitated the continued Europeanization of Siberia. As in the United States, the Russian government encouraged and aided this process, hoping to forestall Chinese pressures in the region and relieve growing population pressures in the more densely settled western lands of the empire.

Variations on a Theme: Industrialization in the United States and Russia

Finding the Main Point: What circumstances led the workers in the United States and Russia to respond to industrial society in very different ways?

Not for long was the Industrial Revolution confined to Britain. It soon spread to continental Western Europe, and by the end of the nineteenth century it was well under way in the United States, Russia, and Japan. The globalization of industrialization had begun. Everywhere it took hold, industrialization bore a range of broadly similar outcomes. New technologies and sources of energy generated vast increases in production and spawned an unprecedented urbanization as well. Class structures changed as aristocrats, artisans, and peasants declined as classes, while the middle classes and a factory working class grew in numbers and social prominence. Middle-class women generally withdrew from paid labor altogether, and their working-class counterparts sought to do so after marriage. Working women usually received lower wages than their male counterparts, had difficulty joining unions, and were accused of taking jobs from men. Working-class frustration and anger gave rise to trade unions and socialist movements, injecting a new element of social conflict into industrial societies.

AP® EXAM TIP

Be prepared to compare examples of industrialization that were state sponsored with those that were not.

BUILDING AP® SKILLS

Argumentation

This would be a good place for students to practice the skills of Continuity and Change and argumentation by creating an LEQ outline. Use released Question 2 from the 2011 exam, which asks students to analyze the continuities and changes in long-distance migrations from 1700 to 1900. Have students create an essay outline and write a thesis statement that answers this prompt. The question can be found on the College Board website, in the AP® World History: Modern Past Exam Questions section. The prompt will need to be updated to match the current format of the AP® Exam. You can change the prompt to the following: Develop an argument that evaluates the extent to which the Industrial Revolution led to changes in long-distance migrations during the period 1750–1900.

TRM LEQ Outline Handout

APPLY THE TIP

As the Industrial Revolution became global, outcomes varied from place to place. You can use the following questions to lead the class in a discussion about the similarities and differences in outcomes as the Industrial Revolution became global. It might be good to wait until after students have also finished Chapter 9 to have this discussion so they will have background on industrialization in Japan.

■ What were the similarities in outcomes of the Industrial Revolution seen in Europe, the United States, Russia, and Japan? *New technologies and sources of energy generated a vast increase in production and spawned unprecedented urbanization. Class structures changed as the middle class and a factory working class began to emerge and grow. Middle-class women generally withdrew from paid labor completely, while working-class women tried to do so once they were married. Working women earned less money than their male counterparts, had difficulty joining unions, and were accused of taking jobs from men. Working-class frustration and anger led to the rise of labor unions and socialist movements.*

■ What differences in outcomes emerged in Europe, the United States, Russia, and Japan? *These states differed in their pace and timing of industrialization, the size and shape of major industries, the role of the state in sponsoring industrialization, and the political expressions of social conflict, along with many other outcomes. For example, Germany focused more on heavy industry than textiles, while Britain focused more on textiles. German industrialization was more concentrated in huge companies and generated a more militant and Marxist-oriented labor movement than did industrialization in Britain.*

■ Why did these differences exist? *The different histories, cultures, and societies caused industrialization to have different effects in these countries.*

BUILDING AP® SKILLS

Making Connections: Comparison and Causation

It's good to have students connect different topics they are learning about in a chapter and unit. As students work through this section on the United States and Russia, think about having them create a comparison chart like the one below listing the causes and effects of migration in the United States and Russia as they went through the process of industrialization. A reproducible version of this chart is available in the Teacher's Resource Materials. (Answers are provided in italics.)

Migration in the United States and Russia

Causes

Similarities	Differences
■ *The governments of both states encouraged and aided the process of migration in their territories, to relieve population pressure and address other issues.*	■ *The United States offered affordable land and industrial jobs, which helped draw in migrants.* ■ *Russia focused more on internal migration into Siberia.*

Effects

Similarities	Differences
■ *New groups of people were formed and were used to expand both nations' hold on territories, as well as spread a European-derived culture across these territories.*	■ *The United States created a myth that the nation was a "melting pot" of the different ideas and cultures of the migrants moving into the country, but in reality, many people were not welcoming to all groups.* ■ *Russia did not create a national myth of a melting pot, but focused more on spreading European-style culture into new areas like Siberia.*

TRM Handout 8.6: Comparison and Causation Chart of Migration in the United States and Russia

---

Nevertheless, different histories, cultures, and societies ensured that the Industrial Revolution unfolded variously. Differences in the pace and timing of industrialization, the size and shape of major industries, the role of the state, the political expression of social conflict, and many other factors have made this process rich in comparative possibilities. French industrialization, for example, occurred more slowly and perhaps less disruptively than did that of Britain. Germany focused initially on heavy industry—iron, steel, and coal—rather than on the textile industry with which Britain had begun. Moreover, German industrialization was far more highly concentrated in huge companies called cartels, and it generated a rather more militant and Marxist-oriented labor movement than in Britain.

Nowhere were the variations in the industrializing process more apparent than in those two vast countries that lay on the periphery of Europe. To the west across the Atlantic Ocean was the United States, a young, vigorous, democratic, expanding country, populated largely by people of European and African descent. To the east was Russia, with its Eastern Orthodox Christianity, an autocratic tsar, a huge population of serfs, and an empire stretching across northern Asia. By the early twentieth century, industrialization had turned the United States into a major global power and had spawned in Russia an enormous revolutionary upheaval that made that country the first outpost of global communism.

The United States: Industrialization without Socialism

American industrialization began in the textile factories of New England during the 1820s but grew explosively in the half century following the conclusion of the Civil War in 1865 (see Map 8.3). The country's huge size, the ready availability of natural resources, its expanding domestic market, and its relative political stability combined to make the United States the world's leading industrial power by 1914. At that time, it produced 36 percent of the world's manufactured goods, compared to 16 percent for Germany, 14 percent for Great Britain, and 6 percent for France. Furthermore, U.S. industrialization was closely linked to that of Europe. About one-third of the capital investment that financed its remarkable growth came from British, French, and German capitalists.

As in other later industrializing countries, the U.S. government played an important role, though less directly than in Germany or Japan. Tax breaks, huge grants of public land to the railroad companies, laws enabling the easy formation of corporations, and the absence of much overt regulation of industry all fostered the rise of very large business enterprises. The U.S. Steel Corporation, for example, by 1901 had an annual budget three times the size of the federal government's budget. In this respect, the United States followed the pattern of Germany but differed from that of France and Britain, where family businesses still predominated.

The United States also pioneered techniques of mass production, using interchangeable parts, the assembly line, and "scientific management" to produce for a mass market. The nation's advertising agencies, Sears Roebuck's and Montgomery

AP®
COMPARISON
How might the political and social backgrounds of the United States and Russia have affected their industrial development?

AP®
COMPARISON
How were the outcomes of the Industrial Revolution similar in Europe, the United States, Russia, and Japan?

AP®
COMPARISON
How did industrialization differ in the United States and Russia?

EXPLORING AP® THEMES

Governance (GOV)

You can get students to think about how the Industrial Revolution in the United States was influenced by and differed from industrialization in Europe by asking them the following questions:

■ How did the U.S. government support industrialization? *The U.S. government offered tax breaks to businesses, gave huge grants of public lands to railroad companies, passed laws enabling the easy formation of corporations, and did not exert much overt regulation of industry. All of this helped foster the rise of very large business enterprises.*

■ How was this pattern similar to or different from how the British government supported industrialization? *Like the U.S. government, the British government supported industrialization by imposing tariffs to protect British businesses, passing laws that made it easy to form companies, and supporting the building of infrastructure. However, the U.S. government's support of business allowed the rise of large business enterprises, while the British government's support of business protected family businesses.*

Map 8.3 The Industrial United States in 1900
By the early twentieth century, manufacturing industries were largely in the Northeast and Midwest, whereas mining operations were more widely scattered across the country.

▲ **AP®**

COMPARISON
Based on your observations of Map 8.3 and Map 8.1 on page 448, compare the advantages of Europe and the United States in the process of industrialization.

Ward's mail-order catalogs, and urban department stores generated a middle-class "culture of consumption." When the industrialist Henry Ford in the early twentieth century began producing the Model T at a price that many ordinary people could afford, he famously declared: "I am going to democratize the automobile." More so than in Europe, with its aristocratic traditions, self-made American industrialists of fabulous wealth such as Henry Ford, Andrew Carnegie, and John D. Rockefeller became cultural heroes, widely admired as models of what anyone could achieve with daring and hard work in a land of endless opportunity.

Nevertheless, well before the first Model T rolled off the assembly line, serious social divisions of a kind common to European industrial societies mounted. Preindustrial America had boasted of a relative social equality, quite unlike that of Europe, but by the end of the nineteenth century a widening gap separated the classes. In Carnegie's Homestead steel plant near Pittsburgh, employees worked every day except Christmas and the Fourth of July, often for twelve hours a day. In Manhattan, where millions of European immigrants disembarked, many lived in

EXPLORING AP® THEMES
Humans and the Environment (ENV)

You can continue a comparison of industrialization in the United States to industrialization in Europe and get students to practice their map analysis skills by having students compare Map 8.3, "The Industrial United States in 1900," to Map 8.1, "The Early Phase of Europe's Industrial Revolution," on page 448. To help guide the comparison, ask students the following questions:

■ Based on your observations of Map 8.3, what is the relationship between areas of natural resources and industrial centers? *While many industrial centers developed near natural resources, as the United States expanded farther west, more areas of natural resources were discovered but industrial centers did not develop in those regions. Industrial centers were mainly focused in the northeastern United States.*

■ How is this relationship similar to or different from the relationship between natural resources and industrial centers in Europe, seen in Map 8.1 on page 448? *Industrial centers in both the United States and Europe developed close to the natural resources needed for industrialization. However, as the United States expanded westward, new sources of natural resources were discovered and shipped back to the industrial centers in the East.*

■ What advantages did the United States have over Europe in the process of industrialization? *The United States had access to more of the natural resources needed for industrialization, especially different forms of fuel, such as coal and oil for factories and transportation.*

■ What advantages did Europe have over the United States in the process of industrialization? *Europe's natural resources were closer to its industrial centers than were the natural resources in the United States, making it easier to quickly move the needed resources to factories and industrial areas.*

five- or six-story buildings with four families and two toilets on each floor. In every large city, such conditions prevailed close by the mansions of elite neighborhoods. To some, the contrast was a betrayal of American ideals, while others saw it as a natural outcome of competition and "the survival of the fittest."

As elsewhere, such conditions generated much labor protest, the formation of unions, strikes, and sometimes violence. In 1877, when the eastern railroads announced a 10 percent wage cut for their workers, strikers disrupted rail service across the eastern half of the country, smashed equipment, and rioted. Both state militias and federal troops were called out to put down the movement. Class consciousness and class conflict were intense in the industrial America of the late nineteenth and early twentieth centuries.

> **AP®**
> CONTEXTUALIZATION
> Why did Marxist socialism fail to flourish in the United States?

Unlike in many European countries, however, no major political party emerged in the United States to represent the interests of the working class. Nor did the ideas of socialism, especially those of Marxism, appeal to American workers nearly as much as they did to European laborers. At its high point, the Socialist Party of America garnered just 6 percent of the vote for its presidential candidate in the 1912 election, whereas socialists at the time held more seats in Germany's Parliament than any other party. Even in the depths of the Great Depression of the 1930s, no major socialist movement emerged to champion American workers. How might we explain the relative weakness of **socialism in the United States**?

One answer lies in the relative conservatism of major American union organizations, especially the American Federation of Labor. Its focus on skilled workers excluded the more radical unskilled laborers, and its refusal to align with any party limited its influence in the political arena. Furthermore, beginning in the 1840s the flow of European migrants increased to a massive degree, creating a very diverse industrial labor force on top of the country's sharp racial divide. This diversity contrasted sharply with the more homogeneous populations of many European countries. Catholics and Protestants; whites and Blacks; English, Irish, Germans, Slavs, Jews, and Italians—such differences undermined the class solidarity of American workers, making it far more difficult to sustain class-oriented political parties and a socialist labor movement. Moreover, the country's remarkable economic growth generated on average a higher standard of living for American workers than their European counterparts experienced. Land was cheaper, and homeownership was more available. Workers with property generally found socialism less attractive than those without. By 1910, a particularly large group of white-collar workers in sales, services, and offices outnumbered factory laborers. Their middle-class aspirations further diluted impulses toward radicalism.

But political challenges to the abuses of capitalist industrialization did arise. In the 1890s, among small farmers in the U.S. South, West, and Midwest, "populists" railed against banks, industrialists, monopolies, the existing money system, and both major political parties, all of which they thought were dominated by the corporate interests of the eastern elites. More successful, especially in the early twentieth century, were the **Progressives**, who pushed for specific reforms,

---

BUILDING AP® SKILLS

Making Connections: Comparison

Students learned earlier in Chapter 8 about reactions to the challenges created by industrialization in Europe. This would be a good place for them to take what they have learned from that section to create a comparison chart on those reactions and the reactions seen in the United States. **Handout 8.7: Comparison Chart for Reactions to Working Conditions in the United States and Europe** contains a completed chart with answers and a blank version for students to complete. You can find the handout in the Teacher's Resource Materials. When students have completed their charts (either on their own or with a partner), ask the following questions to check for understanding:

■ What were the similarities and differences in the reactions of the United States and Europe to the harsh working conditions of the Industrial Revolution? *In both the United States and Europe, workers joined labor or trade unions to bargain for better working conditions and wages. In both places, workers protested. However, in Europe political parties like the Socialist Party formed to represent the interests of the working class. In the United States, there was no similar political movement.*

■ Why did these similarities and differences exist? *Labor and trade unions formed in both regions because they gave workers a way to have a voice in the changes they wanted to see in their working conditions. Political parties representing worker interests and socialism did not gain much of a foothold in the United States because of the relative conservatism of major American unions, along with the diverse industrial workforce — unlike the homogeneous workforce in Europe — and the relatively higher standard of living enjoyed by American workers.*

> **TRM** **Handout 8.7: Comparison Chart for Reactions to Working Conditions in the United States and Europe**

EXPLORING AP® THEMES

Governance (GOV)

Despite the fact that Marxism did not gain as strong a foothold in the United States during the nineteenth century as it did in Europe, other political parties did rise up in the United States in reaction to abuses of industrialization. Students can help one another learn about these different political parties through group presentations. Divide the class into six groups and assign three groups to research the "populist" party and three groups to research the Progressive Party. Pair up each "populist" group with a Progressive group. Let groups know that they will be researching their assigned

party and sharing what they have found with their assigned partner group.

Give students 30–45 minutes to research and put together their information to share with their assigned partner group. Groups should be able to answer the following:

■ What elements of the Industrial Revolution were the political parties reacting to?

■ Which social class gave the most support to these parties?

■ What solutions did the parties offer for the problems of industrialization?

such as wages-and-hours legislation, better sanitation standards, antitrust laws, and greater governmental intervention in the economy. Socialism, however, came to be understood as fundamentally "un-American" in a country that so valued individualism and so feared "big government." It was a distinctive feature of the American response to industrialization.

Russia: Industrialization and Revolution

As a setting for the Industrial Revolution, it would be hard to imagine two more different environments than the United States and Russia. If the United States was the Western world's most exuberant democracy during the nineteenth century, Russia remained the sole outpost of absolute monarchy, in which the state exercised far greater control over individuals and society than anywhere in the Western world.

At the beginning of the twentieth century, Russia still had no national parliament, no legal political parties, and no nationwide elections. The tsar, answerable to God alone, ruled unchecked. Furthermore, Russian society was dominated by a titled nobility of various ranks. Its upper levels included great landowners, who furnished the state with military officers and leading government officials. Until 1861, most Russians were peasant serfs, bound to the estates of their masters, subject to sale, greatly exploited, and largely at the mercy of their owners. Even after

Russian Serfs This 1872 photograph shows a wealthy Russian landowner and his wife being pulled in a cart by serfs, who had been legally freed just eleven years earlier but continued to serve their master. They are attending a high-society wedding of another local estate owner. (© SZ Photo/Scherl/Bridgeman Images)

◀ **AP®**

CLAIMS AND EVIDENCE IN SOURCES
What does the image indicate about the success of Russia's social reforms in the nineteenth century?

	United States	**Russia**
Political	■ The United States was the Western world's most exuberant democracy. ■ The U.S. government had a system of checks and balances to avoid absolute political control. ■ Most male citizens had the right to vote in this period. ■ Multiple political parties represented the interests of the people.	■ Russia was an absolute monarchy with no national parliament, no legal political parties, and no nationwide elections. ■ The tsar ruled the state, unchecked in his power.
Social	■ American society was divided among the upper class, the middle class, and the working class. ■ While a social gap emerged in this period, social changes did bubble up from free farmers, workers, and businessmen.	■ Most Russians were peasant serfs, who were subject to the mercy of their owners, were bound to their estates, and could be sold to a new owner. ■ Social change was usually initiated by the state, such as the abolishment of serfdom in 1861.
Economic	■ Businessmen, merchants, and free farmers had a large amount of economic freedom, and the market activities of production and trade dominated the American economy.	■ Prior to industrialization, Russia was a primarily agrarian economy dependent on peasant serf workers. Economic and industrial change was driven by the state in an attempt to catch up to other industrial states.

TRM Handout 8.8: Comparison Chart for Political, Social, and Economic Characteristics of the United States and Russia emancipation, a vast cultural gulf separated these two classes. Many nobles were highly westernized, some speaking French better than Russian, whereas their serfs were steeped in a backwoods Orthodox Christianity that incorporated pre-Christian spirits, spells, curses, and magic.

A further difference between Russia and the United States lay in the source of social and economic change. In the United States, such change bubbled up from society as free farmers, workers, and businessmen sought new opportunities and operated in a political system that gave them varying degrees of expression. In autocratic Russia, change was far more often initiated by the state, in its continuing efforts to catch up with its more powerful and innovative European competitors. This kind of "transformation from above" found expression in the freeing of the serfs in 1861 by an order from the tsar. Russia's industrial development, which began in the 1860s, was also heavily directed by the state, far more so than was the case in Western Europe or the United States.

By the 1890s, Russia's Industrial Revolution was launched and growing rapidly. It focused particularly on railroads and heavy industry and was fueled by a substantial amount of foreign investment. By 1900, Russia ranked fourth in the world in steel production and had major industries in coal, textiles, and oil. Its industrial enterprises, still modest in comparison to those of Europe, were concentrated in a few major cities—Moscow, St. Petersburg, and Kiev, for example—and took place in factories far larger than in most of Western Europe.

All of this contributed to the explosive social outcomes of Russian industrialization. A growing middle class of businessmen and professionals increasingly took shape. As modern and educated people, many in the middle class objected strongly to the deep conservatism of tsarist Russia and sought a greater role in political life, but they were also dependent on the state for contracts and jobs and for suppressing the growing radicalism of the workers, which they greatly feared. Although factory workers constituted only about 5 percent of Russia's total population, they quickly developed a radical class consciousness, based on harsh conditions and the absence of any legal outlet for their grievances. As in Western Europe, millions flocked to the new centers of industrial development. By 1897, over 70 percent of the population in Moscow and St. Petersburg were recent migrants from the rural areas. Their conditions of life resembled those of industrial migrants in New York or Berlin. One observer wrote: "People live in impossible conditions: filth, stench, suffocating heat. They lie down together barely a few feet apart; there is no division between the sexes and adults sleep with children."[23] Until 1897, a thirteen-hour working day was common, while ruthless discipline and overt disrespect from supervisors created resentment. In the absence of legal unions or political parties, these grievances often erupted in the form of large-scale strikes.

In these conditions, a small but growing number of educated Russians found in Marxist socialism a way of understanding the changes they witnessed daily as well as hope for the future in a revolutionary upheaval of workers. In 1898, they created an illegal Russian Social Democratic Labor Party and quickly became involved in workers' education, union organizing, and, eventually, revolutionary action. By the

---

AP®
CAUSATION
What factors set the stage for the Russian Revolution in the early twentieth century?

AP® EXAM TIP
Comparing responses to the Industrial Revolution is a popular topic on the AP® Exam.

APPLY THE TIP

If you had students create the Comparison chart for reactions to the challenges of industrialization in the United States and Europe on page 462, consider having them add another column to **Handout 8.7: Comparison Chart for Reactions to Working Conditions in the United States and Europe** for Russia. Russia experienced similar challenges from industrialization as the United States and Europe, and students should be able to compare all of their responses. After students have completed the Russian section of the chart, ask the following questions:

■ What were the similarities and differences in working and living conditions in Russia, the United States, and Europe? *Workers in Russia, the United States, and Europe lived in crowded, polluted cities in cramped living quarters. Working conditions were also similar in all three areas: long hours for low wages and poor treatment of workers by management. However, in the United States and Europe, factory owners preferred to hire women and children over men because they could be paid less.*

■ What were the similarities and differences in reactions to industrialization in Russia, the United States, and Europe? *Workers in all three regions declared strikes to get better working conditions, but only workers in the United States and Europe joined labor unions to bargain for better conditions. While political parties supporting worker interests formed only in Europe, socialism gained a foothold in Russia and Europe in reaction to the social and economic changes occurring because of industrialization.*

TRM Handout 8.7: Comparison Chart for Reactions to Working Conditions in the United States and Europe

early twentieth century, the strains of rapid change and the state's continued intransigence had reached the bursting point, and in 1905, following its defeat in a naval war with Japan, Russia erupted in spontaneous insurrection (see Map 8.4). Workers in Moscow and St. Petersburg went on strike and created their own representative councils, called soviets. Peasant uprisings, student demonstrations, revolts of non-Russian nationalities, and mutinies in the military all contributed to the upheaval. Recently formed political parties, representing intellectuals of various persuasions, came out into the open.

The **Russian Revolution of 1905**, though brutally suppressed, forced the tsar's regime to make more substantial reforms than it had ever contemplated. It granted a constitution, legalized both trade unions and political parties, and permitted the election of a national assembly, called the Duma. Censorship was eased, and plans were under way for universal primary education. Industrial development likewise continued at a rapid rate, so that by 1914 Russia stood fifth in the world in terms of overall output. But in the first half of that year, some 1,250,000 workers, representing about 40 percent of the entire industrial workforce, went out on strike.

Thus the tsar's limited political reforms, which had been granted with great reluctance and were often reversed in practice, failed to tame working-class radicalism or to bring social stability to Russia. In Russian political life, the people generally, and even the middle class, had only a very limited voice. Representatives of even the privileged classes had become so alienated by the government's intransigence that many felt revolution was inevitable. Various revolutionary groups, many of them socialist, published pamphlets and newspapers, organized trade unions, and spread their messages among workers and peasants. Particularly in the cities, these revolutionary parties had an impact. They provided a language through which workers could express their grievances; they created links among workers from different factories; and they furnished leaders who were able to act when the revolutionary moment arrived.

World War I provided that moment. The enormous hardships of that war, coupled with the immense social tensions of industrialization within a still autocratic political system, sparked the Russian Revolution of 1917 (see Chapter 11). That massive upheaval quickly brought to power the most radical of the socialist groups operating in the country—the Bolsheviks, led by the charismatic Vladimir Ilyich Ulyanov, better known as Lenin. Only in Russia was industrialization associated

Legend:
- Peasant unrest and land seizures
- ■ Workers' soviets
- ◆ Army mutinies
- ⚓ Naval mutinies
- ▲ Major strikes and armed workers' uprisings

0   150   300 miles
0   300 kilometers

Revel · St. Petersburg · Moscow · Warsaw · Kiev · Sevastopol · Black Sea · Baku · Caspian Sea

R U S S I A N   E M P I R E

Map 8.4 Industrialization and Revolution in Russia, 1905
Only in Russia did industrialization lead to violent revolutionary upheavals, both in 1905 and more successfully in 1917.

▲ **AP**
CAUSATION
What does the map suggest about the connection between industrialization and revolution?

AP EXAM TIP
You must know which empires expanded, which ones contracted, and which ones collapsed during this time.

BUILDING AP® SKILLS

Argumentation

This is a good time to practice writing a timed Long Essay Question. To compare the growth of industrialization in different states, ask students to write an essay on the following prompt:

- In the period 1750–1900, the process of industrialization changed the way in which goods were produced and consumed, which led to a variety of responses in industrialized states, such as Great Britain, the United States, and Russia.
  Develop an argument that evaluates how one or more states reacted to the effects of the Industrial Revolution in this time period.

Either give the prompt to the class ahead of time and allow students to prepare or ask students to write the essay using only what they know about the topic from memory. Give students 40 minutes to write the essay so they can practice writing under timed conditions. *Answers will vary.*

TEACHING IDEA

Exit Slip

As a wrap-up to the Western world's experience with industrialization and an introduction to Latin America's experience, consider asking students: How did the Industrial Revolution lead to Western dominance in the nineteenth century? *The Industrial Revolution helped shift global trade and economic power to the West. The technological innovations of industrialization also boosted the economic and military power of the West. Western nations claimed ownership of other nations as colonies in order to gain natural resources and to open up new markets to which they could sell their manufactured goods.*

AP®
COMPARISON
What was common to industrialization everywhere, and in what ways did it vary from place to place?

AP® EXAM TIP
Make sure you study the ways the Industrial Revolution affected regions beyond Europe and the United States, because these examples are frequently found on the AP® Exam.

AP® EXAM TIP
Know that the same content can be asked in different ways on the AP® Exam. Latin American independence is the same topic as the decline of the Spanish Empire.

with violent social revolution. This was the most distinctive feature of Russia's modern historical development. And only in Russia was a socialist political party, inspired by the teachings of Karl Marx, able to seize power, thus launching the modern world's first socialist society, with enormous implications for the twentieth century.

The Industrial Revolution and Latin America in the Nineteenth Century

> **Finding the Main Point:** How did the rapid industrialization of Europe and the United States transform the economies and cultures of Latin American countries?

Beyond the world of Europe and North America, only Japan underwent a major industrial transformation during the nineteenth century, part of that country's overall response to the threat of European aggression. (See "The Japanese Difference: The Rise of a New East Asian Power" in Chapter 9.) Elsewhere very limited experiments in modern industry were undertaken. In the early nineteenth century, factories to process cotton into cloth and to manufacture modern weapons were established in a quasi-independent Egypt under the leadership of Muhammad Ali. A little later, the modest beginnings of modern shipbuilding, steel, and textile industries took root in colonial India. And China too, in the late nineteenth century, initiated textile, steel, and armaments industries in a belated effort to protect the country from Western aggression. (See "The Failure of Conservative Modernization" in Chapter 9.) But none of these efforts drove the kind of major economic and social transformation that had taken place in Europe, North America, and Japan. However, even in societies that did not experience their own Industrial Revolution, the profound impact of European and North American industrialization was hard to avoid. Such was the case in Latin America during the nineteenth century. (See Snapshot: The Industrial Revolution and the Global Divide.)

After Independence in Latin America

The struggle for independence in Latin America had lasted far longer and proved far more destructive than in North America. Decimated populations, diminished herds of livestock, flooded or closed silver mines, abandoned farms, shrinking international trade and investment capital, and empty national treasuries—these were the conditions that greeted Latin Americans upon independence. Furthermore, the four major administrative units (viceroyalties) of Spanish America ultimately dissolved into eighteen separate countries, and regional revolts wracked Brazil in the early decades of its independent life. A number of international wars in the post-independence century likewise shook these new nations. Peru and Bolivia briefly united and then broke apart in a bitter conflict (1836–1839); Mexico lost huge territories to the United States (1846–1848); and an alliance of Argentina, Brazil, and Uruguay went to war with Paraguay (1864–1870) in a conflict that devastated Paraguay's small population.

APPLY THE TIP

Throughout the year, you will need to talk to students about how some topics and groups can be referred to in multiple ways, and they should be familiar with how the same content can be asked in different ways. For example, Latin American independence is the same topic as the contraction of the Spanish Empire, Native Americans are also called American Indians or Amerindians, and the French and Indian War is also known as the Seven Years' War in Europe. This might also be a good place to note that terminology can also change over time; for example, the nation-state of Turkey changed the spelling of its name to Türkiye as a connection to its roots in the Ottoman Empire.

SNAPSHOT The Industrial Revolution and the Global Divide

During the nineteenth century, the Industrial Revolution generated an enormous and unprecedented economic division in the world, as measured by the share of manufacturing output. What patterns can you see in this table?

SHARE OF TOTAL WORLD MANUFACTURING OUTPUT (percentage)

	1750	1800	1860	1880	1900
EUROPE AS A WHOLE	23.2	28.1	53.2	61.3	62.0
United Kingdom	1.9	4.3	19.9	22.9	18.5
France	4.0	4.2	7.9	7.8	6.8
Germany	2.9	3.5	4.9	8.5	13.2
Russia	5.0	5.6	7.0	7.6	8.8
UNITED STATES	0.1	0.8	7.2	14.7	23.6
JAPAN	3.8	3.5	2.6	2.4	2.4
THE REST OF THE WORLD	73.0	67.7	36.6	20.9	11.0
China	32.8	33.3	19.7	12.5	6.2
South Asia (India/Pakistan)	24.5	19.7	8.6	2.8	1.7

Source: Data from Paul Kennedy, *The Rise and Fall of the Great Powers* (New York: Random House, 1987), 149.

> ◄ **AP**
>
> **CAUSATION**
>
> What conclusions can you draw from this chart about changes in global power structures and imperialism between 1750 and 1900?

Within these new countries, political life was turbulent and unstable. Conservatives favored centralized authority and sought to maintain the social status quo of the colonial era in alliance with the Catholic Church, which at independence owned perhaps half of all productive land. Their often bitter opponents were liberals, who attacked the Church in the name of Enlightenment values, sought at least modest social reforms, and preferred federalism. In many countries, conflicts between these factions, often violent, enabled military strongmen known as *caudillos* (kaw-DEE-yos) to achieve power as defenders of order and property, although they too succeeded one another with great frequency. One of them, Antonio López de Santa Anna of Mexico, was president of his country at least nine separate times between 1833 and 1855. Constitutions too replaced one another with bewildering speed. Bolivia had ten constitutions during the nineteenth century, while Ecuador and Peru each had eight.

But social life did not change fundamentally in the aftermath of independence. As in Europe and North America, women remained disenfranchised and wholly outside of formal political life. Slavery was abolished in most of Latin America by mid-century, although it persisted in both Brazil and Cuba until the late 1880s. Most of the legal distinctions among various racial categories also disappeared, and all free people were considered, at least officially, equal citizens. Nevertheless, productive economic resources such as businesses, ranches, and plantations remained overwhelmingly in the hands of creole white men, who were culturally oriented toward Europe. The military provided an avenue of mobility for a few skilled and ambitious mestizo men, some of whom subsequently became caudillos. Other multiracial men and

> **AP** EXAM TIP
>
> Take notes on this paragraph about social continuities in nineteenth-century Latin America.

---

women found a place in a small middle class as teachers, shopkeepers, or artisans. The vast majority—Blacks, Indigenous peoples, and many multiracial people of both sexes—remained impoverished, working small subsistence farms or laboring in the mines or on the *haciendas* (ah-see-EHN-duhz) (plantations) of the well-to-do. Only rarely did the poor and dispossessed actively rebel against their socioeconomic betters. One such case was the Caste War of Yucatán (1847–1901), a prolonged struggle of the Maya people of Mexico aimed at cleansing their land of European and mestizo intruders.

Facing the World Economy

During the second half of the nineteenth century, a measure of political consolidation took hold in Latin America, and countries such as Mexico, Peru, and Argentina entered periods of greater stability. At the same time, Latin America as a whole became more closely integrated into a world economy driven by the industrialization of Western Europe and North America. The new technology of the steamship cut the sailing time between Britain and Argentina almost in half, while the underwater telegraph instantly brought the latest news and fashions of Europe to Latin America.

The most significant economic outcome of this increasing integration was a rapid growth of Latin American exports to the industrializing countries, which now needed the food products, raw materials, and markets of these new nations. Latin American landowners, businessmen, and governments proved eager to supply those needs, and in the sixty years or so after 1850, a **Latin American export boom** increased the value of goods sold abroad by a factor of ten.

Mexico continued to produce large amounts of silver, providing more than half the world's new supply until 1860. Now added to the list of raw materials flowing out of Latin America were copper from Chile, a metal that the growing electrical industry required; tin from Bolivia, which met the mounting demand for tin cans; wild rubber from the Amazon rain forest, in great demand for bicycle and automobile tires; and nitrates from Chile and guano (bird droppings) from Peru, both of which were used for fertilizer. Bananas from Central America, beef from Argentina, cacao from Ecuador, coffee from Brazil and Guatemala, and sugar from Cuba also found eager markets in industrializing countries. In return for these primary products, Latin Americans imported the textiles, machinery, tools, weapons, and luxury goods of Europe and the United States (see Map 8.5).

Accompanying this burgeoning commerce was large-scale investment of foreign capital in Latin America, most of it from Great Britain but also from France, Germany, Italy, and the United States. By 1910, U.S. business interests controlled 40 percent of Mexico's property and produced half of its oil. Much of this capital was used to build railroads, largely to funnel Latin American exports to the coast, where they were shipped to overseas markets. Mexico had only 390 miles of railroad in 1876; it had 15,000 miles in 1910. By 1915, Argentina, with 22,000 miles of railroad, had more track per person than the United States had.

AP®
CAUSATION
How was Latin America linked to the global economy of the nineteenth century, and what was the impact of those links?

U.S. Interventions

➡ Puerto Rico, 1898–on
➡ Panama, 1903
➡ Cuba, 1898–1902, 1905–09, 1917–21
➡ Haiti, 1915–34
➡ Mexico, 1846–48, 1914, 1916–17
➡ Nicaragua, 1909, 1912–25, 1927–32
➡ Dominican Republic, 1916–24

MEXICO
$1329

CUBA
$471
$11 $16 $44

$99 $42
$19 $12
$61 $28

VENEZUELA
$161

COLOMBIA
$77

ECUADOR $41

PERU
$197

BRAZIL
$1913

BOLIVIA
$59

PARAGUAY
$27

ARGENTINA
$4001

CHILE
$668

$475 URUGUAY

EXPORTS

Bananas		Oil	
Cacao		Rubber	
Cattle		Sheep	
Coffee		Silver	
Copper and tin		Sisal	
Cotton		Sugar	
Guano		Tobacco	
Nitrate		Wheat	

$161 Foreign investment
(in millions of U.S. dollars around 1914)
⟵ European immigration

Map 8.5 Latin America and the World, 1825–1935
During the nineteenth and early twentieth centuries, Latin American countries interacted with the industrializing world via investment, trade, immigration, and military intervention from the United States.

▲ **AP**

CAUSATION
What are some specific causes of the increased global economic connections shown on the map?

EXPLORING AP® THEMES

Humans and the Environment (ENV)

Now is a good time to practice some map-reading skills with your students. Have students look at Map 8.5, "Latin America and the World, 1825–1935." Note the different levels of foreign investment in each of the Latin American nations, and ask: What could explain the high levels of foreign investment and intervention in Latin America from 1825 to 1935? *The raw materials and natural resources of Latin America pushed foreign states to lend money and intervene in Latin America to gain access to these resources.*

Cultural Developments and Interactions (CDI) and Social Interactions and Organization (SIO)

Now is a good time to explain that an ethnic enclave forms where people of the same ethnicity or culture settle in one area of a city or region. Usually the cultural traditions of the native land are preserved by the community living in an ethnic enclave. Then ask students the following questions:

■ Did ethnic enclaves become established in Latin American cities during this period? *Yes. For example, Buenos Aires boasted a large population that mimicked European styles. The city nicknamed itself the "Paris of South America."*

■ How did Latin American cities change by the early twentieth century? *Latin American cities lost their colonial architectural styles and became modern metropolises, with the introduction of modern innovations like streetcars and telephones. Many cities began to mimic European culture and tried to attract more Europeans to move to them.*

■ Why do you think these changes occurred? *Europeans who immigrated to Latin America believed that civilization, progress, and modernity derived from Europe.*

BUILDING AP® SKILLS

Making Connections: Comparison

Students should constantly practice comparison skills. This is a good place to start a discussion comparing the lives of Latin America's working class with the working class in other areas of the world. Ask students the following questions:

■ How were the lives of Latin America's working class and lower class similar to those of the United States and Europe? *The working classes in all three regions made up a majority of the population and worked in manual labor jobs. By the end of the nineteenth century, the working classes of all three regions had organized themselves in a variety of mutual aid societies, but they also began to create unions and engage in labor strikes.*

■ How were the lives of Latin America's working class and lower class different from those of the United States and Europe? *A majority of the lower class in Latin America lived in rural areas, unlike the majority of the lower class in the United States and Europe, who lived in urban areas as they searched for work in the new industrial economy. In Latin America, many lower-class people became dependent laborers or peons on the haciendas of the wealthy and could barely make a living.*

Becoming like Europe?

To the economic elites of Latin America, intent on making their countries resemble Europe or the United States, all of this was progress. Economies were growing, producing more than ever before. The population was also burgeoning; it increased from about 30 million in 1850 to more than 77 million in 1912 as public health measures (such as campaigns to eliminate mosquitoes that carried yellow fever) brought down death rates.

Urbanization also proceeded rapidly. By the early twentieth century, wrote one scholar, "Latin American cities lost their colonial cobblestones, white-plastered walls, and red-tiled roofs. They became modern metropolises, comparable to urban giants anywhere. Streetcars swayed, telephones jangled, and silent movies flickered from Montevideo and Santiago to Mexico City and Havana."[24] Buenos Aires, Argentina's metropolitan center, boasted 750,000 people in 1900 and billed itself as the "Paris of South America." There the educated elite discussed European literature, philosophy, and fashion, usually in French.

To become more like Europe, Latin America sought to attract more Europeans. Because civilization, progress, and modernity apparently derived from Europe, many Latin American countries actively sought to increase their "white" populations by deliberately recruiting impoverished Europeans with the promise, mostly unfulfilled, of a new and prosperous life in the New World. Argentina received the largest wave of European immigrants (some 2.5 million between 1870 and 1915), mostly from Spain and Italy.

Only a quite modest segment of Latin American society saw any great benefits from the export boom and all that followed from it. Upper-class landowners certainly gained as exports flourished and their property values soared. Middle-class urban dwellers — merchants, office workers, lawyers, and other professionals — also grew in numbers and prosperity as their skills proved valuable in a modernizing society. As a percentage of the total population, however, these were small elites. In Mexico in the mid-1890s, for example, the landowning upper class made up no more than 1 percent and the middle classes perhaps 8 percent of the population. All other people were lower class, and most of them were impoverished.[25]

A new but quite small segment of this vast lower class emerged among urban workers who labored in the railroads, ports, mines, and a few factories. They initially organized themselves in a variety of mutual aid societies, but by the end of the nineteenth century they were creating unions and engaging in strikes. To authoritarian governments interested in stability and progress, such activity was highly provocative and threatening, and they acted harshly to crush or repress unions and strikes. In 1907 more than 1,000 men, women, and children were slaughtered by police in the Chilean city of Iquique when nitrate miners protested their wages and working conditions.

The vast majority of the lower class lived in rural areas, where they suffered the most and benefited the least from the export boom. Government attacks on communal landholding and peasant indebtedness to wealthy landowners combined to push many farmers off their land or into remote and poor areas where they could

AP®
COMPARISON
Did Latin America follow or diverge from the historical path of Europe during the nineteenth century?

AP®
COMPARISON
How were the social changes in Latin America similar to or different from the social changes in Europe?

barely make a living. Many wound up as dependent laborers or peons on the haciendas of the wealthy, where their wages were often too meager to support a family. Thus women and children, who had earlier remained at home to tend the family plot, were required to join the men of the family as field laborers.

Although local protests and violence were frequent, only in Mexico did these vast inequalities erupt into a nationwide revolution. There, in the early twentieth century, middle-class reformers joined with workers and peasants to overthrow the long dictatorship of Porfirio Díaz (r. 1876–1911). What followed was a decade of bloody conflict (1910–1920) that cost Mexico some 1 million lives, or roughly 10 percent of the population. Huge peasant armies under charismatic leaders such as Pancho Villa and Emiliano Zapata helped oust Díaz. Intent on seizing land and redistributing it to the peasants, they then went on to attack many of Mexico's large haciendas. But unlike the leaders of the later Russian and Chinese revolutions, whose most radical elements seized state power, Villa and Zapata proved unable to do so on any long-term basis, in part because they were hobbled by factionalism and focused on local or regional issues.

Despite this limitation and its own internal conflicts, the **Mexican Revolution** transformed the country. When the dust settled, Mexico had a new constitution (1917) that proclaimed universal male suffrage; provided for the redistribution of land; stripped the Catholic Church of any role in public education and forbade it to own land; announced unheard-of rights for workers, such as a minimum wage and an eight-hour workday; and placed restrictions on foreign ownership of property. Much of Mexico's history in the twentieth century involved working out the implications of these nationalist and reformist changes. The revolution's direct influence, however, was largely limited to Mexico itself and a few places in Central America and the Andes; the upheaval did not have the wider international impact of the Russian and Chinese revolutions.

Perhaps the most significant outcome of the export boom lay in what did *not* happen, for nowhere in Latin America did it jump-start a thorough Industrial Revolution. The reasons are many. A social structure that relegated some 90 percent of its population to an impoverished lower class generated only a very small market for manufactured goods. Moreover, economically powerful groups such as landowners and cattlemen benefited greatly from exporting agricultural products and had little incentive to invest in manufacturing. Domestic manufacturing enterprises could only have competed with cheaper and higher-quality foreign goods if they had been protected for a time by high tariffs. But Latin American political leaders had thoroughly embraced the popular European doctrine of prosperity through free trade, and many governments depended on taxing imports to fill their treasuries.

Instead of their own Industrial Revolution, Latin Americans developed a form of economic growth that was largely financed by capital from abroad and dependent on European and North American prosperity and decisions. Brazil experienced this kind of dependence when its booming rubber industry suddenly collapsed in 1910–1911, after seeds from the wild rubber tree had been illegally exported to Britain and were used to start competing and cheaper rubber plantations in Malaysia.

AP® EXAM TIP

Be able to compare features of the Mexican Revolution to those of earlier revolutions.

AP® EXAM TIP

Make sure you understand "dependent development" because the concept is sometimes seen on the AP® Exam.

APPLY THE TIP

If you had your students complete **Handout 7.1: Comparison Chart for Atlantic Revolutions** from Chapter 7, have them add a section for the Mexican Revolution of 1910 and take notes on the revolution using pages 471–472.

TRM **Handout 7.1: Comparison Chart for Atlantic Revolutions**

APPLY THE TIP

Students often struggle with vocabulary, especially when they see words that they know the meaning of but do not understand the concept. "Dependent development" is one of those terms that can be seen on an AP® Exam on either MCQs or FRQs. To help students understand the term, ask the following questions.

■ According to your reading, what was "dependent development" in Latin America? *"Dependent development" refers to economic growth in Latin America that was largely financed by capital from abroad and dependent on European and North American prosperity and decisions. Later this dependency was seen as a new form of colonialism, where power was expressed through the decisions of foreign investors.*

■ What are some examples of "dependent development" from this period? *Brazil experienced a collapse in its rubber industry when rubber tree seeds were illegally exported to Malaysia and competing rubber plantations were established there. Brazil depended on foreign investors buying its rubber, and the appearance of a competing group hurt Brazil's industry. Another example was the influence of the United Fruit Company over Central America. The company was connected to politicians and wealthy landowners. It used those connections to pressure Central American governments to maintain conditions favorable to U.S. businesses.*

CHAPTER 8

The Mexican Revolution Women were active participants in the Mexican Revolution. They prepared food, nursed the wounded, washed clothes, and at times served as soldiers on the battlefield, as illustrated in this cover image from a French magazine in 1913. (Apic/Getty Images)

▲ AP®

COMPARISON

Compare the role of women in the Mexican Revolution, pictured here, with the role of women in the French Revolution of the previous era.

Later critics saw this **dependent development** as a new form of colonialism, expressed in the power exercised by foreign investors. The influence of the U.S.-owned United Fruit Company in Central America was a case in point. Allied with large landowners and compliant politicians, the company pressured the governments of these "banana republics" to maintain conditions favorable to U.S. business. This indirect or behind-the-scenes imperialism was supplemented by repeated U.S. military intervention in support of American corporate interests in Cuba, Haiti, the Dominican Republic, Nicaragua, and Mexico. The United States also controlled the Panama Canal and acquired Puerto Rico as a territory in the aftermath of the Spanish-American War (see Map 8.5, page 469).

Thus, despite Latin America's domination by people of European descent and its close ties to the industrializing countries of the Atlantic world, that region's historical trajectory in the nineteenth century diverged considerably from that of Europe and North America.

CONCLUSIONS AND REFLECTIONS

Pondering the Industrial Revolution

Finding the Main Point: What are the debates about the Industrial Revolution's enduring legacy in world history?

Only twice in world history has there been a revolutionary transformation of human life on a planetary scale. The first was the Agricultural Revolution, which began some 12,000 years ago, emerged separately in many places, and over thousands of years gradually encompassed the entire world. The ongoing Industrial Revolution, which is the second major transformation of human life, took shape very differently. It began little more than two centuries ago in a single place (Great Britain) and has already become global. Its significance has been an enduring issue of controversy and debate.

In the European heartland of the early Industrial Revolution, its social and economic transformations attracted the most attention. Technological innovations such as the steam engine enabled the production of goods to soar, though, as always, that unprecedented wealth was very unevenly distributed. Many Europeans viewed their technological mastery as a sure sign of their cultural and racial superiority as they came to use "machines as the measure of men."[26] Equally novel was the large-scale movement of Europeans to the cities or to altogether new homes in the Americas, Australia, South Africa, and elsewhere. With this shift, the landowning aristocracy lost ground to the emerging middle classes and wealthy industrialists, even as rural peasants declined in numbers relative to the growing urban working classes. These new forms of inequality generated sharp social conflict that led to the rise of trade unions and Marxist or socialist movements. Clearly, the Industrial Revolution did not generate social harmony.

Very quickly, industrialization had a global impact beyond Great Britain and Western Europe. Already in the nineteenth century, the United States and Japan initiated substantial industrialization programs of their own, each of them distinctive. So too did Russia, where industrialization led to a vast revolutionary upheaval and the beginnings of world communism. Latin American countries experienced a great expansion in their exports of raw materials and received much European investment, though without generating an Industrial Revolution of their own. Much of Asia and Africa came under European colonial rule as the Industrial Revolution provided Europeans with both the motives and means to exercise power on a global scale.

By the early twenty-first century, public concern about industrialization focused largely on its dire threat to the natural environment. Even as many governments and individuals continued to pursue the dream of greater economic growth through industrialization, profound questions about the sustainability of modern industrial life had prompted the emergence of a global environmental movement. By 2020, widespread discussion about a "climate crisis," "tipping points," and the possible "collapse of civilization" had pushed environmental issues higher on the political agenda. (See "The Environment in the Anthropocene Era" in Chapter 14.)

But such widespread fear about environmental consequences was conspicuous by its absence in the early years of the Industrial Revolution. Scattered European or American scientists, writers, and government officials during the nineteenth century did highlight the negative impact of industrial life—its pollution of air and water, its encroachment on the wilderness, and more. For the most part, however, industrialization was seen as "progress" and its unfortunate byproducts were a price well worth paying. Furthermore, those problems were perceived as local, rather than national or global. Earth systems seemed larger and more stable then, with little sense that human activity could seriously disrupt them. Thus when protests erupted in the early industrial era, they were about social rather than environmental issues.

During the nineteenth century, the Industrial Revolution was widely viewed as hopeful. Karl Marx understood it as ensuring the end of poverty and class conflict, even if he despised the capitalist system in which it was embedded. Even today, many still view industrialization in that positive light, for clearly it has enabled billions of people to live longer, healthier, and more materially abundant lives. But alongside that sensibility, the last fifty years or so has witnessed the emergence of a

TEACHING IDEA

Exit Slip

The Industrial Revolution was the second revolutionary transformation of human life after the Agricultural Revolution, and there is much debate over this ongoing process in human history. Consider having your students read the section "Pondering the Industrial Revolution" on pages 472–474 and having a quick class discussion to answer the "Finding the Main Point" question on page 472. You can use their responses to set the stage for moving into Unit 6 of the AP® World History: Modern curriculum. Answers can be found in the Teacher's Resource Materials.

CHAPTER 8

very different perspective on the industrial era, characterized more by fear than by hope. Navigating that tension will surely be the central task of humankind during the balance of this century.

CHAPTER REVIEW

AP⁰ Key Terms

steam engine, 442
British textile industry, 447
middle-class society, 450
ideology of domesticity, 450
lower middle class, 450
laboring classes, 451
Karl Marx, 453
Labour Party, 456

socialism in the United States, 462
Progressives, 462
Russian Revolution of 1905, 465
caudillos, 467
Latin American export boom, 468
Mexican Revolution, 471
dependent development, 472

Finding the Main Point

1. What were the environmental, demographic, and economic consequences of industrial methods of production?
2. How were traditional social and gender structures transformed during the Industrial Revolution?
3. What were the effects of European migrations on the South Pacific, North and South America, and Russia?
4. What circumstances led the workers in the United States and Russia to respond to industrial society in very different ways?
5. How did the rapid industrialization of Europe and the United States transform the economies and cultures of Latin American countries?
6. What are the debates about the Industrial Revolution's enduring legacy in world history?

AP⁰ Big Picture Questions

1. What did humankind gain from the Industrial Revolution, and what did it lose?
2. In what ways might the Industrial Revolution be understood as a global rather than simply a European phenomenon?
3. The Industrial Revolution transformed social as well as economic life. What evidence might support this statement?
4. How do you think the Industrial Revolution will be viewed 50, 100, or 200 years into the future?
5. **Looking Back** How did the Industrial Revolution interact with the Scientific Revolution and the French Revolution to generate Europe's modern transformation?

TRM Suggested Responses to Questions
You can find suggested responses to the Chapter Review questions in the Teacher's Resource Materials.

ERIC'S
ACTIVITY **8**   **Living the Industrial Revolution**

This is a great place to have students focus on the AP® Theme of Social Interactions and Organization because that theme plays such an important role in the Industrial Revolution. Find the complete activity in the Teacher's Resource Materials.

TRM Eric's Activity 8: Living the Industrial Revolution

Sourcing and Situation in Primary and Secondary Sources

History is a discipline built on the analysis of primary sources. Historians use the information gleaned from primary sources to weave together a story about the past. They also examine the work of other historians based on primary sources; a historian's interpretation and analysis of primary sources are considered a secondary source.

In the first part of this workshop, you will learn how to gather and analyze sourcing for primary sources to more fully engage with the evidence that makes up the fabric of history. In the second part, you will analyze the background of authors, and their perspective, in considering the validity and limitations of secondary sources.

UNDERSTANDING PRIMARY SOURCES AND SOURCING

What a document contains (its content) is as important as who created it, when they created it, and for what or whose purpose. Think about the saying "consider the source" when you get new information. For the purposes of history, when we "consider the source," it is called **sourcing** a document. In other words, we need to look at the situation surrounding the source.

Before discussing sourcing for a primary source, let's define what it is.

> **Primary Source: A piece of evidence created during the time period being discussed or created by someone who experienced the period firsthand**

A primary source can be a book, a letter, a diary, a painting, a statue, an accounting ledger, a building—any cultural artifact. When you analyze a primary source, there are two main things you'll need to analyze: **sourcing** and **content**.

In this workshop, we're focusing on "sourcing," which means uncovering all of the background information you need to better understand the evidence that a primary source offers. Who created the primary source, and what is their point of view on the subject? Is the author a credible source, or likely to be biased? What is the purpose of the source? What is the historical situation underlying the source? Who is the intended audience for this source?

The point of gathering this background information is to see how it might inform (or even skew) the content of the source. On an even more practical level, sourcing your evidence when you write helps your readers know where the evidence comes from and what to take into account as they read it. This usually takes the form of a sentence or two that precedes the evidence, called a "sourcing statement."

Let's take a moment to make sure you understand all of the aspects of sourcing:

Point of view: What was the specific viewpoint of the creator of the source, as influenced by their beliefs, position, historical situation, or other factors?

Purpose: What was the creator of the source hoping to accomplish? What was their intention in creating this source?

TRM AP® Skills Workshop Activity
Handout: Sourcing and Situation in
Primary and Secondary Sources

BUILDING AP® SKILLS

Sourcing and Situation

The AP® skill of Sourcing and Situation is difficult and is a skill that students should practice whenever possible. This skill is the backbone of studying history. Primary sources are what historians use to tell the story of history. Knowing what primary sources are and how to use the aspects of sourcing is an important skill to master for the AP® World History Exam.

Even though mastering the AP® skill of Sourcing and Situation is difficult, it is an easy skill to practice. Use the explanations of primary sources on page 475 to explain the concept of analyzing primary sources to students. Have students use the HIPPY acronym found on page 476 to model sourcing for your students. After you model this skill, have students practice with Activity 1 and Activity 2 found on page 479.

475

Audience: Who was the creator of the source specifically trying to address?

Historical situation: How has the time, place, culture, and other factors influenced the creation of the source?

Credibility: How believable is a source, and what limitations might there be when taking into consideration the writer's background and point of view?

That's a lot to keep in mind as you approach a source, so teachers and students often use the acronym HIPPY:

Historical situation

Intended audience

Point of view

Purpose

Y Why or how the source is relevant to your argument

A Model of Sourcing a Document

Let's demonstrate this series of skills using the primary source document from AP® Looking Again, page 480. The following is from a poem-turned-hymn titled *The Internationale*. It was composed in secret in 1871 by a French working-class activist named Eugène Pottier and translated into English by an American publisher of radical books named Charles Kerr in 1900.

Arise, ye prisoners of starvation!
Arise, ye wretched of the earth!
For justice thunders condemnation,
A better world's in birth!
No more tradition's chains shall bind us,
Arise ye slaves, no more in thrall!
The earth shall rise on new foundations,
We have been nought, we shall be all.

Chorus
'Tis the final conflict,
Let each stand in his place.

The international working class
Shall be the human race. . . .

Behold them seated in their glory
The kings of mine and rail and soil!
What have you read in all their story,
But how they plundered toil?
Fruits of the workers' toil are buried
In the strong coffers of a few;
In working for their restitution
The men will only ask their due. (*Chorus*)

Historical situation: The Industrial Revolution in France caused extreme social change and conflict. One result was the Paris Commune of 1871, when revolutionaries took possession of the city and instituted radical policies based on the French Revolution's ideals of "liberty, equality, fraternity." The French government suppressed the Commune and brutally massacred 20,000 revolutionaries.

Intended audience: This poem was directed to the industrial workers, as well as other revolutionaries in France and elsewhere.

Point of view: The writer of this poem is clearly a supporter of socialist ideals and the movement of workers to rise up against the oppression of the bourgeoisie.

Purpose: To inspire the industrial workers of the world into rising up against the "chains" of oppression and taking their place at the forefront of society.

Here is a model sourcing and analysis statement for this document:

> *The Internationale*, a hymn written in secret by a survivor of the French government's massacre of the Paris Commune in 1871, was intended to inspire industrial workers with socialist ideals, regardless of location, so that they might break the traditional chains of oppression and take their place at the forefront of society. This hymn was meant to express the oppression and hopes of the common people and to work toward the goal of a socialist future.

UNDERSTANDING SECONDARY SOURCES AND SOURCING

So, what is a secondary source, and how is it different from a primary source?

Secondary Source: A source created after the fact, by someone who did not experience the event firsthand; in the study of history, this usually means a historian commenting on historical events or processes

While historians may aim for an objective view of the past, it's not completely possible. Historians are shaped by their time, cultures, and fields of study. These factors inevitably influence the way they interpret primary documents and view the events and processes that make up history. As a result, interpretations of a historical event or process can vary across different times and cultures.

To gain a good insight into what might influence a historian, pay attention to the date when the excerpt was written. Something from the early twenty-first century, for example, is going to look different from something written in the eighteenth century. You will also need to be able to analyze a secondary source to understand how the historians' context and point of view influence their interpretation of the event or process. Take into consideration their educational background and fields of study.

As a student of history and a historian-in-training, you should also be aware of your own context and how it shapes your point of view.

Let's see what sourcing secondary sources looks like by comparing two authors who wrote about the effects of the Industrial Revolution from different perspectives.

> Material life in Britain and in the industrialized world that followed it is far better today than could have been imagined by the most wild-eyed optimistic 18th-century philosophe—and whereas this outcome may have been an unforeseen consequence, most economists, at least, would regard it as an undivided blessing.
>
> — Joel Moykr, historian of European economics for the period 1750–1914,
> *The Enlightened Economy: An Economic History of Britain, 1700–1850*, 2009

> [The Industrial Revolution] begins to look like, at best, a mixed blessing—one that resulted in technologies that have allowed many people to live longer, safer lives, but that has,

BUILDING AP® SKILLS

Sourcing and Situation

Working with secondary sources is primarily looking at the work of other historians. Secondary sources can be tricky because sometimes historians disagree on how to interpret historical events. Understanding what secondary sources are and how to use them is an important skill to master for the AP® World History Exam.

Use the discussions of secondary sources on page 477 to explain what a secondary source is to students. Use the examples found on pages 477 and 478 to model with students how to interpret secondary sources.

Consider having students complete Activity 3 on page 479 to reinforce the skill.

477

simultaneously, destroyed global ecosystems, caused the extinction of many living species, facilitated rampant population growth, and wreaked havoc on climate systems, the effects of which will be an increase in droughts, floods, storms, and erratic weather patterns that threaten most global societies.

— Jeremy Caradonna, historian of science, technology, and environmental studies, "Is 'Progress' Good for Humanity?", *The Atlantic*, 2014

What do you immediately notice about the two texts? While both were written within a five-year time frame in the twenty-first century, the authors' perspectives on the effects of the Industrial Revolution are different. The first text was written by an economic historian who focuses on the benefits of "material life" that emerged as a result of the Industrial Revolution. However, the author of the second text is a historian of technology and the environment. His assessment of the effects of the Industrial Revolution is focused on the environmental damage that resulted from industrialization. Their background and point of view influenced what they wrote about the same topic.

Reading secondary sources from multiple perspectives provides an opportunity for corroboration, an important skill for historians, but the background and point of view of the author may pose a limitation on the use and validity of the source. Therefore, it is always important to *consider the source*.

UNDERSTANDING QUANTITATIVE DATA AS A SECONDARY SOURCE

Quantitative data, which is data expressed in numbers and/or visual representations, is critical to the understanding of history because it allows historians to precisely track historical developments. Analyzing quantitative data and using it to support a historical argument is a necessary skill in the study of history.

It's often said that numbers do not lie. And although it is true that data can be precise, it can also be deceiving, and it needs to be read carefully. For example, who created the information? Is it an agency that could be manipulating numbers, or a source that might be inaccurate? What is the data not showing? How is the data framed or contextualized? This is why knowing the background of the information (sourcing) is so vitally important when working with quantitative data. Historical knowledge can really help put data into context.

PRIMARY AND SECONDARY SOURCES ON THE AP® WORLD HISTORY EXAM

Information garnered from primary and secondary sources will be tested heavily on the AP® Exam. Remember that the Multiple-Choice section contains a minimum of one primary source or one secondary source as a stimulus, or a pair of secondary sources as stimuli, for every set of four to five questions. Short-Answer Questions will also include a primary source and a secondary source, presented as a visual or as quantitative data. Both primary and secondary sources may ask you to determine sourcing. In primary sources, you may be asked to determine the audience or purpose of a primary source document. In secondary sources, you may

BUILDING AP® SKILLS

Sourcing and Situation

Historians use quantitative data to track historical developments. Quantitative data is information that is expressed in numbers or represented visually. Much of the information that historians use is from historical and archeological research, but historians also use information from academic disciplines such as geography, sociology, economics, and political science. Most of the information from these disciplines is represented in the form of tables, charts, graphs, and maps. Using secondary sources such as quantitative data can help students understand the events described by the data. For AP® World History: Modern, students will be tested on their ability to interpret quantitative data on one or more portions of the exam.

AP® CLASSROOM

AP® Topic Questions

If you want to give students practice with quantitative data, you can log in to your AP® Classroom account and assign the AP® Multiple-Choice Topic Questions under Topic 5.9, "English Textile Workers Table MCQ 1 through 3." AP® Classroom allows you to set the questions up digitally or print out a copy for each student. Consider dividing the class into groups of three to four students to discuss the questions together to come to the correct answer.

be asked to compare the point of view of the authors of each source, or you may be asked how the historian's context influenced the argument. You may also need to determine, based on the information in the secondary sources, which source was created first and which second. Questions about how historical context affects the document or how the document is affected by the time and place it was created are often more challenging.

Historical sources are the basis of the Document-Based Question, where you are expected to apply the skills of summarization, evidence gathering, sourcing, and inferencing as you weave documents into an argument addressing the prompt. One requirement of the DBQ essay is for you to "explain **how or why** the document's point of view, purpose, historical situation, and/or audience is relevant to an argument." As such, the "Y" in the HIPPY acronym—standing for "how or why" the sourcing information of a document is insightful in understanding the evidence being presented—is an important step.

Thus, knowing how to determine sourcing for primary sources and secondary sources (including quantitative data) is critical for success on the AP® World History Exam.

BUILDING AP® SKILLS

1. **Activity: Sourcing a Primary Source Document.** Study the primary source written by Vladimir Lenin from AP® Working with Evidence, Document 5 (page 487). Then fill out the box below to identify the key elements of sourcing for the source.

Summary	
H = historical situation	
I = intended audience	
P = point of view of the author	
P = purpose of the document	
Y = why or how	

2. **Activity: Writing a Sourcing Statement for a Primary Source.** After completing the HIPPY analysis in Activity 1, write a paragraph analyzing the document's background. Be sure to address how all of the following elements impacted the creation of the source: point of view, purpose, audience, historical situation, and credibility/limitations. Then, write a sourcing statement that encompasses the most important aspects of your analysis.

3. **Activity: Analyzing a Secondary Source.** Read AP® Historians' Voices 8.2, found on page 491, which is an excerpt by Terry Eagleton on the relevance of Marxism. Next, research the background of Terry Eagleton online. Write a statement describing Eagleton's background and point of view, and how this information both validates and limits the use of his work in historical research.

TRM **Suggested Responses to Questions**
You can find suggested responses to the Building AP® Skills questions in the Teacher's Resource Materials.

479

The Internationale was just one of many expressions of the socialist vision produced by writers and artists during the period. The image in AP® Working with Evidence, Document 7, "Socialist Perspectives in Art," page 489, offers another viewpoint in a different medium. Compare this image to *The Internationale* by answering the following question:

1. In what ways does Document 7, "The Pyramid of the Capitalist System," illustrate the social conflicts and grievances in *The Internationale*?

FURTHER ACTIVITY

Perhaps not surprisingly, *The Internationale* was prominent in the communist world of the twentieth century; it served as the anthem of the Soviet Union until 1944 and as late as 2017 was performed at a National Congress of the Chinese Communist Party. It was also sung during celebrations in Cuba and Vietnam, both communist-governed countries.

But it became a song of resistance to oppression in many settings. In the 1930s, it was sung during the Great Depression in the United States and during the civil war in Spain. Jews in the Warsaw Ghetto sang it during their uprising against the Nazi regime in 1943. The American folk musician and activist Pete Seeger sang it at the Vancouver Folk Festival in 1989. And also in 1989 Chinese demonstrators against communist tyranny sang it shortly before the massacre in Tiananmen Square. "It encouraged us to stand up to the highest authority in China," declared one of those protesters.[27]

In a paragraph, write a response on "The Twentieth-Century Legacy of *The Internationale*." Why does the song have a continuing appeal in times and places far removed from its original setting? You will need to introduce the song as it initially appeared in Western Europe, and you might want to distinguish between its use in established communist regimes and its role in resisting a variety of oppressive systems.

TEACHING IDEA

Class Discussion

If you want to extend students' thinking about *The Internationale* becoming a part of the growing socialist movement and practice sourcing, you can use the question in "Further Activity" on this page to drive a class discussion or debate rather than having students write a paragraph as a response. You will need to provide context, but the discussion should help students understand how events from the past can affect events in the future.

Socialist Visions

Among the ideologies and social movements that grew out of Europe's nineteenth-century Industrial Revolution, none was more important than socialism. Socialists rejected the inequalities created by the competitive and cutthroat capitalism of an industrializing Europe. They also challenged the assumptions of classical liberalism that an unrestricted free market economy generated a good society. Instead they envisioned a society in which the benefits of the new industrial economy were far more equally shared. By the end of the nineteenth century, socialism had become a major element of the political and intellectual life of Europe's industrializing countries, and it enjoyed a modest presence in the United States and Japan and among a handful of intellectuals elsewhere. But socialism was never a single unified movement. Rather, the socialist vision found expression in many ways, as the following sources illustrate.

LOOKING AHEAD

AP® DBQ PRACTICE

As you read through the documents in this collection, remember that the documents are put in chronological order. Think about what these sources have in common, and what is different about them.

DOCUMENT 1   The Utopian Socialists

The first expression of modern socialism emerged during the early nineteenth century in a series of writings advocating the creation of small-scale voluntary and intentional communities based on rational and ethical principles. The French philosopher Charles Fourier (1772–1837) wrote opposing industrial society altogether as cruel, inhumane, and monotonous. In its place he proposed a series of small communities called Phalanstère, where gender equality and sexual freedom could be practiced and where education for children, workshops for adults, gardens, and cultural activities for all would be available. A number of such communities were in fact established, albeit briefly, in Europe and the United States. In the passage that follows, Fourier outlined some of the goals and conditions that would characterize these communities, based on the principles of "attraction" and "societary work."

Source: Charles Fourier, thoughts on societary work in Phalanstere utopian socialist communities, 1822.

If it is to attract the people so forcefully, societary work must have none of the loathsome aspects that make work in the present state so odious. For societary work to become attractive it must fulfill the following conditions:

1. Each worker must be an associate who is compensated by dividend [a share of the profits] and not by wages.

TRM Suggested Responses to Questions
You can find suggested responses to the AP® Working with Evidence questions in the Teacher's Resource Materials.

BUILDING AP® SKILLS

Claims and Evidence in Sources

Interpreting text-based as well as non-text-based sources is an important skill for AP® World History: Modern students. If time is available, have students investigate one of the results of industrialism by using the evidence in "Socialist Visions" beginning on page 483. Consider having students analyze one or more of the sources found on pages 483–489. You can check for understanding by:

■ Using the questions at the end of each source as a discussion starting point.

■ Pairing students to analyze (identify and describe) using the author or creator's point of view, purpose, historical situation, and/or audience. This activity can continue to reinforce sourcing.

■ Assigning a source to a group of three to four students and having them present an overview of the source along with the sourcing to the rest of the class.

■ Having students present an overview of the source, and then having them practice AP® Comparison skills using Question 4 under AP® Doing History on page 490.

483

2. Each person—man, woman, or child—must be paid in proportion to his contribution in capital, work, and talent.

3. Work sessions must be varied about eight times a day because a man cannot remain enthusiastic about his job for more than an hour and a half or two when he is performing an agricultural or manufacturing task. . . .

6. The division of labor must be carried to the supreme degree in order to allot suitable tasks to people of each sex and of every age.

7. The distribution of tasks must assure each man, woman or child the right to work or the right to take part at any time in any kind of work for which he or she is qualified.

X. Finally, in this new order the common people must enjoy a guarantee of well-being, a minimum income sufficient for present and future needs. This guarantee must free them from all anxiety either for their own welfare or that of their dependents.

Question to Consider: Based on the excerpt, what were Fourier's social values?

AP **Analyzing Sources:** Who do you suppose Fourier targets as his main audience? What clues does he provide in the source?

DOCUMENT 2 Socialism According to Marx and Engels

German-born intellectual Karl Marx (1818–1883) lived during the harshest phase of European industrialization, before the benefits of this new and highly productive system were widely shared. In his writings, he praised the productive capacity of the Industrial Revolution while providing devastating criticism of the social inequalities, the economic instability, and the blatant exploitation that accompanied this process.

Document 2 presents excerpts from the most famous of Marx's writings, *The Communist Manifesto*, first published in 1848. In this effort and throughout much of his life, Marx was assisted by another German thinker, Friedrich Engels (1820–1895), the son of a successful textile manufacturer. Engels became radicalized as he witnessed the devastating social results of capitalist industrialization. Their *Manifesto* begins with a summary description of the historical process.

Source: Karl Marx and Friedrich Engels, from *The Communist Manifesto*, 1848.

Society as a whole is more and more splitting up into two great hostile camps, into two great classes directly facing each other—bourgeoisie and proletariat.

The bourgeoisie, wherever it has got the upper hand, has put an end to all feudal, patriarchal, idyllic relations. It has . . . left no other nexus between people than naked self-interest, than callous "cash payment.". . . It has resolved personal worth into exchange value, and in place of the numberless indefeasible chartered freedoms, has set up that single, unconscionable freedom—Free Trade. In one word, for exploitation, veiled by religious and political illusions, it has substituted naked, shameless, direct, brutal exploitation. . . .

But not only has the bourgeoisie forged the weapons that bring death to itself; it has also called into existence the men who are to wield those weapons—the modern working class—the proletarians. . . .

These laborers, who must sell themselves piecemeal, are a commodity, like every other article of commerce, and are consequently exposed to all the vicissitudes of competition, to all the fluctuations of the market.

[T]he first step in the revolution by the working class is to raise the proletariat to the position of ruling class, to win the battle of democracy. The proletariat will use its political supremacy to wrest, by degree, all capital from the bourgeoisie, to centralize all instruments of production in the hands of the state.

Question to Consider: What groups do the authors glorify and demonize? Why?

AP **Analyzing Sources:** How could the background of the two authors influence their claims in the excerpt?

DOCUMENT 3 Socialism in Song

While socialist intellectuals developed a particular understanding of history and capitalism, ordinary workers, many animated by socialist ideals, gave voice to their experience and aspirations in song. The hymn of the socialist movement was *The Internationale*, composed in 1871 by Eugène Pottier, a French working-class activist, poet, and songwriter. Document 3 offers an English translation made in 1900 by Charles Kerr, an American publisher of radical books. He published his translation the following year. The song gave expression to both the oppression and the hopes of ordinary people as they worked for a socialist future. (See AP® Looking Again: *The Internationale*, page 480, for a further analysis of this song.)

Source: Eugène Pottier, *The Internationale*, 1871.

Arise, ye prisoners of starvation!
Arise, ye wretched of the earth!
For justice thunders condemnation,
A better world's in birth!
No more tradition's chains shall bind us,
Arise ye slaves, no more in thrall!
The earth shall rise on new foundations,
We have been nought, we shall be all. (Chorus)

Chorus
'Tis the final conflict,
Let each stand in his place.
The international working class
Shall be the human race.
We want no condescending saviors
To rule us from a judgment hall;
We workers ask not for their favors;
Let us consult for all.

485

Behold them seated in their glory	Fruits of the workers' toil are buried
The kings of mine and rail and soil!	In the strong coffers of a few;
What have you read in all their story,	In working for their restitution
But how they plundered toil?	The men will only ask their due. (Chorus)

Charles H. Kerr, comp. and trans., *Socialist Songs with Music* (Chicago: Charles H. Kerr, 1901), No. 2.

Question to Consider: How does the song depict the working class?

AP **Analyzing Sources:** Why do you think the song compares workers to enslaved people and the owners of "mine and rail and soil" to kings?

DOCUMENT 4 Socialism without Revolution

Organized in various national parties and joined together in international organizations as well, socialists usually referred to themselves as social democrats, for they were seeking to extend the principles of democracy from the political arena (voting rights, for example) into the realm of the economy and society. The chief spokesperson for this group of socialists, known as "revisionists," was Eduard Bernstein (1850–1932), a prominent member of the German Social Democratic Party. His ideas provoked a storm of controversy within European socialist circles. Document 4 is drawn from the preface of Bernstein's 1899 book, *Evolutionary Socialism*.

> **Source: Eduard Bernstein, member of the German Social Democratic Party, from the preface of *Evolutionary Socialism*, 1899.**
>
> I set myself against the notion that we have to expect shortly a collapse of the bourgeois economy. . . .
>
> Social conditions have not developed to such an acute opposition of things and classes as is depicted in the *Manifesto*. It is not only useless, it is the greatest folly to attempt to conceal this from ourselves. The number of members of the possessing classes is today not smaller but larger. The enormous increase of social wealth is not accompanied by a decreasing number of large capitalists but by an increasing number of capitalists of all degrees. The middle classes change their character but they do not disappear from the social scale.
>
> In all advanced countries we see the privileges of the capitalist bourgeoisie yielding step by step to democratic organizations. Under the influence of this, and driven by the movement of the working classes which is daily becoming stronger, a social reaction has set in against the exploiting tendencies of capital. . . . Factory legislation, the democratizing of local government, and the extension of its area of work, the freeing of trade unions and systems of cooperative trading from legal restrictions, the consideration of standard conditions of labor in the work undertaken by public authorities—all these characterize this phase of the evolution.
>
> Eduard Bernstein, *Evolutionary Socialism*, translated by Edith C. Harvey (New York: Schocken Books, 1961), xxiv–xxx.

486

Question to Consider: How does Bernstein seek to achieve the goals of socialism? How does his excerpt differ from previous sources?

AP **Analyzing Sources:** What evidence does Bernstein provide to support his argument that "the capitalist bourgeoisie [is] yielding step by step to democratic organizations"?

DOCUMENT 5 Lenin and Russian Socialism

Vladimir Ilyich Ulyanov, better known as Lenin, then a prominent figure in the small Russian Social Democratic Labor Party established in 1898, was particularly hostile to what he called "economism" or "trade-unionism," which focused on immediate reforms such as higher wages, shorter hours, and better working conditions. In a famous pamphlet titled *What Is to Be Done?,* Lenin addressed many of these issues, well before he became the leader of the world's first successful socialist revolution in 1917.

Source: Lenin, member of the Russian Social Democratic Labor Party, from the political pamphlet *What Is to Be Done*?, 1902.

The political struggle carried on by the Social Democrats is far more extensive and complex than the economic struggle the workers carry on against the employers and the government. Similarly . . . the organization of a revolutionary Social Democratic Party must inevitably differ from the organizations of the workers designed for the latter struggle. A workers' organization . . . must be as wide as possible; and . . . it must be as public as conditions will allow. . . . On the other hand, the organizations of revolutionaries must consist first and foremost of people whose profession is that of a revolutionary. . . . Such an organization must of necessity be not too extensive and as secret as possible. . . .

  I assert:

1. that no movement can be durable without a stable organization of leaders to maintain continuity;

2. that the more widely the masses are spontaneously drawn into the struggle and form the basis of the movement and participate in it, the more necessary is it to have such an organization. . . .

3. that the organization must consist chiefly of persons engaged in revolutionary activities as a profession;

4. that in a country with an autocratic government, the more we restrict the membership of this organization to persons who are engaged in revolutionary activities as a profession and who have been professionally trained in the art of combating the political police, the more difficult will it be to catch the organization. . . .

Question to Consider: What kind of revolutionary movement did Lenin think was necessary to achieve socialism in Russia?

AP Analyzing Sources: Consider the historical situation of Russia, especially its political systems when this document was written. Why might Lenin be opposed to the kind of democratic approach to socialism that Bernstein advocates for Germany in Document 4?

DOCUMENT 6 The Woman Question

Marxist socialism coincided with the emergence of feminism, giving rise to what many socialists called "the woman question." Should socialists treat women as members of an oppressed class or as members of an oppressed sex? Since most socialists believed that the lack of economic independence was the root cause of women's subordination, how should socialist parties relate to middle-class feminists in addressing uniquely female issues such as suffrage, equal pay, education, and maternity insurance? Among the leading figures addressing such issues was Clara Zetkin (1857–1933), a prominent member of the German Social Democratic Party and an ardent feminist. In Document 6, Zetkin describes the party's posture on "the woman question."

Source: Clara Zetkin, feminist and member of the German Social Democratic Party, from *The German Socialist Women's Movement*, 1909.

Socialist women have continued their propaganda in favor of the full political emancipation of their sex. . . . The integral human emancipation of all women depends in consequence on the social emancipation of labor; that can only be realized by the class-war of the exploited majority. Therefore, our Socialist women oppose strongly the bourgeois women righters' credo that the women of all classes must gather into an unpolitical, neutral movement striving exclusively for women's rights. In theory and practice they maintain the conviction that the class antagonisms are much more powerful, effective, and decisive than the social antagonisms between the sexes. . . . [T]hus the working-class women will [only] win their full emancipation . . . in the class war of all the exploited, without difference of sex, against all who exploit, without difference of sex. That does not mean at all that they undervalue the importance of the political emancipation of the female sex. On the contrary, they employ much more energy than the German women-righters to conquer the suffrage. But the vote is, according to their views, not the last word and term of their aspirations, but only a weapon— a means in [the] struggle for a revolutionary aim—the Socialistic order.

Question to Consider: What does Zetkin believe is critical to the success of the women's movement?

AP Analyzing Sources: Why do you think the author pits herself against bourgeois or middle-class feminists?

DOCUMENT 7 Socialist Perspectives in Art: Depicting Capitalist
Society

Socialists expressed their understanding of existing capitalist society in art as well as
writing. This image was published in 1911 in a newspaper of the International Workers
of the World, a trade union established in the United States in 1905 that copied earlier
Russian and Belgian versions.

Source: Industrial Workers of the World, image entitled "The Pyramid of the Capitalist
System," 1911.

IAM/akg-images

Question to Consider: In the poster, who is villainized and who is glorified? How
can you tell?

AP Analyzing Sources: Consider the audience of the poster. How might that
impact the author's decisions while designing it?

489

AP **DOING HISTORY**

1. **DBQ Practice:** Evaluate the extent to which understandings of socialism changed during the period 1800–1950.

2. **Contextualization:** "Socialism developed as an economic theory in response to problems caused by major economic changes in the period 1750–1900." What details can you provide to develop a statement that contextualizes this prompt?

3. **Outside Evidence:** What additional information can you use to support your claims about the changes or continuities regarding understandings of socialism?

4. **Complex Argumentation:** What factors, other than time, could have influenced different expressions of socialist ideology?

The Legacy of Karl Marx in the Twenty-First Century

Approaching 150 years after the death of Marx, scholars and activists alike continue to debate his relevance. Voice 8.1 comes from British educator Allan Todd and explores the relationship between recent events and Marxist ideas. In Voice 8.2, Terry Eagleton, a British professor of literature, argues for the continued usefulness of Marxist thinking.

VOICE 8.1

Allan Todd on Marx and Current History | 2016

The opening words of Marx and Engels' *The Communist Manifesto*, first published in 1848, are: "A spectre is haunting Europe, the spectre of communism." Given the visible collapse of most states claiming to be communist, this "spectre" would appear to have been laid to rest. Certainly the failure of attempts in the Soviet Union and Eastern Europe to construct socialism led to a "retreat from Marxism" in the first decades after the collapse of these regimes.

Yet Marx's analysis had claimed that capitalist globalization was bound to lead to periodic and serious economic crises. . . . And indeed the financial crash of 2008 and the global economic crisis of 2011 . . . along with the ecological crises associated with the unrestricted drive for profit suggest that . . . Marx's theories might still have some relevance for the 21st century.

Thus historians such as E. Hobsbawm have argued that the events of 1989–91 and afterwards do not necessarily mark the end of Marxism or communism. They have pointed out that Marxist theory and communist practice arose from conditions of poverty, the destruction of war, and strong desires for liberty, fairness, and equality.

Other commentators have observed that Marxism . . . was in large part an extension of the French Revolution's ideals of "liberty, equality, and fraternity." . . . Movements calling for the full implementation of these ideals continue to emerge around the globe in the 21st century. Thus it may be rather too early for historians to proclaim the death and funeral of communism [Marxism].

Source: Allan Todd, *The Soviet Union and Post-Soviet Russia* (Cambridge: Cambridge University Press, 2016), 294–96.

VOICE 8.2

Terry Eagleton on the Continuing Relevance of Marx | 2011

Very few thinkers . . . have changed the course of actual history as decisively as [Marx]. . . . He transformed our understanding of human history. . . .

Marx was the first to identify the historical object known as capitalism—to show how it arose, by what laws it worked and how it might be brought to an end. . . . Marx unmasked our everyday life to reveal an imperceptible entity known as the capitalist mode of production. . . .

About Marxism as a moral and cultural critique. . . . Alienation, the "commodification" of social life, a culture of greed, aggression, mindless hedonism . . . , the steady hemorrhage of meaning and value from human existence—it is hard to find an intelligent discussion of these questions that is not indebted to the Marxist tradition. Marxism is a critique of capitalism. . . . It is also the only such critique that has transformed large sectors of the globe. . . . As long as capitalism is in business, Marxism must be as well.

Marx himself predicted a decline of the working class and the steep rise of white collar work. . . . He also foresaw so-called globalization. He is accused of being outdated by champions of a capitalism that is rapidly reverting to Victorian levels of inequality. . . . In our own time, as Marx predicted, inequalities of wealth have dramatically deepened.

Capitalism has brought about great material advances. But though this way of organizing our affairs has had a long time to demonstrate that it is capable of satisfying human demands all around, it seems no closer to doing so than ever.

Source: Terry Eagleton, *Why Marx Was Right* (New Haven, CT: Yale University Press, 2011), x, xi, 2, 3, 8, 10.

AP Analyzing Secondary Sources

1. What events or circumstances does Allan Todd believe have shaped postures toward Marx and Marxism?

2. Why does Terry Eagleton in Voice 8.2 believe that Marx remains relevant in the twenty-first century?

3. **Integrating Primary and Secondary Sources:** What evidence from the primary sources might these authors use to support their arguments?

BUILDING AP® SKILLS

Claims and Evidence in Sources

You can use the "AP® Historians' Voices: The Legacy of Karl Marx in the Twenty-First Century" to help students work on understanding and interpreting secondary sources. Have students read both of the sources found on page 491 and answer Questions 1 and 2. After students have answered the questions on their own, have them discuss their responses as a class. This activity can help students practice reading and interpreting secondary sources, which are found on the MCQ and SAQ sections of the exam.

TRM **Suggested Responses to Questions**
You can find suggested responses to the AP® Analyzing Secondary Sources questions in the Teacher's Resource Materials.

TRM Suggested Responses to Questions

You can find suggested responses to the Chapter 8 AP® Exam Practice questions in the Teacher's Resource Materials.

TEACHING IDEA

AP® Exam Strategies

It's good for students to continually practice their test-taking skills. To help them, project or copy the multiple-choice questions found on pages 492 and 493. This can be done as a bell ringer for practice or as a practice quiz prior to the unit or chapter test. Once students have answered the questions, have the class discuss why the different answer choices were correct or incorrect.

Multiple-Choice Questions   Choose the correct answer for each question.

Questions 1–3 refer to this passage.

> The first step in the revolution by the working class is to raise the proletariat to the position of ruling class to win the battle of democracy. . . . In most advanced countries, the following [means for accomplishing this] will be pretty generally applicable:
>
> 1. Abolition of property in land and application of all rents of land to public purpose. . . .
> 3. Abolition of all rights of inheritance. . . .
> 5. Centralization of credit in the banks of the state, by means of a national bank with state capital and an exclusive monopoly. . . .
> 7. Extension of factories and instruments of production owned by the state; the bringing into cultivation of waste lands, and the improvement of the soil generally in accordance with a common plan.
> 8. Equal obligation of all to work. Establishment of industrial armies, especially for agriculture. . . .
> 10. Free education for all children in public schools. Abolition of children's factory labor in its present form. Combination of education with industrial production, etc.
>
> — Karl Marx and Friedrich Engels, *The Communist Manifesto*, 1848

1. Which of the following conclusions is best supported by the text above and your knowledge of world history?
   a. Industrialized states increased voting rights in efforts to improve industrial production.
   b. New ideologies emerged in response to social and political upheavals.
   c. Public pressures convinced governments to build up their armies.
   d. The middle class declined because of economic instability.

2. Which of these best describes the response of governments in industrialized states to worker demands for political and economic reforms?
   a. The elimination of the privileged classes through higher taxes
   b. The creation of government-run laboring villages to provide workers for factories
   c. The creation of communist governments in Russia and Japan in the nineteenth century
   d. The adoption of labor laws and increased suffrage to help ease some negative effects of industrialization

3. The ideas of Marx and Engels, seen in the passage above, were in response to which of the following issues of industrialization?
   a. A desire by industrialists to create a national tax for all social classes
   b. An increase in the wealth of the overall population in industrialized states
   c. Unsafe working and living conditions for urban workers
   d. The production of more and cheaper goods for the population to purchase

492

Questions 4–6 refer to this table.

SHARE OF TOTAL WORLD MANUFACTURING OUTPUT (percentage)

	1750	1800	1860	1880	1900
EUROPE AS A WHOLE	23.2	28.1	53.2	61.3	62.0
United Kingdom	1.9	4.3	19.9	22.9	18.5
France	4.0	4.2	7.9	7.8	6.8
Germany	2.9	3.5	4.9	8.5	13.2
Russia	5.0	5.6	7.0	7.6	8.8
UNITED STATES	0.1	0.8	7.2	14.7	23.6
JAPAN	3.8	3.5	2.6	2.4	2.4
THE REST OF THE WORLD	73.0	67.7	36.6	20.9	11.0
China	32.8	33.3	19.7	12.5	6.2
South Asia (India/Pakistan)	24.5	19.7	8.6	2.8	1.7

Source: Data from Paul Kennedy, *The Rise and Fall of the Great Powers* (New York: Random House, 1987), 149.

4. Which of the following most directly explains the comparative shift in British and Indian manufacturing levels between 1750 and 1900?
   a. The disruption of global cotton production because of the U.S. Civil War
   b. More restrictive labor laws in South Asia that hindered production
   c. The application of steam power to textile production in Britain
   d. The decline in agricultural production because of the Enclosure Acts in Britain

5. What best enabled the change evident in U.S. manufacturing illustrated in the chart?
   a. The securing of reliable sources of coal outside U.S. borders
   b. The granting of suffrage to a large portion of U.S. citizens
   c. The emancipation of enslaved people so that they could serve as an industrial labor force
   d. A significant increase in migration to the United States from Europe and Asia

6. A historian researching economic systems in the nineteenth century would find the data in the chart most helpful in
   a. understanding the decline of Japan as an imperial power.
   b. comparing the effectiveness of states that practiced laissez-faire economics with those practicing communism.
   c. understanding the causes of European imperialism in the late nineteenth century.
   d. understanding the underlying economic causes of the cold war.

493

BUILDING AP® SKILLS

Argumentation

Students need to practice their writing skills for the AP® Exam on a regular basis. Use the SAQs on pages 494 and 495 for students to write as an "exit ticket" at the end of class to check for understanding. You can also spread the three SAQs across several days or have students write them all at once to practice timing for the AP® Exam. If you choose to have students write them all at once, make certain that students have the correct amount of time for this exercise. On exam day, students will have a total of 40 minutes to write three SAQs.

If you want to try something different with the SAQs, partner the students up and have them write the SAQs together by having one student write the claim or topic sentence for an SAQ and the other student write the supporting evidence for the claim.

Short-Answer Questions
Read each question carefully and write a short response. Use complete sentences.

1. **Use this passage and your knowledge of world history to answer all parts of the question that follows.**

> [The Industrial Revolution's] most serious consequences were social: the transition to the new economy created misery and discontent, the material of social revolution.... Simple minded labourers reacted to the new system by smashing the machines which they thought responsible for their troubles.... The exploitation of labor which kept its incomes at subsistence level, thus enabling the rich to accumulate the profits which financed industrialization, antagonized the proletarian. However, another aspect of this diversion of national income from the poor to the rich, from consumption to investment, also antagonized the small entrepreneur. The great financiers, the tight community of home and foreign "fund-holders" who received what all paid in taxes—something like 8 percent of the entire national income—were perhaps even more unpopular among small businessmen than among labourers, for these knew enough about money and credit to feel a personal rage at their disadvantage.

> — Eric Hobsbawm, Marxist historian from Britain, *The Age of Revolution*, 1962

   A. Identify ONE specific piece of historical evidence that supports the author's claim that the most serious consequences of industrialization were social.
   B. Explain why the response of the lower classes to the situation described above was much different in the Russian Empire than in the United States.
   C. Explain how Hobsbawm's Marxism is reflected in the passage.

2. **Use your knowledge of world history to answer all parts of the question that follows.**
   A. Identify ONE similar social impact of the Industrial Revolution in Europe and Latin America.
   B. Explain the cause for a major change in labor systems during the Industrial Revolution.
   C. Explain ONE significant change in the relationship between nations that industrialized and those that did not.

494

3. Use the map below and your knowledge of world history to answer all parts of the question that follows.

The Early Phase of Europe's Industrial Revolution

A. Identify ONE region of Europe that is an exception to the rise of industrial production.

B. Explain why some areas with abundant ore and coal resources did not develop industrial production at the same rate as other regions with similar resources.

C. Explain ONE effect of the economic transformation shown on the map on regions outside of Europe.

495

9 Empires in Collision
Europe, the Middle East, and East Asia, 1800–1900

AP® Overview for Chapter 9

This chapter corresponds to AP® Unit 6: Consequences of Industrialization, 1750–1900. It focuses on three major non-Western empires that experienced tremendous transformations during the nineteenth century. The shock waves of European imperialism influenced all three, even though the Ottoman Empire, China, and Japan were never directly ruled by European imperialists. In China, this period includes a portion of the "century of humiliation," as some historians term it. This period also sees the last stages of the Ottoman Empire and the first stages of the empire of Japan and its industrialization. The AP® reasoning processes of Causation, Comparison, and especially Continuity and Change are in play when analyzing the content of Chapter 9.

Chapter 9 Essential Activity

Ask students to create a chart of the "Developments of the European Moment in World History" that are noted in the chapter introduction on pages 497–498. A sample chart is provided below. As students work through the chapter, they should note examples of various countries that adopted or confronted one or more of those "European developments." A reproducible version of this chart is available in the Teacher's Resource Materials. (Answers are provided in italics.)

European Developments	Example
Military strength and political ambitions of rival European states	*The carving up of China by imperial powers*
Networks of trade, investment, and migration	*China and the Opium Wars*
Influence of traditional European culture, including language, religion, literature, and philosophy	*The Ottomans became a secular state with a strong Islamic heritage*
Scientific rationalism, including technological achievements, belief in a better future, and ideas of nationalism, socialism, feminism, and individualism	*The industrialization of Japan*

TRM Handout 9.1: Chart for Developments of the European Moment in World History

Chapter 9 Resources

TRM AP® Skills Workshop Activity Handout: Claims and Evidence in Primary Sources

TRM Chapter 9 DBQ Activity Handout

TRM Chapter 9 Guided Reading

TRM Chapter 9 Lecture Presentation Slides

TRM Chapter 9 Outline

TRM Chapter 9 Suggested Responses to Questions

TRM Eric's Activity 9: Comparing Responses to the West

TRM Handout 9.1: Chart for Developments of the European Moment in World History

TRM Handout 9.2: Causation Chart for China's Century of Crisis

TRM Handout 9.3: Comparison Chart for the Decline of the Qing Dynasty and Ottoman Empire

TRM Handout 9.4: OPTIC Chart for Addiction to Opium Photograph

TRM Handout 9.5: Venn Diagram for China and Ottoman Empire Reactions to Pressure from the West

TRM Handout 9.6: Chart for the Tanzimat: Goals and Motivation

TRM Handout 9.7: Comparison Chart for the Chinese and Japanese Class Systems

TRM Handout 9.8: Chart for Political, Economic, and Social Features of the Meiji Restoration

TRM Map 9A: The World

Pacing Guide

Below is a pacing guide for the AP® World History: Modern course beginning in ca. 1200 C.E. This pacing guide is based on a schedule with 120 sessions of 50 minutes each before the AP® Exam. It is meant as a place to start. If you have a different number of sessions before the exam, you can modify the pacing to suit your needs.

Day	Pages Assigned	AP® Topic	AP® Theme	Suggested Assignments	Coverage Notes
1	Read pages 498–502 to "Western Pressures"	5.4 6.5	ECN TEC	Chapter 9 Essential Activity AP® Exam Practice: Multiple-Choice Questions 4–6 on pages 545–546 Building AP® Skills: Making Connections: Causation on page 499	The opening of Chapter 9 helps connect the Industrial Revolution and nineteenth-century imperialism to non-European empires. This will help give context to students as they begin to study the reactions of Japan, the Ottomans, and the Qing dynasty to increasing European power and influence in this era.
2	Read pages 502–508 from "Western Pressures" to "The Ottoman Empire and the West in the Nineteenth Century"	5.6 5.8 6.3 6.5	GOV ECN SIO	Building AP® Skills: Claims and Evidence in Sources on page 503 AP® Exam Practice: Multiple-Choice Questions 1–3 on page 544 AP® Exam Practice: Short-Answer Question 2 on page 546	This entire chapter lends itself well to practicing the comparison skill by looking at the different reactions of older states and empires to industrialization and imperialism, as well as the effects of those reactions. You can also bring in Russia's reactions to industrialization in Chapter 8 to add another society to this comparison.
3	Read pages 508–511 from "The Ottoman Empire and the West in the Nineteenth Century" to "Reform and Its Opponents"	5.4 6.3 6.5	GOV ECN TEC	Apply the Tip on page 508 Exploring AP® Themes: CDI on page 509 Exploring AP® Themes: ENV on page 510	See above.
4	Read pages 511–515 from "Reform and Its Opponents" to "The Japanese Difference: The Rise of a New East Asian Power"	5.6 5.8 6.3 6.4 6.5	ENV GOV ECN SIO	AP® Exam Practice: Short-Answer Question 1 on page 546 Apply the Tip on page 512 Apply the Tip on page 514	See above.
5	Read pages 515–519 from "The Japanese Difference: The Rise of a New East Asian Power" to "Modernization Japanese-Style"	5.4 5.6 5.8	GOV SIO TEC	Building AP® Skills: Making Connections: Comparison on page 517 Apply the Tip on page 518 AP® Historians' Voices: The Sino-Japanese War of 1894–1895 on page 543	If you have your students comparing the reactions of Japan, the Ottoman Empire, and the Qing dynasty to industrialization and imperialism, make sure to emphasize how Japan differed from the other groups. Students also need to know that Japan's reactions through the Meiji reforms allowed the state to become a major power in the second half of the nineteenth century.
6	Read pages 519–526 from "Modernization Japanese-Style" through "Success and Failure in History"			Eric's Activity 9: Comparing Responses to the West on page 524 AP® Exam Practice: Short-Answer Question 3 on page 547 Teaching Idea: Exit Slip on page 526	See above.

Contextualization

Students should practice the skill of contextualization on a regular basis. This French cartoon from the late 1890s is a good chance to practice contextualization with an image. Show students the cartoon and ask the following questions:

▪ Why is France represented by a woman and not by a picture of its government leader? *The president of France during the Third Republic was elected and could change. All the other figures are monarchs.*

▪ Why are the fingernails of the Chinese man so long? *Chinese aristocrats grew their fingernails to show that they did not do manual labor.*

▪ Why do Queen Victoria, Kaiser Wilhelm I, and the Chinese representative appear to look more cartoonish than the other three figures? *The drawing is French, and at the time France had better relations with Russia and Japan than with the other three nations.*

▪ Why does the pie say "Chine" and not "China"? *This cartoon first appeared in a French newspaper.*

TEACHING IDEA

Bell Ringer

Before starting this section of Chapter 9, ask students to name events or circumstances that have troubled China in the past and that might also be expected to appear in this chapter. *Problems include the possibility of revolution within the dynastic cycle, emperors losing touch with their people, emperors not being involved in governing, the court becoming factionalized, and tensions with outside influences.*

Carving Up the Pie of China In this French cartoon from the late 1890s, the Great Powers of the day (from left to right: Great Britain's Queen Victoria, Germany's Kaiser Wilhelm, Russia's Tsar Nicholas II, a female figure representing France, and the Meiji emperor of Japan) participate in dividing China, while a Chinese figure behind them tries helplessly to stop the partition of his country. (Bridgeman Images)

CHAPTER

9

Empires in Collision

Europe, the Middle East, and East Asia

1800–1900

◀ AP®

COMPARISON
To what extent does this image of European powers and Japan competing for "slices" of China depict actions that were similar to those taken by European powers in the Americas in the sixteenth and seventeenth centuries?

CONNECTING PAST AND PRESENT

"Several centuries ago, China was strong. . . . In over 100 years after the 1840 Opium War, China suffered immensely from aggression, wars and chaos."[1] Speaking in early 2017, Chinese president Xi Jinping thus reminded his listeners of Britain's nineteenth-century violent intrusion into China's history bearing shiploads of highly addictive opium. This conflict marked the beginning of what the Chinese still describe as a "century of humiliation." In official Chinese government thinking, it was only the victory of the Chinese Communist Party that enabled China to finally escape from that shameful past. Memories of the Opium War remain a central element of China's "patriotic education" for the young, serving as a warning against uncritical admiration of the West and providing a rejoinder to any Western criticism of China. Approximately 180 years after that clash between the Chinese and British empires, the Opium War retains an emotional resonance for many Chinese and offers a politically useful tool for the country's government. ■

While the Opium Wars dramatically registered the impact of Europe's modern transformation described in Chapters 7 and 8, China was just one of many countries across the globe that confronted an aggressive and industrializing West while avoiding outright incorporation into Western colonial empires. The Ottoman Empire and Japan, for instance, also retained some ability to resist aggression and to reform or transform their own societies, though in quite distinct ways. The range of responses and outcomes experienced by these three major states provides many opportunities for comparison as they all navigated this era of colliding empires. The bulk of this chapter compares developments in China, the Ottoman Empire, and Japan.

But these major states were not the only ones that maintained their independence while encountering the new balance of global power

497

TRM Chapter 9 Guided Reading
You can find a guided reading handout for this chapter in the Teacher's Resource Materials.

TRM Chapter 9 Lecture Slides
You can find curated lecture slides for this chapter in the Teacher's Resource Materials.

TRM Chapter 9 Outline
You can find a chapter outline to model good note-taking for this chapter in the Teacher's Resource Materials.

TRM Suggested Responses to Questions
You can find suggested responses to all of the AP® margin questions in this chapter in the Teacher's Resource Materials.

EXPLORING AP® THEMES

Governance (GOV)

Having students study physical geography is always helpful for periodization and writing skills. Give students a blank world map and ask them to indicate the colonies of Great Britain, France, Germany, and the Netherlands. For a blank world map that you can use with this activity, download **Map 9A: The World** from the Teacher's Resource Materials. After students have completed their maps, ask the following questions:

■ What are some of the reasons the imperial powers engaged in colonization? *Some British possessions came out of the competition with France. The British and the French took some places for strategic reasons, such as supply stations for their fleets. The Dutch took colonies to improve their business activities. Germany's motivation was similar to that of France and Britain — boosting its status as an imperial power.*

■ How did some countries avoid becoming colonized? *Ethiopia adopted Western military technology. The Ottoman Empire, while waning, was still strong enough to resist colonization. Liberia had strong ties to the United States.*

TRM Map 9A: The World

CHAPTER 9 (vertical tab)

resulting from Europe's industrialization. Latin America also belongs in this category (see "The Industrial Revolution and Latin America in the Nineteenth Century" in Chapter 8). So too does Persia (modern Iran), which avoided a European takeover while maneuvering between the rival ambitions of Russia and Great Britain and introducing elements of Western science, technology, education, and culture.

Or consider Ethiopia, an ancient Christian East African state, which decisively defeated Italian imperial ambitions at the Battle of Adowa in 1896 and went on to substantially enlarge its own empire. Under the leadership of Emperor Menelik II (r. 1889–1913), the country began a modest program of modernization to support its independence, developing telegraph, telephone, and electricity services; railroads; modern banking and postal systems; and a new capital of Addis Ababa. By playing off various European powers, Menelik also acquired a substantial arsenal of modern weapons. All of this made Ethiopia a potent symbol of African resistance and resourcefulness.

Something similar occurred in Southeast Asia, where the Kingdom of Siam (later known as Thailand) held off European colonial takeover under the leadership of two remarkable kings, Mongkut (r. 1851–1868) and Chulalongkorn (r. 1868–1910). Unlike Ethiopia, which militarily defeated the Italians, Siam's rulers preserved their country's independence through their willingness to make modest concessions to the Europeans and their ability to maneuver between the rivalries of the British and the French imperialists. They undertook a series of political and social reforms, codifying the country's laws, allowing people to petition the king, ending slavery and other forms of forced labor, and initiating a modern Western-style educational system. Railroads and the country's first electric power–generating plant were also part of Chulalongkorn's modernizing program.

All of these societies faced the immense military might and political ambitions of the major imperial powers. They also became enmeshed in networks of trade, investment, and sometimes migration that accompanied a new world economy centered in an industrializing and capitalist Europe. They were influenced as well by various aspects of traditional European culture, as some among them learned the French, English, or German language; converted to Christianity; or studied European literature and philosophy. They engaged with the culture of modernity—its scientific rationalism; its technological achievements; its belief in a better future; and its ideas of nationalism, socialism, feminism, and individualism. In those epic encounters, they sometimes resisted, at other times accommodated, and almost always adapted what came from the West. At the same time, these societies were dealing with their own internal issues. Population growth and peasant rebellion wracked China; internal social and economic changes eroded the stability of Japanese public life; the great empires of the Islamic world shrank or disappeared; and rivalry among competing elites troubled Latin American societies. These countries were active participants in the global drama of nineteenth-century world history, not simply its passive victims or beneficiaries.

BUILDING AP® SKILLS

Making Connections: Continuity and Change

This is a good time to reinforce the AP® skill of Continuity and Change. The text notes that although a number of states resisted colonization, they still faced challenges, including encounters with the culture of modernity and the ideas of nationalism, socialism, and feminism. These terms appear regularly on the AP® World History: Modern Exam. Divide the class into small groups and ask them to define these concepts and collect examples from previous chapters.

Suggest that they continue to track these ideas in the next chapters. (Answers are provided in italics.)

■ **Nationalism:** *The strong belief that the interests of a nation or nation-state are of primary importance (Nazi Germany). The belief that a people who share a common history, language, and culture should be an independent nation or nation-state (the movement for independence in India).*

■ **Socialism:** *The political ideology and movement that involve social and economic measures, policies, and systems characterized by societal ownership or control of the means of production in some or all sectors of the society (industry in Soviet Russia, socialized medicine in Britain).*

■ **Feminism:** *A range of movements and ideologies that share a goal of achieving equal political, economic, cultural, personal, and social rights for women, including establishing equal opportunities for women in employment and education (the suffragette movements in the United States and Britain).*

AP®
COMPARISON
What differences can you identify in how China, the Ottoman Empire, and Japan experienced Western imperialism and responded to it? How might you account for those differences?

Landmarks for Chapter 9

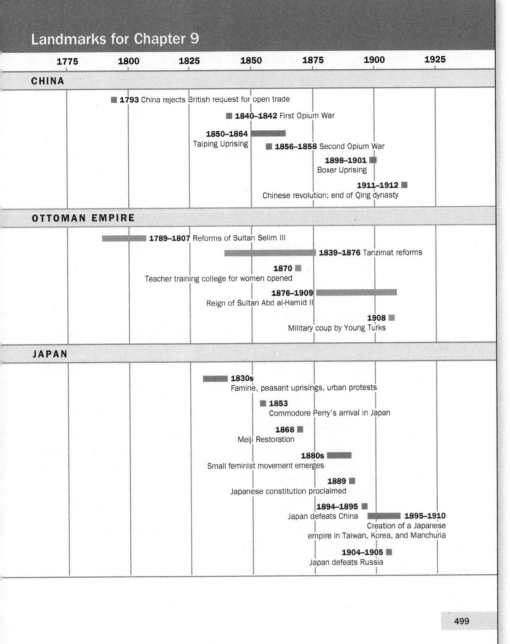

| | 1775 | 1800 | 1825 | 1850 | 1875 | 1900 | 1925 |

CHINA

- **1793** China rejects British request for open trade
- **1840–1842** First Opium War
- **1850–1864** Taiping Uprising
- **1856–1858** Second Opium War
- **1898–1901** Boxer Uprising
- **1911–1912** Chinese revolution; end of Qing dynasty

OTTOMAN EMPIRE

- **1789–1807** Reforms of Sultan Selim III
- **1839–1876** Tanzimat reforms
- **1870** Teacher training college for women opened
- **1876–1909** Reign of Sultan Abd al-Hamid II
- **1908** Military coup by Young Turks

JAPAN

- **1830s** Famine, peasant uprisings, urban protests
- **1853** Commodore Perry's arrival in Japan
- **1868** Meiji Restoration
- **1880s** Small feminist movement emerges
- **1889** Japanese constitution proclaimed
- **1894–1895** Japan defeats China
- **1895–1910** Creation of a Japanese empire in Taiwan, Korea, and Manchuria
- **1904–1905** Japan defeats Russia

499

BUILDING AP® SKILLS

Making Connections: Causation

Ask students to begin a cause-and-effect chart, like the one shown here, using examples from "Landmarks for Chapter 9." As they read this section, they should draw connections between these events and suggest the reasons for those connections. If you are running short on time, consider putting students in groups of three to four to complete one section of the chart and then "jigsaw" the information so that all students have a complete chart. A reproducible version of this chart is available in the Teacher's Resource Materials. (Answers are provided in italics.)

Cause and Effect: China's Century of Crisis

Cause	Effect	Explanation
China rejects British requests for open trade (1793)	*The first Opium War*	*British sale of opium to pay for Chinese tea and silk*
The first Opium War (1840–1842)	*The Taiping Uprising in China (1850–1864)*	*Dissatisfaction with the emperor*
Famine and rebellions in Japan (1830s)	*Meiji Restoration in Japan (1868)*	*Lack of trust in the shogunate and a renewed interest in the emperor in Japan*
Admiral Perry arrives in Japan (1853)	*Meiji Restoration in Japan (1868)*	*Failure of military power, which increases mistrust of the shogunate*
Meiji Restoration in Japan (1868)	■ *Japan defeats China (1894–1895)* ■ *Japan defeats Russia (1904–1905)*	■ *Meiji industrialization, enhancing Japan's ability to wage war and expand its empire* ■ *Prevented Russia from interfering with Japanese expansion and demonstrated Japan's competitive military power*

TRM Handout 9.2: Causation Chart for China's Century of Crisis

BUILDING AP® SKILLS

Contextualization

The quote from Emperor Qianlong rejecting British requests for a more open trade relationship in the first paragraph on page 500 is an excellent opportunity for a quick practice in contextualization. Consider reading the quote from this page out loud to students or projecting the quote for them to read on their own. Then ask students to name another example of negative attitudes toward foreign trade from Chinese history. *The Ming brought an end to the voyages of Zheng He and declared that "nothing larger than a stick of wood shall leave the shores of China." Although there were additional reasons for Zheng He's dismissal, it was an attempt to end trade with outside nations.*

APPLY THE TIP

Students might complain about completing so many charts in this class, but it really is a great way to compile information so that they can understand connections. Consider having your students create a chart, like the one seen below, examining the internal and external factors that led to the decline of the Qing dynasty and the Ottoman Empire in the nineteenth century and their eventual collapse in the twentieth century. A reproducible version of this chart is available in the Teacher's Resource Materials. (Answers are provided in italics.)

AP®

CONTINUITY AND CHANGE
To what extent did the policy of Qianlong continue earlier patterns of interactions between China and those it perceived to be outsiders?

AP® EXAM TIP
Understand how empires during this period fell because of internal factors.

AP®

CAUSATION
How did China's internal and external challenges intersect during the nineteenth century?

AP®

COMPARISON
What was distinctive about the Taiping rebellion in comparison with other Chinese peasant upheavals?

Reversal of Fortune: China's Century of Crisis

Finding the Main Point: What major events and processes shaped Chinese history from the late eighteenth century to the early twentieth century?

In 1793, just a decade after King George III of Britain lost his North American colonies, he received yet another rebuff, this time from China. In a famous letter to the British monarch, the Chinese emperor Qianlong (chyan-loong) sharply rejected British requests for a less restricted trading relationship with his country. "Our Celestial Empire possesses all things in prolific abundance," he declared. "There was therefore no need to import the manufactures of outside barbarians." Qianlong's snub simply continued the pattern of the previous several centuries, during which Chinese authorities had strictly controlled and limited the activities of European missionaries and merchants. But by 1912, little more than a century later, China's long-established imperial state had collapsed, and the country had been transformed from a central presence in the global economy to a weak and dependent participant in a European-dominated world system in which Great Britain was the major economic and political player. It was a stunning reversal of fortune for a country that in Chinese eyes was the civilized center of the entire world—in their terms, the Celestial Empire or the Middle Kingdom.

The Crisis Within

In some ways, China was the victim of its own earlier success. Its robust economy and American food crops had enabled substantial population growth, from about 100 million people in 1685 to some 430 million in 1853. Unlike in Europe, though, where a similar population spurt took place, no Industrial Revolution accompanied this vast increase in the number of people, nor was agricultural production able to keep up. Neither did China's internal expansion to the west and south generate anything like the wealth and resources that derived from Europe's overseas empires. The result was growing pressure on the land, smaller farms for China's huge peasant population, and, in all too many cases, unemployment, impoverishment, misery, and starvation.

Furthermore, China's governing institutions did not keep pace with the growing population. Thus the state was increasingly unable to effectively perform its many functions, such as tax collection, flood control, social welfare, and public security. Gradually the central state lost power to provincial officials and local gentry. Among such officials, corruption was endemic, and harsh treatment of peasants was common. According to an official report issued in 1852, "Day and night soldiers are sent out to harass taxpayers. Sometimes corporal punishments are imposed upon tax delinquents; some of them are so badly beaten to exact the last penny that blood and flesh fly in all directions."[2] Finally, European military pressure and economic penetration during the first half of the nineteenth century disrupted internal trade routes, created substantial unemployment, and raised peasant taxes.

This combination of circumstances, traditionally associated with a declining dynasty, gave rise to growing numbers of bandit gangs roaming the countryside

---

Comparison of the Decline of the Qing Dynasty and Ottoman Empire

Qing Dynasty		Ottoman Empire	
Internal Factors	**External Factors**	**Internal Factors**	**External Factors**
▪ *Agricultural production was unable to keep up with massive population growth* ▪ *Governing institutions did not keep pace with growing population* ▪ *Local officials were corrupt and treated peasants harshly* ▪ *Central government lost power to provincial officials and local gentry* ▪ *Peasant rebellions occurred, like the Taiping Uprising*	▪ *European military and economic pressure disrupted internal trade* ▪ *British opium trade resulted in Opium Wars* ▪ *"Unequal treaties" and informal European imperialism resulted from Opium Wars*	▪ *Provinces throughout empire won independence in the nineteenth century* ▪ *Central government had weakened as provincial authorities and local warlords gained more power* ▪ *Janissaries lost their military edge and became a highly conservative force within the imperial government* ▪ *Government relied on foreign loans* ▪ *Power of Young Turks increased*	▪ *During late eighteenth and throughout nineteenth century, Ottoman Empire lost territory to Russia, Britain, Austria, and France* ▪ *Economy declined due to competition from cheap European goods and economic capitulations made to European states*

TRM Handout 9.3: Comparison Chart for the Decline of the Qing Dynasty and Ottoman Empire

---

and, even more dangerous, to outright peasant rebellion. Beginning in the late eighteenth century, such rebellions drew on a variety of peasant grievances and found leadership in charismatic figures proclaiming a millenarian religious message. Increasingly they also expressed opposition to the Qing dynasty because of its foreign Manchu origins. "We wait only for the northern region to be returned to a Han emperor," declared one rebel group in the early nineteenth century.[3]

China's internal crisis culminated in the **Taiping Uprising**, which set much of the country aflame between 1850 and 1864. This was a different kind of peasant upheaval. Its leaders largely rejected Confucianism, Daoism, and Buddhism alike, finding their primary ideology in a unique form of Christianity. Its leading figure, Hong Xiuquan (hong show-chwaan) (1814–1864), proclaimed himself the younger brother of Jesus, sent to cleanse the world of demons and to establish a "heavenly kingdom of great peace." Nor were these leaders content to restore an idealized Chinese society; instead they insisted on genuinely revolutionary change. They called for the abolition of private property, a radical redistribution of land, the end of prostitution and opium smoking, and the organization of society into sexually segregated military camps of men and women. Hong fiercely denounced the Qing dynasty as foreigners who had "poisoned China" and "defiled the emperor's throne." His cousin, Hong Rengan, developed plans for transforming China into an industrial nation, complete with railroads, health insurance for all, newspapers, and widespread public education.

Among the most revolutionary dimensions of the Taiping Uprising was its posture toward women and gender roles. This outlook reflected its origins among the minority Hakka people of southern China, where women were notably less restricted than Confucian orthodoxy prescribed. During the uprising, Hakka women, whose feet had never been bound, fought as soldiers in their own regiments, and in liberated regions, Taiping officials ordered that the feet of other women be unbound. The Taiping land reform program promised women and men equal shares of land. Women were now permitted to sit for civil service examinations and were appointed to supervisory positions, though usually ones in which they exercised authority over other women rather than men. Mutual attraction rather than family interests was promoted as a basis for marriage.

None of these reforms were consistently implemented during the short period of Taiping power, and the movement's leadership demonstrated considerable ambivalence about equality for women. Hong himself

Taiping Uprising Western powers generally supported the Qing dynasty during the Taiping Uprising and even provided it with some military support. This image shows a group of the Taiping rebels and a British soldier they have captured. (Peter Newark Military Pictures/Bridgeman Images)

AP
CAUSATION
Analyze the internal and external factors that led to the Taiping Uprising.

▼ **AP**
SOURCING AND SITUATION
How does this British painting portray the attitude of the Chinese rebels to the British soldier?

BUILDING AP® SKILLS

Making Connections: Continuity and Change

Use this opportunity to help students practice Continuity and Change. Ask students: How might the succession of rebellions described in the text represent an expected political result according to the Mandate of Heaven? *According to the Mandate of Heaven, when one dynasty no longer served the gods and the country well enough, rebellion was necessary to bring in better leadership.*

EXPLORING AP® THEMES

Governance (GOV)

In the past, essay questions on the AP® World History Exams have asked students to differentiate between the goals and outcomes of a particular event. To help your students understand the difference between a goal and an outcome, ask: How well did the goals of the Taiping Uprising match the outcomes of the rebellion? *The goals of the rebellion included land reform, an end to the opium trade, equality for women, industrialization, and an end to prostitution. The goals of the rebellion were not fulfilled, largely because of divisions and indecisiveness within the leadership and the inability of Taiping leaders to unify with other rebel groups. The Qing dynasty, though weakened, was not defeated, and its more conservative approach remained. Moreover, the devastation and destruction occasioned by this massive civil war seriously disrupted and weakened China's economy.*

AP
CAUSATION
What accounts for the successes and failures of the massive peasant rebellions of nineteenth-century China?

AP
COMPARISON
To what extent were the causes and results of the Taiping Uprising similar to those of the Atlantic revolutions you learned about in Chapter 7?

▼ **AP**
SOURCING AND SITUATION
What aspects of this photograph appear to be posed? What was the photographer's purpose in taking this photo?

reflected a much more traditional understanding of elite women's role when he assembled a large personal harem and declared: "The duty of the palace women is to attend to the needs of their husbands; and it is arranged by Heaven that they are not to learn of the affairs outside."[4] Nonetheless, the Taiping posture toward women represented a sharp challenge to long-established gender roles and contributed to the hostility that the movement generated among many other Chinese, including women.

With a rapidly swelling number of followers, Taiping forces swept out of southern China and established their capital in Nanjing in 1853. For a time, the days of the Qing dynasty appeared to be over. But divisions and indecisiveness within the Taiping leadership, along with the failure of Taiping forces to link up with several other rebel groups also operating separately in China, provided an opening for Qing dynasty loyalists to rally and by 1864 to crush this most unusual of peasant rebellions. Western military support for pro-Qing forces likewise contributed to their victory. It was not, however, the imperial military forces of the central government that defeated the rebels. Instead provincial military leaders, fearing the radicalism of the Taiping program, mobilized their own armies, which in the end crushed the rebel forces.

Thus the Qing dynasty was saved, but it was also weakened as the provincial gentry consolidated their power at the expense of the central state. The intense conservatism of both imperial authorities and their gentry supporters postponed any resolution of China's peasant problem, delayed any real change for China's women, and deferred vigorous efforts at modernization until the communists came to power in the mid-twentieth century. More immediately, the devastation and destruction occasioned by this massive civil war seriously disrupted and weakened China's economy. Estimates of the number of lives lost range from 20 to 30 million. In human terms, it was the most costly conflict in the world during the nineteenth century, and it took China more than a decade to recover from its devastation. China's internal crisis in general and the Taiping Uprising in particular also provided a highly unfavorable setting for the country's encounter with a Europe newly invigorated by the Industrial Revolution.

Addiction to Opium Throughout the nineteenth century, opium imports created a massive addiction problem in China, as this photograph of an opium den from around 1900 suggests. Not until the early twentieth century did the British prove willing to curtail the opium trade from their Indian colony. (Hulton Deutsch/Getty Images)

Western Pressures

Nowhere was the shifting balance of global power in the nineteenth century more evident than in China's changing relationship with Europe, a

SNAPSHOT Chinese/British Trade at Canton, 1835–1836

Calculate opium exports as a percentage of British exports to China, Britain's trade deficit without opium, and its trade surplus with opium. What did this pattern mean for China?

	Item	Value (in Spanish dollars)
British Exports to Canton	Opium	17,904,248
	Cotton	8,357,394
	All other items (sandalwood, lead, iron, tin, cotton yarn and piece goods, tin plates, watches, clocks)	6,164,981
	Total	32,426,623
British Imports from Canton	Tea (black and green)	13,412,243
	Raw silk	3,764,115
	Vermilion	705,000
	All other goods (sugar products, camphor, silver, gold, copper, musk)	5,971,541
	Total	23,852,899

Source: Data from Hsin-Pao Chang, ed., *Commissioner Lin and the Opium War* (New York: W. W. Norton, 1970), 226-27.

▶ **AP**
CLAIMS AND EVIDENCE IN SOURCES
What do the Snapshot figures suggest about the role of opium in British trade with China?

transformation that registered most dramatically in the famous **Opium Wars**. Derived from Arab traders in the eighth century or earlier, opium had long been used on a small scale as a drinkable medicine; it was regarded as a magical cure for dysentery and described by one poet as "fit for Buddha."[5] It did not become a serious problem until the late eighteenth century, when the British began to use opium, grown and processed in India, to cover their persistent trade imbalance with China. By the 1830s, British, American, and other Western merchants had found an enormous, growing, and very profitable market for this highly addictive drug. From 1,000 chests (each weighing roughly 150 pounds) in 1773, China's opium imports exploded to more than 23,000 chests in 1832. (See Snapshot: Chinese/British Trade at Canton, 1835–1836.)

By then, Chinese authorities recognized a mounting problem on many levels. Because opium importation was illegal, it had to be smuggled into China, thus flouting Chinese law. Bribed to turn a blind eye to the illegal trade, many officials were corrupted. Furthermore, a massive outflow of silver to pay for the opium reversed China's centuries-long ability to attract much of the world's silver supply, and this imbalance caused serious economic problems. Finally, China found itself with many millions of addicts—men and women, court officials, students preparing for exams, soldiers going into combat, and common laborers seeking to overcome the pain and drudgery of their work.

Following an extended debate at court in 1836 on whether to legalize the drug or crack down on its use, the emperor decided on suppression. An upright official,

AP EXAM TIP
The Opium Wars were a major turning point leading to China's decline in the nineteenth century.

BUILDING AP® SKILLS

Claims and Evidence in Sources

You can work with students in interpreting secondary sources with this activity. Ask students to read the essay "The First Opium War: The Anglo-Chinese War of 1839–1842" by Peter C. Perdue, which can be found on MIT's Visualizing Cultures website. Students should read the introductory section. Then ask students to answer the following questions:

■ When do historians believe that foreign imperialism with regard to China finally ended? *Imperialism in China ended when Hong Kong reverted from Britain to China in 1997.*

■ Which countries and regions were involved in the opium trade? *Britain, the United States, Turkey, India, and Southeast Asia, as well as domestic Chinese merchants, were involved in the opium trade.*

■ How did China control its trade under the Qing? *Western traders were restricted to conducting trade through Guangzhou, could only stay a short time, and were required to trade through a particular guild of merchants.*

■ How much opium was China importing before the Opium Wars? How much did this amount increase? *Just before the Opium Wars, China was importing 4,000 chests of opium annually. This amount doubled over the next twenty years.*

■ Why did the Chinese court feel that opium had become a problem? *The percentage of opium addicts rose dramatically and included people in the military, opium purchases caused an outflow of silver, and the illegal opium trade did not bring in any taxes.*

ZOOMING IN   Lin Zexu: Confronting the Opium Trade

When the Chinese emperor decided in 1838 on firm measures to suppress the opium trade, he selected Lin Zexu to enforce that policy.[6] Born in 1785, Lin was the son of a rather poor but scholarly father who had never achieved an official position. Lin, however, excelled academically, passing the highest-level examinations in 1811 after two failed attempts and then rising rapidly in the ranks of China's bureaucracy. In the process, he gained a reputation as a strict and honest official; he was immune to bribery, genuinely concerned with the welfare of the peasantry, and unafraid to confront the corruption and decadence of rich and poor alike.

And so in December of 1838, after some nineteen personal audiences with the emperor, Lin found himself in Canton, the center of the opium trade and the only Chinese city legally open to foreign merchants. He was facing the greatest challenge of his professional life. Undertaken with the best of intentions, his actions were unable to

Commissioner Lin Zexu ordering the destruction of opium.

prevent a war with Britain that propelled the country into a century of humiliating subservience to an industrializing Europe and forced growing numbers of Chinese to question their vaunted civilization.

In established Confucian fashion, Lin undertook his enormous task with a combination of moral appeals, reasoned argument, political pressure, and coercion, while hoping to avoid outright armed conflict. It was an approach that focused on both the demand and supply sides of the problem. In dealing with Chinese opium users, Lin emphasized the health hazards of the drug and demanded that people turn in their supplies of opium and the pipes used to smoke it. By mid-1839, he had confiscated some 50,000 pounds of the drug, together with over 70,000 pipes, and arrested some 1,700 dealers. Hundreds of local students were summoned to an assembly where they were invited to identify opium distributors and to suggest ways of dealing with the problem. Opium-using officials became the target of investigations, and five-person teams were established to enforce the ban on opium smoking on one another.

photo: Pictures from History/TopFoto

Commissioner Lin Zexu (lin zuh-SHOO), led the campaign against opium use as a kind of "drug czar." (See Zooming In: Lin Zexu.) The British, offended by the seizure of their property in opium and emboldened by their new military power, sent a large naval expedition to China, determined to end the restrictive conditions under which they had long traded with that country. In the process, they would teach the Chinese a lesson about the virtues of free trade and the "proper" way to conduct relations among countries.

Thus began the first Opium War (1840–1842), in which Britain's industrialized military might proved decisive. (See AP® Working with Evidence: The Opium War, for more on the Opium War.) The Treaty of Nanjing, which ended the war in 1842, largely on British terms, imposed numerous restrictions on Chinese sovereignty

Overview	*A photograph of men in an opium den in China around 1900.*
Parts	*There are three men huddled around a tray with the ingredients for smoking opium. A fourth man on the right appears to have more supplies for the men. He could be an employee of the opium den. A fifth man is on the left and seems to be reading a newspaper to one of the men smoking the opium. These men are native Chinese and are wearing their hair in the long queue that was a requirement of the Qing dynasty.*
Title	*Addiction to Opium.*
Interrelationships	*The three men in the middle of this photograph were involved in smoking opium, emphasizing China's concern with the opium flowing into China from India. Two of the three men seem to be feeling the effects of the drug. The walls of the opium den are decorated with what appear to be Chinese historical events. All of the ingredients and supplies to cook opium are on a tray in the middle of the three men. The two other men in the photograph are possibly employees of the opium den. They do not seem to be smoking the opium but are providing services such as reading the newspaper and bringing supplies to the men.*
Conclusion	*China fought the disastrous effects of Britain's opium trade throughout the nineteenth century. This photograph could possibly be staged as propaganda used by the Qing government to show the disastrous effect that opium had on Chinese society.*

You can use the rest of the documents in "AP® Working with Evidence: The Opium War" on pages 535–541 for additional primary source practice. The AP® Doing History questions on page 542 will help students reinforce the skills practice.

TRM Handout 9.4: OPTIC Chart for Addiction to Opium Photograph

Lin applied a similar mix of methods to the foreign suppliers of opium. A moralistic appeal to Queen Victoria argued that the articles the English imported from China—silk, tea, and rhubarb—were all beneficial. "By what right," he asked, "do [the barbarians] use this poisonous drug to injure Chinese people?" He pointedly reminded Europeans that new regulations, applying to Chinese and foreigners alike, fixed the penalty for dealing in opium at "decapitation or strangling." Then he demanded that foreign traders hand over their opium, and without compensation. When the merchants hesitated, Lin tightened the screws, ordering all Chinese employed by foreigners to leave their jobs and blockading the Europeans in their factories. After six weeks of negotiations, the Europeans capitulated, turning over some 3 million pounds of raw opium to Lin Zexu.

Disposing of the drug was an enormous task. Workers, stripped and searched daily to prevent looting, dug three huge trenches into which they placed the opium mixed with water, salt, and lime and then flushed the concoction into the sea. (See the image in this feature, which shows the commissioner overseeing this process.) Lin also offered a sacrifice to the Sea Spirit, apologizing for introducing this poison into its domain and "advising the Spirit to tell the creatures of the water to move away for a time." He informed the emperor that throngs of local people flocked to witness the destruction of the opium. And foreigners too came to observe the spectacle. Lin reported,

"[The foreigners] do not dare to show any disrespect, and indeed I should judge from their attitudes that they have the decency to feel heartily ashamed."

Had Lin been correct in his appraisal, history would have taken a very different turn. But neither Lin nor his superiors anticipated the response that these actions provoked from the British government. They were also largely unaware that European industrial and military advances had decisively shifted the balance of power between China and the West. Arriving in 1840, a British military expedition quickly demonstrated its superiority and initiated the devastating Opium War that marked Lin's policies in Canton as a failure.

As a punishment for his unsatisfactory performance, the emperor sent Lin to a remote post in western China. Although his career rebounded somewhat after 1845, he died in 1850 while on the way to an appointment aimed at suppressing the Taiping rebellion. While his reputation suffered in the nineteenth century, it recovered in the twentieth as an intensely nationalist China recalled his principled stand against Western imperialism.

QUESTIONS

How might Lin Zexu have handled his task differently or more successfully? Or had he been given an impossible mission?

and opened five ports to European traders. Its provisions reflected the changed balance of global power that had emerged with Britain's Industrial Revolution. To the Chinese, that agreement represented the first of the **unequal treaties** that seriously eroded China's independence by the end of the century.

But it was not the last of those treaties. Britain's victory in a second Opium War (1856–1858) was accompanied by the brutal vandalizing of the emperor's exquisite Summer Palace outside Beijing and resulted in further humiliations. Still more ports were opened to foreign traders. Now those foreigners were allowed to travel freely and buy land in China, to preach Christianity under the protection of Chinese authorities, and to patrol some of China's rivers. Furthermore, the Chinese were forbidden to use the character for "barbarians" to refer to the British in official documents. Following

AP

CAUSATION
How did Western pressures stimulate change in China during the nineteenth century?

EXPLORING AP® THEMES

Economic Systems (ECN)

The idea of "unequal treaties" is often confusing to students when looking at the outcomes of the Opium Wars. To help students understand these treaties, ask: How do the provisions of the treaties at the end of the two Opium Wars reflect social and cultural issues as well as politics? *Foreigners were not bound by Chinese laws and courts or by Chinese customs, so their influence brought changes and tensions. Opening the ports allowed more Western influence throughout the nation in addition to trade goods. Christianity became more influential.*

EXPLORING AP® THEMES

Economic Systems (ECN)

Another term that students often have a problem understanding is "spheres of influence." This is a good opportunity to explain this concept to students. Ask students: What does the text mean when it says that the Western nations, Japan, and Russia "carved out spheres of influence within China"? *These nations gave themselves special economic rights and the right to establish military bases, and they established control over the legal system with regard to foreign citizens.*

BUILDING AP® SKILLS

Argumentation

After students have read the section "Western Pressures," ask them to write a one-paragraph response to the following question to practice their argumentation skills: Evaluate the extent to which the Opium Wars were a major factor in China's decline during the nineteenth century. *Answers will vary.*

BUILDING AP® SKILLS

Making Connections: Continuity and Change

Vocabulary is an important part of any AP® history course. You can help improve students' vocabulary in small ways, such as by asking students to explain what the authors mean by using a specific term. Ask students to explain what the authors mean by "self-strengthening." *The Chinese overhauled the civil service examination system, but it was still based on conservative Confucian principles.*

later military defeats at the hands of the French (1885) and Japanese (1895), China lost control of Vietnam, Korea, and Taiwan. By the end of the century, the Western nations plus Japan and Russia had all carved out spheres of influence within China, granting themselves special privileges to establish military bases, extract raw materials, and build railroads. Many Chinese believed that their country was being "carved up like a melon" (see Map 9.1 and the chapter-opening image).

Coupled with its internal crisis, China's encounter with European imperialism had reduced the proud Middle Kingdom to dependency on the Western powers as it became part of a European-based **informal empire**, an area dominated by Western powers but retaining its own government and a measure of independence. China was no longer the center of civilization to which "barbarians" paid homage and tribute, but just one weak and dependent nation among many others. The Qing dynasty remained in power, but in a weakened condition, which served European interests well and Chinese interests poorly. Restrictions imposed by the unequal treaties clearly inhibited China's industrialization, as foreign goods and foreign investment flooded the country largely unrestricted. Chinese businessmen mostly served foreign firms, rather than developing as an independent capitalist class capable of leading China's own Industrial Revolution.

The Failure of Conservative Modernization

Chinese authorities were not passive in the face of their country's mounting internal and external crises. Known as **self-strengthening**, their policies during the 1860s and 1870s sought to reinvigorate a traditional China while borrowing cautiously from the West. An overhauled examination system, designed to recruit qualified candidates for official positions, sought the "good men" who could cope with the massive reconstruction that China faced in the wake of the Taiping rebellion. Support for landlords and the repair of dikes and irrigation helped restore rural social and economic order. A few industrial factories producing textiles and steel were established, coal mines were expanded, and a telegraph system was initiated. One Chinese general in 1863 confessed his humiliation that "Chinese weapons are far inferior to those of foreign countries."[7] A number of modern arsenals, shipyards, and foreign-language schools sought to remedy this deficiency.

Self-strengthening as an overall program for China's modernization was inhibited by the fears of conservative leaders that urban, industrial, or commercial development would erode the power and privileges of the landlord class. Furthermore, the new industries remained largely dependent on foreigners for machinery, materials, and expertise. And they served to strengthen local authorities, who largely controlled those industries, rather than the central Chinese state.

The general failure of "self-strengthening" became apparent at the end of the century, when China suffered a humiliating military defeat by Japan (1894–1895). This failure was only confirmed when an antiforeign movement known as the **Boxer Uprising** (1898–1901) erupted in northern China. Led by militia organizations

AP®
CAUSATION
What strategies did China adopt to confront its various problems? Why were they so unsuccessful?

AP®
CONTINUITY AND CHANGE
To what extent were these self-strengthening strategies a continuation of Chinese policies toward outsiders, and to what extent were they a change?

MAPPING HISTORY   Map 9.1 **China and the World in the Nineteenth Century**

As China was reeling from massive internal upheavals during the nineteenth century, it also faced external assaults from Russia, Japan, and various European powers. By the end of the century, large parts of China were divided into spheres of influence, each affiliated with one of the major industrial powers of the day.

Reading the Map: Which imperial powers created spheres of influence in China that were adjacent to territories that they already controlled? In which regions of China do the spheres of influence of major powers come into contact? Where would you predict that conflicts between major outside powers might occur in China?

AP **Making Connections:** How might you compare the success of Japanese and European colonialism in Asia?

This is a good time to have students practice their geography skills. Have students look at the inset of Map 9.1, "China and the World in the Nineteenth Century." Ask students: Why did the rebellions occur where they did? *Muslim rebellions occurred in Muslim population centers. The other three occurred in areas with a lot of people, but not in Beijing because of the military power concentrated there.*

calling themselves the Society of Righteous and Harmonious Fists, the "Boxers" killed numerous Europeans and Chinese Christians and laid siege to the foreign embassies in Beijing. When Western powers and Japan occupied Beijing to crush the rebellion and imposed a huge payment on China as a punishment, it was clear that China remained a dependent country, substantially under foreign control.

No wonder, then, that growing numbers of educated Chinese, including many in official elite positions, became highly disillusioned with the Qing dynasty, which was both foreign and ineffective in protecting China. By the late 1890s, such people were organizing a variety of clubs, study groups, and newspapers to examine China's desperate situation and to explore alternative paths. The names of these organizations reflect their outlook—the National Rejuvenation Study Society, Society to Protect the Nation, and Understand the National Shame Society.

These educated people admired not only Western science and technology but also Western political practices that limited the authority of the ruler and permitted wider circles of people to take part in public life. They believed that only a truly unified nation in which rulers and ruled were closely related could save China from dismemberment at the hands of foreign imperialists. Despite the small number of women who took part in these discussions, traditional gender roles became yet another focus of opposition. No one expressed that issue more forcefully than Qiu Jin (1875–1907), the rebellious daughter of a gentry family who started a women's journal, arguing that liberated women were essential for a strong Chinese nation, and became involved in revolutionary politics. Thus was born the immensely powerful force of Chinese nationalism, directed alike against Western imperialists, the foreign Qing dynasty, and aspects of China's traditional culture.

The Qing dynasty response to these new pressures proved inadequate. A flurry of progressive imperial edicts in 1898, known as the Hundred Days of Reform, was soon squelched by conservative forces. More extensive reform in the early twentieth century, including the end of the old examination system and the promise of a national parliament, was a classic case of too little too late. In 1912 the last Chinese emperor abdicated as the ancient imperial order that had governed China for two millennia collapsed, with only a modest nudge from organized revolutionaries. This **Chinese revolution of 1911–1912** marked the end of a long era in China's long history and the beginning of an immense struggle over the country's future.

The Ottoman Empire and the West in the Nineteenth Century

Finding the Main Point: How did the Ottoman experience during the nineteenth century parallel that of China, and how did it diverge from it?

Like China, the Islamic world represented a highly successful civilization that felt little need to learn from the "infidels" or "barbarians" of the West until it collided with an expanding and aggressive Europe in the nineteenth century. Unlike China,

AP EXAM TIP
Be sure to understand how Indigenous groups resisted state expansion in this time period.

AP EXAM TIP
As you study this time period, look for similarities in how states expanded their control of territories through economic or military power.

APPLY THE TIP

Students often learn about the past by finding examples in things that they know in the present. Many Indigenous groups resisted state expansion during this time, and the names of the Indigenous groups play a role in their goals. The text states, "The names of these organizations reflect their outlook—the National Rejuvenation Study Society, Society to Protect the Nation, and Understand the National Shame Society." Ask students to list various groups or clubs in your school whose objectives or goals might be found by examining their names. *Answers will vary.*

APPLY THE TIP

Although the AP® skill of Comparison is often viewed by students as easy, it frequently is more difficult than they imagine. This is a good time for students to compare China's and the Ottoman Empire's reactions to pressure from the West. Have students create a Venn diagram or chart to compare the two. Once they have completed their diagrams or charts, lead the class in a discussion on whether China and the Ottomans were more similar or different in their reactions and why. A reproducible version of this chart is available in the Teacher's Resource Materials. *Answers will vary.*

TRM Handout 9.5: Venn Diagram for China and Ottoman Empire Reactions to Pressure from the West though, Islamic civilization had been a near neighbor to Europe for 1,000 years. Its most prominent state, the Ottoman Empire, had long governed substantial parts of southeastern Europe and had posed a clear military and religious threat to Europe in the sixteenth and seventeenth centuries. But if its encounter with the West was less abrupt than that of China, it was no less consequential. Neither the Ottoman Empire nor China fell under direct colonial rule, but both were much diminished as the changing balance of global power took hold; both launched efforts at "defensive modernization" aimed at strengthening their states and preserving their independence; and in both societies, some people held tightly to old identities and values, even as others embraced new loyalties associated with nationalism and modernity.

"The Sick Man of Europe"

In 1750, the Ottoman Empire was still the central political fixture of a widespread Islamic world. From its Turkish heartland in Anatolia, it ruled over much of the Arab world, from which Islam had come. It protected pilgrims on their way to Mecca, governed Egypt and coastal North Africa, and incorporated millions of Christians in the Balkans. Its ruler, the sultan, claimed the role of caliph, successor to the Prophet Muhammad, and was widely viewed as the leader, defender, and primary representative of the Islamic world. But by the middle, and certainly by the end, of the nineteenth century, the Ottoman Empire was no longer able to deal with Europe from a position of equality, let alone superiority. Among the Great Powers of the West, it was now known as "**the sick man of Europe.**" Within the Muslim world, the Ottoman Empire, once viewed as "the strong sword of Islam," was unable to prevent region after region—India, Indonesia, West Africa, Central Asia—from falling under the control of Christian powers.

The Ottoman Empire's own domains shrank considerably at the hands of Russian, British, Austrian, and French aggression (see Map 9.2). In 1798, Napoleon's invasion of Egypt, which had long been a province of the Ottoman Empire, was a particularly stunning blow. A contemporary observer, Abd al-Rahman al-Jabarti, described the French entry into Cairo:

> The French entered the city like a torrent rushing through the alleys and streets without anything to stop them, like demons of the Devil's army.... And the French trod in the Mosque of al-Azhar with their shoes, carrying swords and rifles....They plundered whatever they found in the mosque.... They treated the books and Quranic volumes as trash....Furthermore, they soiled the mosque, blowing their spit in it, pissing and defecating in it. They guzzled wine and smashed bottles in the central court.[8]

When the French left, a virtually independent Egypt pursued a modernizing and empire-building program of its own during the early and mid-nineteenth century and on one occasion came close to toppling the Ottoman Empire itself.

AP
SOURCING AND SITUATION
In what ways does al-Jabarti's language reveal his point of view about the French entry into Cairo?

Cultural Developments and Interactions (CDI)

Often students get confused with vocabulary terms that they think can mean the same thing but the difference between the terms is very important to understand. The terms "sultan" and "caliph" are two of those terms. Now would be a good opportunity to explain the difference to students by having them research the difference between the terms, including the history of each term. *A caliph is considered the successor of Muhammad as both the political and spiritual leader of the Muslim people (Dar al-Islam), beyond the constraints of particular national boundaries. The Sunni and Shia have different beliefs about how a caliph is selected. The term "sultan" was first used by Mahud of Ghazna and refers to a Muslim ruler who holds full sovereignty over particular lands, known as a sultanate.*

BUILDING AP® SKILLS

Sourcing and Situation

As sourcing is one of the most difficult points to achieve on the DBQ, it's good to practice this skill with students as much as you possibly can. One way to do a quick practice is to use quotes in the text. Have students read the quote on page 509 and then ask: How does the author's language reveal the way he feels about the French entry into Cairo? *His language is strong and full of distaste. From the first sentence, we are told that the invaders are "demons." He portrays the French as vulgar and disrespectful.*

EXPLORING AP® THEMES

Humans and the Environment (ENV)

Have students look at Map 9.2, "The Contraction of the Ottoman Empire," and ask:

- When did the Ottoman Empire begin losing territory? *In 1800–1877.*

- What do the different periods of territorial loss for the Ottoman Empire tell us about the struggles the empire faced in the nineteenth century? *The empire was too large to effectively rule; local groups took power away from Ottoman rulers, and the Ottomans were facing external pressures from European states and Russia.*

BUILDING AP® SKILLS

Making Connections: Causation

The Ottoman Empire declined in the nineteenth century due to a variety of causes, and it can be helpful for students to use the text to distinguish between the primary and secondary causes of Ottoman decline. Answers are provided in the Teacher's Resource Materials.

MAPPING HISTORY   Map 9.2 **The Contraction of the Ottoman Empire**

Foreign aggression and nationalist movements substantially diminished the Ottoman Empire during the nineteenth century, but they also stimulated a variety of efforts to revive and reform Ottoman society.

Reading the Map: Aside from North Africa, where did the Ottoman Empire lose the most territory between 1800 and 1913?

AP **Making Connections:** Compare this map with Map 4.5 The Ottoman Empire. How does the Ottoman Empire in 1800 compare to the empire in 1566? Had the empire already lost major territories before 1800, or does much of the decline seem to have occurred between 1800 and 1913?

AP

CAUSATION

What primary and secondary causes led to the decline of the Ottoman Empire in the nineteenth century?

Beyond territorial losses to stronger European powers, other parts of the empire, such as Greece, Serbia, Bulgaria, and Romania, achieved independence based on their own surging nationalism and support from the British or the Russians. The continued independence of the core region of the Ottoman Empire owed much to the inability of Europe's Great Powers to agree on how to divide it up among themselves.

Behind the contraction of the Ottoman Empire lay other problems. As in China, the central Ottoman state had weakened, particularly in its ability to raise necessary revenue, as provincial authorities and local warlords gained greater power. Moreover, the Janissaries, once the effective and innovative elite infantry units of

Ottoman military forces, lost their military edge, becoming a highly conservative force within the empire. The technological and military gap with the West was clearly growing.

Economically, the earlier centrality of the Ottoman and Arab lands in Afro-Eurasian commerce diminished as Europeans achieved direct oceanic access to the treasures of Asia. Competition from cheap European manufactured goods hit Ottoman artisans hard and led to urban riots protesting foreign imports. Furthermore, a series of agreements, known as capitulations, between European countries and the Ottoman Empire granted Westerners various exemptions from Ottoman law and taxation. Like the unequal treaties with China, these agreements facilitated European penetration of the Ottoman economy and became widely resented. Such measures eroded Ottoman sovereignty and reflected the changing position of that empire relative to Europe. So too did the growing indebtedness of the Ottoman Empire, which came to rely on foreign loans to finance its efforts at economic development. By 1881, its inability to pay the interest on those debts led to foreign control of much of its revenue-generating system, while a similar situation in Egypt led to its outright occupation by the British. Like China, the Ottoman Empire had fallen into a position of considerable dependency on Europe.

Reform and Its Opponents

The leadership of the Ottoman Empire recognized many of its problems and during the nineteenth century mounted increasingly ambitious programs of "defensive modernization" that were earlier, more sustained, and far more vigorous than the timid and halfhearted measures of self-strengthening in China. One reason perhaps lay in the absence of any internal upheaval, such as the Taiping Uprising in China, which threatened the very existence of the ruling dynasty. Nationalist revolts on the empire's periphery, rather than Chinese-style peasant rebellion at the center, represented the primary internal crisis of nineteenth-century Ottoman history. Nor did the Middle East in general experience the explosive population growth that contributed so much to China's nineteenth-century crisis. Furthermore, the long-established Ottoman leadership was Turkic and Muslim, culturally similar to its core population, whereas China's Qing dynasty rulers were widely regarded as foreigners from Manchuria.

Ottoman reforms began in the late eighteenth century when Sultan Selim III (r. 1789–1807) sought to reorganize and update the army, drawing on European advisers and techniques. Even these modest innovations stirred the hostility of powerful factions among both the *ulama* (religious scholars) and the elite military corps of Janissaries, who saw them in conflict with both Islam and their own institutional interests. Opposition to his measures was so strong that Selim was overthrown in 1807 and then murdered. Subsequent sultans, however, crushed the Janissaries and brought the ulama more thoroughly under state control than elsewhere in the Islamic world.

AP®
DEVELOPMENTS AND PROCESSES
In what respects did the Ottoman Empire decline during the nineteenth century?

AP®
COMPARISON
In what ways were China and the Ottoman Empire similarly affected by Western industrialism?

AP® EXAM TIP
While understanding the changes brought on by state expansion in this time period is important, pay attention to political and social continuities as well.

AP®
CAUSATION
In what different ways did the Ottoman state respond to its various problems?

APPLY THE TIP

Since the decline of the Ottoman Empire affected both the nineteenth and twentieth centuries, it is important for students to understand not just the changes but the continuities as well. Ask students: What were the political and social continuities in the Ottoman Empire in this era? *Politically, the leadership remained Turkic and Muslim. The empire did not experience the same kind of internal upheaval as China, in part because it did not experience the same kind of population growth and its people remained primarily Turkic and Muslim like its leadership.*

BUILDING AP® SKILLS

Making Connections: Continuity and Change

It is important for students to understand the reform measures that the Ottoman sultans tried to make during the late eighteenth century. Ask students: What reforms did Ottoman sultans try to implement to strengthen the empire? What were the reactions to these reforms? *Sultan Selim III wanted to reorganize and reform the Ottoman army, using European advisers and techniques to do so. The ulama and Janissaries saw these reforms as conflicting with Islam and their own interests, so they overthrew and murdered Selim in 1807.*

► AP®
CLAIMS AND EVIDENCE
IN SOURCES
What elements of
modernization or
European influence can
you find in this
photograph?

Ottoman Modernization Bustling major cities provided environments where Ottoman modernizers hoped to transform their society and economy. With ships anchored in Constantinople's harbor and the smokestacks of industry to the right, this 1890s colorized image of the Ottoman capital illustrates the outcomes of these modernization efforts. (Universal History Archive/Getty Images)

EXPLORING AP® THEMES

Cultural Developments and Interactions (CDI)

Read or present the excerpt from the 1856 proclamation on page 512. Then ask students: How might this proclamation reflect the Ottoman Empire's drive to become competitive with Western Europe? *Ottoman leaders saw more equality in Western Europe as one of the reasons for Western success, and they used that equality as a model.*

APPLY THE TIP

As the Ottoman sultans tried to stop the decline of the empire, they implemented measures known as Tanzimat (reorganization). Students need to understand how these reforms attempted to stop the ultimate collapse of the empire. Have students create a chart like the one below that lists the goals of the Tanzimat and explains the motivation behind each goal. A reproducible version of this chart is available in the Teacher's Resource Materials. (Answers are provided in italics.)

Then, in the several decades after 1839, more far-reaching reformist measures, known as **Tanzimat** (tahn-zee-MAHT) (reorganization), took shape as the Ottoman leadership sought to provide the economic, social, and legal underpinnings for a strong and newly recentralized state. Factories producing cloth, paper, and armaments; modern mining operations; reclamation and resettlement of agricultural land; telegraphs, steamships, railroads, and a modern postal service; Western-style law codes and courts; new elementary and secondary schools—all of these new departures began a long process of modernization and westernization in the Ottoman Empire.

Even more revolutionary, at least in principle, were changes in the legal status of the empire's diverse communities, which now gave non-Muslims equal rights under the law. An imperial proclamation of 1856 declared:

> Every distinction or designation tending to make any class whatever of the subjects of my Empire inferior to another class, on account of their religion, language or race shall be forever effaced. . . . No subject of my Empire shall be hindered in the exercise of the religion that he professes. . . . All the subjects of my Empire, without distinction of nationality, shall be admissible to public employment.[9]

This declaration represented a dramatic change that challenged the fundamentally Islamic character of the state. Mixed tribunals with representatives from various

AP® EXAM TIP
You need to understand
how measures, like the
Tanzimat reforms, were
attempts to stave off
economic and political
collapse in the face of
Western intrusion.

The Tanzimat: Goals and Motivation

Goal	Motivation
Provide the economic, social, and legal underpinnings for a strong and newly recentralized state	*To remedy problems created by the former weak, disorganized, and corrupt government*
Build factories that produce cloth, paper, and armaments	*To rebuild the economy and rearm the military to prevent Western incursion*
Build modern mining operations, reclaim and resettle agricultural land, and industrialize with telegraphs, steamships, railroads, and a modern postal service	*To strengthen the economy and compete with the West*
Create Western-style law codes and courts as well as new elementary and secondary schools	*To compete intellectually with the West*

TRM Handout 9.6: Chart for the Tanzimat: Goals and Motivation religious groups were established to hear cases involving non-Muslims. More Christians were appointed to high office. A mounting tide of secular legislation and secular schools, drawing heavily on European models, now competed with traditional Islamic institutions.

Although Tanzimat-era reforms did not directly address gender issues, they did stimulate modest educational openings for women, mostly in Constantinople, with a training program for midwives in 1842, a girls' secondary school in 1858, and a teacher training college for women in 1870. Furthermore, the reform-minded class that emerged from the Tanzimat era generally favored greater opportunities for women as a means of strengthening the state, and a number of upper- and middle-class women were involved in these discussions. During the 1870s and 1880s, the prominent female poet Sair Nigar Hanim held weekly "salons" in which reformist intellectuals of both sexes participated.

The reform process raised profound and highly contested questions. What was the Ottoman Empire, and who were its people? Were they Ottoman subjects of a dynastic state, Turkish citizens of a national state, or Muslim believers in a religiously defined state? For decades, the answers oscillated, as few people wanted to choose decisively among these alternative identities.

To those who supported the reforms, the Ottoman Empire was an inclusive state, all of whose people, Muslim and non-Muslim alike, were loyal to the dynasty that ruled it. This was the outlook, sometimes called Ottomanism, of a new class spawned by the reform process itself—lower-level officials, military officers, writers, poets, and journalists, many of whom had a modern Western-style education. Dubbed the **Young Ottomans**, they were active during the middle decades of the nineteenth century, as they sought major changes in the Ottoman political system itself. They favored a more European-style parliamentary and constitutional regime that could curtail the absolute power of the sultan. Only such a political system, they felt, could mobilize the energies of the country to overcome backwardness and preserve the state against European aggression. In religious matters, the Young Ottomans favored Islamic modernism, which also found expression in many parts of the Muslim world in the second half of the century. Muslim societies, the Young Ottomans argued, needed to embrace Western technical and scientific knowledge, while rejecting its materialism. Islam in their view could accommodate a full modernity without sacrificing its essential religious character. After all, the Islamic world had earlier hosted impressive scientific achievements and had incorporated elements of Greek philosophical thinking.

In 1876, the Young Ottomans experienced a short-lived victory when **Sultan Abd al-Hamid II** (r. 1876–1909) accepted a constitution and an elected parliament, but not for long. Under the pressure of war with Russia, the sultan soon suspended the reforms and reverted to an older style of despotic rule for the next thirty years, even renewing the claim that he was the caliph, the successor to the Prophet and the protector of Muslims everywhere.

Opposition to this revived despotism soon surfaced among both military and civilian elites known as the **Young Turks**. Largely abandoning any reference to Islam, they advocated a militantly secular public life, were committed to thorough modernization

AP
COMPARISON
In what different ways did various groups define the Ottoman Empire during the nineteenth century?

AP
COMPARISON
How did the reforms and failures of the Young Ottomans compare with those of the Chinese self-strengthening movement?

EXPLORING AP® THEMES

Cultural Developments and Interactions (CDI)

This is a good place in this chapter to remind students that at the beginning of the chapter, the authors note that even those states that did not become colonies of the West "engaged with the culture of modernity—its scientific rationalism; its technological achievements; its belief in a better future; and its ideas of nationalism, socialism, feminism, and individualism." Then ask: How does the program of the Young Ottomans reflect this engagement with the culture of modernity? *The Young Ottomans felt that Muslim societies could embrace the West's technical and scientific knowledge, while rejecting its materialism. They believed that Islam could accommodate a full modernity without sacrificing its essential religious character.*

EXPLORING AP® THEMES

Governance (GOV)

It is very easy for students to get different political groups mixed up. To help students understand the difference between political groups in the Ottoman Empire, ask: What was the difference between the Young Ottomans and the Young Turks? *The two groups had somewhat similar goals but existed in different periods. The Young Ottomans were active in the mid-nineteenth century. They favored a more European-style parliamentary and constitutional regime that could curtail the absolute power of the sultan. The Young Ottomans argued that Muslim societies needed to embrace the West's technical and scientific knowledge, while rejecting its materialism. The Young Turks, active in the early years of the twentieth century, were more secular and did more for women's rights. They pushed for a radical secularization of schools, courts, and law codes; permitted elections and competing parties; established a single Law of Family Rights for all regardless of religion; and encouraged Turkish as the official language of the empire. They also opened modern schools for women, including giving them access to Istanbul University; allowed women to wear Western clothing; restricted polygamy; and permitted women to obtain divorces in some situations.*

BUILDING AP® SKILLS

Contextualization

Contextualization is a skill that students should constantly practice. Show students the image titled "The First Ottoman Constitution" and read the caption. You may wish to show a larger version, which is available on Wikimedia Commons. Explain to students that this is a Greek lithograph. The Greeks, who were oppressed by the sultanate, were glad to see a new government. As you examine the image, ask the following questions:

■ Why does the image quote from the French Revolution? *The Young Ottomans were trying to create a revolution and admired the spirit of the French Revolution. The French slogan "Liberté, égalité, fraternité" fits with many of the ideas of the Ottoman constitution.*

■ What else do you see? *The banner is in Arabic and Greek, and the writing on the rock in the lower left (visible more fully in the online image) is in Arabic, Greek, and French. The person being freed is a woman, which speaks to a major thrust of the changes. While the officials in the center are in Western dress, the crowd in the background is mixed. The uniform of the man holding the Greek flag represents the anti-Ottoman Greek fighters. The red and green flags represent the split in Turkish thinking—the red flag is for the sultanate (political) and the green is for the caliphate (religious).*

APPLY THE TIP

Many students think that the idea of nationalism only exists in Europe. Nationalism and national identity are extremely important concepts to know and be able to explain on the AP® Exam. To help students understand that nationalism is a global concept, ask them: How were the Young Turks an example of growing nationalism in the Ottoman Empire? *The Young Turks advocated for a militantly secular public life, while abandoning any reference to Islam, and began to think of the Ottoman Empire as a Turkish national state. When they gained more power in 1908, they pushed for the secularization of society and encouraged Turkish nationalism, setting the stage for the later Turkish republic.*

▶ **AP**
CONTEXTUALIZATION
To what extent does this image reflect European Enlightenment ideals? (See Chapter 5.)

The First Ottoman Constitution This Ottoman-era postcard celebrates the short-lived constitutional period of 1876–1878 and the brief political victory of the Young Ottoman reformers. The country is represented by an unveiled woman being released from her chains, while an angel carries a banner inscribed with the slogan of the French Revolution: liberty, equality, fraternity. ("The Ottoman Constitution, December 1895." Color postcard, artist unknown/Visual Connection Archive)

along European lines, and increasingly thought about the Ottoman Empire as a Turkish national state. "There is only one civilization, and that is European civilization," declared Abdullah Cevdet, a prominent figure in the Young Turk movement. "Therefore we must borrow western civilization with both its rose and its thorn."[10]

AP EXAM TIP
Examples of nationalism and of national identity are "must know" concepts on the AP® Exam.

A military coup in 1908 finally allowed the Young Turks to exercise real power. They pushed for a radical secularization of schools, courts, and law codes; permitted elections and competing parties; established a single Law of Family Rights for all regardless of religion; and encouraged Turkish as the official language of the empire. They also opened modern schools for women, including access to Istanbul University; allowed women to wear Western clothing; restricted polygamy; and permitted women to obtain divorces in some situations. Women established a number of publications and organizations, some of them linked to British suffrage groups. In the western cities of the empire, some women abandoned their veils.

But the nationalist Turkish conception of Ottoman identity antagonized non-Turkic peoples and helped stimulate Arab and other nationalisms in response. For some, a secular nationality was becoming the most important public loyalty, with Islam relegated to private life. Nationalist sentiments contributed to the complete disintegration of the Ottoman Empire following World War I, but the secularizing and westernizing principles of the Young Turks informed the policies of the Turkish republic that replaced it.

Outcomes: Comparing China and the Ottoman Empire

By the beginning of the twentieth century, both China and the Ottoman Empire, recently centers of proud and vibrant civilizations, had experienced the consequences of a rapidly shifting balance of global power. Now they were "semi-colonies" within the "informal empires" of Europe. Although they retained sufficient independence for their governments to launch catch-up efforts of defensive modernization, the Ottomans earlier and the Chinese later, neither was able to create the industrial economies or strong states required to fend off European intrusion and restore their former status in the world. Despite their diminished power, however, both China and the Ottoman Empire gave rise to new nationalist conceptions of society that were initially small and limited in appeal but of great significance for the future.

In the early twentieth century, that future witnessed the end of both the Chinese and Ottoman empires. In China, the collapse of the imperial system in 1912 was followed by a vast revolutionary upheaval that by 1949 led to a communist regime within largely the same territorial space as the old empire. By contrast, the collapse of the Ottoman Empire following World War I led to the creation of the new but much smaller nation-state of Turkey in the Anatolian heartland of the old empire, which lost its vast Arab and European provinces.

China's twentieth-century revolutionaries rejected traditional Confucian culture far more thoroughly than the secularizing leaders of modern Turkey rejected Islam. Almost everywhere in the Islamic world, including Turkey, traditional religion retained its hold on the private loyalties of most people and later in the twentieth century became a basis for social renewal in many places. Islamic civilization, unlike its Chinese counterpart, had many independent centers and was never so closely associated with a single state. Furthermore, it was embedded in a deeply religious tradition that was personally meaningful to millions of adherents, in contrast to the more elitist and secular outlook of Confucianism. Many Chinese, however, retained traditional Confucian values such as filial piety, and Confucianism has made something of a comeback in China over the past several decades. Nonetheless, Islam retained a hold on its civilization in the twentieth century rather more firmly than Confucianism did in China.

AP®
COMPARISON
In what ways were the declines of the Chinese and the Ottoman empires similar?

The Japanese Difference: The Rise of a New East Asian Power

Finding the Main Point: In what ways was Japan's history in the nineteenth century shaped by its efforts to respond to European and American imperialism?

AP® EXAM TIP
Be sure to understand how Japan was able to undertake rapid industrialization in this time.

Like China and the Ottoman Empire, the island country of Japan confronted the aggressive power of the West during the nineteenth century. This threat took shape as U.S. commodore Matthew Perry's "black ships" steamed into Tokyo Bay in 1853

BUILDING AP® SKILLS

Making Connections: Comparison

This is a good place to quickly practice comparison skills. Ask students: What were some similarities between China and the Ottoman Empire? *Both were semi-colonies — officially sovereign and independent nations, but dependent on and dominated by another imperialist country or several imperialist countries within the informal empires of Europe. Both retained some measure of independence. Both governments sought to launch catch-up efforts of defensive modernization. Neither was able to create the industrial economies or strong states required to fend off European intrusion and restore its former status in the world. Both gave rise to new nationalist conceptions of society.*

APPLY THE TIP

Japan's transformation in the nineteenth century is considered to be miraculous. To help students understand how Japan was able to accomplish its political, economic, and social reforms during the nineteenth century, ask: What do you think enabled Japan to undergo radical transformation and begin a long period of prosperity? *There was a long period of peace, society was carefully ordered, the country was governed as individual states without too much power given to a central authority, and well-functioning networks of exchange and flourishing cities contributed to economic growth and development.*

EXPLORING AP® THEMES

Economic Systems (ECN)

As you are discussing Japan's amazing transformation with students, ask: Given the various revolutions in China described earlier in this chapter, what might the term "revolution from above" mean? *Japan's revolution, primarily industrial but also social, was driven by the government.*

EXPLORING AP® THEMES

Social Interactions and Organization (SIO)

This is a good point to have your students examine the differences between the Chinese and Japanese class systems. A reproducible version of the chart is available in the Teacher's Resource Materials. (Answers are provided in italics.)

and forcefully demanded that this reclusive nation open up to more "normal" relations with the world. However, the outcome of that encounter differed sharply from the others. In the second half of the nineteenth century, Japan undertook a radical transformation of its society—a "revolution from above," according to some historians—that turned it into a powerful, modern, united, industrialized nation. It was an achievement that neither China nor the Ottoman Empire was able to duplicate. Far from succumbing to Western domination, Japan joined the club of imperialist countries by creating its own East Asian empire at the expense of China and Korea. In building a society that was both modern and distinctly Japanese, Japan demonstrated that modernity was not a uniquely European phenomenon. This "Japanese miracle," as some have called it, was both promising and ominous for the rest of Asia.

The Tokugawa Background

For 250 years prior to Perry's arrival, Japan had been governed by a shogun (a military ruler) from the Tokugawa family who acted in the name of a revered but powerless emperor who lived in Kyoto, 300 miles away from the seat of power in Edo (Tokyo). The chief task of this Tokugawa shogunate was to prevent the return of civil war among some 260 rival feudal lords, known as daimyo, each of whom had a cadre of armed retainers, the famed samurai warriors of Japanese tradition.

Based on their own military power and political skills, successive shoguns gave Japan more than two centuries of internal peace (1600–1850). To control the restive daimyo, they required these local authorities to create second homes in Edo, the country's capital, where they had to live during alternate years. When they left their rural residences, families stayed behind, almost as hostages. Nonetheless, the daimyo, especially the more powerful ones, retained substantial autonomy in their own domains and behaved in some ways like independent states, with separate military forces, law codes, tax systems, and currencies. With no national army, no uniform currency, and little central authority at the local level, **Tokugawa Japan** was "pacified . . . but not really unified."[11] To further stabilize the country, the Tokugawa regime issued highly detailed rules governing the occupation, residence, dress, hairstyles, and behavior of the four hierarchically ranked status groups into which Japanese society was divided—samurai at the top, then peasants, artisans, and, at the bottom, merchants.

During these 250 years of peace, much was changing within Japan in ways that belied the control and orderliness of Tokugawa regulations. For one thing, the samurai, in the absence of wars to fight, evolved into a salaried bureaucratic or administrative class amounting to 5 to 6 percent of the total population, but they remained fiercely devoted to their daimyo lords and to their warrior code of loyalty, honor, and self-sacrifice.

More generally, centuries of peace contributed to a remarkable burst of economic growth, commercialization, and urban development. Entrepreneurial

AP®
CONTINUITY AND CHANGE
In what ways was Japan changing during the Tokugawa era?

	China	Japan
Upper	*Scholar bureaucrats and gentry*	*Warriors: daimyo and samurai*
Middle	*Peasants, artisans, workers, and merchants*	*Peasants and artisans*
Lower	*Soldiers, beggars, and enslaved people*	*Merchants*

After students have completed their charts, ask the following questions:

■ How might the stratification in China have affected the military? *Although the Chinese army could be enormous, because of the social standing of soldiers, men did not make a career of the military, unlike in Rome. Therefore, the Chinese army lacked the depth of experience to make it a good fighting force.*

■ What might have been the effect on the samurai who were forced to move into business to survive? *The reaction was mixed. Some did fine, while others, unable to deal with the loss of status, became impoverished, and a percentage committed seppuku.*

TRM Handout 9.7: Comparison Chart for the Chinese and Japanese Class Systems peasants, using fertilizers and other agricultural innovations, grew more rice than ever before and also engaged in a variety of rural manufacturing enterprises. By 1750, Japan had become perhaps the world's most urbanized country, with about 10 percent of its population living in sizable towns or cities. Edo, with perhaps a million residents, was among the world's largest cities. Well-functioning networks of exchange linked urban and rural areas, marking Japan as an emerging market economy. The influence of Confucianism encouraged education and generated a remarkably literate population, with about 40 percent of men and 15 percent of women able to read and write. Although no one was aware of it at the time, these changes during the Tokugawa era provided a solid foundation for Japan's remarkable industrial growth in the late nineteenth century.

Such changes also undermined the shogunate's efforts to freeze Japanese society in the interests of stability. Some samurai found the lowly but profitable path of commerce too much to resist. "No more shall we have to live by the sword," declared one of them in 1616 while renouncing his samurai status. "I have seen that great profit can be made honorably. I shall brew *sake* and soy sauce, and we shall prosper."[12] Many merchants, though hailing from the lowest-ranking status group, prospered in the new commercial environment and supported a vibrant urban culture, while not a few daimyo found it necessary, if humiliating, to seek loans from these social inferiors. Thus merchants had money, but little status, whereas samurai enjoyed high status but were often indebted to inferior merchants. Both resented their positions.

Despite prohibitions to the contrary, many peasants moved to the cities, becoming artisans or merchants and imitating the ways of their social betters. A decree of 1788 noted that peasants "have become accustomed to luxury and forgetful of their status." They wore inappropriate clothing, used umbrellas rather than straw hats in the rain, and even left the villages for the city. "Henceforth," declared the shogun, "all luxuries should be avoided by the peasants. They are to live simply and devote themselves to farming."[13] This decree, like many others before it, was widely ignored.

More than social change undermined the Tokugawa regime. Corruption was widespread, to the disgust of many. The shogunate's failure to deal successfully with a severe famine in the 1830s eroded confidence in its effectiveness. At the same time, a mounting wave of local peasant uprisings and urban riots expressed the many grievances of the poor. The most striking of these outbursts left the city of Osaka in flames in 1837. Its leader, Oshio Heihachiro, no doubt spoke for many ordinary people when he wrote:

> We must first punish the officials who torment the people so cruelly; then we must execute the haughty and rich Osaka merchants. Then we must distribute the gold, silver, and copper stored in their cellars, and bands of rice hidden in their storehouses.[14]

From the 1830s on, one historian concluded, "there was a growing feeling that the *shogunate* was losing control."[15]

AP
COMPARISON
To what extent was the social and economic status of the merchant class in Japan and China similar?

AP
COMPARISON
To what extent were the factors that led to the downfall of the Tokugawa regime similar to factors that led to the downfall of the Qing dynasty and the Ottoman Empire?

CHAPTER 9

BUILDING AP® SKILLS
Making Connections: Comparison

Students should be practicing AP® skills every day. This is a good place to insert a quick comparison skills practice with urbanization. Students might be surprised that in the United States in 1750, urbanization, that is, the percentage of the population living in cities, was only 5.6 percent. Ask students to compare this figure to the urbanization rate of Japan at the time and to suggest what this difference means. *The urbanization rate in Japan at the time was nearly double that of the United States. In the United States, most colonists made a living from agricultural activities. Japan's economic development was more advanced, people had more opportunities, and the Japanese had some degree of social mobility because of these opportunities.*

BUILDING AP® SKILLS
Making Connections: Causation

The Tenpo famine of 1833–1837 and the increased peasant movement from the country to the cities were some causes of the discontent with the shogunate prior to Matthew Perry's arrival in Japan in the 1850s. Have students research the Tenpo famine and ask if they can find a connection between the flight of peasant farmers to the cities and the fall in food supplies. *The famine, which was caused by weather and crop disease, inspired people to seek alternative employment and additional food sources.*

American Intrusion and the Meiji Restoration

AP® EXAM TIP
The rise of the United States as a world power is an important development in AP® World History.

AP® EXAM TIP
You should understand the political and economic features of the Meiji Restoration.

▶ **AP®**
CLAIMS AND EVIDENCE IN SOURCES
What does this image reveal about the Japanese artist's view of the recently arrived Americans?

It was foreign intervention that brought matters to a head. Since the expulsion of European missionaries and the harsh suppression of Christianity in the early seventeenth century, Japan had deliberately limited its contact with the West to a single port, where only the Dutch were allowed to trade. (See "Asians and Asian Commerce" in Chapter 6.) By the early nineteenth century, however, various European countries and the United States were knocking at the door. All were turned away, and even shipwrecked sailors or whalers were expelled, jailed, or executed. As it happened, it was the United States that forced the issue, sending Commodore Perry in 1853 to demand humane treatment for castaways, the right of American vessels to refuel and buy provisions, and the opening of ports for trade. Authorized to use force if necessary, Perry presented his reluctant hosts with, among other gifts, a white flag for surrender should hostilities follow.

In the end, the Japanese avoided war. Aware of what had happened to China as a result of resisting European demands, Japan agreed to a series of unequal treaties with various Western powers. That humiliating capitulation to the demands of the "foreign devils" further eroded support for the shogunate, triggered a brief civil

The Black Ships of the United States The initial occasion for serious Japanese reflection on the West occurred in 1853–1854, in the context of American commodore Matthew Perry's efforts to "open" Japan to regular commercial relationships with the United States. His nine coal-fired steamships, belching black smoke and carrying a crew of some 1,800 men and more than 100 mounted cannons, became known in Japan as the "black ships." Created around 1854, this image represents perhaps the best known of many such Japanese depictions of the American warships. (Granger, NYC — All rights reserved)

Political Features	Economic Features	Social Features
▪ *The Restoration centralized political power in a national government* ▪ *A national army was created and conscripted soldiers from all social classes* ▪ *The constitution of 1889 was presented as a sacred gift from the emperor and introduced an elected parliament, political parties, and democratic ideas to Japan* ▪ *Political power lay (theoretically) with the emperor; the parliament acted as advisers* ▪ *The Japanese army and navy were modernized*	▪ *The state guided industrialization (established businesses and then sold them to investors)* ▪ *The state built railroads, created a postal service, and established a national currency and banking system* ▪ *"Labor-intensive industrialization" developed that relied on a large workforce rather than machines and capital investment* ▪ *A large part of the workforce in the factories was female laborers*	▪ *Samurai had to relinquish their traditional role as the country's warrior class* ▪ *All Japanese became legally equal as commoners and as subjects of the emperor* ▪ *Many of the old elites (daimyo and samurai) found new positions of power in the army, bureaucracy, or business enterprises* ▪ *Some reformers pushed for more gender equality, but the government did not allow women to play a role in public life despite needing female labor in the factories*

TRM Handout 9.8: Chart for Political, Economic, and Social Features of the Meiji Restoration war, and by 1868 led to a political takeover by a group of young samurai from southern Japan. This decisive turning point in Japan's history was known as the **Meiji Restoration**, for the country's new rulers claimed that they were restoring to power the young emperor, then a fifteen-year-old boy whose throne name was Meiji (MAY-jee), or Enlightened Rule. Despite his youth, he was regarded as the most recent link in a chain of descent that traced the origins of the imperial family back to the sun goddess Amaterasu. Having eliminated the shogunate, the patriotic young men who led the takeover soon made their goals clear—to save Japan from foreign domination not by futile resistance, but by a thorough transformation of Japanese society drawing on all that the modern West had to offer. "Knowledge shall be sought throughout the world," they declared, "so as to strengthen the foundations of imperial rule."

Japan now had a government committed to a decisive break with the past, and it had acquired that government without massive violence or destruction. By contrast, the defeat of the Taiping Uprising had deprived China of any such opportunity for a fresh start, while saddling it with enormous devastation and massive loss of life. Furthermore, Japan was of less interest to Western powers than either China, with its huge potential market and reputation for riches, or the Ottoman Empire, with its strategic location at the crossroads of Asia, Africa, and Europe. The American Civil War and its aftermath likewise deflected U.S. ambitions in the Pacific for a time, further reducing the Western pressure on Japan.

AP
CONTEXTUALIZATION
To what extent were Japanese reformers justified in believing their independence was in danger?

Modernization Japanese-Style

These circumstances gave Japan some breathing space, and its new rulers moved quickly to take advantage of that unique window of opportunity. Thus they launched a cascading wave of dramatic changes that rolled over the country in the last three decades of the nineteenth century. Like the more modest reforms of China and the Ottoman Empire, Japanese modernizing efforts were defensive, based on fears that Japanese independence was in grave danger. Those reforms, however, were revolutionary in their cumulative effect, transforming Japan far more thoroughly than even the most radical of the Ottoman efforts, let alone the limited "self-strengthening" policies of the Chinese.

The first task was genuine national unity, which required an attack on the power and privileges of both the daimyo and the samurai. In a major break with the past, the new regime soon ended the semi-independent domains of the daimyo, replacing them with governors appointed by and responsible to the national government. The central state, not the local authorities, now collected the nation's taxes and raised a national army based on conscription from all social classes.

AP
CONTINUITY AND CHANGE
In what respects was Japan's nineteenth-century transformation revolutionary? And in what ways did it retain earlier Japanese traditions?

Thus the samurai relinquished their ancient role as the country's warrior class and with it their cherished right to carry swords. The old Confucian-based social order with its special privileges for various classes was largely dismantled, and almost all Japanese became legally equal as commoners and as subjects of the emperor.

TEACHING IDEA

Class Discussion

China's and Japan's responses to Western pressure were vastly different, and this difference is something that students need to understand because both of these nations were important in the twentieth century. Ask students: What were differences in how China and Japan responded to Western incursions? *The Chinese rejected European influence when they could. The Chinese did not begin serious industrial development, especially railroads, until after 1890. Even then it was not by choice but because they lost the war with Japan. The Japanese embraced European influence and changed rapidly.*

APPLY THE TIP

Gender roles are always an important topic to understand when preparing for the AP® World History: Modern Exam. Students should understand that despite the important role of women in Japanese industrialization, women still did not play a role in public life. Ask students: What changes occurred in the role of women in Meiji Japan? *Although a reform movement arose, women's roles remained largely the same. The new government did make plans for education that included girls with a gender-specific curriculum. However, women could not play a role in public life, could not take legal action, and had no political rights.*

Limitations on travel and trade likewise fell as a nationwide economy came to parallel the centralized state. Although there was some opposition to these measures, including a brief rebellion of resentful samurai in 1877, it was on the whole a remarkably peaceful process in which a segment of the old ruling class abolished its own privileges. Many, but not all, of these displaced elites found a soft landing in the army, bureaucracy, or business enterprises of the new regime, thus easing a painful transition.

Accompanying these social and political changes was a widespread and eager fascination with almost everything Western. Knowledge about the West—its science and technology; its various political and constitutional arrangements; its legal and educational systems; its dances, clothing, and hairstyles—was enthusiastically sought out by official missions to Europe and the United States, by hundreds of students sent to study abroad, and by many ordinary Japanese at home. Western writers were translated into Japanese. "Civilization and Enlightenment" was the slogan of the time, and both were to be found in the West. The most prominent popularizer of Western knowledge, Fukuzawa Yukichi, summed up the chief lesson of his studies in the mid-1870s—Japan was backward and needed to learn from the West: "If we compare the knowledge of the Japanese and Westerners, in letters, in technique, in commerce, or in industry, from the largest to the smallest matter, there is not one thing in which we excel. . . . In Japan's present condition there is nothing in which we may take pride vis-à-vis the West."[16]

After this initial wave of uncritical enthusiasm for everything Western receded, Japan proceeded to borrow more selectively and to combine foreign and Japanese elements in distinctive ways. For example, drawing heavily on German models, the constitution of 1889 introduced a framework for political representation, including an elected parliament, that many in Japan had been pushing for, but that constitution was presented as a gift from a sacred emperor descended from the sun goddess. The parliament could advise, but ultimate power, and particularly control of the military, lay theoretically with the emperor and in practice with an oligarchy of prominent reformers acting in his name. Likewise, a modern educational system, which achieved universal primary schooling by the early twentieth century, was laced with Confucian-based moral instruction and exhortations of loyalty to the emperor. Christianity made little headway in Meiji Japan, but Shinto, an ancient religious tradition featuring ancestors and nature spirits, was elevated to the status of an official state cult. Japan's experience many centuries before of borrowing massively but selectively from Chinese culture perhaps served it better in these new circumstances than either the Chinese disdain for foreign cultures or the reluctance of many Muslims to see much of value in the infidel West.

AP® EXAM TIP
Understand how industrialization impacted gender roles and other parts of society in Japan in this era.

Like their counterparts in China and the Ottoman Empire, some reformers in Japan—male and female alike—argued that the oppression of women was an obstacle to the country's modernization and that family reform was essential to gaining the respect of the West. Fukuzawa Yukichi, who was widely read, urged an end to concubinage and prostitution, advocated more education for girls, and called for gender equality in matters of marriage, divorce, and property rights. But most male reformers understood women largely in the context of family life, seeing them as "good wife, wise mother." By the 1880s, however, a small feminist movement arose, demanding—and modeling—a more public role for women. Some even sought the right to vote at a time when only a small fraction of men could do so. A leading feminist, Kishida Toshiko, not yet twenty years old, astonished the country in 1882 when she undertook a two-month speaking tour during which she addressed huge audiences. Only "equality and equal rights," she argued, would allow Japan "to build a new society." Japan must rid itself of the ancient habit of "respecting men and despising women."

While the new Japanese government included girls in its plans for universal education, it was with a gender-specific curriculum and in schools segregated by sex. Any thought of women playing a role in public life was harshly suppressed. A Peace Preservation Law of 1887, in effect until 1922, forbade women from joining political parties and even from attending meetings where political matters were discussed. The Civil Code of 1898 accorded absolute authority to the male head of the family, while grouping all wives with "cripples and disabled persons" as those who "cannot undertake any legal action." To the authorities of Meiji Japan, a serious transformation of gender roles was more of a threat than an opportunity.

At the core of Japan's effort at defensive modernization lay its state-guided industrialization program. More than in Europe or the United States, the government itself established a number of enterprises, later selling many of them to private

▼ AP®

COMPARISON
To what extent are the signs of modernization shown in the image similar to those found in the image of "The First Ottoman Constitution" found on page 514?

Japan's Political Modernization This woodblock print shows a meeting of the House of Peers, one of the new institutions created during the Meiji Restoration that was modeled on European institutions. The peers were chosen primarily from Japan's hereditary nobility. Note the Western dress worn by the peerage at this meeting. (Pictures from History/Bridgeman Images)

BUILDING AP® SKILLS

Making Connections: Comparison

This is a good place to practice comparison skills. Have students think back to Chapter 8 and industrialization in the United States. Ask students: How was Japan's Industrial Revolution different from the industrialization that took place in Europe and the United States? *Industrialization was more state-guided in Japan, where the government established a number of businesses and later sold them to private investors. The government also worked to create modern infrastructure, such as railroads and a postal service, throughout the country. Also, unlike Western Europe and the United States, Japan relied more heavily on an abundant workforce to produce industrial goods, rather than replacing human labor with machinery.*

BUILDING AP® SKILLS

Making Connections: Comparison

Another good opportunity to practice comparison skills is with the image found on page 514 titled "The First Ottoman Constitution" and the Japanese woodblock print found on page 521. Project the images together and ask students to find signs of westernization in both prints. *In "The First Ottoman Constitution," men are dressed in Western fashion and the French slogan "Liberté, égalité, fraternité" shows the borrowing of ideas from the French Revolution. The Japanese woodblock print shows a meeting of the House of Peers modeled on European institutions; the men are dressed in Western fashion, and the women in the viewing gallery are dressed in Western fashion as well.*

CONTINUITY AND CHANGE
How could this photograph be used to show changes in the Japanese economy and society? How could it be used to show continuities?

AP®

COMPARISON
To what extent did Japan's industrialization differ from that of Western Europe, Russia, and North America? In what respects was it similar?

Japanese Women Workers Young women were prominent in Japan's emerging textile industry. The women in this photograph from a silk factory around 1900 are spinning silk threads from raw cocoons. (Pictures from History/Bridgeman Images)

investors. It also acted to create a modern infrastructure by building railroads, creating a postal service, and establishing a national currency and banking system. From the 1880s on, the Japanese government developed a distinctive form of "labor-intensive industrialization" that relied more heavily on the country's abundant workforce and less on the replacement of labor by machinery and capital than in Western Europe or North America.[17]

By the early twentieth century, Japan's industrialization, organized around a number of large firms called *zaibatsu*, was thriving in major urban areas. Early zaibatsu included the Mitsubishi corporation, still a manufacturing and exporting business today. Japan quickly became a major exporter of textiles, in part to pay for imports of raw materials, like cotton, that were necessary because Japan had limited natural resources. Soon the country was able to produce its own munitions and industrial goods as well. Its major cities enjoyed mass-circulation newspapers, movie theaters, and electric lights. All of this was accomplished through its own resources and without the massive foreign debt that so afflicted Egypt and the Ottoman Empire. No other country outside of Europe and North America had been able to launch its own Industrial Revolution in the nineteenth century. It was a distinctive feature of Japan's modern transformation.

Less distinctive, however, were the social results of that process. Taxed heavily to pay for Japan's ambitious modernization program, many peasant families slid into poverty. Their sometimes violent protests peaked in 1883–1884 as the Japanese countryside witnessed infanticide, the sale of daughters, and starvation.

While state authorities rigidly excluded women from political life and denied them adult legal status, they badly needed female labor in the country's textile

---

BUILDING AP® SKILLS

Making Connections: Causation

It's important for students to understand the results of Japan's industrialization efforts in the nineteenth century so that they can understand Japan's rise to a global power in the early twentieth century. Ask students: What were the negative and positive results of Japan's industrialization efforts in the nineteenth century? *Japan became a major exporter of textiles and was able to produce its own munitions and industrial goods. The country was able to achieve industrialization through its own resources and without massive foreign debt. However, many peasant families fell into poverty because of the heavy taxes the government used to pay for the modernization and industrialization program. A majority of textile workers were young women who were treated harshly in the factories and were paid poorly. The government repressed workers' efforts to create labor unions and to organize strikes for better conditions.*

industry, which was central to Japan's economic growth. Accordingly, the majority of Japan's textile workers were young women from poor families in the countryside. Recruiters toured rural villages, contracting with parents for their daughters' labor in return for a payment that the girls had to repay from their wages. That pay was low and their working conditions were terrible. Most lived in factory-provided dormitories and worked twelve or more hours per day. While some committed suicide or ran away and many left after earning enough to pay off their contracts, others organized strikes and joined the anarchist or socialist movements that were emerging among a few intellectuals. One such woman, Kanno Sugako, was hanged in 1911 for participating in a plot to assassinate the emperor. Efforts to create unions and organize strikes, both illegal in Japan at the time, were met with harsh repression even as corporate and state authorities sought to depict the company as a family unit to which workers should give their loyalty, all under the beneficent gaze of the divine emperor.

Japan and the World

Japan's modern transformation soon registered internationally. By the early twentieth century, its economic growth, openness to trade, and embrace of "civilization and enlightenment" from the West persuaded the Western powers to revise the unequal treaties in Japan's favor. This had long been a primary goal of the Meiji regime, and the Anglo-Japanese Treaty of 1902 now acknowledged Japan as an equal player among the Great Powers of the world.

Not only did Japan escape from its semi-colonial entanglements with the West, but it also launched its own empire-building enterprise, even as European powers and the United States were carving up much of Asia, Africa, and Pacific Oceania into colonies or spheres of influence. It was what industrializing Great Powers did in the late nineteenth century, and Japan followed suit, in part to compensate for the relative poverty of its natural resource base. A successful war against China (1894–1895) established Japan as a formidable military competitor in East Asia, replacing China as the dominant power in the region. Ten years later in the **Russo-Japanese War** (1904–1905), which was fought over rival imperial ambitions in Korea and Manchuria, Japan became the first Asian state to defeat a major European power. Through those victories, Japan also gained colonial control of Taiwan and Korea and a territorial foothold in Manchuria. And in the aftermath of World War I, Japan acquired a growing influence in China's Shandong Peninsula and control over a number of Micronesian islands under the auspices of the League of Nations.

Japan's entry onto the broader global stage was felt in many places (see Map 9.3). It added yet one more imperialist power to those already burdening a beleaguered China. Defeat at the hands of Japanese upstarts shocked Russia and triggered the 1905 revolution in that country. To Europeans and Americans, Japan was now an economic, political, and military competitor in Asia.

AP®
CONTINUITY AND CHANGE
How did Japan's relationship to the larger world change during its modernization process?

EXPLORING AP® THEMES

Humans and the Environment (ENV)

Continue to have students practice their map analysis skills by asking them to study Map 9.3, "The Rise of Japan." Then ask them to reflect on what they remember seeing on the maps of industrial Europe and the United States from Chapter 8 and use that information, along with their analysis of Map 9.3, to help them answer the following question: What accounts for the location of the major industrial areas in Japan? *Japan, unlike England, has limited natural resources, and industrial areas were placed for the convenience of transportation, mainly shipping. Harbors on the coast are the easiest point for ships to bring in raw materials and load finished products. Similar to early Greece, much of the transportation in Japan's history has been by sea rather than by land. Both Japan and Greece are rugged land areas, but with easy access to the sea.*

Map 9.3 The Rise of Japan
As Japan modernized after the Meiji Restoration, it launched an empire-building program that provided a foundation for further expansion in the 1930s and during World War II.

▲ **AP®**

CONTEXTUALIZATION
To what extent did Japan's geography both limit and facilitate its imperialist policy?

In the world of subject peoples, the rise of Japan and its defeat of Russia generated widespread admiration among those who saw Japan as a model for their own modern development and perhaps as an ally in the struggle against European imperialism. Some Poles, Finns, and Jews viewed the Russian defeat in 1905 as an opening for their own liberation from the Russian Empire and were grateful to Japan for the opportunity. Despite Japan's aggression against their country, many Chinese reformers and nationalists found in the Japanese experience valuable

---

ERIC'S ACTIVITY 9   Comparing Responses to the West

Skill: Comparison

Making meaningful comparisons can be tricky. I find that this chapter provides an ideal place to explore both the strengths and weaknesses of comparison and its relationship to causation in world history. The growing power of the West in the nineteenth century was a global phenomenon affecting regions across the world. But the experience of Western encroachment depended a great deal on local circumstances. To what extent did local factors define possible responses to the West? To what extent do these local factors complicate comparisons between the experiences of China and Japan? I challenge my students to evaluate these questions through the critical examination of a comparative thesis. Find the complete activity in the Teacher's Resource Materials.

TRM Eric's Activity 9: Comparing Responses to the West

lessons for themselves. Thousands flocked to Japan to study its achievements. Newspapers throughout the Islamic world celebrated Japan's victory over Russia as an "awakening of the East" that might herald Muslims' own liberation. Some Turkish women gave their children Japanese names. Indonesian Muslims from Aceh wrote to the Meiji emperor asking for help in their struggle against the Dutch, and Muslim poets wrote odes in his honor. The Egyptian nationalist Mustafa Kamil spoke for many when he declared: "We are amazed by Japan because it is the first Eastern government to utilize Western civilization to resist the shield of European imperialism in Asia."[18]

Those who directly experienced Japanese imperialism in Taiwan or Korea no doubt had a less positive view, for its colonial policies matched or exceeded the brutality of European practices. While Japanese colonial rule of Korea (1910–1945), for example, arguably contributed to Korea's urban, commercial, and industrial growth, many Koreans lost land to Japanese settlers, who controlled over half the arable land by 1932. In 1919 a huge but peaceful Korean protest movement was harshly crushed by Japanese authorities, with some 7,500 Koreans killed and tens of thousands injured or arrested. With the outbreak of the war after 1937, Japanese policy seemed intent on wiping out Korean national identity as Koreans were forced to worship at Shinto shrines and to adopt Japanese names while Korean-language newspapers and magazines were forbidden. And during World War II, the Japanese required thousands of Korean "comfort women" to provide sexual services to men in the Japanese military. Beyond Korea, China and much of Southeast Asia suffered bitterly under Japanese imperial aggression. But both the idea of Japan as a liberator of Asia from the European yoke and the reality of Japan as an oppressive imperial power in its own right derived from the country's remarkable modern transformation and its distinctive response to the provocation of Western intrusion.

CONCLUSIONS AND REFLECTIONS

Success and Failure in History

Finding the Main Point: What measurements could be used when thinking about the success or failure of a state?

In our endless efforts to understand the past, all of us make judgments about success and failure. In 1900, Europeans often congratulated themselves on their successes during the previous century. They had created unprecedented wealth through their industrial technology; their sciences had penetrated the secrets of nature; their empires spanned the globe; and they had bested both the ancient civilization of China and the previously fearsome Ottoman Empire.

By contrast, thoughtful Chinese in 1900 had much to lament as they pondered their country's failures. They had endured a terribly disruptive civil war that killed many millions, and they had suffered numerous military defeats at the hands of

BUILDING AP® SKILLS

Making Connections: Comparison

This is a good time to have students practice their essay-writing skills. You can use released Question 3 from the 2002 exam. This question asks students to analyze and compare the responses of China and Japan to Western penetration in the nineteenth century. If you have students write the full essay, give them 40 minutes to write. The question can be found on the College Board website, in the AP® World History: Modern Past Exam Questions section. You can use the following updated prompt to align this question to the most recent exam redesign:

- In the period 1750–1900, states and empires around the world, like the Ottoman Empire, Qing China, and Tokugawa Japan, began to respond to the increasing power of industrialized states in a variety of ways.

  Develop an argument that evaluates the extent to which older states and empires differed in their responses to the rise of industrialized states in this time period.

Differentiation

While it's good for students to write full essays, especially as they get closer to the AP® Exam, it can also be helpful to have them work on a group essay outline and evaluate their peers' responses. This exercise allows them to see different ways of formulating arguments and to potentially understand what graders are looking for when scoring essays. If you want students to complete a group outline essay with this prompt, consider following the "Must Do, Should Do, Strive For" model below:

- Must Do: Working in groups of four or fewer, students must create an LEQ outline on the provided butcher paper. The outline should include contextualization and a thesis that responds to the prompt, at least two arguments, and at least two pieces of evidence for *each* argument.

- Should Do: Once all the groups have completed their LEQ poster, have students hang them up and do a gallery walk to see how other groups put together this LEQ. As they look at each poster, ask students to leave "I wonder . . ." and "I like . . ." statements about what they see in the outline.

- Strive For: For students who want or need a writing challenge, have them choose one of their arguments from their LEQ poster and write a full argument paragraph on it.

TEACHING IDEA

Class Discussion

This could be a good place to get students to think about how historians and other scholars try to define what "success" means for different events in world history. Ask students to use what they have learned about the Ottoman Empire, Qing China, and Japan's attempts at modernization and answer the following question ("Finding the Main Point" on page 525): What measurements could be used when thinking about the success or failure of a state? Use specific evidence from what you have learned in Chapter 9 to defend your answer. *Answers will vary, but could include ideas such as: The Japanese could be considered successful because they were able to westernize and modernize to the point where they could defeat Russia in war; Qing China could be considered a failure because its attempts at modernizing and expelling Western powers were unsuccessful and sometimes led to more Western control; the Ottoman Empire could be considered a failure because it was reliant on European investment to industrialize and it shrank throughout the nineteenth century.*

You could extend the discussion by asking students to read the "Conclusions and Reflections" section on pages 525–526 and compare what they read to what was discussed with their classmates.

TEACHING IDEA

Exit Slip

As a quick check of what students have learned in Chapter 9, you can have them answer the following question on a piece of paper and turn it in as they leave class: How much freedom of action did the leaders of China, the Ottoman Empire, and Japan really have when making choices about political, social, or economic change? *Answers will vary.*

Europeans and Japanese, forcing the Chinese into humiliating concessions to these foreigners. Their once powerful state had proved unable to prevent these catastrophes.

Like the Chinese, Ottoman observers around 1900 might well have contemplated the failures of the past century. Their empire had shrunk dramatically, was economically dependent on Europe, and had been unable to create a strong state or economy despite implementing a far more robust reform program than China. In the early twentieth century, both of these old imperial systems collapsed.

But many Japanese, on the eve of the twentieth century, had good reason to celebrate their country's successes. They had created an efficient state and an industrialized economy, which had forestalled European aggression and made Japan one of the Great Powers of the world with the beginnings of an empire of its own.

So had Europe and Japan "succeeded" in the nineteenth century, while China, the Ottoman Empire, and the many colonized peoples of the world had "failed"? The historical record is complex, and we might want to be very careful about how we apply these notions to the past.

If the measure of success is national wealth and power, then Europeans and Japanese had reason to boast about their nineteenth-century achievements, while China and the Ottoman Empire had cause for disappointment. But success for whom? Not everyone shared equally in national prosperity. British artisans who lost their livelihood to industrial machines and Japanese women textile workers who suffered through the early stages of industrialization might be forgiven for not appreciating the "success" of their country's transformation, even if their middle-class counterparts and subsequent generations benefited. Furthermore, European and Japanese success as measured by their empires meant defeat, humiliation, and untold suffering for millions of their colonial subjects.

Success is frequently associated with good judgment and wise choices, yet actors in the historical drama are never completely free in making their decisions, and none, of course, have historians' benefit of hindsight. Did the leaders of China and the Ottoman Empire fail to push industrial development more strongly, or were they not in a position to do so? Were Japanese leaders wiser and more astute than their counterparts elsewhere, or did their knowledge of China's earlier experience and their unique national history simply provide them with circumstances more conducive to modern development?

Finally, national wealth and power are surely not the only criteria for success. Modern science and technology have certainly made human life healthier, longer, and more comfortable for millions. Surely a great success! But they have also eroded the face-to-face relationships of village life, undermined the comforts of religious belief, and generated massive environmental changes—global warming in particular—that pose severe threats to modern societies.

Questions about success and failure have no clear-cut answers, but they usefully highlight the ambiguity and uncertainty of historical judgments and foster humility in the face of immense complexity.

CHAPTER REVIEW

AP* Key Terms

Taiping Uprising, 501
Opium Wars, 503
Commissioner Lin Zexu, 504
unequal treaties, 505
informal empires, 506
self-strengthening, 506
Boxer Uprising, 506
Chinese revolution of 1911–1912, 508

"the sick man of Europe," 509
Tanzimat, 512
Young Ottomans, 513
Sultan Abd al-Hamid II, 513
Young Turks, 513
Tokugawa Japan, 516
Meiji Restoration, 519
Russo-Japanese War, 523

Finding the Main Point

1. What major events and processes shaped Chinese history from the late eighteenth century to the early twentieth century?
2. How did the Ottoman experience during the nineteenth century parallel that of China, and how did it diverge from it?
3. In what ways was Japan's history in the nineteenth century shaped by its efforts to respond to European and American imperialism?
4. What measurements could be used when thinking about the success or failure of a state?

AP* Big Picture Questions

1. "The response of each society to European imperialism grew out of its larger historical development and its particular internal problems." What specific evidence might illustrate this statement?
2. Were deliberate government policies or historical circumstances more important in shaping the history of China, the Ottoman Empire, and Japan during the nineteenth century?
3. What kinds of debates, controversies, and conflicts were generated by European intrusion within each of the societies examined in this chapter?
4. **Looking Back** How did the experiences of China, the Ottoman Empire, and Japan compare with those of Latin America during the nineteenth century?

TRM **Suggested Responses to Questions**
You can find suggested responses to the Chapter Review questions in the Teacher's Resource Materials.

BUILDING AP® SKILLS

Claims and Evidence in Sources

It's incredibly important for students to know how to analyze and interpret primary sources for the AP® Exam because primary sources are part of Multiple-Choice Questions and at least one SAQ, as well as making up the documents in the DBQ. The "AP® Skills Workshop" explanation on understanding claims and evidence in primary sources on pages 528 to 531 would be good for students to read through. Consider having them read these pages and discuss the skills taught in them with a partner. You can also have them practice the skills from the workshop using Activity 1 (which would be a quick practice) or Activity 3 (which would be a longer practice) found on page 531.

Claims and Evidence in Primary Sources

As we mentioned in the previous workshop, history is a discipline built on the analysis of primary sources. In this workshop, we'll investigate the information in the source itself and think about what you should be looking for as you analyze the content of a primary source. More specifically, we will be focusing on how to use primary sources as evidence to support a historical claim. We will also discuss how to analyze visual primary sources such as photographs and cartoons.

UNDERSTANDING CLAIMS AND EVIDENCE IN PRIMARY SOURCES

In the previous workshop, we discussed sourcing, which is useful because it can inform our understanding of the content—the information in the primary source itself—and help uncover its historical significance. What is the source communicating directly and indirectly? If it is an argument, what is the claim? Why is the source useful or significant? Sourcing thus works hand in hand with an analysis of the content to build a full understanding of the source. When attempting to understand the content of a primary source document, **always read the source first**. The source may give you the location, time period, and usually some information about the author. This information will help orient your thinking when you begin to read and analyze the document.

When using a primary source as evidence, you will first want to read all the primary source documents for the information each gives you. Then, you will want to start putting the information that is useful as evidence into groups, each of which will be linked to a topic sentence that directly informs your claim. Once you have a general idea of what documentary evidence you want to put where, you will need to reread the documents for the sourcing nuances and add those to your argument. Especially on the Document-Based Question, the information you glean from the seven primary sources will form the basis of your argument and your counterargument. Don't forget, however, that you need to provide at least one piece of outside evidence (not found in the documents) to support your argument. You will also need outside information to contextualize the question, in both the Document-Based Question and Long Essay Question.

Using Inference to Identify Claims and Evidence

Historians draw conclusions about the historical significance of a source's content by using inference:

Inference: A general conclusion drawn from specific evidence

For instance, while the image titled "Carving Up the Pie of China" on page 496 does not say, "China was unable to stop industrialized nations from imperializing Chinese land," a historian could draw that conclusion by looking at this source created by a French cartoonist in 1898. The cartoon depicts caricatures representing different industrialized nations huddled over and dividing a pie that represents China, while a stereotypical caricature of

528

a weaponless Qing official in the background unsuccessfully attempts to stop this from happening.

We can also infer things about the motivations and relationships of the industrialized nations. The woman on the far left is Queen Victoria, representing Britain, and the man next to her is Kaiser Wilhelm, representing Germany. Their eyes are locked and knives are drawn, suggesting conflict regarding land claims in China between Britain and Germany.

The third person from the left is Czar Nicholas II, representing Russia, and the woman behind him represents France. With his knife drawn, Czar Nicholas seems to be looking at a specific piece of land, while France, standing behind him, does not appear to have any land claims in China. The closeness between these two caricatures and the depiction of her hand on his back suggest an alliance. On the far right, we see a caricature representing Japan; with his sword down, he appears to be thinking about which piece to take, illustrating Japan's imperialist intentions in China. When all of these parts are put together, we can infer that industrialized nations like Britain, Germany, Russia, and Japan wanted to imperialize parts of China and the Qing government was unable to prevent that encroachment.

In order to draw those inferences, we have to know some background information on what historical developments were occurring in China, Europe, and Japan in the late nineteenth century. We also want to think about HIPPY—historical situation, intended audience, point of view, purpose, and why or how—regarding the person creating the cartoon (in this case, a French cartoon artist). From there, we can begin to summarize what is happening in the document. This is the flip side of the sourcing skill you learned about in Chapter 8. We also use this skill to identify the limitations of the source. For example, although a painting of a samurai might tell us much about upper-class military culture, it would tell us nothing about the peasants who also lived at the time, other than presuming they would not have had the material wealth or social status displayed in the picture.

Using OPTIC to Identify Claims and Evidence

Visual images can be especially difficult to understand in terms of their content. One way to help structure your investigation of the content of a visual is with an acronym called OPTIC. OPTIC helps you observe the big picture and track the details.

Let's use OPTIC to analyze the photograph of a port in Constantinople on page 512. Let's walk through the information-gathering process and then infer what the painting is telling us.

O = Overview: This is where you tell what you see in the picture in general. So in this case, you would say you see a photograph of a busy port or harbor.

P = Parts: You look at all aspects of the picture, including the caption. There are ships in the harbor, with a large city in the background. There are many people who appear to be working. There is smoke billowing out of smokestacks on the right. There are horses attached to carriages waiting to transport something. Most of the people appear to be men, some in Turkish and others in Western styles of dress.

T = Title: The title of this photograph is "Ottoman Modernization." The title emphasizes the process that is occurring in the picture.

529

I = Interrelationships: Here we try to figure out how the parts relate to one another. Clearly this is a busy port city where commerce is occurring. The horses attached to carriages are waiting to transport the goods from the ships to Constantinople and beyond. The smokestacks on the right suggest that this area has industrialized, but most of the ships on the left do not appear to have steam engines, so perhaps this city is not fully industrialized. The fact that most of the men in this photograph are wearing pants also suggests that Constantinople is going through a process of westernization.

C = Conclusion: This photograph shows a bustling port in Constantinople in the 1890s and illustrates the process of modernization occurring in the Ottoman Empire. Capital acquired through commerce and trade could be used to further modernize the Ottoman Empire. The smokestacks, which illustrate industrialization, and the men wearing pants, which show westernization, further support the idea that the Ottoman Empire was attempting to modernize at the end of the nineteenth century.

PRIMARY SOURCES ON THE AP® WORLD HISTORY EXAM

Information garnered from primary sources will be tested heavily on the AP® Exam. Remember that the Multiple-Choice section contains a primary source as a stimulus for every set of four to five questions. The "easy" questions often ask for a main idea or a summary of a claim in the primary source. Questions about how historical context affects the document or how the document is affected by the time and place it was created (i.e., sourcing) are often more challenging. Additionally, one of the Short-Answer Questions will always be tied to a primary source. Many times, this source is visual, so inferencing is an important skill to know. Most importantly, the Document-Based Question (DBQ) expects you, the novice historian, to apply the skills of summarization, evidence gathering, sourcing, and inferencing as you weave seven documents into an argument addressing the prompt.

When you write the body paragraphs of the DBQ on the AP® Exam, you want to show that you understand the documents by summarizing them (do not use the exact same language from the documents), connecting them to support your arguments, analyzing the source using HIPPY, and offering relevant outside evidence not in the documents that helps answer the prompt.

Below is an outline for a body paragraph you can follow to maximize points on the DBQ. Remember that you want to have two to three body paragraphs in your essay.

Topic Sentence: One of the evidence groups from your thesis

Evidence:

- Summarize two to three documents to show understanding (paraphrase the documents)
- Connect two to three documents to your argument (show how they support the evidence group where you put them)

Analysis (HIPPY for two to three documents):

- Historical situation: What was going on at the time this document was created?
- Intended audience: Who was the document created for, and why?

530

- Purpose: Why was the document made? What did the author want to see happen from this document's creation?
- Point of view: How does this person's background connect to what they are saying?
- Why or how: Why or how is the source important to the argument?

Outside Information:

- Describe and connect outside information (proper nouns/specific facts) that is RELEVANT to the prompt

BUILDING AP® SKILLS

1. **Activity: Analyzing Evidence in a Written Primary Source.** Read the primary source below and then answer the following questions.

   > Every distinction or designation tending to make any class whatever of the subjects of my Empire inferior to another class, on account of their religion, language or race shall be forever effaced. . . . No subject of my Empire shall be hindered in the exercise of the religion that he professes. . . . All the subjects of my Empire, without distinction of nationality, shall be admissible to public employment.
   >
   > — Ottoman Imperial Proclamation of 1856

   a. Summarize the document to show understanding.
   b. Intended audience: Who was the document created for, and why?

2. **Activity: Analyzing a Visual Primary Source Using OPTIC.** Turn to page 514 and look at the Ottoman-era postcard that celebrates the short-lived constitutional period of 1876–1878. Using the table below, analyze the image using the OPTIC strategy we discussed above:

O = Overview	
P = Parts	
T = Title	
I = Interrelationships	
C = Conclusion	

3. **Activity: Creating an Argument Using Primary Sources as Evidence.** Using only the images in this chapter as evidence, write a claim and create the first body paragraph of an essay using the DBQ outline given above based on the prompt below. Be sure to summarize the image, connect it to support your argument, analyze the source using HIPPY, and describe relevant outside evidence that helps answer the prompt.

   Analyze the extent to which modernization programs changed politics and society in Asia in the period 1750–1900.

TRM Suggested Responses to Questions
You can find suggested responses to the Building AP® Skills questions in the Teacher's Resource Materials.

531

Critiquing Westernization:
A Cartoon from Meiji Japan

The political revolution known as the Meiji Restoration of 1868 replaced the shogunate that had ruled Japan for centuries with a new government headed directly by the emperor and committed to a thorough transformation of the country. Particularly among the young, there was an acute awareness of the need to create a new culture that could support a revived Japan and deal with the impingement of Western powers. "We have no history," declared one of these students; "our history begins today."[19]

In this context much that was Western was enthusiastically embraced. The technological side of this borrowing contributed significantly to Japan's remarkable industrialization and was the most obvious expression of westernization. But this borrowing also extended to more purely cultural matters. Eating beef became popular, despite Buddhist objections. Many men adopted Western hairstyles and grew beards, even though the facial hair of Westerners had earlier been portrayed as ugly. In 1872, Western dress was ordered for all official ceremonies.

However, not everyone in Japan was so enthusiastic about the adoption of Western culture. Indeed, beginning in the late 1870s and continuing into the next decade, numerous essays and images satirized the apparently indiscriminate fascination with all things Western. The image entitled Monkey-show reproduced here represents that point of view. Published in 1879, this cartoon was created by Honda Kinkichiro (1850–1921), a Japanese artist who specialized in Western-style painting and taught at the Tokyo Military Academy.

HONDA KINKICHIRO | *Monkey-show* | 1879

Monkey-show.
All the monkeys dressed in European style, and in every respect trying to ape Foreigners.

1 A FIRST LOOK

Begin your analysis by carefully examining the visual elements of the image to better understand the scene created by Honda and those elements of westernization that are the focus of his cartoon. While doing so, answer the following questions:

1. What is going on in this image?

2. What specific aspects of Japan's efforts at westernization is the artist mocking?

2 A SECOND LOOK

Cartoons are often accompanied by captions or other text intended to help the viewer interpret the visual elements of the source. In this case, Honda has included captions in both English and Japanese. Examine the English caption and answer the following:

1. What does the caption add to your understanding of the cartoon?

2. How specifically in his drawing does Honda reinforce the monkey-show theme expressed in the caption?

3. Why might Honda have included a caption in English for his cartoon?

Political cartoons can offer an interesting perspective on historical events for students to study and analyze that they may not get from more traditional images, like paintings or photographs. This would be a good place to have students analyze a political cartoon about the adoption of Western culture in Japan during the Meiji Restoration. Have students study Honda Kinkichiro's cartoon on page 533 and answer the questions under "A First Look" on their own. Then partner students up to share their answers to the first set of questions and to work together on answering the questions under "A Second Look." Once they are finished with those questions, combine the partner pairs into groups of four to work through the questions under "A Third Look" on page 534.

533

BUILDING AP® SKILLS

Sourcing and Situation

Students should continually practice writing sourcing statements throughout the year to build on this skill for the DBQ. You could use the "AP® Activity: Using Visual Sources as Evidence" on this page to get students to work on writing a sourcing statement for Honda Kinkichiro's cartoon.

BUILDING AP® SKILLS

Making Connections: Comparison

If you want to have students work on the skill of Comparison and have them practice the skills learned in the "AP® Skills Workshop" on pages 528–531, consider having them complete the "Further Activity" on this page. You could have students work on their own or with a partner to analyze the three images listed in the activity and write a comparison argument about the viewpoints expressed by the images.

---

3 A THIRD LOOK

Finally, let's consider the caption in Japanese, which reads in part as follows: "Mr. Morse [an American zoologist who introduced Darwin's theory of evolution to Japan in 1877] explains that all human beings were monkeys in the beginning. In the beginning—but even now aren't we still monkeys? When it comes to Western things we think the red beards are the most skillful at everything."[20] While analyzing the caption, answer the following questions:

1. What does this caption add to your understanding of the cartoon? Does it influence your interpretation of the English caption?

2. Why might the artist have used a Western scientific theory (Darwinian evolution) to criticize excessive westernization in Japan?

AP® ACTIVITY USING VISUAL SOURCES AS EVIDENCE

Historians frequently use visual sources as evidence to support their arguments. In this activity, you will use Honda's cartoon to support this thesis: "By the late 1870s some in Japan had come to oppose the indiscriminate copying of Western culture." First, in a sentence or two, create a sourcing statement that introduces Honda's cartoon and the historical situation in which it was created. You may want to use material from "The Japanese Difference: The Rise of a New East Asian Power" (page 515) when creating this sourcing statement. Then in another sentence or two, identify specific evidence from the cartoon—its illustration or captions—that provide evidence in support of the thesis. Be sure to explain to your reader how these specific elements support the thesis.

FURTHER ACTIVITY

Honda's cartoon was just one of many images created by Japanese artists in the second half of the nineteenth century that touch upon Japan's relationship with the West. The images "The Black Ships of the United States" on page 518 and "Japan's Political Modernization" on page 521 offer two further perspectives. Analyze these two images using the approaches and techniques that you employed in analyzing Honda's cartoon. Then summarize in a few paragraphs the variety of viewpoints expressed by these three images using specific features of the visual sources as evidence.

The Opium War

The Opium War of 1840–1842 marked a dramatic turn in China's long history and in its relationship with the wider world. It also indicated the new kinds of cross-cultural encounters that were increasingly taking place as Europe's global power mounted. The seven documents in this section of the chapter allow us to follow the unfolding of that encounter, largely from a Chinese point of view.

By the early nineteenth century, China had long enjoyed a position of unrivaled dominance in East Asia. Furthermore, its wealth and technological innovations had given it a major role in the world economy of the early modern era, reflected in the flow of much of the world's silver into China. At the same time, the island nation of Great Britain was emerging as a major global economic and military power, thanks to its position as the first site of the Industrial Revolution and its increasingly dominant role in India.

At the heart of the emerging conflict between these two countries was trade rather than territory. From the British point of view, the problem lay in the sharp restrictions that the Chinese had long imposed on commerce between the two nations. The British were permitted to trade only in a single city, Canton, and even there they had to deal with an officially approved group of Chinese merchants. This so-called Canton system meant that Europeans had no direct access to the Chinese market. Thus in the early 1790s, the British government sent a major diplomatic mission to China, headed by Lord George Macartney, to seek greater access to the Chinese market.

LOOKING AHEAD

AP DBQ PRACTICE

Evaluate the impact of imperialism in China during the period 1750–1900.

DOCUMENT 1 Macartney Mission

Macartney's mission to China represented a cultural encounter between two civilizations. It included extensive negotiations about the rituals that would accompany Macartney's audience with the Chinese emperor. Hoping to impress the Chinese with British science and technology, Macartney brought telescopes, clocks, weapons, textiles, and other examples of British achievements. He had been instructed to provide the Chinese with "assurances of His Majesty's friendly and pacific inclinations towards the Emperor, and his respect for the reputed mildness of his Administration." Document 1 provides a further excerpt from those instructions.

TRM Suggested Responses to Questions
You can find suggested responses to the AP® Working with Evidence questions in the Teacher's Resource Materials.

BUILDING AP® SKILLS

Claims and Evidence in Sources

Interpreting text-based as well as non-text-based sources is an important skill for AP® World History: Modern students. If time is available, have students investigate the impact of imperialism in China from 1750 to 1900 by using the evidence in "The Opium War" beginning on page 535. Consider having students analyze one or more of the sources found on pages 535–541. Check for understanding by:

■ Using the questions at the end of each source as a discussion starting point.

■ Pairing students to analyze (identify and describe) using author/creator's point of view, purpose, historical situation, and/or audience. This activity can continue to reinforce sourcing.

■ Assigning a source to a group of three or four students and having them present an overview of the source along with the sourcing to the rest of the class.

■ Having students practice an AP® skill of their choice by using one of the activities under "AP® Doing History" on page 542.

Source: Lord Macartney's Commission from Henry Dundas, 1792.

It is necessary you should be on your Guard against one stipulation which, perhaps, will be demanded from you: which is that of the exclusion of the trade of opium from the Chinese dominions as being prohibited by the Laws of the Empire; if this subject should come into discussion, it must be handled with the greatest circumspection. It is beyond a doubt that no inconsiderable portion of the opium raised within our Indian territories actually finds its way to China: but if it should be made a positive requisition or any article of any proposed commercial treaty, that none of that drug should be sent by us to China, you must accede to it, rather than risk any essential benefit by contending for a liberty in this respect in which case the sale of our opium in Bengal must be left to take its chance in an open market, or to find a consumption in the dispersed and circuitous traffic of the eastern Seas.

A due sense of wisdom and justice of the King of Great Britain, which it will be your business to impress, as well as of the wealth and power of this Country, and of the genius and knowledge of its People, may naturally lead to a preferable acceptance of a treaty of friendship and alliance with us, as most worthy of themselves; and in a political light, as most likely to be useful to them, from our naval force, being the only assistance of which they may foresee the occasional importance to them.

Question to Consider: Why do you think Macartney was instructed to agree to the ending of opium imports if it was necessary to achieve a commercial treaty with China?

AP Analyzing Sources: How does the point of view of the source impact how we interpret the document?

DOCUMENT 2 A Chinese Response to Lord Macartney

Despite a polite reception at the Chinese court, Macartney's mission was an almost total failure from the British point of view. At its conclusion the Chinese emperor Qianlong sent a message to the British monarch George III replying to Macartney's requests.

Source: Emperor Qianlong, "Message to King George III," 1793.

Yesterday your Ambassador petitioned my Ministers to memorialize me regarding your trade with China, but his proposal is not consistent with our dynastic usage and cannot be entertained. Hitherto, all European nations, including your own country's barbarian merchants, have carried on their trade with our Celestial Empire at Canton. Such has been the procedure for many years, although our Celestial Empire possesses all things in prolific abundance and lacks no product within its own borders. There was therefore no need to import the manufacturers of outside barbarians in exchange for our own produce. But as the tea, silk, and porcelain which the Celestial Empire produces are absolute necessities to European nations and to yourselves, we have permitted, as a signal mark of favor, that foreign *hongs* should be established at Canton, so that your wants might be supplied and your country thus participate in our beneficence.

But your Ambassador has now put forward new requests which completely fail to recognize the Throne's principle to "treat strangers from afar with indulgence," and to exercise a pacifying control over barbarian tribes, the world over. Moreover, our dynasty, swaying the myriad races of the globe, extends the same benevolence toward all. Your England is not the only nation trading at Canton. If other nations, following your bad example, wrongfully importune my ear with further impossible requests, how will it be possible for me to treat them with easy indulgence? Nevertheless, I do not forget the lonely remoteness of your island, cut off from the world by intervening wastes of sea, nor do I overlook your excusable ignorance of the usages of our Celestial Empire. I have consequently commanded my Ministers to enlighten your Ambassador on the subject, and have ordered the departure of the mission.

"Edict on Trade with Great Britain," in J. O. P. Brand, *Annals and Memoirs of the Court of Peking* (Boston: Houghton Mifflin, 1914), 325–31.

Question to Consider: What does this document reveal about the Chinese view of trade in general?

AP **Analyzing Sources:** In what historical context does the Chinese emperor understand Macartney's mission?

DOCUMENT 3 Debating the Opium Problem

Fearing aggression from revolutionary France, Great Britain made no immediate response to China's 1793 rebuff. But in the several decades following Napoleon's 1815 defeat, the issue reemerged. This time the question was not just trade in general but opium in particular. By the early nineteenth century, that addictive drug was providing a solution to another of Great Britain's problems in its trade relations with China — the difficulty of finding Western goods that the Chinese were willing to buy. This had long meant that the British had to pay for much-desired Chinese products with major exports of silver. Now, however, opium grown in British India proved increasingly attractive in China, and imports soared.

But this solution to a British problem had by the mid-1830s provoked a growing and many-sided crisis for China. The country's legal prohibition on the importing of opium was widely ignored, silver was flowing out of the country to pay for the drug, and addiction was increasing, even among the elite. This dire situation prompted the Chinese emperor Daoguang to seek advice from his senior officials. The responses he received revealed the sharp division within Chinese official circles, with one side advocating legalization and the other counseling suppression. In the memorandum reproduced here, Xu Naiji makes the case for the legalization of opium.

537

Source: Xu Naiji, an argument for opium legalization, 1836.

Xu Naiji, Vice-President of the Sacrificial Court, presents the following memorial in regard to opium, to show that the more severe the interdicts against it are made, the more widely the evils arising therefrom spread.

It will be found, on examination, that the smokers of opium are idle, lazy vagrants, having no useful purpose before them, and are unworthy of regard or even of contempt. And though there are smokers to be found who have overstepped the threshold of age, yet they do not attain to the long life of other men. But new births are daily increasing the population of the empire; and there is no cause to apprehend a diminution therein; while, on the other hand, we cannot adopt too great, or too early, precautions against the annual waste which is taking place in the resources, the very substance of China.

Since then, it will not answer to close our ports against [all trades], and since the laws issued against opium are quite inoperative, the only method left is to revert to the former system, to permit the barbarian merchants to import opium paying duty thereon as a medicine, and to require that, after having passed the Custom-House, it shall be delivered to the Hong merchants only in exchange for merchandise, and that no money be paid for it. The barbarians finding that the amount of dues to be paid on it, is less than what is now spent in bribes, will also gladly comply therein. Foreign money should be placed on the same footing with sycee silver, and the exportation of it should be equally prohibited. Offenders, when caught, should be punished by the entire destruction of the opium they may have, and the confiscation of the money that may be found with them. . . .

It becomes my duty, then, to request that it be enacted, that any officer, scholar, or soldier, found guilty of secretly smoking opium, shall be immediately dismissed from public employ, without being made liable to any other penalty.

"Memorial from Heu-Naetse," in *Blue Book—Correspondence Relating to China* (London, 1840), 56–59.

Question to Consider: Why does Xu Naiji believe that legalization of opium is the best course of action for the Chinese emperor?

AP Analyzing Sources: What is the purpose of the source?

DOCUMENT 4 The Case against the Legalization of Opium

At about the same time that Xu Naiji expressed his support for the legalization of opium, another high official, Yuan Yulin, put forward the case for its suppression. He laid out his thinking in this memo written in response to Emperor Daoguang's request for advice.

Source: Yuan Yulin, an argument for opium suppression, 1836.

I, your minister, believe that the success or failure in government and the prosperity or decay of administration depend largely upon our capacity to distinguish between right and wrong, between what is safe and what is dangerous.

Uniformity is the most important element in the decrees of the Court. Now it has been proposed that the prohibition of opium-smoking would reach the officers of the Government,

538

the scholars, and the military, but not the common people. But it is forgotten that the common people of today will be the officers, scholars, and the military of the future. Should they be allowed to smoke at first and then be prohibited from it in the future? Moreover, the officers, scholars, and the military of today may be degraded to the rank of the common people. In that case, are they to be freed from the prohibition once imposed on them? Prohibition was proclaimed because opium is pernicious. It follows then that the ban should not be abolished until it ceases to be an evil. A partial prohibition or partial legalization is a confusion of rules by the government itself; consequently good faith in its observance can hardly be expected. When the law was all for prohibition, decrees had not been followed. How can the people respect the restrictions or punishments should the law be in confusion? The logical consequence will be the ruin of government and demoralization of our culture.

"Memorial from Yuan Yu-lin," in P. C. Kuo, *A Critical Study of the First Anglo-Chinese War* (Shanghai: Commercial Press, 1935), 211–13.

Question to Consider: What issue does Yulin have with current policy regarding opium in China?

AP Analyzing Sources: What impact does the position of Yuan Yulin have on how we interpret the source?

DOCUMENT 5 A Moral Appeal to Queen Victoria

The Chinese emperor soon decided this debate in favor of suppression and sent a prominent official, Commissioner Lin Zexu, to enforce it. Lin did so vigorously, seizing and destroying millions of pounds of the drug, flushing it out to the sea with a prayer to the local spirit: "[You] who wash away all stains and cleanse all impurities." At the same time (1839), Lin wrote a letter to the British monarch, Queen Victoria, appealing for her assistance in ending this noxious trade.

Source: Chinese Commissioner Lin Zexu, letter to Queen Victoria, 1839.

A communication: magnificently our great Emperor soothes and pacifies China and the foreign countries, regarding all with the same kindness. If there is profit, then he shares it with the people of the world; if there is harm, then he removes it on behalf of the world. We find that your country is sixty or seventy thousand *li* from China. Yet there are barbarian ships that strive to come here for trade for the purpose of making a great profit. The wealth of China is used to profit the barbarians. By what right do they use this poisonous drug to injure the Chinese people?

Let us ask, where is your conscience? I have heard that the smoking of opium is very strictly forbidden by your country; that is because the harm caused by opium is clearly understood. Since it is not permitted to do harm to your country, then even less should you let it be passed on to the harm of other countries—how much less to China! Of all that China exports to foreign countries, there is not a single thing which is not beneficial to people: they are of benefit when eaten, or of benefit when used, or of benefit when resold: all are beneficial. Is there a single article from China which has done any harm to foreign countries? Take tea and rhubarb, for example; the foreign countries cannot get along for a single day without them.

539

If China cuts off these benefits with no sympathy for those who are to suffer, then what can the barbarians rely upon to keep themselves alive? On the other hand, articles coming from the outside to China can only be used as toys. We can take them or get along without them. Nevertheless our Celestial Court lets tea, silk, and other goods be shipped without limit and circulated everywhere without begrudging it in the slightest. This is for no other reason but to share the benefit with the people of the whole world.

Dun J. Li, ed., *China in Transition, 1517–1911* (London: Wadsworth, 1969), 64–67.

Question to Consider: What assumptions about the West does this letter reveal? Which were accurate, and which represented misunderstandings?

AP Analyzing Sources: How does the intended audience impact the source?

DOCUMENT 6 **War and Defeat**

While Queen Victoria and British authorities apparently never received Commissioner Lin's letter and certainly did not respond to it, they did react to the commissioner's actions. Citing the importance of free trade and the violation of British property rights, they launched a major military expedition in which their steamships and heavy guns reflected the impact of the Industrial Revolution on the exercise of British power. This was the first Opium War, and the Chinese lost it badly. One prominent scholar has described it as "the most decisive reversal the Manchus [Qing dynasty] had ever received." The Treaty of Nanjing, which ended that conflict in 1842, was largely imposed by the British. It was the first of many "unequal treaties" that China was required to sign with various European powers and the United States in the decades that followed. While Chinese authorities tried to think about the treaty as a means of "subduing and conciliating" the British, as they had done with other "barbarian" intruders, it represented in fact a new, much diminished, and dependent position for China on the world stage.

Source: *The Treaty of Nanjing*, concluding the first Opium War between the Chinese and the British, 1842.

I. There shall henceforward be peace and friendship between Her Majesty the Queen of the United Kingdom of Great Britain and Ireland and His Majesty the Emperor of China, and between their respective subjects, who shall enjoy full security and protection for their persons and property within the dominions of the other.

II. His Majesty the Emperor of China agrees, that British subjects, with their families and establishments, shall be allowed to reside, for the purposes of carrying on their mercantile pursuits, without molestation or restraint, at the cities and towns of Canton, Amoy, Foochowfoo, Ningpo, and Shanghai. . . .

IV. The Emperor of China agrees to pay the sum of 6,000,000 of dollars, as the value of the opium which was delivered up at Canton in the month of March, 1839, as a ransom for the lives of Her Britannic Majesty's Superintendent and subjects, who had been imprisoned and threatened with death by the Chinese High Officers.

Question to Consider: What provisions of the treaty most clearly challenged traditional Chinese understandings of their place in the world?

AP® Analyzing Sources: What historical events of the period help provide context for the source?

DOCUMENT 7 Addiction to Opium

Throughout the nineteenth century, opium imports created a massive addiction problem in China, as this photograph of an opium den from around 1900 suggests. Not until the early twentieth century did the British prove willing to curtail the opium trade from their Indian colony.

Source: Photograph of men in an opium den in China, ca. 1900.

Hulton Deutsch/Getty Images

Question to Consider: What does this image show of the societal effect of opium in China during the period?

AP® Analyzing Sources: How does the context of China during the period impact how we interpret the image?

541

AP® DOING HISTORY

1. **DBQ Practice:** Evaluate the impact of imperialism in China during the period 1750–1900.

2. **Argumentation:** "The Opium War was about more than opium." How would you support or challenge this statement?

3. **Contextualization:** In what ways might the Opium War be regarded as a clash of cultures? In what respects might it be seen as a clash of interests? Was it an inevitable conflict, or were there missed opportunities for avoiding it?

4. **Comparison:** In the context of British and Chinese views of the world, how do you understand the Treaty of Nanjing? Which country's view of the world is more clearly reflected in that treaty?

5. **Claims and Evidence in Sources:** Based on these documents, how well or how poorly did the Chinese and the British understand one another? How might you account for their misunderstandings?

The Sino-Japanese War of 1894–1895

The war between China and Japan during 1894–1895, fought largely over control of Korea, signaled a radical reversal in the historical relationship of these two East Asian countries. It also marked major turning points in the internal development of both countries. Voice 9.1, from two Chinese historians, David Atwill and Yurong Atwill, describes the significance of that war for China, while historian James Huffman does the same for Japan in Voice 9.2.

VOICE 9.1

David Atwill and Yurong Atwill on the Significance of the War for China | 2010

[N]o military loss affected the Qing court and the Chinese populace quite as much as their defeat at the hands of the Japanese. . . . For centuries China had sat at the center of a vast tributary network, with neighboring countries acknowledging China's dominant military, political and commercial importance. . . . Contemporary observers all assumed Japan would be defeated quickly. It was a horrible shock to China when Japan not only routed Chinese troops dispatched to Korea, but with devastating precision devastated China's navy. These defeats dealt a savage blow to China's national pride. . . .

If the war eroded China's confidence, the peace was excruciating. With the Treaty of Shimonoseki, Japan proved itself fully as capable as its European counterparts at extracting concessions, indemnities, and territories. The Chinese public, who had been sheltered from the Qing's lack of military modernization, were whipped into a frenzy over the defeats and were further enraged at [China's] submissive acceptance of Japan's peace terms. While the Qing dynasty survived for another fifteen years, it would never recover psychologically from the humiliation it received at the hands of the Japanese. This truly marks the beginning of the end for the Qing dynasty.

Source: David G. Atwill and Yurong Y. Atwill, *Sources in Chinese History* (Upper Saddle River, NJ: Prentice Hall, 2010), 89–90.

VOICE 9.2

James L. Huffman on the Significance of the War for Japan | 2010

More important than the victory . . . was the explosion of patriotic fervor the war ignited at home. "The excitement generated among the Japanese people was beyond imagination," the commentator Ubukata Toshiro recalled. . . . By war's end, Japan had become a different place; proud of defeating Asia's giant, confident in its military might, thirsty for more territory.

The postwar years saw a rush of support for this vision of strength, even as Japan's cities became both modern and massive. . . . In part, that reflected a rise in industry—and city jobs—as the Sino-Japanese War indemnity poured more than 300 million yen into the economy. . . . When Japan provided roughly half of the international force that put down China's Boxer Rebellion in 1900, and then shared handsomely in the indemnity, the pride that had marked the Sino-Japanese War was reignited.

Source: James L. Huffman, *Japan in World History* (Oxford: Oxford University Press, 2010), 86, 88.

AP Analyzing Secondary Sources

1. In what ways was the Sino-Japanese War devastating for China?

2. What impact did the Sino-Japanese War have on Japan?

3. **Integrating Primary and Secondary Sources:** Write a paragraph about China's declining fortunes that integrates evidence from Document 6 and Voice 9.1.

You can use this exercise to help students work on improving their analysis skills with secondary sources. Consider having students read both of the sources on the Sino-Japanese War of 1894–1895 and answer Questions 1–3 found on page 543. Discuss their answers as a class. This activity can help students practice reading and interpreting secondary sources on the MCQ and SAQ sections of the exam.

TRM Suggested Responses to Questions
You can find suggested responses to the AP® Analyzing Secondary Sources questions in the Teacher's Resource Materials.

543

Multiple-Choice Questions   Choose the correct answer for each question.

Questions 1–3 refer to this passage.

> We have heard that in your own country opium is prohibited with the utmost strictness
> and severity:—this is a strong proof that you know full well how hurtful opium is to
> humans. . . . You ought not to have this harmful drug transferred to another country, and
> above all others, how much less to us! . . . Has China ever sent you a noxious product
> from its soil? No. But the things that come from your country are only calculated to
> harm our country.
>
> — Qing government commissioner Lin Zexu to Queen Victoria of Great Britain, 1839

1. Based on your knowledge of world history and this excerpt, which of the following best describes
   a result of the Opium Wars between Great Britain and China in the early nineteenth century?
   a. Because of its decisive victory, China was able to renegotiate a more equal trade agreement
      with Britain.
   b. China lost her place as a major economic power because of the total destruction of her land
      in the war.
   c. China and Britain were able to maintain an equal balance of trade for the remainder of the
      nineteenth century.
   d. Because of unequal treaties, European imperial powers carved out spheres of influence in
      China.

2. Which of the following best explains the purpose of Lin Zexu's letter to Queen Victoria?
   a. A request to create a more balanced trade relationship between Britain and China
   b. A plea for the importation of only necessary household goods into China
   c. A demand for the British to stop importing opium into China
   d. A threat to stop all trade with Europe if certain demands were not met

3. Rebellions in China, such as the Taiping Uprising and the Boxer Uprising, were a response to
   a. European powers' colonial takeover of China's government.
   b. continued foreign economic involvement in China and a weakening Qing government.
   c. the increased involvement of China in interregional trade with Japan and Russia.
   d. the perceived weakness of Europe because of World War I.

544

Questions 4–6 refer to this map.

Taiping Uprising, 1853–1863
Nian Rebellion, 1853–1868
Boxer Uprising, 1898–1901
Muslim revolts, 1855–1873

China and the World in the Nineteenth Century

4. The expansion of nineteenth-century European empires into Asia was most likely the result of which of these historical processes?

   a. European industrialization

   b. The rise of communism

   c. The spread of Enlightenment ideas

   d. The creation of military alliances

5. Based on the map and your knowledge of world history, what conclusion about Asian reactions to imperialism in the late nineteenth and early twentieth centuries is most accurate?

a. Most groups in Asia welcomed European colonization.

b. Some groups actively resisted European powers, while some chose to work with the colonial governments.

c. Most Asian groups accepted European rule, unlike groups in the Americas, who fought European incursions in the sixteenth century.

d. Most elites in both Asia and the Americas rejected European rule and led rebellions against Europeans.

6. Which of these comparisons between European expansion in the Americas in the sixteenth century (Chapter 4) and Asia in the late nineteenth and early twentieth centuries is most accurate?

a. There was a greater number of settler colonies in Asia than in the Americas.

b. European imperialism in Asia was mainly focused on economics, but in the Americas imperial powers mainly focused on religion.

c. There was resistance to European imperialism in Asia but not in the Americas.

d. Spain and Portugal played a large role in Latin American expansion, but their role lessened in Asia by the beginning of the twentieth century.

Short-Answer Questions

Read each question carefully and write a short response. Use complete sentences.

1. **Use the passage below and your knowledge of world history to answer all parts of the question that follows.**

> A consequence of intellectual borrowing from Europe [in the mid-nineteenth century] was the emergence of a distinguished group of intellectuals who hoped for an ideal society quite different from the one they inhabited. For conservative Ottoman leaders, this was an awful outcome. Nevertheless, this transformation of Ottoman intellectuals who were exposed to western thinking was a catalyst for social change.
> — M. Sukru Hanioglu, *The Young Turks in Opposition* (Studies in Middle Eastern History), 1995

A. Identify ONE piece of historical evidence that would support the author's main argument.

B. Describe ONE example of political modernization or westernization by the Ottoman Empire in the nineteenth century.

C. Explain ONE effect of the changes described by the author.

2. **Use your knowledge of world history to answer all parts of the question that follows.**

A. Explain ONE cause of European imperialism in Asia in the nineteenth century.

B. Explain ONE example of Asian accommodations to European imperialism in the nineteenth century.

C. Explain ONE example of Asian resistance to European imperialism in the nineteenth century.

BUILDING AP® SKILLS

Argumentation

AP® World History: Modern writing skills need to be practiced on a regular basis. You can use the SAQs on pages 546 and 547 for students to write an "exit ticket" at the end of class to check for understanding. You can also use the SAQs for more traditional timed writing practice, either by spreading the three SAQs across several days or as practice for the AP® Exam by writing them all at once. Make certain that students have the correct amount of time for this exercise. On exam day, students will have a total of 40 minutes to write three SAQs. If you are having them write only one at a time, you'll need to give them about 14 minutes to write it.

3. Use the image and your knowledge of world history to answer all parts of the question that
   follows.

A Russian bear and an English lion fight over the dead dragon labeled "China," while the United States,
Japan, and several European nations look on. From the American satirical magazine *Puck*, 1900.

A. Describe ONE cause that led to the historical situation shown in the image.

B. Explain ONE effect of the historical situation shown in the image.

C. Explain ONE way in which the historical situation shown is similar to that of another state in
   the nineteenth century.

10

Colonial Encounters in Asia, Africa, and Oceania
1750–1950

AP® Overview for Chapter 10

Chapter 10 corresponds with AP® Unit 6: Consequences of Industrialization, 1750–1900. This chapter explores the tighter web of connections brought by the second great wave of colonial expansion in the nineteenth century. The legacies of imperialism have had profound effects on the twentieth and twenty-first centuries. Since the experience of imperialism has shaped ideology, a clear study of it is necessary to understand the causes, effects, and continuity and change from earlier versions of empire building and colonization.

Chapter 10 Essential Activity

The age of imperialism offers a great opportunity for students to work with their sourcing skills on documents representing differing points of view, which students can struggle with throughout the year. The OER Project's activity "Sourcing: Differing Perspectives on Imperialism" offers students an interesting way to work on sourcing and to gain a better understanding of how point of view can affect an author's work. This activity has students compare the perspectives of two European figures on imperialism and walks them through analyzing the documents using point of view, purpose, and significance. You can find the detailed instructions to the activity on the OER Project's World History: AP® curriculum in Unit 6, Topic 6.1: State Expansion and Economic Imperialism.

Chapter 10 Resources

- **TRM** AP® Skills Workshop Activity Handout: Claims and Evidence in Secondary Sources
- **TRM** Chapter 10 DBQ Activity Handout
- **TRM** Chapter 10 Guided Reading
- **TRM** Chapter 10 Lecture Presentation Slides
- **TRM** Chapter 10 Outline
- **TRM** Chapter 10 Suggested Responses to Questions
- **TRM** Eric's Activity 10: Comparing Colonial Systems
- **TRM** Handout 10.1: Continuity and Change Chart for First-Wave and Second-Wave European Conquests

- **TRM** Handout 10.2: Chart for Colonial Powers in Early Twentieth-Century Colonial Asia
- **TRM** Handout 10.3: Chart for Colonial Powers in Early Twentieth-Century Colonial Africa
- **TRM** Handout 10.4: Causation Chart for Imperialism
- **TRM** Handout 10.5: Chart for Anti-Imperial Movements
- **TRM** Handout 10.6: Chart for Nineteenth-Century Indentured Servitude through Documents
- **TRM** Writing Organizer for DBQ

Pacing Guide

Below is a pacing guide for the AP® World History: Modern course beginning in ca. 1200 C.E. This pacing guide is based on a schedule with 120 sessions of 50 minutes each before the AP® Exam. It is meant as a place to start. If you have a different number of sessions before the exam, you can modify the pacing to suit your needs.

Day	Pages Assigned	AP® Topic	AP® Theme	Suggested Assignments	Coverage Notes
1	Read pages 549–556 to "A Second Wave of European Conquests"	6.1	CDI	Teaching Idea: Bell Ringer on page 548 Building AP® Skills: Contextualization on page 550 Building AP® Skills: Claims and Evidence in Sources on page 554	The opening to Chapter 10 is a good transition from the Industrial Revolution to European imperialism in the nineteenth century. This can help give students contextualization to this second "wave" of European expansion. It also gives a good overview of motivations for imperialism in the nineteenth century.
2	Read pages 556–561 through "A Second Wave of European Conquests"	6.2	GOV	Chapter 10 Essential Activity Apply the Tip on page 557 Building AP® Skills: Making Connections: Continuity and Change on page 557	European imperialism goes through two "waves" in world history from 1450 to the present. To help students understand the differences between these "waves" of European imperialism, briefly review and compare what they learned in Chapters 5 and 6 to this section of Chapter 10. Make sure to note the different forms of imperialism in this time period and the new imperial states that arose.
3	Read pages 562–566 from "Under European Rule" to "Ways of Working: Comparing Colonial Economies"	6.2 6.3	GOV	Teaching Idea: Bell Ringer on page 562 Exploring AP® Themes: GOV on page 563 Exploring AP® Themes: SIO on page 564	Students may not understand that people in conquered countries reacted in a variety of ways to European imperialism. Have them work on their comparison skills by looking at the different reactions discussed in this chapter. If students need DBQ practice, consider incorporating the documents from the AP® World History 2009 DBQ into their study of this section.
4	Read pages 566–569 in "Ways of Working: Comparing Colonial Economies"	6.4 6.5	ENV ECN	Building AP® Skills: Argumentation on page 566 Exploring AP® Themes: ECN on page 568	Imperialism and industrialization caused major changes to the global economy, local economies, and labor systems in the nineteenth century. Students can work on their Continuity and Change skills by looking at how these three topics change from the 1450–1750 era to the nineteenth century.
5	Read pages 570–575 to "Believing and Belonging: Identity and Cultural Change"	6.4 6.5 6.6	ENV ECN	AP® Classroom: AP® Topic Questions on page 571 Apply the Tip on page 572 Building AP® Skills: Argumentation on page 574	See above. This section also discusses migration in the nineteenth century, which you may want to combine with the section on migration in Chapter 8.
6	Read pages 575–582 from "Believing and Belonging: Identity and Cultural Change" to "'Race' and 'Tribe'"	6.3	GOV CUL	Teaching Idea: Incorporating Outside Resources on page 576 Building AP® Skills: Contextualization on page 578 Teaching Idea: Class Discussion on page 581	Along with bringing about major economic changes, nineteenth-century imperialism caused cultural changes in conquered societies. Make sure students know these changes and the differing reactions conquered peoples had to them.
7	Read pages 582–585 from "'Race' and 'Tribe'" through "Conclusions and Reflections"	6.3	GOV SOC	Building AP® Skills: Making Connections: Causation on page 583 Teaching Idea: Exit Slip on page 585 Eric's Activity 10: Comparing Colonial Systems on page 585	See above.

Bell Ringer

An interesting way to start this chapter and AP® Unit 6: Consequences of Industrialization with students could be to ask: Could imperialism be considered a change from previous mechanisms of state building? If so, how? *Imperialism continues the pattern of empire building, with expansion of one civilization into another and with stronger nations conquering the weaker and less technologically advanced. During this period, the process intensified; the emergent industrial economies of European countries made imperialism more aggressive.*

EXPLORING AP® THEMES

Governance (GOV)

You can help students work on their image analysis skills by displaying the painting "The Imperial Durbar of 1903" from this page and ask them: How does the painting reflect imperialism? *The British couple on the leading elephant are the viceroy of India and his wife. This painting represents the British Raj. The viceroy and his wife sit in an elaborate seat, while an Indian man protects them from the sun. The front elephant is draped in gold, while the elephants of the Indian leaders are not. The British officials also have more foot escorts.*

The Imperial Durbar of 1903 To mark the coronation of British monarch Edward VII and his installation as the emperor of India, colonial authorities in India mounted an elaborate assembly, or durbar. The durbar was intended to showcase the splendor of the British Empire, and its pageantry included sporting events; a state ball; a huge display of Indian arts, crafts, and jewels; and an enormous parade in which a long line of British officials and Indian princes passed by on bejeweled elephants. (TopFoto)

548

CHAPTER 10

Colonial Encounters in Asia, Africa, and Oceania

1750–1950

◀ **AP**

CLAIMS AND EVIDENCE IN SOURCES
How did the kind of pageantry depicted in this painting contribute to maintaining British rule in India?

CONNECTING PAST AND PRESENT

"We will now . . . officially call these events what they were from today's perspective: a genocide, without sparing or glossing over them."[1] This was a statement by the German foreign minister in May 2021 about a mass slaughter of Africans during the first decade of the twentieth century in what was then the German colony of Southwest Africa. It was, according to many scholars, the first genocide of the twentieth century. At that time, the German military commander in the colony, seeking to suppress a rebellion by the Herero and Nama peoples, had declared that "every Herero, with or without a gun, with or without cattle, will be shot. I will no longer accept [spare] women and children."[2] Some 80 percent of the Herero people and perhaps 50 percent of the Nama perished in that suppression. Since the colony's independence in 1990 as the African state of Namibia, its government has pressed Germany for a recognition of what happened, a formal apology, and compensation. After long negotiations, the Germany government finally agreed to acknowledge its actions as "genocide," to apologize, and to contribute $1.3 billion in development assistance over the next thirty years. Critics in Namibia and elsewhere remained dissatisfied because the Germans did not commit to "reparations" as they had done for Jewish victims of the Holocaust. Thus the colonial past continues to echo in both Germany and Namibia more than a century later. ■

Between roughly 1775 and the mid-twentieth century, foreign rule by Western Europeans, Russians, or Americans was a major new experience for many millions of Africans, Asians, and Pacific islanders. Unlike those living in China, the Ottoman Empire, Japan, or Latin America, as described in Chapter 9, these people were formally incorporated into Western imperial systems.

But no single colonial experience characterized this vast region. Much depended on the cultures and prior history of various colonized peoples,

549

TRM **Chapter 10 Guided Reading**
You can find a guided reading handout for this chapter in the Teacher's Resource Materials.

TRM **Chapter 10 Lecture Slides**
You can find curated lecture slides for this chapter in the Teacher's Resource Materials.

TRM **Chapter 10 Outline**
You can find a chapter outline to model good note-taking for this chapter in the Teacher's Resource Materials.

TRM **Suggested Responses to Questions**
You can find suggested responses to all of the AP® margin questions in this chapter in the Teacher's Resource Materials.

BUILDING AP® SKILLS

Developments and Processes

After students have read Chapter 10, consider having them come back and read the opening paragraph of the chapter. Then ask students: What does the German government's acknowledgment of the 1904–1907 genocide in its Southwest African colony show us about the lasting impacts of imperialism? *It shows how the legacy of nineteenth- and twentieth-century imperialism continues to impact the current age. It shows that nation-states that were former colonies still struggle to gain recognition for the injustices and atrocities committed during imperialism.*

BUILDING AP® SKILLS

Contextualization

The beginning of Chapter 10 would be a great place for students to practice their contextualization writing skills, since the Industrial Revolution played such a significant role in nineteenth-century European imperialism. Ask students to write a contextualization statement (no more than three or four sentences long) for the following LEQ prompt:

■ In the period 1750–1900, industrialized states expanded existing overseas empires and established new colonies in Africa and Asia.

Develop an argument that evaluates the extent to which various factors led to the expansion of empires and the establishment of new colonies in this time period.

BUILDING AP® SKILLS

Making Connections: Continuity and Change

The age of imperialism in the nineteenth century led to changes for both the societies that were colonized and the imperial powers. You can get students to think about some of those changes by having them search for evidence throughout the chapter to support the following statement: European states' desire for raw materials led to major changes in the lives of the people supplying those materials; however, some aspects of their lives remained the same. *Changes included the amount of land and labor employed exclusively in a new enterprise such as banana growing, diamond mining, or tapping for rubber. The economy of the exporting countries, and thus the people living in them, also became linked in new ways to the world market. However, subsistence agriculture continued. Traditional customs remained for a long time, and although people were more connected to the world economically, they were not yet culturally connected.*

AP
MAKING CONNECTIONS
How was colonial rule experienced by the societies that it encompassed? And in what ways did colonized people respond to it?

AP
CONTINUITY AND CHANGE
In what ways did the Industrial Revolution shape the character of nineteenth-century European imperialism?

and the policies of the colonial powers sometimes differed sharply and changed over time. Men and women experienced the colonial era differently, as did traditional elites, Western-educated groups, artisans, peasant farmers, and migrant laborers. Furthermore, the varied actions and reactions of such people, despite their oppression and exploitation, shaped the colonial experience, perhaps as much as the policies, practices, and intentions of their temporary European rulers. All of them—colonizers and colonized alike—were caught up in the flood of change that accompanied this new burst of European empire building.

Industry and Empire

> **Finding the Main Point:** How did capitalist industrialization, nationalism, and pseudoscience contribute to Europe's global imperialism?

Behind much of Europe's nineteenth-century imperial expansion lay the massive fact of its Industrial Revolution, a process that gave rise to new economic needs, many of which found solutions abroad. The enormous productivity of industrial technology and Europe's growing affluence now created the need for extensive raw materials and agricultural products: cotton, opium, and jute from India; rubber from the Congo; gold and diamonds from South Africa; palm oil, cocoa, and peanuts from West Africa; rice and tin from Southeast Asia; wool and meat from New Zealand; and much more. This demand radically changed patterns of economic and social life in their places of origin.

Furthermore, Europe needed to sell its own products abroad, since its factories churned out more goods than its own people could afford to buy. By 1840, for example, Britain was exporting 60 percent of its cotton-cloth production, annually sending 200 million yards to Europe, 300 million yards to Latin America, and 145 million yards to India. Part of European and American fascination with China during the nineteenth and twentieth centuries lay in the enormous market potential represented by its huge population. Much the same could be said for capital, for European and American investors often found it more profitable to invest their money abroad than at home. Between 1910 and 1913, Britain was sending about half of its savings overseas as foreign investment, while the United States became a major investor in Latin America. Large-scale overseas investment continued even after the collapse of European territorial empires in the mid-twentieth century, underpinning what some have termed the "economic imperialism" of the second half of the twentieth century (see Then and Now: Imperialism, page 552).

Wealthy Europeans also saw social benefits to foreign markets because they kept Europe's factories humming and its workers employed. The English imperialist Cecil Rhodes confided his fears to a friend in the late nineteenth century:

> Yesterday I attended a meeting of the unemployed in London and having listened to the wild speeches which were nothing more than a scream for bread, I returned home convinced more than ever of the importance of imperialism. . . . In order to save the 40 million inhabitants of the United Kingdom from a murderous civil war, the colonial politicians must open up

BUILDING AP® SKILLS

Claims and Evidence in Sources

To get students thinking about European states' motivations for imperialism in the nineteenth century, have them read the quote from Cecil Rhodes that starts at the bottom of this page. Then ask: According to Cecil Rhodes, why was imperialism important to Britain? *Rhodes was convinced that without a growing empire to "absorb" Britain's excess population and purchase the manufactured goods Britain produced, the poor of Britain would revolt and a civil war would ensue.*

Landmarks for Chapter 10

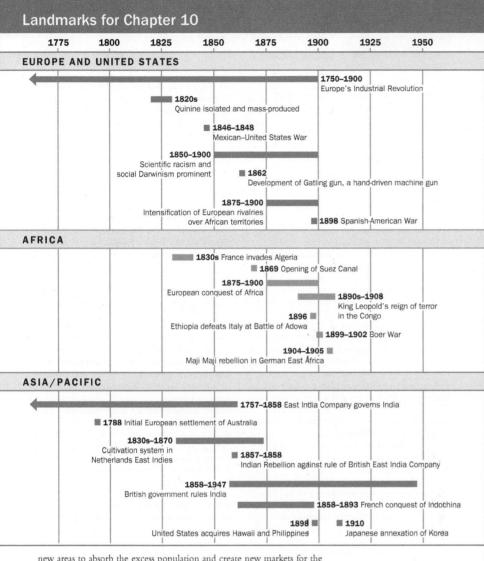

EUROPE AND UNITED STATES

1750–1900 Europe's Industrial Revolution

1820s Quinine isolated and mass-produced

1846–1848 Mexican–United States War

1850–1900 Scientific racism and social Darwinism prominent

1862 Development of Gatling gun, a hand-driven machine gun

1875–1900 Intensification of European rivalries over African territories

1898 Spanish-American War

AFRICA

1830s France invades Algeria

1869 Opening of Suez Canal

1875–1900 European conquest of Africa

1890s–1908 King Leopold's reign of terror in the Congo

1896 Ethiopia defeats Italy at Battle of Adowa

1899–1902 Boer War

1904–1905 Maji Maji rebellion in German East Africa

ASIA/PACIFIC

1757–1858 East India Company governs India

1788 Initial European settlement of Australia

1830s–1870 Cultivation system in Netherlands East Indies

1857–1858 Indian Rebellion against rule of British East India Company

1858–1947 British government rules India

1858–1893 French conquest of Indochina

1898 United States acquires Hawaii and Philippines

1910 Japanese annexation of Korea

new areas to absorb the excess population and create new markets for the products of the mines and factories.[3]

Thus imperialism promised to solve the class conflicts of an industrializing society while avoiding revolution or the serious redistribution of wealth.

551

EXPLORING AP® THEMES

Cultural Developments and Interactions (CDI) and Governance (GOV)

This would be a good place to have students partner up and study "Landmarks for Chapter 10" to answer the following questions together:

■ What events on the timeline could be used to explain the development of European imperialism? *Answers may include quinine (a medicine) being isolated and mass-produced in the 1820s; scientific racism and social Darwinism being prominent from 1850 to 1900; and the development of the Gatling gun in 1862.*

■ What event marks the beginning of European imperialism? *Imperialism began in the 1750s with the British takeover of India.*

■ When did imperialism begin to decline? Who led the movement that started the decline? (Note: Students will have to use outside knowledge to answer the second question.) *Imperialism began to end in the 1920s under the leadership of Gandhi.*

AP® CLASSROOM

AP® Daily Videos

As you begin studying the rationales for imperialism in the nineteenth century in detail, this would be a good time to have students watch both AP® Daily Videos for 6.1. The first video takes a look at social Darwinism and other racially based ideologies as rationales for imperialism, while the second video takes a look at nationalism and the civilizing mission as rationales for imperialism. Both videos also have students work on the skill of contextualization.

Students need to be able to explain how historical events can have long-term impacts on the world. You can have students examine this idea with imperialism by asking them to read "Then and Now: Imperialism" on pages 552 and 553. This section looks at the different types of imperialism that emerged in the nineteenth and twentieth centuries. Use the questions on page 553 to drive a class discussion on how imperialism impacts the twenty-first-century world.

THEN AND NOW   Imperialism

Imperialism thrived in the nineteenth century. The British famously boasted that the sun never set on their global empire. All across Asia, Africa, and Pacific Oceania, Western European powers created territorial empires that brought large lands and many peoples under their formal control. Likewise during this time, Russians expanded into Central Asia, as did the United States across North America, and Japan into parts of East Asia. Almost everywhere, it was a bloody process. But for the colonizing nations and many of their citizens, imperialism was seen as something to celebrate. It confirmed their sense of racial or cultural superiority even as it persuaded many that they were bringing civilization and progress to inferior or less fortunate peoples.

By the late 1970s, however, almost all of this imperialism was gone. Nationalist movements had dissolved empires, bringing many dozens of "new nations" into existence, fifty-four of them in Africa alone. The collapse of the Soviet Union in 1991 brought an end to much of the Russian Empire, creating another fifteen newly independent countries. Only the continental empire of the United States remained intact, though few of its citizens, with the exception of Native Americans, Hawaiians, and Puerto Ricans, thought of their country as an imperial state. Even more startling was the sharp turnaround in thinking about empires. Imperialism had become illegitimate and morally reprehensible, a term of insult rather than praise, a matter of shame rather than pride. This amazing transformation of values registered globally in 1960, when the United Nations acknowledged "the passionate yearning for freedom in all dependent peoples" and declared that colonial rule represented a "denial of fundamental human rights."

So, with the disintegration of territorial empires, had the age of imperialism come to an end? Or had it merely changed its form?

For many observers, the international behavior of the United States and the Soviet Union during the Cold War (1950–1991) was usefully described in terms of empire. The case for a continuing American empire was rooted in multiple factors: its dominant economic power and the global penetration of its multinational corporations; its enormous military capacity, widespread network of military bases, and frequent military interventions such as those in Central America, Korea, Vietnam, Afghanistan, and Iraq; its leadership of many alliances such as the North Atlantic Treaty Organization; its promotion of democracy and capitalist market economies through aid programs like the Peace Corps; and the international spread of its culture (rock and roll, McDonald's, blue jeans, movies).

Something similar generated the notion of a Soviet empire during the Cold War. Certainly the Soviet Union's domination of Eastern Europe; its use of economic and military aid to draw developing countries into its orbit; its military interventions in Hungary, Czechoslovakia, Cuba, and Afghanistan; and its promotion of a communist culture of social equality and anticolonialism parallel the contours of the American empire. Ironically, both the United States and the Soviet Union created new kinds of empires while opposing the older European-style territorial empires.

A third country recently charged with imperial ambitions is China. Begun in 2013, its multitrillion-dollar global infrastructure project, known as the Belt and Road Initiative, envisaged an array of roads, railways, port facilities, and energy pipelines stretching all across the Eastern Hemisphere and parts of Latin America as well. Funded in large part with Chinese capital and involving agreements with some 125 countries, it gave China a global economic footprint. In the eyes of some, it was an "empire-building strategy." Certainly some developing countries that eagerly took Chinese loans came to fear indebtedness and a dependence on China that limited their own sovereignty.

Thus a new vocabulary of "imperialism" has emerged to describe the different ways in which empire has found expression beyond political and territorial aims. "Economic imperialism," sometimes called "neocolonialism," suggests the ability of rich countries to gain advantage over poorer ones without the need to exercise direct political control or use military force. The notion of "cultural imperialism" refers to the domination of foreign cultural patterns over those of one's own country or people. The most prominent target of cultural imperialism has been "Americanization" as critics have deplored the growing influence of American movies, foods, fashion, political practices, manufactured goods, and much more. "Linguistic imperialism" points to the widespread adoption or imposition of particular languages (English, Spanish, French, Russian, Chinese) to the detriment of less widely spoken languages. "Religious imperialism" highlights the decline of local religions as world religions such as Buddhism, Christianity, or Islam have gained converts.

U.S. imperialism has been a frequent subject of political cartoons, such as this one entitled "Yummy!" from 2010. (Wilfred Hildonen via CartoonStock, www.cartoonstock.com/cartoonview.asp?catref=whin209)

Almost all of these uses of "imperialism" in recent decades have been highly critical. They reflect the recent change in values about empire even as they have enlarged the meaning of "imperialism." In contemporary usage, imperialism no longer requires political control or military force, as it did in the nineteenth century. Rather, the term suggests that almost any exercise of unequal power qualifies as "imperialism" and is therefore morally questionable. Is this new understanding useful because it points to the essence of imperialism—inequality, domination, and exploitation? Or does it confuse our understanding of imperialism by lumping together quite different things without making necessary distinctions?

Despite the recent widespread condemnation of imperialism, a kind of "imperial nostalgia" has also surfaced. Turkey's nationalist President Erdogan has linked his country closely to the Ottoman Empire, which is widely celebrated in films and TV programs, while seeking to carve out for Turkey an Ottoman-like centrality in the Middle East. He has also asked that the English spelling of his country's name be changed to Türkiye to better reflect "the culture, civilization, and values of the Turkish nation." In a similar fashion, Russia's President Putin declared the collapse of the Soviet Union the "greatest geopolitical tragedy" of the twentieth century, while Russia's invasion of Ukraine in early 2022 is widely viewed as an attempt to revive an earlier Russian/Soviet empire. And in Western Europe, a recent poll found that some 30 percent of the British and 50 percent of the Dutch were more proud than ashamed of their imperial past.[4] Some British historians, notably Niall Ferguson, have recently written quite favorably about the British Empire, arguing that colonial rule was better for its subjects than their earlier governments. "It's hard to make the case . . . ," Ferguson declared, "that somehow the world would have been better off if the Europeans had stayed home."[5]

So the question remains: did the imperialism of the nineteenth century persist in the twentieth, or did it fundamentally change?

QUESTIONS

What different kinds of imperialism have arisen over the past two centuries? To what extent does it still persist?

TEACHING IDEA

Bell Ringer

For a quick way to start class, consider projecting a picture of one of the many political cartoons about imperialism that can be found on the Web. Use your browser to search for political cartoons or use one of the political cartoons found in this chapter. Ask students: What theme is prevalent in the cartoon? *Themes prevalent in such cartoons include the greed of Western powers and the immorality of carving up an area without regard for the Indigenous people.*

BUILDING AP® SKILLS

Making Connections: Continuity and Change

Students may find it interesting to examine how historical terms and the meaning(s) we give to them can change over time. After reading "Then and Now: Imperialism," you could have students debate how the use of the term "imperialism" has changed from the nineteenth century to the twenty-first century. *Answers will vary.*

BUILDING AP® SKILLS

Claims and Evidence in Sources

The political cartoon on this page, published in *Puck* in 1911, shows a large African man sitting against a tree seemingly asleep, as several European countries are planting flags that represent their claims to Africa. Display this cartoon for students to study, and then ask: What appears to be happening in this cartoon? *Answers will vary. The goal is to guide the students to understand that the Europeans feel that Africa is theirs to divide up among themselves and that the Africans are unimportant.*

Differentiation

If you want to scaffold an image analysis practice for students and provide an opportunity for them to practice writing sourcing statements, consider following the "Must Do, Should Do, Strive For" model below:

■ Must Do: Display the *Puck* political cartoon on page 554 for students to study. Students must explain what they think is happening in the cartoon.

■ Should Do: Students should use evidence gathered from the political cartoon to answer the AP® Sourcing and Situation margin question on page 554.

■ Strive For: Students who want a challenge can choose one part of HIPP (Historical situation, Intended audience, or Point of view, and Purpose) to write a sourcing statement about the *Puck* political cartoon.

APPLY THE TIP

After students complete the "Industry and Empire" section of Chapter 10 as reading home-work, you can pair them up and have them look through their reading notes to find the answer to the following question: What are the important factors that contributed to nineteenth-century imperialism? *Important factors are the mass appeal of nationalism, the rivalries that ensued between the European nations, and the notion that overseas possessions endowed the European nations with Great Power status. In short, imperialism was important socially and economically for the wealthy but important emotionally for the common man, and it was politically and strategically necessary in the game of international power politics.*

▶ **AP®**
SOURCING AND SITUATION
How could a historian use this political cartoon to describe European attitudes toward African societies during the age of imperialism?

Colonial Rivalries This image shows Africa as a sleeping giant, while various European countries stake their rival claims to parts of the continent. It was published in 1911 in *Puck*, a British magazine of humor and satire. (Library of Congress, Prints and Photographs Division, LC-DIG-ppmsca-27783)

AP® EXAM TIP
Take notes on the factors that contributed to nineteenth-century imperialism.

But what made imperialism so broadly popular in Europe, especially in the last quarter of the nineteenth century, was the growth of mass nationalism. By 1871, the unification of Italy and Germany intensified Europe's already competitive international relations. Much of this rivalry spilled over into the struggle for overseas colonies or economic concessions, which became symbols of "Great Power" status for a nation. Their acquisition was a matter of urgency, even if they possessed little immediate economic value. After 1875, it seemed to matter, even to ordinary people, whether some remote corner of Africa or some obscure Pacific island was in British, French, or German hands. Imperialism, in short, appealed on economic and social grounds to the wealthy or ambitious, seemed politically and strategically necessary in the game of international power politics, and was emotionally satisfying to almost everyone. It was a potent mix!

Industrialization also provided new means for achieving those goals. Steam-driven ships moving through the new Suez Canal, completed in 1869, allowed Europeans to reach distant Asian, African, and Pacific ports more quickly and predictably and to penetrate interior rivers as well. The underwater telegraph made possible almost instant communication with far-flung outposts of empire. The discovery of quinine to prevent malaria greatly reduced European death rates in the tropics. Breech-loading rifles and machine guns vastly widened the military gap between Europeans and everyone else.

The nineteenth century also marked a change in the way Europeans perceived themselves and others. In earlier centuries, Europeans had defined others largely in religious terms. "They" were heathen; "we" were Christian. With the advent of the industrial age, however, Europeans developed a secular arrogance that fused with or in some cases replaced their notions of religious superiority. They had, after all, unlocked the secrets of nature, created a society of unprecedented wealth, and used both to produce unsurpassed military power. These became the criteria by which Europeans judged both themselves and the rest of the world.

By such standards, it is not surprising that their opinions of other cultures dropped sharply. The Chinese, who had been highly praised in the eighteenth century, were reduced in the nineteenth century to the image of "John Chinaman"—weak, cunning, obstinately conservative, and, in large numbers, a distinct threat labeled a "yellow peril." African societies, which even in the slave-trade era had been regarded as nations and their leaders as kings, were demoted in nineteenth-century European eyes to the status of tribes led by chiefs as a means of emphasizing their "primitive" qualities.

Peoples of Pacific Oceania and elsewhere could be regarded as "big children," who lived "closer to nature" than their civilized counterparts and correspondingly distant from the high culture with which Europeans congratulated themselves. Upon visiting Tahiti in 1768, the French explorer Bougainville concluded: "I thought I was walking in the Garden of Eden."[6] Such views could be mobilized to criticize the artificiality and materialism of modern European life, but they could also serve to justify the conquest of people who were, apparently, doing little to improve what nature had granted them. Writing in 1854, a European settler in Australia declared: "The question comes to this; which has the better right—the savage, born in a country, which he runs over but can scarcely be said to occupy . . . or the civilized man, who comes to introduce into this . . . unproductive country, the industry which supports life?"[7]

Increasingly, Europeans viewed the culture and achievements of Asian and African peoples through the prism of a new kind of **scientific racism**. Although physical differences had often been a basis of fear or dislike, in the nineteenth century Europeans increasingly used the prestige and

PROGRESSIVE DEVELOPMENT OF MAN.—(a) EVOLUTION ILLUSTRATED WITH THE SIX CORRESPONDING LIVING FORMS.

European Racial Images This nineteenth-century chart, depicting the "Progressive Development of Man" from apes to modern Europeans, reflected the racial categories that were so prominent at the time. It also highlights the influence of Darwin's evolutionary ideas as they were applied to the varied physical features of human beings. (Granger NYC – All rights reserved)

TEACHING IDEA

Incorporating Outside Resources

Students may be interested to dive further into some of the ideas of scientific racism that Europeans used to justify imperialism. You can show students the video *Phrenology: The Weirdest Pseudoscience of Them All? – BBC REEL* to let them dive deeper into one of these ideas. This video looks at how phrenology developed and how it influenced the scientific world over time. You can find this video by searching for it on YouTube. After watching, ask students: How do you think Europeans used phrenology to justify a racial hierarchy in their colonies? *Europeans might have used this pseudoscience to "prove" that European skulls showed they were more advanced than other races and "deserved" to rule over them.*

APPLY THE TIP

After students have learned about scientific racism and social Darwinism, ask them the following question as an exit ticket to gauge student understanding of the topic: How did the concept of social Darwinism apply Darwin's ideas about the survival of the fittest? Students should turn in their answers as they leave the room. *According to social Darwinism, European dominance was an example of the natural order Darwin proposed, by which those who were fittest to survive dominated, displaced, and even eliminated those who were unfit. Proponents of social Darwinism believed that Europeans, or whites, were naturally the most fit to rule.*

AP®
CONTINUITY AND CHANGE
Evaluate how Europeans would use these new views toward non-European societies to separate themselves from their colonial subjects in Asia and Africa.

AP® EXAM TIP
The concept of social Darwinism is important as a justification of imperialism and will likely appear on the AP® Exam.

apparatus of science to support their racial preferences and prejudices. Phrenologists, craniologists, and sometimes physicians used allegedly scientific methods and numerous instruments to classify the size and shape of human skulls and concluded, not surprisingly, that those of whites were larger and therefore more advanced. Nineteenth-century biologists, who classified the varieties of plants and animals, applied these notions of rank to human beings as well. The result was a hierarchy of races, with the whites on top and the less developed "child races" beneath them. Race, in this view, determined human intelligence, moral development, and destiny. "Race is everything," declared the British anatomist Robert Knox in 1850. "Civilization depends on it."[8] Furthermore, as the germ theory of disease took hold in nineteenth-century Europe, it was accompanied by fears that contact with "inferiors" threatened the health and even the biological future of more advanced or "superior" peoples.

These ideas influenced how Europeans viewed their own global expansion. Almost everyone saw it as inevitable, a natural outgrowth of a superior civilization. For many, though, this viewpoint was tempered with a genuine, if condescending, sense of responsibility to the "weaker races" that Europe was fated to dominate. "Superior races have a right, because they have a duty . . . to civilize the inferior races," declared the French politician Jules Ferry in 1883.[9] That **civilizing mission** included bringing Christianity to the heathen, good government to disordered lands, work discipline and production for the market to "lazy natives," a measure of education to the ignorant and illiterate, clothing to the naked, and health care to the sick, all while suppressing "native customs" that ran counter to Western ways of living. In European thinking, this was "progress" and "civilization."

A harsher side to the ideology of imperialism found expression in **social Darwinism**. Its adherents applied Charles Darwin's evolutionary concept of "the survival of the fittest" to human society. This outlook suggested that European dominance inevitably led to the displacement or destruction of backward peoples or "unfit" races. Such views made imperialism, war, and aggression seem both natural and progressive, for weeding out "weaker" peoples of the world would allow the "stronger" to flourish. These were some of the ideas with which industrializing and increasingly powerful Europeans confronted the peoples of Asia and Africa in the nineteenth century.

A Second Wave of European Conquests

Finding the Main Point: In what different ways did various parts of Asia and Africa come to be enveloped within European, American, or Japanese empires?

The imperialism of the long nineteenth century (1750–1900) continued the process of European colonial conquests that had begun with the takeover of the Americas during the sixteenth and seventeenth centuries. Now it was focused in Asia, Africa, and Oceania rather than in the Western Hemisphere. And it featured a number of new players—Germany, Italy, Belgium, the United States, and Japan—who were not at all involved in the earlier phase, while the Spanish and Portuguese now had only minor roles. In general, Europeans preferred informal control, which operated through economic penetration and occasional military intervention but without a wholesale colonial takeover. Such a course was cheaper and less likely to provoke wars. But where rivalry with other European states made it impossible or where local governments were unable or unwilling to cooperate, Europeans proved more than willing to undertake the expense and risk of conquest and outright colonial rule.

Once established in a region, they frequently took advantage of moments of weakness in local societies to strengthen their control. "Each global drought was the green light for an imperialist landrush," wrote one scholar when examining the climatic instability that caused monsoon rains across Asia and parts of Africa to repeatedly fail in the second half of the nineteenth century.[10] Nowhere was this more evident than in Africa, where a drought in the southern part of the continent in 1877 coincided with British success in reining in Zulu independence, and famine in Ethiopia starting in the late 1880s coincided with Italian efforts to subdue the Horn of Africa.

The construction of these new European empires in the Afro-Asian world, like empires everywhere, involved military force or the threat of it. Increasingly in the nineteenth century, Europeans possessed overwhelming advantages in firepower, derived from the recently invented repeating rifles and machine guns. Nonetheless, Europeans had to fight, often long and hard, to create their new empires, as countless wars of conquest attest. In the end, though, they prevailed almost everywhere. Thus gathering and hunting bands in Australia, agricultural village societies or chiefdoms on Pacific islands and in parts of Africa, pastoralists of the Sahara and Central Asia, residents of states large and small, and virtually everyone in the large and complex civilizations of India and Southeast Asia—all of them alike lost the political sovereignty and freedom of action their rulers had previously exercised.

The passage to colonial status occurred in various ways. For the peoples of India and Indonesia, colonial conquest grew out of interaction with European trading firms that were authorized to conduct military operations and exercise political and administrative control over large areas. The British East India Company, rather than the British government directly, played the leading role in the colonial takeover of South Asia. The fragmentation of the Mughal Empire and the absence of any overall sense of cultural or political unity both invited and facilitated European penetration. A similar situation of many small and rival states assisted the Dutch acquisition of Indonesia. However, neither the British nor the Dutch had a clear-cut plan for conquest. Rather, in India it evolved slowly as local authorities and European traders made and unmade a variety of alliances with local states over roughly a century (1750–1850). In Indonesia, a few areas held out until the early twentieth century (see Map 10.1).

AP®

COMPARISON
In what different ways was colonial rule established in the various regions of Africa and Asia?

AP® EXAM TIP
Understand examples of Africans' and Asians' acceptance and rejection of European imperialism.

APPLY THE TIP

The 2009 released Question 1 (the DBQ) focuses on African reactions to European imperialism in the nineteenth century. This would be good to use for students to create a DBQ outline to practice their DBQ writing skills and to help them understand Africans' acceptance and rejection of European imperialism. You can find a copy of the released DBQ on the AP® World History: Modern Past Exam Questions webpage.

To bring Question 1 from the 2009 Exam into alignment with the current DBQ requirements, consider removing Documents 1 and 9. You can also change the prompt to: Evaluate the extent to which African responses to European imperialism <u>differed</u> during the late nineteenth and early twentieth centuries.

TRM Writing Organizer for DBQ

BUILDING AP® SKILLS

Making Connections: Continuity and Change

Students need to be able to make connections between different periods of world history. You can ask them to use their prior knowledge from Unit 4: Transoceanic Interconnections and the information in "A Second Wave of European Conquests" to create a chart that lists the changes and continuities between first-wave and second-wave European conquests. A reproducible version of this chart is available in the Teacher's Resource Materials. (Answers are provided in italics.)

Changes	Continuities
Colonialism during the second wave occurred in the Afro-Asian world rather than in the Western Hemisphere.	*Colonialism involved military force, or the threat of it, by powers that had overwhelming military strength.*
Portugal and Spain were on the margins, while Germany, Italy, Belgium, the United States, and Japan had become colonial powers during the second wave.	*France and Britain had the biggest colonial networks.*
European colonial powers in the second wave tried to rule the colonies indirectly through economic control rather than through formal governmental structures.	*Indigenous people lost political and economic sovereignty.*

TRM Handout 10.1: Continuity and Change Chart for First-Wave and Second-Wave European Conquests

Humans and the Environment (ENV)

Consider having students read the last paragraph on page 557 and using what they learned in it to help them analyze Map 10.1, "Colonial Asia in the Early Twentieth Century." Then have them answer the following question in small groups: Why did it take longer for Europeans to build their empires in Asia than in other areas, like the Americas? *Answers may include: Asian peoples were immune to the diseases Europeans brought with them, unlike the people of the Americas; Europeans were trying to gain territory in areas that were already under the control of centralized governments, which made it harder to conquer new land; Europeans had to contend with other empires in this region of the world, like the Ottomans, Mughals, and Qing dynasty.*

Governance (GOV)

Students may find it helpful to have a "quick reference" chart for which areas in Asia were controlled by which colonial power. You can have them fill in a chart like the one below to help them remember how colonial powers divided Asia. Map 10.1 will be helpful for students as they complete the chart. A reproducible version of this chart is available in the Teacher's Resource Materials. (Answers are provided in italics.)

Colonizing Power	Area "Imperialized"
Japan	*Formosa, Korea*
United States	*Philippines*
France	*French Indochina (Vietnam and Laos)*
Netherlands	*Netherland East Indies (Indonesia)*
Great Britain	*India (Pakistan, India, Myanmar, Bangladesh), Malay States, British North Borneo*

TRM Handout 10.2: Chart for Colonial Powers in Early Twentieth-Century Colonial Asia

MAPPING HISTORY   Map 10.1 Colonial Asia in the Early Twentieth Century

By the early twentieth century, several of the great population centers of Asia had come under the colonial control of Britain, the Netherlands, France, the United States, or Japan.

Reading the Map: Which Southeast Asian kingdom maintained its independence from European colonial powers?

AP **Making Connections:** What geographical and political barriers made direct confrontations between the British Empire in South Asia and the Chinese empire unlikely?

For most of Africa, mainland Southeast Asia, and the Pacific islands, colonial conquest came later, in the second half of the nineteenth century, and rather more abruptly and deliberately than in India or Indonesia. The **scramble for Africa**, for example, pitted half a dozen European powers against one another as they partitioned the entire continent among themselves in only about twenty-five years (1875–1900). (See Working with Evidence: Colonial Conquest, page 594, for various perspectives on the "scramble.") Despite widespread resistance to European conquest, African kingdoms and societies were ultimately unable to overcome Europeans' modern weapons and professional armies. Thus Europeans divided the continent among themselves with little attention to ethnic or linguistic divisions, and by 1914 only Liberia and Ethiopia were free from European control. European leaders themselves were surprised by the intensity of their rivalries and the speed with which they acquired huge territories, about which they knew very little.

That process involved endless but peaceful negotiations among the competing Great Powers about "who got what" and extensive and bloody military action, sometimes lasting decades, to make their control effective on the ground. Among the most difficult to subdue were those decentralized societies without any formal state structure. In such cases, Europeans confronted no central authority with which they could negotiate or that they might decisively defeat. It was a matter of village-by-village conquest against extended resistance. As late as 1925, one British official commented on the process as it operated in central Nigeria: "I shall of course go on walloping them until they surrender. It's a rather piteous sight watching a village being knocked to pieces and I wish there was some other way, but unfortunately there isn't."[11] Another very difficult situation for the British lay in South Africa, where they were initially defeated by a Zulu army in 1879 at the Battle of Isandlwana. And twenty years later, in what became known as the Boer War (1899–1902), the Boers, white descendants of the earlier Dutch settlers in South Africa, fought bitterly for three years before succumbing to British forces (see Map 10.2). In West Africa, Samory Toure, the Muslim ruler of a substantial state, led a military resistance that held off French conquest of the region for almost twenty years. The colonial conquest of Africa was intensely resisted.

Europeans and Americans had been drawn into the world of Pacific Oceania during the eighteenth century through exploration and scientific curiosity, by the missionary impulse for conversion, and by their economic interests in sperm whale oil, coconut oil, guano, mineral nitrates and phosphates, sandalwood, and other products. Primarily in the second half of the nineteenth century, these entanglements morphed into competitive annexations as Britain, France, the Netherlands, Germany, and the United States, now joined by Australia, claimed control of all the islands of Oceania (see Map 10.1). Chile too, in search of valuable guano and nitrates, entered the fray and gained a number of coastal islands as well as Rapa Nui (Easter Island), the easternmost island of Polynesia.

The colonization of the South Pacific territories of Australia and New Zealand, both of which were taken over by the British during the nineteenth century, was more similar to the earlier colonization of North America than to contemporary patterns of Asian and African conquest. In both places, conquest was accompanied by large-scale European settlement and diseases that reduced native numbers by 75 percent or more by 1900. Like Canada and the United States, these became **settler colonies**, "neo-European" societies in the Pacific. Aboriginal Australians constituted only about 2.4 percent of their country's population in the

AP
CAUSATION
What caused the scramble for Africa?

AP
COMPARISON
How was the colonization of Australia in the nineteenth century similar to the colonization of North America in the seventeenth century?

TEACHING IDEA

Incorporating Outside Resources

This would be a good place to show the Crash Course European History episode *Expansion and Resistance*. In this episode, John Green discusses how Europeans expanded into Africa, Asia, and Oceania during the nineteenth century. You can find the video on YouTube. After students watch the video, have them answer the following questions:

■ Why did Asia, Africa, and the Pacific islands become the focus of imperial activity by the mid-nineteenth century? *These regions became the focus of imperialism because they helped Europeans gain trading advantages and acquire more raw materials that could be used in industrialization.*

■ What were the tools of empire that helped Europeans colonize Africa? *Europeans used local people as informants, guides, go-betweens, and negotiators to gain access and territories. Steamships helped Europeans navigate rivers, while railroads helped them get natural resources to ports as quickly as possible. Industrial weaponry gave Europeans an advantage over local groups. Quinine gave Europeans a treatment for malaria, allowing them to invade the interior of Africa.*

■ What were some of the effects of colonialism on both the colonizer and the colonized? *The wealth extracted from the colonies only benefited the colonizers. The ideas about race that were created to justify colonialism are still deeply ingrained in lived human experience around the world.*

Governance (GOV)

If you had students create a "quick reference" chart for colonial powers in Asia on page 558, consider having them make a second one for what parts of Africa were controlled by colonial powers. Students can use Map 10.2 on this page to help them complete the chart. A reproducible version of this chart is available in the Teacher's Resource Materials. (Answers are provided in italics.)

European Power	Area "Imperialized"
Great Britain	*Egypt, Sudan, Kenya, Somalia, Sierra Leone, Gold Coast, Nigeria, Northern and Southern Rhodesia, South Africa, Zanzibar, Gambia, Nyasaland, Bechuanaland*
France	*Morocco, Algeria, Mauritania, Senegal, French Equatorial Africa, French Somaliland, French Congo, Madagascar, Tunisia*
Germany	*Cameroon, German Southwest Africa, German East Africa, Togo*
Italy	*Italian Somaliland, Eritrea, Libya*
Portugal	*Portuguese Guinea, Angola, Mozambique*
Belgium	*Belgian Congo*
Spain	*Spanish Guinea, Spanish Morocco, Rio de Oro*

TRM Handout 10.3: Chart for Colonial Powers in Early Twentieth-Century Colonial Africa

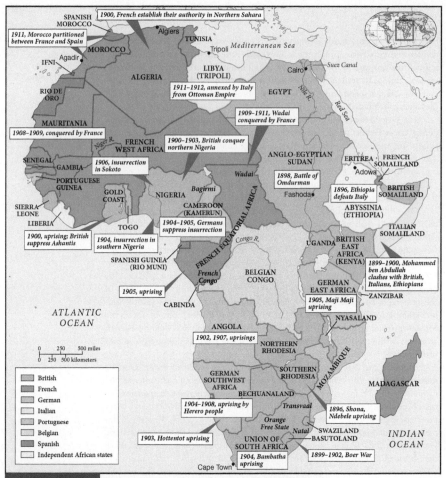

MAPPING HISTORY **Map 10.2 Conquest and Resistance in Colonial Africa**

By the early twentieth century, the map of Africa reflected the outcome of the scramble for Africa, a conquest that was heavily resisted in many places.

Reading the Map: "France's colonial possessions were concentrated in North and West Africa, with Britain's colonies focused in eastern and southern Africa." To what extent is this statement accurate? What problems can you identify with this generalization?

AP Making Connections: Which European colonial powers experienced uprisings and insurrections more frequently than others? What regions of Africa experienced the most uprisings and insurrections? Can you make any generalizations concerning uprisings and insurrections based on these observations?

Claims and Evidence in Sources

This map is good to use for helping students work on their source analysis skills. Show them Map 10.2, "Conquest and Resistance in Colonial Africa," and then ask: What does the map say about African reactions to the scramble for Africa? *There were multiple uprisings around Africa against European conquest and rule, most of which were suppressed. Only Ethiopia, which became completely landlocked, remained independent.*

early twenty-first century, and the indigenous Maori were a minority of about 15 percent in New Zealand. In other previously isolated regions as well—Polynesia, Amazonia, Siberia—disease took a terrible toll on peoples who lacked immunities to European pathogens. For example, the population of Hawaii declined from around 142,000 in 1823 to only 39,000 in 1896. Unlike these remote areas, most African and Asian regions shared with Europe a broadly similar disease environment and so were less susceptible to the pathogens of the conquerors.

Elsewhere other variations on the theme of imperial conquest unfolded. The westward expansion of the United States, for example, overwhelmed Native American populations and involved the country in an imperialist war with Mexico. Seeking territory for white settlement, the United States practiced a policy of removing, sometimes almost exterminating, Indigenous peoples. On the "reservations" to which they were confined and in boarding schools to which many of their children were removed, reformers sought to "civilize" the remaining Native Americans, eradicating tribal life and culture, under the slogan "Kill the Indian and Save the Man."

Japan's takeover of Taiwan and Korea bore marked similarities to European actions, as that East Asian nation joined the imperialist club. Russian penetration of Central Asia brought additional millions under European control as the Russian Empire continued its earlier territorial expansion. Filipinos acquired new colonial rulers when the United States took over from Spain following the Spanish-American War of 1898. Seeking greater freedom than was possible at home, some 13,000 formerly enslaved people from the United States migrated to West Africa, where they became, ironically, a colonizing elite in the land they named Liberia.

These broad patterns of colonial conquest contained thousands of separate encounters as the target societies of Western empire builders were confronted with decisions about how to respond to encroaching European power in the context of their local circumstances. Many initially sought to enlist Europeans in their own internal struggles for power or in their rivalries with neighboring states or peoples. As pressures mounted and European demands escalated, some tried to play off imperial powers against one another, while others resorted to military action. Many societies were sharply divided between those who wanted to fight and those who believed that resistance was futile. After extended resistance against French aggression, the nineteenth-century Vietnamese emperor Tu Duc argued with those who wanted the struggle to go on: "Do you really wish to confront such a power with a pack of [our] cowardly soldiers? . . . With what you presently have, do you really expect to dissolve the enemy's rifles into air or chase his battleships into hell?"[12] Still others negotiated, attempting to preserve as much independence and power as possible. The rulers of the East African kingdom of Buganda, for example, saw opportunity in the British presence and negotiated an arrangement that substantially enlarged their state and personally benefited the kingdom's elite class.

AP EXAM TIP

Be able to compare imperialist motivations and outcomes in the nineteenth and early twentieth century.

BUILDING AP® SKILLS

Claims and Evidence in Sources

This is a good place to assign "Working with Evidence: Colonial Conquest: The Scramble for Africa," on pages 594–599. You could use one or several of the documents for students to work on their DBQ skills. The questions after each source could be used for students to answer as homework or to guide a class discussion.

APPLY THE TIP

You could partner students up and have them read through pages 559 to 561 to complete a chart on some of the causes (motivations) and effects (outcomes) of imperialism. A reproducible version of this chart is available in the Teacher's Resource Materials. (Possible answers are provided in italics.)

Motivations	Outcomes
Territorial expansion	■ *Many Indigenous people fell under the control of new colonizers.*
Changing native culture to be more Western, pressuring Indigenous people to conform to standard norms	■ *Native Americans were placed on reservations in the United States.* ■ *Native American children were removed from families and sent to school to be "civilized." A similar pattern was carried out in Australia.*
Greater freedom	■ *Formerly enslaved people moved from the United States to Liberia, where they became colonizing elites.*

TRM Handout 10.4: Causation Chart for Imperialism

TEACHING IDEA

Class Discussion

Consider dividing the class up into groups of three to four students and having them discuss the following question based on what they have learned from "A Second Wave of European Conquests": What actions did the colonized Indigenous people take to mitigate the encroachment of the Europeans? *Answers will vary, but may focus on how some colonized Indigenous people decided to try to enlist the Europeans in their internal struggles; some tried to play colonizing powers against one another; many resorted to military action and decided to fight, while others considered it futile.*

Sourcing and Situation

For a quick sourcing practice, you can have students read the introduction paragraphs to "Under European Rule" and then ask: How did Vietnamese such as Nguyen Khuyen react to being incorporated into a new culture as a result of French colonization? *People such as Nguyen felt that the new culture repressed the old culture. The pressure was to change and adapt, but leaders such as Nguyen found that the new cultural norms were not as comfortable as the old ones had been.*

Bell Ringer

Consider using the AP® Contextualization margin question on this page as a bell ringer to start class when students are learning about Indigenous responses to imperialism. You could have students brainstorm ideas on their own, before sharing them with a partner or with the entire class.

Under European Rule

Finding the Main Point: In what ways were European colonial empires similar to earlier imperial processes? In what ways were they distinctive?

In many places and for many people, incorporation into European colonial empires was a traumatic experience. Especially for small-scale societies, the loss of life, homes, cattle, crops, and land was devastating. In 1902, a British soldier in East Africa described what happened in a single village: "Every soul was either shot or bayoneted. . . . We burned all the huts and razed the banana plantations to the ground."[13]

For the Vietnamese elite, schooled for centuries in Chinese-style Confucian thinking, conquest meant that the natural harmonies of life had been so badly disrupted that "water flowed uphill." Nguyen Khuyen (1835–1909), a senior Vietnamese official, retired to his ancestral village to farm and write poetry after the French conquest, expressing his anguish at the passing of the world he had known. Many others also withdrew into private life, feigning illness when asked to serve in public office under the French.

Cooperation and Rebellion

Although violence was a prominent feature of colonial life both during conquest and after, various groups and many individuals willingly cooperated with colonial authorities to their own advantage. Many men found employment, status, and security in European-led armed forces. The shortage and expense of European administrators and the difficulties of communicating across cultural boundaries made it necessary for colonial rulers to rely heavily on a range of local intermediaries. Thus Indian princes, Muslim emirs, and African rulers, often from elite or governing families, found it possible to retain much of their earlier status and many of their privileges while gaining considerable wealth by exercising authority, legally and otherwise, at the local level. For example, in French West Africa, an area eight times the size of France and with a population of about 15 million in the late 1930s, the colonial state consisted of just 385 French administrators and more than 50,000 African "chiefs." Thus colonial rule rested on and reinforced the most conservative segments of colonized societies.

AP®
CONTEXTUALIZATION
Why might subject peoples choose to cooperate with or to actively resist the colonial regime? What might prompt them to violent rebellion or resistance?

Both colonial governments and private missionary organizations had an interest in promoting a measure of European education. From this process arose a small Western-educated class, whose members served the colonial state, European businesses, and Christian missions as teachers, clerks, translators, and lower-level administrators. A few received higher education abroad and returned home as lawyers, doctors, engineers, or journalists. As colonial governments and business enterprises became more sophisticated, Europeans increasingly depended on the Western-educated class at the expense of the more traditional elites.

If colonial rule enlisted the willing cooperation of some, it provoked the bitter opposition of many others. Thus periodic rebellions, both large and small, erupted in colonial regimes everywhere. The most famous among them was the **Indian Rebellion of 1857–1858**, triggered by a mutiny among disaffected Indian troops in Meerut, near Delhi. Behind this incident were many groups of people with a whole series of grievances generated by the British colonial presence: troops whose religious beliefs and practices were transgressed, local rulers who had lost power, landlords deprived of their estates or their rent, peasants overtaxed and exploited by urban moneylenders and landlords alike, unemployed weavers displaced by machine-manufactured textiles, and religious leaders outraged by missionary preaching. Soon parts of India were aflame. Some rebel leaders presented their cause as an effort to revive an almost-vanished Mughal Empire. Although it was crushed in 1858, the rebellion greatly widened the racial divide in colonial India. It also convinced the British government to assume direct control over India, ending the era of British East India Company rule in the subcontinent. Fear of provoking another rebellion also made the British more conservative and cautious about deliberately trying to change Indian society.

The westward expansion of the United States likewise generated frequent rebellions, some of them religiously inspired. The Ghost Dance, practiced by multiple Native American societies in the western states, gained strength in the latter part of the nineteenth century. Practitioners believed that the Ghost Dance would reunite the living with the spirits of their ancestors, oust the foreigners, and bring peace, prosperity, and unity to the Native American population in North America.

In colonial Africa, as well, frequent uprisings punctuated the "imperial peace" in the early decades of colonial rule. In Muslim areas, Islam provided an ideology of resistance, supporting rebellions in Algeria, Niger, Somalia, and the Sudan. Elsewhere, traditional religions enabled opposition movements. In German East Africa (now Tanzania), a large-scale uprising, stimulated by the forced growing of cotton, erupted in 1904 among a large number of distinct peoples. Known as the Maji Maji rebellion, it was led by a spirit medium named Kinjikitile who spoke with religious authority and distributed water-medicine (maji) said to make people invulnerable to bullets (for more on this rebellion, see "Economies of Coercion: Forced Labor and the Power of the State" later in the chapter). In colonial Nigeria, a "women's war" (1928–1929) reflected women's opposition to high school fees, corruption among local African chiefs, and especially the threat of direct taxation on women and their market activities. Thousands of women gathered in protest, singing and dancing, sometimes naked, and employing a long-standing tradition known as "sitting on a man." This tradition involved directly confronting African warrant chiefs appointed by the British, shaming them for their bad behavior, damaging their homes, and sometime directly attacking them. Women also destroyed "native courts" and released prisoners from jails. Some fifty-five women were killed by the colonial troops who suppressed the rebellion.

Anti-Imperial Movement	Events of the Movement
Indian Rebellion of 1857–1858	Caused by a variety of grievances against the British in India: local leaders losing power, feelings of disrespect toward religious beliefs and practices, landlords deprived of their lands or rent, overtaxed peasants, and weavers losing their jobs to machine-manufactured textiles. Rebellion was sparked by perceived disrespect toward Sepoy soldiers by British officers and quickly flared up all over India. The rebellion was crushed in 1858 and resulted in the British government taking direct control of India.
Ghost Dance Movement	Religiously inspired movement against the movement of the United States into native territories. Practitioners believed the Ghost Dance would reunite the living with their ancestors' spirits and together they would push out the foreigners in their lands. This would bring peace, prosperity, and unity to the Native American population. Over time, participation in the movement declined due to a fear of continued violence by the United States against those who practiced it.
Maji Maji Rebellion	Rebellion in German East Africa in 1904 that was led by a spirit medium who distributed water-medicine he claimed would make people and rebels invulnerable to bullets. The rebels were defeated by the Germans, but the rebellion resulted in the Germans ending the forced growing of cotton in their colony.
"Women's War" in colonial Nigeria	This rebellion was led in 1928 by Nigerian women who opposed high school fees in the colony, corruption among local African chiefs, and the threat of direct taxation on women and their market activities. The women protested and used a long-standing tradition of directly confronting African warrant chiefs (who had been appointed by the British) by shaming them for their bad behavior, damaging their homes, and sometimes attacking them. They also destroyed "native courts" and released prisoners from jails. Colonial troops eventually suppressed the rebellion in 1929.

TRM Handout 10.5: Chart for Anti-Imperial Movements

Class Discussion

Students often like to debate controversial issues, and imperialism is still a controversial issue in the twenty-first century. To get students to think "outside the box" about imperialism, you can have them read "Colonial Empires with a Difference" and then ask: Did imperialism provide anything positive to Indigenous peoples? Explain your answer. *Because of imperialism, new means of communication and transportation were developed, as were sanitation measures and public health initiatives. However, students may not see these developments as worth the cost of colonialism.*

Social Interactions and Organization (SIO)

Europeans used their own ideas about race, social hierarchies, and gender roles to define their relationships with colonial peoples. To get students to think about this issue, have them discuss the following question with a partner: How did Europeans use social structures and gender systems to classify groups of colonial peoples in this era? *Europeans used social structures and gender systems to classify groups of colonial peoples through tribal distinction, emphasizing female inferiority, keeping European women separate from native men, who were seen as lusting and thus untrustworthy, and depicting certain colonized people as "martial" and recruiting them into the military.*

Colonial Empires with a Difference

At one level, European colonial empires were but the latest in a very long line of imperial creations, all of which had enlisted cooperation and experienced resistance from their subject peoples, but the nineteenth-century European version of empire was distinctive in several remarkable ways. One was the prominence of race in distinguishing rulers as "superior" to the ruled, as the high tide of scientific racism in Europe coincided with the acquisition of Asian and African colonies. In East Africa, for example, white men expected to be addressed as *bwana* (Swahili for "master"), whereas Europeans regularly called African men "boy." Particularly affected by European racism were those whose Western education and aspirations most clearly threatened the racial divide. For example, a proposal in 1883 to allow Indian judges to hear cases involving whites provoked outrage and massive demonstrations among European inhabitants of India.

In those colonies that had a large European settler population, the expression of racial distinctions was much more pronounced than in places that had few permanently settled whites. The most extreme case was South Africa, where a large European population and the widespread use of African labor in mines and industries brought blacks and whites into closer and more prolonged contact than elsewhere. Racial fears among whites resulted in extraordinary efforts to establish race as a legal, not just a customary, feature of South African society. This racial system provided for separate "homelands," educational systems, residential areas, public facilities, and much more. In what was eventually known as apartheid, South African whites attempted the impossible task of creating an industrializing economy based on cheap African labor while limiting African social and political integration in every conceivable fashion.

A further distinctive feature of nineteenth-century European empires lay in the extent to which colonial states were able to penetrate the societies they governed. Centralized tax-collecting bureaucracies, new means of communication and transportation, imposed changes in landholding patterns, integration of colonial economies into a global network of exchange, public health and sanitation measures, and the activities of missionaries—all of this touched the daily lives of many people far more deeply than in earlier empires. Not only were Europeans foreign rulers, but they also bore the seeds of a very different way of life that had grown out of their own modern transformation.

Nineteenth-century European colonizers were extraordinary as well in their penchant for counting and classifying their subject people. With the assistance of anthropologists and missionaries, colonial governments collected a vast amount of information, sought to organize it "scientifically," and used it to manage the unfamiliar, complex, varied, and fluctuating societies that they governed. In India, the British found in classical texts and Brahmin ideology an idealized description of the caste system, based on the notion of four ranked and unchanging varnas. It was a vast simplification of the immense complexity and variety of caste as it actually

AP®

COMPARISON

In what ways were European notions of class in the colonies similar to the Indian caste system?

operated. Thus the British invented or appropriated a Brahmin version of "traditional India" that they favored and sought to preserve, while scorning as "non-Indian" the new elite who had been educated in European schools and were enthusiastic about Western ways of life. This view of India reflected the great influence of Brahmins on British thinking and clearly served the interests of this Indian upper class.

Likewise, within African colonies Europeans identified, and sometimes invented, distinct tribes, each with its own clearly defined territory, language, customs, and chief. The notion of a "tribal Africa" expressed the Western view that African societies were primitive or backward, representing an earlier stage of human development. It was also a convenient idea, for it reduced the enormous complexity and fluidity of African societies to a more manageable state and thus made colonial administration easier.

Gender too entered into the efforts of Europeans to define both themselves and their newly acquired subject peoples. European colonizers—mostly male—took pride in their "active masculinity" while defining the "conquered races" as soft, passive, and feminine. Indian Bengali men, wrote a British official in 1892, "are disqualified for political enfranchisement by the possession of essentially feminine characteristics."[14] By linking the alleged inferiority of women with that of people of color, imperialists joined gender ideology and race prejudice in support of colonial rule.

But the intersection of race, gender, and empire was complex and varied. European men in the colonies often viewed their own women as the bearers and emblems of civilization, "upholding the moral dignity of the white community" amid the darkness of inferior peoples.[15] As such, European women had to be above reproach in sexual matters, protected against the alleged lust of native men by their separation from local societies. Furthermore, certain colonized people, such as the Sikhs and Gurkhas in India, the Kamba in Kenya, and the Hausa in Nigeria, were gendered as masculine or "martial races" and targeted for recruitment into British military or police forces.

Finally, the colonial policies of Europeans contradicted their own core values and their practices at home to an unusual degree. While nineteenth-century Britain and France were becoming more democratic, their colonies were essentially

European Master and Indian Servants This image, dating to 1812, shows a young European gentleman attended by multiple servants in colonial India. It illustrates the exalted status available to quite ordinary Europeans in a colonial setting as well as the sharp racial divide separating Europeans and Indians. (Historia/Shutterstock)

▲ **AP®**
CLAIMS AND EVIDENCE IN SOURCES
What does this image reveal about the relationship of Europeans and Indians in early colonial India?

AP®
CONTEXTUALIZATION
How did European colonial powers contradict the values of the Enlightenment through their treatment of their colonial territories?

TEACHING IDEA
Incorporating Outside Resources

For students who like to read or those who might be interested in digging further into the relationships between Europeans and colonial peoples, you could recommend the novel *A Passage to India* by E. M. Forster (written in 1924). The novel is set in the British Raj and is the story of a friendship between an Indian doctor and his British friend, which cannot survive the false accusation of assault an Englishwoman makes against the Indian doctor. It explores the dark side of colonial power. You could offer extra credit for students to read the novel, or they could watch the 1984 film version of it by director David Lean and write a report on how the story portrays the influence of colonial rule.

BUILDING AP® SKILLS
Sourcing and Situation

You can help students practice their ability to think about different points of view on a historical event by asking: Would colonized people have been aware of the dichotomy between European ideals and the realities of governing colonial empires? *Colonized people who received a Western education, such as Gandhi, were especially aware of the differences between the Enlightenment, with its ideas of human equality, and the colonial system of institutionalized inequality among races, genders, and castes.*

AP® CLASSROOM

AP® Daily Videos

It might be good for students to watch the AP® Daily Video for 6.5, *Economic Imperialism from 1750 to 1900*, before starting to learn about colonial economies. This video takes a look at what economic imperialism is and where it happened, along with helping students work on the skill of contextualization.

APPLY THE TIP

Natural resources played a major role in the motivations European countries had to take over states in Africa and Asia. As a bell ringer when students are learning about economic imperialism, ask them to list out what natural resources European countries received from African and Asian colonies. *Gold, diamonds, copper, tin, rubber, coffee, cotton, sugar, cocoa, hemp, palm oil, etc.*

AP®
CAUSATION
What were the causes of nineteenth-century European imperialism? What were the effects of imperialism on Asian and African societies?

AP® EXAM TIP
Make a list of natural resources that European countries received from African and Asian colonies.

AP®
COMPARISON
In what different ways did the colonial experience reshape the economic lives of Asian and African societies?

dictatorships, where few colonial subjects participated as citizens. Empire, of course, was wholly at odds with European notions of national independence, and ranked racial classifications went against the grain of both Christian and Enlightenment ideas of human equality. Furthermore, many Europeans were distinctly reluctant to encourage within their colonies the kind of modernization—urban growth, industrialization, individual values, religious skepticism—that was sweeping their own societies. They feared that this kind of social change, often vilified as "detribalization," would encourage unrest and challenge colonial rule. As a model for social development, they much preferred "traditional" rural society, with its established authorities and social hierarchies, though shorn of abuses such as slavery and *sati* (widow burning). Such contradictions between what Europeans embraced at home and what they practiced in the colonies became increasingly apparent to many Asians and Africans and played a major role in undermining the foundations of colonial rule in the twentieth century.

Ways of Working: Comparing Colonial Economies

Finding the Main Point: How were societies across Africa and Asia transformed by colonial economic policies?

Colonial rule deeply affected the lives of its subject people, but the most pronounced change was in their ways of working. The colonial state—with its power to tax, to seize land for European enterprises, to compel labor, and to build railroads, ports, and roads—played an important role in these transformations. Even more powerful was the growing integration of colonized societies into a world economy that increasingly demanded their gold, diamonds, copper, tin, rubber, coffee, cotton, sugar, cocoa, and many other products. But the economic transformations born of these twin pressures were far from uniform. Various groups—migrant workers and cash-crop farmers, plantation laborers and domestic servants, urban elites and day laborers, men and women—experienced the colonial era differently as their daily working lives underwent profound changes.

To various degrees, older ways of working were eroded almost everywhere in the colonial world. Subsistence farming, in which peasant families produced largely for their own needs, diminished as growing numbers directed at least some of their energies to working for wages or selling what they produced for a cash income. That money was both necessary to pay taxes and school fees and useful for buying the various products—such as textiles, bicycles, and kerosene—that the industrial economies of Europe sent their way. As in Europe, artisans suffered greatly when cheaper machine-manufactured merchandise displaced their own handmade goods. A flood of inexpensive textiles from Britain's new factories ruined the livelihood of tens of thousands of India's handloom weavers. Iron smelting largely disappeared in Africa, and occupations such as blacksmithing and tanning lost ground.

BUILDING AP® SKILLS

Argumentation

You don't always need to have students write full essays to get them to work on their writing skills throughout the year. You can use the following question as a prompt for students to practice writing an LEQ-style argument paragraph. The paragraph should open with a topic sentence, have at least two pieces of evidence to support it, and use one of the historical reasoning skills (Comparison, Causation, and Continuity and Change) to shape their argument.

■ In what ways did the economics of colonial societies change as a result of

imperialism? *Answers may include: Subsistence farming, in which peasant families produced largely for their own needs, diminished as growing numbers directed at least some of their energies to working for wages or selling what they produced for a cash income; That money was necessary to pay taxes and school fees and useful for buying the various products, such as machine-produced textiles, bicycles, and kerosene, that the industrial economies of Europe sent their way; As*

in Europe, artisans in colonial societies suffered greatly when cheaper machine-manufactured merchandise displaced their own handmade goods; A flood of inexpensive textiles from Britain's new factories ruined the livelihoods of tens of thousands of India's handloom weavers; Iron smelting largely disappeared in Africa, and occupations such as blacksmithing and tanning lost ground.

Furthermore, Asian and African merchants, who had earlier handled the trade between their countries and the wider world, were squeezed out by well-financed European commercial firms. Thus colonial rule facilitated the commercialization of Asian and African economies, requiring growing numbers of people to operate within market-based networks of production and exchange. (See "Commerce and Social Change" in Chapter 6 for earlier examples of this process.)

Economies of Coercion: Forced Labor and the Power of the State

Many of the new ways of working that emerged during the colonial era derived directly from the demands of the colonial state. The most obvious was required and unpaid labor on public projects, such as building railroads, constructing government buildings, and transporting goods. In French Africa, all "natives" were legally obligated to do "statute labor" for ten to twelve days a year, a practice that lasted through 1946. It was much resented. A resident of British West Africa, interviewed in 1996, bitterly recalled this feature of colonial life: "They [British officials] were rude, and they made us work for them a lot. They came to the village and just rounded us up and made us go off and clear the road or carry loads on our heads."[16]

The most infamous cruelties of forced labor occurred during the early twentieth century in the **Congo Free State**, then governed personally by King Leopold II of Belgium. Private companies in the Congo, operating under the authority of the state, forced villagers to collect rubber, which was much in demand for bicycle and automobile tires, with a reign of terror and abuse beginning in the 1890s that cost millions of lives. One refugee from these horrors described the process:

> We were always in the forest to find the rubber vines, to go without food, and our women had to give up cultivating the fields and gardens. Then we starved. . . . We begged the white man to leave us alone, saying we could get no more rubber, but the white men and their soldiers said "Go. You are only beasts yourselves. . . ." When we failed and our rubber was short, the soldiers came to our towns and killed us. Many were shot, some had their ears cut off; others were tied up with ropes round their necks and taken away.[17]

Eventually such outrages were widely publicized in Europe, where they created a scandal, forcing the Belgian government to take control of the Congo in 1908 and ending Leopold's reign of terror.

A variation on the theme of forced labor took shape in the so-called **cultivation system** of the Netherlands East Indies (Indonesia) during the nineteenth century. Peasants were required to cultivate 20 percent or more of their land in cash crops such as sugar or coffee to meet their tax obligation to the state. Sold to government contractors at fixed and low prices, those crops, when resold on the world market, proved highly profitable for Dutch traders as well as for the Dutch state and its citizens.

AP® EXAM TIP

Return to Chapter 6 and compare the plantation systems in the Americas to the colonial economies discussed here.

AP®

COMPARISON

In what ways is the forced labor described here similar to earlier versions of coerced labor, such as the mita (see "The Emergence of the Incas in the Andes" in Chapter 2) and slavery?

APPLY THE TIP

Students can be asked to make comparisons between time periods on the AP® Exam, and it's good to have them practice these comparisons throughout the course. Consider dividing the class into two groups. Ask one group to return to Chapter 6 to review the American plantation system, and ask the other to look up cash-crop agriculture in nineteenth-century Asia. Then have each group create a short presentation (on a poster or digital slides) to present their findings. Once the groups have presented, ask students to describe the similarities and differences of the two systems. *Both systems produced cash crops for the international market and used forced labor. In the American plantation system, the plantation owners used the labor of enslaved people or indentured servants. In the Asian system, private ownership of relatively small farms thrived as a result of rice growing.*

TEACHING IDEA

Incorporating Outside Resources

A different way to get students thinking about the brutalities of the colonial economy is to show them the 5-minute trailer of *King Leopold's Ghost*. This documentary is based on the book by Adam Hochschild about the brutality of the Belgian colonization of the Congo. You can find the trailer on YouTube. After showing the trailer, display the image "Colonial Violence in the Congo" from page 568 and ask students: What do you think motivated the brutality? How do you think the people who enacted such violence justified their actions? *The brutality was motivated by frustration that quotas were not being met for a variety of reasons. The people who carried out the violence could have justified it by seeing the Indigenous people as less than human.*

EXPLORING AP® THEMES

Economic Systems (ECN)

This might be a good point to put students into small groups of three to four to discuss the different examples of forced labor during the colonial era. Have them read through "Economies of Coercion: Forced Labor and the Power of the State" and take notes on their own. After they finish, ask them to discuss the following question with their small group: What are examples of the types of forced labor colonial peoples had to perform? How did these people react to the forced labor? *The types of forced labor were "statute labor" or a kind of labor tax in French Africa, the forcing of villagers in the Congo to collect rubber for private companies, the cultivation system in the Dutch East Indies, and the forced cultivation of cotton in German East Africa. In some places, native peoples rebelled against colonial powers because of their treatment under forced labor.*

Colonial Violence in the Congo Horrific photos of mutilated children had an important impact on public opinion about imperial rule in the Congo Free State. They came to symbolize widespread abuses, including murders, rapes, starvation, and the burning of villages, associated with efforts to obtain supplies of wild rubber for use in industrialized societies. (Universal History Archive/Getty Images)

▲ AP
ARGUMENTATION
How could political and social reformers in the nineteenth century use photographs such as this to promote changes in how governments ruled their colonies?

AP
CAUSATION
Why might local farmers resist the forced cultivation of cash crops?

According to one scholar, the cultivation system "performed a miracle for the Dutch economy," enabling it to avoid taxing its own people and providing capital for its Industrial Revolution.[18] It also enriched and strengthened the position of those "traditional authorities" who enforced the system, often by using lashings and various tortures, on behalf of the Dutch. For the peasants of Java, however, it meant a double burden of obligations to the colonial state as well as to local lords. Many became indebted to moneylenders when they could not meet those obligations. Those demands, coupled with the loss of land and labor now excluded from food production, contributed to a wave of famines during the mid-nineteenth century in which hundreds of thousands perished.

On occasion, the forced cultivation of cash crops was successfully resisted. In German East Africa, for example, colonial authorities in the late nineteenth century imposed the cultivation of cotton, which seriously interfered with production of local food crops. Here is how one man remembered the experience:

> Every village was allotted days on which to cultivate. . . . After arriving you all suffered very greatly. Your back and your buttocks were whipped and there was no rising up once you stooped to dig. . . . And yet he [the German] wanted us to pay him tax. Were we not human beings?[19]

Such conditions prompted the massive rebellion in 1904–1905 known as Maji Maji, which persuaded the Germans to end the forced growing of cotton. Thus the actions of colonized peoples could alter or frustrate the plans of the colonizers.

Economies of Cash-Crop Agriculture: The Pull of the Market

Many Asian and African peoples had produced quite willingly for an international market long before they were enclosed within colonial societies. They offered for trade items such as peanuts and palm oil in West Africa, cotton in Egypt, spices in Indonesia, pepper and textiles in India, and silks in China. In some places, colonial rule created conditions that facilitated and increased **cash-crop production** to the advantage of local farmers. British authorities in Burma, for example, encouraged rice production among small farmers by ending an earlier prohibition on rice exports, providing irrigation and transportation facilities, and enacting land tenure laws that facilitated private ownership of small farms. Under these conditions, the population of the Irrawaddy Delta boomed, migrants from Upper Burma and India poured into the region, and rice exports soared. Local small farmers benefited considerably because they were now able to own their own land, build substantial houses, and buy imported goods. For several decades in the late nineteenth century, standards of living improved sharply, and huge increases in rice production fed millions of people in other parts of Asia and elsewhere. It was a very different situation from that of peasants forced to grow crops that seriously interfered with their food production.

But that kind of colonial development, practiced also in the Mekong River delta of French-ruled Vietnam, had important environmental consequences. It involved the destruction of mangrove forests and swamplands along with the fish and shellfish that supplemented local diets. New dikes and irrigation channels inhibited the depositing of silt from upstream and thus depleted soils in the deltas of these major river systems. And, unknown to anyone at the time, this kind of agriculture generates large amounts of methane gas, a major contributor to global warming.

Profitable cash-crop farming also developed in the southern Gold Coast (present-day Ghana), a British territory in West Africa. Unlike in Burma, it was African farmers themselves who took the initiative to develop export agriculture. Planting cacao trees in huge quantities, they became the world's leading supplier of cocoa, used to make chocolate, by 1911. Cacao was an attractive crop because, unlike cotton, it was compatible with the continued production of foods and did not require as much labor. In the early twentieth century, it brought a new prosperity to many local farmers. But that success brought new problems in its wake. A labor shortage fostered the employment of formerly enslaved people as dependent and exploited workers. It also generated tensions between the sexes when some men married women for their labor but refused to support them adequately. Moreover, the labor shortage brought a huge influx of migrants from the drier interior parts of West Africa, generating ethnic and class tensions. Another problem was that many colonies came to specialize in one or two cash crops, creating an unhealthy dependence when world market prices dropped. Thus African and Asian farmers were increasingly subject to the uncertain rhythms of the international marketplace as well as to those of weather and climate.

Much of the international commerce generated during the colonial era was facilitated by large European corporations such as Lever Brothers (later Unilever), Lipton, the Royal Africa Company, the British South Africa Company, and many others, often supported by colonial governments. Their wealth and power gave them great leverage over the prices paid to Asian and African producers and workers, even as they displaced local merchant communities.

AP®
CONTINUITY AND CHANGE
How did cash-crop agriculture transform the lives of colonized peoples?

EXPLORING AP® THEMES
Humans and the Environment (ENV)

It's good for students to know that economic imperialism and the rise of cash-crop production as described on this page had major environmental impacts on the world. You can get students to think about this by asking them to describe the environmental destruction caused by increased agriculture in various parts of the world in this period. *In Vietnam, agriculture destroyed mangroves and swamplands, depleted fish and shellfish, inhibited the deposit of silt and thus depleted soils, and began the release of methane, a greenhouse gas. In Africa, increased agriculture led to more migration from the dry interior, where farming could not be sustained.*

AP EXAM TIP

The massive migrations in the late nineteenth and early twentieth centuries are a major concept in the AP® course.

Economies of Wage Labor: Migration for Work

Yet another new way of working in colonial societies involved wage labor in some European enterprise. Driven by the need for money, by the loss of land adequate to support their families, or sometimes by the orders of colonial authorities, millions of colonial subjects across Asia, Africa, and Oceania sought employment in European-owned plantations, mines, construction projects, and homes. Often this required migration to distant work sites, many of them overseas. In this process, colonized migrants were joined by millions of Chinese, Japanese, and others who lived in more independent states. Together they generated vast streams of migration that paralleled and at least equaled in numbers the huge movement of Europeans during the nineteenth and early twentieth centuries. For Europeans, Asians, and Africans alike, the globalizing world of the colonial era was one of people in motion. (See the Snapshot on long-distance migration.)

The African segment of this migratory stream moved in several directions. For much of the nineteenth century, the Atlantic slave trade continued, funneling well over 3 million additional people to the Americas, mostly to Brazil. As the slave trade diminished and colonial rule took shape in Africa, internal migration mounted within or among particular colonies. More than in Asia, many Africans lost their land to Europeans and then had to migrate to European-controlled farms or plantations to find work. In the settler colonies of Africa—Algeria, Kenya, Southern Rhodesia (Zimbabwe), and South Africa, for example—permanent European communities, with the help of colonial governments, obtained huge tracts of land, much of which had previously been home to Africans. A 1913 law in South Africa legally defined 88 percent of the land as belonging to whites, who were then about 20 percent of the population. Much of highland Kenya, an enormously rich agricultural region that was home to the Gikuyu and Kamba peoples, was taken over by some 4,000 white farmers. In such places, some Africans stayed on as "squatters," working for the new landowners as the

▶ **AP**
CONTINUITY AND CHANGE
In what ways are the migrations seen in the Snapshot chart different from the patterns of global migrations in the period 1450 to 1750?

SNAPSHOT Long-Distance Migration in an Age of Empire, 1846–1940

The age of empire was also an age of global migration. Beyond the three major patterns of long-distance migration shown here, shorter migrations within particular regions or colonies set millions more into motion.

Origins	Destination	Numbers
Europe	Americas	55–58 million
India, southern China	Southeast Asia, Indian Ocean rim, South Pacific	48–52 million
Northeast Asia, Russia	Manchuria, Siberia, Central Asia, Japan	46–51 million

Source: Data from Adam McKeown, "Global Migration, 1846–1940," *Journal of World History* 15, no. 2 (2004): 156.

BUILDING AP® SKILLS

Claims and Evidence in Sources

You can use the "Snapshot: Long-Distance Migration in an Age of Empire, 1846–1940" to help students begin to examine the mass migration that took place in the nineteenth century. Have students study the chart and then ask the following questions:

■ Which area absorbed the largest number of migrants? *The Americas absorbed the largest number of migrants.*

■ Which area absorbed the fewest migrants? *Manchuria, Siberia, Central Asia, and Japan absorbed the fewest migrants in this period.*

■ Roughly, what is the average number of migrants who traveled long distances per year? *The average number of long-distance migrants per year in this period was 1.6 million.*

It might also be interesting to have students connect the trends they see in this chart with their observations of the information on Map 8.2, "European Migration in the Industrial Age," on page 458 in Chapter 8.

BUILDING AP® SKILLS

Claims and Evidence in Sources

This could be a good place to work on DBQ skills with students using the documents from the 2003 released Question 1 prompt, which focuses on indentured servants in the nineteenth and twentieth centuries. You can find a copy of the released DBQ on the AP® World History: Modern Past Exam Questions webpage. Have students analyze the documents for evidence of the causes and consequences of indentured servitude in the imperial age and record their observations in **Handout 10.6: Chart for Nineteenth-Century Indentured Servitude through Documents**. A reproducible version of this chart can be found in the Teacher's Resource Materials.

TRM Handout 10.6: Chart for Nineteenth-Century Indentured Servitude through Documents price of remaining on what had been their own land. Others were displaced to "native reserves," limited areas that could not support their growing populations. In South Africa, such reserved areas became greatly overcrowded: soil fertility declined, hillsides were cleared, forests shrank, and erosion scarred the land. This kind of ecological degradation forced ever more Africans into wage labor in European enterprises.

The gold and diamond mines of South Africa likewise set in motion a huge pattern of labor migration that encompassed all of Africa south of the Belgian Congo. With skilled and highly paid work reserved for white miners, Africans worked largely as unskilled laborers at a fraction of the wages paid to whites. Furthermore, they were recruited on short-term contracts, lived in all-male prison-like barracks that were often surrounded by barbed wire, and were forced to return home periodically to prevent them from establishing a permanent family life near the mines.

Asians too were in motion and in large numbers. Some 29 million Indians and 19 million Chinese migrated variously to Southeast Asia, the South Pacific, East and South Africa, the Caribbean, or the lands around the Indian Ocean basin, where they generally lived in ethnic enclaves. All across Southeast Asia in the later nineteenth and early twentieth centuries, huge plantations sprouted that were financed from Europe and that grew sugarcane, rubber, tea, tobacco, sisal (used for making rope), and more. Impoverished workers by the hundreds of thousands came from great distances (India and China) to these plantations, where they were subject to strict control, often housed in barracks, and paid poorly, with women receiving 50 to 75 percent of a man's wage. Disease was common, and death rates were at least double that of the colony as a whole. In 1927 in southern Vietnam alone, one in twenty plantation workers died. British colonial authorities facilitated the migration of millions of Indians to worksites elsewhere in the British Empire—Trinidad, Jamaica, Fiji, Malaysia, Ceylon, South Africa, Kenya, and Uganda, among others. Some worked as indentured laborers, receiving free passage and enough money to survive in return for

> **AP®**
> **CONTINUITY AND CHANGE**
> As slave labor declined in the nineteenth century, what forms of labor replaced it?

> ▼ **AP®**
> **CAUSATION**
> What developments might have led people to leave their homeland and work in conditions seen in this image?

Economic Change in the Colonial World These workers at a Malayan tin-mining facility in the early twentieth century were just a few of the millions drawn from as far away as China and India to labor in the mines and on the plantations of Southeast Asia. (© Look and Learn/Bridgeman Images)

EXPLORING AP® THEMES

Governance (GOV) and Humans and the Environment (ENV)

Consider having a quick class discussion on the connections between European colonial policies and nineteenth-century migration. To get the discussion started, ask: How are migrations and European land confiscation linked? *Africans migrated to other areas as their land was confiscated. In 1913, South African law defined 88 percent of the land as belonging to whites, who made up just 20 percent of the population. This meant that many Africans migrated to find work as wage laborers.*

AP® CLASSROOM

AP® Topic Questions

Students should practice their test-taking skills whenever they can throughout the year to become comfortable with the MCQs on the AP® Exam. The three AP® Topic Questions for "Indentured and Non-Indentured Workers MCQ" would be a good set to give students for practice. You can find the questions in your AP® Classroom account under Topics 6.6 and 6.7. Have students answer the questions on their own. Then partner them up to review the questions, discuss the correct answers, and explain why they chose them.

Making Connections: Causation

While students are reading "Economies of Wage Labor: Migration for Work," suggest they make a list of the push and pull factors they see in the reading that contributed to the massive migrations of this time period. After students finish the reading, ask them to share what push and pull factors they found. *Push factors included the following: migrants were driven by the need for money, by the loss of land adequate to support their families, or sometimes by the orders of colonial authorities. Pull factors included the following: millions of colonial subjects across Asia, Africa, and Oceania sought employment in European-owned plantations, mines, construction projects, and homes.*

You can have students read the last paragraph on this page to help them understand the information in the AP® Exam Tip. After they have read it, ask: What are the factors that led to the growth of colonial cities in the era of imperialism? *Answers will include: Cities were seen as places of opportunity; Cities have jobs for all types of workers.*

AP
CONTINUITY AND CHANGE
What kinds of wage labor were available in the colonies, and why might people choose this work? How did doing so affect their lives?

AP EXAM TIP
You should understand the factors that led to the growth of colonial cities in this era.

five to seven years of heavy labor. Others operated as independent merchants. Particularly in the Caribbean region, Indian migration rose as the end of slavery created a need for additional labor. Since the vast majority of these Asian migrants were male, gender ratios were altered on the islands and in their countries of origin, where women faced increased workloads.

Mines were another source of wage labor for many Asians. In the British-ruled Malay States (Malaysia), tin mining accelerated greatly in the late nineteenth century, and by 1895 that colony produced some 55 percent of the world's tin. Operated initially by Chinese and later by European entrepreneurs, Malaysian tin mines drew many millions of impoverished Chinese workers on strictly controlled three-year contracts. Appalling living conditions, disease, and accidents generated extraordinarily high death rates.

Beyond Southeast Asia, Chinese migrants moved north to Manchuria in substantial numbers, encouraged by a Chinese government eager to prevent Russian encroachment in the area. The gold rushes of Australia and California also attracted hundreds of thousands of Chinese, who often found themselves subject to sharp discrimination from local people, including recently arrived European migrants. For example, Dennis Kearney, who led a California anti-immigrant labor organization with the slogan "The Chinese must go," was himself an Irish-born immigrant. In 1882, the United States passed the Chinese Exclusion Act, which made Chinese immigrants ineligible for citizenship and halted Chinese immigration for a decade. It was the first law designed to prevent a specific ethnic group from migrating to the United States. It was repealed only in 1943. And in the South Pacific, a "white Australia policy" sought to prevent non-Europeans, especially Asians and Pacific islanders, from living and working in Australia.

A further destination of African and Asian migrants lay in the rapidly swelling cities of the colonial world—Lagos, Nairobi, Cairo, Calcutta, Rangoon, Batavia, Singapore, and Saigon. Racially segregated, often unsanitary, and greatly overcrowded, these cities nonetheless were seen as meccas of opportunity for people all across the social spectrum. Traditional elites, absentee landlords, and wealthy Chinese businessmen occupied the top rungs of Southeast Asian cities. Western-educated people everywhere found opportunities as teachers, doctors, and professional specialists, but more often as clerks in European business offices and government bureaucracies. Skilled workers on the railways or in the ports represented a working-class elite, while a few labored in the factories that processed agricultural goods or manufactured basic products such as beer, cigarettes, cement, and furniture. Far more numerous were the construction workers, rickshaw drivers, food sellers, domestic servants, prostitutes, and others who made up the urban poor of colonial cities. In 1955, a British report on life in Nairobi, the capital of Kenya, found that low wages, combined with the high cost of housing and food, "makes family life impossible for the majority."[20] After a half century of colonial rule, it was quite an admission.

Women and the Colonial Economy: Examples from Africa

If economic life in European empires varied greatly from place to place, even within the same colony, it also offered a different combination of opportunities and hardships to women than it did to men, as the experience of colonial Africa shows.[21] In precolonial Africa, women were almost everywhere active farmers, with responsibility for planting, weeding, and harvesting in addition to food preparation and child care. Men cleared the land, built houses, herded the cattle, and in some cases assisted with field work. Within this division of labor, women were expected to feed their own families and were usually allocated their own fields for that purpose. Many were also involved in local trading activity. Though clearly subordinate to men, African women nevertheless had a measure of economic autonomy.

As the demands of the colonial economy grew, women's lives increasingly diverged from those of men. In colonies where cash-crop agriculture was dominant, men often withdrew from subsistence production in favor of more lucrative export crops. Among the Ewe people of southern Ghana, for example, men almost completely dominated the highly profitable cacao farming, whereas women assumed nearly total responsibility for domestic food production. Thus when men focused on cash-crop agriculture, the subsistence workload of women increased. One study from Cameroon estimated that women's working hours increased from forty-six per week in precolonial times to more than seventy by 1934.

Further increasing women's workload and differentiating their lives from those of men was labor migration. As growing numbers of men sought employment in the cities, on settler farms, or in the mines, their wives were left to manage the domestic economy almost alone. In many cases, women also had to supply food to men in the cities to compensate for very low urban wages. They often took over such traditionally male tasks as breaking the ground for planting, milking the cows, and supervising the herds, in addition to their normal responsibilities. In South Africa, where the demands of the European economy were particularly heavy, some 40 to 50 percent of able-bodied adult men were absent from the rural areas, and women headed 60 percent of households. In Botswana, which supplied much male labor to South Africa, married couples by the 1930s rarely lived together for more than two months at a time. Increasingly, men and women lived in different worlds, with one focused on the cities and working for wages and the other on village life and subsistence agriculture.

Women coped with these difficult circumstances in a number of ways. Many sought closer relations with their families of birth rather than with their absent husbands' families, as would otherwise have been expected. Among the Luo of Kenya, women introduced laborsaving crops, adopted new farm implements, and earned some money as traders. In the cities, they established a variety of self-help associations, including those for prostitutes and for brewers of beer.

The colonial economy sometimes provided a measure of opportunity for enterprising women, particularly in small-scale trade and marketing. In some parts of West Africa, women came to dominate this sector of the economy by selling foodstuffs, cloth,

EXPLORING AP® THEMES

Social Interactions and Organization (SIO)

To help students understand the changes women in Africa experienced due to imperialism, ask them to describe women's lives in precolonial Africa. *In precolonial Africa, women were active farmers almost everywhere, with responsibility for planting, weeding, and harvesting in addition to food preparation and child care. Women were expected to feed their own families and were usually allocated their own fields for that purpose. Many were also involved in local trading activity. Though clearly subordinate to men, African women nevertheless had a measure of economic autonomy.*

BUILDING AP® SKILLS

Making Connections: Comparison

Gendered divisions in labor have existed since the Neolithic Revolution led to sedentary societies. You can help students think about how those divisions might have been affected by imperialism by asking: How was women's work in the colonial economy different from men's work? *Women's work tended to be centered on benefiting the family by growing food and tending to cotton crops to make clothes, while men's work, traditionally, was growing cash crops, caring for cattle, and breaking new ground for future planting.*

BUILDING AP® SKILLS

Argumentation

This is a good place to pause and have students review the information in this section to write an essay. Give them 40 minutes to write an essay on the following prompt:

- Evaluate the extent to which colonial economic policies led to opportunities and/or barriers for women in Africa during the late nineteenth and early twentieth centuries.

Essays should touch on the following points:

Opportunities

- *Earned money as traders*
- *Introduced laborsaving tools*
- *Made money by selling food*
- *Stayed closer to birth family, instead of following the tradition of moving closer to the husband's family*
- *Became almost autonomous heads of households*

Barriers

- *More responsibilities because men left the villages to work elsewhere*
- *Land and crop production co-opted by men when traditional agricultural crops grown by women became cash crops*

APPLY THE TIP

As students read this portion of the text, you can ask them to take notes on the three main points of "Assessing Colonial Development." This is an important skill for students to learn as they work on improving reading comprehension skills. *Answers should include the following points:*

I. *Colonial rule served to further integrate Asia and Africa into a global network of exchange centered on Europe.*

II. *Europeans brought their modernization to the colonies.*

III. *Because no colonies became industrialized, their economies did not advance and they remained impoverished.*

Women and Peanut Production in Gambia In this photograph from the British colony of Gambia in West Africa, women are threshing peanuts, separating the nuts from the plants on which they grow. Throughout the colonial era, peanuts were the colony's major export crop, and women were heavily involved in their production. (Popperfoto/Getty Images)

▲ **AP®**
CONTINUITY AND CHANGE
Using information learned in this chapter and the image, explain how women's lives both changed and yet remained the same during nineteenth-century colonization.

AP® EXAM TIP
Take notes on this important discussion of the legacies of nineteenth-century imperialism.

and inexpensive imported goods, while men or foreign firms controlled the more profitable wholesale and import-export trade. Such opportunities sometimes gave women considerable economic autonomy. By the 1930s, for example, Nupe women in northern Nigeria had gained sufficient wealth as itinerant traders that they were contributing more to the family income than their husbands and frequently lent money to them. Among some Igbo groups in southern Nigeria, men were responsible for growing the prestigious yams, but women's crops—especially cassava—came to have a cash value during the colonial era, and women were entitled to keep the profits from selling them. "What is man? I have my own money" was a popular saying that expressed the growing economic independence of such women.[22]

At the other end of the social scale, women of impoverished rural families, by necessity, often became virtually independent heads of household in the absence of their husbands. Others took advantage of new opportunities in mission schools, towns, and mines to flee the restrictions of rural patriarchy. Such challenges to patriarchal values elicited various responses from men, including increased accusations of witchcraft against women. Among the Shona in Southern Rhodesia, and no doubt elsewhere, senior African men repeatedly petitioned the colonial authorities for laws and regulations that would criminalize adultery and restrict women's ability to leave their rural villages. The control of women's sexuality and mobility was a common interest of European and African men.

Assessing Colonial Development

Beyond the many and varied changes that transformed the working lives of millions in the colonial world lies the difficult and highly controversial question of the overall economic impact of colonial rule on Asian and African societies. Defenders, both then and now, praise it for jump-starting modern economic growth, but numerous critics cite a record of exploitation and highlight the limitations and unevenness of that growth.

Amid the continuing debates, three things seem reasonably clear. First, colonial rule served, for better or worse, to further the integration of Asian and African economies into a global network of exchange, then centered in Europe. Within the colonial world far more land and labor were devoted to production for the global market at the end of the colonial era than at its beginning. Many colonized groups and individuals benefited from their new access to global markets—Burmese rice farmers and West African cocoa farmers, for example. Others were devastated. In India, large-scale wheat exports to Britain continued unchecked—or even increased—despite a major drought and famine that claimed between 6 and 10 million lives in the late 1870s. A colonial government committed to free market principles and white superiority declined to interfere with those exports or to provide much by way of relief. One senior official declared it "a mistake to spend so much money to save a lot of black fellows."[23]

Second, Europeans could hardly avoid conveying to the colonies some elements of their own modernizing process. It was in their interests to do so, and many felt duty bound to "improve" the societies they briefly governed. Modern administrative and bureaucratic structures facilitated colonial control; transportation and communication infrastructure (railroads, ports, telegraphs, postal services) moved products to the world market; schools trained the army of intermediaries on which colonial rule depended; and modest health care provisions fulfilled some of the "civilizing mission" to which many Europeans felt committed. These elements of modernization made an appearance, however inadequately, during the colonial era.

Third, nowhere in the colonial world did a major breakthrough to modern industrial society occur. When India became independent after two centuries of colonial rule by the world's first industrial society, it was still one of the poorest of the world's developing countries. The British may not have created Indian poverty, but neither did they overcome it to any substantial degree. Scholars continue to debate the reasons for that failure: was it the result of deliberate British policies, or was it due to the conditions of Indian society? The nationalist movements that surged across Asia and Africa in the twentieth century had their own answer. To their many millions of participants, colonial rule, whatever its earlier promise, had become an economic dead end, whereas independence represented a grand opening to new and more hopeful possibilities. Taking off from a famous teaching of Jesus, Kwame Nkrumah, the first prime minister of an independent Ghana, declared, "Seek ye first the political kingdom, and all these other things [schools, factories, hospitals, for example] will be added unto you."

Believing and Belonging: Identity and Cultural Change

Finding the Main Point: How did the cultural and ethnic identities of colonized people change in the face of European imperialism?

Beyond profound economic transformations, the experience of colonial rule—its racism, its exposure to European culture, its social and economic upheavals—also generated new patterns of cultural identity within Asian, African, and Oceanic

AP®

ARGUMENTATION
Did colonial rule bring economic "progress" in its wake? What value assumptions are implicit in this question?

societies. Millions of people underwent substantial and quite rapid changes in what they believed and in how they defined the communities to which they belonged. Those new ways of believing and belonging echoed long after European rule had ended.

Education

For an important minority, it was the acquisition of Western education, obtained through missionary or government schools, that generated a new identity. To previously nonliterate people, the knowledge of reading and writing of any kind often suggested an almost magical power. Within the colonial setting, it could mean an escape from some of the most onerous obligations of living under European control, such as forced labor. More positively, it meant access to better-paying positions in government bureaucracies, mission organizations, or business firms and to the exciting imported goods that their salaries could buy. Moreover, education often provided social mobility and elite status within colonized peoples' own communities and an opportunity to achieve, or at least approach, equality with whites in racially defined societies. An African man from colonial Kenya described an encounter he had as a boy in 1938 with a relative who was a teacher in a mission school:

> Aged about 25, he seems to me like a young god with his smart clothes and shoes, his watch, and a beautiful bicycle. I worshipped in particular his bicycle that day and decided that I must somehow get myself one. As he talked with us, it seemed to me that the secret of his riches came from his education, his knowledge of reading and writing, and that it was essential for me to obtain this power.[24]

Many such people ardently embraced European culture, dressing in European clothes, speaking French or English, building European-style houses, getting married in long white dresses, and otherwise emulating European ways. Some of the early Western-educated Bengalis from northeastern India boasted about dreaming in English and deliberately ate beef, to the consternation of their elders. In a well-known poem titled "A Prayer for Peace," Léopold Senghor, a highly educated West African writer and political leader, enumerated the many crimes of colonialism and yet confessed, "I have a great weakness for France." Asian and African colonial societies now had a new cultural divide: between the small numbers who had mastered to varying degrees the ways of their rulers and the vast majority who had not. Literate Christians in the East African kingdom of Buganda referred with contempt to their "pagan" neighbors as "those who do not read."

Many among the Western-educated elite saw themselves as a modernizing vanguard, leading the regeneration of their societies in association with colonial authorities. For them, at least initially, the colonial enterprise was full of promise for a better future. (See AP® Looking Again: Advocating for Western Education in India, page 591, for an Indian example of this kind of thinking.) The Vietnamese

---

Students can struggle with skimming a passage to find information, so this is a valuable skill for them to learn. To help them work on this skill, have students skim the section titled "Education" on pages 576 to 578 to look for the names of colonial elites who became involved in independence movements in the twentieth century. *Answers will include: Leopold Senghor of West Africa, Nguyen Thai Hoc of Vietnam, Keshub Chunder Sen of India, James Aggrey of West Africa.*

Incorporating Outside Resources

In the Crash Course World History episode *Imperialism*, John Green describes imperialism in the nineteenth century. You can use the video to help sum up what students have learned so far about imperialism. The episode can be found on YouTube. Note that the section on imperialism in Africa begins at 3:37. After watching the video, ask students the following questions:

■ Why did Europeans succeed in colonizing Africa in the nineteenth century? *Modern industrial technology such as Maxim guns, steamships, and quinine allowed Europeans to colonize Africa in this period.*

■ Why did nineteenth-century imperialism rely on local elites to rule the local area? *Local elites kept their power and influence and often profited by having access to Western education for their children.*

AP® Topic Questions

This would be a good point to assign the three AP® Topic Questions for "French Algeria School Image MCQ" for stimulus-based multiple-choice question practice. You can find the questions in your AP® Classroom account under Topics 6.1 and 6.2. You can assign the questions as a bell ringer for students or as a quick check for understanding at the end of class.

teacher and nationalist Nguyen Thai Hoc, while awaiting execution in 1930 by the French for his revolutionary activities, wrote about his earlier hopes: "At the beginning, I had thought to cooperate with the French in Indochina in order to serve my compatriots, my country, and my people, particularly in the areas of cultural and economic development."[25]

In nineteenth-century India, Western-educated men organized a variety of reform societies that drew inspiration from the classic texts of Hinduism while seeking a renewed Indian culture that was free of idolatry, caste restrictions, and other "errors" that had entered Indian life over the centuries. Much of this reform effort centered on improving the status of women. Thus reformers campaigned against *sati*, the ban on remarriage of widows, female infanticide, and child marriages, while advocating women's education and property rights. For a time, some of these Indian reformers saw themselves working in tandem with British colonial authorities. One of them, Keshub Chunder Sen, addressed his fellow Indians in 1877: "You are bound to be loyal to the British government that came to your rescue, as God's ambassador, when your country was sunk in ignorance and

AP® EXAM TIP

The rise of anticolonial nationalism within African and Asian colonies is an important concept in AP® World History.

▼ AP®

MAKING CONNECTIONS

How could a historian use this image to describe the relationship between European colonial powers and native elites?

The Educated Elite Throughout the Afro-Asian world of the nineteenth century, the European presence generated a small group of people who enthusiastically embraced the culture and lifestyle of Europe. Here King Chulalongkorn of Siam poses with the crown prince and other young students, all of them impeccably garbed in European clothing. (Hulton Deutsch/Getty Images)

EXPLORING AP® THEMES

Cultural Developments and Interactions (CDI)

The final paragraph on page 576, which continues onto page 577, starts to look at how Western-educated elites in colonial states saw themselves as the modernizers in their societies. You can get students to analyze this idea by asking: How did education help blend European and native cultures? *Indigenous people often wore Western clothing, spoke and wrote in English, and incorporated European ways of eating. In India, they organized reform societies mainly focused on raising women's rights and level of education. While this was going on, these Indigenous elites fully understood their own cultures, although they sometimes looked at their traditionalist compatriots with contempt.*

BUILDING AP® SKILLS

Claims and Evidence in Sources

Consider displaying the photograph of King Chulalongkorn, known as the modernizing king of Siam and the subject of the musical *The King and I*, for students to study and analyze. Talk to students about how, although his kingdom was one of the few areas that remained independent, he clearly embraced modern Western culture. You could then have students research a short biography of the king of Siam and ask them: Why might the king, who was determined to keep his country's independence, embrace aspects of Western culture as shown in this image? *The king believed that by embracing European ideals he could keep his country independent. Just as the educated elite of colonized societies believed that by embracing European culture they could maintain some level of control, the king believed that by turning himself into a European monarch he could keep his country free.*

superstition. . . . India in her present fallen condition seems destined to sit at the feet of England for many long years, to learn western art and science."[26]

Those who held such hopes for the modernization of their societies within a colonial framework would be bitterly disappointed. Europeans generally declined to treat their Asian and African subjects — even those with a Western education — as equal partners in the enterprise of renewal. The frequent denigration of Asian and African cultures as primitive, backward, or uncivilized certainly rankled, particularly among the well-educated. "My people of Africa," wrote the West African intellectual James Aggrey in the 1920s, "we were created in the image of God, but men have made us think that we are chickens, and we still think we are; but we are eagles. Stretch forth your wings and fly."[27] In the long run, the educated classes in colonial societies everywhere found European rule far more of an obstacle to their countries' development than a means of achieving it. Turning decisively against a now-despised foreign imperialism, they led the many struggles for independence that came to fruition in the second half of the twentieth century.

Religion

Religion too provided the basis for new or transformed identities during the colonial era. Most dramatic were those places where widespread conversion to Christianity took place, such as Pacific Oceania and especially non-Muslim Africa. Some 10,000 missionaries had descended on Africa by 1910; by the 1960s, about 50 million Africans, roughly half of the non-Muslim population, claimed a Christian identity. The attractions of the new faith were many. As in the Americas centuries earlier, military defeat shook confidence in the old gods and local practices, fostering openness to new sources of supernatural power that could operate in the wider world now impinging on Oceanic and African societies. Furthermore, Christianity was widely associated with modern education, and, especially in Africa, mission schools were its primary providers. The young, the poor, and many women — all of them disadvantaged groups in many African societies — found new opportunities and greater freedom in some association with missions. Moreover, the spread of the Christian message was less the work of European missionaries than of those many thousands of African teachers, catechists, and pastors who brought the new faith to remote villages as well as the local communities that begged for a teacher and supplied the labor and materials to build a small church or school. In Oceania, local authorities, such as those in Fiji, Tonga, and Hawaii, sought to strengthen their position by associating with Christian missionaries, widely regarded as linked to the growing influence of European or American power in the region. In many of these small island societies, mission Christianity with its schools, clinics, political counsel, and new social conventions provided a measure of social cohesion for peoples devastated by disease and other disruptions that accompanied Western incursions.

BUILDING AP® SKILLS

Contextualization

For a short contextualization practice, ask students: In what context did Christianity offer positive opportunities for colonial societies? *It offered opportunities for unity and social cohesion. It was divisive where preserving native cultures and maintaining traditional gender norms were preferred.*

But missionary teaching and practice also generated conflict and opposition, particularly when they touched on gender roles. A wide range of issues focusing on the lives of women proved challenging for missionaries and spawned opposition from converts or potential converts. Female nudity offended Western notions of modesty. Polygyny contradicted Christian monogamy, though such prescriptions sat uneasily beside the biblical testimony that Old Testament figures such as Abraham, Jacob, David, and Solomon all had multiple wives. And the question of what male converts should do with their additional wives was always difficult. To many missionaries, bride wealth made marriage seem "a mere mercantile transaction." Marriages between Christians and non-Christians remained problematic. Sexual activity outside of monogamous marriage often resulted in disciplinary action or expulsion from the church. Missionaries' efforts to enforce Western gender norms were in part responsible for considerable turnover in the ranks of African church members.

Among the more explosive issues that agitated nascent Christian communities in colonial Kenya was that of **female circumcision**, now commonly referred to as "female genital mutilation." Involving the excision of a pubescent girl's clitoris and adjacent genital tissue, it was generally undertaken as a part of initiation rites marking her coming-of-age. To the Gikuyu people, among whom it was widely practiced, it was a prerequisite for adult status and marriage. To missionaries, it was physically damaging to girls and brought "unnecessary attention . . . to the non-spiritual aspects of sex."[28] When missionaries in 1929 sought to enforce a ban on the practice among their African converts, outrage ensued. Thousands abandoned mission schools and churches, but they did not abandon Christianity or modern education. Rather, they created a series of independent schools and churches in which they could practice their new faith and pursue their educational goals without missionary intrusion. Some recalled that

AP®
CONTEXTUALIZATION
What were the attractions of Christianity in colonial Africa? What kinds of conflicts did it generate?

▼ **AP®**
SOURCING AND SITUATION
How does this photograph reflect Europeans' beliefs about their role in colonial societies?

The Missionary Factor Among the major change agents of the colonial era were the thousands of Christian missionaries who brought not only a new religion but also elements of European medicine, education, gender roles, and culture. Here is an assembly at a mission school for girls in New Guinea in the early twentieth century. (Library of Congress, Prints & Photographs Division, Reproduction number LC-USZ62-46884 [b&w film copy neg. of half stereo])

BUILDING AP® SKILLS

Making Connections: Causation

Have students practice causation skills by asking: What caused the rift between Europeans and the Gikuyu? *The rift was caused by female circumcision, which for the Gikuyu represented traditional practices that they did not want to give up. The rift did not, however, diminish the impact of Christianity, which was brought to the Gikuyu by Europeans.*

BUILDING AP® SKILLS

Sourcing and Situation

For a quick sourcing practice, have students examine the image titled "The Missionary Factor" and ask: What observations can be made about the photo? *The white man has his hands on his hips; the whites are better dressed and wearing hats; the students are orderly and are holding books; and Papuans significantly outnumber whites.*

CHAPTER 10

ZOOMING IN Vivekananda, a Hindu Monk in America

The modern colonial era is associated with the "westernization" of the peoples of Asia, Africa, and the Middle East. Less frequently noticed has been traffic in the other direction, as Eastern, and especially Indian, religious culture penetrated Europe and the Americas. At his cabin on Walden Pond in the mid-1840s, Henry David Thoreau remarked, "In the morning I bathe my intellect in the stupendous . . . philosophy of the Bhagavad Gita . . . in comparison with which our modern world and its literature seem puny and trivial."[29]

A more seminal moment in the coming of Indian spirituality to the United States occurred in Chicago during September 1893. The occasion was the World's Parliament of Religions, an interfaith gathering that drew representatives from many of the world's religious traditions. The man who made the most vivid impression at the conference was a handsome thirty-

Swami Vivekananda.

photo: akg-images

year-old Hindu monk known as Swami Vivekananda. Appearing in an orange robe and a yellow turban and speaking fluent and eloquent English, he had only recently arrived from India, where he had received an excellent European education as well as a deep immersion in Hindu philosophy and practice.

In his initial speech to the parliament on its opening day, Vivekananda declared, "I am proud to belong to a religion which has taught the world both tolerance and universal acceptance. . . . We accept all religions as true." He concluded with a plea that the parliament might mark the end of sectarianism, fanaticism, and persecution "between persons wending their way to the same goal."

In further speeches at the parliament and in subsequent travels around the country, Vivekananda expressed the major themes of his modernized Hindu outlook: that all human beings possess a divine nature; that awakening to that nature can be pursued through a variety of paths;

Consider dividing the class into two groups. Have one half read about the Africanization of Christianity and the other half read about the new notion of Hinduism. After students have finished reading, have each student create a short presentation on their section and then share it with another student using the "Think, Pair, Share" method.

AP EXAM TIP

Pay attention to how major religions continually adapt to local customs.

the New Testament itself had declared that "circumcision is nothing and uncircumcision is nothing." Accordingly, wrote one angry convert to a local missionary, "Has God spoken to you this time and informed you that those who circumcise will not enter in to God's place? It is better for a European like you to leave off speaking about such things because you can make the Gospel to be evil spoken of."[30]

As elsewhere, Christianity in Africa soon adapted to local cultural patterns. This **Africanization of Christianity** took many forms. Within mission-based churches, many converts continued using protective charms and medicines and consulting local medicine men, all of which caused their missionary mentors to speak frequently of "backsliding." Other converts continued to believe in their old gods and spirits but now deemed them evil and sought their destruction. Furthermore, thousands of separatist movements established a wide array of independent churches that were thoroughly Christian but under African rather than missionary and that spiritual practice and inner experience are far more important than dogma or doctrine. He argued that the disciplines of mind and body that derived from the Hindu tradition represented a psychological, experimental, and almost scientific approach to spiritual development and certainly did not require "conversion" to an alien faith. On occasion, he was sharply critical of Christian missionaries for their emphasis on conversion. "The people of India have more than religion enough," he declared. "What they want is bread." He described England as "the most prosperous Christian nation in the world with her foot on the neck of 250 million Asiatics."

Vivekananda emerged from the parliament a sensation and a celebrity, widely acclaimed but also widely criticized. His critique of Christian missionaries offended many. More conservative Christians objected to his assertion of the equality of all religious traditions. "We believe that Christianity is to supplant all other religions," declared the leading organizer of the parliament.

Vivekananda's time in the United States represented India speaking back to the West. After a century of European missionary activity and colonial rule in his country, he was declaring that India could offer spiritual support to a Western world mired in materialism and militarism. He proclaimed, "The whole of the Western world is a volcano which may burst tomorrow. . . . Now is the time to work so that India's spiritual ideas may penetrate deep into the West."[31]

In exposing Americans to Indian spirituality, Vivekananda's followers did not seek converts, but invited participants to apply Hindu principles and practices within their own religious traditions. They spoke about Jesus with great respect and displayed his image along with that of the Buddha and various Hindu sacred figures. In the early twentieth century, these ideas attracted a modest following among Americans who were disillusioned with the superficiality of modern life as well as with the rigidity of Christian doctrine and the many divisions and conflicts among Christian churches. In the 1960s and later, interest in Eastern religion exploded in the West as hundreds of Indian teachers arrived, many of them bearing the same universal message that Vivekananda had presented in Chicago. The growing numbers of Americans who claim to be "spiritual but not religious" are following in the path of that orange-robed monk.

QUESTION
What accounts for the appeal of Vivekananda's message, and what accounts for opposition to it?

control and that in many cases incorporated African cultural practices and modes of worship. It was a twentieth-century "African Reformation."

In India, where Christianity made only very modest inroads, leading intellectuals and reformers began to define their region's endlessly varied beliefs, practices, sects, rituals, and philosophies as a more distinct, unified, and separate religion, now known as **Hinduism**. It was in part an effort to provide for India a religion wholly equivalent to Christianity, "an accessible tradition and a feeling of historical worth when faced with the humiliation of colonial rule."[32] To Swami **Vivekananda** (1863–1902), one of nineteenth-century India's most influential religious figures, as well as others active in reform movements, a revived Hinduism, shorn of its distortions, offered a means of uplifting the country's village communities, which were the heart of Indian civilization. It also served to distinguish a "spiritual East" from a "materialistic West." (See Zooming In: Vivekananda, a Hindu Monk in America, page 580.)

CHAPTER 10

EXPLORING AP® THEMES

Cultural Developments and Interactions (CDI)

For a quick review on the role of culture in different societies, ask students: In what ways did Eastern religions influence Western culture? *Eastern religions influenced Western culture through Transcendentalism, yoga, and Vedanta.*

TEACHING IDEA

Class Discussion

Nationalism is an important concept for students to understand, and often students struggle with how beliefs can influence historical developments. Ask students: How might religion contribute to a sense of nationalism? Have students give examples to support their answers. *Religion offers a sense of unity and belonging. It is an ideology around which people can unite. In the case of India, Hinduism became a source of pride as India worked to free itself from Christian missionaries. In the case of the African Reformation, Christianity continued, but in a very different form from the missionary Christianity of the Europeans. Religion united Indigenous people and offered an alternative to Western culture that they could rally around.*

AP

CONTINUITY AND CHANGE

How and why did Hinduism emerge as a distinct religious tradition during the colonial era in India?

This new notion of Hinduism provided a cultural foundation for emerging ideas of India as a nation, but it also contributed to a clearer sense of Muslims as a distinct community in India. Before the British takeover, little sense of commonality united the many diverse communities who practiced Islam—urban and rural dwellers; nomads and farmers; artisans, merchants, and state officials. But the British had created one set of inheritance laws for all Muslims and another set for all Hindus; in their census taking, they counted the numbers of people within these now sharply distinguished groups; and they allotted seats in local councils according to these artificial categories. As some anti-British patriots began to cast India in Hindu terms, the idea of Muslims as a separate community that was perhaps threatened by the much larger number of Hindus began to make sense to some who practiced Islam. In the early twentieth century, a young Hindu Bengali schoolboy noticed that "our Muslim school-fellows were beginning to air the fact of their being Muslims rather more consciously than before and with a touch of assertiveness."[33] Here were the beginnings of what became in the twentieth century a profound religious and political division within the South Asian peninsula.

"Race" and "Tribe"

AP   EXAM TIP

Racial identity, the way that groups are viewed by others and how they view themselves, is a crucial theme in the AP® course.

In Africa as well, intellectuals and ordinary people alike forged new ways of belonging as they confronted the upheavals of colonial life. Central to these new identities were notions of race and ethnicity. By the end of the nineteenth century, a number of African thinkers, familiar with Western culture, began to define the idea of an **African identity**. Previously, few if any people on the continent had regarded themselves as Africans. Rather, they were members of particular local communities, usually defined by language; some were also Muslims; and still others inhabited some state or empire. Now, however, influenced by the common experience of colonial oppression and by a highly derogatory European racism, well-educated Africans began to think in broader terms, similar to those of Indian reformers who were developing the notion of Hinduism. It was an effort to revive the cultural self-confidence of their people by articulating a larger, common, and respected "African tradition," equivalent to that of Western culture.

This effort took various shapes. For some, African culture and history in fact possessed the very characteristics that Europeans exalted. Knowing that Europeans valued large empires and complex political systems, African intellectuals pointed with pride to the ancient kingdoms of Axum/Ethiopia, Mali, Songhay, and others. C. A. Diop, a French-educated scholar from Senegal, insisted that Egyptian civilization was in fact the work of black Africans. Reversing European assumptions, Diop argued that Western civilization owed much to Egyptian influence and was therefore derived from Africa. Black people, in short, had a history of achievement fully comparable to that of Europe and therefore deserved just as much respect and admiration.

APPLY THE TIP

Racial identity is an important concept as the study of world history moves into modern and contemporary periods. Ask students what the term "African identity" meant in terms of imperialism. As students respond, point out that as Africans began to think in broader terms they also began to think about the "African tradition" and to make it equal to the idea of "Western culture."

EXPLORING AP® THEMES

Cultural Developments and Interactions (CDI)

After students have discussed racial identity, ask: How did Africans use their history to convince Europeans that African culture deserved respect? *Knowing that Europeans valued large empires and complex political systems, African intellectuals pointed with pride to the ancient kingdoms of Ethiopia, Mali, Songhay, and others. C.A. Diop, a French-educated scholar from Senegal, insisted that Egyptian civilization was in fact the work of Black Africans.*

An alternative approach to defining an African identity lay in praising the differences between African and European cultures. The most influential proponent of such views was **Edward Blyden** (1832–1912), a West African born in the West Indies and educated in the United States who later became a prominent scholar and political official in Liberia. Blyden accepted the assumption that the world's various races were different but argued that each had its own distinctive contribution to make to world civilization. The uniqueness of African culture, Blyden wrote, lay in its communal, cooperative, and egalitarian societies, which contrasted sharply with Europe's highly individualistic, competitive, and class-ridden societies; in its harmonious relationship with nature as opposed to Europe's efforts to dominate and exploit the natural order; and particularly in its profound religious sensibility, which Europeans had lost in centuries of attention to material gain. Like Vivekananda in India, Blyden argued that Africa had a global mission "to be the spiritual conservatory of the world."[34]

In the twentieth century, such ideas resonated with a broader public. Hundreds of thousands of Africans took part in World War I, during which they encountered other Africans as well as Europeans. Some were able to travel widely. Contact with American Black leaders, such as Booker T. Washington, W. E. B. Du Bois, and Marcus Garvey, as well as various West Indian intellectuals further stimulated among a few a sense of belonging to an even larger pan-African world. Such notions underlay the growing nationalist movements that contested colonial rule as the twentieth century unfolded.

For the vast majority, however, the most important new sense of belonging that evolved from the colonial experience was not the notion of "Africa"; rather, it was the **idea of "tribe"** or, in the language of contemporary scholars, that of ethnic identity. African peoples, of course, had long recognized differences among themselves based on language, kinship, clan, village, or state, but these were seldom clearly defined. Boundaries fluctuated and were hazy; local communities often incorporated a variety of culturally different peoples. The idea of an Africa sharply divided into separate and distinct "tribes" was in fact a European notion that facilitated colonial administration and reflected Europeans' belief in African primitiveness. By requiring people to identify their "tribe" on applications for jobs, schools, and identity cards, colonial governments spread the idea of tribe widely within their colonies.

But new ethnic identities were not simply imposed by Europeans, for Africans themselves increasingly found ethnic or tribal labels useful. This was especially true in rapidly growing urban areas. Surrounded by a bewildering variety of people and in a setting where competition for jobs, housing, and education was very intense, migrants to the city found it helpful to categorize themselves and others in larger ethnic terms. Thus, in many colonial cities, people who spoke similar languages, shared a common culture, or came from the same general part of the country began to think of themselves as a single people — a new tribe. They organized a rich variety of ethnic or tribal associations to provide mutual assistance while in the cities

CONTINUITY AND CHANGE
In what ways were "race" and "tribe" new identities in colonial Africa?

CAUSATION
Why did European colonizers create the notion of tribes in Africa? How did Africans find it useful?

BUILDING AP® SKILLS
Making Connections: Causation

After discussing African identity with students, ask: Why did European colonizers create the notion of tribes in Africa, and why did Africans find it useful? *The notion of tribal identity was an artificial creation of Europeans to facilitate governance. Because people had to identify themselves by their tribe on applications for jobs, schools, and identity cards, this notion traveled quickly and then was appropriated by the Africans to help navigate the complexities of the modern world.*

BUILDING AP® SKILLS

Contextualization

As mentioned before, the concept of nationalism is often difficult for students to understand. Consider using the first full paragraph on page 584 to discuss nationalism by asking: How did the Igbo embody the concept of nationalism? *They had a common language but no myth of common ancestry. Once they became Christian, they embraced Western education, discovered what they had in common, and realized how they differed from the other peoples of Nigeria. By the 1940s, Igbos were asked to "sink all differences" for unity and progress.*

TEACHING IDEA

Bell Ringer

To help wrap up the chapter, ask students: What are some legacies of imperialism that you can think of? *The influence of imperialism remains in the languages some countries use as their official language. For example, the official language of some former French colonies in Africa is French. English has become an international language. The boundaries of many countries were set during imperialism. Laws changed and became more European, as did many educational systems.*

and to send money back home to build schools or clinics. Migrant workers, far from home and concerned about protecting their rights to land and to their wives and families, found a sense of security in being part of a recognized tribe, with its chiefs, courts, and established authority.

The Igbo people of southeastern Nigeria represent a case in point. Prior to the twentieth century, they were organized in a series of independently governed village groups. Although they spoke related languages, they had no unifying political system and no myth of common ancestry. Occupying a region of unusually dense population, many of these people eagerly seized on Western education and moved in large numbers to the cities and towns of colonial Nigeria. There they gradually discovered what they had in common and how they differed from the other peoples of Nigeria. By the 1940s, they were organizing on a national level and calling on Igbos everywhere to "sink all differences" to achieve "tribal unity, cooperation, and progress of all the Igbos." Fifty years earlier, however, no one had regarded himself or herself as an Igbo. One historian summed up the process of creating African ethnic identities: "Europeans believed Africans belonged to tribes; Africans built tribes to belong to."[35]

CONCLUSIONS AND REFLECTIONS

Who Makes History?

Finding the Main Point: To what extent did colonized people retain some ability to shape their own history even within the constraints and repression of imperial rule?

Winners may write history, at least temporarily, but they do not make history, at least not alone. Dominant groups everywhere — imperial rulers, upper classes, and men generally — have found their actions constrained and their choices limited by the sheer presence of subordinated people and the ability of those people to act. So it was in the colonial encounters of the long nineteenth century.

European colonial rulers clearly held the upper hand in those encounters. Their military power — repeating rifles and machine guns, for example — made conquest possible almost everywhere, enabled them to compel the labor and taxes of conquered people, and allowed them to create new states with new boundaries. Their industrializing economies drove imperial expansion and shaped the lives of millions as their demand for colonial foodstuffs, raw materials, investment opportunities, and export markets took hold around the world. In the colonies these processes transformed the working lives of colonial subjects as farmers increasingly produced for the world market and laborers migrated to distant sites for jobs in the mines and on the farms or plantations of Europeans. Colonial rulers also imported elements of their culture to the colonies—their languages, their Christian religion, their ideas about gender and sexuality, their racial prejudices, their educational systems, their medical practices, and more.

But colonized peoples were certainly not passive in these encounters, nor were European policies and intentions always realized in practice. Colonial conquest, though ultimately successful, was no cakewalk, as extended military resistance impeded European takeovers in many parts of Asia and Africa. Even after colonial rule was established, frequent rebellions, such as the massive Indian Rebellion of 1857–1858, punctuated the imposed peace of empire. Furthermore, some state authorities actively negotiated with European powers; through such means, Ethiopia and the Kingdom of Siam (Thailand) were able to maintain their precarious independence. Elsewhere, rulers in Buganda and Botswana in Africa and many Indian princes carved out a degree of autonomy for their states. Many individuals joined the administrative service or military forces of their colonial rulers, which permitted established elites to maintain their privileged positions and others to elevate their social position.

In economic life, West African farmers grew cocoa and Burmese farmers grew rice for export to their own economic benefit. But Europeans who sought to make their home countries self-sufficient in cotton by requiring colonized Africans to grow it were generally frustrated as African farmers effectively resisted that onerous and unprofitable work. African women took advantage of opportunities to grow cash crops, engage in small-scale trading, and brew beer in urban areas. In regions such as southern Africa, the absence of men who had left home as migratory workers required women to assume traditionally male roles as heads of households.

Particularly in sub-Saharan Africa, many became Christians, adapting that religion to their own cultures in a massive movement of independent churches. Throughout the colonial world, young people eagerly sought Western education but later, as leaders of nationalist movements, turned it against the colonizers. Colonized peoples also shaped or reshaped their social and cultural identities, as Africans forged new ethnic groupings and Indian intellectuals and reformers generated a modern form of Hinduism. In these and many other ways, colonized people actively shaped the history of the colonial era, even in highly oppressive conditions.

"Men make their own history," Karl Marx famously wrote, "but they do not make it as they please nor under conditions of their own choosing." In the colonial experience of the nineteenth and early twentieth centuries, both the colonizers and the colonized "made history," but neither were able to do so precisely as they pleased.

TEACHING IDEA
Exit Slip

As another way to wrap up this chapter, ask students to write down a brief definition for each concept in the list below, based on what they learned in the chapter. (Answers are provided in italics.)

- **African Reformation:** *The transformation of Western Christianity into African Christianity.*

- **Nationalism:** *The creation of an identity based on common factors such as language, religion, and history; nationalism in Africa transformed into tribal identity.*

- **Imperialism:** *The colonization that ensued after the Industrial Revolution in Europe.*

ERIC'S ACTIVITY 10 Comparing Colonial Systems

Theme 3: Governance

The diversity of experiences in European overseas colonial societies makes teaching this topic a challenge. I like to face this issue head-on through an activity that asks students to explore the varieties of European overseas empires in Period 3 of *Ways of the World*. The purpose of the activity is to provide an opportunity to explore European overseas empires as a distinctive development in state building, expansion, and conflict after 1500. It also offers my students the opportunity to practice their skills in Contextualization and Comparison. Find the complete activity in the Teacher's Resource Materials.

TRM Eric's Activity 10: Comparing Colonial Systems

CHAPTER REVIEW

AP® Key Terms

scientific racism, 555	cash-crop production, 569
civilizing mission, 556	female circumcision, 579
social Darwinism, 556	Africanization of Christianity, 580
scramble for Africa, 558	Hinduism, 581
settler colonies, 559	Vivekananda, 581
Indian Rebellion of 1857–1858, 563	African identity, 582
Congo Free State, 567	Edward Blyden, 583
cultivation system, 567	idea of "tribe," 583

Finding the Main Point

1. How did capitalist industrialization, nationalism, and pseudoscience contribute to Europe's global imperialism?
2. In what different ways did various parts of Asia and Africa come to be enveloped within European, American, or Japanese empires?
3. In what ways were European colonial empires similar to earlier imperial processes? In what ways were they distinctive?
4. How were traditional societies across Africa and Asia transformed by colonial economic policies?
5. How did the cultural and ethnic identities of colonized people change in the face of European imperialism?
6. To what extent did colonized people retain some ability to shape their own history even within the constraints and repression of imperial rule?

AP® Big Picture Questions

1. In what ways did colonial rule rest on violence and coercion, and in what ways did it elicit voluntary cooperation or generate benefits for some people?
2. In what respects were colonized people more than victims of colonial conquest and rule?
3. Was colonial rule a transforming, even a revolutionary, experience, or did it freeze or preserve existing social and economic patterns? What evidence can you find to support both sides of this argument?
4. **Looking Back** How would you compare the colonial experience of Asian and African peoples during the long nineteenth century to the earlier colonial experience in the Americas?

Claims and Evidence in Secondary Sources

In this workshop, you'll learn what to look for when analyzing a secondary source, which usually means looking at the work of other historians. As an emerging historian, you will learn how to glean the thesis from secondary sources as well as determine what evidence may support or refute the author's claim.

UNDERSTANDING CLAIMS AND EVIDENCE IN SECONDARY SOURCES

As a reminder, a secondary source is created after the fact, by someone who did not experience the event firsthand; in the study of history, this usually means a historian commenting on historical events or processes. A secondary source may appear in an academic journal or published as a monograph. Parts of secondary sources may also appear in textbooks on particular subject matters. Each chapter in this textbook contains two secondary sources on the topics covered in that chapter. And your textbook itself is a secondary source.

In a previous workshop (see Chapter 8 AP® Skills Workshop: Sourcing and Situation in Primary and Secondary Sources), we discussed how to evaluate sourcing information for a secondary source. This is a critical first step when examining a source. When was the source written? Who wrote the source? What is that person's background? How might this information influence the value and credibility of that source? No matter which type of source you are examining, **always identify the sourcing information first**.

In this workshop, we are moving to the next step in examining secondary sources: looking for claims and evidence. The claim is the historian's thesis, and it often appears at the beginning of a well-written essay with the evidence following the claim. When examining a secondary source, it is important to determine the claim that the historian is making as well as the evidence they are using to support that claim. For example, take a look at this secondary source excerpt about the origins of the Indian Rebellion of 1857 and extract the historian's claim and supporting evidence:

> Many were warning that the pace of change was too swift. Important groups within Indian society were being too brashly ignored, too completely alienated. The deposed princes poisoned all ears around with talk of the "faithless" British promises and treaties torn to bits by men without honor. The landed aristocrats, whose estates had always been freeholds, were now assailed by low-born [Indian] tax collectors and bullied by beardless [British] young men in a foreign tongue.
>
> — Stanley Wolpert, *India*, 93–94.

Historian's claim: Changes being imposed by the British in India were happening too quickly while important groups of Indians were being ignored.

BUILDING AP® SKILLS

Claims and Evidence in Sources

While it is incredibly important to know how to analyze and interpret primary sources, it is just as important for students to know how to analyze and interpret secondary sources for the AP® Exam. Working with secondary sources is primarily looking at the work of other historians. Secondary sources can be tricky because sometimes historians disagree on how to interpret historical events. Understanding what secondary sources are and how to use them is an important skill to master for AP® World History: Modern. The "AP® Skills Workshop" explanation on understanding claims and evidence in secondary sources on pages 587–589 would be good for students to read through, especially the section on quantitative data. Consider having them read these pages and discuss the skills taught in them with a partner. You can also have them practice the skills from the workshop using Activity 1 or 2 (which would be a quick practice) or Activity 3 (which would incorporate quantitative data) found on page 590.

587

Evidence supporting the claim: Deposed princes complained of the British not delivering on their promises and the landed aristocrats complained of being bullied by lower-caste tax collectors and young British men.

As an emerging historian, you may also need to recall additional evidence that would support or refute the author's claim. Therefore, the next step is to consider additional evidence to **support** this author's claim. For example, the British ignored the religious sensibilities of Muslim and Hindu soldiers when they adopted the Enfield rifle, which utilized gunpowder cartridges that were greased with animal fat from pigs and cows and that had to be torn with one's teeth. In addition, is there any evidence that can **refute** this author's claim? Indeed, universities emerged in major cities like Calcutta and Madras in the mid-nineteenth century and benefited mostly elites and the middle classes, both important groups that were expected to, and often did, support the British occupation of India.

As you can see, secondary sources offer a wealth of information on historical developments, and you will be asked to determine claims and evidence to support as well as refute claims.

UNDERSTANDING CLAIMS AND EVIDENCE IN QUANTITATIVE DATA

As mentioned in a previous workshop, quantitative data is expressed in numbers and/ or visual representations and is critical to the understanding of history because it allows historians to more precisely track historical developments. Historical and archeological research can generate important data (such as population numbers for a given region at a given time), but historians also draw on data from a variety of academic disciplines, including geography, economics, sociology, political science, and more. Many of the statistical findings in these disciplines are best understood when presented in the form of tables, charts, graphs, maps, or other visual representations. This type of secondary source can help students of history gain an overarching understanding of the events described by the data. Thus analyzing quantitative data and using it to support a historical argument are necessary skills in the study of history.

To begin, let's examine this chart from page 570 of the textbook:

Long-Distance Migration in an Age of Empire, 1846–1940

The age of empire was also an age of global migration. Beyond the three major patterns of long-distance migration shown here, shorter migrations within particular regions or colonies set millions more into motion.

Origins	Destination	Numbers
Europe	Americas	55–58 million
India, southern China	Southeast Asia, Indian Ocean rim, South Pacific	48–52 million
Northeast Asia, Russia	Manchuria, Siberia, Central Asia, Japan	46–51 million

Source: Data from Adam McKeown, "Global Migration, 1846-1940," *Journal of World History* 15, no. 2 (2004): 156.

588

What do we see here? Looking at the chart, it appears that approximately 161,000,000 people migrated from one region to another between 1846 and 1940. The largest migration pattern appears to be from Europe to the Americas, although the data doesn't tell us which country in the Americas was the greatest recipient of migrants or where the greater number of migrants generated from within Europe. The next largest migration pattern is from India or southern China to Southeast Asia, the Indian Ocean rim, and the South Pacific, although this chart does not provide the breakdown of precise numbers for India versus southern China. Drawing on background information about imperialism in India, however, we can see that the migration out of India was impacted by the change in economy to benefit the British, which resulted in many out-of-work farmers and artisans embarking on journeys to become indentured servants in other parts of the world. Some drawbacks to the data chart: the numbers of migrants traveling shorter distances is missing (and perhaps unknowable), and it doesn't indicate how many of the people making up these numbers were temporary migrants who moved for work before heading back to their homeland.

As you can see, quantitative data can speak volumes in providing historical data to make determinations about the course of history. However, it is important to also consider the limitations of the data, as this will impact its usefulness in supporting historical analysis.

CLAIMS AND EVIDENCE IN SECONDARY SOURCES, INCLUDING QUANTITATIVE DATA, ON THE AP® WORLD HISTORY EXAM

Secondary source analysis comes into play on the AP® Exam in two important ways. On the Multiple-Choice portion of the exam, a secondary source, or a pair of secondary sources, could serve as the stimulus item for a series of four to five Multiple-Choice Questions. You may need to find the claim of the excerpt or the evidence the author is using to substantiate their claim. You may also be asked to assess additional evidence that can prove or refute the author's claim. In addition, quantitative data will frequently show up as a Multiple-Choice stimulus item.

One of the mandatory Short-Answer Questions is about a secondary source. Again, you may be asked to identify the claim, identify the evidence used to support the historian's argument, explain additional evidence to support and/or refute the author's claim, and analyze the context of the argument. The second question may present a data representation of a historical development. The first prompt may ask you to describe something about the data, to show that you understand the basic information, while the second and third questions will ask you to explain the data by citing evidence and analyzing the significance of the information presented. You may also be asked to discuss a limitation of the data in making historical inferences.

Sometimes, on the Document-Based Question (DBQ), you may encounter a primary source that was once a secondary source, such as an excerpt from a historical text that was written close to the time—for example, a fairly contemporary biography of Napoleon.

589

You may also be presented with data that is relevant to the topic of the prompt. You will need to evaluate how this data set will help you respond to the prompt and whether it is corroborated, modified, or qualified by other sources in the DBQ.

BUILDING AP® SKILLS

1. **Activity: Identifying Claims and Evidence in Secondary Sources.** Using Historians' Voices 10.1, found on page 600, determine the motives for Europe's desire for Africa. What is the claim that Pakenham is making about these motives? What is the evidence?

   Historian's claim:

   Evidence supporting the claim:

2. **Activity: Analyzing a Secondary Source.** Read Historians' Voices 10.2, found on page 600, and determine the African responses to the European scramble for Africa. Why does Boahen think that Africans were unable to prevent colonial conquest? What evidence can you find that supports the historian's claim?

   Historian's claim:

   Evidence supporting the claim:

   Context:

3. **Activity: Identifying and Working with Quantitative Data.** Look at the data chart titled Snapshot: The Industrial Revolution and the Global Divide in Chapter 8, page 467. Respond to the questions below:

   a. Where do you see manufacturing increasing as a share of the global manufacturing output?
   b. Where do you see manufacturing decreasing as a share of the global manufacturing output?
   c. Explain why the percentage of manufacturing for South Asia fell between 1800 and 1900.

Advocating for Western Education in India

Until the late 1850s, Britain's growing involvement with India was organized and led by the British East India Company, a private trading firm that had acquired a charter from the Crown allowing it to exercise military, political, and administrative functions in India as well as its own commercial operations. Responses among Indians to the growing political and administrative control of India by the East India Company varied widely and changed over time, but early on there was significant hope among some that British rule might bring tangible benefits, especially in the realm of education.

In this activity, you will examine the reaction of the Indian intellectual Ram Mohan Roy (1772–1833) to plans by British administrators to establish a school dedicated to the study of Sanskrit texts and traditional Hindu learning in the major East India Company trading center of Calcutta (modern Kolkata). Roy was born and highly educated within a Brahmin Hindu family. He subsequently studied both Arabic and Persian, learned English, came into contact with British Christian missionaries, and found employment with the British East India Company. He emerged in the early nineteenth century as a leading advocate for religious and social reform within India, with a particular interest in ending *sati*, the practice in which widows burned themselves on their husbands' funeral pyres. In 1823, he wrote the letter reproduced here to Lord Amherst, the British governor-general of India, expressing his thoughts on the proposed new school.

1 A FIRST LOOK

Begin by establishing Roy's point of view in this letter by answering these questions:

1. What was Roy's reaction to the plan to found a Sanskrit school in Calcutta?

2. According to Roy, what differentiated Western education from a traditional Indian education? Which type of education was more useful for India's "improvement"? Why?

RAM MOHAN ROY | *Letter to Lord Amherst* | 1823

The establishment of a new Sanskrit School in Calcutta evinces the laudable desire of Government to improve the natives of India by education, a blessing for which they must ever be grateful. . . . When this seminary of learning was proposed . . . we were filled with sanguine hopes that [it would employ] European gentlemen of talent and education to instruct the natives of India in Mathematics, Natural Philosophy, Chemistry, Anatomy, and other useful sciences, which the natives of Europe have carried to a degree of perfection that has raised them above the inhabitants of other parts of the world. . . . Our hearts were filled with mingled feelings of delight and gratitude; we already offered up thanks to Providence for inspiring the most generous and enlightened nations of the West with the glorious ambition of planting in Asia the arts and sciences of Modern Europe.

TRM **Suggested Responses to Questions**
You can find suggested responses to the AP® Looking Again questions in the Teacher's Resource Materials.

591

We find [however] that the Government are establishing a Sanskrit school under Hindu Pandits [scholars] to impart such knowledge as is already current in India. This seminary can only be expected to load the minds of youth with grammatical niceties and metaphysical distinctions of little or no practical use to the possessors or to society. The pupils will there acquire what was known two thousand years ago with the addition of vain and empty subtleties since then produced by speculative men, such as is already commonly taught in all parts of India. . . .

Neither can much improvement arise from such speculations as the following which are the themes suggested by the Vedanta [a branch of Hindu philosophy]: in what manner is the soul absorbed in the Deity? What relation does it bear to the Divine Essence? Nor will youths be fitted to be better members of society by the Vedantic doctrines which teach them to believe that all visible things have no real existence, that as father, brother, etc., have no actual entity, they consequently deserve no real affection, and therefore the sooner we escape from them and leave the world the better. . . .

[T]he Sanskrit system of education would be the best calculated to keep this country in darkness, if such had been the policy of the British legislature. But as the improvement of the native population is the object of the Government, it will consequently promote a more liberal and enlightened system of instruction, embracing Mathematics, Natural Philosophy, Chemistry, Anatomy, with other useful sciences, which may be accomplished with the sums proposed by employing a few gentlemen of talent and learning educated in Europe and providing a College furnished with necessary books, instruments, and other apparatus. In presenting this subject to your Lordship, I conceive myself discharging a solemn duty which I owe to my countrymen, and also to that enlightened sovereign and legislature which have extended their benevolent care to this distant land, actuated by a desire to improve the inhabitants, and therefore humbly trust you will excuse the liberty I have taken in thus expressing my sentiments to your Lordship.

Source: Rammohun Roy, *The English Works of Raja Rammohun Roy* (Allahabad, India: Panini Office, 1906), 471–74.

2 A SECOND LOOK

While Roy's letter focuses on the project to found a new Sanskrit school, it also offers insight into his more general attitude toward British colonial government in India. Reread Roy's letter with an eye to his assessment of British rule, and then answer these questions.

1. How does Roy characterize British motivations and intentions in governing India?

2. What specific goals for India does Roy ascribe to the British?

3. What does this letter reveal about Roy's attitude to both European and Indian culture?

BUILDING AP® SKILLS

Claims and Evidence in Sources

There can never be too much practice with primary sources for students getting ready to take the AP® World History: Modern Exam. Consider having students read Ram Mohan Roy's "Letter to Lord Amherst" written in 1823 and having them answer the questions under "A First Look" on page 591 and "A Second Look" on page 592 on their own. Once they are finished, partner the students up and have them work together to answer the questions under "A Third Look" on page 593. These activities can be an excellent method for DBQ skills practice as well as for working with a primary source.

3 A THIRD LOOK

Next consider how the historical situation in which Roy wrote his letter may have influenced both how he expressed his sentiments toward British rule and what he chose to comment on.

1. Why did Roy write his letter? What did he hope to secure for India by writing it?

2. Who was Roy's intended audience, and how might that audience have influenced the tone of his letter and the arguments that he chose to employ?

3. Roy's letter was written early during Britain's rule in India, which lasted until 1947. How might this fact have shaped Roy's outlook?

4. Roy has been widely regarded as the "father" of modern India. More recently, some supporters of India as a Hindu country have accused Roy of being a "traitor who sold out to the colonizers."[36] How might this letter be used by both sides of this debate? What kind of nation did Roy seek to shape?

AP ACTIVITY CONSIDERING BRITISH COLONIAL RULE

Based on Roy's letter to the British governor-general, write a brief essay in which you describe his assessment of British colonial rule and his hopes for India's future. Be sure to introduce both Roy and the circumstances in which his letter was written.

FURTHER ACTIVITY

In 1909, Mahatma Gandhi wrote a small pamphlet called *Hind Swaraj* (Indian Home Rule) in which he bitterly criticized European civilization for its materialism, its single-minded focus on technological and economic "progress," and its erosion of spiritual life. "The tendency of the Indian civilization," he wrote, "is to elevate the moral being; that of the Western civilization is to propagate immorality. The latter is Godless; the former is based on a belief in God.... [I]t behooves every lover of India to cling to Indian civilization even as a child clings to the mother's breast."[37] Write a brief essay in which you imagine Roy responding to Gandhi's views. Where do your sympathies lie in this debate?

Colonial Conquest: The Scramble for Africa

The centerpiece of Europe's global expansion during the nineteenth century occurred in the so-called scramble for Africa, during which a half dozen or so European countries divided up almost the entire continent into colonial territories (see Map 10.2, page 560). The "scramble" took place very quickly (between roughly 1875 and 1900), surprising even the European leaders who initiated it, as well as the many African societies that suddenly found themselves confronting highly aggressive and well-armed foreign forces. The sources that follow illustrate some of the distinctive features of the scramble for Africa as well as the differing ways in which it was perceived and represented.

LOOKING AHEAD

AP DBQ PRACTICE

As you read through this collection of documents, consider the relationships that existed between the various participants of the scramble for Africa, both European and African, and the different degrees of competition and violence in those relationships.

DOCUMENT 1 From Cape to Cairo

Nowhere did the vaulting ambition of European colonial powers in Africa emerge more clearly than in the British vision of a north-south corridor of British territories along the eastern side of the continent stretching from South Africa to Egypt, or in the popular phrase of the time, "from the Cape to Cairo." A part of this vision was an unbroken railroad line running the entire length of the African continent. That grand idea was popularized by Cecil Rhodes, a British-born businessman and politician who made a fortune in South African diamonds. A famous cartoon, published in a British satirical paper in 1892, portrayed an armed Rhodes bestriding all of Africa with one foot in Egypt and the other in South Africa. An accompanying poem described Rhodes as "o'er Africa striding from dark end to end, to forward black emancipation." Rhodes's enthusiasm for British imperialism, particularly in Africa, is illustrated in the following passage.

> Source: Cecil Rhodes, views on British imperialism in Africa, sent to British journalist William Thomas Stead, 1877.
>
> Why should we not form a secret society with but one object: the furtherance of the British Empire and the bringing of the whole uncivilized world under British rule . . . making the Anglo-Saxon race but one empire. What a dream, but yet it is probable, it is possible. . . .
>
> Put your mind to another train of thought. . . . Africa is still lying ready for us. It is our duty to take it. It is our duty to seize every opportunity of acquiring more territory and we should keep this one idea steadily before our eyes that more territory simply means more of the Anglo-Saxon race, more of the best, the most human, most honourable race the world possesses.

594

TRM Suggested Responses to Questions
You can find suggested responses to the AP® Working with Evidence questions in the Teacher's Resource Materials.

BUILDING AP® SKILLS

Claims and Evidence in Sources

Interpreting text-based as well as non-text-based sources is an important skill for AP® World History: Modern students. If time is available, have students investigate the impact of imperialism in Africa in the late nineteenth and early twentieth centuries by using the evidence in "Colonial Conquest: The Scramble for Africa" beginning on page 594. Consider having students analyze one or more of the sources found on pages 594–599. Check for understanding by:

■ Using the questions at the end of each source as a discussion starting point.

■ Pairing students to analyze (identify and describe) using author/creator's point of view, purpose, historical situation, and/or audience. This activity can continue to reinforce sourcing.

■ Assigning a source to a group of three or four students and having them present an overview of the source along with the sourcing to the rest of the class.

■ Then having students practice an AP® skill of their choice by using one of the activities under "AP® Doing History" on page 599.

Question to Consider: What is Rhodes's attitude toward the people of Africa? As you continue to read, keep this source in mind. How does this attitude help explain European actions in later sources?

AP Analyzing Sources: How do you understand the sense of "duty" that Rhodes articulates? Do you think it was a genuine feeling of obligation or a cover for greed?

DOCUMENT 2 Agreement in Europe

The "scramble" began with the Berlin Conference of 1884–1885, organized by Otto von Bismarck, the first chancellor of Germany. It included most of the other major European nations. The following excerpt from records of the conference outlines its major purposes and by implication reveals prevailing European assumptions about Africa.

Source: General Act of the Berlin West Africa Conference, 1885.

WISHING, in a spirit of good and mutual accord, to regulate the conditions most favourable to the development of trade and civilization in certain regions of Africa, and to assure to all nations the advantages of free navigation on the two chief rivers of Africa flowing into the Atlantic Ocean; BEING DESIROUS, on the other hand, to obviate the misunderstanding and disputes which might in future arise from new acts of occupation . . . on the coast of Africa; and concerned, at the same time, as to the means of furthering the moral and material well-being of the native populations; HAVE RESOLVED, on the invitation addressed to them by the Imperial Government of Germany, in agreement with the Government of the French Republic, to meet for those purposes in Conference at Berlin. . . .

Article 12: In case a serious disagreement originating on the subject of, or in the limits of, the territories mentioned in Article 1, and placed under the free trade system, shall arise between any Signatory Powers of the present Act, or the Powers which may become parties to it, these Powers bind themselves, before appealing to arms, to have recourse to the mediation of one or more of the friendly Powers. In a similar case the same Powers reserve to themselves the option of having recourse to arbitration.

Question to Consider: What seems to be the overriding goal of this conference?

AP Analyzing Sources: What assumptions about Africa are implicit in the document?

DOCUMENT 3 Ethiopia and the Scramble for Africa

The East African state of Ethiopia played an intriguing role during the scramble, for alone in all of Africa, it successfully resisted incorporation into a European empire. Document 3 records Menelik's call to arms in 1895 as Ethiopia prepared for war with Italy, which was making demands on its territory. The famous Battle of Adowa, which followed in 1896, marked a decisive victory for Ethiopia over the Italians. Ethiopia had preserved its independence, becoming a symbol of African resistance and bravery. But Ethiopia also participated in the scramble, almost doubling the size of the country at the expense of neighboring peoples.

595

Enemies have now come upon us to ruin our country and to change our religion. Our enemies have begun the affair by advancing and digging into our country like moles. With the help of God, I will not deliver my country to them. Today, you who are strong, give me your strength, and you who are weak, help me by prayer. Men of my country, up to now I believe I have never wronged you and you have never caused me sorrow. If you refuse to follow me, beware. You will hate me, for I shall not fail to punish you. I swear in the name of Mary that I shall never accept any plea of pardon. . . . Meet me at Were Illu [the place of assembly for Menelik's forces], and may you be there by the middle of [October]. So says Menelik, elect of God, king of kings.

Quoted in Rick Duncan, *Man, Know Thyself* (Bloomington, IN: XLibris, 2013), 1:330.

Question to Consider: How does this proclamation allude to violence, without directly discussing it?

AP **Analyzing Sources:** Why does Menelik II rely so heavily on religion in this call to arms?

DOCUMENT 4   "Pacification" in East Africa

In European eyes, conquest was frequently termed "pacification," with the goal of ending all active resistance to colonial authorities. Document 4 provides a vivid example of what the scramble for Africa meant at the local level. It comes from the diary of a young British soldier who took part in the takeover of what is now Kenya.

Source: British soldier Richard Meinertzhagen, excerpt from his *Kenya Diary*, 1902.

I have performed a most unpleasant duty today. I made a night march to the village at the edge of the forest where the white settler had been so brutally murdered the day before yesterday. Though the war drums were sounding throughout the night, we reached the village without incident and surrounded it. By the light of the fires, we could see savages dancing in the village, and our guides assured me that they were dancing around the mutilated body of the white man.

I gave orders that every living thing except children should be killed without mercy. I hated the work and was anxious to get through with it. So soon as we could see to shoot we closed in. Several of the men tried to break out but were immediately shot. I then assaulted the place before any defense could be prepared. Every soul was either shot or bayoneted, and I am happy to say that there were no children in the village. They, together with the younger women, had already been removed by the villagers to the forest. We burned all the huts and razed the banana plantations to the ground.

Question to Consider: What kinds of violence occur in this source? How is one kind of violence used to respond to a second kind of violence?

AP **Analyzing Sources:** Why does Meinertzhagen use the term "savages" but still emphasize his sympathy toward the villagers?

DOCUMENT 5 **Exploiting African Resources**

Even as the scramble was under way, Europeans began exploiting African resources and people. Nowhere was this more apparent than in the Congo, then governed personally by King Leopold of Belgium. Rich in wild rubber, the Congo attracted investors interested in profiting from this resource. How they did so is revealed in a report issue in 1903. It also provides an authentic African perspective on what the scramble meant.

Source: Report on the Administration of the Independent State of the Congo, 1903.

Q: "How much pay did you get for this [rubber]?"
A: "Our village got cloth and a little salt, but not the people who did the work. Our Chiefs eat up the cloth; the workers got nothing. . . . It used to take ten days to get the twenty baskets of rubber—we were always in the forest and then when we were late we were killed. We had to go further and further into the forest to find the rubber vines, to go without food, and our women had to give up cultivating the fields and gardens. Then we starved. Wild beasts—the leopards—killed some of us when we were working away in the forest, and others got lost or died from exposure and starvation, and we begged the white man to leave us alone, saying we could get no more rubber, but the white men and their soldiers said: 'Go! You are only beasts yourselves, you are nyama (meat).' We tried, always going further into the forest, and when we failed and our rubber was short, the soldiers came to our towns and killed us. Many were shot, some had their ears cut off; others were tied up with ropes around their necks and bodies and taken away."

Question to Consider: What types of violence are portrayed in this document and for what purposes?

AP **Analyzing Sources:** Who is the intended audience of this report, and why do you think the author chose to allow such a candid recording of an African perspective?

DOCUMENT 6 **Empire Building in North Africa**

In North Africa, the primary European rivalries for territory involved Great Britain, France, and Italy. Document 6 portrays two of these rivals—Britain, on the right, and France, on the left—toasting one another while standing on piles of skeletons. This image appeared in the *Cairo Punch*, a British-owned magazine in Egypt published in Arabic, probably around 1910.

597

This image refers specifically to two incidents. On the British side, the cartoon evokes a 1906 quarrel between British soldiers hunting pigeons and local villagers of Denshway that resulted in the death of one of the soldiers. In response, outraged British authorities hanged several people and flogged dozens of others. The following year in Morocco, French civilians building a small railway near the harbor of Casablanca dug up parts of a Muslim cemetery, "churning up piles of bones." When attacks against European laborers followed, killing eight, the French bombarded the Arab quarter of the city, with many casualties—European and Arab alike—in the fighting that ensued. Both incidents stimulated nationalist feelings in these two North African countries.

Source: British and French in North Africa, cartoon from the *Cairo Punch*, ca. 1910.

Library of Congress, Prints & Photographs Division, Reproduction number LC-USZC2-1379 (color film copy slide)

Question to Consider: What different relationships are depicted in the image? What kinds of violence take place in these different relationships?

AP **Analyzing Sources:** The British and French generally saw themselves as rivals in the scramble for Africa. How are they portrayed here? How does the intended audience of the image explain your answer?

DOCUMENT 7 **An African American Voice on the Scramble for Africa**

Writing in 1915, shortly after the outbreak of World War I, the African American scholar and activist W. E. B. Du Bois reflected on the scramble for Africa, arguing that it was a leading cause of the war.

Source: W. E. B. Du Bois, from "The African Roots of War," published in *Atlantic Monthly*, May 1915.

The methods by which this continent has been stolen have been contemptible and dishonest beyond expression. Lying treaties, rivers of rum, murder, assassination, mutilation, rape, and torture have marked the progress of Englishman, German, Frenchman, and Belgian on the dark continent. . . .

The present world war is, then, the result of jealousies engendered by the recent rise of armed [nations] . . . whose aim is the exploitation of the wealth of the world mainly outside the European circle of nations . . . , and particularly in Africa.

Question to Consider: How does Du Bois describe the violence in Africa?

AP **Analyzing Sources:** Why does Du Bois view the violence in Africa differently than most Europeans view the violence?

AP DOING HISTORY

1. **DBQ Practice:** Evaluate the extent to which violence facilitated the European scramble for Africa in the late nineteenth and early twentieth centuries.

2. **Contextualization:** How did industrialization motivate the scramble for Africa? What other factors also played a role in driving the scramble?

3. **Outside Evidence:** In the chapter, you read about both methods of imperialism and responses to imperialism; what facts can you use as evidence to support your argument in Question 1 about the scramble for Africa?

4. **Complex Argumentation:** How might these documents be used to reflect on the moral justification for the scramble . . . or lack of it?

TRM Chapter 10 DBQ Activity Handout

599

AP® HISTORIANS' VOICES

The Invasion of Africa

Two major issues have informed historians' inquiry about the scramble for Africa—the motives of the Europeans and the responses of Africans. Voice 10.1 deals with the first of these issues. It comes from British historian Thomas Pakenham's award-winning history of the scramble. In Voice 10.2 the West African scholar A. Adu Boahen, a pioneer in the field of African history, addresses the second problem.

exploration and evangelization of Central Africa and she felt a proprietary right to most of the continent. . . . As the only great maritime empire, she needed to prevent her rivals obstructing the steamer routes to the East, via Suez and the Cape.

Source: Thomas Pakenham, *The Scramble for Africa* (New York: Avon Books, 1992), xxi–xxiii.

VOICE 10.1

Thomas Pakenham on European Motivations | 1992

Why this undignified rush by the leaders of Europe to build empires in Africa? . . . [T]hey all conceived the crusade in terms of romantic nationalism. To imperialism—a kind of race nationalism—they brought a missionary zeal. Not only would they save Africa from itself. Africa would be the saving of their own countries.

At first, European governments were reluctant to intervene. But to most people in their electorates, there seemed a real chance of missing something. . . . There were dreams of El Dorado, of diamond mines and goldfields crisscrossing the Sahara. There might be new markets out there in this African Garden of Eden and tropical groves where golden fruit could be plucked by willing brown hands. . . .

[O]verseas empire would sooth the *amour proper* [self-esteem] of the French army, humiliated by its collapse in the Franco-Prussian war. And it would no less bolster the pride of the political *parvenus* [newcomers] of Europe [recently united Germany and Italy] . . . and what about a place in the sun for emigrants? . . .

In Britain . . . there was growing resentment toward the intruders. . . . Britain had pioneered the

VOICE 10.2

A. Adu Boahen on African Strategies | 1987

Africans devised three main strategies [for responding to the scramble]. . . . [First] some African rulers readily submitted to the European invaders . . . either because they became aware of the futility and cost of confronting the imperialists or . . . because they themselves urgently needed European protection.

The second main strategy adopted . . . was that of alliance. . . . These African rulers sought to achieve the very sovereignty of their state, and what they saw themselves doing was not collaborating but rather allying with the incoming invaders to achieve this national end.

The third strategy . . . was confrontation . . . and an overwhelming majority of the Africans adopted the military option. . . . Most of these African armies were non-professional and not properly trained. . . . African armies were, in many cases, numerically inferior to European armies. . . . Most of the armies of the European imperialists consisted of African soldiers. . . . Above all, technologically and logistically, African armies were at a great disadvantage.

[And] no African state was strong enough economically to have sustained any protracted warfare. . . . Most African rulers failed to form . . . alliances [among themselves]. Not only did this weaken them

600

militarily, but it also enabled European imperialists to play one African power against the other. . . . It was above all . . . because the Europeans had the maxim gun and the Africans did not that an overwhelming number of African states lost their independence.

Source: A. Adu Boahen, *African Perspectives on Colonialism* (Baltimore, MD: Johns Hopkins University Press, 1987), 39–57.

AP **Analyzing Secondary Sources**

1. What range of European motivations underlay the scramble for Africa according to Voice 10.1?

2. How does Boahen in Voice 10.2 classify African responses to the European intrusion, and why does he believe Africans were unable to maintain their independence?

3. **Integrating Primary and Secondary Sources:** How might Pakenham (Voice 10.1) use the documents in AP® Working with Evidence to substantiate his argument? In which of his three categories of African response to the scramble might Boahen place Menelik in Document 3?

TRM **Suggested Responses to Questions**
You can find suggested responses to the AP® Analyzing Secondary Sources questions in the Teacher's Resource Materials.

601

Multiple-Choice Questions Choose the correct answer for each question.

Questions 1–3 are based on this map and chart.

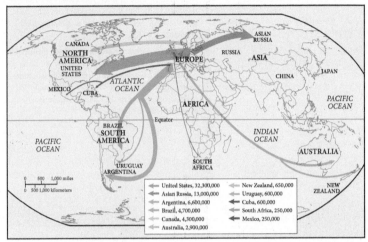

United States, 32,300,000 — New Zealand, 650,000
Asian Russia, 13,000,000 — Uruguay, 600,000
Argentina, 6,600,000 — Cuba, 600,000
Brazil, 4,700,000 — South Africa, 250,000
Canada, 4,300,000 — Mexico, 250,000
Australia, 2,900,000

European Migration in the Industrial Age

Long-Distance Migration in an Age of Empire, 1846–1940

Origins	Destination	Numbers
Europe	Americas	55–58 million
India, southern China	Southeast Asia, Indian Ocean rim, South Pacific	48–52 million
Northeast Asia, Russia	Manchuria, Siberia, Central Asia, Japan	46–51 million

Source: Data from Adam McKeown, "Global Migration, 1846-1940," *Journal of World History* 15, no. 2 (2004): 156.

1. Which of these statements accurately explains why global migration occurred in the nineteenth century, as shown in this map and chart?
   a. Most people migrated to escape religious and political persecution.
   b. Most of the migration in the nineteenth century was because of an increase in unfree labor.
   c. Most migrants moved to South Africa to work in the new mining industry.
   d. Most migrants were motivated by better opportunities to economically support their families.

602

2. Based on your knowledge of world history and this map and chart, the white Australia policy and the Chinese Exclusion Act are evidence of

   a. state regulation of immigration in the nineteenth century.

   b. religious persecution of immigrants in the nineteenth century.

   c. the acceptance of immigrants to Australia and the exclusion of immigrants from China.

   d. the desire to develop international trade agreements.

3. Which of these statements best describes a result of nineteenth-century global migration?

   a. Few migrants adapted to the culture and traditions of the area they migrated to.

   b. Many migrants found political acceptance and voting rights immediately open to them in their new countries.

   c. Migrating peoples often created ethnic and cultural enclaves in new areas in order to maintain a connection to home.

   d. Migrant populations had difficulty finding work, as native workers remained the main labor force.

Questions 4–6 are based on this image.

Women and Peanut Production in Gambia.

AP® CLASSROOM

AP® Personal Progress Check

You can extend the AP® Exam Strategies activity on page 602 by logging into your AP® Classroom account and using the questions in the Progress Check for Unit 6 as more practice for your students. AP® Classroom allows you to set the quiz up digitally or print out a copy for each student. After students take the Progress Check for Unit 6, you can discuss the answers as a class.

When you assign the Topic Questions or Personal Progress Checks, it can be a good idea to put a timer on the question(s) so that students can practice the skill in a timed setting like the AP® Exam.

603

4. The activities seen in the picture above are best understood within the context of which of the following global processes between 1750 and 1900?

   a. New food items that brought richer diets to people in sub-Saharan Africa

   b. The exploitation of colonial labor by European imperialists.

   c. The end of the transatlantic slave trade

   d. The lack of farming technologies in poorer regions of the world

5. Which of the following ideologies would be most likely to justify coercive forms of labor in the late nineteenth century?

   a. Social Darwinism

   b. Mercantilism

   c. Abolitionism

   d. Communism

6. What is most likely the purpose of this picture being produced and circulated by the British?

   a. To sway popular opinion against slavery to end the slave trade

   b. To make a case for new agricultural practices and the introduction of American crops into new areas

   c. To illuminate the rising economies of African societies after their contact with Europeans

   d. To demonstrate the profitability of global colonies and colonial labor

Short-Answer Questions

Read each question carefully and write a short response. Use complete sentences.

1. **Use the images below and your knowledge of world history to answer all parts of the question that follows.**

Charles Ball (ca. 1860), *The History of the Indian Mutiny: Giving a Detailed Account of the Sepoy Insurrection in India; and a Concise History of the Great Military Events Which Have Tended to Consolidate British Empire in Hindostan.* London: The London Printing and Publishing Company

A scene from the Indian Rebellion, showing an attack by rebels on the Redan Battery at Lucknow, India, July 1857.

Argumentation

AP® World History: Modern writing skills need to be practiced on a regular basis. You can use the SAQs on pages 604 and 605 for students to write an "exit ticket" at the end of class to check for understanding. You can also use the SAQs for more traditional timed writing practice, either by spreading the three SAQs across several days or as practice for the AP® Exam by writing them all at once. Make certain that students have the correct amount of time for this exercise. On exam day, students will have a total of 40 minutes to write three SAQs. If you are having them write only one at a time, you'll need to give them about 14 minutes to write it.

An 1857 illustration from the British satirical publication *Punch*, entitled "The British Lion's Vengeance on the Bengal Tiger."

A. Identify ONE historical process taking place in the above images.

B. Explain ONE effect of European imperialism reflected in the images above.

C. Explain ONE way in which India's relationship with Great Britain changed in the twentieth century.

2. **Use the passage below and your knowledge of world history to answer all parts of the question that follows.**

> The European conquest of these territories had been relatively easy, especially during the era of new imperialism, when machine guns, telegraph lines and other forms of technology, and a disregard for African and Asian lives allowed European armies and their local allies to kill or devastate everyone who stood in their way. . . . In most colonies, however, very few colonizers actually remained in place to maintain control, and so they relied on local collaborators to exercise sovereignty. All sorts of reasons, from existing rivalries with other local people and leaders to new possibilities for power, prestige, knowledge, and wealth, led some of the conquered to put up with or accept—even respect or admire—the colonizing authorities.
> —Todd Shepard, *Voices of Decolonization: A Brief History with Documents*, 2015

A. Identify ONE example of how a European colonial power maintained its control as described by the author in the paragraph.

B. Identify ONE example of an African or Asian society that challenges the first argument made by the author about European colonization.

C. Explain how ONE colonial society resisted European colonial rule.

3. **Answer all parts of the question that follows.**

A. Identify ONE motivation for European imperialism in the period ca. 1850–1900.

B. Explain ONE similarity in the effects of nineteenth-century European imperialism on Africa and Asia.

C. Explain ONE difference in the effects of nineteenth-century European imperialism on Africa and Asia.

605

TRM Suggested Responses to Questions
You can find suggested responses to the Period 3 AP® Exam Practice questions in the Teacher's Resource Materials.

TEACHING IDEA

AP® Exam Strategies

The Document-Based Question (DBQ) is an important part of the AP® World History: Modern Exam because it is 25 percent of the overall score on the exam. It also requires practice to master the skills required on the DBQ. Have students write a full-length DBQ using the Document-Based Question found on pages 606–609.

Differentiation

If you want to differentiate the Document-Based Question (DBQ) for Period 3 and give students more practice with writing skills, follow the "Must Do, Should Do, Strive For" model below for a DBQ poster.

■ Must Do: In their groups, students must analyze the documents and decide what two or three arguments they can create out of them. On their provided butcher paper (to create their poster), they need to name their arguments, glue the supporting documents under the corresponding argument, and write a quick analysis next to each document. Finally, students need to create a thesis statement that answers the prompt and write it at the bottom of their poster.

■ Should Do: In their groups, students need to write one or two sourcing statements for each argument (ending with a total of three sourcing statements) and contextualization (which should go above the thesis) on their poster. Once all the groups have completed their DBQ poster, have students hang them up and do a gallery walk to see how other groups put together this DBQ. As they look at each poster, ask students to leave "I wonder . . ." and "I like . . ." statements.

■ Strive For: For students who want or need a writing challenge, have them choose one of their arguments from their DBQ poster and write a full argument paragraph on it.

Document-Based Question

Using these sources and your knowledge of world history, develop an argument in response to the prompt.

1. Evaluate the extent to which industrialization fundamentally altered people's way of life.

Document 1

Source: Documents from the Luddite movement. The first is a threat from a Luddite to an industrialized fabric workshop, ca. 1811. The second is a song entitled "General Ludd's Triumph," explaining the purpose of the Luddite movement.

If you do Not Cause those Dressing Machines to be Remov'd Within the Bounds of Seven Days . . . your factory and all that it Contains Will and Shall Surely Be Set on fire . . . it is Not our Desire to Do you the Least Injury, But We are fully Determin'd to Destroy Both Dressing Machines and Steam Looms.

These Engines of mischief were sentenced to die / By unanimous vote of the Trade / And Ludd who can all opposition defy / Was the Grand executioner made.

Document 2

Source: Elizabeth Bentley, from her testimony before a parliamentary committee assembled to investigate the conditions of factory workers, 1831.

What age are you?
Twenty-three.
Where do you live?
At Leeds.
What time did you begin to work at a factory?
When I was six years old.
What were your hours of labour in that mill?
From 5 in the morning till 9 at night, when they were thronged [busy].
What were your usual hours when you were not so thronged?
From 6 in the morning till 7 at night.
What time was allowed for your meals?
Forty minutes at noon.
Suppose you flagged a little, or were too late, what would they do?
Strap us.
Are they in the habit of strapping those who are last in doffing?
Yes.
Constantly?
Yes.
Girls as well as boys?
Yes.
Have you ever been strapped?
Yes.
Severely?
Yes.
Were the girls struck so as to leave marks upon their skin? —
Yes, they have had black marks many times, and their parents dare not come to him about it, they were afraid of losing their work.

606

Document 3

Source: Map of the world showing migration patterns out of Europe as the world industrialized in the 19th century.

United States, 32,300,000
Asian Russia, 13,000,000
Argentina, 6,600,000
Brazil, 4,700,000
Canada, 4,300,000
Australia, 2,900,000
New Zealand, 650,000
Uruguay, 600,000
Cuba, 600,000
South Africa, 250,000
Mexico, 250,000

Document 4

Source: Friedrich Engels, *The Condition of the Working Class in England in 1844*, published in 1892. Along with Karl Marx, Engels developed the ideology of modern communism.

Manchester contains about four hundred thousand inhabitants....The town itself is peculiarly built, so that a person may live in it for years, and go in and out daily without coming into contact with a working-people's quarter or even with workers, that is, so long as he confines himself to his business or to pleasure walks. This arises chiefly from the fact, that by unconscious tacit agreement, as well as with outspoken conscious determination, the working people's quarters are sharply separated from the sections of the city reserved for the middle-class....

In one of these courts there stands directly at the entrance, at the end of the covered passage, a privy without a door, so dirty that the inhabitants can pass into and out of the court only by passing through foul pools of stagnant urine and excrement....Below it on the river there are several tanneries which fill the whole neighbourhood with the stench of animal putrefaction.

In dry weather, a long string of the most disgusting, blackish-green, slime pools are left standing on this bank, from the depths of which bubbles of miasmatic gas constantly arise and give forth a stench....Above the bridge are tanneries, bone mills, and gasworks, from which all drains and refuse find their way into the Irk, which receives further the contents of all the neighbouring sewers and privies.

Passing along a rough bank, among stakes and washing-lines, one penetrates into this chaos of small one-storied, one-roomed huts, in most of which there is no artificial floor; kitchen, living and sleeping-room all in one. In such a hole, scarcely five feet long by six broad, I found two beds—and such bedsteads and beds!—which, with a staircase and chimney-place, exactly filled the room. . . .

In almost every court one or even several such pens [of pigs] may be found, into which the inhabitants of the court throw all refuse and offal, whence the swine grow fat; and the atmosphere, confined on all four sides, is utterly corrupted by putrefying animal and vegetable substances. . . .

Such is the Old Town of Manchester. . . . Everything which here arouses horror and indignation is of recent origin, belongs to the industrial epoch.

Document 5

Source: *The Communist Manifesto*, written by Karl Marx and Friedrich Engels in response to the devastating social results of industrialization, 1848.

The history of all hitherto existing society is the history of class struggles. . . . Our epoch, the epoch of the bourgeoisie, possesses, however, this distinct feature: it has simplified class antagonisms. Society as a whole is more and more splitting up into two great hostile camps, into two great classes directly facing each other—bourgeoisie and proletariat. The need of a constantly expanding market for its products chases the bourgeoisie over the entire surface of the globe. It must nestle everywhere, settle everywhere, establish connections everywhere. . . . All old-established national industries have been destroyed or are daily being destroyed. They are dislodged by new industries . . . , that [use] raw material drawn from the remotest zones; industries whose products are consumed, not only at home, but in every quarter of the globe.

Document 6

Source: Refugee from King Leopold's Congo, speaking after the invention of the bicycle in Europe increased the demand for rubber, ca. 1895.

We were always in the forest to find the rubber vines, to go without food, and our women had to give up cultivating the fields and gardens. Then we starved. . . . We begged the white man to leave us alone, saying we could get no more rubber, but the white men and their soldiers said "Go. You are only beasts yourselves. . . ." When we failed and our rubber was short, the soldiers came to our towns and killed us. Many were shot, some had their ears cut off; others were tied up with ropes round their necks and taken away.

Document 7

Source: Kang Youwei, Confucian scholar and adviser to the Chinese emperor, appeal to the emperor spelling out his understanding of what China needed, 1898.

After studying ancient and modern institutions, Chinese and foreign, I have found that . . . ancient times were different from today. I hope that Your Majesty will daily read Mencius [a famous Confucian writer] and follow his example of loving the people . . . but it should be remembered that the [present] age of universal unification is different from that of sovereign nations. . . . As to the republican governments of the United States and France and the constitutional governments of Britain and Germany, these countries are far away and their customs are different from ours. . . . Consequently I beg Your Majesty to adopt the purpose of Peter the Great of Russia as our purpose and to take the Meiji Reform of Japan as the model of our reform. The time and place of Japan's reforms are not remote and her religion and customs are somewhat similar to ours. Her success is manifest; her example can be followed.

Long Essay Questions

Using your knowledge of world history, develop an argument in response to one of the following questions.

2. Newly industrialized states often enlarged their empires, conquered new territories, colonized other parts of the world, and established transoceanic relationships.

   Evaluate the extent to which the establishment of empires during the age of industry led to social and political transformations in various parts of the world from 1750 to 1900.

3. The period from 1750 to 1900 was marked by revolutions and rebellions, which led to the development of new nation-states.

   Evaluate the extent to which new political philosophies led to rebellions and revolutions from 1750 to 1900.

4. The rise of capitalism and global empires led to new patterns of long-distance migration.

   Evaluate the extent to which new patterns of long-distance migration led to transformations in host societies in the nineteenth century.

BUILDING AP® SKILLS

Argumentation

The Long Essay Question (LEQ) is an important part of the AP® World History: Modern Exam. The LEQ is 15 percent of the overall score on the exam. Students will pick from one of three prompts. Consider giving students all three prompts and allowing them to choose the prompt they wish to write on. This will mimic the exam layout and give them practice. Students should have 40 minutes to write the LEQ.

Differentiation

If you want to differentiate this activity, follow the "Must Do, Should Do, Strive For" model below.

■ Must Do: Students write a contextualization and a thesis for the prompt.

■ Should Do: Students write two arguments (claims) for the prompt with three pieces of evidence to defend their argument.

■ Strive For: Students write a full-length LEQ in 40 minutes.

Prior AP® World History Exam questions are available on the AP® World History course website. While older DBQs and FRQs are excellent practice for building writing skills in AP® students, it is important to keep in mind that the essay format changed slightly in the 2019–2020 school year. The following questions are relevant for this part of the text. Questions marked with an asterisk (*) are available on the AP® World History course website in a modified version; below are updated versions of the prompts to fit the 2019–2020 model.

Document-Based Questions

■ 2005, Question 1: Evaluate the extent to which Muslim leaders in North Africa and South Asia were similar in how they confronted and/or defined their nationalist sentiments in the twentieth century. (Revised prompt)

■ 2008, Question 1: Evaluate the extent to which various factors shaped the modern Olympic movement from 1892 to 2002. (Revised prompt)

■ 2011, Question 1: Evaluate the extent to which the Green Revolution led to a variety of consequences in the period from 1945 to the present. (Revised prompt)

■ 2012, Question 1: Evaluate the extent to which politics influenced cricket in South Asia between 1880 and 2005. (Revised prompt)

■ 2014, Question 1: Evaluate the extent to which the Chinese Communist Party used differing methods to gain support from peasants during the Chinese civil war between ca. 1925 and ca. 1950. (Revised prompt)

■ 2015, Question 1: Evaluate the extent to which the responses to the spread of influenza differed around the world in the early twentieth century. (Revised prompt)

■ 2016, Question 1: Evaluate the extent to which politics impacted gender roles and relationships in twentieth-century Latin America. (Revised prompt)

■ 2021, Question 1: Evaluate the extent to which economic factors led to the outbreak of the Mexican Revolution (1910–1920).

Long Essay Questions

■ 2004, Question 3: Develop an argument that evaluates the extent to which the First World War affected two or more regions in the period from 1918 through the 1930s. (Revised prompt)

The Long Twentieth Century

1900–present

THE BIG PICTURE

The Long Twentieth Century: A New Period in World History?

The years since roughly 1900 appear to many historians as a new and distinct phase of the human journey, in large part because the pace of change has so sharply accelerated during this relatively brief time. The architecture of global politics changed rapidly in little more than a century. In 1900, European imperial powers were globally dominant. But two world wars, the Great Depression, the rise of fascism and communism, and surging nationalist movements within the colonies ended that dominance. In its place emerged the rivalry of two superpowers (the Soviet Union and the United States) among over 150 independent states during the cold war (1950–1990). Following the collapse

610

(continued)

■ 2006, Question 3: Develop an argument that evaluates the extent to which the goals and outcomes of twentieth-century revolutions differed between two of the following: Mexico, China, and Russia.* (Revised prompt)

■ 2007, Question 2: Develop an argument that evaluates the extent to which the formation of national identities changed in the Middle East, Southeast Asia, or sub-Saharan Africa from 1914 to the current day.* (Revised prompt)

■ 2008, Question 3: Develop an argument that evaluates the extent to which the emergence of nation-states in Latin America in the nineteenth century was similar to the emergence of nation-states in the twentieth century. (Revised prompt)

■ 2017, Question 3: Develop an argument that evaluates the extent to which the global balance of political power changed in the period 1900 to the present. (Revised prompt) ➡

of the Soviet Union in 1991, yet another global system emerged with one global superpower, the United States, challenged by a widening array of other centers of economic, military, and political influence. Accompanying these global political changes was the evolution of military technologies far more powerful than ever before, culminating in nuclear weapons with a completely unprecedented capacity for destruction.

Beneath the surface of these dramatic events, more significant and enduring processes likewise accelerated at an unparalleled rate. Industrialization quickly became a genuinely global phenomenon, accompanied by a massive increase in energy consumption and overall wealth, a soaring population, and rapid urbanization. Furthermore, long-distance migration mixed the world's peoples in novel ways, generating new social patterns and cultural identities. Feminists mounted an unprecedented attack on patriarchal attitudes and practices, while religious fundamentalists renewed their faith, often in opposition to established political and religious authorities.

But the most fundamental of these processes involved an extraordinary and mounting human impact on the environment. The well-known world historian David Christian has written that "the big story of the twentieth century is how one species began to dominate the energy and resources of the biosphere as a whole."[1] By the late twentieth century, that dominance had taken humankind well into what many scientists have been calling the Anthropocene era, the age of man, in which human activity is leaving an enduring and global mark on the

geological, atmospheric, and biological history of the planet itself. All of this has been part of an astonishing and often disorienting rate of change in human life.

A further distinctive feature of the human story during the past 100 years or so is an increasingly thick connectedness or entanglement commonly referred to as "globalization." It found expression in the worldwide empires of major European powers, in a great increase of international trade and investment, in the flow of ideas and cultural patterns around the world, in the large-scale movements of people, and in the global spread of diseases. War, economic crises, communism, fundamentalism, feminism, and the warming of the planet all operated on a global scale. The speed with which this globalizing world took shape and the density of the connections it forged—these too arguably mark the past century or more as a new era in world history.

And yet many of these changes find a place within historical patterns of the more distant past. Interaction among distinct societies, civilizations, and regions has a very long history. "Contact with strangers possessing new and unfamiliar skills," wrote world historian William McNeill, has long been "the principal factor promoting historically significant social change."[2] In that sense, modern globalization has an ancient pedigree. Furthermore, the collapse of empires during the past century resonates with the dissolution of many earlier empires. Technological innovation too has been a feature of human societies since the beginning, and human activity has left its mark on

(continued)

- 2018, Question 4: Develop an argument that evaluates how one or more of these political ideologies—communism, fascism, or nationalism—challenged the existing political and/or social order in the period 1900 to 2001.

- 2019, Question 4: Develop an argument that evaluates the extent to which one or more states controlled their economies in the period 1900 to 2001.

- 2021, Question 4: Develop an argument that evaluates the extent to which governments (other than the U.S. government) changed their economic policies in response to the Great Depression.

- 2022, Question 4: Develop an argument that evaluates the extent to which one or more states controlled their economies in the late twentieth century.

BUILDING AP® SKILLS
Developments and Processes

The AP® World History: Modern Course Framework dates this era from 1900 to the present. Consider challenging students to look at the chapter topics and predict what they might learn about in this era. Consider asking students: Looking at the chapter titles, what are some of the big events of the period? *The big events of the period include World Wars I and II, the Great Depression, the communist revolution in Russia and other revolutions it engendered, the cold war, the struggle for political and economic independence in previously colonized regions, and globalization.*

BUILDING AP® SKILLS
Making Connections: Continuity and Change

If you want to preview Period 4 for students, you can have them read "The Big Picture" and then ask them the following questions regarding continuities and changes in this period:

- What continuities does the book detail for the fourth period in modern world history? *The collapse of empires during the twentieth century resonated with the fall of earlier empires. The traditions of long-established religions are still popular with many people around the world. Humans continue to leave their mark on the environment, through technological innovations and human activity.*

- What changes does the text highlight? *The world wars of the twentieth century were new in the extent to which whole populations were mobilized to fight them and in the enormity of the destruction that they caused. The Russian and Chinese revolutions were the first large-scale revolutions in modern world history and broke radically with the Western capitalist model. Industrialization became a truly global phenomenon, and long-distance migration mixed the world's peoples in new ways.*

BUILDING AP® SKILLS

Making Connections: Continuity and Change

It's good for students to connect the previous periods of history they've studied to what they are currently studying. As you begin globalization, you can get students to think about those connections by asking: Explain in what ways globalization is a continuity and in what ways it represents a change. *Globalization occurred in the past through the Silk Road network; Indian Ocean and trans-Saharan commerce; the spread of religions like Buddhism, Christianity, and Islam; and the Columbian exchange. However, much has also changed. We now have deeper and faster connections to one another through the Internet, radio, and television. This unprecedented network of communication and exchange has allowed more people than ever before to produce products and services for the world market and to depend on that market. Regional conflicts have also become global.*

the planet since our gathering and hunting ancestors decimated a number of large animal species. Billions of people continue to operate in the tradition of long-established religions. Not everything has been new since 1900.

And even if world historians emphasize global networks and connections, what was local, regional, and particular continued to matter. Communism may have been a global phenomenon, but its Russian, Chinese, and Cuban variants were hardly identical. Feminism in the Global North certainly differed from that of the Global South. Economic globalization elicited both a warm embrace among corporate and technological elites and bitter rejection from those whose livelihoods and values were threatened by global linkages. Family, village, city, and nation remain deeply meaningful communities even in an interconnected world. Not everything has been global in this most recent era of world history.

In recounting this history, the four chapters of Period 4 seek to balance what was new, global, and rapidly changing with what persisted from the past and what was unique to particular places. Chapters 11 and 12 highlight the major events or "milestones" of this era and align closely with the major themes of Units 7 and 8 of the AP® World History: Modern course. Chapter 11 focuses on the first half of the twentieth century: the world wars, the Great Depression, the rise of fascist and authoritarian movements and states, and the beginnings of communism in Russia and China, all of this cast in a global context. Chapter 12 then carries this

narrative of events from roughly 1950 to 2022. It examines the postwar recovery of Europe, the Soviet Union, and Japan; the emergence of a distinctive Chinese communism; the cold war; the end of European empires in Asia and Africa; the emergence of dozens of new states on the global stage; the demise of communism; and international tensions in the three decades since the end of the cold war.

With these "milestones" of the past century in mind, Chapters 13 and 14 turn to the larger and perhaps even more consequential processes occurring beneath the major public events of the century, as reflected in Unit 9 of the AP® Course and Exam Description. Chapter 13 treats the enormous acceleration of technological innovation as a decisive driver of a deeply interconnected world economy and of pervasive social change. Chapter 14 then turns the spotlight on the explosive growth of human numbers, on the movement of many people to the cities and to new lives abroad, and on the cultural transformations that accompanied modern life during the past century. The chapter—and the book—conclude by examining the enormous and continuing impact of human activity on the entire biosphere, which represents by far the most significant long-term process of this new era and the most critical challenge of the next century.

The accelerating changes of this globalizing century have elicited a wide range of responses. Some individuals and communities welcomed changes that brought them unheard-of levels of material comfort and opportunities for an enriched personal life. Others resisted, denied, or sought to endure and adapt to changes that produced loss, disappointment, impoverishment, and sometimes horror beyond imagination. Reflecting on the flux and flow of this tumultuous era allows all of us—historians and students of history alike—to assess these recent transformations of the human condition, to locate ourselves in this torrent of change, and to ponder what lies ahead.

FIRST REFLECTIONS

1. **Questioning Chronology** How might you support the idea that the twelve decades since 1900 represent a distinct and novel period of world history? Or is it more useful to consider these years as continuing older patterns of change?

2. **Assessing Markers of Change** Do you think that events (World War I, the Russian Revolution, the end of European empires) or processes (population growth, globalization, technological innovation, climate change) provide the best indicators of new phases of world history?

3. **Comparing Significance** How might you rank the following processes in terms of their impact on the course of world history over the past century: population growth, globalization, technological innovation, and climate change? What criteria did you use to make your assessment?

4. **Looking Back . . . from the Future** What events and processes in the twentieth century do you think will appear as most significant to historians living a hundred years from now? What will likely garner less attention? Why?

BUILDING AP® SKILLS

Argumentation

Any of the questions under "First Reflections" would be good to give students as a practice with argumentation. Partner students up and assign them one of the four questions to answer. Give them time to think of an answer on their own before having them share their response with their partner.

Students should practice their periodization skills as much as possible throughout the year and especially once they get into the long twentieth century, when a huge number of historical events happened. You can ask students to examine the "Landmarks in World History (ca. 1900–present)" timeline and answer the following questions:

■ Which events lasted the longest? *The cold war, military coups in Latin America and Africa, African independence achieved, the Stalin era in the Soviet Union, the League of Nations, assertion of Islamic renewal, emergence of Soviet/Chinese hostility, the civil rights and anti–Vietnam War protests in U.S., and Islamic fundamentalist movements lasted the longest.*

■ Which events extend into the current day? *Islamic renewal and fundamentalist movements, Russia seizes Crimea and invades Ukraine, and COVID-19 pandemic outbreak extend into the present day.*

You can get students to practice their argumentation skills using the information in "Landmarks in World History (ca. 1900–present)" by asking: What is the problem with considering 1900–present a separate period? *One problem lies in the brevity of this period — only 100 years — compared to the many centuries or millennia that define earlier eras. Furthermore, because we are so close to the events we study and obviously ignorant of the future, we cannot know if or when this most recent period of world history will end. Or, as some have argued, has it ended already, perhaps with the collapse of the Soviet Union in 1991, with the attacks of September 11, 2001, or with the global economic crisis beginning in 2008? If so, are we now in yet another phase of historical development?*

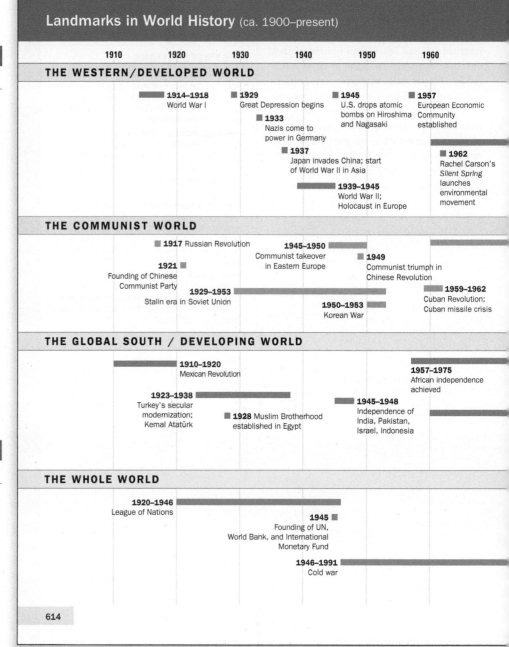

Landmarks in World History (ca. 1900–present)

	1910	1920	1930	1940	1950	1960

THE WESTERN/DEVELOPED WORLD

- 1914–1918 World War I
- 1929 Great Depression begins
- 1933 Nazis come to power in Germany
- 1937 Japan invades China; start of World War II in Asia
- 1939–1945 World War II; Holocaust in Europe
- 1945 U.S. drops atomic bombs on Hiroshima and Nagasaki
- 1957 European Economic Community established
- 1962 Rachel Carson's *Silent Spring* launches environmental movement

THE COMMUNIST WORLD

- 1917 Russian Revolution
- 1921 Founding of Chinese Communist Party
- 1929–1953 Stalin era in Soviet Union
- 1945–1950 Communist takeover in Eastern Europe
- 1949 Communist triumph in Chinese Revolution
- 1950–1953 Korean War
- 1959–1962 Cuban Revolution; Cuban missile crisis

THE GLOBAL SOUTH / DEVELOPING WORLD

- 1910–1920 Mexican Revolution
- 1923–1938 Turkey's secular modernization; Kemal Atatürk
- 1928 Muslim Brotherhood established in Egypt
- 1945–1948 Independence of India, Pakistan, Israel, Indonesia
- 1957–1975 African independence achieved

THE WHOLE WORLD

- 1920–1946 League of Nations
- 1945 Founding of UN, World Bank, and International Monetary Fund
- 1946–1991 Cold war

614

1970   1980   1990   2000   2010   2020

1990 ■
Reunification of Germany

■ **2001**
Attacks on World Trade
Center; "war on terror" begins

1991 ■
Earliest web browser released

■ **2002**
Introduction of the euro

1960s
Civil rights and anti–Vietnam
War protests in U.S.

■ **1993**
Formation of the EU

1991–2001
Yugoslavia civil war and breakup

2020 ■
Britain exits EU

1960s
Emergence of Soviet/
Chinese hostility

■ **1989**
Collapse of communism
in Eastern Europe

1965–1973
Vietnam War

■ **1991** Collapse of Soviet Union

■ **1968**
Prague Spring;
Soviet invasion of
Czechoslovakia

2014–present
Russia seizes Crimea and
invades Ukraine

1978–1989
Deng Xiaoping oversees
liberalizing reforms in China

■ **1979**
Islamic revolution
in Iran

■ **1994** End of apartheid
in South Africa

■ **2011**
Syrian civil war
begins

■ **1967** Six-Day War
between Israel
and Arab states

1979–1989
Soviet war in
Afghanistan

■ **2001** U.S. military
action begins in
Afghanistan and Iraq

■ **2014**
Rise of Islamic
State

1960s–1970s
Many military coups in
Africa and Latin America

1970s–present
Assertion of Islamic renewal; fundamentalist movements

■ **1995**
World Trade
Organization
established

■ **2008**
Global recession begins

2015 ■
Paris Climate
Agreement

1976–1985
UN Decade for Women

2022 ■
World population approaches 8 billion

2020
COVID-19 pandemic outbreak

TEACHING IDEA

Bell Ringer

As a quick start to class, you can ask students to examine the "Landmarks in World History (ca. 1900–present)" and determine whether, in general, events are long-lasting or fairly short. *Events appear to be fairly short. Most events last one year, although their impact may last much longer.*

Class Discussion

Consider having a class discussion to wrap up Unit 9: Globalization. This can help students review what they have learned and allow you to check their understanding of the material. Ask the following question to start the discussion: How has globalization occurred? *Wars have taken shape on a global stage. The emergence of dozens of new nations, arising from the end of empires, has emphatically changed the architecture of world politics. Modern economic development has become a global quest; industrialization and its profoundly disruptive environmental impact likewise have operated globally even as the economies of particular nations have become inextricably connected to one another. Social, cultural, and political movements such as communism, feminism, nationalism, and religious fundamentalism have assumed worldwide dimensions, crossing national or civilizational boundaries.*

Accelerating Global Change and Realignment

In every phase of the human journey, world history focuses attention on the intersections of various peoples, civilizations, and societies. That process, widely known now as globalization, has been especially prominent over the past century or so and is therefore the guiding theme in Period 4 of *Ways of the World*. Wars, both hot and cold, have taken shape on a global stage. Dozens of new nations, arising from the end of empires, emphatically have changed the architecture of world politics. Modern economic development has become a global quest; industrialization and its profoundly disruptive environmental impact likewise have operated globally even as the economies of particular nations have become inextricably connected to one another. Social, cultural, and political movements such as communism, feminism, nationalism, and religious fundamentalism have assumed worldwide dimensions, crossing national or civilizational boundaries. To paraphrase the seventeenth-century English poet John Donne, more than ever before in human affairs, "No man or woman is an island, entire of itself; everyone is a piece of the continent, a part of the main."

1900–present

ENVIRONMENT

Entering the Anthropocene era: global environmental transformations in the 20th century
- Changes in landscape
- Declining biodiversity
- Air, water, soil pollution
- Radioactive waste

Early environmental movements in the 19th and early 20th centuries

Climate change/global warming: origins and outcomes

Nuclear weapons and the environment

Second-wave environmentalism
- In the West
- Role of Rachel Carson
- In the communist world
- In the Global South
- North/South conflict about environmental issues

Environmental issues in the collapse of USSR

Paris Climate Agreement (2015)

CULTURES

Communist Ideology

Fascist ideology

Religious fundamentalism
- Christian
- Hindu
- Islamic

Religious alternatives to fundamentalism

Islam and modernity: westernization in Turkey and Islamic renewal in Iran

Religion and politics in India

Anti-Semitism and the Holocaust

Japanese nationalist ideology

Global culture of liberation

Ideologies of modern feminism

Critique of capitalist globalization emerges

Cultural globalization

GOVERNANCE	ECONOMIES	SOCIAL STRUCTURES	TECHNOLOGY
Russian Revolution	Great Depression in	Global population growth and migration	Development of the weaponry of "total war"
Constructing the Soviet state	▪ Europe	Class, gender, and fascism	Emergence of the automobile
World Wars I and II	▪ United States	Class and gender issues in prewar Japan	Rise of oil and natural gas
Authoritarian states: comparing Italy, Germany, and Japan	▪ The colonies	Urbanization and elite privilege in the USSR	Radio and cinema as media of mass entertainment
League of Nations and United Nations	▪ Latin America	Social outcomes of world wars in the West	Telephone
Chinese Revolution: compared to Russian	▪ Japan	Social transformation in communist revolutions	Atom bomb and arms race
The cold war	Fascist economic policies	Effects of bureaucracy and inequality in Mao's China	New biomedical technologies
Decolonization in Asia and Africa	Communist industrial development: five-year plans	Communist feminism	Television age
Political variations in the Global South	Collectivization of agriculture in USSR and China	Women and Islam: Turkey, Iran, Morocco, Pakistan	Popularization of air and auto travel
▪ Democracy in India	Muslim Brotherhood: economic goals and outcomes	Searching for enemies in USSR and China	Increases in commercial trucking
▪ Military rule in Africa and Latin America	Marshall Plan: recovery of Europe	Changing family structures	New energy sources: nuclear and solar power
▪ Communist states in China, Vietnam, Cuba	Economic development in the Global South: problems, policies, and varying outcomes	Second-wave feminism in the West	Space exploration and competition
Persistence of Communist Party rule in China: Tiananmen Square (1989)	Economic reforms in communist China	Feminism in the Global South	Fiber optics
Cuban revolution	Economic globalization since the 1980s: growth, instability, and inequality	Changing patterns of sexuality	Development of new surgical technologies
End of communism in Eastern Europe	Globalization of industrialization	Ethnicity and political conflict in developing countries	New methods of birth control
Collapse of the Soviet Union	Debating globalization		New agricultural technologies and chemistry associated with the Green Revolution
Globalization of democracy in the late 20th century			Computers and Internet
Debating an American empire			Cellular communications
			Containerized shipping

EXPLORING AP® THEMES

Previewing the time period students are about to study can help them get an idea of the major concepts they need to keep an eye out for as they work through Units 7, 8, and 9. You can ask students to study the events on the thematic chart on pages 616 and 617 and then write a general statement about the patterns they see for each theme in the period. (Suggested answers are provided in italics.)

▪ **Environment:** *This period sees the rise of the environmental movement after record environmental destruction and transformation.*

▪ **Cultures:** *The patterns of this period include extremism such as fascism, ultranationalist ideology, and religious fundamentalism.*

▪ **Governance:** *The patterns of this period include revolutions, decolonization, global warfare (both hot and cold), attempts of supranational organizations to maintain peace, and globalization of democracy.*

▪ **Economies:** *The patterns of this period include globalization, communism, collectivization, the Great Depression, and attempts of smaller groups such as the fascists and the Muslim Brotherhood to regain economic ground.*

▪ **Social Structures:** *In this period, many societies have addressed questions about class, gender, and cultural or ethnic differences. Global migration patterns have played an important part in the transformation of social structures.*

▪ **Technology:** *In this period, new transportation and communication technologies brought the world closer together. New medical and agricultural technologies also revolutionized human lives, allowing more people to survive and thrive.*

11 Milestones of the Past Century

War and Revolution, 1900–1950

AP® Overview for Chapter 11

Chapter 11 corresponds to AP® Unit 7: Global Conflict 1900–present and AP® Unit 8: Cold War and Decolonization 1900–present. It covers both world wars, the Great Depression, and the beginning of the cold war as well as the Russian Revolution and the Chinese Revolution. The material in this chapter is rich with historical information and images that will expose students to the developments that occurred in the first half of the twentieth century. Students should utilize their skills and compare the conflicts discussed in this chapter with earlier conflicts among European powers that occurred during Units 3, 4, 5, and 6. Teachers should encourage students to go deeper into the skills that the AP® World History course seeks to develop.

Chapter 11 Essential Activity

This chapter provides a good opportunity for students to practice writing an essay that uses a number of AP® Themes and Historical Thinking Skills. When students have completed the chapter, ask them to write a 40-minute timed essay on the following prompt:

- In the period from 1900 to 1950, challenges from existing political orders led to military conflicts around the world.
  Develop an argument that evaluates the extent to which the causes of World War II were similar to the causes of World War I.

Students should consider the following two AP® themes:

- Governance
- Economic Systems

Students should also use the following Historical Thinking Skills and Reasoning Processes:

- Argumentation
- Comparison
- Causation

Answers should consider the following points: *Causation includes militarism, imperialism, alliances, and nationalism for World War I and nationalism for World War II. However, in the case of World War II, Germany was the main instigator.* Students may also bring in effects of the world wars: *The effects of both wars included an increased demand among European colonies for their independence and the effects on Germany of losing. Different effects included the rise of the United States as a world power and the cold war with the Soviet Union after World War II.*

Differentiation

While it's good for students to write full essays, especially as they get closer to the AP® Exam, it can also be helpful to have them work on a group essay outline and evaluate their peers' responses. This exercise allows them to see different ways of formulating arguments and potentially understand what graders are looking for when scoring essays. If you want students to complete a group outline essay with this prompt, consider following the "Must Do, Should Do, Strive For" model below:

- Must Do: Working in groups of four or fewer, students must create an LEQ outline on provided butcher paper. The outline should include contextualization and a thesis that responds to the prompt, at least two arguments, and at least two pieces of evidence for *each* argument.

- Should Do: Once all the groups have completed their LEQ poster, have students hang them up and do a gallery walk to see how other groups put together this LEQ. As they look at each poster, ask students to leave "I wonder . . ." and "I like . . ." statements about what they see in the outline.

- Strive For: For students who want or need a writing challenge, have them choose one of their arguments from their LEQ poster and write a full argument paragraph on it.

Chapter 11 Resources

- **TRM** AP® Skills Workshop Activity Handout: Writing an LEQ: Argumentation
- **TRM** Chapter 11 DBQ Activity Handout
- **TRM** Chapter 11 Guided Reading
- **TRM** Chapter 11 Lecture Presentation Slides
- **TRM** Chapter 11 Outline
- **TRM** Chapter 11 Suggested Responses to Questions
- **TRM** Eric's Activity 11: Civil War in the West
- **TRM** Handout 11.1: Causation Chart for Twentieth-Century Global Conflicts
- **TRM** Handout 11.2: Continuity and Change Chart for States Created after World War I and Current Status
- **TRM** Handout 11.3: Comparison Chart for Rise of Authoritarian Governments
- **TRM** Handout 11.4: Comparison Chart for Effects of Authoritarian Governments
- **TRM** Handout 11.5: Sourcing Chart for Analysis of *Mein Kampf*
- **TRM** Handout 11.6: Comparison Chart for the Great Depression in Germany and Japan
- **TRM** Handout 11.7: Graphic Organizer for Communism in China and the USSR
- **TRM** Handout 11.8: Chart for Opportunities and Barriers for Women in Communist Nations
- **TRM** Handout 11.9: Continuity and Change Charts for Global Communism in the Twentieth Century
- **TRM** Map 11A: The World
- **TRM** Writing Organizer for DBQ Practice

Pacing Guide

Below is a pacing guide for the AP® World History: Modern course beginning in ca. 1200 c.e. This pacing guide is based on a schedule with 120 sessions of 50 minutes each before the AP® Exam. It is meant as a place to start. If you have a different number of sessions before the exam, you can modify the pacing to suit your needs

Day	Pages Assigned	AP® Topic	AP® Theme	Suggested Assignments	Coverage Notes
1	Read pages 619–623, completing the paragraph on page 623	7.1 7.2	GOV	Eric's Activity 11: Civil War in the West on page 619 Apply the Tip on page 620 Teaching Idea: Incorporating Outside Resources on page 622	While it may be tempting to jump right into teaching about World War I, spend some time "setting the stage" for the first great war of the twentieth century. Giving context to World War I will help students make the connection between what they learned about the nineteenth century and the events of this era.
2	Read pages 623–626 from the last paragraph on page 623 to the paragraph about social and cultural changes	7.2 7.3	GOV TEC	Building AP® Skills: Claims and Evidence in Sources on page 624 Apply the Tip on page 625 AP® Classroom: AP® Daily Videos on page 626	While the beginning of Chapter 11 does an excellent job of setting the stage for World War I, you will need to give more guidance to students on how the war was fought (especially with the concept of total war).
3	Read pages 626–632 from the paragraph about social and cultural changes to "Capitalism Unraveling: The Great Depression"	7.3 7.5 7.8	GOV SIO TEC	Building AP® Skills: Making Connections: Continuity and Change on page 627 AP® Classroom: AP® Daily Videos on page 629 Building AP® Skills: Claims and Evidence in Sources on page 630	The course framework emphasizes the outcomes of World War I, especially how these outcomes led to later conflicts in the twentieth century. Help students understand how the way World War I ended contributed to these future conflicts.
4	Read pages 632–634 from "Capitalism Unraveling: The Great Depression" to "Democracy Denied: The Authoritarian Alternative"	7.4 7.5	GOV ECN	Apply the Tip on page 632 Building AP® Skills: Claims and Evidence in Sources on page 632 AP® Classroom: AP® Topic Questions on page 633	The Great Depression and the interwar period are a good place to practice causation and comparison skills with students. Have them examine the causes of the Great Depression, along with comparing how different nations reacted to the challenges of the Depression.

➡

Day	Pages Assigned	AP® Topic	AP® Theme	Suggested Assignments	Coverage Notes
5	Read pages 634–636 from "Democracy Denied: The Authoritarian Alternative" to "Hitler and the Nazis"	7.4 7.5 7.6	GOV ECN	Teaching Idea: Incorporating Outside Resources on page 634 Building AP® Skills: Making Connections: Causation on page 635 Exploring AP® Themes: GOV on page 635	See above. This section also begins the discussion on the rise of authoritarian states in the years leading to World War II. Students could practice their comparison skills here by looking at the rise of authoritarianism in Italy, Germany, and Japan during the interwar period.
6	Read pages 636–640 from "Hitler and the Nazis"	7.5 7.6	GOV	Exploring AP® Themes: ECN on page 636 Apply the Tip on page 637 Building AP® Skills: Developments and Processes on page 640	See above.
7	Read pages 641–643	7.5 7.6	GOV	Teaching Idea: Class Discussion on page 641 Building AP® Skills: Making Connections: Comparison on page 642 AP® Classroom: AP® Topic Questions on page 643	See above.
8	Read pages 644–646 to "The Road to War in Europe"	7.6 7.7	GOV	Teaching Idea: Incorporating Outside Resources on page 644 Building AP® Skills: Making Connections: Causation on page 645 AP® Classroom: AP® Daily Videos on page 646	The previous sections can be helpful with contextualization and causation by explaining the causes of World War I. Students can also practice comparison by comparing World War II to World War I with respect to how the wars were conducted and what their results were. Because of how fast the course moves, make sure to not spend too much time on World War II.
9	Read pages 646–649 from "The Road to War in Europe" through the last paragraph about women's roles	7.6 7.7	GOV	AP® Classroom: AP® Topic Questions on page 647 Apply the Tip on page 648 Apply the Tip on page 649	See above.
10	Read pages 649–656 from the first paragraph about the Holocaust through "Conclusions and Reflections"	7.7 7.8	GOV SIO	Teaching Idea: Incorporating Outside Resources on page 649 Apply the Tip on page 652 Teaching Idea: Incorporating Outside Resources on page 653	See above. Genocides throughout the twentieth century are a major topic in the course framework. Use this section's discussion on the Holocaust as a way to lead the students into a broader study of twentieth-century genocides.

NOTES

Global War This British propaganda poster created during World War II and entitled "Together" depicts soldiers from various parts of Britain's far-flung empire marching in unity. While it celebrates an alleged spirit of cooperation between Europeans and their colonial subjects during this global conflict, the war contributed in many ways to the breakup of these empires, as described in Chapter 12. (PhotoQuest/Getty Images)

618

Milestones of the Past Century

War and Revolution

1900–1950

◄ **AP**

**CLAIMS AND EVIDENCE IN
SOURCES**
Based on this picture, how did the
British use their colonial territories
during World War II? What message
did the image seek to convey? Can
you imagine different interpretations
of the relationship between Britain
and its empire?

**CONNECTING
PAST AND
PRESENT**

"The First World War was described at the time as the war to end all wars. It did nothing of the sort."[1] So said UN secretary general Ban Ki-moon at an event in 2014 marking one hundred years since the outbreak of that global conflict. And in 2017, the one-hundredth anniversary of the Russian Revolution, Russian president Vladimir Putin offered a commentary on that event. "Could we not have evolved by way of gradual and consistent forward movement," he asked, "rather than at the cost of destroying our statehood and the ruthless fracturing of millions of human lives?"[2] Both men reflected a widespread and intense sense of disappointment, even futility, about events that had earlier been greeted with great expectations. ■

However they are evaluated, these two immense upheavals—World War I and the Russian Revolution—initiated a chain of events that shaped much of world history during the past century. They were followed by the economic meltdown of the Great Depression, by the rise of Nazi Germany and the horror of the Holocaust, and by an even bloodier and more destructive World War II, a struggle that encompassed much of the world. Among the major outcomes of that war was the Chinese Revolution, which brought a modern Communist Party to power in that ancient land. Within the colonial world of Africa, Asia, and the Middle East, these events set in motion processes of change that would shortly put an end to Europe's global empires. It was, to put it mildly, an eventful half century, and many of its developments had their origins in the First World War and the Russian Revolution.

619

TRM Chapter 11 Guided Reading
You can find a guided reading handout for this chapter in the Teacher's Resource Materials.

TRM Chapter 11 Lecture Slides
You can find curated lecture slides for this chapter in the Teacher's Resource Materials.

TRM Chapter 11 Outline
You can find a chapter outline to model good note-taking for this chapter in the Teacher's Resource Materials.

TRM Suggested Responses to Questions
You can find suggested responses to all of the AP® margin questions in this chapter in the Teacher's Resource Materials.

BUILDING AP® SKILLS

Developments and Processes

Period 4 covers the big events of the twentieth century: the two world wars, the Russian Revolution, the Chinese Revolution, the Great Depression, and the cold war. As a review and an introduction into Period 3, ask students: What were the big events of Period 3, ca. 1750 to ca. 1900? *The big events of Period 3 included the Industrial Revolution, imperialism, the American Revolution, the French Revolution, the Enlightenment, the Haitian Revolution, independence in Latin America, and the rise of Russia and Japan.*

ERIC'S ACTIVITY 11 Civil War in the West

Theme 3: Governance

Students usually study the two world wars and the Great Depression in separate chapters. They also typically study these events through the prism of American history. I like to challenge my students to reconsider what they already know about these developments and consider how a world-historical perspective might change their understanding. By first examining their own ideas about the world wars and then exploring an alternative interpretation, students develop a richer perspective on the period. Find the complete activity in the Teacher's Resource Materials.

TRM Eric's Activity 11: Civil War in the West

AP®

CAUSATION

In what ways were war, depression, and revolution motors of global change during the first half of the twentieth century?

AP® EXAM TIP

Understand how World War I, World War II, and the cold war transformed patterns of global politics.

AP® EXAM TIP

Remember that, like South Asia, Europe was rarely under one unified political system.

AP®

CONTEXTUALIZATION

Before the outbreak of World War I, in which territories did European powers compete, and why were these territories considered valuable?

AP®

CAUSATION

What elements of Europe's earlier history shaped the course of the First World War?

The First World War: A European Crisis with a Global Impact, 1914–1918

Finding the Main Point: What were the major causes and consequences of World War I?

Since 1500, Europe had assumed an increasingly prominent position on the global stage, reflected in its military capacity, its colonial empires, and its Scientific and Industrial Revolutions (see Map 11.1). That unique situation provided the foundation for Europeans' pride, self-confidence, and sense of superiority. In 1900, few could have imagined that this "proud tower" of European dominance would lie shattered less than a half century later. The starting point in that unraveling was the First World War.

Origins: The Beginnings of the Great War

Europe's modern transformation and its global ascendancy were certainly not accompanied by a growing unity or stability among its own peoples—in fact, quite the opposite. The historical rivalries of its competing nation-states further sharpened as both Italy and Germany joined their fragmented territories into two major new powers around 1870. A powerful and rapidly industrializing Germany, seeking its "place in the sun," was a particularly disruptive new element in European political life, especially for the more established powers, such as Britain, France, and Russia. Since the defeat of Napoleon in 1815, a fragile and fluctuating balance of power had generally maintained the peace among Europe's major countries. By the early twentieth century, that balance of power was expressed in two rival alliances, the Triple Alliance of Germany, Italy, and the Austro-Hungarian Empire and the Triple Entente of Russia, France, and Britain. Those commitments, undertaken in the interests of national security, transformed a relatively minor incident in the Balkans (southeastern Europe) into a conflagration that consumed almost all of Europe.

That incident occurred on June 28, 1914, when a Serbian nationalist assassinated the heir to the Austro-Hungarian throne, Archduke Franz Ferdinand. To the rulers of Austria-Hungary, the surging nationalism of Serbian Slavs was a mortal threat to the cohesion of their fragile multinational empire, which included other Slavic peoples as well. Thus they determined to crush it. But behind Austria-Hungary lay its far more powerful ally, Germany; and behind tiny Serbia lay Russia, with its self-proclaimed mission of protecting other Slavic peoples. Allied to Russia were the French and the British. Thus a system of alliances intended to keep the peace created obligations that drew these Great Powers of Europe into a general war by early August 1914 (see Map 11.2).

Landmarks for Chapter 11

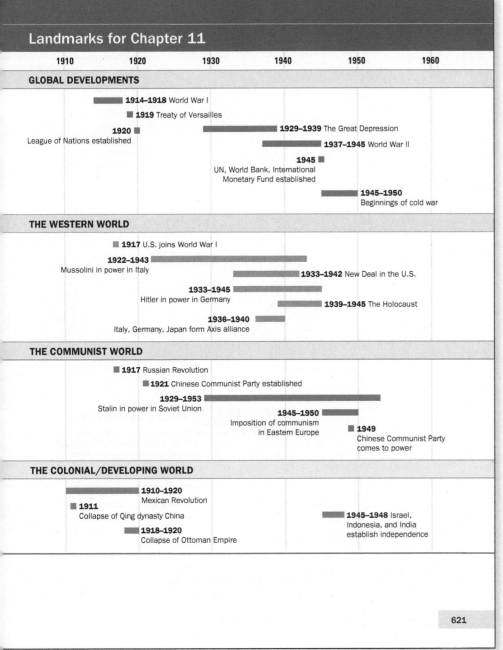

1910   1920   1930   1940   1950   1960

GLOBAL DEVELOPMENTS

1914–1918 World War I

1919 Treaty of Versailles

1920 League of Nations established

1929–1939 The Great Depression

1937–1945 World War II

1945 UN, World Bank, International Monetary Fund established

1945–1950 Beginnings of cold war

THE WESTERN WORLD

1917 U.S. joins World War I

1922–1943 Mussolini in power in Italy

1933–1942 New Deal in the U.S.

1933–1945 Hitler in power in Germany

1939–1945 The Holocaust

1936–1940 Italy, Germany, Japan form Axis alliance

THE COMMUNIST WORLD

1917 Russian Revolution

1921 Chinese Communist Party established

1929–1953 Stalin in power in Soviet Union

1945–1950 Imposition of communism in Eastern Europe

1949 Chinese Communist Party comes to power

THE COLONIAL/DEVELOPING WORLD

1910–1920 Mexican Revolution

1911 Collapse of Qing dynasty China

1945–1948 Israel, Indonesia, and India establish independence

1918–1920 Collapse of Ottoman Empire

621

BUILDING AP® SKILLS

Developments and Processes

Ask students to study the events listed in "Landmarks for Chapter 11." There are many global events between 1900 and 1970. To avoid confusion with students, have them create an annotated map that shows the global events between 1900 and 1970. Students can then see that the global events overlap and can influence one another. You can also make the annotated map a class (rather than an individual) activity. All levels will benefit: advanced students can help the lower-level students, and all students can use this activity to review geography skills. Divide the activity among random groups, making certain to spread advanced and lower-level students equally among groups. Make groups responsible for one regional area and ensure that everyone contributes. The annotated map could be drawn on butcher paper and placed in an area that students can reference during the entire unit.

TEACHING IDEA

Incorporating Outside Resources

Students are often incredibly interested in how World War I began. In the episode *How World War I Started* of Crash Course World History, John Green discusses how World War I began. Find the video on YouTube. After students have watched the video, ask the following questions:

■ What was the immediate trigger of World War I? *The immediate trigger of World War I was the assassination of Archduke Franz Ferdinand.*

■ What were the long-term causes of World War I? *The long-term causes of World War I included militarism, alliances, imperialism, and nationalism.* (You can mention here how students can use the acronym "MAIN" to help them remember the long-term causes of World War I.)

■ Do you see connections between the causes of World War I and the causes of the post-9/11 war on terror? *Answers will vary.*

AP® CLASSROOM

AP® Topic Questions

Now is an excellent opportunity for some practice with multiple-choice questions. You can find a set of questions about the causes of World War I by logging into AP® Classroom, clicking on Unit 7 under Classroom Resources, and then selecting Topic Questions. Look for the questions labeled "Moltke and Giolitti WWI Predictions." You can either assign the questions to the students to complete individually or allow them to partner up to work through the set together.

MAPPING HISTORY   Map 11.1 **The World in 1914**

A map of the world in 1914 shows an unprecedented situation in which one people—Europeans or those of European descent—exercised enormous control and influence over virtually the entire planet.

AP®
CAUSATION
What developments in the nineteenth century were long-term causes of the First World War?

The outbreak of **World War I** was something of an accident, in that none of the major states planned or predicted the archduke's assassination or deliberately sought a prolonged conflict, but the system of rigid alliances made Europe vulnerable to that kind of accident. Moreover, behind those alliances lay other factors that contributed to the eruption of war and shaped its character. One of them was a mounting popular nationalism (see "Nations and Nationalism" in Chapter 7). The rulers of the major countries of Europe saw the world as an arena of conflict and competition among rival nation-states. Schools, mass media, and military service had convinced millions of ordinary Europeans that their national identities were profoundly and personally meaningful. The public pressure of these competing

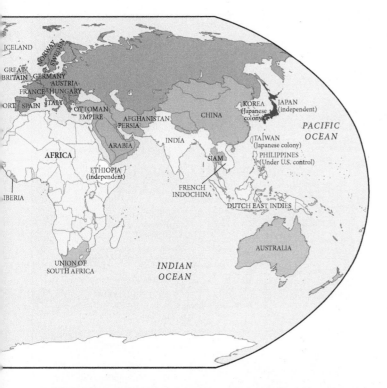

Reading the Map: Identify the two countries that were fully independent in 1914 and were not European-derived states that had once been European colonies.

AP **Making Connections:** Compare this map to Map 6.2: The Global Silver Trade, which depicts European colonial empires in the seventeenth century. On which continents had direct European colonial control expanded or declined?

nationalisms allowed statesmen little room for compromise and ensured widespread popular support, at least initially, for the decision to go to war. Many men rushed to recruiting offices, fearing that the war might end before they could enlist, and celebratory parades sent them off to the front. For conservative governments, the prospect of war was a welcome occasion for national unity in the face of the mounting class- and gender-based conflicts in European societies.

Also contributing to the war was an industrialized militarism. Europe's armed rivalries had long ensured that military men enjoyed great social prestige, and most heads of state wore uniforms in public. All of the Great Powers had substantial standing armies and, except for Britain, relied on conscription (compulsory military service)

AP **EXAM TIP**
On the exam, the causes and consequences of global conflicts are much more important than a military history of these wars.

CHAPTER 11

Making Connections: Causation

One of the causes of World War I was imperialism. Ask students: Before the outbreak of World War I, which territories did European powers fight over, and why were these territories so valuable? *European powers fought over China, Samoa, and Morocco. These territories served as a source of raw materials to fuel European industrialization, as well as strategic ports for military vessels.*

APPLY THE TIP

Have students create a chart like the one below so that they can keep track of the causes and consequences of global conflicts of the twentieth century. A reproducible version of this chart is available in the Teacher's Resource Materials. (Answers are provided in italics.)

Conflict	Cause(s)	Consequences(s)
World War I	*Militarism, alliances, imperialism, nationalism, assassination of Archduke Franz Ferdinand (trigger)*	*Loss of empire resulting in newly independent states in Europe and the Middle East, economic depression, social changes, colonial unrest*
World War II	*Issues stemming from the Treaty of Versailles (failure of the League of Nations and harsh treatment of Germany), global economic depression, rise of fascism*	*Colonies gaining independence, rise of the United States and the USSR as superpowers*
Cold War	*Post-WWII disagreements on division of Europe and free elections, democracy vs. communism, rise of U.S. and USSR as new global superpowers*	*Fear of nuclear war, space race, rise in tensions between NATO members and Warsaw Pact, Truman Doctrine and the domino theory*

TRM Handout 11.1: Causation Chart for Twentieth-Century Global Conflicts

Claims and Evidence in Sources

This is a great opportunity to have students look for evidence in images. Show students the political cartoon titled "The Crime of the Ages: Who Did It?" by artist John T. McCutcheon. Ask students: What is the cartoonist's message, and what historical evidence supports his message? *The cartoonist is showing the various nations involved in the war blaming one another for starting the war. The cartoon seems to indicate that with everyone laying the blame on someone else, there will be no agreement. Evidence to support this message is the web of alliances that were formed before the war and the competition that grew with imperialism among rival nation-states. The text also discusses how competing nationalism and rigid alliances supported an inclination toward war.*

Governance (GOV)

Have students look at Map 11.2, "Europe on the Eve of World War I." Ask students to explain why Europe at that time was a "powder keg." *In the years leading up to the war, technological advancements and a mounting arms race contributed to the growth of both British and German naval power and the development of new war tools, including tanks, submarines, airplanes, poison gas, machine guns, and barbed wire. In addition, major states had developed elaborate war plans to prepare for the possibility of war.*

▲ AP®
CONTEXTUALIZATION
How does the map explain why a war between two nations of Europe could lead to a European-wide war?

Map 11.2 Europe on the Eve of World War I

Despite many elements of common culture, Europe in 1914 was a powder keg, with its major states armed to the teeth and divided into two rival alliances. In the early stages of the war, Italy changed sides to join the French, British, and Russians.

to staff them. Furthermore, each of the major states had developed elaborate "war plans" that spelled out in great detail the movement of men and materials that should occur immediately upon the outbreak of war. Such plans created a hair-trigger mentality because each country had an incentive to strike first so that its particular strategy could be implemented on schedule and without interruption or surprise. The rapid industrialization of warfare generated an array of novel weapons, including submarines, tanks, airplanes, poison gas, machine guns, and barbed wire. This new military technology contributed to the staggering casualties of the war, including some 10 million deaths, the vast majority male; perhaps twice that number were wounded, severely blistered by poison gas, or lost limbs. For countless women, as a result, there would be no husbands or children.

Europe's imperial reach around the world likewise shaped the scope and conduct of the war. It funneled colonial troops and laborers by the hundreds of thousands into the war effort, with men from Africa, India, China, Southeast Asia, Australia, New Zealand, and Canada taking part in the conflict. British and French forces seized German colonies in Africa and the South Pacific. Japan, allied with Britain, took various German possessions in China and the Pacific and demanded territorial and economic concessions from China itself. The Ottoman Empire, which entered the conflict on the side of Germany, became the site of intense military actions and witnessed an Arab revolt against Ottoman Turkish control. Finally, the United States, after initially seeking to avoid involvement in European quarrels, joined the war in 1917 when German submarines threatened American shipping. Thus the war, though centered in Europe, had global dimensions and certainly merited its title as a "world war."

Outcomes: Legacies of the Great War

The Great War shattered almost every expectation. Most Europeans believed in the late summer of 1914 that "the boys will be home by Christmas," but instead the war ground relentlessly on for more than four years before ending in a German defeat in November 1918. Moreover, it had become a **total war**, requiring the mobilization of each country's entire population. Thus the authority of governments expanded greatly. As the German state, for example, assumed further control over the economy, its policies became known as "war socialism," thus continuing a long-term strengthening of state power across much of Europe. Vast propaganda campaigns sought to arouse citizens by depicting a cruel and inhuman enemy who killed innocent children and violated women. Labor unions agreed to suspend strikes and accept sacrifices for the common good, while women, replacing the men who had left the factories for the

Women and the Great War World War I temporarily brought a halt to the women's suffrage movement as well as to women's activities on behalf of international peace. Most women on both sides actively supported their countries' war efforts, as suggested by this French wartime poster, showing women contributing to the war effort in industrial, agricultural, and domestic settings. (Library of Congress, Prints & Photographs Division, Reproduction number LC-USZC2-4067 [color film copy slide])

▲ **AP®**
MAKING CONNECTIONS
How does this image portray the role of women during the Great War?

AP® EXAM TIP
Understand how propaganda posters were one strategy used by governments to mobilize populations.

AP® CLASSROOM

AP® Daily Videos

This is an excellent opportunity to have students watch Daily Videos for Topic 7.3: Conducting World War I, located on AP® Classroom. You can find the two videos for Topic 7.3 by logging into AP® Classroom, clicking on Unit 7 under Classroom Resources, and then selecting Daily Videos. The two videos for Topic 7.3: Conducting World War I focus on total war, mobilization, and new military technology and work on the skill of identifying evidence used in a source to support an argument.

APPLY THE TIP

After discussing the importance of the Treaty of Versailles with students, you should focus on how the unresolved tensions after World War I led to other developments in the twentieth century. The OER Project's activity "Quick Sourcing: Unresolved Tensions" offers a unique way to practice sourcing skills. This lesson uses the OER Project's "Quick-Sourcing Tool" technique to practice unpacking document collections, and this tool helps students succeed on both the SAQ and DBQ Free-Response Questions. You can find the detailed instructions to the activity as well as the "Quick-Sourcing Tool" instructions on the OER Project's World History: AP® Curriculum in Unit 7, Topic 7.3: From World War I to World War II.

AP®
CONTINUITY AND CHANGE
In what ways did World War I mark new departures in the history of the twentieth century?

battlefront, temporarily abandoned the struggle for the vote. (See AP® Working with Evidence, page 667, for the various ways in which the Great War was experienced.)

No less surprising were the longer-term outcomes of the war. In the European cockpit of that conflict, unprecedented casualties, particularly among elite and well-educated groups, and physical destruction, especially in France, led to a widespread disillusionment among intellectuals with their own civilization. (See AP® Looking Again: Depicting the Aftermath of War, page 664, for an artistic expression of this sensibility.) For many, the war seemed to mock the Enlightenment values of progress, tolerance, and rationality, and some began to doubt that the West was superior or that its vaunted science and technology were unquestionably good things. In the most famous novel to emerge from the war, the German veteran Erich Maria Remarque's *All Quiet on the Western Front*, one soldier expressed what many no doubt felt: "It must all be lies and of no account when the culture of a thousand years could not prevent this stream of blood being poured out."

The aftermath of war also brought substantial social and cultural changes to ordinary Europeans and Americans. Women were urged to leave the factory work they had taken up during the war and return to their homes, where they would not compete against returning veterans for "men's jobs." Nonetheless, the war had loosened the hold of tradition in various ways. Enormous casualties promoted social mobility, allowing the less exalted to move into positions previously dominated by the upper classes. As the war ended, suffrage movements revived and women received the right to vote in a number of countries—Britain, the United States, Germany, the Soviet Union, Hungary, and Poland—in part perhaps because of the sacrifices they had made during the conflict. Young middle-class women, sometimes known as "flappers," began to flout convention by appearing at nightclubs, smoking, dancing, drinking hard liquor, cutting their hair short, wearing revealing clothing, and generally expressing a more open sexuality. Technological innovations, mass production, and pent-up demand after the austerities of wartime fostered a new consumerism, particularly in the United States, encouraging those who could to acquire cars, washing machines, vacuum cleaners, electric irons, gas ovens, and other newly available products. Radio and the movies now became vehicles of popular culture, transmitting American jazz to Europe and turning Hollywood stars into international celebrities.

AP® EXAM TIP
Make sure to understand how the unresolved tensions after World War I led to other developments in the twentieth century, like the Great Depression, World War II, and decolonization.

The war also transformed international political life. From the collapse of the German, Russian, and Austro-Hungarian empires emerged a new map of Central Europe with an independent Poland, Czechoslovakia, Yugoslavia, and other nations (see Map 11.3). Such new states were based on the principle of "national self-determination," a concept championed by U.S. president Woodrow Wilson, but each of them also contained dissatisfied ethnic minorities who claimed the same principle. By the **Treaty of Versailles**, which formally concluded the war in 1919, Germany lost its colonial empire and 15 percent of its European territory, was required to pay heavy reparations to the winners, had its military forces severely restricted, and was required to accept sole responsibility for the outbreak of the

MAPPING HISTORY   Map 11.3 **Europe and the Middle East after World War I**

The Great War brought into existence a number of new states that were carved out of the old German, Austro-Hungarian, Russian, and Ottoman empires. Some were independent, while others were administered by Britain or France as mandates of the League of Nations.

Reading the Map: In which regions were new countries created in the aftermath of World War I? Which of the new states were independent, and which were administered by Britain and France as mandates of the League of Nations?

AP **Making Connections:** "The peace settlement at the end of World War I brought an end to empires in Europe and the Middle East." To what extent does the map support this assertion?

BUILDING AP® SKILLS

Making Connections: Continuity and Change

The end of World War I brought about massive changes to the political landscape of Europe and the Middle East. To identify these changes, have students look at Map 11.3, "Europe and the Middle East after World War I," on page 627. Have students create a chart like the one shown below, listing the newly created states as outlined on the map and noting which still exist today by referring to the world map at the beginning of the book. A reproducible version of this chart is available in the Teacher's Resource Materials. (Answers are provided in italics.)

Newly Created State	Current Status
Finland	*Similar to post–World War I*
Estonia	*Similar to post–World War I*
Latvia	*Similar to post–World War I*
Lithuania	*Similar to post–World War I*
Poland	*Changed since World War I; post–World War II borders shrank in the east and grew slightly in the west*
Czechoslovakia	*Divided into the Czech Republic and Slovakia*
Hungary	*Similar to post–World War I*
Romania	*Similar to post–World War I*
Yugoslavia	*Divided into Slovenia, Croatia, Serbia, Bosnia and Herzegovina, Montenegro, Kosovo, and Macedonia*
Turkey	*Similar to post–World War I*
Syria	*Similar to post–World War I*
Iraq	*Similar to post–World War I*
Palestine	*Left British mandate to become Israel*
Transjordan	*Became Jordan*
Kuwait	*Similar to post–World War I*

TRM Handout 11.2: Continuity and Change Chart for States Created after World War I and Current Status

EXPLORING AP® THEMES

Governance (GOV)

Have students look at Map 11.3, "Europe and the Middle East after World War I." Ask students to speculate about which areas of postwar Europe and the Middle East were likely to see future conflict and why. *Central Europe and the Middle East are two areas that were likely to see problems. The many newly created states did not have a history of unity and self-government. Eastern European states shared a border with Russia, which was unsettled and militaristic. In the Middle East, tribal and religious conflicts and desirable resources, such as oil, created instability.*

war. All of this created immense resentment in Germany. One of the country's many demobilized and disillusioned soldiers declared in 1922: "It cannot be that two million Germans should have fallen in vain. . . . No, we do not pardon, we demand—vengeance."[3] His name was Adolf Hitler, and within two decades he had begun to exact that vengeance.

The Great War generated profound changes in the world beyond Europe as well. During the conflict, Ottoman authorities, suspecting that some of their Armenian subjects were collaborating with the Russian enemy, massacred or deported an estimated 1 million Armenians. Although the term "genocide" had not yet been invented, some historians have applied it to those atrocities, arguing that they established a precedent on which the Nazis later built. The war also brought a final end to a declining Ottoman Empire, creating the modern map of the Middle East, with the new states of Turkey, Syria, Iraq, Transjordan, and Palestine. Thus Arabs emerged from Turkish rule, but many of them were governed for a time by the British or French, as "mandates" of the League of Nations (see Map 11.3). Conflicting British promises to both Arabs and Jews regarding Palestine set the stage for an enduring struggle over that ancient and holy land.

And in the world of European colonies, the war echoed loudly. Millions of Asian and African men had watched Europeans butcher one another without mercy, had gained new military skills and political awareness, and returned home with less respect for their rulers and with expectations for better treatment as a reward for their service. To gain Indian support for the war, the British had publicly promised to put that colony on the road to self-government, an announcement that set the stage for the independence struggle that followed. In East Asia, Japan emerged strengthened from the war, with European support for its claim to take over German territory and privileges in China. That news enraged Chinese nationalists, particularly among the young, and pushed many of them into a more revolutionary posture, as it seemed to signify the continuation of an arrogant imperialist attitude among Europeans toward the Chinese people.

Furthermore, the First World War brought the United States to center stage as a global power. Its manpower had contributed much to the defeat of Germany, and its financial resources turned the United States from a debtor nation into Europe's creditor. When the American president Woodrow Wilson arrived in Paris for the peace conference in 1919, he was greeted with an almost religious enthusiasm. His famous Fourteen Points seemed to herald a new kind of international life, one based on moral principles rather than secret deals and imperialist machinations. Particularly appealing to many was his idea for the League of Nations, a new international peacekeeping organization committed to the principle of "collective security" and intended to avoid any repetition of the horrors that had just ended. Wilson's idealistic vision largely failed, however. Germany was treated more harshly than he had wished. National self-determination in the multiethnic states of Europe and elsewhere was very difficult, and Wilson's rhetoric inspired hopes in the colonies that could not be immediately fulfilled. In his own country, the U.S. Senate refused

AP® EXAM TIP
Understand key political, social, and economic causes and effects of twentieth-century world wars.

APPLY THE TIP

Divide the class into three groups. Assign one group to list the social effects of World War II, another group to list the political effects of World War II, and the third group to list the economic effects of World War II. Have each group share their results with the rest of the class. As students are sharing their results, compile a complete class list. *Answers should consider the social effects of the Holocaust, the mass displacement of people, and the death toll; the political effects of the emergence of the United States as a world power, the loss of British colonies, and tensions between the Soviet Union and the United States; and the economic effects of the financial cost of the war, the employment that came with the war, and the rationing that continued during and after the war.*

to join the League, which was established in 1920, fearing that Americans would be forced to bow to "the will of other nations." That refusal seriously weakened the League of Nations as a vehicle for Wilson's new international order.

The Russian Revolution and Soviet Communism

Among the most significant outcomes of World War I was the beginning of world communism, which played such an enormous role in the history of the twentieth century. Modern communism found its political and philosophical roots in nineteenth-century European socialism, inspired by the teachings of Karl Marx. Most European socialists had come to believe that they could achieve their goals peacefully and through the democratic process, but not so in Russia, where democracy barely existed. Many Russian socialists therefore advocated uncompromising revolution as the only possible route to a socialist future. That revolution occurred during World War I in 1917. (For the background to the Russian Revolution, see "Russia: Industrialization and Revolution" in Chapter 8.)

The catalyst for the **Russian Revolution** was World War I, which was going very badly for the Russians. Under this pressure the accumulated tensions of Russian society exploded. Workers—men and women alike, along with the wives of soldiers—took to the streets to express their outrage at the incompetence and privileges of the elites. Activists organized demonstrations, published newspapers, and plotted revolution. By early 1917, Tsar Nicholas II had lost almost all support and was forced to abdicate the throne, thus ending the Romanov dynasty, which had ruled Russia for more than three centuries. What followed was a Provisional Government, led by major political figures from various parties. But the Russian Revolution had only begun.

The tsar's abdication opened the door for a massive social upheaval. Ordinary soldiers, seeking an end to a terrible war and despising their upper-class officers, deserted in substantial numbers. In major industrial centers such as St. Petersburg and Moscow, new trade unions arose to defend workers' interests, and some workers seized control of their factories. Grassroots organizations of workers and soldiers, known as soviets, emerged to speak for ordinary people. Peasants, many of whom had been serfs only a generation or two earlier, seized landlords' estates, burned their manor houses, and redistributed the land among themselves. Non-Russian nationalists in Ukraine, Poland, Muslim Central Asia, and the Baltic region demanded greater autonomy or even independence.

This was social revolution, and it provided an environment in which a small socialist party called the Bolsheviks was able to seize power by the end of 1917 under the leadership of its determined and charismatic leader, Vladimir Ilyich Ulyanov, more commonly known as **Lenin**. In the desperate circumstances of 1917, his party's message—an end to the war, land for the peasants, workers' control of factories, self-determination for non-Russian nationalities—resonated with an increasingly rebellious public mood, particularly in the major cities.

AP® EXAM TIP

Look back at Marx's theories in Chapter 8 and note their twentieth-century outcomes. Also remember that the rise, fall, and features of communism are some of the most important developments in the twentieth century.

AP®

CAUSATION

What factors contributed to the Russian Revolution and the victory of the Bolsheviks?

APPLY THE TIP

This is a good time to review the origins of the Marxist ideology covered in Chapter 8. Ask students to begin a list of the features of Marxist ideology as they appear throughout Chapter 11 in communist societies. *Some of the features of Marxist ideology that appear in communist societies are social equality, collective living, and lack of private property.*

AP® CLASSROOM

AP® Daily Videos

This is an excellent opportunity to have students watch Topic 7.1: Daily Video 2: Shifting Power after 1900, located on AP® Classroom. You can find the second video for Topic 7.1 by logging into AP® Classroom, clicking on Unit 7 under Classroom Resources, and then selecting Daily Videos. The second video for Topic 7.1: Shifting Power after 1900 focuses on the internal and external factors that led to the Russian Revolution as well as the skill of contextualization.

The Russian Civil War through Bolshevik Eyes This Bolshevik poster from 1921, titled "Electrification and Counterrevolution," presents a communist view of the civil war that followed the Russian Revolution. It shows a worker bringing electricity and more generally the light of modernity and progress to a backward country, while depicting his opponents, which include a priest, a general, and a businessman, as seeking to extinguish that light. (The New York Public Library/Art Resource, NY)

▲ **AP**

COMPARISON
Based on this poster, in what way was the Bolsheviks' view of their revolutionary role similar to that of the French revolutionaries of the late eighteenth century?

AP

DEVELOPMENTS AND PROCESSES
What were the major features of Soviet communism during the Stalin era?

AP

COMPARISON
How was the process of industrialization in Soviet Russia different from that in Western Europe and the United States?

BUILDING AP® SKILLS

Claims and Evidence in Sources

Propaganda has been a useful tool of governments and revolutionaries. The Soviets used propaganda to demonize their enemies and gain support for their programs and policies. Have students read the caption and look at the propaganda poster titled "Electrification and Counterrevolution." Ask students why a communist promise of a light bulb would appeal to rank-and-file Russians in the early twentieth century. *Electricity in homes was an unheard-of luxury for many people around the world, including the Russians at the time.*

EXPLORING AP® THEMES

Governance (GOV)

As students have learned in previous chapters, gathering support for a revolution is fairly easy, especially when the conditions are ripe for change. However, holding on to the power gained after achieving control is much more difficult. Ask students to work in pairs to create a list of the ways the Bolsheviks successfully held on to their power. *They ended Russian involvement in World War I by signing a separate peace treaty with Germany. They suppressed nationalist rebellions. They integrated lower-class men into the Red Army and local governments, which gave them social mobility. In fighting international troops, the Bolsheviks claimed to be defending Russia from foreign takeover.*

A three-year civil war followed in which the Bolsheviks, now officially calling their party "communist," battled an assortment of enemies—tsarist officials, landlords, disaffected socialists, and regional nationalist forces, as well as troops from the United States, Britain, France, and Japan, all of which were eager to crush the fledgling communist regime. Remarkably, the Bolsheviks held on and by 1921 had staggered to victory over their divided and uncoordinated opponents. They renamed their country the Union of Soviet Socialist Republics (USSR or Soviet Union) and set about its transformation. For the next twenty-five years, the Soviet Union remained a communist island in a capitalist sea.

Once they had consolidated power and resolved their leadership struggles, Soviet communists soon began the task of constructing a socialist society under the control of Joseph **Stalin** (1878–1953), who emerged as the principal Soviet leader by the late 1920s. To Stalin and communists generally, building socialism meant first of all the modernization and industrialization of their country's backward society. They sought, however, a distinctly socialist modernity with an emphasis on social equality and the promotion of cultural values of selflessness and collectivism.

Those imperatives generated a political system thoroughly dominated by the Communist Party. Top-ranking party members enjoyed various privileges but were expected to be exemplars of socialism in the making by being disciplined, selfless, and utterly loyal to their country's Marxist ideology. The party itself penetrated society in ways that Western scholars called "totalitarian," for other parties were forbidden, the state controlled almost the entire economy, and political authorities ensured that the arts, education, and the media conformed to approved ways of thinking. Mass organizations for women, workers, students, and various professional groups operated under party control, with none of the independence that characterized civil society in the West.

In the rural areas, building socialism meant the end of private ownership of land and the **collectivization of agriculture**. Between 1928 and 1933, peasants were forced, often against great resistance, into large-scale collective farms, which were supposedly more productive and better able to utilize modern agricultural machinery than the small family farms that had emerged from the revolution.

Stalin singled out the richer peasants, known as *kulaks* (koo-LAHKS), for exclusion from the new collective farms. Some were killed, and many others were deported to remote areas of the country. With little support or experience in the countryside, the urban activists who enforced collectivization were viewed as intrusive outsiders in Russian peasant villages. A terrible famine ensued, particularly in Ukraine, with some 5 million deaths from starvation or malnutrition.

In the cities, the task was rapid industrialization. The Soviet approach to industrial development, so different from that of the capitalist West, involved state ownership of property, centralized planning embodied in successive five-year plans, priority to heavy industry, massive mobilization of the nation's human and material resources, and intrusive Communist Party control of the entire process. For a time, it worked. During the 1930s, while the capitalist world floundered amid the massive unemployment of the Great Depression, the Soviet Union largely eliminated unemployment and constructed the foundations of an industrial society that proved itself in the victory over Nazi Germany in World War II. In addition, the USSR achieved massive improvements in literacy rates and educational opportunities, allowing far greater social mobility for millions of people than ever before. As in the West, industrialization fostered rapid urbanization, exploitation of the countryside to provide resources for modern industry in the cities, and the growth of a privileged bureaucratic and technological elite intent on pursuing their own careers and passing on their new status to their children.

Despite its totalitarian tendencies, the communist society of the Soviet Union was laced with conflict. Under Stalin's leadership, those conflicts erupted in a search for enemies that terribly disfigured Soviet life. An elastic concept of "enemy" came to include not only surviving remnants from the prerevolutionary elites but also, and more surprisingly, high-ranking members and longtime supporters of the Communist Party, who allegedly had been corrupted by bourgeois ideas, as evidenced by their opposition to some of Stalin's harsh policies. Refracted through the lens of Marxist thinking, these people became "class enemies" who had betrayed the revolution and were engaged in a vast conspiracy, often linked to foreign imperialists, to subvert the socialist enterprise and restore capitalism.

That process culminated in Stalin's Terror, or the Great Purges, of the late 1930s, which enveloped tens of thousands of prominent communists, including virtually

Mobilizing Women for Communism As the Soviet Union mobilized for rapid economic development in the 1930s, women entered the workforce in great numbers. Here two young women are mastering the skills of driving a tractor on one of the large collective farms that replaced the country's private agriculture. (Sovfoto/Getty Images)

▲ **AP®**
CONTINUITY AND CHANGE
What major changes to Russian society are represented in this photograph?

AP® EXAM TIP
Understand the features of communist-led planned economies.

EXPLORING AP® THEMES

Social Interactions and Organization (SIO)

Show students the photo titled "Mobilizing Women for Communism" and read the caption. Ask students why learning to drive a tractor could be considered an advancement of feminist ideas. *Driving anything (car, truck, or tractor) was usually considered man's work in the early twentieth century.*

APPLY THE TIP

Ask students to list the features of communist-led planned economies. *The features of communist-led planned economies include state ownership of property, centralized planning, priority on heavy industry, mobilization of human and material resources, and Communist Party control of the entire process.*

all of Lenin's top associates, and millions of more ordinary people. Based on suspicious associations in the past, denunciations by colleagues, connections to foreign countries, or simply bad luck, such people were arrested, usually in the dead of night, and then tried and sentenced either to death or to long years in harsh and remote labor camps known as the gulag. A series of show trials publicized the menace that these "enemies of the people" allegedly posed to the country and its revolution. Close to 1 million people were executed between 1936 and 1941. An additional 4 or 5 million were sent to the gulag, where they were forced to work in horrendous conditions and died in appalling numbers. Such were among the outcomes of the world's first experiment with communism.

Capitalism Unraveling: The Great Depression

Finding the Main Point: How did the Great Depression impact economies around the world?

AP® EXAM TIP
Political responses to the Great Depression around the world are "must know" information for the AP® Exam.

While the Soviet Union was constructing the world's first communist society, the capitalist world languished in the **Great Depression**, which began with an abrupt stock market crash in October 1929 and then lasted for a decade. If World War I represented the political collapse of Europe, this economic catastrophe suggested that Western capitalism was likewise failing, as Marx had predicted. All across the Euro-American heartland of the industrialized capitalist world, this vaunted economic system seemed to unravel. For the rich, it meant contracting stock prices that wiped out paper fortunes almost overnight. Banks closed, and many people lost their life savings. Investment dried up, world trade dropped by 62 percent within a few years, and businesses contracted or closed. Unemployment soared everywhere, and in both Germany and the United States it reached 25 percent or more by 1933. Vacant factories, soup kitchens, bread lines, shantytowns, and beggars came to symbolize the human reality of this economic disaster.

AP®
DEVELOPMENTS AND PROCESSES
In what respects was the Great Depression a global phenomenon?

This economic breakdown began in the United States, which had experienced a booming economy during the 1920s. By the end of that decade, its farms and factories were producing more goods than could be sold, either at home or abroad. Meanwhile, a speculative stock market frenzy had driven up stock prices to an unsustainable level. When that bubble burst in late 1929, its ripple effects quickly encompassed the industrialized economies of Europe, which were intimately connected to the United States through ties of trade, debt, and investment.

Much as Europe's worldwide empires had globalized the Great War, so too its economic linkages globalized the Great Depression. Countries or colonies tied to exporting one or two products were especially hard-hit. Colonial Southeast Asia, the world's major rubber-producing region, saw the demand for its primary export drop dramatically as automobile sales in Europe and the United States were cut in half. In Britain's West African colony of the Gold Coast (present-day Ghana), farmers who had staked their economic lives on producing cocoa for the world market

---

APPLY THE TIP

Although the causes of the Great Depression are complicated and continue to be investigated and discussed by economists and historians, students should be aware of the effects of the Great Depression and some of the political responses. As students finish reading this section, ask them to list the effects and responses to the Great Depression globally. (Answers are provided in italics.)

Effects

- *Those who had invested in the stock market lost almost everything.*

- *Unemployment rose to an all-time high.*

- *People could not afford to keep their homes and feed their families.*

- *European nations were connected to the United States through ties of trade, debt, and investment and therefore suffered.*

Political Responses

- *Import substitution by Latin American nations*

- *Democratic Socialism in France, Britain, and Scandinavia*

- *FDR's New Deal in the United States*

- *European fascism*

- *Japanese militarism*

BUILDING AP® SKILLS

Claims and Evidence in Sources

As the Great Depression is a cause for the start of World War II, it is a good idea to focus on the economy in the interwar period. The OER Project's activity "Quick Sourcing: Economy in the Interwar Period" offers a unique way to practice sourcing skills. This lesson uses the OER Project's "Quick-Sourcing Tool" technique to practice unpacking document collections. This tool can help students succeed on both the SAQ and DBQ Free-Response Questions. You can find the detailed instructions to the activity as well as the "Quick-Sourcing Tool" instructions on the OER Project's World History: AP® Curriculum in Unit 7, Topic 7.3: From World War I to World War II.

Contrasts of the Great Depression This 1937 *Life* magazine image by famed photographer Margaret Bourke-White shows black victims of a flood in Louisville, Kentucky, standing in a breadline during the Depression while behind them rises a billboard depicting a happy and prosperous white family. (Margaret Bourke-White/Time & Life Pictures/Getty Images)

were badly hurt by the collapse of commodity prices. Latin American countries saw the value of their exports cut by half, generating widespread unemployment and social tensions. In response to these problems, governments sought to steer their economies away from exports and toward producing for the internal market, a policy known as import substitution. In Mexico, the Depression opened the way to reviving the principles of the Mexican Revolution under the leadership of Lázaro Cárdenas (1934–1940), who pushed land reform, favored Mexican workers against foreign interests, and nationalized an oil industry dominated by American capital.

The Great Depression also sharply challenged the governments of industrialized capitalist countries. The apparent failure of a market economy to self-correct led many people to look twice at the Soviet Union. There, the dispossession of the propertied classes and a state-controlled economy had generated an impressive economic growth with almost no unemployment in the 1930s, even as the capitalist world was reeling. No Western country opted for the dictatorial and draconian socialism of the Soviet Union, but in Britain, France, and Scandinavia, the Depression energized a "democratic socialism" that sought greater regulation of the economy and a more

▲ **AP®**
SOURCING AND
SITUATION
What contrasts does this image show? What message was *Life* magazine seeking to convey in publishing it?

AP®
CAUSATION
How did the Great Depression affect the relationship between governments and their citizens?

AP® CLASSROOM

AP® Daily Videos

This is an excellent opportunity to have students watch the Daily Videos for Topic 7.4: Economy in the Interwar Period, located on AP® Classroom. You can find the three videos for Topic 7.4 by logging into AP® Classroom, clicking on Unit 7 under Classroom Resources, and then selecting Daily Videos. The three videos for Topic 7.4: Economy in the Interwar Period focus on how the United States (Video 1), Italy and Germany (Video 2), and Russia (Video 3) reacted to the Great Depression, as well as focusing on writing skills.

AP® CLASSROOM

AP® Topic Questions

This is a great time for some practice with multiple-choice questions. You can find a set of questions about the economy in the interwar period by logging into AP® Classroom, clicking on Unit 7 under Classroom Resources, and then selecting Topic Questions. Look for the questions labeled "Brazilian Government Document." You can either assign the questions to the students to complete individually or allow them to partner up to work through the set together.

CHAPTER 11

TEACHING IDEA

Incorporating Outside Resources

For a good overview of fascism, consider showing the OER Project's short video on fascism. You can find the video on the OER Project's World History: AP® Curriculum in Unit 7, Topic 7.3: From World War I to World War II. After students watch the video, use these questions to start a class discussion.

■ Why is it important for everyone to know and understand the history and meaning of fascism? *So we can notice when it is beginning to appear and when fascists begin to acquire power.*

■ What is fascism according to the historian Robert O. Paxton? *A form of political behavior*

■ How do fascists convince people to let them change society? *Fascists spread misinformation, promise improvements, and tell stories about who is a member of the community and who is not.*

■ How do fascists justify violence? *As a way to exclude or eliminate those perceived as outsiders*

■ How did Hitler and Mussolini claim they could eliminate class conflict? *National unification, racial cleansing, a return to traditional "roles" and values, and state-controlled or corporatist economies*

■ What was the elevation of the state supposed to do? *Pull a country together*

■ Who generally benefited from fascism? *Capitalist owners and industries as well as traditional elites*

■ Why do fascists like violence and war? *It allows them to solve perceived problems that cannot be solved in normal ways.*

■ Why do fascists use staged events, symbolic imagery, and propaganda? *To increase their appeal*

■ What is not fascism? *Authoritarianism, populism*

APPLY THE TIP

Between the end of World War I and the beginning of World War II, authoritarian governments rose up in Italy, Germany, and Japan. Ask students to create a chart, like the one below, to compare the causes for the rise of authoritarian governments in these states. (Answers are in italics.)

---

equal distribution of wealth through peaceful means and electoral politics. The Great Depression, like the world wars, strengthened the power of the state.

The United States illustrated this trend as President Franklin Roosevelt's New Deal (1933–1942) took shape, permanently altering the relationship among government, the private economy, and individual citizens. The New Deal involved immediate programs of public spending (for dams, highways, bridges, and parks); longer-term reforms, such as the Social Security system, the minimum wage, and various relief and welfare programs; support for labor unions; and subsidies for farmers. A mounting number of government agencies marked a new degree of federal regulation and supervision of the economy.

Ultimately, the New Deal's programs were unable to bring the Great Depression to an end. Not until the massive government spending required by World War II kicked in did economic disaster abate in the United States. The most successful efforts to cope with the Depression came from unlikely places—Nazi Germany and an increasingly militaristic Japan.

Democracy Denied: The Authoritarian Alternative

Finding the Main Point: What is an authoritarian government, and what different kinds of authoritarian governments arose by the mid-twentieth century?

AP® EXAM TIP
You need to know the effects of the rise of authoritarian governments in the twentieth century.

Despite the victory of the democratic powers in World War I—Britain, France, and the United States—their democratic political ideals and their cultural values celebrating individual freedom came under sharp attack in the aftermath of that bloody conflict. One challenge derived from communism, which was initiated in the Russian Revolution of 1917. In the 1920s and 1930s, however, the more immediate challenge to the victors in the Great War came from highly authoritarian, intensely nationalistic, territorially aggressive, and ferociously anticommunist regimes, particularly those that took shape in Italy, Germany, and Japan. The common political goals of these three countries drew them together by 1936–1937 in an alliance directed against the Soviet Union and international communism. In 1940, they solidified their relationship in a formal military alliance, creating the so-called Axis powers. Within this alliance, Germany and Japan clearly stand out, though in quite different ways, in terms of their impact on the larger patterns of world history, for it was their efforts to "establish and maintain a new order of things," as the Axis Pact put it, that generated the Second World War both in East Asia and in Europe.

European Fascism

Between 1919 and 1945, a new political ideology, known as **fascism**, found expression across parts of Europe. While communists celebrated class conflict as the driving force of history, for fascists it was the conflict of nations. Fascism was intensely

---

(continued)

Causes for the Rise of Authoritarian Government in Italy	Causes for the Rise of Authoritarian Government in Germany	Causes for the Rise of Authoritarian Government in Japan
■ *Dissatisfaction with the Treaty of Versailles* ■ *Lack of a democratic tradition* ■ *Fear of communism* ■ *Economic pressures from high unemployment*	■ *War-guilt clause of the Treaty of Versailles* ■ *Lack of a democratic tradition* ■ *Hyperinflation of the early 1920s* ■ *Global depression* ■ *High unemployment*	■ *Dissatisfaction with the Treaty of Versailles* ■ *Needed resources to fuel industrialization* ■ *Return to the "Japanese Way"* ■ *Military gains prominence in the government*

TRM Handout 11.3: Comparison Chart for Rise of Authoritarian Governments nationalistic, seeking to revitalize and "purify" the nation and to mobilize its people for some grand task. Its spokesmen praised violence against enemies as a renewing force in society, celebrated action rather than reflection, and placed their faith in a charismatic leader. Fascists also bitterly condemned individualism, liberalism, feminism, parliamentary democracy, and communism, all of which, they argued, divided and weakened the nation. In their determination to overthrow existing regimes, they were revolutionary; in their embrace of traditional values and their opposition to much of modern life, however, they were conservative or reactionary.

Such ideas appealed to aggrieved people all across the social spectrum. In the devastation that followed the First World War, the numbers of such people grew substantially. Some among the middle and upper classes felt the rise of socialism and communism as a dire threat; small-scale merchants, artisans, and farmers feared the loss of their independence to either big business or socialist revolution; demobilized soldiers had few prospects and nursed many resentments; and intellectuals were appalled by the materialism and artificiality of modern life. Such people had lost faith in the capacity of liberal democracy and capitalism to create a good society and to protect their interests. Some among them proved a receptive audience for the message of fascism. Fascist or other highly authoritarian movements appeared in many European countries, such as Spain, Romania, and Hungary, and some in Latin America, but it was in Italy and Germany that such movements achieved prolonged power in major states, with devastating consequences for Europe and the world.

The fascist alternative took shape first in Italy. That nation had become a unified state only in 1870 and had not yet developed a thoroughly industrialized economy or a solidly democratic culture. The First World War gave rise to resentful veterans, many of them unemployed, and to patriots who believed that Italy had not gained the territory it deserved from the Treaty of Versailles. During the serious economic downturn after World War I, trade unions, peasant movements, and various communist and socialist parties threatened the established social order with a wave of strikes and land seizures.

Into this setting stepped a charismatic orator and a former journalist with a socialist background, Benito **Mussolini** (1883–1945). With the help of a private army of disillusioned veterans and jobless men known as the Black Shirts, Mussolini swept to power in 1922 amid considerable violence, promising an alternative to communism, order in the streets, an end to bickering party-based politics, and the maintenance of the traditional social order. That Mussolini's government allegedly made the trains run on time became evidence that these promises might be fulfilled.

In Mussolini's thinking, fascism was resolutely anticommunist, "the complete opposite . . . of Marxist socialism," and equally antidemocratic. "Fascism combats the whole complex system of democratic ideology, and repudiates it," he wrote. At the core of Mussolini's fascism was his conception of the state. "Fascism conceives of the State as an absolute, in comparison with which all individuals and groups are relative, only to be conceived of in their relation to the State." The state was a conscious entity with "a will and a personality" that represented the "spirit of the nation." Its expansion in war and empire building was "an essential manifestation of vitality."

BUILDING AP® SKILLS

Making Connections: Causation

The AP® Causation question in the student edition could make a great comprehension check for students. Ask them: What are some of the factors that led to the rise of fascism in Italy? *Factors that led to the rise of fascism in Italy include tension between an industrial working class and a substantial middle class, resentful veterans from World War I, high unemployment, and nationalists who believed Italy did not get a fair share of land from the Treaty of Versailles.*

EXPLORING AP® THEMES

Governance (GOV)

Divide the class into six or seven groups and assign each group one item of Italian fascist propaganda directed toward youth from the collection "Italian Youth Organizations," which can be found at the University of Wisconsin–Madison in the Fry Collection. Have students visit the University of Wisconsin Libraries Online Exhibits site and search for "Italian Life under Fascism." Students will need the explanatory notes also provided on the website beneath the images. Give the class 5 minutes to brainstorm on these items, and then ask each group to describe their item and why it might have been effective propaganda for the fascist movement to use with youth. *Answers will vary.*

Mussolini's government suspended democracy and imprisoned, deported, or sometimes executed opponents. Italy's fascist regime also disbanded independent labor unions and peasant groups as well as all opposing political parties. In economic life, a "corporate state" took shape, at least in theory, in which workers, employers, and various professional groups were organized into "corporations" that were supposed to settle their disagreements and determine economic policy under the supervision of the state.

Culturally, fascists invoked various aspects of traditional Italian life. Though personally an atheist, Mussolini embraced the Catholic culture of Italy in a series of agreements with the Church, known as the Lateran Accords of 1929, that made the Vatican a sovereign state and Catholicism Italy's national religion. In fascist propaganda, women were portrayed in highly traditional domestic terms, particularly as mothers creating new citizens for the fascist state, with no hint of equality or liberation. Nationalists were delighted when Italy invaded Ethiopia in 1935, avenging the embarrassing defeat that Italians suffered at the hands of Ethiopians in 1896. In the eyes of Mussolini and fascist believers, all of this was the beginning of a "new Roman Empire" that would revitalize Italian society and give it a global mission.

Hitler and the Nazis

Far more important in the long run was the German expression of European fascism, which took shape as the **Nazi Party** under the leadership of Adolf **Hitler** (1889–1945). In many respects, it was similar to its Italian counterpart. Both espoused an extreme nationalism, openly advocated the use of violence as a political tool, generated a single-party dictatorship, were led by charismatic figures, despised parliamentary democracy, hated communism, and viewed war as a positive and ennobling experience.[4] The circumstances that gave rise to the Nazi movement were likewise broadly similar to those of Italian fascism, although the Nazis did not achieve national power until 1933. Germany too was a new European nation, lacking a long-term democratic tradition. As in Italy, resentment about the Treaty of Versailles was widespread, especially among unemployed veterans. Fear of socialism or communism was prevalent among middle- and upper-class groups. But it was the Great Depression that provided the essential context for the victory of German fascism. The German economy largely ground to a halt in the early 1930s amid massive unemployment among workers and the middle class alike. Everyone demanded decisive action from the state.

This was the context in which Adolf Hitler's National Socialist, or Nazi, Party gained growing public support. Its message expressed an intense German nationalism cast in terms of racial superiority, bitter hatred for Jews as an alien presence, passionate opposition to communism, a determination to rescue Germany from the humiliating requirements of the Treaty of Versailles, and a willingness to

---

AP EXAM TIP

Pay close attention to how the rise of authoritarian governments in the early twentieth century led to World War II.

AP CONTEXTUALIZATION

What was distinctive about the German expression of fascism? How were Nazis able to gain widespread popular support?

EXPLORING AP® THEMES

Economic Systems (ECN)

Ask students to list some of the economic challenges that faced Germany before Hitler rose to power. *Severe inflation in 1923 was followed by the Great Depression. The German economy largely ground to a halt in the early 1930s amid massive unemployment among workers and the middle class. Everyone demanded decisive action from the state.*

APPLY THE TIP

Between the end of World War I and the beginning of World War II, authoritarian governments rose up in Italy, Germany, and Japan. Ask students to create a chart, like the one below, to compare the effects of the rise of authoritarian government in the twentieth century.

Effects of Authoritarian Government in Italy	Effects of Authoritarian Government in Germany	Effects of Authoritarian Government in Japan
▪ Fascism, extreme nationalism	▪ Fascism, extreme nationalism	▪ Extreme nationalism and dedication to elite leadership
▪ Suspended democracy	▪ Violence as a political tool	▪ More dominant role of the military
▪ Disbanded independent labor unions and all opposing political parties	▪ Single-party dictatorship	▪ Government censorship
▪ Creation of the "corporate state"	▪ Feeling of racial superiority, extreme anti-Semitism	▪ Extreme imperial ambitions
▪ Focus on traditional gender roles	▪ Traditional roles for women	

TRM Handout 11.4: Comparison Chart for Effects of Authoritarian Governments

◀ **AP**
SOURCING AND
SITUATION
In what way do the
camera angle and
composition of this
photograph complement
fascist ideology?

Nationalism and Nazi Ideology A critical element of Nazi fascist ideology was the promotion of fierce nationalism cast in terms of racial superiority. In this image, Adolf Hitler salutes a mass gathering of the Hitler Youth, an organization whose purpose in part was to instill national fervor in Germany's children and adolescents. (Corbis/Getty Images.)

decisively tackle the country's economic problems. All of this resonated widely, enabling the Nazis to win 37 percent of the vote in the election of 1932. The following year, Hitler was legally installed as the chancellor of the German government. Thus a weak democratic regime that never gained broad support gave way to the Third Reich.

Once in power, Hitler moved quickly to consolidate Nazi control of Germany. All other political parties were outlawed; independent labor unions were ended; thousands of opponents were arrested; and the press and radio came under state control. Far more thoroughly than Mussolini in Italy, Hitler and the Nazis established their control over German society.

By the late 1930s, Hitler apparently had the support of a considerable majority of the population, in large measure because his policies successfully brought Germany out of the Depression. The government invested heavily in projects such as superhighways, bridges, canals, and public buildings and, after 1935, in rebuilding and rearming the country's diminished military forces. These policies drove down the number of unemployed Germans from 6.2 million in 1932 to fewer

AP EXAM TIP
Take notes on how
fascist governments
dealt with economic
problems of the Great
Depression.

BUILDING AP® SKILLS

Claims and Evidence in Sources

Show students the photo of Hitler saluting a mass gathering of the Hitler youth. Ask: What features of this photo glorify Hitler? *Hitler is the only one standing in the vehicle and so is placed above his subordinates. The camera is angled so that the sun appears to be shining only on Hitler. Hitler is dressed in a military uniform, and the Hitler youth are all showing their respect to him with a Nazi salute.*

APPLY THE TIP

Ask students to list the ways that fascist governments dealt with the economic problems of the Great Depression. *Government investment in infrastructure projects, state supervision of economic policy.*

Making Connections: Causation

Have the class read the quote from Erna Kranz at the top of page 638. Ask students why Erna Kranz was so willing to give Hitler unwavering support. *Kranz was happy there was employment and order after the chaos of World War I and the Great Depression.*

Sourcing and Situation

The Document-Based Question (DBQ) requires students to analyze the intended audience, purpose, point of view, and historical context of three of the seven presented documents. Students can practice these skills by analyzing the following quote from Hitler's *Mein Kampf* using a table like the one here. A reproducible version of this chart is available in the Teacher's Resource Materials. (Answers are provided in italics.)

■ "He lacks completely the most essential requirement for a cultured people, the idealistic attitude. . . . The Jew is led by nothing but the naked egoism of the individual. With satanic joy in his face, the blackhaired Jewish youth lurks in wait for the unsuspecting girl whom he defiles with his blood, thus stealing her from her people. With every means he tries to destroy the racial foundations of the people he has set out to subjugate. . . . And in politics he begins to replace the idea of democracy by the dictatorship of the proletariat."

Intended Audience	*German Aryan people*
Purpose	*Unite Aryan Germans against a common enemy*
Point of View	*Gain power by playing on people's fears*
Historical Context	*The Treaty of Versailles and the Great Depression*

TRM Handout 11.5: Sourcing Chart for Analysis of *Mein Kampf*

The Ideal Nazi Family This painting by Wolfgang Willrich, a prominent Nazi artist, portrays the highly romanticized Nazi image of an ideal Aryan family. They have four children; most are dressed in plain peasant-style clothing; the mother wears her hair in a bun and does not use makeup; they live in a rural agricultural setting; the boy is wearing a Hitler Youth uniform; and all of them are blonde, with athletic bodies and ruddy complexions. (bpk Bildagentur/Art Resource, NY)

▲ AP®

CLAIMS AND EVIDENCE IN SOURCES
What specific aspects of German family life are romanticized in this painting? What does it imply about the kind of society that the Nazis sought to create?

than 500,000 in 1937. Two years later Germany had a labor shortage. Erna Kranz, a teenager in the 1930s, later remembered the early years of Nazi rule as "a glimmer of hope . . . not just for the unemployed but for everybody because we all knew that we were downtrodden. . . . It was a good time . . . there was order and discipline."[5] Millions agreed with her.

Other factors as well contributed to Nazi popularity. Like Italian fascists, Hitler appealed to rural and traditional values that many Germans feared losing as their country modernized. In Hitler's thinking and in Nazi propaganda, Jews became the symbol of the urban, capitalist, and foreign influences that were undermining traditional German culture. Thus the Nazis reflected and reinforced a broader and long-established current of anti-Semitism that had deep roots in much of Europe. In his book *Mein Kampf* (My Struggle), Hitler outlined his case against the Jews and his call for the racial purification of Germany in vitriolic terms.

Far more than in Italy or elsewhere, this insistence on a racial revolution was a central feature of the Nazi program. Upon coming to power, Hitler implemented policies that increasingly restricted Jewish life. Soon Jews were excluded from universities, professional organizations, and civil employment. In 1935, the Nuremberg Laws ended German citizenship for Jews and forbade marriage or sexual relations between Jews and Germans. On the night of November 9, 1938, known as Kristallnacht ("Night of Crystal" or "Night of Broken Glass"), persecution gave way to terror, when Nazis smashed and looted Jewish shops. Such actions made clear the Nazis' determination to rid Germany of its Jewish population, thus putting into effect the most radical element of Hitler's program. Still, it was not yet apparent that this "racial revolution" would mean the mass killing of Europe's Jews. That horrendous development emerged only in the context of World War II.

Beyond race, gender too figured prominently in Nazi thought and policies. While Soviet communists sought to enroll women in the country's industrialization effort, Nazis wanted to limit women largely to the home, removing them from the paid workforce. To Hitler, the state was the natural domain of men, while the home was the realm of women. "Woman in the workplace is an oppressed and tormented being," declared a Nazi publication. Concerned about declining birthrates, Italy and Germany alike promoted a cult of motherhood, glorifying and rewarding women who produced children for the state. Accordingly, fascist regimes in both countries generally opposed abortion, contraception, family planning, and sex education, all of which were associated with feminist thinking. Yet such an outlook did not necessarily coincide with conservative or puritanical sexual attitudes. In Germany, a state-sponsored system of brothels was initiated in the mid-1930s, for it was assumed that virile men would be promiscuous and that soldiers required a sexual outlet if they were to contribute to the nation's military strength.

Also sustaining Nazi rule were massive torchlight ceremonies celebrating the superiority of the German race and its folk culture. In these settings, Hitler was the mystical leader, the Führer, a mesmerizing orator who would lead Germany to national greatness and individual Germans to personal fulfillment.

If World War I and the Great Depression brought about the political and economic collapse of Europe, the Nazi phenomenon represented a rejection of some of the values—rationalism, tolerance, democracy, human equality—that for many people had defined the core of Western civilization since the Enlightenment. On the other hand, Nazis claimed the legacy of modern science, particularly in their concern to classify and rank various human groups. Thus they drew heavily on the "scientific racism" of the late nineteenth century and its expression in phrenology, which linked the size and shape of the skull to human behavior and personality (see "Industry and Empire" in Chapter 10). Moreover, in their effort to "purify" German society, the Nazis reflected the Enlightenment confidence in the perfectibility of humankind and in the social engineering necessary to achieve it.

By 1940, the European political landscape had altered dramatically from what it had been just a few decades earlier. At the beginning of the twentieth century, major European countries had embraced largely capitalist economies and to varying degrees increasingly democratic political systems with multiple parties and elected parliaments. But by the time World War II broke out, Europe's largest country, the Soviet Union, had altogether rejected capitalism in favor of a state-controlled economy and a political system dominated by a single communist political party. The fascist states of Germany and Italy likewise dismantled multiparty democracies, replacing them with highly authoritarian dictatorships. While these dictatorships retained major private ownership of property, the state played a large role in economic affairs. Communist and fascist states alike rejected the individualistic liberalism of the remaining democracies, celebrating the collective identities of "class" in the case of the Soviet Union and of nation or race in Italy and Germany. (See Snapshot: Comparing German Fascism and Soviet Communism, page 640.)

AP EXAM TIP

You should be able to cite examples of genocide against minority groups in the twentieth century, like that of Jews in Europe.

APPLY THE TIP

Have students read and take notes on the two paragraphs about the Holocaust on page 649 to better understand an example of the repression of minority groups in Europe during the twentieth century. After students have taken notes, ask: Can you think of any other minority groups that were repressed by European states or governments during the twentieth century? *Answers will vary.*

BUILDING AP® SKILLS

Sourcing and Situation

Ask students to choose one of the Nazi propaganda images found at the United States Holocaust Memorial Museum's website. The propaganda images can be found by typing "Nazi Propaganda Posters" in the site's search and filtering by images. Students should write a short description of the image, note the intended audience and author's purpose, and analyze its emotional appeal. *Answers will vary.*

CHAPTER 11

BUILDING AP® SKILLS

Developments and Processes

The difference between communism and fascism is often confusing for students. Consider using the Snapshot Chart and the OER Project's activity "Communism vs Fascism" to practice comparison skills. You can find the detailed instructions to the activity on the OER Project's World History: AP® Curriculum in Unit 7, Topic 7.3: From World War I to World War II.

BUILDING AP® SKILLS

Making Connections: Comparison

This is a good time to have students practice their essay writing skills. Use the prompt below comparing communism and fascism. Students can use evidence from the Snapshot: Comparing German Fascism and Soviet Communism to help them write the essay.

- In the period 1900–present, governments responded to economic uncertainty and global tensions by turning to communism and fascism.

  Develop an argument that evaluates the extent to which Soviet communism and fascism differed in their political practices and ideologies.

Differentiation

While it's good for students to write full essays, especially as they get closer to the AP® Exam, it can also be helpful to have them work on a group essay outline and evaluate their peers' responses. This exercise allows them to see different ways of formulating arguments and to potentially understand what graders are looking for when scoring essays. If you want students to complete a group outline essay with this prompt, consider following the "Must Do, Should Do, Strive For" model below:

- Must Do: Working in groups of four or fewer, students should create an LEQ outline on the provided butcher paper. The outline should include contextualization and a thesis that responds to the prompt, at least two arguments, and at least two pieces of evidence for *each* argument.

SNAPSHOT Comparing German Fascism and Soviet Communism

COMMONALITIES BETWEEN GERMAN FASCISM AND SOVIET COMMUNISM

- Intense opposition to liberal democratic ideology and practice in the West
- A party-dominated state seeking to penetrate and control society and individuals
- Elimination of competing political parties
- A transformational and utopian ideology seeking personal and social regeneration
- Leadership by a single highly celebrated individual with enormous personal power
- Contraction of private or civic life; expansion of collective or public life
- Mobilization of mass support for the regime
- Extensive use of violence against perceived enemies

DIFFERENCES

Theme	German Fascism	Soviet Communism
Ideology	• Focus on race and nation • Superiority of German peoples • Desire to purify Germany of "alien" Jewish presence • Desire to avenge humiliation of the Versailles treaty • Territorial expansion for increased living space	• Focus on class conflict, leading to revolution and socialism • Russia as initial breakthrough to international communism • Industrialization needed to provide foundation for socialism
Theory of state	• The state as an absolute value • Individuals and groups defined by their relationship to the state	• State to "wither away" in time (in practice, the state grew large, powerful, and intrusive)
Economic system	• Retained major elements of capitalism: private property, profit motive, market exchange • State intervened to regulate, control, and direct	• Eliminated capitalism and private property • Agriculture collectivized and industry owned by the state • Expressed in "five-year plans" for entire economy
Posture toward women	• Deeply antifeminist; sought to limit women to home as their "natural domain" • Opposed abortion and contraception	• Liberation of women; legal equality in marriage; mobilized women for production as workers
Modern life	• Ambivalent about modernity • Romanticized Aryan racial purity and traditional German peasant communities • Embraced science, technology, and industry	• Thoroughly modernist • No romanticism about the past; peasant Russia viewed as in need of modernization • Valued all things industrial and urban
Religion	• Monitored and controlled churches; no frontal attack on Christianity • Severe persecution of Jehovah's Witnesses and Jews	• Major effort to eliminate religion and promote atheism

---

(*continued*)

- Should Do: Once all the groups have completed their LEQ poster, have students hang them up and do a gallery walk to see how other groups put together this LEQ. As they look at each poster, ask students to leave "I wonder . . ." and "I like . . ." statements about what they see in the outline.

- Strive For: For students who want or need a writing challenge, have them choose one of the arguments from their LEQ poster and write a full argument paragraph on it.

Japanese Authoritarianism

In various ways, the modern history of Japan paralleled that of Italy and Germany. All three were newcomers to Great Power status, with Japan joining the club of industrializing and empire-building states only in the late nineteenth century as its sole Asian member (see "The Japanese Difference" in Chapter 9). Like Italy and Germany, Japan had a rather limited experience with democratic politics, for its elected parliament was constrained by a very small electorate (only 1.5 million men in 1917) and by the exalted position of a semi-divine emperor and his small coterie of elite advisers. During the 1930s, Japan too moved toward authoritarian government and a denial of democracy at home, even as it launched an aggressive program of territorial expansion in East Asia. But in sharp contrast to Italy and Germany, Japan's participation in World War I was minimal, and its economy grew considerably as other industrialized countries were consumed by the European conflict. At the peace conference ending that war, Japan was seated as an equal participant, allied with the winning side of democratic countries such as Britain, France, and the United States.

During the 1920s, Japan seemed to be moving toward more democratic politics and Western cultural values. Universal male suffrage was achieved in 1925, and a two-party system began to emerge. Supporters of these developments, mostly urban and well-to-do, generally embraced the dignity of the individual, free expression of ideas, and greater gender equality. Education expanded; an urban consumer society developed; middle-class women entered new professions; and young women known as *moga* (modern girls) sported short hair and short skirts, while dancing with *mobo* (modern boys) at jazz clubs and cabarets. To such people, the Japanese were becoming global citizens and their country was becoming "a province of the world" as they participated increasingly in a cosmopolitan and international culture.

In this environment, the accumulated tensions of Japan's modernizing and industrializing processes found expression. "Rice riots" in 1918 brought more than a million people into the streets of urban Japan to protest the rising price of that essential staple. Union membership tripled in the 1920s as some factory workers began to think in terms of entitlements and workers' rights rather than the benevolence of their employers. In rural areas, tenant unions multiplied, and disputes with landowners increased amid demands for a reduction in rents. A mounting women's movement advocated a variety of feminist issues, including suffrage and the end of legalized prostitution. "All the sleeping women are now awake and moving," declared Yosano Akiko, a well-known poet, feminist, and social critic, in 1911. A number of "proletarian (working-class) parties"—the Labor-Farmer Party, the Socialist People's Party, and a small Japan Communist Party—promised in various ways to promote radical social change.

For many people in established elite circles—bureaucrats, landowners, industrialists, military officials—all of this was both appalling and alarming, suggesting echoes of the Russian Revolution of 1917. As in Germany, however, it was the

◄ AP®

SOURCING AND SITUATION

Does the chart on the facing page favor the view that fascist and communist states were equally "totalitarian"? Or does it suggest sharp differences between them?

AP®

CAUSATION

Understand how political instability in Japan in the early twentieth century led to conflict in East Asia and eventually to World War II.

AP®

COMPARISON

How did Japan's experience during the 1920s and 1930s resemble that of Germany, and how did it differ?

AP®

CAUSATION

What explains the rise and the limits of right-wing politics in Japan?

BUILDING AP® SKILLS

Making Connections: Causation

Ask students to list the sources of political, economic, and social tensions in the early twentieth century that led to political instability in Japan. *Since the Meiji Restoration, Japan had been industrializing and needed resources from China in order to industrialize. Japan invaded China in the early twentieth century, which led to conflict with the United States. The emperor took on the role of dictator while trying to modernize Japan.*

TEACHING IDEA

Class Discussion

Ask students to recall what they learned about Japan's rise as a modern industrial power in Chapter 9. *In 1854, the United States forced Japan to open up to foreign trade. The Meiji Restoration occurred, and power was placed with the emperor. Japan quickly industrialized by studying the methods of the industrialized West.*

BUILDING AP® SKILLS

Making Connections: Comparison

Ask students to create a table like the one below to compare the similarities and differences in reactions to the Great Depression in Germany and Japan. A reproducible version of this chart is available in the Teacher's Resource Materials. (Answers are provided in italics.)

Similarities	Differences
■ *Both Germany and Japan became more authoritarian.* ■ *In Japan, Radical Nationalism or the "Revolutionary Right" was similar to the Third Reich of Nazi Germany.*	■ *No right-wing fascist group took over Japan, as it did in Germany.* ■ *Japan did not produce a charismatic leader like Hitler.* ■ *People arrested for political offenses were not exterminated in Japan, as they were in Germany.* ■ *There was not a widespread fascist movement in Japan.*

TRM **Handout 11.6: Comparison Chart for Reactions to the Great Depression in Germany and Japan**

EXPLORING AP® THEMES

Governance (GOV)

Ask students: What was the purpose of the Cherry Blossom Society? *To honor the emperor and exhibit nationalism*

---

impact of the Great Depression that paved the way for harsher and more authoritarian action. That worldwide economic catastrophe hit Japan hard. Shrinking world demand for silk impoverished millions of rural dwellers who raised silkworms. Japan's exports fell by half between 1929 and 1931, leaving a million or more urban workers unemployed. Many young workers returned to their rural villages only to find food scarce, families forced to sell their daughters to urban brothels, and neighbors unable to offer the customary money for the funerals of their friends. In these desperate circumstances, many began to doubt the ability of parliamentary democracy and capitalism to address Japan's "national emergency." Such conditions energized a growing movement in Japanese political life known as Radical Nationalism or the **Revolutionary Right**. Expressed in dozens of small groups, it was especially appealing to younger army officers. The movement's many separate organizations shared an extreme nationalism, hostility to parliamentary democracy, a commitment to elite leadership focused around an exalted emperor, and dedication to foreign expansion. The manifesto of one of those organizations, the Cherry Blossom Society, expressed these sentiments clearly in 1930:

> As we observe recent social trends, top leaders engage in immoral conduct, political parties are corrupt, capitalists and aristocrats have no understanding of the masses, farming villages are devastated, unemployment and depression are serious. . . . The rulers neglect the long term interests of the nation, strive to win only the pleasure of foreign powers and possess no enthusiasm for external expansion. . . . The people are with us in craving the appearance of a vigorous and clean government that is truly based upon the masses, and is genuinely centered around the Emperor.[6]

AP®
COMPARISON
What did Italian fascism, German Nazism, and Japanese authoritarianism have in common? How did they differ?

In sharp contrast to developments in Italy and Germany, however, no right-wing or fascist party gained wide popular support in Japan, and no such party was able to seize power. Nor did Japan produce any charismatic leader on the order of Mussolini or Hitler. People arrested for political offenses were neither criminalized nor exterminated, as in Germany, but instead were subjected to a process of "resocialization" that brought the vast majority of them to renounce their "errors" and return to the "Japanese way." Japan's established institutions of government were sufficiently strong, and traditional notions of the nation as a family headed by the emperor were sufficiently intact, to prevent the development of a widespread fascist movement able to take control of the country.

In the 1930s, though, Japanese public life clearly changed in ways that reflected the growth of right-wing nationalist thinking. The military in particular came to exercise a more dominant role in Japanese political life, reflecting the long-standing Japanese respect for the samurai warrior class. Censorship limited the possibilities of free expression, and a single news agency was granted the right to distribute all national and most international news to the country's newspapers and radio stations.

Established authorities also adopted many of the ideological themes of the Revolutionary Right. In 1937, the Ministry of Education issued a new textbook, *Cardinal Principles of the National Entity of Japan*, for use in all Japanese schools. That document proclaimed the Japanese to be "intrinsically quite different from the so-called citizens of Occidental [Western] countries." Those nations were "conglomerations of separate individuals" with "no deep foundation between ruler and citizen to unite them." In Japan, by contrast, an emperor of divine origin related to his subjects as a father to his children. It was a natural, not a contractual, relationship, expressed most fully in the "sacrifice of the life of a subject for the Emperor."

The state's success in quickly bringing the country out of the Depression likewise fostered popular support. As in Nazi Germany, state-financed credit, large-scale spending on armaments, and public works projects enabled Japan to emerge from the Depression more rapidly and more fully than major Western countries. "By the end of 1937," noted one Japanese laborer, "everybody in the country was working."[7] By the mid-1930s, the government increasingly assumed a supervisory or managerial role in economic affairs. Private property, however, was retained, and the huge industrial enterprises called *zaibatsu* continued to dominate the economic landscape.

Although Japan during the 1930s shared some common features with fascist Italy and Nazi Germany, it remained, at least internally, a less repressive and more pluralistic society than either of those European states. Japanese intellectuals and writers had to contend with government censorship, but they retained some influence in the country. Generals and admirals exercised great political authority as the role of an elected parliament declined, but they did not govern alone. Political prisoners were few and were not subjected to execution or deportation as in European fascist states. Japanese conceptions of their racial purity and uniqueness were directed largely against foreigners rather than an internal minority. Nevertheless, like Germany and Italy, Japan developed extensive imperial ambitions. Those projects of conquest and empire building collided with the interests of established imperial powers such as the United States and Britain, launching a second, and even more terrible, global war.

The Growth of Japanese Militarism This poster celebrating the Japanese navy was created by the National Defense Women's Association in 1938. It reflects the increasing role of the military in Japanese national life and seeks to encourage female support for it. (Pictures from History/Bridgeman Images)

▲ **AP®**

CLAIMS AND EVIDENCE IN SOURCES
What does the poster suggest about how women were used to promote Japanese militarization?

EXPLORING AP® THEMES

Governance (GOV)

Ask students: How did Japanese public life change in the 1930s? *In the 1930s, Japanese public life clearly changed in ways that reflected the growth of right-wing nationalist thinking. Major cabinet positions went to prominent bureaucratic or military figures rather than to party leaders. The military came to exercise a more dominant role in Japanese political life. Censorship limited the possibilities of free expression, and a single news agency was granted the right to distribute all national and most international news to the country's newspapers and radio stations. An Industrial Patriotic Federation replaced independent trade unions with factory-based "discussion councils" to resolve local disputes between workers and managers.*

AP® CLASSROOM

AP® Topic Questions

Now is an excellent opportunity for some practice with multiple-choice questions. You can find a set of questions about Japan's dissatisfaction with the Treaty of Versailles by logging into AP® Classroom, clicking on Unit 7 under Classroom Resources, and then selecting Topic Questions. Look for the questions labeled "Shigenobu on Japanese Grievance." You can either assign the questions to the students to complete individually or allow them to partner up to work through the set together.

A Second World War, 1937–1945

Finding the Main Point: What are the main similarities and differences between World War II in Asia and in Europe?

World War II, even more than the Great War, was a genuinely global conflict with independent origins in both Asia and Europe. Dissatisfied states in both continents sought to fundamentally alter the international arrangements that had emerged from World War I. Many Japanese, like their counterparts in Italy and Germany, felt stymied by Britain and the United States as they sought empires that they regarded as essential for their national greatness and economic well-being.

The Road to War in Asia

AP®
COMPARISON
How did the origins, course, and outcomes of World War II differ from those of World War I?

World War II began in Asia before it occurred in Europe. In the late 1920s and the 1930s, Japanese imperial ambitions mounted as the military became more powerful in Japan's political life and as an earlier cultural cosmopolitanism gave way to more nationalist sentiments. An initial problem was the rise of Chinese nationalism, which seemed to threaten Japan's sphere of influence in Manchuria, acquired by Japan after the Russo-Japanese War of 1904–1905. Acting independently of civilian authorities in Tokyo, units of the Japanese military seized control of Manchuria in 1931 and established a puppet state called Manchukuo, which Japan called a Greater East Asia Co-Prosperity Sphere. This action was condemned by China, the United States, and the League of Nations alike, but there was no effective military response to the Japanese aggression. The condemnation, however, prompted Japan to withdraw from the League of Nations and in 1936 to align more closely with Germany and Italy. By that time, relations with an increasingly nationalist China had deteriorated further, leading to a full-scale attack on heartland China in 1937 and escalating a bitter conflict that would last another eight years. **World War II in Asia** had begun (see Map 11.4).

As Japan's war against China unfolded, the view of the world held by Japanese authorities and many ordinary people hardened. Increasingly, they felt isolated, surrounded, and threatened. Anti-Japanese immigration policies in the United States convinced some Japanese that racism prevented the West from acknowledging Japan as an equal power. Furthermore, Japan was quite dependent on foreign and especially American sources of strategic goods — oil, for example — even as the United States was becoming increasingly hostile to Japanese ambitions in Asia. Moreover, Western imperialist powers — the British, French, and Dutch — controlled resource-rich colonies in Southeast Asia. Finally, the Soviet Union, proclaiming an alien communist ideology, loomed large in northern Asia. To growing numbers of Japanese, their national survival was at stake.

Thus in 1940–1941, Japan extended its military operations to the French, British, Dutch, and American colonies of Southeast Asia — Malaya, Burma, Indonesia, Indochina, and the Philippines — in an effort to acquire those resources that would free it from dependence on the West. In carving out this Pacific empire,

---

Incorporating Outside Resources

In the episode *World War II* of Crash Course World History, John Green argues that World War II started when Japan invaded Manchuria in 1931 or when Japan invaded China. He also touches on the many different theaters of war. Find the video on YouTube. After students watch the video, ask the following questions:

■ How did Japan's invasion of China begin the Pacific theater of war? *Japan violated the League of Nations agreements when it invaded China in the 1930s. The Western powers were threatened by Japan's presence in China, and they did not want to lose control of the iron ore they were getting from Manchuria.*

■ What was Germany's Hunger Plan? *Take Poland, Ukraine, and eastern Russia and resettle them with Germans so that Germany could feed her people.*

■ Why were civilians targeted in World War II? *World War II was a total war, which meant that everyone's role was important. Most civilians involved in the war effort were helping to sustain the war primarily in industrial roles.*

BUILDING AP® SKILLS

Making Connections: Causation

Divide the class into three groups. Assign one group to list the social effects of World War II, another group to list the political effects of World War II, and the third group to list the economic effects of World War II. Have each group share their results with the rest of the class. As students are sharing their results, compile a complete class list. *Answers should consider the social effects of the Holocaust, the mass displacement of people, and the death toll; the economic effects of the financial cost of the war, the employment that came with the war, and the rationing that continued during and after the war; and the political effects of the emergence of the United States as a world power, the loss of British colonies, and tensions between the Soviet Union and the United States.*

BUILDING AP® SKILLS

Argumentation

Ask students to write a paragraph on the following prompt. You may wish to make this a timed response of 10–15 minutes in class or assign it for homework.

■ Refute, support, or modify this statement: "World War II began in Asia before it occurred in Europe." Answers should touch on the following points: *In the 1930s, Japan began to expand and* *extend its influence, and then it invaded China. This break from the League of Nations began the conflict between Japan and Western nations. Japan then aligned with Germany and Italy. Although Japan was expanding before Germany did, the rise of authoritarian rule in Germany and Italy could actually be considered the beginning of the war.*

Map 11.4 World War II in Asia and the Pacific
Japanese aggression temporarily dislodged the British, French, Dutch, and Americans from their colonial possessions in Asia, while inflicting vast devastation on China. Much of the American counterattack involved "island hopping" across the Pacific until the dropping of the atomic bombs on Hiroshima and Nagasaki finally forced the Japanese surrender in August 1945.

▲ **AP®**
COMPARISON
Compare this map with Map 11.5. How were Allied strategies fundamentally different in the Pacific than in Europe?

the Japanese presented themselves as liberators and modernizers, creating an "Asia for Asians" and freeing their continent from European and American dominance. Experience soon showed that Japan's concern was far more for Asia's resources than for its liberation and that Japanese rule exceeded in brutality even that of the Europeans.

EXPLORING AP® THEMES
Humans and the Environment (ENV)

In the article titled "Pacific and Philippines" on the Sky History UK website, students can read about the involvement of these areas in the war. Have students search "Pacific and Philippines" for the article. After students read the article, ask them to work in pairs and use Map 11.4, "World War II in Asia and the Pacific," to locate each island discussed in the article.

BUILDING AP® SKILLS
Making Connections: Causation

Have students draw a "bubble" thinking map with Pearl Harbor in the middle circle. The students will then draw four or five circles sprouting from the center circle; in these circles they should include the various events that contributed to the invasion of Pearl Harbor. *Circles may include Japan's invasion of China, Japan's military operations in Southeast Asia, Japan's feeling of being slighted by Western powers, Japan's reliance on American resources, and the U.S. oil embargo.*

A decisive step in the development of World War II in Asia lay in the Japanese attack on the United States at Pearl Harbor in Hawaii in December 1941. Japanese authorities undertook that attack with reluctance and only after negotiations to end American hostility to Japan's empire-building enterprise proved fruitless and an American oil embargo was imposed on Japan in July 1941. In the face of this hostility, Japan's leaders felt that the alternatives for their country boiled down to either an acceptance of American terms, which they feared would reduce Japan to a second- or third-rank power, or a war with an uncertain outcome. Given those choices, the decision for war was made more with foreboding than with enthusiasm. A leading Japanese admiral made the case for war in this way in late 1941: "The government has decided that if there were no war the fate of the nation is sealed. Even if there is a war, the country may be ruined. Nevertheless a nation that does not fight in this plight has lost its spirit and is doomed."[8]

As a consequence of the attack on Pearl Harbor, the United States entered the war in the Pacific, beginning a long and bloody struggle that ended only with the use of atomic bombs against Hiroshima and Nagasaki in 1945. Since Japan was allied with Germany and Italy, the Pearl Harbor action also joined the Asian theater of the war with the ongoing conflict in Europe into a single global struggle that pitted Germany, Italy, and Japan (the Axis powers) against the United States, Britain, and the Soviet Union (the Allies).

The Road to War in Europe

If Japan was the dissatisfied power in Asia, Nazi Germany occupied that role in Europe. As a consequence of their defeat in World War I and the harsh terms of the Treaty of Versailles, many Germans harbored deep resentments about their country's position in the international arena. Taking advantage of those resentments, the Nazis pledged to rectify the treaty's perceived injustices. Thus, to most historians, the origins of **World War II in Europe** lie squarely in German aggression, although with many twists and turns and encouraged by the initial unwillingness of Britain, France, or the Soviet Union to confront that aggression forcefully. If World War I was accidental and unintended, World War II was deliberate and planned—perhaps even desired—by the German leadership and by Hitler in particular.

Slowly at first and then more aggressively, Hitler rearmed the country for war as he also pursued territorial expansion, annexing Austria and the German-speaking parts of Czechoslovakia. At a famous conference in Munich in 1938, the British and the French gave these actions their reluctant blessing, hoping that this "appeasement" of Hitler could satisfy his demands and avoid all-out war. But it did not. On September 1, 1939, Germany unleashed a devastating attack on Poland, triggering the Second World War in Europe, as Britain and France declared war on Germany. Quickly defeating France, the Germans launched a destructive air war against Britain and in 1941 turned their war machine loose on the Soviet Union. By then, most of Europe was under Nazi control (see Map 11.5).

AP®
COMPARISON
How did the origins of World War II in Europe differ from those of the war in Asia?

Map 11.5 World War II in Europe and Africa
For a brief moment during World War II, Nazi Germany came close to bringing all of Europe and North Africa under its rule. Then in late 1942, the Allies began a series of counterattacks that led to German surrender in May 1945.

▲ **AP®**
CLAIMS AND EVIDENCE IN SOURCES
According to the map, which nation took the most territory from Nazi Germany in the final two years of the war?

The Second World War was quite different from the first. It was not welcomed with the kind of mass enthusiasm across Europe that had accompanied the opening of World War I in 1914. The bitter experience of the Great War suggested to most people that only suffering lay ahead. The conduct of the two wars likewise

EXPLORING AP® THEMES
Humans and the Environment (ENV)

Show students Map 11.5, "World War II in Europe and Africa." Ask students: Why do you think the Allies chose a "Germany first" strategy in conducting the war, over a "Japan first" strategy? *Because of Germany's location, the Allies believed that Germany was a more imminent threat to the remaining unconquered European states than Japan was.*

AP® CLASSROOM
AP® Topic Questions

Consider this an excellent opportunity for practice with an SAQ. You can find an SAQ over the causes of World War II by logging into AP® Classroom, clicking on Unit 7 under Classroom Resources, and then selecting Topic Questions. Look for the questions labeled "Moser Great Depression and WWII Secondary." By this time in the course, students should be able to write an SAQ within the time limit of approximately 14 minutes.

differed. The first war had quickly bogged down in trench warfare that emphasized defense, whereas in the second war the German tactic of *blitzkrieg* (lightning war) coordinated the rapid movement of infantry, tanks, and airpower over very large areas.

Such military tactics were initially successful and allowed German forces, aided by their Italian allies, to sweep over Europe, the western Soviet Union, and North Africa. The tide began to turn in 1942 when the Soviet Union absorbed the German onslaught and then began to counterattack, slowly and painfully moving westward toward the German heartland. The United States, with its enormous material and human resources, joined the struggle against Germany in 1942 and led the invasion of northern France in 1944, opening a long-awaited second front in the struggle against Hitler's Germany. Years of bitter fighting ensued before these two huge military movements ensured German defeat in May 1945.

Consequences: The Outcomes of a Second Global Conflict

AP® EXAM TIP
Understand the effects of technology on twentieth-century warfare casualties.

AP®
COMPARISON
How did the military use of technology in World War II differ from the military use of technology in World War I?

The Second World War was the most destructive conflict in world history, with total deaths estimated at around 60 million, some six times that of World War I. More than half of those casualties were civilians. Partly responsible for this horrendous toll were the new technologies of warfare — heavy bombers, jet fighters, missiles, and atomic weapons. Equally significant, though, was the almost complete blurring of the traditional line between civilian and military targets, as entire cities and whole populations came to be defined as the enemy. Nowhere was that blurring more complete than in the Soviet Union, which accounted for more than 40 percent of the total deaths in the war — probably around 25 million, with an equal number made homeless and thousands of towns, villages, and industrial enterprises destroyed. In China as well, perhaps 15 million deaths and uncounted refugees grew out of prolonged Chinese resistance and the shattering Japanese response, including the killing of every person and every animal in many villages. Within a few months, during the infamous Rape of Nanjing in 1937–1938, some 200,000 to 300,000 Chinese civilians were killed and often mutilated, and countless women were sexually assaulted. Indiscriminate German bombing of British cities and the Allied firebombing of Japanese and German cities likewise reflected the new morality of total war, as did the dropping of atomic bombs on Hiroshima and Nagasaki, which in a single instant vaporized tens of thousands of people. Many survivors subsequently contracted radiation-related diseases such as leukemia and other forms of cancer. Profound psychological distress, based on the feeling of having experienced "the destruction of everything," likewise accompanied the aftermath of these bombings. This was total war with a scale, intensity, and indiscriminate brutality that exceeded even the horrors of World War I. (See Zooming In: Hiroshima.)

APPLY THE TIP

This is an excellent opportunity to have students watch Topic 7.7: Daily Video 3: Conducting World War II, located on AP® Classroom. You can find the third video for Topic 7.7 by logging into AP® Classroom, clicking on Unit 7 under Classroom Resources, and then selecting Daily Videos. The third video for Topic 7.7: Conducting World War II focuses on the new military technology used in fighting World War II and the skill of identifying and explaining evidence used in a source to support an argument.

BUILDING AP® SKILLS

Making Connections: Comparison

Ask students to research the Rape of Nanjing and explain why the atrocities in Nanjing are not as well publicized as the genocide of the Holocaust. *Answers may include: Asian victims were viewed as less important in Western media due to racism; The Rape of Nanjing was not as long as the Holocaust; The survivors did not spread throughout the world to share their stories; Shortly after World War II, China became communist and was largely closed off to the rest of the world.*

AP® CLASSROOM

AP® Topic Questions

Now is an excellent opportunity for some practice with multiple-choice questions. You can find a set of questions about conducting World War II by logging into AP® Classroom, clicking on Unit 7 under Classroom Resources, and then selecting Topic Questions. Look for the questions labeled "Franck on Nuclear Weapons." You can either assign the questions to the students to complete individually or allow them to partner up to work through the set together.

A further dimension of total war lay in governments' efforts to mobilize their economies, their people, and their propaganda machines even more extensively than before. Colonial resources were harnessed once again. The British in particular made extensive use of colonial troops and laborers from India and Africa. Japan compelled several hundred thousand women from Korea, China, and elsewhere to serve the sexual needs of Japanese troops as so-called comfort women, who often accommodated twenty to thirty men a day.

As in World War I, though on a much larger scale, the needs of the war drew huge numbers of women into both industry and the military. In the United States, "Rosie the Riveter" represented those women who now took on heavy industrial jobs, which previously had been reserved for men. In the Soviet Union, women constituted more than half of the industrial workforce by 1945 and almost completely dominated agricultural production. Soviet women also participated actively in combat, with some 100,000 of them winning military honors. A much smaller percentage of German and Japanese women were mobilized for factory work, but a Greater Japan Women's Society enrolled some 19 million members, who did volunteer work and promised to lay aside their gold jewelry and abandon extravagant weddings. As always, war heightened the prestige of masculinity, and given the immense sacrifices that men had made, few women were inclined to directly challenge the practices of patriarchy immediately following the war.

Among the most haunting outcomes of the war was the **Holocaust**. The outbreak of war closed off certain possibilities, such as forced emigration, for implementing the Nazi dream of ridding Germany of its Jewish population. It also brought millions of additional Jews in Poland and the Soviet Union under German control and triggered among Hitler's enthusiastic subordinates various schemes for a "final solution" to the Jewish question. From this emerged the death camps that included Auschwitz, Treblinka, and Sobibór. Altogether, the Nazis killed some 6 million Jews in a technologically sophisticated form of mass murder that set a new standard for human depravity. The Nazis likewise murdered millions of non-Jewish civilians whom they deemed inferior, undesirable, or dangerous—Russians, Poles, and other Slavs; the Roma people; those with mental or physical disabilities; gay men; communists; and Jehovah's Witnesses—as part of Germany's efforts at racial purification.

Although the Holocaust was concentrated in Germany, its significance in twentieth-century world history has been huge. It has haunted postwar Germany in particular and the Western world in general. How could such a thing have occurred in a Europe bearing the legacy of both Christianity and the Enlightenment? More specifically, it sent many of Europe's remaining Jews fleeing to Israel and gave urgency to the establishment of a modern Jewish nation in the ancient Jewish homeland. That action outraged many Arabs, some of whom were displaced by the arrival of the Jews, and has fostered an enduring conflict in the Middle East. Furthermore, the Holocaust defined a new category of crimes against humanity—genocide, the attempted elimination of entire peoples.

AP
CAUSATION
What were the major consequences of World War II?

AP **EXAM TIP**
The twentieth-century concept of "total war," including its effect on women's roles, is an important one in the AP® course.

APPLY THE TIP

Ask students to explain what is meant by the term "total war." *Distinctions between the military and civilians were blurred, and war involved all the resources of the nations.* Then ask students to describe the effect of "total war" on women's roles. *Women worked in industry and in other capacities in the United States, Great Britain, and the Soviet Union. A smaller percentage of women worked in factories in Germany and Japan. The Soviet Union used women in combat.*

TEACHING IDEA

Incorporating Outside Resources

Have students go to the United States Holocaust Memorial Museum site. On the home page, have students click on "Introduction to the Holocaust" and read the information. After giving students time to read the article, ask the following questions:

■ In addition to Jews, what other groups were persecuted? *Other persecuted groups included developmentally disabled people, gypsies, Soviet prisoners of war, homosexuals, Jehovah's Witnesses, communists, and socialists.*

■ What was the "final solution"? *The final solution began by rounding up Jewish citizens and putting them in ghettos and then deporting millions to extermination camps, where they were murdered in gas chambers. In addition, Hitler used mobile killing units to carry out mass-murder operations against targeted groups behind German lines.*

ZOOMING IN | Hiroshima

"If the radiance of a thousand suns were to burst at once into the sky, that would be the splendor of the Mighty One."[9] This passage from the Bhagavad Gita, an ancient Hindu sacred text, occurred to J. Robert Oppenheimer, a leading scientist behind the American push to create a nuclear bomb, as he watched the first successful test of a nuclear weapon in the desert south of Santa Fe, New Mexico, on the evening of July 16, 1945. Years later, he recalled that another verse from the same sacred text had also entered his mind: "I am become Death, the shatterer of worlds." And so the atomic age was born amid Oppenheimer's thoughts of divine splendor and divine destruction.

A mother and child, victims of Hiroshima, on the floor of a makeshift hospital, two months after the attack.

Several weeks later, the whole world became aware of this new era when American forces destroyed the Japanese cities of Hiroshima and Nagasaki with nuclear bombs. The U.S. government decided to use this powerful new weapon partially to hasten the end of World War II, but also to strengthen the United States' position in relation to the Soviet Union in the postwar world. Whether the bomb was necessary to force Japan to surrender is a question of some historical debate. What is not in dispute was the horrific destruction and human suffering wrought by the two bombs. The centers of both cities were flattened, and as many as 80,000 inhabitants of Hiroshima and 40,000 of Nagasaki perished almost instantly from the force and intense heat of the explosions.

The harrowing accounts of survivors offer some sense of the suffering that followed. Iwao Nakamura, a

photo: AP Images

AP CAUSATION
How did World War II lead to decolonization in Africa and Asia?

AP EXAM TIP
Note that Europe's colonial power was greatly diminished after World War II.

On an even larger scale than World War I, this second global conflict rearranged the architecture of world politics. As the war ended, Europe was impoverished, its industrial infrastructure shattered, many of its great cities in ruins, and millions of its people homeless or displaced. Within a few years, this much-weakened Europe was effectively divided, with its western half operating willingly under an American security umbrella and the eastern half subject to Soviet control, but less willingly. It was clear that Europe's dominance in world affairs was finished. Not only had the war weakened both the will and the ability of European powers to hold on to their colonies, but it had also emboldened nationalist and anticolonial movements everywhere (see "Toward Independence in Asia and Africa" in Chapter 12). Japanese victories in Southeast Asia had certainly damaged European prestige. Furthermore, tens of thousands of Africans had fought for the British or the French, had seen white people die, schoolboy in Hiroshima who lived through the attack, recalled "old people pleading for water, tiny children seeking help, students unconsciously calling for their parents." He remembered that "there was a mother prostrate on the ground, moaning with pain but with one arm still tightly embracing her dead baby."[10] But for many of these survivors, the suffering had only begun. It is estimated that by 1950 as many as 200,000 additional victims had succumbed to their injuries, especially burns and the terrible effects of radiation. Cancer and genetic deformations caused by exposure to radiation continue to affect survivors and their descendants today.

Human suffering on a massive scale was a defining feature of total war during the first half of the twentieth century. In this sense, the atomic bomb was just the latest development in an arms race that drew on advances in manufacturing, technology, and science to create ever more horrific weapons of mass destruction. But no other weapon from that period was as revolutionary as the atomic bomb, which made use of recent discoveries in theoretical physics to harness the fundamental forces of the universe for war. The subsequent development of those weapons has cast an enormous shadow on the world ever since.

That shadow lay in a capacity for destruction previously associated only with an apocalypse of divine origin. Now human beings have acquired that capacity. A single bomb in a single instant can obliterate any major city in the world, and the detonation of even a small fraction of the weapons in existence today would reduce much of the world to radioactive rubble and social chaos. The destructive power of nuclear weapons has led responsible scientists to contemplate the possible extinction of our species—by our own hands. It is hardly surprising that the ongoing threat of nuclear war has led many survivors of the Hiroshima and Nagasaki bombings to push for a world free of nuclear weapons by highlighting the human suffering that they cause. In a speech to a United Nations Special Session on Disarmament in 1982, Senji Yamaguchi, a survivor of the Nagasaki bombing, pleaded for those present to look at his burnt face and hands, before calling for "no more Hiroshimas, no more Nagasakis, no more war, no more [survivors of nuclear attacks]."[11]

QUESTION

How might you define both the short- and long-term outcomes of the Hiroshima bombing?

had developed relationships with white women, and had returned home with very different ideas about white superiority and the permanence of colonial rule. Colonial subjects everywhere were very much aware that U.S. president Franklin Roosevelt and British prime minister Winston Churchill had solemnly declared in 1941 that "we respect the right of all peoples to choose the form of government under which they will live." Increasingly, Asian and African leaders demanded that such principles should apply to them as well.

The horrors of two world wars within a single generation prompted a renewed interest in international efforts to maintain the peace in a world of competing and sovereign states. The chief outcome was the United Nations (UN), established in 1945 as a successor to the moribund League of Nations. As a political body dependent on agreement among its most powerful members, the UN proved more effective as a forum for international opinion than as a means

AP° EXAM TIP

Understand examples of international peacekeeping organizations in the twentieth century, such as the United Nations.

AP°

DEVELOPMENTS AND PROCESSES

Is it more useful to consider World Wars I and II as separate and distinct conflicts or as a single briefly interrupted phenomenon?

APPLY THE TIP

Ask students: What was the purpose of the formation of the United Nations? *To maintain peace in the world.*

of resolving the major conflicts of the postwar world, particularly the Soviet/American hostility during the cold war decades. Further evidence for a growing internationalism lay in the creation in late 1945 of the World Bank and International Monetary Fund, whose purpose was to regulate the global economy, prevent another depression, and stimulate economic growth, especially in the poorer nations. What these initiatives shared was the dominant presence of the United States, as the half century following the end of World War II witnessed its emergence as a global superpower. This was among the major outcomes of the Second World War and a chief reason for the remarkable recovery of a badly damaged and discredited Western civilization.

Communist Consolidation and Expansion: The Chinese Revolution

Yet another outcome of World War II lay in the consolidation and extension of the communist world. The Soviet victory over the Nazis, though bought at an unimaginable cost in blood and treasure, gave immense credibility to that communist regime and to its leader, Joseph Stalin. Whatever atrocities he had committed, many in the Soviet Union credited Stalin with leading the country's heroic struggle against Nazi aggression. Furthermore, Stalin also presided over a major expansion of communist control in Eastern Europe, much of which was occupied by Soviet forces as the war ended. He insisted that Soviet security required "friendly" governments in the region to permanently end the threat of invasion from the West. Stalin also feared that large-scale American aid for Europe's economic recovery, which began in 1948, sought to incorporate Eastern Europe into a Western and capitalist economic network. Thus he acted to install fully communist governments, loyal to himself, in Poland, East Germany, Czechoslovakia, Hungary, Romania, and Bulgaria. Backed by the pressure and presence of the Soviet army, **communism in Eastern Europe** was largely imposed from the outside rather than growing out of a domestic revolution, as had happened in Russia itself. The situation in Yugoslavia differed sharply from the rest of Eastern Europe. There a genuinely popular communist movement had played a leading role in the struggle against Nazi occupation and came to power on its own with little Soviet help. Its leader, Josef Broz, known as Tito, openly defied Soviet efforts to control Yugoslav communism, claiming that "our goal is that everyone should be master in his own house."

In Asia too, communism took root after World War II. Following Japan's defeat, its Korean colony was partitioned, with the northern half coming under Soviet and therefore communist control. In Vietnam, a much more locally based communist movement, active since the mid-1920s under the leadership of **Ho Chi Minh** (1890–1969), embodied both a socialist vision and Vietnamese nationalism

---

APPLY THE TIP

You could have students create posters for a quick gallery walk to help them learn about how the end of World War II set the stage for the cold war. Divide the class up into five groups and assign each group one of the following events that helped lead to the cold war: (1) ideological differences between the Allies (Britain, U.S., and USSR) in World War II; (2) delay of the second front invasion in Europe in World War II; (3) Potsdam and Yalta conferences; (4) Stalin's plans for Eastern Europe after the war; (5) creation and use of the atomic bomb. Each group should create a poster, including images, that briefly explains what happened during the event and how it led to the cold war. When the groups have finished their posters, place them in the hallway and have students do a gallery walk to get the information about each event. After students get the information, consider having a quick class discussion on which event they believe had the greatest impact on the start of the cold war.

APPLY THE TIP

When thinking of communist states in the twentieth century, students may automatically think of the Soviet Union (Russia) and China, but they also need to know that communist movements took place in other states as well. It may help students to partner them up and ask them to work with their partner to identify at least two other communist movements using the information from the first two paragraphs of "Communist Consolidation and Expansion: The Chinese Revolution." *Possible answers are: Stalin imposed communism in Eastern European states like Poland, East Germany, Czechoslovakia, Hungary, Romania, and Bulgaria; A popular movement led to the rise of communism in Yugoslavia; After Korea was partitioned at the end of World War II, the northern part came under communist control (influenced by the Soviet Union); Vietnam had a communist movement since the 1920s that eventually established control over the entire country in 1975; Communist parties took power in the mid-1970s in Cambodia and Laos.*

as it battled Japanese, French, and later American invaders and established communist control first in the northern half of the country and after 1975 throughout the whole country. The victory of the Vietnamese communists spilled over into neighboring Laos and Cambodia, where communist parties took power in the mid-1970s.

Far and away the most striking expansion of communism occurred in China, where that country's Communist Party triumphantly seized power in 1949. As in Russia, that victory came on the heels of war and domestic upheaval. But the **Chinese Revolution of 1949**, which was a struggle of decades rather than a single year, was far different from its earlier Russian counterpart. The Chinese imperial system had collapsed in 1911 under the pressure of foreign imperialism, its own inadequacies, and mounting internal opposition (see "The Failure of Conservative Modernization" in Chapter 9). Unlike in Russia, where intellectuals had been discussing socialism for half a century or more before the revolution, the ideas of Karl Marx were barely known in China in the early twentieth century. Not until 1921 was a small Chinese Communist Party (CCP) founded, aimed initially at organizing the country's minuscule urban working class.

Over the next twenty-eight years, that small party, with an initial membership of only sixty people, grew enormously, transformed its strategy, found a charismatic leader in **Mao Zedong** (1893–1976), engaged in an epic struggle with its opponents, fought the Japanese heroically, and in 1949 emerged victorious as the rulers of the world's most populous country. That victory was all the more surprising because the CCP faced a far more formidable foe than the weak Provisional Government over which the Bolsheviks had triumphed in Russia. That opponent was the **Guomindang** (GWOH-mihn-dahng) (Nationalist Party), which governed China after 1928. Led by a military officer, Chiang Kai-shek, that party promoted a measure of modern development (railroads, light industry, banking, airline services) in the decade that followed. However, the impact of these achievements was limited largely to the cities, leaving the rural areas, where most people lived, still impoverished. The Guomindang's base of support was also narrow, deriving from urban elites, rural landlords, and Western powers.

Whereas the Bolsheviks had found their primary audience among workers in Russia's major cities, Chinese communists, in a striking adaptation of European Marxism, increasingly looked to the country's peasant villages for support. But Chinese peasants did not rise up spontaneously against their landlords, as Russian peasants had. Instead, years of guerrilla warfare, experiments with land reform in areas under communist control, and the creation of a communist military force to protect liberated areas slowly gained for the CCP a growing measure of respect and support among China's peasants, particularly during the 1930s. In the process, Mao Zedong, the son of a prosperous Chinese peasant family and a professional revolutionary since the early 1920s, emerged as the party's leader. A central event in Mao's rise to prominence was the Long March of 1934–1935,

AP EXAM TIP
Compare the causes of the French (in Chapter 7), Russian, and Chinese revolutions to chart how revolutions begin.

AP COMPARISON
Compare the features of communism in China and the USSR.

AP CAUSATION
How might you explain the success of the Chinese Communist Party in coming to power by 1949?

AP EXAM TIP
Understand the ways that communism in China was similar to and different from communism in Russia.

TEACHING IDEA

Incorporating Outside Resources

In the episode *Communists, Nationalists, and China's Revolutions* of Crash Course World History, John Green discusses China's revolutions in the early twentieth century. While war consumed most of the rest of the world, China was changing the dynastic system that had ruled it for millennia. China's twentieth-century revolutions were extremely disruptive and lasted until after World War II. Chairman Mao's various programs to purify the Communist Party and build up the new People's Republic of China had mixed results. You can find the video on YouTube. Consider either assigning the video as homework or showing it in class. Then ask students the following questions as they watch it.

■ What made the 1911 revolution more successful than the revolts that had preceded it? *The army joined the rebellion because it wanted to become more modern.*

■ Why did the Communists win out over the Nationalists in China? *The Nationalists failed to defeat the Japanese and had to rely on Communist help. The Communists exploited the problems of the Nationalists and gained control in 1949 as the Nationalists fled to the island of Taiwan.*

BUILDING AP® SKILLS

Making Connections: Comparison

Students need to understand the similarities and differences in communist systems as they developed in the USSR and in China. You can have students work to create a Venn diagram similar to the table below. A reproducible version of the diagram is available in the Teacher's Resource Materials. (Answers are provided in italics.)

Communism in China	Similarities	Communism in USSR
■ *Communism replaced the post-revolutionary government after a long civil war interrupted by Japan's invasion in 1937.* ■ *Very few Chinese knew about the ideas of Marx.* ■ *The communists focused on peasants (farmers).*	■ *Both experienced social, political, and economic instability for many years preceding the revolution.* ■ *The communists appealed to women to gain their support.*	■ *The communist revolution took place in one year.* ■ *Marx's teachings were well known to the educated of Russia.* ■ *The communists focused on the working class (proletariat).*

TRM Handout 11.7: Graphic Organizer for Communism in China and the USSR

BUILDING AP® SKILLS

Claims and Evidence in Sources

Students often have difficulty understanding the Chinese Revolution, and the event they have the most difficulty understanding is the Long March. The Long March was the "make it or break it" event of the Chinese communist revolution. In the end, the Long March helped Mao Zedong gather support for communism and turned the revolution in its favor. This would be a good place to explain this event to students, and then ask them to study the photograph of Mao Zedong on his horse for the 6,000-mile journey displayed on this page. Then ask students whether they think this photograph was posed for propaganda purposes or was a spontaneous news photograph. *Students should agree that it is a spontaneous photograph because Mao is not positioned in a heroic pose and the photo is not framed in a way that carefully glorifies Mao as you might expect from a staged propaganda photo; for example, his fellow marchers are not looking up at him.*

After discussing the photograph, ask students: How could this photograph help Mao gain supporters? *Answers will vary.*

EXPLORING AP® THEMES

Social Interactions and Organization (SIO)

Communism was very appealing to many women because it seemed to give women more opportunities than previous regimes had. It would be good for students to know the opportunities communism offered to women and the barriers communism created for women. Consider asking students to list the opportunities and barriers that existed for women in communist nations. Students can keep track of these in a chart like **Handout 11.8: Chart for Opportunities and Barriers for Women in Communist Nations**. A reproducible version of this chart is available in the Teacher's Resource Materials.

TRM Handout 11.8: Chart for Opportunities and Barriers for Women in Communist Nations

Mao Zedong and the Long March An early member of China's then-minuscule Communist Party, Mao rose to a position of dominant leadership during the Long March of 1934–1935, when beleaguered communists from southeastern China trekked to a new base area in the north. This photograph shows Mao on his horse during that epic journey. (© Collection J. A. Fox/Magnum Photos)

▶ **AP**
CONTEXTUALIZATION
What does this image suggest about the early prospects of the Chinese Communist Party coming to power?

AP
CAUSATION
In what way did World War II contribute to the rise of the Chinese Communist Party?

AP **EXAM TIP**
Understand that most revolutions since the French Revolution have promised some type of land reform.

when beleaguered communist forces in southern China made a harrowing but successful retreat to a new base area in the northwest of the country, an epic journey of some 5,600 miles that soon acquired mythical dimensions in communist lore.

To recruit women for the revolution, communists drew on a theoretical commitment to their liberation and in the areas under their control established a Marriage Law that outlawed arranged or "purchased" marriages, made divorce easier, and gave women the right to vote and own property. Women's associations enrolled hundreds of thousands of women and promoted literacy, fostered discussions of women's issues, and encouraged handicraft production such as making clothing, blankets, and shoes, so essential for the revolutionary forces. But resistance to such radical measures from more traditional rural villagers, especially the male peasants and soldiers on whom the communists depended, persuaded the party leaders to modify these measures. Women were not permitted to seek divorce from men on active military duty. Women's land deeds were often given to male family heads and were regarded as family property. Female party members found themselves limited to work with women or children.

It was Japan's brutal invasion of China that gave the CCP a decisive opening, for that attack destroyed Guomindang control over much of the country and forced it to retreat to the interior, where it became even more dependent on conservative landlords. The CCP, by contrast, grew from just 40,000 members

APPLY THE TIP

Since the French Revolution, revolutionary leaders have typically promised land reform, especially to gain support from the people. You can help students connect this idea to the twentieth century by asking them to list the land reforms made by the Soviet Union and China after their revolutions. (Answers are provided in italics.)

■ Soviet Union: *Under Lenin, the spontaneous redistribution of land to the peasants was ratified by the government. Under Stalin, collective agriculture ended private property ownership.*

■ China: *A long, difficult process to redistribute land began in the 1950s. By the late 1950s, collectivization was occurring in China.*

in 1937 to more than 1.2 million in 1945, while the communist-led People's Liberation Army mushroomed to 900,000 men, supported by an additional 2 million militia troops. Much of this growing support derived from the vigor with which the CCP waged war against the Japanese invaders. Using guerrilla warfare techniques learned in the struggle against the Guomindang, communist forces established themselves behind enemy lines and, despite periodic setbacks, offered a measure of security to many Chinese faced with Japanese atrocities. The Guomindang, by contrast, sometimes seemed to be more interested in eliminating the communists than in actively fighting the Japanese. Furthermore, in the areas it controlled, the CCP reduced rents, taxes, and interest payments for peasants; taught literacy to adults; and mobilized women for the struggle. As the war drew to a close, more radical action followed. Teams of activists encouraged poor peasants to "speak bitterness" in public meetings, to "struggle" with landlords, and to "settle accounts" with them.

Thus the CCP frontally addressed both of China's major problems—foreign imperialism and peasant exploitation. It expressed Chinese nationalism as well as a demand for radical social change. It gained a reputation for honesty that contrasted sharply with the massive corruption of Guomindang officials. It put down deep roots among the peasantry in a way that the Russian Bolsheviks never did. And whereas the Bolsheviks gained support by urging Russian withdrawal from the highly unpopular First World War, the CCP won support by aggressively pursuing the struggle against Japanese invaders during World War II. In 1949, four years after the war's end, the Chinese communists swept to victory over the Guomindang, many of whose followers fled to Taiwan. Mao Zedong announced triumphantly that "the Chinese people have stood up."

CONCLUSIONS AND REFLECTIONS

Historical Intersections and Their Implications

Finding the Main Point: Do you think it is possible to "learn lessons" from the upheaval of the early twentieth century?

Major historical events, such as the world wars, the Russian and Chinese revolutions, and the Great Depression, did not turn on a dime. Rather they emerged at intersections or crossroads where multiple paths converged, where many factors played a role, and where the aspirations of various individuals and groups encountered one another.

World War I, for example, was shaped by the unstable balance of power among the major countries of Europe, by the growth of mass nationalism, by the highly destructive weaponry born of the Scientific and Industrial Revolutions, and by the rivalry of Europe's global empires. The Russian Revolution occurred when the immediate pressures of World War I were coupled with the long-term inequalities

BUILDING AP® SKILLS

Argumentation

Students don't always need to write full essays to practice their writing skills. This would be a good place to pause and have students work on their DBQ writing skills using the released Question 1 from the 2014 AP® Exam. This prompt asks students to analyze the relationship between the Chinese Communist Party and Chinese peasants from 1925 to 1950. You can find the essay question on the AP® World History page at AP® Central.

Give students a set of the documents and then give them 15 minutes to analyze the documents. They should also brainstorm at least two arguments they could use to answer the prompt with the documents. After the 15 minutes is over, ask them to write one DBQ-style argument paragraph using one of the arguments they brainstormed. The paragraph should include a topic sentence, evidence from two or three documents, and a sourcing statement on one document. You could also ask students to complete a DBQ Organizer after analyzing the documents.

To bring this DBQ into alignment with the current DBQ requirements, consider removing Documents 3 and 4. You can also change the prompt to: Evaluate the extent to which the Chinese Communist Party used a variety of methods to gain the support of Chinese peasants from ca. 1925 to ca. 1950.

TRM Writing Organizer for DBQ Practice

BUILDING AP® SKILLS

Making Connections: Comparison

Students should be able to compare the revolutions of the twentieth century. Graphic organizers are a useful tool for students to create and use for review throughout their study of world history. As students get ready to study the chapter on global communism, it could be good to ask them to complete the charts below for the Russian Revolution and the Chinese Revolution. Students will continue to work on these charts in Chapter 12 and can use them for a later comparison activity or discussion. Find sample completed charts for **Handout 11.9: Continuity and Change Charts for Global Communism in the Twentieth Century** in the Teacher's Resource Materials.

Russian Revolution

Event	Impetus for Change	Effects of Change	Continuities
February Revolution			
Bolshevik Revolution			
Collapse of the Soviet Union			

Chinese Revolution

Event	Impetus for Change	Effects of Change	Continuities
1911 Revolution			
Civil War			
Mao's Regime			
Post 1976			

TRM Handout 11.9: Continuity and Change Charts for Global Communism in the Twentieth Century

TEACHING IDEA

Class Discussion

After students have learned about the massive upheaval the world experienced in the first half of the twentieth century, consider having a class discussion on how the events of this period influenced one another. It may be interesting to see the connections students can make between these events. *Answers will vary, but may include ideas like: The economic and personal losses Russia experienced in World War I contributed to the revolutions of 1917; The legacy of World War I aggravated the long-term instabilities of capitalism and contributed to the start of the Great Depression; Resentments from World War I and the Treaty of Versailles led to the rise of authoritarians in Italy, Germany, and Japan; Events from World War II led to the start of the cold war.*

TEACHING IDEA

Class Discussion

Have students provide evidence to support both arguments found in the last sentence in the quote by Adam Gopnik: "The First [World War] teaches us never to rush into a fight, the Second [World War] never to back down from a bully." *The alliance system that was in place prior to World War I led the world into a terrible bloodbath after the assassination of the archduke. European powers were too ready for war, and very little was gained after four years of fighting. Conversely, the appeasement of Adolf Hitler during the mid-1930s led to the Holocaust and World War II.*

of Russian society and the more recent development of an aggrieved group of industrial workers. The legacy of World War I—debt, protectionism, and reparations demanded of Germany—also aggravated the long-term instabilities of capitalism to generate the Great Depression, which spread across the world along the economic linkages of globalization. Among the factors that facilitated the rise of the Nazis were the resentments following World War I, the economic tragedy of the Great Depression, and fear of Soviet communism.

And what about the role of particular people as they intersected with major events of the twentieth century? How much did the personal qualities of Lenin in Russia, Hitler in Germany, or Mao in China contribute to the movements they led? Ordinary people as well—hungry Russian women, impoverished Chinese peasants, millions of soldiers—also decided how to act amid these vast upheavals. Historians continue to debate the relationship between larger historical processes and the actions of individuals.

An awareness of this immense complexity has had implications for how historians respond to several commonplace notions about the past. One of them is the idea that history has "lessons" that can be applied in the present. About this, many historians are skeptical. The historical record, after all, is sufficiently rich and multifaceted to allow people to draw quite different lessons from it. The world wars of the twentieth century represent a case in point, as writer Adam Gopnik has pointed out:

> The First World War teaches that territorial compromise is better than full-scale war, that an "honor-bound" allegiance of the great powers to small nations is a recipe for mass killing, and that it is crazy to let the blind mechanism of armies and alliances trump common sense. The Second [World War] teaches that searching for an accommodation with tyranny by selling out small nations only encourages the tyrant, that refusing to fight now leads to a worse fight later on. . . . The First teaches us never to rush into a fight, the Second never to back down from a bully.[12]

History offers a rich reservoir of past experiences to ponder, but their lessons are not always clear or consistent to those seeking to learn from them.

A second notion to which historians bring considerable skepticism is that "history repeats itself." While historians often notice repetitive patterns in the past—wars, revolutions, and empires, for example—they usually focus more sharply on the complexity and distinctiveness of particular events such as World War I or the Chinese Revolution. They are also acutely aware of the surprising nature of historical events. Few people in 1914 anticipated the duration and carnage of World War I. The Holocaust was literally unimaginable when Hitler took power in 1933 or even at the outbreak of the Second World War in 1939. So while all of us quite naturally look to the past as we try to imagine the future, for many scholars history repeats itself most certainly in its unexpectedness.

TEACHING IDEA

Exit Ticket

To wrap up Chapter 11, you can ask students: Do you think history repeats itself? Students can either participate in a class discussion or turn in a written response as they leave the room. *Answers will vary.*

CHAPTER REVIEW

AP® Key Terms

World War I, 622
total war, 625
Treaty of Versailles, 626
Russian Revolution, 629
Lenin, 629
Stalin, 630
collectivization of agriculture, 630
Great Depression, 632
fascism, 634
Mussolini, 635
Nazi Party, 636

Hitler, 636
Revolutionary Right (Japan), 642
World War II in Asia, 644
World War II in Europe, 646
Holocaust, 649
communism in Eastern Europe, 652
Ho Chi Minh, 652
Chinese Revolution of 1949, 653
Mao Zedong, 653
Guomindang, 653

Finding the Main Point

1. What were the major causes and consequences of World War I?
2. How did the Great Depression impact economies around the world?
3. What is an authoritarian government, and what different kinds of authoritarian governments arose by the mid-twentieth century?
4. What are the main similarities and differences between World War II in Asia and in Europe?
5. Do you think it is possible to "learn lessons" from the upheaval of the early twentieth century?

AP® Big Picture Questions

1. The disasters that befell Europe in the first half of the twentieth century derived from fundamental flaws in its civilization. Do you agree? Why or why not?
2. To what extent did the two world wars settle the issues that caused them? What legacies for the future did they leave?
3. In what ways did Europe's internal conflicts between 1914 and 1945 have global implications?
4. How did communism shape world history in the first half of the twentieth century?
5. **Looking Back** In what ways were the major phenomena of the first half of the twentieth century—world wars, communist revolutions, the Great Depression, fascism, the Holocaust, the emergence of the United States as a global power—rooted in earlier times?

TRM **Suggested Responses to Questions**
You can find suggested responses to the Chapter Review questions in the Teacher's Resource Materials.

Writing an LEQ: Argumentation

In this workshop, we'll begin to put together all of the building blocks of claim, evidence, and reasoning and start to develop a full historical argument, such as you would have to write on the Long Essay Question on the AP® Exam. In later workshops, we'll add in documentary evidence to help prepare you for the Document-Based Question.

UNDERSTANDING ARGUMENTATION

In order to build a historical argument, historians begin by making a claim, or stating a thesis, that is based on historical reasoning—such as comparison, causation, or continuity and change. Historians support that claim with appropriate and historically defensible evidence. They then take into consideration any counterarguments (evidence that contradicts the claim) or qualifications (evidence that might modify their claim). Those are the key components to building a historical argument. Most of these terms should be familiar to you from previous workshops in this book, but in this workshop we'll go into them in more detail and show you specifically how to use them to succeed on the AP® Exam.

ARGUMENTATION ON THE AP® WORLD HISTORY EXAM

On the AP® Exam, you will be asked to write two historical arguments. One is the Document-Based Question (DBQ), and the other the Long Essay Question (LEQ). The DBQ is worth 25 percent of the exam and will require you to read seven documents from which you will create an argument in response to a prompt. Since the DBQ is based on primary source information, much of the evidence you will use to support your argument is provided for you. However, you need to contextualize your argument by setting the stage, historically speaking, for what was going on around the time mentioned in the prompt. You also need to know history well enough that you can create a solid argument for which you will use the documents. These documents should be used in service of your thesis, which should then provide the roadmap for your essay. You should have strong topic sentences that dive into the things mentioned in your thesis, and then use documentary evidence to support your reasoning. According to the College Board, you should use at least six documents accurately and describe them, not just quote from them. Refer to the workshops in Chapters 8 and 9 to review how to use primary source documents as evidence.

The LEQ is worth 15 percent of the overall score. You will have a choice of three prompts for this question. The prompts will be very similar for all three choices but will focus on different time periods. Make sure you choose the time period you know the most about so you can create a strong argument supported by lots of specific pieces of evidence. In this essay, the entirety of the information comes from you. You will need to know the historical reasoning skill you wish to use in answering the prompt, and you will also need to have all the pieces of evidence you wish to use memorized. This means you need to read your history book! That is the only way to build the content knowledge you need to tackle this essay. Just like on the DBQ, you will need to begin your essay by contextualizing the prompt and then creating a solid thesis statement that addresses the prompt and provides a roadmap for your essay, which will make use of one of the historical reasoning skills. You will need to write topic sentences that refer back to the thesis and address one portion of the prompt specifically. You will then weave evidence into the body of each paragraph, making sure you stick with your line of reasoning while acknowledging that there may be more than one way to interpret the evidence. This seems like a hard thing to do, but since you have only 35 minutes to write this essay, the essay does not have to be very long and complex. Rather, in a page or two, it needs to answer the "question" posed by the prompt and support that answer with solid evidence.

Writing a Historical Argument

To write an effective historical argument, you need to include the following components. Each of these components is worth a certain number of points on the AP® Exam:

Contextualization (0–1 point): Contextualization can be placed in many different areas of the essay, but since it is supposed to set the stage for the answer you are crafting with your thesis and evidence, it makes sense to contextualize in your introductory paragraph. In this section of your argument, you are establishing the historical context for your argument. What is the situation that leads to your claim?

Claim/Thesis (0–1 point): The claim is the main idea of your argument. The thesis is the formal statement of that claim. An effective thesis should do the following things:

- address the prompt or answer the question posed by the prompt
- be accurate
- establish your reasoning (comparison, continuity and change, or causation)
- establish the structure of your essay by previewing the points you'll make
- address the counterargument

That's a lot for one sentence, but it's an important sentence. Your thesis statement should be in the opening paragraph of the essay, although you should also restate it in the conclusion.

Let's look at a model thesis as an example. Consider the following prompt:

Evaluate the extent to which governments took a more active role in the economy between 1900 and 1937.

We can use the template below to create a thesis that responds to this prompt:

Although [address counterargument], [state claim that includes reasoning], [preview two topics].

BUILDING AP® SKILLS

Argumentation

If your students are struggling with writing arguments for LEQs, this AP® Skills Workshop may help them work on their writing skills. You could have students start with reading the section "Writing a Historical Argument" on pages 659 and 660 to get an overview of the different parts of an LEQ argument. Then consider reprinting the sample essay from pages 661 and 662 (without the annotations) for students to analyze and identify the different points of the LEQ rubric they see in the essay. After they score the essay, have a class discussion on what points they gave the essay and why.

If you want students to practice writing an LEQ argument, consider extending this activity by having them complete Activity 3 on page 663.

659

This model thesis is taken from the sample essay later in this workshop:

> Although both governments allowed for some private control of the economy to different extents, Russia and the United States increased government control in their respective economies between 1900 and 1937, such as by the introduction of communism in Russia and the New Deal in the United States.

Review the full sample essay in the "A Model of a Historical Argument" section to see how the author hit these points.

Evidence (0–2 points on the LEQ, 0–3 points on the DBQ): Evidence works a little differently on the LEQ than on the DBQ. On the LEQ, you can earn up to 2 points for use of evidence: one for using specific evidence, and another for tying the evidence back to the thesis. On the DBQ, you can score up to 3 points: 2 points for supporting your argument with at least six documents, and 1 more point for supporting your argument with a piece of evidence beyond the documents. Overall, the key to earning these points is to create a cohesive argument, selecting good evidence to support your argument, and then adding analysis/commentary after every piece of evidence to tie it directly back to your thesis. We cannot stress this enough. Evidence can be interpreted in more than one way. It is up to you to demonstrate how your evidence supports your thesis.

This is why it is critically important to write a thesis statement that sets the stage for the essay and then use topic sentences that build on the structure established in the thesis. The thesis and topic sentences are the basic structure of your argument. Your evidence supports that structure and creates a cohesive argument. If you do that, and supply accurate evidence that supports your argument, you might just earn all of the points!

Analysis and Reasoning (0–2 points): The analysis and reasoning within your argument, which are set up by your thesis statement, are where you show how the evidence relates to the claim. Here you use one of three historical reasoning skills—comparison, continuity and change, or causation—to answer the prompt. You should only use ONE reasoning skill and stick with it throughout the essay. This is critical to scoring this point on the exam. Many of the prompts you will encounter on the exam could be answered using more than one reasoning skill. Your job is to decide which one you want to use and then stick to it. Doing so in a well-structured argument will earn you this 1 point. To earn the other point, you will need to demonstrate your ability to acknowledge the existence of multiple perspectives within your argument—nuance. Although there are many ways to do that, the most obvious way is to discuss changes as well as continuities when writing a continuity and change essay, similarities as well as differences in a comparison essay, or multiple causes (or causes as well as effects) if using causation as the reasoning skill.

The most subjective point for exam graders is the "complexity" point, which asks that students demonstrate a complex understanding of the subject matter by using evidence to "corroborate, qualify, or modify" an argument. Having a good counterargument will help with this, but it will also help if you avoid absolutes. "X caused Y" ignores all other viewpoints. "X greatly contributed to Y" leaves room to discuss what else contributed. Using language that is not absolute is called qualifying your argument, and it's something you should practice in every discipline, because it allows you to recognize the complexity of the subject matter.

A Model of a Historical Argument

What do these components look like when they are all put together into an essay written for the AP® World History Exam? Below is a model using the prompt that was introduced in the "Claim/Thesis" section:

> Evaluate the extent to which governments took a more active role in the economy between 1900 and 1937.

You will note that we have annotated each of the elements outlined above.

World War I and the Great Depression had a dramatic impact on Russia and the United States. In Russia, World War I was so unpopular that many Russian soldiers began to desert their posts and public support of tsarist rule began to be challenged. In the United States, a short economic burst after World War I was followed by a stock market collapse that left many impoverished and unemployed. Although both governments allowed for some private control of the economy to different extents, Russia and the United States increased government control in their respective economies between 1900 and 1937, such as by the introduction of communism in Russia and the New Deal in the United States.

Contextualization

Thesis

Russia's government involvement in the economy increased significantly after 1917 when Russia became a communist state. Led by Lenin, the Bolsheviks took over the Russian government and instituted communism. Communism is an ideology created by Karl Marx where there is common ownership of the means of production and no social classes. Under communism, the government controls the economy. This illustrates a clear shift toward a government-controlled economy. Although Lenin created a communist economy where the government had an increased role in economic decisions, after years of famine and civil war, Lenin enacted the New Economic Policy in 1921. This program introduced elements of capitalism into the Soviet economy, allowing farmers to buy and sell crops in markets, lessening government control of the economy. This helped increase agricultural productivity and halt famine and food shortages. Even though the NEP relaxed some communist economic policies, the Soviet Union's control over the economy would increase dramatically under Stalin's five-year plans and collectivization of farms. Russia's shift from tsarist rule under Nicholas II to communism under Lenin and Stalin shows a clear change in domestic policy that expanded the Russian government's control over its economy.

Topic sentence

Evidence

Tying evidence to support thesis

Evidence qualifying argument

Evidence

Historical reasoning: change

661

Topic sentence	The United States enacted the New Deal under President Roosevelt to respond to the economic hardships caused by the Great Depression. The New Deal was an
Evidence	economic program based on Keynesian economics that sought to create programs to help unemployed Americans and regulate the banking industry to prevent another
Tying evidence to support thesis	economic crash. These programs and regulations illustrate a dramatic increase in the U.S. government's control over the economy. Programs such as the Civilian Conser-
Evidence	vation Corps and Social Security Administration were created to address unemploy- ment and financial support for the elderly. These programs were a direct result of the
Historical reasoning: change	problems brought on by the stock market crash in 1929. The New Deal illustrates a change in American domestic policy from laissez-faire economics to a more govern- ment-regulated economy.

Conclusion restating thesis — Roosevelt's New Deal, focused on government assistance to deal with the economic problems created by the Great Depression, and Russia's shift to communism both illustrate a change in how states controlled their economies in the time period after 1900.

BUILDING AP® SKILLS

1. **Activity: Identifying a Historical Argument.** Read AP® Historians' Voices 11.1: John Keegan on the legacies of World War I, 2000 (page 674), and identify the components of the historical argument listed below:

   Claim/Thesis:

   Pieces of evidence that support the thesis:

   Type of reasoning:

   The counterargument, or contradictory evidence:

2. **Activity: Building a Historical Argument Paragraph.** Below we have given you the prompt and thesis for a historical argument. We then provide a topic sentence for one paragraph of that argument. Find evidence from the section titled "Outcomes: Legacies of the Great War" on pages 625–629, and apply the reasoning skill evident in the thesis to create one paragraph of a historical argument.

   When you are done, explain what you have learned about the structure of a good argument.

   Prompt: Evaluate the extent to which gender norms changed as a result of World War I.

   Thesis: The extent to which gender norms changed as a result of World War I varied. Although patriarchy was still prevalent in many locations, World War I led to women

662

TRM **Suggested Responses to Questions**
You can find suggested responses to the Building AP® Skills questions in the Teacher's Resource Materials.

working in jobs that were traditionally male dominated and after World War I, suffrage for women in the United States and Britain.

Evidence from the text that could be used to support the topic sentence:

Type of reasoning:

3. **Activity: Creating a Historical Argument.** Using evidence from this chapter, create a historical argument based on the prompt below. Before you begin, outline your argument by filling in the blanks below with a thesis statement and at least two topic sentences that clearly link to the thesis. (You are not limited to two paragraphs.)

Prompt: Evaluate the extent to which governments utilized total war to mobilize their civilian populations during World War I and World War II.

Historical reasoning skill I want to use to answer this prompt:

Thesis statement based on reasoning skill and prompt:

Topic sentence for paragraph 1:

Evidence for paragraph 1:

Topic sentence for paragraph 2:

Evidence for paragraph 2:

Type of reasoning:

663

Depicting the Aftermath of War

Among the many outcomes of World War I was the presence in every European country of disillusioned, maimed, and disfigured veterans, many of them literally "men
without faces." Often neglected or overlooked, such men were reminders of a terrible
past that others wanted to forget. But some intellectuals and artists sought to highlight
these veterans' suffering as one of the tragic outcomes of the fundamentally flawed civilization that had given rise to such terrible carnage.

OTTO DIX | *Prague Street* | 1920

Prägerstrasse, 1920 (oil on canvas) by Otto Dix (1891-1969)/Peter Willi/Staatsgalerie, Stuttgart, Germany/Bridgeman Images/© 2022 Artists Rights Society (ARS), New York/VG Bild-Kunst, Bonn

One such artist was Otto Dix (1891–1969), a German painter who served in his country's military forces throughout the war and was seriously wounded. The horror of that experience generated recurrent nightmares, what we might now call post-traumatic stress disorder, and pushed him to express his outrage through his art. In 1924, he joined with other artists to mount an exhibition entitled "No More War." His antiwar activism later earned Dix the enmity of the Nazi regime, which called his work "degenerate," fired him from his academic position, and destroyed some of his paintings. Artistically Dix worked in a style known as the "new objectivity," which focused heavily on the horrendous outcomes of war and, as Dix put it, "the dimension of ugliness." His painting made little attempt to create a unified image, preferring to present disconnected "particles of experience." In this activity you will analyze and interpret one of Dix's most famous paintings, entitled *Prager Strasse* (Prague Street), named after an upscale shopping street in the German city of Dresden, where the scene is set. He created this painting in 1920, just two years after the war ended.

1 A FIRST LOOK

Let's begin by examining the veterans with missing limbs, the primary focus of the painting, by answering the following questions:

1. How would you describe the veteran in the center of the image in the yellow straw boater hat? What physical injuries has he suffered? What psychological traumas can you imagine he experienced? What evidence does the image provide about his life since his military service?

2. How would you describe the second veteran in the green bowler hat with a war medal on his chest, who is pulling himself along on a wheeled trolley? What similarities and differences can you identify between him and the veteran in the straw hat? Be sure to consider his dress and demeanor.

3. A third victim of the war appears in the lower left as a high-quality prosthetic hand leaning on a cane and apparently wearing a white shirt. What class differences are represented in these three figures? Why might Dix have wanted to show these differences?

4. Do you think that these veterans are hanging out together, or merely crossing paths on a city street? Why?

2 A SECOND LOOK

Now take a closer look at the physical setting in which Dix has placed the veterans. Answer these questions to organize your analysis:

1. On the extreme upper left of the image the well-dressed arm of a man drops a stamp (used as money at the time) into the outstretched hand of the veteran in the straw hat, while on the far right, a well-dressed woman in a pink dress and high heels walks by with her dog. What do these figures add to the portrayal of the veterans at the center of the image?

665

2. Now turn your attention to the store window in the background, with the young girl in front of it scribbling on its wall with chalk. What does it sell, and why might Dix have chosen to include this specific shop in the painting? How do the items available in the shop compare to those used by the veteran in the straw hat sitting in front of it?

3. Notice how Dix's fluid use of perspective encourages the viewer's eye to shift from point to point in the image rather than take in the image as a whole. How does the disconnected or fragmentary style of the painting contribute to its tone and message?

3 A THIRD LOOK

Finally, notice the leaflet under the trolley of the legless veteran. Its headline reads "Juden raus" or "Jews out." It evokes a widely held scapegoat theory seeking to explain Germany's defeat in the war. In this view, Jewish industrialists had profited from the war and in doing so had fatally undermined Germany's military might. In seeking to understand this element of the painting, consider these questions:

1. What does it suggest about the political views of the figures represented in the painting?

2. Why might disillusioned veterans have embraced such a theory?

3. Why might Dix have included this element in his painting?

AP ACTIVITY USING ART AS EVIDENCE

Historians often use artistic works as primary sources that provide information and evidence about the artists who created them and the societies in which they worked. In a paragraph or two, place Dix's painting in its historical situation and explain the various ways in which the painting provides evidence about the experiences of German veterans after World War I. Be sure to use specific evidence from the painting to sustain your claims.

FURTHER ACTIVITY

Otto Dix created his painting in 1920, years before Adolf Hitler and the Nazis began their rise to prominence. Drawing on the information in this activity and the chapter narrative, write a short essay about how Dix's painting offers evidence about those elements of postwar German society that facilitated Hitler's rise to power. Keep in mind that Hitler, although not maimed, was a disillusioned veteran of World War I, as were many of his early followers.

BUILDING AP® SKILLS

Argumentation

Students should practice their argumentation writing skills frequently throughout the year. You can help students tie what they saw in Otto Dix's *Prague Street* with the rise of authoritarianism in Germany by asking them to complete the "Further Activity" on this page.

AP® WORKING WITH EVIDENCE

Experiencing World War I

The history of World War I is often told in terms of diplomatic maneuvering, international alliances, altered borders, negotiated treaties, military strategies, battles, and new technologies of war. Here, however, we set aside these important matters to focus on the experience of the Great War as reflected in the accounts of particular individuals, most of them quite ordinary and unknown beyond the circle of their families and friends. Of course, the experience of the war varied greatly. Men and women; Europeans, Asians, and Africans; officers and enlisted men; refugees and prisoners of war; pacifists and militarists—all of these and many others as well encountered the war in quite different ways. Furthermore, the enthusiasm for the war that characterized many at its beginning soon turned to horror and despair as it became apparent that the conflict would drag bloodily on for years. From this immense variety, the following sources provide just a glimpse of the powerful impact of World War I on a number of individuals.

LOOKING AHEAD Evaluate the extent to which national origins impacted individual experiences in World War I.

AP® DBQ PRACTICE

DOCUMENT 1 | In the Trenches

A prominent feature of World War I involved "trench warfare," in which lines of entrenched men, often not far apart, periodically went "over the top," only to gain a few yards of bloody ground before being thrown back with enormous casualties on both sides. Document 1 derives from a letter that British officer Julian Grenfell wrote to his parents, describing the early stages of trench warfare.

Source: Julian Grenfell, letter from a British officer in the trenches, November 18, 1914.

They had us out again for 48 hours [in the] trenches. After the shells, after a day of them, one's nerves are really absolutely beat down. I can understand now why our infantry have to retreat sometimes; a sight which came as a shock to me at first, after being brought up in the belief that the English infantry cannot retreat.

[We are] in a dripping sodden wood, with the German trench in some places 40 yards ahead. We had been worried by snipers all along and I had always been asking for leave to go out and have a try myself. Well, on Tuesday . . . they gave me leave. Off I crawled through sodden clay and trenches going about a yard a minute. Then I saw the Hun trench . . . so I crawled on again very slowly to the parapet of the trench. Then the German behind me put his head up again. He was laughing and talking. I saw his teeth glistening against my foresight, and I pulled the trigger very slowly. He just grunted and crumpled up.

[Something similar happened the next day.] I went back at a sort of galloping crawl to our lines and sent a message to the 10th that the Germans were moving up their way in some

---

TRM Suggested Responses to Questions
You can find suggested responses to the AP® Working with Evidence questions in the Teacher's Resource Materials.

BUILDING AP® SKILLS

Claims and Evidence in Sources

Interpreting text-based as well as non-text-based sources is an important skill for AP® World History: Modern students. If time is available, have students investigate the individual experiences of people in World War I by using the evidence in "Experiencing World War I" beginning on page 667. Consider having students analyze one or more of the sources found on pages 667–673. You can check for understanding by:

■ Using the questions at the end of each source as a discussion starting point.

■ Pairing students to analyze (identify and describe) using author/creator's point of view, purpose, historical situation, and/or audience. This activity can continue to reinforce sourcing.

■ Assigning a source to a group of three to four students and having them present an overview of the source along with the sourcing to the rest of the class.

■ Having students practice AP® skills using any of the activities under "Doing History" on page 673.

numbers. Half an hour afterward, they attacked the 10th and our right, in massed formation, advancing slowly to within 10 yards of the trenches. We simply mowed them down. It was rather horrible.

Laurence Housman, ed., *War Letters of Fallen Englishmen* (London: E. P. Dutton, 1930), 119–20.

Question to Consider: What insights about the experience of fighting in World War I might you derive from the source?

AP Analyzing Sources: What additional information would provide valuable historical context for the source?

DOCUMENT 2 Reading the Letters of the Enemy

Modern warfare has been a generally impersonal affair, with men killing other unknown men at a distance. Occasionally, however, circumstances allowed a more personal encounter between soldiers on opposing sides of the war. Such was the case of Hugo Mueller, a young German soldier in World War I who was able to read the letters of dead or captured French soldiers. The following excerpt describes his reaction to this unusual experience.

Source: Hugo Mueller, letter from a German soldier on the western front, 1915.

It has been extremely interesting to study the contents of the letter-cases of French killed and prisoners. The question frequently recurs, just as it does with us: "When will it all end?" To my astonishment I practically never found any expressions of hatred or abuse of Germany or German soldiers. On the other hand, many letters from relations revealed an absolute conviction of the justice of their cause and sometimes also of confidence in victory. In every letter, mother, fiancée, children, friends . . . spoke of a joyful return and speedy meeting—and now they are all lying dead and hardly even buried between the trenches, while over them bullets and shells sing their gruesome dirge.

War hardens one's heart and blunts one's feelings, making a man indifferent to everything that formerly affected and moved him; but these qualities of hardness and indifference towards fate and death are necessary in the fierce battle to which trench warfare leads. Anybody who allowed himself to realize the whole tragedy of some of the daily occurrences in our life here would either lose his reason or be forced to bolt across the enemy's trench with his arms high in the air.

Philipp Witkop, ed., *German Students' War Letters*, translated by Anne F. Wedd (London: Methuen, 1929), 278–79.

Question to Consider: What does this extract convey about the impact of the war on Mueller's outlook?

AP Analyzing Sources: How might you understand the contradiction between Mueller's feelings of empathy for French soldiers and his recognition of the "hardness and indifference" that war generated?

DOCUMENT 3 | On the Home Front

World War I is often described as an early example of "total war," in which the civilian population was both mobilized for the struggle and deeply affected by it. With so many men away from home, women were engaged with the war in any number of ways. Tens of thousands joined the military in support roles, particularly nursing, while in Russia several "women's battalions," all-female combat forces, were created in 1917, in part to encourage war-weary men to continue the fight. This British propaganda poster from 1915, aimed at recruiting men for military service, speaks to the moral expectation for women in wartime.

Source: British propaganda poster, "Women of Britain Say—'GO!,'" 1915.

669

Question to Consider: For what purposes did male authorities seek to mobilize women during the war?

AP Analyzing Sources: How does the intended audience impact what is depicted in the source?

DOCUMENT 4 An Indian Soldier in World War I

More than a million soldiers from South Asia served in World War I as the British mobilized the manpower of their Indian colony to support the war effort. Some 74,000 of them died in that conflict. Beyond the normal horrors of wartime, these soldiers had a distinctive experience based on their status as colonial subjects, racially and culturally different from European soldiers. In an excerpt from a letter he wrote, one of those soldiers, Behari Lal, commented on that experience.

> Source: Behari Lal, letter from a soldier in the British Indian army, 1917.
>
> There is no likelihood of our getting rest during the winter. I am sure German prisoners could not be worse off in any way than we are. I had to go three nights without sleep, as I was on a motor lorry, and the lorry fellows, being Europeans, did not like to sleep with me, being an Indian. [The] cold was terrible, and it was raining hard; not being able to sleep on the ground in the open, I had to pass the whole night sitting on the outward lorry seats. I am sorry the hatred between Europeans and Indians is increasing instead of decreasing, and I am sure that the fault is not with the Indians. I am sorry to write this, which is not a hundredth part of what is in mind, but this increasing hatred and continued ill-treatment has compelled me to give you a hint.
>
> David Omussi, ed., *Indian Voices of the Great War* (New York: St. Martin's Press, 1999), 336–37.

Question to Consider: What was distinctive about Behari Lal's experience in World War I compared to that of European soldiers?

AP Analyzing Sources: How might Lal's service in the British Indian army impact his point of view about the war?

DOCUMENT 5 A Senegalese Veteran's Oral Testimony

The experience of Nar Diouf, one of some 140,000 West Africans who served with French forces during World War I, provides another illustration of the impact of the war on colonial subjects. When he returned home to the French colony of Senegal after the war, he found that his outlook and status had changed substantially.

Source: Oral testimony of Nar Diouf, a Senegalese veteran of World War I, 1919.

I received many lasting things from the war. I demonstrated my dignity and courage, and [I] won the respect of the people and the [colonial] government. And whenever the people of the village had something to contest [with the French]—and they didn't dare do it [themselves] because they were afraid of them—I used to do it for them. And many times when people had problems with the government, I used to go with my decorations and arrange the situation for [them]. Because whenever the *Tubabs* [Europeans] saw your decorations, they knew that they [were dealing with] a very important person. . . And I gained this ability—of obtaining justice over a *Tubab*—from the war.

   [For example], one day a *Tubab* came here [to the village]—(he was a kind of doctor)—to make an examination of the people. So he came here, and there was a small boy who was blind. And [the boy] was walking, [but] he couldn't see, and he bumped into the *Tubab*. And the *Tubab* turned and pushed the boy [down]. And when I saw that, I came and said to the *Tubab*: "Why have you pushed this boy? [Can't] you see that he is blind?" And the *Tubab* said: "Oh, *pardon, pardon*. I did not know. I will never do it again, excuse me." [But] before the war, [no matter what they did], it would not have been possible to do that with a *Tubab*.

Joe Lunn, *Memories of the Maelstrom: A Senegalese Oral History of the First World War* (Portsmouth, NH: Heinemann, 1999), 232.

Question to Consider: How had the war changed Nar Diouf's self-image and his relationship with the European rulers of his country?

AP **Analyzing Sources:** How might you explain the differences between the experiences of Diouf and Behari Lal?

DOCUMENT 6 Nationalism and War

Nationalism was a central element in the origin and conduct of World War I. In the following passage, Ernst Junger, a German officer who served on the western front for four years, comments on this fundamental loyalty as he experienced it.

Source: German officer Ernst Junger, from *Storm of Steel*, 1920.

I took an entrenching party from the Altenburg Redoubt to C sector. One of them, Landsturms-man Diener, climbed on to a ledge in the side of the trench to shovel earth over the top. He was scarce up when a shot fired from the sap got him in the skull and laid him dead on the floor of the trench. He was married and had four children. His comrades lay in wait a long while behind the parapet to take vengeance. They sobbed with rage. It is remarkable how little they grasp the war as an objective thing. They seem to regard the Englishman who fired the fatal shot as a personal enemy. I can understand it.

   It has always been my ideal in war to eliminate all feelings of hatred and to treat my enemy as an enemy only in battle and to honour him as a man according to his courage. It

671

is exactly in this that I have found many kindred souls among British officers. It depends, of course, on not letting oneself be blinded by an excessive national feeling, as the case generally is between the French and the Germans. The consciousness of the importance of one's own nation ought to reside as a matter of course and unobtrusively in everybody, just as an unconditional sense of honour does in the gentleman. Without this it is impossible to give others their due.

Question to Consider: What is Junger's view on the nationalistic motive of war?

AP Analyzing Sources: Why is Junger critical of those who sought vengeance over the death of one of their comrades?

DOCUMENT 7 In the Aftermath of the Great War

Beyond the enormous political, social, and economic changes wrought by World War I lay those transformations of consciousness, outlook, and expectation that registered in the work of artists and writers as well as in the sensibilities of individual people. Document 7 derives from the most famous novel to emerge from the war. Written by the German war veteran Erich Maria Remarque, *All Quiet on the Western Front* describes the experience of a young German soldier and his classmates during the war. Published in 1929, it captured the sense of disillusionment and hopelessness that many returning veterans surely felt as they reentered civilian society. "Bombardment, barrage, curtain-fire, mines, gas, tanks, machine guns, hand grenades—words, words, but they hold the horror of the world." Such was the strained effort of Remarque to find language to describe what he and millions of others had experienced on the battlefield.

Source: German World War I veteran Erich Maria Remarque, from his novel *All Quiet on the Western Front*, 1929.

Had we returned home in 1916, out of the suffering and the strength of our experiences we might have unleashed a storm. Now if we go back we will be weary, broken, burnt out, rootless, and without hope. We will not be able to find our way anymore.

And men will not understand us, for the generation that grew up before us, though it has passed these years with us, already had a home and a calling; now it will return to its old occupations, and the war will be forgotten; and the generation that has grown up after us will be strange to us and push us aside. We will be superfluous even to ourselves, we will grow older, a few will adapt themselves, some others will merely submit, and most will be bewildered; the years will pass by and in the end we shall fall into ruin.

But perhaps all this that I think is mere melancholy and dismay, which will fly away as the dust, when I stand once again beneath the poplars and listen to the rustling of their leaves. It cannot be that it has gone, the yearning that made our blood unquiet, the unknown, the perplexing, the oncoming things, the thousand faces of the future, the melodies from dreams and from books, the whispers and divinations of women; it cannot be that this has vanished in bombardment, in despair, in brothels. . . .

672

I stand up. I am very quiet. Let the months and years come, they can take nothing from me, they can take nothing more. I am so alone, and so without hope that I can confront them without fear.

Question to Consider: How does Remarque describe the sensibility of those soldiers about to return to ordinary life? How did Remarque's response to returning home differ from that of Nar Diouf in Document 5?

AP Analyzing Sources: In describing the purpose of his book, Remarque wrote: "It will try simply to tell of a generation of men who, even though they may have escaped its shells, were destroyed by the war." How does this passage reflect that purpose?

AP DOING HISTORY

1. **DBQ Practice:** Evaluate the extent to which national origins impacted individual experiences in World War 1.

TRM Chapter 11 DBQ Activity Handout

2. **Comparison:** Based on these sources, how would you define the novel or distinctive features of World War I compared to earlier European conflicts?

3. **Making Connections:** How do you think the creators of these sources might have responded to the idea of "the perfectibility of humanity" described by Condorcet during the European Enlightenment of the eighteenth century?

4. **Sourcing and Situation:** What perspectives on the war are not reflected in these sources? Where might you look to find those perspectives?

5. **Contextualization:** What specific historical processes before this period led to the interconnectedness of Europe to countries such as India and Senegal?

You can use this exercise to help students work on improving skills with secondary sources. Consider having students read both of the sources and answer Questions 1–3 on this page. Then discuss students' answers to the questions as a class. This activity can help students practice reading and interpreting secondary sources found on the MCQ and SAQ sections of the AP® Exam.

TRM **Suggested Responses to Questions**

You can find suggested responses to the AP® Analyzing Secondary Sources questions in the Teacher's Resource Materials.

The Legacies of World War I

World War I has had a profound impact on many aspects of world history over the last century. The voices in this feature explore two of the Great War's most important legacies. In Voice 11.1, John Keegan, a prominent military historian, makes the case that World War II should be considered as part of the legacy of World War I. Then in Voice 11.2 the world historian Peter Frankopan explores how World War I began a process that brought an end to the "age of empires" in Europe.

VOICE 11.1

John Keegan on the Legacies of World War I | 2000

The First World War was a tragic and unnecessary conflict. Unnecessary because the train of events that led to its outbreak might have been broken at any point during the five weeks of crisis that preceded the first clash of arms, had prudence or common goodwill found a voice; tragic because the consequences of the first clash ended the lives of ten million human beings, tortured the emotional lives of millions more, destroyed the benevolent and optimistic culture of the European continent and left, when the guns at last fell silent four years later, a legacy of political rancour and racial hatred so intense that no explanation of the causes of the Second World War can stand without reference to those roots. The Second World War, five times more destructive in human life and incalculably more costly in material terms, was the direct outcome of the First. On 18 September 1922, Adolf Hitler, the demobilised front fighter, threw down a challenge to defeated Germany that he would realise seventeen year later: "It cannot be that two million Germans should have fallen in vain . . . No, we do not pardon, we demand—vengeance!"

Source: John Keegan, *The First World War* (New York: Vintage, 2000), 3.

VOICE 11.2

Peter Frankopan on World War I and the Decline of Empire | 2015

[In 1914], Europe was a continent of empires. Italy, France, Austro-Hungary, Germany, Russia, Ottoman Turkey, Britain, Portugal, the Netherlands, even tiny Belgium, only formed in 1831, controlled vast territories across the world. [World War I was when] the process of turning them back into local powers began. Within a matter of years, gone were the emperors, who had sailed on each other's yachts and appointed each other to grand chivalric orders; gone were some colonies and dominions overseas—and others were starting to go in an inexorable progression to independence.

In the course of four years, perhaps 10 million were dead from fighting, and half the same again from disease and famine. Over $200 billion had been spent by the Allies and the Central Powers fighting each other. European economies were shattered by the unparalleled expenditures that were exacerbated by falling productivity. Countries engaged in the fighting posted deficits and clocked up debts at a furious pace—debts they could not afford. The great empires that had dominated the world for four centuries did not slip away overnight. But it was the beginning of the end. Dusk was beginning to descend. The veil of shadows from behind which western Europe had emerged a few centuries earlier was starting to fall once again.

Source: Peter Frankopan, *The Silk Roads: A New History of the World* (New York: Vintage, 2015), 309–10.

AP® Analyzing Secondary Sources

1. Why does Keegan include the destruction wrought in the Second World War as an integral part of the terrible legacy of World War I?

2. According to Frankopan, why did European empires decline in the decades after World War I?

3. **Integrating Primary and Secondary Sources:** How might you construct an essay on the legacies of World War I that incorporates both of these Voices with Otto Dix's painting *Prague Street*; AP® Working with Evidence, Document 5: A Senegalese Veteran's Oral Testimony; and Document 7: In the Aftermath of the Great War?

CHAPTER 11 [AP®] EXAM PRACTICE

Multiple-Choice Questions Choose the correct answer for each question.

Questions 1–3 refer to this graph.

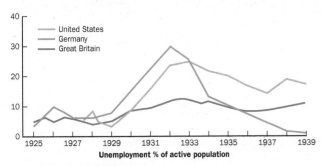

Unemployment % of active population

Comparing the Impact of the Depression

1. Based on your knowledge of world history and the graph, which of these best explains the increased rate of unemployment in the United States, Germany, and Great Britain seen in the chart?

    a. The decrease in manufacturing and agricultural production at the end of World War I

    b. An increased reliance on colonial workers, rather than local workers, in the new industrial age

    c. Soldiers reentering the workforce after World War I and displacing female workers

    d. The global economic devastation resulting from World War I and the U.S. stock market crash

2. Which of these best demonstrates differing responses to the hardships of the Great Depression?

    a. The replacement of communism with free-market economics in Eastern Europe

    b. Increases in government programs in the United Kingdom and the United States and the rise of absolutist political parties in Italy and Germany

    c. The buildup of militaries in the United States and the USSR and the beginnings of decolonization in the British Empire

    d. Increased imperialistic seizure of colonies in Africa and Asia

3. Using the graph and your knowledge of world history, which of these would best explain the dramatic decrease in Germany's unemployment rate by 1936?

    a. The military buildup caused by the Nazi Party's rise to power

    b. The final reparation payment made to the United Kingdom and France

    c. The introduction of new agricultural techniques from the United States

    d. The global dependence on German coal and iron

TRM **Suggested Responses to Questions**
You can find suggested responses to the Chapter 11 AP® Exam Practice questions in the Teacher's Resource Materials.

TEACHING IDEA

AP® Exam Strategies

You should continue to offer opportunities to students to practice test-taking skills, especially as you get closer to the AP® Exam. Project or copy the stimulus-based multiple-choice questions found on pages 675 to 676. It might be good to give students the questions as a practice quiz prior to the unit or chapter test. You could have students discuss why their answer choice was correct or incorrect with a partner after they check their answers.

675

For extra practice with multiple-choice questions, consider assigning the Unit 7 Personal Progress Check to students. This can act as a wrap-up to Chapter 11 and Unit 7, as well as help students practice their test-taking skills. You can find the questions in your AP® Classroom account under the Progress Checks for Unit 7.

BUILDING AP® SKILLS

Argumentation

AP® World History: Modern writing skills need to be practiced on a regular basis. You can use the SAQs on pages 676 and 677 for students to write an "exit ticket" at the end of class to check for understanding. You can also use the SAQs for more traditional timed writing practice, either by spreading the three SAQs across several days or as practice for the AP® Exam by writing them all at once. Make certain that students have the correct amount of time for this exercise. On exam day, students will have a total of 40 minutes to write three SAQs. If you are having them write only one at a time, you'll need to give them about 14 minutes to write it.

Differentiation

If you want to challenge students with writing an SAQ and developing evidence, consider following the "Must Do, Should Do, Strive For" model below for Question 3 on page 677. Students will need to work with a partner for this activity.

■ Must Do: On their own, students must write a topic sentence that states a clear argument answering Part A of Question 3.

■ Should Do: Students should switch their response with their partner and write evidence and analysis for the topic sentence their partner created.

■ Strive For: Students should repeat the process for Parts B and C of Question 3 with their partner. After they finish, they should discuss the SAQ answers they created together.

Questions 4–6 refer to this passage.

> I consider that the League of Nations at present is entirely useless. The Great Powers have simply gone ahead and arranged the world to suit themselves. England and France have gotten out of the Treaty everything that they wanted, and the League of Nations can do nothing to alter any of the unjust clauses of the Treaty except by unanimous consent of the members of the League, and the Great Powers will never give their consent to changes in the interests of weaker peoples.
>
> — Private comments by Robert Lansing, a U.S. diplomat at the Versailles peace conference in 1919, to U.S. diplomat William Bullitt. Bullitt made these comments public without Lansing's permission.

4. Based on the passage and your knowledge of world history, what was a consequence of the "unjust clauses" mentioned by Lansing?
   a. A decrease in nationalist fervor across Europe
   b. The stock market crash and ensuing Great Depression
   c. The goals of the United States being written into the Treaty of Versailles
   d. The rise of fascism in Europe

5. What pre–World War I situation would represent a continuity immediately after the war?
   a. European imperialism
   b. The central role of the United States in international diplomacy
   c. The industrial power of Germany
   d. International organizations as the primary instruments of negotiation

6. Based on the context of the passage, which of these conclusions is most likely true?
   a. Lansing did not want the United States involved in international diplomacy.
   b. Bullitt wished to sabotage the passing of the Versailles peace treaty.
   c. Lansing and Bullitt had very different opinions of the League of Nations.
   d. Bullitt sought to use the peace conference to end colonialism.

Short-Answer Questions

Read each question carefully and write a short response. Use complete sentences.

1. **Use the passage below and your knowledge of world history to answer all parts of the question that follows.**

> All revolutions have liberté, egalité, fraternité, and other noble slogans inscribed on their banners. All revolutionaries are enthusiasts, zealots; all are utopians, with dreams of creating a new world in which the injustice, corruption, and apathy of the old world are banished forever. They are intolerant of disagreement; incapable of compromise; mesmerized by big, distant goals; violent, suspicious, and destructive. Revolutionaries are unrealistic and inexperienced in government; their institutions and procedures are extemporized. They have the intoxicating illusion of personifying the will of the people, which means they assume the people is monolithic. They are Manicheans, dividing the world into two camps: light and darkness, the revolution and its enemies. They despise all traditions, received wisdom, icons, and superstition.
>
> — Sheila Fitzpatrick, *The Russian Revolution*, 2017

676

A. Describe ONE revolution in the period 1750 to 1900 that has the characteristics described in the passage.

B. Explain how ONE movement in the twentieth century supports the author's contention that revolutionaries seek to overcome injustice and corruption.

C. Explain how a global conflict in the twentieth century contributed to the success of a revolutionary movement.

2. **Use this image and your knowledge of world history to answer all parts of the question that follows.**

"Day of the African Army and Colonial Troops," First World War Poster, 1914-1918 (color litho)/Charles Fouqueray (1872-1956)/MICHEL TOULET/Private Collection/Bridgeman Images

First World War poster: "Day of the African Army and Colonial Troops"

A. Describe ONE aspect of the image that supports the argument that the First World War was a truly global war.

B. Explain ONE historical process that explains why the First World War was very likely to become a global war rather than a local European conflict.

C. Explain ONE long-term effect of the development illustrated in the image.

3. **Use your knowledge of world history to answer all parts of the question that follows.**

A. Explain how ONE cause of the First World War was also a cause of the Second World War.

B. Explain ONE way the First and Second World Wars represent a change from previous conflicts and wars.

C. Explain ONE way the First or Second World War transformed global politics.

677

12

Milestones of the Past Century

A Changing Global Landscape, 1950–present

AP® Overview for Chapter 12

Chapter 12 corresponds to AP® Unit 8: Cold War and Decolonization, 1900–Present. It considers the major changes to the global landscape after the end of World War II, with the focus on twentieth-century communism and decolonization in the empires that were established in the nineteenth century. It views communism through the lens of the cold war and the end of communist policies at the close of the twentieth century, while also examining the process and effects of decolonization throughout this period. Such an approach to communism and decolonization fits well into the historical reasoning skills of Contextualization, Comparison, and Continuity and Change.

Chapter 12 Essential Activity

Students should be able to compare the revolutions and major political movements of the twentieth century, especially communism and decolonization. Graphic organizers are a useful tool for students to create and use for review throughout their study of world history. As students study the chapter on global communism and decolonization, you can ask them to complete the charts below for Communism in the Soviet Union, Communism in China, and Decolonization. Find reproducible blank charts and sample completed charts in **Handout 12.1: Charts for Global Communism and Decolonization in the Twentieth Century** in the Teacher's Resource Materials.

Communism in the Soviet Union

Event	Impetus for Change	Effects of Change	Remained Unchanged
Bolshevik Revolution			
Cold War			
Collapse of the Soviet Union			

Communism in China

Event	Impetus for Change	Effects of Change	Remained Unchanged
Civil War			
Mao's Regime			
Post 1976			

Decolonization

Event	Impetus for Change	Effects of Change	Remained Unchanged
Vietnam			
India			
Gold Coast (Ghana)			
Algeria			

When students have completed their charts, ask them to use the information to write a timed essay of 40 minutes answering one of the following prompts:

- In the period 1900–2001, various challenges to the existing political and social order led to military conflicts around the world. Develop an argument that evaluates the extent to which shifts in the global balance of power after World War II led to global or regional military conflicts.

- In the period 1900–2001, emerging anti-imperialist ideas led to the dissolution of empires around the world. Develop an argument that evaluates the extent to which anti-imperialist ideas led to the dissolution of empires or restructuring of states in this time period.

TRM Handout 12.1: Charts for Global Communism and Decolonization in the Twentieth Century

Differentiation

If you want to help students scaffold the skills needed to complete the Chapter 12 Essential Activity, consider following the "Must Do, Should Do, Strive For" model below:

- Must Do: Students must complete the Charts for Global Communism and Decolonization in the Twentieth Century.

- Should Do: Working on their own or with a partner, students should create an LEQ outline that answers one of the prompts from above.

- Strive For: Using the ideas they put together on their LEQ outlines, students should write a timed essay answering one of the prompts from above.

Chapter 12 Resources

TRM AP® Skills Workshop Activity Handout: Writing a DBQ: Causation Arguments

TRM Chapter 12 DBQ Activity Handout

TRM Chapter 12 Guided Reading

TRM Chapter 12 Lecture Presentation Slides

TRM Chapter 12 Outline

TRM Chapter 12 Suggested Responses to Questions

TRM Eric's Activity 12: Communism in World History

TRM Handout 12.1: Charts for Global Communism and Decolonization in the Twentieth Century

TRM Handout 12.2: Comparison Chart for Political and Economic Outcomes of World Wars

TRM Handout 12.3: OPTIC Chart for Soviet Invasion, Prague Photograph

TRM Handout 12.4: Chart for African and Asian Independence

TRM Handout 12.5: Chart for Ideologies of Nationalist Independence Movements

TRM Handout 12.6: Graphic Organizer for Postcolonial Latin America and Africa

TRM Handout 12.7: Comparison Chart for the Declines of the USSR and Great Britain

TRM Handout 12.8: Chart for Sources of Conflict in the Middle East

TRM Map 12A: The World

Pacing Guide

Below is a pacing guide for the AP® World History: Modern course beginning in ca. 1200 C.E. This pacing guide is based on a schedule with 120 sessions of 50 minutes each before the AP® Exam. It is meant as a place to start. If you have a different number of sessions before the exam, you can modify the pacing to suit your needs.

Day	Pages Assigned	AP® Topic	AP® Theme	Suggested Assignments	Coverage Notes
1	Read pages 679–683 to "Communism Chinese-Style"	8.1	GOV	Building AP® Skills: Making Connections: Continuity and Change on page 679 Building AP® Skills: Sourcing and Situation on page 680 Apply the Tip on page 683	This opening section is a good transition between the end of World War II and the major events of the second half of the twentieth century, such as the cold war and decolonization.
2	Read pages 683–687 from "Communism Chinese-Style" to "East versus West: A Global Divide and a Cold War"	8.4	ECN	Chapter 12 Essential Activity Teaching Idea: Incorporating Outside Resources on page 683 Building AP® Skills: Argumentation on page 684 Building AP® Skills: Claims and Evidence in Sources on page 686	It would be good to review the Chinese communist revolution from Chapter 11 with students as they start this section. If you want students to work on their comparison skills, have them compare the development of Chinese communism discussed here with the development of Russian communism from Chapter 11.

Day	Pages Assigned	AP® Topic	AP® Theme	Suggested Assignments	Coverage Notes
3	Read pages 687–690 from "East versus West: A Global Divide and a Cold War"	8.2 8.3	CDI GOV	Chapter 12 Essential Activity AP® Classroom: AP® Daily Videos on page 689 Exploring AP® Themes: ENV and GOV on page 688 Building AP® Skills: Argumentation on page 688	While the cold war dominated the second half of the twentieth century, students need to know that the conflict impacted more than just the United States and the Soviet Union. This chapter will help them gain a more global view of the conflict and see how decolonization was affected by it.
4	Read pages 691–694 to "The Cold War and the Superpowers"	8.2 8.3 8.4	CDI GOV SIO	Building AP® Skills: Developments and Processes on page 691 Teaching Idea: Incorporating Outside Resources on page 693	See above.
5	Read pages 694–696 from "The Cold War and the Superpowers" to "Toward Freedom: Struggles for Independence"	8.2 8.3	CDI GOV	Chapter 12 Essential Activity Building AP® Skills: Claims and Evidence in Sources on page 694 Building AP® Skills: Claims and Evidence in Sources on page 695	See above.
6	Read pages 696–697 from "Toward Freedom: Struggles for Independence"	8.5 8.7	CDI GOV	Chapter 12 Essential Activity Exploring AP® Themes: GOV on page 696 Apply the Tip on page 697	The collapse of empires in world history is not a new topic for students; however, the influence of nationalism, World War I, and World War II on twentieth-century decolonization does create differences in the collapse of contemporary empires compared with earlier empires. You can use this section to help students contextualize the collapse of empires in the twentieth century.
7	Read pages 698–702 to the second paragraph about the Indian National Congress	8.5 8.7	CDI GOV	Chapter 12 Essential Activity Building AP® Skills: Argumentation on page 700 Apply the Tip on page 701	Decolonization in the twentieth century is a vast topic. Students need to know that not all decolonization movements were the same and that former colonies experienced a wide variety of outcomes once they gained independence. If you have time, this would be a good topic to spend an extra day or two on.
8	Read pages 702–703 from the second paragraph about the Indian National Congress to the third paragraph on tactics	8.5 8.6 8.7	CDI GOV	Chapter 12 Essential Activity Apply the Tip on page 702	See above.
9	Read pages 703–704 from the third paragraph on tactics to "After Freedom"	8.5 8.7	CDI GOV	Chapter 12 Essential Activity Apply the Tip on page 704 AP® Classroom: AP® Exam Question on page 704	See above.
10	Read pages 704–706 from "After Freedom" to "The End of the Communist Era"	8.6 8.7	CDI GOV ECN	Chapter 12 Essential Activity Apply the Tip on page 705 Building AP® Skills: Making Connections: Causation on page 706	See above.

Day	Pages Assigned	AP® Topic	AP® Theme	Suggested Assignments	Coverage Notes
11	Read pages 706–711 from "The End of the Communist Era"	8.3 8.8	GOV	Chapter 12 Essential Activity Building AP® Skills: Contextualization on page 707 Apply the Tip on page 711 AP® Classroom: AP® Topic Question on page 711	This section teaches students the different responses of Soviet and Chinese leaders to the challenges faced by their states in the 1970s and 1980s, along with explaining how Chinese communism survived while Russian communism did not.
12	Read pages 712–716	8.3	GOV	Exploring AP® Themes: GOV on page 714 Building AP® Skills: Argumentation on page 716 Eric's Activity 12: Communism in World History on page 716	The final section of Chapter 12 helps students understand how the end of the cold war and what happened afterward affect global events in the twenty-first century. This could be a good place to have students practice contextualization and causation.

African Independence Achieved This poster depicts an Independence Day celebration in the new West African nation of Ghana in 1957. Its exuberance reflects the sense of great achievement that came with the defeat of colonial rule and the immense hopes for the future that independence raised. (© Look and Learn/Bridgeman Images)

678

CHAPTER 12

Milestones of the Past Century

A Changing Global Landscape

1950–present

◀ **AP**

CONTEXTUALIZATION
What major global shifts facilitated the independence movements of the mid- to late twentieth century?

CONNECTING PAST AND PRESENT

"What good is independence in the age of neocolonialism? Europe still plays the flute and our government dances. We owe billions to the World Bank and the International Monetary Fund. Western nonprofits arrive at a steady speed to improve our education and health care systems. Chinese interests have descended on our resources, taking away the livelihoods of many."[1] This was the view of Imbolo Mbue, a Cameroonian novelist writing in early 2020. She was describing the situation in her Central African country sixty years after its independence from colonial rule in 1960.

A rather different view of the six decades since independence comes from Omar Victor Diop, a photographer from Senegal in West Africa, also writing in 2020: "I have faith in our ability to forgive ourselves for not being where we thought we'd be, 60 years after 1960; building a nation and a functioning republic takes time. I have faith in our ability to see that we've done great things, staying together in peace being the greatest among them. . . . I will have the honor to witness the greatness of my hopeful, elegant and future-loving people."[2] ■

Despite their diverging opinions, both of these individuals experienced the end of European empires as an event of great personal significance even as it marked a dramatic change in the political landscape of the world in the second half of the twentieth century. But this epic transformation intersected with other profound changes during these years. A devastated Europe rebuilt its modern economy and moved toward greater union. Communism expanded its reach into Eastern Europe, China, Southeast Asia, and Cuba. A cold war between the United States and the Soviet Union, both of them armed with nuclear weapons of unprecedented destructive power, structured much of international life until the communist experiment largely collapsed at the end of the twentieth century. By the early twenty-first century, China had become a powerful and

679

BUILDING AP® SKILLS

Making Connections: Continuity and Change

Consider having students "preview" the major events of Chapter 12 and AP® Unit 8: Cold War and Decolonization by asking them to read the opening paragraph to the chapter on pages 679 and 680. After they have read it, ask: What dramatic changes to the political landscape did the world experience during the second half of the twentieth century? *Europe rebuilt its economy and moved toward greater union following World War II, while communism expanded its reach into new areas such as Eastern Europe, China, Southeast Asia, and Cuba. The United States and the Soviet Union "fought" a cold war that influenced international life and relations until the collapse of the Soviet Union at the end of the twentieth century. By the twenty-first century, China had become a powerful global player, while the Middle East became a center of conflict and instability.*

APPLY THE TIP

Students need to be able to compare the world wars of the early twentieth century and understand how their outcomes influenced future events. You can ask students to create a chart to compare the outcomes of World War I and World War II. When students have finished their charts, ask: What are some of the differences between the outcomes of World War I and World War II? Find a reproducible chart in the Teacher's Resource Materials.

TRM Handout 12.2: Comparison Chart for Political and Economic Outcomes of World Wars

APPLY THE TIP

Consider having a quick class discussion with students about conflicts in Europe and the significance of the European Union in the twentieth and twenty-first centuries. Ask students to list as many examples as they can of European conflict from Units 4, 5, and 6. *Answers may include the mercantilist policies during the early sixteenth-century colonization of the New World, the Seven Years' War, Napoleon's expansion and the Napoleonic Wars, the Crimean War, the revolutions of 1848, and the Berlin Conference.*

Then point out to students that European Union countries have not experienced a major intercontinental conflict since World War II because of the unity provided by the European Union. Students may be surprised to learn that the past seventy-seven years are the longest period of relative peace in European history.

AP°
CONTINUITY AND CHANGE
In what ways has the structure of global political life changed in the decades since the end of World War II?

AP° EXAM TIP
You need to know the differences between the political and economic outcomes of World War I and World War II.

AP° EXAM TIP
It's important to note that the European Union is a rare example in history of some measure of unity on the European continent.

AP°
CAUSATION
In the late twentieth century, how did the establishment of the EEC support economic recovery and growth in Europe?

prominent player in the global arena, challenging the dominance of the United States, while the Middle East emerged as a major exporter of oil and a center of conflict and instability. Few of these changes were apparent as World War II drew to a close in 1945. But taken together they have substantially transformed the world for billions of individuals over the past seventy-five years.

Recovering from the War

Finding the Main Point: What internal and external factors accounted for Europe's remarkable recovery after the devastation of World War II?

The tragedies that afflicted Europe in the first half of the twentieth century—fratricidal war, economic collapse, the Holocaust—were wholly self-inflicted, and yet that civilization had not permanently collapsed. In the twentieth century's second half, Europeans rebuilt their industrial economies and revived their democratic political systems. Three factors help to explain this astonishing recovery. One is the apparent resiliency of an industrial society, once it has been established. The knowledge, skills, and habits of mind that enabled industrial societies to operate effectively remained intact, even if the physical infrastructure had been substantially destroyed. Thus even the most terribly damaged countries—Germany, the Soviet Union, and Japan—had largely recovered by 1960, amid a worldwide economic boom during the 1950s.

A second factor lay in the ability of the major Western European countries to integrate their recovering economies, putting aside some of their prickly nationalism in return for enduring peace and common prosperity. That process took shape during the 1950s, giving rise to the **European Economic Community** (EEC), established in 1957, whose members reduced their tariffs and developed common trade policies. Over the next half century, the EEC expanded its membership to include almost all of Europe, including many former communist states. In 1993, the EEC was renamed the European Union (see Map 12.1), and in 2002 twelve of its members, later increased to twenty, adopted a common currency, the euro. All of this sustained Europe's remarkable economic recovery and expressed a larger European identity.

A third element of European recovery lay in the United States, which emerged after 1945 as the dominant center of Western civilization and a global superpower. An early indication of the United States' intention to exercise global leadership took shape in its effort to rebuild and reshape shattered European economies. Known as the **Marshall Plan**, that effort funneled into Europe some $12 billion (roughly $121 billion in 2017 dollars), together with numerous advisers and technicians. It was motivated by some combination of genuine humanitarian concern, a desire to prevent a new depression by creating overseas customers for American industrial goods, and an interest in undermining the growing appeal of European communist parties. This economic recovery plan, along with access to American

---

BUILDING AP° SKILLS

Sourcing and Situation

The cold war era offers a variety of political cartoons for students to practice document analysis and sourcing. This would be a good place to show students the political cartoon by Herb Block titled "It's the Same Thing without Mechanical Problems," which can be found in the "Tick-Tock" section of Herblock's History exhibit section of the Library of Congress website. Have them study the cartoon and then ask: What is the point of view and purpose of the author of the cartoon? *The purpose is to increase support for the Marshall Plan among Americans by*

depicting the Soviets as brutal tyrants. The piece has a sarcastic tone; the point of view is negative toward communism, while the author supports the rebuilding efforts of the United States.

Differentiation

If your students are struggling with sourcing documents, consider following the "Must Do, Should Do, Strive For" model below to build up students' skills:

■ Must Do: Students must explain the main message of the political cartoon

and the history surrounding the event it depicts.

■ Should Do: Students should work with a partner to identify the point of view and purpose of the cartoon, and then write a sourcing statement together. Have students share what they write with the rest of the class.

■ Strive For: For students who have mastered the sourcing skill, ask them to pick another of Herb Block's political cartoons from the Library of Congress exhibit and write a sourcing statement for it.

Landmarks for Chapter 12

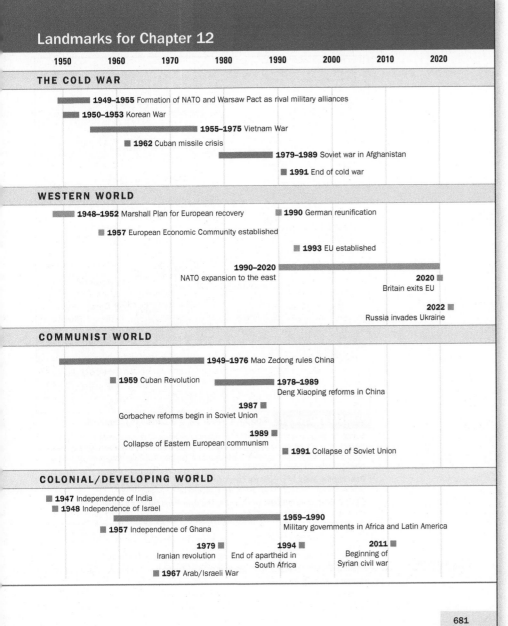

1950 1960 1970 1980 1990 2000 2010 2020

THE COLD WAR

1949–1955 Formation of NATO and Warsaw Pact as rival military alliances

1950–1953 Korean War

1955–1975 Vietnam War

1962 Cuban missile crisis

1979–1989 Soviet war in Afghanistan

1991 End of cold war

WESTERN WORLD

1948–1952 Marshall Plan for European recovery   **1990** German reunification

1957 European Economic Community established

1993 EU established

1990–2020
NATO expansion to the east

2020
Britain exits EU

2022
Russia invades Ukraine

COMMUNIST WORLD

1949–1976 Mao Zedong rules China

1959 Cuban Revolution   **1978–1989**
Deng Xiaoping reforms in China

1987
Gorbachev reforms begin in Soviet Union

1989
Collapse of Eastern European communism

1991 Collapse of Soviet Union

COLONIAL/DEVELOPING WORLD

1947 Independence of India
1948 Independence of Israel

1959–1990
Military governments in Africa and Latin America

1957 Independence of Ghana

1979
Iranian revolution   **1994**
End of apartheid in
South Africa   **2011**
Beginning of
Syrian civil war

1967 Arab/Israeli War

681

Making Connections: Causation

As part of a lesson on the positive and negative consequences of global political movements, you could ask students to study the events in "Landmarks for Chapter 12" and determine which events seem to indicate positive consequences and which seem to indicate negative consequences. (Answers are provided in italics.)

Positive
Increased political cooperation and political freedom events, such as:

- *1947: Independence of India*
- *1948–1952: Marshall Plan for European recovery*
- *1949: Formation of NATO*
- *1957: Independence of Ghana*
- *1957: European Economic Community established*
- *1978–1989: Deng Xiaoping reforms in China*
- *1987: Gorbachev reforms begin in Soviet Union*
- *1989: Collapse of Eastern European communism*
- *1990: German reunification*
- *1990–2020: NATO expansion to the east*
- *1991: Collapse of Soviet Union; End of cold war*
- *1993: EU established*
- *1994: End of apartheid in South Africa*

Negative
Increased political tension events, such as:

- *1949–1955: Formation of NATO and Warsaw Pact as rival military alliances*
- *1950–1953: Korean War*
- *1955–1975: Vietnam War*
- *1959: Cuban Revolution*
- *1959–1990: Military governments in Africa and Latin America*
- *1962: Cuban missile crisis*
- *1979: Revolution in Iran*
- *1979–1989: Soviet war in Afghanistan*
- *2011: Beginning of Syrian civil war*
- *2020: Britain exits EU*
- *2022: Russia invades Ukraine*

Making Connections: Causation

For a quick overview of the major events that pertain to communism and decolonization in the twentieth century, it could be helpful to ask students to work with a partner to research one event listed on "Landmarks for Chapter 12." Allow them 10–15 minutes to research and prepare a short report on that event. As students report on their event to their classmates, ask them to state what impact this event had on the global political landscape in the second half of the twentieth century. *Answers will vary.*

EXPLORING AP® THEMES

Governance (GOV)

It could be interesting to have students brainstorm some ideas for why certain states haven't been admitted to the European Union, using prior knowledge or logical thinking to develop their answers. Show students Map 12.1, "The Growth of European Integration." Then ask: What are some possible reasons that candidate countries have not yet been admitted to the European Union? *Reasons that candidate countries have not yet been admitted to the European Union include political and economic instability, their status as newly developed nations, or religious differences.*

MAPPING HISTORY   Map 12.1 **The Growth of European Integration**

During the second half of the twentieth century, Europeans gradually put aside their bitter rivalries and entered into various forms of economic cooperation with one another, although these efforts fell short of complete political union. This map illustrates the growth of what is now called the European Union (EU).

Reading the Map: Where did the European Union start, and into which regions did it expand? How would you describe the growth of the European Union through time?

AP **Making Connections:** Why might Russia have found the recent growth of the European Union threatening to its interests?

AP° EXAM TIP

NATO is an important example of a military alliance in the twentieth century.

markets, was successful beyond all expectations. Between 1948 and the early 1970s, Western European economies grew rapidly, generating a widespread prosperity and improving living standards.

Beyond economic assistance, the American commitment to Europe soon came to include political and military security against the distant possibility of renewed

German aggression and the more immediate communist threat from the Soviet Union. Thus was born the military and political alliance known as the North Atlantic Treaty Organization (NATO) in 1949. It committed the United States and its nuclear arsenal to the defense of Europe against the Soviet Union, and it firmly anchored West Germany within the Western alliance. It also allowed Western Europe to avoid heavy military expenditures.

A parallel process in Japan, which was under American occupation between 1945 and 1952, likewise revived that country's devastated but already industrialized economy. In the two decades following the occupation, Japan's economy grew remarkably, and the nation became an economic giant on the world stage. The democratic constitution imposed on Japan by American occupation authorities required that "land, sea, and air forces, as well as other war potential, will never be maintained." This meant that Japan, even more so than Europe, depended on the United States for its military security.

Recovery in the Soviet Union, so terribly damaged by the war, occurred under very different conditions from that of Japan and Western Europe. The last years of Stalin's rule (1945–1953) were extraordinarily harsh, with no tolerance for dissent of any kind. One result was a huge and growing convict labor force of 3 to 4 million people who provided a major source of cheap labor for the recovery effort. Furthermore, that program was a wholly state-planned effort that favored heavy industry, agricultural production, and military expenditure at the expense of basic consumer goods, such as shoes and clothing. But Stalin's regime did gain some popular support by substantially lowering the price of bread and other essentials. Finally, the Soviet Union benefited greatly from its seizure of industrial complexes, agricultural goods, raw materials, gold, and European art from Germany, Poland, and elsewhere. Viewed as looting or plunder in the West, this appropriation in Soviet eyes was seen as the "spoils of war" and was justified by the massive damage, both human and material, that the Nazi invasion had caused in the USSR. By the mid-1950s, economic recovery was well under way.

Communism Chinese-Style

> **Finding the Main Point:** What measures did Mao take to forge China's own version of communism?

While Europe, Japan, and the Soviet Union were emerging from the chaos of World War II, China was likewise recovering from decades of civil war and from its devastating struggle against Japanese imperialism. And it was doing so under the direction of the Chinese Communist Party and its leader **Mao Zedong**. In a longer-term perspective, China's revolution represented the real beginning of that country's emergence from a century of imperialist humiliation and semi-colonial rule, the development of a distinctive Chinese approach to modern development, and its return to a position of prominence on the global stage.

AP® EXAM TIP
Be sure to note the differing responses to the effects of World War II in different countries.

APPLY THE TIP

To help students practice their comparison skills, ask them to work in small groups (three to four students) to compare American-sponsored post–World War II rebuilding programs in Japan to those in Europe. *Answers should include: The Marshall Plan in Europe rebuilt the infrastructure of nations devastated by war, and the $2 billion given to Japan did the same. The United States took a larger role in political affairs in Japan than it did in Western Europe. Japan was forced to create a democratic constitution and could not have a large military; it thus had to rely on the United States for military security.*

Then ask: How did the recovery efforts in the Soviet Union after World War II differ from the efforts seen in Japan and Western Europe? *Answers should include: A state-planned effort for recovery emerged in the Soviet Union after the war that favored heavy industry, agricultural production, and military expenditure at the expense of basic consumer goods and that took place during the last years of Stalin's rule, which were incredibly harsh. The Soviet Union also benefited in its recovery efforts from its seizure of industrial complexes, agricultural goods, raw materials, gold, and European art from occupied areas.*

TEACHING IDEA

Incorporating Outside Resources

The episode *Communists, Nationalists, and China's Revolutions* of Crash Course World History could be a good review of the Chinese communist revolution and a preview of what happened to China during Mao's rule. In this episode, John Green discusses China's revolutions. While war consumed most of the rest of the world, China was changing the dynastic system that had ruled it for millennia. China's twentieth-century revolutions were extremely disruptive and lasted until after

World War II. Chairman Mao's various programs to purify the Communist Party and build up the new People's Republic of China had mixed results. The video can be found on YouTube. You can either assign the video as homework or show it in class and ask students the following questions:

■ Why did the Communists win out over the Nationalists, or Guomindang, in China? *The Guomindang failed to defeat the Japanese and had to rely on Communist help. The Communists exploited*

the problems of the Guomindang and gained control in 1949 as the Guomindang fled to the island of Taiwan.

■ What were the results of the Great Leap Forward? *The Great Leap Forward brought more suffering for the peasants, more deaths and famine, and no increase in industrial production.*

■ What were the results of the Cultural Revolution? *Millions of people were persecuted, and many historical and religious artifacts were destroyed.*

BUILDING AP® SKILLS

Claims and Evidence in Sources

As a part of teaching about the Great Leap Forward, consider showing students the propaganda poster on this page and have them read the caption for it. Then explain that this poster was created in 1960, after many disastrous effects of the Great Leap Forward were already being felt. Ask students to identify elements of the propaganda poster that reflect the reality of life under communism but that also remain optimistic about the goals of the Great Leap Forward. *The large figure of the male communist supporter with a steel beam is projecting strength, and the large figure of the female communist supporter with a bundle of wheat is projecting prosperity. The smaller figures in the foreground are all actively embracing the revolution. However, the caption also guides citizens to "practice thrift" because of a scarcity of resources.*

BUILDING AP® SKILLS

Argumentation

If you want to have your students practice writing SAQs, you could give them 14 minutes to respond to the prompts below:

A. Explain ONE way in which the construction of socialist societies <u>differed</u> between the Soviet Union in the 1920s and China in the 1950s and 1960s.

B. Explain ONE way in which the construction of socialist societies was <u>similar</u> between the Soviet Union in the 1920s and China in the 1950s and 1960s.

Answers can include the following points:

Differences in the Construction of Socialist Societies in the Soviet Union and China

▪ *Chinese revolutionaries had decades of government experience; the Soviets came to power without experience.*

▪ *The support for Chinese communism was very strong in the rural areas; support for the Soviets was strongest in urban areas.*

▪ *China had a larger, less literate population than the Soviet Union.*

▪ *China did not have the same industrial base or availability of agricultural land as the Soviets.*

AP®
COMPARISON
What was distinctive about the Chinese experience of communism compared to that of the Soviet Union?

▼ AP®
SOURCING AND SITUATION
How does the poster reflect China's approach to economic progress? How effective was this policy?

The Great Leap Forward This Chinese poster from 1960 celebrates both the agricultural and industrial efforts of the Great Leap Forward. The caption reads: "Start the movement to increase production and practice thrift, with foodstuffs and steel at the center, with great force!" The great famine that accompanied this "great leap" belied the optimistic outlook of the poster. (Stefan R. Landsberger Collections/International Institute of Social History, Amsterdam/www.chineseposters.net)

As a communist country, China began its task of "building socialism" in a very different international environment than its Soviet counterpart had experienced. In 1917 Russian Bolsheviks faced a hostile capitalist world alone, while Chinese communists, coming to power over thirty years later, had an established Soviet Union as a friendly northern neighbor and ally. Furthermore, Chinese revolutionaries had actually governed parts of their huge country for decades, gaining experience that the new Soviet rulers had altogether lacked, since they had come to power so quickly. And the Chinese communists were firmly rooted in the rural areas and among the country's vast peasant population, while their Russian counterparts had found their support mainly in the cities.

If these comparisons generally favored China in its efforts to "build socialism," in economic terms that country faced even more daunting prospects than did the Soviet Union. Its population was far greater, its industrial base far smaller, and the availability of new agricultural land far more limited than in the Soviet Union. China's literacy and modern education, as well as its transportation network, were likewise much less developed. Even more than the Soviets, Chinese communists had to build a modern society from the ground up.

Building a Modern Society

Initially China sought to follow the Soviet model of socialist modernization, though with important variations. In sharp contrast to the Soviet experience, the collectivization of agriculture in China during the 1950s was a generally peaceful process, owing much to the close relationship between the Chinese Communist Party and the peasantry that had been established during three decades of struggle. China, however, pushed collectivization even further than the Soviet Union did, particularly in huge "people's communes" in the late 1950s. It was an effort to mobilize China's enormous population for rapid development and at the same time to move toward a more fully communist society with an even greater degree of social equality and collective living. (See AP® Working with Evidence, Documents 1 and 3, pages 726 and 727.)

(continued)

▪ *The Soviet transportation network was far more developed than the Chinese transportation network.*

Similarities in the Construction of Socialist Societies in the Soviet Union and China

▪ *Both sought modernization and industrialization of underdeveloped societies.*

▪ *Both attacked long-standing inequalities of class and gender.*

▪ *Both promoted cultural values of selflessness and collectivism that could support a socialist society.*

▪ *Both fostered totalitarian governments that held control of politics, the economy, the arts, education, and the media.*

▪ *Both promoted mass organizations for women, workers, students, and various professional groups.*

China's industrialization program was also modeled on the earlier Soviet experience, with an emphasis on large-scale heavy industries, urban-based factories, centralized planning by state and party authorities, and the mobilization of women for the task of development. As in the Soviet Union, impressive economic growth followed, as did substantial migration to the cities and the emergence of a bureaucratic elite of planners, managers, scientists, and engineers (see Snapshot). And both countries favored urban over rural areas and privileged an educated, technically trained elite over workers and peasants. Stalin and his successors largely accepted these inequalities, while Mao certainly did not. Rather, he launched recurrent efforts

SNAPSHOT China under Mao, 1949–1976

The following table reveals some of the achievements, limitations, and tragedies of China's communist experience during the era of Mao Zedong.

Steel production	from 1.3 million to 23 million tons
Coal production	from 66 million to 448 million tons
Electric power generation	from 7 million to 133 billion kilowatt-hours
Fertilizer production	from 0.2 million to 28 million tons
Cement production	from 3 million to 49 million tons
Industrial workers	from 3 million to 50 million
Scientists and technicians	from 50,000 to 5 million
"Barefoot doctors" posted to countryside	1 million
Annual growth rate of industrial output	11 percent
Annual growth rate of agricultural output	2.3 percent
Total population	from 542 million to 1 billion
Average population growth rate per year	2 percent
Per capita consumption of rural dwellers	from 62 to 124 yuan annually
Per capita consumption of urban dwellers	from 148 to 324 yuan annually
Overall life expectancy	from 35 to 65 years
Counterrevolutionaries killed (1949–1952)	between 1 million and 3 million
People labeled "rightists" in 1957	550,000
Deaths from famine during Great Leap Forward	30 million to 45 million
Deaths during Cultural Revolution	500,000
Officials sent down to rural labor camps during Cultural Revolution	3 million or more
Urban youth sent down to countryside	17 million (1967–1976)

Source: Such figures are often highly controversial. See Maurice Meisner, *Mao's China and After* (New York: Free Press, 1999), 413–25; Roderick MacFarquhar, ed., *The Politics of China* (Cambridge: Cambridge University Press, 1997), 243–45.

◀ **AP**
CLAIMS AND EVIDENCE IN SOURCES
Based on this chart, in what areas did Mao's programs achieve the greatest success? What methods were used to maintain control of the nation?

AP® CLASSROOM

AP® Topic Questions

This would be a good point to assign the three AP® Topic Questions for "Li Zhisui Great Leap Forward MCQ" for stimulus-based multiple-choice question practice after students learn about the Great Leap Forward. You can find the questions in your AP® Classroom account under Topic 8.4. You can assign the questions as a bell ringer for students or as a quick check for understanding at the end of class.

BUILDING AP® SKILLS

Making Connections: Comparison

It can be helpful to let students work collaboratively to practice skills, as they can encourage one another and build on one another's ideas. Consider dividing students into groups of three to four and have each group work together to divide the events in "Snapshot: China under Mao, 1949–1976" into three lists: achievements, limitations, and tragedies under Mao. Let students know that some of the items could fit into two or more categories. After students have created their lists, ask them to compare the lists with their group and discuss which items overlap. After students have finished the comparison, have them write a one-paragraph response explaining why the items are overlapping. *Answers will vary.*

BUILDING AP® SKILLS

Claims and Evidence in Sources

China pushed collectivization even further than the Soviet Union did. This was an effort to mobilize China's enormous population for rapid agricultural development and social change. To help students understand how China's collectivization developed as well as the differences between the planned idea and the reality of what actually happened, ask them to analyze and discuss "AP® Working with Evidence, Document 3: Socialism in the Countryside" on pages 727–728. Use the questions on page 728 to guide a class discussion, or assign them to students as homework.

BUILDING AP® SKILLS

Claims and Evidence in Sources

As Chairman Mao tried to distance China from being a "copycat" of the Soviet Union, he also tried to keep the revolutionary spirit alive in China. Both the Great Leap Forward and the Cultural Revolution had disastrous effects on China's population. You can have students examine some of those effects by looking at the following two photo-essays on China for this activity:

■ Henri Cartier-Bresson's photo-essay "The Great Leap Forward, China, 1958," found on Life.com as "'Red China' In Color, 1958."

■ Li Zhensheng's photographs from the Cultural Revolution, found on the Lens Blog post "A Panoramic View of China's Cultural Revolution" on the *New York Times* website.

If time is short, choose two photographs from each photo-essay and use those for the activity. Consider using the Library of Congress's "Teacher's Guide for Analyzing Photographs and Prints," found on the Library of Congress Teachers Program website. Click "Getting Started with Primary Sources," then "Teacher's Guides and Analysis Tool," and locate the guide for Analyzing Photographs and Prints. As students are viewing the photo-essays, have them answer the following questions:

■ Who is the photographer? *Either Henri Cartier-Bresson or Li Zhensheng*

■ Describe what you see. What do you notice first? *Answers will vary depending on the photograph.*

■ What in the caption allows you to understand what is taking place in the photograph? *Answers will vary depending on the photograph.*

■ What about these photographs allows you to understand what takes place in communal life in China? *Answers should include: All of the people are working or making decisions together. Those that are not part of the group are viewed as "enemies" and punished.*

Differentiation

Another way to work with the photo-essays is to start with a "Think, Pair, Share" activity and work students up to a one-paragraph response using the "Must Do, Should Do, Strive For" model below:

■ Must Do: Students will be assigned one photo to analyze from one of the photo-essays. After they've analyzed it, they should share what they found with another student

to combat these perhaps inevitable tendencies of any industrializing process and to revive and preserve the revolutionary spirit that had animated the Communist Party during its long struggle for power.

By the mid-1950s, Mao and some of his followers had become persuaded that the Soviet model of industrialization was leading China away from socialism and toward new forms of inequality, toward individualistic and careerist values, and toward an urban bias that favored the cities at the expense of the countryside. The **Great Leap Forward** of 1958–1960 marked Mao's first response to these distortions of Chinese socialism. His plan called for simultaneous growth in both agriculture and industry. It promoted small-scale industrialization in the rural areas rather than focusing wholly on large enterprises in the cities; it tried to foster widespread and practical technological education for all rather than relying on a small elite of highly trained technical experts; and it envisaged an immediate transition to full communism in the "people's communes" rather than waiting for industrial development to provide the economic basis for that transition. Private property was abolished in the communes; collective living arrangements were established; and all services (such as education and health care) were provided by the commune. Citizens were even encouraged to create backyard furnaces for steel production. Ultimately, the Great Leap Forward failed, temporarily discrediting Mao's radicalism. Poor-quality steel and industrial goods undermined Mao's lofty goals. Administrative chaos, disruption of marketing networks, bad weather, and crop failures combined to produce a massive famine, the worst in human history according to some scholars, that killed some 30 million people or more between 1959 and 1962, dwarfing the earlier Soviet famine. The failure of the Great Leap Forward caused Mao to step down from his role as head of state, but he remained party chairman.

Nonetheless, in the mid-1960s, Mao launched yet another campaign—the Great Proletarian **Cultural Revolution**—to combat the capitalist tendencies that he believed had penetrated even the highest ranks of the Communist Party itself. The Cultural Revolution also involved new efforts to bring health care and education to the countryside and to reinvigorate earlier attempts at rural industrialization under local rather than central control. In these ways, Mao struggled, though without great success, to overcome the inequalities associated with China's modern development and to create a model of socialist modernity quite distinct from that of the Soviet Union. (See AP® Working with Evidence: Mao's China, pages 726–731, for more on China's Cultural Revolution.)

Confronting Enemies

China under Mao, like the Soviet Union under Stalin, found itself caught up in a gigantic search for enemies beginning in the 1950s. In the Soviet Union, that process occurred under the clear control of state authorities. In China, however, it became much more public, escaping the control of the leadership, particularly during the most intense phase of the Cultural Revolution (1966–1969). Convinced that many within the Communist Party had been seduced by capitalist values of self-seeking and materialism, Mao called for rebellion against the Communist Party itself. He

---

(continued)

in a "Think, Pair, Share" activity. Have students repeat the process until they've learned about at least five photos.

■ Should Do: Students should use what they learned from the "Think, Pair, Share" of the photos to participate in a class discussion on this question: What about these photographs allows you to understand what takes place in communal life in China?

■ Strive For: Students can write a response to the following prompt to demonstrate what they have learned from their reading homework, the photo-essays, and class discussion:

   ■ Which program do you feel had more severe consequences for China: the Great Leap Forward or the Cultural Revolution? Provide specific, accurate evidence to back up your opinion.

purged the party leadership of skeptical officials, replacing them with people who sided with Mao's radical program. Millions of young people responded to the call for revolution, and, organized as Red Guards, they set out to rid China of those who were "taking the capitalist road." Following gigantic and ecstatic rallies in Beijing, they fanned out across the country and attacked local party and government officials, teachers, intellectuals, factory managers, and others they defined as enemies. Many were "sent down" to the countryside for hard physical labor and to "learn from the peasants." Others were humiliated, beaten, and sometimes killed. (See AP® Working with Evidence, Document 7, page 730.) Rival revolutionary groups soon began fighting with one another, violence erupted throughout the country, and civil war threatened China. Mao was forced to call in the military to restore order and Communist Party control. Both Stalin's Terror and the Chinese Cultural Revolution badly discredited the very idea of revolutionary socialism and contributed to the ultimate collapse of the communist experiment at the end of the century.

East versus West: A Global Divide and a Cold War

Finding the Main Point: In what ways did the ideological struggle between the United States and the Soviet Union manifest itself across the globe in the decades after the Second World War?

Not only did communist regimes bring revolutionary changes to the societies they governed, but their very existence launched a global conflict that restructured international life and touched the lives of almost everyone, particularly in the twentieth century's second half. That rift had begun soon after the Russian Revolution when the new communist government became a source of fear and loathing to many in the Western capitalist world. The common threat of Nazi Germany temporarily made unlikely allies of the Soviet Union, Britain, and the United States, but a few years after World War II ended, that division erupted again in what became known as the **cold war**. Underlying that conflict were the geopolitical and ideological realities of the postwar world. The Soviet Union and the United States were now the world's major political and military powers, replacing the shattered and diminished states of Western Europe, but they represented sharply opposed views of history, society, politics, and international relations. In retrospect, conflict seemed almost inevitable, as both sides felt they were riding the tides of historical progress.

Military Conflict and the Cold War

The initial arena of the cold war was Eastern Europe, where Soviet insistence on security and control clashed with American and British desires for open and democratic societies with ties to the capitalist world economy. What resulted were rival military alliances. The **North Atlantic Treaty Organization (NATO)**, created in 1949, brought the United States and various West European countries together

AP®
COMPARISON
In what different ways was the cold war expressed and experienced?

BUILDING AP® SKILLS
Claims and Evidence in Sources

Both the Soviet Union and China used propaganda to gain support and weed out their perceived "enemies." You can help students better understand how China used the Cultural Revolution to weed out its perceived "enemies" by asking them to analyze and discuss "AP® Working with Evidence, Document 5: A Vision of the New China," on page 729, along with "AP® Working with Evidence, Document 7: Experiencing the Cultural Revolution," on pages 730–731. Use the questions on pages 729 and 731 to guide a class discussion on the different experiences people had during the Cultural Revolution.

TEACHING IDEA
Class Discussion

Students are typically fascinated with Joseph Stalin and his rule of the USSR. If you have the time, this would be a good time to supplement information about Stalin and his leadership of the Soviet Union. Have students start by reading the biography of Stalin that can be found on History.com. Then talk to them about how, to Russians, Stalin has a mixed legacy. To see the differences, have students read the 2006 article "Why Russia Still Loves Stalin" by Nina L. Khrushcheva, which can be found on the *Washington Post* website. These readings will help students understand that historical figures are multifaceted. You can assign the readings as homework or have students read them in class.

This is also an excellent chance to practice using appropriate, factual historical evidence in an essay as well as to practice writing point of view (POV) statements for the DBQ. After reading the two selections, ask students to respond to the following question:

■ Do you feel that Stalin was good or bad for the Soviet Union? Why do you think that Stalin has such a mixed legacy? Defend your answer with evidence from the articles. *Answers will vary.*

TEACHING IDEA
Bell Ringer

A good way to wrap up Chinese communism and connect it with what students learned in Chapter 11 is to ask students to write a thesis statement for the following prompt:

■ Evaluate the extent to which communism in the USSR and communism in China differed from 1900 to the present.

Thesis statements can include the following elements:

■ **Similarities**

■ *Both countries went through revolutions to raise communism up in their state.*

■ *Both countries replaced existing governments with a communist government.*

■ **Differences**

■ *The USSR's communism focused on the working class (proletariat).*

■ *China's communism focused on the peasants in the countryside.*

EXPLORING AP® THEMES

Humans and the Environment (ENV) and Governance (GOV)

Students need to understand the divisions of the cold war era. Give students a blank outline map of the world and have them label Canada, the United States, Mexico, South America, Africa, the United Kingdom, Portugal, Spain, Turkey, the Soviet Union, Finland, Iraq, Iran, Pakistan, India, China, North Korea, South Korea, and Taiwan. After students finish labeling their map, ask them to identify NATO countries by shading them blue, Warsaw Pact countries by shading them red, and the other communist countries by shading them green. Have students identify the cold war crisis areas with a star. As they identify the cold war crisis areas, have them annotate the map with the dates the crisis occurred. For a blank world map that you can use with this activity, download **Map 12A: The World** from the Teacher's Resource Materials.

TRM Map 12A: The World

BUILDING AP® SKILLS

Argumentation

You can extend student analysis of Map 12.2, "The Global Cold War," by asking them to use the map to identify the two continents that contain the greatest number of neutral countries. Then have students either write a response to the following question or discuss it as a class: Does the fact that [insert continents students chose] had the most neutral countries mean that the cold war did not affect them? If not, why not? *South America and Africa appear neutral on the map, which did not mean that the cold war did not affect them. The United States and the USSR tried to gain influence within the different countries so they could gain access to the natural wealth there. Countries such as South Africa were closely aligned with the United States, whereas countries such as Ethiopia were closely aligned with the USSR. Other countries, such as Chile and Egypt, changed sides either as a diplomatic strategy or as the result of a change in leadership. Still other nations, such as Angola or Mozambique, were torn by brutal civil wars in which one side aligned with the United States and the other with the USSR.*

Map 12.2 The Global Cold War

The cold war witnessed a sharp division between the communist world and the Western democratic world. It also divided the continent of Europe; the countries of China, Korea, Vietnam, and Germany; and the city of Berlin. In many places, it also sparked crises that brought the nuclear-armed superpowers of the United States and the USSR to the brink of war, although in every case they managed to avoid direct military conflict between themselves. Many countries in Africa and Asia claimed membership in a Non-Aligned Movement that sought to avoid entanglements in cold war conflicts.

 AP®

CONTEXTUALIZATION
Identify the continents that contained the greatest number of neutral countries. What effects did the cold war have on these regions?

to defend themselves against the threat of Soviet aggression. Then in 1955 the **Warsaw Pact** joined the Soviet Union and East European communist countries in an alliance intended to provide a counterweight to NATO and to prevent Western influence in the communist bloc. These alliances created a largely voluntary American

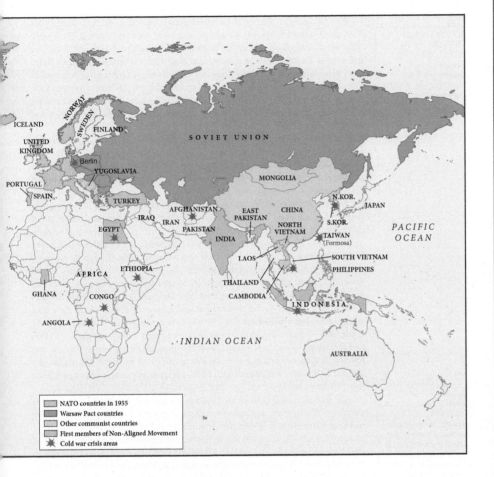

NATO countries in 1955
Warsaw Pact countries
Other communist countries
First members of Non-Aligned Movement
Cold war crisis areas

sphere of influence in Western Europe and an imposed Soviet sphere in Eastern Europe. The heavily fortified border between Eastern and Western Europe came to be known as the Iron Curtain. Thus Europe was bitterly divided. But although tensions flared across this dividing line, particularly in Berlin, no shooting war occurred between the two sides (see Map 12.2).

CHAPTER 12

EXPLORING AP® THEMES
Governance (GOV)

You can have students practice their map analysis skills by showing them Map 12.2, "The Global Cold War," and having them use what they see to answer the following questions:

■ Which NATO members and U.S. allies directly bordered communist states? *West Germany, Turkey, Greece, Iran, Pakistan, Thailand, South Vietnam, and South Korea.*

■ What potential issues might arise from these countries' being bordered by a communist state? *Communism could spread, leading to conflicts in those areas.*

AP® CLASSROOM
AP® Daily Videos

Both AP® Daily Videos for Topic 8.2: The Cold War can offer students an overview of the causes and effects of the cold war, along with helping students practice sourcing primary documents. Consider assigning these videos as homework or watch them in class to "preteach" the cold war. You can find the two videos for Topic 8.2 by logging into AP® Classroom, clicking on Unit 8 under Classroom Resources, and then selecting Daily Videos.

EXPLORING AP® THEMES

Governance (GOV)

Students need to understand that while the cold war never resulted in direct fighting between the United States and the Soviet Union, "proxy wars" (conflicts between two nations where neither directly fights the other; the "wars" take place between surrogate countries) were an important part of tensions in the cold war. It can be helpful to students to ask them to read the three paragraphs on this page and list examples of heightened tensions. *The Korean War, the Cuban missile crisis, Soviet intervention in Afghanistan, American involvement in Vietnam.*

BUILDING AP® SKILLS

Sourcing and Situation

You can show students the political cartoon of Kennedy and Khrushchev arm-wrestling as a wrap-up to them reading about the Cuban missile crisis. The political cartoon can be found on the "Teaching the Cuban Missile Crisis" entry on the Teaching History site. Ask students if they can guess the nationality of the artist who drew the cartoon. Most students will probably answer "American." However, a British artist drew the cartoon, and it was first published on October 29, 1963, one day after Khrushchev announced that he was withdrawing the missiles from Cuba. After telling students about the context of the cartoon, ask: What is significant about the fact that this cartoon was drawn by a British artist? *The cartoon is an example of how the events of the cold war affected the entire world.*

AP®
CONTINUITY AND CHANGE
In what different ways was the cold war experienced by the member states of NATO, the Warsaw Pact, and nonaligned nations?

AP®
CAUSATION
How did the differing ideologies of the United States and the Soviet Union impact global interactions in the late twentieth century?

By contrast, the extension of communism into Asia—China, Korea, and Vietnam—globalized the cold war and occasioned its most destructive and prolonged "hot wars," sometimes referred to as "proxy wars" because Soviet and American forces never directly fought one another. A North Korean invasion of South Korea in 1950 led to both Chinese and American involvement in a bitter three-year conflict (1950–1953), which ended in an essential standoff that left the Korean peninsula still divided in the early twenty-first century. Likewise in Vietnam, military efforts by South Vietnamese communists and the already communist North Vietnamese government to unify their country prompted massive American intervention in the 1960s. American authorities believed that a communist victory would open the door to further communist expansion in Asia and beyond. Armed and supported by the Soviets and Chinese and willing to endure enormous losses, the Vietnamese communists bested the Americans, who were hobbled by growing protest at home. The Vietnamese united their country under communist control by 1975.

A third major military conflict of the cold war era occurred in Afghanistan, where a Marxist party had taken power in 1978. Soviet leaders were delighted at this extension of communism on their southern border, but radical land reforms and efforts to liberate Afghan women soon alienated much of this conservative Muslim country and led to a mounting opposition movement. Fearing the overthrow of a new communist state and its replacement by Islamic radicals, Soviet forces intervened militarily and were soon bogged down in a war they could not win. The Afghan Mujahideen (Arabic for "the strugglers") used guerrilla-style tactics against Soviet troops and received financial aid and supplies from the American government. For a full decade (1979–1989), that war was a "bleeding wound." Under widespread international pressure, Soviet forces finally withdrew in 1989, and the Afghan communist regime soon collapsed, creating a power vacuum that resulted in civil war and the eventual rise to power of extremist groups like the Taliban. In Vietnam and Afghanistan, both superpowers painfully experienced the limits of their power.

The most haunting battle of the cold war era was one that never happened. The setting was Cuba, where a communist regime under the leadership of Fidel Castro had emerged by the early 1960s. (See Zooming In: Fidel Castro and the Cuban Revolution.) Intense American hostility to this nearby outpost of communism prompted the Soviet leader Nikita Khrushchev (KROOSH-chef), who had risen to power after Stalin's death in 1953, to secretly deploy nuclear-tipped Soviet missiles to Cuba, believing that this would deter further U.S. action against Castro. When the missiles were discovered in October 1962, the world held its breath for thirteen days as American forces blockaded the island and prepared for an invasion. A nuclear exchange between the superpowers seemed imminent, but that catastrophe was averted by a compromise between Khrushchev and U.S. president John F. Kennedy. Under its terms, the Soviets removed their missiles from Cuba in return for an American promise not to invade the island. That promise was kept and a communist regime persisted in Cuba, though much changed, well into the twenty-first century.

Nuclear Standoff and Rivalry in the Developing World

The **Cuban missile crisis** gave concrete expression to the most novel and dangerous dimension of the cold war—the arms race in nuclear weapons. An initial American monopoly on those weapons prompted the Soviet Union to redouble its efforts to acquire them, and in 1949 it succeeded. Over the next forty years, the world moved from a mere handful of nuclear weapons to a global arsenal of close to 60,000 warheads. Delivery systems included submarines, bomber aircraft, and missiles that could rapidly propel numerous warheads across whole continents and oceans with accuracies measured in hundreds of feet. During those decades, the entire world lived in the shadow of weapons whose destructive power is scarcely within the bounds of human imagination.

Awareness of this power is surely the primary reason that no shooting war of any kind occurred between the two superpowers, for leaders on both sides knew beyond any doubt that a nuclear war would produce only losers and utter catastrophe. Already in 1949, Stalin had observed that "atomic weapons can hardly be used

AP® EXAM TIP

Cold war tensions around the globe are an important subject in the AP® course.

◄ AP®

CAUSATION

How might the widespread development of nuclear weapons have prevented direct conflict between the United States and Soviet Union in the cold war era?

The Hydrogen Bomb During the 1950s and early 1960s, tests in the atmosphere of ever larger and more sophisticated hydrogen bombs made images of enormous fireballs and mushroom-shaped clouds the universal symbol of these weapons, which were immensely more powerful than the atomic bombs dropped on Japan. The American test pictured here took place in 1957. (Photo courtesy of National Nuclear Security Administration/Nevada Site Office)

BUILDING AP® SKILLS

Developments and Processes

Consider using the picture "The Hydrogen Bomb" and the accompanying caption to start a class discussion on the impact of the threat of atomic weapons on the world. After students have studied the picture and read the caption, ask: Why did the world become so frightened of the effects of atomic weapons? *The destructive power of atomic weapons had the potential to inflict more damage to life and the environment than any previous weapon. People feared that power struggles between the United States and the Soviets would lead to the use of these weapons and destroy the planet.*

TEACHING IDEA

Incorporating Outside Resources

Students might be interested in the short film *Duck and Cover*, the civil defense training on what to do during a nuclear attack, and what it tells them about nuclear fears during the cold war. You could show students the original TV advertisement for the film as a follow-up to your discussion of the Building AP® Skills: Developments and Processes question in the activity above. You can find the original TV advertisement for *Duck and Cover* on YouTube.

BUILDING AP® SKILLS

Sourcing and Situation

To help students continue to prepare for the different skills needed to write a DBQ essay, ask them to read the statement from Anastas Mikoyan in the first two sentences of "Zooming In: Fidel Castro and the Cuban Revolution." Then ask them to create a point of view (POV) statement for Mikoyan's comment. *Answers should include the idea of Mikoyan's feelings of triumph and elation regarding the success of the revolution.*

ZOOMING IN   Fidel Castro and the Cuban Revolution

"You Americans must realize what Cuba means to us old Bolsheviks," declared a high-ranking Soviet official, Anastas Mikoyan, in 1960. "We have been waiting all our lives for a country to go communist without the Red Army. It has happened in Cuba, and it makes us feel like boys again."[3] The triumph of the Cuban revolutionaries must have been exhilarating for communists everywhere because it occurred in such an unlikely place. Located just ninety miles from Florida, Cuba had been a virtual protectorate of the United States in the decades following its independence from Spain in 1902. Moreover, U.S. companies had long exerted considerable influence over the weak and corrupt Cuban government and dominated key sectors of the economy, including sugar, the island's most important export. Nonetheless, Fidel Castro, son of a wealthy sugar plantation owner, led a successful popular insurrection that transformed Cuba into a Marxist socialist state just off the southern coast of the United States.

The armed revolt began disastrously. In 1953, the Cuban army defeated Castro and 123 of his supporters when they attacked two army barracks in what was

Fidel Castro fighting in the mountains of Cuba in 1957.

their first major military operation. Castro himself was captured, sentenced to jail, and then released into exile. However, fortunes shifted in 1956, when Castro slipped back into Cuba and succeeded in bringing together many opponents of the current regime in an armed nationalist insurgency dedicated to radical economic and social reform. Upon seizing power in 1959, Castro and his government acted decisively to implement their revolutionary agenda. Within a year, they had effectively redistributed 15 percent of the nation's wealth by granting land to the poor, increasing wages, and lowering rents. In the following year, the new government nationalized the property of both wealthy Cubans and U.S. corporations. Many Cubans, particularly among the elite, fled into exile. "The revolution," declared Castro, "is the dictatorship of the exploited against the exploiters."[4]

Economic and political pressure from the United States followed, culminating in the Bay of Pigs, a failed invasion of the island in 1961 by Cuban exiles with covert

photo: Peter Newark American Pictures/Bridgeman Images

without spelling the end of the world."[5] Particularly after the frightening Cuban missile crisis of 1962, both sides carefully avoided further nuclear provocation, even while continuing to build up their respective arsenals. Moreover, because they feared that a conventional war would escalate to the nuclear level, they implicitly agreed to sidestep any direct military confrontation at all.

Still, opportunities for conflict abounded as the U.S.–Soviet rivalry spanned the globe. Using military and economic aid, educational opportunities, political pressure, and covert action, both sides courted countries emerging from colonial rule. The Soviet Union aided anticolonial and revolutionary movements in many support from the U.S. government. American hostility pushed the revolutionary nationalist Castro closer to the Soviet Union, and gradually he began to think of himself and his revolution as Marxist. In response to Cuban pleas for support against American aggression, the Soviet premier Khrushchev deployed nuclear missiles on the island, sparking the Cuban missile crisis. While the compromise reached between the two superpowers resulted in the withdrawal of the missiles, it did include assurances from the United States that it would not attack Cuba.

In the decades that followed, Cuba sought to export its brand of revolution beyond its borders, especially in Latin America and Africa. Che Guevara, an Argentine who had fought in the Cuban Revolution, declared, "Our revolution is endangering all American possessions in Latin America. We are telling these countries to make their own revolution."[6] Cuba supported revolutionary movements in many regions; however, none succeeded in creating a lasting Cuban-style regime.

The legacy of the Cuban Revolution has been mixed. The new government devoted considerable resources to improving health and education on the island. By the mid-1980s, Cuba possessed both the highest literacy rate and the lowest infant mortality rate in Latin America. Over the same period, life expectancy increased from fifty-eight to seventy-three years, putting Cuba on a par with the United States. Living standards for most improved as well. Indeed, Cuba became a model for development in other Latin American countries.

However, earlier promises to establish a truly democratic system never materialized. Castro declared in 1959 that elections were unneeded because "this democracy . . . has found its expression, directly, in the intimate union and identification of the government with the people."[7] The state placed limits on free expression and arrested opponents or forced them into exile. Cuba has also failed to achieve the economic development originally envisioned at the time of the revolution. Sugar remains its chief export crop, and by the 1980s Cuba had become almost as economically dependent on the Soviet Union as it had been upon the United States. Desperate consequences followed when the Cuban economy shrank by a third following the collapse of the Soviet Union.

Like communist experiments in the Soviet Union and China, Cuba experienced real improvements in living standards, especially for the poor, but these gains were accompanied by sharp restraints on personal freedoms and mixed results in the economy. Such have been the ambivalent outcomes of many revolutionary upheavals.

QUESTIONS

Compare the Cuban Revolution to those in Russia and China. What are the similarities and differences? How might you assess the successes and failures of the Cuban Revolution?

---

places, including South Africa, Mozambique, Vietnam, and Cuba. Cold war fears of communist penetration prompted U.S. intervention, sometimes openly and often secretly, in Iran, the Philippines, Guatemala, El Salvador, Chile, the Congo, and elsewhere. In the process the United States frequently supported anticommunist but corrupt and authoritarian regimes. However, neither superpower was able to completely dominate its supposed allies, many of whom resisted the role of pawns in superpower rivalries. Some countries, such as India, Indonesia, Ghana, and Egypt, took a posture of nonalignment in the cold war. And when circumstances allowed, countries sometimes tried to play off the superpowers against each other. Indonesia

BUILDING AP® SKILLS

Making Connections: Causation

You could ask students to list the positive and negative results of the Cuban Revolution after reading "Zooming In: Fidel Castro and the Cuban Revolution." This will help them practice their Causation skill, which is the recommended reasoning skill for AP® Unit 8. (Answers are provided in italics.)

■ **Positive:** *The literacy rate rose to the highest in Latin America, and health care improved so that by the 1980s Cuba had the lowest infant mortality rate in Latin America and life expectancy increased from fifty-eight to seventy-three years. Living standards initially improved for the poor.*

■ **Negative:** *Promises for democracy never materialized, economic growth has stagnated, living conditions remain poor compared to most of the developed world, free expression is limited, other personal freedoms are restricted, and economic dependency on the Soviet Union caused great hardship when the Soviet Union collapsed.*

After students have created their lists, have them discuss the following question as a class: Was the revolution more positive or negative in its impacts on the Cuban people? *Answers will vary.*

TEACHING IDEA

Incorporating Outside Resources

Students should understand that the cold war impacted decolonization movements in the twentieth century with the actions taken by the United States and the USSR. Consider showing students the OER Project videos *Decolonization and the Cold War: Through a Caribbean Lens* and *Decolonization and the Cold War: Through an Asian Lens* to help them see how this interaction happened. You can find the videos on the OER Project's World History: AP® Curriculum in Unit 8, Topic 8.1: The Cold War and Decolonization. If you choose to have students watch the videos in class, have them pause at the key ideas and discuss the questions as a class or in small groups.

BUILDING AP® SKILLS

Claims and Evidence in Sources

Students may find the May 15, 1950, cover of *Time* magazine an interesting representation of the United States' influence in the world during the twentieth century, and showing it to them could be a good way to start class while teaching the cold war. The cover shows a globe drinking from a Coke bottle. The cover can be found by going to "The TIME Vault" section of the Time website and selecting 1950 in the "Browse by Year" dropdown. Show students the cover and then ask them to describe what they think the message of the cover is. *American culture became very popular after World War II: music, movies, food, and even slang terms spread rapidly. The globe drinking from the Coke bottle represents the global popularity of American culture and the influence of the American economy on the world.*

EXPLORING AP® THEMES

Governance (GOV)

During the cold war, many Americans believed that all communist states were allies of the Soviet Union and were under Soviet control, but that was not always the case. Students may also have that misconception, so you can help challenge it by having students read through "The Cold War and the Superpowers" and write down examples of divides in the communist world during the second half of the twentieth century. (Answers provided in italics.)

■ *Following Stalin's death, the Soviet leadership in the mid-1950s revealed Stalin's many crimes, which shocked faithful communists around the world.*

■ *Reform movements in Hungary, Czechoslovakia, and Poland led protests against highly repressive and Soviet-dominated communist governments.*

■ *Yugoslav leaders rejected Soviet domination of their state's affairs early on and created their own independent road to socialism.*

■ *The Sino-Soviet split developed because of territorial disputes, ideological differences, and rivalry for communist leadership between China and the Soviet Union.*

received large amounts of Soviet and Eastern European aid, but that did not prevent it from destroying the Indonesian Communist Party in 1965, killing half a million suspected communists in the process. When the Americans refused to assist Egypt in building the Aswan Dam in the mid-1950s, that country developed a close relationship with the Soviet Union. Later, in 1972, Egypt expelled 21,000 Soviet advisers, following disagreements over the extent of Soviet military aid, and again aligned more clearly with the United States.

The Cold War and the Superpowers

World War II and the cold war provided the context for the emergence of the United States as a global superpower. Much of that effort was driven by the perceived demands of the cold war, during which the United States spearheaded the Western effort to contain a worldwide communist movement that seemed to be advancing. By 1970, one writer observed, "the United States had more than 1,000,000 soldiers in 30 countries, was a member of four regional defense alliances and an active participant in a fifth, had mutual defense treaties with 42 nations, was a member of 53 international organizations, and was furnishing military or economic aid to nearly 100 nations across the face of the globe."[8] Sustaining this immense international effort was a flourishing U.S. economy and an increasingly middle-class society. The United States was the only major industrial country to escape the physical devastation of war on its own soil. As World War II ended with Europe, the Soviet Union, and Japan in ruins, the United States was clearly the world's most productive economy.

On the communist side, the cold war was accompanied by considerable turmoil within and among the various communist states. In the Soviet Union, the superpower of the communist world, the mid-1950s witnessed devastating revelations of Stalin's many crimes, shocking the communist faithful everywhere. And in Hungary (1956–1957), Czechoslovakia (1968), and Poland (early 1980s), various reform movements registered sharp protest against highly repressive and Soviet-dominated communist governments.

Many in the West had initially viewed world communism as a monolithic force whose disciplined members meekly followed Soviet dictates in cold war solidarity against the West. And Marxists everywhere contended that revolutionary socialism would erode national loyalties as the "workers of the world" united in common opposition to global capitalism. Nonetheless, the communist world experienced far more bitter and divisive conflict than did the Western alliance, which was composed of supposedly warlike, greedy, and highly competitive nations.

In Eastern Europe, Yugoslav leaders early on had rejected Soviet domination of their internal affairs and charted their own independent road to socialism. Fearing that reform might lead to contagious defections from the communist bloc, Soviet forces actually invaded their supposed allies in Hungary and Czechoslovakia to crush such movements, and they threatened to do so in Poland. Such actions gave

AP®
CAUSATION
What factors enabled the rise of the United States as a global superpower?

AP®
DEVELOPMENTS AND PROCESSES
What divisions surfaced within the communist world during the cold war years?

▶ **AP**
DEVELOPMENTS AND PROCESSES
What does the image tell us about growing factions within the communist world?

Soviet Invasion, Prague In the 1950s and 1960s, the Soviet Union sent troops into supposedly allied countries in Eastern Europe to crush nascent reform movements. In this image from 1968, protesters in Prague, Czechoslovakia, swarm around and on top of Russian military equipment in a doomed effort to oppose a Russian crackdown. (AP Photo/Libor Hajsky/CTK)

APPLY THE TIP
If you had students create a list of divides in the communist world on page 694, this could be a good place to pause and draw their attention to the Sino-Soviet split. The History Matters channel on YouTube has a good short video on the Sino-Soviet split that you can show to students. Find the video by searching for *The Sino Soviet Split: Explained* on YouTube. After they watch the video, ask: How were the Soviet Union and communist China opposed to each other, despite their early alliance? *Answers may include: The two communist powers were divided by issues such as territorial disputes, ideological differences, and rivalry for communist leadership in the world; Both states developed atomic bombs and threatened nuclear strikes on each other.*

credibility to Western perceptions of the cold war as a struggle between tyranny and freedom and badly tarnished the image of Soviet communism as an attractive alternative to capitalism.

Even more startling, the two communist giants, the Soviet Union and China, found themselves sharply opposed, owing to territorial disputes, ideological differences, and rivalry for communist leadership. In 1960, the Soviet Union backed away from an earlier promise to provide China with the prototype of an atomic bomb and abruptly withdrew all Soviet advisers and technicians who had been assisting Chinese development. By the late 1960s, China on its own had developed a modest nuclear capability, and the two countries were at the brink of war, with the Soviet Union hinting at a possible nuclear strike on Chinese military targets. Beyond this central conflict, communist China in fact went to war against communist Vietnam in 1979, even as Vietnam invaded communist Cambodia. Nationalism, in short, proved more powerful than communist solidarity, even in the face of cold war hostilities with the capitalist West.

Despite its many internal conflicts, world communism remained a powerful global presence during the 1970s, achieving its greatest territorial reach. China was emerging from the chaos of the Cultural Revolution, while the Soviet Union

AP **EXAM TIP**
Be sure to note examples of differences among communist nations.

BUILDING AP® SKILLS

Claims and Evidence in Sources

Students will benefit from frequent image analysis practice, especially to help them prepare for the SAQ and the DBQ. Consider having them complete an OPTIC chart for the photograph of the Soviet invasion of Czechoslovakia on this page to work on image analysis. A reproducible version of this chart can be found in the Teacher's Resource Materials. (Answers are provided in italics.)

Overview	*A photograph of Czech protesters during the Prague Spring in 1968.*
Parts	*There are Soviet tanks and possibly Soviet soldiers surrounded by Czech protesters. The protesters are dressed in "everyday" clothes, showing that they aren't part of the military, and are carrying the Czech flag. Some protesters are standing on a Soviet military vehicle.*
Title	*The photograph doesn't have an official title but could be called "Protest of the Soviet Invasion of Czechoslovakia."*
Interrelationships	*The Czech protesters on top of the military vehicle are carrying the Czech flag, emphasizing their desire to keep Czechoslovakia independent of the Soviet Union. The protesters throughout the photo appear to be peaceful, and the Soviet soldiers don't seem to feel very threatened by them based on their body language. It could also be that the Soviet soldiers are waiting for orders and don't feel the need to engage with the Czech protesters.*
Conclusion	*This photograph demonstrates how Eastern European states tried to resist Soviet influence, especially through popular protests, even if the efforts did not succeed. It could have been created as propaganda to draw more Czech people into the protest against the Soviet invasion.*

TRM **Handout 12.3: OPTIC Chart for Soviet Invasion, Prague Photograph**

had matched U.S. military might. Despite American hostility, Cuba remained a communist outpost in the Western Hemisphere, with impressive achievements in education and health care for its people and a commitment to supporting revolutionary movements in Africa and Latin America. Communism triumphed in Vietnam, dealing a major setback to the United States. A number of African countries also affirmed their commitment to Marxism. Few people anywhere expected that within two decades most of the twentieth century's experiment with communism would be gone.

Toward Freedom: Struggles for Independence

Finding the Main Point: What external factors facilitated the anticolonial movements of the twentieth century, and what internal factors complicated them?

From an American or Soviet perspective, cold war struggles dominated international life from the 1940s through the early 1990s. But viewed from the world of Asia and Africa, a rather different global struggle was unfolding. Its central focus was colonial rule, subordination, poverty, and racism. Variously called the struggle for independence or **decolonization**, that process marked a dramatic change in the world's political architecture, as nation-states triumphed over the empires that had structured much of the world's political life in the nineteenth and early twentieth centuries. It mobilized millions of people, thrusting them into political activity and sometimes into violence and warfare. Decolonization signaled the declining legitimacy of both empire and race as a credible basis for political or social life. It promised not only national freedom but also personal dignity, opportunity, and prosperity.

In 1900, European colonial empires in Africa, Asia, the Caribbean region, and Pacific Oceania appeared as enduring features of the world's political landscape. Well before the end of the twentieth century, they were gone. The first major breakthroughs occurred in Asia and the Middle East in the late 1940s, when the Philippines, India, Pakistan, Burma, Indonesia, Syria, Iraq, Jordan, and Israel achieved independence. The decades from the mid-1950s through the mid-1970s were an age of African independence as colony after colony, more than fifty in total, emerged into what was then seen as the bright light of freedom. During the 1970s, many of the island societies of Pacific Oceania — Samoa, Fiji, Tonga, the Solomon Islands, Kiribati — joined the ranks of independent states, almost entirely peacefully and without much struggle as the various colonial powers willingly abandoned their right to rule. Hawaiians, however, sought incorporation as a state within the United States, rather than independence. Finally, a number of Caribbean societies — the Bahamas, Barbados, Belize, Jamaica, and Trinidad and Tobago — achieved independence during the 1960s and 1970s, informed by a growing awareness of a distinctive Caribbean culture. Cuba, although formally independent since 1902, dramatically declared its rejection of American control in its revolutionary upheaval in 1959. By 1983 the Caribbean region hosted sixteen separate independent states.

TEACHING IDEA

Bell Ringer

The breakup of empires is not a new concept in world history, but the way it takes place during the twentieth century is different from previous eras of world history. To help students grasp this idea, ask: What are previous examples of decolonization and the end of empires in world history? *Answers may include:*

- **Decolonization:** *The American Revolution, the Haitian Revolution, Venezuela and Argentina in the 1800s, Mexico's War for Independence*

- **End of Empires:** *Fall of Roman Empire, Collapse of Han dynasty*

EXPLORING AP® THEMES

Governance (GOV)

It would be useful for students to create a reference map of independence movements in the twentieth century and label them based on the time they gained independence. Give students a world map and ask them to create a key based on the waves of twentieth-century independence (the 1940s, the 1950s, the 1960s, the 1970s, and the 1980s). Next, ask students to color the areas according to the description in the text. *The first major breakthroughs occurred in Asia and the Middle East in the late* **1940s***, when the Philippines, India, Pakistan, Burma, Indonesia, Syria, Iraq, Jordan, and Israel achieved independence. The period from the* **mid-1950s through the mid-1970s** *was an age of African independence as colony after colony, more than fifty in total, emerged into what was then seen as the bright light of freedom.* **During the 1970s,** *many of the island societies of Pacific Oceania — Samoa, Fiji, Tonga, the Solomon Islands, Kiribati — joined the ranks of independent states, almost entirely peacefully and without much struggle as the various colonial powers willingly abandoned their right to rule.* **By 1983** *the Caribbean region hosted sixteen separate independent states.*

For a blank world map that you can use with this activity, download **Map 12A: The World** from the Teacher's Resource Materials.

TRM Map 12A: The World

The End of Empire in World History

At one level, this vast process was but the latest case of imperial dissolution, a fate that had overtaken earlier empires, including those of the Assyrians, Romans, Arabs, and Mongols. But never before had the end of empire been so associated with the mobilization of the masses around a nationalist ideology. More comparable perhaps was that earlier decolonization in which the European colonies in the Americas had thrown off British, French, Spanish, or Portuguese rule during the late eighteenth and early nineteenth centuries (see Chapter 7). Like their earlier counterparts, the new nations of the mid- to late twentieth century claimed an international status equivalent to that of their former rulers. In the Americas, however, many of the colonized people were themselves of European origin, sharing much of their culture with their colonial rulers. In that respect, the freedom struggles of the twentieth century were very different, for they not only asserted political independence but also affirmed the vitality of cultures that had been submerged and denigrated during the colonial era.

The twentieth century witnessed the demise of many empires. The Austrian and Ottoman empires collapsed following World War I, giving rise to a number of new states in Europe and the Middle East. The Russian Empire also unraveled, although it was soon reassembled under the auspices of the Soviet Union. World War II ended the German and Japanese empires. African and Asian movements for independence shared with these other end-of-empire stories the ideal of national self-determination. This novel idea—that humankind was naturally divided into distinct peoples or nations, each of which deserved an independent state of its own—was loudly proclaimed by the winning side of both world wars. It gained a global acceptance, particularly in the colonial world, during the twentieth century and rendered empire illegitimate in the eyes of many people.

Empires without territory, such as the powerful influence that the United States exercised in Latin America, likewise came under attack from highly nationalist governments. An intrusive U.S. presence was certainly one factor stimulating the Mexican Revolution, which began in 1910. One of the outcomes of that upheaval was the nationalization in 1937 of Mexico's oil industry, much of which was owned by American and British investors. Similar actions accompanied Cuba's revolution of 1959–1960 and also occurred in other places throughout Latin America and elsewhere. National self-determination and freedom from Soviet control likewise lay behind the Eastern European revolutions of 1989. The disintegration of the Soviet Union itself in 1991 brought to an inglorious end one of the last major territorial empires of the twentieth century and the birth of fifteen new national states. China's Central Asian empire, however, remained intact despite considerable resistance in Tibet and elsewhere. Although the winning of political independence for Europe's African and Asian colonies was perhaps the most spectacular challenge to empire in the twentieth century, that process was part of a larger pattern in modern world history (see Map 12.3).

AP® EXAM TIP
Take notes on these examples of similarities in empire collapse in world history.

AP® COMPARISON
How did the decolonization movement of the late twentieth century differ from earlier independence movements?

AP® CAUSATION
In what ways were the American, Soviet, and Chinese empires challenged during the twentieth century?

APPLY THE TIP

After students finish "The End of Empire in World History" and before they begin learning about twentieth-century decolonization, consider having them use their class notes to have a class discussion using the following question: Based on your reading, what is the cause for the end of empire in world history? *According to the text, empire in world history has ended because of mobilization of the masses around nationalist ideologies. The world contains a plethora of nation-states, each claiming an equal place in a world of nation-states. The idea that humankind was naturally divided into distinct peoples or nations, each of which deserved an independent state of its own, gained global acceptance, especially in the colonial world, during the twentieth century and rendered empires illegitimate in the eyes of growing numbers of people.*

BUILDING AP® SKILLS

Making Connections: Continuity and Change

This would be a good place to pause and have students see what they remember about the collapse of empires during Unit 7. Have students "Think, Pair, Share" the following question with a partner: What empires collapsed during the first half of the twentieth century? *The Qing Empire fell to the nationalist revolution in China in 1912. The Austrian and Ottoman empires collapsed after World War I. The Russian Empire fell toward the end of World War I, but was "revived" under the Soviet Union. World War II led to the end of the German and Japanese empires.*

EXPLORING AP® THEMES

Governance (GOV)

Students need to know that while countries like Great Britain and France ruled or controlled a majority of the countries and territories that gained independence during this time period, they were not the only ones. Consider having students use Map 12.3, "The End of Empire in Africa and Asia," to create a quick-reference chart like the one below to list the countries that gained independence from "other" states. Students should locate the light purple areas labeled "other" on the map and list when each of them gained their independence and from whom on their chart. A reproducible version of this chart is available in the Teacher's Resource Materials. (Answers are provided in italics.)

Country and Independence Date	Former Imperial Power
Namibia, 1985	South Africa
Western Sahara, 1975	Spain
Liberia, 1820s	United States
Equatorial Guinea, 1968	Spain
North and South Korea, 1948	Japan
Papua New Guinea, 1975	Australia

TRM Handout 12.4: Chart for African and Asian Independence

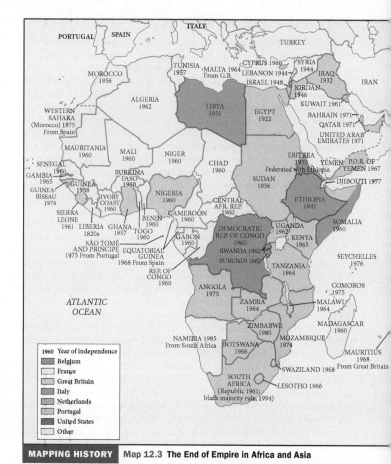

MAPPING HISTORY Map 12.3 **The End of Empire in Africa and Asia**

In the second half of the twentieth century, under pressure from nationalist movements, Europe's Asian and African empires dissolved into dozens of new independent states, dramatically altering the structure of international life.

Toward Independence in Asia and Africa

As the twentieth century closed, the end of European empires seemed in retrospect almost inevitable, for colonial rule had lost any credibility as a form of political order.

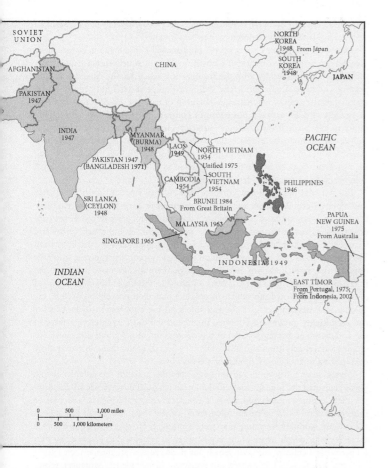

Reading the Map: Which European colonial power gave up its colonies late in the decolonization process?

AP **Making Connections:** Compare this map with Maps 10.1 and 10.2. To what extent did the colonial era provide the framework for the postcolonial political boundaries of Africa, South Asia, and Southeast Asia?

What could be more natural than for people to seek to rule themselves? Yet at the beginning of the century, few observers were predicting the collapse of these empires, and the idea that "the only legitimate government is national self-government" was not nearly as widespread as it subsequently became. How might historians explain

---

TEACHING IDEA

Incorporating Outside Resources

The Crash Course World History episode *Decolonization and Nationalism Triumphant* might be interesting to students as an introduction to decolonization in the twentieth century. In this episode, John Green discusses the breakup of European empires following World War II. He also touches on how independence was nonviolent in some states, while in others independence was violent and not orderly. Find the video on YouTube. You can assign the video as homework to students or watch it as a class. While students watch the video, they should answer the following questions:

■ How did World War II contribute to the breakup of empires following the war? *European empires called on their colonies to help them fight the war, and the defeat of the Nazis discredited the idea of empire. Also, the war weakened many of the big imperial powers, which would make it difficult for them to continue holding on to their colonies.*

■ What were the similar characteristics of decolonization in the post–World War II world? *1. Since decolonization took place during the cold war, many newly independent states had to choose between socialist and capitalist influences; 2. While many of the new states eventually adopted democracy, their road to it was rocky; 3. Decolonization often involved violence, mainly to overthrow the colonial elites.*

■ How did the legacies of colonialism cause problems for newly independent states in Africa? *Colonial boundaries became the borders of new nations, which did not account for the historical divisions of tribes and ethnicities in Africa. African nations did not have the institutions needed to thrive in the postwar industrial world after European empires left; for example, during imperialism, Europeans focused on resource extraction rather than on long-term economic growth. There were few schools and universities to educate the needed political and economic leaders for the new nations. Local leaders who had worked with imperial powers were distrusted by the people after independence, which led to the rise of strongmen as the new leaders. However, many African nations have shown consistent signs of growth since decolonization, despite these challenges.*

BUILDING AP® SKILLS

Argumentation

It can be fun to challenge students to create lists of what they believe to be the most important causes, results, and impacts of a historical event and then have them compare their list to what their classmates came up with. This exercise also helps them develop their argumentation skills. You could ask students, in small groups or individually, to create a list of five or six causes of decolonization and then rank them in importance. Once they finish, have students discuss their findings with the rest of the class. (Rankings will vary; make sure students justify their choices. Suggested answers are provided in italics.)

1. *The rhetoric of Christianity, Enlightenment thought, and material progress sat awkwardly with the realities of colonial racism, exploitation, and poverty.*

2. *The increasingly democratic values of European states ran counter to the dictatorial nature of colonial rule.*

3. *The ideal of national self-determination was profoundly at odds with the possession of colonies that were denied the opportunity to express their own national character.*

4. *The enormously powerful force of nationalism, having earlier driven the process of European empire building, now played a major role in its disintegration.*

5. *Both the United States and the Soviet Union, the new global superpowers, generally opposed the older European colonial empires, even as they created empire-like international relationships of their own.*

6. *By the early twentieth century in Asia and the mid-twentieth century in Africa, a second or third generation of Western-educated elites, largely male, rose throughout the colonial world. These young men were familiar with European culture, were deeply aware of the gap between its values and its practices, did not feel colonial rule was beneficial as their fathers had, and increasingly insisted on immediate independence.*

AP®
CAUSATION
What factors contributed to the end of European colonial empires in Africa and Asia?

the rapid collapse of European colonial empires and the emergence of a transformed international landscape with dozens of new nation-states?

One approach focuses attention on fundamental contradictions in the entire colonial enterprise. The rhetoric of Christianity, Enlightenment thought, and material progress sat awkwardly with the realities of colonial racism, exploitation, and poverty. The increasingly democratic values of European states ran counter to the essential dictatorship of colonial rule. The ideal of national self-determination was profoundly at odds with the possession of colonies that were denied any opportunity to express their own national character. The enormously powerful force of nationalism, having earlier driven the process of European empire building, now played a major role in its disintegration. From this perspective, colonial rule dug its own grave because its practice ran counter to established European values of democracy and national self-determination.

But why did this "fatal flaw" of European colonial rule lead to independence in the post–World War II decades rather than earlier or later? Here, historians have found useful the notion of "conjuncture": the coming together of several separate developments at a particular time. At the international level, the world wars had weakened Europe while discrediting any sense of European moral superiority. Both the United States and the Soviet Union, the new global superpowers, generally opposed the older European colonial empires, even as they created empire-like international relationships of their own. Meanwhile, the United Nations provided a prestigious platform from which to conduct anticolonial agitation. Within the colonies, the dependence of European rulers on the cooperation of local elites, and increasingly on Western-educated men, rendered those empires vulnerable to the withdrawal of that support. All of this contributed to the global illegitimacy of empire, a novel and stunning transformation of social values that was enormously encouraging to anticolonial movements everywhere.

At the same time, social and economic processes within the colonies themselves generated the human raw material for anticolonial movements. By the early twentieth century in Asia and the mid-twentieth century in Africa, a second or third generation of Western-educated elites, largely male, had arisen throughout the colonial world. These young men were thoroughly familiar with European culture; they were deeply aware of the gap between its values and its practices; they no longer viewed colonial rule as a vehicle for their peoples' progress as their fathers had; and they increasingly insisted on immediate independence. Moreover, growing numbers of ordinary people — women and men alike — were receptive to this message. Veterans of the world wars; young people with some education but few jobs commensurate with their expectations; a small class of urban workers who were increasingly aware of their exploitation; small-scale female traders resentful of European privileges; rural dwellers who had lost land or suffered from forced labor; impoverished and insecure newcomers to the cities — all of these groups had reason to believe that independence held great promise. And as populations grew across the colonial world, the pressure of numbers enhanced these grievances.

TEACHING IDEA

Class Discussion

Try to point out terms in the textbook, tests, or primary documents that students may be unfamiliar with and work with them to define and discuss those words. This exercise will help them feel more comfortable approaching questions on the AP® Exam. The second full paragraph on this page refers to the notion of "conjuncture," which might be a term students don't know. Ask students to use the paragraph to answer the following question: What does the term "conjuncture" mean, and how does it relate to the end of empire?

Conjuncture is the coming together of several separate developments at a particular time. At the international level, the world wars had weakened Europe, while discrediting any sense of European moral superiority. Both the United States and the Soviet Union, the new global superpowers, generally opposed the older European colonial empires, even as they created empire-like international relationships of their own. Meanwhile, the United Nations provided a prestigious platform from which to conduct anticolonial agitation.

Such pressures increasingly placed colonial rulers on the defensive. As the twentieth century wore on, these colonial rulers began to plan—tentatively at first—for a new political relationship with their Asian and African subjects. The colonies had been integrated into a global economic network, and local elites were largely committed to maintaining those links. In these circumstances, Europeans could imagine retaining profitable economic interests in Asia, Africa, and Oceania without the expense and trouble of formal colonial governments. Deliberate planning for decolonization included gradual political reforms; investments in railroads, ports, and telegraph lines; the holding of elections; and the writing of constitutions. To some observers, it seemed as if independence was granted by colonial rulers rather than gained or seized by anticolonial initiatives.

But these reforms, and independence itself, occurred only under considerable pressure from mounting nationalist movements. Creating such movements was no easy task. Leaders, drawn everywhere from the ranks of the educated few and almost always male, organized political parties, recruited members, plotted strategy, developed an ideology, and negotiated with one another and with the colonial state. The most prominent among them became the "fathers" of their new countries as independence dawned—Gandhi and Nehru in India, Sukarno in Indonesia, Ho Chi Minh in Vietnam, Nkrumah in Ghana, and Mandela in South Africa. In places where colonial rule was particularly intransigent—settler-dominated colonies such as Algeria, Kenya, and Rhodesia and Portuguese territories, for example—leaders also directed military operations and administered liberated areas. While such movements drew on memories of earlier, more localized forms of resistance, nationalist leaders did not seek to restore a vanished past. Rather, they looked forward to joining the world of independent nation-states, to membership in the United Nations, and to the wealth and power that modern technology promised.

A further common task of the nationalist leadership involved recruiting a mass following, and to varying degrees, they did. Millions of ordinary men and women joined Gandhi's nonviolent campaigns in India; tens of thousands of freedom fighters waged guerrilla warfare in Algeria, Kenya, Mozambique, and Zimbabwe; in West Africa workers went on strike and market women joined political parties, as did students, farmers, and the unemployed.

But struggles for independence were rarely if ever cohesive movements of uniformly oppressed people. More often, they were fragile alliances representing different classes, ethnic groups, religions, or regions. Beneath the common goal of independence,

Military Struggles for Independence While many colonies won their independence through peaceful political pressure, others found it necessary to adopt a military strategy. This photograph from 1975 shows a nationalist Rhodesian fighter training for the long-running guerrilla war against British rule. In 1980, South Rhodesia finally won its independence, becoming modern Zimbabwe. (AFP Contributor/Getty Images)

▲ AP®

CAUSATION

Why did some nationalist movements turn to violence while others achieved independence through peaceful protest?

AP® EXAM TIP

Be able to compare the educational and socioeconomic backgrounds of leaders of independence movements in Asia and Africa in the twentieth century.

AP®

ARGUMENTATION

What evidence supports the authors' claim that independence movements were fragile alliances representing different classes, ethnic groups, religions, or regions?

BUILDING AP® SKILLS

Making Connections: Causation

You can ask students the following question for a quick causation practice on decolonization: How did European leaders respond to the increasing nationalist pressures in their colonies? *They began to see an opportunity to maintain the economic connections with their colonies without the expenses of a formal colonial government. Eventually they began to plan for decolonization, including making gradual political reforms; investing in railroads, ports, and telegraph lines; holding elections; and writing constitutions.*

APPLY THE TIP

It's helpful to have students jigsaw information when there are several topics that need to be covered at the same time, like looking at decolonization movements or decolonization leaders. If you want students to examine the leaders of independence movements and their impacts, divide the class into six groups. Assign each group one of the following leaders: Mahatma Gandhi (India), Jawaharlal Nehru (India), Sukarno (Indonesia), Ho Chi Minh (Vietnam), Kwame Nkrumah (Ghana), and Nelson Mandela (South Africa). Each group should research the background of their assigned leader, focusing on his socioeconomic background and how he became involved in their independence movement, and then create a short presentation on him. After the groups are done researching, have them present what they found to their classmates. Then ask each student to, on their own, pick two of the leaders and write a comparison paragraph on their backgrounds.

Differentiation

If you don't have time for students to research and present the leaders or have a group of students who need a little more support on finding information, consider following the "Must Do, Should Do, Strive For" model below:

■ Must Do: Students must gather information on the six leaders from a "gallery walk" and put the information in a chart.

■ Should Do: Students should be able to use the information from the "gallery walk" to participate in a class discussion comparing the backgrounds of the different leaders.

■ Strive For: For students who need a writing challenge, ask them to pick at least two of the leaders and write a comparison paragraph on them. The paragraph should focus on their backgrounds and how those backgrounds impacted their leadership of their independence movement.

EXPLORING AP® THEMES

Governance (GOV)

As with the revolutions of the nineteenth century, not all participants in decolonization movements were happy with their leaders or with the direction the movement took. You can get students to think about this idea by first asking them to create a chart like the one below, listing the guiding ideology of each of the nationalist independence movements. A reproducible version of this chart is available in the Teacher's Resource Materials. (Answers provided in italics.)

Region	Ideology of Independence Movement
India	*Religion: Hinduism and Islam*
Middle East	*Religion: Islam*
Indonesia	*Religion: Islam; Marxism*
Vietnam	*Marxism*
China	*Marxism*

After students have completed their charts, ask them to read the first paragraph on this page (it begins at the bottom of page 701) and discuss the following question with a partner: How could conflicts or disagreements emerge in the independence movements of the twentieth century? *Answers will vary, but may include: Religious differences in a state could lead to disagreements; Fear of persecution from the leading ideology in a movement could lead to conflict; Differences in political ideologies, like Marxism, could contribute to arguments between factions in an independence movement.*

TRM Handout 12.5: Chart for Ideologies of Nationalist Independence Movements

APPLY THE TIP

The AP® Daily Video for Topic 8.6: Newly Independent States examines how new states were created by redrawing political boundaries. One of the new states discussed in the video is Pakistan, which was created during the partitioning of India in 1947. This video could be good to show students or have them watch on their own to better understand what happened to India after its independence from Great Britain. The video also helps students practice using evidence to support a claim. You can find the video for Topic 8.6 by logging into AP® Classroom, clicking on Unit 8 under Classroom Resources, and then selecting Daily Videos.

---

they struggled with one another over questions of leadership, power, strategy, ideology, and the distribution of material benefits, even as they fought and negotiated with their colonial rulers. Sometimes the relationship between nationalist leaders and their followers was fraught with tension. One such Indonesian leader, educated in Holland, spoke of his difficulty in relating to the common people: "Why am I vexed by the things that fill their lives, and to which they are so attached? Why are the things that contain beauty for them . . . only senseless and displeasing for me? We intellectuals here are much closer to Europe or America than we are to the primitive Islamic culture of Java and Sumatra."[9] In colonial Nigeria, the independence movement took shape as three major political parties, each of them identified primarily with a particular ethnic group: Igbo, Yoruba, or Hausa. Thus the very notion of "national self-government" posed obvious but often contentious questions: What group of people constituted the "nation" that deserved to rule itself? And who should speak for it?

India's independence movement, which found expression in the **Indian National Congress** or Congress Party, provides a compelling example of these divisions and controversies. Its primary leader, **Mohandas Gandhi**, rejected modern industrialization as a goal for his country, while his own chief lieutenant, Jawaharlal Nehru, thoroughly embraced science, technology, and industry as essential to India's future. (See AP® Working with Evidence for Chapter 13, Document 3, for this debate between Nehru and Gandhi.) Nor did everyone accept Gandhi's nonviolent philosophy or his inclusive definition of India as embracing all religions, regions, and castes. Some believed that Gandhi's efforts to improve the position of women or untouchables were a distraction from the chief task of gaining independence. Whether to participate in British-sponsored legislative bodies prior to complete independence also became a divisive issue. Furthermore, a number of smaller parties advocated on behalf of particular regions or castes.

By far the most serious threat to a unified movement derived from the growing divide between the country's Hindu and Muslim populations. As a distinct minority within India, some Muslims feared that their voice could be swamped by numerically dominant Hindus, despite Gandhi's inclusive sensibility. Some Hindu politicians confirmed those fears when they cast the nationalist struggle in Hindu religious terms, hailing their country, for example, as a goddess, Bande Mataram (Mother India). This approach, as well as Hindu efforts to protect cows from slaughter, antagonized Muslims. Their growing skepticism about the possibility of a single Indian state found expression in the **Muslim League**, whose leader, Muhammad Ali Jinnah (JIN-uh), argued that those parts of India that had a Muslim majority should have a separate political status. They called it Pakistan, the land of the pure. In this view, India was not a single nation, as Gandhi had long argued. Jinnah put his case succinctly: "The Muslims and Hindus belong to two different religious philosophies, social customs, and literatures. They neither intermarry nor interdine [eat] together and, indeed, they belong to two different civilizations."[10] With great reluctance and amid mounting violence, Gandhi and the Congress Party finally agreed to partition as the British declared their intention to leave India after World War II.

AP® CONTINUITY AND CHANGE

In what way did the Indian National Congress represent a continuity in Indian culture? In what way was it a change?

AP® EXAM TIP

You need to know the names of some twentieth-century independence leaders, such as Gandhi, and what country they represented.

AP® EXAM TIP

You should know the features of India's independence movement and the meaning of "partition" in relation to the division of India after its independence.

TEACHING IDEA

Incorporating Outside Resources

One interesting element of twentieth-century history is the ability to find recordings or videos of eyewitnesses to historical events, which can help students gain a better understanding of what an event was like for the people who went through it (moving away from "big man" history). Students might be interested in the four-minute BBC interview of a man who witnessed the aftermath of Indian partition. You can find the interview to show to your class by searching for "Partition of India: My memories" on the BBC News website. Although the event is reported from the Hindu point of view, the narration makes clear that Muslims were equally victimized by the mass migration that followed. After students watch the interview, ask them if this story is similar to other historical events they have heard about. *Some similar events include the Trail of Tears, the Jewish diaspora, and Armenian relocation.*

If you want to make a pop culture connection, let the students know that the Disney+ show *Ms. Marvel* incorporates the aftermath of the partition of India into the story.

Thus colonial India became independent in 1947 as two countries—a Muslim Pakistan, itself divided into two wings 1,000 miles apart, and a mostly Hindu India governed by a secular state. Dividing colonial India in this fashion was horrendously painful. A million people or more died in the communal violence that accompanied partition, and some 12 million refugees moved from one country to the other to join their religious compatriots. Gandhi himself, desperately trying to stem the mounting tide of violence, refused to attend the independence celebrations. Only a year after independence, he was assassinated by a Hindu extremist. The great triumph of independence, secured from the powerful British Empire, was overshadowed by the great tragedy of violent partition.

Beyond their internal divisions, nationalist movements seeking independence differed sharply from one another. In some places, that struggle, once begun, produced independence within a few years, four in the case of the Belgian Congo. Elsewhere it was measured in decades. Nationalism had surfaced in Vietnam in the early 1900s, but the country achieved full political independence only in the mid-1970s, having fought French colonial rulers, Japanese invaders during World War II, and U.S. military forces in the 1960s and 1970s, as well as Chinese forces during a brief war in 1979. And the struggle in South Africa was distinctive in many ways. It was not waged against a distant colonial power, but against a white settler minority representing about 20 percent of the population that had already been granted independence from Great Britain in 1910. It took place in a mature industrialized and urbanized nation and in the face of the world's most rigid and racially repressive regime, known as apartheid. These factors help to explain why South Africa gained its "independence" from colonial oppression only in 1994.

Tactics too varied considerably. In many places, such as West Africa, nationalists relied on peaceful political pressure—demonstrations, strikes, mass mobilization, and negotiations—to achieve independence. Elsewhere armed struggle was required. Eight years of bitter guerrilla warfare preceded Algerian independence from France in 1962, while Angolan nationalists waged a war of independence from Portugal for thirteen years (1961–1974).

While all nationalist movements sought political independence for modern states, their ideologies and outlooks also differed. Many in

AP®
COMPARISON
What were the economic differences between India and South Africa around the time of independence?

AP®
CONTEXTUALIZATION
What features of South African society hindered independence in the nation?

Mahatma Gandhi on the Salt March The most widely recognized and admired figure in the global struggle against colonial rule was Mohandas Gandhi, often known as Mahatma, or "Great Soul." He is shown here with his granddaughter Ava (left) and his personal physician Dr. Sushila Nayar (right). (Bettmann/Getty Images)

TEACHING IDEA

Incorporating Outside Resources

To help students understand the bloody struggle of apartheid that took place in South Africa throughout the twentieth century, you can have them read about it on the South African History Online website. In the "Biographies" page, students will find a section titled "Lives of Courage." Divide students into groups to study some of the people listed in "Lives of Courage," or simply give them an opportunity to search and explore the following category links: "Political executions," "June 16 Soweto Youth Uprising casualties," "Political assassinations 1974–1994," "Political prisoners," "Robben Island political prisoners." Have students look at facts such as dates, numbers of people, and types of ways people died as they go through the different sections and articles. After they are finished, have them reflect on the violence of the uprising by answering the following questions:

■ What proof is there on the website that opposition to apartheid was violent? *Facts show accidental deaths, assassinations, and long-term imprisonment with hard labor as the punishment.*

■ In light of these facts and figures, why would a person who remembered these events feel that Nelson Mandela's election was so momentous? *Not long before his election as president, Mandela was considered an enemy of the state and sentenced to prison for the rest of his life.*

TEACHING IDEA

Class Discussion

As you end this section on independence movements, it would be good to talk to students about how independence in South Africa was different from independence for other states. Use the following question to start a class discussion on it: What made the struggle for independence in South Africa distinctive from other independence movements? *Independence from Britain was granted to a government wholly controlled by a white settler minority, which represented less than 20 percent of the total population, through the policy* of apartheid. The country's Black African majority had no political rights whatsoever within the central state. Economically, the most prominent whites were of British descent and had arrived in the nineteenth century. The politically dominant section of the white community, known as Boers or Afrikaners, was descended from the early Dutch settlers, who had arrived in the mid-seventeenth century.

Students may need to do a little outside research on South Africa's independence movement before starting the class discussion.

India and the Islamic world viewed their new nations through the prism of religion, while elsewhere more secular outlooks prevailed. In Indonesia an early nationalist organization, the Islamic Union, appealed on the basis of religion, while later groups espoused Marxism. Indonesia's primary nationalist leader, Sukarno, sought to embrace and reconcile these various outlooks. "What is Sukarno?" he asked. "A nationalist? An Islamist? A Marxist? . . . Sukarno is a mixture of all these isms."[11] Nationalist movements led by communist parties, such as those in Vietnam and China, sought major social transformations as well as freedom from foreign rule, while those in most of Africa focused on ending racial discrimination and achieving political independence with little concern about emerging patterns of domestic class inequality.

However they were achieved, the collapse of colonial rule and the emergence of these new nations onto the world stage as independent and assertive actors have been distinguishing features of world history in this most recent century.

After Freedom

Having achieved the long-sought status of independent nation-states, how would those states be governed? And how would they undertake the tasks of nation building and modern development? Those were the questions that confronted both the former colonies and those already independent, such as China, Thailand, Ethiopia, Iran, Turkey, and Central and South America. Together they formed the bloc of nations known variously as the third world, the developing countries, or the Global South.

All across the developing world, efforts to create a new political order had to contend with a set of common conditions. Populations were exploding, and expectations for independence ran very high, often exceeding the available resources. Many developing countries were culturally very diverse, with little loyalty to a central state. Nonetheless, public employment mushroomed as the state assumed greater responsibility for economic development. In conditions of widespread poverty and weak private economies, groups and individuals sought to capture the state, or parts of it, both for the salaries and status it offered and for the opportunities for private enrichment that public office provided.

This was the formidable setting in which developing countries had to hammer out new political systems. The range of that effort was immense: Communist Party control in China, Vietnam, and Cuba; multiparty democracy in India and South Africa; one-party democracy in Mexico, Tanzania, and Senegal; military regimes for a time in much of Latin America, Africa, and the Middle East; personal dictatorships in Iraq, Uganda, and the Philippines. In many places, one kind of political system followed another in kaleidoscopic succession.

As colonial rule drew to a close, European authorities in many places attempted to transplant democratic institutions to colonies they had long governed with such a heavy and authoritarian hand. They established legislatures, permitted elections, allowed political parties to operate, and in general anticipated the development of constitutional, parliamentary, multiparty democracies similar to their own.

Sidebar notes

AP COMPARISON
What were the similarities and differences among the independence movements that arose in the various regions of Africa and Asia?

AP EXAM TIP
Pay attention to examples of struggles faced by emerging independent countries in the twentieth century.

AP CAUSATION
What caused governments in newly independent states to take a strong role in guiding economic life?

AP COMPARISON
To what extent did Western-style democracy take root in the newly independent states?

APPLY THE TIP

The opening two paragraphs in the "After Freedom" section would be good for students to use to make a list of challenges that emerging independent countries faced. Have students share their lists with the class when they finish to compare what they found. *Challenges that emerging independent countries faced included quickly rising population, economic dependence despite political independence, cost of education, and high unemployment rate.*

AP® CLASSROOM

AP® Exam Question

One challenge many newly independent states faced was how to navigate a world dominated by the cold war. Consider assigning the "Africa in Cold War DBQ" from AP® Classroom to get students to analyze the challenges African states faced when trying to conduct independent policies during the cold war. Students can create a DBQ outline using the documents, or you can have them write a timed DBQ. If you choose to have them write the full DBQ, give them 60 minutes to do so. You can find this DBQ by searching for it in the Question Bank in AP® Classroom.

It was in India that such a political system established its deepest roots. There Western-style democracy, including regular elections, multiple parties, civil liberties, and peaceful changes in government, has been practiced almost continuously since independence. Elsewhere in the colonial world, democracy proved a far more fragile transplant.

Among the new states of Africa, for example, few retained their democratic institutions beyond the initial post-independence decade. Many of the apparently popular political parties that had led the struggle for independence lost mass support and were swept away by military coups, one-party systems, or "big man" dictatorships. Across much of Africa, economic disappointments, class resentments, and ethnic conflicts provided the context for numerous military takeovers. By the early 1980s, the military had intervened in at least thirty of Africa's forty-six independent states and actively governed more than half of them. Army officers swept aside the old political parties and constitutions and vowed to begin anew, while promising to return power to civilians and restore democracy at some point in the future.

A similar wave of military interventions swept over Latin America during the 1960s and 1970s, leaving Brazil, Argentina, Peru, Chile, Uruguay, Bolivia, the Dominican Republic, and other countries governed at times by their military officers. However, the circumstances in Latin America were quite different from those in Africa. While military rule was something new and unexpected in Africa, Latin American armed forces had long intervened in political life. The region had also largely escaped the bitter ethnic conflicts that afflicted so many African states, though its class antagonisms were more clearly defined and expressed. Furthermore, Latin American societies in general were far more modernized and urbanized than those of Africa. And while newly independent African states remained linked to their former European rulers, long-independent Latin American states lived in the shadow of a dominant United States.

The late twentieth century, however, witnessed a remarkable political reversal, a **globalization of democracy** that brought popular movements, multiparty elections, and new constitutions to many countries all around the world. This included the end of military and autocratic rule in Spain, Portugal, and Greece as well as the stunning rise of democratic movements, parties, and institutions amid the collapse of communism in the Soviet Union and Eastern Europe. But the most extensive expression of this global reemergence of democracy lay in the developing countries. By 2000, almost all Latin American countries had abandoned their military-controlled regimes and returned to some form of democratic governance. So too did most African states previously ruled by soldiers, dictators, or single parties. In Asia, authoritarian regimes, some long established, gave way to more pluralistic and participatory political systems in South Korea, Taiwan, Thailand, the Philippines, Iraq, and Indonesia. And in 2011, in what came to be called the Arab Spring, mass movements in various Arab countries—Tunisia, Egypt, Libya, Syria, Bahrain, Yemen—challenged the hold of entrenched, corrupt, and autocratic rulers, while proclaiming their commitment to democracy, human dignity, and honest government.

AP **EXAM TIP**

Take notes comparing post-independence conditions in Africa and Latin America.

BUILDING AP® SKILLS

Making Connections: Comparison

This would be a good place to pause and have a class discussion on how India differed from other states following independence. Ask students to explain why India's postcolonial experiences were different from the experiences of other former colonies in Africa and Asia. *Answers may include: India experienced a longer transition to self-rule; India's Congress Party united several diverse groups, whereas in many other former colonies, party unity was rare; Africa had huge problems with democracy because governing a country that had been divided according to tribal differences by colonizers intent on separating Indigenous peoples proved terribly difficult; Often, dictatorships emerged because it seemed that the only way to keep a country together was through violence.*

APPLY THE TIP

Students may find it helpful to create a Venn diagram similar to the table below to compare the postcolonial governments of Latin American and African states. A reproducible version of the diagram can be found in the Teacher's Resource Materials.

Latin America	Similarities	Africa
■ More class conflicts	■ Military interventions occurred in newly independent states	■ More ethnic conflicts
■ Armed forces had long intervened in political life	■ Struggle with government stability	■ Military intervention in political life was new and unexpected
■ More modernized and urbanized societies	■ Economic disappointments led to struggle with governments	■ Less modernized and urbanized societies
■ Lived in the shadow of the United States, rather than former European rulers		■ Remained linked to former European rulers

TRM Handout 12.6: Graphic Organizer for Postcolonial Latin America and Africa

BUILDING AP® SKILLS

Making Connections: Causation

To get students to practice their LEQ writing skills, you can have them read the section on the globalization of democracy, which starts with the last paragraph on page 705 and ends with the first paragraph on page 706. After they finish reading it, have them use what they have learned about twentieth-century decolonization and this section to write a thesis and one body paragraph that answers the prompt below:

■ Develop an argument that evaluates the extent to which various factors led to the global reemergence of democracy in the late nineteenth and early twentieth centuries. *Answers may include the following arguments: Communism was found not to work after the collapse of the Soviet Union. Running repressive governments was more expensive than fragile economies could afford. Colonial conflicts were far enough removed that some of the earlier divisions were gone. Economic policies furthered by autocratic governments succeeded in redistributing enough resources to allow for working democracies.*

BUILDING AP® SKILLS

Argumentation

If you had students complete the LEQ practice above, it could be interesting to have a brief class discussion on whether they believe the wave of democratization that swept the world is strong or fragile. They should use their knowledge of current events and the information in the second and third paragraphs on this page to help support their answer. *Answers will vary.*

AP®
CAUSATION
Why did Latin American and African countries return to democratic governments in the late twentieth and early twenty-first centuries?

AP®
CONTEXTUALIZATION
What challenges were faced by newly democratic nations in the late twentieth and early twenty-first centuries?

AP® EXAM TIP
Create a timeline of the fall of global communism.

APPLY THE TIP

Timelines can make good reference points for students as they study events that take place across multiple regions. Have students use the first paragraph on page 707 to make a list of major events in the fall of global communism from the 1960s to the early 1990s to preview the end of the cold war. *In 1976, Chairman Mao died, which allowed the CCP to abandon almost everything associated with Mao communism. In 1989, popular movements toppled communist governments in Eastern Europe. In December 1991, the Soviet Union fell apart.*

By the final quarter of the twentieth century, democracy was increasingly viewed as a universal political principle to which all could aspire rather than an alien and imposed system deriving from the West. It was therefore more available as a vehicle for social protest in the rest of the world. Meanwhile, established authoritarian governments had often failed abysmally to promote economic growth or to curb pervasive corruption. Many no doubt agreed with the West African critic George Ayittey when he labeled various African governments as "vampire states" led by "gangsters, thugs and crooks . . . who use the state to enrich themselves."[12] Growing numbers of people were outraged. The growth of civil society with its numerous voluntary groups provided a social foundation, independent of the state, for demanding change. Disaffected students, professionals, urban workers, religious organizations, women's groups, and more joined in a variety of grassroots movements, some of them mobilized through social media, to insist on democratic change as a means to a better life.

But the consolidation of democratic practice was an uncertain and highly variable process. Some elected leaders, such as Hugo Chávez in Venezuela, Vladimir Putin in Russia, and Recep Erdogan in Turkey, turned authoritarian once in office. Even where parliaments existed, they were often quite circumscribed in their powers. Outright electoral fraud tainted democratic institutions in many places, while established elites and oligarchies found it possible to exercise considerable influence even in formal democracies. Chinese authorities brutally crushed a democratic movement in 1989. The Algerian military sponsored elections in 1992 and then abruptly canceled them when an Islamic party seemed poised to win. And the political future of the Arab Spring remained highly uncertain, as a military strongman became a civilian politician and returned to power in Egypt in 2014 and Syria degenerated into brutal civil war. While no longer exclusively Western, democracy remained a fragile experiment in many parts of the world.

Even in the West, democracy was not necessarily secure. In Hungary and Poland, right-wing populist movements had shifted their countries' political systems in an authoritarian direction by 2020. And in the United States, a violent assault on the capitol in January 2021 sought to undermine the election of Joe Biden as president and represented a sharp challenge to one of the oldest democracies.

The End of the Communist Era

> **Finding the Main Point:** To what extent had the communist era ended by the early twenty-first century? And how might this phenomenon be explained?

As the emergence of dozens of "new nations" from colonial rule reshaped the international political landscape during the second half of the twentieth century, so too did the demise of world communism during the last quarter of that century. It effectively ended the cold war (at least temporarily), diminished the threat of a nuclear holocaust, and marked the birth of another twenty or so new nation-states.

Surprisingly enough, the communist era came to an end far more peacefully than it had begun. That ending might be viewed as a drama in three acts. Act One began in China during the late 1970s, following the death of its towering revolutionary leader Mao Zedong in 1976. Over the next several decades, the CCP gradually abandoned almost everything that had been associated with Maoist communism, even as the party retained its political control of the country. Act Two took place in Eastern Europe in the "miracle year" of 1989, when popular movements toppled despised communist governments one after another all across the region. The climactic act in this "end of communism" drama occurred in 1991 in the Soviet Union, where the entire "play" had opened seventy-four years earlier. There the reformist leader Mikhail Gorbachev (GORE-beh-CHOF) had come to power in 1985 intending to revive and save Soviet socialism from its accumulated dysfunctions. Those efforts, however, only exacerbated the country's many difficulties and led to the political disintegration of the Soviet Union on Christmas Day 1991. The curtain had fallen on the communist era.

Behind these separate stories lay two general failures of the communist experiment, measured both by communists' own standards and by those of the larger world. The first was economic. Despite their early successes, communist economies by the late 1970s showed no signs of catching up to the more advanced capitalist countries. The highly regimented Soviet economy in particular was largely stagnant; its citizens were forced to stand in long lines for consumer goods and complained endlessly about their poor quality and declining availability. This was enormously embarrassing, for it had been the proud boast of communist leaders everywhere that they had found a better route to modern prosperity than their capitalist rivals. Furthermore, these unflattering comparisons were increasingly well known, thanks to the global information revolution. A lagging economy had political and national security implications as well, for economic growth, even more than military capacity, was increasingly the measure of state power and widely expected among the general population as consumerism took hold around the world.

The second failure was moral. The horrors of Stalin's Terror and the gulag, of Mao's Cultural Revolution, of something approaching genocide in communist Cambodia—all of this wore away at communist claims to moral superiority over capitalism. Moreover, this erosion occurred as global political culture more widely embraced democracy and human rights as the universal legacy of humankind, rather than the exclusive possession of the capitalist West. In both economic and moral terms, the communist path to the modern world was increasingly seen as a road to nowhere.

Communist leaders were not ignorant of these problems, and particularly in China and the Soviet Union, they moved aggressively to address them. But their approach to doing so varied greatly, as did the outcomes of those efforts. Thus, much as the Russian and Chinese revolutions differed and their approaches to building socialism diverged, so too did these communist giants chart distinct paths during the final years of the communist experiment.

AP®
COMPARISON
What were the defining characteristics associated with democratic nations compared to the characteristics of communist states?

BUILDING AP® SKILLS
Contextualization

You can have students practice their contextualization skills with the end of the communist era and the cold war by asking: What two general failures led to the idea that the communist experiment was no longer a path that states would be willing to take in the modern world? *First, the failure of communist economies to catch up to more advanced capitalist economies, along with the stagnation of communist economies like the Soviet Union, was seen as embarrassing to communist states that believed their system was the best route to prosperity. Second, the horrors of Stalin's Terror and the gulags in the Soviet Union, of Mao's Cultural Revolution, and of the genocide in communist Cambodia wore away at communist claims to moral superiority over capitalism.*

CONTINUITY AND CHANGE
What major cultural changes occurred in China during the twentieth century? What cultural continuities reemerged with the decline of communist economic policies?

Beyond Mao in China

In China the reform process took shape under the leadership of **Deng Xiaoping** (dung shee-yao-ping), who emerged as China's "paramount leader" in 1978, following the death of Mao Zedong. Particularly dramatic were Deng's dismantling of the country's system of collectivized farming and a return to something close to small-scale private agriculture. Impoverished Chinese peasants eagerly embraced these new opportunities and pushed them even further than the government had intended. Industrial reform proceeded more gradually. Managers of state enterprises were given greater authority and encouraged to act like private owners, making many of their own decisions and seeking profits. China opened itself to the world economy and welcomed foreign investment in "special enterprise zones" along the coast, where foreign capitalists received tax breaks and other inducements. Local governments and private entrepreneurs joined forces in thousands of flourishing "township and village enterprises" that produced food, clothing, building materials, and much more.

The outcome of these reforms was stunning economic growth and a new prosperity for millions. Better diets, lower mortality rates, declining poverty, massive urban construction, and surging exports—all of this accompanied China's state-directed rejoining of the world economy and contributed to a much-improved material life for millions of its citizens. China was the rising economic giant of the twenty-first century. That economic success provided the foundation for China's emergence as one of the Great Powers of the new century, able to challenge American dominance in eastern Asia and the Pacific.

On the other hand, the country's burgeoning economy also generated massive corruption among Chinese officials, sharp inequalities between the coast and the interior, a huge problem of urban overcrowding, terrible pollution in major cities, and periodic inflation as the state loosened its controls over the economy. Urban vices such as street crime, prostitution, gambling, drug addiction, and a criminal underworld, which had been largely eliminated after 1949, surfaced again in China's booming cities. Nonetheless, something remarkable had occurred in

After Communism in China Although the Communist Party still governed China in the early twenty-first century, communist values of selflessness, community, and simplicity had been substantially replaced for many by Western-style consumerism. This New Year's Good Luck poster from 1993 illustrates the new interest in material wealth in the form of American dollars and the return of older Chinese cultural patterns represented by the traditional gods of wealth, happiness, and longevity. The caption reads: "The gods of wealth enter the home from everywhere." (Zhejiang People's Art Publishing House/Stefan R. Landsberger Collections/International Institute of Social History, Amsterdam/www.chineseposters.net)

Incorporating Outside Resources

In the Crash Course World History 2 episode *Democracy, Authoritarian Capitalism, and China*, John Green takes a look at the successes of "authoritarian capitalism" as it is practiced in China and Singapore. This episode also examines what happened in China after the death of Mao Zedong. You can find the video on YouTube. Consider either assigning the video as homework or showing it in class. After students watch it, ask them the following questions:

■ Why might democracy be falling out of favor in parts of the world? *Leaders are seeing that they can have economic prosperity without representative democracy, such as in the People's Republic of China, parts of the Middle East, and Singapore.*

■ Why would knowing that the ruling party would win elections allow Singapore's politicians to focus on other things? *If there are no worries about a change in government, then politicians can focus on long-term planning for Singapore.*

■ What message is being sent when Chinese state-owned companies build large buildings in Africa? *China has a system by which people can get things done despite the repressive government.*

■ What are some of the drawbacks to authoritarian capitalism? *Some of the drawbacks are that the economy is not responsive to investors, corruption makes it hard to do business and to retain the profits of hard work, too much reliance on government subsidies distorts the market, and there is no support for the freedom of expression that helps fuel cultural and intellectual industries.*

Claims and Evidence in Sources

The New Year's Good Luck poster from 1993 on this page provides an interesting source for students to analyze to see how Chinese attitudes have changed since the rise of communism in the country. You can show students the poster and then ask: What changes in Chinese attitudes are portrayed in this poster? *The poster reflects an interest in material wealth, personal happiness, and a return to the traditions of the past, as indicated by the traditional Chinese portrayal of Confucius.*

China: a largely capitalist economy had been restored, and by none other than the Communist Party itself. Mao's worst fears had been realized, as China "took the capitalist road."

Although the party was willing to abandon many communist economic policies, it was adamantly unwilling to relinquish its political monopoly or to promote democracy at the national level. "Talk about democracy in the abstract," Deng Xiaoping declared, "will inevitably lead to the unchecked spread of ultra-democracy and anarchism, to the complete disruption of political stability, and to the total failure of our modernization program. . . . China will once again be plunged into chaos, division, retrogression, and darkness."[13] Such attitudes associated democracy with the chaos and uncontrolled mass action of the Cultural Revolution. Thus, when a democracy movement spearheaded by university and secondary school students surfaced in the late 1980s, Deng ordered the brutal crushing of its brazen demonstration in Beijing's Tiananmen Square before the television cameras of the world.

The Collapse of the Soviet Union

A parallel reform process unfolded quite differently in the USSR under the leadership of **Mikhail Gorbachev**, beginning in the mid-1980s. Like Deng Xiaoping in China, Gorbachev was committed to aggressively tackling the country's many problems—economic stagnation, a flourishing black market, public apathy, and cynicism about the party. His economic program, launched in 1987 and known as *perestroika* (per-uh-STROI-kuh) (restructuring), paralleled aspects of the Chinese approach by freeing state enterprises from the heavy hand of government regulation, permitting small-scale private businesses called cooperatives, offering opportunities for private farming, and cautiously welcoming foreign investment in joint enterprises.

But in cultural and political affairs, Gorbachev moved far beyond Chinese reforms. His policy of *glasnost* (GLAHS-nohst) (openness) now permitted an unprecedented range of cultural and intellectual freedoms. In the late 1980s, glasnost hit the Soviet Union like a bomb. Newspapers and TV exposed social pathologies—crime, prostitution, child abuse, suicide, elite corruption, and homelessness—that previously had been presented solely as the product of capitalism. "Like an excited boy reads a note from his girl," wrote one poet, "that's how we read the papers today."[14] Plays, poems, films, and novels that had long been buried "in the drawer" were now released to a public that virtually devoured them. Films broke the ban on nudity and explicit sex. Soviet history was also reexamined as revelations of Stalin's crimes poured out of the media. The Bible and the Quran became more widely available, atheistic propaganda largely ceased, and thousands of churches and mosques were returned to believers and opened for worship. And beyond glasnost lay democratization and a new parliament with real powers, chosen in competitive elections. When those elections occurred in 1989, dozens of leading

AP COMPARISON
In what different ways was the erosion of communism experienced in China and the Soviet Union?

AP EXAM TIP
Take notes on the factors that led to more economic freedom in communist China starting in the late twentieth century.

AP EXAM TIP
Understand examples of resistance to authoritarian governments in the twentieth century.

AP CAUSATION
What factors help to explain the collapse of the Soviet Union?

BUILDING AP® SKILLS

Argumentation

Consider having students work on their writing skills here by having them write a short response to a prompt and then peer-grade a classmate's response. Grading another person's response can help students understand what is being looked for in their essays. Students should write a one- to two-paragraph response to the following prompt:

■ Evaluate the extent to which the reforms in China that began in the late 1970s had a positive and/or negative effect on the people. (Possible answers are provided in italics.)

■ **Positive:** *Better diets, lower mortality rates, declining poverty, urban construction, rejoining the global economy*

■ **Negative:** *Massive corruption among Chinese officials, inequalities between the coastal urban areas and interior rural areas, horrible pollution, urban overcrowding, periodic inflation, prostitution, drug addiction*

Once students have finished, partner them up with a classmate and have them peer-grade each other's responses. They can use the phrases "I like . . ." and "I wonder . . ." to guide their feedback to their partner.

APPLY THE TIP

Students should understand different types of resistance to authoritarian government in the twentieth century. Ask students to name some examples. *Answers should include: Bloody Sunday in Russia, the 1917 Bolshevik Revolution in Russia, the Prague Spring in Czechoslovakia, the 1911 Chinese revolution, the 1910 Mexican Revolution, the Cuban Revolution, and the failed Bay of Pigs invasion by the United States in 1961.*

BUILDING AP® SKILLS

Claims and Evidence in Sources

To help students understand that the effects of Gorbachev's policies of glasnost and perestroika led to the breakup of the Soviet Union, use the cartoon titled "Gorbachev Beholds a Shattered Hammer and Sickle," located on the Library of Congress website. Scroll down the page to find the cartoon. After showing the cartoon, ask what it symbolizes. *An unhappy Gorbachev looks at what was once a globally recognized symbol of Soviet power and unity. This image shows how Gorbachev presided over the breakup of the Soviet Union.*

TEACHING IDEA

Class Discussion

As you continue to examine the collapse of the Soviet Union, ask students to list the demands that the new freedoms seemed to unleash among the people of the Soviet Union. *People sought more democratic representation and a more market-based economy. Independent labor unions began to form, nationalist movements sprang up, and Western culture became more pervasive.*

AP®

COMPARISON
How did the decline of communism in the Soviet Union compare to the decline of communism in China?

▶ **AP®**

CAUSATION
What events in the Soviet Union facilitated the dismantling of the Berlin Wall?

communists were rejected at the polls. In foreign affairs, Gorbachev moved to end the cold war by making unilateral cuts in Soviet military forces, engaging in arms control negotiations with the United States, and refusing to intervene as communist governments in Eastern Europe were overthrown.

But almost nothing worked out as Gorbachev had anticipated. Far from strengthening socialism and reviving a stagnant Soviet Union, the reforms led to its further weakening and collapse. In a dramatic contrast with China's booming economy, the Soviet Union spun into a sharp decline as its planned economy was dismantled before a functioning market-based system could emerge. Inflation mounted; consumer goods were in short supply, and ration coupons reappeared; many feared the loss of their jobs. Unlike Chinese peasants, few Soviet farmers were willing to risk the jump into private farming, and few foreign investors found the Soviet Union a tempting place to do business.

Furthermore, the new freedoms provoked demands that went far beyond what Gorbachev had intended. A democracy movement of unofficial groups and parties now sprang to life, many of them seeking a full multiparty democracy and a market-based economy. They were joined by independent labor unions, which actually went on strike, something unheard of in the "workers' state." Most corrosively, a multitude of nationalist movements used the new freedoms to insist on greater autonomy, or even independence, from the Soviet Union. In the face of

Breaching the Berlin Wall In November 1989, anticommunist protesters broke through the Berlin Wall dividing the eastern and western sections of the city, even as East Berlin citizens joyfully entered their city's western zone. That event has become an iconic symbol of the collapse of communism in Eastern Europe and heralded the reunification of Germany and the end of the cold war, which had divided Europe since the late 1940s. (Tom Stoddart/Reportage via Getty Images)

these mounting demands, Gorbachev resolutely refused to use force to crush the protesters, another sharp contrast with the Chinese experience.

Events in Eastern Europe intersected with those in the Soviet Union. Gorbachev's reforms had lit a fuse in these Soviet satellites, where communism had been imposed and maintained from outside. If the USSR could practice glasnost and hold competitive elections, why not Eastern Europe as well? In Poland, for example, the political activist Lech Walesa had established the Solidarity labor union in 1980. This was the first trade union created in any Warsaw Pact nation that was not under the control of the Communist Party. During the 1980s, Solidarity fought for workers' rights by using civil resistance tactics, often operating underground even as it received support from the United States and Pope John Paul II. Despite government oppression, public support of the union grew. In 1989 Poland held semi-free elections, and in 1990 Walesa was elected president of Poland.

This kind of growing opposition to communist regimes in Eastern Europe was the background for the "miracle year" of 1989. Massive demonstrations, last-minute efforts at reforms, the breaching of the Berlin Wall, the surfacing of new political groups—all of this and more overwhelmed the highly unpopular communist regimes of Poland, Hungary, East Germany, Bulgaria, Czechoslovakia, and Romania, which were quickly swept away. This success then emboldened nationalists and democrats in the Soviet Union. If communism had been overthrown in Eastern Europe, perhaps it could be overthrown in the USSR as well. Soviet conservatives and patriots, however, were outraged. To them, Gorbachev had stood idly by while the political gains of World War II, for which the Soviet Union had paid in rivers of blood, vanished before their eyes. It was nothing less than treason.

A brief and unsuccessful attempt to restore the old order through a military coup in August 1991 triggered the end of the Soviet Union and its communist regime. From the wreckage there emerged fifteen new and independent states, following the internal political divisions of the USSR. Arguably the Soviet Union had collapsed less because of its multiple problems and more from the unexpected consequences of Gorbachev's efforts to address them.

The Soviet collapse represented a unique phenomenon in the world of the late twentieth century. Simultaneously, the world's largest state and its last territorial empire vanished; the world's first Communist Party disintegrated; a powerful command economy broke down; an official socialist ideology was repudiated; and a forty-five-year global struggle between the East and the West ended, at least temporarily. In Europe, Germany was reunited, and a number of former communist states joined NATO and the European Union, ending the division of the continent. At least for the moment, capitalism and democracy seemed to triumph over socialism and authoritarian governments. In many places, the end of communism allowed simmering ethnic tensions to explode into open conflict. Beyond the disintegration of the Soviet Union, both Yugoslavia and Czechoslovakia fragmented. Chechens in Russia, Abkhazians in Georgia, Russians in the Baltic states and Ukraine, Tibetans and Uighurs in China—all of these minorities found themselves in opposition to the states in which they lived.

Compare the internal and external forces that led to the fall of the USSR with those that led to the fall of earlier empires.

AP® CLASSROOM

AP® Topic Question

Now is an excellent opportunity for some practice with multiple-choice questions. You can find a set of questions about the breakup of the Soviet Union by logging into AP® Classroom, clicking on Unit 8 under Classroom Resources, and then selecting Topic Questions. Look for the questions labeled "Soviet Cartoon of Red Square Parades." You can either assign the questions to the students to complete individually or allow them to partner up to work through the set together.

APPLY THE TIP

Ask students to complete a chart like the one here, comparing the decline of the USSR with the decline of the British Empire in the twentieth century. Students should consider both the external and internal forces. A reproducible version of this chart is available in the Teacher's Resource Materials. (Answers are provided in italics.)

	USSR	Great Britain
Internal Factors That Led to the Decline	*Glasnost and perestroika*; *Protests by "labor unions"*; *Growing unrest in the Soviet republics*	*War loans*; *Lack of financial and military resources to maintain the colonies*
External Forces That Led to the Decline	*Cold war expenses*; *Pressures from the U.S. because of the cold war*; *Demonstrations from the communist satellite states in Eastern Europe*	*World War I*; *Great Depression*; *World War II*; *Protests and resistance by colonial subjects*

TRM Handout 12.7: Comparison Chart for the Declines of the USSR and Great Britain

Economic Systems (ECN)

As you wrap up looking at the breakup of the Soviet Union, ask students: How does the current economic situation in former communist states reflect the challenges of trying to recover from decades of communist control over the country's economy? *Russia's economy contracted and did not recover until 2006. China embraced a market economy, which has been successful but is currently undergoing some contraction. Cuba, after losing Soviet subsidies, allowed some privatization of its economy; recent reestablishment of diplomatic relations with the United States may allow for the economy to improve. There have been no changes in North Korea.*

Sourcing and Situation

To help students understand the radical nature of the new ideas of cultural openness as in Cuba, ask them to read the *New York Times* article "Socialism's Sacred Cows Suffer Zombie Attack in Popular Cuban Film" by Victoria Burnett. After they have read the article, ask students: How might this film reflect the changes occurring in Cuba as a result of loosening communism? *The film shows that there is now some freedom of expression since it makes fun of some of the elements of Cuban communism and even displays some humor directed toward Fidel Castro. This would not have been possible in the past.*

After Communism

As the twenty-first century dawned, the communist world had shrunk considerably from its high point just three decades earlier. In the Soviet Union and Eastern Europe, communism had disappeared entirely as the governing authority and dominant ideology. In the immediate aftermath of the Soviet collapse, Russia experienced a sharply contracting economy, widespread poverty and inequality, and declining life expectancy. Not until 2006 did its economy recover to the level of 1991. By contrast, as China abandoned its communist economic policies, a market economy took shape, spurring remarkable economic growth. By 2010 China had become the world's second largest economy and by various accounts seemed on track to overtake the United States in the not-too-distant future.

Like China, Vietnam and Laos remained officially communist, even while they pursued Chinese-style reforms, though more cautiously. Even Cuba, which was beset by economic crisis in the 1990s after massive Soviet subsidies ended, allowed small businesses, private food markets, and tourism to grow, while harshly suppressing opposition political groups. Cubans were increasingly engaged in private enterprise, able to buy and sell cars and houses, and enthusiastically embracing mobile phones and computers. In 2015 diplomatic relations with the United States were restored after more than a half century of hostility between the two countries. An impoverished and highly nationalistic North Korea, armed with nuclear weapons, remained the most unreformed and repressive of the surviving communist countries. But either as a primary source of international conflict or as a compelling path to modernity and social justice, communism was effectively dead. The brief communist era in world history had ended.

The end of the cold war and the thorough discrediting of communism, however, did not usher in any extended period of international tranquility as many had hoped, for the rivalries of the Great Powers had certainly not ended. As the bipolar world of the cold war era faded away, the United States emerged as the world's sole superpower, but Russia and China alike continued to challenge American dominance in world affairs. Russian president Vladimir Putin deeply resented the loss of his country's international stature after the breakup of the Soviet Union and what he regarded as U.S. or Western efforts to threaten Russia's security in the region. Putin objected to the eastward expansion of NATO to include many Eastern European countries (Poland, Hungary, and the Czech Republic, for example) that had once been members of the Soviet-led Warsaw Pact. Particularly offensive to the Russian president was the incorporation into NATO of the former Soviet Baltic republics of Estonia, Latvia, and Lithuania. These issues came to a head as Ukraine expressed interest in NATO membership and its political culture increasingly embraced Western-style democracy. Russia's annexation of Crimea in 2014 and especially its invasion of Ukraine in early 2022 represented an attempt to overturn the post–cold war security arrangements in Europe. This effort to re-establish a Russian sphere of influence in Eastern Europe, and Western resistance to it, brought the relationship of Russia and the United States to something resembling cold war–era hostility.

AP®
CONTINUITY AND CHANGE
In what ways did international life change following the end of the communist era?

China too became an increasingly prominent player on the global stage. Its remarkable economic growth suggested to many that the next hundred years would be the "Chinese century," much as the twentieth century had been dubbed the "American century." China's hosting of the 2008 Summer Olympics and the 2022 Winter Olympics affirmed its arrival as one of the world's most modern and culturally influential countries. Militarily, China now ranks third in the world, surpassed only by the United States and Russia, with a growing array of modern high-tech weapons systems, including long-range missiles. China's growing economic and military clout has enabled the country to assert geopolitical dominance in its region, to become a major presence all across Asia, and to emerge as one of the "Great Powers" of the world. Much as Russia challenged American dominance in Eastern Europe, so too did China in the Pacific, with a particular focus on recovering control of Taiwan.

Furthermore, in 2013 China launched a multitrillion-dollar global infrastructure project known as the **Belt and Road Initiative**, sometimes called the New Silk Road. It envisaged an array of roads, railways, port facilities, and energy pipelines stretching all across the Eastern Hemisphere and parts of Latin America as well. Involving agreements with some 125 countries, it was a bid to give China a global economic footprint. Chinese president Xi Jinping declared in 2017 that China under communist party leadership was "moving closer to centre stage" in global affairs.[15] In the United States, accustomed to its role as the essential and dominant global superpower, many have come to see China as a global rival and a menace to American interests and values. "China is the greatest long-term threat to the U.S. way of life," declared an American Defense Department official in 2019.[16]

Beyond the continuing antagonisms among the major world powers, the Middle East emerged as a vortex of instability and conflict that echoed widely across the world. The struggles between the new Jewish state of Israel, granted independence in 1948, and the adjacent Palestinian Muslim territories generated periodic wars and upheavals that have persisted into the post–cold war era. Near neighbors, such as Syria, Jordan, Turkey, and Egypt, as well as distant powers, such as the United States and Russia, have been drawn into the **Israeli-Palestinian conflict** on both sides.

The **Iranian revolution** of 1979 overthrew more than 2,000 years of Persian monarchy, replacing it with a theocratic republic under the control of the Shia religious leader Ayatollah Khomeini. (See "Religion and Global Modernity" in Chapter 14 for more on the Iranian revolution.) That upheaval established a radically Islamist government in Iran, helped to trigger a long and bloody war with neighboring Iraq during the 1980s, posed a serious threat

The Middle East, ca. 2000

AP®
CONTINUITY AND CHANGE
How did China's relation with the world change between the rule of Mao Zedong and the present?

AP® EXAM TIP
Be sure to note the major global conflicts of the early twenty-first century.

EXPLORING AP® THEMES

Economic Systems (ECN)

China's booming economy in the late twentieth and early twenty-first centuries has changed the dynamics of global trade. Have students read "China's $900 Billion New Silk Road: What You Need to Know," found on the World Economic Forum website. After students read the article, ask the following questions:

■ What is China calling this massive endeavor, and what is its goal? *The Belt and Road Initiative Plan. "Belt" refers to land routes and "Road" refers to maritime routes. The goal is to trade relationships with infrastructure investments.*

■ How will this plan benefit China? *China's influence will increase globally, and many Chinese companies will see profits rise from the investments. China also feels that it can be viewed as a global superpower.*

■ Which countries, other than China, will gain from this initiative? *Sixty-two countries, including India, Russia, Indonesia, Iran, Egypt, the Philippines, and Pakistan.*

APPLY THE TIP

Ask students to name examples of major global conflicts in the early twenty-first century. *Russia's annexation of the Crimea, the Syrian civil war and the involvement of rival states on both sides of the war, U.S. military intervention and wars in Afghanistan and Iraq, and Russia's invasion of Ukraine.*

AP®

CAUSATION

In the twenty-first century, what factors led to the continuation of conflict in the Middle East and North Africa?

to Israel, and launched a continuing rivalry with Saudi Arabia for dominant influence in the region. A contentiously negotiated international agreement in 2015 brought to a halt Iran's alleged efforts to acquire nuclear weapons capability, but the unilateral withdrawal of the United States from the agreement in 2018 and the subsequent restarting of the Iran nuclear program put the agreement in doubt.

The most globally unsettling and novel aspect of post–cold war international life has been the proliferation of "terrorist" attacks undertaken by small radical Islamist groups such as the Taliban, al-Qaeda, Boko Haram, and the Islamic State or by individuals inspired by their message. (See "Religion and Global Modernity" in Chapter 14 for more on various forms of Islamic radicalism.) The random character of these attacks, their unpredictability, and their targeting of civilians have generated immense fear and insecurity in many places. In terms of their international consequences, the most significant of these attacks was that launched against several U.S. targets, including the World Trade Center, in September of 2001, for that event prompted large-scale U.S. military intervention and prolonged wars in both Afghanistan and Iraq. The complete withdrawal of U.S. military forces from Afghanistan in July 2021, after a twenty-year effort at "nation building," reflected once again the limited ability of Great Powers to impose their will on smaller nations.

But the United States has certainly not been the sole target of terrorist violence. Many European and Russian cities have experienced such attacks in the twenty-first century, and terrorism has claimed far more victims in the Islamic world itself, as Muslim radicals have sought to oust what they view as corrupt and un-Islamic governments. Despite their small numbers and minority status within the larger Islamic world, those who have undertaken these attacks have generated intense antagonism toward Islam and Muslims among some circles in the West. Thus terrorism and the so-called war on terrorism have become a global issue in the post–cold war era.

A final source of international tension deriving from the Middle East has been the flood of refugees from war-torn and economically desperate societies in the region and adjacent African states, many of them headed for Europe. The **Syrian civil war**, beginning in 2011, had by itself generated over 12 million refugees by mid-2016, with about 1 million seeking asylum in Europe, almost 5 million relocated to Turkey and other neighboring

The Syrian Refugee Crisis Among the most wrenching aspects of the Syrian civil war were the millions of refugees that it generated, many of them fleeing to Turkey or Europe and winding up in refugee camps. This photograph shows an anguished woman arriving on the Greek island of Lesbos, having survived a hazardous crossing of the Aegean Sea from Turkey in late 2015. Five other migrants had died during that crossing. (DIMITAR DILKOFF/Getty Images)

EXPLORING AP® THEMES

Governance (GOV)

Have students create a chart, like the one seen below, and take notes on the various sources of tension emerging from the Middle East during the twentieth and twenty-first centuries. A reproducible version of this chart is available in the Teacher's Resource Materials. (Answers are provided in italics.)

Formation of Israel in 1948	*Since the formation of the new Jewish state of Israel in 1948, Israel and the adjacent Palestinian Muslim territories have fought periodic wars during and after the cold war. Neighboring states, like Syria, Jordan, Turkey, and Egypt, as well as distant powers, like the United States and Russia, have been involved in the Israeli-Palestinian conflict on both sides.*
Iranian Revolution of 1979	*This revolution established a radically Islamist government, helped trigger a long and bloody war with Iraq during the 1980s, posed a serious threat to Israel, and started a continuing rivalry with Saudi Arabia for dominant influence in the Middle East. More recently, Iran's efforts to acquire nuclear weapons have led to global worries about its ability to do so and resulted in a negotiated international agreement in 2015 to prevent that possibility.*
Rise of Terrorist Groups	*In the post–cold war era, international life has been shaken by "terrorist" attacks undertaken by groups such as the Taliban, al-Qaeda, Boko Haram, the Islamic State, and individuals inspired by their message. The randomness of these attacks, their unpredictability, and the willingness to target civilians have generated immense fear and insecurity in many places. The September 2001 attacks on the United States led to the so-called war on terrorism, which has also become a global issue in the post–cold war era.*
Syria's Civil War	*The Syrian civil war has added to the flood of refugees fleeing to Europe—it had created over 12 million refugees by mid-2016—while also becoming an international conflict as Russia, the United States, and various Muslim governments and radical groups have taken sides. The conflict has also sharpened the regional rivalry between Iran and Saudi Arabia.*

TRM Handout 12.8: Chart for Sources of Conflict in the Middle East countries, and another 6.5 million displaced within Syria. That conflict became thoroughly internationalized as Russia, the United States, and various Muslim governments and radical groups took sides. It also sharpened the regional rivalry between Iran and Saudi Arabia, which contained both an ethnic Persian/Arab dimension and a religious Shia/Sunni element.

Beyond the Middle East, conflicts between India and Pakistan, between North Korea and its various neighbors, and between China and Taiwan continued to roil the waters of international life. That all of these countries except Taiwan possessed nuclear weapons compounded the potential dangers of these conflicts. Furthermore, the East-West struggles of the cold war era gave way to tension between the wealthy countries of the Global North and the developing countries of the Global South, led by such emerging powers as India, Indonesia, Brazil, Mexico, and South Africa.

The pattern of global military spending in the postcommunist era reflected all of these continuing or emerging tensions in international life. After a brief drop during the 1990s, global military spending rose during the early twenty-first century to exceed cold war levels by 2010. The United States led this global pattern, with sharp spending increases after the attacks of 2001, as the "war on terror" took hold. Although the United States accounted for roughly 35 to 40 percent of this spending in the twenty-first century, China has steadily increased its military budget during this time and is now second only to the United States in expenditures for war. Clearly, no prolonged period of international stability and no lasting "peace dividend" accompanied the passing of the cold war into history as many had hoped.

CONCLUSIONS AND REFLECTIONS

On Judgment and Ambiguity: Considering Communism

Finding the Main Point: What complexities arise in assessing the legacy of communism in history?

Among the major shapers of twentieth-century world history was the phenomenon of global communism, beginning with its initial breakthrough in the Russian Revolution of 1917. Communist regimes everywhere sought a radical transformation of their societies as they set about "building socialism." Fear and hatred of communism were major factors in the ideology and appeal of fascist movements in Italy, Germany, and elsewhere. Communism likewise motivated American aid to a recovering Western Europe as well as the creation of NATO as an anticommunist alliance.

Communism and Western opposition to it gave rise to the cold war and the various military conflicts that it spawned, such as in Korea, Vietnam, Cuba, and Afghanistan. The decades-long rivalry between the communist Soviet Union and the democratic capitalist United States generated the arms race in nuclear weapons, which hung like a dark cloud over the entire world for over forty years.

BUILDING AP® SKILLS

Making Connections: Continuity and Change

Students should understand that global tensions have changed since the end of the cold war era. Ask students: How have global tensions changed from the East-West struggles of the cold war era? *In the post-cold war era, tensions have been between the wealthy countries of the Global North and the developing countries of the Global South, along with a number of civil wars and ethnically based separatist movements around the world.*

TEACHING IDEA

Exit Ticket

After students read "On Judgment and Ambiguity: Considering Communism," post the following question and ask students to respond to it. You could also turn this into a silent discussion activity by writing the question on the board and having students respond to it by writing their responses on Post-it notes.

▪ **To what extent have both communist and democratic counties committed crimes against humanity?** *Crimes against humanity exist in democracies. For example, Native Americans were forced from their traditional lands with the idea of Manifest Destiny in the nineteenth century. Many American reputations were ruined in the communist witch-hunts of the McCarthy era. South Korea is technically a democracy, but there are still limits on freedom of expression.*

BUILDING AP® SKILLS

Argumentation

This is a good time to have students practice their essay writing skills and the OER Project's Unit 8 LEQ prompt. This prompt is an excellent wrap-up to Chapter 12, "Milestones of the Past Century," because it asks students to evaluate how decolonization and the cold war were interconnected in two of three choices of countries. You can find the prompt on the OER Project's Unit 8 page.

Differentiation

While it's good for students to write full essays, especially as they get closer to the AP® Exam, it can also be helpful to have them work on a group essay outline and evaluate their peers' responses. This exercise allows them to see different ways of formulating arguments and better understand what graders are looking for when scoring essays. If you want students to complete a group outline essay with this prompt, consider following the "Must Do, Should Do, Strive For" model below:

▪ **Must Do:** Working in groups of four or fewer, students must create an LEQ outline on the provided butcher paper. The outline should include contextualization and a thesis that responds to the prompt, at least two arguments, and at least two pieces of evidence for *each* argument.

▪ **Should Do:** Once all the groups have completed their LEQ poster, have students hang them up and do a gallery walk to see how other groups put together this LEQ. As they look at each poster, ask students to leave "I wonder . . ." and "I like . . ." statements about what they see in the outline.

▪ **Strive For:** For students who want or need a writing challenge, have them choose one of their arguments from their LEQ poster and write a full argument paragraph on it.

Communism and cold war rivalries also intersected with the end of European empires. Both the Soviet Union and the United States opposed European-style colonial empires, thus encouraging independence movements in Asia and Africa. But both sides also sought allies among the "new nations" of Asia and Africa. Resistance to these efforts gave rise to the idea of a "third world" consisting of countries seeking to avoid entanglement in Great Power rivalries, while focusing on their own economic development. China, itself a communist country after 1949, aspired to a major role in the developing world even as it challenged the Soviet Union for leadership in the communist world. And for a time, a number of countries (Cuba, Vietnam, India, Ethiopia, Mozambique) adopted a Marxist or communist approach to governing their countries.

The collapse of communism, particularly in the Soviet Union and Eastern Europe, also had global geopolitical implications, largely ending the ideological cold war, though not the rivalry between China, Russia, and the United States. It also gave birth to about two dozen new states and many ethnic conflicts. Of the remaining communist states, North Korea remains a flashpoint of global tension, while China has embraced many elements of a market economy even as it is still governed by a Communist Party.

Particularly during the cold war, efforts to study communism encountered many obstacles. In the United States, which lacks a major socialist tradition, sometimes saying anything positive about communism or even noting its appeal to millions of people has brought charges of whitewashing the crimes of the most brutal communist leaders. Within the communist world, even modest criticism of the government was usually regarded as counterrevolutionary and was largely forbidden and harshly punished. Certainly few observers were neutral in their assessment of the communist experiment.

Were the Russian and Chinese revolutions a blow for human freedom and a cry for justice on the part of oppressed people, or did they simply replace one tyranny with another? Did Stalin and Mao lead successful efforts to industrialize backward countries or a ferocious assault on their moral and social fabric? Did Chinese reforms of the late twentieth century represent a return to sensible policies of modernization, a continued denial of basic democratic rights, or an opening to capitalist inequalities, corruption, and acquisitiveness? Passionate debate continues on all of these questions. Communism, like many human projects, has been an ambiguous enterprise. On the one hand, communism brought hope to millions by addressing the manifest injustices of the past; by providing new opportunities for women, workers, and peasants; by promoting rapid industrial development; and by challenging Western domination. On the other hand, communism was responsible for mountains of crimes—millions killed and wrongly imprisoned; massive famines partly caused by radical policies; human rights violated on an enormous scale; lives uprooted and distorted by efforts to achieve the impossible.

Studying communism challenges our inclination to want definitive answers and clear moral judgments. Can we hold contradictory elements in some kind of tension? Can we affirm our own values while acknowledging the ambiguities of life, both past and present? Doing so is arguably among the essential tasks of growing up and achieving a measure of intellectual maturity. In that undertaking, history can be helpful.

ERIC'S ACTIVITY 12 — Communism in World History

Skill: Continuity and Change

The rise and collapse of communism in the twentieth century provide me with the opportunity to explore the impact of large-scale developments in the course of world history. Students readily see the importance of the communist experiment and can identify how it affected the course of history in the twentieth century. But what will be communism's lasting historical impact? Exploring this question in both small groups and as a class challenges my students to evaluate different ways of thinking about continuity and change in world history. Find the complete activity in the Teacher's Resource Materials.

TRM Eric's Activity 12: Communism in World History

CHAPTER REVIEW

AP® Key Terms

European Economic Community, 680

Marshall Plan, 680

Mao Zedong, 683

Great Leap Forward, 686

Cultural Revolution, 686

cold war, 687

North Atlantic Treaty Organization (NATO), 687

Warsaw Pact, 688

Cuban missile crisis, 691

decolonization, 696

Indian National Congress, 702

Mohandas Gandhi, 702

Muslim League, 702

globalization of democracy, 705

Deng Xiaoping, 708

Mikhail Gorbachev, 709

Belt and Road Initiative, 713

Israeli-Palestinian conflict, 713

Iranian revolution, 713

Syrian civil war, 714

Finding the Main Point

1. What internal and external factors accounted for Europe's remarkable recovery after the devastation of World War II?

2. What measures did Mao take to forge China's own version of communism?

3. In what ways did the ideological struggle between the United States and the Soviet Union manifest itself across the globe in the decades after the Second World War?

4. What external factors facilitated the anticolonial movements of the twentieth century, and what internal factors complicated them?

5. To what extent had the communist era ended by the early twenty-first century? And how might this phenomenon be explained?

6. What complexities arise in assessing the legacy of communism in history?

AP® Big Picture Questions

1. Two major international conflicts shaped the second half of the twentieth century: the cold war struggle between the communist and capitalist worlds and the anticolonial struggles of Afro-Asian peoples against the Western imperial powers. How might you compare these two conflicts, and how did they intersect with one another?

2. How would you compare the historical experiences of India and China since World War II?

3. In what ways did the struggle for independence shape the agenda of developing countries in the second half of the twentieth century?

4. "The end of communism was as revolutionary as its beginning." Do you agree with this statement? Explain your thinking.

5. **Looking Back** To what extent did the struggle for independence and the postcolonial experience of African and Asian peoples in the twentieth century parallel or diverge from the experience of the earlier "new nations" in the Americas in the eighteenth and nineteenth centuries?

TRM **Suggested Responses to Questions**

You can find suggested responses to the Chapter Review questions in the Teacher's Resource Materials.

Writing a DBQ: Causation Arguments

In this workshop, we'll continue to work on source-based arguments in preparation for the Document-Based Question on the AP® Exam, this time focusing on the skill of causation.

UNDERSTANDING CAUSATION ARGUMENTS

Historians create causation arguments when they look at the relationship between causes and effects in history. The purpose of a causation argument is not just to show that one thing led to another (which could lead you to a continuity and change argument), but **what the relationship is between a cause and an effect**. Are the causes major, minor, direct, or indirect? Are there other causes that are more significant? This sounds relatively simple, but in fact it can become quite complex because there tend to be many direct and indirect causes of any given event or process, and one cause might lead, potentially, to many different effects. Often, it is the conjuncture, or coming together, of various factors at the same time that generates a particular outcome. In addition, like pushing over a row of dominoes, an effect can become a cause, setting off a chain of events. And like most things in history, a cause or an effect might be interpreted in multiple ways. For instance, what one historian might see as a major effect, another might argue is minor in comparison to another effect. The point is that **nuance** is especially important in creating an effective causation argument. Recognizing the complexity of the situation without losing focus is the key.

A Model of a Causation Argument

Let's see how the authors of this book use causation to create an argument on page 680 of this chapter. Keep in mind that the structure varies from what would be expected of you on the exam, since this is from a textbook, and thus less formulaic. However, like a document-based essay, you have a contextualization and thesis/claim in an opening paragraph:

> Contextuali-
> zation
>
> The tragedies that afflicted Europe in the first half of the twentieth century—fratricidal war, economic collapse, the Holocaust—were wholly self-inflicted, and yet that civilization had not permanently collapsed. In the twentieth century's second half, Europeans rebuilt their industrial economies and revived their democratic political systems.
>
> First
> causation
> claim
>
> Three factors help to explain this astonishing recovery. One is the apparent resiliency of an industrial society, once it has been established. The knowledge, skills,
>
> Evidence on
> what helped
> parts of
> Europe and
> Japan recover
>
> and habits of mind that enabled industrial societies to operate effectively remained intact, even if the physical infrastructure had been substantially destroyed. Thus even the most terribly damaged countries—Germany, the Soviet Union, and Japan—had largely recovered by 1960, amid a worldwide economic boom during the 1950s.
>
> 718

BUILDING AP® SKILLS

Argumentation

Students often struggle with writing arguments for DBQs. This AP® Skills Workshop focuses on the skill of causation and will be a good opportunity to help your students work on these skills. You can begin by having students read the section "Causation Arguments on the AP® World History Exam" on pages 719–721 for an overview of what a causation argument should look like. You can reprint the sample essay from pages 718–719 (without annotations) for students to analyze and identify the causation claims.

If you would like to have students practice writing a source-based causation argument, consider extending this activity by having them complete Activity 3 on page 722.

A second factor lay in the ability of the major Western European countries to integrate their recovering economies, putting aside some of their prickly nationalism in return for enduring peace and common prosperity. That process took shape during the 1950s, giving rise to the **European Economic Community** (EEC), established in 1957, whose members reduced their tariffs and developed common trade policies. Over the next half century, the EEC expanded its membership to include almost all of Europe, including many former communist states. In 1993, the EEC was renamed the European Union (see Map 12.1), and in 2002 twelve of its members, later increased to nineteen, adopted a common currency, the euro. All of this sustained Europe's remarkable economic recovery and expressed a larger European identity.

Topic sentence: second causation claim

Evidence on how Western Europeans established cooperation to aid recovery

The authors then go on to consider a third factor that aided in the recovery from the war, namely, the role that the United States played as a global leader in helping Europe rebuild through the Marshall Plan.

CAUSATION ARGUMENTS ON THE AP® WORLD HISTORY EXAM

On the AP® Exam, causation is one of three reasoning processes that will be tested on the Document-Based Question (DBQ) and the Long Essay Question (LEQ). These two essays make up 40 percent of the exam, so knowing how to create a causation argument is critical. The aim of this workshop is to help you develop a causation argument in the DBQ essay.

Writing a Causation Argument

Rule 1 when writing a causation argument is to avoid just listing events in chronological order. This should be an argument, not a list. Your purpose is to state a claim about which causes you think are most significant, and to explain why you believe that. Also keep in mind that the cause-effect relationship should not always be seen as positive, with a predetermined outcome, or based on the narrative of "progress."

As we mentioned in the introduction, causation arguments require nuance, and nuance means recognizing complexity and qualifying your argument. Writing a causation argument on the AP® Exam requires the same specific moves that we mentioned in the previous workshops:

- contextualization in an intro paragraph
- claim/thesis that addresses the prompt using a specific historical reasoning skill
- topic sentences at the beginning of each paragraph that tie back to the thesis (i.e., each claim in a thesis statement typically has its own paragraph with the topic sentence laying out the claim)
- evidence that supports the thesis
- analysis/reasoning that shows how/why the evidence supports the thesis

719

Structuring Your Causation Argument

Just as with the other essays, you need to determine how you want to structure your causation essay. The best way to do this is to have one paragraph for each cause that you list in your thesis.

As an example, let's say you're looking at a DBQ with a prompt asking you to evaluate the causes behind the end of empires and the process of decolonization in the twentieth century. You may choose to write a thesis that states:

> Although the more immediate reasons for the end of empires and the process of decolonization were the nationalist ambitions that arose among the Western-educated elite of the colonies and the general opposition of the new global superpowers to colonialism of the traditional kind, the most important cause was the long-term racism and exploitation experienced by colonial peoples at the hands of the colonial powers.

You would then spend three paragraphs discussing each of the three causes listed in the thesis. However, first notice the nuance in this thesis. There is a discussion of immediate versus long-term causes, with the latter being deemed most important in this case. Keep in mind that another writer may deem another cause as more important. Either way, the onus is on the writer to prove his or her claims by making good use of the documents provided as well as bringing in outside knowledge to bolster the arguments.

Using a Document in Support of a Causation Argument

Let's use a document to further the argument about causes for the end of empires and the process of decolonization. As already mentioned, one cause of the end of empires was the nationalist ambition that arose among the Western-educated elite of the colonies. How would you go about supporting your claim with evidence from a document? Read this document to see how it supports your assertion:

Document 1

> **Source: "Declaration of the Granting of Independence to Colonial Countries and Peoples," adopted by the United Nations, December 14, 1960.**
>
> Convinced that all peoples have an inalienable right to complete freedom, the exercise of their sovereignty and the integrity of their national territory,
>
> [The United Nations] . . . proclaims the necessity of bringing a speedy and unconditional end to colonialism in all its forms and manifestations;
>
> And to this end Declares that:
>
> 2. All peoples have the right to self-determination: by virtue of that right they freely determine their political status and freely pursue their economic, social, and cultural development.

One way to build a causation argument, using this document as evidence, would be to follow the model outlined earlier of topic sentence/claim, evidence from document, and analysis/reasoning to show how/why the textual evidence supports the claim. Here is an example of what that can look like:

An immediate reason for the end of empires and the process of decolonization was the nationalist ambition that arose among the Western-educated elite of the colonies. Many of the elites that agitated for independence in the colonies were exposed to Enlightenment thought and the ideals of nationalism, including the notion of self-determination, through their education at Western schools or missionary schools. In addition, the prestigious United Nations, in the "Declaration of the Granting of Independence," stated that self-determination is a natural right that people had to determine what their political, economic, social, and cultural state would look like (Document 1). With this educational background and support from the prestigious multinational platform, the elite began the work of severing the ties of their lands from the "mother" country to build a new nation, often with themselves at the helm. The intention was to join the global roster of independent nation-states and gain the wealth and power that modern nations enjoyed. In effect, however, the political and economic fruits of self-determination were often limited to those at the very top of the power hierarchy and only if they managed to maintain control using authoritarian measures.

In conclusion, remember to build your causation arguments with the understanding that cause-effect relationships are seldom simple in nature and therefore use nuance to make the best possible argument you can in your essays.

BUILDING AP® SKILLS

1. **Activity: Writing a Causation Thesis.** Using the information in the section "The Collapse of the Soviet Union" on pages 709–711 as your evidence, write a thesis statement for the prompt that follows. Remember that a good thesis needs to: answer the prompt, be specific, take a stance, be historically defensible, provide a roadmap for the essay, and include a counterargument.

   Prompt: Evaluate the extent to which domestic factors led to the collapse of the Soviet Union.

TRM **Suggested Responses to Questionss**
You can find suggested responses to the Building AP® Skills questions in the Teacher's Resource Materials.

721

2. **Activity: Building a Causation Argument Paragraph.** Using the thesis statement you wrote in response to the prompt in activity 1, create one causal paragraph of your argument. Use evidence from the section "The Collapse of the Soviet Union" on pages 709–711:

> Prompt: Evaluate the extent to which international factors led to the collapse of the Soviet Union.

> Thesis:
> Topic sentence 1:
>   Evidence A:
>   Evidence B:
>   Evidence C:

3. **Activity: Creating a Source-Based Causation Argument.** Based on the prompt below, use the AP® Working with Evidence section of this chapter (pages 726–731) to create a contextualizing introduction, a thesis, and two topic sentences for paragraphs. Then, select the evidence in the documents you would use to support your argument.

> Prompt: Using the documents provided, evaluate the extent to which Chinese Communist Party (CCP) policies led to a new Chinese society.

This prompt could be answered by making a change and continuity argument, but because we are working on causation, try to stick to creating an argument with causes and/or effects.

> Contextualizing intro:
> Thesis:
> Topic sentence 1:
>   Evidence A:
>   Evidence B:
>   Evidence C:
>   Analysis:
> Topic sentence 2:
>   Evidence A:
>   Evidence B:
>   Evidence C:
>   Analysis:

Kwame Nkrumah's Vision
of Postcolonial Africa

For millions of people in Africa, the achievement of political independence from colonial rule brought with it the possibility of building new lives and new societies. Many of the most ambitious goals subsequently went unfulfilled or were betrayed, fueling immense disappointment. Nonetheless, it is worth reflecting on the ambitious visions for the future put forward in the immediate aftermath of independence, for they capture the fervent hopes of many Africans looking forward to a fresh beginning as the new postcolonial era dawned.

For Kwame Nkrumah (1909–1972), independence meant an opportunity to challenge the common assumption that Europe's African colonies should become nation-states within their existing borders. The leader of Ghana's anticolonial movement and the new West African country's first president, Nkrumah was convinced that only by forming a much larger union could the African continent achieve substantial economic development and genuine political independence. In constructing his vision, Nkrumah drew on the notion of a broader African identity, Pan-Africanism, that had emerged among some highly educated Africans during the colonial era. In this activity, you will read passages from Nkrumah's famous book *Africa Must Unite*, first published in 1963, where he lays out the case for a united Africa even while recognizing the challenges that stood in the way of its formation.

1 A FIRST LOOK

To start, read Nkrumah's vision of African unification with an eye to identifying the specific changes that he advocates and the economic and political benefits that he believed would result from his plan. Then answer the following questions:

1. How does he envision the coordination of Africa's economic life? What benefits would Africans enjoy from economic unification?

2. What type of political unification does Nkrumah envision? What specific efficiencies or savings would political unification bring?

3. What weaknesses or problems caused by economic and political fragmentation does Nkrumah believe African unification would mitigate or remedy?

KWAME NKRUMAH | *Africa Must Unite* | 1963

There are those who maintain that Africa cannot unite because we lack the three necessary ingredients for unity, a common race, culture, and language. It is true that we have for centuries been divided. The territorial boundaries dividing us were fixed long ago, often quite arbitrarily, by the colonial powers. Some of us are Moslems, some Christians; many believe in traditional, tribal gods. Some of us speak French, some English, some Portuguese, not

TRM Suggested Responses to Questions
You can find suggested responses to the AP® Looking Again questions in the Teacher's Resource Materials.

BUILDING AP® SKILLS

Claims and Evidence in Sources

As the leader of Ghana's anticolonial movement, Kwame Nkrumah had a vision of an African identity he referred to as Pan-Africanism. You can have students practice their document analysis skills by having them read "Africa Must Unite" and answering the question under "A First Look" and "A Second Look" on pages 723 and 724 individually. Once students finish answering those questions, use the questions under "A Third Look" on page 725 to have a class discussion on why Nkrumah's vision was never realized.

723

to mention the millions who speak only one of the hundreds of different African languages. We have acquired cultural differences which affect our outlook and condition our political development. . . .

In the early flush of independence, some of the new African states are jealous of their sovereignty and tend to exaggerate their separatism in a historical period that demands Africa's unity in order that their independence may be safeguarded. . . .

[A] united Africa — that is, the political and economic unification of the African Continent — should seek three objectives: Firstly, we should have an overall economic planning on a continental basis. This would increase the industrial and economic power of Africa. So long as we remain balkanized, regionally or territorially, we shall be at the mercy of colonialism and imperialism. The lesson of the South American Republics vis-à-vis the strength and solidarity of the United States of America is there for all to see.

The resources of Africa can be used to the best advantage and the maximum benefit to all only if they are set within an overall framework of a continentally planned development. An overall economic plan, covering an Africa united on a continental basis, would increase our total industrial and economic power. We should therefore be thinking seriously now of ways and means of building up a Common Market of a United Africa and not allow ourselves to be lured by the dubious advantages of association with the so-called European Common Market. . . .

Secondly, we should aim at the establishment of a unified military and defense strategy. . . . For young African States, who are in great need of capital for internal development, it is ridiculous — indeed suicidal — for each State separately and individually to assume such a heavy burden of self-defense, when the weight of this burden could be easily lightened by sharing it among themselves. . . .

The third objective: [I]t will be necessary for us to adopt a unified foreign policy and diplomacy to give political direction to our joint efforts for the protection and economic development of our continent. . . . The burden of separate diplomatic representation by each State on the Continent of Africa alone would be crushing, not to mention representation outside Africa. The desirability of a common foreign policy which will enable us to speak with one voice in the councils of the world, is so obvious, vital and imperative that comment is hardly necessary. . . .

Under a major political union of Africa there could emerge a United Africa, great and powerful, in which the territorial boundaries which are the relics of colonialism will become obsolete and superfluous, working for the complete and total mobilization of the economic planning organization under a unified political direction. The forces that unite us are far greater than the difficulties that divide us at present, and our goal must be the establishment of Africa's dignity, progress, and prosperity.

Source: Kwame Nkrumah, *Africa Must Unite* (London: Heinemann, 1963), 132, 148, 218–21.

2 | A SECOND LOOK

If his vision of a unified Africa was to become a reality, Nkrumah recognized that Africans would have to overcome a variety of historical, cultural, and political circumstances that divided them. Reread the passages from *Africa Must Unite* to identify these factors, and then answer these questions.

1. For Nkrumah, what cultural factors had historically divided Africans and therefore made unification more difficult?

2. What new challenges to unity emerged when Africans achieved political independence from colonial powers?

3. What is Nkrumah's posture or tone toward these challenges?

3 A THIRD LOOK

Finally, reread the passage with an eye to what Nkrumah's United States of Africa might look like if it were fully implemented, and then answer these questions.

1. What does Nkrumah mean when he argues that economically Africa would look more like the United States of America than South America?

2. If Nkrumah's vision of unification were achieved, what would ultimately happen to existing African nation-states and their territorial boundaries? What implications might this have for the political loyalties of individuals?

3. Obviously Nkrumah's vision was never realized, as there are currently over fifty separate and independent countries on the African continent, most of them following colonial boundaries and each with its own economic development plan, military forces, and foreign policy. How might you account for the failure of Nkrumah's vision? Why did Africa go the way of Latin America rather than the United States? (See "Latin American Revolutions," pages 402–405, in Chapter 7 and "Toward Independence in Asia and Africa," pages 698–704, and "After Freedom," pages 704–706, in this chapter.)

AP ACTIVITY SUMMARIZING AN ARGUMENT

In two paragraphs, summarize in your own words the major points of Nkrumah's vision for Africa's future and the challenges that it faced. In the first, summarize the potential gains that Nkrumah argued Africans would enjoy from economic and political union. In the second, identify the major hurdles standing in the way of African unity. Be sure to open your first paragraph with a sourcing statement that identifies Nkrumah and places him in his historical context.

FURTHER ACTIVITY

Nkrumah's vision for Africa was revolutionary, and his plan, if implemented, would have unified the continent as never before. Nonetheless, this vision of a radically different future was also in part a reaction to the recent past. In a short essay, analyze the ways in which the experience of European imperialism and colonialism influenced Nkrumah's thinking about Africa's future. Be sure to draw directly upon passages from his text to sustain your argument.

BUILDING AP® SKILLS

Argumentation

Students should practice their argumentation writing skills frequently throughout the year. You can help students understand why Nkrumah's vision was not achieved by asking them to complete the "Further Activity" on this page.

725

BUILDING AP® SKILLS

Claims and Evidence in Sources

Interpreting text-based as well as non-text-based sources is an important skill for AP® World History: Modern students. If time is available, have students investigate the experiences of the Chinese during the decades of Mao Zedong's power by using the evidence in "Mao's China" beginning on page 726. Consider having students analyze one or more of the sources found on pages 726–731. You can check for understanding by:

■ Using the questions at the end of each source as a discussion starting point.

■ Pairing students to analyze (identify and describe) using author/creator's point of view, purpose, historical situation, and/or audience. This activity can continue to reinforce sourcing.

■ Assigning a source to a group of three to four students and having them present an overview of the source along with the sourcing to the rest of the class.

■ Having students practice AP® skills using any of the activities under "Doing History" on page 731.

Mao's China

Within the communist world of the twentieth century, the experience of the Chinese people was distinctive, particularly during the decades when Mao Zedong led the country (1949–1976). The sources that follow provide a glimpse into those tumultuous decades, at times hopeful for some and at other times tragic for many.

LOOKING AHEAD

AP® **DBQ PRACTICE**

As you read through the documents in this collection, pay special attention to the women in the documents. What was their role in communist China? Did communism in China offer women new opportunities in society, or did it limit them?

DOCUMENT 1 **Revolution in Long Bow Village**

The Chinese Revolution occurred in thousands of separate villages as Communist Party activists called "cadres" encouraged peasants to "speak the bitterness" of their personal experience, to "struggle" with their landlords, and to "settle accounts" with them. American farmer and activist William Hinton personally observed and described one such struggle in Long Bow Village.

Source: American activist William Hinton describing Long Bow villagers confronting a landlord, 1948.

There was no holding back. . . . So vicious had been Ching-ho's practices and so widespread his influence that more than half the families in the village had scores to settle with him. Old women who had never spoken in public before stood up to accuse him. Even Li Mao's wife—a woman so pitiable she hardly dared look anyone in the face—shook her fist before his nose and cried out, "Once I went to glean wheat on your lands but you cursed me . . . and beat me. Why did you seize the wheat I had gleaned?" Altogether over 180 opinions were raised. Ching-ho had no answer to any of them. He stood there with his head bowed. . . .

William Hinton, *Fanshen* (New York: Random House, 1966), 137–38, 158.

Question to Consider: What opportunities were afforded to women during the Chinese Revolution that may not have been available previously?

AP® **Analyzing Sources:** Consider the characteristics of the author. How could those details impact the way he frames the story?

DOCUMENT 2 **Marriage Law**

In May 1950, the Chinese Communist Party (CCP) promulgated this Marriage Law, one of several important social reforms of the period.

726

Source: The Chinese Communist Party's Marriage Law, May 1950.

Article 1
The feudal marriage system based on the arbitrary and compulsory arrangements and supreme act of man over woman, and in the disregard of the interests of children, is abolished.

Article 2
Bigamy, concubinage, interference in re-marriage of widows and the extraction of money or gifts in connection with marriages are prohibited.

Article 3
Marriage is based upon the complete willingness of the two parties. Neither party shall use compulsion and no third party is allowed to interfere.

Article 4
A marriage can be contracted only after the man has reached 20 years of age and the woman 18 years of age.

Article 10
Husband and wife have equal rights in the possession and management of the family property.

Article 17
Divorce is granted when husband and wife both desire it. In the event of neither the husband or the wife alone insisting upon divorce, it may be granted only when mediation by the district people's government and the judicial organ has failed to bring about a reconciliation.

https://www.bannedthought.net/China/MaoEra/Women-Family/MarriageLawOfThePRC-1950-OCR-sm.pdf.

Question to Consider: How might these new laws have protected women? How might they have harmed women?

AP Analyzing Sources: Think about the timing of these new laws. Why might a new communist government establish them?

DOCUMENT 3 Socialism in the Countryside

The centerpiece of Mao's plans for the vast Chinese countryside lay in the "people's communes." Established during the Great Leap Forward in the late 1950s, these were huge political and economic units intended to work the land more efficiently and collectively, to undertake large-scale projects such as building dams and irrigation systems, to create small-scale industries in rural areas, and to promote local self-reliance. Document 3 contains Mao's vision of these communes, expressed at a party conference in 1958.

727

The characteristics of the people's communes are (1) big and (2) public. [They have] vast areas of land and abundant resources [as well as] a large population . . . [and] they will gradually eradicate the vestiges of capitalism—for example the eradication of private plots and private livestock rearing and the running of public mess halls, nurseries, and tailoring groups so that all working women can be liberated. They will implement a wage system and agricultural factories [in which] every single man, woman, old person and youth receives his own wage, in contrast to the former [system of] distribution to the head of household. . . . This eradicates the patriarchal system and the system of bourgeois rights. Another advantage of [communes] being public is that labor efficiency can be raised. . . .

Roderick MacFarquhar, Timothy Cheek, and Eugene Wu, eds., *The Secret Speeches of Chairman Mao* (Cambridge, MA: Council on East Asian Studies/Harvard University, 1989), 431.

Question to Consider: What kind of society does this document imagine for rural China? What were its implications for women?

AP Analyzing Sources: What role does the author play in the communist government of China? How might that influence the audience?

DOCUMENT 4 Generational Division

Fan Cao was a teenager during the Cultural Revolution who later, as a high school student, denounced her parents. In her 2005 memoir *Under the Red Sun*, she describes her experiences.

Source: Fan Cao, a teenage Chinese girl during Mao's Cultural Revolution, describes denouncing her parents in 1968, from her memoir *Under the Red Sun*, 2005.

I was a 7th grader when the Great Cultural Revolution broke out. Growing up in the "New China" we were fed with revolutionary ideas bathed in the red sunlight of Mao. We worshiped Mao the same way pious Christians worship their God, and we were completely devoted to him. . . .

I was not allowed to join the Red Guards, simply because my grandparents were rich before the communists took away their land, and my parents were considered intellectuals, which automatically made them anti-revolutionists, regardless of the fact that they had been following Mao's idealism since their early adulthood. . . .

Despite this unbearable life, I did not dare challenge my belief in the revolution. Instead, I wondered if it might be my parents who had done something wrong. I wrote a dazibao denouncing them to show my loyalty to Mao. My naivety deeply wounded the feelings between my parents and me.

Question to Consider: How are women treated (protected, elevated, harmed) in this document?

AP **Analyzing Sources:** How might the time difference between the authorship of the document and the events described have impacted the author's description?

DOCUMENT 5 A Vision of the New China

In the eyes of its leaders, the Chinese Communist Party's victory in 1949 by no means meant the end of the struggle with enemies. What the party called the "Four Olds"—old customs, cultures, habits, and ideas—had to be destroyed so that a wholly "new world" might take shape. Document 5, a poster from the Cultural Revolution era (1966–1976), effectively presented the major features of this imagined new society. Its caption urged everyone to "encourage late marriage, plan for birth, and work hard for the new age."

Source: Chinese Communist Party propaganda poster, "Work Hard for a New Age," 1970s.

Question to Consider: What does this image suggest about the place of women in the new society of communist China?

AP **Analyzing Sources:** Who is the likely audience of this poster? How might it explain the depictions of different women?

729

Writing in her 1986 autobiography *Wild Swans: Three Daughters of China*, Jung Chang explains how her mother became involved with the CCP during the 1940s.

Source: Jung Chang on her mother's involvement with the Chinese Communist Party, from her autobiography *Wild Swans: Three Daughters of China*, 1986.

When my mother heard that her cousin Hu had been killed by the Guomindang she approached Yu-wu about working for the Communists. He turned her down, on the grounds that she was too young. My mother had become quite prominent at her school and she was hoping that the Communists would approach her. They did. . . .

Her first job was to distribute literature like Mao Zedong's *On Coalition Government*, and pamphlets on land reform and other Communist policies. These had to be smuggled into the city, usually hidden in big bundles of sorghum stalks which were to be used for fuel. The pamphlets were then repacked, often rolled up inside big green peppers. Sometimes Yu-lin's wife would buy the peppers and keep a lookout in the street when my mother's associates came to collect the literature. She also helped hide the pamphlets in the ashes of various stoves, heaps of Chinese medicines, or piles of fuel. The students had to read this literature in secret.

Question to Consider: What kinds of opportunities existed for women during China's revolution? What limitations were placed on the author's mother?

AP **Analyzing Sources:** Think about the historical context of this text. Why did Jung Chang's mother decide to get involved in Communist Party activities?

DOCUMENT 7 **Experiencing the Cultural Revolution**

As the Cultural Revolution unfolded, teachers and other intellectuals became a particular target of the young revolutionary Red Guards, who publicly humiliated, tortured, or killed those they believed to be enemies of Mao and the revolution. Document 7 contains an account of such confrontations or "struggle meetings." It was written by Gao Yuan some twenty years after it occurred.

Source: Gao Yuan describing struggle meetings, from his autobiography *Born Red*, 1987.

At struggle meetings, students would often force teachers into the "jet-plane" position. Two people would stand on either side of the accused, push him to his knees, pull back his head by the hair, and hold his arms out in back like airplane wings. We tried it on each other and found it caused great strain on the back and neck. . . .

A young teacher from a worker's family was charged with emphasizing academics over politics and a young woman of poor peasant origin was criticized for wearing high heels, proof that she had betrayed her class. Each apologized in a public meeting.

730

Question to Consider: How and why does this document seem to contradict many of the other documents found in this set?

AP Analyzing Sources: Why might the Chinese Communist Party have adopted these practices during the Cultural Revolution?

AP DOING HISTORY

1. **DBQ Practice:** Evaluate the extent to which the rise of communism affected the role of women in Chinese society after 1940.

2. **Contextualization:** Why was communism created, and how did the development of communism impact gender roles in other communist societies?

3. **Outside Evidence:** What additional information can you use to support your claim about women and Chinese communism?

4. **Complex Argumentation:** Incorporate continuity and change over time into your argument about the effect of communism on the role of women in Chinese society.

TRM Chapter 12 DBQ Activity Handout

731

Assessing Mao

You can use this exercise to help students work on improving skills with secondary sources. Consider having students read both of the sources and answer Questions 1–3 on page 733. Then discuss students' answers to the questions as a class. This activity can help students practice reading and interpreting secondary sources found on the MCQ and SAQ sections of the AP® Exam.

The towering significance of Mao Zedong in China's recent history has led to no end of effort to assess his role and legacy. By some mysterious mathematical reckoning, the Chinese Communist Party declared him 70 percent correct and 30 percent wrong. Historians too have weighed in on the question. Voice 12.1 by Maurice Meisner, a prominent historian of modern China, highlights Mao's role as a modernizing figure in China's history, while lamenting his limitations as a builder of democratic socialism. In Voice 12.2, the Dutch historian of China, Frank Dikotter, proclaims Mao's responsibility for perhaps the greatest famine in world history, which emerged from the Great Leap Forward.

industrial values of economic rationality and bureaucratic professionalism became the dominant social norms, subordinating the socialist goals [of equality, selflessness, service to the collective]. . . . The Maoist state machine became increasingly separated from the society it ruled . . . and the division between rulers and ruled became ever more pronounced. . . . Maoism . . . was not a doctrine that recognized popular democracy as both the necessary means to realize socialism and one of its essential ends as well.

Source: Maurice Meisner, *Mao's China and After* (New York: Free Press, 1999), 414–15, 417–19, 421–22.

VOICE 12.1

Maurice Meisner on Mao, Modernization, and Socialism | 1999

Mao Zedong was far more successful as an economic modernizer than as a builder of socialism. . . . Between 1952 . . . and 1977, the output of Chinese industry increased at an average annual rate of 11.3 percent, as rapid a pace of industrialization as has ever been achieved by any country in a comparable period in modern world history. . . . [T]he Maoist era was the time of China's modern industrial revolution. . . . It is a record that compares favorably with comparable stages in the industrialization of Germany, Japan and Russia. . . . Maoist industrialization proceeded without benefit of foreign loans or investment. . . . The near doubling of average life expectancy over the quarter century of Mao's rule . . . offers dramatic statistical evidence for the material and social gains that the Communist revolution brought to the great majority of the Chinese people.

More questionable . . . is his lingering, if tarnished, image as the builder of a socialist society. . . . As industrial development proceeded, new bureaucratic and technological elites emerged. The rural areas were exploited for the benefit of the cities. . . . And

VOICE 12.2

Frank Dikotter on Mao's Great Famine | 2011

Between 1958 and 1962 China descended into hell. Mao Zedong . . . threw his country into a frenzy with the Great Leap Forward, an attempt to catch up with and overtake Britain in less than 15 years. By unleashing China's greatest asset, a labor force that was counted in the hundreds of millions, Mao thought he could catapult his country past its competitors. . . . In pursuit of a utopian paradise, everything was collectivized as villagers were herded together in giant communes which heralded the advent of communism. People in the countryside were robbed of their work, their home, their land, their belongings, and their livelihood. Food, distributed by the spoonful in collective canteens according to merit, became a weapon to force people to follow the party's every dictate. Irrigation campaigns forced up to half the villagers to work for weeks on end on giant water conservancy projects, often far from home, without adequate food and rest. The experiment ended in the greatest catastrophe the country had ever known, destroying tens of millions of lives. . . . [A]t least 45 million people died unnecessarily between 1958 and 1962. . . .

[A] vision of promised abundance . . . also inflicted unprecedented damage on agriculture, trade, industry, and transportation. Pots, pans, and tools were thrown into backyard furnaces to increase the country's steel output, which was seen as one of the magic markers of progress. Livestock declined precipitously . . . despite extravagant schemes for giant piggeries that would bring meat to every table. . . . As everyone cut corners in the relentless pursuit of higher output, factories spewed out inferior goods. . . . Corruption seeped into the fabric of life, tainting everything from soy sauce to hydraulic dams.

Source: Frank Dikotter, *Mao's Great Famine* (London: Bloomsbury, 2011), xi–xiii.

AP® Analyzing Secondary Sources

1. In what respects was Mao a successful modernizer and a failed builder of socialism according to Meisner?

2. How does Dikotter explain the "great famine" of 1958–1962?

3. **Integrating Primary and Secondary Sources:** How might the primary sources in AP® Working with Evidence be used to support or challenge the arguments of Meisner and Dikotter?

TRM Suggested Responses to Questions
You can find suggested responses to the AP® Analyzing Secondary Sources questions in the Teacher's Resource Materials.

733

Multiple-Choice Questions Choose the correct answer for each question.

Questions 1–3 refer to these two images.

1958 propaganda poster: "Brave the Wind and the Waves, Everything Has Remarkable Abilities."

Private Collection, International Institute of Social History (Amsterdam)

TRM Suggested Responses to Questions
You can find suggested responses to the Chapter 12 AP® Exam Practice questions in the Teacher's Resource Materials.

TEACHING IDEA

AP® Exam Strategies

You should continue to offer opportunities to students to practice test-taking skills, especially as you get closer to the AP® Exam. Project or copy the stimulus-based multiple-choice questions found on pages 734 through 737. It might be good to give students the questions as a practice quiz prior to the unit or chapter test. You could have students discuss why their answer choice was correct or incorrect with a partner after they check their answers.

Stefan R. Landsberger Collections, International Institute of Social History (Amsterdam)

1985 propaganda poster: "Dragons Rise over the Divine Land."

1. Which of these comparisons between the two posters is most accurate?

   a. Both posters emphasize traditional Buddhist values concerning social hierarchies and government bureaucracies.

   b. While the "Dragons Rise over the Divine Land" poster shows the success of Mao's policies, the "Brave the Wind" poster provides a commentary on the failure of capitalism.

   c. The "Brave the Wind" poster emphasizes the equality of society, while the "Dragons Rise over the Divine Land" poster shows more of an emphasis on consumerism.

   d. Both posters celebrate the success of collectivization and rapid industrialization brought about by Mao's policies.

2. The context for the "Brave the Wind" poster is the Great Leap Forward. Based on your knowledge of world history, what was the result of Mao's Great Leap Forward in the People's Republic of China?

   a. The Great Leap Forward caused significant economic hardship for the people, including a major famine.

   b. The Great Leap Forward allowed China to produce enough food for its entire population.

   c. The Great Leap Forward was successful in turning China into a modern industrial power.

   d. The success of the Great Leap Forward helped the international spread of communism.

3. What global pattern of communism in the late twentieth century is best represented in the second poster?

   a. A worldwide trend toward the creation of communist states continued to gain strength.

   b. Communist economies focused increasingly on industrialization.

   c. Communist political parties failed and were abandoned.

   d. Many communist countries began to turn toward more capitalist economic policies.

735

Questions 4–6 refer to this map.

The Global Cold War

4. Based on the map and your knowledge of world history, which of the European countries was not a member of either NATO or the Warsaw Pact?

   a. Turkey

   b. Yugoslavia

   c. Norway

   d. Poland

5. A historian researching the cold war period would most likely find this map useful as a source of information about what?

   a. The formation of new regional economic organizations during the cold war era

   b. The position of major nuclear sites during the cold war era

   c. The location of proxy wars fought during the cold war era

   d. The extent of global patterns of decolonization during the cold war era

6. Which of these was a direct result of the formation of the Western bloc and the Eastern bloc during the cold war?

   a. Many Asian, African, and Latin American nations claimed membership in the Non-Aligned Movement.

   b. Western bloc nations and Eastern bloc nations frequently engaged in small military clashes in order to advance their agendas.

   c. Nations around the world began to sign nuclear nonproliferation agreements out of fear of global nuclear war.

   d. Poland was divided into two separate zones of occupation and served as the physical representation of the cold war division.

736

In the early flush of independence, some of the new African states are jealous of their sovereignty and tend to exaggerate their separatism in a historical period that demands Africa's unity. . . .

[A] united Africa . . . should seek three objectives: Firstly, we should have an overall economic planning on a continental basis. . . .

Secondly, we should aim at the establishment of a unified military and defense strategy. . . .

The third objective: [I]t will be necessary for us to adopt a unified foreign policy and diplomacy.

— Kwame Nkrumah, *Africa Must Unite*

7. The passage is an example of what transnational movement?

   a. Pan-Slavism

   b. African Separatist

   c. Pan-Africanism

   d. Communism

8. Which of these accurately describes independence movements in Africa after the end of World War II?

   a. All of these independence movements peacefully negotiated their nations' independence.

   b. While a majority of African independence movements gained independence through peaceful means, some of them undertook armed resistance against imperial powers.

   c. All African independence movements fought violent rebellions to gain independence.

   d. European imperial powers maintained their African colonies until the end of the cold war in order to prevent the spread of communism into Africa.

9. Which of these best explains Kwame Nkrumah's use of the words "united" and "unified" in the excerpt?

   a Nkrumah wanted to create one nation out of the African continent to prevent further incursions from Asia.

   b. Having studied the history of the United States, Nkrumah argued that the African union should reject America as a model.

   c. To prevent potential ethnic conflicts, Nkrumah encouraged the different communities in Africa to minimize contact with their neighbors.

   d. Nkrumah was encouraging Africa to unify in order to help move into a modern age, as Africa had been divided among different ethnic and cultural groups.

737

Argumentation

AP® World History: Modern writing skills need to be practiced on a regular basis. You can use the SAQs on pages 738 and 739 for students to write an "exit ticket" at the end of class to check for understanding. You can also use the SAQs for more traditional timed writing practice, either by spreading the three SAQs across several days or as practice for the AP® Exam by writing them all at once. Make certain that students have the correct amount of time for this exercise. On exam day, students will have a total of 40 minutes to write three SAQs. If you are having them write only one at a time, you should to give them about 14 minutes to write it.

Differentiation

If you want to challenge students with writing an SAQ and developing evidence, consider following the "Must Do, Should Do, Strive For" model below for Question 3 on page 739. Students will need to work with a partner for this activity.

■ Must Do: On their own, students must write a topic sentence that states a clear argument answering Part A of Question 3.

■ Should Do: Students should switch their response with their partner and write evidence and analysis for the topic sentence their partner created.

■ Strive For: Students should repeat the process for Parts B and C of Question 3 with their partner. After they finish, they should discuss the SAQ answers they created together.

Short-Answer Questions

Read each question carefully and write a short response. Use complete sentences.

1. Use this image and your knowledge of world history to answer all parts of the question that follows.

AFP/Getty Images

The Handshake in Space. American astronaut Stafford shakes hands with Soviet cosmonaut Leonov during the Apollo-Soyuz mission of 1975. The Apollo-Soyuz mission was the first U.S.-Soviet joint space flight.

A. Identify ONE way in which the event depicted reflects a POLITICAL change in international relationships in the late twentieth century.

B. Explain ONE development of the late twentieth century that facilitated the event depicted.

C. Explain ONE event in the late twentieth century that would challenge this image of cooperation between the United States and the Soviet Union.

738

2. **Use the passage below and your knowledge of world history to answer all parts of the question that follows.**

> The great crime of colonialism went beyond expropriating [taking land away from] the native, the name it gave to the indigenous population. The greater crime was to politicize . . . [being indigenous] in the first place: first negatively, as a settler libel of the native; but then positively, as a native response, as a self-assertion. The dialectic of the settler and the native did not end with colonialism and political independence. To understand the logic of genocide, I argue, it is necessary to think through the political world that colonialism set into motion. This was the world of the settler and the native, a world organized around a binary preoccupation that was as compelling as it was confining.
> — Mamood Mamdani, *When Victims Become Killers: Colonialism, Nativism and the Genocide in Rwanda*, 2001

A. Identify ONE example of mass violence committed by pre-twentieth-century colonial governments on a native population that would support Mamdani's argument.

B. Identify ONE example of mass violence that was the result of independence movements of the twentieth century that would support Mamdani's argument.

C. Explain ONE development of the twentieth century that facilitated independence movements.

3. **Use your knowledge of world history to answer all parts of the question that follows.**

A. Identify ONE similarity in decolonization movements in a country in Africa and a country in Asia during the twentieth century.

B. Identify ONE difference in decolonization movements in a country in Africa and a country in Asia during the twentieth century.

C. Explain the reason for ONE similarity or difference identified in A or B.

739

13 Global Processes
Technology, Economy, and Society, 1900–present

AP® Overview for Chapter 13

Chapter 13 corresponds with AP® Unit 9: Globalization, 1900–Present. It covers the acceleration of globalization from 1945 to the present. The chapter includes the transformation of global technology, the global economy, and global feminism in the modern world. The material in this chapter is rich with historical information and images that will expose students to the development and impact of globalization in various regions of the world. Students should use their skills and assess the change and continuity among social, economic, and technological trends during and before this time period. Teachers should encourage students to go deeper into the skills that the AP® World History course seeks to develop.

Chapter 13 Essential Activity

"Chalk talk" is a simple activity that helps students think, discuss, make connections, and write—all completed silently. This activity is also a way to ensure that all student voices are heard. Choose eight to ten questions or statements based on the AP® World History Course Framework. Print them out, cut them apart, and glue them onto poster paper. You can put the poster paper on tables or in a hallway so that students can walk around and make their comments. Make certain that you provide students with clear instructions. This activity only works if everyone is writing and responding to the prompts. Make it clear that everyone is responsible for writing comments, reading other students' comments, and responding to those comments; there should be no talking. The time limit should be set by the teacher; the chalk talk can be as long as you want. As the facilitator, you can walk around, read, and make written comments to guide students in the direction you want them to go. To end the chalk talk, either have a class discussion about what students learned or have them write a short response to a prompt. Questions and instructions are included in **Handout 13.1: Chapter 13 Essential Activity**, found in the Teacher's Resource Materials.

TRM Handout 13.1: Chapter 13 Essential Activity

Chapter 13 Resources

TRM AP® Skills Workshop Activity Handout: Writing a DBQ: Continuity and Change Arguments

TRM Chapter 13 DBQ Activity Handout

TRM Chapter 13 Guided Reading

TRM Chapter 13 Lecture Presentation Slides

TRM Chapter 13 Outline

TRM Chapter 13 Suggested Responses to Questions

TRM Eric's Activity 13: Debating Globalization

TRM Handout 13.1: Chapter 13 Essential Activity

TRM Handout 13.2: Chart for Technological Innovations

TRM Handout 13.3: Chart for the 2008 Economic Crisis

TRM Handout 13.4: Continuities and Changes Chart for Nineteenth- to Twentieth-Century Industrial Workers

TRM Handout 13.5: Chart for Government Influence on Population Growth

TRM Handout 13.6: OPTIC Chart for One-Child Family Billboard

Pacing Guide

Below is a pacing guide for the AP® World History: Modern course beginning in ca. 1200 C.E. This pacing guide is based on a schedule with 120 sessions of 50 minutes each before the AP® Exam. It is meant as a place to start. If you have a different number of sessions before the exam, you can modify the pacing to suit your needs.

Day	Pages Assigned	AP® Topic	AP® Theme	Suggested Assignments	Coverage Notes
1	Read pages 741–750 to "The Global Economy: The Acceleration of Entanglement"	9.1	TEC	AP® Classroom: AP® Daily Videos on page 742 Exploring AP® Themes: TEC on page 746 Teaching Idea: Incorporating Outside Resources on page 749	Chapter 13 is set up more thematically than chronologically. This format will help students understand these larger topics related to globalization in the twentieth and twenty-first centuries. This chapter focuses on how new technologies bring the world and the global economy closer together, along with the effects and reactions to those technologies.
2	Read pages 750–759 from "The Global Economy: The Acceleration of Entanglement" to "Producing and Consuming: The Shapes of Modern Societies"	9.4 9.7	CDI ECN	AP® Classroom: AP® Daily Videos on page 752 Eric's Activity 13: Debating Globalization on page 754 Building AP® Skills: Argumentation on page 758	See above.
3	Read pages 759–766 from "Producing and Consuming: The Shapes of Modern Societies" to "Getting Personal: Transformations of Private Life"	9.4	ECN	Building AP® Skills: Sourcing and Situation on page 760 Building AP® Skills: Making Connections: Continuity and Change on page 762 Teaching Idea: AP® Exam Strategies on page 764	See above.
4	Read pages 766–775 from "Getting Personal: Transformations of Private Life" through "Conclusions and Reflections"	9.1 9.5 9.8	SIO TEC GOV	Building AP® Skills: Claims and Evidence in Sources on page 766 Exploring AP® Themes: SIO on page 770 Teaching Idea: Exit Ticket on page 775	See above.

Technological Globalization In 2019 a Kenyan woman uses her cell phone following prayers marking the end of the Muslim holy month of Ramadan. This image illustrates the intersection of tradition and modernity for billions across the globe who have integrated contemporary technologies into the rhythms of their everyday lives. (SIMON MAINA/AFP/Getty Images)

740

CHAPTER 13

Global Processes

Technology, Economy, and Society

1900–present

◀ **AP**

CLAIMS AND EVIDENCE IN SOURCES
How does this image reflect the
integration of modernity and tradition?

CONNECTING PAST AND PRESENT

Around 2012, Bella, an eighteen-year-old Indonesian girl seeking to escape a difficult family situation at home, applied for a job as a "sales promotion girl" on a distant island. There she found herself trapped as a sex worker in a night club, where she became indebted and was terribly abused. "They turned women into animals," reported Bella's mother. "[They] claimed they owed debts that they obviously could not repay. The women there were helpless."[1]

At roughly the same time, another Indonesian, a fisherman named Samysuddin, found his livelihood threatened as coral reefs degraded in the face of global warming and fish became scarce. "If the reefs continue to degrade," he declared, "then there won't be any fish here. There won't be anything left for us to do." [2]

Yet a third Indonesian whose life was shaped by the changing conditions of a globalized world was Arfian Faudi, a young engineer, who with only a vocational high school education built a successful high-tech firm, DTech Engineering. In an international design contest sponsored by General Electric, he and his younger brother twice won first place, winning a prize of $7,000 in 2013. "We created products that were basically non-existent in the market," he remarked. "As long as we got the opportunity, we were willing to learn."[3] ■

For all three of these Indonesians, life in the early twenty-first century was defined not so much by war, revolution, or liberation struggles, but by powerful though less visible processes such as migration and sex trafficking for Bella, climate change and impoverishment for Samysuddin, and technological innovation and economic globalization for Arfian. And so it has been for billions of others during the past century. Therefore, the

741

TRM **Chapter 13 Guided Reading**
You can find a guided reading handout
for this chapter in the Teacher's Resource
Materials.

TRM **Chapter 13 Lecture Slides**
You can find curated lecture slides for this
chapter in the Teacher's Resource Materials.

TRM **Chapter 13 Outline**
You can find a chapter outline to model good
note-taking for this chapter in the Teacher's
Resource Materials.

TRM **Suggested Responses to Questions**
You can find suggested responses to all of
the AP® margin questions in this chapter in
the Teacher's Resource Materials.

BUILDING AP® SKILLS

Contextualization

Have students read the opening paragraph on page 741. Ask students to use contextualization skills to answer this question: What social and economic issues can be found in the story of Bella? *The young woman crossed borders to find work; migration is a part of globalization. Unfortunately, she became a victim of sex trafficking, a serious social problem that has emerged with the new international networks as part of globalization.*

Technology and Innovations (TEC)

Ask students: Why did modern technological breakthroughs happen in the West and Japan? *Answers should include: The Industrial Revolution first took place in Western Europe, the United States, and Japan; The wealth from the first Industrial Revolution allowed these areas to maintain their momentum into the twenty-first century.*

AP® Daily Videos

This is an excellent opportunity to have students watch AP® Daily Videos for Topic 9.1: Advances in Technology and Exchange after 1900, located on AP® Classroom. You can find the video for Topic 9.1 by logging into AP® Classroom, clicking on Unit 9 under Classroom Resources, and then selecting Daily Videos. The video for Topic 9.1: Advances in Technology and Exchange after 1900 focuses on examining new technologies of the twentieth century and identifying continuities and changes associated with the new technological advancements.

two final chapters of Period 4 turn the historical spotlight away from the dominant events of the past century, recounted in Chapters 11 and 12, to focus more explicitly on such immensely transformative processes, all of which have played out on a deeply interconnected global stage.

Science and Technology: The Acceleration of Innovation

Finding the Main Point: What were the most important technological innovations of the twentieth century? What drove the accelerating pace of technological change?

Behind both the major events and the global processes of the past century lay the decisive power of scientific discovery and technological innovation. Breakthroughs in both domains initially occurred largely within the Western world, where the Scientific and Industrial Revolutions had first taken shape. The accumulated wealth and experience derived from these earlier processes enabled this region to maintain its momentum as the primary source of global innovation well into the twentieth century. By the end of the century, however, the science and technology enterprise had become global, with major expressions in Mexico, Brazil, China, Vietnam, India, Indonesia, South Africa, and elsewhere.

Particularly after World War II, a potent combination of universities, governments, and large corporations relentlessly drove the process of scientific and technological development. University-based scientific research provided the foundational knowledge from which new conceptions of the universe and all manner of technical applications emerged. Governments enmeshed in wars and concerned about national security funded some basic scientific research and were particularly interested in military applications such as weaponry, medicine, communications, aircraft, rocketry, and computing. And large corporations, eager for profits and motivated to create or meet consumer demand, invested heavily in both basic science and new products. Thus advances in chemistry generated the plastics industry; developments in physics enabled nuclear weapons and aerospace technologies; and new understandings in biology gave rise to many medical advances (antibiotics and vaccines) and various forms of genetic engineering such as those increasing the resilience, nutritional value, and growth rate of crops.

A Second Scientific Revolution

Like the Scientific Revolution of the sixteenth and seventeenth centuries, the scientific breakthroughs of the past century in astronomy, physics, biochemistry, and biology have given rise to profound changes in our understanding of the cosmos, with important cultural implications. In the first place, this new picture of the universe is one of mind-bending dimensions. We are now aware of the enormous duration of the universe — 13.8 billion years and counting. We now measure

AP®

CAUSATION

In what ways was technology a major driver of economic and social change during the past century?

AP®

MAKING CONNECTIONS

How were the scientific breakthroughs of the twentieth century similar to or different from those of the first Scientific Revolution?

AP® EXAM TIP

Make sure to understand the major intended (and unintended) effects of these scientific breakthroughs.

Landmarks for Chapter 13

| 1900 | 1920 | 1940 | 1960 | 1980 | 2000 | 2020 |

THE DEVELOPED INDUSTRIAL WORLD / GLOBAL NORTH

1882–1920 Electric grids developed in industrial countries

■ **1908** Mass production of automobiles begins

1940s Earliest digital computers

1960 Birth control pill approved in U.S.

1960s Second-wave feminism begins

1983 ■ Earliest cell phone

■ **1991** Earliest web browser released

1999 ■ Seattle protests against the WTO

2000–present Rapid growth of solar energy

■ **2008** Housing bubble collapse in U.S.

2020 ■ Britain exits EU

2017 ■ U.S. withdraws from Trans-Pacific Partnership

THE DEVELOPING WORLD / GLOBAL SOUTH

1920–1940 Land reform in Mexico

1923–1938 Women's emancipation in Turkey

1970s Developing countries demand "new international economic order"

1978–2013 Rapid economic growth in China

■ **1979** Islamic revolution in Iran

1980–2014 China's one-child family policy

2004 ■ Morocco's Family Law Code advances women's rights

THE WHOLE WORLD

1929–1940 The Great Depression

1930s–1960s Green Revolution technologies developed and applied

1945–1970 Postwar economic boom

■ **1975** United Nations: International Women's Year

2006 ■ UN Convention on the Elimination of All Forms of Discrimination against Women ratified by 183 nations

743

EXPLORING AP® THEMES

Humans and the Environment (ENV)

Ask students to study the events listed in "Landmarks for Chapter 13." Give students a map of the world on 11 by 17 paper. Have students note on the map where the landmarks occurred. Creating this map will allow students to understand the differences between the events occurring in the developed world versus the developing world. As students create the map, have them take notes on the events to create an annotated map. You can also make this a class activity rather than an individual activity. Divide the landmarks between random groups, with each group responsible for one regional area. The annotated map could be drawn on butcher paper and placed in an area that students can reference during the entire unit.

EXPLORING AP® THEMES

Technology and Innovations (TEC)

Understanding the origins and effects of the Scientific Revolution in the fourteenth through eighteenth centuries is important to understanding the technological breakthroughs of the twentieth and twenty-first centuries. Make certain that students understand the origins and effects of the Scientific Revolution by asking the following questions.

■ Why did the Scientific Revolution begin around the same time as the Renaissance? *The new ideas in art, architecture, and literature allowed scientists to begin theorizing about observations in the world around them. The publication of Nicolaus Copernicus's On the Revolutions of the Heavenly Spheres is often used as a starting point.*

■ What were the positive and negative effects of the Scientific Revolution? *Positive effects include: gain in knowledge, greater toleration (both religious and scientific), less superstition and more scientific answers, freedom to deviate from established theories, allowing further developments. Negative effects include: loss of traditional faith, loss of faith in Heaven, earth no longer regarded as the center of the universe, etc.*

astronomical distance in light years, just one of which is about 5.879 trillion miles. Our Milky Way galaxy alone measures about 100,000 light years across. And the universe contains an estimated 100 to 200 billion galaxies, each of which contains hundreds of millions or even billions of stars. Such numbers are merely educated guesses by scientists, but at this level they almost exceed our ability to feel them as meaningful. Our universe is incomprehensibly large.

Furthermore, the world we know through modern science is one of constant flux or change. The current "big bang" theory imagines a singular beginning of things, in an explosion of unimaginable power and temperature, perhaps only the most recent of many "big bangs" and many universes. In this understanding of the cosmos, everything changes, constantly. Even stars are born, generate in their fusion furnaces the elements known to students of chemistry, and eventually use up their fuel and die. For billions of years, the universe itself has been expanding very rapidly and, according to some, at accelerating rates. As one science writer put it: "The eternal heavens aren't. We are the first generation to live in a dynamic universe."[4] We have discovered, in short, that the cosmos has a history.

So too does the earth, which initially took shape some 4.5 billion years ago, along with its neighboring planets. One aspect of that history, discovered only in the 1960s and 1970s, is "plate tectonics," which explains how the continents have migrated across the surface of the earth for at least 2.5 billion years, how mountain chains arose, and how earthquakes function. Climate has also changed, as ice ages with extensive glaciation have alternated with warmer periods. The most significant change on earth was the emergence of life from the chemical soup of the early planet about 3.5 billion years ago. And life also changed or evolved, particularly in the past 600 million years, when larger multicelled plants and animals became abundant. New species arose, changed, and died out in periodic "extinction events." At the tail end of this enormous unfolding of cosmic and planetary evolution, just several hundred thousand years ago, human life emerged. In this new picture of the world, humankind is embedded in grand unfolding natural processes, and everything changes.

Those changes seem to move toward greater complexity, from simple hydrogen and helium atoms, to the development of stars, to the emergence of life on earth embodied in cells. "Even the simplest cell is far more complex than any inanimate object," wrote a leading astrophysicist.[5] Each cell membrane encloses many millions of molecules that are constantly interacting with one another. And then cells began to coordinate and work together, sharing information and giving rise to trees, whales, and people. "The human brain," writes the American physicist Michio Kaku, "has 100 billion neurons [nerve cells], each neuron connected to 10,000 other neurons. Sitting on your shoulders is the most complicated object in the known universe."[6]

In addition to this picture of increasing complexity, recent science has disclosed the connectivity of things. Everything, it seems, is connected to everything else; nothing can be understood by itself. Matter and energy, Einstein declared, are two manifestations of the same thing. Atoms, molecules, cells, and organs are entangled in vast networks of relationships in our bodies. Plants, animals, and the environment are linked in ecologies of interaction. Trees communicate and cooperate. And humankind is intimately connected to both cosmic and planetary history.

This novel understanding of the world has invited a reconsideration of old questions in a new context with profound cultural implications. Does the world exhibit purpose, direction, coherence, or unity? What is the significance of human consciousness in the face of cosmic vastness? Has science undermined religion or enhanced our experience of wonder, awe, and mystery? About such cultural matters, there is endless debate. What is not controversial, however, is the enormous role that science has played in seeding the massive acceleration of technological innovation that has so decisively shaped the history of the past century.

Fossil Fuel Breakthroughs

None of those technologies have been more significant than those related to energy production. Access to the stored energy of fossil fuels—coal, oil, and natural gas—has provided the foundation of the modern world economy, beginning with the Industrial Revolution in the nineteenth century. As their consumption skyrocketed, the twentieth century became the **age of fossil fuels** (see Figure 13.1 and AP® Looking Again). Coal production increased by some 700 percent during that century, and in its second half oil overtook coal as the dominant source of energy. Natural gas became a growing element in the energy equation in the latter decades of the century. In 2019 fossil fuels provided about 84 percent of the energy that powered the world economy.

Technological innovations allowed humankind to turn the potential energy of fossil fuels into useful energy, particularly the generation of electricity, the basic principles of which were discovered in the early nineteenth century in Great Britain. The subsequent development of coal-, oil-, or gas-fired power stations, alternating current, transformers, and batteries permitted electricity to be generated on a commercial scale, moved across great distances, and stored.

This more widespread availability of electricity was the product of electric grids, which generated power and transmitted it widely to homes and businesses. The development of such grids began in the late nineteenth century in the already industrialized

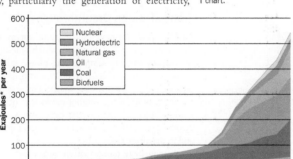

*An exajoule is a large-scale unit of energy.

Figure 13.1 Sources of World Energy Consumption, 1820–2010
Access to fossil fuels allowed world energy production to skyrocket during the twentieth century. (Data from Gail Tverberg, OurFiniteWorld.com, from https://ourfiniteworld.com/2012/03/12/world-energy-consumption-since-1820-in-charts)

TEACHING IDEA

Class Discussion

Ask students: What does "the age of fossil fuel" refer to? *The increased consumption of coal, oil, and natural gas, which allowed humans to turn potential energy into useful energy.*

BUILDING AP® SKILLS

Sourcing and Situation

For some quick practice on interpreting charts and graphs, have students look at Figure 13.1 and ask the following questions:

■ What helps explain the massive growth in energy production during the twentieth century? *The increased access to and use of fossil fuels, such as coal, oil, and natural gas, as an energy source.*

■ Increased concerns over the use of fossil fuels as an energy source have led some scientists and groups to find alternative energy sources. What alternative sources of energy are represented in the graph? *Nuclear power and hydroelectric power.*

countries, but it spread rapidly in capitalist, communist, colonial, and developing countries alike. By 2016, some 87 percent of the world's population had access to electricity, though not always reliably. Europe, Russia, North America, and Japan achieved 100 percent electrification first, but China, North Africa, Latin America, and parts of India achieved or approached that figure in the early twenty-first century.[7] By any historical standard, global electrification represents a very rapid transition to new ways of living.

Electrification lit up the world, especially at night, and much more cheaply than oil or gas lighting, allowing students to study, people to play, and employees to work around the clock. Electric motors powered all manner of industrial machinery far more productively than steam engines, and they made possible a vast array of consumer goods. Electrification became a crucial component of all economic development planning.

Another breakthrough in the generation of useful energy via fossil fuels was the gasoline- or oil-driven internal combustion engine, pioneered in the late nineteenth century in Western Europe and applied widely throughout the world in the twentieth century. That innovation created a huge new industry that became central to modern economic life; it led to a sharp decline in the use of horses; it enabled the far more rapid and efficient movement of goods and people, transforming the patterns of daily life for much of humankind; and it has been a potent source of the greenhouse gases that have driven climate change. Together, electricity and the internal combustion engine have enormously increased the energy available to humankind, even as access to that energy has favored the most highly industrialized economies (see Map 13.1).

Transportation Breakthroughs

Nowhere did this new availability of energy register more dramatically than in the technology of transportation, which built upon the revolutionary development of railroads and steamships in the nineteenth century. To those innovations, the twentieth century added cars, buses, and trucks; containerized shipping and super-tankers; and airplanes and air freight. This was the technological infrastructure that has made possible the surging movement of goods and people in the globalized world of recent times. By the early twenty-first century, the planet was densely crisscrossed on land by roads, railways, and pipelines, on the seas by shipping routes, and in the air by flight patterns.

Among these transportation technologies, none achieved a greater social and cultural impact than the automobile. In 1900, there were only about 10,000 cars in the global inventory, all of them expensive luxury items for the rich and most of them driven by steam or electric power. But the growing availability of cheap gasoline established the internal combustion engine as the means of propulsion for cars for the next century. It was Henry Ford's Model T, initially built in 1908, that launched the democratization of the automobile and made the United States the first country to market cars for the masses, followed by European countries and

AP
CAUSATION
How did electricity and the internal combustion engine transform human life during the past century?

AP
CAUSATION
Explain how transportation methods impacted the environment.

AP
CONTINUITY AND CHANGE
How did the acceleration of technological innovation contribute to globalization in the twenty-first century? How did this recent phase of globalization differ from earlier forms of transregional interaction?

EXPLORING AP® THEMES

Technology and Innovations (TEC)

Make certain that students understand how the development of new technologies changed the world in the twentieth century. Assign students pages 742–750 in Chapter 13. As students read the information, have them create a chart to keep track of the technological innovations of the last 120 years. The chart should look like the one below:

Fossil Fuel Breakthroughs	Transportation Breakthroughs	Communication and Information Breakthroughs	Military Breakthroughs
Coal, oil, natural gas, wind, solar, electricity, batteries	Internal combustion engine, cars, buses, trucks, shipping, airplanes	Transistors, integrated circuits, microprocessors, fiber-optic cables, cell/smart phones, radio, television, motion pictures, personal computers	Machine guns, submarines, tanks, poison gas, military aircraft, radar, jet engines, atomic weapons, space exploration

TRM Handout 13.2: Chart for Technological Innovations

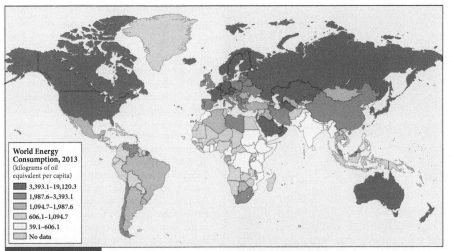

World Energy Consumption, 2013
(kilograms of oil equivalent per capita)

- 3,393.1–19,120.3
- 1,987.6–3,393.1
- 1,094.7–1,987.6
- 606.1–1,094.7
- 59.1–606.1
- No data

MAPPING HISTORY   Map 13.1 **World Energy Consumption per Capita, 2013**

While global energy production soared during the past century, access to that energy remained highly uneven in the early twenty-first century when measured on a per-person basis. (Data from World Bank)

Reading the Map: Which continents used the least amount of energy per capita in 2013? Was energy consumption relatively uniform on these continents, or were there significant variations between countries in these lower-use regions?

AP **Making Connections:** Compare this map with Map 11.1: The World in 1914. What might you infer about the legacy of colonialism by comparing relative energy consumption in 2013 in former imperial countries and their colonies?

Japan after World War II. By 2010, the world had over 1 billion cars, with developing countries contributing substantially to that number. China and India alone produced 28 percent of the world's cars in that year. The age of the automobile had become a global phenomenon.

Cars have shaped modern society and culture in many ways. Ownership of a car conveyed a sense of freedom, individuality, personal empowerment, and status. Like electrification, the car linked remote rural areas more firmly into national life. A farmwife in Georgia wrote to Henry Ford in 1918 about the Model T: "Your car lifted us out of the mud. It brought joy into our lives."[8] In urban areas, car ownership facilitated the growth of burgeoning suburbs. In doing so, it also created pervasive traffic jams and contributed much to air pollution, greenhouse gas emissions, and traffic fatalities. Like most technologies, the car conveyed both great benefits and heavy costs, but the world's love affair with the automobile has shown few signs of waning.

Technology and Innovations (TEC)

Make certain that students understand how new modes of communication reduced the geographic distance between people and continents. Ask them to brainstorm advancements in the nineteenth and twentieth centuries that led to mass communication between people. *Answers will include: telegraph, telephone, radios, television, computers, cell phones.*

The Automobile In the early twentieth century, the automobile represented unparalleled freedom of movement. The early driver was a mounted knight, observed the British intellectual Kenneth Boulding, while pedestrians were mere peasants. This French poster dating from around 1920 catches something of the car's mystique by depicting an automobile hurtling across the landscape guided by the ancient Greek messenger god Mercury wearing his winged helmet and sandals. (Popperfoto/Getty Images)

▲ **AP®**

SOURCING AND SITUATION

Why would the advertiser want to use Mercury in this poster? How does the poster reflect a mixture of technological progress and tradition?

Communication and Information Breakthroughs

The past century has also witnessed a flurry of innovations in communication and information that have transformed life for almost everyone. The modern **communication revolution**, like that of transportation, began in the nineteenth century with the telegraph and telephone, both of them using electricity to transmit information along a wire. In the twentieth century, innovation piled on innovation: vacuum tubes, transistors, integrated circuits, microprocessors, and fiber-optic cables. These novel technologies enabled radios, motion pictures, televisions, and most recently computers, cell phones, and the Internet. While these technologies and products were initially created in the West or Japan, they have taken root globally in less than a century, albeit unevenly. Radios have spread most widely, with over 75 percent of households in developing countries having access to a radio in 2012. TV coverage is more variable but surprisingly widespread. In much of Latin America, North Africa, the Middle East, and East Asia, 90 percent or more of households had a TV in the early twenty-first century. Internet access has soared globally since the introduction of web browsers in 1991, connecting about 59 percent of the world's population by 2020. The availability of cell phones has also spread very rapidly since the first mobile call in 1973 and the first smart phone in 1992. In much of Africa, for example, close to 80 percent of adults had access to a cell phone in 2017, allowing much of the continent to avoid installing more expensive land lines.

These communication technologies have reshaped human life across the planet and have spawned numerous debates about their consequences. Radio enabled even remote villagers to become aware of national and international events, even as it empowered authoritarian and democratic governments alike. Hitler's minister of propaganda, Joseph Goebbels, claimed in 1933 that "it would not have been possible for us [Nazis] to take power or to use it in the ways we have without the radio."[9] And Franklin Roosevelt used his radio "fireside chats" to reassure the American public during the Depression and World War II. But radio also challenged governments that sought to restrict their people's access to information. The availability of short-wave radio broadcasts from Europe and the United States eroded the capacity of the Soviet regime to monopolize the mass media and contributed to the collapse of Communist Party rule in the Soviet Union.

Television and the movies have generated a particularly sharp debate. Supporters have praised their ability to inform, educate, and entertain, but critics fear that American or Western domination of the media might erode local or national cultures, regret the generally low cultural level of TV programming, lament the effects of TV violence on children, and argue about the portrayal of women, minorities, Muslims, and others. Some states have sought to restrict the access of their citizens to these technologies. In 1994, Iran, for instance, passed a law that banned the production, sale, and assembly of satellite dishes in an effort to tightly control what Iranians could watch on TV.

The impact of personal computers and their numerous uses (the Internet, e-mail, social media, cell phones) has been pervasive and contested ever since they began to be widely available, at least in the West, during the 1980s. They made possible virtually unlimited access to information, enabling people the world over to participate creatively in this technological revolution. Education in many parts of the world has been transformed as online courses, "smart" classrooms, and digital books have proliferated, while computer science has become a major new field of study. Computer applications have become central to almost every aspect of business and economic life, spawning entirely new industries and forms of commerce. In many African countries, mobile banking has allowed millions to access financial services, with over two-thirds of Kenyans using their cell phones for this purpose in 2018. Online commerce has grown rapidly in the twenty-first century, with Alibaba in China and Amazon in the United States emerging as the leading online retailers.

Computer applications have also transformed personal life as online dating has spread to urban areas all around the world. Internet pornography has also become pervasive, though it is legally banned in China, India, the Islamic world, and elsewhere. By 2021 Facebook, launched in

AP
CAUSATION
What impact has modern communication technology had on the world in the past century?

▼ AP
CONTINUITY AND CHANGE
How does this image reflect the blending of tradition and modernity?

Computers and Camels The global penetration of computer technology is illustrated in this 2012 image of two Tunisian Bedouins consulting their laptop in the Sahara Desert. (akg-images/UIG/Godong)

TEACHING IDEA

Class Discussion

Ask students to read the last paragraph on page 748 and the first full paragraph on page 749 and make a list of how communication technology has reshaped life in the twentieth and twenty-first centuries. *Answers will include: Radio allowed isolated areas to keep up with national and international events; The radio also allowed both authoritarian and democratic leaders to reach and influence their people; Governments that attempted to restrict their people have been challenged by radios; Television and motion pictures have shared cultural traditions on a global scale.*

TEACHING IDEA

Incorporating Outside Resources

Personal computers have become the norm for almost everyone. Most students have technology at their fingertips. Over the last one hundred years, computers and computing have changed tremendously. If students are interested in this topic, have them watch *The Computer and Turing*, Crash Course History of Science 36 found on YouTube. After students watch the video, ask the following questions:

■ What is a "computer," and how has that word changed over the years? *Prior to 1950, the term "computer" referred to someone (usually a woman) who was able to complete mathematical computations. Since 1950, a computer is a machine that can be programmed to perform logical tasks.*

■ What modern company developed out of the Punch Card Tabulating Machine? *IBM.*

■ Who was Alan Turing? *A famous code breaker and mathematician whose work during World War II led to the later invention of the general-purpose computer and even artificial intelligence.*

2004, had connected some 2.89 billion active users, over a third of the world's population, to an array of "friends," generating intense controversy about privacy, censorship, "fake news," and the dissemination of misinformation. Recreation also has been transformed as computer-based gaming has spread globally, with China emerging as the largest video game market in the world.

These information technologies have generated anxieties and criticism. Individuals fear being bullied by peers, monitored and controlled by governments, and manipulated by corporations able to track their buying preferences. Debate has arisen as to whether the Internet facilitates or undermines personal relationships. Hacking of government records and corporate secrets has raised concerns about cyber-warfare, while the entire complex system remains vulnerable to outages, sabotage, and natural disaster. Democratic countries have increasingly worried about cyber interference in their elections.

Military Weapons Breakthroughs

A final example of accelerated innovation lies in technologies of destruction. The late nineteenth-century development of high-power explosives such as dynamite as well as machine guns found application in World War I, along with other new technologies such as submarines, tanks, poison gas, radio, and military aircraft. World War II refined and enhanced these technologies, while adding radar, computers, jet engines, battle tanks, fighter aircraft, aircraft carriers, and atomic bombs to the mix. The cold war generated ever more sophisticated nuclear weapons, from enormous hydrogen bombs to smaller tactical nuclear weapons. New means of delivering them with almost pinpoint accuracy also emerged, using ballistic missiles launched from airplanes, land-based silos, or submarines. At the height of the cold war and ever since, we have been able to imagine, realistically, a nuclear war that would result in instant death for tens of millions of people, the collapse of modern civilization, and perhaps the extinction of the human species. Military technologies, of course, have also had numerous civilian spin-offs, including radar, nuclear power plants, the Internet, space exploration, and communication satellites.

The Global Economy: The Acceleration of Entanglement

> **Finding the Main Point:** What were the major drivers of globalization over the past century? How did this enormous process reshape world history?

Accelerating technological innovation decisively shaped the world economy of the past century, enabling what we now refer to as **economic globalization**, particularly during the seven decades following World War II. A central element of that process has been the spread of industrialization among the peoples of the Global South.

Industrial Globalization: Development in the Global South

As decolonization, independence, and revolution rolled over much of Africa, Asia, and Latin America, economic development and industrialization became a central priority everywhere. They were an essential promise of all revolutions and independence struggles, and they were increasingly the standard by which people measured and granted legitimacy to their governments.

Achieving economic development, however, was no easy or automatic task for societies sharply divided by class, religion, ethnic group, and gender and facing explosive population growth. In many places, colonial rule had provided only the most slender foundations for modern development, as new nations often came to independence with low rates of literacy, few people with managerial experience, a weak private economy, and little industrial infrastructure. Furthermore, the entire effort occurred in a world split by rival superpowers and economically dominated by the powerful capitalist economies of the West.

Beyond these difficulties lay the vexing question of what strategies to pursue. Should state authorities take the lead, or was it wiser to rely on private enterprise and the market? Should industrial production be aimed at the domestic market in an "import substitution" approach, or was it more effective to specialize in particular products, such as cars, clothing, or electronics, for an export market?

For developing countries, it was an experimental process, and the outcomes varied considerably. (See Snapshot, page 756.) In general, East Asian countries that produced products primarily for export have had the strongest record of economic growth. South Korea, Taiwan, Singapore, and Hong Kong were dubbed **Asian Tigers** or newly industrialized countries. Following the death of Mao Zedong in 1976, China soon became a spectacular economic success story, boasting the most rapid economic growth in the world by the end of the twentieth century while replacing Japan as the world's second-largest economy and edging up on the United States. In the 1990s, Asia's other giant, India, opened itself more fully to the world market and launched rapid economic growth with a powerful high-tech sector and major steel, chemical, automotive, and pharmaceutical industries. Oil-producing countries reaped a bonanza when they were able to demand much higher prices for that essential commodity in the 1970s and after. By 2016, Mexico, Turkey, Malaysia, Thailand, Vietnam, India, and Indonesia numbered in the top twenty of the most competitive manufacturing countries, with China ranking number one. Limited principally to Europe, North America, and Japan in the nineteenth century, industrialization and modern economic growth had become a global phenomenon by the early twenty-first century. It was also an uneven process, as much of Africa and various other countries (such as Afghanistan, Myanmar, Yemen, and Haiti) lagged behind.

Economic Globalization: Deepening Connections

Accompanying the worldwide spread of modern development and industrial growth was a tightening network of global economic relationships that cut across the world's separate countries and regions, binding them together more closely, but

AP EXAM TIP

Make sure you can identify the impact of globalization on the Global South in the second half of the twentieth century.

AP

COMPARISON

How has global industrial development varied across the world during the past century?

AP

CAUSATION

In what ways have global economic connections deepened during the past century? What have been the consequences of these deepening connections?

APPLY THE TIP

You could have students view the map in the AP® World History: Modern Course and Exam Description Guide to review the regions of the Global South.

BUILDING AP® SKILLS

Making Connections: Continuity and Change

The late twentieth century is not the first time civilizations and distant cultures were connected. Ask students to name previous examples of cross-cultural connections. *In the past, cultures became connected through the spread of empires, such as the Roman, Byzantine, and Mongolian empires. Trade routes such as the Silk Road were another mechanism for the connection of distant civilizations and cultures. Finally, cultures also became connected through colonization.*

BUILDING AP® SKILLS

Developments and Processes

Ask students: Given that there are many examples of previous global encounters, why is the post–World War II era labeled the era of globalization? *Global interaction quickened its pace after World War II through networks of communication and transportation that advanced rapidly with technology. The development of international economic and social organization that began to appear at that time has also increased the pace of globalization.*

AP® CLASSROOM

AP® Daily Videos

This is an excellent opportunity to have students watch AP® Daily Videos for Topic 9.4: Economics in the Global Age, located on AP® Classroom. You can find the video for Topic 9.4 by logging into AP® Classroom, clicking on Unit 9 under Classroom Resources, and then selecting Daily Videos. Daily Video 1 for Topic 9.4: Economics in the Global Age looks at the skills of sourcing and situation to understand the significance of primary sources, while Daily Video 2 looks at the skills of sourcing and situation to understand the significance of secondary sources.

Containerized Shipping The growth of global trade has been facilitated by containerized shipping, a highly mechanized process of moving goods that requires far fewer workers and has substantially reduced transportation costs. This photograph illustrates that process as it occurred in the Chinese port of Qingdao in mid-2017. (STR/Getty Images)

▲ AP®
CAUSATION
What are the social and economic effects of the type of trade pictured in this image?

AP® EXAM TIP
You need to know examples of governments that promoted free-market economies, like Britain under Margaret Thatcher or China under Deng Xiaoping.

also more contentiously, during the second half of the twentieth century. It signaled a renewal and a great acceleration of earlier trends that had linked the economies of the world.

The capitalist victors in World War II, led by the United States, were determined to avoid any return to the kind of economic contraction and nationalist excesses associated with World War I and the Great Depression. At a conference in Bretton Woods, New Hampshire, in 1944, they forged a set of agreements and institutions (the World Bank and the International Monetary Fund [IMF]) that laid the foundation for postwar globalization. This **Bretton Woods system** negotiated the rules for commercial and financial dealings among the major capitalist countries, while promoting relatively free trade, stable currency values linked to the U.S. dollar, and high levels of capital investment.

By the 1980s, leading figures in capitalist countries such as President Ronald Reagan in the United States and Prime Minister Margaret Thatcher of Great Britain, as well as in major international lending agencies such as the World Bank, increasingly viewed the entire world as a single market. This approach to the world economy, widely known as neoliberalism, favored the reduction of tariffs, the free global movement of capital, a mobile and temporary workforce, the privatization of many state-run enterprises, the curtailing of government efforts to regulate the economy, and both tax and spending cuts. In this view, the market, operating both globally and within nations, was the most effective means of generating the holy grail of economic growth. As communism collapsed by the end of the twentieth century, "capitalism was global and the globe was capitalist."[10]

Such policies, together with major changes in transportation and communication technology, accompanied a dramatic quickening of global economic transactions after World War II, expressed in the accelerating circulation of both goods and capital. World trade, for example, skyrocketed from a value of some $57 billion in 1947 to about $18.3 trillion in 2012. For those with enough money, it meant access to the goods of the world. It also meant employment. In the United States in 2008, exports supported some 10 million jobs and represented about 13 percent of the country's gross domestic product (GDP). Many developing countries, however, were far more dependent on exports, usually raw materials and agricultural products. Ghana, for example, relied on exports for 44 percent of its GDP in 2014, mostly gold, cocoa beans, and timber products. Cocoa alone supported some 700,000 farming families. Mounting trade entangled the peoples of the world to an unprecedented degree.

Economic entanglement was financial as well as commercial. "Foreign direct investment," whereby a firm in, say, the United States opens a factory in China or Mexico, exploded after 1960 as companies in rich countries sought to take advantage of cheap labor, tax breaks, and looser environmental regulations in developing countries. Money also surged around the planet as investors and financiers annually spent trillions of dollars purchasing foreign currencies or stocks that were likely to increase in value and often selling them quickly thereafter, with unsettling consequences. The personal funds of individuals likewise achieved a new mobility as international credit cards took hold almost everywhere.

Central to the acceleration of economic globalization have been huge global businesses known as **transnational corporations** (TNCs), which produce goods or deliver services simultaneously in many countries. Toyota, the world's largest automaker in 2016, sold cars around the world and had manufacturing facilities in some twenty-eight countries on five continents. Burgeoning in number since the 1960s, TNCs such as Shell based in the Netherlands, Nissan in Japan, General Motors in the United States, and Mahindra and Mahindra in India often were so enormous and had such economic clout that their assets and power dwarfed those of many countries. By 2000, fifty-one of the world's hundred largest economic units were in fact TNCs, not countries. In the permissive economic climate of recent decades, such firms have been able to move their facilities quickly from place to place in search of the lowest labor costs or the least restrictive environmental regulations. During one five-year period, for example, Nike closed twenty factories and opened thirty-five others, often thousands of miles apart.

Growth, Instability, and Inequality

The impact of these tightening economic linkages has prompted enormous debate and controversy. (See Controversies: Debating Globalization, page 754.) Amid the swirl of contending opinion, one thing seemed reasonably clear: economic globalization accompanied, and arguably helped generate, the most remarkable spurt of economic growth in world history. On a global level, total world output grew from a value of $7 trillion in 1950 to $73 trillion in 2009 and on a per capita basis from $2,652 to $10,728.[11] While world population quadrupled during the twentieth century, the output of the world economy grew by a factor of 14 and industrial output by a factor of 40. This represents an immense, rapid, and unprecedented creation of wealth with a demonstrable impact on human welfare. Everywhere people lived longer. Global average life expectancy has more than doubled since 1900, to 73.2 years in 2020. Everywhere, far fewer children died before the age of five: in 1960 the global average was 18.2 percent; in 2018, 3.8 percent. And everywhere more people were literate. Some 80 percent of adults could read and write

CONTROVERSIES | Debating Globalization

By the early 1990s, "globalization" had become a buzz-word among scholars, journalists, and ordinary people alike because it succinctly captured something of the deeply connected and entangled world of the late twentieth century. The economists, sociologists, and political scientists who first embraced the term presented "globalization" as novel and unprecedented: the world was becoming "a single place," and human history was entering a wholly new era of global connectedness and global consciousness.

World historians, however, were not so sure about the novelty of "globalization." They had, after all, long traced patterns of interaction, communication, and exchange among distant regions and civilizations: the Silk Road commercial networks across Eurasia; the movement of technologies and disease; the transcontinental spread of Buddhism, Christianity, and Islam; the making of an Atlantic world linking Europe, Africa, and the Americas; and the globe-spanning empires of Europe. Did all of this count as "globalization," pushing its origins deep into the past?

Yet another controversy involved the "drivers" of globalization. For some, they were impersonal forces—"the inexorable integration of markets, nation-states, and technologies"—according to leading journalist Thomas Friedman. In such a view, no one was in control, and the process, once begun, was inevitable and unstoppable. Others believed that powerful economic elites and political leaders, acting from a free market ideology, deliberately shaped policies (such as low tariffs) and institutions (the World Trade Organization, for example) that opened the door to corporate globalization.

The economic outcomes of recent globalization have also generated much debate. Did globalization increase or reduce inequality? Answers depend very much on what is being measured. If the measure is income, most economists think that inequality on a global level has substantially increased. One study concluded that the per capita income gap between the United States and various regions of the Global South roughly tripled since 1960.[12] The rich were getter richer much faster than the poor were gaining income.

But if the measure of economic outcomes involves "quality of life indicators," the picture changes considerably. Average global life expectancy, for example, more than doubled since 1900, reaching 73.2 years in 2020. By 2019 many countries in the Global South approached the 79-year life span of U.S. citizens: China, 77 years; Brazil, 76; India, 70. Even poorer countries have dramatically increased their life expectancies, with sub-Saharan African rates improving from 40 years in 1960 to 61.6 years in 2019.[13] Clearly, despite growing inequality in income, inequality in longevity has lessened. So which is the more important measure of inequality: income measured in dollars or life expectancy measured in years?

Yet another controversy involves the impact of globalization on nation-states. Many elements of the globalized world have arguably diminished the ability of nation-states to act freely in their own interests—agreements favoring free trade and the power of huge transnational corporations, for example. The more enthusiastic advocates of globalization have imagined a future in which the nation-state has vanished, or at least greatly weakened, in the face of global flows of people, capital, goods, services, and ideas.

Others, however, view such opinions as exaggerated. It was, after all, the decisions of some states that created a free trade international system after World War II, even as other states, especially in the communist bloc, refused to take part in it. And what states create they can also change. China joined the World Trade Organization in 2001 after decades of declining to take part in the global marketplace; the United Kingdom decided in 2020 to leave the European Union; the Trump administration in the United States announced American withdrawal

AP

CAUSATION
Explain how an economic crisis in one country can affect multiple nations.

at some level by 2000, while only 21 percent could do so in 1900. The UN Human Development Report in 1997 concluded that "in the past 50 years, poverty has fallen more than in the previous 500."

Far more problematic have been the instability of this emerging world economy and the distribution of the immense wealth it has generated. Amid overall economic

ERIC'S ACTIVITY 13 Debating Globalization

"Globalization" is a term that regularly elicits strong reactions from my students, who tend to see it as either a positive or negative development. This activity uses the Controversies feature of this chapter as the starting point for a discussion designed to highlight the mixed impact of globalization on humankind. Through this discussion students develop skills in interpretation as they grapple with a process that defies easy generalization. Find the complete activity in the Teacher's Resource Materials.

TRM Eric's Activity 13: Debating Globalization

from the Trans-Pacific Partnership agreement in early 2017. Even developing countries have some leverage. Both Mexico and Cuba nationalized American industries in their countries in the twentieth century. And the oil-producing states of the Middle East upended the global markets in the 1970s when they refused to sell oil to the United States for six months and dramatically raised the price of oil. All of this testifies to the continuing power of state action to shape the world economy.

Cultural globalization too prompted debate and controversy. Has the world become more culturally homogeneous in the global age? Many feared that the answer was "yes" as "cultural imperialism" in the shape of westernization or Americanization swept the planet, displacing many established cultural patterns and ways of living. The prevalence of English and modern science; the pervasive presence of global brands such as Coca-Cola; the popularity of McDonald's, blue jeans, Barbie dolls, and American films; shopping malls and Western-style consumerism across the world; cell phones and the Internet—all of this and much more suggested the emergence of a "global culture."

But perhaps globalization produces or reinforces cultural difference as well as commonality. The rise of Islamic fundamentalism represented strong resistance to the intrusion of Western secular culture. French efforts to prevent the importation of too many American films or TV programs and to prohibit the wearing of headscarves by Muslim women likewise reflected a desire to preserve major elements of French national culture in an age of globalization. A proliferation of ethnic nationalist movements articulated demands to ensure the integrity of particular and local cultures. Furthermore, a phenomenon known as "glocalization" refers to the process by which foreign products or practices are adapted to local cultural patterns. Yoga in the West often became a form of exercise or relaxation, losing much of its original spiritual

significance, while McDonald's restaurants in India and China now include various rice-based menu offerings.

Globalization is commonly regarded as a still-unfolding process leading to an uncertain destination, often called "globality" or "entanglement on a global scale." Two prominent historians have recently contested this understanding, arguing that "globality" has long been a "done deal," a condition already achieved. The question then is not whether to participate in this globalized world, but rather "how to change in order to keep pace with, hold out against, or adapt to a world of continuous and inescapable interactivity."[14]

And yet, is it possible to imagine global connections unraveling? Is globalization really a "done deal"? Various events of the early twenty-first century have caused many to wonder: the global recession of 2008; the sharp economic contraction during the COVID-19 pandemic of the early 2020s; the exit of Great Britain from the European Union; the U.S. election of Donald Trump promising that "Americanism not globalism will be our credo"; the reaction against immigration in the United States and Western Europe; the Russian invasion of Ukraine; and the rise of assertive nationalist movements in much of Europe, Turkey, Iran, China, India, and elsewhere. Does this mean that globalization is in retreat? The debate continues, as it does for almost everything related to globalization.

QUESTIONS TO CONSIDER

1. How might you describe in your own words the major debates and controversies that are associated with the concept of globalization? Can you think of other questions that arise from the use of this term?

2. How do you think the authors of this book have answered those questions in Chapter 13? Or have they avoided doing so?

growth, periodic crises and setbacks have shaped recent world history. Soaring oil prices in 1973–1974 resulted in several years of economic stagnation for many industrialized countries, great hardship for many developing countries, and an economic windfall for oil-producing countries. Inability to repay mounting debts triggered a major financial crisis in Latin America during the 1980s and resulted in a "lost decade"

BUILDING AP® SKILLS

Argumentation

This is a good time to practice a long essay on globalization. You can use the released LEQ Question 4 from the 2022 exam. This prompt can be found under the Exam tab on the AP® World History homepage located on AP® Central.

Differentiation

While it's good for students to write full essays, especially as they get closer to the AP® Exam, it can also be helpful to have them work on a group essay outline and evaluate their peers' responses. This exercise allows them to see different ways of formulating arguments and potentially understand what graders are looking for when scoring essays. If you want students to complete a group outline essay with this prompt, consider following the "Must Do, Should Do, Strive For" model below:

■ Must Do: Working in groups of four or fewer, students should create an LEQ outline on the provided butcher paper. The outline should include contextualization and a thesis that responds to the prompt, at least two arguments, and at least two pieces of evidence for *each* argument.

■ Should Do: Once all the groups have completed their LEQ poster, have students hang them up and do a gallery walk to see how other groups put together this LEQ. As they look at each poster, ask students to leave "I wonder . . ." and "I like . . ." statements about what they see in the outline.

■ Strive For: For students who want or need a writing challenge, have them choose one of their arguments from their LEQ poster and write a full argument paragraph on it.

Making Connections: Causation

The multiple-choice section of the exam will have questions that are anchored to a stimulus, such as the "Snapshot: Global Development and Inequality, 2011." Ask students the following multiple-choice question: Which of the following was a consequence of the information shown in the chart?

a. Movements throughout the world protested the negative economic consequences of global integration.
b. The International Monetary Fund was formed.
c. Western nations moved to recolonize the nations with the lowest income.
d. Migration came to a near halt to minimize income disparity.

Answer: a. Movements throughout the world protested the negative economic consequences of global integration.

Making Connections: Contextualization

Show students "Snapshot: Global Development and Inequality, 2011." Discuss the information on the chart as a class. Ask students what statistic they find most surprising and why. *Answers will vary.*

SNAPSHOT Global Development and Inequality, 2011

This table shows thirteen commonly used indicators of "development" and their variations in 2011 across four major groups of countries defined by average level of per capita income. In which areas has the Global South most nearly caught up with the Global North?

	GROSS NATIONAL INCOME PER CAPITA (SAMPLE COUNTRIES)			
	Low Income: $995 or Less (Congo, Kenya, Ethiopia, Afghanistan, Myanmar)	Lower-Middle Income: $996–$3,945 (India, China, Egypt, Algeria, Indonesia, Nigeria)	Upper-Middle Income: $3,946–$12,195 (Mexico, Brazil, Turkey, Russia, Iran)	Upper Income: $12,196 or More (USA, Western Europe, Japan, South Korea, Australia)
Life expectancy: M/F in years	58/60	66/70	68/75	77/83
Deaths under age 5 per 1,000 live births	120	60	24	7
Deaths from infectious disease: %	36	14	11	7
Access to toilets: %	35	50	84	99
Years of education	7.9	10.3	13.8	14.5
Literacy rate: %	66	80	93	99
Population growth: % annual	2.27	1.27	.96	.39
Urban population: %	27	41	74	78
Cell phones per 100 people	22	47	92	106
Internet users per 100 people	2.3	13.7	29.9	68.3
Personal computers per 100 people	1.2	4.3	11.9	60.4
Cars per 1,000 people	5.8	20.3	125.2	435.1
Carbon dioxide emissions: metric tons per capita	1	3	5	13

Data from "Map Supplement," *National Geographic* (Washington, DC: National Geographic Society, March 2011).

▲ **AP**

CONTEXTUALIZATION
What can we infer about a country by studying its access to toilets and cell phones? Why is population growth smaller in the wealthiest regions?

in terms of economic development. Another financial crisis in Asia during the late 1990s resulted in the collapse of many businesses, widespread unemployment, and political upheaval in Indonesia and Thailand. And in 2008 an inflated housing market—or "bubble"—in the United States collapsed, triggering millions of home foreclosures, growing unemployment, the tightening of credit, and declining consumer spending. Soon this crisis rippled around the world. In Sierra Leone, some 90 percent of the country's diamond-mine workers lost their jobs. Impoverished Central American and Caribbean families, dependent on money sent home by family members working abroad, suffered further as those remittances dropped sharply. Contracting economies contributed to debt crises in Greece, Italy, and Spain and threatened to unravel European economic integration. Whatever the overall benefits of globalization, economic stability and steady progress were not among them.

Nor did globalization resolve the problem of inequality. (See Snapshot, page 756.) Despite substantial gains in life expectancy, infant mortality, literacy, and the reduction of poverty, economic inequality on a global level has been stubbornly persistent and by some measures growing. In 1870 the average per capita income in the world's ten richest countries was six times that of the ten poorest countries. By 2002 that ratio was 42 to 1.[15] That gap has been evident, often tragically, in great disparities in incomes, medical care, availability of clean drinking water, educational and employment opportunities, access to the Internet, and dozens of other ways. It has shaped the life chances of practically everyone. Even among developing countries, great inequalities were apparent. The oil-rich economies of the Middle East had little in common with the banana-producing countries of Central America. The rapidly industrializing states of China, India, and South Korea had quite different economic agendas than impoverished African countries.

Economic globalization has contributed to inequalities not only among countries and regions, but also within individual nations, rich and poor alike. In the United States, for example, income inequality has sharply increased since the late 1970s. The American economy shed millions of manufacturing jobs, with some companies moving their operations to Asia or Latin America, where labor costs were lower. More important, however, was automation. The U.S. steel industry, for example, lost 75 percent of its workforce between 1962 and 2005, while producing roughly the same amount of steel. This left many American workers in the lurch, forcing them to work in the low-wage service sector, even as other Americans were growing prosperous in emerging high-tech industries. Globalization divided Mexico as well. The northern part of the country, with close business and manufacturing ties to the United States, grew much more prosperous than the south, which was a largely rural agricultural area and had a far more slowly growing economy. China's rapid economic growth likewise fostered mounting inequality between its rural households and those in its burgeoning cities, where income by 2000 was three times that of the countryside. Economic globalization may have brought people together as never before, but it has also divided them sharply.

Pushback: Resistance to Economic Globalization

Those who felt unfairly treated, left behind, or overwhelmed by a tsunami of change increasingly pushed back. One expression of this resistance derived from the Global South, a term that refers to the less industrialized countries, most of which were located south of the wealthier countries of the Global North. As the East/West division of capitalism and communism faded, differences between the rich nations of the Global North and the developing countries of the Global South assumed greater

AP
CONTEXTUALIZATION
What criticisms of economic globalization have emerged, and from what sources do they derive?

EXPLORING AP® THEMES

Economic Systems (ECN)

Ask students to complete a chart like the one below by indicating how the worldwide economic crisis of 2008 affected various regions. A reproducible version of this chart is available in the Teacher's Resource Materials. (Answers are provided in italics.)

Region	Impact of Economic Crisis
United States	*Millions of home foreclosures, unemployment, declining consumer spending*
Europe	*Bank failures, debt crisis*
Africa	*Reduced demand for exports, unemployment*
Central America	*Families dependent on money sent home suffered economically*
Asia	*High unemployment in China*

TRM Handout 13.3: Chart for the 2008 Economic Crisis

TEACHING IDEA

Incorporating Outside Resources

In the episode *Globalization II: Good or Bad?* of Crash Course World History, John Green discusses globalization and whether or not globalization is positive for humanity. While globalization has created a lot of wealth, it has also had negative effects on the environment and with the spread of disease. You can find the video on YouTube. Ask students to take notes on the key features of the negative aspects of globalization, and then have them analyze whether or not globalization is truly beneficial. *Globalization can lead to a rise in the standard of living via employment for many countries and provides developing countries with goods and services. Globalization can also have disastrous environmental effects and lead to pandemics.*

BUILDING AP® SKILLS

Argumentation

In preparation for the exam, students should know the negative impacts as well as the positive impacts of globalization. Use the following short-answer-style questions to develop a more nuanced understanding of globalization and to practice citing evidence for the short-answer questions on the exam.

■ Some historians stress the negative impact that globalization has had on developing nations. Provide two pieces of evidence that support the assertion that globalization has had a negative impact on developing nations. *Globalization has led to environmental damage, the westernization of the world, and poor working conditions for some people.*

■ Some historians stress the positive impact that globalization has had on developing nations. Provide at least two pieces of evidence that support the assertion that globalization has had a positive impact on developing nations. *Globalization provides goods and jobs to many parts of the world. It has increased the technology available to people in developing nations. It has increased the availability of medical care and improved living conditions for some impoverished people. Globalization has raised the awareness of poverty and improved the standard of living for many.*

BUILDING AP® SKILLS

Sourcing and Situation

Using all available opportunities to practice sourcing is wise the closer the exam date gets. Ask students to look at the photograph and ask: What is the significance of the activist wearing the HAZMAT protective gear? *Answers will vary.*

prominence in world affairs. Highly contentious issues have included the rules for world trade, availability of and terms for foreign aid, representation in international economic organizations, the mounting problem of indebtedness, and environmental and labor standards. In the 1970s, for example, a large group of developing countries joined together to demand a "new international economic order" that was more favorable to the poor countries, though with little success. Developing countries have often contested protectionist restrictions on their agricultural exports imposed by the rich countries seeking to safeguard their own politically powerful farmers.

In the 1990s a growing popular movement, featuring a highly critical posture toward globalization, emerged as an international coalition of political activists, concerned scholars and students, trade unions, women's and religious organizations, environmental groups, and others, hailing from rich and poor countries alike. Though reflecting a variety of viewpoints, that opposition largely agreed that market-driven corporate globalization had lowered labor standards, fostered ecological degradation, prevented poor countries from protecting themselves against financial speculators, ignored local cultures, disregarded human rights, and enhanced global inequality, while favoring the interests of large corporations and rich countries.

▼ **AP**
COMPARISON
How are the criticisms of globalization similar to the criticisms of capitalism?

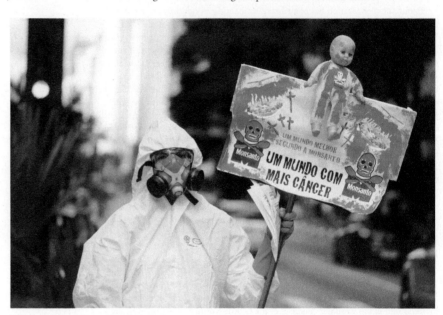

Anti-Globalization Protest A demonstrator in São Paulo, Brazil, in 2013, part of a worldwide protest against the biotech giant Monsanto, holds a sign reading: "A better world according to Monsanto is a world with more cancer." (Nelson Antoine/AP Images)

This movement appeared dramatically on the world's radar screen in 1999 in Seattle at a meeting of the **World Trade Organization (WTO)**. An international body founded in 1995 and now representing 164 nations, the WTO has sought to negotiate the rules for global commerce and to promote free trade. Increasingly, it became a major target of globalization critics. "The central idea of the WTO," argued one such critic, "is that *free trade*—actually the values and interests of global corporations—should supersede all other values."[16] Tens of thousands of protesters from all over the world descended on Seattle in what became a violent, chaotic, and much-publicized protest. Such protests stimulated the creation in 2001 of the World Social Forum, an annual gathering of alternative globalization activists to coordinate strategy, exchange ideas, and share experiences, under the slogan "Another world is possible."

Local activists in various places likewise resisted the impact of globalization. In 1994 in southern Mexico, peasant resentment boiled over against the Mexican government and its privatizing of communally held land, which was related to the country's 1984 entry into the **North American Free Trade Agreement (NAFTA)**. The leader of this peasant upheaval referred to globalization as a "process to eliminate that multitude of people who are not useful to the powerful." Likewise in southern India, activist farmers during the late 1990s organized protests against the opening of Kentucky Fried Chicken outlets as well as against the giant American chemical corporation Monsanto, uprooting and burning fields where Monsanto grew genetically modified cotton.

Opposition to globalization also emerged from more conservative circles, especially after the sharp economic downturn beginning in 2008. Britain's decision to leave the European Union in 2020 clearly represented a backlash against globalization, even as movements hostile to a more united Europe gained support in many countries. So too did the U.S. election of 2016, in which all of the candidates expressed reservations about international trade agreements as threatening American jobs. The most vociferous voice was that of the winner, Donald Trump, who withdrew the United States from the Trans-Pacific Partnership trade agreement and renegotiated NAFTA, replacing it with the United States–Mexico–Canada Agreement in 2020. Elsewhere as well—in Turkey, Russia, China, and India, for example—political leaders increasingly appealed to national pride and cultural purity. Observers wondered if this represented a rejection of earlier assumptions that international cooperation in reducing trade barriers fostered peace and prosperity for all concerned.

Producing and Consuming: The Shapes of Modern Societies

Finding the Main Point: How did societies around the world change in the twentieth and twenty-first centuries?

Technological innovation and economic globalization during the past century have dramatically reshaped human societies around the world. Further contributing to this reshaping of social structures have been the actions of state authorities through

TEACHING IDEA

Class Discussion

Ask students: What is the significance of the World Social Forum? *Answers will include: It supports protest against the WTO and fosters alternative ideas of globalization.*

AP® CLASSROOM

AP® Topic Questions

Now is an excellent opportunity for some practice with multiple-choice questions. You can find a set of questions about free trade markets by logging into AP® Classroom, clicking on Unit 9 under Classroom Resources, and then selecting Topic Questions. Look for the questions labeled "Deng Xiaoping." You can either assign the questions to the students to complete individually or allow them to partner up to work through the set together.

their laws, regulations, and policies. Broad global patterns such as the declining role of peasant farmers and the growing role of middle-class professionals found expression in many variations across the multiple divides of the modern world.

Life on the Land: The Decline of the Peasantry

A little over 20 percent of the world's population farmed full time in 2000, a dramatic drop from 66 percent in 1950 and around 80 percent in many preindustrial agricultural societies. One historian has described this development as "the death of the peasantry," which has allowed "an absurdly tiny percentage" of the population "to flood . . . the world with untold quantities of food."[17]

A major factor in this decline was mechanization, as machinery such as tractors and combines made farmers more productive, earlier in North America and Australia and later elsewhere in the world. Furthermore, many farmers in the Global North and some regions of the Global South (India, Argentina, and Brazil) also embraced Green Revolution innovations, including chemical fertilizers and new types of seed, that were initially developed between the 1930s and the late 1960s. By the 1970s a corn farmer in the United States was between 100 and 1,000 times more productive than his nineteenth-century counterpart, but costs were also much higher as expenditures on machinery, fertilizer, and diesel fuel soared. Describing the impact of technology on his work, Ken Grimsdell, whose company raised crops in the Midlands of England, noted in 2015: "A tractor can be controlled by satellite, drones can fly over a crop, record pictures and send them back to the office. The technology has made for better farming."[18] It also made for fewer farmers.

Many of the most mechanized and efficient farms in the world remained dependent on seasonal labor at crucial moments in the agricultural year. The work of migrant laborers, often organized into teams that moved from place to place, was intense, repetitive, and sometimes dangerous, especially as the use of toxic pesticides increased with the Green Revolution. Migrant workers typically were outsiders in the communities where they worked and in the United States were often undocumented or possessed temporary work visas. Nevertheless, this difficult life attracted millions of Latin American and Caribbean migrants to the fields of the United States, as well as similar numbers of Eastern Europeans to the farms of Western Europe following the enlargement of the European Union in the early twenty-first century.

Ever cheaper transportation costs created an increasingly global market for food, forcing farmers, often on different continents, to compete with one another. Trade deals exposed small-scale farmers in the Global South to the mechanized and heavily subsidized farming industries of the Global North. In 1994, NAFTA allowed corn from the United States to flood the Mexican market, forcing 2 million small farmers in Mexico to abandon its cultivation. In 2006, Tirso Alvares Correa worried that no one would be left to work land that his family had tilled for generations. "Free trade has been a disaster for us. . . . Corn from abroad is taking a toll. . . . We can't sell our corn anymore."[19] Some displaced farmers found work on large estates

---

Ask students the following question: *What caused the decline of the peasantry in the twentieth century? Answers will vary, but should include: mechanization, scientific advancements in farming techniques, the Green Revolution, etc.*

BUILDING AP® SKILLS
Sourcing and Situation

To examine the effects of the Green Revolution on the declining peasantry, consider using Document 7 from the 2011 AP® World History Exam. Document 7 is from *Focus*, the Food and Agriculture Organization (FAO) newsletter, and can be used to help students practice sourcing for the DBQ. Copy or project the document and ask students to complete a HIPP exercise for the selection. *Suggested answers:*

■ **Historical Situation:** *The newsletter was published thirty years after the start of the Green Revolution, when scholars and scientists had begun to see more of the long-term effects of the revolution.*

■ **Intended Audience:** *The FAO intended for this report to show the social effects of the Green Revolution to the governments of different countries that were participating in the revolution.*

■ **Purpose:** *The article was written for the newsletter to explain to governments the negative social effects of the Green Revolution to make sure no group was being hurt or "left behind" by the revolution.*

■ **Point of View:** *The FAO is a specialized agency within the UN dedicated to ensuring food security for everyone and ensuring that people can lead active lives, which is why it was concerned with the impact of the Green Revolution on rural women.*

geared toward raising crops like avocados for export. Many others immigrated to the United States, with some finding work on American farms.

While farmers as a percentage of the population declined dramatically in the second half of the twentieth century, nearly 27 percent of the world's population, about 2 billion people, still earned their living from the land in 2016, more than the total world population in 1850. Most remained small-scale or subsistence cultivators. In some regions, farming populations grew rapidly, paralleling the growth of population generally. Land reform movements in Mexico, Ethiopia, Iran, India, and elsewhere during the twentieth century contributed to this trend by distributing small plots of land to farming families. Collectivization movements in the communist world also employed large numbers in agriculture as private ownership of land ended. Nonetheless, after millennia during which 80 percent or more of people toiled on the land, the past century has witnessed those who farm shrink to a distinct minority of humankind.

The Changing Lives of Industrial Workers

The opening decades of the twentieth century brought considerable changes to the lives of millions who labored in factories. American industry pioneered the moving production line and "scientific management" that broke down more complex activities into simple steps. While increasing productivity substantially, these changes fundamentally altered the pace and nature of factory work. More jobs became repetitive and boring. The moving assembly line removed nearly all control over the pace of work from those who performed it. Some employers, like the car manufacturer Henry Ford, offered better pay and somewhat shorter hours to his workers to entice them into his factories, while union movements and social reformers pressed for worker's rights, sometimes through strikes. Elements of these American innovations spread to factories in Europe, the Soviet Union, and to a lesser extent Japan by the 1930s.

In many heavily unionized industries, the two-day weekend became standard by the 1920s and along with higher wages created a growing culture of leisure and consumption, often called **consumerism**. "Industrial cities," wrote one scholar, "became places of leisure as well as labor."[20] Shopping at department stores and attending movies or sporting events emerged as popular pastimes among working-class families, who also increasingly purchased prepared foods rather than cooking. Fish and chips (French fries) became a particular favorite of the British working class, with over 30,000 shops across the country offering this new convenience food by the 1920s.

Plant closures during the Great Depression significantly disrupted the lives of factory workers, as did World War II through the rationing and physical destruction of wartime. But the shortage of wartime labor drew women into factories across the industrialized world in unprecedented numbers and also allowed them to fill positions traditionally reserved for men. After the war many women were forced

AP®

CAUSATION
What effects does a consumer society have on social relationships?

Argumentation

This is a good time for an activity to help students practice finding thesis statements or arguments and supporting evidence. Have students read the first full paragraph on this page (the paragraph ends on page 763). As they read the paragraph, they should identify the thesis or argument of the paragraph and list the supporting evidence for the thesis. (Answers are provided in italics.)

- **Thesis:** *Multiple changes to manufacturing in the late twentieth century led to the decline of many well-established industrial centers in parts of Western Europe and the United State and the displacement of many low-income workers.*

- **Evidence:** *Many state-owned manufacturing enterprises collapsed or declined in the former Soviet Union, and China opened up to global trade in the 1990s. A new factory working class in China formed in its coastal regions when foreign investors created new industrial operations there. Factory closures around the world led many workers to seek better employment opportunities elsewhere. New, more efficient automated manufacturing has allowed factories in some heavily industrialized regions to survive and compete in the global market, but with far fewer workers.*

Making Connections: Continuity and Change

Ask students to complete the chart below, which examines the changes and continuities between the lives of industrial workers in the nineteenth century and industrial workers in the twentieth century. Use the section titled "The Changing Lives of Industrial Workers" (pages 761 to 763) to gather the information. A reproducible version of this chart is available in the Teacher's Resource Materials. (Answers are provided in italics.)

to leave the factories altogether or at least abandon "male" jobs. In the 1950s and 1960s, stable and well-paid workforces often represented by strong unions typified the industrial sectors of Japan, the United States, and Western Europe. After decades of depression and wartime scarcity, industrial workers everywhere reacted to the good times by embracing consumerism. By 1970 nearly all urban households in Japan owned the "big three"—a television, washing machine, and refrigerator. Between 1945 and 1960 companies in the United States quadrupled their collective advertising expenditure, reflecting the buying power of the American worker. Europeans consumed more but also emphasized leisure, as one month of paid annual vacation became standard in many industries. In the communist world, large factory workforces enjoyed similar job security, even if their economies proved unable to produce the variety of consumer goods available to workers elsewhere.

Further changes awaited factory workers in the later twentieth century. Liberalization of global trade, automation and robots, relocation of factories to places with cheaper labor costs, and the rapid growth of manufacturing in the Global South—all of this led to the decline or "rusting out" of many well-established industrial centers in parts of Western Europe and the United States and the displacement of many less skilled workers. As the former Soviet Union and China opened up to global trade in the 1990s, many state-owned manufacturing enterprises collapsed or fell into decline, displacing many workers, even as a new factory working class formed in China's coastal regions, where foreign investors had created new industrial operations. Closure of factories around the world tore at the social fabric of communities and led many to seek better employment opportunities elsewhere. Speaking

▶ **AP**
SOURCING AND SITUATION
What economic factors led to the situation depicted in the photograph?

Closed Factories and Displaced Industrial Workers As automation and outsourcing swept across the industrialized West, factories closed, employees lost their jobs, communities were disrupted, and protests ensued. Workers at a Goodyear tire plant in northern France responded to the company's plans to close the facility, eliminating some 1,000 jobs, by holding two managers hostage and setting fire to numerous tires in early 2014. (DENIS CHARLET/Getty Images)

Nineteenth-Century Industrialized Workers	Twentieth-Century Industrialized Workers	Continuities
▪ *Working 6.5 days a week*	▪ *Working 5 days a week*	▪ *Working long hours using repetitive movements*
▪ *Lack of safety measures in factories*	▪ *More women working in factories after World War II*	▪ *Union protection*
▪ *Laws limiting the number of hours children could work*	▪ *Laws requiring safety measures in factories*	▪ *Child labor continues in many parts of the world*

TRM Handout 13.4: Continuities and Changes Chart for Nineteenth- to Twentieth-Century Industrial Workers in 2015 about his two teenage daughters, Mark Semande, a former worker at the closed Maytag appliance plant in Galesburg, Illinois, mused: "Maybe they could find jobs and live in the community but not if they want to do as well as [my wife and I]."[21] Nonetheless, in some heavily industrialized regions, new, more efficient automated manufacturing allowed factories to survive and compete in the global market, but with far fewer and more highly skilled workers.

Even as manufacturing declined in many of its traditional heartlands in the later twentieth century, it took root and thrived in new regions. Between 1980 and 2007 the global manufacturing workforce grew from 1.9 to 3.1 billion people, offering many new employment opportunities, especially in the developing world. Countries competed to attract manufacturers, luring them with weak labor laws, low wages, tax incentives, and special **export-processing zones (EPZs)** where international companies could operate with expedited building permits, exemptions from certain taxes and customs duties, and other benefits.

Many of the conditions for these workers remained much as they had been during the first Industrial Revolution. The use of child labor, for example, has been common in parts of sub-Saharan Africa, South Asia, and Latin America as it was in early industrial England. Similarly, women made up an important part of the global industrial workforce and typically earned less than men. At the turn of the twenty-first century, around 74 percent of the workers in the Philippine EPZs were women who earned on average 54 percent of what their male counterparts did. Also mirroring the first Industrial Revolution, workers frequently labored in dangerous conditions that resulted in tragedies like the collapse of the Rana Plaza garment factory in Bangladesh in April 2013, which killed 1,135 workers and injured a further 2,500. In some regions like South Africa during the apartheid era or China during the 1980s and 1990s, migrants from the countryside who worked in industrial zones commonly lacked official residency and work privileges, limiting their ability to oppose the demands of their employers and access services like education or health care. But as manufacturing became established in new regions, workers often voiced dissatisfaction and sought better pay and working conditions. In Brazil, South Africa, and South Korea, labor movements emerged within a generation of the auto industry establishing major production facilities.

The Service Sector and the Informal Economy

Beyond farm and factory, employment opportunities grew significantly in service industries and sales. A significant part of the service sector involved what is often called the "knowledge economy," which included government, medicine, education, finance, communication, information technology, and media. It flourished to some extent everywhere but especially in the more highly developed countries of North America, Western Europe, and Japan. Growth in these areas was driven in part by an emerging consumerism and increasing population and was encouraged by new communication and computational technologies, including the typewriter, telephone, and later the computer and the Internet. Some of these **service sector** enterprises employed highly educated, well-paid workers such as doctors, computer coders, and bankers, but many more were lower-skilled, lower-paid workers such as cleaners, shopkeepers, taxi drivers, secretaries, and typists. Everywhere race and gender pay differentials existed, with jobs gendered female — manicurist, nurse, teacher — paying less than those gendered male — plumber, bank manager, engineer.

The last decades of the twentieth century witnessed a trend toward less stable employment in service industries and the knowledge economies of more developed regions as employers outsourced jobs to freelancers, independent contractors, contract workers, and temporary staffing agencies. Advances in telecommunications and the Internet allowed companies to relocate jobs in the service industry (call centers, data entry) and knowledge economy (computer coding, editing) to lower-wage countries. At the opening of the twenty-first century, zero-hour contracts, which required employees to be on call without any guarantee of work, grew more common in the retail sector, and new ride-sharing apps competed with taxi firms. In what has been described as the new "gig economy," jobs came with greater flexibility for workers but also less security, fewer fringe benefits, looser relationships with employers, and often longer workdays. The COVID-19 pandemic beginning in 2019 further changed the working lives of many in the service sector and the knowledge economy, at least temporarily. Virtual collaboration via video conferencing replaced business travel and meetings; "work from home" alternatives made "commuting to the office" optional rather than the norm; and e-commerce and delivery services surged while in-person shopping fell sharply.

The **informal economy** (or "shadow" economy), which operated "off the books" and largely outside government regulation and taxation, grew rapidly as fewer employees worked in stable, permanent jobs. This growth occurred most notably in the Global South, where new immigrants to rapidly expanding cities often found employment as day laborers or small-scale traders and lived in crowded shantytowns, but it was also evident in the Global North. Greece's black market reached 20 to 25 percent of its total economy in 2017, and in the United States, an estimated \$2 trillion of unreported income in 2012 suggested a substantial shadow economy. The expansion of such informal economies over the past several decades has led some scholars to conclude that the stable and well-defined workplaces in the mid-twentieth-century industrialized North were an aberration rather than a new norm in the world of work.

Global Middle Classes and Life at the Top

A prosperous middle class in the Global North was a defining feature of the twentieth century. By the 1950s factory workers, tradesmen, and increasing numbers of service, sales, clerical, and knowledge economy workers came to view themselves as "middle class," for they were earning stable wages that allowed them to live comfortably, own their homes, and secure access to health care, education, entertainment, and travel. In much of the Global South, "middle class" was defined differently — as those households

---

TEACHING IDEA

AP® Exam Strategies

To emphasize the use of new technology to relocate jobs in the service industry, have students look at Multiple-Choice Questions 4 to 6 on pages 794 and 795.

TEACHING IDEA

Class Discussion

For this "Think, Pair, Share" activity, have students write down what they think the term "middle-class" means. Then have students share their definition with a partner and come up with a combined definition. Share the definitions with the class and discuss.

earning significantly above the poverty line but less than the highest earners in their communities. In most developing countries, a large middle class of this kind only emerged at the opening of the twenty-first century. But by 2009, an estimated 1.8 billion people globally were "middle class."[22] The shifting of manufacturing and some service and knowledge economy employment to the Global South was an important driver in this remarkable growth.

However, at the opening of the twenty-first century, many in the global middle class felt that their position in society was insecure or under threat. In Europe, the United States, Japan, and other places in the industrial North, the middle class as a proportion of society has been stagnant or shrinking since the 1970s, and the living standards of many declined even as economic growth continued in these regions. As one Chicago steelworker whose plant shut down in the 1980s put it: "I'm working harder, making less money, got less of a future."[24] Less secure employment, the loss of manufacturing jobs, immigration, and the decline of labor unions have all taken their toll on the middle class, sparking populist political backlashes such as Britain's exit from the European Union in 2020 and the election of President Donald Trump in the United States in 2016. In the Global South as well, many in the middle class find their positions precarious. More than 60 percent of the middle class in Bolivia, Brazil, Chile, and Mexico work within the informal economy, often running their own very small businesses.

The last several decades also produced economic winners. Never before had the richest 1 percent controlled so much wealth as they did at the opening of the twenty-first century. In 2016 an OXFAM study concluded that the eight richest people in the world possessed roughly the same amount of wealth as the poorest 3.5 billion. The gap between the pay of top executives and employees at major firms has widened dramatically. One commentator in 2011 described it as "the winner-take-most economy," in which a small number of "superstar" performers enjoyed most of the newly generated wealth.[25]

The richest 1 percent looked very different in 2000 than a century earlier. More were self-made, with fewer having inherited their wealth. In the West and some other places, the globalization and deregulation of the financial industry from the 1980s on allowed some in the banking, private equity, and hedge fund industries to make

Middle-Class Life in Nigeria One sign of an emerging middle class in the Global South was the proliferation of malls and huge retail outlets such as this Shoprite store, located in the new Delta Mall in Warri, Nigeria. Shoprite is Africa's largest food retailer, selling food, liquor, household goods, and small appliances. A recent customer commented: "A middle-class person can come into this mall and feel a sense of belonging."[23] (GLENNA GORDON/© The New York Times/Redux)

▲ **AP®**

CLAIMS AND EVIDENCE IN SOURCING
What aspects of this photo reflect a growing middle class?

BUILDING AP® SKILLS

Sourcing and Situation

Ask students to look at the photograph "Middle-Class Life in Nigeria" and ask students what similarities to shopping in the United States they see in the photograph. *Answers will vary, but should include: massive ads trying to influence consumers to buy something, long lines, checkout aisles, plastic shopping bags, etc.*

fortunes even as a series of financial bubbles and collapses made finance more risky. At the same time, the remarkable growth of high-tech and especially Internet businesses made billionaires out of a lucky few. Following decolonization in the Global South, some 1 percenters made their fortunes by taking over the structures of the state, often profiting through embezzlement, kickbacks, and other forms of direct corruption. In Nigeria, for instance, billions in oil revenues were siphoned off into the personal accounts of officials. Similarly, following the collapse of the Soviet Union, well-connected individuals who frequently had held elite positions in the former regime purchased state assets on the cheap, becoming billionaires in the process.

The newly enriched rubbed shoulders with one another and with more traditional elites while living global lifestyles almost unimaginable to the rest. Owning multiple houses in desirable locations—London, Dubai, Hong Kong, New York—and moving between them on private jets or on luxury yachts established their place in the new elite, as did participation in exclusive gatherings like the annual Davos summit in Switzerland. More so than in the past, the superrich possessed a shared international outlook, educational background, and experiences that made them a self-conscious global class. "A person in Africa who runs a big African bank and went to Harvard Business School has more in common with me than he does with his neighbors, and I have more in common with him than I do with my neighbors," observed the private equity banker Glen Hutchins.[26] At the opening of the twenty-first century, humankind had never been so collectively wealthy. That wealth lifted billions out of poverty and created a growing global middle class, but it also accumulated in the hands of a privileged few, creating an unprecedentedly wealthy global plutocracy.

Getting Personal: Transformations of Private Life

Finding the Main Point: How did views on gender roles and sexuality change in the twentieth and twenty-first centuries?

The public face of social life, expressed in work, class, income, and wealth, has a more private counterpart, experienced in marriage, family, sexuality, and gender roles. These elements of personal life also changed dramatically amid the technological and economic transformations of the past century. Increasingly, individuals were able to make choices about intimate matters that were previously regarded as determined by custom or law—who to marry, how many children to raise, when to begin sexual activity, and how to define gender roles and sexual identity. Amid much diversity and variation, many people the world over have experienced and celebrated those changes as liberation from ancient constraints and social oppression, while many others have felt them as an assault on the natural order of things and a threat to ways of living sanctioned by religion and tradition. These diverse reactions have driven matters long considered private or unspeakable into the public sphere of controversy, debate, and political action.

AP
COMPARISON
How did the wealthy global elite in the twentieth and twenty-first centuries differ from the factory owners of the Industrial Revolution?

BUILDING AP® SKILLS

Claims and Evidence in Sources

Ask students to read the United Nations Universal Declaration of Human Rights, located on the United Nations website. Then ask the following questions:

■ What was the historical context of the document? *The horror of the Holocaust was the primary inspiration for the document. The genocide associated with the Holocaust was well documented visually, which inspired many nations to attempt to ensure that the "final solution" could never happen again.*

■ Which rights particularly affect women? *Women are especially affected by employment, property, and voting rights. Women are also affected by the declaration that marriages should be entered into with the consent of both individuals. (Articles 16 and 17)*

Modernity and Personal Life

Among the agents of change in personal life, none have been more fundamental than the multiple processes widely associated with modernity—science and technology, industrialization and urbanization, and globalization and migration. Consider, for example, their impact on family life, experienced earlier and most fully in the industrialized societies of Europe, North America, and Japan, but also more recently in the Global South.

As industrial and urban life took hold across the world during the past two centuries, large business enterprises and the state took over functions that families had previously performed. Production moved from family farms and workshops to factories, offices, and large-scale agricultural enterprises, and opportunities for work outside the home beckoned to growing numbers of women as well as men. Education became the task of state-run schools rather than families, and the primary role of children became that of student rather than worker. Families increasingly functioned primarily to provide emotional and financial security in a turbulent and rapidly changing world. In this setting, modern families became smaller as children were increasingly seen as economic burdens and as both men and women married later. Furthermore, family life grew less stable as divorce became far more frequent and the stigma attached to it diminished. Modern life also witnessed an increasing variety of family patterns across the world: patriarchal families of several generations living together; small nuclear families of mother, father, and children; single-parent families, usually headed by women; unmarried couples living together, sometimes with children and often without; blended families as a result of second marriages; polygamous families; and LGBTQ families.

These broad patterns of change in family life at the global level hide a great deal of diversity. While family size has dropped sharply in much of Asia and Latin America during the past century, it has remained quite high in sub-Saharan Africa, where women in the early twenty-first century gave birth to an average of 5 children during their reproductive years, compared to a global average of 2.5.

Divorce rates too varied widely in the early twenty-first century, with 50 percent or more of marriages ending in divorce in the United States, France, Spain, Cuba, Hungary, and the Czech Republic, compared to much lower rates in Chile (3 percent), Brazil (21 percent), Egypt (17 percent), Iran (22 percent), and South Africa (17 percent). Since the mid-1990s, China has experienced a dramatic increase in divorce, prompting the Chinese government to intervene to address the issue.

Most of the world's marriages during the past century have involved one man and one woman, though polygamy remains legal in much of Africa and the Islamic Middle East. And same-sex marriages have gained a measure of acceptance at least in some cultures in recent decades. While the past century has generally favored free choice or "love" marriages, many families in India and elsewhere still arrange marriages for their children.

Modern life has also deeply impacted sexuality. Technologies of contraception—condoms, IUDs, diaphragms, and above all "the pill"—have allowed many people to

AP

CONTINUITY AND CHANGE
In what ways has personal or private life been transformed over the past century?

TEACHING IDEA

Class Discussion

Understanding the term "modernity" is paramount to understanding the changes that took place during the twentieth century. Ask students to write down what they think modernity means. Then have students look at the first paragraph under "Modernity and Personal Life" and compare their answer with the textbook. Have a class discussion on the processes that are associated with the term "modernity."

BUILDING AP® SKILLS

Making Connections: Continuity and Change

Ask students to brainstorm what changes to family life have occurred in the last century. *Answers will vary, but should include: Family size has shrunk in some areas but has remained high in other areas; Families are less stable as divorce rates have increased; Education has become the responsibility of the state rather than the family; Family patterns have become more varied.*

CHAPTER 13

separate sexual life from reproduction. Access to more effective forms of birth control gave women, especially in the Global North, greater control over their fertility and led to a decreased family size in middle-class households in the late twentieth century.

Especially since the 1960s, this change has contributed to the emergence of a highly sexualized public culture in many parts of the world, expressed in advertising and in an enormous pornography industry with a global reach. One investigator reported on a remote village in the West African country of Ghana: "The village has no electricity, but that doesn't stop a generator from being wheeled in, turning a mud hut into an impromptu porn cinema."[27] Sex tourism has also become big business, with major destinations in Thailand, Indonesia, the Philippines, Colombia, Brazil, and the Netherlands. Men from the Global North have been among the primary consumers of porn and the drivers of sex tourism. Movies, TV, newspapers, and magazines openly display or discuss all manner of sexual topics that would have been largely forbidden in public discourse only a century ago: premarital sex, homosexuality, gay marriage, LGBTQ rights, sexually transmitted diseases, birth control, abortion, teen pregnancy, and much more. Sex education in schools has spread globally to varying degrees, while provoking sharp controversy in many places.

Sex, in short, has become a less taboo topic and has found a far more visible and pervasive expression in public life during the past century. Unsurprisingly, this has been associated with a considerable increase in premarital sex in many parts of the world, with the vast majority of Americans and Europeans participating in such activity by the late 1960s. A rapidly industrializing China has witnessed the frequency of premarital sex skyrocket since 1989, approaching levels in the United States.

But all of this has occurred in the face of much controversy and opposition. The hierarchies of the Catholic Church and many fundamentalist or evangelical Christian leaders have remained steadfastly opposed to the "sexual revolution" of the past century, even as many of their parishioners participate in it. Despite the sexual revolution, over 90 percent of Muslims in Indonesia, Jordan, Pakistan, Turkey, and Egypt found premarital sex unacceptable in the early twenty-first century, while fewer than 10 percent of the people in France, Germany, and Spain felt the same way.[28] Even as there has been greater openness and assertiveness among the LGBTQ community, anti-LGBTQ activists have triggered new and increased legal action, especially in Africa, where many countries have passed harsh antigay legislation, citing the AIDS crisis, a defense of traditional marriage, and the supposedly "un-African" character of homosexuality.

AP®

CAUSATION

In what different ways did the policies of governments shape personal life during the past century?

The State and Personal Life

States too shaped personal life in the past century, as they grew more powerful and intrusive and as matters of marriage, family, gender, and sexuality became ever more entangled with politics. Nazi Germany, for example, prohibited birth control and rewarded large families during the 1930s in an effort to produce as many "good Germans" as possible. At the same time, they sterilized or executed those deemed "undesirable" and forbade marriage or sexual relations between Jews and Germans to prevent "contamination" of the Aryan race. For similar racial reasons, South Africa under the apartheid regime legally prohibited both sexual relationships and marriage between whites and people of other races. In the aftermath of World War II, the Soviet Union sharply limited access to all contraception in an effort to rebuild a population devastated by war.

But as concerns about population growth mounted in the 1970s and beyond, some states moved to limit the numbers of their people. Acting under a state of emergency, the government of India sterilized some 11 million men and women between 1975 and 1977, using a combination of incentives and compulsion to gain consent. China pursued population control on an even larger scale through its **one-child family policy**, which lasted from 1980 until 2014. Under the pressure of financial incentives and penalties and intense pressure from local authorities, over 300 million women "agreed" to have IUD devices implanted, over 100 million were sterilized, and many were persuaded or forced to undergo abortions.

Communist regimes intervened in personal life in other ways as well. Among the earliest and most revolutionary actions of the new communist government in the Soviet Union were efforts at liberating and mobilizing women. Almost immediately upon coming to power, communist authorities in the Soviet Union declared full legal and political equality for women; marriage became a civil procedure among freely consenting adults; divorce was legalized and made easier, as was abortion; illegitimacy was abolished; women no longer had to take their husbands' surnames; pregnancy leave for employed women was mandated; and women were actively mobilized as workers in the country's drive to industrialization. (See Zooming In: Anna Dubova, a Russian Woman, and the Soviet State, page 770.) During the 1920s, a special party organization called the **Women's Department** (Zhenotdel) organized numerous conferences for women, trained women to run day-care centers and medical clinics, published newspapers and magazines aimed at a female audience, provided literacy and prenatal classes, and encouraged Muslim women to take off their veils.

▼ **AP**

CAUSATION
What have been some of the consequences of the policy depicted in this image?

China's One-Child Family China's vigorous efforts to limit its population growth represented a radical intrusion of state power into the private lives of its people. It was accompanied by a massive propaganda effort, illustrated by this urban billboard. (Barry Lewis/Alamy)

EXPLORING AP® THEMES

Governance (GOV) and Social Interactions and Organization (SIO)

You can help students work on their writing skills by having them write a quick response to the following question after they read "The State and Personal Life": How did the Soviet Union use different methods to liberate and mobilize women? *Answers should include: Full legal and political equality was declared for men and women, marriage became a civil procedure rather than a religious event, women no longer had to take their husband's name, divorce and abortion were legalized, and women were considered important in the USSR's progress to greater industrialization.*

BUILDING AP® SKILLS

Claims and Evidence in Sources

Students can benefit from frequent image analysis practice, especially to help them prepare for the SAQ and the DBQ. Consider having them complete an OPTIC chart for the billboard of China's One-Child Family on this page to work on image analysis. A reproducible version of this chart can be found in the Teacher's Resource Materials. (Answers are provided in italics.)

Overview	*A billboard in a Chinese city depicting a one-child family.*
Parts	*There is a mother, a father, and a child, possibly sitting in a field. There might be balloons behind the family.*
Title	*The photograph doesn't have an official title but could be called "The Ideal Family."*
Interrelationships	*The family appear to be on an outing, maybe to a party or an outdoor park. They look happy and content together, suggesting they have a good life and aren't struggling.*
Conclusion	*This billboard is promoting the ideal family as imagined by the Chinese government, showing people how happy they could be if they followed the government's policy. This is a piece of propaganda to promote China's one-child family policy.*

TRM Handout 13.6: OPTIC Chart for One-Child Family Billboard

EXPLORING AP® THEMES

Social Interactions and Organization (SIO)

Students need to be able to apply what they have learned to help them with interpreting a source. Have students read "Zooming In: Anna Dubova, a Russian Woman, and the Soviet State" and then show them the photograph of a Soviet woman factory worker in 1941 on this page. Then ask the following questions:

■ What can you say about the woman based on her body language? *She appears to be happy with her job.*

■ How does this photo compare to Anna Dubova's experiences in "Zooming In"? *The woman in the photograph appears to be happy with her job and life, while Anna Dubova seemed to always be scared of what might happen to her should her origins as a kulak be discovered.*

■ What types of goods do you think the women in the photograph are producing? *Since the date on the photograph is 1941, the women must be producing goods for the Soviet war effort.*

AP® CLASSROOM

AP® Daily Videos

This would be a good place to pause and have students watch the second AP® Daily Video for Topic 9.5: Calls for Reforms and Responses after 1900. This video focuses on the calls for reform and responses after 1900 that related to women, including women gaining the right to vote around the world. The video will also help students practice the skill of contextualization. You can find the second video for Topic 9.5 by logging into AP® Classroom, clicking on Unit 9 under Classroom Resources, and then selecting Daily Videos.

ZOOMING IN   Anna Dubova, a Russian Woman, and the Soviet State

Born into a large peasant family near Smolensk in western Russia in 1916, Anna Dubova lived through the entire communist period in her country.[29] Her experience illustrates the impact of state policies on the life of one woman, as well as Anna's efforts to find her own way within a sometimes dangerous and often oppressive society.

Anna was one of fourteen children, of whom seven survived. Her family was dominated by a strict, hardworking, and highly religious father, who was choirmaster of the local church. Anna's father was suspicious of the communists when they came to power the year after Anna's birth, but her grandmother was more forthright. "The forces of the Antichrist have triumphed," she declared. Nonetheless, her father accepted an appointment in 1922 as chairman of the village soviet, the new communist organ of local government. During the 1920s, the village and Anna's family flourished under Lenin's New Economic Policy, which briefly permitted a considerable measure of private enterprise and profit

A 1941 image of a woman factory worker in Moscow.

making. Her father even opened a small shop in the village, where he sold goods purchased in the city.

By 1928, however, everything changed as the Soviet regime, now under Joseph Stalin's leadership, abruptly moved to collectivize agriculture and root out kulaks, supposedly wealthy peasants who were thought to bear the germ of a hated capitalism. Because of her father's shop, the family was labeled as kulak and their property was confiscated. "I remember so well how Mama sat and cried when they took away the cow," Anna recalled years later. The family forestalled their expected deportation to the far north of the Soviet Union only by promising Anna, then just thirteen, in marriage to the local Communist Party secretary. The marriage never took place, however, and the family was forced to leave. Later, Anna was permitted to join her older sister in Moscow, but approval for that much-coveted move came at a very high price. Anna recalled, "I had to write out an official

photo: Library of Congress, Prints and Photographs Division, LC-USW33-024241-C (P&P)

AP®

CONTINUITY AND CHANGE

In what ways did Atatürk change Turkish society as it moved from being the center of the Ottoman Empire to being a nation-state?

Elsewhere as well, states acted in favor of women's rights and gender equality, with Brazil granting the vote to women in 1932, Turkey in 1934, and India in 1947. Turkey, a thoroughly Muslim country that had emerged as an independent state from the ashes of the Ottoman Empire following World War I, acted decisively on women's issues during the 1920s and 1930s. In the view of Turkey's first leader Kemal Atatürk, the emancipation of women was a cornerstone of the new Turkey and a mark of the country's modernization. In a much-quoted speech, he declared: "If henceforward the women do not share in the social life of the nation . . . we shall remain irremediably backward, incapable of treating on equal terms with the civilizations of the West."[30] Thus polygamy was abolished and women were granted equal rights in divorce, inheritance, and child custody. Public beaches were opened statement that I renounced my parents, that I no longer had any ties with them."

Thus Anna, a rural teenage girl, joined millions of other young women who flocked to the city to pursue the new opportunities that became available as the Soviet Union launched its industrialization drive, which required the labor of men and women alike. In Moscow, she gained a basic education, pursued a vocation in cake decorating, which she enjoyed, and did a brief stint as a mechanic and chauffeur, which she detested. All the while the shadow of her kulak label followed her. Had it been discovered, she could have lost her job and her permission to live in Moscow. And so she married a party activist from a poor peasant family, she explained years later, "just so I could cover up my background." Her husband drank heavily, leaving her with a daughter when he went off to war in 1941.

In the Soviet Union, the late 1930s witnessed the Terror when millions of alleged "enemies of the people" were arrested and hauled off to execution or labor camps. Anna recalled what it was like: "You'd come home and they'd say, Yesterday they took away Uncle Lesha. . . . You'd go to see a girlfriend, they'd say, We have an empty room now; they've exiled Andreitsev." Like most people not directly involved, Anna believed in the guilt of these people. And she feared that she herself might be mistakenly accused, for those with a kulak label were particular targets of the search for enemies.

Beyond her kulak background, Anna also felt compelled to hide a deep religious sensibility derived from her childhood. She remembered the disappearance of the village priest, the looting of the churches, and the destruction of icons. And so she never entered a church or prayed in front of others. But she wore a cross under her clothing. "I never stopped [believing]," she recalled. "But I concealed it. Deep down . . . I believed." Nor did she ever seek to join the Communist Party, though it may well have advanced her career prospects and standard of living.

In the decades following World War II and especially after Stalin's death in 1953, Anna's life seemed to stabilize. She entered into a thirty-year relationship with a man and found satisfying work in a construction design office, though the lack of higher education and party connections prevented her from moving into higher-paid jobs. Despite Anna's ability to forge a life for herself in an industrializing and repressive Soviet Union, she had come to value, perhaps nostalgically, the life of a peasant over that of an urban worker. "[As a peasant,] I would have lived on the fruits of my labor," she reflected. ". . . [Instead,] I've lived someone else's life."

QUESTIONS

In what ways did state policies shape Anna's life? What deliberate actions did she and her family take to make a life for themselves within the communist system?

---

to women, and Atatürk encouraged them to discard the veil or head covering, long associated with Muslim piety, in favor of Western styles of dress. As in the early Soviet Union, this was a state-directed feminism, responsive to Atatürk's modern views, rather than reflecting popular demands from women themselves.

But what the state granted to women, the state could also take away, as it did in Iran in the years following that country's Islamic revolution in 1979. The country's new Islamic government, headed by the Ayatollah Khomeini, moved to sharply tighten religiously inspired restrictions on women, while branding feminism and women's rights as a Western evil. By 1983, all women were required to wear loose-fitting clothing and the head covering known as hijab, a regulation enforced by roving groups of militants, or "revolutionary guards." Sexual segregation was

AP
CONTINUITY AND CHANGE
What changes and continuities in women's lives resulted from the Iranian revolution?

TEACHING IDEA

Class Discussion

To help students get a more personalized view of how state policies can affect a woman's life, have them read "Zooming In: Anna Dubova, a Russian Woman, and the Soviet State." You can use the questions at the end of the section to help guide a class discussion on what they read.

BUILDING AP® SKILLS

Making Connections: Comparison

You should try to give students opportunities throughout the year to practice writing parts of an LEQ or DBQ without having them write a full essay. Have students read the last two paragraphs of "The State and Personal Life" on pages 770–772 about the differences between Turkey's (Türkiye) and Iran's treatment of women. After they finish the paragraphs, ask them to use what they learned to write a thesis statement that answers the following prompt:

■ Develop an argument that evaluates the extent to which the state's involvement in women's personal lives differed between Turkey (Türkiye) and Iran during the twentieth century.

Answers should include the following ideas: Turkey (Türkiye) offered women equal rights in divorce, inheritance, and child custody, along with loosening traditional religious restrictions on them and granting them the right to vote. Iran, after the 1979 revolution, tightened religiously inspired restrictions on women: women were required to wear loose-fitting clothing and hijabs; segregation based on gender was imposed in schools, parks, beaches, and public transportation; the legal age of marriage for girls was lowered; and married women could no longer file for divorce.

imposed in schools, parks, beaches, and public transportation. The legal age of marriage for girls, set at eighteen under the prerevolutionary regime, was reduced to nine with parental consent. Married women could no longer file for divorce or attend school. Yet, despite such restrictions, many women supported the revolution and over the next several decades found far greater opportunities for employment and higher education than before. By the early twenty-first century, almost 60 percent of university students were women, women's right to vote remained intact, and some loosening of earlier restrictions on women had become apparent.

Feminism and Personal Life

A third source of change in personal life during the past century derived from social movements committed to liberation from ancient patterns of inequality and oppression. No expression of this global culture of liberation held a more profound potential for social change than feminism, for it represented a sharp challenge to patriarchy or male dominance, which had been a central feature of most civilizations for a very long time. Although feminism had begun in the West in the nineteenth century, it became global in the twentieth, as organized efforts to address the concerns of women took shape across the world.

AP®
DEVELOPMENTS AND PROCESSES
What social, political, and cultural norms were challenged by women in the twentieth century?

AP®
CAUSATION
What drove global feminism since the 1960s?

Western feminism had lost momentum as an organized movement by the end of the 1920s, when many countries in Western Europe and North America had achieved women's suffrage. But it revived in the 1960s with a quite different agenda as women's participation in the paid workforce mounted rapidly. Millions of American women responded to Betty Friedan's book, *The Feminine Mystique* (1963), which disclosed the identity crisis of educated women, unfulfilled by marriage and motherhood. Some adherents of this **second-wave feminism** took up the equal rights agenda of their nineteenth-century predecessors, but with an emphasis now on employment and education rather than voting rights. A more radical expression of American feminism, widely known as "women's liberation," took broader aim at patriarchy as a system of domination, similar to those of race and class. One manifesto from 1969 declared:

> We are exploited as sex objects, breeders, domestic servants, and cheap labor. We are considered inferior beings, whose only purpose is to enhance men's lives. . . . Because we live so intimately with our oppressors, we have been kept from seeing our personal suffering as a political condition.[31]

Thus liberation for women meant becoming aware of their own oppression, a process that took place in thousands of consciousness-raising groups across the United States and Europe. Women also brought into open discussion issues involving sexuality, insisting that free love, lesbianism, and celibacy should be accorded the same respect as heterosexual marriage.

Yet another strand of Western feminism emerged from women of color. For many of them, the concerns of white, usually middle-class, feminists were hardly relevant to their oppression. Black women had always worked outside the home and so felt little need to be liberated from the chains of homemaking. Whereas white women might find the family oppressive, African American women viewed it as a secure base from which to resist racism and poverty. Solidarity with Black men, rather than separation from them, was essential in confronting racism.

As women mobilized across Asia, Africa, and Latin America, they faced very different situations than did white women in the United States and Europe. The predominant issues for **feminism in the Global South**—colonialism, racism, poverty, development, political oppression, and sometimes revolution—were not always directly related to gender. To many African feminists in the 1970s and later, the concerns of their American or European sisters were too individualistic, too focused on sexuality, and insufficiently concerned with issues of motherhood, marriage, and poverty to be of much use. Furthermore, they resented Western feminists' insistent interest in cultural matters such as female genital mutilation and polygamy, which sometimes echoed the concerns of colonial-era missionaries and administrators. Western feminism could easily be seen as a new form of cultural imperialism.

AP®

COMPARISON
How was feminism different in the Global South than it was in the Global North?

During the colonial era, much of women's political activity was aligned with the struggle for independence. Later, women's movements in the Global South took shape around a wide range of issues. In the East African country of Kenya, a major form of mobilization was the "women's group" movement. Some 27,000 small associations of women, an outgrowth of traditional self-help groups, enabled women to provide personal support for one another and took on community projects, such as building water cisterns, schools, and dispensaries. Some groups became revolving loan societies or bought land or businesses. One woman testified to the sense of empowerment she derived from membership in her group:

> I am a free woman. I bought this piece of land through my group. I can lie on it, work on it, keep goats or cows. What more do I want? My husband cannot sell it. It is mine.[32]

Elsewhere, other issues and approaches predominated. In the North African Islamic kingdom of Morocco, a more centrally directed and nationally focused feminist movement targeted the country's Family Law Code, which still defined women as minors. In 2004, a long campaign by Morocco's feminist movement, often with the help of supportive men and a liberal king, resulted in a new Family Law Code that recognized women as equals to their husbands and allowed them to initiate divorce and to claim child custody, all of which had previously been denied.

In Chile, a women's movement emerged as part of a national struggle against the military dictatorship of General Augusto Pinochet, who ruled the country from 1973 to 1990. Because they were largely regarded as "invisible" in the public sphere, women were able to organize extensively, despite the repression of the Pinochet regime. From this explosion of organizing activity emerged a women's movement that crossed class lines and party affiliations. Poor urban women by the tens of thousands organized soup kitchens, craft workshops, and shopping collectives, all

BUILDING AP® SKILLS

Making Connections: Comparison

It's important to make sure that students don't think the movements that swept across the globe in the twentieth century, like feminism, were monolithic movements about which every member agreed. You can help them by asking students to compare the issues that were important to Western feminists to the issues that were important to the women from the Global South. *Women in the Global South felt oppressed not just by men or patriarchy, but by women of the Western countries who had colonized them. Women in the West wanted to focus on political or economic rights.*

BUILDING AP® SKILLS

Sourcing and Situation

A quick way to get students to practice their sourcing skills is to pull quotes from the textbook and have students analyze them. The quote from the woman testifying about her newfound empowerment on the bottom half of this page would be a good one to pull for students to work with. Ask students to read the quote and analyze the speaker's point of view and state where, according to the speaker, her power comes from. *The woman associates freedom with ownership of land and property. She wants to ensure legal entitlement for her property.*

If you had students complete the Comparison activity on page 773, you could extend the idea that movements are not monolithic even in specific regions by asking students to read the information about feminism in the Global South on pages 773 and 774. After they finish reading, start a class discussion using the following question: What issues kept feminists in the Global South from uniting in their cause? *Answers will include: Women in the Global South were affected by divergent issues, including colonialism, racism, national independence, and poverty; Their causes were dependent on their circumstances; In Kenya, women formed self-help groups in which members provided support for one another during times of need and took on community projects; In Morocco, feminists initiated the Family Law Code, which recognized women as equals to their husbands and allowed them to initiate divorce; In Chile, feminists struggled against a military dictatorship.*

While feminism is a major movement in the twentieth and twenty-first centuries, not everyone has supported it. You can help students think about why people might have pushed back against feminism by asking: What are some of the objections to feminism? *Some people feel that its radical agenda undermined family life, the "proper" relationship of men and women, and civilization generally. In the Islamic world, Western-style feminism, with its claims of gender equality and open sexuality, was highly offensive to many and fueled movements of religious revivalism that invited or compelled women to wear the veil and sometimes to lead highly restricted lives. The Vatican and some Catholic and Muslim countries took strong exception to aspects of global feminism, particularly its emphasis on reproductive rights, including access to abortion and birth control.*

aimed at the economic survival of their families. Smaller numbers of middle-class women brought more distinctly feminist perspectives to the movement and argued pointedly for "democracy in the country and in the home." This diverse women's movement was an important part of the larger national protest that returned Chile to democratic government in 1990.

Perhaps the most impressive achievement of feminism in the twentieth century was its ability to project the "woman question" as a global issue and to gain international recognition for the view that "women's rights are human rights." Like slavery and empire before it, patriarchy lost at least some of its legitimacy during this most recent century. Feminism registered as a global issue when the United Nations (UN), under pressure from women activists, declared 1975 as International Women's Year and the next ten years as the Decade for Women. By 2006, 183 nations, though not the United States, had ratified a UN Convention on the Elimination of All Forms of Discrimination against Women. Clearly, this international attention to women's issues set a global standard to which feminists operating in their own countries could aspire.

But feminism generated a global backlash among those who felt that its agenda undermined family life, the proper relationship of men and women, and civilization generally. To Phyllis Schlafly, a prominent American opponent of equal rights for women, feminism was a "disease" that brought in its wake "fear, sickness, pain, anger, hatred, danger, violence, and all manner of ugliness."[33] In the Islamic world, Western-style feminism, with its claims of gender equality and open sexuality, was highly offensive to many and fueled movements of religious revivalism that invited or compelled women to wear the veil and sometimes to lead highly restricted lives. The Vatican, some Catholic and Muslim countries, and at times the U.S. government took strong exception to aspects of global feminism, particularly its emphasis on reproductive rights, including access to abortion and birth control. Many African governments and many African men defined feminism of any kind as "un-African" and associated with a hated colonialism. Feminist support for gay and lesbian rights only solidified opposition to women's rights activists within socially conservative circles internationally. Thus feminism was global as the twenty-first century dawned, but it was very diverse and much contested.

On Contemporary History

Finding the Main Point: Why is it difficult for historians to study and explain modern history?

Most of the history we study involves stories that have more or less clear endings, such as the Spanish conquest of the Aztec Empire, the Haitian Revolution, or the First World War. We also know something of their legacies, which often continue to resonate decades or even centuries after the event. But when dealing with more recent historical processes, our accounts of the past bump up directly against the present and extend into the future. In this situation, we know neither their ending point nor their legacies. This is contemporary history.

Scientific and technological innovation, for example, has accelerated sharply since World War II, with no end in sight, generating new conceptions of the universe, new sources of energy, new breakthroughs in medicine, and virtually endless applications in manufacturing, transportation, communication, and the military. These innovations continue to drive deepening economic entanglement all across the planet, reflected in the globalization of industrialization, in skyrocketing volumes of world trade and investment, and in the ever-growing activities of multinational corporations. In response to these processes, social life too has changed dramatically over the past century. Full-time farmers have declined sharply in numbers; many industrial workers have been displaced by technology or outsourcing; the already rich have increased their share of the world's wealth; sexual expression has become more open and varied; and feminism has generated many new possibilities for women. Each of these patterns seems likely to continue into the foreseeable future. Opposition to all of this likewise persists, based variously on environmental or social justice concerns, or fears that cherished cultural values are eroding.

In dealing with such contemporary matters, historians are often uneasy. That discomfort derives in part from the belief that only time can provide perspective. In writing about ongoing and unfinished processes, historians worry that they may lack enough distance to identify what is truly significant as opposed to what is of only passing interest. They may also lack sufficient detachment. Can historians write "objectively" or in some balanced fashion about matters in which they have been witnesses or even participants and about which they have strong personal opinions?

Yet another source of discomfort about contemporary history arises from questions about the future. Should historians speculate about "what's next"? Many people think that some understanding of the past gives historians a unique insight into the future. But historians themselves are often rather cautious about predictions because they are so aware that historical change can be unexpected and surprising. At the end of World War II, who could have anticipated the Internet, the collapse of the Soviet Union, or China's massive industrial growth?

Nevertheless, the study of contemporary history offers some larger frameworks for the news of the day. Such contexts disclose where there is continuity with the past, as well as highlight where there is a departure from it. At its best, an understanding of contemporary history also provides a corrective to the self-serving uses of the past—and the outright lies—to which politicians are prone. Current issues also encourage historians to look at the past in different ways. It is surely no accident that as feminism and environmentalism have achieved global prominence, women's history and environmental history have flourished in recent decades.

Finally, for those seeking direction for our personal lives and our societies, historical context is one of the few resources we have. So, like everyone before us, we stumble forward, using the past as guidance, as we feel our way into an always uncertain future.

TEACHING IDEA

Exit Ticket

It might be fun for students to use what they have learned from this chapter to speculate about the future. As an exit ticket one day during Unit 9, ask students to write down what they think will happen in the next century in regards to the globalization of economics, technology, and societies. They should turn in their responses as they leave the room, or you could have them share their responses at the start of class the next day.

TRM Suggested Responses to Questions
You can find suggested responses to the Chapter Review questions in the Teacher's Resource Materials.

CHAPTER REVIEW

AP Key Terms

age of fossil fuels, 745
communication revolution, 748
economic globalization, 750
Asian Tigers, 751
Bretton Woods system, 752
transnational corporations, 753
World Trade Organization (WTO), 759
North American Free Trade Agreement (NAFTA), 759

consumerism, 761
export-processing zones (EPZs), 763
service sector, 764
informal economy, 764
one-child family policy (China), 769
Women's Department (USSR), 769
second-wave feminism, 772
feminism in the Global South, 773

Finding the Main Point

1. What were the most important technological innovations of the twentieth century? What drove the accelerating pace of technological change?
2. What were the major drivers of globalization over the past century? How did this enormous process reshape world history?
3. How did societies around the world change in the twentieth and twenty-first centuries?
4. How did views on gender roles and sexuality change in the twentieth and twenty-first centuries?
5. Why is it difficult for historians to study and explain modern history?

AP Big Picture Questions

1. In shaping the history of the past century, how might you assess the relative importance of the deliberate actions of human beings (such as social movements and government policies) and impersonal forces (such as technological innovation or economic change)?
2. How might you assess the costs and benefits of the processes discussed in this chapter?
3. How have the global developments examined in this chapter shaped your own life and community?
4. **Looking Back** How did the processes discussed in this chapter (energy revolution, technological change, globalization, and feminism) have an impact on the major events of the past century explored in Chapters 11 and 12 (war, revolution, fascism, communism, the cold war, and decolonization)?

Writing a DBQ: Continuity and Change Arguments

TRM AP® Skills Workshop Activity Handout: Writing a DBQ: Continuity and Change Arguments

In this workshop, we will work with primary sources in order to develop a source-based continuity and change argument, in preparation for the Document-Based Question on the AP® Exam.

UNDERSTANDING CONTINUITY AND CHANGE ARGUMENTS

Historians create a continuity and change argument when they want to evaluate how processes, events, or civilizations have changed or stayed the same. One historian might argue that there are more changes than continuities, for example, while another might conclude that there are more continuities than changes.

A continuity and change argument is not merely a listing of changes and continuities. It is, rather, analytical and evaluative. This means that it takes a position. For example, you might argue that trade has changed more than it has stayed the same over a one-hundred-year span. Or you could argue for what you think the most interesting or significant change was over that period. What you wouldn't argue is that trade changed over that period. That's obvious and doesn't need to be argued.

You would then find evidence and build your argument. But keep in mind that historians don't pick and choose only the evidence that supports their argument. They see what's out there and allow the evidence to support, qualify, or even modify their argument. One way to do this is to bundle evidence into two categories: the main argument and the counterargument. Often, the counterargument is signaled in the thesis statement with words such as "although" and "however."

CONTINUITY AND CHANGE ARGUMENTS ON THE AP® WORLD HISTORY EXAM

On the AP® Exam, continuity and change over time is one of three reasoning skills that will be tested on the Document-Based Question (DBQ) and the Long Essay Question (LEQ). As you will remember from the workshop on building a historical argument (in Chapter 11), the difference between these two essay types is that the DBQ requires you to use the primary source documents that are provided to weave together an argument (along with one outside piece of evidence, if you want to score that extra point), while the LEQ will require you to use the information you have learned in the world history course as evidence. These two essays make up 40 percent of the exam. Thus, knowing how to create a continuity and change argument is critical.

BUILDING AP® SKILLS

Making Connections: Continuity and Change

Continuity and change is a skill that historians frequently use. When historians want to evaluate how processes, events, or civilizations have changed yet stayed the same, they create a continuity and change argument. Continuity and change arguments are deceptive to the beginning historian. They are not simply a list; they are analytical and evaluative. Continuity and change arguments take positions. On the AP® World History: Modern Exam, continuity and change is one of the reasoning skills that will be tested. As continuity and change can be used in both DBQs and LEQs, it's crucial for students to understand how to write this type of argument.

You can use the explanations on pages 777 to 779 to explain how to write a continuity and change argument to your students. One of the three activities found under Building AP® Skills on pages 779 to 780 would also be a good follow-up activity to this AP® Skills Workshop for students to practice putting together a continuity and change argument.

777

Writing a Continuity and Change Argument

As you will remember from the workshop on historical arguments, creating an argument (especially one for the AP® Exam) involves several specific moves:

- contextualization in an intro paragraph
- thesis that addresses the prompt using a specific historical reasoning skill
- topic sentences at the beginning of each paragraph that tie back to the thesis
- evidence that supports the thesis
- analysis/reasoning that shows how the evidence supports the thesis

Structuring Your Continuity and Change Argument

Continuity and change arguments have the counterargument built right in: if you're arguing that there is more continuity, then the counterargument should address the changes, and vice versa. As a result, there are two common options for structuring a continuity and change argument:

- Option 1 is that you have one paragraph on continuities, and one paragraph on changes.
- Option 2 is having one paragraph showing continuity and change on a single topic, and the second paragraph showing continuity and change on a second topic.

As an example, let's say you're discussing the changes and continuities of Chinese culture as it transitioned from the Ming to the Qing dynasty. If you take Option 1, you would first discuss continuities in Chinese culture as the dynasties transitioned from Ming rule to Qing rule, and then discuss the changes in the next paragraph. Or, if you take Option 2, you might discuss the continuities and changes in political structures in the first paragraph and then continuities and changes in social structures in the second paragraph. Remember that Option 2 has to be by *topic*. But, be careful! You are not comparing the Chinese under the Qing to the Chinese under the Ming. This is not simply a comparison. You are detailing how Chinese culture has continued and changed.

A Model of a Continuity and Change Argument

Let's look at an example of a continuity and change argument:

Contextualization — Advancements in science and technology have radically transformed how the world uses energy for production and day-to-day life, beginning with the coal-powered engines of the Industrial Revolution in the nineteenth century.

Claim of change — The source of energy for production and electricity has changed from coal to other fossil fuels, nuclear energy, and sustainable green energies.

Evidence of change — The use of fossil fuels like oil and natural gas has increased worldwide in both developed and developing nations. The widespread use of the internal combustion engine, mainly in transportation vehicles, is a factor that has caused the use and demand for oil to grow globally. Also, nuclear energy and green energies like wind and solar power have been developed as sources of energy that decrease the carbon footprint.

778

Although energy now comes from a variety of fossil fuels and alternative green energies, coal is still the largest source of electricity production globally.

Counter-argument addressing continuity

This paragraph is a continuity and change argument in miniature. The authors set up the context and put forth the claim that new energy sources, other than coal, have been developed and utilized globally. They then give evidence to support this claim. Last, the authors address the counterargument in the form of a continuity. If you wish to expand upon this with more context, perhaps write a separate paragraph for changes with more evidence and discussion, and then make the continuity counterargument its own paragraph. Add a conclusion summarizing your findings, and you have a LEQ response that is fit for the AP® Exam.

If you are working on the DBQ, setting up your essay will be essentially the same as what we have discussed, with the difference being that your paragraphs have to speak to the evidence found in the documents in addition to addressing the prompt.

BUILDING AP® SKILLS

1. **Activity: Writing Continuity and Change Thesis Statements.** Using the information in the section "Feminism and Personal Life" on pages 772–774 as your evidence, write a thesis statement for the prompt that follows. Remember that a good thesis needs to answer the prompt, be argumentative, provide a roadmap for the essay, and address the counterargument.

   Prompt: Evaluate the extent to which global feminism has resulted in widespread societal change.

2. **Activity: Building a Continuity and Change Argument Paragraph.** Based on the thesis statement addressing the prompt that follows, create one body paragraph of a continuity and change argument essay. You will need to decide whether you want to create a paragraph of continuities, a paragraph of changes, or a paragraph centered on a topic that encompasses both continuities and changes. Begin by filling in the template below using the information in the section called "Life on the Land: The Decline of the Peasantry" that begins on page 760 for your evidence. Then write the paragraph, being sure to analyze every piece of evidence to show how it connects back to the thesis.

   Prompt: Evaluate the extent to which agricultural technology changed in the twentieth century.

   Thesis: Although agriculture remains seasonally dependent on human labor, such as migrant labor, the number of people needed to grow crops globally has dramatically decreased due to the use of mechanization, such as tractors and combines, and through Green Revolution innovations like chemical fertilizers and new types of seeds.

TRM **Suggested Responses to Questions**
You can find suggested responses to the Building AP® Skills questions in the Teacher's Resource Materials.

779

Topic sentence:
    Evidence A:
    Evidence B:
    Evidence C:
    Analysis:

3. **Activity: Creating a Source-Based Continuity and Change Argument.** Based on the following prompt, use the "Economic Globalization: Deepening Connections" section of this chapter (pages 751–753) to create a contextualizing intro, a thesis, and two topic sentences for paragraphs that include at least three points of evidence and an analysis that shows how the evidence supports the thesis. Then, select the evidence in the documents you would use to support your argument.

Prompt: Evaluate the changes in the global economy from 1900 to the present.

Intro/Context:

Thesis:

Topic sentence 1:
    Evidence A:
    Evidence B:
    Evidence C:
    Analysis:

Topic sentence 2:
    Evidence A:
    Evidence B:
    Evidence C:
    Analysis:

Analyzing Energy Consumption over Time

Energy derived primarily from the burning of fossil fuels has driven both global economic growth and climate change since at least the beginning of the Industrial Revolution, and especially since 1950. But the consumption of energy has evolved over time in terms of both the mix of fuels used to produce it and the overall amount of energy consumed. In this activity, you will examine energy consumption data from 1965 to 2018 in order to identify continuities and changes in energy usage in recent decades.

This graph is based on population data from the World Bank and data compiled for the Statistical Review of World Energy created by British Petroleum, one of the largest energy companies in the world. The graph is specifically designed to show change over time between 1965 and 2018 in terms of the types and amounts of energy consumed. It also provides data on the per capita consumption of energy through time — that is, consumption of energy per person. Note that the base unit used to compare different types of energy is "million tons oil equivalent," an amount of energy equivalent to that released by the burning of 1 million tons of oil.

Graph of Energy Consumption by Type, 1965–2018

World Energy Consumption, 1965-2018. Data from BP Statistical Review of World Energy; population data from World Bank.

BUILDING AP® SKILLS

Claims and Evidence in Sources

The beginning of Chapter 13 focuses on the new technologies of the twentieth century, including energy technologies. The "AP® Looking Again: Analyzing Energy Consumption over Time" would be a good activity to have students complete as they work through the section "Fossil Fuel Breakthroughs" to help them practice breaking down a source. Have students start off by analyzing the "Graph of Energy Consumption by Type, 1965–2018" and then answering the questions under "A First Look" and "A Second Look" on page 782 on their own. When they've finished answering those questions on their own, divide the class into groups of three to four students and have them discuss their answers with one another. Then have them work as a group to answer the questions under "A Third Look."

781

1 A FIRST LOOK

Start by carefully examining the graph and how it conveys information. Then test your understanding by answering these questions:

1. Which color corresponds to which source of energy on this graph?

2. What information is conveyed along the horizontal axis below the graph?

3. What information is conveyed on the vertical axes to the right and left of the graph?

2 A SECOND LOOK

Now that you have oriented yourself to how the graph conveys its data, use it to analyze total global energy consumption and the mix of energy sources used across the world between 1965 and 2018. Structure your analysis of the data by answering the following questions:

1. How would you describe the general trend in total energy consumption between 1965 and 2018?

2. How has the mix of energy sources consumed changed between 1965 and 2018?

3. Oil, gas, and coal are all fossil fuels that emit climate-warming gases when burned, while nuclear, hydro, and renewables (wind, solar, etc.) do not. How did the mix between energy sources that generated global warming gases and those that did not change between 1965 and 2018?

3 A THIRD LOOK

Beyond the change in overall consumption through time, this graph also offers information about consumption of energy per person, that is, per capita consumption. Return to the graph and identify in the key how per capita consumption is represented through time, and establish which vertical axis refers to tons of oil equivalent emissions per capita. Then answer the following questions:

1. How would you describe the overall trend in per capita consumption between 1965 and 2018?

2. In the early 1970s oil prices spiked for a number of years, leading to significant fuel economy initiatives in industrialized countries. Do the data conveyed in this graph indicate that these developments may have had an impact on per capita consumption during this period?

3. How do you personally assess the data in this chart? How does the chart affect your thinking about the future and the tasks that lie ahead for people of your generation?

AP' ACTIVITY **MAKING AN ARGUMENT**

In a brief essay, identify specfic data from the graph to support each part of the following three-part argument: (1) Despite the growth in the use of nuclear, hydro, and renewable energy sources (2) and a fall in per capita energy consumption, (3) humankind burned more climate-changing fossil fuels in 2018 than it did in 1965. Conclude your essay by seeking to explain this apparent contradiction. You might look at the Snapshot in Chapter 14, page 802, for help in answering this question.

FURTHER ACTIVITY

Using the graph, calculate how many more millions of tons of oil equivalent energy would need to have been produced from nuclear, hydro, and renewable energy sources in 2018 to reduce fossil fuel consumption to 1965 levels. How does this total compare to the actual total of nuclear, hydro, and renewable energy production in 2018?

BUILDING AP® SKILLS

Argumentation

You can help students practice their argumentation skills as a follow-up to "AP® Looking Again: Analyzing Energy Consumption over Time." Ask students to write a short essay that provides evidence for the arguments in the "AP® Activity: Making an Argument" on this page.

783

BUILDING AP® SKILLS

Claims and Evidence in Sources

Interpreting text-based as well as non-text-based sources is an important skill for AP® World History: Modern students. If time is available, have students complete a further investigation into how technology has affected contemporary life by using the evidence in "Reflections on Technology" beginning on page 784. Consider having students analyze one or more of the sources found on pages 784–790. You can check for student understanding by:

■ Using the questions at the end of each source as a discussion starting point.

■ Pairing students to analyze (identify and describe) the author/creator's point of view, purpose, historical situation, and/or audience. This activity can continue to reinforce sourcing.

■ Assigning a source to a group of three to four students and having them present an overview of the source along with the sourcing to the rest of the class.

■ After students present an overview of the source, have them practice AP® skills using any of the activities under "AP® Doing History" on page 790.

Reflections on Technology

The past century has witnessed an astonishing pace of technological innovation, transforming practically every domain of human life: work and play; making war and making love; transportation and communication; commerce and consumption; politics and private life. Accompanying these transformations has been an endless commentary on all matters technological that took shape variously as celebration and criticism, as prediction and propaganda, and as professorial essays and parental warnings. The sources that follow provide just a tiny sample of this vast conversation about the role of technology in contemporary life since 1900.

LOOKING AHEAD   Evaluate the extent to which technology has impacted contemporary life
AP® **DBQ PRACTICE**   since 1900.

DOCUMENT 1 **Imagining the Future of Technology from a Western Viewpoint**

The turn of the twentieth century prompted widespread speculation about the shape of the future that focused heavily on technology, at least in the West. In 1900, an article in the *Ladies' Home Journal*, an American women's magazine, predicted "What May Happen in the Next Hundred Years."

Source: John E. Watkins Jr., "What May Happen in the Next Hundred Years," published in American magazine *Ladies' Home Journal*, 1900.

There will probably be from 350,000,000 to 500,000,000 people in America.

The American will be taller by from one to two inches. He will live fifty years instead of thirty-five at present. The trip from suburban home to office will require only a few minutes.

Automobiles will have been substituted for every horse vehicle now known. There will be air-ships, but they will not successfully compete with surface cars and water vehicles for passenger or freight traffic.

Man will see around the world. Persons and things of all kinds will be brought within focus of cameras connected electrically, thousands of miles at a span. Grand Opera will be telephoned to private homes.

Peas and beans will be as large as beets are today. Strawberries as large as apples.

A university education will be free to every man and woman.

Question to Consider: What posture toward technology does the document reflect?

AP® **Analyzing Sources:** How do the technological changes of the time period in which the source was written impact the author's view of technology in the future?

784

DOCUMENT 2 **Communism and Technology**

If technological optimism characterized the capitalist world, twentieth-century communists were no less enamored. In 1920, Lenin had famously declared that "communism is Soviet power plus the electrification of the whole country." And in a report on the Soviet Union's first five-year plan, delivered in 1933, Stalin boasted that the country had recently created a long list of industries—iron and steel, tractors, automobiles, machine tools, chemicals, agricultural machinery, electric power, oil and coal—all of them the products of modern technology. Accompanying the printed version of Stalin's report was a series of images that illustrated the country's technological and industrial successes. One of those images is presented here.

Source: Illustration depicting Soviet industry and technology that accompanied Stalin's first five-year plan, 1933.

Question to Consider: How does the source reflect the distinctive Soviet approach to industrialization in the 1930s?

AP **Analyzing Sources:** What was the purpose of the source?

Nehru and Gandhi on Technology and Industry

The leaders of anticolonial movements throughout Asia and Africa were virtually unanimous that modern technology, science, and industrialization were essential for the new nations they sought to create. No one expressed these sentiments more clearly than Jawaharlal Nehru, a leading figure in India's independence movement and the country's first prime minister. But Nehru had to take into account the rather different views held by his leader and mentor, Mahatma Gandhi. Almost alone among major political figures, Gandhi was highly skeptical about industrialization and "the machine": "Industrialization is, I am afraid, going to be a curse for mankind," he declared. "God forbid that India should ever take to industrialism after the manner of the West." He also stated that "it is machinery that has impoverished India." Document 3, taken from Nehru's book, *The Discovery of India*, was written while he and Gandhi were in prison during World War II because of their political activity. In this passage, Nehru outlines his own hopes for technology in India.

Source: India's first prime minister, Jawaharlal Nehru, on the importance of industrialization for Indian independence, from his book *The Discovery of India*, 1946.

It can hardly be challenged that, in the context of the modern world, no country can be politically and economically independent, even within the framework of international interdependence, unless it is highly industrialized and has developed its power resources to the utmost. Nor can it achieve or maintain high standards of living and liquidate poverty without the aid of modern technology in almost every sphere of life. An industrially backward country will continually upset the world equilibrium and encourage the aggressive tendencies of more developed countries. Thus an attempt to build up a country's economy largely on the basis of cottage and small-scale industries is doomed to failure. It will not solve the basic problems of the country or maintain freedom, nor will it fit in with the world framework, except as a colonial appendage.

The economy based on the latest technical achievements of the day must necessarily be the dominating one. If technology demands the big machine, as it does today in a large measure, then the big machine with all its implications and consequences must be accepted. Where it is possible, in terms of that technology, to decentralize production, this would be desirable. But, in any event, the latest technique has to be followed, and to adhere to outworn and out-of-date methods of production, except as a temporary and stop gap measure, is to arrest growth and development.

Question to Consider: Why does Nehru feel that industry and modern technology are essential for India's future as an independent country?

AP Analyzing Sources: How might events in India during this period have influenced the source?

DOCUMENT 4 "Technology with a Human Face"

By the mid-twentieth century, a highly positive and optimistic view of modern technology had become firmly inscribed in global culture—in capitalist, communist, and colonial and developing countries alike—and to a large extent it has remained so to the present day. And no wonder! For billions of individuals, this technology has lengthened life spans substantially, improved health, enabled travel and communication, diminished poverty, and greatly enriched the material conditions of life. For businesses large and small, that technology has created vast markets and spawned no end of profit-making possibilities. For governments, it has enhanced military power and international prestige, while generating economic growth, which has become a major source of legitimacy and popularity for political elites everywhere.

And yet, as the twentieth century wore on in its second half and as the twenty-first dawned, more skeptical voices appeared, even as technological innovations of all kinds multiplied many times over. In 1972, for example, an international think tank, the Club of Rome, published the highly controversial *The Limits to Growth*, a report that sharply challenged "technological optimism" and questioned the earth's ability to accommodate continued economic and population growth.

A year later, the German-born British economist E. F. Schumacher published his classic text, *Small Is Beautiful*. Widely read around the world, it was dubbed one of the hundred most influential books since World War II. Challenging what he called "gigantism," "mass production," and "unlimited economic growth," Schumacher called for "technology with a human face" and "economics as if people mattered."

Source: British economist E. F. Schumacher on "intermediate technology" from his book *Small Is Beautiful*, 1973.

The system of *mass production*, based on sophisticated, highly capital-intensive, high energy input dependent, and human labour-saving technology, presupposes that you are already rich, for a great deal of capital investment is needed to establish one single workplace. The system of *production by the masses* mobilises the priceless resources which are possessed by all human beings, their clever brains and skillful hands, and supports them with first-class tools. The technology of *mass production* is inherently violent, ecologically damaging, self-defeating in terms of non-renewable resources, and stultifying for the human person. The technology of *production by the masses*, making use of the best of modern knowledge and experience, is conducive to decentralisation, compatible with the laws of ecology, gentle in its use of scarce resources, and designed to serve the human person instead of making him the servant of machines. I have named it intermediate technology to signify that it is vastly superior to the primitive technology of bygone ages but at the same time much simpler, cheaper, and freer than the super-technology of the rich. One can also call it self-help technology, or democratic or people's technology—a technology to which everybody can gain admittance and which is not reserved to those already rich and powerful.

Question to Consider: What is Schumacher's critique of the prevailing technology he observed?

AP Analyzing Sources: For what audience was this source likely intended?

787

DOCUMENT 5 Nuclear Technology and Fears of a Nuclear Holocaust

Yet another source of anxiety and skepticism about modern technology derived from growing fears about nuclear weapons and their likely consequences. During the 1980s as a nuclear arms race, driven by cold war hostilities, picked up speed, such concerns found expression in a variety of grass roots campaigns like the "nuclear freeze" movement in the United States that called for a Soviet-American "freeze on testing, production, and further deployment of nuclear weapons." The scientific case for the fearful consequences of a major nuclear war appeared in the prestigious American periodical *Scientific American* in 1984.

Source: From the article "The Climatic Effects of Nuclear War," published in *Scientific American*, 1984.

Recent findings by our group, confirmed by [scientific] workers in Europe, the U.S. and the U.S.S.R. suggest that the long term climatic effects of a major nuclear war are likely to be much severer and farther-reaching than had been supposed. In the aftermath of such a war, vast areas of the earth could be subjected to prolonged darkness, abnormally low temperatures, violent windstorms, toxic smog and persistent radioactive fallout—in short the combination of conditions that has come to be known as "nuclear winter." The physical effects of nuclear war would be compounded by the widespread breakdown of transportation systems, power grids, agricultural production, food processing, medical care, sanitation, civil service and central government. Even in regions far from the conflict, the survivors would be imperiled by starvation, hypothermia, radiation sickness, weakening of the human immune system, epidemics, and other dire consequences. Under some circumstances, a number of biologists and ecologists contend, the extinction of many species of organisms—including the human species—is a real possibility.

Question to Consider: What outcomes of a large-scale nuclear war do these authors predict?

AP Analyzing Sources: How might events of the postwar era have influenced this source?

DOCUMENT 6 Technology and Climate Change

By the early 1990s the cold war had ended and at least temporarily the danger of nuclear war had receded. But that existential threat to the planet and its many inhabitants—human and otherwise—was soon replaced by another such threat: climate change or global warming. Like nuclear war, climate change is also rooted in the vast capacities of modern technology and holds the very real possibility of social collapse on a massive scale.

Many observers argue that any effective response to global warming will require major adjustments and painful sacrifices in both personal and public life. These include, potentially, lower standards of living, higher taxes, greater regulations, less driving and flying, wealth transfers from the rich to the poor, and most fundamentally, changes in modern values and habits of thought that have led us into an unsustainable way of living.

Such an outlook is reflected in a recent book by Jeffrey Kiehl, a prominent American climate scientist and a Jungian analyst.

Source: American climate scientist Jeffrey T. Kiehl on reducing fossil fuel dependence, from his book *Facing Climate Change*, 2016.

Our commitment to burning fossil fuels arises from our need for more and more energy. The critical social factors that drive this need are the increasing number of people on the planet, the increasing consumption of energy, and technological innovations that require more energy. . . . The explosion of consumerism has led to owning more things that require energy. . . . Until we rein in this desire to consume recklessly we will continue to place the world out of balance. . . .

We need to imagine a world without fossil fuels, a world where we tread lightly on the earth, and in which food is distributed more equally. A world where we are living in cooperation, rather than competition, with nature. . . . We have drifted far away from seeing a living world, and we view the material world as existing to serve our endless needs and wants. . . . It is time to recognize our active participation in a fully animate world. . . . To live a balanced life requires us to consider how we relate to the world around us. . . .

We require a transformation unique in human civilization, a transformation in which we relinquish our dependence on something to which we are highly addicted. It is for this reason that we need to look beyond a technological transformation. . . . We need to look toward a transformation of consciousness; our behavior toward the world and toward one another needs to change. We need to recognize our interconnectedness. . . . We need to enter onto a path of *compassionate action* to avoid the worst consequences of human-induced climate change.

Question to Consider: When Jeffrey Kiehl says that "we need to look beyond a technological transformation," what kinds of changes does he envision?

AP Analyzing Sources: To what contemporary developments does this source respond?

DOCUMENT 7 **Debating Artificial Intelligence**

Yet another technological innovation that has generated great controversy is that of artificial intelligence. Abbreviated as AI, this outgrowth of computer science seeks to create smart machines that can undertake tasks that normally require a human agent. This technology has found applications in business, science, education, government, and the military. To its proponents, such technology holds great promise. Its ability to recognize patterns in huge data sets enables it to make useful predictions, to undertake highly complex tasks, and to drive smarter decision making. Furthermore, AI robots can perform tasks too dangerous for humans in both civilian and military life. And AI can "work" twenty-four hours a day, while human workers need rest, get sick, and require regular payment. And yet AI technology has generated intense anxiety, as the following excerpt by a well-known AI specialist indicates.

789

Source: Artificial intelligence analyst Ron Schmelzer, "Should We Be Afraid of AI?," from *Forbes* magazine, October 2019.

People don't like machines that get too smart, because we fear we can't control it. . . . Another major fear of AI is rooted in the idea of mass unemployment of human workers due to their replacement by AI workers. . . . AI systems will make us increasingly uncomfortable; applied to warfare, surveillance, law enforcement, and other purposes. . . . Probably the biggest fear of AI . . . is that of super intelligence or that AI will reach a point where it doesn't care for or about the existence of humanity anymore.

Question to Consider: What reservations or anxieties about AI technology are expressed in this extract?

AP **Analyzing Sources:** Who was likely the intended audience for this source?

AP® DOING HISTORY

1. **DBQ Practice:** Evaluate the extent to which technology has impacted contemporary life since 1900.

2. **Contextualization:** What changes in attitudes toward technology since 1900 do these sources reveal? How might you account for these changes?

3. **Comparison:** To what extent are differing postures toward technology more about human uses of these innovations than about the nature of the technologies themselves?

4. **Making Connections:** Construct a conversation among the authors or creators of these sources. What issues or arguments might arise? What areas of agreement might surface?

5. **Sourcing and Situation:** Collectively, to what extent were the sources a response to the situations in which they were created?

Technological Change in the Twentieth Century

The rapid pace of technological change over the course of the twentieth century transformed the lives of people across the planet in increasingly profound ways and played a central role in ushering in the Anthropocene—the "age of man." The two voices that follow take stock of the global impact of these developments at two different points in the century. In Voice 13.1, Trevor I. Williams, a scientist and historian writing in the 1980s, assesses the impact of technological change on humankind by the mid-twentieth century. In Voice 13.2, J. R. McNeill, one of the most prominent environmental historians of his generation, assesses the historical constraints on humankind that had been overcome during the twentieth century and the new constraints that had emerged by the end of the century.

VOICE 13.1

Trevor Williams on the Impacts of Technology in the First Half of the Twentieth Century | 1982

First, . . . was a very great increase in man's material wealth. For many this encouraged the hope that the long-sought brotherhood of mankind would be brought demonstrably nearer; the elimination of poverty and disease, it was argued, would remove the main causes of strife and create a milieu favourable to universal peace. In the event no such thing happened: nine years of our half-century were given over to two World Wars and the peace between and after was uneasy in both the military and the industrial sphere. The new wealth was not evenly distributed: if anything the rich became richer and the poor became poorer. . . . Understandably, new technology brought not only the fear but also the reality of unemployment, and led to bitter disputes not only between unions and employers but also between unions. . . . While it can be argued convincingly that new technology created rather than diminished employment, in the sense that at mid-century a very large number of people worked in industries that in 1900 did not even exist, individuals made redundant were often unfitted by age or training to grasp the new opportunities. . . .

Equally important was the fact that wealth provided a degree of security that made it possible to stand back and question the means by which it had been created. Technology was no longer satisfying merely basic needs—food, clothing, shelter—for a growing population, but had created new ones. Abundant and sophisticated foods out of season; non-stop entertainment by radio and, later, television; . . . were all pleasant new adjuncts to life but certainly not necessities. Paradoxically perhaps, the first half of this century witnessed the beginning of an anti-technology movement that was quickly to represent a political force too powerful to be ignored.

Source: Trevor I. Williams, *A Short History of Twentieth-Century Technology c. 1900–c. 1950* (Oxford: Clarendon, 1982), 397.

VOICE 13.2

J. R. McNeill on Challenges Overcome and Challenges Created in the Twentieth Century | 2000

According to the Hebrew Bible, on the fifth day of creation God enjoined humankind to fill and subdue the earth and to have dominion over every living thing. For most of history, our species failed to live up to these . . . injunctions, not for want of trying so much as for want of power. But in the twentieth century the harnessing of fossil fuels, unprecedented population growth, and a myriad of technological changes made it more nearly possible to fulfill these instructions. The prevailing political and economic systems made it seem imprudent not to try: most societies, and all the big ones, sought to maximize their current formidability and wealth at the risk of sacrificing ecological buffers and tomorrow's resilience. The general policy of the twentieth century was to try to make the most of resources, make Nature perform to the utmost, and hope for the best.

Claims and Evidence in Sources

You can use this exercise to help students work on improving skills with secondary sources. This activity can help students practice reading and interpreting secondary sources found on the MCQ and SAQ sections of the AP® Exam. Consider having students read both of the sources found on pages 791 and 792 and answer Questions 1–3 on page 792. When students have finished, discuss their answers as a class.

Differentiation

If students have been struggling with analyzing and interpreting secondary sources, consider following the "Must Do, Should Do, Strive For" model below:

■ Must Do: Divide the class into two groups. Assign one group Voice 13.1 and the other group Voice 13.2 to read and summarize the main ideas of the passage.

■ Should Do: Pair the students up based on what they read; each pairing should have one student who read Voice 13.1 and one who read Voice 13.2. Students should share their summaries of the passage they read with their partner and then work together to answer Questions 1 and 2 on page 792.

■ Strive For: For students who seem comfortable working with primary and secondary sources and want a writing challenge, ask them to write a 1- to 2-paragraph response to Question 3 on page 792.

With our new powers we banished some historical constraints on health and population, food production, energy use, and consumption generally. Few who know anything about life with these constraints regret their passing. But in banishing them we invited other constraints in the form of the planet's capacity to absorb the wastes, by-products, and impacts of our actions. These latter constraints had pinched occasionally in the past, but only locally. By the end of the twentieth century they seemed to restrict our options globally. Our negotiations with these constraints will shape the future as our struggles against them shaped our past.

Source: J. R. McNeill, *Something New under the Sun: An Environmental History of the Twentieth-Century World* (New York: W. W. Norton, 2000), 361–62.

AP **Analyzing Secondary Sources**

1. What do these two assessments share, and where do they differ?

2. According to McNeill, how have natural constraints on humankind changed over the past century?

3. **Integrating Primary and Secondary Sources:** How might Williams and McNeill use the sources in this feature to support their arguments?

792

Multiple-Choice Questions Choose the correct answer for each question.

Questions 1–3 refer to this passage.

> The apparent truth, which speaks to the paradox at the core of this book, is that the tendencies of both Jihad [referring to local, ethnic, or national identities] and McWorld [referring to global patterns of communication and exchange] are at work, both visible sometimes in the same country at the very same instant. Iranian zealots keep one ear tuned to the mullahs urging holy war and the other cocked to Rupert Murdoch's Star television beaming in *Dynasty*, *Donahue* and *The Simpsons* from hovering satellites. Serbian assassins wear Adidas sneakers and listen to Madonna on Walkman headphones as they take aim through their gunscopes at scurrying Sarajevo civilians looking to fill family watercans. . . . Jihad not only revolts against but abets McWorld, while McWorld not only imperils but re-creates and reinforces Jihad. McWorld is a product of popular culture driven by expansionist commerce. Its template is American, its form style. Japan has, for example, become more culturally insistent on its own traditions in recent years even as its people seek an ever greater purchase on McWorld.
>
> —Benjamin Barber, *Jihad vs. McWorld*, 1995

1. According to the passage, which of these is a consequence of globalization?
   a. Acceleration of the cold war
   b. Promotion of nonviolence to bring about political change
   c. New communication and transportation technologies
   d. An increase in nationalism

2. The ideas expressed in the passage occurred in the context of which of the following?
   a. Popular and consumer culture becoming more global in the second half of the twentieth century
   b. Military conflicts that occurred on an unprecedented global scale
   c. The rise and diffusion of Enlightenment thought
   d. The development of imperial societies using social Darwinism to justify imperialism

3. Which of these led to the dichotomy presented in the passage?
   a. The onset of the Great Depression
   b. The support by many governments of free market economic policies and economic liberalization
   c. The collapse of the older, land-based empires such as the Ottoman and Qing empires
   d. The Mexican Revolution and a desire to redistribute land

TEACHING IDEA

AP® Exam Strategies

You should continue to give students opportunities to practice test-taking skills. You can project or copy the stimulus-based multiple-choice questions found on pages 793 to 795. Give students the question as a practice quiz prior to the unit or chapter test. Have students discuss why their answer choice was correct or incorrect. Another way to use the multiple-choice questions is to gauge student learning of a topic after initial teaching.

Here employees in an Indian-based call center in Patna, a major city in northeastern India, undergo voice training in order to communicate more effectively with their English-speaking callers.

4. Which of the following best explains this image?

   a. New modes of communication reducing the problem of geographic distance, allowing for international call centers

   b. The desire of developing nations to increase their industrial strength by importing new technologies

   c. International organizations' encouragement of education and increasing literacy rates around the world

   d. An increased desire to break down old cultural and social barriers in order to facilitate modernization

5. A historian would most likely see which of these processes occurring in this India-based call center?

   a. Industrialization

   b. Collectivization

   c. Religious syncretism

   d. Globalization

6. Following the end of the cold war, free market economic theories became more widespread. The spread of these theories is best represented by an increase in which of these?

   a. Environmental protection organizations

   b. Multinational corporations

   c. Corporate monopolies

   d. International political organizations

Short-Answer Questions

Read each question carefully and write a short response. Use complete sentences.

1. **Use these passages and your knowledge of world history to answer all parts of the question that follows.**

   Never before in the history of the world has there been such a concentration and centralization of capital in so few nations and in the hands of so few people. Five hundred multinational corporations account for 80 percent of world trade and . . . half of all multinational corporations are based in the United States. But worse was still to come. Something happened that to me seemed impossible at one time. . . . I have taken to wearing blue jeans and Nike shoes. . . . But in the third-world, films, TV, and other media have increased the percentage of smokers. I saw half-starved kids in a marketplace in Mali buying single imported Benson & Hedges cigarettes and smoking.

   — Sherif Hetata, *Dollarization*, 1998

   If critics of globalization were less obsessed with "Cocacolonization," they might notice a rich feast of cultural mixing that belies fears about Americanized uniformity. Algerians in Paris practice Thai boxing; Asian rappers in London snack on Turkish pizza; Salman Rushdie delights readers everywhere with his Anglo-Indian tales. Although there can be downsides to cultural globalization, this cross-fertilization is overwhelmingly a force for good.

   — Philippe Legrain, *Cultural Globalization Is Not Americanization*, 2003

795

BUILDING AP® SKILLS

Argumentation

AP® World History: Modern writing skills should be practiced on a regular basis. Consider using the SAQs on pages 795–797 for students to write an "exit ticket" at the end of class to check for understanding. You can also use the SAQs for more traditional timed writing practice, either by spreading the three SAQs across several days or as practice for the AP® Exam by writing them all at once. Make certain that students have the correct amount of time for this exercise. On exam day, students will have a total of 40 minutes to write three SAQs. If you are having them write only one at a time, you'll need to give them about 14 minutes to write it.

A. Describe ONE major difference between Hetata's and Legrain's historical interpretation of globalization.

B. Explain how ONE specific historical event or development that is not explicitly mentioned in the excerpts could be used to support Hetata's argument.

C. Explain how ONE specific historical event or development that is not explicitly mentioned in the excerpts could be used to support Legrain's argument.

2 . Use this map and your knowledge of world history to answer all parts of the question that follows.

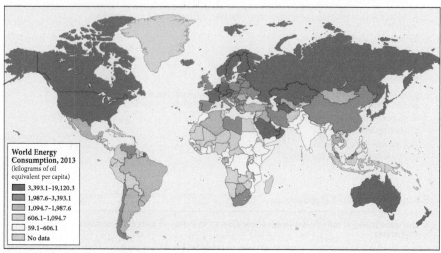

World Energy Consumption per Capita, 2013

A. Identify ONE development from 1945 to the present that contributed to the world energy consumption depicted in the map.

B. Identify ANOTHER development from 1945 to the present that contributed to the world energy consumption depicted in the map.

C. Explain a consequence of the world energy consumption depicted in the map.

3. **Use your knowledge of world history to answer all parts of the question that follows.**

   A. Identify ONE specific historical difference between the impact of feminism and globalization on women in the Global North and their impact on women in the Global South.

   B. Identify ONE specific historical similarity between the impact of feminism and globalization on women in the Global North and their impact on women in the Global South.

   C. Explain ONE reason for either the difference or similarity between the impact of feminism and globalization on women in the Global North and their impact on women in the Global South.

797

14 Global Processes

Demography, Culture, and the Environment, 1900–present

AP® Overview for Chapter 14

Chapter 14 covers the effects of globalization from 1900 to the present. The chapter includes the increase in global migration, the growth of cultural identity, and the changing interactions between humans and the environment in the modern world. The material in this chapter is rich with historical information and images that will expose students to the differing reactions to globalization in various regions of the world. Students should utilize their skills and assess the change and continuity among social, cultural, and environmental trends during and before this time period. You should encourage students to go deeper into the skills that the AP® World History: Modern course seeks to develop.

Chapter 14 Essential Activity

By this point in the year, it's almost time for the AP® Exam. Chapter 14, as the final chapter, would be a good place to have students write one last LEQ or DBQ before the exam. The OER Project has a great DBQ in Unit 9 of its World History: AP® course that asks students to evaluate whether globalization brought positive effects to all people in the contemporary era. Students will have to call on what they have learned from Chapters 13 and 14 to help them analyze the documents and write their essay. Give students 60 minutes to read the documents and write their DBQ. You can find the prompt and documents in Topic 9.3: Global Culture, Resistance and Reforms of the OER Project's World History: AP® Curriculum in Unit 9.

Differentiation

If you want to help students scaffold the skills needed to complete the Chapter 14 Essential Activity, consider following the "Must Do, Should Do, Strive For" model below:

- **Must Do:** Students must complete a DBQ organizer that responds to the OER Project's prompt. Find a printable version of the Writing Organizer DBQ in the Teacher's Resource Materials.
- **Should Do:** After completing the organizer, students should pick the argument they feel most comfortable with and write an argumentative body paragraph.
- **Strive For:** Using the ideas they put together on their DBQ outlines (but not the organizer itself), students should write a timed essay answering the prompt from the OER Project.

TRM Writing Organizer for DBQ Practice

Chapter 14 Resources

- **TRM** AP® Skills Workshop Activity Handout: Writing a DBQ: Comparative Arguments
- **TRM** Chapter 14 DBQ Activity Handout
- **TRM** Chapter 14 Guided Reading
- **TRM** Chapter 14 Lecture Presentation Slides
- **TRM** Chapter 14 Outline
- **TRM** Chapter 14 Suggested Responses to Questions
- **TRM** Eric's Activity 14.1: Generalizing about Islam
- **TRM** Eric's Activity 14.2: Living in the Anthropocene
- **TRM** Handout 14.1: Chart for Effects of Globalization
- **TRM** Handout 14.2: OPTIC Chart for Slums and Skyscrapers Photo
- **TRM** Handout 14.3: Comparison Chart for Nineteenth- and Twentieth-Century Migrations
- **TRM** Handout 14.4: Chart for Demographic Effects of Twentieth-Century Political Changes

- **TRM** Handout 14.5: OPTIC Chart for Mexican Migrant Workers Photo
- **TRM** Handout 14.6: Chart for Twentieth-Century Political Ideologies
- **TRM** Handout 14.7: Continuity and Change Chart for Religion in the Twentieth Century
- **TRM** Handout 14.8: Chart for Religious Fundamentalist Movements
- **TRM** Handout 14.9: Chart for Environmental Impacts in Holocene and Anthropocene Eras
- **TRM** Handout 14.10: Chart for Initiatives to Combat Environmental Damage
- **TRM** Map 14A: The World
- **TRM** Writing Organizer for DBQ Practice

Pacing Guide

Below is a pacing guide for the AP® World History: Modern course beginning in ca. 1200 C.E. This pacing guide is based on a schedule with 120 sessions of 50 minutes each before the AP® Exam. It is meant as a place to start. If you have a different number of sessions before the exam, you can modify the pacing to suit your needs.

Day	Pages Assigned	AP® Topic	AP® Theme	Suggested Assignments	Coverage Notes
1	Read pages 799–811 to "Cultural Identity in an Entangled World"	9.1 9.2	ENV TEC	Exploring AP® Themes: ENV on page 800 Apply the Tip on page 800 Building AP® Skills: Making Connections: Continuity and Change on page 807 AP® Classroom: AP® Daily Video on page 811	Like Chapter 13, Chapter 14 is set up more thematically than chronologically. This is going to help students understand these larger topics related to globalization in the past century. This chapter focuses on the increase in global migration in the past century, along with cultural diffusion and identity in an increasingly globalized world.
2	Read pages 811–822 from "Cultural Identity in an Entangled World"	9.5 9.6 9.7	CDI SIO	Chapter 14 Essential Activity Building AP® Skills: Argumentation on page 814 Exploring AP® Themes: CDI on page 815 Building AP® Skills: Making Connections: Continuity and Change on page 816 Eric's Activity 14.1: Generalizing about Islam on page 822	See above.
3	Read pages 823–828 to "Protecting the Planet: The Rise of Environmentalism"	9.1 9.3	ENV TEC	Teaching Idea: Incorporating Outside Resources on page 823 Eric's Activity 14.2: Living in the Anthropocene on page 825 Building AP® Skills: Claims and Evidence in Sources on page 826 Teaching Idea: Incorporating Outside Resources on page 828	This final section of Chapter 14 focuses heavily on the first theme of this course, Humans and the Environment, by looking at how the environment has changed due to modern human behavior and the growth of the environmental movement.
4	Read pages 828–835 from "Protecting the Planet: The Rise of Environmentalism"	9.3 9.5	ENV SIO	Teaching Idea: Class Discussion on page 830 Exploring AP® Themes: ENV on page 833 Building AP® Skills: Argumentation on page 834	See above.

One World This composite NASA photograph, showing both the earth and the moon, reveals none of the national, ethnic, religious, or linguistic boundaries that have long divided humankind. Such pictures have both reflected and helped create a new planetary consciousness among growing numbers of people. (Image created by Reto Stockli, Nazmi El Saleous, and Marit Jentoft-Nilsen, NASA GSFC)

798

Global Processes

Demography, Culture, and the Environment

1900–present

◀ **AP**

ARGUMENTATION
Explain how images like this could be used to support environmental and international peace movements. What does it evoke for you?

CONNECTING PAST AND PRESENT

In the early twenty-first century, a forty-five-year-old vege-table grower named Omar Imma Assayar moved with his wife and ten children from their rural village of some 400 people in the West African country of Chad to the capital city of N'Djamena with a population of over a million. His decision to move was prompted by the death of all his cattle during a severe drought. Furthermore, while living in the village, he had to get up early and carry his produce by bicycle to the market in the city. "My life is easier now," he explained. "I live right next to the market. I have more time to be with my family, and I can get a better price for my vegetables as well. . . . My one big wish is for my children to go to school."[1] ■

Omar and his family have both witnessed and participated in some of the major drivers of world history during the past century. His ten children have contributed to the enormous increase in human numbers. In moving to the capital of Chad, Omar joined millions of others in Africa, Asia, and Latin America who are seeking a better life in the city. In his desire to educate his children, he has also taken part in the vast expansion of literacy that has swept the planet during the past century. Not far from his new home is Lake Chad, which has shrunk drastically in response to climate change and overuse, linking his country to global patterns of environmental degradation. The life of this single individual then is connected to the global processes that conclude this account of the human journey during the twentieth century and beyond—massive population growth, widespread movement of people, changing patterns of cultural identity, and unprecedented human impact on the environment.

799

TRM **Chapter 14 Guided Reading**
You can find a guided reading handout for this chapter in the Teacher's Resource Materials.

TRM **Chapter 14 Lecture Slides**
You can find curated lecture slides for this chapter in the Teacher's Resource Materials.

TRM **Chapter 14 Outline**
You can find a chapter outline to model good note-taking for this chapter in the Teacher's Resource Materials.

TRM **Suggested Responses to Questions**
You can find suggested responses to all of the AP® margin questions in this chapter in the Teacher's Resource Materials.

BUILDING AP® SKILLS

Developments and Processes

You should try to give students opportunities to read the stories of "everyday" people throughout the course, especially during the twentieth and twenty-first centuries. It's good for them to see a different view of historical events. The opening to Chapter 14 offers a good opportunity. Ask students to read the opening about Omar Imma Assayar and have them list examples of how Omar's story reflects globalization in the contemporary age. (Answers provided in italics.)

■ *His ten children reflect the massive population growth that happened in the twentieth century.*

■ *His family's move from a rural village in Chad to the capital city, N'Djamena, reflects the migration of millions to urban areas. The population growth of major cities is also going to affect the surrounding environment.*

■ *Omar's desire to have his children go to school reflects the massive expansion of literacy across the globe in the twentieth century.*

This is a good time to assign released Question 1 from the 2011 exam to help students understand the effects of the Green Revolution. In this Document-Based Question, students are asked to analyze the causes and the consequences of the Green Revolution from approximately 1945 through the present day. Ask students to analyze the documents as homework to see how they could use them to answer the prompt, and discuss answers as a class the next day. The question and associated materials can be found on the College Board website, in the AP® World History: Modern Past Exam Questions section. If you choose to have students write this essay, keep in mind that it does not match the redesigned essay format. You will need to delete one document to bring it in line with the new format (we recommend deleting Document 6). You will also need to update the prompt: Evaluate the extent to which the Green Revolution led to a variety of consequences in the period from 1945 to the present.

Humans and the Environment (ENV)

The world experienced massive demographic change in the twentieth and twenty-first centuries. You can get students to explore these changes and their effects by dividing them into groups to create a list of the causes and effects of human population growth since 1900. Also ask them to connect the population increase in the twentieth century to a previous population increase. Ask: How does the population growth of the twentieth century compare to previous population growths? *Answers may include: Population increases have occurred because of advances in medicine and sanitation, and because of Green Revolution technologies, which have increased food production; The effects include more consumption of the earth's resources, massive urbanization, and global migration.*

Differentiation

If you want to get students to practice multiple historical reasoning skills with this activity, consider following the "Must Do, Should Do, Strive For" model below:

■ Must Do: Students must work with their groups to create a list of the causes and effects of human population growth since 1900.

AP®
CAUSATION
What has enabled the demographic, cultural, and environmental changes of the past century?

AP® EXAM TIP
You should be able to explain a variety of effects of the Green Revolution.

AP®
CAUSATION
What factors led to the slowing rate of global population growth toward the end of the twentieth century?

More People: Quadrupling Human Numbers

Finding the Main Point: Why did the rate of global population growth increase so dramatically from 1900 to the present?

From about 1.65 billion people in 1900, world population soared to almost 8 billion in 2022. In 120 years, the human species had more than quadrupled its numbers. It had taken humankind several hundred thousand years to reach 1 billion people in the early nineteenth century. That number then reached 2 billion in roughly 1930, 4 billion in 1975, 6 billion in 1999, and 7 billion by 2012. The speed and extent of this **population explosion** have no parallel in the human past or in the history of primate life on the planet.[2] Equally striking is the distribution of this massive growth, as some 90 percent of it occurred in the developing countries of Asia, Africa, the Middle East, and Latin America. (See Snapshot: World Population Growth, 1950–2100, page 802.)

The explanation for this massive demographic change lies in lower death rates, while birth rates have remained high. In 1945 roughly 20 people died each year for every 1,000 people in the world's population. By 2014 that figure was 8.[3] Infant mortality dropped even more quickly, especially after the 1960s. New medical technologies such as antibiotics, as well as widespread public health programs, played a major role in this unprecedented change. Various mosquito control measures sharply reduced death from malaria and yellow fever, while extensive vaccination campaigns eradicated smallpox by 1977.

As populations grew, innovations in agriculture enabled food production globally to keep up with, and even exceed, growing human numbers. A new **Green Revolution** greatly increased agricultural output through the use of tractors and mechanical harvesters; the massive application of chemical fertilizers, pesticides, and herbicides; and the development of high-yielding varieties of wheat and rice. All of this sustained the enormous population growth in developing countries.

By the end of the twentieth century, the rate of global population growth had begun to slow, as birth rates dropped all around the world. This transition to fewer births had occurred first in the more industrialized countries, where birth control measures were widely available, women were educated and pursuing careers, and large families were economically burdensome. By 1975, births in Europe had fallen below the replacement rate. More recently, this pattern has begun to take hold in developing countries as well, associated with urbanization, with growing educational opportunities for girls, and with vigorous family-planning programs in many places. China's famous one-child family policy, introduced in 1980, was the most dramatic of these efforts. Nonetheless, the world's population has continued to rise and according to statistical projections is expected to reach 9.6 billion in 2050 and 10.9 billion in 2100.

(continued)

■ Should Do: Students should work with their groups to compare the population increase of the twentieth century to previous growths in population. *Previous increases in human population were associated with increases in food production, including population growth during both the Neolithic era and the Columbian exchange. Unlike in previous population growths, a major factor in twentieth-century population growth was the use of science and medicine to save lives.*

■ Strive For: Students can use what they learned about population increase in the twentieth century to answer the SAQ below.

A. Identify ONE reason for population growth in the twentieth century.

B. Explain ONE way in which population growth in the twentieth century affected the environment.

C. Explain ONE way in which population growth in the twentieth century was similar to population growth in a previous period of history.

Landmarks for Chapter 14

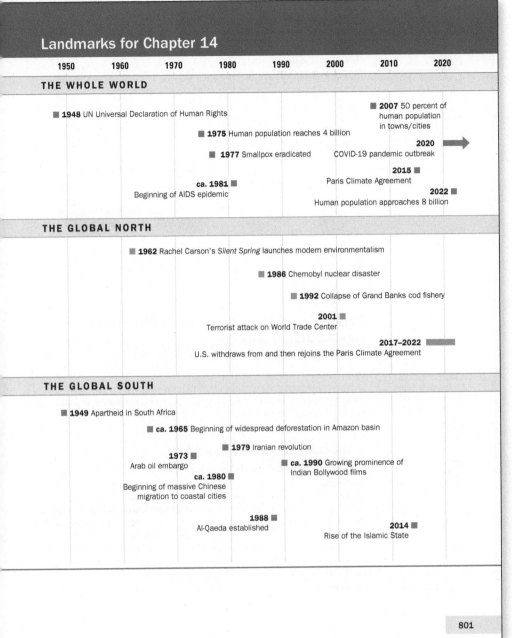

| 1950 | 1960 | 1970 | 1980 | 1990 | 2000 | 2010 | 2020 |

THE WHOLE WORLD

■ **1948** UN Universal Declaration of Human Rights

■ **2007** 50 percent of human population in towns/cities

■ **1975** Human population reaches 4 billion

2020
COVID-19 pandemic outbreak

■ **1977** Smallpox eradicated

2015 ■
Paris Climate Agreement

ca. 1981 ■
Beginning of AIDS epidemic

2022 ■
Human population approaches 8 billion

THE GLOBAL NORTH

■ **1962** Rachel Carson's *Silent Spring* launches modern environmentalism

■ **1986** Chernobyl nuclear disaster

■ **1992** Collapse of Grand Banks cod fishery

2001 ■
Terrorist attack on World Trade Center

2017–2022
U.S. withdraws from and then rejoins the Paris Climate Agreement

THE GLOBAL SOUTH

■ **1949** Apartheid in South Africa

■ **ca. 1965** Beginning of widespread deforestation in Amazon basin

■ **1979** Iranian revolution

1973 ■
Arab oil embargo

ca. 1990 Growing prominence of Indian Bollywood films

ca. 1980 ■
Beginning of massive Chinese migration to coastal cities

1988 ■
Al-Qaeda established

2014 ■
Rise of the Islamic State

801

BUILDING AP® SKILLS

Making Connections

Chapter 14 examines the interactions and effects of globalization on three major topics: Migration and Population, Culture and Identity, and the Environment. To preview the more detailed subjects students will learn about, you can ask them to sort the events from "Landmarks for Chapter 14" into a thematic chart like the one below. (Answers provided in italics.)

Migration and Population	Culture and Identity	The Environment
■ *1970: Human population reaches 4 billion*	■ *1948: UN Universal Declaration of Human Rights*	■ *1962: Rachel Carson's Silent Spring launches modern environmentalism*
■ *1977: Smallpox eradicated*	■ *1949: Apartheid in South Africa*	■ *ca. 1965: Beginning of widespread deforestation in Amazon basin*
■ *ca. 1980: Beginning of massive Chinese migration to coastal cities*	■ *1979: Iranian revolution*	■ *1973: Arab oil embargo*
■ *ca. 1981: Beginning of AIDS epidemic*	■ *1988: Al-Qaeda established*	■ *1986: Chernobyl nuclear disaster*
■ *2007: 50% of human population in towns/cities*	■ *ca. 1990: Growing prominence of Indian Bollywood films*	■ *1992: Collapse of Grand Banks cod fishery*
■ *2020: COVID-19 pandemic outbreak*	■ *2001: Terrorist attack on World Trade Center*	■ *2015: Paris Climate Agreement*
■ *2022: Human population approaches 8 billion*	■ *2014: Rise of the Islamic State*	■ *2017: U.S. withdraws from and then rejoins the Paris Climate Agreement*

TRM Handout 14.1: Chart for Effects of Globalization

SNAPSHOT World Population Growth, 1950–2100 (projected)

Shares according to UN medium fertility
variant projection.

| 1950 | 2010 | 2050 | 2100 |
| 2.5 billion | 6.9 billion | 9.6 billion | 10.9 billion |

Data from the European Environment Agency.

People in Motion: Patterns of Migration

Finding the Main Point: What factors shaped migration patterns since 1900, and what effects did migrations have on the receiving nations?

Growing numbers pushed more people to move. War, famine, climate change, poverty, industrialization, and urban growth drove migration, while new forms of transportation — steamships, trains, buses, cars, trucks, airplanes — facilitated this vast circulation of people.

To the Cities: Global Urbanization

In the early twenty-first century, humankind reached a remarkable, though largely unnoticed, milestone. For the first time more people around the world lived in towns and cities than in the countryside. Although urban populations had been slowly increasing for centuries, it was massive **global urbanization**, the explosive growth of cities after 1900, that made the world an "urban place."[4] City-dwellers made up 15 percent of the world's population in 1900, about 25 percent in 1950 before doubling again to 50 percent by 2007, and over 56 percent in 2021.

Mechanized farming and the Green Revolution had reduced the need for rural labor, even as population was growing rapidly, pushing many to migrate to cities. Opportunities for employment in manufacturing, commerce, government, and the service industry drew such people to urban centers, where life expectancies were rising because of improving infrastructure and health care. "These shifts in population," wrote historian Michael Hunt, "stripped villages of healthy young men and young, unmarried women. Their departure tore the social fabric of villages, leaving wives, young children, and the elderly behind."[5]

The timing of this movement to the cities varied. Europe and North America led the way, with about half their populations urbanized by 1950. Latin America, Africa, and Asia followed this general pattern in subsequent decades. And many of the urban centers to which people moved were large **megacities** with populations of over 10 million. In 1950, only New York and Tokyo had reached megacity status, but by 2020 the world counted thirty-seven such megacities on five continents. Joining Tokyo among the top five by population were Shanghai in China, Delhi in India, São Paolo in Brazil, and Mexico City in Mexico. From the 1970s on, the decline in manufacturing in some regions of the developed world prompted many industrial cities to reinvent themselves as hubs for education, health care, logistics, information technology, and other services. And as industrialization took hold in the Global South after 1950, cities grew at around twice the rate of already industrialized regions. In the 1980s, the Chinese government loosened residency restrictions that had kept much of the population in the countryside, unleashing an unprecedented wave of urban migrants, so that by 2018 nearly 60 percent of China's population lived in cities, dramatically up from 26 percent in 1990. Everywhere, cities attracted primarily young people from the countryside looking for better job prospects and educational, social, and cultural opportunities.

Even the most modern, well-managed cities had profound impacts on the environment, as large concentrations of people consumed huge amounts of food, energy, and water and in turn emitted enormous amounts of sewage, garbage, carbon dioxide, and toxic substances. Certainly, the poorly serviced slums and loosely regulated manufacturing enterprises of many cities across the planet created ecological disasters that destroyed local environments and damaged the health of residents, while elite neighborhoods boasted safe water, sewage systems, electricity,

▼ **AP**

CLAIMS AND EVIDENCE IN SOURCES

How does this image reflect the social disparities caused by urbanization?

Slums and Skyscrapers The enormous disparities that have accompanied urbanization in Latin America and elsewhere are illustrated in this photograph from São Paulo, Brazil. (Florian Kopp/imageBROKER/AGE Fotostock)

Overview	*A photograph that juxtaposes the wealth of major cities like São Paulo against the inequalities that exist side by side with them.*
Parts	*The background of the photograph features the skyscrapers of the city, representing modernization and growth. The foreground is a slum on the edges of São Paulo, where the buildings and homes are put together out of what seems to be scrap material and don't seem very stable. A family are walking on the sidewalk by the slum—they could possibly be residents of it.*
Title	*The photograph doesn't have an official title but could be called "The Slums and Skyscrapers of São Paulo."*
Interrelationships	*The placement of the two parts of São Paulo are trying to show the two realities of major urban areas and to bring recognition to the slums, which are not always acknowledged in conversations about urbanization.*
Conclusion	*This photograph is trying to illustrate how extreme poverty and inequality can exist side by side with modernization in urban areas.*

TRM Handout 14.2: OPTIC Chart for Slums and Skyscrapers Photo

BUILDING AP® SKILLS

Sourcing and Situation

The quote from the visitor to the Kibera slum in Nairobi in 2006 from the end of the first full paragraph provides students a good opportunity to practice their sourcing skills. You can ask students to read the quote. Then have them write down what they think this quote tells them about the speaker's views on how the Kenyan government has responded to inequality in urban areas. Once they have all finished, ask them to share what they wrote with the class. *The visitor believes the government has done nothing to help the people living in the slums or to end inequality, specifically mentioning that the state gives the people nothing, "no sanitation, no roads, no hospitals."*

APPLY THE TIP

Consider having a class discussion here about the changes between long-distance migrations during the nineteenth and twentieth centuries. To help students prepare for the discussion, ask them to create a chart on the characteristics of migration for both time periods. Students will need to use the sections on migration in Chapters 8 and 10 to complete the characteristics of migration in the nineteenth century. A reproducible version of the chart can be found in the Teacher's Resource Materials.

TRM Handout 14.3: Comparison Chart for Nineteenth- and Twentieth-Century Migrations

and fire and police services. On a per person basis, however, city living sometimes reduced electricity consumption and carbon emissions because public transportation, energy-efficient residences, and smaller families lessened the impact of humans on the environment.

Everywhere, wealth was concentrated in cities, but inequality was all the more apparent because the rich and poor often lived in close proximity, with luxury apartment buildings, office blocks, and malls overlooking slums and shantytowns. Improvements in public and private transport in the twentieth century allowed cities to spread out as never before. In the early twentieth century some cities, like Munich, Chicago, Sydney, and Cape Town, had large middle-class suburban communities composed of single-family houses, and after midcentury similar communities developed in cities across the globe where incomes and transportation networks allowed. In other cities, like Jakarta, Rio de Janeiro, Nairobi, and Lagos, rapid urban sprawl was driven primarily by recent arrivals who settled in slums on empty pieces of land with few public services, often at the edges of cities or in marginal spaces like steep hillsides or areas prone to flooding. In 2006, a visitor described the Kibera slum in Nairobi as "a squeezed square mile . . . home to nearly one million people. . . . Most of them live in one-room mud or wattle huts or in wooden or basic stone houses often windowless. . . . The Kenyan state provides the huge, illegal sprawl with nothing—no sanitation, no roads, no hospitals. It is a massive ditch of mud and filth, with a brown dribble of a stream running through it."[6] Clearly population growth and the rise of cities did not solve, and probably exacerbated in many places, the problem of urban poverty.

Moving Abroad: Long-Distance Migration

AP® EXAM TIP
You should be able to compare the long-distance migrations of the nineteenth century (Chapters 8 and 10) and the twentieth century.

AP®
CONTINUITY AND CHANGE
How did patterns of international migration change during the past century, and with what results?

While most "people in motion" traveled to nearby cities, a growing number moved abroad. (See Map 14.1.) Older patterns of migration, from Europe to the Americas, for example, continued and even accelerated in the early twentieth century, but migration patterns changed as the century unfolded. (For earlier patterns of migration, see "Europeans in Motion" in Chapter 8 and "Economies of Wage Labor: Migration for Work" in Chapter 10.) The number of migrants from Asia, Africa, and Latin America grew significantly, while Europe, earlier a leading source of long-distance emigrants, instead became an important destination for immigrants. From the 1920s on, the percentage of female migrants steadily grew, and in 2016 women constituted nearly half of all international migrants.

During the twentieth century states increasingly sought to control the flow of migrants across their borders, requiring travelers to possess passports and creating numerous administrative categories to describe migrants—asylum seekers, guest workers, tourists, students, undocumented persons, and refugees fleeing war, political oppression, climate catastrophes, religious persecution, or ethnic and cultural discrimination. Since World War II, these efforts to regulate borders have helped create enormous increases in refugees as desperate individuals find routes for flight shut off, leaving many millions living in refugee camps, often for generations.

The twentieth century also witnessed new patterns of human migration driven by war, revolution, the end of empire, and the emergence of new nation-states—many of which proved less tolerant of ethnic minorities than the empires that they replaced. The collapse of the Ottoman Empire following World War I prompted a large-scale exchange of populations as over a million Greek Orthodox Christians from Turkey relocated to Greece, while some 400,000 Turkish-speaking Muslims living in Greece moved in the other direction. Fleeing anti-Semitism, fascism, and the Holocaust, Jews immigrated to what is now Israel in large numbers, generating in the process a flow of Palestinian refugees to settlements in neighboring countries. Indian independence from Britain in 1947 resulted in the partition of the region along sectarian lines, forcing millions to migrate. In Rwanda, massacres by Hutus in July 1994 required over a million Tutsis to flee their homes, while the ultimate victory of the Tutsis sparked an even larger exodus of Hutus. Still other peoples moved as refugees fleeing violence or political oppression in places such as Vietnam, Cambodia, Sudan, Uganda, Cuba, Haiti, Venezuela, Iraq, Afghanistan, Syria, and most recently Ukraine.

Perhaps the most significant pattern of global migration since the 1960s has featured a vast movement of people from the developing countries of Asia, Africa, and Latin America to the industrialized world of Europe and North America, with smaller flows to Australia and the oil-rich states of the Persian Gulf. Pakistanis, Indians, and West Indians have moved to Great Britain; Algerians and West Africans to France; Turks and Kurds to Germany; Filipinos, Koreans, Cubans, Mexicans, and Haitians to the United States; and Egyptians, Pakistanis, Bangladeshis, and smaller numbers of highly skilled Westerners to the Persian Gulf states.

Much of this movement has involved **labor migration**, as people have moved, often without permission from government authorities and with few employable skills, to escape poverty in their own lands, drawn by a belief that employment opportunities and a better future await them in the developed countries. Often their journeys have been dangerous, as migrants have confronted long treks through burning deserts in the American Southwest or braved dangerous crossings of the Mediterranean Sea to Europe in rickety and overcrowded vessels. Many have depended on expensive and sometimes unreliable human smugglers. Smaller numbers of highly skilled and university-trained people, such as doctors and computer scientists, have come in search of professional opportunities less available in their own countries.

Everywhere migrants have struggled to find a place in their adopted communities. In some regions immigrant groups have for centuries assimilated into local societies without fully losing their distinct identities, a pattern that persisted into the twentieth century. Indians in East Africa, Chinese in Southeast Asia, and Japanese in Peru took advantage of their outsider status to become middlemen, forging links between existing groups in society as merchants, traders, or financiers.

AP® EXAM TIP
How the end of colonial empires in the twentieth century impacted migration is an important concept in the AP® course.

AP® EXAM TIP
You should know about the relationship between demographic and political changes in the 1900s.

AP® EXAM TIP
Take notes on this discussion of the reactions to migrants in different countries throughout the past century.

APPLY THE TIP

This would be a good place to pause and help students make connections between time periods. Remind students of previous reactions to migrants from Unit 6, like the Chinese Exclusion Act and the White Australia Policy, and let them know that these reactions both continued and changed in the twentieth century. Then ask them to read and take notes on the reactions to migrants in the 1900s using the information on pages 805 and 808. After they have taken notes, ask them to write a one-paragraph LEQ-style response to the following question: Evaluate the extent to which attitudes and reactions toward migrants changed throughout the twentieth century.

APPLY THE TIP

It's good to have students make connections between different themes. You can help students make connections between politics and demography by asking them to create a chart, like the one below, to explain the demographic effects of major political changes in the twentieth century. You can find a reproducible version of the chart in the Teacher's Resources Materials. (Answers are provided in italics.)

Political Change	Demographic Effects
Collapse of Ottoman Empire	*After the collapse of the Ottoman Empire following World War I, over a million Greek Orthodox Christians living in Turkey relocated to Greece, while about 400,000 Turkish-speaking Muslims living in Greece relocated to Turkey.*
Holocaust and Jewish Migration to Palestine	*Jews fleeing from anti-Semitism, fascism, and the Holocaust immigrated to Israel in large numbers, leading to a flow of Palestinian refugees to settlements in neighboring countries in the Middle East.*
Indian Independence and the Partition of India	*When India gained its independence in 1947, the British partitioned their former colony along sectarian lines (Hindu and Muslim), forcing millions to migrate from India to Pakistan and vice versa.*
1994 Rwandan Genocide	*The genocide forced over a million Tutsis to flee their homes in 1994, but when the Tutsis were ultimately victorious in the conflict, an even larger exodus of Hutus fled their homes.*
Political Oppression around the World	*Refugees fled political oppression or violence in places such as Vietnam, Cambodia, Sudan, Uganda, Cuba, Haiti, Iraq, Afghanistan, and Syria throughout the twentieth century.*

TRM Handout 14.4: Chart for Demographic Effects of Twentieth-Century Political Changes

EXPLORING AP® THEMES

Humans and the Environment (ENV)

You can get students to use what they've learned from their reading to analyze a map, chart, or image. Have students read through the information on page 805 about the causes of migration in the twentieth century and connect it to Map 14.1, "Global Migration Patterns, 1990–2005." Then ask: Which historical events from the twentieth century could be used to help explain the migration patterns seen in the map? *Answers may include: Conflicts and wars would lead people to seek better lives in other countries; Industrialization would have drawn people from developing countries to industrialized countries looking for work; Decolonization would lead to people seeking asylum or better living conditions.*

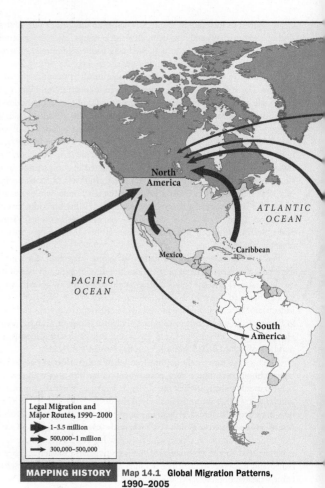

Legal Migration and Major Routes, 1990–2000

➤ 1–3.5 million
➤ 500,000–1 million
➤ 300,000–500,000

MAPPING HISTORY   **Map 14.1 Global Migration Patterns, 1990–2005**

The late twentieth and early twenty-first centuries witnessed a large-scale movement of people, primarily from the Global South to the Global North.

(Data from United Nations, World Bank, 2005; OEDC, 2001)

Countries Experiencing Net Outward Migration, 2005
- Countries with large-scale emigration (+15% of population living abroad)
- Countries with significant emigration (5–15% of population living abroad)

Countries Experiencing Net Inward Migration, 2005
- Countries with large-scale immigration (+15% of population born abroad)
- Countries with significant immigration (5–15% of population born abroad)

Reading the Map: Which regions produced the most emigrants in total numbers? Which regions produced the most outward migration measured as a percentage of the region's population? Do areas where the largest number of emigrants originated always correlate with regions with the highest percentage of outward migration?

AP Making Connections: Does this map offer any evidence to support the idea that migration patterns at the end of the twentieth century were still influenced by older links between Europe and its overseas empires?

BUILDING AP® SKILLS

Making Connections: Continuity and Change

The recommended historical reasoning skill for Unit 9 is Continuity and Change, and having students examine how migration patterns have changed throughout world history would be a good way to practice the skill. Give students a blank outline map of the world, available in the Teacher's Resource Materials, and then have them trace the migration patterns of the nineteenth century in one color and the migration patterns of the twentieth century in another color. Students should use Map 8.2 on page 453, "Snapshot: Long-Distance Migration in an Age of Empire, 1846–1940" on page 570, and Map 14.1 on pages 806–807 to help them trace the patterns on their map. After students have completed their maps, ask:

■ What changed in migration patterns between the two centuries? *Answers will vary, but may include: There was less migration from Europe compared to the age of empire; There was an increase in migration from the Global South to the Global North; The Gulf States experienced a large influx of migrants at the end of the twentieth century into the twenty-first.*

■ Why have these changes happened? *Answers will vary, but may include: The end of imperialism, the cold war, and the economic growth of the Global North influenced where groups migrated to; New technologies facilitated the mass movement of peoples around the globe.*

■ What has stayed the same with migration patterns? *Answers will vary, but may include: Western countries, like the United States and states in Western Europe, continue to see a large amount of immigration coming into their states; Industrialized states probably continue to be a major draw for migration.*

TRM Map 14A: The World

However, with the emergence or strengthening of national identities during the twentieth century, some of these minorities faced persecution. In Indonesia, huge numbers of ethnic Chinese who had lived in the region for generations were killed or driven from the country in 1965 by authorities suspicious that they held communist sympathies.

The most important countries of arrival for twentieth-century migrants—the United States, Canada, Australia, and, since the 1960s, Western Europe—all expected that immigrants would assimilate into their societies by adopting the language, political values, and cultural norms of the host society. Many migrants agreed, viewing assimilation as a pathway to better economic opportunities and social status even if it often took several generations for a migrant family to fully integrate into the host society. Despite this pressure toward assimilation, migrants also maintained aspects of their homelands' cultures, some of which were embraced by their new communities. Immigrants often opened eateries featuring dishes from their countries of origin, such as a Mexican tamale food truck in Los Angeles, an Indian curry house in London, or a Chinese noodle café in Sydney.

BUILDING AP® SKILLS

Argumentation

Consider having students complete an SAQ here to describe reactions to migrants in the twentieth century. If you want to time students, give them 14 minutes to respond to the prompt below.

A. Identify ONE piece of technology that facilitated the movement of migrants around the world in the twentieth century.

B. Explain ONE way in which one or more nations reacted to the arrival of migrants in the twentieth century.

C. Explain ONE way in which twentieth-century migrants were able to maintain aspects of their homeland's culture in their new communities.

▶ AP

MAKING CONNECTIONS
How were patterns of migration, as depicted in this image, related to significant global events in the twentieth century?

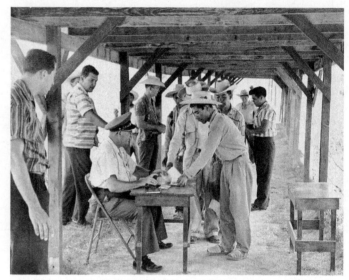

Mexican Migrant Workers Since the early twentieth century, U.S. growers had employed migrant Mexican workers. But the acute labor shortage associated with World War II prompted a formal agreement between the governments of the two countries. Known as the Bracero (migrant labor) program, it brought some 4.5 million agricultural workers to the United States between 1942 and 1964. This image shows some of these workers being processed at a labor center in Hidalgo, Texas, in 1959. (AP Photo)

BUILDING AP® SKILLS

Claims and Evidence in Sources

Consider having students complete an OPTIC chart for the "Mexican Migrant Workers" photo on this page to work on image analysis. A reproducible version of this chart can be found in the Teacher's Resource Materials. (Answers are provided in italics.)

Overview	*Mexican migrant workers are being processed at a labor center in Texas.*
Parts	*Migrant workers are lined up by a registration table; an official, either local police or possibly military, is checking in the workers; the processing center is more of a covering over the line of men than a formal building; other Americans in the background are monitoring the workers being processed.*
Title	*This photo could be titled "Processing Migrant Workers in the United States."*
Interrelationships	*The photo is meant to show the cooperation between the United States and Mexico through the Bracero program. There is a clear process for workers entering the United States, shown by the organization of the processing center, with the workers having a designated place to check in with American officials.*
Conclusion	*This photograph was meant to illustrate the success of the Bracero program and show how the process of migrant workers coming into the United States worked.*

TRM Handout 14.5: OPTIC Chart for Mexican Migrant Workers Photo

The expectation of assimilation also brought tensions and conflict, particularly over cultural integration. In France, for instance, the immigration of Muslims, mostly from North Africa, has sparked controversy over women's clothing. A French law in 2004 forbade the practice of wearing headscarves in public schools on the grounds that it compromised the secularism of French education and represented the repression of women. But many Muslim women strongly objected to the law, arguing that it undermined their freedom of religion and violated their cultural traditions. As one woman put it, "France is supposed to be a free country. Nowadays women have the right to take their clothes off but not put them on."[7] In the United States, large-scale migration from Latin America in recent decades has led some to demand that English be designated the official language of the country. More recently, fears that immigrants openly hostile to Western values might bring terrorism to host societies have led to calls to limit or refuse admission to refugees from some Islamic countries. At the same time, other voices have advocated the benefits of multiculturalism for the globalized and knowledge-based societies and economies of the twenty-first century.

A final category of long-distance migrants has encompassed those engaged in short-term travel. International tourist arrivals grew from 25 million in 1950 to 1.4 billion in 2018 and then dropped sharply to just 399 million in 2020, owing to travel restrictions associated with the COVID-19 pandemic.[8] Businesspeople in search of profits and students in search of education have crisscrossed the world in large numbers. These travelers have participated in "an unprecedented new era of transnational ties and mobility" that is only a few decades old.[9]

Microbes in Motion: Disease and Recent History

People in motion have carried not only their cultures but also their microbes. Everywhere growing populations, urban living, and unprecedented mobility have created more efficient pathways for deadly diseases to mutate and spread across the globe. Even before the emergence of commercial air travel, the early twentieth century witnessed one of the worst pandemics in human history when three waves of an **influenza pandemic** swept across the globe in 1918 and 1919, carried by soldiers, refugees, and other people dislocated by World War I. Infecting about one-third of the world's population, this pandemic killed at least 50 million people.

Another new pathogen, human immunodeficiency virus (HIV), which causes acquired immune deficiency syndrome (AIDS), sparked a second global pandemic beginning in the 1980s. Unlike the airborne influenza virus of 1918, **HIV/AIDS** spread primarily through sexual contact, contaminated blood products, or the sharing of needles by intravenous drug users. Nonetheless, the disease has spread rapidly across the globe. In 2018 nearly 38 million people lived with HIV, while some 32 million have died since the 1980s of AIDS or its complications. In sub-Saharan Africa, where the disease first emerged—and where nearly 70 percent of those currently infected reside—the disease was spread in part by

AP
CONTINUITY AND CHANGE
How have global responses to diseases and pandemics changed over the past century?

AP
COMPARISON
What differences can you notice among major pandemics of the past century?

EXPLORING AP® THEMES

Technology and Innovations (TEC)

You could ask students to read through the information on this page and have them take notes on how technologies and innovations in the twentieth and twenty-first centuries have impacted disease. After they finish their notes, lead them in a class discussion on the following question: *How have innovations in transportation and communications technologies both facilitated and slowed the spread of diseases like HIV/AIDS, Ebola, and COVID-19? Transportation technologies like long-haul trucks have helped facilitate the spread of HIV/AIDS in sub-Saharan Africa, and airplanes helped spread COVID-19 around the world but have also helped get treatments for the diseases to regions that need it. Communication technologies have helped with responses to disease outbreaks. Governments and communities can take action to limit the spread of disease by ordering border checks and quarantines. National and international organizations can use these technologies to coordinate their efforts to combat diseases around the world, like the international effort to track and stop the spread of the 2014 Ebola outbreak.*

APPLY THE TIP

You can give students an opportunity to work on their map-reading skills here by displaying maps of incidence rates for the following diseases around the world: Alzheimer's disease, heart disease, cholera, diabetes, malaria, tuberculosis. After students have studied the maps, ask: Do you see any trends with these maps? What global events can help explain the trends seen on these maps? *Answers will vary.*

You can find maps on incidence rates for these diseases at:

■ Wikimedia Commons, in the category "Mortality rate maps of the world": Alzheimer's disease, cardiovascular diseases, diabetes

■ The World Health Organization website, Map Gallery page: cholera, malaria, tuberculosis

long-distance truck drivers and the commercial sex workers they frequented on their travels. When the disease arrived in wealthier countries, drug companies responded by producing treatments, which have transformed this disease from a major killer into a serious but chronic and manageable disease for those with access to the latest medicines.

The twentieth century saw humankind mobilize its resources as never before to combat deadly pandemics, with better results in the richer Global North than the Global South. Polio, for instance, was virtually eradicated from much of the world, including the United States and other Western nations, following the development of an effective vaccine in the 1950s. But despite a concerted and sustained global campaign, some regions of the Global South, including Pakistan, Afghanistan, and Nigeria, have never halted the transmission of the virus, in part because of distrust of vaccination efforts. Malaria is another disease that has not been completely eradicated despite global efforts to stop its spread. According to the World Health Organization (WHO), nearly one-half of the world's population, mostly in the Global South, is at risk of malaria.

Modern communication has meant that reports of new diseases spread faster than ever before. Concerned communities and their governments have taken action to try to keep diseases out or limit their spread by ordering measures like border checks and quarantines. Recognizing the potentially destabilizing economic, social, and political effects of pandemics, governments created both national and international institutions, like the World Health Organization in 1948, to help coordinate efforts to combat disease within national borders and beyond. In the early twenty-first century, new threats—severe acute respiratory syndrome (SARS), the Ebola virus, and the Zika virus, among others—prompted large-scale international efforts to identify, track, and stop their spread.

But despite these unprecedented advances in public health, starting in late 2019 much of the world was overwhelmed by COVID-19, a disease that for the first time became endemic in humans and that spread easily from person to person. First emerging in Wuhan, China, it traveled across the globe in a matter of months as air travel quickly dispersed infected people to distant parts of the world. Governments almost everywhere issued travel restrictions and shelter-at-home decrees that brought with them great social and economic costs as many businesses and schools closed or operated remotely. By 2021, effective vaccines had emerged, but were most readily available in the more highly developed countries of the Global North and much less so in the developing countries. Even in the rich countries, resistance to vaccination and the wearing of masks, sometimes politically inspired, prolonged the pandemic and added to the mounting global death toll, numbering in the many millions. The coronavirus provided a sobering reminder of the limits of human control over disease and the vulnerabilities to pandemics that come with our more highly entangled and urbanized world, our growing human population, and our ever-increasing intrusion into the shrinking domain of wild animals.

> **AP® EXAM TIP**
>
> Along with knowing examples of new epidemic diseases, it is important for you to know examples of diseases associated with poverty (e.g., malaria) and diseases associated with humans' longevity and changing lifestyles (e.g., heart disease).

The deadly consequences of global inequality also came into sharp relief during the COVID-19 pandemic. In addition to uneven access to vaccines, the poor, particularly those working in the service sector or casually for daily wages in the informal sector, lost employment and income far more than middle-class professionals, many of whom could work from home. And beyond COVID, the diseases of the rich and poor have increasingly diverged. Malaria, tuberculosis, cholera, measles, pneumonia, and diarrhea, often accompanied by malnutrition, are known as "diseases of poverty" and are prominent and often fatal in developing countries. Among those better off everywhere, it is lifestyle diseases and those associated with longevity, such as heart attacks, strokes, lung cancer, type 2 diabetes, and Alzheimer's, that are of greatest concern.

The COVID-19 Pandemic Many schools that initially closed in the face of the COVID-19 pandemic reopened after scrambling to institute measures that made their classrooms safer. This photograph taken in June 2020 depicts students attending a high school in Cape Town, South Africa. They practice social distancing with their desks spaced widely apart and they wear masks. (Gallo Images/Getty Images)

Cultural Identity in an Entangled World

Finding the Main Point: How have modern societies been united and divided by notions of race, nationalism, religion, and the globalization of culture?

Large and impersonal global processes (industrialization, migration, and urbanization, for example) have had a profound and personal impact at the level of individual identity—how people define the communities to which they belong, the religions with which they affiliate, and even the food they eat, the clothes they wear, and the music they enjoy. Certainly older patterns of identity have been challenged as individuals have come up against people and cultures quite different from their own. Secular ideas and values were often at odds with traditional religious outlooks; feminist ideas confronted patriarchal assumptions; socialist or communist thinking undermined the legitimacy of deeply rooted social hierarchies. Among the identities in question during the past century, those of political and religious loyalty loomed large.

Race, Nation, and Ethnicity

Nineteenth-century Europe gave rise to an elaborate ideology of "race" as a fundamental distinction among human communities based on allegedly permanent biological characteristics. (See "Ways of Working" in Chapter 10.) But it was in the

AP® CLASSROOM

AP® Daily Video

Consider showing the AP® Daily Video for Topic 9.2: Technological Advances and Limitations after 1900: Disease, as a wrap-up to this section. This video focuses on the impact that diseases had during the twentieth century, along with helping students connect that impact to the major themes of AP® World History: Modern. You can find the video for Topic 9.2 by logging into AP® Classroom, clicking on Unit 9 under Classroom Resources, and then selecting Daily Videos.

▲ **AP®**

CLAIMS AND EVIDENCE IN SOURCES
How does this image help explain global responses to epidemic and pandemic diseases?

AP® EXAM TIP
Pay close attention to the different ideologies used to unite groups of people throughout the twentieth century.

AP®
CONTINUITY AND CHANGE
In what ways have race, nation, and ethnicity found expression and played a role in world history during the past century?

APPLY THE TIP

It could be helpful for students to have a quick-reference chart on ideologies (or "-isms") that united groups during the twentieth century. Ask them to create a chart like the one below to help them find examples of the different ideologies of the twentieth century. A reproducible version of this chart can be found in the Teacher's Resource Materials. (Answers are provided in italics.)

	Example of Ideology
Nationalism	*Independence movements in Africa and Asia; nationalism uniting countries during World War I and World War II; Nazi regime in Germany; pan-Africanism; pan-Arabism*
Communism	*Communist International (Comintern), the international communist group formed after the creation of the Soviet Union; the Warsaw Pact; Council for Mutual Economic Assistance (COMECON)*
Democracy	*North Atlantic Treaty Organization (NATO); the United States during the cold war; democracy movements leading to end of authoritarian governments in the 1980s and 1990s*
Globalization	*League of Nations; United Nations*

TRM **Handout 14.6: Chart for Twentieth-Century Political Ideologies**

CHAPTER 14

This would be a good place to have students make connections between what they are learning here and what they have learned about previous periods of world history. Review the development of the ideology of "race," discussed in Chapter 10 (pages 582–584), with the students. Then ask: How was the ideology of race put into practice in the twentieth century? *Answers may include: Nazi Germany's genocide of Jews and persecution of other "non-Aryan" groups during the Holocaust; the southern United States from the 1890s to the 1950s sanctioning racist ideologies, prohibiting interracial marriage, legislating social segregation, denying political rights to Blacks, and deliberately keeping Blacks in poverty; Apartheid-era South Africa (which ended in 1994) sanctioning racist ideologies, prohibiting marriage across racial lines, legislating social segregation, denying political rights to Blacks, and deliberately keeping Blacks in poverty.*

twentieth century that such ideas achieved their greatest prominence, shaping individual behavior, institutional practices, and government policies alike. Three societies in particular stand out as openly racist regimes: Nazi Germany, the southern United States from the 1890s to the 1950s, and apartheid-era South Africa. All of them officially sanctioned explicitly racist ideologies, prohibited marriage across racial lines, legislated extreme forms of social segregation, denied political rights to Jews or Blacks, and deliberately kept them in poverty.

In many other places, race was a pervasive reality, though perhaps racist thinking was less officially endorsed. Racial distinctions and white supremacy were prominent in European thinking and central features within all of the European colonies in Africa and Asia, generating in turn a new racial awareness among many colonized people. Aime Cesaire, a poet from the French island of Martinique in the Caribbean region, coined the term "negritude," which he defined in 1939 as "the simple recognition of the fact that one is black."[10] Black, Native American, and multiracial people in Latin America and the United States clearly experienced discrimination and disadvantage in relationship to whites or Europeans, even in the absence of legal constraints.

During the second half of the twentieth century, race lost much of its public legitimacy as a social distinction, discredited in part by the horrors of the Nazi regime. As the American author Barbara Ehrenreich put it: "Hitler gave race a bad name." Furthermore, scholars thoroughly debunked the connection between biology and culture or behavior, which was so central to racial thinking. But perhaps most importantly, the sharp critique of white bigotry and discrimination that accompanied the surging independence movements across Asia and Africa made overt racism globally illegitimate. The 1948 UN Universal Declaration of Human Rights inscribed this rejection of racism as a new global moral standard.

Nonetheless, race remained a social reality in many places and continued to generate serious conflict. Even after the end of apartheid in South Africa, pervasive inequalities between whites and Blacks in wealth, housing, jobs, and educational opportunities remained front and center in the life of the country. In the United States, the civil rights movement made important gains in the 1960s for Black Americans in terms of voting rights, education, and employment. But deeply rooted cultural and social attitudes based on race persisted. For example, these attitudes, combined with long-established wealth inequalities, found expression in institutional practices that hindered access to mortgages to buy homes and capital to start businesses. Black Americans were also disproportionately subjected to arbitrary arrest and police brutality, giving rise to the Black Lives Matter movement beginning in 2013.

In Europe as well, racial tensions grew as increasing numbers of Africans and Asians migrated to the continent after World War II. Immigrants often faced discrimination in employment and housing, and efforts by European countries to encourage cultural and social assimilation were a source of further tension. Calls for a greater reckoning with Europe's imperial and slave-trading past have also provided a focus for disagreement. Despite their loss of public legitimacy, entrenched racial attitudes have persisted, together with economic inequalities, as a social reality in many parts of the world.

Even more pervasive than race as a form of individual identity and political loyalty has been nationalism, and the two have sometimes overlapped. Loyalty to national states and their presumed interests drove the world wars of the past century and undermined empires around the globe. But if nation-states and national loyalties largely triumphed during the past century, they also faced challenges. Transnationalism appealed to those seeking a larger identity and loyalty beyond particular nation-states. Pan-Arabism, for example, called for military and economic cooperation among Arabic-speaking peoples in North African and Middle Eastern states in the 1950s and 1960s. And pan-Africanism invoked the common history, culture, and destiny of all the peoples of Africa as well as those of African descent living outside the continent. Unlike pan-Arabism or pan-Africanism, which seldom achieved effective political expression, the European Union gave concrete political and economic structure to the idea of "Europe" in the aftermath of two disastrous wars. (For more on the European Union, see "Recovering from the War" in Chapter 12.) By the early twenty-first century the Union appeared shaky in the face of rising nationalist sentiments and the British decision to withdraw from it. But Russia's invasion of Ukraine in 2022 renewed for many the ideals of the European Union (democracy and human rights, for example) and the notion of a wider European identity.

Globalization too challenged national loyalties as visions of a world without borders and destructive national rivalries appealed to many. The League of Nations and the United Nations gave expression to such visions. The growth of international economic linkages and an increasing global awareness of problems common to all of humankind generated for some a sense of global citizenship, a cosmopolitan feeling of being at home in the world as a whole. Pictures of the earth viewed from the moon or outer space—a beautiful but solitary planet in an immense cosmos—came to symbolize this one-world sensibility (see the "One World" image at the opening of the chapter).

If globalization represented an external challenge to national loyalties and existing nation-states, a serious internal challenge took shape as ethnically based separatist movements. Most of the world's states, after all, contained several, and sometimes many, culturally distinct peoples. Such peoples readily adopted the rhetoric and logic of nationalism, arguing that they too deserved some separate political status, such as greater autonomy or full independence. Under the pressure of such movements, a number of states have in fact disintegrated. British India dissolved immediately upon independence into a Muslim Pakistan and largely Hindu India. In the 1990s, the multinational states of the Soviet Union, Czechoslovakia, and Yugoslavia dissolved into many separate ethnically based states. In northeastern Africa, Eritrea seceded from Ethiopia in 1993, and in 2011 South Sudan claimed independence from the Republic of Sudan, both of them following decades of civil war. Even

AP EXAM TIP

How transnational movements like pan-Africanism and pan-Arabism have united groups is an important concept in the AP® course.

AP EXAM TIP

You should be able to explain how international organizations that formed during the past century have helped promote international cooperation.

APPLY THE TIP

You should try to have students practice writing sections of an essay throughout the year to help them work on specific skills. You could ask students to write a one- to two-paragraph response to the following prompt: Evaluate the extent to which organizations such as the League of Nations and the United Nations have helped promote international cooperation in the twentieth and twenty-first centuries. *Answers may include: The League of Nations was meant to be an international peacekeeping organization dedicated to maintaining peace and preventing another global war. However, the U.S. refusal to join the League severely weakened it, and the League was unable to stop the aggressive actions of Japan, Italy, and Germany in the 1930s. The United Nations was established in 1945 as a successor to the League of Nations. The UN's different organs, like the General Assembly, Security Council, Economic and Social Council, and International Court of Justice, were more successful at facilitating international cooperation during the twentieth century. While it has not always been successful at resolving conflicts, the UN has kept the international community together through debate and certain actions.*

APPLY THE TIP

Students are probably not going to be familiar with the Pan-African and the Pan-Arab movements during the twentieth century. To help students learn the basics of these two movements, have them work with a partner to define and explain the impact they had. Students may need to do online research to find more information. After they finish their research, have students share what they found with the class. (Answers provided in italics.)

■ **Pan-Africanism:** *This is the idea that peoples of African descent have common interests and should be unified. It led to a Pan-African Congress, representing people of African descent from all over the world, meeting several times throughout the twentieth century. Following World War II, the Pan-African movement became more concerned with the issues and affairs of the African continent, especially as independence movements grew across the continent. In 2002, the African Union was created to promote the further integration of Africa.*

■ **Pan-Arabism:** *This ideology promoted cultural and political unity among Arab states, especially after their independence from the Ottoman Empire and European powers in the twentieth century. It led to the founding of the Arab League in 1945 to strengthen the ties between the different states and to promote their political, cultural, economic, and social interests.*

BUILDING AP® SKILLS

Argumentation

To help students practice finding thesis statements or arguments and supporting evidence, have them read the first paragraph on this page (it begins on page 813). As they read the paragraph, they should identify the thesis or argument of the paragraph and list the supporting evidence for the thesis. (Answers provided in italics.)

■ **Thesis:** *Ethnically based separatist movements are a serious internal challenge to national loyalties and existing nation-states.*

■ **Evidence:** *British India was divided immediately after independence into a Muslim Pakistan and largely Hindu India; Czechoslovakia and Yugoslavia fragmented along ethnic lines in the early 1990s; Eritrea seceded from Ethiopia in 1993; South Sudan declared independence from the Republic of Sudan in 2011; Kurds living in Iraq, Iran, Syria, and Turkey want to form an independent Kurdistan; Ethnic separatist movements (Scotland from the United Kingdom, Quebec from Canada, Tibet from China, the Basques from Spain, Igbo-speaking peoples from Nigeria, and the Moro people from the Philippines) have tried to break away from existing nation-states, but have not succeeded yet; Some Russian speakers in eastern Ukraine sought annexation by Russia even before the 2022 Russian invasion of Ukraine.*

TEACHING IDEA

Class Discussion

While students have a good understanding of what genocide is, they sometimes do not understand the difference between genocide and ethnic cleansing. This would be a good place to pause and ask students to research both terms before discussing with a partner what they found.

AP®
CONTINUITY AND CHANGE
In what ways were traditional ideas on nationalism challenged throughout the twentieth century?

▼ **AP®**
CONTEXTUALIZATION
Explain how nationalism and nationalist ideologies contributed to the event depicted in the image.

where a separate state was not achieved, ethnic separatist movements have threatened the integrity of existing nation-states. Scotland has sought to exit from the United Kingdom, Quebec from Canada, Tibet from China, the Basques from Spain, Igbo-speaking peoples from Nigeria, and the Moro people from the Philippines. Some Russian speakers in eastern Ukraine had sought annexation by Russia even before Russia's full-scale invasion of Ukraine in 2022, and many Kurds living in Iraq, Iran, Syria, and Turkey aspire to an independent Kurdistan.

These various cultural identities—racial, national, ethnic, and global—have become politically and personally meaningful for much of the world's population even as they have mixed and mingled in many ways. German nationalism in the Nazi era found expression in racial terms. Some people found it possible to embrace both an ethnic heritage and loyalty to a larger nation with little contradiction, as many Irish, Italians, Hispanics, and Americans of African descent have done in the United States. A sense of global citizenship, in the struggle against climate change, for example, remains compatible with loyalty to a particular country.

Ethnic Cleansing in Vukovar, Croatia The disintegration of the multiethnic state of Yugoslavia in southeastern Europe during the 1990s gave rise to numerous violent conflicts among its various ethnic groups. This photograph shows Croatians making their way through the rubble of the city of Vukovar, from which some 20,000 of them had been expelled by Serbian troops. The city was almost completely destroyed and largely "cleansed" of its non-Serb population. (Ron Haviv/VII/Redux)

Popular Culture on the Move

Related to these cultural and political identities have been the many elements of popular culture that have increasingly permeated social life during the past century. They too have been on the move around the world in a many-sided process widely known as **cultural globalization**, with the heaviest currents moving from the West to the rest of the world. American films, TV, music (jazz, rock and roll, rap), and fast-food chains such as McDonald's and KFC, for instance, have all shaped patterns of taste globally. Furthermore, English has become a world language; Western sports such as soccer, cricket, basketball, and baseball have an international presence; and Western fashions—jeans, suits and ties, miniskirts, white wedding dresses—have become common in many places, sometimes losing their direct association with the West.

All of this has been driven by the dominance of the West in world affairs over the past several centuries and the impulse of many to imitate the ways of the powerful. But the assimilation of Western cultural forms has also come to symbolize modernity, inclusion in an emerging global culture, and sometimes liberation or rebellion, especially among the young. Such a sensibility informed Kemal Atatürk's desire for "civilized, international dress" for Turkish men when he sought to impose Western-style clothing on them during the 1920s and 1930s. The outlook was similar for young women in Japan who imitated the dress style of Western "flappers" during the same time. They were *moga* or "modern girls" whose country was becoming a "province of the world."

The global spread of Western culture has raised fears in many places about cultural homogenization or "cultural imperialism" threatening local or national cultures, values, and traditions. Like other forms of globalization, the cultural variant of this larger process has witnessed not only enthusiastic embrace but also push-back, much of which has targeted the outsized American influence in the world. Communist Party officials in the Soviet Union, for example, were suspicious of the growing popularity of American jazz and later rock and roll. Associating these musical forms with Western individualistic values of spontaneity, open sexuality, and opposition to authority, they tried periodically to suppress them, though without much success. A number of Western social media platforms have been blocked in China, such as Facebook and Twitter, allowing China's locally developed platforms (WeChat, Weibo, and Bilibili, for example) to grow rapidly.

In the Islamic world, pushback against cultural "contamination" from the West has been particularly prominent, especially in religiously fundamentalist circles. The Ayatollah Khomeini, architect of Iran's Islamic revolution, strongly expressed this outlook:

> Just what is the social life we are talking about? Is it those hotbeds of immorality called theatres, cinemas, dancing, and music? Is it the promiscuous presence in the streets of lusting young men and women with arms, chests, and thighs bared? Is it the ludicrous wearing of a hat like the Europeans or the imitation of their habit of wine drinking . . . [or] the disrobed women to be seen on the thoroughfares and in swimming pools?[11]

AP®
CONTINUITY AND CHANGE
What elements of popular culture have moved globally during the past century?

AP® EXAM TIP
Keep in mind examples of how popular culture and consumer culture have become more global during the past century.

AP®
CAUSATION
What conflicts have emerged because of cultural globalization?

TEACHING IDEA

Bell Ringer

Before students start the section "Popular Culture on the Move," consider giving them two minutes to brainstorm as many examples of global culture as they can think of. After time is up, have them share what they wrote down with the class. *Answers will vary, but may include: Bollywood, Chinese/Asian market influence on Hollywood films, soccer, cricket, the Olympics, foreign-language covers of pop songs, popularity of K-pop groups, global spread of American fast-food restaurants.*

EXPLORING AP® THEMES

Cultural Developments and Interactions (CDI)

To help illustrate global culture for students in a fun way, you can put together a PowerPoint of examples of Western and American cultural iconography in foreign countries. Have students guess what country they think each example is from. Suggested examples:

- McDonald's
- Starbucks
- Coca-Cola
- Harry Potter
- A Marvel movie poster
- KFC

EXPLORING AP® THEMES

Cultural Developments and Interactions (CDI)

While the globalization of culture is widely accepted by groups around the world, some groups, organizations, and communities oppose it out of fear of what this global culture will do to their local culture. Consider using the AP® Causation question on page 815 to start a class discussion on the opposition to cultural globalization.

CHAPTER 14

AP® Topic Questions

The end of "Popular Culture on the Move" would be an excellent opportunity for some practice with multiple-choice questions. You can find a set of questions examining a Subway menu in India by logging into AP® Classroom, clicking on Unit 9 under Classroom Resources, and then selecting Topic Questions. Look for the questions labeled "Subway Menu India Globalization MCQ." You can either assign the questions to the students to complete individually or allow them to work through the set with a partner.

APPLY THE TIP

It could be fun for students to think about what examples of non-Western cultural influences they see in their local community. You could ask students to brainstorm examples and then discuss them with a partner. Afterwards, you can extend on their response by having students read through the second paragraph on this page and find other examples of non-Western influences. Have students share what they found with the class. *Answers may include: Americans and Europeans have received Chinese, Indian, Thai, Mexican, and Ethiopian cuisine; Yoga has become a form of exercise or relaxation in the West after its adoption from India; India-based Ayurvedic medicine and traditional Chinese medicine have become forms of "alternative" medical treatment in the West; Latin American telenovelas have gained audiences around the world; Korean popular culture has taken hold in East and Southeast Asia; Jamaican-based reggae music has extended around the world.*

Yoga in the United States The cultural dimension of globalization is illustrated in the spread of yoga, a mind-body practice from India that has become a part of global culture. This photo shows an outdoor yoga class held in New York's Time's Square to celebrate the summer solstice in 2017. (Brazil Photo Press/Alamy)

▲ AP®
ARGUMENTATION
Use the image to develop an argument that evaluates the impact of cultural globalization on American culture.

AP® EXAM TIP
You should be able to explain how the globalization of culture was also influenced by non-Western cultures.

AP®
CONTINUITY AND CHANGE
What continuities and changes can be seen within religions during the past century?

Efforts to protect national languages have also prompted resistance to cultural globalization. The French Academy, for example, has long been on the lookout for English terms that have crept into general usage while urging their replacement by French equivalents. Chinese authorities have sought to require foreign firms to use Chinese terms for their products, and in 2012 over 100 Chinese scholars urged the removal of English words from a prominent Chinese dictionary.

But the cultural flows of the past century have moved in many directions, not simply outward from the United States and Europe. In exchange for Big Macs, Americans and Europeans have received Chinese, Indian, Thai, Mexican, and Ethiopian cuisine. Yoga, originally a mind-body practice of Indian origin, has taken hold widely in the West and elsewhere, losing much of its earlier association with spiritual practice and becoming a form of exercise or relaxation. India's huge film industry, known as Bollywood, has had a major cultural impact in the Soviet Union, Western Europe, the United States, and Latin America. India-based Ayurvedic medicine and traditional Chinese medicine, including acupuncture, have become widely used "alternative" treatments in Europe and North America. Japanese and Chinese martial arts have attracted numerous participants in the West and have been featured in many highly popular films. Latin American telenovelas or "soap operas" have enthralled audiences around the world, and Korean popular culture, including TV dramas, movies, and music, has also spread far beyond Korean borders. Congolese music, sometimes blended with Latin American dance rhythms, has spread widely throughout Africa and by the 1980s attracted eager audiences in Europe as well. Jamaican-based reggae music has extended around the world, while its superstar Bob Marley became an international icon. In short, cultural traffic in the entangled world of the past century has never been a one-way street.

Religion and Global Modernity

Among the various expressions of cultural identity during the past century, religion has provoked perhaps the deepest personal response among individuals and has provided a potent source of identity in social and political life. Some of these responses were highly critical of religion, while others affirmed and sought to renew or revitalize religious belief and practice.

Making Connections: Continuity and Change

Consider having students create a continuity and change chart like the one here on religion in the twentieth century. A reproducible version of the chart can be found in the Teacher's Resource Materials. (Answers are provided in italics.)

Differentiation

If you want students to extend their understanding of the material in the chart, consider following the "Must Do, Should Do, Strive For" model below:

■ **Must Do:** Students must complete the continuity and change chart on religion in the twentieth century.

■ **Should Do:** Once they finish their chart, they should discuss their findings in small groups of three to four.

■ **Strive For:** For students who need or want a writing challenge, have them write a thesis statement and an argument paragraph that responds to the following prompt: Develop an argument that evaluates the extent to which globalization led to religious changes in the twentieth and twenty-first centuries.

On the critical side, many of the most "advanced" thinkers of the past several hundred years—Enlightenment writers in the eighteenth century, Karl Marx in the nineteenth, and many academics and secular-minded intellectuals in the twentieth—believed that religion was headed for extinction in the face of modernity, science, communism, or globalization. In some respects, that prediction seemed to come true during the twentieth century and beyond. Soviet authorities, viewing religion as a backward-looking bulwark of an exploiting feudal or capitalist class, closed many churches and seminaries, promoted atheism in public education, prohibited any display of religion in public or the media, and denied believers access to better jobs and official positions. In several modernizing Islamic countries, the role of religion in public life was sharply restricted. Kemal Atatürk in Turkey sought to relegate Islam to the personal and private realm, arguing that "Islam will be elevated, if it will cease to be a political instrument." (See AP® Working with Evidence, Document 1, page 843.)

Even without such state action, religious belief and practice during the past century declined sharply in the major European countries such as Britain, France, Italy, and the Netherlands. A 2019 poll found that 26 percent of Americans defined themselves as religiously unaffiliated, while only 31 percent claimed to attend religious services every week.[12] Moreover, the spread of a scientific culture around the world persuaded small minorities everywhere, often among the most highly educated, that the only realities worth considering were those that could be measured with the techniques of science. To such people, all else was superstition, born of ignorance.

Nevertheless, the far more prominent trends of the last century have involved the further spread of major world religions, their resurgence in new forms, their opposition to elements of a secular and global modernity, and their political role as a source of community identity and conflict. Contrary to earlier expectations, religion has played an unexpectedly powerful role in this most recent century.

Buddhism, Christianity, and Islam had long functioned as transregional cultures and continued to do so in the twentieth century. Buddhist ideas and practices such as meditation found a warm reception in the West, and Buddhism has been reviving in China since the 1970s. Christianity of various kinds spread widely in non-Muslim Africa and South Korea, less extensively in parts of India, and after 1975 was growing even in China. By 2019 Christianity was no longer a primarily European or North American religion, as some 67 percent of its adherents lived in Asia, Africa, Oceania, and Latin America. Islam too continued its

AP® EXAM TIP

Understand how religious movements affected the relationship between people and their governments.

AP® EXAM TIP

Pay attention to the philosophical disagreements among Islamic leaders in the twentieth century

▼ **AP®**
SOURCING AND SITUATION

What was the Soviet government's motivation in creating and distributing this postcard?

Religion and Soviet Communism This postcard from the 1930s illustrates Soviet hostility to religion as it depicts a Soviet worker against the background of modern industrial life smashing stereotyped symbols of Muslim, Christian, and Jewish religion. (Bridgeman Images)

APPLY THE TIP

The "AP® Working with Evidence: Contending for Islam" on pages 843–849 gives students a great opportunity to examine the philosophical disagreements among Islamic leaders. You could place students into groups of four and have them take notes on what the documents tell them about continuity and change in religious practice. The questions at the end of the documents provide a good guide for taking notes. When the groups have finished examining the documents, lead the students in a class discussion on what differences they saw between the ideas and philosophies of the documents.

(continued)

Continuities in Religion in Twentieth Century	Changes in Religion in Twentieth Century
■ *Major world religions continued to spread around the world and played a role in creating community identity and conflict*	■ *States restricted the role of religion in public life, as in Turkey, or prohibited public displays of religion, as in the Soviet Union*
■ *Religions have continued to oppose elements of secular and global modernity*	■ *Religious belief and practice declined in major European countries and the United States during the second half of the twentieth century and the beginning of the twenty-first century*
■ *Buddhism, Christianity, and Islam continued to function as transregional cultures*	■ *Spread of scientific culture around the world persuaded some that the only realities worth believing were those that could be scientifically measured*
	■ *Religious fundamentalism arose as a reaction to a modernizing and globalizing world*

TRM **Handout 14.7: Continuity and Change Chart for Religion in the Twentieth Century**

Cultural Developments and Interactions (CDI)

Before students look at religious fundamentalism in the twentieth century, it would be good to have them identify the factors that helped lead to its rise. You can ask students to identify the features of the modern world that may be considered a threat to religious values and practices. Discuss these as a class and compare student answers with the answers in the text on this page. *Features of the modern world that may be considered a threat to religious values and practices include the media, sexual promiscuity, and changing family structures. The text includes the scientific and secular focus on modernity, capitalism, industrialization, and globalization, all of which have affected family and gender relationships.*

Cultural Developments and Interactions (CDI)

Consider having students work with a partner to create a chart like the one below on the characteristics of the religious fundamentalist movements that are discussed on pages 818–822. They could use this chart to discuss the similarities and differences between the movements that emerged in the twentieth century. You can find a reproducible version of the chart in the Teacher's Resource Materials. (Answers are provided in italics.)

AP®
COMPARISON
In what different ways have religious believers responded to the challenges of modern life?

AP®
DEVELOPMENTS AND PROCESSES
Why did similar "fundamentalist" movements emerge in different religious traditions across the globe in the twentieth century?

AP®
CONTEXTUALIZATION
Explain the relationship between "religious fundamentalist" groups and politics.

centuries-long spread in Asia and Africa, while migrants from the Islamic world have planted their religion solidly in the West, constructing 2,769 mosques in the United States by 2020. Sufi mystical practices have attracted the attention of many in the West who have grown disillusioned with conventional religion.

Religious vitality in the twentieth century was expressed also in the vigorous response of those traditions to the modernizing and globalizing world. One such response has been widely called **religious fundamentalism**—a militant piety hostile to secularism and religious pluralism—that took shape to some extent within every major religious tradition. Many features of the modern world, after all, appeared threatening to established religion. The scientific and secular focus of global modernity challenged the core beliefs of religion, with its focus on an unseen realm of reality. Furthermore, the social upheavals connected with capitalism, industrialization, imperialism, and globalization thoroughly upset customary class, family, and gender relationships that had long been sanctified by religious tradition.

To such threats deriving from a globalized modern culture, fundamentalism represented a religious response, characterized by one scholar as "embattled forms of spirituality . . . experienced as a cosmic war between the forces of good and evil."[13] The term "fundamentalism" came from the United States, where religious conservatives in the early twentieth century were outraged and threatened by many recent developments: the growth of secularism; critical and "scientific" approaches to the Bible; Darwin's concept of evolution; liberal versions of Christianity that emphasized ethical behavior rather than personal salvation; the triumph of communism in the Soviet Union, which adopted atheism as its official doctrine; and postwar labor strikes that carried echoes of the Russian Revolution to many conservatives.

Feeling that Christianity itself was at stake, they called for a return to the "fundamentals" of the faith, which included a belief in the literal truthfulness of the scriptures, in the virgin birth and physical resurrection of Jesus, and in miracles. After World War II, American Protestant fundamentalists came to oppose political liberalism and "big government," the sexual revolution of the 1960s, LGBTQ rights, abortion rights, and secular humanism generally. From the 1970s on, they entered the political arena as the "religious right," determined to return America to a "godly path."

In the very different setting of independent India, another fundamentalist movement—known as **Hindutva** (Hindu nationalism)—took shape during the 1980s. Like American fundamentalism, it represented a politicization of religion within a democratic context. To its advocates, India was, and always had been, an essentially Hindu land, even though it had been overwhelmed in recent centuries by Muslim invaders, then by the Christian British, and most recently by the secular state of the post-independence decades. The leaders of modern India, they argued, and particularly its first prime minister, Jawaharlal Nehru, were "the self-proclaimed secularists who . . . seek to remake India in the Western image," while repudiating its basically Hindu religious character. The Hindutva movement took political shape in an increasingly popular party called the Bharatiya Janata Party (BJP),

Fundamentalist Movement	Characteristics of Movement
Christian Fundamentalism in the United States	■ *Religious conservatives felt threatened by recent developments in the early twentieth century, including the growth of secularism and critical or "scientific" approaches to the Bible* ■ *Called for a return to the "fundamentals" of the faith* ■ *Beliefs include a belief in literal truthfulness of the scriptures, in the virgin birth and resurrection of Jesus, and in miracles* ■ *After World War II, fundamentalists became more involved in opposing political liberalism and "big government"*
Hindutva in India	■ *Is based on the idea that India has always been an essentially Hindu land and that political leaders were trying to repudiate the country's Hindu religious character* ■ *Took political shape in the Bharatiya Janata Party (BJP), which promoted a distinctly Hindu identity in education, culture, and religion* ■ *Sometimes defined Muslims as outsiders, more loyal to Muslim Pakistan than Hindu India*

promoting a distinctly Hindu identity in education, culture, and religion. Muslims in particular were sometimes defined as outsiders, potentially more loyal to a Muslim Pakistan than to India. The BJP's sweeping victories in the 2014 and 2019 national elections offer evidence of substantial support for Hindu nationalism in twenty-first-century India.

Nowhere were fundamentalist religious responses to political, social, and cultural change more intense or varied than within the Muslim world. Conquest and colonial rule; awareness of the huge technological and economic gap between Islamic and European civilizations; the disappearance of the Ottoman Empire, long the chief Islamic state; elite enchantment with Western culture; the retreat of Islam for many to the realm of private life—all of this had sapped the cultural self-confidence of many Muslims by the mid-twentieth century. Political independence for former colonies certainly represented a victory for Islamic societies, but it had given rise to major states—Egypt, Pakistan, Indonesia, Iraq, Algeria, and others—that pursued essentially Western and secular policies of nationalism, socialism, and economic development, often with only lip service to an Islamic identity.

Even worse, these policies were not very successful. Vastly overcrowded cities with few services, widespread unemployment, pervasive corruption, slow economic growth, a mounting gap between the rich and poor—all of this flew in the face of the great expectations that had accompanied the struggle against European domination. Despite formal independence, foreign intrusion still persisted. Israel, widely regarded as an outpost of the West, had been reestablished as a Jewish state in the very center of the Islamic world in 1948. In 1967, Israel inflicted a devastating defeat on Arab forces in the Six-Day War and seized various Arab territories, including the holy city of Jerusalem. Furthermore, broader signs of Western cultural penetration persisted—secular schools, alcohol, Barbie dolls, European and American movies, miniskirts, and more. (See Zooming In: Barbie and Her Competitors in the Muslim World.)

To all of this, many Muslims objected strongly. An emerging fundamentalist movement argued that it was the departure from Islamic principles that had led the Islamic world into its sorry state, and only a return to the "straight path of Islam" would ensure a revival of Muslim societies. To politically militant Islamists, this meant the overthrow of those Muslim governments that had allowed these tragedies and their replacement by regimes that would purify Islamic practice while enforcing Islamic law and piety in public life. One of the leaders of an Egyptian Islamist group put the matter succinctly: "The first battlefield for jihad is the extermination of these infidel leaders and to replace them by a complete Islamic Order."[14] (See AP® Working with Evidence: Contending for Islam, pages 843–849.)

Islamic fundamentalists won a significant victory in 1979 when the Iranian revolution chased out the country's long-reigning monarch, the shah of Iran, who had aligned his country with the West. The leader of the revolution, the Ayatollah Khomeini, believed that the purpose of government was to apply the law of Allah as expressed in the *sharia*. The secular law codes under which the shah's

AP®

CAUSATION

What factors help to explain the rise of Islamic fundamentalism? In what different ways has it been expressed?

BUILDING AP® SKILLS

Contextualization

The section on the Bharatiya Janata Party on pages 818 and 819 is a good place to pause and have students practice their contextualization skills. To help them with this, ask students to identify what constellation of events led to the formation of the Bharatiya Janata Party (BJP). *The events that led to the formation of the BJP included a resurgence of Indian nationalism, recent centuries of Muslim invaders, India's recognition of members of the lower caste, and modern globalism. The goals of the BJP party included promoting Hindu identity in education, culture, and religion.*

(continued)

Islamic Fundamentalism	■ Reaction to rise of secular society in the Muslim world, especially after decolonization, and foreign intrusion
	■ Emerging fundamentalist movement in the second half of the twentieth century argued that only a return to the "straight path of Islam" would ensure revival of Muslim societies
	■ Some groups within the movement were politically militant and advocated for the overthrow of Muslim governments that allowed for a rise in secularism, replacing them with governments that would enforce Islamic practices in public life
	■ Violence was not the only response; Islamic renewal movements around the world created organizations that provided social services and that sought to embed elements of modernity within a more distinctly Islamic culture

TRM Handout 14.8: Chart for Religious Fundamentalist Movements

820   PERIOD 4 • The Long Twentieth Century, 1900–present

BUILDING AP® SKILLS

Making Connections: Comparison

Students might find it interesting to look at how Barbie, a toy from their own childhoods, is received by different groups around the world. Consider starting the activity by reading "Zooming In: Barbie and Her Competitors in the Muslim World." After they've read the "Zooming In," show them the short CBS news clip *Barbie in China*, which can be found on YouTube, and lead them in a quick discussion comparing the reactions of the Iranians and the Chinese to Barbie. You can follow up the class discussion by asking students: What does this tell us about globalization? What is the historical context of the Chinese and Iranian reactions to Barbie? *While the Iranians are fighting the presence of Barbie, the Chinese have welcomed her. The Iranians have become progressively anti-Western since the 1979 revolution, and the Chinese have become more open to Western culture since the death of Mao.*

ZOOMING IN Barbie and Her Competitors in the Muslim World

"I think every Barbie doll is more harmful than an American missile," declared Iranian toy seller Masoumeh Rahimi in 2002. To Rahimi, Barbie's revealing clothing, her shapely appearance, and her close association with Ken, her longtime unmarried companion, were "foreign to Iran's culture."[15]

Thus Rahimi warmly welcomed the arrival in 2002 of Sara and Dara, Iranian Muslim dolls meant to counteract the negative influence of Barbie, who had long dominated Iran's toy market. Created by the Iranian government, Sara and her brother, Dara, represented eight-year-old twins and were intended to replace Barbie and Ken, which the authorities had officially banned in the mid-1990s because they represented a "Trojan horse" for Western values. Sara came complete with a headscarf to cover her hair in modest Muslim fashion and a full-length white chador enveloping her from head to toe. She and her brother were described as helping each other solve problems, while looking to

A Syrian girl examining Fulla dolls at a toy store in Damascus in 2005.

photo: Khaled al-Hariri/Reuters/Newscom

their loving parents for guidance, hardly the message that Barbie and Ken conveyed.

In 2003, a toy company based in Syria introduced Fulla, a doll depicting a young Muslim woman about the same age as Barbie, perhaps a grown-up version of Sara. Dressed modestly in a manner that reflected the norms of each national market, Fulla was described by her creator as representing "Muslim values." Unlike Barbie, with her boyfriend and a remarkable range of careers, including astronaut and president of the United States, Fulla was modeled on the ideal traditional Arab woman. She interacted with male family members rather than a boyfriend and was depicted only as a teacher or a doctor, both respected professions for women in the Islamic world. But she did share an eye for fashion with Barbie. Underneath her modest outer dress, Fulla wore stylish

---

government had operated were discarded in favor of those based solely on Islamic precedents. Some 200 universities and colleges closed for two years while textbooks, curricula, and faculty were "purified" of un-Islamic influences. Afterwards the history of Islam and Iran's revolution predominated in schools and the mass media. Sharp restriction of the lives of women represented a major element of this religious revolution. (See AP® Historians' Voices: Perspectives on the Iranian Revolution, page 850.)

A further expression of **Islamic radicalism** lay in violent attacks, largely against civilian targets, undertaken by radical groups such as al-Qaeda, the Taliban, Boko Haram, and the Islamic State. The most widely known of these attacks occurred on September 11, 2001, when the World Trade Center in New York and other targets were attacked. Subsequent assaults targeted various European and Russian cities, but this kind of terrorist violence was directed far more often and with far clothing, although it was less revealing than that of her American counterpart, and, like Barbie, she chose from an extensive wardrobe, sold separately of course. "This isn't just about putting the hijab [a headscarf covering a woman's hair and chest] on a Barbie doll," Fawaz Abidin, the Fulla brand manager, noted. "You have to create a character that parents and children want to relate to."[16]

Fulla proved far more popular than Sara among Muslim girls, becoming one of the best-selling dolls in the Islamic world. In part, the adoption by Fulla's creators of Western marketing techniques, similar to those that had been used to promote Barbie for decades, lay behind the doll's remarkable success. Fulla-themed magazines appeared on newsstands, and commercials advertising Fulla dolls and their accessories permeated children's television programming in the Muslim world. "When you take Fulla out of the house, don't forget her new spring abaya [a long, robe-like full-body covering]!" admonished one advertisement. Fulla's image was used to market an endless number of other licensed products, including branded stationery, backpacks, prayer rugs, bikes, and breakfast cereals, all in trademark "Fulla pink." In this respect, Fulla and Barbie shared a great deal.

Despite Fulla's success, Barbie has continued to enjoy a loyal following in the region, in part because of her exotic qualities. "All my friends have Fulla now, but I still like Barbie the best," one ten-year-old Saudi girl stated. "She has blonde hair and cool clothes. Every single girl in Saudi looks like Fulla....What's so special about that?"

The widespread availability of Barbie in the Muslim world provides one small example of the power of global commerce in the world of the early twenty-first century. But Sara and Fulla illustrate resistance to the cultural values associated with this American product. Still, Sara, Fulla, and Barbie had something in common: nearly all were manufactured in East Asian factories. Indeed, the same factories frequently manufactured the rival dolls. This triangular relationship of the United States, the Muslim world, and East Asia symbolized the growing integration of world economies and cultures as well as their divergences and conflicts. These linked but contrasting patterns involve much more than dolls in the early twenty-first century, for they define major features of our entangled world.

QUESTIONS

What can Barbie, Sara, and Fulla tell us about the globalized world of the twenty-first century? What different values and sensibilities do they convey?

---

greater casualties against targets in the Islamic world itself, including Iraq, Pakistan, Afghanistan, Saudi Arabia, India, Indonesia, Yemen, Somalia, and Nigeria.

Violence, however, was not the only response of Islamic fundamentalists or radicals. All over the Muslim world, from North Africa to Indonesia, Islamic renewal movements spawned organizations that operated legally to provide social services—schools, clinics, youth centers, legal-aid societies, financial institutions, publishing houses—that the state offered inadequately or not at all. Islamic activists took leadership roles in unions and professional organizations of teachers, journalists, engineers, doctors, and lawyers. Such people embraced modern science and technology but sought to embed these elements of modernity within a more distinctly Islamic culture. Some served in official government positions or entered political life and contested elections where it was possible to do so. The Algerian Islamic Salvation Front was poised to win elections in 1992, when a frightened military

AP EXAM TIP
You should know the different ways that religious groups have reacted to global modernity.

APPLY THE TIP

You can help students examine the different ways that religious groups have reacted to globalization by asking them to read the article "Globalization and the Middle East, Part One: Why Islamic Societies of the Middle East Are So Opposed to Globalization" by Middle East expert Barry Rubin, which can be found on the YaleGlobal Online website. After students read the article, ask them to describe at least three reasons that many Islamic societies of the Middle East are opposed to globalization. *Answers should include: Globalization means westernization; Globalization is modernization and a threat to tradition; It is perceived as destroying local society; Globalization may contradict Islam.*

Confronting Islamic Radicalism The Nigerian Islamic radical group Boko Haram ("Western influence is a sacrilege") has waged a violent campaign of terror in support of a highly restrictive version of sharia law, killing thousands and displacing millions in northeastern Nigeria. In 2014 the group abducted over 200 schoolgirls, prompting this demonstration in Lagos to "bring back our girls." (Xinhua/Alamy)

▲ AP

MAKING CONNECTIONS
How could a historian use this picture to explain the response to Islamic radicalism?

government intervened to cancel it, an action that plunged the country into a decade of bitter civil war. Egypt's Muslim Brotherhood did come to power peacefully in 2012, but it was removed by the military a year later amid widespread protests against its policies.

Militant fundamentalism has certainly not been the only religious response to modernity and globalization within the Islamic world. (See AP® Working with Evidence: Contending for Islam, Documents 5 and 7.) Considerable debate among Muslims has raised questions about the proper role of the state; the difference between the eternal law of God (sharia) and the human interpretations of it; the rights of women; the possibility of democracy; and many other issues. In 1996, Anwar Ibrahim, a major political and intellectual figure in Malaysia, insisted:

> Southeast Asian Muslims . . . would rather strive to improve the welfare of the women and children in their midst than spend their days elaborately defining the nature and institutions of the ideal Islamic state. They do not believe it makes one less of a Muslim to promote economic growth, to master the information revolution, and to demand justice for women.[17]

In 2004 and 2005 scholars from all major schools of Islamic thought called for Islamic unity, condemned terrorism, forbade Muslims from declaring one another as "apostate" or nonbelievers, and emphasized the commonalities shared by Muslims, Christians, and Jews.

Within other religious traditions as well, believers found various ways of responding to global modernity. A number of liberal and mainstream Christian groups spoke to the ethical issues arising from economic globalization and climate change. Many Christian organizations, for example, were active in agitating for debt relief for poor countries and the rights of immigrants. Adherents of "liberation theology," particularly in Latin America, sought a Christian basis for action in the areas of social justice, poverty, and human rights, while viewing Jesus as liberator as well as savior. In Asia, a growing movement known as socially engaged Buddhism addressed the needs of the poor through social reform, educational programs, health services, and peacemaking action during times of conflict and war. In short, religious responses to global modernity were articulated in many voices.

BUILDING AP® SKILLS

Sourcing and Situation

You can use quotes from the text to get students to practice their sourcing skills, like the one from Anwar Ibrahim on this page. It's good to try this activity frequently throughout the year because sourcing is one of the more difficult skills of the DBQ that students need to master. Display the quote from Anwar Ibrahim for students to read. Then ask them to identify the historical situation, intended audience, purpose, and point of view of the author (HIPP). (Answers are provided in italics.)

■ **Historical Situation:** *The author is writing in the context of the growth of militant or radical Islam in the second half of the twentieth century.*

■ **Intended Audience:** *The author is writing for the citizens of Malaysia and Muslims worldwide. He may also be attempting to reach Western countries to assure them that not all Muslims are radical or against modernity.*

■ **Purpose and Point of View of the Author:** *As a major political and intellectual figure in Malaysia, the author wants to convince Muslims that they can be concerned about the economy and women's rights while still being a Muslim. He may be attempting to convince Muslims not to be radicalized.*

ERIC'S ACTIVITY 14.1 Generalizing about Islam

Skill: Argumentation

In this chapter, "AP® Working with Evidence: Contending for Islam," starting on page 843, provides an ideal opportunity to explore approaches to constructing historical arguments that acknowledge a multiplicity of viewpoints. Formative exercises in small groups are followed by a summative writing assignment to challenge students to evaluate and synthesize conflicting historical evidence into a single narrative that reflects the rich diversity of the modern worlds of Islam. At the same time, students gain an appreciation of the various, often conflicting, understandings of Islam present in the world today. Find the complete activity in the Teacher's Resource Materials.

TRM Eric's Activity 14.1: Generalizing about Islam

The Environment in the Anthropocene Era

Finding the Main Point: What have been the consequences of humanity's interaction with the environment in modern times, and how have societies responded to these consequences?

The fossil fuel revolution and rapid technological innovation; industrialization and economic growth; urbanization and consumerism; population growth and migration; nationalism and global citizenship—all of these accelerating global processes of the past century connect with what is surely the most distinctive feature of that century: the human impact on the environment. As environmental historian J. R. McNeill put it: "This is the first time in human history that we have altered ecosystems with such intensity, on such a scale, and with such speed.... The human race, without intending anything of the sort, has undertaken a gigantic uncontrolled experiment on the earth."[18]

The Global Environment Transformed

By the early twenty-first century, that "experiment" had acquired a name: the **Anthropocene era** or the age of humankind. Many scientists and environmental historians now use this term to designate the contemporary era since the advent of the Industrial Revolution and more dramatically since 1950. It emphatically calls attention to the enduring impact of recent human activity on the planet. Species extinctions; mounting carbon dioxide emissions and climate change; the depletion of groundwater reserves; accumulating radioactive isotopes in the earth's surface; the enlargement of deserts; dead zones in the oceans; the prevalence of concrete and plastics—these and other environmental changes, all of them generated by human actions, will be apparent to archeologists many thousands of years in the future, should they be around to reflect on them. A prominent geologist recently declared: "We are the dominant geologic force shaping the planet. It's not so much river or ice or wind anymore. It's humans."[19]

As geologists reckon time, humankind has been living for the past 12,000 years in the **Holocene era**, a warmer and often wetter period that began following the end of the last Ice Age. During this Holocene era, environmental conditions were uniquely favorable for human thriving. It was, according to prominent earth scientist Johan Rockstrom, a "Garden of Eden" era, providing "a stable equilibrium of forests, savannahs, coral reefs, grasslands, fish, mammals, bacteria, air quality, ice cover, temperatures, fresh water availability, and productive soils."[20] These conditions enabled the development of agriculture, significant population growth, and the creation of complex civilizations. Human activity during the Holocene era certainly transformed the environment in many ways, as plants and animals were domesticated, as native vegetation and forests gave way to agricultural fields and grazing land, as soils were eroded or became salty, as cities grew, and in many other ways. However, these environmental impacts were limited, local, and sometimes temporary.

AP® EXAM TIP

How humans changed their interactions with the environment throughout the twentieth century is a major concept in the AP® course.

AP®

ARGUMENTATION
What evidence might support the notion that the earth has moved into the "age of humankind"?

APPLY THE TIP

Before starting "The Environment in the Anthropocene Era," think about guiding students in a quick class discussion on human-environment interactions in the twentieth and twenty-first centuries. Ask: How have humans changed their interactions with the environment during the twentieth and twenty-first centuries? *Due to the Industrial Revolution, new fossil fuels, a growing population,* *rapid urbanization, and new technologies, humans have drastically changed their interactions with the environment. Because of these changes, more species have gone extinct; there are higher carbon dioxide emissions and climate change is intensifying; groundwater reserves are depleted; deserts are being enlarged; and there is an increase in dead zones in the oceans.*

TEACHING IDEA

Incorporating Outside Resources

"Anthropocene era" is a term many students are not going to be familiar with. The Crash Course Big History episode *The Anthropocene and the Near Future* could be an interesting way to introduce students to this new age of history. In this episode, John Green, Hank Green, and Emily Graslie examine what the Anthropocene era is and the pros and cons of the progress made during this time. Find the video on YouTube. As students watch the video, have them take notes on the pros and cons of the progress made during the Anthropocene era.

■ **Pros:** *Since 1970, manufacturing jobs have lifted approximately 600 million people out of poverty. Modern technologies can now feed and clothe more humans than ever before. Standards of living are increasing on average. We have managed to harness a lot of energy with our use of coal and oil and nuclear power. Advances in medicine, agriculture, and genetic engineering have in the past 200 years lowered the death rate and freed billions of people from the cycles of starvation and famine that affected agrarian civilizations. Economic development in different countries has meant that people can have fewer children, more children can be educated, and more adults can have a variety of opportunities to choose from.*

■ **Cons:** *More people in the developing world are forced from traditional ways of life and into factory jobs with poor safety standards, long hours, and low wages. Many of the goods produced in the developing world go overseas to enhance the standard of living of the developed world. Despite an increase in the average standard of living, the wealth inequality gap is getting wider and wider. Current modes of production rely heavily on nonrenewable resources that are bad for the environment. We're accelerating the rate of extinction of plant and animal species that don't happen to be useful to us. Climate change that affects the amount of arable land we have to farm on and rapidly growing populations in parts of the world mean we could be facing a major overpopulation problem soon.*

AP®

CAUSATION

What impact has the Anthropocene era had on the environment?

That began to change as industrialization and population growth took hold first in Europe, North America, and Japan during the nineteenth century, in the Soviet Union during the 1930s, and then after 1950 in many other parts of the world. Everywhere, the idea of economic growth or "development" as something possible and highly desirable took hold, in capitalist, communist, and developing countries alike. Thus, human impact on the environment has become pervasive, global, and permanent, eroding the "Garden of Eden" conditions of the Holocene era.

Among the chief indicators of the Anthropocene era were multiple transformations of the landscape.[21] The growing numbers of the poor and the growing consumption of the rich led to the doubling of cropland and pasturelands during the twentieth century. By 2015, some 40 percent of the world's land area was used to produce food for humans and their domesticated animals, whereas in 1750 that figure was only 4 percent. As grasslands and swampland contracted, so too did the world's forests. The most dramatic deforestation took place in tropical regions of Latin America, Africa, and Southeast Asia, making way for timbering and farming, even as some reforestation took hold in Europe, North America, and Japan. Furthermore, huge urban complexes have transformed the landscape in many places into wholly artificial environments of concrete, asphalt, steel, and glass. China alone lost some 6.7 million hectares of farmland, over 5 percent of its available agricultural land, to urban growth between 1996 and 2003.[22]

These human incursions reduced the habitat available to wild plants and animals, leading to the extinction of numerous species and declining biodiversity. Extinction is, of course, a natural phenomenon, but by the early twenty-first century the pace of species extinction had spiked far beyond the natural or "background rate" because of human interventions in the form of agriculture, lumbering, and urban growth. Tropical rain forest habitats, home to a far richer diversity of species than more temperate environments, were particularly susceptible to human intrusion.

This loss of biodiversity extended to the seas of the world as well. Fishing with industrial-style equipment has led to the collapse or near collapse of fisheries around the world. The 1992 breakdown of the Grand Banks cod fishery off the coast of Newfoundland persuaded the Canadian government to place a moratorium on further fishing in that area. By the early 1960s, most whale species were on the verge of extinction, though many have begun to recover as restrictions on whaling have been put in place. "For the first time since the demise of the dinosaurs 65 million years ago," wrote the director of the World Wildlife Federation, "we face a global mass extinction of wildlife."[23]

The global spread of modern industry, heavily dependent on fossil fuels, has generated dramatic changes in the air, water, soil, and atmosphere, with profound impacts on human life. China's spectacular economic growth since the 1980s, fueled largely by coal, has resulted in an equally spectacular pall of air pollution in its major cities. In 2004, the World Bank reported that twelve of the world's twenty most polluted cities were in China. Degradation of the world's rivers, seas, and oceans has also mounted, as pesticides, herbicides, chemical fertilizers, detergents,

BUILDING AP® SKILLS

Making Connections: Comparison

Humans have constantly been affecting the environment around them, but their impact has drastically changed in the past 150 years. This would be a good place to ask students to create a chart on the human impact on the environment during the Holocene era to the human impact on the environment during the Anthropocene era. When students are finished, you could have them share what they found with a partner and compare the impact the two eras had on the environment. You can find a reproducible version of the chart in the Teacher's Resource Materials. (Answers provided in italics.)

Environmental Impact during Holocene Era	Environmental Impact during Anthropocene Era
■ *Plants and animals were domesticated*	■ *More animal and plant species have become extinct*
■ *Native vegetation and forests gave way to agricultural fields and grazing land*	■ *Carbon dioxide levels have risen due to the use of fossil fuels, contributing to climate change*
■ *In agricultural and grazing areas, soils were eroded or became salty*	■ *Groundwater reserves have been depleted*
■ *Growing cities changed the environments around them*	■ *Radioactive isotopes have accumulated on the earth's surface*
■ *The environmental impacts of this era were limited, local, and sometimes temporary*	■ *Deserts and dead zones in the oceans have been enlarged*
	■ *Massive deforestation and other transformations to the landscape have occurred*
	■ *Changes have happened due to increased human activity and will be apparent for many years to come*

TRM Handout 14.9: Chart for Environmental Impacts in Holocene and Anthropocene Eras oil, sewage, industrial waste, and plastics have made their way from land to water. The Great Pacific Garbage Patch, an area of about 7 million square miles in the North Pacific, has trapped an enormous quantity of debris, mostly plastics, endangering oceanic food webs and proving deadly to creatures of the sea, which ingest or become entangled in this human garbage. Industrial pollution in the Soviet Union rendered about half of the country's rivers severely polluted by the late 1980s, while fully 20 percent of its population lived in regions defined as "ecological disasters." The release of chemicals known as chlorofluorocarbons thinned the ozone layer, which protects the earth from excessive ultraviolet radiation, before an international agreement put an end to the practice.

Urban Pollution in Beijing Deriving from auto exhausts, coal burning, and dust storms, the air pollution in China's capital city of Beijing has long been horrendous. In this photograph from early 2014, teenagers wear face masks to protect themselves from inhaling the noxious particles in the air. Many thousands of people across the globe die daily from the long-term effects of air pollution. (Rolex Dela Pena/EPA/Shutterstock)

In other ways as well, human activity has left a lasting mark on the planet during the past century. Radioactive residue from the testing of nuclear weapons and from the storage of nuclear waste produced by power plants can remain detectable for tens or hundreds of thousands of years. Mining has also created a vast underground network of shafts and tunnels and above-ground scarring of open-pit mines and quarries. As the demand for water to serve growing populations, industries, and irrigation needs increased by 900 percent during the twentieth century, many of the planet's aquifers became substantially depleted. A number of large cities—Beijing, Mexico City, Bangkok, Tokyo, Houston, Jakarta, and Manila—have been measurably sinking over the past century due in part to groundwater depletion. All of these environmental changes deriving from human activity will be apparent to our descendants for a long time to come.

Changing the Climate

By the early twenty-first century, **climate change** had become the world's most pressing environmental issue. Since the Industrial Revolution took hold in Western Europe, higher concentrations of carbon dioxide and methane, generated by the burning of fossil fuels, as well as nitrous oxide derived largely from fertilizers, began to accumulate in the atmosphere, slowly at first and then much more rapidly after 1950. These so-called greenhouse gases act as a blanket around the world, limiting

▲ AP
CLAIMS AND EVIDENCE IN SOURCES
How would a historian use this image to explain the environmental impact of industrialization and the Anthropocene era?

AP EXAM TIP
Pay attention to how human activity has led to deforestation, desertification, and air and water pollution.

ERIC'S ACTIVITY 14.2   Living in the Anthropocene

Theme 1: Humans and the Environment

We live in extraordinary times. Only in the last century or so has our species come to dominate our environment on a global scale. My students are active participants in this process, and the implications of the Anthropocene will directly affect their lives. I use data from the last century to ask my students to explore the promise and challenges for the next century of the Anthropocene. In the process, my students gain valuable skills in analyzing data. Find the complete activity in the Teacher's Resource Materials.

TRM Eric's Activity 14.2: Living in the Anthropocene

Incorporating Outside Resources

In *Climate 101 with Bill Nye* from the Climate Reality Project, Bill Nye explains the basics of climate change. This video could be a good introduction to the section "Changing the Climate" and help give students an overview of the topic. Find the video on YouTube. After students have watched it, ask them to write two short-answer quiz questions based on what they've learned from the video and quiz a partner. *Answers will vary.*

Claims and Evidence in Sources

To give students an overview of the different sides of the debate on climate change, consider asking them to read the article "Is Human Activity Primarily Responsible for Global Climate Change?" You can find the article on the Britannica ProCon website. Pair students up and have one student read about the Pro arguments and the other read about the Con arguments. After they have read the article, have them share what they found with their partner.

▶ **AP®**

CONTEXTUALIZATION
What global and regional events can help explain the trends seen in Figures 14.1 and 14.2 on carbon dioxide emissions?

Figure 14.1 Carbon Dioxide Concentrations, 1750–2020
Rising concentrations of carbon dioxide in the atmosphere have been matched by a marked increase in global temperatures. (Data from Scripps Institution of Oceanography at the University of California San Diego)

AP®

CAUSATION
In what ways has global warming affected life on earth?

the escape of infrared energy from the earth's surface and so warming the planet. Carbon dioxide concentrations have increased substantially since 1900, and even more rapidly since 1950, reaching 421 parts per million (ppm) by the summer of 2022, a level well beyond the 350 ppm generally considered "safe" and greater than at any time during the over 200,000 years of human life on the planet. (See Figure 14.1 and Figure 14.2.) Paralleling this growing accumulation of carbon dioxide in the atmosphere has been a clear rise in average global temperature of 1.2°C. The years between 2011 and 2020 represent the warmest decade on record, and temperature projections into the near future are alarming. While this temperature increase may seem numerically small, its consequences have already been substantial and are intensifying.

Scientists have associated this warming of the planet with all manner of environmental changes. One of them involves the accelerating melting of glaciers and polar ice caps. Arctic temperatures, unprecedented in the past 44,000 years, have been melting glaciers and sea ice at record levels. Coupled with expanded sea volumes as the oceans warm, this rapid melting has raised sea levels by 8 to 9 inches since 1880. The rising oceans have particularly threatened to inundate a number of small island nations in Oceania—Tuvalu and Kiribati in particular. Coastal communities everywhere have become more vulnerable to storm surges, and many of the world's largest cities are located on the coast. Low-lying regions of Bangladesh and the Philippines already flood almost every year and more catastrophically during particularly strong storms, which seem to occur with increasing frequency and power as the planet warms. The first decade of the twenty-first century witnessed eight Category 5 hurricanes in the Atlantic Ocean, the most for any decade on record.

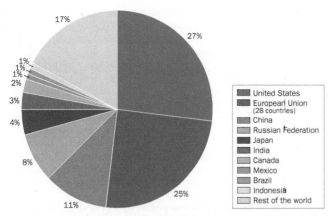

Figure 14.2 Distribution of Total World Carbon Dioxide Emissions, 1850–2011
The various regions or countries of the world have contributed very unevenly to carbon dioxide emissions over the past 160 years. By 2014, however, industrializing Asian economies had become major emitters, with China responsible for some 30 percent of global carbon dioxide discharges into the atmosphere in that year. (Data from World Resources Institute)

While global warming has exacerbated storms and rainfall in some regions, it has increased the prevalence and duration of droughts in others. Since the 1970s, droughts have been longer and more extreme in parts of Africa, the Middle East, southern Asia, and the western United States. In 2010 and 2011, extreme weather conditions characteristic of global warming—droughts, dust storms, fires, heavy rainfall—afflicted many grain-producing regions of the world, including Canada, Russia, China, Argentina, and Australia, causing a sharp spike in grain prices on the world market. The Middle East and North Africa, heavily dependent on grain imports, experienced sharply rising food prices, arguably aggravating social unrest and contributing to the political protests of the Arab Spring. In various parts of Africa, surging populations, record high temperatures, and prolonged drought have generated crop failures, devastation of livestock herds, and local conflicts over land and water. These pressures have turned many people into "climate refugees" who migrate to urban areas or northward toward Europe.

Climate change has also disrupted many aquatic ecosystems, as the world's oceans and lakes have become warmer and more acidic, absorbing some 25 percent of human-generated carbon dioxide. While this absorption has limited the extent of atmospheric warming to date, the resulting carbonic acid has damaged any number of marine organisms with calcium shells, such as oysters, clams, sea urchins, and plankton, and places entire aquatic food chains in jeopardy. The world's coral reefs have been especially vulnerable. Record-high oceanic temperatures in 2016 killed

Incorporating Outside Resources

The OER Project has a Making Claims activity on how globalization affects the environment that could be a good wrap-up for students on this section of Chapter 14. In this activity, students are asked to make two claims and one counterclaim, along with providing evidence to support the claims, about the environmental impacts of globalization. Consider giving students an extra challenge by partnering them up and having them provide evidence for the claims their partner wrote. You can find the "Making Claims: Globalization" activity in Topic 9.1: Technology and the Environment, of the OER Project's World History: AP® Curriculum in Unit 9.

Class Discussion

Give students four to five minutes to list as many environmental groups as they can think of. Once time is up, have students share what they came up with. *Answers will vary, but may include Greenpeace, World Wildlife Fund, the Environmental Protection Agency, the Sierra Club.*

67 percent of the coral in some areas of Australia's Great Barrier Reef. "The coral was cooked," declared one of the scientists studying this phenomenon.[24]

Nor have land-based communities of living organisms been spared the impact of global warming. Drier conditions, for example, have meant more forest fires. Those in the western United States have increased fourfold since 1970, and the fire season has been extended by more than two months. Both plants and animals adapted to a particular temperature range have been forced to migrate or die as temperatures have increased. In Ethiopia, this has meant that mosquitos bearing malaria have migrated higher up the country's mountains, bringing the disease to people who never knew it before. Warmer temperatures in western North America have enabled bark beetles, which cause great damage as they feed on the bark and wood of trees, to survive the less intense winters and move to new environments. They have killed over 150,000 square miles of trees in recent decades. Polar bears have become an iconic image of the impact of global warming, as the sea ice on which they depend vanishes.

Clearly climate change as a marker of the Anthropocene era is in its early stages, with more, much more, to follow if these emissions continue more or less unchecked. Projections to the year 2100, although subject to much dispute and controversy, paint a bleak picture: there will be carbon dioxide concentrations of 600 ppm and up; temperature increases of 1.8°C to 4°C; massive melting of glaciers and sea ice with sea level rise in the range of 2.5 to 6 feet; millions of homes and hundreds of cities at least partially under water; drought and falling food production in parts of Africa, leading to mass migrations; widespread species extinction of up to half of earth's higher life forms by one estimate; and frequent international conflicts over dwindling freshwater supplies. Under these conditions, serious observers have begun to speak about the possibility of a major collapse of modern civilization. Can humans restrain their activities enough to stop climate change when the world has never experienced anything like this in the past? (See Then and Now: Humanity and Nature, page 830.) In the face of such current conditions and future threats, a large number of environmental movements have arisen over the past century.

Protecting the Planet: The Rise of Environmentalism

Long before climate change emerged as a global issue, a growing awareness of ecological damage and a desire to counteract it accompanied human entry into the Anthropocene era.[25] In the late eighteenth and early nineteenth centuries, Romantic English poets such as William Blake and William Wordsworth denounced the industrial era's "dark satanic mills," which threatened the "green and pleasant land" of an earlier England. In opposing the extension of railroads, the British writer John Ruskin declared in 1876 that "the frenzy of avarice is daily drowning our sailors, suffocating our miners, poisoning our children and blasting the cultivable surface of England into a treeless waste of ashes."[26] Another element in early environmentalism, especially prominent in the United States and Germany, derived from a concern with deforestation, drought, and desertification as pioneering settlers, lumbermen, miners, and colonial plantation owners inflicted terrible damage on the woodlands and pasturelands of the world. Articulated primarily by scientists often working in the colonial world, this approach sought to mobilize scientific expertise and state control to manage, contain, and tame modern assaults on the environment.

Protecting remaining wilderness areas was yet another piece of early environmentalism. The first international environmental conference, held in London in 1900, aimed at preserving African wildlife from voracious European hunters. In the United States it was the opening of the west to European settlers that threatened the natural order. "With no eye to the future," wrote naturalist John Muir in 1897, "these pious destroyers waged interminable forest wars . . . , spreading ruthless devastation ever wider and further. . . . Wilderness is a necessity . . . not only as fountains of timber and irrigating rivers, but as fountains of life."[27] This kind of sensibility found expression in the American national parks, the first of which, Yellowstone, was established in 1872.

These early examples of environmental awareness were distinctly limited, largely a product of literary figures, scientists, and some government officials. None of them attracted a mass following or elicited a global response. But **second-wave environmentalism**, beginning in the 1960s, certainly did. It began, arguably, with the publication in 1962 of Rachel Carson's *Silent Spring*, which exposed the chemical contamination of the environment with a particular emphasis on the use of pesticides. Ten years later, the Club of Rome, a global think tank, issued a report called *Limits to Growth*, which warned of resource exhaustion and the collapse of industrial society in the face of unrelenting economic and population growth. Soon a mounting wave of environmental books, articles, treatises, and conferences emerged in Europe and North America, pushing back in various ways against the postwar emphasis on "development," consumerism, and unending economic growth. That sensibility was aptly captured in the title of a best-selling book by British economist E. F. Schumacher in 1973, *Small Is Beautiful* (see AP® Working with Evidence, Document 4, in Chapter 13).

But what most clearly distinguished second-wave environmentalism was widespread grassroots involvement and activism. By the late 1990s, millions of people in North America, Europe, Japan, Australia, and New Zealand had joined one of the rapidly proliferating environmental organizations, many of them local. The issues addressed in these burgeoning movements were many and various: pollution, resource depletion, toxic waste, protecting wildlife habitats, nuclear power and nuclear testing, limiting development, and increasingly at the top of the agenda in the twenty-first century, climate change. Beyond particular issues, proponents of "deep ecology" argued that human beings should no longer be considered central but understood as occupying a place of equivalence with other species. Those supporting an "environmental justice" outlook were more concerned with the impact of environmental devastation on the poor, minorities, and developing countries.

 AP®
COMPARISON
In what different ways has environmentalism been expressed?

AP® EXAM TIP
You should be able to explain the growth and impact of the environmental movement in the second half of the twentieth century.

CHAPTER 14

TEACHING IDEA

Class Discussion

Have students read "Then and Now: Humanity and Nature" and work with a partner to answer the questions on page 831. After students complete this activity, use these questions to begin a class discussion on the arguments presented in this essay. *Answers will vary but should provide an excellent discussion for the class.*

THEN AND NOW Humanity and Nature

Homo sapiens, like all other living creatures, are a product of the natural world. The earth's environment has sustained our kind even as we have learned more and more how to harness and redirect its resources for our needs and desires. Natural challenges have repeatedly shaped our historical trajectory. Global warming at the end of the last Ice Age, for instance, enabled the emergence of agriculture, while tiny microbes carried by Europeans and Africans decimated Native American peoples in the sixteenth century.

Two ancient and persistent patterns have featured prominently in humankind's relationship with the natural world. First, humans have long been inspired by nature's impressive power and immense grandeur and understood themselves as deeply connected to it. Paleolithic cave art, Australian Dreamtime mythology, Chinese landscape paintings, and many religious traditions reflect this reverence for nature, often celebrating its ancient rhythms while inspiring practices that preserve elements of the natural world.

At the same time, humans have also long sought to use nature for their own benefit, often altering, degrading, or destroying the environment in the process. The arrival of the earliest human settlers in many places brought the rapid extinction of some species and the reshaping of environments to meet human needs through practices such as controlled burns, where humans intentionally set fires to parts of their environment to help favored species thrive. Then starting some 10,000 years ago, the spread of agriculture allowed humankind to harness ever more of nature's resources. But doing so often imposed great environmental costs, including deforestation, water pollution, and soil degradation.

For many centuries, the environmental impact of human activity remained limited and local. Very recently, however, humankind's relationship with nature has changed profoundly. Starting about two centuries ago but accelerating markedly over the past seventy years, we have increasingly entered a new era—the Anthropocene, or "age of humankind." For the first time in the history of our planet, a single species—us—has "acquired such control over the biosphere that it dominates change on the surface of the Earth."[28] This is what separates our relationship with the natural world now from all that has come before.

So what has caused this dramatic change in balance between humankind and nature in such a short time? Human numbers certainly played a role. Unprecedented in human history, our population expanded from 1 billion in the early nineteenth century to almost 8 billion in 2022. And energy use, associated with industrialization on a global scale, has increased even more quickly than the population, so that humankind today consumes twenty-five times more energy than it did in 1800, mostly thanks to the burning of fossil fuels.

Thus population and economic growth have granted humankind the means to drive change on an unprecedented scale. Humans now move more earth for construction, road building, and other projects than do all the natural processes of the planet, including erosion and glaciation. Greenhouse gas emissions far beyond anything in human history have melted glaciers and polar ice caps, raising sea levels by at least three inches since 1993. Species extinction rates are 1,000 times greater today than the average over the last few million years. As one leading scholar has recently put it, "we humans have become a planet-changing species."[29]

Already in the opening decades of the twentieth century, many predicted that the shifting balance between nature and humankind would continue and accelerate. The British science fiction author H. G. Wells envisioned futures in which humans became god-like masters of nature and thus their own fate. "The final goal . . . is a profound rearrangement of the entire living world," declared the communist Soviet intellectual Nikolai Kashchenko in 1929. "All living nature will live, thrive and die at none other than the will of humans and according to their designs."[30]

While some viewed this future as full of promise, other observers struck a more cautious tone. Was humankind really up to creating nature in its image? The German philosopher and intellectual Ludvig Klages expressed his doubts when he wrote that "in no conceivable case

Electric lights have overturned night's limitations on humankind but also consume the earth's fuel. (Matthias Kulka/Getty Images)

will human beings ever meet with success in their attempt to 'correct' nature."[31] And as the impact of human activity on the environment became more apparent over the course of the twentieth century, a growing number of scientists and environmentalists warned that mistreating and overwhelming nature might bring terrible repercussions. Already by 1948, the American conservationist and environmentalist Aldo Leopold gave expression to what later was dubbed a "deep ecology" outlook. "We abuse land," he wrote, "because we regard it as a commodity belonging to us. When we see land as a community to which we belong, we may begin to use it with love and respect."[32] In the 1960s, a growing environmentalist movement emerged that was dedicated to limiting humankind's imprint on the natural world and conserving the natural environment; notable successes included the improvement of air and water quality in many regions and the protection of some endangered species.

But in the 2020s it remains an open question whether humankind will be able to slow, let alone stop, its unprecedented assault on the natural order, which is driven by powerful forces beyond the control of any single person or government: a rising human population, the universal desire for economic growth, the imperatives of capitalism, and the technological capacity to overcome limitations imposed by nature. The past offers us few lessons about the future, for our age has no parallel in our planet's 4.5-billion-year history. Never before has a single species gained a large element of control over change on earth. Can we recover a sense of ourselves as a part of the natural order rather than the masters of it? In short, can humanity restrain itself?

Or will nature restrain humankind? The COVID-19 pandemic provides a timely reminder of human vulnerability in the face of nature. In just a matter of months, the coronavirus jumped species through human contact with wild animals and then rode along modern transportation routes and became established almost everywhere. Another natural phenomenon, global warming, could prove an even greater constraint than disease. The burning of fossil fuels, which has been critical to humans' control over their environment, threatens to cause catastrophic climate changes that calls into question the viability of our current way of life. The Anthropocene has arrived, but the duration and course of this "age of humankind" remain unclear, as the future always is.

QUESTIONS

What separates humankind's relationship with the natural environment today from its relationship in the more distant past? Is the Anthropocene a permanent break from the past, or might the relationship between humankind and the natural environment return to older patterns in the future?

This social justice perspective informed Pope Francis's 2015 environmental encyclical, which commanded global attention, as the world's most prominent Christian leader called for humankind to "care for our common home."

The tactics of these movements were as varied as the issues they addressed. Much attention was given to public education and to lobbying governments and corporations, often through professionally run organizations such as Greenpeace, the Worldwide Fund for Nature, and the Citizens Climate Lobby. In Germany, New Zealand, and Australia, environmentalists created Green parties, which contested elections and on occasion shared power. Teach-ins, demonstrations, street protests, and various local actions also played a role in the strategies of environmental activists.

In the communist world, environmentalism was constrained by highly authoritarian states that were committed to large-scale development. In the late 1980s, the Chinese government, for example, sharply repressed groups critical of the enormous Three Gorges Dam project across the Yangzi River. By the early twenty-first century, however, a grassroots environmental movement had taken root in China, expressed in hundreds of private groups and in state-sponsored organizations as well. Many of these grounded their activism in Buddhist or Daoist traditions that stressed the harmony of humankind and the natural order. In the Soviet Union during the 1970s and after, environmentalists were able to voice their concerns about the shrinking of the Aral Sea, pollution threats to Lake Baikal in Siberia, and poor air quality in many cities. After the nuclear disaster at Chernobyl in 1986, Gorbachev's policy of *glasnost* allowed greater freedom of expression as environmentalist concerns became part of a broader challenge to communism and Russian domination.

Quite quickly, during the 1970s and 1980s, environmentalism also took root in the Global South, where it frequently assumed a distinctive character compared to the more industrialized countries. There it was more locally based, with less connection to global issues or large national organizations than in the West; it involved more poor people in direct action rather than in political lobbying and corporate strategies; it was more concerned with issues of food security, health, and basic survival than with the rights of nature or wilderness protection; and it was more closely connected to movements for social justice. Thus, whereas Western environmentalists defended forests where few people lived, the Chikpo, or "tree-hugging," movement in India sought to protect the livelihood of farmers, artisans, and herders living in areas subject to extensive deforestation. A massive movement to prevent or limit the damming of India's Narmada River derived from the displacement of local people; similar anti-dam protests in the American Northwest were more concerned with protecting salmon runs.

In the Global South, this "environmentalism of the poor" took shape in various ways, often in opposition to the gigantic development projects of national governments. Residents of the Brazilian Amazon basin, facing the loss of their livelihood to lumbering interests, ranchers, and government road-building projects, joined

AP EXAM TIP

Movements that protested the inequality that resulted from global environmental problems are an important concept in the AP® course.

AP

COMPARISON

How does environmentalism in the Global South differ from environmentalism in more industrialized states?

---

hands and directly confronted workers sent to cut down trees with their chain-saws. When the Thai government sought to create huge eucalyptus plantations, largely to supply Japanese-owned paper mills, Buddhist teachers, known as "ecology monks," mobilized subsistence farmers to put their case to public officials. In the Philippines, coalitions of numerous local groups mobilized large-scale grassroots movements against foreign-owned mining companies. Kenya's Green Belt Movement, led by Nobel Peace Prize winner Wangari Maathai, organized groups of village women to plant millions of trees to forestall the growth of deserts and protect the soil.

By the early twenty-first century, environmentalism had become a matter of global concern and had prompted action at many levels. A growing market for solar and wind power helped drive its cost sharply lower, moving it closer to being competitive with conventional forms of electric generation like coal or oil. Governments acted to curtail pollution and to foster the use of renewable energy sources. Germany, for example, increased the proportion of its electricity from renewable sources from 6.3 percent in 2000 to 46 percent in 2020. China has enacted a large body of environmental laws and regulations and invested heavily in solar power. Brazil and Canada derive the bulk of their electricity from renewables, primarily hydropower. Some 6,000 national parks in over 100 countries served to protect wildlife and natural beauty.

Many businesses found it commercially useful and therefore profitable to brand themselves as "green." Reforestation programs were under way in China, Honduras, Kenya, and elsewhere. International agreements have come close to eliminating the introduction of ozone-depleting substances into the atmosphere. And after extensive negotiations, the **Paris Climate Agreement** of 2015 committed some 195 countries, 700 cities, and many companies to reduce greenhouse gas emissions sufficiently to avoid a 2°C increase in global temperatures. Furthermore, millions of individuals altered their ways of life, agreeing to recycle, to install solar panels, to buy fuel-efficient cars, to shop in local markets, and to forgo the use of plastic bags.

But resistance has also surfaced, partly because moving toward a clean energy economy would require lifestyle adjustment for citizens in the Global North and for elites everywhere. Powerful and entrenched interests in fossil fuel industries likewise generate resistance. Furthermore, large-scale international agreement on

Environmentalism in Action Many environmental activists have channeled their energies into direct action at the local level. In this photograph taken in 2020, two volunteers in kayaks—part of a flotilla of about 300 small craft—take part in a waste removal and cleanup campaign in Cairo, Egypt. The group that sponsored this event claims to have collected some thirty-seven tons of garbage from the Nile River over a three-year period. (Khaled Desouki/Getty Images)

 AP

CLAIMS AND EVIDENCE IN SOURCES

How does this image reflect the changes that emerged from second-wave environmentalism?

AP

CONTINUITY AND CHANGE

Explain the changes to the environmentalist movement in the twenty-first century.

EXPLORING AP® THEMES

Humans and the Environment (ENV)

Ask students to read the quote by the Malaysian official. Then ask students: How is this representative of the Global South's view the Global North's attitude toward environmental initiatives? *The official believes the Global North put profit above the environment for years and caused the environmental crisis.*

BUILDING AP® SKILLS

Argumentation

Ask students to read "Conclusions and Reflections: World History and the Making of Meaning." After they have read the article, ask them to write a one-paragraph response to the following question: After learning about global history during this school year, what meaning do you give history? *Answers will vary.*

global warming has come up against sharp conflicts between the Global North and South. Both activists and governments in the developing countries have often felt that Northern initiatives to address atmospheric pollution and global warming would curtail their industrial development, leaving the North/South gap intact. A Malaysian official put the dispute succinctly: "The developed countries don't want to give up their extravagant lifestyles, but plan to curtail our development."[33]

Since signing the Paris Agreement in 2016, U.S. government policy toward climate change has shifted more dramatically between engagement and resistance than in any other major country in the world. In 2017 the new Trump administration began to partially dismantle existing climate change regulations and stunned the world by announcing U.S. withdrawal from the Paris Agreement. Then in 2021 the United States changed course under President Joe Biden by rejoining the agreement and beginning the process of reversing other actions taken by his predecessor. As one of the largest producers of greenhouse gases in the world, the path charted by the United States in coming years will have a critical impact on the success or failure of efforts to limit global warming.

More than any other widespread movement, global environmentalism has come to symbolize a focus on the common plight of humankind across the artificial boundaries of nation-states. It also marked a challenge to modernity itself, particularly its overriding commitment to endless growth and consumption. The ideas of sustainability and restraint, certainly not prominent in any list of modern values, entered global discourse and marked the beginnings of a new environmental ethic. This change in thinking, although limited, was perhaps the most significant achievement of global environmentalism.

CONCLUSIONS AND REFLECTIONS

World History and the Making of Meaning

Finding the Main Point: In what ways do historians deal with the question of meaning in human life?

Humans everywhere are meaning-making creatures. We find meaning in relationship with others, in causes and common efforts, in religious or spiritual experience, and in perceiving pattern or purpose both in the world generally and in our individual lives. In the absence of meaning, we do not flourish.

A large part of the historian's task involves identifying and describing the multiple meanings that individuals and societies in the past have ascribed to their world and to their behavior. Over the last century, for example, religiously committed people, pummeled by the multiple assaults of modern life, have sought meaning and a sense of belonging by returning to what they believed were earlier and more authentic forms of Hinduism, Christianity, or Islam. For many others, identification with a particular racial, national, or ethnic group has provided that sense of meaning, as in Nazi Germany and apartheid South Africa. Still others have found significance in a sense of world citizenship or membership in larger international communities, such as a pan-African community, the European Union, or a global scientific association. Amid many signs of serious damage to the planet, environmentalists too have understood the world in ways that give meaning to what they see and what they value.

But historians are more than observers of past meanings. They also join the rest of humankind in creating meaning as they give definition to the human past. World historians, for example, have sometimes pointed to a broad trend toward greater social complexity and more connectivity among regions and peoples, especially in the twentieth century. They give some meaning to human tragedies such as wars and genocide by explaining their origins and development. In defining the past century as a new and distinctive age in world history, the "Anthropocene," historians assert that a special significance or meaning attaches to this period. In identifying particular patterns within the recent past — unprecedented population growth, widespread urbanization, international migration, recurring pandemics, cultural globalization, and global warming — historians seek to impose some shape and significance on the chaos of random events.

In doing so, they are insisting that history is more than "one damned thing after another," that it is possible to find a measure of coherence in the record of humankind. Some might argue that any such "shape" is an illusion, an artificial product of human self-serving. Certainly historians' formulations are endlessly contested and debated. But we are apparently impelled to seek pattern, structure, or meaning in the past. An infinite array of miscellaneous historical "facts" is neither satisfying nor useful.

The study of world history can also be helpful for each of us as we seek to make meaning in our own lives. As we witness the broad contours of the human journey and learn more about the wider world, we can more readily locate ourselves individually in the larger stream of that story. In short, world history provides context, which is so essential to the creation of meaning. If we base our understanding of the world only on what we personally experience in our own brief and limited lives, we render ourselves both impoverished and ineffective.

World history opens a marvelous window into the unfamiliar. It confronts us with the "ways of the world," the whole panorama of human achievement, tragedy, and sensibility. It allows us some modest entry into the lives of people far removed from us in time and place. And it offers us company for the journey of our own lives. Pondering the global past with a receptive heart and an open mind can assist us in enlarging and deepening our sense of self. In exposing us to the wider experience of "all under Heaven," as the Chinese put it, world history can aid us in constructing more meaningful lives. That is among the many gifts that the study of the global past offers to us all.

TEACHING IDEA

Exit Slip

Remind students that this chapter has considered relatively current events. Ask students to imagine that they are in a classroom 100 years from now. Ask them: Will history look back at any of the events discussed in this chapter and consider them less important? More important? *Answers will vary.*

CHAPTER REVIEW

AP Key Terms

population explosion, 800

Green Revolution, 800

global urbanization, 802

megacities, 803

labor migration, 805

influenza pandemic, 809

HIV/AIDS, 809

cultural globalization, 815

religious fundamentalism, 818

Hindutva, 818

Islamic radicalism, 820

Anthropocene era, 823

Holocene era, 823

climate change, 825

second-wave environmentalism, 829

Paris Climate Agreement, 833

Finding the Main Point

1. Why did the rate of global population growth increase so dramatically from 1900 to the present?
2. What factors shaped migration patterns since 1900, and what effects did migrations have on the receiving nations?
3. How have modern societies been united and divided by notions of race, nationalism, religion, and the globalization of culture?
4. What have been the consequences of humanity's interaction with the environment in modern times, and how have societies responded to these consequences?
5. In what ways do historians deal with the question of meaning in human life?

AP Big Picture Questions

1. In what ways has population growth shaped the movement of people and the human impact on the environment?
2. How have cultural patterns evolved over the past century? What broader processes have contributed to those cultural changes?
3. To what extent do the changes described in these last two chapters justify considering the past century a new phase of world history?
4. How have the technological and economic changes explored in the previous chapter shaped the demographic, cultural, and environmental processes discussed in this chapter?
5. **Looking Back** To what extent are the dramatic changes of the world after 1900 rooted in earlier centuries?

TRM Suggested Responses to Questions

You can find suggested responses to the Chapter Review questions in the Teacher's Resource Materials.

Writing a DBQ: Comparative Arguments

In this workshop, we will work with primary sources to develop a source-based comparison argument in preparation for the Document-Based Question on the AP® Exam.

UNDERSTANDING COMPARATIVE ARGUMENTS

Historians create a comparative argument when they want to evaluate how two or more events, civilizations, or processes are similar and different. As mentioned in the Chapter 7 workshop on responding to comparison questions, comparisons are usually best constructed by looking thematically at several cases together while identifying and pointing out similarities and differences, rather than by discussing each case separately one after another.

WRITING A COMPARATIVE ARGUMENT

As you will remember from the Chapter 11 workshop on argumentation, creating an argument (especially one for the AP® Exam) involves several specific moves:

- contextualization in an intro paragraph
- thesis that addresses the prompt using a specific historical reasoning skill
- topic sentences that tie back to the thesis
- evidence that supports the thesis
- analysis/reasoning that shows how or why the evidence supports the thesis

Structuring Your Comparative Argument

You need to make certain decisions as you plan your comparative essay. First, you need to decide, based on the prompt and the evidence, whether you will argue that two or more things are *substantially similar* despite some differences, or whether you will argue that two or more things are *substantially different* despite some similarities. Will you write more of a comparison, or a contrast?

Then, you need to determine your paragraph structure. You have two basic options:

- Option 1 is that you have one paragraph on similarities, and one paragraph on differences.
- Option 2 is having one paragraph comparing and contrasting on a single topic, and the second paragraph comparing and contrasting on a second topic.

As an example, let's say you're comparing the structure of British imperialism and French imperialism. If you take Option 1, you would first discuss similarities of state building in those two empires, and then discuss differences of state building in the next paragraph. Or, if you take Option 2, you might compare political structures in the first paragraph

837

TRM AP® Skills Workshop Activity Handout: Writing a DBQ: Comparative Arguments

BUILDING AP® SKILLS

Making Connections: Comparison

Historians work with comparison frequently. Anytime historians want to evaluate two or more events, societies, or processes, they create a comparative argument. For AP® World History: Modern, students must be able to look at both similarities and differences as a whole, not simply discuss similarities and then differences. You can begin by having students read the section "Writing a Comparative Argument" on pages 837–839 for an overview of what a comparative argument should look like. Often students feel that comparative arguments are easy to write, but they can be deceptively difficult. As comparison can be used in both DBQs and LEQs, it's important for students to understand how to write this type of argument.

If you would like to have students practice writing a comparative argument, consider extending this activity by having students complete one of the three activities found in Building AP® Skills on page 840.

and then growth of cities in the second paragraph. Remember that Option 2 has to be by topic. What you must not do is just talk about the British Empire in the first paragraph and then about the French Empire in the next paragraph, because you are not comparing when you do that.

If you choose Option 1, then your essay would consist of the following:

Intro paragraph with context and thesis
Paragraph 1 on similarities
Paragraph 2 on differences
Conclusion

If you choose Option 2, then it might look like this:

Intro paragraph with context and thesis
Paragraph 1 on political structure, detailing similarities and differences
Paragraph 2 on growth of cities, detailing similarities and differences
Conclusion

A Model of a Comparative Argument

Let's look at an example of a comparative argument from pages 829 and 832, which begins with a single broad similarity between environmentalism in the Global North and South. Then it focuses on differences within the Global North and between the North and South.

Claim focusing on similarities

But what most clearly distinguished second-wave environmentalism was widespread grassroots involvement and activism. By the late 1990s, millions of people in North America, Europe, Japan, Australia, and New Zealand had joined one of the rapidly proliferating environmental organizations, many of them local. The issues addressed in these burgeoning movements were many and various: pollution, resource depletion, toxic waste, protecting wildlife habitats, nuclear power and nuclear testing, limiting development, and increasingly at the top of the agenda in the twenty-first century, climate change. Beyond particular issues, proponents of "deep ecology" argued that human beings should no longer be considered central but understood as occupying a place of equivalence with other species. Those supporting an "environmental justice" outlook were more concerned with the impact of environmental devastation on the poor, minorities, and developing countries. This social justice perspective informed Pope Francis's 2015 environmental encyclical, which commanded global attention, as the world's most prominent Christian leader called for humankind to "care for our common home."

Variations within the Global North

838

Quite quickly, during the 1970s and 1980s, environmentalism also took root in the Global South, where it frequently assumed a distinctive character compared to the more industrialized countries. There it was more locally based, with less connection to global issues or large national organizations than in the West; it involved more poor people in direct action rather than in political lobbying and corporate strategies; it was more concerned with issues of food security, health, and basic survival than with the rights of nature or wilderness protection; and it was more closely connected to movements for social justice. Thus, whereas Western environmentalists defended forests where few people lived, the Chikpo, or "tree-hugging," movement in India sought to protect the livelihood of farmers, artisans, and herders living in areas subject to extensive deforestation. A massive movement to prevent or limit the damming of India's Narmada River derived from the displacement of local people; similar anti-dam protests in the American Northwest were more concerned with protecting salmon runs.

Topic sentence introducing contrast between Global North and South

Evidence of contrasts

In this case, the authors discuss the reactions to environmental issues by comparing the development of movements but contrasting the tactics used to address the issues in different geographic areas. Movements had a common base, even though some, such as the deep ecology movement and the environmental justice movement, focused more on a particular set of issues.

If you were to expand this into an essay on the AP® Exam, you might use comparative language to clearly show what you are trying to do (ex: "similarly"). In addition, you can use contrasting language to clearly identify where you are showing different approaches (ex: "on the other hand").

COMPARATIVE ARGUMENTS ON THE AP® WORLD HISTORY EXAM

With only three reasoning skills to choose from, prompts calling for a comparative argument are extremely common on the AP® World History Exam, both for the Document-Based Question (DBQ) and the Long Essay Question (LEQ). As you will remember from the Chapter 11 workshop on argumentation, the difference between these two essay types is that the DBQ requires you to use primary source documents that are provided for you in order to weave together an argument (along with one outside piece of evidence, if you want to score that extra point), while the LEQ requires you to use the information you have learned in the world history course as evidence. These two essays make up 40 percent of the exam, so knowing how to create a comparative argument is critical.

839

BUILDING AP® SKILLS

1. **Activity: Writing a Strong Comparative Thesis.** Using the information in the section "Moving Abroad: Long-Distance Migration" on pages 804–809 as your evidence, write a thesis statement for the prompt that follows. Remember that a good thesis needs to answer the prompt, be argumentative, provide a road map for the essay, address the historical thinking skill (in this case comparison), and address the counterargument.

   Prompt: Evaluate the extent to which global migration followed similar patterns throughout the nineteenth and twentieth centuries.

2. **Activity: Building a Comparative Argument Paragraph.** Based on the prompt below, create one body paragraph of an essay. You will need to decide whether you want to create a paragraph of similarities or a paragraph of differences, or whether you want to create a paragraph centered on a topic that encompasses both similarities and differences. Use the section "Religion and Global Modernity" on pages 816–822 for your evidence.

   Thesis: Evaluate the extent to which various religious traditions responded similarly to global modernity.

   Contextualizing intro:
   Topic sentence:
   Evidence A:
   Evidence B:
   Evidence C:

3. **Activity: Creating a Comparative Argument.** Based on the prompt below, use AP® Working with Evidence: Contending for Islam (pages 843–849) in this chapter to create a contextualizing intro, a thesis, and two topic sentences for paragraphs. Then, select at least three pieces of evidence and analysis to support each topic sentence.

   Prompt: Evaluate the extent to which there have been differing views on the role of Islam in public life from 1900 to the present.

   Note that you could approach this essay with any of the three historical reasoning skills, but since we are practicing comparison, please focus on creating a comparative argument. Use examples of context statements and thesis statements in this and the earlier workshops to help guide you.

840

The Anthropocene: A Modern Historian's Assessment

No other development of the twentieth century was more important than the emergence of the Anthropocene—or "age of man." Only accelerating after midcentury, the rapid pace of technological change, explosive growth of human numbers, and unprecedented increase in the consumption of natural resources dramatically altered the relationship between humankind and the natural environment. The Anthropocene has already profoundly changed the world we live in, and its impact will likely only increase in the coming decades.

1 A FIRST LOOK

At the turn of the twenty-first century, the prominent environmental historian J. R. McNeill examined the emergence of the Anthropocene over the previous century in his important book *Something New under the Sun: An Environmental History of the Twentieth-Century World*. In the passage from this work reproduced here, McNeill takes a big-picture view by summarizing both the benefits and challenges of the Anthropocene for humankind.

To break down McNeill's wide-ranging argument into more manageable parts, start by identifying the specific changes that he identifies and the forces that facilitated these changes by answering the following questions:

1. According to McNeill, how did the relationship between humankind and the natural environment change during the twentieth century?

2. What developments allowed humans to gain greater control over the natural world than ever before?

J. R. McNEILL | *Something New under the Sun* | 2000

According to the Hebrew Bible, on the fifth day of creation God enjoined humankind to fill and subdue the earth and to have dominion over every living thing. For most of history, our species failed to live up to these . . . injunctions, not for want of trying so much as for want of power. But in the twentieth century the harnessing of fossil fuels, unprecedented population growth, and a myriad of technological changes made it more nearly possible to fulfill these instructions. The prevailing political and economic systems made it seem imprudent not to try: most societies, and all the big ones, sought to maximize their current formidability and wealth at the risk of sacrificing ecological buffers and tomorrow's resilience. The general policy of the twentieth century was to try to make the most of resources, make Nature perform to the utmost, and hope for the best.

With our new powers we banished some historical constraints on health and population, food production, energy use, and consumption generally. Few who know anything about life with these constraints regret their passing. But in banishing them we invited other constraints in the form of the planet's capacity to absorb the wastes, by-products, and impacts of our actions. These latter constraints had pinched occasionally in the past, but only locally. By

841

TRM Suggested Responses to Questions
You can find suggested responses to the AP® Looking Again questions in the Teacher's Resource Materials.

BUILDING AP® SKILLS

Claims and Evidence in Sources

The emergence of the Anthropocene, or "age of man," is one of the most important developments of the twentieth century. You can have students investigate this modern historical development and practice their document analysis skills by having them read "Something New under the Sun" and answering the questions under "A First Look" and "A Second Look" on pages 841 and 842 individually. Once students finish answering those questions, use the questions under "A Third Look" on page 842 to have a class discussion on McNeill's general statements.

the end of the twentieth century they seemed to restrict our options globally. Our negotiations with these constraints will shape the future as our struggles against them shaped our past.

Source: J. R. McNeill, *Something New under the Sun: An Environmental History of the Twentieth-Century World* (New York: W. W. Norton, 2000), 361–62.

2 A SECOND LOOK

In humankind's new relationship with the natural world, McNeill identifies both benefits in the form of older constraints overcome and challenges in the form of new constraints. Read the passage a second time to identify benefits that humankind enjoyed, at least initially, from overcoming long-established constraints imposed by the natural environment. Then answer the following questions:

1. What specific constraints did humankind overcome during the twentieth century?

2. What benefits did humankind derive from increased control over the natural environment?

3. McNeill writes in general terms. Can you provide some specific examples that illustrate his argument?

3 A THIRD LOOK

Finally, read McNeill's passage for a third time with the following questions in mind.

1. What new challenges and constraints did humankind face because of its increased control over the natural environment?

2. What protections offered by nature were degraded or sacrificed while seeking to maximize the wealth and power of human societies?

3. What formerly localized constraints became global problems?

4. Again, can you provide some specific illustrations of McNeill's general statements?

AP ACTIVITY USING SECONDARY SOURCES

Historians frequently draw on the scholarship of other historians to support their own arguments. In this activity you will use McNeill's passage to support this thesis: "During the twentieth century humankind gained greater control over the natural world than ever before, and this control brought with it new problems and limitations for humankind." First create a sourcing statement for J. R. McNeill explaining to your reader why you are citing him and why his conclusions should be taken seriously. Then identify a direct quote from the McNeill passage or summarize in your own words a part of his argument that sustains the thesis.

FURTHER ACTIVITY

When writing about the Anthropocene, historians must describe an ongoing process whose outcomes are unknown and unknowable. In a paragraph or two, reflect on whether a historian should focus only on what has already happened when writing about the Anthropocene, or whether there is merit in also addressing what may happen next, since the Anthropocene has just begun and its most profound impacts likely still lie in future.

842

BUILDING AP® SKILLS

Argumentation

Students should practice their argumentation writing skills frequently throughout the year. You can help students understand the Anthropocene by asking them to complete the "Further Activity" on this page.

Contending for Islam

Over the past century, the growing intrusion of the West and of modern secular culture into the Islamic world has prompted acute and highly visible debate among Muslims. Which ideas and influences flowing from the West could Muslims safely utilize, and which should they decisively reject? The sources that follow illustrate some of these controversies.

LOOKING AHEAD

[AP] DBQ PRACTICE

As you read the sources that follow, pay close attention to the various expressions of Islam, and consider whether they demonstrate a change or continuity in religious practice.

DOCUMENT 1 **A Secular State for an Islamic Society**

Modern Turkey emerged from the ashes of the Ottoman Empire after World War I, adopting a distinctive path under the leadership of Mustafa Kemal Atatürk (see "Religion and Global Modernity" earlier in the chapter). In a speech delivered in 1927, Atatürk explained and justified this path, which went against the grain of much Islamic thinking.

> **Source: Mustafa Kemal Atatürk, *Speech to the General Congress of the Republican Party*, 1927.**
>
> [Our Ottoman rulers] hoped to unite the entire Islamic world in one body, to lead it and to govern it. For this purpose, [they] assumed the title of Caliph [successor to the Prophet Muhammad]. . . . It is an unrealizable aim to attempt to unite in one tribe the various races existing on the earth, thereby abolishing all boundaries. . . .
>
> [The current constitution] laid down as the first duty of the Grand National Assembly that "the prescriptions of the Shari'a [Islamic law] should be put into force. . . ." [But] if a state, having among its subjects elements professing different religions and being compelled to act justly and impartially toward all of them . . . , it is obliged to respect freedom of opinion and conscience. . . . The Muslim religion includes freedom of religious opinion. . . . Will not every grown-up person in the new Turkish state be free to select his own religion? . . . When the first favorable opportunity arises, the nation must act to eliminate these superfluities [the enforcement of sharia] from our Constitution. . . .

Question to Consider: How does the author contrast his own views against those of Islamic rulers before him?

[AP] Analyzing Sources: What historical events took place in Turkey that could lead to the author's reticence to adapt traditional Islamic political structures?

843

BUILDING AP® SKILLS

Claims and Evidence in Sources

Interpreting text-based as well as non-text-based sources is an important skill for AP® World History: Modern students. If time is available, have students complete a further investigation into the challenges Islam is facing in the twenty-first century by using the evidence in "Contending for Islam" beginning on page 843. Consider having students analyze one or more of the sources found on pages 843–849. You can check for student understanding by:

■ Using the questions at the end of each source as a discussion starting point.

■ Pairing students to analyze (identify and describe) the author or creator's point of view, purpose, historical situation, and/or audience. This activity can continue to reinforce sourcing.

■ Assigning a source to a group of three to four students and having them present an overview of the source along with the sourcing to the rest of the class.

■ After students present an overview of the source, have them practice AP® skills using any of the activities under "AP® Doing History" on page 849.

Toward an Islamic Society

Founded in 1928 by impoverished Egyptian schoolteacher Hassan al-Banna (1906–1949), the Muslim Brotherhood argued in favor of "government that will act in conformity to the law and Islamic principles." As the earliest mass movement in the Islamic world advocating such ideas, the Brotherhood soon attracted a substantial following, including many poor urban residents recently arrived from the countryside. In 1936, it published a pamphlet, addressed to Egyptian and other Arab political leaders, that spelled out its views about the direction toward which a proper Islamic society should move.

Source: The Muslim Brotherhood, *Towards the Light*, 1936.

After having studied the ideals which ought to inspire a renascent nation on the spiritual level, we wish to offer, in conclusion, some practical suggestions. . . .

I. In the political, judicial, and administrative fields:
   2nd. To reform the law . . . [to] be entirely in accordance with Islamic legal practice;
   5th. To propagate an Islamic spirit within the civil administration . . .
   6th. To supervise the personal conduct of officials . . .

II. In the fields of social and everyday practical life:
   2nd. To find a solution for the problems of women, a solution that will allow her to progress and which will protect her while conforming to Islamic principles.
   3rd. To root out clandestine or public prostitution and to consider fornication as a reprehensible crime . . .
   5th. To stop the use of alcohol and intoxicants
   10th. To close dance halls; to forbid dancing;
   11th. To censor theater productions and films;
   14th. To confiscate malicious articles and books as well as magazines displaying a grotesque character or spreading frivolity;
   19th. To bring to trial those who break the laws of Islam, who do not fast, who do not pray, and who insult religion;
   24th. . . . Absolute priority to be given to Arabic over foreign languages;

III. The economic field:
   2nd. To prevent the practice of usury [charging interest on loans]
   3rd. To facilitate and to increase the number of economic enterprises and to employ the jobless . . . ,
   7th. To encourage agricultural and industrial works, to improve the situation of the peasants and industrial workers[.]

Hassan al-Banna, "Towards the Light," in Robert Landen, *The Emergence of the Modern Middle East* (New York: Van Nostrand Reinhold, 1970), 261–64.

Question to Consider: How do the views of this source contrast with the views in Document 1?

AP Analyzing Sources: Consider the audience of this document. Why might members of the urban poor find the message of the Muslim Brotherhood appealing?

DOCUMENT 3 **The Ideas of the Ayatollah Khomeini**

While the Muslim Brotherhood was never able to seize control of the state in Egypt, an Islamic revolution in Iran brought to power in 1979 a government committed to similar ideas about the role of Islam in public life. That revolution had been inspired and led by the Ayatollah Khomeini (1902–1989), an Iranian religious scholar, who outlines here his argument about the role of Islam in the social and political life of Iran.

Source: Ayatollah Khomeini, *Sayings of the Ayatollah Khomeini*, 1980.

What do you understand of the harmony between social life and religious principles? And more important, just what is the social life we are talking about? Is it those hotbeds of immorality called theaters, cinemas, dancing, and music? Is it the promiscuous presence in the streets of lusting young men and women with arms, chests, and thighs bared? Is it the ludicrous wearing of a hat like the Europeans or the imitation of their habit of wine drinking? We are convinced that you have been made to lose your ability to distinguish between good and evil, in exchange for a few radio sets and ludicrous Western hats. Your attention has been attracted to the disrobed women to be seen on thoroughfares and in swimming pools. Let these shameful practices come to an end, so that the dawn of a new life may break!

We [clergy] forcefully affirm that refusal to wear the veil is against the law of Allah and the Prophet, and a material and moral affront to the entire country. We affirm that the ludicrous use of the Western hat stands in the way of our independence and is contrary to the will of Allah. We affirm that coeducational schools are an obstacle to a wholesome life; they are a material and moral affront to the country and contrary to the divine will. We affirm that music engenders immorality, lust, and licentiousness, and stifles courage, valor, and the chivalrous spirit; it is forbidden by Qur'anic law and must not be taught in the schools. Radio Tehran, by broadcasting Western, Oriental, and Iranian music, plays a nefarious role by introducing immorality and licentiousness into respectable families.

Question to Consider: What arguments does Khomeini make about the role of Islam in modern society?

AP Analyzing Sources: Why might Khomeini be so adamantly opposed to Western influence, especially by 1980?

845

Islamic Feminism

For a few women, exposure to Western gender norms and liberal thought has occasioned the abandonment of Islam altogether. Far more common have been efforts to root gender equality in both personal and public life within the traditions of Islam. Such was the argument of Benazir Bhutto, several times the prime minister of Pakistan, in a speech delivered to a United Nations conference on women in 1995.

Source: Benazir Bhutto, *Politics and the Muslim Woman*, 1995.

I stand before you not only as a Prime Minister but as a woman and a mother proud of her cultural and religious heritage. . . . Muslim women have a special responsibility to help distinguish between Islamic teachings and social taboos spun by the traditions of a patriarchal society. . . .

[W]e must remember that Islam forbids injustice; injustice against people, against nations, against women. It shuns race, colour, and gender as a basis of distinction amongst fellow men. It enshrines piety as the sole criteria for judging humankind. It treats women as human beings in their own right, not as chattels. A woman can inherit, divorce, receive alimony and child custody. Women were intellectuals, poets, jurists and even took part in war. . . . Prophet Muhammad (peace be upon him) emphatically condemned and put an end to the practice of female infanticide in pre-Islamic Arabia. . . .

How tragic it is that the pre-Islamic practice of female infanticide still haunts a world we regard as modern and civilized. . . . Statistics show that men now increasingly outnumber women in more than 15 Asian nations. . . . Boys are wanted to satisfy the ego: they carry on the father's name in this world. Yet too often we forget that for Muslims on the Day of Judgement, each person will be called not by their father's name but by the mother's name. . . . The rights Islam gave Muslim women have too often been denied.

United Nations, Fourth World Conference on Women, September 4, 1995, http://www.un.org/esa/gopher-data/conf/fwcw/conf/gov/950904202603.txt, made available by the United Nations.

Question to Consider: In what ways does the author rely on Islamic history to make her arguments about the role of Islam in modern society?

AP **Analyzing Sources:** Why do you think the author relied on Islamic history to make her arguments about modern society?

Progressive Islam

All across the Islamic world, many Muslims sought to balance their distinctive religious sensibility with democracy, women's rights, technological progress, freedom of thought, and religious pluralism. One viewpoint was expressed in a pamphlet composed in 2009 by a leading American Muslim scholar, translator, and teacher, Kabir Helminski. He was listed then as one of the 500 most influential Muslims in the world.

Source: Kabir Helminski, *Islam and Human Values*, 2009.

If the word "Islam" gives rise to fear or mistrust today, it is urgent that American Muslims clarify what we believe Islam stands for in order to dispel the idea that there is a fundamental conflict between the best values of Western civilization and the essential values of Islam. . . .

[One issue] is the problem of violence. . . . Thousands of Muslim institutions and leaders, the great majority of the world's billion or more Muslims, have unequivocally condemned the hateful and violent ideologies that kill innocents and violate the dignity of all humanity. . . .

Islamic civilizations have a long history of encouraging religious tolerance and guaranteeing the rights of religious minorities. . . .

Jerusalem, under almost continuous Islamic rule for nearly fourteen centuries, has been a place where Christians and Jews have lived side by side with Muslims, their holy sites and religious freedom preserved. Medieval Spain also created a high level of civilization as a multi-cultural society under Islamic rule for several centuries. . . . It was the Ottoman sultan who gave sanctuary to the Jews expelled from Catholic Spain. India was governed for centuries by Muslims, even while the majority of its people practiced Hinduism. . . .

Islam is not an alien religion. It does not claim a monopoly on virtue or truth. . . . It continues on the Way of the great Prophets and Messengers of all sacred traditions.

Selections from Kabir Helminski, *Islam and Human Values*, unpublished pamphlet, 2009.

Question to Consider: What is Helminski's argument about the compatibility of Islam and modern life?

AP® Analyzing Sources: What does this text suggest about its intended audience?

DOCUMENT 6 Debating the Burqa

When the French government in 2011 began to enforce a law forbidding the concealment of the face in public, it was widely understood to be a prohibition of the burqa, the head-to-toe covering worn by some Muslim women. To many French people, the burqa represented a security risk and violated the secularism of French life, while banning it prevented women from being forced by their families to wear it. But the new law prompted considerable protest in many places. One such protester outside Notre Dame Cathedral in Paris said: "We view this ban as an assault on our human rights."[34] Document 6 shows a group of Muslim women in Britain, clad in black burqas, protesting the law outside the French embassy in London.

847

Source: *Protests in London against French Ban of Face Concealment, 2011.*

Question to Consider: How does this image demonstrate the conflict between Islamic ideas of freedom and Western ideas of freedom?

AP **Analyzing Sources:** How does the protestors' purpose influence the language on their posters?

DOCUMENT 7 **The Sufi Alternative**

Sufis represent the more spiritual or mystical dimension of Islam. While most Sufis participate in conventional Islamic practices, they are generally more sharply focused on interior spiritual experience than on the precise prescriptions of the law. Thus they have resisted the legalistic prescriptions of Islamic radicals. India's prime minister Narendra Modi delivered an important message to the Sufi World Forum in Delhi in 2016. That it came from a prominent Hindu figure in India made the message all the more striking, given the historical tension between Muslims and Hindus.

Source: Narendra Modi, *Sufism and Islamic Radicalism*, 2016.

At a time when the dark shadow of violence is becoming longer, you [Sufis] are the noor, or the light of hope. . . . And, you represent the rich diversity of the Islamic civilization that stands on the solid bedrock of a great religion. . . . It is a civilization that reached great heights by the 15th century in science, medicine, literature, art, architecture and commerce. . . . And, this is the message of Sufism, one of the greatest contributions of Islam to this world. . . .

For the Sufis, therefore, service to God meant service to humanity. . . . And, its humanism also upheld the place and status of women in society. Above all, Sufism is a celebration of diversity and pluralism. . . . Sufism is the voice of peace, co-existence, compassion and equality; a call to universal brotherhood.

Indeed, when terrorism and extremism have become the most destructive force of our times, the message of Sufism has global relevance. . . . Every year, we spend over 100 billion dollars on securing the world from terrorism, money that should have been spent on building lives of the poor. . . . [W]e must reject any link between terrorism and religion. Those who spread terror in the name of religion are anti-religious. . . . And, we must advance the message of Sufism that stands for the principles of Islam and the highest human values.

Question to Consider: In what ways does Modi's argument represent a criticism of Islamic fundamentalism?

AP Analyzing Sources: How does the religious and ethnic identity of the author impact the way an audience member might listen to this speech?

AP DOING HISTORY

1. **DBQ Practice:** Evaluate the extent to which characteristics of modern society impacted the beliefs and practices of Islam after 1900.

TRM Chapter 14 DBQ Activity Handout

2. **Contextualization:** In the period leading up to the twentieth century, what changes occurred in world history that created a global shift in power, leading to the rise of Western states and the decline of Islamic states?

3. **Outside Evidence:** Recall Chapter 1. What key components of Islam do you remember that could improve one of your arguments?

4. **Complex Argumentation:** How can you incorporate comparisons or causation relationships into your argument?

849

Perspectives on the Iranian Revolution

The Iranian revolution of 1979 gave rise to a religiously inspired government that has sought to inscribe Islamist principles in the political, economic, and social fabric of a major Middle Eastern nation. In Voice 14.1, Francis Robinson, a prominent British historian of the Islamic world, describes the modern Islamic renewal movements that provide the larger context for the Iranian revolution. Then in Voice 14.2, John Esposito, a highly regarded American scholar of modern Islam, reflects on the specific conditions that gave rise to the Iranian revolution.

of Islam as a system, an ideology is new in Islamic history. So too . . . is the complete merger between religion and political power.

Islamist movements . . . have brought Islam closer to the centre of political identity of Muslim peoples. In some places, such as Iran . . . , they have taken power.

Source: Francis Robinson, *The Cambridge Illustrated History of the Islamic World* (Cambridge: Cambridge University Press, 1996), 292, 293, 296.

VOICE 14.1

Francis Robinson on Islamic Renewal Movements | 1996

A powerful movement of religious renewal has animated all parts of the Muslim world since the eighteenth century. . . .

Since the 1970s the desire to effect renewal has been more powerfully expressed in the Islamist movements. Often led by western-educated professionals and run by university students, these movements have aimed to fill the vacuum created by the failures of the state at the local level in cities and towns through much of the Islamic world. By providing schools, clinics, welfare, and psychological support, they have served the needs of urban communities disrupted by the penetration of the modern state and the international economy. They have also attracted the millions who have flocked to the cities in recent decades from the countryside. The rhetoric of these movements is profoundly opposed to western culture and western power. Their programmes, which start from the premise that the Quran and the holy law are sufficient for all human circumstances, aim to establish an Islamic system to match those of capitalism or socialism. They are to be implemented by seizing power in the modern nation state. This understanding

VOICE 14.2

John Esposito on the Source of the Iranian Revolution | 1999

Iran [in 1979] captured the imagination of many throughout the Muslim world and the West. . . . A seemingly modern, enlightened and invincible shah was overthrown by a movement led by an ayatollah [a high-ranking religious scholar] in exile in France. Intellectuals, merchants, students, and journalists as well as clergy mobilized under the banner of Islam. Islam was . . . also a symbol of protest for all who opposed the shah. . . . Islamic symbols, rhetoric, and institutions provided the infrastructure for organization, protest, and mobilization of a coalition of forces calling for reform and in the end for revolution. . . .

Although the shah's modernization program did improve the lot of many, the benefits of modernization tended to favor disproportionately a minority of elites and urban centers. Economic, educational and military reforms were not accompanied by political liberalization. Traditional merchants and religious leaders . . . were alienated by the shah's religious and economic reforms. State control of religious affairs . . . and a tilt toward western markets and the corporate sector threatened their interests, authority, and power. Many modern educated academics, professionals, and

---

You can use this exercise to help students work on improving skills with secondary sources. This activity can help students practice reading and interpreting secondary sources found on the MCQ and SAQ sections of the AP® Exam. Consider having students read both of the sources found on pages 850–851 and answer Questions 1–3 on page 851. When students have finished, discuss their answers as a class.

Differentiation

If students have been struggling with analyzing and interpreting secondary sources, consider following the "Must Do, Should Do, Strive For" model below:

■ **Must Do:** Divide the class into two groups. Assign one group Voice 14.1 and the other group Voice 14.2 to read and summarize the main ideas of the passage.

■ **Should Do:** Pair the students up based on what they read; each pairing should have one student who read Voice 14.1 and one who read Voice 14.2. Students should share their summaries of the passage they read with their partner and then work together to answer Questions 1 and 2 on page 851.

■ **Strive For:** For students who seem comfortable working with primary and secondary sources and want a writing challenge, ask them to write a 1- to 2-paragraph response to Question 3 on page 851.

journalists increasingly expressed concerns over the excessive dependence of Iran on the West. . . . Some . . . spoke of the dangers of "Westoxification," an excessive dependence on the West that threatened to rob Iranians of their independence and cultural identity. These were issues that resonated across many sectors of society.

Source: John Esposito, *The Oxford History of Islam* (Oxford: Oxford University Press, 1999), 661–62.

AP® Analyzing Secondary Sources

1. How does Francis Robinson in Voice 14.1 explain the appeal of Islamist renewal movements since the 1970s?

2. According to John Esposito in Voice 14.2, what conditions within Iran provided the raw material for revolution?

3. **Integrating Primary and Secondary Sources:** How might both of these authors use the primary sources to illustrate or support their arguments?

TRM Suggested Responses to Questions
You can find suggested responses to the AP® Analyzing Secondary Sources questions in the Teacher's Resource Materials.

851

TEACHING IDEA

AP® Exam Strategies

You should continue to give students opportunities to practice test-taking skills. You can project or copy the stimulus-based multiple-choice questions found on pages 852 to 854. Give students the question as a practice quiz prior to the unit or chapter test. Have students discuss why their answer choice was correct or incorrect. Another way to use the multiple-choice questions is to use them to gauge student learning of a topic after initial teaching.

CHAPTER 14 AP® EXAM PRACTICE

Multiple-Choice Questions Choose the correct answer for each question.

Questions 1–3 refer to this table.

	GROSS NATIONAL INCOME PER CAPITA (SAMPLE COUNTRIES)			
	Low Income (Congo, Kenya, Ethiopia)	Lower-Middle Income (India, China, Egypt)	Upper-Middle Income (Mexico, Brazil, Russia)	Upper Income (USA, Japan, South Korea)
Life expectancy: Male/Female in years	58/60	66/70	68/75	77/83
Deaths under age 5 per 1,000 live births	120	60	24	7
Deaths from infectious disease: %	36	14	11	7
Years of education	7.9	10.3	13.8	14.5
Literacy rate: %	66	80	93	99
Population growth: % annual	2.27	1.27	.96	.39
Urban population: %	27	41	74	78
Cell phones per 100 people	22	47	92	106
Carbon dioxide emissions: metric tons per capita	1	3	5	13

1. Based on your knowledge of world history and the chart, what conclusion can you make about carbon dioxide emissions in the early twenty-first century?
   a. The per capita income of a region has no effect on the amount of its carbon dioxide emissions.
   b. Carbon dioxide emissions have grown exponentially around the globe, leading to calls for all nations to cut back on their emissions.
   c. The higher the per capita income of a region, the higher the level of carbon dioxide emissions in that region.
   d. The Kyoto Protocol focuses on lowering carbon dioxide levels among developing nations.

2. Which of the following conclusions about population growth is supported by the information in the table?
   a. Even though birth control is more available, populations all over the world have continued to increase.
   b. In areas where birth control is more accessible, population growth has slowed.
   c. Deaths due to infectious disease have increased with the increase in years of education in a given region.
   d. Infant mortality rates have decreased in certain regions, while deaths due to infectious diseases in those regions have increased.

852

3. Based on your knowledge of world history and the chart, which of the following best explains an increase in life expectancy in countries with higher incomes?

a. New dietary restrictions and guidelines

b. New labor laws creating safer workplaces

c. New building codes requiring air conditioning in all new construction

d. New medical discoveries such as x-rays and vaccines

Questions 4–6 refer to these images.

A McDonald's restaurant in Moscow, Russia, 2010.

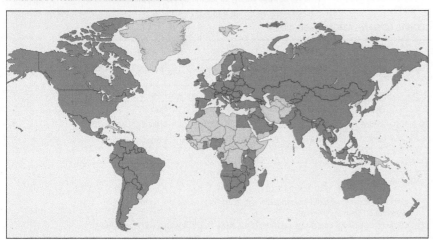

Countries with Kentucky Fried Chicken Restaurants, 2019.

853

AP® CLASSROOM

AP® Personal Progress Check

For extra practice with multiple-choice questions, consider assigning the Unit 9 Personal Progress Check to students. This can act as a wrap-up to Chapter 14 and Unit 9, as well as help students practice their test-taking skills. You can find the questions in your AP® Classroom account under the Progress Checks for Unit 9.

4. Which of the following was most important for accelerating the economic changes depicted in these images?

a. The end of the cold war in the later part of the twentieth century

b. The increase in global food supply due to the Green Revolution

c. The increase of governments' roles in planning national economies and global commerce

d. New modes of communication and transportation technologies that have led to a universalization of culture

5. The corporations represented in the images best represent which of the following economic ideologies?

a. Utilitarianism and Malthusian theory

b. Communism and collectivization

c. Capitalism and free market economies

d. Socialism and militarized Keynesianism

6. While the images represent the influence of Western cultures in the world, which of the following best demonstrates the spread of culture from the Global South to the Global North?

a. The global popularity of Hollywood movies

b. The global participation in World Cup soccer

c. The spread of Daoism around the world

d. The practice of yoga around the world

Short-Answer Questions
Read each question carefully and write a short response. Use complete sentences.

1. **Use this table and your knowledge of world history to answer all parts of the question that follows.**

GLOBAL URBANIZATION, 1950–2014

Rank	1950			2014		
	City	Country	Population in Millions	City	Country	Population in Millions
1	New York City	USA	12.3	Tokyo	Japan	37.8
2	Tokyo	Japan	11.3	Delhi	India	24.9
3	London	UK	8.4	Shanghai	China	23.0
4	Paris	France	6.5	Mexico City	Mexico	20.84
5	Moscow	USSR	5.6	São Paulo	Brazil	20.83

From 1950 to 2014, the percentage of the world's population that lived in urban areas changed from 29.6 percent to 54 percent.

A. Identify ONE development between 1950 and 2014 that caused the trends in global urbanization seen in this chart.

B. Explain ONE environmental consequence of the demographic trends seen in this chart.

C. Explain ONE limitation this chart would have for scholars researching urbanization patterns in contemporary nations today.

854

BUILDING AP® SKILLS

Argumentation

AP® World History: Modern writing skills need to be practiced on a regular basis. You can use the SAQs on pages 854 and 855 for students to write an "exit ticket" at the end of class to check for understanding. You can also use the SAQs for more traditional timed writing practice, either by spreading the three SAQs across several days or as practice for the AP® Exam by writing them all at once. Make certain that students have the correct amount of time for this exercise. On exam day, students will have a total of 40 minutes to write three SAQs. If you are having them write only one at a time, you should give them about 14 minutes to write it.

Differentiation

If you want to challenge students with writing an SAQ and developing evidence, consider following the "Must Do, Should Do, Strive For" model below for Question 3 on page 855. Students will need to work with a partner for this activity.

▪ Must Do: On their own, students must write a topic sentence that states a clear argument answering Part A of Question 3.

▪ Should Do: Students should switch their response with their partner and write evidence and analysis for the topic sentence their partner created.

▪ Strive For: Students should repeat the process for Parts B and C of Question 3 with their partner. After they finish, they should discuss the SAQ answers they created together.

2. **Use this passage and your knowledge of world history to answer all parts of the question that follows.**

> The rise of America, and the globalization of war, politics, trade, and communications during the twentieth century, are mirrored by the rise of Coca-Cola, the world's most valuable and widely recognized brand, which is universally regarded as the embodiment of America and its values. For those who approve of the United States, that means economic and political freedom of choice, consumerism and democracy, the American dream; for those who disapprove, it stands for ruthless global capitalism, the hegemony of global corporations and brands, and the dilution of local cultures and values into homogenized and Americanized mediocrity.
>
> — Tom Standage, *A History of the World in 6 Glasses*, 2005

A. Identify ONE historical example of an American brand other than the one mentioned in the passage that would support Standage's argument.

B. Explain ONE historical example of a group or movement that would support Standage's argument regarding the disapproval of the United States' influence.

C. Explain ONE development in the first half of the twentieth century that likely shaped Standage's view of the United States' place in globalization.

3. **Use your knowledge of world history to answer all parts of the question that follows.**

A. Explain ONE way in which new technological innovations contributed to globalization in the twentieth century.

B. Explain ONE way in which the global economy changed because of globalization in the twentieth century.

C. Explain ONE way in which culture changed because of globalization in the twentieth century.

855

Document-Based Question Using these documents and your knowledge of world history, develop an argument in response to the prompt.

1. **Evaluate the extent to which new ideologies affected the growth of independence movements in the twentieth century.**

Document 1

Source: Photo of Mahatma Gandhi on the Salt March, 1930. Gandhi and his followers marched to the ocean to produce salt from the water as a nonviolent protest of the salt tax imposed by the British authorities.

Bettmann/Getty Images

Document 2

Source: Ho Chi Minh, leader of the Vietnamese independence movement and of the Vietnamese Communist Party, "Declaration of Independence of the Democratic Republic of Vietnam," September 2, 1945.

"All men are created equal. They are endowed by their Creator with certain inalienable rights, among them are Life, Liberty, and the pursuit of Happiness."

In a broader sense, this means: All the peoples on the earth are equal from birth, all the peoples have a right to live, to be happy and free.

The Declaration of the French Revolution made in 1791 on the Rights of Man and the Citizen also states: "All men are born free and with equal rights, and must always remain free and have equal rights."...

Nevertheless, for more than eighty years, the French imperialists, abusing the standard of Liberty, Equality, and Fraternity, have violated our Fatherland and oppressed our fellow-citizens. They have acted contrary to the ideals of humanity and justice.

... [W]e, members of the Provisional Government, representing the whole Vietnamese people, declare that from now on we break off all relations of a colonial character with France; we repeal all the international obligations that France has so far subscribed to on behalf of Vietnam and we abolish all the special rights the French have unlawfully acquired in our Fatherland.

Document 3

Source: A group of Algerian women who were involved in the Algerian independence movement, statement to a mostly male nationalist gathering at the Casablanca Labour Exchange, 1958.

You make a revolution, you fight colonialist oppression but you maintain the oppression of women; beware, another revolution will certainly occur after Algeria's independence: a women's revolution!

Document 4

Source: "Declaration on the Granting of Independence to Colonial Countries and Peoples," adopted by the United Nations, December 14, 1960.

Convinced that all peoples have an inalienable right to complete freedom, the exercise of their sovereignty and the integrity of their national territory,

[The United Nations] ... proclaims the necessity of bringing a speedy and unconditional end to colonialism in all its forms and manifestations;

And to this end Declares that:

1. The subjection of peoples to alien subjugation, domination and exploitation constitutes a denial of fundamental human rights....

2. All peoples have the right to self-determination; by virtue of that right they freely determine their political status and freely pursue their economic, social and cultural development.

Document 5

Source: Egyptian president Gamal Abdel Nasser, *Charter of National Action*, 1962.

[E]very individual shall have a chance and an opportunity. This is what I mean when I talk about dissolving class barriers.... Instead, there shall be equality and freedom for each individual in this nation.... I want a society in which class distinctions are dissolved through equality of opportunities to all citizens. I want a society in which the free individual can determine his own position by himself, on the basis of his efficiency, capacity and character.

Document 6

Source: Kwame Nkrumah, president of Ghana, speech to the inaugural meeting of the Organization of African Unity, attended by many leaders of newly independent African nations, 1963.

Our people supported us in our fight for independence because they believed that African Governments could cure the ills of the past in a way which could never be accomplished under colonial rule. If, therefore, now that we are independent we allow the same conditions to exist that existed in colonial days, all the resentment which overthrew colonialism will be mobilised against us.

The resources are there. . . . Unless we establish African Unity now, we who are sitting here today shall tomorrow be the victims and martyrs of neo-colonialism.

Document 7

Source: Julius Nyerere, president of Tanzania, speech to the Sixth Pan-African Congress, June 1974.

The Pan-African movement was born as a reaction to racialism. And racialism still exists. . . . In large areas of Africa it is now proclaimed as a state philosophy, and imposed ruthlessly on the black majority of the population. The evil which required the birth of the Pan-African movement has not yet made meetings like this irrelevant.

Let us make it quite clear. We oppose racial thinking. But as long as black people anywhere continue to be oppressed on the grounds of their color, black people everywhere will stand together in opposition to that oppression.

Long Essay Questions

Using your knowledge of world history, develop an argument in response to one of the following questions.

2. Rapid progress in science and technology has revolutionized our understanding of the universe and led to significant changes in industry, agriculture, and social life.

   Develop an argument in which you evaluate the extent to which developments in science and technology have led to changes in social life from 1900 to the present.

3. Challenges to existing states and social structures have arisen in various parts of the world.

   Develop an argument in which you evaluate the extent to which patterns of social protest have been continuous from 1900 to the present.

4. The role of states in national economic systems and in global economic development intensified in the twentieth century.

   Develop an argument in which you evaluate the extent to which the role of the state in economic development has changed since 1900.

BUILDING AP® SKILLS

Argumentation

The Long Essay Question (LEQ) is an important part of the AP® World History: Modern Exam. The LEQ is 15 percent of the overall score on the exam. Students will pick one of three prompts. Consider giving students all three prompts and allowing them to choose the prompt they wish to write. This will mimic the exam layout to give them practice. Students should have 40 minutes to write the LEQ.

Differentiation

If you want to differentiate this activity, follow the "Must Do, Should Do, Strive For" model below.

■ Must Do: Students write a contextualization and a thesis for the prompt.

■ Should Do: Students write two arguments (claims) for the prompt with three pieces of evidence to defend their arguments.

■ Strive For: Students write a full-length LEQ in 40 minutes.

Multiple-Choice Questions

Questions 1–2 refer to this map.

The Early Phase of Europe's Industrial Revolution

1. Based on the map and your knowledge of world history, which of the following best represents an environmental cause of industrialization in the era beginning ca. 1750?

   a. Europe's lack of significant ports and increased pollution

   b. Europe's location on major water routes and the geographical distribution of coal and iron

   c. An abundance of railroads and soaring population increases

   d. Government-sponsored programs to protect the environment

2. Which of the following statements best explains how new technologies were used to transport large amounts of raw materials to industrial centers in the first half of the nineteenth century?

a. Horse-drawn wagons were still being used because they were in abundant supply.

b. New canals were dug to take advantage of steamships.

c. Railroads were used because they were quicker and could carry more than traditional methods could.

d. Even though most roads were not paved, automobiles and trucks were used because they were the newest technology.

Questions 3–4 are based on this map.

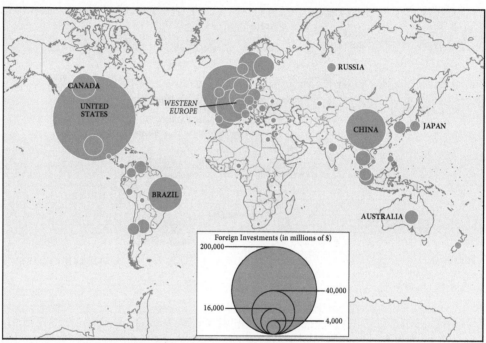

Globalization in Action: Countries Receiving Foreign Investment in the Late Twentieth Century

3. The map above is best understood in the context of

a. the global rise in tariffs on imports after the financial crisis of 2008.

b. the rise of transnational businesses after World War II.

c. the increase in global migration into cities.

d. the rapid increase in global population during the twentieth century.

4. Late twentieth- and early twenty-first-century opposition to trends such as those seen in the map above included

a. anticommunist resistance movements in Eastern and Central Europe.

b. anti–nuclear proliferation protests in Western Europe.

c. prodemocracy protests in China in 1989.

d. protests against regional trade agreements and multinational corporations.

Questions 5–6 refer to this passage.

There shall be for the Union of South Africa a department, to be known as the department of Public Health, which shall be under the control of a Minister and in respect of which there shall be a portfolio of Public Health. The functions of the department of Public Health shall . . . be to prevent, or safeguard against, the introduction of infectious disease into the Union from outside, to promote the public health and the prevention, limitation or suppression of . . . diseases within the Union, to advise and assist provincial administrations and local authorities in regard to matters affecting the public health; to promote or carry out researches and investigations in connection with . . . human diseases.

—The Union of South Africa, *Bill to Make Provision for the Public Health,* January 6, 1919

5. A historian researching the role of governments in the twentieth century would most likely find the excerpt above most useful in understanding how governments responded to

    a. public health crises.   c. economic depressions.

    b. worker rights protests.   d. increasing pollution.

6. The excerpt above is most clearly an example of which of the following?

    a. A global response to a local crisis   c. A local response to World War I

    b. A global response to World War I   d. A local response to a global crisis

Questions 7–8 refer to this map.

The Russian Empire

7. Which of the following statements about the era ca. 1450–1750 can be supported by the map?

a. Land-based empires, such as the Russian Empire, were able to expand more extensively than maritime empires in this era.

b. Control of land-based trade routes was a major motivation for the expansion of empires in this era.

c. The expansion of the Russian Empire in this era accelerated as the Russian military adopted firearms.

d. After rapid expansion to the east, the Russian Empire experienced westward expansion at the end of this era.

8. Which of the following was a major difference between the rise of the Russian Empire, pictured in the map, and that of imperial China in this time period?

a. Unlike the Russian Empire, the Chinese empire was sometimes ruled by ethnic minorities who originated outside the civilization's center.

b. The Russian Empire was strictly a land-based empire, while the Chinese empire incorporated vast maritime conquests.

c. Native peoples in both regions quickly surrendered to the invaders, but the Chinese were more determined to force the assimilation of conquered people into their culture.

d. The Chinese empire limited government positions to ethnic Chinese, while the Russians were more tolerant of non-Russians in their bureaucracy.

Question 9–11 refer to this table.

WORLD POPULATION ESTIMATES, ca. 1200 c.e.–ca. 2000 c.e.

(Population in Millions and as a Percentage of World Total)

Year	Eurasia	Africa	North America	South America	Australia/ Oceania	Total World
ca. 1200	352.41 (79.2%)	45.29 (10.2%)	22.96 (5.2%)	22.72 (5.1%)	1.37 (0.3%)	444.75
ca. 1600	435.63 (84.5%)	68.17 (13.2%)	3.81 (0.7%)	6.38 (1.2%)	1.76 (0.3%)	515.75
ca. 2000	4,466.50 (72.7%)	810.98 (13.2%)	486.12 (7.9%)	348.41 (5.7%)	31.43 (0.5%)	6,140

Data from https://ourworldindata.org/grapher/population?time=1200..latest.

9. Which region experienced the largest gain as a percentage of world population between ca. 1200 and ca. 2000?

a. Eurasia

b. Africa

c. North America

d. South America

10. In which region and era can the demographic effects of disease pathogens most clearly be seen in the data?

a. Eurasia between 1200 and 1600

b. Eurasia between 1600 and 2000

c. South America between 1200 and 1600

d. North America between 1600 and 2000

11. Which of the following factors best explains the transformation of North America's population between ca. 1600 and ca. 2000 as seen in the chart?

    a. Decolonization and the rise of global trade networks

    b. European colonization and major labor migrations

    c. The fall of the Soviet Union and the spread of capitalist practices

    d. The mercantilist practices of maritime empires from the sixteenth to the eighteenth centuries

Questions 12–15 refer to these two images.

This woodprint shows Commodore Perry's gift of a small-scale train to the Japanese in 1853.

Japanese women in a factory spinning silk threads from raw cocoons, ca. 1900.

12. According to the second picture and your knowledge of world history, what was a similarity in the industrial societies of Britain and Japan in the nineteenth century?

a. The power of landowning elites increased.

b. Large segments of society were drawn into the labor pool.

c. Middle-class women in both societies made gains in their status and social positions.

d. Economic opportunities for women increased after they were granted suffrage.

13. The two pictures could best be used to describe which of the following changes made to Japanese society as a result of U.S. and European influence?

a. All Japanese citizens quickly embraced Western technology and culture.

b. While most Japanese embraced Western technology, they rejected Western culture, such as literature and fashion.

c. The majority of the elite in Japanese society rapidly embraced Western culture, such as literature and fashion.

d. Japan largely rejected Western culture in an attempt to protect its traditional beliefs.

14. Which of these comparisons between nineteenth-century Japan and Qing China most accurately describes their reactions to influences from the West?

a. Both Qing China and Japan successfully adopted widespread changes based on Western technology in an attempt to regain control of East Asian trade.

b. Qing China's attempts at modernization were largely unsuccessful, while Japan's attempts resulted in it becoming a political and economic power by 1900.

c. Japan's modernization efforts focused solely on political reform, while Qing China focused solely on economic reform.

d. Both Qing China and Japan vehemently rejected westernization, modernization, and industrialization.

15. What best explains of the purpose of the second photograph?

a. To highlight the higher status of women in Japan compared to those in Western Europe and the United States

b. To challenge China by showing Japan's ability to produce luxury goods

c. To justify the increased roles of women in Japan's political system

d. To showcase Japan's industrial efficiency after significant government reforms

Questions 16–18 refer to this passage.

> The central division within Mughal India was religious. . . . Emperor Akbar . . . acted deliberately to accommodate the Hindu majority. . . . Akbar married several Hindu princesses but did not require them to convert to Islam. . . . He built Hindu temples as well as Muslim mosques and palaces. But Akbar softened some Hindu restrictions on women, discouraged child marriages and *sati* (the practice in which a widow followed her husband to death by throwing herself on his funeral pyre), and persuaded merchants to set aside special market days for women. In other religious matters, Akbar imposed a policy of toleration, removing the special tax (*jizya*) on non–Muslims.
>
> — Robert W. Strayer and Eric W. Nelson, *Ways of the World*

16. The excerpt reveals which of the following about Akbar's policies?

    a. He sought to impose a strict Islamic state in Mughal India.

    b. Like other major religions, Islam adapted to local cultural conditions.

    c. Akbar was deeply uninformed about Hindu tenets.

    d. Akbar did not consider Hindus to be "people of the book."

17. Akbar's policies toward the cultures of his subjects were most similar to the policies of which of the following?

    a. Iran after the late twentieth-century revolution

    b. The Aztecs before the arrival of Europeans

    c. The Ottoman Empire

    d. The Spanish after the *reconquista*

18. Based on the passage above and your knowledge of world history, what was a major political similarity between the Mughal and Qing empires?

    a. Both adopted Islam as an official state belief system to legitimize their rule.

    b. Both empires were ruled by ethnic minorities.

    c. Both of them exploited cultural differences to centralize their power.

    d. Both gave significant rights to women.

Questions 19–21 refer to these two images.

Stefan R. Landsberger Collections/International Institute of Social History, Amsterdam/www.chineseposters.net

Chinese poster, 1960. The text reads, "Start the Movement to increase production and practice thrift, with foodstuffs and steel at the center, with great force!"

Zhejiang People's Art Publishing House/Stefan R. Landsberger Collections/ International Institute of Social History, Amsterdam/www.chineseposters.net

Chinese poster, 1993. The text reads: "The gods of wealth enter the home from everywhere."

19. What aspect of Chinese socialism is reflected in the first poster?

    a. A gradual approach to building socialism

    b. Promotion of gender equality

    c. Dependence on foreign investment and credit

    d. Chinese communism as a response to the economic devastation of the First World War

20. What global pattern of communism in the late twentieth century is best represented in the second poster?

    a. A worldwide trend toward communist states continued to expand.

    b. Most communist economies sought to isolate themselves from global trading.

    c. Communism failed and was abandoned in all nations.

    d. Many communist countries began to turn toward more capitalist economic policies.

21. What is the best explanation for the Chinese government's production of the second poster above?

    a. To justify China's economic isolationism with the rest of the world

    b. To celebrate the completion of the Great Leap Forward

    c. To promote a Chinese alliance with the United States

    d. To herald the success of communist practices in China

Questions 22–23 refer to this map.

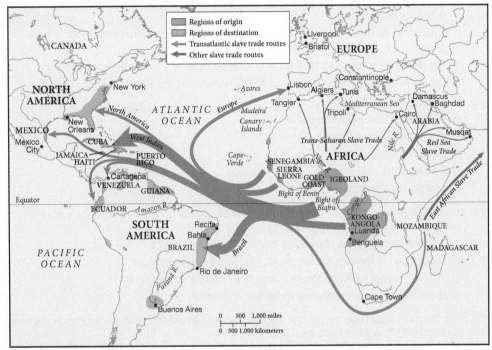

The Transatlantic Slave System

22. Which of the following was an effect in South America and the Caribbean of the historical process shown in the map?

   a. The creation of a social hierarchy called the *casta* system

   b. Constant warfare between newly arrived Africans and Native Americans

   c. A sudden rise in the social status of enslaved Africans within Latin American culture

   d. A new wave of epidemics brought in from Africa that killed Native Americans and Europeans in roughly equal numbers

23. Which of the following was an effect in West Africa of the historical process shown in the map?

   a. Increased unification among West African groups against European exploitation

   b. Increased cultural borrowing of European political systems

   c. Decreased trade in nonhuman goods with Europeans

   d. A decreased male population in West Africa

Questions 24–27 refer to this passage.

> Yesterday I attended a meeting of the unemployed in London and having listened to the wild speeches which were nothing more than a scream for bread, I returned home convinced more than ever of the importance of imperialism. . . . In order to save the 40 million inhabitants of the United Kingdom from a murderous civil war, the colonial politicians must open up new areas to absorb the excess population and create new markets for the products of the mines and factories.
>
> — British imperialist Cecil Rhodes, 1895

24. Which of these was a major factor that led to the meeting described in the excerpt?
    a. Effects of the Industrial Revolution, which included overcrowded urban centers with high levels of poverty
    b. The British Parliament's refusal to allow anyone other than elites to vote for public office
    c. The British government's confiscation of food supplies to ship to markets overseas
    d. The British government's use of propaganda to incite the masses to start a civil war

25. Cecil Rhodes's description of social tensions in the passage best supports which interpretation of industrial economies?
    a. The capitalist interpretation
    b. The Marxist interpretation
    c. A mercantilist interpretation
    d. A social Darwinist interpretation

26. What nineteenth-century cultural development most directly contributed to the concepts of racial hierarchy that were popular among imperialists?
    a. Enlightenment theories concerning the nature of governments
    b. Social contract theories declaring that "all men are created equal"
    c. Darwin's natural selection theories regarding "survival of the fittest"
    d. Abolition movements promoting expansion of slavery

27. How did many urban poor respond to the conditions cited by Rhodes in the excerpt in the late nineteenth and early twentieth centuries?
    a. They willingly migrated overseas, seeking better living conditions.
    b. They moved to the suburbs, where living conditions were more comfortable.
    c. They overthrew Western European governments and established communism.
    d. They rejected Christianity in favor of utopian philosophies.

Questions 28–29 refer to these passages.

> Inside the city . . . there are many abbeys and churches of the Idolaters. . . . Both men and women clothe themselves in silk, so vast is the supply of the material. . . . The crowd of people . . . is so vast that no one would believe it possible to [feed them all]. . . . All the squares are crammed with traders who have brought in stores . . . by land or water. . . . And [they are] free from all jealously or suspicion of the conduct of their women. These they treat with the greatest respect.
>
> — Italian explorer Marco Polo, *The Book of Sir Marco Polo the Venetian Concerning the Kingdoms and Marvels of the East*, 13th century

> The garments of [the town's] inhabitants, most of whom belong to the Massufa tribe, are of fine Egyptian fabrics. . . . [T]heir women show no bashfulness before men and do not veil themselves, though they are assiduous in attending the prayers. . . . A traveller in this country carries no provisions, whether plain food or seasonings, and neither gold nor silver. . . . When he comes to a village the womenfolk of the blacks bring out millet, milk, chickens, pulped lotus fruit, rice, . . . and pounded haricot beans.
>
> — Moroccan explorer Ibn Battuta, *Travels in Asia and Africa 1325–1354*

28. Which of the following is the most likely reason for similarities in Marco Polo's and Ibn Battuta's accounts of their travels in the thirteenth and fourteenth centuries?

    a. Historians believe they may have met each other on their journeys and compared observations.

    b. Both the areas observed participated in significant long-distance trade.

    c. Both the areas observed were highly influenced by Confucian teachings.

    d. The travelers had the same religious background and perspectives.

29. Which of these accurately describes the political status of China in Marco Polo's time?

    a. China was under the foreign influence of European commercial interests.

    b. China was experiencing a series of civil wars led by regional warlords.

    c. China was under the control of Mongol rulers.

    d. China was controlled by religious leaders, who chose the emperor.

Questions 30–32 refer to this passage.

> Now it has been proposed that the prohibition of opium-smoking would reach the officers of the Government, the scholars, and the military, but not the common people. But it is forgotten that the common people of today will be the officers, scholars, and the military of the future. Should they be allowed to smoke at first and then be prohibited from it in the future? Moreover, the officers, scholars, and the military of today may be degraded to the rank of the common people. In that case, are they to be freed from the prohibition once imposed on them? Prohibition was proclaimed because opium is pernicious. It follows then that the ban should not be abolished until it ceases to be an evil. A partial prohibition or partial legalization is a confusion of rules by the government itself.
>
> — Yuan Yulin, a high-ranking Qing official, in a court argument over foreign trade, 1836

30. The argument of Yuan Yulin is based upon what continuity in Chinese history?

    a. The filial piety that nurtured respect for elders and the deceased

    b. The syncretic blend of Daoism and Confucianism that encouraged family bonds

    c. The high regard in which Confucian scholars held the merchant class

    d. The use of academic exams that allowed for class mobility

31. The resolution of the issues debated in the passage had what direct consequence in Chinese history?

    a. China's division into spheres of influence by other empires

    b. The success of Mao Zedong in China's civil war

    c. A reluctant acceptance of the presence of foreigners in China

    d. A reform movement that successfully industrialized China

32. The debate between Yuan Yulin and his opponents is best understood in the context of

    a. a wave of opium addictions that swept the globe in the early nineteenth century.

    b. the decline of traditional societies relative to industrial nations.

    c. an increase in communist societies pushing back against capitalism.

    d. China's role as a provider of cheap labor in global economic markets.

Questions 33–34 refer to this passage.

> Non-violence means conscious suffering. It does not mean meek submission to the will of the evil-doer, but it means the pitting of one's whole soul against the will of the tyrant. It is possible for a single individual to defy the whole might of an unjust empire to save his honour, his religion, his soul.
>
> — Mohandas K. Gandhi, 1920

33. The excerpt is best understood in the context of
    a. struggles for independence following World Wars I and II.
    b. the Green Revolution of the 1950s–1970s.
    c. a global increase in violence against religious minorities beginning in the 1970s.
    d. the proclaiming of a "new world order" after the cold war at the end of the twentieth century.

34. What was a long-term consequence of the political goals expressed in the passage?
    a. The spread of socialism across Asia
    b. The religious partitioning of South Asia
    c. A peaceful process of decolonization in South Asia
    d. Independent India's siding with the Soviet Union during the cold war

Questions 35–36 refer to this image.

Hughes Hervé/AGE Fotostock

Peruvian Catholic Christians participating in a religious procession.

35. The image indicates which of the following?
    a. A syncretic form of Christianity, blended with Indigenous American traditions
    b. Increased levels of anti-Western protest movements in the late twentieth century
    c. Decreased participation in religious practices caused by the Columbian exchange
    d. The influence of Protestantism in Latin America in the era ca. 1450–ca. 1750

36. What is the most likely reason that Native Americans generally accepted Christianity, whereas East Asian cultures generally did not, in the era ca. 1450–1750?

   a. The cultures of the Americas had already accepted Christianity by the beginning of this era.

   b. Native American cultures were generally receptive to outside influences, whereas all East Asian cultures rejected outside influences.

   c. East Asian cultures had widely accepted Christians in an earlier era.

   d. Europeans were more successful in imposing their culture in the Americas, but Asian cultures proved more resistant.

Questions 37–38 refer to this image.

An image of the Buddha and accompanying bodhisattvas found near Dunhuang, China. Carved in caves between ca. 400 and 1400 C.E.

37. Which of the following claims about the diffusion of Buddhism is supported by the image?

   a. As Buddhism spread, its adherents grew to see the Buddha as a single god.

   b. As Buddhism spread, it adopted the material values of the Chinese culture.

   c. By the fifteenth century, Theravada Buddhism had become the dominant branch in China.

   d. As Buddhism diffused across China, it borrowed Chinese concepts of filial piety.

38. How did the spread of Buddhism compare to the spread of Islam by 1500?

   a. Like Islam, Buddhism accepted women in positions of spiritual authority.

   b. Islam spread across Afro-Eurasia through trade networks and military conquest, while Buddhism mainly spread only through trade networks.

   c. Buddhism had far more adherents than Islam.

   d. Like Buddhism, Islam was more popular in its place of origin than outside its place of origin.

Questions 39–42 refer to this passage.

> [Latin] Americans . . . who live within the Spanish system occupy a position in society as mere consumers. Yet even this status is surrounded with galling restrictions, such as being forbidden to grow European crops, or to store products that are royal monopolies, or to establish factories of a type that the Peninsula itself does not possess. To this, add the exclusive trading privileges, even in articles of prime necessity.
>
> In short, do you wish to know what our future held [under Spanish rule]? The cultivation of fields of indigo, grain, coffee, sugarcane, cacao, and cotton; cattle raising on the broad plains; hunting wild game in the jungles; digging in the earth to mine its gold.
>
> — Letter written by Latin American revolutionary leader Simón Bolívar, Jamaica, 1815

39. The economic system described by Bolívar in the document is best understood in the context of

   a. free trade, which in the nineteenth century sought to reduce international economic barriers.

   b. communism, which in the nineteenth century sought economic equality for all.

   c. the doctrine of laissez-faire, which in the nineteenth century sought no government oversight of trade.

   d. mercantilism, which in the nineteenth century sought to increase a nation's wealth through access to colonial raw materials.

40. Leaders of nineteenth-century Latin American revolutions were most often

   a. revolutionaries from the lower classes who promised to destroy inequalities in the political and economic systems.

   b. members of the long-ruling political class who promised to step down once independence from Spain was achieved.

   c. members of the Creole upper class who promised land reform and equality under the law.

   d. students who studied the political lessons learned from the French Revolution of the eighteenth century.

41. To what extent were the social, political, and economic promises made by leaders of these Latin American revolutions fulfilled by the end of the nineteenth century?

   a. Almost all promises made by leaders of Latin American revolutions were fulfilled by the end of the nineteenth century.

   b. Most promises made by leaders of Latin American revolutions, except for the end of slavery, were fulfilled by the end of the nineteenth century.

   c. Some promises made by leaders of Latin American revolutions, such as limited land and education reform, were fulfilled by the end of the nineteenth century.

   d. No promises were fulfilled by leaders of Latin American revolutions once they gained power.

42. What did Bolívar's letter have in common with the Declaration of Independence and the Declaration of the Rights of Man?

   a. All of them made arguments for colonial independence from the rule of kings.

   b. All of them had economic independence as their primary goal.

   c. All of them inspired revolutions that brought social equality.

   d. All of them drew inspiration from Enlightenment principles.

Questions 43–44 refer to this image.

A gathering of Turkish men at an Ottoman coffeehouse, ca. 16th century.

43. The individuals and activities seen in this image of a coffeehouse indicate what feature of Islamic culture?

   a. There were highly unified standards of dress in Islamic culture.

   b. "Untouchables" were required to serve their superiors in public places.

   c. Islamic culture was multiethnic.

   d. Women and men freely occupied all public spaces.

44. The scene of drinking coffee and smoking tobacco featured in the image was made possible by

   a. interconnections of global trade, which introduced new products to the Islamic world.

   b. a weakening of Islamic rules of behavior as the faith blended with other religions.

   c. Muslim trade connections with Southeast Asia, where tobacco originated.

   d. Chinese merchants, who first introduced the Muslim world to coffee and tobacco.

Questions 45–46 refer to this image.

"Day of the African Army and Colonial Troops," First World War Poster, 1914–1918 (color litho)/Charles Fouqueray (1872–1956)/MICHEL TOULET/Private Collection/Bridgeman Images

"Day of the African Army and Colonial Tropps," First World War poster, 1914–1918.

45. What event in the nineteenth century most directly led to the circumstances portrayed in the image?

    a. The rise of indentured servitude
    b. The Sepoy Rebellion
    c. The Opium War
    d. The Great Scramble for Africa

46. The end of World War II had what effect on European imperial powers?

    a. Imperial powers immediately withdrew from their colonies after the end of World War II.
    b. Nationalist parties in Asia and Africa led the way toward gaining independence from imperial powers.
    c. Imperial powers used their victory at the end of the war to gain even more colonies.
    d. The League of Nations called for "self-determination" for all peoples.

Questions 47–48 refer to this passage.

The silkworms have finished their third sleep and are famished. The family is poor, without cash to buy the mulberry leaves to feed them. Hungry silkworms do not produce silk. What can they do? . . . The daughter is twenty but does not have wedding clothes. The [tax collectors] are like tigers. If the family has no clothes to dress their daughter, they can postpone a wedding. If they have no silk to turn over to the government, they will go bankrupt.

—Wen-hsiang, 13th-century Chinese writer

47. Which of these statements best describes the status of China's economy in the thirteenth century?
   a. The economy was slowly recovering after the warring states period.
   b. The economy continued to be the most powerful in the world.
   c. The economy was coming under European influence after the unequal treaties.
   d. The economy rapidly declined at the hands of the Mongol Empire.

48. In what larger historical process was the family's work participating?
   a. An unfree labor system like indentured servitude
   b. Factory work involving an assembly line
   c. Government-supervised production as in a socialist system
   d. Production of goods for distribution across transregional markets

Questions 49–51 refer to this passage.

Everyone is entitled to all the rights and freedoms set forth in this Declaration. . . .
Everyone has the right to seek and to enjoy in other countries asylum from persecution. . . .
Men and women of full age . . . have the right to marry and to found a family. . . .
Marriage shall be entered into only with the free and full consent of the intending spouses. . . .
Everyone has the right to freedom of thought, conscience and religion; . . .
. . . and the right to security in the event of . . . circumstances beyond his control.
Motherhood and childhood are entitled to special care and assistance. . . .
Everyone has the right to education. Education shall be free, at least in the elementary and fundamental stages.

— *The Universal Declaration of Human Rights*, General Assembly
of the United Nations, adopted December 10, 1948

49. *The Universal Declaration of Human Rights* is most clearly an example of which of the following?
   a. A response to the horrors of World War II and a growing Western belief in certain human rights
   b. A reaction to the increased number of women voters immediately after World War II
   c. The push by the West to stop the spread of communism during the cold war
   d. The move toward decolonization after World War II

50. Which of the following conclusions about the twentieth century is most directly supported by the passage?

   a. The idea of global free trade spread after World War II.

   b. United Nations forces were authorized to invade any nation that did not support the *Universal Declaration of Human Rights*.

   c. There was a growing movement following World War II to protect the rights of women, children, and refugees.

   d. After World War II, there were fewer attempts to create international political and economic organizations.

51. After the end of World War II, the world became more interdependent. This change was facilitated most directly by

   a. the global increase in tariffs on imported goods.

   b. the elimination of international borders.

   c. the decline of industrial economic powers.

   d. the creation of new international organizations.

Questions 52–55 refer to this map.

Religion and Commerce in the Afro-Eurasian World, ca. 1200–1450

52. Based on the map and your knowledge of world history, the area that saw the greatest reduction in Muslim political control between the years 1200 and 1450 was

    a. South Asia, because of opposition to Islam by Hindu political leaders.

    b. Anatolia, because of opposition to Islam by Mongol invaders.

    c. Ethiopia, because of opposition by Christian political leaders.

    d. Spain, because of opposition by Christian political leaders.

53. The revival of trade routes on the map connecting East Asia and the Middle East in the thirteenth century was a result of which of the following developments?

    a. The expansion of the Mongol Empire

    b. The use of silk as a form of currency

    c. An increased demand for European luxury goods in China

    d. The fracturing of the Abbasid caliphate

54. Which of these statements best explains the existence of continuous trade routes across diverse faith regions in the fifteenth century?

    a. Empires from Western Europe to East Asia signed agreements to keep the trade routes open.

    b. The financial incentives provided by trade goods outweighed divisions over religious beliefs.

    c. Major global trade corporations kept open all trade routes using private military forces.

    d. Superior European technology and imperialist motives dominated Asian and African trade routes.

55. What advantage did Muslim merchants have over their European and East Asian counterparts?

    a. Muslim merchants enjoyed exclusive use of camels for long-distance caravans.

    b. Islam's comparatively stronger belief system gave it a competitive edge when dealing with Christians and Buddhists.

    c. Islam's central position between European and East Asian markets facilitated its exchanges with both regions.

    d. Muslim navigation skills and technology far exceeded those of East Asians and Europeans.

Short-Answer Questions

Time: 40 minutes

Directions: Answer question 1 **and** question 2. Answer **either** question 3 **or** question 4.

In your responses, be sure to address all parts of the questions you answer. Use complete sentences; an outline or bulleted list is not acceptable.

1. Use the passage below and your knowledge of history to answer all parts of the question that follows.

    Communism, like many human projects, has been an ambiguous enterprise. On the one hand, communism brought hope to millions by addressing the manifest injustices of the past; by providing new opportunities for women, workers, and peasants; by promoting rapid industrial development; and by ending Western domination. On the other hand, communism was responsible for mountains of crimes—millions killed and wrongly imprisoned; massive famines partly caused by radical policies; human rights violated on an enormous scale; lives uprooted and distorted by efforts to achieve the impossible.

    —Robert W. Strayer and Eric W. Nelson, *Ways of the World*

A. Identify ONE specific piece of historical evidence that supports the authors' statement that communism brought hope to millions of people.

B. Explain ONE twentieth-century development that supports the authors' statement that communism was responsible for many crimes.

C. Explain ONE reason for the collapse of communism in Europe at the end of the twentieth century.

2. Use the map below to answer all parts of the question that follows.

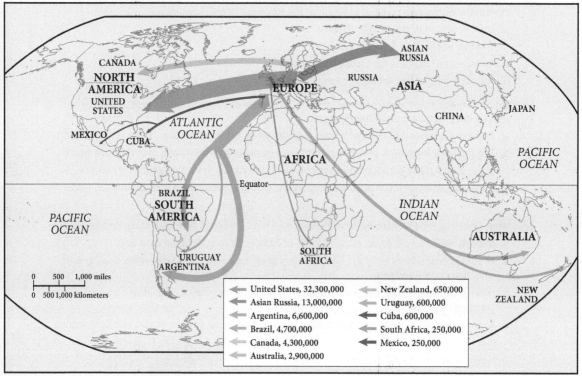

Migrations during the Industrial Period

A. Identify ONE reason for the migrations from Europe to the Americas shown on this map.

B. Explain ONE reason why global patterns of migration from 1500 to 1800 were different than the patterns shown on this map.

C. Explain ONE continuity in migrations between the era 1500 to 1800 and the era shown on this map.

Directions: Answer **either** question 3 **or** question 4.

3. Answer all parts of the question that follows.

A. Identify ONE similarity in how governments maintained power in East Asia and the Middle East in the era ca. 1200–ca. 1450.

B. Explain ONE difference in how governments maintained power in East Asia and the Middle East in the era ca. 1200–ca. 1450.

C. Explain ONE weakness in methods used by governments to maintain power between ca. 1200 and ca. 1450.

4. Answer all parts of the question that follows.

   A. Identify ONE strategy used by <u>land-based</u> empires to deal with ethnic or cultural diversity in the period 1450–1750.

   B. Explain ONE method used by <u>land-based</u> empires to legitimize political authority in the period 1450–1750.

   C. Explain ONE method used by <u>maritime empires</u> to maintain imperial control in areas far from their imperial homelands.

Document-Based Question

Suggested reading and writing time: 1 hour (15 minutes reading, 45 minutes writing)

Directions: Question 1 is based on the accompanying documents. The documents have been edited for the purpose of this exercise.

In your response you should do the following.

- Respond to the prompt with a historically defensible thesis or claim that establishes a line of reasoning.
- Describe a broader historical context relevant to the prompt.
- Use the content of at least three documents to address the topic of the prompt (1 point) OR support an argument in response to the prompt using at least six documents (2 points).
- Use at least one additional piece of historical evidence (beyond that found in the documents) that is relevant to an argument about the prompt.
- For at least three documents, explain how or why the document's point of view, purpose, historical situation, and/or audience is relevant to an argument.
- Use evidence to corroborate, qualify, or modify an argument that addresses the prompt. (Complexity)

1. Evaluate the extent to which nationalism affected the construction of the Suez and Panama canals in the late nineteenth and early twentieth centuries.

The map above shows the locations of the Suez and Panama canals.

Document 1

Source: Ferdinand de Lesseps, chief developer of the Suez Canal project for France, to Muhammad Said Pasha, leader of Egypt, appointed by the Ottoman Empire. Conversation in front of witnesses, Libyan desert, 1854.

A canal at Suez will show that Egypt can still be a potent force in world affairs, and can add a brilliant page to the history of world civilization. The names of the Egyptian pharaohs who built the pyramids will be ignored. . . . The name of the ruler who opens a grand canal through Egypt will be blessed century after century for securing the safe passage to Mecca and Medina for the faithful and place Egypt at the center of world trade between Europe, India and China.

Document 2

Source: Lord Palmerston, prime minister of Great Britain, speech in Parliament, 1857.

For the last fifteen years Her Majesty's Government has used all its influence with the Ottoman Sultan and the Egyptian leaders to prevent this French scheme of [digging a canal] from being carried out. It is impractical, immensely expensive and unprofitable. Even if it could be done, it would lead to a power shift between the Ottomans and Egypt that would damage British political and commercial interests.

Document 3

Source: Ismail Pasha, newly appointed leader of Egypt chosen by the Ottoman Empire, letter to European diplomats, 1863.

I oppose the use of abusive and exploitative *corvée* [a system of government-sanctioned forced labor] imposed on sixty thousand of my country men to build the canal. This system must be abolished because it is abusive and exploitative. It robs my people of their rights as human beings. However, I also believe this labor system is still essential for the grand work of building the canal and I pledge to push the project to its completion.

Document 4

Source: New York *Herald* newspaper editorial, 1902.

All the objections to building a canal through the Americas have been submitted by scientific authorities, but their weight is nothing compared with the conviction that the canal project is so deeply rooted in the American nation, conceived by Americans, sustained by Americans, and if constructed, operated by Americans according to American ideas and American needs. In one word, it is a national enterprise.

Document 5

Source: French newspaper cartoon depicting the completion of the Suez Canal, ca. 1870. De Lesseps is depicted as the biblical figure Samson, dividing Egypt from the rest of Africa.

AKG Images

Document 6

Source: Ruben Dario, Nicaraguan poet, poem titled, "To Roosevelt," 1904.

You are the United States, you are the future invader of the native
America that has Indian blood. . . .
You think that wherever you shoot,
you hit the future. No! . . .
Be careful. Viva Spanish America!
There are a thousand cubs loosed from the Spanish lion.
Roosevelt—the rifleman and hunter—
you would have to be God Himself to manage
to grab us in your iron claws.
And although you count on everything, you lack one thing: God!

Document 7

> Source: Dr. William Gorgas, U.S. Army colonel and chief medical officer at the Panama Canal construction site. Supply request to the U.S. government, 1904. The cost was $1,000,000.
>
> | Supplies | Amount |
> | --- | --- |
> | Insecticide powder | 300 tons |
> | Garbage cans | 3,000 |
> | Buckets | 4,000 |
> | Brooms | 1,000 |
> | Kerosene oil for smoke | 600,000 gallons |
> | Fumigation pots | 1,200 |
> | Wire screens | $90,000–worth |
> | Workers to do the above tasks | 4,000 |

Long Essay Questions

Suggested writing time: 40 minutes
Directions: Answer question 2 **or** 3 **or** 4.

In your response you should do the following:

- Respond to the prompt with a historically defensible thesis or claim that establishes a line of reasoning.
- Describe a broader historical context relevant to the prompt.
- Support an argument in response to the prompt using specific and relevant examples of evidence.
- Use historical reasoning (e.g., comparison, causation, continuity or change) to frame or structure an argument that addresses the prompt.
- Use evidence to corroborate, qualify, or modify an argument that addresses the prompt.

2. Between 1200 and 1450, powerful societies emerged that changed the way people produced and exchanged goods.

   Develop an argument that evaluates the extent to which centralized states contributed to networks of exchanges in this era.

3. Between 1450 and 1750, large states expanded and maintained order through a variety of administrative policies, procedures, and institutions.

   Develop an argument that evaluates the extent to which the expansion of land-based empires in this era changed social structures.

4. As empires grew between 1750 and 1900, they were affected by the ways they produced, exchanged, and consumed goods and services.

   Develop an argument that evaluates the extent to which economic changes affected imperial practices in this era.

Glossary/Glosario

Glossary	Glosario

A

Abbasid caliphate An Arab dynasty of caliphs (successors to the Prophet) who governed much of the Islamic world from its capital in Baghdad beginning in 750 C.E. After 900 C.E. that empire increasingly fragmented until its overthrow by the Mongols in 1258. (p. 83)

Califato abasí Dinastía de califas árabes (sucesores del profeta) que gobernaron la mayoría del mundo islámico desde su capital en Bagdad a partir del año 750 E. C. Después del 900 E. C., el imperio se fragmentó hasta ser derrocado por los mongoles en 1258. (p. 83)

Abd al-Hamid II Ottoman sultan (r. 1876–1909) who accepted a reform constitution but then quickly suppressed it, ruling as a despotic monarch for the rest of his long reign. (p. 513)

Abdul Hamid II Sultán otomano (r. 1876–1909) que aceptó una constitución de reforma para después suprimirla. Reinó como un monarca despótico durante el resto de su largo reinado. (p. 513)

abdicate As a ruler, to renounce power and position. (p. 508)

abdicar Como gobernante, renunciar al poder y al cargo. (p. 508)

abolitionist movement An international movement that condemned slavery as morally repugnant and contributed much to ending slavery in the Western world during the nineteenth century; the movement was especially prominent in Britain and the United States beginning in the late eighteenth century. (p. 407)

movimiento abolicionista Movimiento internacional que condenó a la esclavitud como moralmente repugnante y contribuyó en gran medida a terminar con la esclavitud en el mundo occidental durante el siglo XIX; el movimiento fue especialmente prominente a principios del siglo XVIII en Bretaña y en los Estados Unidos. (p. 407)

Aboriginal The earliest known or indigenous inhabitants of an area. Today the most common use of the term is used for Aboriginal Australians. (p. 10)

Aborigen Primeros habitantes conocidos o indígenas de una región. En la actualidad, el uso más habitual del término es para referirse a los aborígenes australianos. (p. 10)

accumulation The collecting or gathering of something over time. (p. 134)

acumulación Acopio o acaparamiento de algo a lo largo del tiempo. (p. 134)

adaptation A change made in order to adjust and improve function in a situation. (p. 97)

adaptación Cambio realizado para amoldarse y mejorar el desempeño en una situación. (p. 97)

adherent A strong supporter of something such as a leader. (p. 43)

adepto Partidario entusiasta de algo o de alguien, como un líder. (p. 43)

aesthetically Being tasteful or pleasing to the eye; beautifully. (p. 75)

estéticamente Con buen gusto y resultando agradable a la vista; bellamente. (p. 75)

African diaspora The global spread of African peoples via the slave trade. (p. 338)

diáspora africana Difusión global de los pueblos africanos a través de la trata de esclavos. (p. 338)

African identity A new way of thinking about belonging that emerged by the end of the nineteenth century among well-educated Africans; it was influenced by the common experience of colonial oppression and European racism and was an effort to revive the cultural self-confidence of their people. (p. 582)

identidad africana Nueva forma de pensar en la pertenencia que surgió a finales del siglo XIX entre africanos con altos niveles de educación; tuvo como influencia la experiencia común de la opresión colonial y el racism europeo y buscó revivir la confianza de los pueblos africanos en sí mismos. (p. 582)

Africanization of Christianity Process that occurred in non-Muslim Africa, where many who converted to Christianity sought to incorporate older traditions, values, and practices into their understanding of Christianity; often expressed in the creation of churches and schools that operated independently of the missionary and colonial establishment. (p. 580)

africanización del cristianismo Proceso que ocurrió en las regiones no musulmanas de África, donde muchas personas que se convirtieron al cristianismo buscaron incorporar tradiciones, valores y prácticas más antiguas a su forma de entender el cristianismo; se manifiesta la creación de iglesias y escuelas que operaban independientemente del establecimiento misionero y colonial. (p. 580)

883

age of fossil fuels Twentieth-century shift in energy production with increased use of coal, oil, and natural gas, resulting in the widespread availability of electricity and the internal combustion engine; a major source of the greenhouse gases that drive climate change. (p. 745)

era de los combustibles fósiles Durante el siglo veinte, cambio en la producción de energía con un incremento del uso de carbón, petróleo y gas natural, que dio como resultado una amplia disponibilidad de electricidad y el motor de combustión interna; una importante fuente de gases de invernadero que inciden en el cambio climático. (p. 745)

agrarian Relating to agriculture or land. (p. 15)

agrario Relacionado con la agricultura o la tierra. (p. 15)

agricultural labor Work done manually or by hand such as farming. (p. 91)

trabajo agrícola Crabajo realizado manualmente, como la labranza. (p. 91)

Agricultural Revolution Perhaps the most transformative process in all of human history, these terms refer to the domestication of plants and animals, which led to both farming and pastoral societies. (p. 13)

Revolución agraria Quizá uno de los procesos que más cambiaron la historia de la humanidad. Este término se refiere a la domesticación de plantas y animales, que conllevó a las sociedades agrícolas y pastorales. (p. 13)

Akbar The most famous emperor of India's Mughal Empire (r. 1556–1605); his policies are noted for their efforts at religious tolerance and inclusion. (p. 236)

Akbar Emperador más famoso del Imperio mogol de la India (r. 1556–1605); sus políticas destacaron por sus esfuerzos en buscar la tolerancia e inclusión religiosas. (p. 236)

alchemy Popular in the Middle Ages, a type of chemistry that aimed to transform common metals to gold or a substance that would produce an elixir of life. (p. 102)

alquimia Tipo de química popular en la Edad Media, cuyo objetivo consistía en transformar los metales comunes en oro o en una sustancia que permitiera producir un elixir de la vida. (p. 102)

alliance An agreement between parties, or sometimes nations, to work together under certain circumstances. (p. 106)

alianza Acuerdo entre partes, u ocasionalmente entre naciones, con el propósito de trabajar conjuntamente bajo determinadas circunstancias. (p. 106)

ambivalence A feeling of uncertainty due to conflicting emotions or thoughts on a subject. (p. 501)

ambivalencia Sentimiento de incertidumbre debido a emociones o pensamientos encontrados respecto de un tema. (p. 501)

American Revolution Successful rebellion against British rule conducted by the European settlers in the thirteen colonies of British North America, starting in 1775; a conservative revolution whose success preserved property rights and class distinctions but established republican government in place of monarchy. (p. 391)

Revolución americana Rebelión exitosa contra el reinado británico dirigida por los pobladores europeos de las trece colonias de Norteamérica británica en 1775; fue una revolución conservadora cuyo éxito mantuvo los derechos de propiedad y las distinciones de clase pero estableció un gobierno republicano en lugar de una monarquía. (p. 391)

American web A term used to describe the network of trade that linked parts of the pre-Columbian Americas; although less densely woven than the Afro-Eurasian trade networks, this web nonetheless provided a means of exchange for luxury goods and ideas over large areas. (p. 167)

Red americana Término empleado para describir la red de comercio que unió partes de América precolombina; aunque no fue tan compleja como las redes de comercio afroeuroasiáticas, esta red ofreció un medio de intercambio de bienes de lujo e ideas a lo largo de grandes extensiones de territorio. (p. 167)

al-Andalus Arabic name for Spain, most of which was conquered by Arab and Berber forces between 711 and 718 C.E. Muslim Spain represented a point of encounter between the Islamic world and Christian Europe. (p. 87)

al-Ándalus Nombre árabe para España, que fue conquistada en su mayoría por fuerzas árabes y bereberes entre 711 y 718 E. C. La España musulmana representó un punto de encuentro entre el mundo islámico y la Europa cristiana. (p. 87)

Angkor Wat The largest religious structure in the premodern world, this temple was built by the powerful Angkor kingdom (located in modern Cambodia) in the twelfth century C.E. to express a Hindu understanding of the cosmos centered on a mythical Mount Meru, the home of the gods in Hindu tradition. It was later used by Buddhists as well. (p. 81)

Angkor Wat Este templo, que es la estructura religiosa más grande del mundo premoderno, fue construido por el reino Angkor (ubicado en el territorio del país conocido actualmente como Camboya) en el siglo XII E. C. para expresar una perspectiva hindú del cosmos centrada en el mítico monte Meru, cuna de los dioses de tradición hindú. Posteriormente fue utilizado también por budistas. (p. 81)

Anthropocene era A recently coined term denoting the "age of man," in general since the Industrial Revolution and more specifically since the mid-twentieth century. It refers to the unprecedented and enduring impact of human activity on the atmosphere, the geosphere, and the biosphere. (p. 823)

Antropoceno Este término acuñado en tiempos recientes significa "la era del hombre", que se inició a grandes rasgos en la Revolución Industrial y más específicamente en la segunda mitad del siglo XX. Se refiere al impacto duradero y nunca antes visto de la actividad humana en la atmósfera, la geosfera y la biosfera. (p. 823)

anthropologist A person who specializes in the study of the cultural and social aspects of humanity. (p. 16)

antropólogo Persona que se especializa en el estudio de los aspectos culturales y sociales de la humanidad. (p. 16)

Apartheid A political system formerly imposed in South Africa that instilled racial segregation. (p. 564)

Apartheid Sistema político impuesto en el pasado en Sudáfrica que inculcaba la segregación racial. (p. 564)

aphrodisiac A substance, typically a drug or food, that is supposed to arouse sexual desire. (p. 318)

afrodisíaco Sustancia, generalmente una droga o un alimento, que supuestamente incrementa el deseo sexual. (p. 318)

Arabian camel Introduced to North Africa and the Sahara in the early centuries of the Common Era, this animal made trans-Saharan commerce possible by 300 to 400 C.E. (p. 157)

camello árabe Introducido en África del Norte y el Sahara en los primeros siglos de la era común, este animal logró que el comercio transahariano fuera posible para el 300 hasta el 400 E. C. (p. 157)

archeologist A person who specializes in the study of ancient peoples and cultures by examining discovered artifacts such as tools, buildings, and inscriptions. (p. 12)

arqueólogo Persona que se especializa en el estudio de los pueblos y las culturas antiguas a través del examen de reliquias descubiertas, como herramientas, edificaciones e inscripciones. (p. 12)

architecture The design and construction of buildings and other large structures. (p. 17)

arquitectura Diseño y construcción de edificios y otras estructuras grandes. (p. 17)

armament Military equipment or the process of being prepared for military battle. (p. 466)

armamento Equipo militar o el proceso de preparación para una batalla. (p. 466)

artisan A skilled worker that makes a product by hand. (p. 17)

artesano Trabajador calificado que hace un producto a mano. (p. 17)

arts Demonstration of what is perceived as beautiful through means such as painting, sculpture, or performance. (p. 17)

artes Demostración de lo que se percibe como bello mediante expresiones como la pintura, la escultura o la interpretación. (p. 17)

ascendancy Having or growing in political dominance, such as on a global stage. (p. 94)

ascendiente Que tiene o que desarrolla un dominio político, como por ejemplo a nivel global. (p. 94)

Asian Tigers Nickname for the East Asian countries of South Korea, Taiwan, Singapore, and Hong Kong, which experienced remarkable export-driven economic growth in the late twentieth century. (p. 751)

Tigres asiáticos Sobrenombre que reciben los países del este de Asia Corea del Sur, Taiwán, Singapur y Hong Kong por el notable crecimiento económico que vivieron gracias a las exportaciones a finales del siglo XX. (p. 751)

assimilation The adoption of other qualities or habits in order to become similar to something else. (p. 32)

asimilación Adopción de cualidades o hábitos para parecerse a otro. (p. 32)

Aurangzeb Mughal emperor (r. 1658–1707) who reversed his predecessors' policies of religious tolerance and attempted to impose Islamic supremacy. (pron. ow-rang-ZEHB) (p. 237)

Aurangzeb Emperador mogol (r. 1658–1707) que revirtió las políticas de tolerancia religiosa de sus predecesores y buscó imponer la supremacía islámica. (pron. au-rang-ZEB) (p. 237)

auspices Support or encouragement; approval. (p. 523)

auspicios Apoyo o fomento; aprobación. (p. 523)

austere Severe and strict discipline such as through psychological teachings. (p. 138)

austero Disciplina severa y estricta, por ejemplo la inculcada mediante enseñanzas psicológicas. (p. 138)

autocracy Form of government with an absolute monarch or small group which has unlimited power. (p. 226)

autocracia Forma de gobierno en la que un monarca absoluto o un grupo pequeño tiene poder ilimitado. (p. 226)

autonomy The state of independence. (p. 84)

autonomía Estado de independencia. (p. 84)

Aztec Empire Major state that developed in what is now Mexico in the fourteenth and fifteenth centuries; dominated by the semi-nomadic Mexica, who had migrated into the region from northern Mexico. (p. 106)

Imperio azteca Estado principal que se desarrolló en los siglos XIV y XV en el territorio actualmente conocido como México; fue dominado por los mexicas que eran seminomádicos y habían llegado a la región desde el norte de México. (p. 106)

B

beleaguered Surrounded with troubles and in some instances military forces. (p. 262)

asediado Rodeado de problemas y, en algunos casos, fuerzas militares. (p. 262)

Belt and Road Initiative An early twenty-first-century initiative of the Chinese government to create a global infrastructure of roads, railways, port facilities, and energy pipelines. Sometimes called a New Silk Road. (p. 713)

Iniciativa de la franja y la ruta Una iniciativa del gobierno chino a principios del siglo veintiuno para crear una infraestructura global de vías, ferrocarriles, puertos y ductos de energía. A veces, es llamada la nueva ruta de la seda. (p. 713)

Benin West African kingdom (in what is now Nigeria) whose strong kings for a time sharply limited engagement with the slave trade. (p. 348)

Benín Reino de África Occidental (en lo que ahora es Nigeria) cuyos reyes poderosos limitaron considerablemente la interacción con la trata de esclavos. (p. 348)

***bhakti* movement** Meaning "worship," this Hindu movement began in south India and moved northward between 600 and 1300 C.E.; it involved the intense adoration of and identification with a particular deity through songs, prayers, and rituals. (pron. BAHK-tee) (p. 31)

movimiento bhakti Este movimiento hinduista, que significa "adoración" se inició en el sur de la India y se desplazó hacia el norte entre el año 600 y 1300 E. C.; consistió en la adoración e identificación con una deidad particular a través de cantos, oraciones y ritos. (pron. bak-TI) (p. 31)

biologist A person who specializes in the study of living things. (p. 556)

biólogo Persona que se especializa en el estudio de los seres vivos. (p. 556)

Black Death A massive pandemic that swept through Eurasia in the early fourteenth century, spreading along the trade routes within and beyond the Mongol Empire and reaching the Middle East and Western Europe by 1347. Associated with a massive loss of life. (p. 148)

Peste negra Pandemia que arrasó Eurasia a principios del siglo XIV y se diseminó por las rutas comerciales dentro y más allá del Imperio mongol hasta alcanzar en 1347 el Oriente Medio y el oeste de Europa. La peste negra ha sido relacionada con la pérdida masiva de vidas humanas. (p. 148)

Blyden, Edward (1832–1912) Prominent West African scholar and political leader who argued that each civilization, including that of Africa, has its own unique contribution to make to the world. (p. 583)

Blyden, Edward (1832–1912) Destacado académico y líder político de África Occidental que argumentó que cada civilización, incluyendo la de África, aporta una contribución única al resto del mundo. (p. 583)

bodhisattvas In Buddhism, a person who chooses to postpone nirvana to help others. (p. 29)

bodhisattvas En el Budismo, persona que decide posponer su entrada en el nirvana para ayudar a otros. (p. 29)

botanist A person who specializes in the study of plant life. (p. 88)

botánico Persona que se especializa en el estudio de la vida vegetal. (p. 88)

bourgeois Relating to the middle class of society. (p. 457)

burgués Relativo a la clase media de la sociedad. (p. 457)

Boxer Uprising Antiforeign movement (1898–1901) led by Chinese militia organizations, in which large numbers of Europeans and Chinese Christians were killed. It resulted in military intervention by Western powers and the imposition of a huge payment as punishment. (p. 506)

Levantamiento de los bóxers Movimiento contra la influencia extranjera (1898-1901) dirigido por milicias chinas en el cual murieron un gran número de cristianos chinos y europeos. Dio lugar a la intervención de poderes occidentales y a la imposición de un pago enorme como castigo. (p. 506)

Bretton Woods system Name for the agreements and institutions (including the World Bank and the International Monetary Fund) set up in 1944 to regulate commercial and financial dealings among the major capitalist countries. (p. 752)

sistema de Bretton Woods Nombre que reciben los acuerdos y las instituciones (inclusive el Banco Mundial y el Fondo Monetario Internacional) establecidos en 1944 para regular las transacciones comerciales y financieras entre los países capitalistas más importantes. (p. 752)

British East India Company Private trading company chartered by the English government around 1600, mainly focused on India; it was given a monopoly on Indian Ocean trade, including the right to make war and to rule conquered peoples. (p. 324)

Compañía Británica de las Indias Orientales Compañía privada comercial constituida por el gobierno inglés hacia 1600 y centrada principalmente en India; recibió el monopolio del comercio en el océano Índico, incluido el derecho de hacer la guerra y de gobernar los pueblos conquistados. (p. 324)

British textile industry The site of the initial technological breakthroughs of the Industrial Revolution in eighteenth-century Britain, where multiple innovations transformed cotton textile production, resulting in an enormous increase in output. (p. 447)

industria textil británica Sector en el que se encontraron los primeros avances tecnológicos de la Revolución Industrial en la Gran Bretaña del siglo XVIII y en el que múltiples innovaciones transformaron la producción textil de algodón, lo que tuvo como resultado un aumento considerable de la producción. (p. 447)

brothel A house or other location that plays host to prostitution. (p. 219)

burdel Casa u otro lugar en el que se ejerce la prostitución. (p. 219)

bureaucracy Government run through various departments and administrators. (p. 17)

burocracia Gobierno ejercido a través de diversos ministerios y administraciones. (p. 17)

burgeoning Developing or expanding quickly, such as regarding cities. (p. 468)

floreciente Que se desarrolla o expande rápidamente, por ejemplo, una ciudad. (p. 468)

bushido The "way of the warrior," referring to the martial values of the Japanese samurai, including bravery, loyalty, and an emphasis on death over surrender. (pron. boo-shee-doh) (p. 78)

bushido "Camino del guerrero", se refiere a los valores militares de los samuráis japoneses; incluye el coraje, la lealtad, y pone la muerte por encima de la rendición. (pron. bu-SHI-do) (p. 78)

Byzantine Empire One of the main centers of Christendom during the medieval centuries, the Byzantine Empire was a continuation of the eastern portion of the Roman Empire. It lasted for a thousand years after the collapse of Roman rule in the West, until its conquest by Muslim forces in 1453. (p. 92)

Imperio bizantino Uno de los principales centros de la cristiandad durante los siglos medievales. El Imperio Bizantino fue la continuación de la porción oriental del Imperio Romano. Duró mil años después del colapso del dominio romano en el oeste, hasta que fue conquistado por fuerzas musulmanas en 1453. (p. 92)

C

cadaver A dead human body that is intended for dissection and research. (p. 284)

cadáver Cuerpo humano sin vida destinado a la disección y la investigación. (p. 284)

cadre A group specially trained for specific aspects of the armed forces or other large organization. (p. 326)

cuadro Grupo entrenado especialmente para aspectos específicos de las fuerzas armadas o de otra organización grande. (p. 326)

caravan A group that travels together in hopes of passing safely through dangerous territory. (p. 136)

caravana Grupo de personas que viajan juntas con la esperanza de atravesar un territorio peligroso de manera segura. (p. 136)

cash-crop production Agricultural production of crops for sale in the market rather than for consumption by the farmers themselves; operated at the level of both individual farmers and large-scale plantations. (p. 569)

producción comercial de cultivos Producción agrícola de cultivos destinada a la venta en el mercado en lugar de ser consumidos por los agricultores mismos; se aplica tanto a nivel de agricultores individuales como a nivel de plantaciones a gran escala. (p. 569)

Caste A social position held in Indian society that is a part of the Caste System. (p. 7)

Casta Posición social dentro de la sociedad de la India que es parte del sistema de castas. (p. 7)

caudillos Military strongmen who seized control of a government in nineteenth-century Latin America, and were frequently replaced. (pron. kow-DEE-yos) (p. 467)

caudillos Hombres fuertes militares que tomaban el control del gobierno por la fuerza en la América Latina del siglo XIX y que eran a menudo sustituidos. (pron. kau-DI-yos) (p. 467)

celibacy Choosing a life of remaining unmarried and maintaining sexual abstinence. (p. 265)

celibato Elección de vida según la cual la persona no se casa y practica la abstinencia sexual. (p. 265)

Chaco Phenomenon Name given to a major process of settlement and societal organization that occurred in the period 860–1130 C.E. among the peoples of Chaco Canyon, in what is now northwestern New Mexico; the society formed is notable for its settlement in large pueblos and for the building of hundreds of miles of roads, the purpose of which is not known. (p. 168)

fenómeno del Chaco Nombre que recibe el mayor proceso de asentamiento y organización social que tuvo lugar entre 860 y 1130 E. C. entre los habitantes del Cañón del Chaco, en lo que hoy es el noroeste de Nuevo México; la sociedad que se formó es notable por su asentamiento en grandes pueblos y por construir cientos de miles de carreteras, cuyo objetivo es desconocido. (p. 168)

China's economic revolution A major rise in prosperity that took place in China under the Song dynasty (960–1279); was marked by rapid population growth, urbanization, economic specialization, the development of an immense network of internal waterways, and a great increase in industrial production and technological innovation. (p. 73)

Revolución económica china Aumento importante en la prosperidad que tuvo lugar en China bajo la dinastía Song (960–1279) caracterizado por el crecimiento rápido de la población, la urbanización, la especialización económica, el desarrollo de una inmensa red de vías navegables internas, así como el incremento pronunciado de la producción industrial y la innovación tecnológica. (p. 73)

Chinese revolution of 1911–1912 The collapse of China's imperial order, officially at the hands of organized revolutionaries but for the most part under the weight of the troubles that had overwhelmed the imperial government for the previous century. (p. 508)

Revolución china de 1911–1912 Colapso del orden imperial chino, oficialmente a cargo de revolucionarios organizados pero en su mayor parte lastrado por los problemas que habían sobrepasado al gobierno imperial el siglo anterior. (p. 508)

Chinese Revolution of 1949 An event that marks the coming to power of the Chinese Communist Party under the leadership of Mao Zedong, following a decades-long struggle against both domestic opponents and Japanese imperialism. (p. 653)

Revolución china de 1949 Acontecimiento que marca la llegada al poder del Partido Comunista de China bajo el liderazgo de Mao Zedong después de varias décadas de lucha contra la oposición interna y el imperialismo japonés. (p. 653)

chu nom A variation of Chinese writing developed in Vietnam that became the basis for an independent national literature; "southern script." (p. 80)

chu nom Variación del sistema de escritura china desarrollada en Vietnam que se convirtió en la base de una literatura nacional independiente; "caracteres del sur." (p. 80)

civilizing mission A European understanding of empire that emphasized Europeans' duty to "civilize inferior races" by bringing Christianity, good government, education, work discipline, and production for the market to colonized peoples, while suppressing "native customs," such as polygamy, that ran counter to Western ways of living. (p. 556)

misión civilizadora Concepción europea del imperio que ponía el énfasis en el deber de los europeos de "civilizer a las razas inferiores" llevando al cristianismo, el buen gobierno, la educación, la disciplina en el trabajo y la producción mercantil a los pueblos colonizados y suprimiendo "costumbres nativas" como la poligamia, que iba en contra del modo de vida occidental. (p. 556)

cleric A leader in a church and member of the clergy. (p. 159)

clérigo Líder de una iglesia y miembro del clero. (p. 159)

climate Weather patterns around the world that include temperature, air pressure, and precipitation. These statistics can be gathered and averaged over time to determine the overall climate of the region under examination. (p. 96)

clima Patrones del tiempo en todo el mundo que incluyen la temperatura, la presión del aire y la precipitación. Estas estadísticas se pueden reunir y promediar a lo largo del tiempo para determinar el clima general de la región examinada. (p. 96)

climate change The warming of the planet, largely caused by higher concentrations of "greenhouse gases" generated by the burning of fossil fuels. It has become the most pressing environmental issue of the early twenty-first century. (p. 825)

cambio climático Calentamiento del planeta causado principalmente por altas concentraciones de "gases de efecto invernadero" generadas por la quema de combustibles fósiles. Se ha convertido en el problema medioambiental más urgente de principios del siglo XXI. (p. 825)

codification The systematic arranging of information into a code. (p. 498)

codificación Disposición sistemática de la información en forma de código. (p. 498)

coercive Forcefully persuading someone to do something. (p. 213)

coercitivo Persuadir por la fuerza a alguien para que haga algo. (p. 213)

cohesion Being tightly held together or united. (p. 196)

cohesión Fuertemente unidos o compenetrados. (p. 196)

cold war Geopolitical and ideological conflict between communist regimes and capitalist powers after World War II, spreading from Eastern Europe through Asia; characterized by the avoidance of direct military conflict between the USSR and the United States and an arms race in nuclear weapons. (p. 687)

Guerra Fría Conflicto geopolítico e ideológico entre regímenes comunistas y poderes capitalistas después de la Segunda Guerra Mundial que se extendió desde Europa del Este y por Asia; evitó el conflicto militar directo entre la URSS y los Estados Unidos y dio lugar a una carrera armamentista nuclear. (p. 687)

collectivization of agriculture Communist policies that ended private ownership of land by incorporating peasants from small family farms into large-scale collective farms. Implemented forcibly in the Soviet Union (1928–1933), it led to a terrible famine and 5 million deaths; a similar process occurred much more peacefully in China during the 1950s. (p. 630)

colectivización de la agricultura Políticas comunistas que acabaron con la propiedad privada de la tierra incorporando a campesinos de pequeñas granjas familiares a granjas colectivas de gran escala. Implementada por la fuerza por la Unión Soviética (1928–1933), condujo a una hambruna terrible y a 5 millones de muertes; un proceso similar ocurrió de manera más pacífica en China durante los años 50. (p. 630)

Columbian exchange The enormous network of transatlantic communication, migration, trade, and the transfer of diseases, plants, and animals that began in the period of European exploration and colonization of the Americas. (p. 212)

Intercambio colombino Inmensa red transatlántica de comunicación, migración, comercio e intercambio de enfermedades, plantas y animales que se inició en el período de exploración europeo y de colonización de las Américas. (p. 212)

commensurate To correspond in a suitable amount. (p. 700)

acorde Que corresponde con una cantidad adecuada. (p. 700)

commodity An object that can be placed in the market to be bought, sold, or traded. (p. 136)

mercancía Objeto que puede colocarse en el mercado para su compra, venta o comercialización. (p. 136)

communication The exchange of thoughts or information between people through various means such as spoken or written words. (p. 44)

comunicación Intercambio de ideas o información entre personas a través de diversos medios, como el discurso oral o la palabra escrita. (p. 44)

communication revolution Modern transformation of communication technology, from the nineteenth-century telegraph to the present-day smart phone. (p. 748)

revolución de la comunicación Transformación moderna de la tecnología de la comunicación desde el telégrafo del siglo XIX hasta el teléfono inteligente de la época actual. (p. 748)

communism in Eastern Europe Expansion of post–World War II communism to Poland, East Germany, Czechoslovakia, Hungary, Romania, and Bulgaria, imposed with Soviet pressure rather than growing out of domestic revolution. (p. 652)

comunismo de Europa del Este Expansión del comunismo después de la Segunda Guerra Mundial a Polonia, Alemania del Este, Checoslovaquia, Hungría, Rumanía y Bulgaria, que fue impuesta por la presión soviética más que por la revolución interna. (p. 652)

compartmentalize To divide into separate parts or categories. (p. 285)

compartimentar Dividir en partes o categorías separadas. (p. 285)

concubine A low social status held by women who participate in a sexual relationship and often live with someone they are not married to. (p. 80)

concubina Estatus social bajo de las mujeres que mantienen una relación sexual y que a menudo viven con alguien con quien no están casadas. (p. 80)

Condorcet The Marquis de Condorcet (1743–1794) was a French philosopher who argued that society was moving into an era of near-infinite improvability and could be perfected by human reason. (p. 288)

Condorcet El marqués de Condorcet (1743–1794) fue un filósofo francés que sostenía que la sociedad se estaba moviendo hacia una época de mejora casi infinita que podría ser perfeccionada por la razón humana. (p. 288)

conflagration A large, destructive event usually in the form of fire. (p. 620)

conflagración Suceso importante y destructivo, generalmente un incendio. (p. 620)

Confucianism The Chinese philosophy first enunciated by Confucius, advocating the moral example of superiors as the key element of social order. (p. 32)

confucianismo Primera filosofía china articulada por Confucio que aboga por el ejemplo moral de los superiores como el elemento clave del orden social. (p. 32)

Congo Free State A private colony ruled personally by Leopold II, king of Belgium; it was the site of widespread forced labor and killing to ensure the collection of wild rubber; by 1908 these abuses led to reforms that transferred control to the Belgian government. (p. 567)

Estado libre del Congo Colonia privada gobernada por Leopoldo II, rey de Bélgica; fue el sitio de trabajos forzados y asesinatos que sirvieron para asegurar la recolección de caucho silvestre; en 1908 estos abusos condujeron a reformas que cedieron el control al gobierno belga. (p. 567)

conquistador A Spanish soldier of the sixteenth and seventeenth centuries that explored the Americas as well as conquered the Indigenous peoples that lived there. (p. 104)

conquistador Soldado español de los siglos XVI y XVII que exploró las Américas y que conquistó a los pueblos indígenas que vivían allí. (p. 104)

consolidate To bring together or unite separate parts. (p. 97)

consolidar Juntar o unir partes separadas. (p. 97)

Constantinople New capital for the eastern half of the Roman Empire; Constantinople's highly defensible and economically important site helped ensure the city's cultural and strategic importance for many centuries. (p. 84)

Constantinopla Nueva capital de la parte oriental del Imperio romano; económicamente importante y altamente defendible, Constantinopla ayudó a garantizar el peso cultural y estratégico de la ciudad durante varios siglos. (p. 84)

consternation Feeling of anger or confusion due to something sudden or unexpected. (p. 576)

consternación Sensación de enojo o confusión a causa de algo repentino o imprevisto. (p. 576)

constraint Restraint or limitation of action. (p. 69)

restricción Limitación de acción. (p. 69)

consumerism A culture of leisure and consumption that developed during the past century or so in tandem with global economic growth and an enlarged middle class; emerged first in the Western world and later elsewhere. (p. 761)

consumismo Cultura del ocio y del consumo que se desarrolló durante el siglo pasado más o menos a la par del crecimiento económico mundial y el incremento de la clase media; apareció primero en el mundo occidental y luego en otras partes del mundo. (p. 761)

Copernicus, Nicolaus (1473–1543) Polish mathematician and astronomer who was the first to argue in 1543 for the existence of a sun-centered universe, helping to spark the Scientific Revolution. (p. 282)

Copérnico, Nicolás (1473–1543) Matemático y astrónomo polaco que fue la primera persona en defender, en 1543, la idea de que el sol está en el centro del universo; Copérnico fue una pieza clave en la Revolución científica. (p. 282)

Cortés, Hernán Spanish conquistador who led the expedition that conquered the Aztec Empire in modern Mexico. (p. 207)

Cortés, Hernán Conquistador español que dirigió la expedición que conquistó el Imperio azteca en el México moderno. (p. 207)

cosmopolitan Being multicultural and showing aspects or experience from across the world. (p. 8)

cosmopolita Multicultural y que muestra aspectos o experiencias de todo el mundo. (p. 8)

Counter-Reformation An internal reform of the Catholic Church in the sixteenth century stimulated in part by the Protestant Reformation; at the Council of Trent (1545–1563), Catholic leaders clarified doctrine, corrected abuses and corruption, and put a new emphasis on education and accountability. (p. 266)

Contrarreforma Reforma interna de la Iglesia católica en el siglo XVI impulsada en parte por la Reforma protestante; en el concilio de Trento (1545–1563) los líderes católicos aclaraban la doctrina, corregían los abusos y la corrupción, y pusieron un énfasis nuevo en la educación y la responsabilidad. (p. 266)

courtesans Similar to prostitutes, women of high social class that had sexual relations with men of important status for money. (p. 75)

cortesanas Similares a las prostitutas, mujeres de clase social alta que mantenían relaciones sexuales con hombres de estatus importante a cambio de dinero. (p. 75)

credit Method of purchasing something without directly paying at the time and instead paying later. (p. 74)

crédito Método que permite comprar algo sin pagar directamente en el momento sino más adelante. (p. 74)

crop rotation Used in medieval and early-modern Europe, the seasonal planting and growing of different kinds of crops in the same agricultural area. (p. 7)

rotación de cultivos Plantación y cuidado de distintos cultivos en una misma área agrícola, según las estaciones, habitual en los tiempos medievales y a principios de la Europa moderna. (p. 7)

crops Plants that are cultivated from the ground, such as fruits, vegetables, and grains. (p. 7)

cultivos Plantas que se cultivan en la tierra, como frutas, verduras y granos. (p. 7)

Crusades A term used to describe the "holy wars" waged by Western Christendom, especially against the forces of Islam in the eastern Mediterranean from 1095 to 1291 and on the Iberian Peninsula into the fifteenth century. Further Crusades were also conducted in non-Christian regions of Eastern Europe from about 1150 on. Crusades could be declared only by the pope; participants swore a vow and received in return an indulgence removing the penalty for confessed sins. (p. 163)

cruzadas Término empleado para describir las "guerras santas" llevadas a cabo por la Europa Occidental cristiana, particularmente contra las fuerzas islámicas en el Mediterráneo oriental desde 1095 hasta 1291 y en la península ibérica hasta entrado el siglo XV. Otras cruzadas también tuvieron lugar en regiones no cristianas de Europa del Este de aproximadamente el año 1150 en adelante. Las cruzadas solo podían ser declaradas por el papa; los cruzados tomaban votos y en cambio se les concedía la indulgencia por los pecados confesados. (p. 163)

Cuban missile crisis Major standoff between the United States and the Soviet Union in 1962 over Soviet deployment of nuclear missiles in Cuba; the confrontation ended in compromise, with the USSR removing its missiles in exchange for the United States agreeing not to invade Cuba. (p. 691)

Crisis de los misiles en Cuba Mayor enfrentamiento entre los Estados Unidos y la Unión Soviética en 1962 por el despliegue soviético de misiles nucleares en Cuba; el conflicto terminó en un acuerdo en el que la URSS debía retirar sus misiles y los Estados Unidos, en cambio, aceptaban no invadir Cuba. (p. 691)

cultivation system System of forced labor used in the Netherlands East Indies in the nineteenth century; peasants were required to cultivate at least 20 percent of their land in cash crops, such as sugar or coffee, for sale at low and fixed prices to government contractors, who then earned enormous profits from resale of the crops. (p. 567)

sistema de cultivo Sistema de trabajo forzado empleado en las Indias Orientales Neerlandesas en el siglo XIX; los campesinos tenían que cultivar al menos un 20 % de sus tierras para cultivos comerciales, tales como el azúcar o el café, que se vendían a precios bajos y fijos a contratistas del gobierno, los cuales obtenían beneficios colosales en la reventa de dichos cultivos. (p. 567)

cultural globalization The global spread of elements of popular culture such as film, language, and music from various places of origin, especially the spread of Western cultural forms to the rest of the world; has come to symbolize modernity, inclusion in global culture, and liberation or rebellion. It has prompted pushback from those who feel that established cultural traditions have been threatened. (p. 815)

mundialización de la cultura Difusión mundial de elementos de la cultura popular como las películas, los idiomas y la música de varios lugares, especialmente de las formas culturales occidentales al resto del mundo; se ha convertido en el símbolo de la modernidad, la inclusión de la cultura mundial y la liberación o rebelión. Ha sido rechazada por sectores que sienten que las tradiciones culturales establecidas están siendo amenazadas. (p. 815)

Cultural Revolution China's Great Proletarian Cultural Revolution was a massive campaign launched by Mao Zedong in the mid-1960s to combat the capitalist tendencies that he believed reached into even the highest ranks of the Communist Party; the campaign threw China into chaos. (p. 686)

Revolución Cultural La Gran Revolución Cultural Proletaria en China fue una campaña de masas organizada por Mao Zedong a mediados de la década de 1960 para luchar contra las tendencias capitalistas que según él llegaban incluso hasta los altos cargos del Partido Comunista; la campaña condujo a China al caos. (p. 686)

culture The way of life of a certain people that is shown through various traditions such as religion, art, and behavior. (p. 10)

cultura Forma de vida de determinadas personas que se ve reflejada en diversas tradiciones, como la religión, el arte y el comportamiento. (p. 10)

currency Money in circulation used for exchange. (p. 137)

moneda Dinero en circulación que se usa para el comercio. (p. 137)

D	
Dahomey West African kingdom in which the slave trade became a major state-controlled industry. (pron. deh-HOH-mee) (p. 346)	**Dahomey** Reino de África Occidental en el que el tráfico de esclavos se convirtió en una importante industria controlada por el Estado. (pron. dao-MEI) (p. 346)
Daoism A Chinese philosophy or popular religion that advocates a simple and unpretentious way of living and alignment with the natural world, founded by the legendary figure Laozi. (pron. dow-ism) (p. 34)	**Taoísmo** Filosofía o religión popular china que aboga por una manera de vivir sencilla y sin pretenciones, y alineada con el mundo natural. Fue fundada por la figura legendaria Lao-Tse. (p. 34)
decimate To kill or damage a large number of something. (p. 104)	**diezmar** Matar o dañar a un gran número. (p. 104)
Declaration of the Rights of Man and Citizen Charter of political liberties, drawn up by the French National Assembly in 1789, that proclaimed the equal rights of all male citizens; the declaration gave expression to the essential outlook of the French Revolution and became the preamble to the French constitution completed in 1791. (p. 395)	**Declaración de los Derechos del Hombre y del Ciudadano** Declaración de libertades políticas redactada por la Asamblea Nacional francesa en 1789 que proclamó la igualdad de derechos de todos los hombres; la declaración dio expresión a las perspectivas esenciales de la Revolución francesa y fue el prefacio a la Constitución francesa de 1791. (p. 395)
decolonization Process in which many African and Asian states won their independence from Western colonial rule, in most cases by negotiated settlement and in some cases through violent military confrontations. (p. 696)	**descolonización** Proceso con el que muchos estados africanos y asiáticos obtuvieron su independencia del dominio colonial occidental negociando acuerdos en la mayoría de los casos, y, en algunos casos, por medio de enfrentamientos militares violentos. (p. 696)
deforestation Cutting or clearing away large amounts of trees in a forested area. (p. 6)	**deforestación** Tala o extracción de gran cantidad de árboles de un área forestada. (p. 6)
demographic Relating to a certain statistic of the human population. (p. 20)	**demográfico** Relativo a cierta estadística de la población humana. (p. 20)
Deng Xiaoping (1904–1997) Leader of China from 1978 to 1997 whose reforms dismantled many of the distinctly communist elements of the Chinese economy. (pron. dung shee-yao-ping) (p. 708)	**Deng Xiaoping (1904–1997)** Líder de China entre 1978 y 1997 cuyas reformas desmantelaron varios elementos comunistas clave de la economía china. (pron. deng-shio-PING) (p. 708)
dependent development Term used to describe Latin America's economic growth in the nineteenth century, which was largely financed by foreign capital and dependent on European and North American prosperity and decisions; also viewed as a new form of colonialism. (p. 472)	**desarrollo dependiente** Término empleado para describir el crecimiento económico de América Latina en el siglo XIX que era principalmente financiado por el capital extranjero y dependía de la prosperidad y las decisiones de Europa y América del Norte; también se consideraba una nueva forma de colonialismo. (p. 472)
derogatory Degrading or criticizing. (p. 219)	**despectivo** Degradante o crítico. (p. 219)
desertification Process of fertile land becoming a desert. This can be caused by frequent agricultural use, deforestation, or drought. (p. 829)	**desertificación** Proceso por el cual un terreno fértil se convierte en un desierto. Esto puede deberse al uso agrícola frecuente, la deforestación o la sequía. (p. 829)
despotic Having absolute power as a ruler that is often taken advantage of. (p. 513)	**despótico** Que tiene poder absoluto como gobernante y a menudo se aprovecha de eso. (p. 513)
devshirme A term that means "collection or gathering"; it refers to the Ottoman Empire's practice of removing young boys from their Christian subjects and training them for service in the civil administration or in the elite Janissary infantry corps. (pron. devv-shirr-MEH) (p. 233)	*devshirme* Término que significa "recogida o recolección" y que se refiere a la práctica del Imperio otomano de separar a los chicos jóvenes de sus súbditos cristianos con el fin de entrenarlos para servir en su administración civil o en los cuerpos de jenízaros de élite. (pron. dev-SHIR-me) (p. 233)
diffusion The scattering or spreading of something. (p. 5)	**difusión** Divulgación o propagación de algo. (p. 5)

dignitary A person of high rank or social authority such as a government official. (p. 236)

dignatario Persona de alto rango o autoridad social, como un funcionario del gobierno. (p. 236)

diphtheria A type of disease that causes weakness of the body as well as fever and difficulty breathing. This can lead to issues of the heart and nervous system. (p. 162)

difteria Tipo de enfermedad que causa debilidad del cuerpo, fiebre y dificultades respiratorias. Esto puede provocar complicaciones cardíacas y del sistema nervioso. (p. 162)

disdain Dislike due to unworthiness. (p. 265)

desdén Desagrado a causa del poco valor de algo. (p. 265)

disease Condition of the body or its parts that have a negative impact and often the potential to spread either internally or externally. (p. 13)

enfermedad Alteración en el cuerpo o en una de sus partes que tiene un impacto negativo y que a menudo puede propagarse interna o externamente. (p. 13)

dispensaries Locations such as hospitals or schools that serve the community by supplying inexpensive medical care. (p. 773)

dispensarios Lugares como hospitales o escuelas que sirven a la comunidad proporcionando atención médica a bajo costo. (p. 773)

dissemination The spread of something such as information or ideas. (p. 12)

divulgación Propagación de algo, como información o ideas. (p. 12)

dogmatic Strong assertion of rules or beliefs. (p. 581)

dogmático Reivindicación de reglas o creencias. (p. 581)

dowry Money, property, or goods given to a man by his wife's parents. (p. 276)

dote Dinero, propiedades o bienes que un hombre entrega a los padres de su esposa. (p. 276)

Dream of the Red Chamber, The Book written by Cao Xueqin that explores the life of an elite family with connections to the court; it was the most famous popular novel of mid-eighteenth-century China. (p. 278)

Sueño en el pabellón rojo Obra escrita por Cao Xueqin que explora la vida de una familia de élite vinculada con la corte; fue la novela popular más famosa de mediados del siglo XVIII en China. (p. 278)

drudgery Tedious, boring, or unpleasant work. (p. 414)

trabajo soporífero Trabajo tedioso, aburrido o desagradable. (p. 414)

Dunhuang A major commercial city on the Silk Road trading network and a center of Buddhist learning and art. Located in western China. (p. 136)

Dunhuang Una de las ciudades comerciales más importantes de la red comercial de la Ruta de la Seda y un centro de aprendizaje y arte budista. Ubicada en el oeste de China. (p. 136)

Dutch East India Company Private trading company chartered by the Netherlands around 1600, mainly focused on Indonesia; it was given a monopoly on Indian Ocean trade, including the right to make war and to rule conquered peoples. (p. 324)

Compañía Neerlandesa de las Indias Orientales Compañía comercial privada fundada por los holandeses en el año 1600 aproximadamente que se dedicaba principalmente al comercio con Indonesia. Recibió el monopolio del comercio en el océano Índico, inclusive el derecho de hacer la guerra y de gobernar a los pueblos conquistados. (p. 324)

dynasty A sequential series of rulers who pass on leadership from generation to generation in their own family line. (p. 3)

dinastía Secuencia de gobernantes que pasan el liderazgo de generación en generación dentro de su propia familia. (p. 3)

E

Eastern Orthodox Christianity Branch of Christianity that developed in the eastern part of the Roman Empire and gradually separated, mostly on matters of practice, from the branch of Christianity dominant in Western Europe; noted for the subordination of the Church to political authorities, a married clergy, the use of leavened bread in the Eucharist, and a sharp rejection of the authority of Roman popes. (p. 95)

cristianismo ortodoxo oriental Rama del cristianismo que se desarrolló en la parte oriental del Imperio romano y que se separó paulatinamente, especialmente en cuestiones de práctica, de la rama dominante del cristianismo en Europa Occidental; conocido por la subordinación de la Iglesia a las autoridades políticas, el matrimonio del clero, el pan con levadura en la eucaristía y un profundo rechazo a la autoridad de los papas de Roma. (p. 95)

ecological Relating to the relationships between organisms and their environment, as well as other organisms. (p. 20)

ecológico Relativo a las relaciones que existen entre los organismos, su medio ambiente y otros organismos. (p. 20)

economic globalization The deepening economic entanglement of the world's peoples, especially since 1950; accompanied by the spread of industrialization in the Global South and extraordinary economic growth following World War II; the process has also generated various forms of inequality and resistance as well as increasing living standards for many. (p. 750)

globalización económica Mayor enredo económico que afecta a todas las naciones del mundo, particularmente desde el año 1950; incluye la expansión industrial del Sur global y un crecimiento económico extraordinario después de la Segunda Guerra Mundial; este proceso también ha causado varias formas de desigualdad y de resistencia, y ha aumentado el nivel de vida de muchas personas. (p. 750)

egalitarian A social view in which all citizens are equal in all aspects of life. (p. 10)

igualitario Visión social en la que todos los ciudadanos son iguales en todos los aspectos de la vida. (p. 10)

embryonic Undeveloped, being in the early stage of progress. (p. 81)

embrionario Sin desarrollar, que se encuentra en la primera etapa del desarrollo. (p. 81)

encroachment Gradually taking control or passing certain limits. (p. 323)

invasión Que gradualmente toma el control o pasa ciertos límites. (p. 323)

endemic Affecting a particular area or people group. (p. 326)

endémico Que afecta un área o a un grupo de personas en particular. (p. 326)

ennobling To make progress in terms of nobility or respect. (p. 636)

ennoblecer Progresar en términos de nobleza o de respeto. (p. 636)

entrench To firmly establish or defend something. (p. 247)

afianzar Establecer o defender algo con firmeza. (p. 247)

entrepreneur Someone who takes a risk by opening and managing a business themselves. (p. 104)

emprendedor Alguien que corre un riesgo al crear y administrar su propia empresa. (p. 104)

equitable Considered to be just and fair; equal. (p. 395)

equitativo Considerado como justo y decente; igualitario. (p. 395)

ethno-linguistic Relating to the language, culture, and worldly perceptions of people. (p. 235)

etnolingüística Relativo al lenguaje, la cultura y las percepciones mundanas de las personas. (p. 235)

eunuch A man who has had his sexual organs removed or, in other words, been castrated. (p. 155)

eunuco Hombre a quien le han extraído su órganos sexuales o que, en otras palabras, ha sido castrado. (p. 155)

European Economic Community An alliance formed in 1957 by six Western European countries dedicated to developing common trade policies and reduced tariffs; it gradually developed into the larger European Union. (p. 680)

Comunidad Económica Europea Unión formada en 1957 por seis países de Europa Occidental destinada a desarrollar políticas comerciales comunes y tarifas reducidas; se convirtió gradualmente en la Unión Europea. (p. 680)

European Enlightenment European intellectual movement of the eighteenth century that applied the principles of the Scientific Revolution to human affairs and was noted for its commitment to open-mindedness and inquiry and the belief that knowledge could transform human society. (p. 286)

Ilustración Movimiento intelectual europeo del siglo XVIII que aplicaba los principios de la Revolución científica a las cuestiones humanas y que fue conocido por su compromiso con la tolerancia y la investigación, así como por la creencia de que el conocimiento podía transformar la sociedad humana. (p. 286)

European Renaissance A "rebirth" of classical learning that is most often associated with the cultural blossoming of Italy in the period 1350–1500 and that included not just a rediscovery of Greek and Roman learning but also major developments in art, as well as growing secularism in society. It spread to Northern Europe after 1400. (p. 103)

Renacimiento "Renacimiento" del saber clásico que se asocia con el Renacimiento italiano de 1350–1500 y que no solo incluyó un redescubrimiento de los saberes griegos y romanos, sino también un importante desarrollo de las artes y un crecimiento del secularismo en la sociedad. Se extendió a Europa del Norte después del año 1400. (p. 103)

exacerbate To worsen in quality or escalate in violence or severity. (p. 707)

exacerbar Disminuir la calidad o bien aumentar el grado de violencia o gravedad. (p. 707)

explicit Being clearly defined or presented. (p. 398)

explícito Que se define o se presenta con claridad. (p. 398)

exploitation To be used for profit or advantage, often unfairly. (p. 40)

explotación Que se usa para obtener una ganancia o una ventaja, a menudo injustamente. (p. 40)

export-processing zones (EPZs) Areas where international companies can operate with tax and other benefits, offered as an incentive to attract manufacturers. (p. 763)

zonas de libre comercio (ZLC) Áreas en las que empresas internacionales pueden operar con beneficios fiscales y otros tipos de beneficios que son ofrecidos para atraer a productores. (p. 763)

expulsion Being forced out or expelled. (p. 324)

expulsión Ser obligado a salir o a abandonar un lugar. (p. 324)

F

factionalism A large group being divided into subgroups that have slight variations. (p. 145)

faccionalismo Grupo grande dividido en subgrupos que tienen pequeñas diferencias entre sí. (p. 145)

fascism Political ideology that considered the conflict of nations to be the driving force of history; marked by intense nationalism and an appeal to post–World War I discontent. Fascists praised violence against enemies as a renewing force in society, celebrated action rather than reflection, and placed their faith in a charismatic leader. Fascists also bitterly condemned individualism, liberalism, feminism, parliamentary democracy, and communism. (p. 634)

fascismo Ideología política que consideraba que el conflicto entre naciones era la fuerza motriz de la historia; fue marcada por un nacionalismo intenso y por su descontento después de la Primera Guerra Mundial. Los fascistas alababan la violencia contra los enemigos como una fuerza renovada en la sociedad, celebraban la acción más que la reflexión y ponían su fe en un líder carismático. Los fascistas condenaban implacablemente el individualismo, el liberalismo, el feminismo, la democracia parlamentaria y el comunismo. (p. 634)

female circumcision The excision of a pubescent girl's clitoris and adjacent genital tissue as part of initiation rites marking her coming-of-age; missionary efforts to end the practice sparked a widespread exodus from mission churches in colonial Kenya. (p. 579)

ablación genital femenina Escisión del clítoris y tejido genital de una niña pubescente como parte de un ritual de iniciación a la vida adulta; los esfuerzos de los misioneros por acabar con esta práctica desencadenaron un éxodo considerable de seguidores de las iglesias misioneras en la Kenia colonial. (p. 579)

feminism in the Global South Mobilization of women across Asia, Africa, and Latin America; distinct from Western feminism because of its focus on issues such as colonialism, racism, and poverty, rather than those exclusively related to gender. (p. 773)

feminismo en el Sur global Movilización de las mujeres a través de Asia, África y América Latina; se distingue del feminismo occidental porque se concentra en cuestiones de colonialismo, de racismo y de pobreza más que concentrarse exclusivamente en las cuestiones de género. (p. 773)

feudalism A highly fragmented and decentralized society in which power was held by the landowning warrior elite. In this highly competitive system, lesser lords and knights swore allegiance to greater lords or kings and thus became their vassals, frequently receiving lands and plunder in return for military service. (p. 97)

feudalismo Una sociedad descentralizada y muy fragmentada en la que el poder estaba en manos de una élite de terratenientes guerreros. En este sistema tan competitivo, los señores y caballeros secundarios le juraban lealtad a los señores y caballeros de mayor rango, y así se convertían en sus vasallos. Con frecuencia, estos recibían tierras y botines a cambio de servicios militares. (p. 97)

Filipino A person who originates from the Philippines. (p. 323)

Filipino Persona originaria de las Filipinas. (p. 323)

finance Management of a person's or organization's money and investments. (p. 25)

finanzas Administración del dinero y las inversiones de una persona o de una organización. (p. 25)

financial instrument A tradeable asset such as cash or bonds. (p. 74)

instrumento financiero Activo negociable, como el dinero en efectivo o los bonos. (p. 74)

foot binding The Chinese practice of tightly wrapping girls' feet to keep them small, prevalent in the Song dynasty and later; an emphasis on small size and delicacy was central to views of female beauty. (p. 75)

vendado de pies Práctica china, frecuente a partir de la dinastía Song, que consistía en vendar los pies de las niñas para prevenir su crecimiento; los pies pequeños y la delicadeza eran aspectos centrales en la concepción de la belleza femenina. (p. 75)

French Revolution Massive upheaval of French society (1789–1815) that overthrew the monarchy, ended the legal privileges of the nobility, and for a time outlawed the Catholic Church. The French Revolution proceeded in stages, becoming increasingly radical and violent until the period known as the Terror in 1793–1794, after which it became more conservative, especially under Napoleon Bonaparte (r. 1799–1815). (p. 395)

Revolución francesa Agitación masiva de la sociedad francesa (1789–1815) que derrocó la monarquía, acabó con los privilegios legales de la nobleza y declaró ilegal a la Iglesia católica durante un tiempo. La Revolución francesa se llevó a cabo por etapas y se hizo cada vez más radical y violenta hasta el período conocido como el Terror en 1793–1794, después del cual se volvió más conservadora, particularmente bajo Napoleón Bonaparte (r. 1799–1815). (p. 395)

frontier An area that lies along or beyond a known border. (p. 43)

frontera Área que se encuentra a lo largo de un límite conocido o en sus alrededores. (p. 43)

fur trade A global industry in which French, British, and Dutch traders exported fur from North America to Europe, using Native American labor and with great environmental cost to the Americas. A parallel commerce in furs operated under Russian control in Siberia. (p. 331)

comercio de pieles Industria global en la que los comerciantes franceses, británicos y holandeses exportaban pieles desde América del Norte hasta Europa, empleando la mano de obra nativa americana y generando un coste medioambiental importante a las Américas. Un comercio paralelo de pieles se desarrolló en Siberia bajo el control ruso. (p. 331)

G

Galileo (1564–1642) An Italian scientist who developed an improved telescope in 1609, with which he made many observations that undermined established understandings of the cosmos. (pron. gal-uh-LAY-oh) (p. 283)

Galileo (1564–1642) Científico italiano que, en 1609, mejoró el telescopio y lo usó para hacer observaciones que derrumbaron los conocimientos establecidos sobre el cosmos. (pron. ga-li-LE-o) (p. 283)

Gandhi, Mohandas (1869–1948) Often known as "Mahatma" or "Great Soul," the political leader of the Indian drive for independence from Great Britain; rejected the goal of modern industrialization and advocated nonviolence. (p. 702)

Gandhi, Mohandas (1869–1948) A menudo llamado "Mahatma" o "Alma Grande", el líder político de los indios impulsó su independencia de Gran Bretaña; rechazaba la industrialización moderna y defendía el pacifismo. (p. 702)

garrisoned city Place used as a home base for troops who originally guarded that particular area. (p. 144)

ciudad de guarnición Lugar establecido como base de las tropas que originalmente protegían un área determinada. (p. 144)

gender Socially constructed characteristics that distinguish between masculinity and femininity. (p. 7)

género Características socialmente construidas que distinguen a la masculinidad de la feminidad. (p. 7)

General Crisis The near-record cold winters experienced in much of China, Europe, and North America in the mid-seventeenth century, sparked by the Little Ice Age; extreme weather conditions led to famines, uprisings, and wars. (p. 210)

crisis del siglo XVII Unos de los inviernos más fríos registrados en la mayor parte de China, Europa y América del Norte a mediados del siglo XVII denominados la Pequeña Edad de Hielo; las condiciones meteorológicas extremas llevaron a hambrunas, levantamientos y guerras. (p. 210)

gentry A high social class that in England represents those just below nobility. (p. 221)

alta burguesía Clase social alta que en Inglaterra representa a aquellos que se encuentran justo por debajo de la nobleza.

germs Microorganisms that spread various pathogens and diseases. (p. 134)

gérmenes Microorganismos que propagan diversos agentes patógenos y enfermedades. (p. 134)

glaciation Period in which ice and glaciers form and cover the earth's surface. (p. 744)

glaciación Periodo en el que el hielo y los glaciares cubren la superficie de la Tierra. (p. 744)

glasnost Part of Mikhail Gorbachev's reform agenda for the Soviet Union during the late 1980s, glasnost (openness) permitted an unprecedented range of cultural and intellectual freedoms in the media, in education, in politics, and in religious life. (p. 709)

glásnost Como parte de la agenda de reformas de Mikhail Gorbachev para la Unión Soviética a finales de la década de 1980, el glasnot (apertura) permitió una variedad sin precedentes de libertades culturales en los medios de comunicación, la educación, la política y la vida religiosa. (p. 709)

globalization of democracy Late twentieth-century political shift that brought popular movements, multiparty elections, and new constitutions to countries around the world. (p. 705)

globalización de la democracia Cambio político de finales del siglo XX que llevó movimientos populares, elecciones multipartidistas y nuevas constituciones a países alrededor del mundo. (p. 705)

global urbanization The explosive growth of cities after 1900, caused by the reduced need for rural labor and more opportunities for employment in manufacturing, commerce, government, and the service industry. (p. 802)

urbanización global Crecimiento explosivo de las ciudades después del año 1900 causado por la necesidad reducida de mano de obra rural y el aumento de oportunidades laborales en la manufactura, el comercio, el gobierno y el sector servicios. (p. 802)

Gorbachev, Mikhail (1931–2022) Leader of the Soviet Union from 1985 to 1991 whose efforts to reform the USSR led to its collapse. (pron. GORE-beh-CHOF) (p. 709)

Gorbachov, Mijaíl (1931–2022) Líder de la Unión Soviética desde 1985 hasta 1991 cuyos esfuerzos por reformar la URSS la llevaron al colapso. (pron. gor-ba-CHOV) (p. 709)

Great Depression Worldwide economic contraction that began in 1929 with a stock market crash in the United States and continued in many areas until the outbreak of World War II. (p. 632)

Gran Depresión Crisis económica mundial que comenzó en 1929 con la caída de la bolsa en Estados Unidos y que se extendió a numerosos países hasta que estalló la Segunda Guerra Mundial. (p. 632)

Great Dying Term used to describe the devastating demographic impact of European-borne epidemic diseases on the Americas; in many cases, up to 90 percent of the pre-Columbian population died. (p. 210)

catástrofe demográfica en América Término empleado para describir el impacto demográfico devastador que tuvieron epidemias de origen europeo en las Américas; en muchos casos, murió hasta el 90 % de la población precolombina. (p. 210)

Great Jamaica Revolt Slave rebellion in the British West Indies (1831–1832) in which around 60,000 enslaved people attacked several hundred plantations; inspired by the Haitian Revolution, the discontent of the enslaved population and the brutality of the British response helped sway the British public to support the abolition of slavery. (p. 406)

Gran Rebelión jamaiquina Rebelión de esclavos en las Indias Occidentales Británicas (1831–1832) inspirada por la revolución haitiana en la que unos 60 000 esclavos destruyeron cientos de plantaciones; el descontento de los esclavos y la brutal respuesta de los británicos persuadió al pueblo británico de que apoyara la abolición de la esclavitud. (p. 406)

Great Leap Forward Communist push for collectivization that created "people's communes" and aimed to mobilize China's population for rapid development. (p. 686)

Gran Salto Adelante Campaña comunista a favor de la colectivización que creó "comunas populares" y cuyo objetivo era movilizar a la población china para conseguir un desarrollo rápido. (p. 686)

Great Zimbabwe A powerful state in the southern African interior that apparently emerged from the growing trade in gold to the East African coast; flourished between 1250 and 1350 C.E. (p. 152)

Gran Zimbabue Poderosa nación en el sur de África que aparentemente surgió del creciente comercio de oro con la costa de África Oriental; floreció entre 1250 y 1350 E. C. (p. 152)

Green Revolution Innovations in agriculture during the twentieth century, such as mechanical harvesters, chemical fertilizers, and the development of high-yielding crops, that enabled global food production to keep up with, and even exceed, growing human numbers. (p. 800)

Revolución verde Innovaciones en la agricultura durante el siglo XX, tales como cosechadoras mecánicas, fertilizantes químicos y el desarrollo de cultivos de gran rendimiento, que permitieron a la producción alimentaria mundial seguir el ritmo, o incluso superarlo, del crecimiento humano. (p. 800)

Guomindang The Chinese Nationalist Party led by Chiang Kai-shek that governed from 1928 until its overthrow by the communists in 1949. (pron. GWOH-mihn-dahng) (p. 653)

Kuomintang Partido Nacionalista Chino liderado por Chiang Kai-shek que gobernó desde 1928 hasta el derrocamiento de los comunistas en 1949. (pron. KUO-mintang) (p. 653)

H

Haitian Revolution The only fully successful slave rebellion in world history; the uprising in the French Caribbean colony of Saint Domingue (later renamed Haiti, which means "mountainous" or "rugged" in the native Taino language) was sparked by the French Revolution and led to the establishment of an independent state after a long and bloody war (1791–1804). Its first leader was Toussaint Louverture, a former enslaved person. (p. 401)

revolución haitiana Única rebelión de esclavos exitosa de la historia; el levantamiento en la colonia francesa de Santo Domingo (más adelante renombrada Haití, lo cual significa "tierra montañosa" en criollo haitiano) fue provocado por la Revolución francesa y llevó a la proclamación de un estado independiente a raíz de una larga y sangrienta guerra (1791–1804). Su primer líder fue Toussaint Louverture, un antiguo esclavo. (p. 401)

Han dynasty The Chinese dynasty (206 B.C.E.–220 C.E.) that emerged after the Qin dynasty collapsed, establishing political and cultural patterns that lasted into the twentieth century. (p. 32)

dinastía Han Dinastía china (206 a. E. C.–220 E. C.) que siguió a la dinastía Qin y estableció modelos políticos y culturales que duraron hasta entrado el siglo XX. (p. 32)

hangul A phonetic alphabet developed in Korea in the fifteenth century in a move toward greater cultural independence from China. (pron. HAHN-gool) (p. 76)

hangul Alfabeto fonético desarrollado en Corea en el siglo XV con el fin de conseguir una mayor independencia cultural de China. (pron. han-GUL) (p. 76)

Hangzhou China's capital during the Song dynasty, with a population at its height of more than a million people. (p. 73)

Hangzhou Capital de China durante la dinastía Song que llegó a tener más de un millón de habitantes. (p. 73)

hashish A type of narcotic and intoxicant drug that is illegal in most countries. (p. 276)

hachís Tipo de droga narcótica y estupefaciente que es ilegal en la mayoría de los países. (p. 276)

havoc Chaos after destruction. (p. 478)

estragos Caos que sigue a la destrucción. (p. 478)

heresy Belief that is contrary to the established beliefs and accepted doctrine of a religious system. (p. 235)

herejía Creencia que es contraria a las creencias establecidas y a la doctrina aceptada de un sistema religioso. (p. 235)

Hidalgo-Morelos rebellion Socially radical peasant rebellion in Mexico (1810) led by the priests Miguel Hidalgo and José Morelos. (p. 403)

rebelión de Hidalgo y Morelos Rebelión campesina socialmente radical que tuvo lugar en México (1810) y que fue liderada por los curas Miguel Hidalgo y José Morelos. (p. 403)

Hinduism A religion based on the many beliefs, practices, sects, rituals, and philosophies in India; in the thinking of nineteenth-century Indian reformers, it was expressed as a distinctive tradition, an Indian religion wholly equivalent to Christianity. (pp. 26, 581)

hinduismo Religión basada en numerosas creencias, prácticas, sectas, rituales y filosofías de la India; en la opinión de los reformadores indios del siglo XIX, representaba una tradición distintiva, una religión india que era el equivalente absoluto del cristianismo. (págs. 26, 581)

Hindutva A Hindu nationalist movement that became politically important in India in the 1980s; advocated a distinct Hindu identity and decried government efforts to accommodate other faith communities, particularly Islamic. (p. 818)

Hindutva Movimiento nacionalista hindú que cobró importancia en la India en el década de 1980; abogaba por una identidad hindú distinta y condenaba los esfuerzos del gobierno por admitir a otras comunidades de fe, particularmente la islámica. (p. 818)

Hitler, Adolf (1889–1945) Leader of the German Nazi Party and Germany's head of state from 1933 until his death. (p. 636)

Hitler, Adolf (1889–1945) Líder del Partido Nazi alemán y jefe del Estado alemán desde 1933 hasta su muerte. (p. 636)

HIV/AIDS A pathogen that spreads primarily through sexual contact, contaminated blood products, or the sharing of needles; after sparking a global pandemic in the 1980s, it spread rapidly across the globe and caused tens of millions of deaths. (p. 809)

VIH/sida Enfermedad que se transmite principalmente por contacto sexual, con productos sanguíneos contaminados o al compartir jeringas; después de provocar una pandemia mundial en la década de 1980, se propagó rápidamente por el mundo y causó decenas de millones de muertes. (p. 809)

Ho Chi Minh (1890–1969) Leader of the Vietnamese communist movement that established control first in the north and then the whole of Vietnam after 1975. (p. 652)

Ho Chi Minh (1890–1969) Líder del movimiento comunista vietnamita que primero tomó control del norte del país y luego de todo Vietnam después de 1975. (p. 652)

Holocaust Name commonly used for the Nazi genocide of Jews and other "undesirables" in German society. (p. 649)

Holocausto Nombre comúnmente dado al genocidio nazi de los judíos y otros "indeseables" en la sociedad alemana. (p. 649)

Holocene era A warmer and often a wetter period that began approximately 12,000 years ago following the end of the last Ice Age. These environmental conditions were uniquely favorable for human thriving and enabled the development of agriculture, significant population growth, and the creation of complex civilizations. (p. 823)

House of Wisdom An academic center for research and translation of foreign texts that was established in Baghdad in 830 C.E. by the Abbasid caliph al-Mamun. (p. 161)

Holoceno Período más cálido y más húmedo que empezó unos 12 000 años después de la última glaciación. Las condiciones medioambientales eran excepcionalmente favorables para el crecimiento humano y posibilitó el desarrollo de la agricultura, un crecimiento significativo de la población y la creación de civilizaciones complejas. (p. 823)

Casa de la sabiduría Centro académico de investigación y traducción de textos extranjeros que fue establecido en Bagdad en 830 E. C. por el califa abasí al-Mamún. (p. 161)

I

idea of "tribe" A new sense of clearly defined ethnic identities that emerged in twentieth-century Africa, often initiated by Europeans intent on showing the primitive nature of their colonial subjects, but widely adopted by Africans themselves as a way of responding to the upheavals of modern life. (p. 583)

idea de "tribu" Nuevo significado dado por los europeos a las identidades étnicas claramente definidas que aparecieron en el siglo XX en África con la intención de mostrar la naturaleza primitiva de sus súbditos coloniales, pero que los africanos mismos adoptaron como modo de respuesta a la agitación de la vida moderna. (p. 583)

ideology Set of thoughts, conscious and unconscious, that compose a person's beliefs. (p. 11)

ideología Conjunto de ideas, conscientes e inconscientes, que componen las creencias de una persona. (p. 11)

ideology of domesticity A set of ideas and values that defined the ideal role of middle-class women in nineteenth-century Europe, focusing their activity on homemaking, child rearing, charitable endeavors, and "refined" activities as the proper sphere for women. (p. 450)

ideología de la domesticidad Conjunto de ideas y valores que definían el papel ideal de las mujeres europeas de clase media del siglo XIX cuya actividad debía centrarse en las tareas del hogar, la crianza, labores caritativas y actividades "refinadas" propias de las mujeres. (p. 450)

immigrant A person who permanently moves to another country. (p. 208)

inmigrante Persona que se establece en otro país de manera definitiva. (p. 208)

impinging Impressing or having an impact. (p. 333)

incidir Causar una impresión o un impacto. (p. 333)

impoverished Being poverty stricken; very poor and weak. (p. 142)

empobrecido Víctima de la pobreza; muy pobre y débil. (p. 142)

Inca Empire The Western Hemisphere's largest imperial state in the fifteenth and early sixteenth centuries. Built by a relatively small community of Quechua-speaking people (the Incas), the empire stretched some 2,500 miles along the Andes Mountains, which run nearly the entire length of the west coast of South America, and contained perhaps 10 million subjects. (p. 108)

Imperio Inca Imperio más grande del hemisferio occidental en el siglo XV y a principios del siglo XVI. Construido por una comunidad relativamente pequeña de hablantes de quechua (los Incas), el imperio se extendía unas 2 500 millas a lo largo de la Cordillera de los Andes, lo que representaba casi la totalidad de la costa occidental de América del Sur, y contaba con quizás 10 millones de súbditos. (p. 108)

inclusivity Accepting and including participants. (p. 37)

inclusividad Aceptar e incluir participantes. (p. 37)

incursion The sudden and aggressive entrance to another's territory; an invasion. (p. 22)

incursión Ingreso repentino y agresivo en el territorio de otro; invasión. (p. 22)

Indian National Congress The political party led by Mahatma Gandhi that succeeded in bringing about Indian independence from Britain in 1947. (p. 702)

Congreso Nacional Indio Partido político liderado por Mahatma Gandhi que logró la independencia india de Gran Bretaña en 1947. (p. 702)

Indian Ocean commercial network The massive, interconnected web of commerce in premodern times between the lands that bordered the Indian Ocean (including East Africa, India, and Southeast Asia); the network was transformed as Europeans entered it in the centuries following 1500. (p. 320)

red de comercio del océano Índico Inmensa red interconectada de comercio de los tiempos premodernos entre las naciones del océano Índico (incluye África Oriental, India y el Sudeste Asiático); la red fue transformada a medida que la integraban los europeos en los siglos después de 1500. (p. 320)

Indian Rebellion of 1857–1858 Massive uprising of parts of India against British rule caused by the introduction to the colony's military forces of a new cartridge smeared with animal fat from pigs and cows, which caused strife among Muslims, who regarded pigs as unclean, and Hindus, who venerated cows. It came to express a variety of grievances against the colonial order. (p. 563)

rebelión en la India de 1857–1858 Gran levantamiento de algunas partes de India contra el dominio británico. Fue producido por la introducción en las fuerzas militares coloniales de un nuevo cartucho recubierto de grasa animal proveniente de cerdos y vacas, lo que produjo revuelo entre los musulmanes, que consideran al cerdo un animal impuro, y los hindús, que veneran a las vacas. Terminó por expresar una variedad de reclamos en contra del orden colonial. (p. 563)

Indigenous The natural and native inhabitants or organisms to a certain area. (p. 81)

Autóctonos Habitantes u organismos naturales nativos de determinada área. (p. 81)

infanticide The killing of newborn babies. (p. 330)

infanticidio Asesinato de bebés recién nacidos. (p. 330)

infidel Someone with opposing beliefs that does not accept a particular faith. (p. 87)

infiel Alguien con creencias opuestas que no acepta una fe en particular. (p. 87)

influenza pandemic One of the worst pandemics in human history, caused by three waves of influenza that swept across the globe in 1918 and 1919, carried by demobilized soldiers, refugees, and other dislocated people returning home from World War I; at least 50 million people died in the pandemic. (p. 809)

pandemia de gripe Una de las peores pandemias en la historia de la humanidad, fue producida por tres olas de influenza que recorrieron el globo en 1918 y 1919. La transmitieron los solados desmovilizados, los refugiados y otras personas que regresaban de la Primera Guerra Mundial; al menos 50 millones de personas murieron en la pandemia. (p. 809)

informal economy Also known as the "shadow" economy; refers to unofficial, unregulated, and untaxed economic activity. (p. 764)

economía informal También denominada economía "en la sombra"; hace referencia a la actividad económica no oficial, no regulada y libre de impuestos. (p. 764)

informal empires Term commonly used to describe areas that were dominated by Western powers in the nineteenth century but retained their own governments and a measure of independence (e.g., China). (p. 506)

imperios informales Término comúnmente empleado para describir las zonas controladas por los poderes occidentales en el siglo XIX que conservaban sus propios gobiernos y algo de independencia (P. Ej. China). (p. 506)

innovation Introduction of something new or different. (p. 3)

innovación Presentación de algo nuevo o diferente. (p. 3)

insurance Protective coverage of potential expenses due to physical losses or death that is proportionally paid for by a client. (p. 444)

seguro Cobertura de protección contra posibles gastos provocados por pérdidas físicas o a la muerte que el cliente paga de manera proporcional. (p. 444)

insurgency Violent rebellion against an instated government. (p. 403)

insurgencia Rebelión violenta contra el gobierno establecido. (p. 403)

intermediary A person who works with two opposing sides by acting as a go-between. (p. 145)

intermediario Persona que actúa como nexo entre dos sectores opuestos. (p. 145)

interventionist Becoming involved or interfering with another country's affairs. (p. 155)

intervencionista Que se involucra o que interfiere en los asuntos de otro país. (p. 155)

intransigence Being inflexible and unwilling to compromise. (p. 465)

intransigencia Inflexible y poco dispuesto a llegar a un acuerdo. (p. 465)

invasion Entering with armed forces into a place; intruding. (p. 5)

invasión Ingresar a un lugar con las fuerzas armadas; inmiscuirse. (p. 5)

Iranian revolution Establishment of a radically Islamist government in Iran in 1979; helped trigger a war with Iraq in the 1980s. (p. 713)

Revolución iraní Establecimiento de un gobierno islamista radical en Irán en 1979; desencadenó una guerra con Irak en la década de 1980. (p. 713)

Islamic radicalism Movements that promote strict adherence to the Quran and the sharia, often in opposition to key elements of Western culture. Particularly prominent since the 1970s, such movements often present themselves as returning to an earlier expression of Islam. Examples include the Iranian revolution, Taliban, al-Qaeda, and Islamic State. (p. 820)

fundamentalismo islámico Movimientos que promueven el respeto riguroso del Corán y de la sharia que se oponen a elementos clave de la cultura occidental. Particularmente importantes en la década de 1970, estos movimientos suelen presentarse como partidarios de una interpretación clásica del Islam. Algunos ejemplos incluyen la Revolución iraní, los talibanes, Al Qaeda y el Estado Islámico. (p. 820)

Israeli-Palestinian conflict Struggle between the Jewish state of Israel and the adjacent Palestinian Muslim territories that has generated periodic wars and upheavals since 1948. (p. 713)

conflicto israelí-palestino Lucha entre el Estado judío de Israel y los Territorios Palestinos musulmanes colindantes que ha generado guerras y levantamientos periódicos desde 1948. (p. 713)

J

Jesuits in China Series of Jesuit missionaries from 1550 to 1800 who, inspired by the work of Matteo Ricci, sought to understand and become integrated into Chinese culture as part of their efforts to convert the Chinese elite, although with limited success. (p. 273)

jesuitas en China Conjunto de misioneros jesuitas desde 1550 hasta 1800 que, inspirados por el trabajo de Matteo Ricci, trataron de entender la cultura china e integrarse en la misma con el fin de convertir a las élites chinas, aunque sin mucho éxito. (p. 273)

Jesus of Nazareth A peasant/artisan "wisdom teacher" and Jewish mystic (ca. 4 B.C.E.–29 C.E.) whose life, teachings, death, and alleged resurrection gave rise to the new religion of Christianity. (p. 36)

Jesús de Nazaret Campesino/artesano, "maestro de sabiduría" y místico judío (hacia los años 4 a. E. C.–29 E. C.) cuya vida, enseñanzas, muerte y supuesta resurrección dieron origen a una nueva religión: el cristianismo. (p. 36)

jizya Special tax paid by *dhimmis* (protected but second-class subjects) in Muslim-ruled territory in return for freedom to practice their own religion. (p. 86)

yizia Impuesto especial que pagan los *dhimmíes* (súbditos protegidos, pero de segunda clase) en los territorios gobernados por musulmanes a cambio de poder practicar su propia religión. (p. 86)

Judaism The monotheistic religion developed in the Middle East by the Hebrews, emphasizing a sole personal god (Yahweh) with concerns for social justice. (p. 35)

judaísmo Religión monoteísta desarrollada en el Oriente Medio por los hebreos que pone énfasis en un dios personal único (Yahveh) que se preocupa por la justicia social. (p. 35)

K

kaleidoscopic Continuously and rapidly changing. (p. 704)

caleidoscópico Que cambia continua y rápidamente. (p. 704)

kaozheng Literally, "research based on evidence"; Chinese intellectual movement whose practitioners were critical of conventional Confucian philosophy and instead emphasized the importance of evidence and analysis, applied especially to historical documents. (p. 289)

kaozheng Literalmente "investigación basada en la evidencia", fue un movimiento intelectual chino cuyos miembros criticaban el confucianismo convencional y ponían el énfasis en la importancia de la evidencia y el análisis, particularmente en documentos históricos. (p. 289)

Khubilai Khan Grandson of Chinggis Khan who ruled China from 1271 to 1294. (pron. koo-buh-l'eye kahn) (p. 144)

Kublai Kan Nieto de Gengis Kan que gobernó China de 1271 a 1294. (pron. ku-blai KAN) (p. 144)

Kievan Rus A culturally diverse civilization that emerged around the city of Kiev in the ninth century C.E. and adopted Christianity in the tenth, thus linking this emerging Russian state to the world of Eastern Orthodoxy. (p. 94)

Rus de Kiev Civilización culturalmente distinta que apareció alrededor de la ciudad de Kiev en el siglo IX E. C. y que adoptó el cristianismo en el sigo X, vinculando así el Estado ruso emergente con el mundo de la ortodoxia oriental. (p. 94)

kinship Maintaining similarities to others, particularly through family relationships. (p. 10)

parentesco Que presenta semejanzas con otros, especialmente por relaciones familiares. (p. 10)

L

laboring classes The majority of Britain's nineteenth-century population, which included manual workers in the mines, ports, factories, construction sites, workshops, and farms of Britain's industrializing and urbanizing society; this class suffered the most and at least initially gained the least from the transformations of the Industrial Revolution. (p. 451)

clase obrera Gran parte de la población británica del siglo XIX, que incluía trabajadores manuales en minas, puertos, fábricas, obras, talleres y granjas de la sociedad en proceso de industrialización y urbanización británica; esta clase fue la que más sufrió y la que menos se benefició, al menos al principio, de las transformaciones generadas por la Revolución Industrial. (p. 451)

labor migration The movement of people, often illegally, into another country to escape poverty or violence and to seek opportunities for work that are less available in their own countries. (p. 805)

migración laboral Traslado de personas, a menudo ilegal, a otro país con el fin de escapar de la pobreza o la violencia así como de buscar oportunidades de trabajo menos disponibles en sus países de origen. (p. 805)

Labour Party British working-class political party established in the 1890s and dedicated to reforms and a peaceful transition to socialism, in time providing a viable alternative to the revolutionary emphasis of Marxism. (p. 456)

Partido Laborista Partido político establecido en la década de 1890 que representaba la clase obrera británica y se dedicaba a impulsar reformas y asegurar una transición pacífica al socialismo, proporcionando con el tiempo una alternativa viable al énfasis revolucionario del marxismo. (p. 456)

Latin American export boom Large-scale increase in Latin American exports (mostly raw materials and food-stuffs) to industrializing countries in the second half of the nineteenth century, made possible by major improvements in shipping; the boom mostly benefited the upper and middle classes. (p. 468)

boom de exportaciones de América Latina Aumento a gran escala de las exportaciones de América Latina (principalmente de materias primas y de productos alimenticios) a países en proceso de industrialización en la segunda mitad del siglo XIX que fue posible gracias a mejoras importantes en el transporte; las clases medias y altas fueron las que principalmente se beneficiaron del boom. (p. 468)

Latin American revolutions Series of risings in the Spanish and Portuguese colonies of Latin America (1808–1825) that established the independence of new states from European rule but that for the most part retained the privileges of the elites despite efforts at more radical social change by the lower classes. (p. 402)

revoluciones latinoamericanas Sucesión de levantamientos en las colonias españolas y portuguesas de América Latina (1808–1825) que lograron la independencia de nuevos estados del dominio europeo, pero que en su mayoría conservaron los privilegios de las élites a pesar de los esfuerzos de las clases más bajas por producir cambios sociales más drásticos. (p. 402)

Lenin (1870–1924) Born Vladimir Ilyich Ulyanov, leader of the Russian Bolshevik (later Communist) Party in 1917, when it seized power. (p. 629)

Lenin (1870–1924) Alias de Vladímir Ilich Uliánov, líder de Partido Bolchevique (más adelante comunista) ruso en 1917, año en el que tomó el poder. (p. 629)

liability Something to be held responsible for. (p. 334)

responsabilidad Algo por lo que uno debe rendir cuentas. (p. 334)

liberation The gaining of equal rights and opportunities; granting freedom. (p. 27)

liberación Obtención de igualdad de derechos y oportunidades; concesión de la libertad. (p. 27)

linguist A person who studies and speaks various languages. (p. 12)

lingüista Persona que estudia y habla diversos idiomas. (p. 12)

Lin Zexu, Commissioner Royal official charged with ending the opium trade in China; his concerted efforts to seize and destroy opium imports provoked the Opium Wars. (pron. lin zuh-SHOO) (p. 504)

Lin Hse Tsu, Comisionado Funcionario de la Casa Real encargado de acabar con el comercio de opio en China; sus esfuerzos concertados por detener y destruir las importaciones de opio provocaron las guerras del Opio. (pron. lin se tsu) (p. 504)

Little Ice Age A period of unusually cool temperatures from the thirteenth to nineteenth centuries, most prominently in the Northern Hemisphere. (p. 210)

Pequeña Edad de Hielo Período con temperaturas excepcionalmente frías desde el siglo XII hasta el siglo XIX, principalmente en el hemisferio norte. (p. 210)

lower middle class Social stratum that developed in Britain in the nineteenth century and that consisted of people employed in the service sector as clerks, salespeople, secretaries, police officers, and the like; by 1900, this group made up about 20 percent of Britain's population. (p. 450)

clase media baja Estrato social que se desarrolló en Gran Bretaña en el siglo XIX y que constaba de personas contratadas en el sector servicios como empleados, dependientes, secretarios, agentes de policía y demás; para el año 1900 este grupo constituía el 20 % de la población británica. (p. 450)

Luther, Martin (1483–1546) German priest who issued the Ninety-Five Theses and began the Protestant Reformation with his public criticism of the Catholic Church's theology and practice. (p. 263)

Lutero, Martín (1483–1546) Sacerdote alemán que escribió las noventa y cinco tesis e inició la Reforma protestante con su crítica pública de la teología y la práctica de la Iglesia católica. (p. 263)

lynching Most often regarding hanging, an execution outside of legal terms. (p. 408)

linchamiento Generalmente referido al uso de la horca, ejecución ilegal. (p. 408)

M	
Madjapahit A significant Southeast Asian state that assimilated Hindu religious ideas. It was located primarily on the island of Java and was at the peak of its power in the fourteenth century. (p. 81)	**Mayapahit** Importante estado del sureste asiático que asimiló ideas religiosas hinduístas. Estaba ubicado principalmente en la isla de Java y estuvo en la cúspide del poder en el siglo catorce. (p. 81)
madrassas Formal colleges for higher instruction in the teachings of Islam as well as in secular subjects like law, established throughout the Islamic world beginning in the eleventh century. (p. 42)	**madrasas** Universidades formales de instrucción superior sobre las enseñanzas del Islam y algunas materias seculares como el derecho. Fueron establecidas en todo el mundo islámico a partir del siglo once. (p. 42)
Mahayana Buddhism "Great Vehicle," the popular development of Buddhism in the early centuries of the Common Era, which gives a much greater role to supernatural beings and to compassion and proved to be more popular than original (Theravada) Buddhism. (p. 29)	**budismo Mahayana** "Gran Vehículo", el desarrollo popular del budismo en los primeros siglos de la era común, el cual concedía un papel más importante a los seres sobrenaturales y a la compasión y resultó ser más popular que el budismo original (Theravada). (p. 29)
malaria A type of disease transferred by mosquitoes into the human bloodstream as well as other animals. (p. 209)	**malaria** Tipo de enfermedad que los mosquitos transmiten al torrente sanguíneo de los seres humanos y de otros animales. (p. 209)
Mali A prominent state within West African civilization; it was established in 1235 C.E. and flourished for several centuries. Mali monopolized the import of horses and metals as part of the trans-Saharan trade; it was a large-scale producer of gold; and its most famous ruler, Mansa Musa, led a large group of Muslims on the pilgrimage to Mecca in 1324–1325. (p. 90)	**Mali** Estado importante de la civilización del África Occidental; fue establecido en 1235 E. C. y floreció durante varios siglos. Mali monopolizó las importaciones de caballos y de metales dentro del comercio transahariano; fue un gran productor de oro; y su gobernante más famoso, Mansa Musa, guió a un gran número de musulmanes en la peregrinación a La Meca en 1324–1325. (p. 90)
Manila The capital of the colonial Philippines, which by 1600 had become a flourishing and culturally diverse city; the site of violent clashes between the Spanish and Chinese residents. (p. 324)	**Manila** Capital de las Filipinas coloniales que para el año 1600 se había convertido en una ciudad próspera y culturalmente diversa; sitio de enfrentamientos violentos entre los españoles y los chinos. (p. 324)
Mao Zedong (1893–1976) Chairman of China's Communist Party and de facto ruler of China from 1949 until his death. (pp. 653, 683)	**Mao Zedong (1893–1976)** Presidente del Partido Comunista de China y gobernante de facto de China desde 1949 hasta su muerte. (págs. 653, 683)
marginalize To give very limited power, making someone seem unimportant. (p. 36)	**marginar** Dar un poder muy limitado, hacer que alguien parezca de poca importancia. (p. 36)
maroon societies / Palmares Free communities of formerly enslaved people in remote regions of South America and the Caribbean; the largest such settlement was Palmares in Brazil, which housed 10,000 or more people for most of the seventeenth century. (p. 344)	**cimarrones y palenques** Comunidades libres de antiguos esclavos provenientes de regiones remotas de América del Sur y del Caribe; el asentamiento más grande se ubicó en Palmares, en Brasil, en la que habitaban 10 000 o más personas durante casi todo el siglo XVII. (p. 344)
Marshall Plan Huge U.S. government initiative to aid in the post–World War II recovery of Western Europe that was put into effect in 1948. (p. 680)	**Plan Marshall** Gran iniciativa de Estados Unidos para ayudar en la recuperación de Europa Occidental después de la Segunda Guerra Mundial que entró en vigor en 1948. (p. 680)
marten A weasel-like animal found in forests of the northern hemisphere, particularly in Europe. (p. 331)	**marta** Animal similar a la comadreja que se encuentra en los bosques del hemisferio norte, especialmente en Europa. (p. 331)
Marx, Karl (1818–1883) The most influential proponent of socialism, Marx was a German expatriate in England who predicted working-class revolution as the key to creating an ideal communist future. (p. 453)	**Marx, Karl (1818–1883)** El exponente más influyente del socialismo, Marx fue un expatriado alemán en Inglaterra que predijo que una revolución de la clase trabajadora era la clave para crear un futuro comunista ideal. (p. 453)

maternal feminism Movement that claimed that women have value in society not because of an abstract notion of equality but because women have a distinctive and vital role as mothers; its exponents argued that women have the right to intervene in civil and political life because of their duty to watch over the future of their children. (p. 415)

feminismo materno Movimiento que afirmaba que las mujeres tienen un valor en la sociedad no a causa de una idea abstracta de igualdad, sino porque las mujeres tienen un papel vital y distintivo como madres; sus exponentes sostenían que las mujeres disponen del derecho de intervenir en la vida civil y política debido a su deber de velar por el futuro de sus hijos. (p. 415)

Maya civilization A major civilization of Mesoamerica known for the most elaborate writing system in the Americas and other intellectual and artistic achievements; flourished from 250 to 900 C.E. (p. 106)

civilización maya Civilización importante de Mesoamérica conocida por tener el sistema de escritura más elaborado de las Américas y por otros logros intelectuales y artísticos; floreció entre el año 250 y el 900 E. C. (p. 106)

Mecca The birth city of Muhammad that acts as the spiritual base for Islam (Mecca); also can be a place people hope to visit or often visit (mecca). (p. 5)

Meca Ciudad en la que nació Mahoma, que constituye el centro espiritual del Islam (La Meca); también puede ser un lugar que las personas esperan poder visitar alguna vez o que recibe a muchos visitantes (meca). (p. 5)

medicine A substance used to aid in illness through treatment and/or prevention of disease, or the science of using such substances. (p. 17)

medicina Sustancia usada para aliviar una enfermedad mediante un tratamiento o la prevención, o bien la ciencia del uso de dichas sustancias. (p. 17)

megacities Very large urban centers with populations of over 10 million; by 2020, there were thirty-seven such cities on five continents. (p. 803)

megaciudades Centros urbanos muy grandes con poblaciones de más de 10 millones de habitantes; para 2020 existían 37 megaciudades en cinco continentes. (p. 803)

Meiji Restoration The political takeover of Japan in 1868 by a group of young samurai from southern Japan. The samurai eliminated the shogun and claimed they were restoring to power the young emperor, Meiji. The new government was committed to saving Japan from foreign domination by drawing upon what the modern West had to offer to transform Japanese society. (pron. MAY-jee) (p. 519)

Restauración Meiji Toma política de Japón en 1868 por un grupo de jóvenes samuráis provenientes del sur del país. Los samuráis destituyeron al shogun y declararon que estaban devolviendo el poder al joven emperador, Meiji. El nuevo gobierno se comprometía a salvar Japón del dominio extranjero usando lo que el Occidente moderno ofreciera para transformar la sociedad japonesa. (pron. MEI-dji) (p. 519)

Melaka Muslim port city that came to prominence on the waterway between Sumatra and Malaya in the fifteenth century C.E.; it was the springboard for the spread of a syncretic form of Islam throughout the region. (p. 153)

Malaca Ciudad portuaria musulmana que ganó prominencia en la vía marítima entre Sumatra y Malasia en el siglo quince E. C.; fue la plataforma de lanzamiento de una forma de sincretismo del Islam hacia el resto de la región. (p. 153)

mercantilism The economic theory that governments served their countries' economic interests best by encouraging exports and accumulating bullion (precious metals such as silver and gold); helped fuel European colonialism. (p. 213)

mercantilismo Teoría económica que expone que los gobiernos sirven mejor a los intereses económicos de sus países promoviendo las exportaciones y acumulando metales preciosos (como la plata y el oro); impulsó el colonialismo europeo. (p. 213)

mercenary Person who partakes in military force for personal gain, often working for a foreign party. (p. 86)

mercenario Persona que participa de las fuerzas militares a cambio de ganancias personales, y que a menudo trabaja para un bando extranjero. (p. 86)

merchant A person who earns a living by buying and selling goods. (p. 7)

comerciante Persona que se gana la vida comprando y vendiendo bienes. (p. 7)

mestizo A term used to describe the multiracial population of Spanish colonial societies in the Americas. Recently, the word has been criticized for being associated with colonialism and racial stratification. (pron. mehs-TEE-zoh) (p. 215)

mestizo Término usado para describir la población multiracial de las sociedades coloniales españolas en las Américas. Recientemente, esta palabra ha sido criticada por estar asociada con el colonialismo y la estratificación racial. (p. 215)

Mexican Revolution Long and bloody war (1910–1920) in which Mexican reformers from the middle class joined with workers and peasants to overthrow the dictator Porfirio Díaz and create a new, much more democratic political order. (p. 471)

Revolución mexicana Larga y sangrienta guerra (1910–1920) durante la cual los reformadores mexicanos de la clase media se unieron a trabajadores y campesinos con el fin de derrocar al dictador Porfirio Díaz y crear un orden político nuevo y mucho más democrático. (p. 471)

middle-class society British social stratum developed in the nineteenth century, composed of small businessmen, doctors, lawyers, engineers, teachers, and other professionals required in an industrial society; politically liberal, they favored constitutional government, private property, free trade, and social reform within limits; had ideas of thrift, hard work, rigid morality, "respectability," and cleanliness. (p. 450)

sociedad de clase media Estrato social británico que se desarrolló en el siglo XIX, compuesto por pequeños hombres de negocios, doctores, abogados, ingenieros, profesores y otros profesionales requeridos en una sociedad industrial; políticamente liberales, favorecían el gobierno constitucional, la propiedad privada, el libre comercio y la reforma social dentro de ciertos límites; valoraban el ahorro, el trabajo duro, la moralidad rígida, la "respetabilidad" y la limpieza. (p. 450)

midwife Someone, usually a woman, who is trained to help women during childbirth despite not being a doctor. (p. 101)

partera Persona, generalmente una mujer, que está capacitada para ayudar a las mujeres durante el parto, a pesar de no ser médico. (p. 101)

millennium A time period of one thousand years. (p. 22)

milenio Periodo de mil años. (p. 22)

Ming dynasty Chinese dynasty (1368–1644) that succeeded the Yuan dynasty of the Mongols; noted for its return to traditional Chinese ways and restoration of the land after the destructiveness of the Mongols. (pp. 145, 226)

dinastía Ming Dinastía china (1368–1644) que sucedió a la dinastía mongol Yuan; conocida por su regreso a las costumbres tradicionales chinas y la restauración de la tierra tras las destructividad de los mongoles. (págs. 145, 226)

Mirabai (1498–1547) One of India's most beloved bhakti poets, who transgressed the barriers of caste and tradition. (p. 279)

Mirabai (1498–1547) Una de las poetas del bhakti más queridas de la India, sobrepasó las barreras de las castas y de la tradición. (p. 279)

missionary A person who goes somewhere, often a foreign country, to share their religious beliefs with others. (p. 26)

misionero Persona que va a determinado lugar, a menudo un país extranjero, para compartir sus creencias religiosas con otros. (p. 26)

mobilize To prepare for action in a certain situation. (p. 102)

movilizar Prepararse para la acción en cierta situación. (p. 102)

monastery The secluded house of residence for monks that also serves as their place of worship. (p. 29)

monasterio Residencia aislada de los monjes que también funciona como su lugar de adoración. (p. 29)

Mongol world war Term used to describe half a century of military campaigns, massive killing, and empire building pursued by Chinggis Khan and his successors in Eurasia after 1209. (p. 142)

guerra mundial de los mongoles Término empleado para describir medio siglo de campañas militares, asesinatos en masa y la construcción de un imperio por Gengis Kan y sus sucesores en Eurasia después de 1209. (p. 142)

monogamous A marital or sexual relationship that is held with only one person at a time. (p. 579)

monógama Relación marital o sexual que se mantiene con una sola persona en todo momento. (p. 579)

monolithic Acting as a solid and massive whole. (p. 694)

monolítico Que funciona como un todo sólido y macizo. (p. 694)

monopoly The exclusive control of a particular item or service on the market. (p. 76)

monopolio Control exclusivo de un determinado elemento o servicio en el mercado. (p. 76)

moratorium A designated time period for suspending activity or delaying something such as payment. (p. 824)

moratoria Periodo designado para suspender una actividad o retrasar algo, como el pago de algo. (p. 824)

moribund Making no advances or progress. (p. 651)

moribundo Que no avanza ni progresa. (p. 651)

Mughal Empire A successful state founded by Muslim Turkic-speaking peoples who invaded India and provided a rare period of relative political unity (1526–1707); their rule was noted for efforts to create partnerships between Hindus and Muslims. (pron. MOO-guhl) (p. 235)

Imperio mogol Próspero estado fundado por los musulmanes hablantes de lenguas túrquicas que invadieron la India y proporcionaron un período de una relativa e insólita unidad política (1526–1707); su reinado era conocido por sus esfuerzos por crear colaboraciones entre los hindúes y los musulmanes. (p. 235)

Muhammad (570–632 C.E.) The Prophet and founder of Islam whose religious revelations became the Quran, bringing a radically monotheistic religion to Arabia and the world. (p. 39)

Mahoma (570–632 E. C.) Profeta y fundador del islam cuyas revelaciones religiosas se convirtieron en el Corán, llevando una religión monoteísta radical a Arabia y al mundo. (p. 39)

mulattoes A derogatory term commonly used to describe people of mixed African and European origin. (p. 219)

mulatos Término despectivo usado comúnmente para describir personas de origen mixto entre africano y europeo. (p. 219)

munition War equipment such as weapons or ammunition. (p. 522)

munición Equipo bélico, como las armas o las municiones. (p. 522)

Muslim League Political group formed in response to the Indian National Congress in India's struggle for independence from Britain; the League's leader, Muhammad Ali Jinnah, argued that regions of India with a Muslim majority should form a separate state called Pakistan. (p. 702)

Liga Musulmana Grupo político formado en respuesta a la lucha del Congreso Nacional Indio por la independencia india de Gran Bretaña; el líder de la Liga, Muhammed Ali Jinnah, sostenía que las regiones de la India que contaban con una mayoría musulmana deberían formar un estado separado llamado Pakistán. (p. 702)

Mussolini, Benito (1883–1945) Charismatic leader of the Italian Fascist Party who came to power in 1922 and ruled until his death. (p. 635)

Mussolini, Benito (1883–1945) Carismático líder del Partido Fascista Italiano que llegó al poder en 1922 y gobernó el país hasta su muerte. (p. 635)

N

Napoleon Bonaparte French head of state and general (r. 1799–1815); Napoleon preserved much of the French Revolution under a military dictatorship and was responsible for the spread of revolutionary ideals through his conquest of much of Europe. (p. 398)

Napoleón Bonaparte Jefe del Estado francés y general (r. 1799–1815); Napoleón mantuvo gran parte de la Revolución francesa bajo una dictadura militar y fue responsable de la difusión de las ideas revolucionarias durante su conquista de gran parte de Europa. (p. 398)

nationalism The focusing of citizens' loyalty on the notion that they are part of a "nation" that merits an independent political life, with a unique culture, territory, and common experience; first became a prominent element of political culture in nineteenth-century Europe and the Americas. (p. 410)

nacionalismo Se centra en la idea de que los ciudadanos forman parte de una "nación" con una cultura y un territorio únicos y una experiencia común, lo cual es digno de una vida política independiente; se convirtió en un elemento destacado de la cultura política en Europa y las Américas en el siglo XIX. (p. 410)

Nazi Party German political party that established a fascist state dedicated to extreme nationalism, territorial expansion, and the purification of the German state. (p. 636)

Partido Nazi Partido político alemán que estableció un estado fascista dedicado al nacionalismo extremo, la expansión del territorio y la purificación del Estado alemán. (p. 636)

neoliberalism In the late 1900s, a political theory focused in the United States that limited the government and maximized personal liberty in regards to trading markets. (p. 752)

neoliberalismo Teoría política centrada en los Estados Unidos a fines del siglo XX que limitaba al gobierno y que maximizaba la libertad personal en los mercados comerciales. (p. 752)

Newton, Isaac (1642–1727) English scientist whose formulation of the laws of motion and mechanics is regarded as the culmination of the Scientific Revolution. (p. 283)

Newton, Isaac (1642–1727) Científico inglés cuya formulación de las leyes del movimiento y de la mecánica es considerada como la culminación de la Revolución científica. (p. 283)

niche A place that is well suited for someone or something. (p. 13)

nicho Lugar apropiado para alguien o para algo. (p. 13)

nobility A distinguished social class which includes those of high birth such as dukes and duchesses, and barons and baronesses. (p. 98)

nobleza Clase social distinguida que incluye a personas de alcurnia como los duques y las duquesas, y los barones y las baronesas. (p. 98)

North American Free Trade Agreement (NAFTA) Free trade agreement between the United States, Mexico, and Canada, established in 1984. It was replaced in 2020 by a new agreement among the United States, Mexico, and Canada. (p. 759)

Tratado de Libre Comercio de América del Norte (TLCAN) Acuerdo de libre comercio entre los Estados Unidos, México y Canadá establecido en 1984. Fue reemplazado en 2020 por un nuevo acuerdo entre Estados Unidos, México y Canadá. (p. 759)

North Atlantic Treaty Organization (NATO) A military alliance, created in 1949, between the United States and various European countries; largely aimed at defending against the threat of Soviet aggression during the cold war. (p. 687)

Organización del Tratado del Atlántico Norte (OTAN) Alianza militar, creada en 1949, entre los Estados Unidos y varios países europeos; su objetivo principal consistía en defenderse de la amenaza de agresión soviética durante la Guerra Fría. (p. 687)

O

oligarchy Government in which only a few people are in command. (p. 520)

oligarquía Gobierno en el que solo unas pocas personas están a cargo. (p. 520)

one-child family policy (China) Chinese policy of population control that lasted from 1980 to 2014; used financial incentives and penalties to promote birth control, sterilization, and abortions in an effort to limit most families to a single child. (p. 769)

política de hijo único (China) Política china de control de la población que duró desde 1980 hasta 2014; utilizaba incentivos y sanciones financieros para promover la anticoncepción, la esterilización, y los abortos con el fin de establecer un límite de un hijo por familia. (p. 769)

onerous Oppressive or troublesome; something that has more costs than advantages. (p. 452)

oneroso Opresivo o problemático; algo cuyos costos superan a las ventajas. (p. 452)

Opium Wars Two wars fought between Western powers and China (1840–1842 and 1856–1858) after China tried to restrict the importation of foreign goods, especially opium; China lost both wars and was forced to make major concessions. (p. 503)

guerras del Opio Dos guerras que tuvieron lugar entre las potencias occidentales y China (1840–1842 y 1856–1858) después de que China intentara restringir las importaciones de productos extranjeros, especialmente el opio; China perdió ambas guerras y se vio obligada a hacer mayores concesiones. (p. 503)

Ottoman Empire Major Islamic state centered on Anatolia that came to include the Balkans, parts of the Middle East, and much of North Africa; lasted in one form or another from the fourteenth to the early twentieth century. (pp. 84, 230)

Imperio otomano Importante estado islámico ubicado en Anatolia que llegó a incluir la península balcánica, partes del Oriente Medio y gran parte de África del Norte; de alguna manera duró desde el siglo XIV hasta principios del siglo XX. (págs. 84, 230)

Ottoman seizure of Constantinople The city of Constantinople, the capital and almost the only outpost left of the Byzantine Empire, fell to the army of the Ottoman sultan Mehmed II "the Conqueror" in 1453, an event that marked the end of Christian Byzantium. (p. 94)

Toma otomana de Constantinopla La ciudad de Constantinopla, capital y casi el único bastión que le quedaba al Imperio Bizantino, cayó ante el ejército del sultán otomano Mehmed II "El conquistador" en 1453. Este evento marcó el fin del Bizancio cristiano. (p. 94)

P

paganism Religiously believing in multiple gods. (p. 39)

paganismo Creencia religiosa en múltiples dioses. (p. 39)

Paleolithic era The long period during which human societies sustained themselves through gathering, hunting, and fishing without the practice of agriculture. Such ways of living persisted well after the advent of agriculture in many places. (p. 10)

Paleolítico Período largo durante el cual las sociedades humanas se sostenían gracias a la recolección, la caza y la pesca sin la ayuda de la agricultura. Estas formas de vida continuaron hasta mucho después de la aparición de la agricultura en varios lugares. (p. 10)

palm oil An oil extracted from palm leaves, nuts, and fruit that can be used for cooking purposes, as well as in making soaps, candles, and cosmetics. (p. 550)

aceite de palma Aceite que se extrae de las hojas, los cocos y los frutos de las palmas, y que se usa para cocinar, así como también para fabricar jabones, velas y cosméticos. (p. 550)

pantheon Place dedicated to all the gods of a religion or other highly important idols or heroes. (p. 32)

panteón Lugar dedicado a todos los dioses de una religión, o a otros ídolos o héroes importantes. (p. 32)

paradox Something that may be true despite its apparent contradictions. (p. 69)

paradoja Algo que puede ser cierto a pesar de sus aparentes contradicciones. (p. 69)

Paris Climate Agreement An international agreement negotiated in 2015 among some 195 countries, 700 cities, and many companies to reduce greenhouse gas emissions sufficiently to avoid a 2°C increase in global temperatures. (p. 833)

Acuerdo de París Acuerdo internacional negociado en 2015 entre unos 195 países, 700 ciudades y varias empresas con el fin de reducir las emisiones de gas de efecto invernadero suficientemente para evitar un aumento de 2 C en las temperaturas globales. (p. 833)

pastoral societies Based on an alternative kind of food-producing economy focused on the raising of livestock, pastoral societies emerged in the Afro-Eurasian world where settled agriculture was difficult or impossible. Pastoral peoples often led their animals to seasonal grazing grounds rather than settling permanently in a single location. (p. 14)

sociedad pastoril Basadas en una economía alternative dedicada a la producción de alimentos y al incremento del ganado, las sociedades pastoriles aparecieron en el mundo euroasiáticoafricano en el que la agricultura sedentaria era difícil o imposible. Más que asentarse en un solo lugar, los pueblos pastoriles llevaban a sus animales a zonas de pastoreo estacionales. (p. 14)

patriarchy A social system in which women have been made subordinate to men in the family and in society; often linked to the development of plow-based agriculture, intensive warfare, and private property. (p. 22)

patriarcado Sistema social en el cual las mujeres están subordinadas a los hombres de la familia y de la sociedad; se le relaciona con el desarrollo de la agricultura del arado, conflictos intensos y la propiedad privada. (p. 22)

patrilineal The focus on ancestry through the male line of descent. (p. 153)

por línea paterna Enfoque de la ascendencia por la rama masculina. (p. 153)

Paul, Saint An early convert and missionary (ca. 6–67 C.E.) and the first great popularizer of Christianity, especially to Gentile (non-Jewish) communities. (p. 36)

Pablo, San Converso, misionero (hacia los años 6–67 E. C.) y primer gran divulgador del cristianismo, especialmente entre las comunidades paganas (no judías). (p. 36)

periphery The boundary or outer edge of an area. (p. 39)

periferia Límites o los alrededores de un área. (p. 39)

Perpetua Christian martyr (181–203 C.E.) from an upper-class Roman family in Carthage. Her refusal to renounce her faith made her an inspiration for other early Christians. (p. 37)

Perpetua Mártir cristiana (181–203 E. C.) proveniente de una familia de clase alta romana en Cartago. Su negación a renunciar a su fe la convirtió en inspiración para otros cristianos antiguos. (p. 37)

pharmacology The science concerning medicine and the study of the effects of drugs on the body. (p. 103)

farmacología ciencia que se especializa en las medicinas y el estudio de los efectos de las drogas en el cuerpo. (p. 103)

philanthropist A person who focuses money and other means to help others. (p. 347)

filántropo Persona que destina dinero y otros medios a la ayuda de otras personas. (p. 347)

Philippines An archipelago of Pacific islands colonized by Spain in a relatively bloodless process that extended for the century or so after 1565, a process accompanied by a major effort at evangelization; the Spanish named them the Philippine Islands in honor of King Philip II of Spain. (p. 323)

Filipinas Archipiélago de las islas del Pacífico que fue colonizado por España en un proceso relativamente sangriento que duró más o menos un siglo a partir de 1565, proceso que fue acompañado de importantes intentos de evangelización; los españoles les llamaron las islas Filipinas en honor al rey Felipe II de España. (p. 323)

philosophy The study of general theories, ideas, and aspects of life. (p. 17)

filosofía Estudio de teorías, ideas y aspectos de la vida en general. (p. 17)

piece of eight The standard Spanish silver coin used by merchants in North America, Europe, India, Russia, West Africa, and China. (p. 329)

real de a 8 Moneda de plata española usada por los comerciantes de América del Norte, Europa, India, Rusia, África Occidental y China. (p. 329)

pochteca Professional merchants among the Aztecs who undertook large-scale trading expeditions in the fifteenth century C.E. (pron. pohch-TEH-cah) (p. 169)

pochtecas Comerciantes profesionales del Imperio azteca que llevaron a cabo expediciones comerciales de gran escala en el siglo XV E. C. (pron. poch-TE-cas) (p. 169)

population explosion An extraordinarily rapid growth in human population during the twentieth and twenty-first centuries that quadrupled human numbers in little more than a century. Experienced primarily in the Global South. (p. 800)

explosión demográfica Un crecimiento extraordinariamente rápido de la población humana durante los siglos veinte y veintiuno, en los que se cuadruplicó el número de humanos en poco más de un siglo. Tuvo lugar principalmente en el Sur global. (p. 800)

Potosí City that developed high in the Andes (in present-day Bolivia) at the site of the world's largest silver mine and that became the largest city in the Americas, with a population of some 160,000 in the 1570s. (p. 329)

Potosí Ciudad que se desarrolló en las alturas de la cordillera de los Andes (en lo que hoy es Bolivia) en el lugar en el que se situaba la mina de plata más grande del mundo y que se convirtió en la ciudad más grande de las Américas, con una población de unos 160 000 habitantes en la década de 1570. (p. 329)

prestigious Maintaining honor, esteem, or noble status. (p. 16)

prestigioso Que posee honor, estima o título de nobleza. (p. 16)

profit A monetary gain made after the sale of something for a higher price than what the seller originally paid. (p. 125)

ganancia Beneficio económico que se obtiene tras la venta de algo por un precio mayor del que se pagó originalmente.

Progressives Followers of an American political movement (progressivism) in the period around 1900 that advocated reform measures such as wages-and-hours legislation to correct the ills of industrialization. (p. 462)

progresistas Seguidores de un movimiento político americano (progresismo) alrededor del año 1900 que abogaban por medidas reformistas tales como leyes laborales para corregir los males de la industrialización. (p. 462)

proliferate To spread greatly and quickly multiply. (p. 31)

proliferar Extenderse en gran medida y multiplicarse rápidamente. (p. 31)

prolific Highly reproductive; fruitful in offspring. (p. 162)

prolífico Altamente productivo; fructífero. (p. 162)

prominence Maintaining importance and being very noticeable. (p. 6)

prominencia Que tiene importancia y que es muy notorio. (p. 6)

propagating Producing something new from a parent and spreading. This can regard a plant, or even an idea. (p. 255)

propagarse Producir algo nuevo a partir de un padre y extenderse. Puede referirse a una planta o incluso a una idea. (p. 255)

Protestant Reformation Massive schism within Christianity that had its formal beginning in 1517 with the German priest Martin Luther; the movement was radically innovative in its challenge to church authority and its endorsement of salvation by faith alone, and also came to express a variety of political, economic, and social tensions. (p. 262)

Reforma protestante Gran cisma del cristianismo que se inició en 1517 con el sacerdote alemán Martín Lutero; el movimiento fue radicalmente innovador por desafiar la autoridad de la Iglesia y respaldar la idea de la salvación solo por la fe, y generó diversas tensiones políticas, económicas y sociales. (p. 262)

Pueblo Revolt A major revolt of Native American peoples against Spanish colonial rule in late-seventeenth-century New Mexico. (p. 239)

Rebelión de los Pueblo Importante rebelión de los pueblos nativos norteamericanos contra el dominio colonial español a finales del siglo diecisiete en Nuevo México. (p. 239)

Q

Qing expansion The growth of Qing dynasty China during the seventeenth and eighteenth centuries into a Central Asian empire that added a small but important minority of non-Chinese people to the empire's population and essentially created the borders of contemporary China. (p. 228)

expansión de la dinastía Qing Crecimiento de la dinastía Qing durante los siglos XVII y XVIII hacia un imperio centroasiático que agregó a una pequeña pero importante minoría no china a la población del imperio y creó las fronteras de la China moderna. (p. 228)

Quran Also transliterated as Qur'án and Koran, this is the most holy text of Islam, which records the words of God through revelations given to the Prophet Muhammad. (p. 40)

Corán También transliterado como Qurán o Korán, es el texto más sagrado del islam que documenta la palabra de Dios a través de las revelaciones hechas al profeta Mahoma. (p. 40)

R

railroad Mode of transportation that travels over the ground by use of parallel steel rails that act as a track for wheeled locomotives. (p. 133)

ferrocarril Medio de transporte terrestre que consiste en el uso de rieles de acero paralelos que sirven de guía a las ruedas de las locomotoras. (p. 133)

regicide The killing of a king or royal figure. (p. 396)

regicidio Asesinato de un rey o de un miembro de la realeza. (p. 396)

rejoinder A quick response. (p. 497)

réplica Respuesta rápida. (p. 497)

religious fundamentalism Occurring within all the major world religions, fundamentalism is a self-proclaimed return to the alleged "fundamentals" of a religion and is marked by a militant piety, exclusivism, and a sense of threat from the modern secular world. (p. 818)

fundamentalismo religioso Dado en las principales religiones del mundo, el fundamentalismo es un autoproclamado retorno a los supuestos "fundamentos" de una religión y se caracteriza por su piedad militante, exclusivismo y un sentido de amenaza desde el mundo moderno secular. (p. 818)

repository A storage place. (p. 91)

depósito Lugar de almacenamiento. (p. 91)

repudiate To refuse acceptance or reject authority. (p. 635)

repudiar Negarse a aceptar o rechazar la autoridad. (p. 635)

revival Restoration of strength or consciousness, often in terms of religious beliefs. (p. 9)

resurgimiento Restauración de la fuerza o la consciencia, a menudo en términos de creencias religiosas. (p. 9)

Revolutionary Right (Japan) Also known as Radical Nationalism, this was a movement in Japanese political life during the Great Depression that was marked by extreme nationalism, a commitment to elite leadership focused around the emperor, and dedication to foreign expansion. (p. 642)

derecha revolucionaria (Japón) También conocido como Nacionalismo Radical, fue un movimiento en la vida política japonesa durante la Gran Depresión que se caracterizaba por su nacionalismo extremo, compromiso con el liderazgo de las élites articulado en torno al emperador y dedicación a la expansión en el extranjero. (p. 642)

Robespierre, Maximilien (1758–1794) Leader of the French Revolution during the Terror; his Committee of Public Safety executed tens of thousands of enemies of the revolution until he was arrested and guillotined. (pron. ROHBS-pee-air) (p. 396)

Robespierre, Maximilien (1758–1794) Líder de la Revolución francesa durante el Terror; su Comité de Salvación Pública ejecutó a decenas de miles de enemigos de la revolución hasta ser detenido y sentenciado a la guillotina. (pron. ro-bes-PIER) (p. 396)

Roman Catholic Church Western European branch of Christianity that gradually defined itself as separate from Eastern Orthodoxy, with a major break occurring in 1054 c.e. that still has not been overcome. By the eleventh century, Western Christendom was centered on the pope as the ultimate authority in matters of doctrine. The Church struggled to remain independent of established political authorities. (p. 98)

Iglesia católica romana Rama del cristianismo en Europa Occidental que se separó de la ortodoxia oriental con un importante cisma en el año 1054 e. c. que aún no ha sido superado. Llegado el siglo XI, la Europa Occidental cristiana consideraba el papa como la autoridad última en materia de doctrina. La Iglesia se esforzaba por permanecer independiente frente a las autoridades políticas establecidas. (p. 98)

Russian Empire A Christian state centered on Moscow that emerged from centuries of Mongol rule in 1480; by 1800, it had expanded into northern Asia and westward into the Baltics and Eastern Europe. (p. 223)

Imperio ruso Estado cristiano ubicado en Moscú que surgió tras siglos de dominio mongol en 1480; para el año 1800 se había expandido hasta Asia del Norte, los países bálticos y Europa del Este. (p. 223)

Russian Revolution Massive revolutionary upheaval in 1917 that overthrew the Romanov dynasty in Russia and ended with the seizure of power by communists under the leadership of Lenin. (p. 629)

Revolución rusa Agitación revolucionaria masiva en 1917 que derrocó la dinastía Romanov en Rusia y al término de la cual los comunistas tomaron el poder bajo el liderazgo de Lenin. (p. 629)

Russian Revolution of 1905 Spontaneous rebellion that erupted in Russia after the country's defeat at the hands of Japan in 1905; the revolution was suppressed, but it forced the government to make substantial reforms. (p. 465)

Revolución rusa de 1905 Rebelión espontánea que estalló en Rusia tras la derrota del país en manos de Japón en 1905; la revolución fue sofocada, pero obligó al gobierno a realizar reformas sustanciales. (p. 465)

Russo-Japanese War (1904–1905) Fought over rival ambitions in Korea and Manchuria, this conflict ended in a Japanese victory, establishing Japan as a formidable military competitor in East Asia. The war marked the first time that an Asian country defeated a European power in battle, and it precipitated the Russian Revolution of 1905. (p. 523)

guerra ruso-japonesa (1904–1905) Librado por ambiciones encontradas en Corea y Manchuria, este conflicto acabó con la victoria de Japón, quién se erigió como un formidable competidor militar en el este de Asia. Marcó un hito al ser la primera vez que un país asiático derrotaba a una potencia europea en el campo de batalla y precipitó la Revolución rusa de 1905. (p. 523)

S

sable A weasel-like animal from colder forested regions that has highly valued fur. (p. 225)	**marta cibelina** Animal parecido a la comadreja; vive en regiones boscosas frías y tiene una piel muy valiosa. (p. 225)
sacrament A religious act or ceremony that is considered important. (p. 264)	**sacramento** Acto o ceremonia religiosa que se considera importante. (p. 264)
sacrosanct Unquestionable due to importance. (p. 390)	**sacrosanto** Incuestionable debido a su importancia. (p. 390)
Safavid Empire Major Turkic empire established in Persia in the early sixteenth century and notable for its efforts to convert its people to Shia Islam. (pron. SAH-fah-vid) (p. 235)	**Imperio safávida** Gran Imperio túrquico establecido en Persia a principios del siglo XVI y conocido por sus esfuerzos por convertir a este pueblo al islam chií. (pron. sa-FA-bi-da) (p. 235)
Sand Roads A term used to describe the routes of the trans-Saharan trade, which linked interior West Africa to the Mediterranean and North African world. (pp. 45, 156)	**rutas de las caravanas** Término empleado para describir las rutas de comercio transahariano que unían el interior del África Occidental con el mundo mediterráneo del África septentrional. (págs. 45, 156)
schism A division of opposing parties that were originally of the same group. (p. 264)	**cisma** División de partidos enfrentados que originalmente formaban parte del mismo grupo. (p. 264)
scientific racism A new kind of racism that emerged in the nineteenth century that increasingly used the prestige and apparatus of science to support European racial prejudices and preferences. (p. 555)	**racismo científico** Nuevo tipo de racismo surgido en el siglo XIX que empleaba cada vez más el prestigio y el aparato científico para sustentar los prejuicios y preferencias raciales de los europeos. (p. 555)
Scientific Revolution The intellectual and cultural transformation that shaped a new conception of the material world between the mid-sixteenth and early eighteenth centuries in Europe; instead of relying on the authority of religion or tradition, its leading figures believed that knowledge was acquired through rational inquiry based on evidence, the product of human minds alone. (p. 280)	**Revolución científica** Transformación intelectual y cultural que moldeó una nueva concepción del mundo material entre la mitad del siglo XVI y principios del siglo XVIII en Europa; en lugar de confiar en la autoridad de la religión o la tradición, sus figuras destacadas creían que el conocimiento se adquiría a través de la investigación racional basada en la experiencia, producto únicamente de la mente humana. (p. 280)
scramble for Africa The process by which European countries partitioned the continent of Africa among themselves in the period 1875–1900. (p. 558)	**reparto de África** Proceso por el que los países europeos se repartieron el continente de África en el período de 1875 a 1900. (p. 558)
Sea Roads The world's largest sea-based system of communication and exchange before 1500 C.E. Centered on India, it stretched from southern China to eastern Africa. (pp. 45, 150)	**rutas marítimas** El sistema de comunicación e intercambio por mar más extenso del mundo antes del año 1500 E. C. Centrado en India, abarcaba desde el sur de China hasta el África Oriental. (págs. 45, 150)
second-wave environmentalism A movement that began in the 1960s and triggered environmental movements in Europe and North America. It was characterized by widespread grassroots involvement focused on issues such as pollution, resource depletion, protection of wildlife habitats, and nuclear power. (p. 829)	**segunda ola del ambientalismo** Movimiento que comenzó en la década de 1960 y desencadenó otros movimientos ecologistas en Europa y Norteamérica. Se caracterizó por una extendida implicación comunitaria focalizada en torno a problemas como la contaminación, el agotamiento de los recursos, la protección de los habitats naturales y la energía nuclear. (p. 829)
second-wave feminism Women's rights movement that revived in the 1960s with a different agenda from earlier women's suffrage movements; second-wave feminists demanded equal rights for women in employment and education, women's right to control their own bodies, and the end of patriarchal domination. (p. 772)	**segunda ola del feminismo** Movimiento por los derechos de la mujer que resurgió en la década de 1960 con una agenda distinta a los movimientos sufragistas anteriores; las feministas de segunda ola demandaban igualdad de derechos para las mujeres en empleo y educación, el derecho de las mujeres de decidir sobre sus cuerpos y el fin del dominio patriarcal. (p. 772)

self-strengthening China's program of internal reform in the 1860s and 1870s, based on vigorous application of traditional principles and limited borrowing from the West. (p. 506)

movimiento de autofortalecimiento Programa de reforma interna de China en las décadas de 1860 y 1870 basado en la enérgica aplicación de principios tradicionales y en la limitación de préstamos de Occidente. (p. 506)

Seljuk Turkic Empire An empire of the eleventh and twelfth centuries, centered in Persia and present-day Iraq. Seljuk rulers adopted the Muslim title of *sultan* (ruler) as part of their conversion to Islam. (p. 84)

Imperio selyúcida Imperio de los siglos XI y XII, extendido por Persia y el actual Irak. Los gobernantes selyúcidas adoptaron el título musulmán de sultán (gobernante) como parte de su conversión al islam. (p. 84)

service sector Industries like government, medicine, education, finance, and communication that have grown due to increasing consumerism, population, and communication technologies. (p. 764)

sector servicios Industrias como la administración pública, la medicina, la educación, las finanzas y las comunicaciones que han crecido debido al incremento del consumismo, la población y las tecnologías de la información. (p. 764)

settler colonies Imperial territories in which Europeans settled permanently in substantial numbers. Examples include British North America, Portuguese Brazil, Spanish Mexico and Peru, Australia, New Zealand, Algeria, and South Africa. (pp. 222, 559)

colonias Territorios imperiales en los que los europeos se instalaron permanentemente y en grandes cantidades. Algunos ejemplos son la América del Norte Británica, el Brasil portugués, el México y el Perú español, Australia, Nueva Zelanda, Argelia y Suráfrica. (págs. 222, 559)

shantytown Area around a city that is settled by the poor, characterized by small, rickety buildings. (p. 632)

barriadas pobres Área en las afueras de una ciudad en la que se establecen los pobres, que se caracteriza por sus edificaciones pequeñas y destartaladas. (p. 632)

sharia Islamic law, dealing with political, economic, social, and religious life. It literally translates as "a path to water," which is considered the source of all life. (pron. shah-REE-ah) (p. 42)

sharia Ley islámica que incluye la vida política, económica, social y religiosa. Literalmente, significa "un paso de agua", pues se considera la fuente de toda la vida. (p. 42)

shogunate The rule of a Japanese military dictator, or shogun. (p. 198)

shogunato El gobierno de un dictador militar japonés, o *shogun*. (p. 198)

sickle Developed in the Middle East, a handheld tool used for harvesting grain. (p. 10)

hoz Herramienta manual creada en el Medio Oriente usada para cosechar granos. (p. 10)

"the sick man of Europe" Western Europe's description of the Ottoman Empire in the nineteenth and early twentieth centuries, based on the empire's economic and military weakness and its apparent inability to prevent the shrinking of its territory. (p. 509)

"hombre enfermo de Europa" Descripción del Imperio otomano por parte de la Europa Occidental en el siglo XIX y principios del siglo XX basada en la debilidad económica y militar del imperio y su aparente incapacidad para impedir el colapso de su territorio. (p. 509)

Siddhartha Gautama (the Buddha) The Indian prince whose exposure to human suffering led him to develop a path to Enlightenment that became the basis for the emerging religious tradition of Buddhism; lived ca. 566–ca. 486 B.C.E. (pron. sidd-ARTH-uh gow-TAHM-uh) (p. 28)

Siddhartha Gautama (el Buda) Príncipe indio cuya exposición al sufrimiento humano le llevó a desarrollar un camino hacia la iluminación absoluta que se convirtió en la base para la emergente tradición religiosa del budismo; vivió allá por los años 566 y 486 a. E. C. (pron. si-DAR-ta gau-TA-ma) (p. 28)

signares The small number of African women who were able to exercise power and accumulate wealth through marriage to European traders. (p. 346)

signares Grupo reducido de mujeres africanas que fueron capaces de ejercer poder y acumular riquezas a través del matrimonio con comerciantes europeos. (p. 346)

Sikhism Religious tradition of northern India founded by Guru Nanak (1469–1539); combines elements of Hinduism and Islam and proclaims the brotherhood of all humans and the equality of men and women. (p. 279)

sijismo Tradición religiosa del norte de la India fundada por Gurú Nanak (1469–1539); combina elementos del hinduismo y del islam y proclama la hermandad de todos los humanos y la igualdad entre hombre y mujer. (p. 279)

Silk Roads Land-based trade routes that linked many regions of Eurasia. They were named after the most famous product traded along these routes. (pp. 44, 134)

Rutas de la seda Rutas comerciales por tierra que conectaban muchas regiones de Eurasia. Se llamaban así por el producto más famoso con el que se comerciaba a lo largo de ellas. (págs. 44, 134)

"silver drain" Term often used to describe the siphoning of money from Europe to pay for the luxury products of the East, a process exacerbated by the fact that Europe had few trade goods that were desirable in Eastern markets; eventually, the bulk of the world's silver supply made its way to China. (p. 328)

"fuga de plata" Término empleado para describir el desvío de dinero de Europa para pagar productos lujosos de Oriente, proceso agravado por el hecho de que Europa tenia pocas mercancías atractivas para los mercados orientales; finalmente, el grueso de suministro de plata mundial se fue a China. (p. 328)

smallpox A highly contagious and deadly disease that was eradicated throughout the world by a vaccine. (p. 162)

viruela Enfermedad muy contagiosa y mortal que logró erradicarse del mundo gracias a una vacuna. (p. 162)

social Darwinism An outlook that suggested that European dominance inevitably led to the displacement or destruction of backward peoples or "unfit" races; this view made imperialism, war, and aggression seem both natural and progressive. (p. 556)

darwinismo social Perspectiva que sugería que el dominio europeo llevaría inexorablemente al desplazamiento o destrucción de pueblos atrasados o razas "no aptas"; esta visión hizo que el imperialismo, la guerra y la hostilidad parecieran algo tanto natural como progresista. (p. 556)

socialism in the United States Fairly minor political movement in the United States; at its height in 1912, it gained 6 percent of the vote for its presidential candidate. (p. 462)

socialismo en los Estados Unidos Movimiento politico bastante minoritario en los Estados Unidos; en su apogee en 1912, su candidato presidencial consiguió un 6 % de los sufragios. (p. 462)

"soft gold" Nickname used in the early modern period for animal furs, highly valued for their warmth and as symbols of elite status. (p. 335)

"oro suave" Apelativo empleado en la Edad Moderna para las pieles de animal, altamente valoradas por su calidez y como símbolos de un estatus social elevado. (p. 335)

Song dynasty The Chinese dynasty (960–1279) that rose to power after the Tang dynasty. During the Song dynasty, an explosion of scholarship gave rise to Neo-Confucianism, and a revolution in agricultural and industrial production made China the richest and most populated country on the planet. (p. 70)

dinastía Song Dinastía china (960–1279) que alcanzó el poder tras la dinastía Tang. Durante la dinastía Song, una eclosión de erudición dio lugar al neoconfucianismo y a una revolución en la producción agrícola e industrial que convirtió a China en el país más rico y poblado de la Tierra. (p. 70)

Songhay Empire Major Islamic state of West Africa that formed in the second half of the fifteenth century. (pron. song-GAH-ee) (p. 237)

Imperio Songhai Importante estado islámico en África Occidental en la segunda mitad del siglo quince. (p. 237)

sprawl To spread and stretch out in a disorganized and awkward manner, such as some cities. (p. 804)

expansión no planificada Propagarse y extenderse de manera desorganizada y compleja, tal como ocurre con algunas ciudades. (p. 804)

squalid Lowly, repulsive and neglected. (p. 342)

miserable Humilde, repulsivo y desatendido. (p. 342)

Srivijaya A Malay kingdom that dominated the critical choke point in Indian Ocean trade at the Strait of Melaka between 670 and 1025 C.E. Like other places in Southeast Asia, Srivijaya absorbed various cultural influences from India. (pron. SREE-vih-juh-yuh) (p. 80)

Srivijaya Reino malayo que dominó el cuello de botella clave del comercio del océano Índico en el estrecho de Malaca entre el 670 y el 1025 c.e. Al igual que otros lugares del Sudeste Asiático, Srivijaya absorbió variadas influencias culturales de India. (pron. es-RI-vi-ja-ya) (p. 80)

Stalin, Joseph (1878–1953) Leader of the Soviet Union from the late 1920s until his death. (p. 630)

Stalin, Josef (1878–1953) Líder de la Unión Soviética desde los últimos años de la década de 1920 hasta su muerte. (p. 630)

Stanton, Elizabeth Cady (1815–1902) Leading figure of the early women's rights movement in the United States. At the first Women's Rights Convention in Seneca Falls, New York, in 1848, she drafted a statement paraphrasing the Declaration of Independence, stating that men and women were created equal. (p. 414)

Stanton, Elizabeth Cady (1815–1902) Figura destacada de los primeros movimientos para los derechos de la mujer en Estados Unidos. En la primera convención sobre derechos de la mujer de 1848 en Seneca Falls (Nueva York), redactó un documento que parafrasea la Declaración de Independencia y en el que se proclama que el hombre y la mujer fueron creados iguales. (p. 414)

steam engine The great breakthrough of the Industrial Revolution, the coal-fired steam engine provided an almost limitless source of power and could be used to drive any number of machines as well as locomotives and ships; the introduction of the steam engine allowed a hitherto un-imagined increase in productivity and made the Industrial Revolution possible. (p. 442)

máquina de vapor Gran hallazgo de la Revolución Industrial, la máquina de vapor alimentada por carbón proporcionaba una casi ilimitada fuente de potencia y podía usarse para impulsar cualquier número de vehículos además de locomotoras y embarcaciones; la introducción de la máquina de vapor permitió un incremento impensable hasta entonces en la productividad e hizo posible la Revolución Industrial. (p. 442)

steppe A treeless plain that covers a wide area with grass. (p. 84)

estepa Área plana y amplia que no tiene árboles y que está cubierta de hierba. (p. 84)

stimulate To encourage growth or activity. (p. 26)

estimular Incentivar el crecimiento o la actividad. (p. 26)

stratification Being arranged into separate parts or layers. (p. 95)

estratificación Organización en partes o capas separadas. (p. 95)

stymied To be prevented from completing a task or goal. (p. 644)

obstaculizado Verse impedido de completar una tarea o lograr una meta. (p. 644)

succumb To accept defeat in regard to something you once opposed or resisted. (p. 516)

sucumbir Darse por vencido y aceptar algo a lo que uno antes se oponía o resistía. (p. 516)

Sufi A Muslim person dedicated to a life of prayer and meditation in order to unite with God. (p. 43)

Sufí Musulmán que dedica su vida a la plegaria y la meditación para unirse con Dios. (p. 43)

Sufism An understanding of the Islamic faith that saw the worldly success of Islamic civilization as a distraction and deviation from the purer spirituality of Muhammad's time. By renouncing the material world, meditating on the words of the Quran, chanting the names of God, using music and dance, and venerating Muhammad and various "saints," Sufis pursued an interior life, seeking to tame the ego and achieve spiritual union with Allah. (p. 43)

sufismo Concepción de la fe islámica que consideraba el éxito terrenal de la civilización islámica como distracción y desviación de la espiritualidad más pura de los tiempos de Mahoma. Mediante la renuncia al mundo material, la meditación sobre la palabra del Corán, el canto de los nombres de Dios, la música y el baile, y la veneración a Mahoma y a los distintos "santos", los sufistas perseguían una vida interior en la que buscaban contener su ego y alcanzar la unión espiritual con Alá. (p. 43)

Swahili civilization An East African civilization that emerged in the eighth century C.E. as a set of commercial city-states linked into the Indian Ocean trading network. Combining African Bantu and Islamic cultural patterns, these competing city-states accumulated goods from the interior and exchanged them for the products of distant civilizations. (p. 88)

civilización suajili Civilización del África Oriental que surgió en el siglo VIII E. C. como una serie de ciudades-Estado comerciales relacionadas con la red de comercio del océano Índico. Estas ciudades-estado rivales, que combinaban patrones culturales del África bantú y del Islam, acumulaban bienes del interior y los intercambiaban por productos de civilizaciones más lejanas. (p. 88)

Syrian civil war Conflict beginning in 2011 that generated over 12 million refugees and asylum seekers by mid-2016 and engaged both regional and world powers on various sides of the conflict. (p. 714)

guerra civil siria Conflicto bélico iniciado en 2011 que ha generado más de 12 millones de refugiados y solicitantes de asilo hasta mediados de 2016 e implicado tanto a potencias regionales como mundiales en varios frentes del conflicto. (p. 714)

T

taboo Something avoided or forbidden due to unacceptable, inappropriate qualities, or sacredness. (p. 415)

tabú Algo que se evita o se prohíbe debido a sus cualidades inaceptables e inapropiadas, o a su calidad de sagrado. (p. 415)

Taiping Uprising Massive Chinese rebellion against the ruling Qing dynasty that devastated much of the country between 1850 and 1864; it was based on the millenarian teachings of Hong Xiuquan. (p. 501)

Rebelión Taiping Significativa rebelión china contra la reinante dinastía Qing que devastó gran parte del país entre 1850 y 1864; se basó en las enseñanzas milenarias de Hong Xiuquan. (p. 501)

Taki Onqoy Literally, "dancing sickness"; a religious revival movement in central Peru in the 1560s whose members preached the imminent destruction of Christianity and of the Europeans and the restoration of an imagined Andean golden age. (p. 272)

Tanzimat Important reform measures undertaken in the Ottoman Empire beginning in 1839; the term "Tanzimat" means "reorganization." (pron. tahn-zee-MAHT) (p. 512)

Temujin (Chinggis Khan) Birth name of the Mongol leader better known as Chinggis Khan (1162–1227), or "universal ruler," a name he acquired after unifying the Mongols. (pron. TEM-oo-chin) (p. 142)

Theravada Buddhism "Teaching of the Elders," the early form of Buddhism according to which the Buddha was a wise teacher but not divine; emphasizes practices rather than beliefs. (pron. THAIR-ah-VAH-dah) (p. 29)

Thirty Years' War Catholic-Protestant struggle (1618–1648) that was the culmination of European religious conflict, brought to an end by the Peace of Westphalia and an agreement that each state was sovereign, authorized to control religious affairs within its own territory. (p. 266)

Timbuktu A major commercial city of West African civilization and a noted center of Islamic scholarship and education by the sixteenth century. (p. 92)

Tokugawa Japan A period of internal peace in Japan (1600–1850) that prevented civil war but did not fully unify the country; led by military rulers, or shoguns, from the Tokugawa family, who established a "closed door" policy toward European encroachments. (p. 516)

total war War that requires each country involved to mobilize its entire population in the effort to defeat the enemy. (p. 625)

trading post empire Form of imperial dominance based on control of trade through military power rather than on control of peoples or territories. (p. 322)

transatlantic slave system Between 1500 and 1866, this trade in human beings took an estimated 12.5 million people from African societies, shipped them across the Atlantic in the Middle Passage, and deposited some 10.7 million of them in the Americas as enslaved people; approximately 1.8 million died during the transatlantic crossing. (p. 335)

transnational corporations Global businesses that produce goods or deliver services simultaneously in many countries; growing in number since the 1960s, some have more assets and power than many countries. (p. 753)

Taki Unquy Literalmente "enfermedad de la danza", fue un movimiento de reavivamiento religioso en el centro del Perú en la década de 1560 cuyos miembros predicaban la inminente destrucción del cristianismo y de los europeos, así como la restauración de una edad de oro andina imaginada. (p. 272)

Tanzimat Importantes medidas reformistas llevadas a cabo en el Imperio otomano e iniciadas en 1839; el término "Tanzimat" significa "reorganización". (pron. tan-ci-MAT) (p. 512)

Temuyín (Gengis Kan) Nombre de pila del líder mongol mejor conocido como Gengis Kan (1162–1227), o "príncipe universal", denominación que adquirió tras unificar a los mongoles. (pron. te-mu-YIN) (p. 142)

budismo Theravada "Doctrina de los antiguos", es la escuela más antigua del budismo según la cual Buda fue un maestro sabio pero no divino; pone el énfasis en la práctica más que en las creencias. (pron. te-ra-VA-da) (p. 29)

guerra de los Treinta Años Lucha católica-protestante (1618–1648), culminación del conflicto religioso europeo, que llegó a su fin con la Paz de Westfalia y un acuerdo por el que cada Estado era soberano y estaba autorizado a manejar asuntos religiosos dentro de su propio territorio. (p. 266)

Tombuctú Importante ciudad comercial en la civilización del África Occidental y notable foco de erudición e intelectualidad islámicas en el siglo XVI. (p. 92)

Japón Tokugawa Período de paz interna en Japón (1600–1850) que impidió la guerra civil pero no unificó el país totalmente; fue liderado por dirigentes militares, o sogunes, del clan Tokugawa, que establecieron una política "de puertas cerradas" hacia las intrusiones europeas. (p. 516)

guerra total Guerra que requiere que cada país involucrado movilice a toda su población en el esfuerzo por vencer al enemigo. (p. 625)

imperio de puestos comerciales Forma de dominio imperial basada en el control del comercio por medio de la fuerza militar en lugar del control de pueblos o territorios. (p. 322)

sistema transatlántico de esclavos Entre 1500 y 1866, este comercio de seres humanos capturó aproximadamente a 12.5 millones personas de sociedades africanas y las transportó por barco a través del océano Atlántico en el pasaje medio, de las cuales algo más de 10.7 millones fueron finalmente depositadas en América como esclavos; aproximadamente 1.8 millones personas murieron durante la travesía transatlántica. (p. 335)

empresas multinacionales Negocios globales que producen bienes o prestan servicios simultáneamente en muchos países; creciendo en número desde la década de 1960, algunas acumulan más activos y poder que muchos países. (p. 753)

trans-Saharan slave trade A fairly small-scale commerce in enslaved people that flourished especially from 1100 to 1400, exporting enslaved West Africans across the Sahara for sale in Islamic North Africa. (p. 91)

comercio transahariano de esclavos Comercio a pequeña escala de personas esclavizadas que floreció especialmente desde el año 1100 hasta el año 1400 en el que se exportaban esclavos del África Occidental a través del Sáhara para su venta en el África islámica septentrional. (p. 91)

Treaty of Versailles The 1919 treaty that officially ended World War I; the immense penalties it placed on Germany are regarded as one of the causes of World War II. (p. 626)

Tratado de Versalles Tratado de 1919 que puso fin de manera oficial a la Primera Guerra Mundial; las enormes sanciones impuestas a Alemania son consideradas una de las causas de la Segunda Guerra Mundial. (p. 626)

tribute system A set of practices that required a show of subordination from all non-Chinese authorities and the payment of tribute—products of value from their countries—to the Chinese emperor. In return, China would grant trading rights to foreigners and offer gifts even more valuable than the tribute itself. (p. 79)

sistema de tributos Un conjunto de prácticas que imponían que las autoridades no chinas mostraran subordinación y pagaran un tributo (productos de valor de sus países) al emperador chino. A cambio, China les otorgaba derechos comerciales a los extranejros y regalos aún más valiosos que el tributo mismo. (p. 79)

tuberculosis A disease with the potential to affect most of the body, particularly the lungs. (p. 811)

tuberculosis Enfermedad que puede afectar la mayor parte del cuerpo, en especial los pulmones. (p. 811)

tumultuous Being noisy or confused; commotion. (p. 612)

tumultuoso Ruidoso o confuso; conmoción. (p. 612)

Tupac Amaru Leader of a Native American rebellion in Peru in the early 1780s, claiming the last Inca emperor as an ancestor. (p. 404)

Túpac Amaru II Líder de la rebelión nativa americana del Perú en los primeros años de la década de 1780 que reclamaba ser descendiente del último emperador inca. (p. 404)

U

ulama Islamic religious scholars, both Sunni and Shia, who shaped and transmitted the core teachings of Islamic civilization. (p. 42)

ulema Académicos religiosos islámicos, tanto suníes como chiíes, que moldearon y transmitieron las enseñanzas básicas de la civilización islámica. (p. 42)

umma The community of all believers in Islam, bound by common belief rather than territory, language, or tribe. (pron. OOM-mah) (p. 40)

umma Comunidad de todos los creyentes del islam unidos por su creencia común en lugar de por su territorio, lengua o tribu. (pron. U-ma) (p. 40)

unequal treaties Series of nineteenth-century treaties in which China made major concessions to Western powers. (p. 505)

Tratados Desiguales Conjunto de tratados del siglo XIX en los que China hizo grandes concesiones a potencias de Occidente. (p. 505)

Upanishads Indian mystical and philosophical works written between 800 and 400 B.C.E. (pron. oo-PAHN-ee-shahds) (p. 27)

Upanishad Textos místicos y filosóficos indios escritos entre el año 800 y el 400 a. E. C. (pron. u-PA-ni-sad) (p. 27)

V

variegated Being diverse, varied, and colorful. (p. 26)

abigarrado Diverso, variado y colorido. (p. 26)

varna The collective Hindu castes. (p. 564)

varna Colectivo de las castas hindúes.

veneration Treating with honor or respect. (p. 39)

veneración Tratamiento honorífico o respetuoso. (p. 39)

Vindication of the Rights of Woman Written in 1792 by Mary Wollstonecraft, this tract was one of the earliest expressions of feminist consciousness. (p. 413)

Vindicación de los derechos de la mujer Escrito en 1792 por Mary Wollstonecraft, este tratado es una de las primeras expresiones de la conciencia feminista. (p. 413)

viscount Member of the European nobility that lies between an earl and a baron. (p. 449)

vizconde Miembro de la nobleza europea que se encuentra entre un conde y un barón. (p. 449)

Vivekananda (1863–1902) Leading religious figure of nineteenth-century India; advocate of a revived Hinduism and its mission to reach out to the spiritually impoverished West. (p. 581)

Vivekananda, Svami (1863–1902) Líder religioso en la India del siglo XIX; defensor de un hinduismo revitalizado y de su misión de conectar con un Occidente espiritualmente empobrecido. (p. 581)

vociferous Expressing beliefs or complaints loudly and repeatedly. (p. 406)

vociferante Que expresa creencias o quejas de manera ruidosa y reiterativa. (p. 406)

Voltaire The pen name of François-Marie Arouet (1694–1778), a French writer whose work is often taken as a model of the Enlightenment's outlook; noted for his deism and his criticism of traditional religion. (p. 286)

Voltaire Pseudónimo de François-Marie Arouet (1694–1778), escritor francés cuyo trabajo se toma como modelo de la Ilustración; célebre por su deísmo y su crítica a la religión tradicional. (p. 286)

W

Wahhabi Islam Major Islamic movement led by the Muslim theologian Muhammad Ibn Abd al-Wahhab (1703–1792) that advocated an austere lifestyle and strict adherence to the Islamic law; became an expansive state in central Arabia. (p. 276)

wahabismo Importante corriente islámica liderada por el teólogo musulmán Muhammad ibn Abd al-Wahhab (1703–1792) que abogaba por un estilo de vida austero y un estricto cumplimiento de la ley islámica; se convirtió en un amplio Estado en Arabia central. (p. 276)

Wang Yangming Influential Ming thinker (1472–1529) who argued that anyone could achieve a virtuous life by introspection and contemplation, without the extended education and study of traditional Confucianism. (p. 277)

Wang Yangming Influyente pensador Ming (1472–1529) que sostenía que cualquiera podría alcanzar una vida virtuosa por medio de la introspección y la contemplación y sin la educación y el estudio prolongados del confucianismo tradicional. (p. 277)

warfare Engaging in battle or strongly competing with fighting executed through use of weaponry. (p. 14)

guerra Entablar combate o luchar enérgicamente mediante el uso de armas. (p. 14)

Warsaw Pact A military alliance between the Soviet Union and communist states in Eastern Europe, created in 1955 as a counterweight to NATO; expressed the tensions of the cold war in Europe. (p. 688)

Pacto de Varsovia Alianza militar entre la Unión Soviética y los países comunistas de Europa del Este creada en 1955 como contrapeso a la OTAN; expresó las tensiones de la Guerra Fría en Europa. (p. 688)

water cistern Container for catching and holding rainwater. (p. 773)

cisterna Recipiente para recolectar y conservar el agua de lluvia. (p. 773)

West African civilization A series of important states that developed in the region stretching from the Atlantic coast to Lake Chad in the period 500 to 1600 C.E. Developed in response to the economic opportunities of trans-Saharan trade (especially control of gold production), it included the states of Ghana, Mali, Songhay, and Kanem-Bornu, as well as numerous towns and cities. (p. 90)

civilización del África Occidental Conjunto de importantes Estados desarrollados en la región que abarca desde la costa atlántica hasta el lago Chad en el período entre el año 500 y el 1600 E. C. Desarrollado en respuesta a las oportunidades económicas del comercio transahariano (especialmente en cuanto al control de la producción de oro), incluía los Estados de Ghana, Malí, Songhai y Kanem, además de numerosos pueblos y ciudades. (p. 90)

Western Christendom Western European branch of Christianity, also known as Roman Catholicism, that gradually defined itself as separate from Eastern Orthodoxy, with a major break occurring in 1054 C.E.; characterized by its relative independence from the state and its recognition of the authority of the pope. (p. 96)

cristiandad occidental Rama del cristianismo en Europa Occidental, también conocida como catolicismo romano, que se definió gradualmente como forma separada de la ortodoxia oriental, con un importante cisma en el año 1054 E. C.; caracterizada por la independencia relativa del Estado y el reconocimiento de la autoridad del papa. (p. 96)

whaling The hunting of whales for meat and oil. (p. 824)

caza de ballenas Matanza de ballenas por su carne y aceite. (p. 824)

Women's Department (USSR) A distinctive organization, known as Zhenotdel, within the Communist Party of the Soviet Union that worked to promote equality for women in the 1920s with conferences, publications, and education. (p. 769)

Departamento de Mujeres Conocida como Jenotdel, organización paralela dentro del Partido Comunista de la Unión Soviética que trabajaba por promulgar la igualdad para las mujeres en la década de 1920 con conferencias, publicaciones y cursos. (p. 769)

World Trade Organization (WTO) An international body now representing 164 nations and charged with negotiating the rules for global commerce and promoting free trade; its meetings have been the site of major anti-globalization protests since 1999. (p. 759)

Organización Mundial del Comercio (OMC) Organismo internacional que representa a 164 naciones encargado de negociar las reglas del comercio global y promover el libre comercio; sus cumbres han sido objeto de importantes protestas antiglobalización desde 1999. (p. 759)

World War I The "Great War" (1914–1918), in essence a European civil war with a global reach that was marked by massive casualties, trench warfare, and mobilization of entire populations. It triggered the Russian Revolution, led to widespread disillusionment among intellectuals, and rearranged the political map of Eastern Europe and the Middle East. (p. 622)

Primera Guerra Mundial La "Gran Guerra" (1914–1918), fue en esencia una guerra civil europea con un alcance global que estuvo marcada por numerosos damnificados, guerra de trincheras y éxodo de poblaciones enteras. Desencadenó la Revolución rusa, provocó un extendido sentimiento de desilusión entre los intelectuales y reordenó el mapa político de Europa del Este y Oriente Medio. (p. 622)

World War II in Asia A struggle to halt Japanese imperial expansion in Asia, fought by primarily Chinese and American forces. (p. 644)

Segunda Guerra Mundial en Asia Lucha por detener la expansión imperialista japonesa en Asia. Intervinieron principalmente fuerzas chinas y estadounidenses. (p. 644)

World War II in Europe A struggle to halt German imperial expansion in Europe, fought by a coalition of allies that included Great Britain, the Soviet Union, and the United States. (p. 646)

Segunda Guerra Mundial en Europa Lucha por detener la expansión imperial de Alemania en Europa mantenida por una coalición de aliados que incluía a Gran Bretaña, la Unión Soviética y los Estados Unidos. (p. 646)

Y

yasak Tribute that Russian rulers demanded from the Indigenous peoples of Siberia, most often in the form of furs. (p. 224)

yasak Tributo que los gobernantes rusos exigían a los pueblos indígenas de Siberia, la mayoría de las veces en forma de pieles. (p. 224)

Young Ottomans Group of would-be reformers in the mid-nineteenth-century Ottoman Empire that included lower-level officials, military officers, and writers; they urged the extension of westernizing reforms to the political system. (p. 513)

Jóvenes Otomanos Grupo de potenciales reformistas en el Imperio otomano de mediados del siglo XIX que incluía a funcionarios de bajo rango, oficiales militares y escritores; urgían la extensión de las reformas occidentalizadoras al sistema político. (p. 513)

Young Turks Movement of Turkish military and civilian elites that advocated a militantly secular public life and a Turkish national identity; came to power through a coup in 1908. (p. 513)

Jóvenes Turcos Movimiento de las élites militares y civiles turcas que abogaba por una vida pública radicalmente secularizada y una identidad nacional turca; llegaron al poder por medio de un golpe de estado en 1908. (p. 513)

Z

zamindars An elite class of the Mughal Empire whose members controlled large tracts of land and collected taxes on behalf of the imperial court. (p. 235)

zamindar Una élite del Imperio Mogol, cuyos miembros controlaban grandes extensiones de tierra y recolectaban los impuestos en nombre de la corte imperial. (p. 235)

Zheng He Great Chinese admiral who commanded a huge fleet of ships in a series of voyages in the Indian Ocean that began in 1405. Intended to enroll distant peoples and states in the Chinese tribute system, those voyages ended abruptly in 1433 and led to no lasting Chinese imperial presence in the region. (pron. JUHNG-huh) (p. 155)

Zheng He Gran almirante chino que comandó una gran flota de barcos en una serie de viajes al océano Índico que comenzaron en 1405. Planeadas para que pueblos y Estados lejanos se adhirieran al sistema tributario chino, estas expediciones acabaron de forma abrupta en 1433 sin dejar presencia imperial china duradera en la región. (pron. sheng-E) (p. 155)

Notes

Prologue

1. See David Christian, *Maps of Time* (Berkeley: University of California Press, 2004).
2. Voltaire, *Treatise on Toleration*, chap. 22.
3. See David Christian, "World History in Context," *Journal of World History* 14, no. 4 (December 2003): 437–58.

Chapter 1

1. "Birthday of Confucius . . . ," China View, September 28, 2009, http://news.xinhuanet.com/english/2009-09/28/content_12123115.htm.
2. Charles V. Langlois and Charles Seignobos, *Introduction to the Study of History*, translated by G. G. Berry (New York: Holt, 1898), 17.
3. David Christian, Cynthia Stokes Brown, and Craig Benjamin, *Big History: Between Nothing and Everything* (New York: McGraw-Hill, 2014), 2.
4. William H. McNeill, "History and the Scientific Worldview," *History and Theory* 37, no. 1 (1998): 12.
5. Christian et al., *Big History*, 4.
6. David Christian, *Maps of Time: An Introduction to Big History* (Berkeley: University of California Press, 2004), 1–5.
7. *The Epic of Gilgamesh*, translated and edited by Benjamin R. Foster (New York: W. W. Norton, 2001), 10, tablet 1: 232.
8. Quoted in Anthony Penna, *The Human Footprint* (Oxford: Wiley-Blackwell, 2010), 151.
9. Quoted in Mark Elvin, *The Retreat of the Elephants* (New Haven, CT: Yale University Press, 2004), 19.
10. Quoted in Eric L. Jones, *Revealed Biodiversity: An Economic History of the Human Impact* (Singapore: World Scientific Publishing, 2014), 152.
11. Richard E. W. Adams, *Ancient Civilizations of the New World* (Boulder, CO: Westview Press, 1997), 53–56; T. Patrick Culbert, "The New Maya," *Archeology* 51, no. 5 (1998): 47–51.
12. I Samuel 8:11–17.
13. The Laws of Manu, in *The Sacred Books of the East*, vol. 25, translated by G. Bühler (Oxford: Clarendon Press, 1886), 195.
14. Quoted in Vivian-Lee Nyitray, "Confucian Complexities: China, Japan, Korea, and Vietnam," in *A Companion to Gender History*, edited by Teresa A. Meade and Merry E. Wiesner-Hanks (Oxford: Blackwell's, 2006), 278.
15. Quoted in Karen Offen, *European Feminisms 1700–1950* (Stanford, CA: Stanford University Press, 2000), 66.
16. Deborah Simonton, *Women in European Culture and Society: A Sourcebook* (New York: Routledge, 2014), 99.
17. Phyllis Schlafly, *The Power of the Christian Woman* (Cincinnati, OH: Standard Publishers, 1981), 117.
18. Quoted in Fred W. Clothey, *Religion in India* (London: Routledge, 2006), 92.
19. A. L. Basham, *The Wonder That Was India* (London: Sidgwick and Jackson, 1967), 309.
20. "The Martyrdom of Saints Perpetua and Felicitas," *Frontline*, "From Jesus to Christ," PBS, April 1998, http://www.pbs.org/wgbh/pages/frontline/shows/religion/maps/primary/perpetua.html.
21. Quoted in Berthold Spuler, *The Muslim World*, vol. 1, *The Age of the Caliph* (Leiden: E. J. Brill, 1960), 29.
22. Bernard Lewis, *Islam and the West* (New York: Oxford University Press, 1993), 157.
23. See J. R. McNeill and William McNeill, *The Human Web* (New York: Norton, 2003), 108–113, 153.
24. William Theodore de Bary and Irene Bloom, eds., *Sources of Chinese Tradition*, 2nd ed., vol. 1 (New York: Columbia University Press, 1999), 326–29.

Chapter 2

1. Bryan Nelson, "Becoming One with Nature," Mother Nature Network, http://www.mnn.com/earth-matters/wilderness-resources/photos/7-people-who-gave-up-on-civilization-to-live-in-the-wild-0.
2. William McNeill, *The Pursuit of Power* (Chicago: University of Chicago Press, 1984), 50.
3. Marco Polo, *The Travels of Marco Polo*, translated by Henry Yule (Toronto: General, 1993), 2:185.
4. Mark Elvin, *The Pattern of the Chinese Past* (London: Eyre Methuen, 1973), 55.
5. J. R. McNeill and William H. McNeill, *The Human Web* (New York: Norton, 2003), 123.
6. Quoted in Francesca Bray, *Technology and Gender: Fabrics of Power in Late Imperial China* (Berkeley: University of California Press, 1997), 116.
7. Patricia Buckley Ebrey, *The Inner Quarters* (Berkeley: University of California Press, 1993), 6.
8. Susan Mann, "Women in East Asia," in *Women's History in Global Perspective*, edited by Bonnie Smith (Urbana: University of Illinois Press, 2005), 2:53–56.
9. Quoted in McNeill, *Pursuit of Power*, 40.
10. John K. Fairbank et al., *East Asia: Tradition and Transformation* (Boston: Houghton Mifflin, 1978), 353.
11. Kenneth R. Hall, *Maritime Trade and State Development in Early Southeast Asia* (Honolulu: University of Hawaii Press, 1985), 101.
12. Craig A. Lockard, *Southeast Asia in World History* (Oxford: Oxford University Press, 2009), 45.
13. Domingos Paes, "Narrative of Domingos Paes of Things Which I Saw and Contrived to Learn Concerning the Kingdom of Narasimga," in Robert Sewell, *A Forgotten Empire (Vijayangar), a Contribution to the History of India*, 2nd Indian ed. (New Delhi: National Book Trust, 1970), 247–48.
14. Marc Jason Gilbert, *South Asia in World History* (Oxford: Oxford University Press, 2017), 57.
15. Jane I. Smith, "Islam and Christendom," in *The Oxford History of Islam*, edited by John L. Esposito (Oxford: Oxford University Press, 1999), 320.
16. Ross Dunn, *The Adventures of Ibn Battuta* (Berkeley: University of California Press, 1986), 124.

17. Nehemia Levtzion and Jay Spaulding, eds., *Medieval West Africa: Views from Arab Scholars and Merchants* (Princeton, NJ: Marcus Wiener, 2003), 5.

18. David Schoenbrun, "Gendered Themes in Early African History," in *A Companion to Gender History*, edited by Teresa Meade and Merry Wiesner-Hanks (Oxford: Blackwell, 2004), 263.

19. Quoted in John Iliffe, *Africans: The History of a Continent* (Cambridge: Cambridge University Press, 1995), 75–76.

20. Leo Africanus, *History and Description of Africa* (London: The Hakluyt Society, 1896), 824–25.

21. Quoted in C. R. N. Routh, *They Saw It Happen in Europe: An Anthology of Eyewitnesses' Accounts of Events in European History, 1450–1600* (Oxford: Blackwell, 1965), 386.

22. Quoted in John M. Hobson, *The Eastern Origins of Western Civilization* (New York: Cambridge University Press, 2004), 113.

23. Quoted in Richard C. Hoffman, "Economic Development and Aquatic Ecosystems in Medieval Europe," *American Historical Review* 101, no. 3 (1996): 648.

24. See Toby Huff, *The Rise of Early Modern Science* (Cambridge: Cambridge University Press, 1993).

25. Quoted in Edward Grant, *God and Reason in the Middle Ages* (Cambridge: Cambridge University Press, 2001), 70.

26. Quoted in Stuart B. Schwartz, ed., *Victors and Vanquished* (Boston: Bedford/St. Martin's, 2000), 8.

27. Michael E. Smith, *The Aztecs* (London: Blackwell, 2003), 220.

28. For a summary of this practice among the Aztecs and Incas, see Karen Vieira Powers, *Women in the Crucible of Conquest* (Albuquerque: University of New Mexico Press, 2005), chap. 1.

29. Powers, *Women in the Crucible*, 25.

30. Marvin Harris, ed., *Cannibals and Kings* (New York: Vintage, 1978), 102.

Chapter 3

1. "China Unveils Action Plan on Belt and Road Initiative," China.org.cn, March 28, 2015, http://www.china.org.cn/china/2015-03/28/content_35181779.htm.

2. Quoted in Edwin O. Reischauer, *Ennin's Travels in Tang China* (New York: Ronald Press, 1955), 221–24.

3. David Christian, *A History of Russia, Central Asia, and Mongolia* (London: Blackwell, 1998), 1:385.

4. Chinggis Khan, "Letter to Changchun," in E. Bretschneider, *Mediaeval Researches from Eastern Asiatic Sources* (London: Kegan, Paul, Trench, Trübner, 1875), 1:37–39.

5. Thomas T. Allsen, *Mongol Imperialism* (Berkeley: University of California Press, 1987), 6.

6. Jack Weatherford, *Genghis Khan and the Making of the Modern World* (New York: Crown, 2004), 111.

7. Quoted in Daniel Baraz, *Medieval Cruelty: Changing Perceptions, Late Antiquity to the Early Modern Period* (Ithaca, NY: Cornell University Press, 2019), 118.

8. Thomas Allsen, *Culture and Conquest in Mongol Eurasia* (Cambridge: Cambridge University Press, 2001), 211.

9. Quoted in Allsen, *Culture*, 121.

10. Quoted in John Aberth, *The Black Death: The Great Mortality of 1348–1350* (Boston: Bedford/St. Martin's, 2005), 84–85.

11. For the Middle East, see Michael Dols, *The Black Death in the Middle East* (Princeton, NJ: Princeton University Press, 1977), 212, 223. For Europe, see James Belich, "The Black Death and the Spread of Europe," in *The Prospect of Global History*, edited by James Belich, John Darwin, Margret Frenz, and Chris Wickham (Oxford: Oxford University Press, 2016), 93–96.

12. Quoted in John Aberth, *A Knight at the Movies: Medieval History on Film* (New York: Routledge, 2003), 225.

13. Quoted in Dols, *Black Death in the Middle East*, 67.

14. Andre Gunder Frank, *ReOrient: Global Economy in the Asian Age* (Berkeley: University of California Press, 1998), 256.

15. Arnold Pacey, *Technology in World Civilization* (Cambridge, MA: MIT Press, 1990), 62.

16. Kenneth McPherson, *The Indian Ocean* (Oxford: Oxford University Press, 1993), 15.

17. McPherson, *Indian Ocean*, 97.

18. Christopher Ehret, *The Civilizations of Africa* (Charlottesville: University of Virginia Press, 2002), 255.

19. Excerpt from Zhou Dagun, *A Record of Cambodia: The Land and Its People*, https://www.virtualangkor.com/tradediplomacy.

20. Quoted in Craig A. Lockard, *Southeast Asia in World History* (Oxford: Oxford University Press, 2009), 67. This account of Melaka draws on Lockard's book and on Craig A. Lockard, "The Sea Common to Us All," *Journal of World History* 21, no. 2 (June 2010): 228–32.

21. Quoted in Patricia Risso, *Merchants and Faith* (Boulder, CO: Westview Press, 1995), 49.

22. Louise Levanthes, *When China Ruled the Seas* (New York: Simon and Schuster, 1994), 175.

23. Ross Dunn, *The Adventures of Ibn Battuta* (Berkeley: University of California Press, 1986), 300.

24. Quoted in Patricia Crone, "The Rise of Islam in the World," in *The Cambridge Illustrated History of the Islamic World*, edited by Francis Robinson (Cambridge: Cambridge University Press, 1996), 11.

25. Christopher Tyerman, *Fighting for Christendom: Holy Wars and the Crusades* (Oxford: Oxford University Press, 2004), 16.

26. Quoted in Charles Warren Hollister, *Medieval History: A Short History* (New York: McGraw-Hill, 1990), 179.

27. Quoted in Aman Y. Nadhiri, *Saracens and Franks in 12th–15th Century European and Near Eastern Literature: Perceptions of Self and the Other* (New York: Routledge, 2017), 145.

28. Christopher Marlowe, "Tamburlaine the Great," in *The Chief Elizabethan Dramatists Excluding Shakespeare*, edited by William Allan Neilson (London: Houghton Mifflin, 1939), 69.

29. J. R. McNeill and William McNeill, *The Human Web* (New York: W. W. Norton, 2003), 160.

30. Brian M. Fagan, *Ancient North America* (London: Thames and Hudson, 2005), 475.

31. Quoted in Michael E. Smith, *The Aztecs* (London: Blackwell, 2003), 108.

32. William H. McNeill, "The Changing Shape of World History," *History and Theory* 34, no. 2 (May 1995): 18.

Chapter 4

1. Thomas Escritt and Andrew Osborn, "Ukrainian Leader Says Putin Wants His Whole Country, Asks for NATO Help," Reuters, November 29, 2018, https://www.reuters.com/article/us-ukraine-crisis-russia/ukrainian-leader-says-putin-wants-his-whole-country-asks-for-nato-help-idUSKCN1NY1K5.

2. Claude Salhani, "One More Twist in Erdogan's Imperial Mindset," *Ahval*, January 17, 2020, https://ahvalnews.com/libya-turkey/one-more-twist-erdogans-imperial-mindset.

3. Quoted in Thomas E. Skidmore and Peter H. Smith, *Modern Latin America* (New York: Oxford University Press, 2001), 15.

4. Quoted in Carlo Cipolla, *Before the Industrial Revolution* (New York: Norton, 1976), 207.

5. George Raudzens, ed., *Technology, Disease, and Colonial Conquest* (Boston: Brill Academic, 2003), xiv.

6. Quoted in Noble David Cook, *Born to Die: Disease and the New World Conquest* (Cambridge: Cambridge University Press, 1998), 202.

7. Quoted in Cook, *Born to Die*, 206.

8. Quoted in Charles C. Mann, *1491: New Revelations of the Americas before Columbus* (New York: Alfred A. Knopf, 2005), 56.

9. Quoted in Geoffrey Parker, *Global Crisis* (New Haven, CT: Yale University Press, 2013), 464.

10. Quoted in Charles C. Mann, *1493: Uncovering the New World Columbus Created* (New York: Alfred A. Knopf, 2011), 165.

11. Felipe Fernandez-Armesto, "Empires in Their Global Context," in *The Atlantic in Global History*, edited by Jorge Canizares-Esguerra and Erik R. Seeman (Upper Saddle River, NJ: Prentice Hall, 2007), 105.

12. Quoted in Alejandro Lugo, *Fragmented Lives; Assembled Parts* (Austin: University of Texas Press, 2008), 53.

13. Quoted in Anthony Padgen, "Identity Formation in Spanish America," in *Colonial Identity in the Atlantic World, 1500–1800*, edited by Nicholas Canny and Anthony Padgen (Princeton, NJ: Princeton University Press, 1987), 56.

14. Quoted in James Lockhart and Stuart B. Schwartz, *Early Latin America* (Cambridge: Cambridge University Press, 1983), 206.

15. Mary Prince, *The History of Mary Prince* (1831; Project Gutenberg, 2006), http://www.gutenberg.org/ebooks/17851.

16. Quoted in Kevin Reilly et al., eds., *Racism: A Global Reader* (Armonk, NY: M. E. Sharpe, 2003), 136–37.

17. Benjamin Wadsworth, *The Well-Ordered Family* (1712), 39.

18. Willard Sutherland, *Taming the Wild Fields: Colonization and Empire on the Russian Steppe* (Ithaca, NY: Cornell University Press, 2004), 223–24.

19. Michael Khodarkovsky, *Russia's Steppe Frontier* (Bloomington: Indiana University Press, 2002), 222.

20. Geoffrey Hosking, "The Freudian Frontier," *Times Literary Supplement*, March 10, 1995, 27.

21. Peter Perdue, *China Marches West: The Qing Conquest of Central Eurasia* (Cambridge, MA: Harvard University Press, 2005), 10–11.

22. Quoted in Lewis Melville, *Lady Mary Wortley Montagu: Her Life and Letters* (Whitefish, MT: Kessinger, 2004), 88.

23. Jane I. Smith, "Islam and Christendom," in *The Oxford History of Islam*, edited by John Esposito (Oxford: Oxford University Press, 1999), 342.

24. Charles Thornton Forester and F. H. Blackburne Daniell, *The Life and Letters of Ogier Ghiselin de Busbecq* (London: C. Kegan Paul, 1881), 1:405–6.

25. Jean Bodin, "The Rise and Fall of Commonwealths," Chapter VII, Constitution Society, accessed February 21, 2012, http://www.constitution.org/bodin/bodin_4.htm.

26. Quoted in John J. Saunders, ed., *The Muslim World on the Eve of Europe's Expansion* (Englewood Cliffs, NJ: Prentice Hall, 1966), 41–43.

27. Quoted in P. Lewis, *Pirs, Shrines, and Pakistani Islam* (Rawalpindi, Pakistan: Christian Study Centre, 1985), 84.

28. Quoted in Stanley Wolpert, *A New History of India* (New York: Oxford University Press, 1993), 160.

29. Leo Africanus, *History and Description of Africa* (London: The Hakluyt Society, 1896), 824–25.

30. Quoted in Deno John Geanakoplos, *Byzantium: Church, Society, and Civilization Seen through Contemporary Eyes* (Chicago: University of Chicago Press, 1984), 389.

31. Miguel Leon-Portilla, *The Broken Spears: The Aztec Account of the Conquest of Mexico*, 2nd ed. (Boston: Beacon Press, 1992), 80–81.

32. Quoted in Donna Martinez and Jennifer L. Williams Bordeaux, *50 Events That Shaped American Indian History* (Santa Barbara, Calif.: Greenwood, 2017), 120.

Chapter 5

1. Lily Kuo, "Spread the Word: Africa's 'Reverse Missionaries' Are Bringing Christianity Back to the United Kingdom," *Quartz Africa*, October 11, 2017.

2. Quoted in Armin Siedlecki and Perry Brown, "Preachers and Printers," *Christian History*, Issue 118 (2016): 22.

3. Quoted in Glenn J. Ames, *Vasco da Gama: Renaissance Crusader* (New York: Pearson/Longman, 2005), 50.

4. Quoted in Marysa Navarro et al., *Women in Latin America and the Caribbean* (Bloomington: Indiana University Press, 1999), 37.

5. Quoted in James Rinehart, *Apocalyptic Faith and Political Violence* (New York: Palgrave Macmillan, 2006), 42.

6. Quoted in Nicolas Griffiths, *The Cross and the Serpent* (Norman: University of Oklahoma Press, 1996), 263.

7. Richard M. Eaton, "Islamic History as Global History," in *Islamic and European Expansion*, edited by Michael Adas (Philadelphia: Temple University Press, 1993), 25.

8. Patricia Buckley Ebrey, ed. and trans., *Chinese Civilization: A Sourcebook* (New York: Free Press, 1993), 257.

9. Quoted in Steven Shapin, *The Scientific Revolution* (Chicago: University of Chicago Press, 1996), 66.

10. Francis Bacon, *The Works of Francis Bacon*, edited by James Spedding, Robert Leslie Ellis, and Douglas Denon Heath (London: Longman, 1875), 114.

11. Girolamo Cardano, *The Book of My Life*, translated by Jean Stoner (London: J. M. Dent, 1931), 189.

12. Quoted in Kapil Raj, *Relocating Modern Science: Circulation and the Construction of Knowledge in South Asia and Europe, 1650–1900* (Basingstoke: Palgrave, 2007), 40.

13. Toby E. Huff, *The Rise of Early Modern Science* (Cambridge: Cambridge University Press, 2003), 339.

14. Quoted in Shapin, *Scientific Revolution*, 28.

15. Isaac Newton, *Sir Isaac Newton's Mathematical Principles of Natural Philosophy and His System of the World*, translated by Florian Cajori (Berkeley: University of California Press, 1966), 2:399.

16. Quoted in Shapin, *Scientific Revolution*, 33.

17. Quoted in Andrew Lossky, *The Seventeenth Century: Sources in Western Civilization* (New York: Free Press, 1967), 72.

18. For this observation, see Clifford R. Backman, *The Cultures of the West: A History* (Oxford: Oxford University Press, 2013), 473.

19. Pope John Paul II, "Faith Can Never Conflict with Reason," *L'Osservatore Romano*, November 4, 1992.

20. Quoted in Lossky, *Seventeenth Century*, 88.

21. H. S. Thayer, ed., *Newton's Philosophy of Nature: Selections from His Writings* (New York: Hafner Library of Classics, 1953), 42.

22. Immanuel Kant, "What Is Enlightenment?" translated by Peter Gay, in *Introduction to Contemporary Civilization in the West* (New York: Columbia University Press, 1954), 1071.

23. Voltaire, *Treatise on Tolerance* (1763), chap. 22, http://www .constitution.org/volt/tolerance.htm.

24. Quoted in Margaret C. Jacob, *The Enlightenment* (Boston: Bedford/St. Martin's, 2001), 103.

25. Quoted in Lynn Hunt et al., *The Making of the West: Peoples and Cultures* (Boston: Bedford/St. Martin's, 2012), 594.

26. Quoted in Hunt et al., 594.

27. Quoted in Karen Offen, *European Feminisms, 1700–1950* (Stanford, CA: Stanford University Press, 2000), 39.

28. Quoted in Alfred J. Andrea and James H. Overfield, *The Human Record: Sources of Global History* (Boston: Cengage, 2015), 2:141.

29. Mary Wollstonecraft, *A Vindication of the Rights of Men; with a Vindication of the Rights of Woman* (Cambridge: Cambridge University Press, 1995), 94 and 111.

30. Quoted in David R. Ringrose, *Expansion and Global Interaction, 1200–1700* (New York: Longman, 2001), 188.

31. Steven Weinberg, *To Explain the World: The Discovery of Modern Science* (New York: HarperCollins, 2015), xiii.

32. Weinberg, xi.

33. Quoted in David Wooton, *The Invention of Science: A New History of the Scientific Revolution* (New York: Harper Perennial, 2016), 163.

Chapter 6

1. Vanessa Mbonu, " 'Humbling,' 'Unforgettable,' Participants Reflect on Their Jamestown to Jamestown Experience as the Journey Comes to a Close," *NAACP*, August 27, 2019.

2. Quoted in M. N. Pearson, ed., *Spices in the Indian Ocean World* (Aldershot, UK: Valorium, 1996), xv.

3. Quoted in Paul Lunde, "The Coming of the Portuguese," *Saudi Aramco World*, July/August 2005, 56.

4. Quoted in Patricio N. Abinales and Donna J. Amoroso, *State and Society in the Philippines* (Lanham, MD: Rowman and Littlefield, 2005), 50.

5. Quoted in Craig A. Lockard, *Southeast Asia in World History* (Oxford: Oxford University Press, 2009), 85.

6. Anthony Reid, *Southeast Asia in the Age of Commerce, 1450–1680* (New Haven, CT: Yale University Press, 1993), 2:274, 290.

7. Anthony Reid, *Charting the Shape of Early Modern Southeast Asia* (Chiang Mai, Thailand: Silkworm Books, 1999), 227.

8. Quoted in Adam Clulow, "Like Lambs in Japan and Devils outside Their Land: Diplomacy, Violence, and Japanese Merchants in Southeast Asia," *Journal of World History* 24, no. 2 (2013): 343.

9. Kenneth Pomeranz and Steven Topik, *The World That Trade Created* (Armonk, NY: M. E. Sharpe, 2006), 28.

10. Quoted in Makrand Mehta, *Indian Merchants and Entrepreneurs in Historical Perspective* (Delhi: Academic Foundation, 1991), 54–58.

11. Andre Gunder Frank, *ReOrient: Global Economy in the Asian Age* (Berkeley: University of California Press, 1998), 131.

12. Quoted in Richard von Glahn, "Myth and Reality of China's Seventeenth Century Monetary Crisis," *Journal of Economic History* 56, no. 2 (1996): 132.

13. Quoted in Pomeranz and Topik, *The World That Trade Created*, 165.

14. Quoted in John Hemming, *The Conquest of the Inca* (New York: Harcourt, 1970), 372.

15. Dennis O. Flynn and Arturo Giraldez, "Born with a 'Silver Spoon,'" *Journal of World History* 6, no. 2 (1995): 210.

16. Quoted in Mark Elvin, *The Retreat of the Elephants* (New Haven, CT: Yale University Press, 2004), 37.

17. Quoted in Robert Marks, *The Origins of the Modern World* (Lanham, MD: Rowman and Littlefield, 2002), 81.

18. See John Richards, *The Endless Frontier* (Berkeley: University of California Press, 2003), pt. 4. Much of this section is drawn from this source.

19. Quoted in Elspeth M. Veale, *The English Fur Trade in the Later Middle Ages* (Oxford: Clarendon Press, 1966), 141.

20. Quoted in Herbert Milton Sylvester, *Indian Wars of New England* (Cleveland, 1910), 1:386.

21. Quoted in Timothy Brook, *Vermeer's Hat: The Seventeenth Century and the Dawn of the Global World* (London: Bloomsbury, 2008), 44.

22. Quoted in Richards, *Endless Frontier*, 499.

23. Richards, 504.

24. Quoted in Jeff Crane, *The Environment in American History* (New York: Routledge, 2015), 68.

25. Pamela McVay, *Envisioning Women in World History* (New York: McGraw-Hill, 2009), 86.

26. These figures derive from the Trans-Atlantic Slave Trade Database, accessed December 26, 2017, http://www .slavevoyages.org/assessment/estimates.

27. Quoted in Charles E. Curran, *Change in Official Catholic Moral Teaching* (Mahwah, NJ: Paulist Press, 2003), 67.

28. David Brion Davis, *Challenging the Boundaries of Slavery* (Cambridge, MA: Harvard University Press, 2003), 13.

29. Quoted in Bernard Lewis, *Race and Slavery in the Middle East* (New York: Oxford University Press, 1990), 52–53.

30. Audrey Smedley, *Race in North America* (Boulder, CO: Westview Press, 1993), 57.

31. Kevin Reilly et al., eds., *Racism: A Global Reader* (Armonk, NY: M. E. Sharpe, 2003), 131.

32. Quoted in Donald R. Wright, *The World and a Very Small Place in Africa* (Armonk, NY: M. E. Sharpe, 1997), 109–10.

33. John Thornton, *Africa and Africans in the Making of the Atlantic World* (Cambridge: Cambridge University Press, 1998), 72.

34. Thomas Phillips, "A Journal of a Voyage Made in the Hannibal of London in 1694," in *Documents Illustrative of the History of the*

Slave Trade to America, edited by Elizabeth Donnan (Washington, DC: Carnegie Institute, 1930), 399–410.

35. Erik Gilbert and Jonathan T. Reynolds, *Africa in World History* (Upper Saddle River, NJ: Pearson Educational, 2004), 160.

36. This account is based largely on Thomas Bluett, *Some Memoirs of the Life of Job . . .* (London, 1734), http://docsouth.unc.edu/neh/bluett/bluett.html/; and James T. Campbell, *Middle Passages* (New York: Penguin Books, 2007), 1–14.

37. Francis Moore, *Travels into the Inland Parts of Africa* (London, 1755), 146–47.

38. Anne Bailey, *African Voices in the Atlantic Slave Trade* (Boston: Beacon Press, 2005), 153–54.

39. Regine Mathias, "Japan in the Seventeenth Century: Labour Relations and Work Ethics," *International Review of Social History* 56, no. 19 (2011): 217–43.

40. Robert Jütte, *Poverty and Deviance in Early Modern Europe* (Cambridge: Cambridge University Press, 1994), 143.

41. James Grehan, "Smoking and 'Early Modern' Sociability: The Great Tobacco Debate in the Ottoman Middle East (Seventeenth to Eighteenth Centuries)," *American Historical Review* 111, no. 5 (2006): 1352–77.

Period 3

1. William H. McNeill, "*The Rise of the West* after 25 Years," *Journal of World History* 1, no. 1 (1990): 7.

Chapter 7

1. Robert Zaretsky, "The Old Regime and the Yellow Revolution," *Foreign Policy*, January 15, 2019, https://foreignpolicy.com/2019/01/15/the-yellow-revolution-france-macron/.

2. Quoted in Keith M. Baker, "A World Transformed," *Wilson Quarterly* (Summer 1989): 37.

3. Quoted in Thomas Benjamin et al., *The Atlantic World in the Age of Empire* (Boston: Houghton Mifflin, 2001), 205.

4. Quoted in Jack P. Greene, "The American Revolution," *American Historical Review* 105, no. 1 (2000): 96–97.

5. Quoted in Greene, "American Revolution," 102.

6. Quoted in Susan Dunn, *Sister Revolutions* (New York: Faber and Faber, 1999), 11, 12.

7. Quoted in Dunn, *Sister Revolutions*, 9.

8. Quoted in Lynn Hunt et al., *The Making of the West* (Boston: Bedford/St. Martin's, 2003), 625.

9. Quoted in Lynn Hunt, ed., *The French Revolution and Human Rights* (Boston: Bedford, 1996), 123.

10. Bonnie S. Anderson and Judith P. Zinsser, *A History of Their Own* (New York: Harper and Row, 1988), 283.

11. Hunt, *French Revolution*, 29.

12. From James Leith, "Music for Mass Persuasion during the Terror," copyright James A. Leith, Queen's University Kingston.

13. Franklin W. Knight, "The Haitian Revolution," *American Historical Review* 105, no. 1 (2000): 103.

14. Quoted in David P. Geggus, *Haitian Revolutionary Studies* (Bloomington: Indiana University Press, 2002), 27.

15. Peter Winn, *Americas: The Changing Face of Latin America and the Caribbean* (Berkeley: University of California Press, 2006), 83.

16. Quoted in Thomas E. Skidmore and Peter H. Smith, *Modern Latin America* (New York: Oxford University Press, 2001), 33.

17. Quoted in David Armitage and Sanjay Subrahmanyam, eds., *The Age of Revolutions in Global Context, c. 1760–1840* (New York: Palgrave Macmillan, 2010), xxiii.

18. James Walvin, "The Public Campaign in England against Slavery," in *The Abolition of the Atlantic Slave Trade*, edited by David Eltis and James Walvin (Madison: University of Wisconsin Press, 1981), 76.

19. Michael Craton, "Slave Revolts and the End of Slavery," in *The Atlantic Slave Trade*, edited by David Northrup (Boston: Houghton Mifflin, 2002), 200.

20. Joseph Dupuis, *Journal of a Residence in Ashantee* (London: Henry Colburn, 1824), 162–64.

21. Eric Foner, *Nothing but Freedom* (Baton Rouge: Louisiana State University Press, 1983).

22. Quoted in Daniel Moran and Arthur Waldron, eds., *The People in Arms: Military Myth and National Mobilization since the French Revolution* (Cambridge: Cambridge University Press, 2003), 14.

23. Barbara Winslow, "Feminist Movements: Gender and Sexual Equality," in *A Companion to Gender History*, edited by Teresa A. Meade and Merry E. Wiesner-Hanks (London: Blackwell, 2004), 186.

24. Quoted in Claire G. Moses, *French Feminism in the Nineteenth Century* (Albany: SUNY Press, 1984), 135.

25. Raden Adjeng Kartini, *Letters of a Javanese Princess* (New York: W. W. Norton, 1964). Unless otherwise noted, all quotes come from this source.

26. Quoted in Jooste Cote, "Raden Ajeng Kartini," in *Gender, Colonialism and Education*, edited by Joyce Goodman and Jayne Martin (London: Woburn Press, 2002), 204.

27. Jean-Denis Lanjuinais, "Discussion of Citizenship under the Proposed New Constitution," in Hunt, *The French Revolution and Human Rights*, 133.

Chapter 8

1. http://news.xinhuanet.com/english/2017-06/05/c_136342098.htm.

2. https://citifmonline.com/2017/06/07/webster-university-holds-public-lecture-on-africa-china-relations/.

3. Edmund Burke III and Kenneth Pomeranz, eds., *The Environment and World History* (Berkeley: University of California Press, 2009), 41.

4. Gregory T. Cushman, *Guano and the Opening of the Pacific World* (Cambridge: Cambridge University Press, 2013), chaps. 1–3.

5. Ricardo Duchesne, *The Uniqueness of Western Civilization* (Leiden: Brill, 2011).

6. Eric Jones, *The European Miracle: Environments, Economics and Geopolitics in the History of Europe and Asia* (Cambridge: Cambridge University Press, 1981).

7. Kenneth Pomeranz, *The Great Divergence* (Princeton, NJ: Princeton University Press, 2000); Pier Vries, "Are Coal and Colonies Really Crucial?" *Journal of World History* 12 (2001): 411.

8. Peter Stearns, *The Industrial Revolution in World History*, 3rd ed. (Boulder, CO: Westview Press, 2007), 47.

9. Charles Dickens, *Barnaby Rudge: A Tale of the Riots of 'Eighty and Hard Times for These Times* (Boston: Chapman and Hall, 1858), 2:223.

10. Eric Hopkins, *Industrialization and Society* (London: Routledge, 2000), 2.

11. Joel Mokyr, *The Lever of Riches* (New York: Oxford University Press, 1990), 81.

12. Eric Hobsbawm, *Industry and Empire* (New York: New Press, 1999), 58. This section draws heavily on Hobsbawm's celebrated account of British industrialization.

13. Samuel Smiles, *Thrift* (London: John Murray, 1875), 39–40.

14. Quoted in Bonnie S. Anderson and Judith P. Zinsser, *A History of Their Own* (New York: Harper and Row, 1988), 2:131.

15. Benjamin Disraeli, *Sybil or the Two Nations* (New York: Routledge, 1845), 76.

16. Hobsbawm, *Industry and Empire*, 65.

17. Quoted in Peter Stearns and John H. Hinshaw, *Companion to the Industrial Revolution* (Santa Barbara, CA: ABC-CLIO, 1996), 150.

18. Quoted in Herbert Vere Evatt, *The Tolpuddle Martyrs* (Sydney: Sydney University Press, 2009), 49.

19. Much of this feature draws from E. P. Thompson, *The Making of the English Working Class* (New York: Vintage Books, 1966).

20. Hobsbawm, *Industry and Empire*, 171.

21. Dirk Hoeder, *Cultures in Contact* (Durham, NC: Duke University Press, 2002), 331–32.

22. Carl Guarneri, *America in the World* (Boston: McGraw-Hill, 2007), 180.

23. Quoted in Hoeder, *Cultures in Contact*, 318.

24. John Charles Chasteen, *Born in Blood and Fire* (New York: W. W. Norton, 2006), 181.

25. Peter Bakewell, *A History of Latin America* (Oxford: Blackwell, 1997), 425.

26. Michael Adas, *Machines as the Measure of Men* (Ithaca, NY: Cornell University Press, 1990).

27. Joanna T. Pecore, Ken Schweitzer, and Yang Fan, "The *Internationale* at Tiananmen Square," *Education about Asia* 4, no. 1 (Spring 1999): 30.

Chapter 9

1. Xi Jinping, "Xi Jinping: UN Climate Deal 'Must Not Be Derailed,'" *Climate Home News*, January 19, 2017, http://www.climatechangenews.com/2017/01/19/xi-jinping-un-climate-deal-must-not-be-derailed/.

2. Quoted in Dun J. Li, ed., *China in Transition, 1517–1911* (New York: Van Nostrand Reinhold, 1969), 112.

3. Quoted in Jonathan D. Spence, *The Search for Modern China* (New York: W. W. Norton, 1999), 169.

4. Quoted in Vincent Shih, *The Taiping Ideology: Its Sources, Interpretations, and Influences* (Seattle: University of Washington Press, 1967), 73.

5. Barbara Hodgson, *Opium: A Portrait of the Heavenly Demon* (San Francisco: Chronicle Books, 1999), 32.

6. This account of Lin Zexu draws from Spence, *Search for Modern China*; and Arthur Waley, *The Opium War through Chinese Eyes* (London: George Allen and Unwin, 1968).

7. Quoted in Teng Ssu and John K. Fairbanks, eds. and trans., *China's Response to the West* (New York: Atheneum, 1963), 69.

8. Quoted in Magali Morsy, *North Africa: 1800–1900* (London: Longman, 1984), 79.

9. Quoted in E. D. G. Prime, *Forty Years in the Turkish Empire; or, Memoirs of Rev. William Goodell* (New York: Carter and Brothers, 1875), 487.

10. Quoted in M. Sukru Hanioglu, *The Young Turks in Opposition* (New York: Oxford University Press, 1995), 17.

11. Marius B. Jansen, *The Making of Modern Japan* (Cambridge, MA: Harvard University Press, 2002), 33.

12. Quoted in Carol Gluck, "Themes in Japanese History," in *Asia in Western and World History*, edited by Ainslie T. Embree and Carol Gluck (Armonk, NY: M. E. Sharpe, 1997), 754.

13. Quoted in S. Hanley and K. Yamamura, *Economic and Demographic Change in Pre-Industrial Japan* (Princeton, NJ: Princeton University Press, 1977), 88–90.

14. Quoted in Harold Bolitho, "The Tempo Crisis," in *The Cambridge History of Japan*, vol. 5, *The Nineteenth Century*, edited by Marius B. Jansen (Cambridge: Cambridge University Press, 1989), 230.

15. Kenneth Henshall, *A History of Japan* (New York: Palgrave, 2004), 67.

16. Quoted in James L. McClain, *Japan: A Modern History* (New York: W. W. Norton, 2002), 177.

17. Kaoru Sugihara, "Global Industrialization: A Multipolar Perspective," in *The Cambridge World History* (Cambridge: Cambridge University Press, 2015), 7:117.

18. Quoted in Renée Worringer, *Ottomans Imagining Japan* (New York: Palgrave Macmillan, 2014), 59.

19. Quoted in Marius B. Jansen, *The Making of Modern Japan* (Cambridge, MA: Harvard University Press, 2000), 460.

20. Quoted in Julia Meech-Pekarik, *The World of the Meiji Print: Impressions of a New Civilization* (New York: Weatherhill, 1986), 182.

Chapter 10

1. "Germany Apologizes for Colonial-Era Genocide in Namibia," *Reuters*, May 28, 2021, https://www.reuters.com/world/africa/germany-officially-calls-colonial-era-killings-namibia-genocide-2021-05-28/.

2. Quoted in Marvin Perry, *Sources of the Western Tradition* (Boston: Wadsworth Cengage Learning, 2012), 2:256.

3. Quoted in Heinz Gollwitzer, *Europe in the Age of Imperialism* (London: Thames and Hudson, 1969), 136.

4. Robert Booth, "UK More Nostalgic for Empire than Other Ex-colonial Powers," *The Guardian*, March 11, 2020.

5. William Skidelsky, "Niall Ferguson: 'Westerners Don't Understand How Vulnerable Freedom Is,'" *The Guardian*, February 19, 2011, https://www.theguardian.com/books/2011/feb/20/niall-ferguson-interview-civilization.

6. Quoted in Steven Roger Fischer, *A History of the Pacific Islands* (New York: Palgrave Macmillan, 2013), 112.

7. Charles Griffith, *The Present State and Prospects of the Port Phillips District . . .* (Dublin: William Curry and Company, 1845), 169.

8. Robert Knox, *Races of Man* (Philadelphia: Lea and Blanchard, 1850), v.

9. Quoted in Ralph Austen, ed., *Modern Imperialism* (Lexington, MA: D. C. Heath, 1969), 70–73.

10. Mike Davis, *Late Victorian Holocausts: El Niño Famines and the Making of the Third World* (New York: Verso, 2001), 12.

11. Quoted in John Iliffe, *Africans: The History of a Continent* (Cambridge: Cambridge University Press, 1995), 191.

12. Quoted in Nicholas Tarling, "The Establishment of Colonial Regimes," in *The Cambridge History of Southeast Asia*, edited by Nicholas Tarling (Cambridge: Cambridge University Press, 1992), 2:76.

13. R. Meinertzhagen, *Kenya Diary* (London: Oliver and Boyd, 1957), 51–52.

14. Mrinalini Sinha, *Colonial Masculinity* (Manchester: Manchester University Press, 1995), 35; Jane Burbank and Frederick Cooper, *Empires in World History* (Princeton, NJ: Princeton University Press, 2010), 308–9.

15. Nupur Chaudhuri, "Clash of Cultures," in *A Companion to Gender History*, edited by Teresa A. Meade and Merry E. Wiesner-Hanks (London: Blackwell, 2004), 437.

16. Quoted in Donald R. Wright, *The World and a Very Small Place in Africa* (Armonk, NY: M. E. Sharpe, 2004), 170.

17. Quoted in Scott B. Cook, *Colonial Encounters in the Age of High Imperialism* (New York: HarperCollins, 1996), 53.

18. D. R. SarDesai, *Southeast Asia: Past and Present* (Boulder, CO: Westview Press, 1997), 95–98.

19. Quoted in G. C. K. Gwassa and John Iliffe, *Records of the Maji Maji Rising* (Nairobi: East African Publishing House, 1967), 1:4–5.

20. Quoted in Basil Davidson, *Modern Africa* (London: Longman, 1983), 79, 81.

21. This section draws heavily on Margaret Jean Hay and Sharon Stichter, eds., *African Women South of the Sahara* (London: Longman, 1984), especially chaps. 1–5.

22. Quoted in Robert A. Levine, "Sex Roles and Economic Change in Africa," in *Black Africa*, edited by John Middleton (London: Macmillan, 1970), 178.

23. Quoted in Davis, *Late Victorian Holocausts*, 37.

24. Josiah Kariuki, *Mau Mau Detainee* (London: Oxford University Press, 1963), 5.

25. Quoted in Harry Benda and John Larkin, *The World of Southeast Asia* (New York: Harper and Row, 1967), 182–85.

26. Quoted in William Theodore de Bary, *Sources of Indian Tradition* (New York: Columbia University Press, 1958), 619.

27. Quoted in Edward W. Smith, *Aggrey of Africa* (London: SCM Press, 1929).

28. Robert Strayer, *The Making of Mission Communities in East Africa* (London: Heinemann, 1978), 137.

29. Unless otherwise noted, this essay and all the quotes derive from Philip Goldberg, *American Vedas* (New York: Harmony Books, 2010), 47–66; and Diana L. Eck, *A New Religious America* (New York: HarperCollins, 2001), 94–104.

30. Strayer, *The Making of Mission Communities*, 139.

31. Quoted in William Theodore de Bary, *Sources of Indian Tradition* (New York: Columbia University Press, 1958), 652.

32. C. A. Bayly, *The Birth of the Modern World* (Oxford: Blackwell, 2004), 343.

33. Nirad Chaudhuri, *Autobiography of an Unknown Indian* (London: John Farquharson, 1968), 229.

34. Edward Blyden, *Christianity, Islam, and the Negro Race* (Edinburgh: Edinburgh University Press, 1967), 124.

35. John Iliffe, *A Modern History of Tanganyika* (Cambridge: Cambridge University Press, 1979), 324.

36. See "Ram Mohan Roy: Christian Converted British Spy?," *Kreately*, August 6, 2020, https://kreately.in/ram-mohan-roy-christian-converted-british-spy/.

37. Mohandas Gandhi, *Indian Home Rule* (Madras: Ganesh, 1922), 13.

Period 4

1. David Christian et al., *Big History* (New York: McGraw-Hill, 2014), 283.

2. William McNeill, "*The Rise of the West* after 25 Years," *Journal of World History* 1, no. 1 (1990): 2.

Chapter 11

1. UN Secretary General, "Remarks to General Assembly . . . ," July 8, 2014, https://www.un.org/sg/en/content/sg/speeches/2014-07-08/remarks-general-assembly-commemoration-100th-anniversary-outbreak.

2. Andrew Osborn, "Putin, Wary of Political Tumult, Shuns Russian Revolution Centenary," Reuters, November 7, 2017, https://www.reuters.com/article/us-russia-revolution-anniversary/putin-wary-of-political-tumult-shuns-russian-revolution-centenary-idUSKBN1D71QA.

3. Quoted in John Keegan, *The First World War* (New York: Vintage Books, 1998), 3.

4. Stanley Payne, *History of Fascism, 1914–1945* (Madison: University of Wisconsin Press, 1995), 208.

5. Quoted in Claudia Koonz, *Mothers in the Fatherland* (New York: St. Martin's Press, 1987), 75.

6. Quoted in James L. McClain, *Japan: A Modern History* (New York: W. W. Norton, 2002), 414.

7. Quoted in Marius B. Jansen, *The Making of Modern Japan* (Cambridge, MA: Harvard University Press, 2000), 607.

8. Quoted in Jansen, *The Making of Modern Japan*, 639.

9. Quoted in Lincoln Barnett, "J. Robert Oppenheimer," *Life Magazine*, October 10, 1949, 133.

10. Quoted in Merry E. Wiesner-Hanks et al., *Discovering the Global Past*, 3rd ed. (Boston: Houghton Mifflin, 2007), 422.

11. Quoted in "A-Bomb Survivor, Anti-Nuclear Movement Leader Senji Yamaguchi Dies at 82," *Japanese Times*, July 6, 2013, https://www.japantimes.co.jp/news/2013/07/06/national/a-bomb-survivor-anti-nuclear-movement-leader-senji-yamaguchi-dies-at-82/.

12. Adam Gopnik, "The Big One: Historians Rethink the War to End All Wars," *New Yorker*, August 23, 2004, 78.

13. Benito Mussolini, *The Political and Social Doctrine of Fascism* (London: Hogarth Press, 1933), 25.

14. Quoted in Christopher Kelly, *The Roman Empire* (Oxford: Oxford University Press, 2006), 124.

Chapter 12

1. Quoted in "A Continent Remade: Reflections on 1960, the Year of Africa," *New York Times*, February 7, 2020, https://www.nytimes.com/interactive/2020/02/06/world/africa/africa-independence-year.html#mbue.

2. Quoted in "A Continent Remade: Reflections on 1960, the Year of Africa," *New York Times*, February 7, 2020, https://www.nytimes.com/interactive/2020/02/06/world/africa/africa-independence-year.html#diop.

3. Quoted in Dean Rusk, *As I Saw It* (New York: W. W. Norton, 1990), 245.

4. Quoted in Frank Mankiewicz and Kirby Jones, *With Fidel: A Portrait of Castro and Cuba* (New York: Ballantine Books, 1976), 83.

5. Quoted in John L. Gaddis, *The Cold War: A New History* (New York: Penguin Press, 2005), 57.

6. Quoted in Paul Mason, *Cuba* (New York: Marshall Cavendish, 2010), 14.

7. Quoted in Peter Roman, *People's Power: Cuba's Experience with Representative Government* (Lanham, MD: Rowman and Littlefield, 2003), 63.

8. Ronald Steel, *Pax Americana* (New York: Viking Press, 1970), 254.

9. Quoted in Craig A. Lockard, *Southeast Asia in World History* (Oxford: Oxford University Press, 2009), 138–39.

10. Quoted in Stanley Wolpert, *A New History of India* (Oxford: Oxford University Press, 1993), 331.

11. Quoted in J. D. Legge, *Sukarno: A Political Biography* (New York: Praeger, 1972), 341.

12. George B. N. Ayittey, "Why Africa Is Poor," 2002, http://ieas.unideb.hu/admin/file_6845.pdf.

13. Deng Xiaoping, "The Necessity of Upholding the Four Cardinal Principles in the Drive for the Four Modernizations," in *Major Documents of the People's Republic of China* (Beijing: Foreign Language Press, 1991), 54.

14. Quoted in Abraham Brumberg, *Chronicle of a Revolution* (New York: Pantheon Books, 1990), 225–26.

15. Tom Phillips, "Xi Jinping Heralds 'New Era' of Chinese Power at Communist Party Congress," *The Guardian*, October 18, 2017, https://www.theguardian.com/toitsworld/2017/oct/18/xi-jinping-speech-new-era-chinese-power-party-congress.

16. Terri Moon Cronk, "China Poses Largest Long-Term Threat to U.S., DOD Policy Chief Says." Press release, U.S. Department of Defense, September 23, 2019, https://www.defense.gov/Explore/News/Article/Article/1968704/china-poses-largest-long-term-threat-to-us-dod-policy-chief-says/.

Chapter 13

1. Australian Embassy, Indonesia, "Human Trafficking (Remains) Rampant, Concealed in Various Guises," https://indonesia.embassy.gov.au/jakt/AR15-005.html#main.

2. Climate and Migration Coalition, "Moving Stories: Indonesia," September 26, 2013, http://climatemigration.org.uk/moving-stories-indonesia/.

3. Forbes Indonesia, "Solving the Impossible," June 2018, https://www.magzter.com/article/Business/Forbes-Indonesia/Solving-The-Impossible.

4. Paul R. Fleischman, *Wonder* (Amherst, MA: Small Batch Books, 2013), 333.

5. Alexei V. Filippenko, "Exploding Stars and the Accelerating Universe," *Bulletin of the American Academy of Arts and Sciences* (Winter 2016), https://www.amacad.org/news/exploding-stars-and-accelerating-universe.

6. Quoted in Nicole M. Gage and Bernard Baars, *Fundamentals of Cognitive Neuroscience* (London: Academic Press, 2018), 17.

7. International Energy Agency, "World Energy Outlook," 2015, http://www.worldenergyoutlook.org/resources/energydevelopment/energyaccessdatabase/; The World Bank, "World Development Indicators," http://databank.worldbank.org/data/reports.aspx?source=2&series=EG.ELC.ACCS.ZS&country=.

8. Quoted in Douglas Brinkley, *Wheels for the World* (New York: Viking, 2003), 118.

9. Quoted in Maja Adena et al., "Radio and the Rise of the Nazis in Pre-War Germany," *Quarterly Journal of Economics* 130, no. 4 (2015): 2.

10. Jeffrey Frieden, *Global Capitalism* (New York: W. W. Norton, 2006), 476.

11. "Gross World Product, 1950–2009," in *World on the Edge*, by Lester R. Brown (New York: W. W. Norton, 2011).

12. Jason Hickel, "Global Inequality May Be Much Worse Than We Think," *The Guardian*, April 8, 2016.

13. The World Bank, "Life Expectancy at Birth," 2019, https://data.worldbank.org/indicator/SP.DYN.LE00.IN?name_desc=false.

14. Charles Bright and Michael Geyer, "Benchmarks of Globalization," in *A Companion to World History*, edited by Douglas Northrup (New York: Wiley-Blackwell, 2012), 290.

15. Branko Milanovic, "Global Income Inequality: What It Is and Why It Matters?" United Nations Department of Economic and Social Affairs, 2006, 9, www.un.org/esa/desa/papers/2006/wp26_2006.pdf.

16. Quoted in Frieden, *Global Capitalism*, 459.

17. Eric Hobsbawm, *The Age of Extremes: A History of the World, 1914–1991* (New York: Vintage, 1996), 289, 290, 292.

18. Quoted in John Vidal, "Hi-Tech Agriculture Is Freeing the Farmer from His Fields," *The Guardian*, October 20, 2015, https://www.theguardian.com/environment/2015/oct/20/hi-tech-agriculture-is-freeing-farmer-from-his-fields.

19. Quoted in Amy Clark, "Is NAFTA Good for Mexico's Farmers?" CBS Evening News, July 1, 2006, http://www.cbsnews.com/news/is-nafta-good-for-mexicos-farmers/.

20. Merry Wiesner-Hanks, *The Concise History of the World* (Cambridge: Cambridge University Press, 2015), 308.

21. Quoted in Binyamin Appelbaum, "Perils of Globalization When Factories Close and Towns Struggle," *New York Times*, May 17, 2015, https://www.nytimes.com/2015/05/18/business/a-decade-later-loss-of-maytag-factory-still-resonates.html?_r=0.

22. The Organisation for Economic Co-operation and Development (OECD) defined middle class as living in a household with a daily per capita income of between 10 and 100 U.S. dollars; Homi Kharas, *The Emerging Middle Class in Developing Countries*, Working Paper No. 285 (Paris: OECD, 2009), 6.

23. Norimitsu Onishi, "Nigeria Goes to the Mall," *New York Times*, January 5, 2016.

24. Studs Terkel, *The Great Divide: Second Thoughts on the American Dream* (New York: Pantheon, 1988), 175.

25. Chrystia Freeland, "The Rise of the New Global Elite," *Atlantic*, January/February 2011, https://www.theatlantic.com/magazine/archive/2011/01/the-rise-of-the-new-global-elite/308343/.

26. Quoted in Chrystia Freeland, *Plutocrats: The Rise of the New Global Super-Rich and the Fall of Everyone Else* (New York: Penguin, 2012), 59.

27. Tim Samuels, "Africa Goes Hardcore," *The Guardian*, August 30, 2009.

28. "Global Views on Premarital Sex 2013," Statista, https://www.statista.com/statistics/297288/global-views-on-premarital-sex/.

29. Barbara Engel and Anastasia Posadskaya-Vanderbeck, eds., *A Revolution of Their Own* (Boulder, CO: Westview Press, 1998), 17–46.

30. Quoted in Patrick B. Kinross, *Ataturk: A Biography of Mustafa Kemal* (New York: Morrow, 1965), 390.

31. Quoted in Sarah Shaver Hughes and Brady Hughes, *Women in World History* (Armonk, NY: M. E. Sharpe, 1997), 2:268.

32. Quoted in Wilhelmina Oduol and Wanjiku Mukabi Kabira, "The Mother of Warriors and Her Daughters: The Women's Movement in Kenya," in *Global Feminisms since 1945*, edited by Bonnie G. Smith (London: Routledge, 2000), 111.

33. Phyllis Schlafly, *The Power of the Christian Woman* (Cincinnati: Standard Publishers, 1981), 117.

Chapter 14

1. "Chad Urban Migrant's Story," *BBC*, http://news.bbc.co.uk/2/shared/spl/hi/picture_gallery/06/africa_chad_urban_migrant0s_story/html/2.stm.

2. J. R. McNeill, "Energy, Population and Environmental Change since 1750," in *The Cambridge World History*, edited by J. R. McNeill and Kenneth Pomeranz (Cambridge: Cambridge University Press, 2015), vol. 7, part 1, 63–67.

3. World Bank, "Death Rate, Crude," http://data.worldbank.org/indicator/SP.DYN.CDRT.IN.

4. David Clark, *Urban World/Global City* (London: Routledge, 1996), 1.

5. Michael H. Hunt, *The World Transformed: 1945 to the Present*, 2nd ed. (New York: Oxford University Press, 2016), 443.

6. Gareth McLean, "Where We're Headed," *The Guardian*, April 1, 2006.

7. Lizzy Davis, "The Young French Women Fighting to Defend the Full Face Veil," *The Guardian*, January 31, 2010.

8. Statista, "Number of International Tourist Arrivals . . . ," https://www.statista.com/statistics/209334/total-number-of-international-tourist-arrivals/.

9. Jose C. Moya and Adam McKeown, *World Migration in the Long Twentieth Century* (Washington, DC: American Historical Association, 2011), 39.

10. Quoted in John J. Simon, "Aime F. Cesaire: The Clarity of Struggle," *Monthly Review* 60 (2008): 2.

11. *Sayings of Ayatollah Khomeini* (New York: Bantam Books, 1980), 4.

12. Pew Research Center, "In U.S., Decline of Christianity Continues at Rapid Pace," 2019, https://www.pewforum.org/2019/10/17/in-u-s-decline-of-christianity-continues-at-rapid-pace/.

13. Karen Armstrong, *The Battle for God* (New York: Alfred A. Knopf, 2000), xi.

14. Quoted in John Esposito, *Unholy War* (Oxford: Oxford University Press, 2002), 63.

15. "Muslim Dolls Tackle 'Wanton' Barbie," *BBC News*, March 5, 2002, http://news.bbc.co.uk/2/hi/middle_east/1856558.stm.

16. Quoted in Katherine Zoepf, "Barbie Pushed Aside in Mideast Cultural Shift. Little Girls Obsessed with Fulla in Scarf," *International Herald Tribune*, September 22, 2005, 2. The passages concerning Fulla are largely drawn from this article.

17. Quoted in John Esposito and John Voll, *Makers of Contemporary Islam* (New York: Oxford University Press, 2001), 193.

18. J. R. McNeill, *Something New under the Sun* (New York: W. W. Norton, 2001), 3–4.

19. Ker Than, "The Atomic Age Ushered In the Anthropocene, Scientists Say," *Smithsonian.com*, January 7, 2016, http://www.smithsonianmag.com/science-nature/scientists-anthropocene-officially-thing-180957742/.

20. Johan Rockstrom et al., *Big World, Small Planet* (New Haven, CT: Yale University Press, 2015), 33.

21. This section draws heavily on the work of John McNeill, a leading environmental historian. See McNeill, "Energy, Population," 72–77; and McNeill, *Something New.*

22. George J. Gilboy and Eric Heginbotham, "The Latin Americanization of China," *Current History*, September 2004, 258.

23. "Sixth Wildlife Mass Extinction May Happen in 2020, Experts Say," *Nature World News*, November 27, 2016, http://www.natureworldnews.com/articles/30805/20161027/year-2020-era-wildlife-mass-extinction.htm.

24. Hywel Griffith, "Great Barrier Reef Suffered Worst Bleaching on Record in 2016, Report Finds," *BBC News*, November 28, 2016, http://www.bbc.com/news/world-australia-38127320.

25. See Ramachandra Guha, *Environmentalism: A Global History* (New York: Longmans, 2000).

26. Quoted in Guha, 14.

27. Quoted in Guha, 50, 53.

28. David Christian, "The Anthropocene Epic," in *The Oxford Illustrated History of the World*, ed. Felipe Fernández-Armesto (Oxford: Oxford University Press, 2019), 340.

29. Christian, 340.

30. Quoted in Douglas Weiner, "The Predatory Tribute-Taking State: A Framework for Understanding Russian Environmental History," in *The Environment and World History*, ed. Edmund Burke III and Kenneth Pomeranz (Berkeley: University of California Press, 2009), 290.

31. Quoted in Edward Ross Dickinson, *The World in the Long Twentieth Century: An Interpretive History* (Berkeley: University of California Press, 2018), 328.

32. Quoted in Dickinson, 328.

33. Quoted in Shiraz Sidhva, "Saving the Planet: Imperialism in a Green Garb," *UNESCO Courier*, April 2001, 41–43.

34. Peter Allen, "Burka Ban," *Daily Mail.com*, April 11, 2011.

Acknowledgments

Chapter 1

Excerpt from Ibn Battuta beginning "Thus we reached the town of Iwalatan after a journey": Ibn Battuta, *Travels in Asia and Africa, 1325–1354*, translated and edited by H.A.R. Gibb (London: Broadway House, 1929), 319-34. Used by permission of David Higham on behalf of the Hakluyt Society.

Chapter 2

Excerpt from Imagawa Ryoshun beginning "As you do not understand the Arts of Peace": Carl Steenstrup, transl., "The Imagawa Letter," *Monumenta Nipponica* 28, no. 3 (1973), 295–316. Copyright © 1973 by Sophia University. Reproduced with permission of Sophia University.

Excerpt beginning "As soon as a baby can recognize": Yen Chih-T'ui, *Family Instructions for the Yen Clan*, Teng Ssu-Yü (translator) (Leiden: Brill, 1968), pp. 3–5, 16, 18–20. Copyright © 1968 by Brill Academic Publishers. Republished with permission of Brill Academic Publishers. Permission conveyed through Copyright Clearance Center, Inc.

Chapter 3

Excerpt from Ma Huan beginning "In the fifth year of the Yung-lo": Ma Huan, *Ying-Yai Sheng-Lan — The Overall Survey of the Ocean Shores 1433*. Translated by Ch'eng Chun. (London: Hakluyt Society, 1970), pp. 138, 140–141, 143, 145. Used with permission of David Higham on behalf of Hakluyt Society.

Chapter 4

Excerpt beginning "One of the things most to be envied": Pedro de Cieza de León, *The Incas of Pedro de Cieze de León*. © 1959 by University of Oklahoma Press. Republished with permission of University of Oklahoma Press. Permission conveyed through Copyright Clearance Center, Inc.

Chapter 5

Excerpt beginning "Then with the true God": Ralph L. Roys et al., trans, *Book of Chilam Balam of Chumayel*. © 1967 University of Oklahoma Press. Republished with permission of University of Oklahoma Press. Permission conveyed through Copyright Clearance Center, Inc.

Chapter 6

Excerpt from Ihara Saikaku beginning "Fashions have changed": Donald Shively, "Sumptuary Regulation and Status in early Tokugawa Japan," *Harvard Journal of Asiatic Studies* 25 (1964–1965), pp. 124–125, DOI:10.2307/2718340. Used with permission.

Poems from Cheng Cong's *The Tobacco Manual*: Timothy Brook, *Vermeer's Hat: The Seventeenth Century and the Dawn of the Global World*. Copyright © 2008 by Timothy Brook. Used with Permission.

Chapter 7

Declaration of the Rights of Man and Citizen: Lynn Hunt, *The French Revolution and Human Rights: A Brief History with Documents*, 2nd ed. by Lynn Hunt. Copyright © 2016 by Bedford/St. Martin's. All rights reserved. Used by permission of the publisher, Macmillan Learning.

Excerpt from "The Jamaica Letter" beginning "These laws favor": *Francisco Javier Yanes y Cristóbal Mendoza Montilla: Colección de documentos relativos a la vida pública del Libertador de Colombia y del Perú Simón Bolívar para servir a la historia de la independencia de Suramérica, Caracas, 1833*, T. XXII, pp. 207–29. Translated by Suzanne Sturn. Used by permission of Suzanne Sturn.

Chapter 8

Excerpt from Charles Fourier beginning "If it is to attract": Jonathan Beecher and Richard Bienvenu, trans. and eds., *The Utopian Vision of Charles Fourier*. Copyright © 1971 by Jonathan Beecher and Richard Bienvenu. Reprinted by permission of Beacon Press, Boston.

Chapter 11

Excerpt from A Senegalese Veteran's Oral Testimony, 1919: Joe Lunn, *Memories of the Maelstrom: A Senegalese Oral History of the First World War* (Portsmouth, NH: Heinemann, 1999), 232. Used by permission of the author.

Chapter 12

Excerpt from William Hinton beginning "There was no holding back": William Hinton, *Fanshen: A Documentary of Revolution in a Chinese Village*. Republished with permission of Monthly Review Press. Permission conveyed through Copyright Clearance Center, Inc.

Chapter 13

Excerpt beginning "Recent findings by our group": Richard P. Turco et. al., "The Climatic Effects of Nuclear War," *Scientific American*, 251:2, August 1984. Copyright © 1984 SCIENTIFIC AMERICAN, Inc. Reproduced with permission. All rights reserved.

Excerpt from Jeffrey T. Kiel beginning "Our commitment": From *Facing Climate Change*, by Jeffrey T. Kiehl. Copyright © 2016 Columbia University Press. Used with permission of Columbia University Press, permission conveyed through Copyright Clearance Center, Inc.

Chapter 14

Selections from Kabir Helminski, "Islam and Human Values," unpublished pamphlet, 2009. Used by permission of the author.

AP° Practice Exam

Excerpt from "The Jamaica Letter" beginning "[Latin] Americans . . . who live within the Spanish system": *Francisco Javier Yanes y Cristóbal Mendoza Montilla: Colección de documentos relativos a la vida pública del Libertador de Colombia y del Perú Simón Bolívar para servir a la historia de la independencia de Suramérica, Caracas, 1833*, T. XXII, pp. 207–29. Translated by Suzanne Sturn. Used by permission of Suzanne Sturn.

Index

Arab Empire. *See also* Islam and Muslims
  Christianity and, 163–166
  cross-cultural interactions in, 44
  geographic scope of, 38, 41*(m)*, 82
  pastoralists and, 39
  trade and, 151–152
Arabia. *See* Arabs and Arab world
Arabic language, 87, 89, 103, 159, 161, 275
Arabs and Arab world. *See also* Arab Empire; Islam and Muslims
  agriculture in, 39
  Byzantine Empire and, 39, 93, 93*(m)*, 163
  camels in, 157, 157*(i)*
  Christianity in, 39, 163–166
  Israel and, 819
  Jews in, 39, 649
  Ottomans Empire and, 231, 509, 514, 625
  pan-Arabism, 813
  pastoralists in, 15, 39
  sugar industry in, 217
  trade in, 39, 151–152
  tribal and clan structure of, 40
  World War I and, 628
  Zoroastrians in, 39
Arab Spring, 391, 705, 827
Aral Sea, shrinking of, 832
Architecture. *See also* Monumental architecture
  Byzantine, 96
  in early civilizations, 17
  in Mughal Empire, 236, 236*(i)*
  in Southeast Asia, 152
Arctic region, climate change in, 826
Argentina
  European migrants in, 458, 470
  exports from, 468
  military rule in, 705
  Paraguay conflict with, 410, 466
  railroads in, 468
  voting rights in, 406
Aristocracy. *See also* Nobility
  in England, 449
  in France, 395
  in Japan, 78
  in Korea, 76, 140
  in Vietnam, 79
Aristotle (Greece), 103, 281, 282
Armenians
  Christianity of, 30*(m)*, 37, 232
  genocide against, 628
  in trade, 349

Armies. *See* Military
Arms and armaments. *See* Weapons
Arranged marriages, 654, 767
Art. *See also* Painting; Sculpture; *specific works and artists*
  in agricultural societies, 15
  Buddhist, 138, 138*(i)*
  in early civilizations, 17
  Mayan, 106
  in Mughal Empire, 299, 300*(i)*
  "new objectivity" style of, 665
  in Paleolithic era, 10, 830
  in Renaissance, 103–104, 233
  Romantic movement in, 288
  of Seljuk Turks, 84*(i)*
  socialist, 456*(i)*, 489*(i)*
  in Southeast Asia, 152
Artifacts, dating techniques for, 12
Artificial intelligence (AI), 789, 790*(d)*
Artillery. *See* Weapons
Artisans and craftspeople
  in Aztec Empire, 169
  in early civilizations, 17
  Indigenous peoples as, 334
  in Japan, 516, 517
  in Mongol Empire, 143, 146
  in Ottoman Empire, 511
  social protest by, 453
Asante kingdom (West Africa), 408
Ascetics, Hindu, 27*(i)*, 28
Asia. *See also* Afro-Eurasia; Eurasia; *specific regions and countries*
  in 15th century, 154*(m)*
  agriculture in, 12
  authoritarianism in, 705
  Buddhism in, 28–32, 30*(m)*, 80–81, 137–138, 152, 262, 822
  Christianity in, 30*(m)*, 44, 195, 262, 273–274, 302, 817
  civilizations of, 16, 69–70, 72–81
  colonialism in, 556–558, 558*(m)*, 561–562
  communism in, 652, 679, 690
  Europeans and, 318, 320–327, 321*(m)*
  family size in, 767
  feminism in, 773
  financial crisis in, 756
  Hinduism in, 26–28, 80, 81, 152, 262
  independence in, 696–704, 698–699*(m)*
  Islam in, 22, 42, 44, 82, 229, 275–276
  migration from, 571–572, 804, 805
  population of, 800, 802*(t)*
  Sufism in, 43

  trade in, 153–155, 318, 320–327
  World War II in, 644–646, 645*(m)*
  "Asia for Asians," Japanese on, 645
Asian Tigers (newly industrialized countries), 751
Askiya Dawud (Songhay Empire), 238
Askiya Muhammad (Songhay Empire), 238
Aslan, Reza (historian), 61*(d)*
Assayar, Omar Imma (Chad), 799
Assembly line production, 460, 461, 761
Assimilation
  Buddhism and, 32, 78, 139
  in China, 228, 274, 289
  Christianity and, 272
  of enslaved people, 339
  Hinduism and, 32
  of migrants, 459, 805, 808–809, 812
  in Persia, 145
Astrolabes, 151
Astronomy
  in China, 273
  Islamic, 17, 161*(i)*, 162
  in Mongol world, 147
  Scientific Revolution and, 282–285
  second Scientific Revolution and, 742, 744
  telescopes and, 283*(i)*, 284
Aswan Dam (Egypt), 694
Atahualpa (Inca), 207
Atatürk, Mustafa Kemal (Turkey), 770–771, 815, 817, 843, 843*(d)*
Athens (Greece), 20, 22
Atlantic Ocean region. *See also* Atlantic revolutions; *specific locations*
  debates regarding, 336–337
  hurricanes in, 826
  slave trade in, 195, 218, 302, 316*(i)*, 335–348, 338*(m)*, 343*(f)*, 343*(t)*
Atlantic revolutions, 387–419. *See also* French Revolution
  abolition of slavery after, 406–409
  American, 387, 391–394, 392*(m)*, 434–435*(d)*
  feminism and, 387, 390, 412–416
  in global context, 388, 390–391
  Haitian, 337, 387, 400–402, 401*(i)*, 429
  intellectual thought in, 390
  Latin American, 387, 402–405, 403*(m)*
  nationalism and, 387, 390, 409–410, 412
  outcomes of, 417–419
  rights and, 426–433